UNIVERSITY CASEBOOK SERIES

ELEMENTS

OF

CIVIL PROCEDURE

CASES AND MATERIALS

By

MAURICE ROSENBERG
Harold R. Medina Professor of Procedural Jurisprudence Emeritus,
Columbia University

HANS SMIT
Stanley H. Fuld Professor of Law
Director, Parker School of Foreign and Comparative Law,
Columbia University

ROCHELLE COOPER DREYFUSS
Professor of Law, New York University

FIFTH EDITION

Westbury, New York
THE FOUNDATION PRESS, INC.
1990

Library of Congress Cataloging-in-Publication Data

Rosenberg, Maurice, 1919–
     Elements of civil procedure, cases and materials / by Maurice
Rosenberg, Hans Smit, and Rochelle Cooper Dreyfuss. — 5th ed.
        p.   cm. — (University casebook series)
     ISBN 0–88277–797–1
     1. Civil procedure—United States—Cases. I. Smit, Hans.
II. Dreyfuss, Rochelle Cooper, 1947–   . III. Title. IV. Series.
KF8839.R6 1990
347.73'05—dc20
[347.3075]   90–3266
                                                     CIP

    R., S. & D.–Cs. Civ.Proc. 5th Ed. UCB
    4th Reprint—1998

PREFACE

The aim of this Fifth Edition is to prepare students for civil dispute resolution in the 21st century. It combines new materials with well-tested approaches. These approaches include the objective of helping students to focus their critical powers on evaluating both the theoretical premises and the actual operations of modern rules of civil procedure. This edition adds recent Supreme Court decisions in such areas as jurisdiction, res judicata, joinder, and federalism. It also examines recent changes and proposed changes to the Federal Rules of Civil Procedure and the important developments in regard to summary judgment and Rule 11 practice. The earlier editions' accent on judicial management and alternative dispute resolution processes is strengthened. To deal with the increasing number of complex cases involving widely dispersed injuries, we have expanded the treatment of the *Agent Orange* litigation, providing a setting in which to examine the special challenges to the courts and society posed by disasters that produce mass tort cases.

This edition continues to view procedure from a number of basic vantage points:

The *historical* perspective finds expression, not only in essays on the writ system and the evolution of today's procedural law, but also in contemporary cases that demonstrate the significance of history for modern problems. Among these are the right to trial by jury and the availability of noncompensatory remedies for newly created rights. These developments make clear to the student that civil procedure is a dynamic pursuit, changing in response to evolving societal needs.

The *functional* perspective is brought to bear in the consideration of such terms as "cause of action," "substance," and "procedure." The search for the meaning of these terms carries Holmes' famous message that procedural concepts are not crystals of invariant content: as to every one, purpose informs meaning.

The *value* perspective is implicit in much of the material. Civil Procedure should not be understood as an esoteric collection of mechanical commands. Rather, values that animate other public debates are often at issue here. The responsibility of the community to its poorest members is discussed in the chapter on access to courts and lawyers; the needs of modern business rub against those of the individual in such areas as jurisdiction and joinder; privacy interests are at stake throughout the discovery and trial process; and issues relating to class actions pit efficiency objectives against demands for individualized justice. Of course, values that are special to procedure are also stressed; for instance, rules protecting the social interest in repose and the integrity of the adversarial process.

PREFACE

The *empirical* perspective surfaces in several contexts, such as the judges' appraisal of the strengths, weaknesses and desirability of the civil jury, the impact of the pretrial conference, and the efficacy of pretrial discovery. The empirical studies in the book underscore the point that rules of procedure are designed to serve practical ends. We are concerned to explore whether the rule works in practice, not merely in theory.

Finally, the *systemic* perspective is conveyed by materials that impart the idea that the courts are but one part of a dispute resolution system and that other means exist to resolve legal controversies. As mediation, arbitration, and newer mechanisms such as mini-trials, rent-a-judge schemes, and summary jury trials are explored, students are encouraged to consider how to make the "forum fit the fuss," and to weigh the extent to which the public's interest in the judicial process is served or disserved by procedural devices tailored more closely to the needs of individual litigants.

Procedure shapes the students' conception of the legal profession, their roles as counselors, their duties to the court, and their positions as citizens with specialized understanding of the problems and limitations of the judiciary. Naturally, we consider it the most exciting course in the first year curriculum.

We extend our thanks to the colleagues in law teaching who have given us valuable suggestions for improving this book. We are grateful to students at the Columbia and New York University Schools of Law who aided us in preparing this revision. They include Tzvi Hirshaut and Tiziana Tabucchi, of the Columbia class of 1991, and Lisa Bialkin, N.Y.U. 1991. We greatly appreciate the assistance of Sheryl Jackson; and the excellent work of Carol Murray in handling many demanding tasks at all phases of the work with great skill, patience and good humor.

Maurice Rosenberg
Hans Smit
Rochelle Cooper Dreyfuss

June, 1990

SUMMARY OF CONTENTS

SUMMARY OF CONTENTS

PART VII. EFFORTS TO CONTROL DECISION MAKERS

TABLE OF CONTENTS

TABLE OF CONTENTS

xi

TABLE OF CONTENTS

PART IV. PRELIMINARIES TO THE TRIAL

*

TABLE OF STATUTES

TABLE OF STATUTES

TABLE OF STATUTES

TABLE OF STATUTES

*

TABLE OF CASES

Principal cases are in italic type. Non-principal cases are in roman type. References are to Pages.

TABLE OF BOOKS AND ARTICLES

Books

li

Miscellaneous Articles

ELEMENTS

OF

CIVIL PROCEDURE

CASES AND MATERIALS

*

Part I

CIVIL PROCEDURE AS A STUDIED ENTERPRISE

Chapter One

CHARACTERISTICS OF CIVIL PROCEDURE

SECTION 1. THE SOCIAL GOALS OF PROCEDURAL LAW

Rules of civil procedure regulate the formal actions of persons engaged in litigating controversies that have been lodged in the courts. The rules are often technical in their nature and deal with matters that are outside common experience. At times they are difficult to understand. Unlike substantive norms, which often turn on competing social values that are readily recognizable to lay persons, procedural rules are usually based on policies and values that lie outside of daily experience. As a result the uninitiated tend to regard procedural rules as entirely mechanical or technical—necessary to preserve order but unworthy of the exertions of real thinkers. This is a misconception it is important to put aside at the very start. Civil procedure is laden with value conflicts and trade-offs. It can be understood only by carefully assessing the many ends and policies that give shape and meaning to its specific details.

A good way to approach this subject is to seek a wider perspective by standing back from the detailed rules of pleading, trial, and appeal and examining the major goals and values of the system. The first question is: What goals does the civil-justice court system try to advance in our society? A facile answer is that the civil courts attempt to resolve legal disputes in a just manner. What, on closer analysis, does that noble sentiment mean? For instance, is it the courts' purpose to learn the *truth,* come what may, when it conducts hearings and takes evidence? Or should the courts limit their search for the truth if necessary to accommodate other social values, such as preserving confidential relations, protecting human dignity or promoting social tranquility by preventing relitigation of issues previously determined?

The adjudicatory process that civil procedure regulates has three main functions. First, it is designed to bring a peaceful end to legal disputes. No organized society could long endure without rules for bringing to a close controversies that are disruptive of the social

1

harmony that rules of law generally seek to achieve. Second, judicial tribunals not only decide who is in the right and who is in the wrong, they also provide state-enforced types of relief. They thus ensure that corrective measures will be taken to remedy wrongs done. Third, courts not only apply law, they also enunciate it. They are not, as Montesquieu wanted us to believe, merely "the mouths that speak the words of the law." In many instances, and increasingly, they avowedly make law.

The merits of rules of procedure depend directly on their capacity to serve these principal functions justly, speedily, and without undue expense. Rule 1 of the Federal Rules of Civil Procedure virtually proclaims these as the very purposes of the procedural enterprise. However, while these end goals exercise a pervasive influence on procedure, there are many other social policies that may collide and require accommodation. These policies are highly diverse. Some are wholly unrelated to processing a dispute through the courts. For example, the substantive concept that negligence claims should be to some extent discouraged may find expression through a procedural rule imposing on the plaintiff the burden of proving the absence of contributory negligence. Usually, however, the operative competing values are more directly related to the process of litigation and adjudication. One example is the recurrent tension between the objective of deciding disputes on their legal merit and the sometimes competing goal of permitting the parties and their counsel to decide what issues to argue and what evidence to produce. Another example is the limitation put upon the reach of pre-trial discovery by the rules protecting privileged communications and materials obtained by adversary counsel in preparation for trial.

The diversity of social values that may be involved in procedural rules underlines the necessity of delineating and weighing them properly. The circumstance that these values may not be immediately apparent provides a special and stimulating challenge to the student of procedure.

The grist of the mills which civil procedural rules regulate consists of legal disputes of a non-criminal kind. These are controversies that rest upon opposed claims of legal entitlement. Someone asserts that another person or the government has infringed an entitlement that is grounded in a legal right and the battle is on. The "right" relied upon may be one that has become well settled by the time of the suit; it may be based upon a constitution, a statute, or a court decision. Or it may be an inchoate right that no one knows for certain exists until a litigant asserts it and is vindicated.

The result is that legal disputes are protean in their form. Nearly every controversy can be transformed into a legal dispute. It requires only that there be a legal rule governing the matter. If there is no already-declared legal rule to cover the claim or defense, the courts can devise one on the spot. Thus the subject matter to which the rules of civil procedure apply is as broad as the law-givers of the society are prepared to acknowledge. It is not an overstatement to say that the domain of civil procedure has been expanding swiftly in recent years, as the adjudicatory process is used for an ever-growing range of disputes. Are there limits? Should there be? Why? What should they be?

GEORGIA HIGH SCHOOL ASSOCIATION v. WADDELL

Supreme Court of Georgia, 1981.
248 Ga. 542, 285 S.E.2d 7.

PER CURIAM.

On October 23, 1981, a football game was played between R.L. Osborne and Lithia Springs High Schools, members of region 5 AAAA established by the Georgia High School Association. The winner of this game would be in the play-offs, beginning with Campbell High School.

The score was 7 to 6 in favor of Osborne. With 7 minutes, 1 second, remaining in the game, Osborne had the ball on its 47 yard line, 4th down and 21 yards to go for a first down. Osborne punted but "roughing the kicker" was called on Lithia Springs. The referee officiating the game with the approval and sanction of the Georgia High School Association assessed the 15 yard penalty, placed the ball on the Lithia Springs 38 yard line, and declared it was 4th down and 6 yards to go.

The rules of the National Federation of State High School Associations provide that the penalty for roughing the kicker shall be 15 yards *and* 1st down. There is a dispute as to whether the Osborne coaches properly protested to the referee, before the ball was put in play, the error in the referee's failing to declare a 1st down.

From Lithia Springs' 38, Osborne punted again. Lithia Springs received the punt and drove down the field to score a field goal. Now 2 points behind, Osborne passed. Lithia Springs intercepted and scored again. The final score was Lithia Springs over Osborne, 16 to 7.

On October 26, Osborne filed a written protest with the Executive Secretary of the Georgia High School Association who is charged with making initial decisions of protests. The Executive Secretary conducted an investigation and denied the protest on November 5 on the ground that, notwithstanding the admitted error, no official protest was made to the referee by the Osborne coaches immediately following the play in question.

On appeal by Osborne to the Hardship Committee of GHSA, that committee approved the Executive Secretary's decision on November 8. On appeal, the state Executive Committee of GHSA approved the Hardship Committee's decision on November 11, 1981.

On November 12, suit was filed in the Superior Court of Cobb County by parents of Osborne players against the GHSA. Hearing was held on November 13. The court found that it had jurisdiction, found that the referee erred in failing to declare an automatic first down, and found that a protest was lodged with the proper officials of GHSA. The court found that the plaintiffs have a property right in the game of football being played according to the rules and that the referee denied plaintiffs and their sons this property right and equal protection of the laws by failing to correctly apply the rules.

The court then entered its order on November 13 cancelling the play-off game between Lithia Springs and Campbell High School scheduled for 8 p.m. that evening and ordered " * * * that Lithia Springs High School and R.L. Osborne High School meet on the football field on November 14, 1981 at an agreed upon time between the parties and resume play at the Lithia Springs thirty eight yard line with the ball being in the possession of R.L. Osborne High School and it be first down and ten yards to go for a first down and that the clock be set at seven minutes one second to play and that the quarter be designated as the fourth quarter."

Asserting that the trial court's order was erroneous under Smith v. Crim, 240 Ga. 390, 240 S.E.2d 884 (1977), and would disrupt the play-off games not only between Lithia Springs and Campbell but succeeding play-offs, the GHSA filed a motion for supersedeas in this court on November 13, 1981, and the court entered its order suspending the trial court's order, pending further order of this court.

In Smith v. Crim, supra, we held that a high school football player has no right to participate in interscholastic sports and has no protectable property interest which would give rise to a due process claim. Pretermitting the question of "state action" which is the threshold of the 14th Amendment, we held that Smith was not denied equal protection by the rule of GHSA there involved. Similarly we find no denial of equal protection by the referee's error here. Were our decision to be otherwise, every error in the trial courts would constitute a denial of equal protection. We now go further and hold that courts of equity in this state are without authority to review decisions of football referees because those decisions do not present judicial controversies. The stay granted by this court on November 13, 1981, is hereby reaffirmed.

All the Justices concur.

SECTION 2.   THE ROLE AND FUNCTIONS OF COURTS

The *Waddell* case does not typify the response of American courts to new claims of legal entitlement. Many, if not most, new types of legal claims are upheld as "judicial controversies," whether or not the claims ultimately are upheld. Among the urgent questions looming for lawyers in the 21st century are these: Added to the large volume of new types of claims created by legislation, the widened domain of legally-based disputes has led to a great expansion in the demand for dispute-resolving machinery. In the 21st century this phenomenon of

American society will confront lawmakers with unavoidable questions: Which disputes are fit for courts? Which are not? What alternative means shall society employ to resolve classes of disputes that are not best decided in courts? To respond to those questions requires identifying what courts do and do not do effectively. A poor mark for effectiveness may not foreclose the possibility that the courts may nevertheless be the best forum for a particular type of dispute, but it will at least make us aware that there are weaknesses in the judicial process that need to be compensated for. Some further sense of the limits on courts' ability to handle some types of claims is suggested by the opinion that follows.

CUDAHY JUNIOR CHAMBER OF COMMERCE v. QUIRK

Supreme Court of Wisconsin, 1969.
41 Wis.2d 698, 165 N.W.2d 116.

Appeal from a judgment of the county court of Milwaukee county: ELLIOT N. WALSTEAD, JUDGE. Reversed.

FACTS

In the spring election of 1966, the voters of the city of Cudahy were to decide by referendum whether the community water supply was to be fluoridated. A leading proponent of fluoridation was the Cudahy Junior Chamber of Commerce. A leading foe of fluoridating the water was James Quirk working as or through The Greater Milwaukee Committee Against Fluoridation.

In the midst of the spirited campaign, Quirk "challenged" the Jaycees, offering to give them $1,000 " * * * if a daily dose of four glasses [of fluoridated water] cannot cause 'dermatologic, gastrointestinal and neurological disorders' " and adding, "If the Jaycees should find that we have misrepresented matters in this paper, we will then also pay the sum of $1,000." The Jaycees did some checking, so found to their satisfaction, demanded payment by Quirk of $1,000. When payment was refused, the Jaycees brought this action, seeking (1) a court finding that Quirk did misrepresent matters in his brochure; (2) a court finding that four glasses of fluoridated water cannot cause the mentioned disorders; (3) a court judgment for $1,000. Trial was had to a jury. The jury found misrepresentation. Judgment was granted on the verdict. Motions after verdict were denied. Defendant Quirk appeals.

ROBERT W. HANSEN, J. This case revolves around a question and answer that headed up a two-page brochure that James Quirk distributed in Cudahy, urging a "No" vote in the April election on the question of whether the public water supply should be fluoridated. Here's the question and here's the answer:

"(Q) Is it true, as Dr. Chelius has once again told the people of Cudahy that 'A person would have to drink the equivalent of fifty bathtubs of water at once to get a harmful dose of fluoride?'

"(A) So preposterous is that statement that we shall give $1,000 to the Jaycees for fluoridation promotion if a daily dose of four glasses cannot cause 'dermatologic, gastrointestinal and neurological disorders.' If the Jaycees should find that we have misrepresented matters in this paper, we will then also pay the sum of $1,000."

WHAT HAVE WE HERE?

In the eyes of the law, exactly what is this sort of challenge made in the heat of an election campaign? Was it an offer that, upon acceptance, became a binding contract? Was it a reward, analogous to the sums of money offered for information leading to the arrest and conviction of the perpetrator of a crime? Was it a bet, a wagering of $1,000 against the possibility that one might be wrong?

In Restatement, Contracts, pp. 1008, sec. 520, comment c, the following is stated: "A wager may relate to a trial of skill or to *proof of an actual fact* or even to a certain point that happened in the past." (Emphasis supplied.) The Restatement gives this example of a wager:

"A promises B one hundred dollars if B can give ocular demonstration of the rotundity of the earth, to the satisfaction of C; in consideration of which B promises to pay a similar amount if he fails. B, by sights established over a large lake, satisfies C. A does not believe when he enters into the transaction that B can make the proof. B knows he can. Though condition is not fortuitous, the transaction is a wager."

The only difference between the example given and the case before us is that the Jaycees were not required to risk their $1,000 or any other amount of money to accept the bet or take up the challenge. It can be contended that the time, effort and expense involved in seeking to prove the defendant wrong supply the element of consideration, a something lost if the effort to prove the defendant wrong should fail. This would make the accepted challenge a contract, but would not change the nature of such contract. It would remain a wager, unenforceable as against public policy. In essence the Quirk challenge was a wager—"I'll gamble my $1,000 against your efforts to prove me wrong that my statements are correct." It is not close kin to a bet that the Green Bay Packers will best the Chicago Bears in their next gridiron encounter. It is, however, a twin to the bet that Babe Ruth once pitched for the Boston Red Sox. It is the essential nature of a transaction, rather than the label attached to it by the parties, that determines whether it is in truth and fact a wager. See 38 Am.Jur.2d, Gambling, pp. 242–43, sec. 189.

WHO WON THE BET?

The jury's finding, which was sustained by the trial court, was that the Jaycees won the wager. This amounted to an acceptance of the credibility of the testimony offered by the Jaycees that Quirk had "misrepresented matters" in his brochure. We do not reach the issue of fact as to who won and who lost the wager. Our holding is that the participants in a wager may not use the court to settle their dispute because gambling debts cannot be established or collected in the courts.

THE QUESTION OF PUBLIC POLICY

In addition to the judicial reluctance to hold the stakes or decide the winner in a betting situation, there are sound reasons of public policy for not having court or jury decide whose gloved fist is to be lifted in victory in this dispute. It is clear that, while $1,000 would be a welcome addition to club coffers, the primary concern of the Jaycees is to vindicate the rightness of their position that fluoridation of the Cudahy water supply involves no harmful side effects. It is at least as clear that James Quirk's principal interest is in seeking court confirmation of his contention that fluoridation of a community's drinking water risks harmful consequences. He appeared as his own counsel, and his brief and oral argument dealt only with the rightness of his anti-fluoridation stance. In fact, in rejecting the demand for payment of the Jaycees, he wrote, with copies to local press, "Top promoters of fluoridation will turn aghast at airing the harm and stupidity of fluoridation in open court. We welcome the opportunity of a court hearing." The time-honored explanation, "It isn't the money. It's the principle of the thing" describes both the intensity of conviction and explains the gap between the points of view of the parties to this action.

If disputants on the issue of the harmful effects of fluoridation can by the process of challenge and acceptance bring their dispute on this issue of public concern to the courts for adjudication, the list of matters in which litigants could seek determinations by the court of questions of public policy would be a long one. Dedicated crusaders for varying points of view, pro and con, by the process of challenge and response, could have courts rule on whether birth control pills have harmful side-effects, whether cigarettes cause cancer, whether sugar substitutes alter chromosomes. If there are ways of bringing such controversies to court, putting up $1,000 to be paid to anyone who can prove you wrong does not make the courts the forum or the referee. Here the true controversy is as to the effects of fluoridation. We have grave doubts as to whether this is a justiciable issue—one appropriate for judicial inquiry. See Baker v. Carr, 369 U.S. 186, 82 S.Ct. 691, 7 L.Ed.2d 663 (1962).

THE ISSUE OF PUBLIC DEBATE

It is to be remembered that the brochure in which the claimed misrepresentation was printed was a part of the public debate of a public issue in a public referendum. It is pertinent that " * * * more than 900 referendums on fluoridation have been held in the United States since 1950 * * * Probably no issue of science and public policy has involved as much emotional fervor as fluoridation of public drinking water." (From Saturday Review March 1, 1969, p. 56.) This case must be considered against the background of what has been termed " * * * a profound national commitment to the principle that debate on public issues should be uninhibited, robust, and wide-open." New York Times v. Sullivan, 376 U.S. 254, 84 S.Ct. 710, 11 L.Ed.2d 686 (1963).

While there may be situations in which the courts are required to intervene, as in cases of libel or slander, it is clear that there is a wide latitude constitutionally assured to participants in the political process of persuading an electorate to vote, Yes, or, No, in a referendum election. It includes the right to be wrong, as one side almost always is in a debate of a public issue.

It is understandable that the Jaycees, a civic organization of young men with an established record for effective participation in civic enterprises, would want to have its presentation of facts found to be accurate, and that of its principal adversary found to be false, misleading and misrepresented. It is not the role or function of the judicial branch of our government to make that determination. Some may see it as a weakness but it is the heart of the referendum law and the democratic process that, in this situation, the voters, not judge or jury, are to bring in the verdict. We can with propriety commend all individuals and all groups who participate in securing the expressed will of an informed electorate, but it is not for us to determine whose presentation had either the greatest accuracy or greatest persuasiveness. The cases, affirmative and negative, were submitted to the jury at the polls. They were not for a jury in a courtroom to affirm or reverse.

The what, why, when and where of this case require that the judgment be reversed and the case dismissed.

By the Court:—Judgment reversed and cause remanded with directions to dismiss the complaint.

NOTES

1. If lessee Roe asserts he has a right to put the premises to a use which the landlord maintains the lease excludes, Roe may ask the court to pronounce a declaratory judgment settling their dispute and it will ordinarily be granted. If neighbors tell Jones they will sue him in nuisance if he persists in his plan to raise chickens in the backyard, Jones will likely be able to obtain a declaration of his rights from a court. In either case, Roe and Jones might have gone ahead with the proposed action and thereupon sued for a judicial declaration that the action was legally correct. Other relief could have been sought in conjunction with the declaratory judgment, including an injunction or damages for harassment and interference with the rights in question. Do those cases differ from the Cudahy fluoridation dispute?

2. For additional material on problems of justiciability see Chapter 5 infra.

There is clearly a legally-based dispute in the *Cudahy* case, but it was deemed inappropriate for the courts, as was the issue in the *Waddell* case. Significant questions are suggested by these cases. What *is* the proper role of a court? What *are* the proper functions of a court? When a group of members of the U.S. Congress were disappointed that the Congress voted against restricting President Reagan's actions in Central America as they thought necessary, they brought suit against the President, asking the court to declare his policy illegal under certain war powers legislation. That case raised a question regarding the proper role and relationship of the courts vis-à-vis other branches of government. Similar questions might arise regarding the courts' role in relation to private institutions or actors. A noteworthy fact is that the courts alone exercise the power of deciding *who* decides, what *procedures* must be followed and what *substantive rules* must be applied.

As American courts do their work of deciding disputes, they encounter the very hard problem of riding two horses that do not want to travel in the same direction. One judicial aim is to achieve stability in human affairs by affirming the rules of the past; the other is to facilitate change by anticipating the needs of the future. A vigorous debate has been raging between those who believe the courts are too much oriented to stability and the status quo and those who believe the courts are too active in fostering change. The question is not whether courts have been correct in the degree of their activism or in their decisions, but whether they have been correct in determining that they, the courts, are the proper tribunals for certain kinds of disputes, regardless of what results are reached. Can it be that there are agencies and institutions that are better able than courts to resolve some types of disputes, from the viewpoints of both the litigants and the society? Is that conceivable? Are not courts society's most civilized arenas? Can any other institution be better than a court to decide a dispute? Some Americans reflexively answer that courts are the very best forum and they resist removing any disputes from the courts or preventing any disputes from entering the courts. But to say that courts should handle *all* legal disputes would be to say that courts should handle virtually all human controversy. That might mean everything except wars, elections, lovers' quarrels, and a few other forms of disagreement. Surely, that would go too far. There are various reasons for concluding that courts are not the appropriate forum for many kinds of dispute.

In the first place, courts operate by the adversarial-adjudicative process. That imposes limitations on how well the courts can function in situations that do not present the classical form of legal dispute. The classical form has distinctive characteristics and dynamics. It is based on the parties' assuming the "I'm right, you're wrong!" posture and contending to the maximum to that effect. The outcome is in the form usually of a winner-loser determination—a zero-sum result. It was in response to the needs of such disputes of the classical legal type that the adversary-adjudicative process evolved, took on its characteristic features and became the standard modus operandi of the courts. However, not all disputes that can be framed in terms of legal entitlements and responses are well served by that mode of conducting the dispute.

In the second place, courts are expensive. They are costly for the public that maintains them and for the litigants who use them. A study of fiscal year 1982 public court costs in several state and federal courts disclosed that a case that requires one hearing, two conferences and a nonjury trial cost the government from $4,225 to $4,501 in California and from $4,503 to $14,698 in the U.S. district court, depending on the type of case. The figures for a jury-tried case went above $8,000 in California and ran from $8,422 to $15,028 in the U.S. district court. (Report for 1989–90, The Institute for Civil Justice, p. 47). These costs are acceptable for cases that raise questions of public interest, but much less so when they involve only narrow, private disputes.

Thirdly, increasing numbers of cases are not in the traditional form of a bipolar dispute, A suing B for damages, divorce or disseizin. They tend rather to be polycentric controversies involving vast webs of interrelated interests. Deciding them inevitably affects the rights of large groups of people; many possible outcomes are conceivable; wide direct consequences radiate from the decision; and large social or political stakes are implicated in them. They frequently require masses of complex, difficult-to-get data. Legislatures are in many respects better equipped to deal with disputes of this kind than courts.

Finally, there are structural limitations that argue against indefinitely expanding the number of courts and judges. While adding judges at the trial level presents no grave problems of a structural kind, expanding the size of the appellate courts does generate difficulties. It becomes nearly impossible to harmonize the varying views of randomly composed panels of appellate judges sitting at the same levels in our court systems. For those reasons, caution is called for in channeling all disputes to the courts.

SECTION 3.   ALTERNATIVES TO COURTS

SANDER, FRANK E.A., VARIETIES OF DISPUTE PROCESSING
70 F.R.D. 79 (1976).

[To control the rate of growth of cases:] we can try to prevent disputes[1] from arising in the first place through appropriate changes in the substantive law, such as the adoption of a no-fault principle for automobile injuries or the removal of a criminal sanction for certain conduct. A less obvious substantive law issue that may have a bearing on the extent of litigation that arises is whether we opt for a discretionary rule or for one that aims to fix more or less firmly the consequences that will follow upon certain facts. For example, if a statute says that marital property on divorce will be divided in the court's discretion there is likely to be far more litigation than if the rule is, as in the community property states, that such property will normally be divided 50–50. I wonder whether legislatures and law revision commissions are sufficiently aware of this aspect of their work.

* * *

A second way of reducing the judicial caseload is to explore alternative ways of resolving disputes outside the courts, and it is to this topic that I wish to devote my primary attention. By and large we lawyers and law teachers have been far too single-minded when it comes to dispute resolution. Of course, as pointed out earlier, good lawyers have always tried to prevent disputes from coming about, but when that was not possible, we have tended to assume that the courts are the natural and obvious dispute resolvers. In point of fact there is a rich variety of different processes, which, I would submit, singly or in combination, may provide far more "effective" conflict resolution.

Let me turn now to the two questions with which I wish to concern myself:

(1) What are the significant characteristics of various alternative dispute resolution mechanisms (such as adjudication by courts, arbitration, mediation, negotiation, and various blends of these and other devices)?

(2) How can these characteristics be utilized so that, given the variety of disputes that presently arise, we can begin to develop some rational criteria for allocating various types of disputes to different dispute resolution processes?

One consequence of an answer to these questions is that we will have a better sense of what cases ought to be left in the courts for resolution,

---

1. For present purposes I use the word "dispute" to describe a matured controversy, as distinguished, for example, from a "grievance" which may be inchoate and unexpressed. [Footnote renumbered; other footnotes omitted. Eds.]

and which should be "processed" in some other way. But since this inquiry essentially addresses itself to developing the most effective method of handling disputes it should be noted in passing that one by-product may be not only to divert some matters now handled by the courts into other processes but also that it will make available those processes for grievances that are presently not being aired at all. We know very little about why some individuals complain and others do not, or about the social and psychological costs of remaining silent. It is important to realize, however, that by establishing new dispute resolution mechanisms, or improving existing ones, we may be encouraging the ventilation of grievances that are now being suppressed. Whether that will be good (in terms of supplying a constructive outlet for suppressed anger and frustration) or whether it will simply waste scarce societal resources (by validating grievances that might otherwise have remained dormant) we do not know. The important thing to note is that there is a clear trade-off: the price of an improved scheme of dispute processing may well be a vast increase in the number of disputes being processed.

The Range of Available Alternatives

There seems to be little doubt that we are increasingly making greater and greater demands on the courts to resolve disputes that used to be handled by other institutions of society. Much as the police have been looked to to "solve" racial, school and neighborly disputes, so, too, the courts have been expected to fill the void created by the decline of church and family. Not only has there been a waning of traditional dispute resolution mechanisms, but with the complexity of modern society, many new potential sources of controversy have emerged as a result of the immense growth of government at all levels, and the rising expectations that have been created.

Quite obviously, the courts cannot continue to respond effectively to these accelerating demands. It becomes essential therefore to examine other alternatives.

GREEN, A COMPREHENSIVE APPROACH TO THE THEORY AND PRACTICE OF DISPUTE RESOLUTION
34 J.Legal Educ. 245, 247–48 (1984).*

[T]he focus in law schools on "disputes" as "litigation" ignores the more fundamental question of whether a dispute ought to be adjudicated rather than arbitrated, mediated, negotiated, investigated by a body of fact finders, or submitted to a "Mini-Trial." Worse, the assumption that "dispute" means "adjudication" also tends to foreclose debate on how scarce resources ought to be allocated among dispute resolution systems. The automatic response by many to problems of court conges-

* Footnotes omitted.

tion and delay is to suggest that we build more courts and appoint more judges. But, while we may need more courts and judges, a broader and more comprehensive policy analysis would first inquire whether the public would be better served instead by hiring public mediators, providing free arbitration, or training law students and laymen to be better negotiators.

To correct this narrowness of vision, lawyers and policymakers must begin to think comprehensively and strategically about "disputes" rather than about "litigation," or, for that matter, about mediation, negotiation, arbitration, or any other single dispute resolution process. To think strategically and comprehensively about dispute resolution, one must first understand the characteristics, dynamics, advantages, disadvantages, costs, and benefits of each dispute resolution process and how each process interacts with the others. One must also understand how each process fulfills or reflects larger political, cultural, and social values, and the practical barriers to the use of each process.

THE ROLE OF COURTS IN AMERICAN SOCIETY
(J. Lieberman ed. 1984, 94–101)*

IV. COURTS IN RELATION TO OTHER DISPUTE-RESOLVING MECHANISMS AND INSTITUTIONS

A. INTRODUCTION

More and more, people have expressed the desire to channel disputes to the institution or mechanism best suited to resolve them. To judge which is best suited for which disputes we need to know how alternative mechanisms differ from courts and from each other. We must analyze the needs implicit in various kinds of disputes in order to compare each to the capabilities of alternative mechanisms, which differ in objectives, values, and functioning.

The capabilities of adjudication can be summarized in these terms: (1) It decides disputes according to law. (2) It declares legal norms as a byproduct of the decision. (3) It casts a "shadow" over others in the community; that is, it lays down guidelines in the form of rules so that others can bargain knowing what the end result will be if they do not reach an agreed settlement and find that they have to turn to the courtroom. (4) It helps educate the public in the decencies of disputing, especially in criminal cases but also in civil ones. (5) Adjudication serves other ends and advances other values besides truth-seeking; for example, it teaches respect for confidential communications, it enforces evidentiary exclusions, statutes of limitations (for repose in the community), and *res judicata* (to prevent repetition). In this section, we

* Footnotes omitted.

compare these values and functions to those served by other means of resolving disputes.

B. THE MECHANISMS COMPARED

At least eight other mechanisms are available.

1. Arbitration

Arbitration is a species of adjudication, not a distinct form. It can be divided into two types: (1) when the parties voluntarily submit to it; for example, by signing a general grievance clause in a contract or by consenting after a dispute has arisen; and (2) when the state requires certain types of cases to be submitted initially to arbitration. Both types are distinguished by the relaxation of the usual rules of procedure and evidence, but they differ in the nature of the judge (the consensual arbitrator is private; the arbitrator imposed on the parties is at least quasi-public) and in the extent of finality (virtually complete in voluntary arbitration; subject to de novo review in compulsory arbitration).

While it has been suggested that arbitration serves mainly as a system to give the lion's share to the lion, it actually has worthier objectives and values; e.g., to: (1) achieve speedier, simpler, final resolution of disputes; (2) do so privately, conveniently, less formally; (3) give the parties more control over the scheduling and bounds of the proceeding (they may limit what the arbitrator may do and decide); and (4) render a decision through experts rather than lay persons or in any event non-experts.

Arbitration is arguably preferable to court adjudication from the parties' viewpoint when speedy resolution is urgently needed, when the legal positions are unclear and not susceptible to definitive determination, when privacy is important and discovery unimportant, when finality is more desirable than a chance to obtain appellate review for correctness, and when the parties do not require judicially-enforceable precedent to be created. From the public's point of view, arbitration is preferable when the disposition of individual cases in the manner outlined is more important than the announcement of rules to guide future cases. Moreover, because arbitration stresses adversariness far less than litigation, an arbitrated disposition will usually serve far better than a court to preserve pre-existing and ongoing relationships, such as those in labor-management and contractor-subcontractor disputes.

2. Mediation

Mediation and adjudication differ in three basic respects: (1) Unlike a judge or arbitrator, a mediator lacks power to decide a dispute by imposing a solution. (2) The mediator attempts to bring about a negotiated resolution by proposing solutions, communicating the parties' positions and priorities each to the other, and facilitating discovery of common ground. The parties thus have total control over both decision and process * * *. (3) The outcome need not be principled, in the sense that it accords with some prior rational standard. Subject to the following caveat, a "correct" result in mediation is whatever the parties will accept. The caveat is this: Increasing numbers of professional mediators believe that they ought not be party to an overreaching agreement, such as a one-sided divorce settlement, arrived at through the ignorance or powerlessness of one of the parties.

Compared to adjudication and other forms of dispute resolution, mediation has four benefits: (1) It gives the parties greater control over the process than they have in adjudication. (2) It permits the parties to arrive at flexible solutions. (3) The process itself can educate the parties and in so doing help preserve an ongoing relationship by helping them learn to deal with future disputes. (4) The evidence suggests that the rate of compliance is higher for mediated agreements than for other types.

Mediation is preferable to adjudication or arbitration, therefore, when the claim of legal entitlement is missing or weak, when a rational, controlling principle is absent or only dimly fits the situation. It is particularly useful in those situations that Fuller termed "polycentric" or "many centered"; i.e., those in which "there is no single solution, or simple set of solutions, toward which the parties meeting in open court could address themselves." When no authoritative legal standard exists or can be fashioned, nothing in the logic of adjudication permits a judge to pick and choose an "ideal" solution from among the calculus of preferences. Examples are decisions about the positions that football players on a team will play (in the absence of a contract entitling the promisee to a particular spot) and setting wages and prices.

Mediation is often used in situations—such as a strike by public employees against a municipal transit company for higher wages—when it is meaningful to talk of the fairness or justice of the settlement beyond the perspective of the immediate parties, since its terms can have fiscal repercussions for local taxpayers and users. Nevertheless, the correctness of the outcome is ultimately what the parties agree on. As Fuller puts it: "The morality of mediation lies in the optimum settlement, a settlement in which each party gives up what he values less, in return for what he values more. The morality of arbitration lies in a decision according to the law of contract." And, it could be added, the morality of adjudication lies in a decision according to law.

3. Conciliation

Conciliation is a weak form of mediation. Unlike the mediator, the conciliator has no authority to propose his own solutions or suggest new ideas as a means of breaking an impasse in negotiations. In essence, the conciliator is a facilitator of negotiation between the parties. Like the mediator, the conciliator will pass on the parties' positions and priorities and will facilitate the search for common ground.

4. Negotiation

In negotiation, the parties dispense with a third-party adjudicator or facilitator and seek to resolve the dispute privately between themselves. Negotiation has all the advantages just enumerated for mediation, to which the parties need repair only if they cannot themselves negotiate an agreement.

Of course, negotiation in the form of bargaining is a fundamental means of interchange among individuals; it takes place over virtually the whole range of human activities and need not arise solely in the context of a dispute. Nor are negotiations and other forms of dispute resolution mutually exclusive. Often negotiation is the first process in a sequence of dispute resolution mechanisms (for example, labor agreements that contain a clause requiring the parties to negotiate face to face). But negotiation also is closely intertwined with adjudication, because the parties often need to be pushed into negotiation—when, for example, one party has overwhelming power. With its coercive process, a court can equalize power and alter the circumstances sufficiently that the parties will sit down at the bargaining table and negotiate, hoping to find a mutual resolution superior to that which the court will impose.

5. Consultation

Consultation is akin to adjudication but lacks the norm of "strong responsiveness." A decision maker must assure the affected parties the opportunity to present reasoned arguments and proofs, and he must attend to them, but he is not obligated to rely on or respond to them in reaching his decision. "The decision maker may base his decision solely on evidence he has himself collected, on his own experience, on his institutional preferences, and on rules neither adduced nor addressed by the parties." Consultation is preferable to adjudication when it is desirable for the decision maker to possess discretion to declare new legal norms. * * *

6. Inquisitorial Approach

A proceeding is inquisitorial when the decision-maker can reach out to seize hold of the controversy by initiating the inquiry and defining its scope. Legislative committee hearings are a familiar example of the inquisitorial approach. The committee may listen to whomever it pleases, no one has a legal right to appear before it, and it may take whatever action it chooses—for example, to issue a subpoena or move to the floor of the legislature a bill of impeachment—or take no action, regardless of the arguments of those who appeared before it.

In the context of resolving individual disputes, the "benign" version of the inquisitorial model, and the one that has sparked the most interest, is the *ombudsman.* Proponents see the ombudsman as preferable to judges to test centralized administrative decisions because under these circumstances adversary presentation of proofs and reasoned arguments is frequently impossible (in large part because of the disparities between the parties in sophistication, economic power, and relative position). . . . Because full-scale adversary proceedings can disrupt ongoing relationships within institutions, many observers are beginning to recognize that in some contexts (including determination of public welfare benefits, school discipline, and correction of prison conditions), a more suitable process for dispute resolution must be found, such as the ombudsman or some form of administrative grievance mechanism. It should be noted that normally the ombudsman has no power to compel resolution of grievances.

7. Administration

Administrative proceedings can take two principal forms: administrative (adjudicatory) hearings and rule-making. The principles of adjudication applicable in court apply in the main to administrative hearings also. But when a governmental agency sits down to shape public policy by devising rules, the process is different. Under administrative procedures, the parties may be consulted but often are in control neither of process nor decision. Lack of party control is not universally true: in many instances statutes give parties to administrative proceedings as much control over process as they would have in court. Regardless of the range of process control, the administrative decision maker has a far greater capacity than the judge to define a problem systematically. Like legislation, administration need not deal with narrowly-focused legal disputes. The administrator has greater flexibility in selecting relevant information: "To act wisely, the economic manager must take into account every circumstance relevant to his decision and must make himself assume the initiative in discovering what circumstances are relevant. . . . The judge, on the other hand, acts upon those facts that are in advance deemed relevant under declared principles of decision."

In defining a solution, moreover, the administrator can seek the optimum solution; the judge is often restricted to ordering the minimal solution legally acceptable. In reaching his decision, the administrator may act in the absence of authoritative standards, whereas the judge is usually constrained from doing so. . . .

8. Legislation

Legislation is the form of governmental power that in a democratic society sweeps most broadly and generally in dealing with the society's needs and problems; it is a power that enacts general norms and specific rules that courts apply, creates institutional structures, and provides finances to operate them. A legislature does not ordinarily proceed on a case-by-case basis, and it need not await action by citizens or organizations to set its processes in motion. In short, a legislature is self-activating and establishes its own agenda.

The legislative process neither requires nor contemplates that all those generally affected will participate by proofs and arguments directly in making laws. Virtual representation is acceptable. Neither a complete factual record nor an evidentiary hearing must precede action. Legislators are not bound by any authoritative standard (although they are bound by constitutional prohibitions); within fairly broad limits they are free to pursue any aim or social goal of their choice. This choice need not be rational in the sense that the means chosen can be shown to produce the desired goal. In an assembly of equals with different views of means and ends there need not be, and often cannot be, a rational and principled way to rank and accommodate competing priorities. In pursuing their programs, legislators can exercise the power of the purse in a manner that courts, no matter how creative and imaginative, cannot duplicate, and they can mobilize public support for their initiatives and programs by communicating with the public in ways denied to the courts.

SECTION 4. THE ADVERSARY PROCESS

In a famous phrase, Mr. Justice Jackson declared that "a common law trial is and always should be an adversary proceeding." See Hickman v. Taylor, 329 U.S. 495, 516, 67 S.Ct. 385, 396, 91 L.Ed. 451, 465 (1947). While lacking a precise and authoritative definition, the term "adversary proceeding" is usually regarded as the English-speaking world's characteristic process of resolving legal disputes by assigning to the lawyers the functions of initiating and molding the questions requiring decision, adducing the evidence and furnishing the momentum for the contest. The judges are expected to decide questions as and when the lawyers present them, to control the tempo of the lawsuit, to direct its progress and to see to it that lawyers, jurors, witnesses and other actors function as the law intends.

The term "adversary process" generally conveys the idea of combat: usually a contest of trained champions in a forensic setting. That connotation has an easily understood basis. The most vivid historical antecedent of the modern American courtroom contest is the ancient common-law trial by battle, with its image of clashing gladiators in fights to the finish. In the dictionary definition the impression created by the gladiatorial image is manifest. Adversary is defined as

> "involving the Anglo-American system of procedure for conducting trials under strict rules of evidence with the right of cross-examination and argument, one party with his witnesses striving to prove the facts essential to his case the other party striving to disprove those facts or to establish an affirmative defense." (See Webster's Third New International Dictionary, 1961.)

While correct in a general way, the picture of contentious gladiators championing their clients' causes overlooks two other aspects of the adversary process that are central to this discussion. One has to do with the power of the litigants in relation to the power of the court and can be conveyed in overstated terms in the phrase "active advocates, passive judges." The other is the privilege the adversary process accords each side to shun, withhold or even obscure the truth instead of being bound to reveal it fully. An epitomizing phrase would be: "A trial is a contest of wits, not a search for the truth." Sometimes this is called the sporting theory of justice.

To say the lawyer is to serve as the client's champion does not reveal which rules the champion must obey in defending his principal's interests. Is the lawyer's primary duty to advance the client's cause or to unearth the factual truth and the legal right of the matter? The answer is: at times one, at times the other. Particularly with regard to the facts, in many circumstances the rules of engagement for legal gladiators permit them to hold back parts of the truth, and most particularly in defending a person accused of crime. At other times the rules require the lawyer to reveal information that damages a client's interests. That is to say, giving a lawyer the status of gladiator does not carry with it the implication that the lawyer is freed from the obligation to try to unearth the truth even while striving to advance a client's cause.

In the same way, the party-control aspect of the adversary process does not necessarily coincide with the truth-limiting privilege. The system at times gives the adversaries a large measure of control over the scope of a lawsuit yet sternly limits their privilege to withhold the truth about a matter once it has been put in issue. A district attorney, for example, wields a large measure of control over the case in deciding whether to seek an indictment, what counts to charge, which suspects to name as defendants, which witnesses to call at the trial and what questions to ask. At the same time he is duty-bound to reveal evidence favorable to the defense. That is a common example of the system's combining at one time a high level of control of the case with a stern duty to aid the search for truth. This also occurs in civil cases, where both sides often find themselves on the one hand free to control the initiation, formulation and progress of the lawsuit and on the other hand bound to reveal a good deal of evidence they would not volunteer and even some that badly damages their clients' interests.

The British also embrace the adversary process, particularly with regard to permitting parties to control the lawsuit. And despite prevalent myths about the "inquisitorial" procedures that are supposed to flourish in civil-law countries, the fact is that most of them accord a large measure of responsibility and control to the lawyers. Judges are not free in those countries to pursue truth and justice by initiating or carrying on spontaneous investigations. Perhaps the least adversarial approach to be found in any highly developed country is that of Japan, where the desirability of maintaining harmony in human affairs is one of the most deeply held values. As a result, conciliation and mediation have a much higher standing and litigation a much lower standing in their approach to resolving legal disputes.

In this country the adversary process reaches nearly the level of constitutional imperative. The Supreme Court has said that "concrete adverseness" is necessary because it "sharpens the presentation of the issues upon which the courts so largely depend for illumination of difficult * * * questions." Without it, the dispute may not be entertainable in the federal courts as a case or controversy. (See Baker v. Carr, 369 U.S. 186, 204, 82 S.Ct. 691, 703, 7 L.Ed.2d 663 (1962).)

WEBSTER EISENLOHR, INC. v. KALODNER, 145 F.2d 316 (3d Cir.1944), cert. denied 325 U.S. 867, 65 S.Ct. 1404, 89 L.Ed. 1986 (1945): Speese, a preferred stockholder of Webster Eisenlohr, brought a class action on behalf of himself and other preferred shareholders, claiming the preferred stock was entitled to exclusive voting power in the company and requesting equitable relief. While the suit was pending, the company offered to purchase the preferred stock. The plaintiff and stockholders for whom he was proxy sold their shares to the company and counsel for Speese at a hearing informed the court that he no longer had a client. Displeased, Judge Kalodner appointed a master to look into the matter, including the circumstances of the company's offer to the preferred stockholders, the possibility of violation of the securities laws and other possible improprieties. In issuing a writ of mandamus against the judge, the Court of Appeals found that he had exceeded his power because (145 F.2d at 319–20):

> "None of these stockholders was under guardianship; all had the full legal power to sell their shares under such circumstances as it pleased them to sell. If any one felt that he had been deceived, he could take the steps necessary to protect his rights. There was no indication that any party to the transaction was complaining. We think that neither the report to the stockholders nor the sale of their stock was involved in the litigation. It was therefore outside the scope of investigation both by the Special Master and the court itself.
>
> We do not think this view imposes unduly restrictive limitations upon courts. The judicial power is limited to deciding controversies. That has been its function historically; that is its function under the Constitution of the United States. No doubt a great deal goes on in the world which ought not to go on. If courts had general investigatory powers, they might discover some of these things and possibly right them. Whether they would do as well in this respect as officers or bodies expressly set up for that purpose may be doubted, but until the concept of judicial power is widened to something quite different from what it now is courts will better serve their public function in limiting themselves to the controversies presented by parties in litigation."

THE JUDGE'S RESPONSIBILITY

As the caseloads of courts change, so do the judicial tasks. The leisurely practices of a rural court would be absurd in a high-volume urban court. The complex calendar-management routines of a crowded city court are useless without long lists of cases. Procedures to handle complex antitrust suits obviously are unneeded in a district that has no antitrust cases. But beyond differences wrought by changes in the business of the courts, there has been a continuing examination of the question of how civil judges should function. In the case of the trial judge, the problem is two-fold: the judicial role vis-à-vis the lawyers before the court and the judge's role in relation to appellate courts. Is the judge to be an umpire or referee, taking no active hand in formulating or advancing issues the litigants choose to present?

———

Seaman Johnson sued under the Jones Act for injuries sustained on shipboard when a heavy block fell on him as he was bending over. He was unable to tell much about how the accident happened, and did not call a fellow seaman, Dudder, who had been holding the block and could have filled out the story. Dissenting from the Supreme Court's decision to allow recovery, Frankfurter, J., said (Johnson v. United States, 333 U.S. 46, 53–54, 68 S.Ct. 391, 395–96, 92 L.Ed. 468 (1948)):

"While a court room is not a laboratory for the scientific pursuit of truth, a trial judge is surely not confined to an account, obviously fragmentary, of the circumstances of a happening, * * * when he has at his command the means of exploring them fully, or at least more fully, before passing legal judgment. A trial is not a game of blind man's bluff; and the trial judge—particularly in a case where he himself is the trier of the facts upon which he is to pronounce the law—need not blindfold himself by failing to call an available vital witness simply because the parties, for reasons of trial tactics, choose to withhold his testimony.

"* * * a Federal judge * * * has the power to call and examine witnesses to elicit the truth (citation omitted). He surely has the duty to do so before resorting to guesswork in establishing liability for fault."

NOTES

(1) Federal Rules of Evidence, Rule 614, covering the calling and interrogation of witnesses by the court, provides:

"(a) **Calling by court.** The court may, on its own motion or at the suggestion of a party, call witnesses, and all parties are entitled to cross-examine witnesses thus called.

(b) **Interrogation by court.** The court may interrogate witnesses, whether called by itself or by a party.

(c) **Objections.** Objections to the calling of witnesses by the court or to interrogation by it may be made at the time or at the next available opportunity when the jury is not present."

(2) Under Rule 614, when is an objection well taken to the court's calling or interrogating a witness? If both sides (for different reasons) oppose putting a person on the witness stand, should the court ask what the reasons are and perchance reject them? Does the judge have a positive responsibility to try to unearth the truth, rather than viewing the case "from a peak of Olympian ignorance"? See Frankel, The Search For Truth: An Umpireal View, 123 U.Pa.L.Rev. 1031, 1042–43 (1975); compare Uviller, The Advocate, the Truth, and Judicial Hackles: A Reaction to Judge Frankel's Idea, 123 U.Pa.L.Rev. 1067 (1975); Weinstein, Some Difficulties in Devising Rules for Determining Truth in Judicial Trials, 66 Colum.L.Rev. 223 (1966).

FRUMMER v. HILTON HOTELS INTERNATIONAL, INC.

Supreme Court, Kings County, 1969.
60 Misc.2d 840, 304 N.Y.S.2d 335.

MANGANO, J. In this negligence action the jury has returned a verdict in favor of the defendant, and the court has been asked by the plaintiff to set aside that determination and grant a new trial. Before discussing the basis of this post-trial motion, the evidence at the trial should be briefly outlined.

On June 9, 1963, plaintiff registered as a guest at the Hilton Hotel in London, England. That night, upon returning to his room, he took a bath. The following night he followed the same procedure. On the third day of his visit, however, he came back to his room late and decided to go to bed immediately. The next morning, June 12, when he arose, he took a shower. While soaping himself he slipped in the bathtub, fell and sustained serious injuries.[1]

At the trial plaintiff sought to charge the defendant[2] with liability on three separate bases: (1) Failing to provide a rubber shower mat even after it had been specifically requested; (2) failing to install grab bars on the wall immediately adjacent to the overhead shower, and (3) not constructing the base of the tub so as to minimize the risk of a person losing his footing. Hilton Limited's position was that it had acted properly in providing all necessary safety devices and that in any case it was plaintiff's own carelessness that was the true cause of the accident. Evidence was offered by the plaintiff to establish each of his theories of liability, while Hilton countered with expert evidence tending to support its position that it had done all that reasonable care required. It may fairly be said that the evidence presented an issue of

---

1. This action was brought in this court in August 1963 against three defendants, one of whom, Hilton Hotels (U.K.) Limited, was the operator of the hotel. A serious question of this court's jurisdiction over this defendant was raised and ultimately resolved in favor of jurisdiction by the Court of Appeals (19 N.Y.2d 533).

2. References in this opinion to the defendant are to Hilton Hotels (U.K.) Limited.

fact which was for the jury to resolve and which it has—in defendants' favor.

The motion to set aside the judgment entered upon the jury's verdict is based upon two grounds. The first is that the court failed to charge properly the relevant provisions of English law, particularly the Occupiers' Liability Act of 1957 (5 and 6 Eliz. 2, C. 31), and second, that certain photographic evidence was improperly excluded.

The latter point requires only brief comment and therefore will be dealt with first. The defendant called as a witness one Del Como, who on direct testified as to the safety practices of the hotel and the hotel industry in England generally. On cross-examination of the witness plaintiff's counsel sought to introduce photographs showing that grab bars had been installed in the bathtub. It is conceded that these photographs were taken and represent a circumstance which existed only after the accident. Under settled law, the photographs were inadmissible, as they constitute evidence of subsequent repairs (Richardson on Evidence [3rd Ed., Prince], § 173). * * *

Alternatively, plaintiff's counsel argued that the photographic evidence was admissible to show how the bathtub might easily have been constructed with this added safety precaution. Had such evidence been offered as part of the plaintiff's principal case and in a manner that would have left the jury unaware that changes had in fact been made in the hotel after the accident, the court's ruling would have been otherwise. Instead, the evidence was offered in a manner calculated to bring to the jury's attention the subsequent repairs. This would have unfairly prejudiced the defendant, making hindsight rather than foresight the test of liability.

[As to the effect of the English Occupiers' Liability Act, the court concluded that the Hotel's duty was not materially affected by the statute.]

* * * Consequently, the moving papers do not establish any basis for the granting of the relief requested. Nevertheless, this discussion cannot terminate here.

During the course of the court's research on the Occupiers' Liability Act, the court became aware of an issue not raised by plaintiff's counsel. It is that contributory negligence is not a defense to this action under English law. That country has adopted a comparative negligence statute which reduces a plaintiff's damages to the extent that plaintiff can be said to be responsible for his own injuries. The statute—entitled the Law Reform (Contributory Negligence) Act (8 and 9 Geo. VI., c. 28)—became law in 1945, and provides in pertinent part (S. 1) as follows:

"(I) Where any person suffers damage as the result partly of his own fault and partly of the fault of any other person or persons, a claim in respect of that damage shall not be defeated by reason of the fault of the person suffering the damage, but the damages recoverable in respect thereof shall be reduced to such extent as the court thinks just and equitable having regard to the claimant's share in the responsibility for the damage."

Here the jury was charged in accordance with established New York law, that any negligence on the part of the plaintiff contributing to the accident required a verdict for the defendant. Three questions are thus raised: (1) Assuming that the English statute applies, was the failure to charge the provisions of that statute prejudicial? (2) If the answer to the first question is affirmative, then is the English law the proper controlling rule? (3) Again, if the answer to the latter question be in the affirmative, does plaintiff's failure to bring the matter to the court's attention preclude relief?

Reviewing the record as a whole, it cannot be gainsaid that the issue of contributory fault was important. It may well have been the decisive consideration in the jury's deliberations. This is so despite the fact that the court charged the jury that momentary forgetfulness by the plaintiff of the risk of slipping did not require a finding of contributory negligence. The defendant strenuously argued to the jury—and now in opposition to the present motion again urges—that the plaintiff, by proceeding to shower without the mat he claims he asked for, was guilty of contributory negligence as a matter of law. In light of plaintiff's fairly substantial evidence of negligence, it is reasonable to assume that this argument of the defendant carried much if not conclusive weight with the jury. There is, therefore, a strong probability that had England's comparative negligence doctrine been applied, the jury would have returned a verdict in plaintiff's favor—albeit in an amount reduced by the jury's assessment of the respective responsibilities of the plaintiff and the defendant for the accident.

[On the question of whether English rather than New York law should supply the controlling rule on the effect of the plaintiff's contributory fault, the court decided that the English comparative negligence rule should have been applied. This was based on application of the relatively new "governmental interests" analysis, the upshot of which was that New York's interest in seeing its own rule applied was in this case outweighed by its interest in applying the English rule.]

Finally, we deal with plaintiff's failure to bring the Law Reform Act to the court's attention which should normally bar any consideration of the statute's application at this point. In James v. Powell (19 N.Y.2d 249), the Court of Appeals, *sua sponte,* raised a conflict of law question which neither side had briefed or argued; but James involved the laws of a jurisdiction of the United States, of whose laws our courts are required to take judicial notice (CPLR 4511[a]). We are here dealing with the law of a foreign country where the court is authorized to take judicial notice but is not required to do so unless the party seeking to have the court invoke foreign law presents the necessary data to the court (CPLR 4511[b]). On the other hand this court has the power—which the Court of Appeals does not—to order a new trial in the interests of justice (CPLR 4404[a]), and the court is quite convinced that this is such a case. The action has been in litigation many years. A costly appeal to the Court of Appeals on the question of jurisdiction has taken place. The court elects, therefore, to take judicial notice of England's Law Reform Act of 1945.

In the court's opinion, to allow the judgment to stand would not conform with the interests of justice. Accordingly, motion for a new trial is granted.

Settle order on notice.

In Arnstein v. Porter, 154 F.2d 464 (2d Cir.1946) page 634 infra, a famous case on summary judgment, two of the Court of Appeals judges consulted the musical ken of outsiders to the record. The case turned on whether Cole Porter had plagiarized some of his most successful tunes—"Night and Day," "Begin the Beguine," and "My Heart Belongs to Daddy," for example—from the plaintiff, a little-known songwriter and well-known litigator. Both judges played it by ear. One found support for the claim of similarity in his secretary's reaction to hearing the tunes. The other found the claim fantastic after consulting the musical ear of not only his secretary but his law clerk and the organist at Yale. See Schick, Judicial Relations on the Second Circuit, 1941–1951, 44 N.Y.U.L.Rev. 939, 944 (1969). Is it proper for a judge to consult "experts" on an ex parte basis in this fashion? One of the judges in the Arnstein case objected acidly to his colleague's doing so: "Although in the old civilian practice the witnesses were heard in secret, at least each party knew who the witnesses were and was allowed to address interrogatories to them." (Quoted, id., at p. 945.)

NOTES

(1) The judges' practice of seeking reactions of law professors to knotty questions, even sensitive ones, is endemic in American appellate processes. If a losing litigant could uncover evidence that such a consultation influenced a judge's decision against him, should a rehearing be allowed before another panel of judges? Is consultation with a professor any worse than reading the same scholar's latest article on the subject? To consult with non-court personnel without notifying the parties may constitute a breach of judicial ethics. Code of Judicial Conduct for United States Judges, Canon 3A(4) (1973); Weinstein & Bonvillian, A Part-Time Clerkship Program in Federal Courts for Law Students, 68 F.R.D. 265, 273 (1975).

(2) Would it be preferable to set up a procedure by which law professors might be invited to file briefs as amici curiae? This would give the litigants an opportunity to respond to professorial errors. Cf. Denecke, The Judiciary Needs Your Help, Teachers, 22 J.Legal Ed. 197, 303 (1970). Such a system was urged by Chief Justice Roger Traynor of the Supreme Court of California. See Badlands in an Appellate Judge's Realm of Reason, 7 Utah L.Rev. 157, 170 (1960): "There is no reason why courts should not request in complicated cases the disinterested expert opinion of scholars, whether in law schools or law

offices. They could appear as amici curiae so that all members of the court and counsel for the parties would have the benefit of their views and the opportunity to present questions to them. We might well develop a tradition of regarding such public service as one of the most honorable responsibilities of the profession."

————

The Lawyer's Responsibility

An action is brought on behalf of a three-year-old child for serious injuries she sustained in a fall from the defendant's porch, allegedly because of the defendant's negligence. The plaintiff's attorney was unable to find an eye witness. The plaintiff's case consisted of testimony describing the porch and its surroundings, the finding of the injured plaintiff by a passerby and the nature and extent of the injuries. The case was dismissed at the close of the plaintiff's proof on the ground that the plaintiff had not made out a sufficient case by the circumstantial evidence.

During the presentation of the case the defendant's lawyer knew of an eye witness to the accident who was actually present in the courtroom, but did not mention the fact to the plaintiff's lawyer or to the court. The trial judge was unaware of the fact that there was an eye witness to the accident and that he was present in court.

Was the defendant's lawyer guilty of improper professional conduct in failing to disclose the information about the eye witness? Cf. Opinions of the Committees on Professional Ethics of the Association of the Bar of the City of New York and the New York County Lawyers' Ass'n 708 (1956), holding in the negative on similar facts. Would the answer be the same under the Model Rules of Professional Conduct adopted by the American Bar Association in August, 1983?

————

MODEL RULES OF PROFESSIONAL CONDUCT

RULE 1.6 Confidentiality of Information

(a) A lawyer shall not reveal information relating to representation of a client unless the client consents after consultation, except for disclosures that are impliedly authorized in order to carry out the representation, and except as stated in paragraph (b).

(b) A lawyer may reveal such information to the extent the lawyer reasonably believes necessary:

(1) to prevent the client from committing a criminal act that the lawyer believes is likely to result in imminent death or substantial bodily harm; or

(2) to establish a claim or defense on behalf of the lawyer in a controversy between the lawyer and the client, to establish a defense to a criminal charge or civil claim against the lawyer based upon conduct

in which the client was involved, or to respond to allegations in any proceeding concerning the lawyer's representation of the client.

*   *   *

RULE 3.3   Candor Toward the Tribunal

(a) A lawyer shall not knowingly:

(1) make a false statement of fact or law to a tribunal, or fail to disclose a fact in circumstances where the failure to make the disclosure is the equivalent of the lawyer's making a material misrepresentation;

(2) fail to make a disclosure of fact necessary to prevent a fraud on the tribunal;

(3) fail to disclose to the tribunal legal authority in the controlling jurisdiction known to the lawyer to be directly adverse to the position of the client and not disclosed by opposing counsel; or

(4) offer evidence that the lawyer knows to be false. If a lawyer has offered material evidence and comes to know of its falsity, the lawyer shall take reasonable remedial measures.

(b) The duties in paragraph (a) continue to the conclusion of the proceeding, and apply even if compliance requires disclosure of information otherwise confidential under Rule 1.6.

(c) A lawyer may refuse to offer evidence that the lawyer reasonably believes is false.

(d) In an ex parte proceeding, a lawyer shall inform the tribunal of all relevant facts known to the lawyer that should be disclosed to permit the tribunal to make an informed decision, whether or not the facts are adverse.

Caveat: Constitutional law defining the right to assistance of counsel in criminal cases may supersede the obligations stated in this Rule.

RULE 3.4   Fairness to Opposing Party and Counsel

A lawyer shall not:

(a) unlawfully obstruct another party's access to evidence or alter, destroy or conceal a document or other material that the lawyer knows or reasonably should know is relevant to a pending proceeding or one that is reasonably foreseeable. A lawyer shall not counsel or assist another person to do any such act;

(b) fabricate evidence, counsel or assist a witness to testify falsely, or offer an inducement to a witness that is prohibited by law;

(c) knowingly disobey an obligation under the rules of a tribunal except for an open refusal based on an assertion that no valid obligation exists;

(d) in pretrial procedure, make a discovery request that has no reasonable basis, or fail to make reasonably diligent effort to comply with a legally proper discovery request by an opposing party;

(e) in trial, allude to any matter that the lawyer does not reasonably believe is relevant or that will not be supported by admissible evidence, assert personal knowledge of facts in issue except when testifying as a witness, or state a personal opinion as to the justness of a cause, the credibility of a witness, the culpability of a civil litigant or the guilt or innocence of an accused; or

(f) request a person other than a client to refrain from voluntarily giving relevant information to another party unless:

(1) the person is a relative or an employee or other agent of a client; and

(2) it is reasonable to believe that the person's interest will not be adversely affected by refraining from giving such information.

RULE 3.5   Impartiality and Decorum of the Tribunal

A lawyer shall not:

(a) seek to influence a judge, juror, prospective juror or other decision-maker by means prohibited by law;

(b) communicate ex parte with such a person except as permitted by law; or

(c) engage in conduct intended to disrupt a tribunal.

———

M. FRANKEL, PARTISAN JUSTICE
128–29 (1980).

In an ideal world, the advocate would be zealously contentious, stretching his imagination and energies to vindicate his cause. He would not lie, however, help the client to lie, conceal evidence, help to conceal evidence, attempt to make a truthful witness seem a liar, or perform the similar daily functions of lawyers that aren't taught in law school. It is not absurdly visionary to speak of such an ideal world. Thousands of lawyers function in it already. The elementary requirements of honesty—for example, revealing to the other side pertinent evidence hurtful to one's position—are enforced against, and appear largely to be obeyed by, government lawyers. Nobody doubts that the lawyer in public service, consistently with the obligations of candor and fairness, may scale heights of effective advocacy. It is within the bounds of reason to expect similar performance generally from people united by professional canons that teach the worth of more than bread alone. And there is reason to hope that the nobler canons would be more effective in a profession less heavily influenced by the profit motive.

––––––––

M. FRANKEL, THE SEARCH FOR TRUTH CONTINUED: MORE DISCLOSURE, LESS PRIVILEGE
54 U.Colo.L.Rev. 51 (1982).

Should a lawyer help to conceal evidence or fail to disclose it? Should a lawyer assist a client to lie by leading the client through testimony the lawyer knows to be false? To what extent are affirmative answers to these questions required by the lawyer's duty to preserve client confidences or the attorney-client privilege? To what extent should affirmative answers be so required? * * *

My suggestion, stated briefly and divided into two segments for easier refutation, is this:

(1) Counsel should be under a duty in civil litigation to disclose all material evidence favorable to the other side.

(2) This requirement should not be obstructed or limited by either the professional rule protecting client confidences or the attorney-client privilege.

I make this proposal in an effort to support and implement the broader thesis that we lawyers should be pursuing the truth more than we do—and concealing it less than we do. It is my hope that others will improve upon, or destroy and replace, this particular proposal, finding better and more practical means to foster truth-telling in the courtroom.

––––––––

M. FREEDMAN, LAWYERS' ETHICS IN AN ADVERSARY SYSTEM
27–30 (1975).*

Is it ever proper for a criminal defense lawyer to present perjured testimony?

One's instinctive response is in the negative. On analysis, however, it becomes apparent that the question is an exceedingly perplexing one. My own answer is in the affirmative.

At the outset, we should dispose of some common question-begging responses. The attorney, we are told, is an officer of the court, and participates in a search for truth. Those propositions, however, merely serve to state the problem in different words: As an officer of the court, participating in a search for truth, what is the attorney obligated to do when faced with perjured testimony? That question cannot be answered properly without an appreciation of the fact that the attorney

* Footnotes omitted.

functions in an adversary system of criminal justice which * * * imposes special responsibilities upon the advocate.

First, the lawyer is required to determine "all relevant facts known to the accused", because "counsel cannot properly perform their duties without knowing the truth". * * *

Second, the lawyer must hold in strictest confidence the disclosures made by the client in the course of the professional relationship. * * *

Third, the lawyer is an officer of the court, and his or her conduct before the court "should be characterized by candor".

As soon as one begins to think about those responsibilities, it becomes apparent that the conscientious attorney is faced with what we may call a trilemma—that is, the lawyer is required to know everything, to keep it in confidence, and to reveal it to the court. Moreover, the difficulties presented by those conflicting obligations are particularly acute in the criminal defense area because of the presumption of innocence, the burden upon the state to prove its case beyond a reasonable doubt, and the right to put the prosecution to its proof. * * *

If we recognize that professional responsibility requires that an advocate have full knowledge of every pertinent fact, then the lawyer must seek the truth from the client, not shun it. That means that the attorney will have to dig and pry and cajole, and, even then, the lawyer will not be successful without convincing the client that full disclosure to the lawyer will never result in prejudice to the client by any word or action of the attorney. That is particularly true in the case of the indigent defendant, who meets the lawyer for the first time in the cell block or the rotunda of the jail. The client did not choose the lawyer, who comes as a stranger sent by the judge, and who therefore appears to be part of the system that is attempting to punish the defendant. It is no easy task to persuade that client to talk freely without fear of harm.

However, the inclination to mislead one's lawyer is not restricted to the indigent or even to the criminal defendant. Randolph Paul has observed a similar phenomenon among a wealthier class in a far more congenial atmosphere. The tax adviser, notes Mr. Paul, will sometimes have to "dynamite the facts of his case out of unwilling witnesses on his own side—witnesses who are nervous, witnesses who are confused about their own interest, witnesses who try to be too smart for their own good, and witnesses who subconsciously do not want to understand what has happened despite the fact that they must if they are to testify coherently". Mr. Paul goes on to explain that the truth can be obtained only by persuading the client that it would be a violation of a sacred obligation for the lawyer ever to reveal a client's confidence. Of course, once the lawyer has thus persuaded the client of the obligation of confidentiality, that obligation must be respected scrupulously.

In contrast to the Frankel and Freedman approaches, Professor A. Kenneth Pye suggests that "the most appropriate way of dealing with the problem is primarily through re-examination and alteration of evidentiary and procedural law, not through ethical proscriptions that would preclude counsel from asserting rights that are available to his client under law." Pye, The Role of Counsel in the Suppression of Truth, 1978 Duke L.J. 921, 925.

Which position is soundest? Why?

SECTION 5.   THE USUAL COURSE OF A CIVIL ACTION

Proper Court: Before commencing an action, the lawyer must consider what court or courts have authority to adjudicate it. This question is complicated in the United States by the fact that in addition to each state having its own system of courts there is a nationwide system of federal courts represented, at the trial court level, by one or more United States district courts sitting within each state. The "subject matter" of the adjudicatory authority of the federal courts is limited, as a general matter, to cases and controversies arising under the United States Constitution and laws (commonly called "federal question" cases) or between citizens of different states ("diversity" cases). That of the state systems extends to all types of cases, thus including concurrent authority over cases suable in the federal courts, except for special classes of "federal question" cases over which the authority of the federal courts is exclusive. Thus in many cases the plaintiff will have a choice between a federal and state court, and in most such instances if the choice is made to bring it in a state court the defendant is entitled to "remove" it to a federal court.

In addition to such adjudicatory authority or "jurisdiction" over the subject matter, the state in which the court sits must ordinarily have some close enough relation to the defendant or property involved in the suit to make it reasonable for the court to decide the case. The defendant must be given reasonable notice of the action and an opportunity to defend against the plaintiff's claim before the court can proceed.

Summons and Complaint. The action is formally commenced by service of a summons and complaint or, in some states, a summons alone with the complaint ordinarily required to be served soon thereafter. Service of the summons has a symbolic function of subjecting the defendant to the court's power—a more civilized counterpart of the earlier common law practice of the sheriff taking him into actual physical custody—and a practical one of giving him the fair notice and opportunity to be heard in opposition to the claim against him that is required by due process. The rules governing the permissible modes of service are prescribed by statute or rule in each state and by Rule 4 of the Federal Rules of Civil Procedure.

Pleadings. That complaint is a statement of the plaintiff's claim. In times past it was commonly called a declaration. It contains allegations of the events and circumstances which plaintiff contends amount to a breach of a legal obligation by the defendant and a demand for the remedy or relief to which the plaintiff believes is due. The complaint must apprise the defendant of the nature of the claim with enough clarity to permit framing a response.

If the defendant does not "appear" in response to the summons, or summons and complaint, within specified time limits a judgment by default may be entered. The response may raise objections to the court's jurisdiction or point to some other formal defect such as an improper joinder of parties or may challenge the claim "on the merits." A response on the merits may take one or more of three forms: (1) the defendant may challenge the complaint's "legal sufficiency"—i.e., whether under the applicable law the events and circumstances alleged do in law give rise to a valid claim to judicial relief; (2) deny the truth of the allegations, or (3) assert additional events and circumstances which defeat the legal effect of those alleged in the complaint even if these are true and otherwise legally sufficient—e.g., that if the defendant assaulted the plaintiff, it was done in self-defense. This type of challenge is sometimes referred to as a plea in "confession and avoidance," its traditional common law name, or as the allegation of "new matter" or, when thus asserted against the complaint, an "affirmative defense." Finally, the defendant may seek affirmative relief in the answer through a counterclaim.

The type of challenge listed first was made at common law by a "demurrer", another term that remains familiar today though its function has been taken over by a motion to dismiss. It raises an issue of law which the court may rule upon forthwith and which, if decided in defendant's favor, may dispose of the case immediately and without the need for a trial. Usually, though, after a successful challenge of this kind, the plaintiff is given at least one more chance to attempt to frame a legally sufficient complaint by amending it.

The second and third kinds of challenge are usually raised in the defendant's "answer." The second—a denial—raises an issue of fact which will require a trial unless one party can demonstrate by appropriate procedures—e.g., a motion for "summary judgment,"—that the other lacks sufficient evidentiary support for essential factual contentions to raise a bona fide issue.

The third type of challenge raises neither an issue of law nor of fact. Instead it calls upon the plaintiff to respond to the affirmative defense in a manner analogous to one or more of the same three types of challenge—demurrer (or motion to strike the defense for legal insufficiency); denial; or "confession and avoidance." The second and third may be made by the plaintiff in a pleading called a "reply," though in some jurisdictions they are deemed made automatically and the pleading stage ends with the answer unless the court orders otherwise.

The defensive moves just outlined are set out in an American Bar Association handbook entitled "Law and the Courts" (1974) which summarizes those and other pretrial procedures as follows at pp. 6–7:

Preparation for Trial

The plaintiff and defendant, through their respective attorneys, attempt to marshal all of the pertinent facts bearing upon the case. The defendant may begin his defense by filing certain pleadings, which may include one or more of the following:

Motion to Quash Service of Summons. Questions whether the defendant has been served with summons as provided by law.

Motion to Strike. Asks the court to rule whether the plaintiff's petition contains irrelevant, prejudicial or other improper matter. If it does, the court may order such matter deleted.

Motion to Make More Definite and Certain. Requires the plaintiff to set out the facts of his complaint more specifically, or to describe his injury or damages in greater detail, so that the defendant can answer more precisely.

Demurrer. Asks whether the plaintiff's petition states a legally sound cause of action against the defendant, even admitting for the purpose of the pleading that all of the facts set out by the plaintiff in his petition are true.

Answer. This statement by the defendant denies the allegations in the plaintiff's petition, or admits some and denies others, or admits all and pleads an excuse.

Cross-petition or Cross-complaint. May be filed by the defendant either separately or as part of his answer. It asks for relief or damages on the part of the defendant against the original plaintiff, and perhaps others. When a cross-petition is filed, the plaintiff may then file any of the previously-mentioned motions to the cross-petition, except a motion to quash service of summons.

Reply. Either party in the case may file a reply, which constitutes an answer to any new allegations raised by the other party in prior pleadings.

Note: A *plea* or *pleading* refers to an answer or other formal document filed in the action. The words should not be used to describe an argument made in court by a lawyer.

Taking of Depositions. A *deposition* is an out-of-court statement of a witness under oath, intended for use in court or in preparation for trial. Under prevailing statutes and rules in most jurisdictions, either of the parties in a civil action may take the deposition of the other party, or of any witness.

Depositions frequently are necessary to preserve the testimony of important witnesses who cannot appear in court or who reside in another state or jurisdiction. This might be the testimony of a friendly witness—one whose evidence is considered helpful to the plaintiff or defendant, as the case may be. Or it might involve an adverse witness whose statements are taken, by one side or the other, to determine the nature of the evidence he would give if summoned as a witness in the trial.

The deposition may take the form of answers to written questions or of oral examination followed by cross-examination.

A deposition is not a public record, and is not available to the press, until it is made so by court order.

A state may not compel the presence at a civil trial of a witness who is outside the state or who is in another county of the same state. When the testimony of such a witness is sought, the procedure is for the party seeking the testimony to apply to the court in which the case is pending for the issuance of a commission—commonly called *letters rogatory*. This is directed to an official or attorney in the jurisdiction where the witness is, empowering him to take the witness's deposition and forward it to the court.

In some states, it is not necessary to secure the issuance of a commission, but only to serve notice of the taking of the deposition upon opposing attorneys.

If a witness is absent from the jurisdiction or is unable to attend the trial in person, his deposition may be read in evidence. If a person who has given a deposition also appears as a witness at the trial, his deposition may be used to attack his credibility, if his oral testimony at the trial is inconsistent with that contained in the deposition.

Discovery. In addition to taking depositions in an attempt to ascertain the facts upon which another party relies, either party may submit written questions, called *interrogatories,* to the other party and require that such be answered under oath.

Other methods of discovery are: Requiring adverse parties to produce books, records and documents for inspection, to submit to a physical examination, or to admit or deny the genuineness of documents.

Pre-Trial Conference

After all the pleadings of both parties have been filed and the case is *at issue,* many courts then set the case for a pre-trial hearing. At this hearing, the attorneys appear, generally without their clients, and in the presence of the judge seek to agree on undisputed facts, called *stipulations.* These may include such matters as time and place in the case of an accident, the use of pictures, maps or sketches, and other matters, including points of law.

The objective of the pre-trial hearing is to shorten the actual trial time without infringing upon the rights of either party.

Pre-trial procedure, used extensively in the federal district courts, frequently results in the settlement of the case without trial. If it does not, the court assigns a specific trial date for the case, following the pre-trial hearing.

———

The ABA handbook continues with a description of the trial stage and subsequent proceedings, pointing out significant differences between civil and criminal trials that generally are applicable in courts throughout this country (pp. 13–19):

Officers of the Court

The *Judge* is the officer who is either elected or appointed to preside over the court. If the case is tried before a jury, the judge rules upon points of law dealing with trial procedure, presentation of the evidence and the law of the case. If the case is tried before the judge alone, he will determine the facts in addition to performing the aforementioned duties.

The *court clerk* is an officer of the court, also either elected or appointed, who at the beginning of the trial, upon the judge's instruction, gives the entire panel of prospective jurors (*veniremen*) an oath. By this oath, the venireman promises that, if called, he will truly answer any question concerning his qualifications to sit as a juror in the case.

Any venireman who is disqualified by law, or has a valid reason to be excused under the law, ordinarily is excused by the judge at this time. A person may be disqualified from jury duty because he is not a resident voter or householder, because of age, hearing defects, or because he has served recently on a jury.

Then the court clerk will draw names of the remaining veniremen from a box, and they will take seats in the jury box. After twelve veniremen have been approved as jurors by the judge and the attorneys, the court clerk will administer an oath to the persons so chosen "to well and truly try the cause."

The *bailiff* is an officer of the court whose duties are to keep order in the courtroom, to call witnesses, and to take charge of the jury as instructed by the court at such times as the jury may not be in the courtroom, and particularly when, having received the case, the jury is deliberating upon its decision. It is the duty of the bailiff to see that no one talks with or attempts to influence the jurors in any manner.

The *court reporter* has the duty of recording all proceedings in the courtroom, including testimony of the witnesses, objections made to evidence by the attorneys and the rulings of the court thereon, and listing and marking for identification any exhibits offered or introduced into evidence. In some states, the clerk of the court has charge of exhibits.

The *attorneys* are officers of the court whose duties are to represent their respective clients and present the evidence on their behalf, so that the jury or the judge may reach a just verdict or decision.

The role of the attorney is sometimes misunderstood, particularly in criminal proceedings. Our system of criminal jurisprudence presumes every defendant to be innocent until proved guilty beyond *a reasonable doubt.* . . .

Jury List

The trial jury in either a civil or criminal case is called a *petit jury.* It is chosen by lot by the court clerk from a previously compiled list called a *venire,* or in some places the *jury array.*

The methods of selecting names of persons for the venire vary among court jurisdictions. The lists in many states are comprised of tax assessment rolls or voter registration lists.

The law in many states requires a preliminary screening by a court official to eliminate persons unqualified or ineligible under the provisions of applicable state laws. In the federal courts, the court clerk is assisted in compiling the list by a *jury commissioner* appointed by the presiding judge.

Many persons are exempted from jury duty by reason of their occupations. These exemptions differ from state to state, but in some jurisdictions those automatically exempted include lawyers, physicians, dentists, pharmacists, teachers and clergymen. In a number of others, nurses, journalists, printers, railroad, telephone and telegraph employees, government officials, firemen and policemen are among the exempt occupational groups.

On occasion, the qualification of all the jurors may be challenged. This is called a *challenge to the array* and generally is based on the allegation that the officers charged with selecting the jurors did so in an illegal manner.

Selecting the Jury

In most cases, a jury of twelve is required in . . . [a] criminal proceeding.* In some courts, alternate jurors are selected to take the places of members of the regular panel who may become disabled during the trial. These alternate jurors hear the evidence just as do the regular jurors, but do not participate in the deliberations unless a regular juror or jurors become disabled.

The jury selection begins with the calling by the court clerk of twelve veniremen whose names are selected at random from a box, to take their places in the jury enclosure. The attorneys for the parties,

---

* Most civil actions in federal courts are tried before 6-member juries.

or sometimes the judge, may then make a brief statement of the facts involved, for the purpose of acquainting the jurors with sufficient facts so that they may intelligently answer the questions put to them by the judge and the attorneys. The questions elicit information such as the name, the occupation, the place of business and residence of the prospective juror, and any personal knowledge he may have of the case. This questioning of the jurors is known as the *voir dire.*

If the venireman expresses an opinion or prejudice which will affect his judgment in the case, the court will dismiss him for *cause,* and a substitute juror will be called by the court clerk. There is no limit on the number of jurors who may be excused for *cause.*

In addition to the challenges for cause, each party has the right to exercise a specific number of *peremptory challenges.* This permits an attorney to excuse a particular juror without having to state a cause. If a peremptory challenge is exercised, another juror then is called until attorneys on both sides have exercised all of the peremptory challenges permitted by law, or they have waived further challenges. The number of peremptory challenges is limited and varies with the type of case.

Thus, the jury is selected and then is sworn in by the court clerk to try the case. The remaining members of the jury panel are excused and directed to report at a future date when another case will be called, or excused and directed to report to another court in session at the time.

Separating the Witnesses

In certain cases, civil or criminal, the attorney on either side may advise the court that he is *calling for the rule* on witnesses. This means that, except for the plaintiff or complaining witness and the defendant, all witnesses who may testify for either party will be excluded from the courtroom until they are called to testify. These witnesses are admonished by the judge not to discuss the case or their testimony with other witnesses or persons, except the attorneys. This is sometimes called a *separation of witnesses.* If the rule is not called for, the witnesses may remain in the courtroom if they desire.

Opening Statements

After selection of the jury, the plaintiff's attorney, or attorney for the state in a criminal case, may make an opening statement to advise the jury what he intends to prove in the case. This statement must be confined to facts intended to be elicited in evidence and cannot be argumentative. The attorney for the defendant also may make an opening statement for the same purpose or, in some states, may reserve the opening statement until the end of the plaintiff's or state's case. Either party may waive his opening statement if he desires.

Presentation of Evidence

The plaintiff in a civil case, or the state in a criminal case, will begin the presentation of evidence with their *witnesses*. These usually will include the plaintiff in a civil case or complaining witness in a criminal case, although they are not required to testify.

A witness may testify to a matter of fact. He can tell what he saw, heard (unless it is hearsay as explained below), felt, smelled or touched through the use of his physical senses.

A witness also may be used to identify documents, pictures or other physical exhibits in the trial.

Generally he cannot state his opinion or give his conclusion unless he is an expert or especially qualified to do so. In some instances, a witness may be permitted to express an opinion, for example, as to the speed an auto was traveling or whether a person was intoxicated.

A witness who has been qualified in a particular field as an *expert* may give his opinion based upon the facts in evidence and may state the reasons for that opinion. Sometimes the facts in evidence are put to the expert in a question called a *hypothetical question*. The question assumes the truth of the facts contained in it. Other times, an expert is asked to state an opinion based on personal knowledge of the facts through his own examination or investigation.

Generally, a witness cannot testify to *hearsay,* that is, what someone else has told him outside the presence of the parties to the action.

Also, a witness is not permitted to testify about matters that are too remote to have any bearing on the decision of the case, or matters that are irrelevant or immaterial.

Usually, an attorney may not ask *leading questions* of his own witness, although an attorney is sometimes allowed to elicit routine, noncontroversial information. A leading question is one which suggests the answer desired.

Objections may be made by the opposing counsel to leading questions, or to questions that call for an opinion or conclusion on the part of the witness, or require an answer based on hearsay. There are many other reasons for objections under the rules of evidence.

Objections are often made in the following form: "I object to that question on the ground that it is irrelevant and immaterial and for the further reason that it calls for an opinion and conclusion of the witness." Many jurisdictions require that the objection specify why the question is not proper. The judge will thereupon sustain or deny the objection. If sustained, another question must then be asked, or the same question be rephrased in proper form.

If an objection to a question is sustained on either direct or cross-examination, the attorney asking the question may make an *offer to prove.* This offer is dictated to the court reporter away from the hearing of the jury. In it, the attorney states the answer which the witness would have given if permitted. The offer forms part of the record if the case is subsequently appealed.

If the objection is overruled, the witness may then answer. The attorney who made the objection may thereupon take an *exception,* which simply means that he is preserving a record so that, if the case is appealed, he may argue that the court erred in overruling the objection. In some states, the rules permit an automatic exception to an adverse ruling without its being asked for in each instance.

Cross-examination

When plaintiff's attorney or the state's attorney has finished his direct examination of the witness, the defendant's attorney or opposing counsel may then cross-examine the witness on any matter about which the witness has been questioned initially in direct examination. The cross-examining attorney may ask leading questions for the purpose of inducing the witness to testify about matters which he may otherwise have chosen to ignore.

On cross-examination, the attorney may try to bring out prejudice or bias of the witness, such as his relationship or friendship to the party, or other interest in the case. The witness can be asked if he has been convicted of a felony or crime involving moral turpitude, since this bears upon his credibility. *dishonesty*

The plaintiff's attorney may object to certain questions asked on cross-examination on previously mentioned grounds or because they deal with facts not touched upon in direct examination.

Re-Direct Examination

After the opposing attorney is finished with his cross-examination, the attorney who called the witness has the right to ask questions on *re-direct examination.* The re-direct examination covers new matters brought out on cross-examination and generally is an effort to rehabilitate a witness whose testimony on direct examination has been weakened by cross-examination.

Then the opposing attorney may recross-examine.

Demurrer to Plaintiff's or State's Case, or Motion for Directed Verdict

At the conclusion of the plaintiff's or state's evidence, the attorney will announce that the plaintiff or state *rests.*

Then, away from the presence of the jury, the defendant's counsel may demur to the plaintiff's or state's case on the ground that a cause of action or that the commission of a crime has not been proven. In many states, this is known as a *motion for a directed verdict,* that is, a verdict which the judge orders the jury to return.

The judge will either sustain or overrule the demurrer or motion. If it is sustained, the case is concluded. If it is overruled, the defendant then is given the opportunity to present his evidence.

Presentation of Evidence by the Defendant

The defense attorney may elect to present no evidence, or he may present certain evidence but not place the defendant upon the stand.

In a criminal case, the defendant need not take the stand unless he wishes to do so. The defendant has constitutional protection against self-incrimination. He is not required to prove his innocence. The plaintiff or the state has the *burden of proof.*

In a civil case, the plaintiff must prove his case by a *preponderance of the evidence.* This means the greater weight of the evidence.

In a criminal case, the evidence of guilt must be *beyond a reasonable doubt.* . . .

The defense attorney may feel that the burden of proof has not been sustained, or that presentation of the defendant's witnesses might strengthen the plaintiff's case. If the defendant does present evidence, he does so in the same manner as the plaintiff or the state, as described above, and the plaintiff or state will cross-examine the defendant's witnesses.

Rebuttal Evidence

At the conclusion of the defendant's case, the plaintiff or state's attorney may then present rebuttal witnesses or evidence designed to refute the testimony and evidence presented by the defendant. The matter covered is evidence on which the plaintiff or state did not present evidence in its *case in chief* initially; or it may be a new witness to contradict the defendant's witness. If there is a so-called *surprise witness,* this is often where you will find him.

After rebuttal evidence, the defendant may present additional evidence to contradict it.

Final Motions

At the conclusion of all the evidence, the defendant may again renew his demurrer or motion for directed verdict. The motion is made away from the presence of the jury. If the demurrer or motion is sustained, the case is concluded. If overruled, the trial proceeds.

Thus, the case has now been concluded on the evidence, and it is ready to be submitted to the jury.

Conferences During the Trial

Occasionally during the trial, the lawyers will ask permission to approach the bench and speak to the judge, or the judge may call them to the bench. They whisper about admissibility of certain evidence, irregularities in the trial or other matters. The judge and lawyers speak in inaudible tones because the jurors might be prejudiced by what they hear. The question of admissibility of evidence is a matter of law for the judge, not the jury, to decide. If the ruling cannot be made quickly, the judge will order the jury to retire, and will hear the attorneys' arguments outside the jury's presence.

Whenever the jury leaves the courtroom, the judge will admonish them not to form or express an opinion or discuss the case with anyone.

Closing Arguments

The attorney for the plaintiff or state will present the first argument in closing the case. Generally, he will summarize and comment on the evidence in the most favorable light for his side. He may talk about the facts and properly drawn inferences.

He cannot talk about issues outside the case or about evidence that was not presented. He is not allowed to comment on the defendant's failure to take the stand as a witness in a criminal case.

If he does talk about improper matters, the opposing attorney may object, and the judge will rule on the objection. If the offending remarks are deemed seriously prejudicial, the opposing attorney will ask that the jury be instructed to disregard them, and in some instances may move for a *mistrial,* that is, ask that the present trial be terminated and the case be set for retrial at a later date.

Ordinarily, before closing arguments, the judge will indicate to the attorneys the instructions he will give the jury, and it is proper for the attorneys in closing argument to comment on them and to relate them to the evidence.

The defendant's attorney will next present his arguments. He usually answers statements made in opening argument, points out defects in the plaintiff's case, and summarizes the facts favorable to his client.

Then the plaintiff or state is entitled to the concluding argument to answer the defendant's argument and to make a final appeal to the jury.

*   *   *

Instructions to the Jury

Although giving instructions to the jury is the function of the judge, in many states attorneys for each side submit a number of instructions designed to apply the law to the facts in evidence. The judge will indicate which instructions he will accept and which he will refuse. The attorneys may make objections to such rulings for the purpose of the record in any appeal.

The judge reads these instructions to the jury. This is commonly referred to as the judge's *charge* to the jury. The instructions cover the law as applicable to the case.

In most cases, only the judge may determine what the law is. In some states, however, in criminal cases the jurors are judges of both the facts and the law.

In giving the instructions, the judge will state the issues in the case and define any terms or words necessary. He will tell the jury what it must decide on the issues. If it is to find for the plaintiff or state, or for the defendant. He will advise the jury that it is the sole judge of the facts and of the credibility of witnesses; that upon leaving the courtroom to reach a verdict, it must elect a *foreman* of the jury and then reach a decision based upon the judgment of each individual juror. In some states, the first juror chosen automatically becomes the foreman.

In the Jury Room

After the instructions, the bailiff will take the jury to the jury room to begin deliberations.

The bailiff will sit outside and not permit anyone to enter or leave the jury room. No one may attempt to *tamper* with the jury in any way while it is deliberating.

Ordinarily, the court furnishes the jury with written forms of all possible verdicts so that when a decision is reached, the jury can choose the proper verdict form.

The decision will be signed by the foreman of the jury and be returned to the courtroom.

          *   *   *

If the jurors cannot agree on a verdict, the jury is called a *hung jury,* and the case may be retried before a new jury at a later date.

In some states, the jury may take the judge's instructions and the exhibits introduced in evidence to the jury room.

If necessary, the jury may return to the courtroom in the presence of counsel to ask a question of the judge about his instructions. In such instances, the judge may reread all or certain of the instructions previously given, or supplement or clarify them by further instructions.

If the jury is out overnight, the members often will be housed in a hotel and secluded from all contacts with other persons. In many cases, the jury will be excused to go home at night, especially if there is no objection by either party.

Verdict

Upon reaching a verdict, the jury returns to the courtroom with the bailiff and, in the presence of the judge, the parties and their respective attorneys, the verdict is read or announced aloud in open court. The reading or announcement may be made by the jury foreman or the court clerk.

Attorneys for either party, but usually the losing party, may ask that the jury be *polled,* in which case each individual juror will be asked if the verdict is his verdict. It is rare for a juror to say that it is not his verdict.

When the verdict is read and accepted by the court, the jury is dismissed, and the trial is concluded.

Motions After Verdict

Motions permitted to be made after the verdict is rendered will vary from state to state.

A *motion in arrest of judgment* attacks the sufficiency of the indictment or information in a criminal case.

A *motion for judgment non obstante veredicto* may be made after the verdict and before the judgment. This motion requests the judge to enter a judgment for one party, notwithstanding the verdict of the jury in favor of the other side. Ordinarily, this motion raises the same questions as could be raised by a motion for directed verdict.

A *motion for a new trial* sets out alleged errors committed in the trial and asks the trial judge to grant a new trial. In some states, the filing of a motion for a new trial is a condition precedent to an appeal.

Judgment

The verdict of the jury is ineffective until the judge enters *judgment* upon the verdict. In a civil damage action, this judgment might read:

> "It is, therefore, ordered, adjudged and decreed that the plaintiff do have and recover the sum of $1,000 from the defendant."

At the request of the plaintiff's lawyer, the clerk of the court in such a case will deliver a paper called an *execution* to the sheriff, commanding him to take and sell the property of the defendant and apply the proceeds to the amount of the judgment.

Sentencing

In a criminal case, if the defendant is convicted, the judge will set a date for sentencing. At that time, the judge may consider mitigating facts in determining the appropriate sentence.

In the great majority of states and in the federal courts, the function of imposing sentence is exclusively that of the judge. But in some states the jury is called upon to determine the sentences for some, or all, crimes. In these states, the judge merely imposes the sentence as determined by the jury.

Rights of Appeal

In a civil case, either party may appeal to a higher court. But in a criminal case this right is limited to the defendant. Appeals in either civil or criminal cases may be on such grounds as errors in trial procedure and errors in *substantive law*—that is, in the interpretation of the law by the trial judge. These are the most common grounds for appeals to higher courts, although there are others.

* * *

Criminal defendants have a further appellate safeguard. Those convicted in state courts may appeal to the federal courts on grounds of violation of constitutional rights, if such grounds exist. This privilege serves to impose the powerful check of the federal judicial system upon abuses that may occur in state criminal procedures.

The record on appeal consists of the papers filed in the trial court and the court reporter's transcript of the evidence. The latter is called a *bill of exceptions* or *transcript on appeal* and must be certified . . . to be true and correct. In most states, only that much of the record need be included as will properly present the questions to be raised on appeal.

Appeal

Statutes or rules of court provide for procedure on appeals. Ordinarily, the party appealing is called the *appellant,* and the other party the *appellee.*

The appeal is initiated by filing the transcript of the trial court record with the appellate court within the time prescribed. This filing marks the beginning of the time period within which the appellant must file his *brief* setting forth the reasons and the law upon which he relies in seeking a reversal of the trial court.

The appellee then has a specified time within which to file his answer brief. Following this, the appellant may file a second brief, or brief in reply to the appellee's brief.

When the appeal has been fully briefed, the case may be set for hearing on *oral argument* before the appellate court. Sometimes the court itself will ask for argument; otherwise, one of the parties may petition for it. Often, appeals are submitted *on the briefs* without argument.

Courts of appeal do not hear further evidence,* and it is unusual for any of the parties to the case to attend the hearing of the oral argument.

Generally, the case has been assigned to one of the judges of the appellate court, although the full court will hear the argument. Thereafter, it is customary for all the judges to confer on the issues presented, and then the judge who has been assigned the case will write an opinion. If a judge or judges disagree with the result, they may dissent and file a *dissenting opinion.* In many states, a written opinion is required.

An appellate court will not weigh evidence and generally will reverse a trial court for errors of law only.

Not every error of law will warrant a reversal. Some are *harmless errors*—that is, the rights of a party to a fair trial were not prejudiced by them.

However, an error of law, such as the admission of improper and persuasive evidence on a material issue, may and often does constitute a *prejudicial* and *reversible error.*

* There are very rare exceptions. [Eds.]

After the opinion is *handed down* and time for the filing of a petition for rehearing—or a petition for transfer, or a petition for *writ of certiorari* (if there is a higher appellate court)—has expired, the appellate court will send its *mandate* to the trial court for further action in the case.

If the lower court is *affirmed,* the case is ended; if reversed, the appellate court may direct that a new trial be held, or that the judgment of the trial court be modified and corrected as prescribed in the opinion.

The taking of an appeal ordinarily does not suspend the operation of a judgment obtained in a civil action in a trial court. Thus, the party prevailing in the trial court may order an execution issued on the judgment, unless the party appealing files an *appeal* or *supersedeas bond,* which binds the party and his surety to pay or perform the judgment in the event it is affirmed on appeal. The filing of this bond will *stay* further action on the judgment until the appeal has been concluded.

Part II

TRANSLATING RIGHTS INTO REMEDIES

Chapter Two

ACCESS TO COURT AND LAWYER

SECTION 1. INTRODUCTION

Legal rights do not enforce themselves. A citizen who is harmed in a way for which society has chosen to provide a remedy through law may have to seek the remedy in the courts. However attractive that path appears to be, lay persons may feel lost without the help of a lawyer. Courts and lawyers are the keys to justice.

The American citizen's access to the courts is one of the pillars of a government of laws. "Access to the courts" must mean more than some abstract or theoretical right to use the courts. It means they must be accessible in the practical sense of being financially affordable as well as physically approachable. People are entitled to pursue their claims or interpose their defenses for financial outlays that are not terrifyingly high or disproportionate to the stakes. Furthermore, the pace of the proceedings should be as rapid as a deliberative process can fairly attain. The right of access is illusory if the judicial system does not respond within a reasonable time of being invoked.

In recent years the ability of judicial systems in this country to respond with affordable and timely justice has been seriously questioned. Delay in the courts has always been a problem, but its extent and seriousness in recent decades have become egregiously troublesome. As for court costs, of late they have risen so steeply they have priced court justice out of reach in large numbers of cases of substantial importance to the ordinary citizen.

There is sound evidence that the expense of litigating—for both defendants and plaintiffs—warps the substantive law, contorts the face of justice, and, in some cases, essentially bars the courthouse door. There also is evidence that the problem is most acute when a litigant with a worthy cause is not entitled to legal aid, but must face legal expenses out of proportion to the amount at stake. Cases involving sums in the range of $1,000 to $25,000 are the hardest hit. When ordinary damage cases of that size are litigated to a conclusion, the lawyers' fees on both sides soon devour a substantial fraction of the

46

disputed amount. The plaintiff's alternative is to abandon the claim or settle under pressure, while the defendant can choose between surrendering or bargaining away a good defense on the merits because the cost of presenting it is too great. For both sides, the bright promise held up by the American justice system is frequently a chimera.

Although the professed goal of modern procedural rules is to lead to determinations that are "inexpensive" (see Fed.R.Civ.P. 1), its achievement can hardly be called an accomplished fact. Even lawyers who charge at moderate rates often price professional legal assistance beyond the reach of the average citizen. Worse still, even small-scale court charges may form insurmountable obstacles for the impecunious litigant. These circumstances threaten the ideal of keeping the courts open to every citizen.

To be sure, the way to the court is paved with rules facilitating access. Important among these is the rule permitting a civil litigant to act for herself or himself without retaining a lawyer. This rule stands in strong contrast to the prevailing rule in most countries requiring that, at least in other than minor matters, a litigant be represented by a lawyer. Also, the contingent-fee arrangement very effectively affords access to lawyer and court for rich and poor alike, in those cases in which is it available. On contingent fees, see pp. 58–59 infra. When contingent-fee arrangements are unavailable because of the nature of the case and there is no prospect of recovering attorneys' fees even if successful, a person having little money or only moderate means may not be able to afford to sue. In this country, unlike the situation in many other industralized societies, a civil litigant without the money to retain a private lawyer has not found help through public resources.

For many years the provision of legal assistance to indigents in civil actions was almost exclusively the province of the Legal Aid Society, which depended on private contributions for its financial resources. Other private organizations have grown up to serve particular constituencies in civil actions, for instance, children, tenants and minority-group members. Various public agencies providing civil legal services have had fitful careers because of their vulnerability to political cross-fire. On various legal service programs, see Pye, The Role of Legal Services in the Antipoverty Program, 31 Law & Contemp.Prob. 211 (1966); Brickman, Of Arterial Passageways Through the Legal Process: The Right of Universal Access to Courts and Lawyering Services, 48 N.Y.U.L.Rev. 595 (1973).

The traditional "American Rule" does not require a losing litigant to compensate the winner for the cost of legal representation: each side pays its own attorney and fees are not shifted as part of the judgment. There is continual agitation to change to a fee-shifting regime, either in favor of plaintiffs only (see Leubsdorf, Recovering Attorney Fees as Damages, 38 Rutgers L.Rev. 439 (1986)), or a reciprocal system. While at first blush the idea of a loser-pays rule has great appeal, close examination of its practical effects has led many observers to doubt its desirability. A leading student of the subject has analyzed the subject comprehensively in Rowe, Predicting the Effects of Attorney Fee Shifting, 47 Law & Contemp.Probs. 139 (Winter 1984). See, also, Katz, Measuring the Demand for Litigation: Is the English Rule Really Cheaper? 3 J.L.Econ. & Org. 143 (1987), considering whether fee-shifting may make litigation more costly.

SECTION 2. ACCESS TO COURT

The significance of the problem of access to courts and lawyers depends, of course, on the extent to which civil litigation is perceived as the optimal means of resolving the problems presented. If other means appear more appropriate, the pressure for facilitated access to the courts diminishes. The courts' prestige and relative insulation from political pressures (especially when staffed by judges who enjoy life tenure) make the courts most attractive to those who seek relief that the body politic may not be ready to grant. This tendency grows and stimulates resort to the courts whenever other governmental bodies do not appear to cope satisfactorily with the problems involved.

The materials that follow treat three different means of improving access to the courts for persons who would find the costs of litigating an insuperable hurdle to using the judicial process.

BODDIE v. CONNECTICUT

Supreme Court of the United States, 1971.
401 U.S. 371, 91 S.Ct. 780, 28 L.Ed.2d 113.

Mr. Justice Harlan delivered the opinion of the Court.*

Appellants, welfare recipients residing in the State of Connecticut, brought this action in the Federal District Court for the District of Connecticut on behalf of themselves and others similarly situated, challenging, as applied to them, certain state procedures for the commencement of litigation, including requirements for payment of court fees and costs for service of process, that restrict their access to the courts in their effort to bring an action for divorce.

It appears from the briefs and oral argument that the average cost to a litigant for bringing an action for divorce is $60. Section 52–259 of the Connecticut General Statutes provides: "There shall be paid to the clerks of the supreme court or the superior court, for entering each civil cause, forty-five dollars * * *." An additional $15 is usually required for the service of process by the sheriff, although as much as $40 or $50 may be necessary where notice must be accomplished by publication.

---

* Footnotes omitted.

There is no dispute as to the inability of the named appellants in the present case to pay either the court fees required by statute or the cost incurred for the service of process. The affidavits in the record establish that appellants' welfare income in each instance barely suffices to meet the costs of the daily essentials of life and includes no allotment that could be budgeted for the expense to gain access to the courts in order to obtain a divorce. Also undisputed is appellants' "good faith" in seeking a divorce.

Assuming, as we must on this motion to dismiss the complaint, the truth of the *undisputed* allegations made by the appellants, it appears that they were unsuccessful in their attempt to bring their divorce actions in the Connecticut courts, simply by reason of their indigency. The clerk of the Superior Court returned their papers "on the ground that he could not accept them until an entry fee had been paid." App. 8–9. Subsequent efforts to obtain a judicial waiver of the fee requirement and to have the court effect service of process were to no avail. Id., at 9.

Appellants thereafter commenced this action in the Federal District Court seeking a judgment declaring that Connecticut's statute and service of process provisions, "requiring payment of court fees and expenses as a condition precedent to obtaining court relief [are] unconstitutional [as] applied to these indigent [appellants] and all other members of the class which they represent." As further relief, appellants requested the entry of an injunction ordering the appropriate officials to permit them "to proceed with their divorce actions without payment of fees and costs." A three-judge court was convened pursuant to 28 U.S.C. § 2281, and on July 16, 1968, that court concluded that "a state [may] limit access to its civil courts and particularly in this instance, to its divorce courts, by the requirement of a filing fee or other fees which effectively bar persons on relief from commencing actions therein." 286 F.Supp. 968, 972.

*　*　* We now reverse. Our conclusion is that, given the basic position of the marriage relationship in this society's hierarchy of values and the concomitant state monopolization of the means for legally dissolving this relationship, due process does prohibit a State from denying, solely because of inability to pay, access to its courts to individuals who seek judicial dissolution of their marriages.

I

At its core, the right to due process reflects a fundamental value in our American constitutional system. Our understanding of that value is the basis upon which we have resolved this case.

Perhaps no characteristic of an organized and cohesive society is more fundamental than its erection and enforcement of a system of rules defining the various rights and duties of its members, enabling them to govern their affairs and definitively settle their differences in an orderly, predictable manner. Without such a "legal system," social organization and cohesion are virtually impossible; with the ability to seek regularized resolution of conflicts individuals are capable of interdependent action that enables them to strive for achievements without the anxieties that would beset them in a disorganized society. Put more succinctly, it is this injection of the rule of law that allows society to reap the benefits of rejecting what political theorists call the "state of nature."

American society, of course, bottoms its systematic definition of individual rights and duties, as well as its machinery for dispute settlement, not on custom or the will of strategically placed individuals, but on the common-law model. It is to courts, or other quasi-judicial official bodies, that we ultimately look for the implementation of a regularized, orderly process of dispute settlement. Within this framework, those who wrote our original Constitution, in the Fifth Amendment, and later those who drafted the Fourteenth Amendment, recognized the centrality of the concept of due process in the operation of this system. Without this guarantee that one may not be deprived of his rights, neither liberty nor property, without due process of law, the State's monopoly over techniques for binding conflict resolution could hardly be said to be acceptable under our scheme of things. Only by providing that the social enforcement mechanism must function strictly within these bounds can we hope to maintain an ordered society that is also just. It is upon this premise that this Court has through years of adjudication put flesh upon the due process principle.

Such litigation has, however, typically involved rights of defendants—not, as here, persons seeking access to the judicial process in the first instance. * * *

* * * [W]e think appellants' plight, because resort to the state courts is the only avenue to dissolution of their marriages, is akin to that of defendants faced with exclusion from the only forum effectively empowered to settle their disputes. Resort to the judicial process by these plaintiffs is no more voluntary in a realistic sense than that of the defendant called upon to defend his interests in court. * * *

IV

In concluding that the Due Process Clause of the Fourteenth Amendment requires that these appellants be afforded an opportunity to go into court to obtain a divorce, we wish to re-emphasize that we go no further than necessary to dispose of the case before us, a case where the *bona fides* of both appellants' indigency and desire for divorce are here beyond dispute. We do not decide that access for all individuals to the courts is a right that is, in all circumstances, guaranteed by the Due Process Clause of the Fourteenth Amendment so that its exercise may not be placed beyond the reach of any individual, for, as we have already noted, in the case before us this right is the exclusive precondition to the adjustment of a fundamental human relationship. The requirement that these appellants resort to the judicial process is entirely a state-created matter. Thus we hold only that a State may not, consistent with the obligations imposed on it by the Due Process Clause of the Fourteenth Amendment, pre-empt the right to dissolve this legal relationship without affording all citizens access to the means it has prescribed for doing so.

Reversed.

[Concurring opinion by JUSTICE DOUGLAS and dissenting opinion by JUSTICE BLACK omitted.]

NOTES

(1) Shortly after the decision in the principal case, eight additional cases raising similar questions reached the Supreme Court. They are described summarily in Justice Black's dissent from the denial of certiorari in five of these cases. Meltzer v. C. Buck LeCraw & Co., 402 U.S. 954, 91 S.Ct. 1624, 29 L.Ed.2d 124 (1971):

"One case, Sloatman v. Gibbons, No. 5067, is distinguishable from *Boddie* only by the fact that Arizona permits an extension of time for an indigent to pay the statutory fee when filing for a divorce. In re Garland, No. 5971, involves the right of a bankrupt to file a petition for discharge in bankruptcy without payment of the $50 statutory fee. Meltzer v. LeCraw & Co., No. 5048, involves a slightly more subtle form of handicap to the indigent seeking judicial resolution of a dispute. In that case a tenant who fights his eviction by resort to the judicial process risks the penalty of a judgment for double the rent due during the litigation if he loses. Two other cases, Frederick v. Schwartz, No. 5050, and Bourbeau v. Lancaster, No. 5054, involve indigents who have lost civil cases—a welfare claim and child guardianship claim—and who cannot afford to pay the fees for docketing an appeal. Beverly v. Scotland Urban Enterprises, Inc., No. 5208, and Lindsey v. Normet, No. 6158, involve indigents who cannot post the penalty bonds required to appeal from adverse judgments in housing-eviction cases. And finally, Kaufman v. Carter, No. 6375, is perhaps the most surprising of all eight cases because in that case an indigent mother was denied court-appointed counsel to defend herself against a state civil suit to declare her an unfit mother and take five of her seven children away from her.

The Court has decided to note probable jurisdiction in No. 6158, Lindsey v. Normet. Review will be denied in five of the other cases—Nos. 5048, 5208, 5054, 5971, and 6375—while the judgments in the two remaining cases are to be vacated and the cases remanded for reconsideration in light of the decision in *Boddie*."

Justice Black, although the only dissenter in Boddie, thought that Boddie required review or outright reversal of all eight cases.

(2) In Lindsey v. Normet, 405 U.S. 56, 92 S.Ct. 862, 31 L.Ed.2d 36 (1972), the Court held that the requirement that the tenant who wished to contest an eviction put up a bond for twice the rent violated the equal protection clause.

UNITED STATES v. KRAS

Supreme Court of the United States, 1973.
409 U.S. 434, 93 S.Ct. 631, 34 L.Ed.2d 626.

MR. JUSTICE BLACKMUN delivered the opinion of the Court.*

The Bankruptcy Act and one of this Court's complementary Orders in Bankruptcy impose fees and make the payment of those fees a condition to a discharge in voluntary bankruptcy.

Appellee Kras, an indigent petitioner in bankruptcy, challenged the fees on Fifth Amendment grounds. [Three charges totaling $50 are payable on filing the petition, except that in voluntary bankruptcy the fees may be paid in installments over six months with a possible three-month extension. Kras' household consisted of six persons (three adults and three small children) living in a 2½-room apartment on $366 a month in public assistance.]

* * *

5. Kras seeks a discharge in bankruptcy of $6,428.69 in total indebtedness in order to relieve himself and his family of the distress of financial insolvency and creditor harassment and in order to make a new start in life. It is especially important that he obtain a discharge of his debt to Metropolitan soon "because until that is cleared up Metropolitan will continue to falsely charge me with fraud and give me bad references which prevent my getting employment."

The District Court's opinion contains an order, 331 F.Supp., at 1215, granting Kras' motion for leave to file his petition in bankruptcy without prepayment of fees. He was adjudged a bankrupt on September 13, 1971. Later, the referee, upon consent of the parties, entered an order allowing Kras to conduct all necessary proceedings in bankruptcy up to but not including discharge. The referee stayed the discharge pending disposition of this appeal.

The District Court [held], that the prescribed fees, payment of which was required as a condition precedent to discharge, served to deny Kras "his Fifth Amendment right of due process, including equal protection." Id., at 1212. It held that a discharge in bankruptcy was a "fundamental interest" that could be denied only when a "compelling government interest" was demonstrated. It noted, . . . that provision should be made by the referee for the survival, beyond bankruptcy, of the bankrupt's obligation to pay the fees. The court rested its decision primarily upon Boddie v. Connecticut, 401 U.S. 371, 91 S.Ct. 780, 28 L.Ed.2d 113 (1971), which came down after the First Circuit's decision in *Garland,* supra. A number of other district courts and bankruptcy referees have reached the same result.

Kras contends that his case falls squarely within *Boddie.* The Government, on the other hand, stresses the differences between divorce (with which *Boddie* was concerned) and bankruptcy, and claims

---

* Footnotes omitted.

that *Boddie* is not controlling and that the fee requirements constitute a reasonable exercise of Congress' plenary power over bankruptcy.

* * *

B. The appellants in *Boddie,* on the one hand, and Robert Kras, on the other, stand in materially different postures. The denial of access to the judicial forum in *Boddie* touched directly, as has been noted, on the marital relationship and on the associational interests that surround the establishment and dissolution of that relationship. * * * Kras' alleged interest in the elimination of his debt burden, and in obtaining his desired new start in life, although important and so recognized by the enactment of the Bankruptcy Act, does not rise to the same constitutional level. * * * If Kras is not discharged in bankruptcy, his position will not be materially altered in any constitutional sense. Gaining or not gaining a discharge will effect no change with respect to basic necessities. We see no fundamental interest that is gained or lost depending on the availability of a discharge in bankruptcy.

C. Nor is the Government's control over the establishment, enforcement, or dissolution of debts nearly so exclusive as Connecticut's control over the marriage relationship in *Boddie.* * * *

However unrealistic the remedy may be in a particular situation, a debtor, in theory, and often in actuality, may adjust his debts by negotiated agreement with his creditors. At times the happy passage of the applicable limitation period, or other acceptable creditor arrangement, will provide the answer. * * *

D. We are also of the opinion that the filing fee requirement does not deny Kras the equal protection of the laws. Bankruptcy is hardly akin to free speech or marriage or to those other rights, so many of which are imbedded in the First Amendment, that the Court has come to regard as fundamental and that demand the lofty requirement of a compelling governmental interest before they may be significantly regulated. * * *

E. There is no constitutional right to obtain a discharge of one's debts in bankruptcy. The Constitution, Art. I, § 8, cl. 4, merely authorizes the Congress to "establish * * * uniform Laws on the subject of Bankruptcies throughout the United States." * * * *full force*

F. The rational basis for the fee requirement is readily apparent. Congressional power over bankruptcy, of course, is plenary and exclusive. * * * It sought to make the system self-sustaining and paid for by those who use it rather than by tax revenues drawn from the public at large. * * *

G. If the $50 filing fees are paid in installments over six months as General Order No. 35(4) permits on a proper showing, the required average weekly payment is $1.92. If the payment period is extended for the additional three months as the Order permits, the average weekly payment is lowered to $1.28. This is a sum less than the payments Kras makes on his couch of negligible value in storage, and less than the price of a movie and little more than the cost of a pack or two of cigarettes. If, as Kras alleges in his affidavit, a discharge in bankruptcy will afford him that new start he so desires, and the Metropolitan then no longer will charge him with fraud and give him bad references, and if he really needs and desires that discharge, this much available revenue should be within his able-bodied reach when the adjudication in bankruptcy has stayed collection and has brought to a halt whatever harassment, if any, he may have sustained from creditors.

VI

* * *

We decline to extend the principle of *Boddie* to the no-asset bankruptcy proceeding. That relief, if it is to be forthcoming, should originate with Congress. See Shaeffer, Proceedings in Bankruptcy In Forma Pauperis, 69 Col.L.Rev. 1203 (1969).

Reversed.

MR. CHIEF JUSTICE BURGER, concurring. [Omitted.]

* * *

MR. JUSTICE STEWART, with whom MR. JUSTICE DOUGLAS, MR. JUSTICE BRENNAN, and MR. JUSTICE MARSHALL join, dissenting. [Omitted.]

* * *

MR. JUSTICE DOUGLAS and MR. JUSTICE BRENNAN, dissenting. [Omitted.]

* * *

MR. JUSTICE MARSHALL, dissenting.

The dissent of Mr. Justice Stewart, in which I have joined, makes clear the majority's failure to distinguish this case from Boddie v. Connecticut, 401 U.S. 371, 91 S.Ct. 780, 28 L.Ed.2d 113 (1971). I add only some comments on the extraordinary route by which the majority reaches its conclusion.

A. The majority notes that the minimum amount that appellee Kras must pay each week if he is permitted to pay the filing fees in installments is only $1.28. It says that "this much available revenue should be within his able-bodied reach." * * *

* * * I cannot agree with the majority that it is so easy for the desperately poor to save $1.92 *each week* over the course of six months. The 1970 Census found that over 800,000 families in the Nation had annual incomes of less than $1,000 or $19.23 a week. U.S. Bureau of Census, Current Population Reports, series P–60, No. 80; U.S. Bureau of Census, Statistical Abstract of the United States 1972, p. 323. I see no reason to require that families in such straits sacrifice over 5% of their annual income as a prerequisite to getting a discharge in bankruptcy.

It may be easy for some people to think that weekly savings of less than $2 are no burden. But no one who has had close contact with poor people can fail to understand how close to the margin of survival many of them are. A sudden illness, for example, may destroy whatever savings they may have accumulated, and by eliminating a sense of security may destroy the incentive to save in the future. A pack or two of cigarettes may be, for them, not a routine purchase but a luxury indulged in only rarely. The desperately poor almost never go to see a movie, which the majority seems to believe is an almost weekly activity. They have more important things to do with what little money they have—like attempting to provide some comforts for a gravely ill child, as Kras must do.

It is perfectly proper for judges to disagree about what the Constitution requires. But it is disgraceful for an interpretation of the Constitution to be premised upon unfounded assumptions about how people live. * * * If the case is to turn on distinctions between the role of courts in divorce cases and their role in bankruptcy cases, I agree with Mr. Justice Stewart that this case and *Boddie* cannot be distinguished; the role of the Government in standing ready to enforce an otherwise continuing obligation is the same.

However, I would go further than Mr. Justice Stewart. I view the case as involving the right of access to the courts, the opportunity to be heard when one claims a legal right, and not just the right to a discharge in bankruptcy. When a person raises a claim of right or entitlement under the laws, the only forum in our legal system empowered to determine that claim is a court. Kras, for example, claims that he has a right under the Bankruptcy Act to be free of any duty to pay his creditors. There is no way to determine whether he has such a right except by adjudicating his claim. Failure to do so denies him access to the courts.

The legal system is, of course, not so pervasive as to preclude private resolution of disputes. But private settlements do not determine the validity of claims of right. Such questions can be authoritatively resolved only in courts. It is in that sense, I believe, that we should consider the emphasis in *Boddie* on the exclusiveness of the judicial forum—and give Kras his day in court.

NOTES

(1) In Ortwein v. Schwab, 410 U.S. 656, 93 S.Ct. 1172, 35 L.Ed.2d 572 (1973), rehearing denied 411 U.S. 922, 93 S.Ct. 1551, 36 L.Ed.2d 315, the Supreme Court held, on the authority of *Kras*, that a welfare recipient was not constitutionally entitled to waiver of a $25 appellate court filing fee in order to permit appeal from an order reducing welfare benefits. Justices Stewart, Douglas, Brennan and Marshall found Boddie controlling and dissented. See also Hill v. Michigan, 488 F.2d 609 (6th Cir.1973), cert. denied 416 U.S. 973, 94 S.Ct. 1999, 40 L.Ed.2d 563 (appellant denied constitutional right to waiver of filing fee and free transcript in proceeding contesting propriety of his dismissal on the ground that his case was frivolous).

(2) After *Kras* and *Ortwein*, to what extent does the Constitution guarantee access to court? Which is the proper constitutional basis, due process or equal protection? What is the likelihood that Boddie will be given an expansive interpretation? See Smit, Constitutional Guarantees in Civil Litigation in the

United States of America, in Fundamental Guarantees of the Parties in Civil Litigation 419, 429–431 (Cappelletti & Tallon, eds., 1973); Comment, The Heirs of Boddie: Court Access for Indigents After Kras and Ortwein, 8 Harv.Civ.Rt.L. Rev. 571 (1973); Note, U.S. v. Kras: Justice at a Price, 40 Bklyn.L.Rev. 147 (1973).

SECTION 3. ACCESS TO LAWYERS

A. THE RIGHT TO COUNSEL

The right to retained counsel must be distinguished from that to assigned counsel. Thus far, whether a civil litigant has the right to be assisted by a lawyer he has hired has not given rise to problems. To the extent that a fair hearing is impossible without the assistance of retained counsel, this right appears to have good claims to constitutional protection. Cf. Goldberg v. Kelly, 397 U.S. 254, 90 S.Ct. 1011, 25 L.Ed.2d 287 (1970) (welfare recipient entitled to hearing with retained attorney before benefits can be terminated); Powell v. Alabama, 287 U.S. 45, 53 S.Ct. 55, 77 L.Ed. 158 (1932) (arbitrary refusal to hear party by counsel denial of due process) (dictum).

A considerably more difficult problem is to what extent a civil litigant has a right to assigned counsel. Since such a right is ordinarily not recognized by statute, it would have to be derived from constitutional premises. Thus far, the Supreme Court has not spoken with a clear voice on this problem. It is part of the broader problem of whether and to what extent constitutional law (federal or state) recognizes not only a right to enter through the court doors, but also to have all forms of assistance without which a litigant cannot adequately protect his interests once he is in court. The increased activism on behalf of poor litigants makes it likely that the Supreme Court will continue to be asked to determine which of these forms of assistance are essential ingredients of the constitutional right to a fair hearing. See also the dissenting opinions of Justice Black in Goldberg v. Kelly, 397 U.S. 254, 90 S.Ct. 1011, 25 L.Ed.2d 287 (1970) (" * * * it is difficult to believe that the same reasoning process [i.e., that recognizing a constitutional right to retained counsel] would not require the appointment of counsel, for otherwise the right to counsel is a meaningless one since these people are too poor to hire their own advocates") (397 U.S. at 278–279, 90 S.Ct. at 1025–1026), and in Meltzer v. C. Buck LeCraw & Co., 402 U.S. 954, 91 S.Ct. 1624, 29 L.Ed.2d 124 (1971) (the crucial foundation upon which *Boddie* rests also entitles an indigent litigant to waiver of fees on appeal, to representation by competent counsel, and to a state-furnished record on appeal). Note, The Indigent's Right to Counsel in Civil Cases, 76 Yale L.J. 545 (1967); Note, The Right to Counsel in Civil Litigation, 66 Colum.L.Rev. 1322 (1966).

The *Kras* and *Ortwein* cases, pp. 52–55 supra, indicate a disposition by the Supreme Court to treat constitutional claims in this area with circumspection. In criminal cases, the Court also took a rather reluctant approach in the beginning and gradually came around to recognition of a broad constitutional right to state-furnished legal assistance. Of course, in criminal cases, a most important interest, the litigant's personal liberty, is normally at stake. The Court's stress on the interests involved in *Boddie, Kras,* and *Ortwein* underlines the importance of this distinction. But if history were to repeat itself and Boddie were expanded broadly, it would mark the beginning of a revolution in the provision of legal aid in civil cases. See generally Smit, Constitutional Guarantees in Civil Litigation in the United States of America, in Fundamental Guarantees of the Parties in Civil Litigation 419, 426–431, 451–459, 471–472 (Cappelletti & Tallon, eds., 1973).

B. INSTITUTIONAL PROVISION OF LEGAL SERVICES

Increasingly, organizations in various fields of endeavor try to make professional legal assistance available to their members. They can either refer them to lawyers with whom they have agreed on rates to be charged or employ lawyers whose services they make available to members at reasonable rates. A variant of the latter arrangement, actively studied today, is to provide legal services insurance, the so-called prepaid legal services plan. Local bar associations may frown on these forms of law practice on the ground that they endanger the professional independence of lawyers and involve the unauthorized practice of law. See, e.g., Rhode Island Bar Association v. Automobile Service Association, 55 R.I. 122, 179 A. 139 (1935) and Chicago Bar Association v. Chicago Motor Club, 362 Ill. 50, 199 N.E. 1 (1935) (motorists' associations may not offer free legal services to members). However, constitutional principles impose limitations on the extent to which the states may limit the provision of legal services. The landmark case is NAACP v. Button, 371 U.S. 415, 83 S.Ct. 328, 9 L.Ed. 2d 405 (1963), in which the Supreme Court held unconstitutional as applied to the NAACP, a Virginia statute, which forbade the solicitation of legal business by a "runner" or "capper" (i.e., someone soliciting business for a lawyer) and which had been amended to include in the definition of "runner" or "capper" an agent for an individual or organization which retains a lawyer in connection with an action to which it is not a party and in which it has no pecuniary right or liability. The amendment had specifically been adopted to reach the activities of the NAACP. The Supreme Court held that "the activities of the NAACP, its affiliates and legal staff shown on this record are modes of expression and association protected by the First and Fourteenth Amendments."

The doctrine of the *Button* case has expanded. In Brotherhood of R.R. Trainmen v. Virginia ex rel., 377 U.S. 1, 84 S.Ct. 1113, 12 L.Ed.2d

89 (1964), rehearing denied 377 U.S. 960, 84 S.Ct. 1625, 12 L.Ed.2d 505, on remand 207 Va. 182, 149 S.E.2d 265 (1966), cert. denied 385 U.S. 1027, 87 S.Ct. 754, 17 L.Ed.2d 675 (1967), the Supreme Court held that Virginia could not forbid the Brotherhood from advising members on where to obtain legal assistance and from recommending particular lawyers. In United Mine Workers of America v. Illinois State Bar Association, 389 U.S. 217, 221–222, 88 S.Ct. 353, 19 L.Ed.2d 426 (1967), this holding was extended:

> " * * * We hold that the freedom of speech, assembly, and petition guaranteed by the First and Fourteenth Amendments gives petitioner [the Union] the right to hire attorneys on a salary basis to assist its members in the assertion of their legal rights."

NOTES

(1) In United Transportation Union v. State Bar of Michigan, 401 U.S. 576, 91 S.Ct. 1076, 28 L.Ed.2d 339 (1971), the union recommended to its members particular attorneys from whom it had obtained a commitment not to charge in excess of 25 per cent of any recovery and reimbursed its employees for transporting injured employees to these attorneys' offices. The Supreme Court struck down the state court's injunction of these activities on the authority of *Button* and *Trainmen.*

(2) For a description of prepaid legal services plans and their reception by the legal profession, see Application of Feinstein, 45 A.D.2d 440, 357 N.Y.S.2d 516 (1974), reversed Feinstein v. Attorney General, 36 N.Y.2d 199, 366 N.Y.S.2d 613, 326 N.E.2d 288 (1975) (dissenting opinion).

(3) Minimum fee schedules promulgated by bar associations are invalid under the antitrust laws. Goldfarb v. Virginia State Bar, 421 U.S. 773, 95 S.Ct. 2004, 44 L.Ed.2d 572 (1975).

————

C. CONTINGENT FEES

A contingent fee arrangement exists when a client agrees that the lawyer's remuneration will consist of a share of the amount recovered. Of course, such an arrangement is likely to be acceptable to a lawyer only when there appears to be a reasonably good prospect of recovery. Contingent fee arrangements are standard on the plaintiff's side in personal injury cases.

At common law, contingent fee agreements were invalid as constituting either maintenance, champerty, or barratry. Maintenance is maintaining, supporting, or promoting the litigation of another. Champerty is a special form of maintenance. It is a bargain to divide the proceeds of litigation between the owner of a claim and a person supporting or enforcing the litigation. Closely related to maintenance and champerty is barratry, which consists of habitually or frequently moving, exciting, or maintaining quarrels, whether at law or otherwise. See Blackstone, Commentaries 134–136 (3d ed. 1884); Draper v. Zebec,

219 Ind. 362, 37 N.E.2d 952 (1941), rehearing denied 219 Ind. 362, 38 N.E.2d 995 (1942). All were considered crimes from early times on and survive in modified form in modern statutes. See, e.g., 220 Ann.Laws of Mass. 8 (1931); 17 Me.Rev.Stat.Ann. 801 (1964); N.Y. Judiciary Law § 474 (1963).

In the United States, contingent fee arrangements are generally valid. Maine, which was one of the last states to relinquish the common law rule, specifically amended its statute prohibiting maintenance and champerty in 1965 to provide that it "shall not apply to agreements between attorney and client to bring, prosecute, or defend a civil action on a contingent fee basis."

Contingent fee agreements are sometimes invalidated for stimulating socially undesirable results. At one time contingent fee agreements in divorce cases were struck down on the ground that they unduly promote divorces, but these holdings appear to be on the wane. Cf. Note, Contingent Fee Contracts: Contract Related to Divorce Action Upheld, 56 Minn.L.Rev. 979 (1972).

While generally permitting contingent fee agreements, the courts have asserted broad powers of scrutiny over the propriety of their contents. Thus, some courts have declared unenforceable clauses requiring the consent of the attorney for settlement or compromise of the claim. Others have struck down provisions granting the attorney an unreasonable share of the recovery. See, *e.g.*, In re Ace Sales Co., 357 F.Supp. 936 (E.D.Mo.1973).

The First Department of the Appellate Division of the New York Supreme Court has limited fees in personal injury and wrongful death cases to 50% of the first $1,000, 40% of the next $2,000, 35% of the next $22,000, 25% of any amount over $25,000 of the recovery; or, alternatively to one third of the total recovery whatever the amount. Its power to do so was upheld in Gair v. Peck, 6 N.Y.2d 97, 188 N.Y.S.2d 491, 160 N.E.2d 43 (1959), cert. denied and appeal dismissed 361 U.S. 374, 80 S.Ct. 401, 4 L.Ed.2d 380 (1960). See also American Trial Lawyers Association, New Jersey Branch v. New Jersey Supreme Court, 126 N.J.Super. 577, 316 A.2d 19 (1974) (50% of first $1,000, 40% of next $2,000, 33$\frac{1}{3}$% of next $47,000, 20% of next $50,000, and 10% of any amount over $100,000).

Rule 1.5(c) of the ABA's Model Rules of Professional Conduct states:

> A fee may be contingent on the outcome of the matter for which the service is rendered, except in a matter in which a contingent fee is prohibited by law. A contingent fee agreement shall be in writing and shall state the method by which the fee is to be determined, including the percentage or percentages that shall accrue to the lawyer in the event of settlement, trial or appeal, expenses to be deducted from the recovery, and whether expenses are to be deducted before or after the contingent fee is calculated. Upon conclusion of a

contingent fee matter, the lawyer shall provide the client with a written statement stating the outcome of the matter and, if there is a recovery, showing the remittance to the client and the method of its determination.

On contingent fees generally, see MacKinnon, Contingent Fees for Legal Services (1964). See also Comment, Of Ethics and Economics: Contingent Percentage Fees for Legal Services, 16 Akron L.Rev. 747 (1983); Note, The Contingent Fee: Disciplinary Rule, Ethical Consideration, or Free Competition?, 1979 Utah L.Rev. 547; Corboy, Contingency Fees: The Individual's Key to the Courthouse Door, 2:4 Litigation 27 (1976). Schwartz & Mitchell, Economic Analysis of the Contingent Fee in Personal-Injury Litigation, 22 Stan.L.Rev. 1125 (1970).

Chapter Three

FINAL REMEDIES

INTRODUCTION

The law of remedies lies midway between the substantive law (which regulates person to person conduct) and procedural law (which regulates what litigants do when they become embroiled in legal controversy). These three bodies of law function in tandem, reacting to each other. Thus, the law of remedies cannot be broadened without regard to the results this has upon the balance of social interests achieved by existing substantive and procedural rules. For example, giving a landlord a right to immediate repossession of leased premises, as an alternative to money damages, may substantially change the balance of bargaining power between landlords and tenants.

When lawmakers consider throwing open the door to broader and more flexible remedies, they must also have in mind that some remedies pose more difficult problems of judicial administration than others. A decree compelling defendant to perform specifically his contract to construct a large building may have much to commend it in theory, but it may involve the court in continuing supervision of a large business activity, with obvious practical problems.

When the tide of events points to the need for broader remedies, the question arises, who should change the law of remedies: judges or legislators? The latter have advantages over judges, including broad powers of investigating the need for, and projecting the possible future impact of, the changes. Does that mean that all modifications in this area should await legislative action?

In studying the following material, try to determine to what extent historical traditions affect the formulation of the applicable rule.

SECTION 1. HISTORICAL BACKGROUND: ENGLISH

A. THE GROWTH OF THE FORMULARY SYSTEM

When, in 1066, William made his conquest, he found in existence a rather elaborate system of local courts, including county courts, manorial courts, hundred courts, and others. Initially, the new King did not interfere with litigation in these courts. He might issue a writ ordering a feudal lord or a sheriff to do justice, or send out his officers to hear a case in a local court, or even evoke a case before his own court, but these interferences were far from systematic and followed no particular patterns.

Gradually, however, the King began to issue his writ in an increasing number of cases. The notions that in a feudal society all disputes affecting land ultimately concern the King and that violations of the law naturally tend to breach the King's peace—a subject of his legitimate concern—furnished the premises for extension of the King's legislative and judicial reach.

At first, the King drew writs to fit particular cases presented to him, but gradually certain patterns emerged, and writs came to be cast in fixed formulae. And as early as the twelfth century, everyone who could bring his case within one of the established formulae could avail himself of royal justice by obtaining, upon payment of a fee, the appropriate writ from the royal chancery. In addition to these writs of course (*brevia de cursu*), which came to be collected in a Register kept in the chancery, the King freely drew new writs to meet new contingencies.

The barons looked askance at this expanding assertion of royal power. Their opposition led to insertion of a provision in *Magna Carta* that, when the tenement was held of a mesne lord, the King could issue only a writ of right (*breve de recto tenendo*) commanding the mesne lord to do justice in his court rather than a writ bringing the case before the royal court (*praecipe in capite*). And shortly thereafter, by the Provisions of Oxford (1258), the Chancellor was forbidden altogether from issuing new writs without the consent of the King and his Council. The practical result of this prohibition was that new writs were no longer issued.

Indeed, the system became frozen to such an extent that a special statute, the Statute of Westminster II (1285), became necessary to empower the Chancellor to issue writs not only in the exact case contemplated by an existing formula, but also in a case that was similar (*in consimili casu*). Initially, even this statute was used rather rarely, but according to the views of leading, although not uncontested, historians, it did provide the authority for variation of the writ of trespass to fit special situations. These variations in time became a new form, trespass on the case, which became not only the appropriate writ for cases sounding in negligence, but also developed into such special forms as assumpsit, trover, deceit, and action on the case for defamation. In this manner, the King, although forbidden to issue new writs on his own, nevertheless managed greatly to expand the reach of royal justice. And in time, when no writ could be found or adjusted to suit a particular case, the King's power in equity complemented his legal powers so as to permit his Chancellor to grant a remedy in equitable proceedings.

NOTES

(1) On English developments generally, see Ames, Lectures on Legal History (1913); Fifoot, English Law and Its Background (1932); Goebel, Development of Legal Institutions (1946); Holdsworth, A History of English Law (1909); Jenks, Short History of English Law (1934); Plucknett, A Concise History of the Common Law (15th ed. 1956); Pollock & Maitland, History of English Law (2d reissued ed. 1968); Smith, Development of Legal Institutions (1965).

(2) The formulary system of actions of the common law greatly resembles the system of *legis actiones* developed by the classical Roman law. Indeed, common law procedure is considerably more Roman in structure than procedure in the civil law countries that trace their heritage directly to Roman law institutions. On the similarity between common law and Roman law procedure, see Clark, Code Pleading 5–9 (2d ed. 1947); Cappelletti & Perillo, Civil Procedure in Italy 25–31 (1965).

B. ROYAL AND ECCLESIASTICAL COURTS

Originally, royal justice was dispensed by the King in Council. But as the number of cases increased, the King's Council split into sections that dealt with particular kinds of cases. These became the King's Bench, the Court of Common Pleas, and the Exchequer, each with a specially defined competence.

Originally, the Common Bench or Court of Common Pleas heard ordinary civil disputes between subjects of the King (*communia placita*). Controversies that directly affected the King (*placita coronae*), including trespass *vi et armis*, were heard by the King's Bench. And controversies relating to the King's debts, including debts to the King's debtor, were adjudicated by the Court of Exchequer. But procedures and expenses in these courts differed, and litigants naturally attempted to bring their actions in the court that offered the particular advantages they sought. In this search for advantage, both the King's Bench and Exchequer managed to expand their adjudicatory powers, mostly at the expense of the Court of Common Pleas. Fictions were employed to serve their purposes. The King's Bench had power to adjudicate controversies involving its prisoners. If a case was to be commenced before it in which it would not normally have adjudicatory power—for example, an action of debt—, it was first fictionally alleged that the defendant had committed a trespass. The King's Bench was then asked to issue a writ to the sheriff of Middlesex where the court was sitting (a so-called Bill of Middlesex), ordering him to produce B to answer. If B were in Middlesex, he would either be arrested or give bail for his appearance. Either event would put him in the Court's custody and thus give the Court power to hear the personal action of debt on the ground that it had power to hear all personal actions against persons in its custody. If the defendant was not in Middlesex, the Court would issue a *labitat* to the sheriff in the county in which B was known to be, and the case proceeded in the same way.

The Court of Common Pleas sought to defend itself against this encroachment upon its verge by resorting to another fiction. It permitted the use of a writ *quare clausum fregit* to bring the defendant into court and then allowed the plaintiff to sue the defendant on a new writ under the bail the latter had given on the original one.

While this struggle, that in the end left the King's Bench largely victorious, continued, the Exchequer availed itself of the opportunity to enlarge its powers. To give the Exchequer power to hear an action, the plaintiff pretended that he was the King's debtor and alleged that the defendant failed to pay the money due him, as a result of which he was less (*quo minus*) able to pay his debt to the King. This fiction became known as *quo minus*. The courts' manoeuvres to expand their powers continued until in the nineteenth century all were combined in one Supreme Court.

In the course of time, royal judicial powers were also exercised by the Court of Chancery and other courts, such as the Court of the Star Chamber, the Court of Requests, the Court of Admiralty, and the Court of Wards and Liveries.

Religious matters were adjudicated in ecclesiastical courts, which had been separated from the common law courts by the Ordinance of William the Conqueror (1072). This development exercised a profound influence on the development of the law, because the ecclesiastical courts dealt with matters affecting the family, including marital matters, descent and distribution, wills, probate, administration of estates, and the like. Insofar as these latter categories are concerned, this separation explains the continued existence today of surrogate and probate courts in the United States and the reluctance of federal courts to decide matters of this nature. See Spindel v. Spindel, 283 F.Supp. 797 (E.D.N.Y.1968).

C. THE REAL ACTIONS

Real actions, which concern rights to real property, originally existed in large numbers, each tailored to suit a particular situation. They became mixed when, in addition to seeking a right in real property, they sought personal relief such as damages. There were two kinds of real actions: the proprietary, in which the claim was based on a proprietary interest, and the possessory, in which the plaintiff's right of possession formed the premise for the claim.

The distinctions between many of the real actions were frequently almost imperceptible. Furthermore, the proceedings in many were highly technical and afforded ample opportunities for delay. These circumstances prompted the development under which the action of ejectment, because of its procedural advantages, was given a much broader thrust and evolved into the favorite device for asserting a proprietary or possessory interest in real estate. This development

[Handwritten at top: NOT ON FINAL]

culminated in the Real Property Limitations Act of 1833, 384 Wm. IV, c. 27, § 36 (1833) which provided that some sixty specifically named real and mixed actions could no longer be brought after December 31, 1834, and in the Common Law Procedure Act of 1860, 23 & 24 Vict. c. 126, § 26 (1860), which abolished some of the old writs that had not been affected by the 1833 legislation. The action of ejectment was spared from this wholesale abolition, however, and, in streamlined form, continued its existence until all forms of actions were abolished by the Supreme Court of Judicature Act of 1873, 36 & 37 Vict., c. 76 (1873) and 38 & 39 Vict., c. 77 (1875) and the Rules promulgated thereunder. As will be seen below, this action continues to form the basis for the statutory action of ejectment prescribed in procedural laws in the United States.

D. THE PERSONAL ACTIONS

Originally, the personal forms of action developed alongside the real and mixed actions. But as the ancient real forms of actions fell into disuse, the personal forms of actions evolved into the principal common law actions.

MAITLAND, THE FORMS OF ACTION AT COMMON LAW

57-58, 61-71 (1962).*

We may say that they were nine in number, (1) Replevin, (2) Detinue, (3) Debt, (4) Account, (5) Covenant, (6) Trespass, (7) Case, (8) Trover, and (9) Assumpsit. *[handwritten: — action for breach of promise or contract]*

Replevin we may quickly put aside. Its importance in the middle ages was very great, but it was not capable of much development. It is an action founded upon a wrongful distraint—the distrainee offers security that he will contest the distrainor's rights in court, and thereupon the distrainor is bound to surrender the goods—usually cattle. If he does not do so the sheriff is to raise the *posse comitatus* and retake them. An action beginning thus with a demand for replevin (i.e. that the goods be 'repledged' pending action) becomes the normal mode of trying the rightfulness of distraint, and such actions are of very common occurrence in the middle ages.

     * * *

Detinue. This is a very old action. The defendant is charged with an unjust detainer (not, be it noted, an unjust taking)—*injuste detinet.* This action looks very like a real action. The writ originating it bears a close similarity with the writ of right (*praecipe in capite*), but in the first place the mesne process is not *in rem*, and in the second (and this is very important) the defendant when worsted is always allowed the

[handwritten marginal notes: "recover lost prop.", "recover damages from lost prop", "to recover property", "agreement", "violence", "action", "lost property", "improper seizure of prop.", "a group of citizens to help sheriff", "against (k?) thing"]

-----

* Footnotes omitted.

option of surrendering the goods or paying assessed damages. The reason of this may perhaps be found partly in the perishable character of medieval moveables, and the consequent feeling that the court could not accept the task of restoring them to their owners, and partly in the idea that all things had a 'legal price' which, if the plaintiff gets, is enough for him.

*   *   *

Debt. An action for a fixed sum of money due for any reason, and own sister to Detinue. Here also we have a *praecipe quod reddat.* *Praecipe quod reddat* (1) *terram*, (2) *catalla*, (3) *pecunia* are the writs of right (for land), of detinue, and of debt respectively.

Its first and chief use was for the recovery of money lent—a sense in which the word 'recovery' is still used. The difference between *commodatum* and *mutuum*—the loan to be returned and the loan to be repaid—was hardly seen. It is hardly seen to-day by the vulgar. 'My money at the bank,' is a phrase in common use. Another use of the action of debt was for the recovery of the price upon a sale, and another the recovery of rent due. There were other *causae debendi,* and gradually the progress towards generalization got to be expressed in the phrase that debt would lie for a fixed sum of money if there were a *quid pro quo* or, later, if there were 'consideration.' Thus Debt, originally conceived as recuperatory, like Detinue, becomes capable of being used for the enforcement of contracts of sorts. One limitation, however, remained—the untranscendible limit—the claim must be for a fixed sum. Debt can not be used to obtain compensation for breach of contract.

*   *   *

Account. The action of Account is another *praecipe,* originally granted against manorial bailiffs. *Praecipe quod reddat compotum.* Auditors were appointed to supervise the account. At a later stage it was extended to some other classes, thus it could be used between partners, but partnership is uncommon and unimportant in the England of the middle ages. A few modern instances of its use are recorded, but the common law action of account remains at a low level of development because of the fact that it was in practice superseded by the equitable jurisdiction of the Chancellor, who in the Bill for account had a more modern remedy operating under a more favourable and convenient procedure.

Covenant. This action is also an old one. Its writ directs *quod conventio teneatur.* The earliest use of the action is for the protection of the termor; at one time it is the lessee's only remedy. It early sends off a branch which is reckoned a real action because land is recovered, in other cases the action results in money being obtained. It appears for a time as if covenant might be of general use wherever there is an agreement (*conventio*), might become, in fact, a general action for breach of contract; but the practice of the thirteenth century decides that there must be a sealed writing. A sacramental importance was attached to the use of the seal—*collatio sigilli*—and it was finally adopted as the only acceptable evidence of a covenant. Thus we come to the English formal contract, the Covenant under Seal. One curious limitation appears, and is maintained until the seventeenth century; Covenant can not be brought for the recovery of a debt, though attested under seal. This action remains useful but in its own narrow sphere.

Trespass. All the other personal actions branch out from one, namely Trespass. *Trespass* appears *circ.* 1250 as a means of charging a defendant with violence but no felony. The writ, as we have seen, contains the words *vi et armis contra pacem*, the procedure is enforced by a threat of outlawry, imprisonment is resorted to by way of mesne process, and the vanquished defendant is punished for his offence. He is not merely *in misericordia*, he is liable to a *capias pro fine*. There is a trifurcation, the writ varying according as the violence is done (1) to land, (2) to the body, or (3) to chattels. Speaking of trespass to land let us once more remember how trespass *quare clausum fregit* sends out the action for ejectment as a branch.

Trespass to the body (assaults and batteries) covered the whole ground of personal injury, and no great development was possible here. Trespass to goods, trespass *de bonis asportatis* is an action which results in damages, never return of the goods, for carrying goods off from the plaintiff's possession—and therefore the bailee can bring it. * * * Gradually during Edward III's reign we find a few writs occurring which in form are extremely like writs of trespass—and they are actually called writs of trespass—but the wrong complained of does not always consist of a direct application of unlawful physical force to the body, lands, or goods of the plaintiff; sometimes the words *vi et armis* do not appear. Sometimes there is no mention of the king's peace. Still they are spoken of as writs of trespass, they appear in the Chancery Register as writs of trespass, mixed up with the writs which charge the defendant with violent assaults and asportations. The plaintiff is said to bring an action upon his case, or upon the special case, and gradually it becomes apparent that really a new and a very elastic form of action has thus been created. I think that lawyers were becoming conscious of this about the end of the fourteenth century. Certain procedural differences have made their appearance—when there is *vi et armis* in the writ, then the defendant if he will not appear may be taken by *capias ad respondendum* or may be outlawed—this can not be if there is no talk of force and arms or the king's peace. Thus Case falls apart from Trespass—during the fifteenth century the line between them becomes always better marked. In 1503 (19 Hen. VII, c. 9) a statute takes note of the distinction; the process of *capias* is given in 'actions upon the case.' Under Henry VIII Fitzherbert in his *Abridgment* and his *Natura Brevium* treats of the 'Action sur la Case' as something different from the action of trespass—each has its precedents. The title of Case covers very miscellaneous wrongs—specially we may notice slander and libel (for which, however, there are but few precedents during the middle ages, since bad words are dealt with by the local courts, and defamation by the ecclesiastical courts), also damage caused by negligence, also deceit.

Case becomes a sort of general residuary action; much, particularly, of the modern law of negligence developed within it. Sometimes it is difficult to mark off case from trespass. The importance of the somewhat shadowy line between them was originally due to the fact that where *vis* and *arma* were not alleged there was no imprisonment in mesne process, nor was the defeated defendant liable to the judgment *quod capiatur pro fine.* ＊ ＊ ＊

Sub-forms of Case become marked off, *e.g.* Case for negligence, for deceit, for words (slander and libel); but two great branches were thrown out which gain an independent life, and are generally important, *viz.* Assumpsit and Trover.

Assumpsit. The most curious offshoot of Case is Assumpsit and the great interest of this action lies in the fact that it becomes the general form by which contracts not under seal can be enforced by way of action for damages. Under the old law the contracts are formal, or 'real,' the form required being the instrument under seal, the bond or covenant, and the 'real' contracts—the word 'real' being used in the sense of general jurisprudence—are protected by Debt–Detinue without it being seen that contract is the basis. Gradually however within the delictual action of Case various precedents collect in which the allegation is made that the defendant had undertaken to do something and then hurt the plaintiff either in his person or in his goods by doing it badly—by misfeasance.

Further an important element in this progress is the idea of breach of contract as being deceit—the plaintiff suffers detriment by relying on the promise of the defendant. ＊ ＊ ＊

The having undertaken (*assumpsit*) to do something, makes its appearance as part of the cause of action in various writs upon the case. Thus we find an early group of cases, from Edward III's reign, in which the plaintiff seeks to recover compensation for some damage done to his person or goods by the active misconduct of the defendant, but still the defendant can not be charged with a breach of the peace, as the plaintiff has put his person or his goods into the defendant's care. The defendant, for example, is a surgeon, and has unskillfully treated the plaintiff or his animals so that he or they have suffered some physical harm. In such cases we find an assumpsit alleged. It is necessary to allege that the defendant undertook the cure—had it not been so, according to the notions of the time, it might well have been urged that the harm was occasioned by the plaintiff's own folly in going to an inexpert doctor. A little later, in the fifteenth century, we have actions against bailees for negligence in the custody of goods intrusted to them, and here also it was necessary to allege an assumpsit. Again, there is another class of cases in which an undertaking is alleged—a seller has sold goods warranting them sound, and they have turned out unsound; the cause of action is regarded not as breach of contract, but as deceit.

Thus in divers directions the law was finding materials for a generalisation, namely, that breach of an undertaking, an assumpsit, for which there was valuable consideration was a cause of action.

Gradually the line between mis-feasance and non-feasance was transcended, and gradually lawyers awoke to the fact that by extending an action of tort they had in effect created a new action by which parol contracts could be enforced. It is, I think, about the beginning of the sixteenth century that they begin to regard Assumpsit as a different form from Case, a form with precedents of its own and rules of its own. Then begins a new struggle to make Assumpsit do the work of Debt. Plaintiffs wish for this result because they desire to avoid that wager of law which is allowed in Debt, and defendants may fairly argue that according to the law of the land they are entitled to this ancient mode of proof. * * * Through the sixteenth century, an actual express agreement alone gives rise to Assumpsit, and therefore if Assumpsit is to be used to enforce a debt, for example for the price of goods sold and delivered, a new promise—a promise to pay that debt—must be alleged and proved. However, in 1602, *Slade's case* (4 Rep. 92 b) decides that Assumpsit may be brought where Debt would lie, and thenceforth Assumpsit supplants Debt as a means for recovering liquidated sums. In that case such a new promise had been alleged and the jury by a special verdict had found the bargain and sale to be proved but that 'there was no promise or taking upon him, besides the bargain aforesaid.' Upon this finding the case was argued in the King's Bench and the action in Assumpsit was held to lie, the Court resolving that 'Every contract executory imports in itself an *assumpsit,* for when one agrees to pay money or to deliver anything, thereby he assumes or promises to pay or deliver it.' Thenceforth the proof of the new promise becomes unnecessary. This form of Assumpsit takes the name of Indebitatus Assumpsit.

Some seven years later we have this action extended from cases of express executory contract to cases where the original bargain was an implied contract, in the sense that a contract is really to be implied from the facts of the case, for example, cases of actions for *Quantum meruit.*

Lastly, at some date between 1673 and 1705, Indebitatus Assumpsit is extended to actions upon Quasi–Contracts in which the element of contract is purely fictitious.

As we have already seen, this action of Assumpsit, which at least seems to us as of delictual origin, becomes the general mode of enforcing contracts even when a sum certain has to be recovered, and thus Assumpsit becomes a rival to and a substitute for Debt in which latter action the defendant may still wage his law. * * *

Trover. One other great branch is thrown out by Case, namely Trover. * * * This also is an action for damages based upon a fictitious loss and finding and a subsequent conversion to the use of the defendant. Here there is no trespass, the defendant may be a perfectly innocent purchaser from the original wrongdoer; and there is no 'recuperation'—the gist of the action is the conversion.

    *   *   *

Meanwhile in 1832 a partial assault had been made on the personal forms.   *   *   * By 2 Will. IV, c. 39 (1832) 'Uniformity of Process Act'— the process in these personal actions was reduced to uniformity. The old original writs were abolished and a new form of writ provided. In this writ, however, the plaintiff had to insert a mention of one of the known forms of action. Another heavy blow was struck in 1852 by the Common Law Procedure Act, 15 and 16 Vic., c. 76. It was expressly provided (sec. 3) that it should not be necessary to mention any form or cause of action in any writ of summons. But still this blow was not heavy enough—the several personal forms were still considered as distinct.

The final blow was struck by the Judicature Act of 1873 and the rules made thereunder, which came into force in 1875. This did much more than finally abolish the forms of actions known to the common law for it provided that equity and law should be administered concurrently. Since that time we have had what might fairly be called a Code of Civil Procedure.

E. PROCEDURE

MAITLAND, THE FORMS OF ACTION AT COMMON LAW
2–4 (1962).

Let it be granted that one man has been wronged by another; the first thing that he or his advisers have to consider is what form of action he shall bring. It is not enough that in some way or another he should compel his adversary to appear in court and should then state in the words that naturally occur to him the facts on which he relies and the remedy to which he thinks himself entitled. No, English law knows a certain number of forms of action, each with its own uncouth name, a writ of right, an assize of novel disseisin or of *mort d'ancestor,* a writ of entry *sur disseisin* in the *per* and *cui,* a writ of *besaiel,* of *quare impedit,* an action of covenant, debt, detinue, replevin, trespass, assumpsit, ejectment, case. This choice is not merely a choice between a number of queer technical terms, it is a choice between methods of procedure adapted to cases of different kinds. Let us notice some of the many points that are implied in it.

(i) There is the competence of the court. For very many of the ordinary civil cases each of the three courts which have grown out of the king's court of early days, the King's Bench, Common Pleas and Exchequer is equally competent, though it is only by means of elaborate and curious fictions that the King's Bench and the Exchequer can entertain these matters, and the Common Pleas still retains a monopoly of those actions which are known as real.

(ii) A court chosen, one must make one's adversary appear; but what is the first step towards this end? In some actions one ought to begin by having him summoned, in others one can at once have him attached, he can be compelled to find gage and pledge for his appearance. In the assize of novel disseisin it is enough to attach his bailiff.

(iii) Suppose him contumacious, what can one do? Can one have his body seized? If he can not be found, can one have him outlawed? This stringent procedure has been extending itself from one form of action to another. Again, can one have the thing in dispute seized? This is possible in some actions, impossible in others.

(iv) Can one obtain a judgment by default, obtain what one wants though the adversary continues in his contumacy? Yes in some forms, no in others.

(v) It comes to pleading, and here each form of action has some rules of its own. For instance the person attacked—the tenant he is called in some cases, the defendant in others—wishes to oppose the attacker—the demandant he is called in some actions, the plaintiff in others—by a mere general denial, casting upon him the burden of proving his own case, what is he to say? In other words, what is the general issue appropriate to this action? In one form it is *Nihil debet,* in another *Non assumpsit,* in another 'Not guilty,' in others, *Nul tort, nul disseisin.*

(vi) There is to be a trial; but what mode of trial? Very generally of course a trial by jury. But it may be trial by a grand or petty assize, which is not quite the same thing as trial by jury; or in Blackstone's day it may still conceivably be a trial by battle. Again in some forms of action the defendant may betake himself to the world-old process of compurgation or wager of law. Again there are a few issues which are tried without a jury by the judges who hear witnesses.

(vii) Judgment goes against the defendant, what is the appropriate form of execution? Can one be put into possession of the thing that has been in dispute? Can one imprison the defendant? Can one have him made an outlaw? or can he merely be distrained?

(viii) Judgment goes against the defendant. It is not enough that he should satisfy the plaintiff's just demand; he must also be punished for his breach of the law—such at all events is the theory. What form shall this punishment take? Will an amercement suffice, or shall there be fine or imprisonment? Here also there have been differences.

(ix) Some actions are much more dilatory than others; the dilatory ones have gone out of use, but still they exist. In these oldest forms— forms invented when as yet the parties had to appear in person and could only appoint attorneys by the king's special leave—the action may drag on for years, for the parties enjoy a power of sending essoins, that is, excuses for non-appearance. The medieval law of essoins is vast in bulk; time is allowed for almost every kind of excuse for non-appearance—a short essoin *de malo veniendi,* a long essoin *de malo lecti.* Now-a-days all is regulated by general rules with a wide discretion left in the Court. In the Middle Ages discretion is entirely excluded; all is to be fixed by iron rules. This question of essoins has been very important—in some forms, the oldest and solemnest, a party may betake himself to his bed and remain there for year and day and meanwhile the action is suspended.

F. THE RISE OF EQUITY

MAITLAND, EQUITY, ALSO THE FORMS OF ACTION AT COMMON LAW
3–11 (1926).

At the head of the Chancery stands the Chancellor, usually a bishop; he is we may say the king's secretary of state for all departments, he keeps the king's great seal and all the already great mass of writing that has to be done in the king's name has to be done under his supervision.

He is not as yet a judge, but already he by himself or his subordinates has a great deal of work to do which brings him into a close connection with the administration of justice. One of the duties of that great staff of clerks over which he presides is to draw up and issue those writs whereby actions are begun in the courts of law—such writs are sealed with the king's seal. A man who wishes to begin an action must go to the Chancery and obtain a writ. * * * This however is not judicial business. The Chancellor does not hear both sides of the story, he only hears the plaintiff's application, and if he grants a writ the courts of law may afterwards quash that writ as being contrary to the law of the land.

But by another route the Chancellor is brought into still closer contact with the administration of justice. Though these great courts of law have been established there is still a reserve of justice in the king. Those who can not get relief elsewhere present their petitions to the king and his council praying for some remedy. Already by the end of the thirteenth century the number of such petitions presented in every year is very large, and the work of reading them and considering them is very laborious. In practice a great share of this labour falls on the Chancellor. He is the king's prime minister, he is a member of the council, and the specially learned member of the council. It is in dealing with these petitions that the Chancellor begins to develop his judicial powers.

In course of time his judicial powers are classified as being of two kinds. It begins to be said that the Court of Chancery, 'Curia Cancellariae'—for the phrase is used in the fourteenth century—has two sides, a common law side and an equity side, or a Latin side and an English side. Let us look for a moment at the origin of these two kinds of powers, and first at that which concerns us least.

(1) Many of these petitions of which I have spoken seek for justice not merely from the king but against the king. If anybody is to be called the wrong doer, it is the king himself. For example, he is in possession of land which has been seized by his officers as an escheat while really the late tenant has left an heir. Now the king can not be sued by action—no writ will go against him; the heir if he wants justice must petition for it humbly. Such matters as these are referred to the Chancellor. Proceedings are taken before him; the heir, it may be, proves his case and gets his land. The number of such cases, cases in which the king is concerned, is very large—kings are always seizing land on very slight pretexts—and forcing other people to prove their titles. Gradually a quite regular and ordinary procedure is established for such cases—a procedure very like that of the three courts of law. The proceedings are enrolled in Latin—just as the proceedings of the three courts of law are enrolled in Latin (hence the name 'Latin side' of the Court of Chancery)—and if a question of fact be raised, it is tried by jury. The Chancellor himself does not summon the jury or preside at the trial, he sends the question for trial to the King's Bench. All this is by no means unimportant, but it does not concern us very much at the present time.

(2) Very often the petitioner requires some relief at the expense of some other person. He complains that for some reason or another he can not get a remedy in the ordinary course of justice and yet he is entitled to a remedy. He is poor, he is old, he is sick, his adversary is rich and powerful, will bribe or will intimidate jurors, or has by some trick or some accident acquired an advantage of which the ordinary courts with their formal procedure will not deprive him. The petition is often couched in piteous terms, the king is asked to find a remedy for the love of God and in the way of charity. Such petitions are referred by the king to the Chancellor. Gradually in the course of the fourteenth century petitioners, instead of going to the king, will go straight to the Chancellor, will address their complaints to him and adjure him to do what is right for the love of God and in the way of charity. Now one thing that the Chancellor may do in such a case is to invent a new writ and so provide the complainant with a means of bringing an action in a court of law. But in the fourteenth century the courts of law have become very conservative and are given to quashing writs which differ in material points from those already in use. But another thing that the Chancellor can do is to send for the complainant's adversary and examine him concerning the charge that has been made against him. Gradually a procedure is established. The Chancellor having considered the petition, or 'bill' as it is called, orders the adversary to come before him and answer the complaint. The writ whereby he does this is called a subpoena—because it orders the man to appear upon pain of forfeiting a sum of money, *e.g. subpoena centum librarum.* It is very different from the old writs whereby actions are begun in the courts of law. They tell the defendant what is the cause of action against him— he is to answer why he assaulted and beat the plaintiff, why he

trespassed on the plaintiff's land, why he detains a chattel which belongs to the plaintiff. The subpoena, on the other hand, will tell him merely that he has got to come before the Chancellor and answer complaints made against him by A.B. Then when he comes before the Chancellor he will have to answer on oath, and sentence by sentence, the bill of the plaintiff. This procedure is rather like that of the ecclesiastical courts and the canon law than like that of our old English courts of law. It was in fact borrowed from the ecclesiastical courts, not from their ordinary procedure but from the summary procedure of those courts introduced for the suppression of heresy. The defendant will be examined upon oath and the Chancellor will decide questions of fact as well as questions of law. * * *

In the second half of the sixteenth century the jurisprudence of the court is becoming settled. The day for ecclesiastical Chancellors is passing away. Wolsey is the last of the great ecclesiastical Chancellors, though in Charles I's day we have one more divine in the person of Dr. Williams. Ellesmere, Bacon, Coventry, begin to administer an established set of rules which is becoming known to the public in the shape of reports and they begin to publish rules of procedure. In James I's day occurred the great quarrel between Lord Chancellor Ellesmere and Chief Justice Coke which finally decided that the Court of Chancery was to have the upper hand over the courts of law. If the Chancery was to carry out its maxims about trust and fraud it was essential that it should have a power to prevent men from going into the courts of law and to prevent men from putting in execution the judgments that they had obtained in courts of law. In fraud or in breach of trust you obtain a judgment against me in a court of law; I complain to the Chancellor, and he after hearing what you have to say enjoins you not to put in force your judgment, says in effect that if you do put your judgment in force you will be sent to prison. Understand well that the Court of Chancery never asserted that it was superior to the courts of law; it never presumed to send to them such mandates as the Court of King's Bench habitually sent to the inferior courts, telling them that they must do this or must not do that or quashing their proceedings—the Chancellor's injunction was in theory a very different thing from a mandamus, a prohibition, a certiorari, or the like. It was addressed not to the judges, but to the party. You in breach of trust have obtained a judgment—the Chancellor does not say that this judgment was wrongly granted, he does not annul it, he tells you that for reasons personal to yourself it will be inequitable for you to enforce that judgment, and that you are not to enforce it. For all this, however, it was natural that the judges should take umbrage at this treatment of their judgments. Coke declared that the man who obtained such an injunction was guilty of the offence denounced by the Statutes of Praemunire, that of calling in question the judgments of the king's courts in other courts (these statutes had been aimed at the Papal curia). King James had now a wished-for opportunity of appearing as supreme over all his judges, and all his courts, and acting on the advice of Bacon and other great lawyers he issued a decree in favor of the Chancery. From this time forward the Chancery had the upper hand. It did not claim to be superior to the courts of law, but it could prevent men from going to those courts, whereas those courts could not prevent men from going to it.

Its independence being thus secured, the court became an extremely busy court.

NOTE

For a more detailed discussion of the famed Coke–Ellesmere dispute, see Dawson, Coke and Ellesmere Disinterred: The Attack on the Chancery in 1616, 36 Ill.L.Rev. 127 (1941).

NOTE ON THE DEVELOPMENT OF EQUITY JURISDICTION

There apparently was no conscious purpose in the fourteenth century to create a new competing system of law in chancery. But the development of "uses" in the fourteenth through sixteenth centuries to avoid the feudal incidents of land ownership and the rigors of common law transfers perpetuated the distinction. The law courts refused to recognize uses for any purpose, so that only chancery could protect the cestui que use or beneficiary.

a. *Enforcement of Trusts.* The enforcement of trusts was the first major area in which the chancellor used his judicial powers. In addition to enforcing explicit trusts, equity imposed a "constructive trust" in cases in which property was held by a defendant that equitably belonged or should be transferred to the plaintiff. See Restatement of Restitution § 160 (1937).

b. *Contracts.* The second area in which equity provided needed relief was contracts. The law courts did not grant relief for breach of a contract that was not under seal and created no debt for a fixed sum. The chancellor provided needed relief in this situation by enforcing contracts that, in the interest of good faith and honest dealings, should be enforced. When the common law courts responded to this assertion of equitable jurisdiction by developing the action of assumpsit (see p. 74 supra), the chancellor continued to exercise jurisdiction to grant specific performance when damages were not an adequate remedy.

In addition, equity provided equitable defenses to contract actions when the enforcement of strict legal rights based on the contract would have been unfair or inequitable. The chief grounds of defense developed by equity were fraud, forgery, and duress; accident and mistake; and relief against penalties. Since originally these defenses could not be interposed in the law courts, the defendant could seek rescission or cancellation of contracts tainted by such defects in the chancery court.

c. *Financial accountings.* The organization and procedure of the court of chancery made it a much more efficient tribunal than the

When 3rd person assumed liability for debtor's debts

common law courts for the investigation and settlement of matters of account. Partnerships, the administration of decedents' estates, receiverships, and suretyships all became for this reason important heads of equitable jurisdiction. Ultimately, equity acquired jurisdiction over the guardianship of infants and persons of unsound mind and over various special matters, including bankruptcy.

d. *Suits to quiet title or to remove a cloud.* Equity aided a possessor of land subjected to repeated unsuccessful ejectment actions by entertaining a bill to quiet title. See Wehrman v. Conklin, 155 U.S. 314, 321–23, 15 S.Ct. 129, 131–132, 39 L.Ed. 167, 172 (1894). In time, this form of relief was extended to other situations in which a party in possession of land, and sometimes out of possession, sought to remove a cloud on his title caused by an outstanding deed, lien, or other asserted interest in the land. Such suits are now regulated by statute in many states. See Leubsdorf, Remedies for Uncertainty, 61 B.U.L.Rev. 132 (1981); Howard, Bills to Remove Cloud from Title, 25 W.Va.L.Rev. 4 (1917).

e. *New remedies.* The court of chancery not only provided needed relief in cases in which the law courts failed to do so, it also developed new and flexible remedies to fit the situations presented. The decree of specific performance, the mandatory or prohibitive injunction, and the enforcement of discovery of documents by commitment are important examples. The power of the court of equity to enforce its decrees by sanctions operating on the person of the defendant (*aequitas agit in personam*) through fine and commitment for contempt made these new remedies particular effective.

SECTION 2.　HISTORICAL BACKGROUND: AMERICAN

A.　IN COLONIAL AND STATE COURTS

In most American systems, the reception of English procedural law was accomplished long before England abolished the formulary system of actions and united the courts of law and equity. Indeed, the first encompassing reforms were enacted in the United States rather than in England, with New York State forming the vanguard. Responding to the call of a leading scholar, David Dudley Field, New York, in its Constitution of 1846, abolished the Chancery Court which previously had had exclusive authority in equity actions and provided for the trial of civil cases, both in law and equity, in the Supreme Court.

The 1846 Constitution also gave the legislature a mandate to appoint three commissioners "to revise, reform, simplify and abridge the rules and practice, pleadings, form and proceedings of the courts of record." N.Y. Const., art. VI, § 24 (1846).

Pursuant to this mandate, the New York legislature, in 1848, adopted a Code of Procedure, generally referred to as the "Field Code," containing the following provision (N.Y.Code of Procedure § 69 [1848]):

"The distinctions between actions at law and suits in equity, and the forms of all such actions and suits heretofore existing, are abolished; and there shall be in this State hereafter but one form of action for the enforcement or protection of private rights and the redress of private wrongs, which shall be denominated a civil action."

The 1848 Code of Procedure purported to accomplish the following major reforms: first, the substitution of a single action, the "civil action," for all the different forms of action then existing at law and in equity; second, the substitution of the equitable rules of parties, pleading and final judgment for the technical common law rules; and, third, the consolidation of procedure at law and in equity, the principal courts becoming courts of law and equity, without difference in action or procedure except that certain legal institutions, mainly trial by jury, were expressly preserved, and except as differences in procedure necessarily continued in enforcing different forms of relief.

It was the New York example that was widely followed in the States and also, although in somewhat different form, in England. But in the states that did not enact a code patterned upon the Field Code, in the main, the common law procedures, changed to various extents, continued to be followed. And in a number of states, a formulary system of actions, of which the rigors were frequently substantially modified, continued its existence even into modern times. Many states also retained separate courts of law and equity, although others, such as Massachusetts and Pennsylvania, had earlier repudiated equity, which was grounded in the hated royal perogative, altogether.

The Federal Rules of Civil Procedure, introduced for the federal district courts in 1938, represented the next major innovative step. They carried forward the improvements introduced by the Field Code and brought many additional improvements. The trend has been towards adoption by the states of procedural rules patterned upon the Federal Rules of Civil Procedure, and the Federal Rules, with local modification, now prevail in the majority of the states.

B. IN THE FEDERAL COURTS

Until 1938, proceedings in the federal courts were conducted under two sets of rules. When a federal court was sitting in equity, it applied rules that were uniform for the whole country. Since 1842, these were formulated by the Supreme Court which had been given rule-making power for this purpose. The Federal Equity Rules of 1912 were the last edition of these rules before adoption of the Federal Rules of Civil Procedure in 1938.

When a federal court was sitting in law, however, a federal statute required conformity, as of a specified date, with the practice of the state. Statutes of this kind successively advanced the crucial date until Congress enacted the Conformity Act of 1872 which required the procedure in the federal court to "conform as near as may be," to the contemporaneous practice in the courts of the state in which the court was sitting. The substantive analogue of the Conformity Act was Section 34 of the original Judiciary Act of 1789, commonly known as the Rules of Decision Act, which provided that the laws of the several states shall be regarded as rules of decisions in the courts of the United States in cases where they apply. In the same year in which the Supreme Court decided Erie Railroad Co. v. Tompkins, 304 U.S. 64, 58 S.Ct. 817, 82 L.Ed. 1188 (1938), dissatisfaction with the Conformity Act had culminated in its repeal and adoption by the Supreme Court, under rule-making power granted by the Enabling Act of 1934, now 28 U.S. C.A. § 2072, of uniform rules of procedure in the federal district courts for actions both at law and in equity. The influence of these rules, which were drafted by an Advisory Committee to which Judge Charles E. Clark was the Reporter, cannot be overestimated. Not only do they govern proceedings in the federal district court and have they been adopted, with varying modifications, in the majority of the states, they also have exercised considerable influence on the development of procedural laws in England and elsewhere.

SECTION 3.   REMEDIES TO–DAY

A.   INTRODUCTION

The developments described above make clear the historical interdependence between substantive rights and judicial remedies: Substantive rights were originally recognized only by writs and bills issued for their protection in individual cases; and the procedure followed and the relief granted in such cases depended on the particular writ or bill issued. These historical developments continue to make their influence felt today.

Constitutional and statutory provisions guaranteeing the right to trial by jury in actions historically brought by writs at law continue to make the availability of so important a right as that to trial by jury depend on what the appropriate writ was at the common law. Furthermore, even in the absence of specific legislative directives, historical traditions continue to determine contemporary legal remedies: The remedy available today is often determined by whether it was the proper remedy under the form of action or bill in equity that was issued to redress the particular wrong complained of at common law.

NOTE

By far the greater number of disputes about legal rights and duties end without resort to the courts. Even when lawsuits are started, formal adjudication ensues in only a minority of the cases. Shaping the outcome of settlements stands the whole panoply of substantive and procedural law and the rules of judicial remedies. Also of consequence are the practical problems of litigation—the trouble, the expense and the ennui of litigating. Of all these factors, the focus in this chapter is upon judicial remedies. Judges have far from unlimited power to award whatever forms of redress they choose. In many legal controversies courts may not act at all; in others, their powers are narrowly confined. At times their lack of power flows from constitutional, statutory or common law sources, as, for example, the inhibitions upon the grant of "advisory opinions" or the enforcement of illegal bargains. Examples are decisions of the Supreme Court of the United States construing the equal protection clause of the Fourteenth Amendment to prohibit state courts' specifically enforcing racially restrictive covenants in land sale contracts (Shelley v. Kraemer, 334 U.S. 1, 68 S.Ct. 836, 92 L.Ed. 1161 (1948)), or awarding damages for breach of such a covenant (Barrows v. Jackson, 346 U.S. 249, 73 S.Ct. 1031, 97 L.Ed. 1586 (1953)).

Private parties may likewise set limits on the court's choice of remedies, for instance, by providing in their contracts for stipulated or "liquidated" damages as the sole remedy for breach; or even that their mutual promises are not to be enforceable at all, but to be treated merely as a "gentleman's agreement." Rose & Frank v. Crompton, 2 K.B. 261 (1923), affirmed L.R. (1925) A.C. 445; see also 6A Corbin on Contracts, §§ 1431, 1442, 1445, 1446 (1962 & Supp.1984). They may also, and commonly do, provide for arbitration rather than judicial determination of disputes arising under their contracts.

B. MONEY JUDGMENT

McCORMICK, DAMAGES

1935.

§ 1. The law of damages consists of the rules, standards, and methods used by the courts for measuring in money the compensation given for losses and injuries. It plays an unusually large part in Anglo–American law because of two distinctive features of the English judicial machinery. First is the presence of the jury, who award the damages under the judge's supervision and control. The rules and formulas used in the exercise of that control make up a substantial part of the law of damages. Second, in dividing jurisdiction between courts of law and courts of equity, the tradition was established that resort must be had to compensation by money damages in preference to specific relief, unless such damages are affirmatively shown to be inadequate for the just protection of the plaintiff's interest. It results from this traditional rule that a judgment for money damages is the normal and preferred remedy in our courts.

§ 137. Occasionally in tort cases an award by way of punishment may be made, but normally in all kinds of cases the truism remains true that the primary aim in measuring damages is to arrive at *compensation,* no more and no less. In a case of tort—the breach of some duty which the law imposes on every one—the general purpose of compensation is to give a sum of money to the person wronged which, as nearly as possible, will restore him to the position he would be in if the wrong had not been committed. In the case of a breach of contract, the goal of compensation is not the mere restoration to a former position, as in tort, but the awarding of a sum which is the equivalent of performance of the bargain—the attempt to place the plaintiff in the position he would be in if the contract had been fulfilled. This distinction finds frequent expression and application in the decisions, but of course these wide generalizations are not adequate formulas for placing before juries the standards of compensation nor for testing and regulating the amount of damages to be given for wrongs and breaches of contract. Other principles have been developed, which serve as limitations upon the extent of liability in these cases. Of these, the most constantly used are the principle which in contract cases restricts the damages to those which were in the "contemplation" of the parties when the contract was made, and the other principle, finding its chief employment in tort cases, which bars recovery for consequences not "proximately" caused by the defendant's conduct. Both of these doctrines give effect to major policies governing the larger outlines of risk or liability which the courts are willing to impose for given conduct.

NOTES

(1) In Groves v. John Wunder Co., 205 Minn. 163, 286 N.W. 235 (1939), the plaintiff sued to recover for the breach of a contract to grade his land. The court, stressing the deliberate character of the breach, held that the plaintiff could recover the cost of the grading of the land rather than the difference in value between the graded and the ungraded land. The cost of grading the land was about $60,000. The value of the land, if properly graded, would have been only about $12,000. Do you agree with this result? Was the plaintiff, after he had received the $60,000, obliged to spend it on the grading of his land?

(2) Whether the plaintiff can recover compensation for his injury or the equivalent of the benefit to the defendant may also depend on whether he could have maintained an action in assumpsit under the formulary system of actions. In Raven Red Ash Coal Co. v. Ball, 185 Va. 534, 39 S.E.2d 231 (1946), plaintiff sought to recover for unauthorized transportation of coal over his land. There was considerable authority for the rule that the plaintiff could recover in assumpsit, which would have entitled him to the monetary equivalent of the benefit to the defendant, only if the defendant had taken something from the land. The court, stressing the deliberate character of the defendant's transgression and rejecting the requirement that the illegal use of the land should involve the taking of something from it, permitted the plaintiff to recover the value of the benefit to the defendant.

(3) The principle laid down by Lord Ellenborough in Baker v. Bolton, 1 Camp. 493, 170 Eng.Rep. 1033 (1808), that "In a civil court, the death of a

human being could not be complained of as an injury" was abrogated in England by passage of the Fatal Accidents Act ("Lord Campbell's Act") in 1846. All American states now have statutes permitting recovery for wrongful death. "Wrongful death" statutes create new causes of action in designated persons or classes of beneficiaries for their losses resulting from tortious death. Recovery is not usually regarded as an asset of the decedent's estate and is not generally available to his creditors. "Survival" statutes annul the common law rule that death ends the victim's cause of action for personal injury and transmits his rights to his personal representative as an asset of his estate. Some states permit both remedies, while others limit their recovery to either "wrongful death" or "survival" benefits. See Duffey, The Maldistribution of Damages in Wrongful Death, 19 Ohio St. L.J. 264 (1958); Schumacher, Rights of Action Under Death and Survival Statutes, 23 Mich.L.Rev. 114 (1924). Several states set a maximum limit on the amount recoverable for tortious death.

(4) The proper elements and the correct measure of damages, and such issues as causation, foreseeability, remoteness and mitigation, are habitually treated in greater detail in courses on torts and contracts. They are therefore not treated more elaborately here.

(5) In Bankers Life and Casualty Co. v. Crenshaw, 486 U.S. 71, 108 S.Ct. 1645, 100 L.Ed.2d 62 (1988), the Supreme Court ruled that the question of whether the imposition of punitive damages could violate the Eighth Amendment and the Due Process Clause presented a question of "moment and difficulty." The Court refused to decide the question, since it had not been presented properly in the court below. However, the court has since ruled that an award of punitive damages does not run afoul of the Eighth Amendment, and particularly does not violate the excessive fines clause. Browning–Ferris Industries of Vermont v. Kelco Disposal, ___ U.S. ___, 109 S.Ct. 2909, 106 L.Ed. 2d 219 (1989).

(6) To what extent can punitive damages be awarded in contract cases? See, e.g., Seaman's Direct Burying Service, Inc. v. Standard Oil Co., 36 Cal.3d 752, 206 Cal.Rptr. 354, 686 P.2d 1158 (1984). Readiness to award punitive damages in contract cases appears to be greatest in cases of insurance companies that refuse to pay benefits. The courts have held that these companies are guilty of violation of an independent obligation of fair dealing which constitutes a tort. Is this a helpful analysis?

C. RECOVERY OF SPECIFIC PROPERTY

1. REPLEVIN AND DETINUE

Replevin and detinue (after it branched away from debt) were the only common law forms of action by which a person might obtain the return of personal property of whose possession he was being wrongfully deprived. At first replevin and detinue were distinct in major respects, but in time they came to be almost alternative actions. Finally replevin won out because of its procedural advantages to plaintiffs. In most American states these remedies have been replaced by a statutory action which is still called "replevin" or "an action in claim and delivery" or an "action to recover a chattel." In the Federal courts rule 64 of the Federal Rules of Civil Procedure makes available, inter alia, the provisional remedy of seizure of the property "at the commencement of" or "during the course of" a replevin action "for the purpose of securing satisfaction of the judgment ultimately to be entered in the action . . . under the circumstances and in the manner provided by the law of the state in which the district court is held, existing at the time the remedy is sought."

The judgment in both common law replevin and its modern equivalents awards the prevailing party possession of the chattel if it is extant (otherwise, its value), together with damages. Some states allow the plaintiff an election as to possession or value. Disagreement persists as to the point in time at which the value of the property should be assessed. The alternatives are the times of: taking, demand and refusal, filing of suit, rendition of verdict, or final judgment. Nice questions also arise as to the proper measure of damages for disturbance of possession.

Replevin often fails in practice to accomplish its purpose as a specific remedy. To seize the property, the sheriff must find it, and usually the law does not constrain cooperation on the defendant's part. Even if the location of the property is known, the sheriff faces delicate problems because of such rules as those forbidding molestation of the person, breaking of outer doors. As indicated in Chapter 4 infra, a series of Supreme Court decisions beginning with Sniadach v. Family Finance Corp. of Bay View, 395 U.S. 337, 89 S.Ct. 1820, 23 L.Ed.2d 349 (1969), expanded the category of cases in which notice and an opportunity to be heard must precede pre-judgment seizure. Indeed, in the view of the Restatement of Torts, "In many cases, depending upon the provisions for release on bond, the probability that replevin or a modern equivalent would successfully function as a specific remedy for the recovery of the chattel may be so slight that the remedy should be appraised in its alternative character as a damage remedy. . . ." See Restatement (Second) of Torts § 946, Comments a and b (1979).

NOTE

Charlotte Barber Supply Co. v. Branham, 184 S.C. 184, 191 S.E. 891 (1937): Action of claim and delivery for the recovery of certain chairs and other equipment for a barber shop to the possession of which plaintiff claimed to be entitled because of defendant's breach of the conditional sale contract by which plaintiff had sold them to defendant. There was some evidence at the trial that their then value was about $850. The trial judge directed a verdict for plaintiff but submitted the question of the value of the property to the jury, which returned the following verdict: "We find for the plaintiff the possession of the property . . ., and in case possession cannot be had; then for its value, to wit: Two Hundred Dollars." Defendant then offered to pay the value of the property as found by the jury, and moved that upon such payment the lien of the conditional sale contract on the property be discharged and his bondsmen be released. Plaintiff, on the other hand, moved for an order directing the defendant to deliver the property to plaintiff. The judge, holding that defendant "had the right to pay the value found by the jury only in the event such property had been destroyed or irremediably lost so that its possession could not be had," denied defendant's motion and granted plaintiff's motion. Affirmed. "In actions of claim and delivery . . ., the first object . . . is to protect the rights of the true owner in obtaining possession of his property in specie, if practicable." He therefore has the right and should be given the opportunity to exhaust every lawful means to locate and gain possession of his property before being required to accept its value as found by the jury. Defendant "overlooks the vital point that he may pay the value only in the event possession of the property cannot be had."

Judgment on the verdict was rendered for plaintiff on Oct. 28, 1936, and on that October night all of the articles "disappeared" from defendant's barber shop. On November 29 execution was issued on the judgment but the sheriff returned that the property could not be found at defendant's shop and that defendant disclaimed knowledge of its whereabouts. On November 2 a second execution was issued with like result. Plaintiff then moved that defendant be adjudged in contempt but the motion was dismissed as premature because defendant had not previously been examined in supplementary proceedings. Plaintiff then examined defendant in supplementary proceedings and he testified that the property was taken from his shop on October 28 and that he did not have it or know where it was. Plaintiff then obtained the appointment of a receiver of the property whom the court directed to secure possession of it. Thereafter, in consequence of a report by the receiver, the court issued a rule requiring defendant to show cause why he should not disclose the whereabouts of and immediately deliver the property to plaintiff and, if he failed to do so, be adjudged in contempt. However, this rule and the order appointing the receiver were subsequently vacated because plaintiff had appealed before they were issued, thus depriving the court of jurisdiction of the matter.

2. ORDER TO DELIVER PROPERTY

DUKE OF SOMERSET v. COOKSON
Court of Chancery, 1735.
3 Peere Williams 390.

The duke of Somerset, as lord of the manor of Corbridge, in Northumberland, (part of the estate of the Piercys late earls of Northumberland) was intitled to an old altar-piece made of silver, remarkable for a Greek inscription and dedication to Hercules. His grace became intitled to it as treasure trove within his said manor. This altar-piece had been sold by one who had got the possession of it, to the defendant, a goldsmith at Newcastle, but who had notice of the duke's claim thereto. The duke brought a bill in equity to compel the delivery of this altar-piece in specie, undefaced.

The defendant demurred as to part of the bill, for that the plaintiff had his remedy at law, by an action of *trover* or *detinue*, and ought not to bring his bill in equity; that it was true, for writings savouring of the realty a bill would lie, but not for any thing merely personal; any more than it would for a horse or a cow. So, a bill might lie for an heirloom; as in the case of Pusey versus Pusey, 1 Vern. 273. And though in *trover* the plaintiff could have only damages, yet in *detinue* the thing itself, if it can be found, is to be recovered; and if such bills as the present were to be allowed, half the actions of *trover* would be turned into bills in chancery.

On the other side it was urged, that the thing here sued for, was matter of curiosity and antiquity; and though at law, only the intrinsic value is to be recovered, yet it would be very hard that one who comes by such a piece of antiquity by wrong, or it may be as a trespasser, should have it in his power to keep the thing, paying only the intrinsic value of it; which is like a trespasser's forcing the right owner to part with a curiosity, or matter of antiquity, or ornament, *nolens volens.* Besides, the bill is to prevent the defendant from defacing the altar-piece, which is one way of depreciating it; and the defacing may be with an intention that it may not be known, by taking out, or erasing some of the marks and figures of it; and though the answer had denied the defacing of the altar-piece, yet such answer could not help the demurrer; that in itself nothing can be more reasonable than that the man who by wrong detains my property, should be compelled to restore it to me again in specie; and the law being defective in this particular, such defect is properly supplied in equity.

Wherefore it was prayed that the demurrer might be over-ruled, and it was over-ruled accordingly.

NOTES

(1) Raftery v. World Film Corporation, 180 App.Div. 475, 482–483, 167 N.Y.S. 1027 (1st Dep't 1917): After expiration of a contract for the exhibition by defendant of a motion picture called "The Head Hunters," plaintiff sued for an accounting of profits and to compel defendant to return the photographic prints. The court held that damages for the cost of making the prints would be inadequate relief because the property was of "unique character" and might be used by others for profit. After pointing out that the legal remedies of replevin and detinue are subject to defects of procedure which prevent the successful plaintiff from invariably recovering possession of the chattel, the court declared: "The plaintiff is entitled to the command of an equity judgment that the defendant return these prints, and to an enforcement of that judgment by proceedings for contempt." See also Chabert v. Robert & Co., 273 App.Div. 237, 76 N.Y.S.2d 400, 401 (1st Dep't 1948).

(2) Broomfield v. Checkoway, 310 Mass. 68, 38 N.E.2d 563 (1941): Plaintiff's bill, described as one for "equitable replevin," alleged and the judge found that defendant prevented plaintiff from removing certain machinery belonging to plaintiff from a building which was owned by defendant and in which the machinery was stored, by locking and barring the entrance to the building. Mass.G.L. (Ter.Ed.1932) c. 214, § 3(1), gives courts of equity jurisdiction over "suits to compel the re-delivery of goods or chattels taken or detained from the owner, and so secreted or withheld that they cannot be replevied." Defendant demurred to the bill on the ground that it did not state a cause of action under this statute because "an officer armed with a writ of replevin would have a right forcibly to remove the locks and bars and to seize the machinery." Demurrer overruled and decree rendered ordering defendant to deliver the machinery to plaintiff. Affirmed. Within the meaning of the statute, chattels are "so secreted or withheld that they cannot be replevied," if there is "a probable inability as a practical matter to obtain relief by replevin." While "an officer may break into a building, such as that here involved, for the purpose of seizing a chattel upon a writ of replevin," the attempt to do so is

attended by "uncertainty and danger" which "present a case within the statute."

(3) In Maxham v. Day, 16 Gray 213, 77 Am.Dec. 409 (Mass.1860), the court held that a sheriff may not, and therefore need not, seize articles of dress or personal adornment in order to execute a writ of replevin if, when he attempts to execute it, defendant is wearing them. "The necessity of securing immunity to the person from unreasonable searches and seizures and the impolicy of allowing an unlimited power to an officer to take on civil process articles worn on the person, forbid the extension of the remedy of replevin to property so used and situated. A bill in equity for property unlawfully withheld affords an ample remedy to recover possession of property of such a nature."

3. EJECTMENT *to recover real property*

NOTES

(1) While at present there is only one form of civil action, an action to recover the possession of real property is still referred to as ejectment. The principal characteristics of the action, other than the mode of pleading, are on the whole the same as those of its common law forebear, including the right to trial by jury.

tangible

(2) The action may be maintained only if it involves real property which is corporeal rather than incorporeal, that is, land or things such as growing crops so attached thereto as in legal contemplation to partake of its nature. Nichols v. Lewis, 15 Conn. 137 (1842); Note, 116 Am.St.Rep. 568 (1907). Accordingly, the action will not lie to recover intangible property, such as an easement, although real (Smith v. Wiggin, 48 N.H. 105 (1868); Lessee of Black v. Hepburne, 2 Yeates 331 (Pa.1798)), or personal property, although tangible. This condition of maintaining the action is often expressed by saying that it lies only to recover real property upon which an entry can actually be made or of which a sheriff can deliver possession. However, it is not essential that the encroachment should rest on or be under the soil; it suffices if a part of defendant's building projects over plaintiff's land. Murphy v. Bolger, 60 Vt. 723, 15 A. 365 (1888).

(3) Ejectment continues to be regarded as an action at law. Hence, it is still generally the case that only one who has a legal right to the immediate possession of the property which he seeks to recover can maintain the action and that in ejectment a legal title will prevail over an equitable one. Lincoln v. French, 105 U.S. (15 Otto) 614, 26 L.Ed. 1189 (1882); Taylor v. Russell, 65 W.Va. 632, 64 S.E. 923 (1909); Laurisinni v. Doe ex dem. Corquette, 25 Miss. 177, 57 Am.Dec. 200 (1852). Cf. Kingsnorth v. Baker, 213 Mich. 294, 182 N.W. 108 (1921).

(4) It is still said that in ejectment a plaintiff must recover upon the strength of his own title rather than upon the weakness of the defendant's, but this condition of maintaining the action has been judicially interpreted somewhat differently from, and with greater uniformity than, the like condition of maintaining replevin. See Philbrick, Seisin and Possession as the Basis of Legal Title, 24 Iowa L.Rev. 268, 277 et seq. (1939); Wiren, The Plea of the Ius Tertii in Ejectment, 41 L.Q.Rev. 139 (1925). In order to understand how most courts have construed it, we must realize that the possession of real property has both legal and evidential significance and that its protection has been a special concern of the courts; and we must distinguish between cases in which

plaintiffs in ejectment have, and those in which they have not, been dispossessed by the defendants. Statements in opinions "in a case where legal title is being tried cannot be properly applied to a case where only possession is at stake; and statements in a case involving mere possession are not applicable where title is drawn into question." Metzger, Real Property—Interest Necessary to Maintain Ejectment, 1954 U.Ill.L.F. 513, 517 (1954).

By the great weight of authority, a plaintiff who has been ousted from possession by a "mere intruder" (as to who is a "mere intruder" or a "mere trespasser," see Tapia v. Williams, 172 Ala. 18, 54 So. 613 (1911)) is entitled to regain it in ejectment, even though he may have acquired it wrongfully. See Bradshaw v. Ashley, 180 U.S. 59, 21 S.Ct. 297, 45 L.Ed. 423 (1901); Casey v. Kimmel, 181 Ill. 154, 54 N.E. 905 (1899); but see Cahill v. Cahill, 75 Conn. 522, 54 A. 201, 60 L.R.A. 706 (1903). This is either on the theory that possession is itself a species of title and, although the lowest species, better than no title at all, or on the theory that it creates a presumption of title which the defendant cannot rebut because, by hypothesis, he cannot establish that he himself has any title whatever and because he is not permitted to take advantage of the ius tertii, that is, to show that one who is legally a stranger to him has title. See Bradshaw v. Ashley, supra; Casey v. Kimmel, supra; Note, 28 Mich.L.Rev. 184 (1929). If, however, the defendant is not a mere trespasser, if he entered upon property peaceably and in good faith, under claim of right or color of title, a concession is made to him for the purpose, as it is said, of protecting his possession: He may rebut the presumption of title in the plaintiff by establishing a title either in himself or in a stranger (Note, 28 Mich.L.Rev. 184 (1929); see Tapia v. Williams, supra), and, if he succeeds in doing so, the plaintiff can no longer rely solely upon his prior possession. He must now prove that he has a right to possession which is superior to that of the defendant or of the stranger, as the case may be. And, of course, that is the plaintiff's predicament in all cases in which he has not been dispossessed by the defendant, for in such cases there is no presumption of title operating in his favor. See Goodtitle dem. Parker v. Baldwin, 11 East 488 (K.B.1809); Colston v. M'Vay, 8 Ky. (1 A.K. Marsh) 250 (1818). In all such cases, therefore, he must in the first instance introduce evidence to establish that he is entitled to immediate possession of the property.

(5) Ejectment does not lie against a defendant not in possession of the land plaintiff claims. The appropriate remedy in such a case is by action to quiet title.

HEROUX v. KATT

Supreme Court of Rhode Island, 1949.
76 R.I. 122, 68 A.2d 25, 12 A.L.R.2d 1186.

FLYNN, CHIEF JUSTICE. This action in trespass and ejectment was brought by a lessee for years to obtain possession of a portion of the demised premises alleged to be occupied by the defendants and wrongfully detained by them from the plaintiff. In the superior court, at the conclusion of the evidence for the plaintiff, the defendants rested their case and each party then moved for a directed verdict. The trial justice granted the plaintiff's motion and denied that of the defendants. The case is before us on defendants' exception to each of these rulings, all other exceptions being waived.

The following undisputed facts appear in the evidence. The land described in the writ and declaration is located at the corner of Broad and Babcock streets in the city of Providence and is owned in fee simple by George A. and Elizabeth Follett. By a lease in writing, said premises were demised by these owners to the plaintiff Joseph F. Heroux for a period of five years from April 27, 1948, the lease also containing a privilege of renewal for an additional period of five years on the same terms and conditions.

At the time this lease was executed the defendants were the owners of land adjoining the demised premises and were the occupants of a building located in part upon their own land and in part upon the land leased by the plaintiff. The portion of the building thus upon the leased land measures approximately 22.50 feet long by 20.05 feet wide.

The defendants were aware that such part of this building was located upon land that did not belong to them. Indeed, they had deliberately erected the building knowing that it encroached upon the land belonging to the Folletts. However, neither of the Folletts nor the plaintiff was aware at any time prior to entering into the lease that such building encroached upon the demised premises. Only after plaintiff had a survey of the premises made did it become known to him and the owners of the land that a portion of the defendants' building approximately 451 square feet in area was wrongfully located and maintained upon a part of the leased premises.

When the defendants refused to deliver possession of the land to the plaintiff the instant action was commenced in the district court by a writ of trespass and ejectment. The writ and declaration plainly described the premises as they appear in the lease and further alleged that the plaintiff by virtue of the lease, which was specifically identified therein, had an immediate right of entry to and possession of said land, a portion of which was being forcibly and wrongfully detained from him by the defendants. Defendants filed no special or equitable plea either in the district or superior court but relied solely upon a plea of the general issue.

* * *

In our opinion the trial justice was correct in directing a verdict for the plaintiff and in denying defendants' motion for a directed verdict. In support of their first contention that the plaintiff was restricted to a suit in equity to enjoin them from a continuing trespass and that only a court of equity had jurisdiction to give relief in the circumstances of record the defendants have cited several cases from other jurisdictions and rely strongly on the case of Rasch v. Noth, 99 Wis. 285, 74 N.W. 820, 40 L.R.A. 577, 67 Am.St.Rep. 858. However, most, if not all, such cases relate generally to suits brought in equity where the respondents sought to defeat equity's jurisdiction by contending that there was an adequate remedy at law. The Courts therein rightly held that equity jurisdiction can be justified where the remedy at law is found to be inadequate, as for example in a case of a continuing trespass or nuisance. But in our opinion none of those cases hold that equity is the *exclusive* forum where relief can be had in circumstances like those in the instant case. Undoubtedly equity could have taken and justified its jurisdiction and perhaps might have granted more effective and complete relief. Nevertheless it does not follow from that potentiality that the law court must be ousted of its ordinary jurisdiction if the plaintiff elected to pursue his legal remedy in trespass and ejectment. Such an election is a matter for plaintiff's consideration and not one of defense to the action in trespass and ejectment.

The case of Rasch v. Noth, supra, concerned projecting eaves without actual interference with the physical possession of the land. While there is a statement concerning equity jurisdiction which might seem to give support to defendants' contention, the reason therefor is clearly confined to the nature and issues of the case. See McCourt v. Eckstein, 22 Wis. 153, 94 Am.Dec. 594. In any event later cases in that jurisdiction make it entirely and expressly clear that the court in that case really did not mean to hold that equity had exclusive jurisdiction in all cases of encroachment. Such cases make it clear that trespass and ejectment may be inadequate and thereby justify resort to equity jurisdiction but not that trespass and ejectment could never be maintained where there has been an ouster by a tangible structure. See Beck v. Ashland Cigar & Tobacco Co., 146 Wis. 324, 130 N.W. 464, Ann. Cas.1912C, 239; Fisher v. Goodman, 205 Wis. 286, 288, 237 N.W. 93.

Even where it appears that the ability of a sheriff to deliver possession upon serving an execution is accepted as a test of whether the action of trespass and ejectment may properly be brought, it has been held that ejectment will lie because there is a disseisin measured by the size of the visible and tangible encroachment; and the sheriff can physically remove the structure and thereby restore the owner to possession. Butler v. Frontier Telephone Co., 186 N.Y. 486, 79 N.E. 716, 11 L.R.A.,N.S., 920, 116 Am.St.Rep. 563, 9 Ann.Cas. 858. See also Wachstein v. Christopher, 128 Ga. 229, 57 S.E. 511, 11 L.R.A.,N.S., 917, 19 Am.St.Rep. 381; Murphy v. Bolger Brothers, 60 Vt. 723, 15 A. 365, 1 L.R.A. 309. The defendants' first contention is without merit.

Nor do we agree with his second contention to the effect that only the owner of the fee in reversion may maintain an action of trespass and ejectment against an admitted trespasser who is wrongfully detaining a portion of the premises from the possession of a lessee. . . . As plaintiff points out, a lessee for years in this state has a right to bring trespass and ejectment against such strangers under General Laws 1938, chap. 435, § 10, and G.L.1938, chap. 538, § 12.

*   *   *

Moreover, this statute seems to carry out the concepts of the old action of ejectment. . . . Tyler on Ejectment, at page 169. . . . To a similar effect, see 2 Taylor's Landlord and Tenant, 9th Ed., 310, § 698; Tiedeman on Real Property, 3d Ed., 165, § 131.

. . . Therefore, whether we consider the instant case under our statute or at common law, we think there is ample authority for a plaintiff lessee for years to bring an action of trespass and ejectment to vindicate his rights of entry and immediate possession against one who wrongfully detains from him possession of a portion of the leased premises.

We find no merit in the defendants' third contention to the effect that the plaintiff and his partner doing an automobile business on the leased premises were in actual possession and therefore the only proper plaintiffs. The defendants overlook the fact that the person entitled to bring an action of trespass and ejectment is the person who is *legally* entitled to enter upon and have the immediate and exclusive possession of the premises against any stranger or trespasser. Only the plaintiff here had that legal right.

The defendants' exceptions are overruled, and the case is remitted to the superior court for entry of judgment for the plaintiff on the verdict as directed.

NOTES

(1) In the principal case, what consequences would follow if on execution the sheriff should remove too large a portion of defendants' encroaching building? Cf. Fisher v. Goodman, p. 95, Note (3), infra. If the sheriff found it impracticable to remove the encroachment, could plaintiff maintain a suit in equity for an injunction? See Hahl v. Sugo, 169 N.Y. 109, 62 N.E. 135 (1901); Restatement (Second) of Judgments §§ 24–26 (1982). What procedural or practical reasons can there be for suing in ejectment instead of for an injunction in equity?

(2) Procedures in an ejectment action, or its statutory equivalent, an action to recover real property, are, as already noted, essentially the same as in any other form of action. Complex statutory provisions deal with such matters as parties and the effect of a judgment, but they are often substantive in nature. See, e.g., N.Y.Real Prop.A. & P.L., Art. 6, particularly § 625 (action by reversioner or remainderman after tenant's death); cf. N.Y. Real Prop.A. & P.L., Art. 9, action for partition; McKinney's N.Y. Real Property Law, Art. 14, action for dower; McKinney's N.Y. Real Property Law, Art. 15, action to compel the determination of a claim to real property.

(3) Sometimes wholly different procedures are available. Consider, for example, Article 7 of the N.Y. Real Prop.A. & P.L. which provides a summary proceeding to recover possession of real property and recover damages for its use wholly different from that available in civil actions generally. It is available in such cases as those involving landlord-tenant, forcible entry, squatters and premises used for vice.

D. ORDER TO DO OR REFRAIN FROM DOING A SPECIFIC ACT

In systems that provide for a single form of action, the distinctions between actions at law and suits in equity nevertheless continue to be of prime importance. As will be seen below, the right to trial by jury may depend on whether the new action can be categorized as one in which formerly relief would have been given at law. And in the field of remedies, the availability of specific relief, such as specific performance or a mandatory or prohibitive injunction, still continues to depend largely on whether available relief at law is adequate.

A unique characteristic of equitable relief is that it operates against the person of the defendant (*aequitas agit in personam*). If he fails to comply with the decree, he may be punished for contempt by fine and imprisonment. Judgments at law declare impersonally that the plaintiff recover a sum of money or specified real or personal property. The defendant who does not pay or surrender the property must suffer the consequences, which may be levy of execution on his property or seizure of the things awarded to the plaintiff by the sheriff, but he does not render himself punishable for failure to obey the judgment.

Another characteristic of equitable relief is that it need not be cast in the stereotyped forms of relief available in actions at law, but may be tailored to the exigencies of the particular case.

To what extent, if any, should the availability of these advantages today depend on the historical distinctions between actions at law and suits in equity? And what role do they play in the shaping of a litigant's judgment as to the mold into which he should cast his action?

BOOMER v. ATLANTIC CEMENT COMPANY, INC.

Court of Appeals, New York *, 1970.
26 N.Y.2d 219, 309 N.Y.S.2d 312, 257 N.E.2d 870.

BERGAN, J. Defendant operates a large cement plant near Albany. These are actions for injunction and damages by neighboring land owners alleging injury to property from dirt, smoke and vibration emanating from the plant. A nuisance has been found after trial, temporary damages have been allowed, but an injunction has been denied.

The public concern with air pollution arising from many sources in industry and in transportation is currently accorded ever wider recognition accompanied by a growing sense of responsibility in State and Federal Governments to control it. Cement plants are obvious sources of air pollution in the neighborhoods where they operate.

* The last three footnotes have been omitted.

But there is now before the court private litigation in which individual property owners have sought specific relief from a single plant operation.

* * *

It seems apparent that the amelioration of air pollution will depend on technical research in great depth; on a carefully balanced consideration of the economic impact of close regulation, and of the actual effect on public health. It is likely to require massive public expenditure and to demand more than any local community can accomplish and to depend on regional and interstate controls.

A court should not try to do this on its own as a by-product of private litigation, and it seems manifest that the judicial establishment is neither equipped in the limited nature of any judgment it can pronounce nor prepared to lay down and implement an effective policy for the elimination of air pollution. This is an area beyond the circumference of one private lawsuit. It is a direct responsibility for government and should not thus be undertaken as an incident to solving a dispute between property owners and a single cement plant— one of many—in the Hudson River valley.

* * *

The ground for the denial of injunction, notwithstanding the finding both that there is a nuisance and that plaintiffs have been damaged substantially, is the large disparity in economic consequences of the nuisance and of the injunction. This theory cannot, however, be sustained without overruling a doctrine which has been consistently reaffirmed in several leading cases in this court and which has never been disavowed here, namely that where a nuisance has been found and where there has been any substantial damage shown by the party complaining an injunction will be granted.

* * *

[The Court's discussion of prior cases has been omitted.]

Although the court at Special Term and the Appellate Division held that injunction should be denied, it was found that plaintiffs had been damaged in various specific amounts up to the time of the trial and damages to the respective plaintiffs was awarded for those amounts. The effect of this was, injunction having been denied, plaintiffs could maintain successive actions at law for damages thereafter as further damage was incurred.

The court at Special Term also found the amount of permanent damage attributable to each plaintiff, for the guidance of the parties in the event both sides stipulated to the payment and acceptance of such permanent damage as a settlement of all the controversies among the parties. The total of permanent damages to all plaintiffs thus found was $185,000. This basis of adjustment has not resulted in any stipulation by the parties.

This result at Special Term and at the Appellate Division is a departure from a rule that has become settled; but to follow the rule literally in these cases would be to close down the plant at once. This court is fully agreed to avoid that immediately drastic remedy; the difference in view is how best to avoid it.*

One alternative is to grant the injunction but postpone its effect to a specified future date to give opportunity for technical advances to permit defendant to eliminate the nuisance; another is to grant the injunction conditioned on the payment of permanent damages to plaintiffs which would compensate them for the total economic loss to their property present and future caused by defendant's operations. For reasons which will be developed the court chooses the latter alternative.

If the injunction were to be granted unless within a short period, e.g., 18 months, the nuisance be abated by improved methods, there would be no assurance that any significant technical improvement would occur.

The parties could settle this private litigation at any time if defendant paid enough money and the imminent threat of closing the plant would build up the pressure on defendant. If there were no improved techniques found, there would inevitably be applications to the court at Special Term for extensions of time to perform on showing of good faith efforts to find such techniques.

Moreover, techniques to eliminate dust and other annoying by-products of cement making are unlikely to be developed by any research the defendant can undertake within any short period, but will depend on the total resources of the cement industry nationwide and throughout the world. The problem is universal wherever cement is made.

For obvious reasons the rate of the research is beyond control of defendant. If at the end of eighteen months the whole industry has not found a technical solution a court would be hard put to close down this one cement plant if due regard be given to equitable principles.

On the other hand, to grant the injunction unless defendant pays plaintiffs such permanent damages as may be fixed by the court seems to do justice between the contending parties. All of the attributions of economic loss to the properties on which plaintiffs' complaints are based will have been redressed.

The nuisance complained of by these plaintiffs may have other public or private consequences, but these particular parties are the only ones who have sought remedies and the judgment proposed will fully redress them. The limitation of relief granted is a limitation only within the four corners of these actions and does not foreclose public health or other public agencies from seeking proper relief in a proper court.

---

* Respondent's investment in the plant is in excess of $45,000,000. There are over 300 people employed there.

It seems reasonable to think that the risk of being required to pay permanent damages to injured property owners by cement plant owners would itself be a reasonably effective spur to research for improved techniques to minimize nuisance.

The power of the court to condition on equitable grounds the continuance of an injunction on the payment of permanent damages seems undoubted. . . .

* * *

to burden P's land for P's benefit

Thus it seems fair to both sides to grant permanent damages to plaintiffs which will terminate this private litigation. The theory of damage is the "servitude on land" of plaintiffs imposed by defendant's nuisance. (See United States v. Causby, 328 U.S. 256, 261, 262, 267, 66 S.Ct. 1062, 90 L.Ed. 1206 where the term "servitude" addressed to the land was used by Justice Douglas relating to the effect of airplane noise on property near an airport.)

The judgment, by allowance of permanent damages imposing a servitude on land, which is the basis of the actions, would preclude future recovery by plaintiffs or their grantees. . . .

This should be placed beyond debate by a provision of the judgment that the payment by defendant and the acceptance by plaintiffs of permanent damages found by the court shall be in compensation for a servitude on the land.

Although the Special Term has found permanent damages as a possible basis of settlement of the litigation, on remission the court should be entirely free to re-examine this subject. It may again find the permanent damage already found; or make new findings.

The orders should be reversed, without costs, and the cases remitted to Special Term to grant an injunction which shall be vacated upon payment by defendant of such amounts of permanent damage to the respective plaintiffs as shall for this purpose be determined by the court.

JASEN, J. (dissenting)—I agree with the majority that a reversal is required here, but I do not subscribe to the newly enunciated doctrine of assessment of permanent damages, in lieu of an injunction, where substantial property rights have been impaired by the creation of a nuisance.

It has long been the rule in this state, as the majority acknowledges, that a nuisance which results in substantial continuing damage to neighbors must be enjoined (Whalen v. Union Bag & Paper Co., 208 N.Y. 1, 101 N.E. 805; Campbell v. Seaman, 63 N.Y. 568; see, also, Kennedy v. Moog, 21 N.Y.2d 966). To now change the rule to permit the cement company to continue polluting the air indefinitely upon the payment of permanent damages is, in my opinion, compounding the magnitude of a very serious problem in our state and nation today.

I see grave dangers in overruling our long-established rule of granting an injunction where a nuisance results in substantial continuing damage. In permitting the injunction to become inoperative upon the payment of permanent damages, the majority is, in effect, licensing a continuing wrong. It is the same as saying to the cement company, you may continue to do harm to your neighbors so long as you pay a fee for it. Furthermore, once such permanent damages are assessed and paid, the incentive to alleviate the wrong would be eliminated, thereby continuing air pollution of an area without abatement.

It is true that some courts have sanctioned the remedy here proposed by the majority in a number of cases, but none of the authorities relied upon by the majority are analogous to the situation before us. In those cases, the courts, in denying an injunction and awarding money damages, grounded their decision on a showing that the use to which the property was intended to be put was primarily for the public benefit. Here, on the other hand, it is clearly established that the cement company is creating a continuing air pollution nuisance primarily for its own private interest with no public benefit.

This kind of inverse condemnation (Ferguson v. Village of Hamburg, 272 N.Y. 234, 5 N.E.2d 801) may not be invoked by a private person or corporation for private gain or advantage. Inverse condemnation should only be permitted when the public is primarily served in the taking or impairment of property (Matter of N.Y.C. Housing Auth. v. Muller, 270 N.Y. 333, 343, 1 N.E.2d 153, 156; The Pocantico Water Works Co. v. Bird, 130 N.Y. 249, 258, 29 N.E. 246, 248.) The promotion of the interests of the polluting cement company has, in my opinion, no public use or benefit.

Accordingly, the orders of the Appellate Division, in so far as they denied the injunction, should be reversed and the actions remitted to Special Term to grant an injunction to take effect eighteen months hence, unless the nuisance is abated by improved techniques prior to said date.

In each action:

Order reversed, without costs, and the case remitted to Supreme Court, Albany County, for further proceedings in accordance with the opinion herein. Opinion by Bergan, J. All concur except Jasen, J., who dissents in part and votes to reverse in an opinion. Breitel and Gibson, JJ., taking no part.

NOTES

(1) The traditional rule is that a court of equity grants equitable relief only when, upon balancing the parties' competing interests, it finds such relief to be proper. A statute may exclude such judicial balancing and make equitable relief mandatory. See TVA v. Hill, 437 U.S. 153, 98 S.Ct. 2279, 57 L.Ed.2d 117 (1978) (holding that an imminent violation of the Endangered Species Act, threatening the extinction of the snail darter, made injunctive relief mandatory). However, statutory exclusion of equitable discretion is not readily to be assumed. See Weinberger v. Romero–Barcelo, 456 U.S. 305, 102 S.Ct. 1798, 72 L.Ed.2d 91 (1982) (holding that the Navy's violating of the Federal Water Pollution Control Act did not make the issuance of an injunction mandatory).

(2) Are private suits for injunctions efficacious to control use of land in an industrialized, swiftly changing civilization? Land zoning and legislative restrictions upon use have multiplied in recent years and with them prolific litigation over their administration by public bodies charged with revising use zones and passing upon requests for relief or "variances". How much may land use be restricted by the state on esthetic grounds? See, e.g., N.Y.S. Thruway Authority v. Ashley Motor Court, 10 N.Y.2d 151, 218 N.Y.S.2d 640, 176 N.E.2d 566 (1961) (billboards).

(3) Fisher v. Goodman, 205 Wis. 286, 289–290, 237 N.W. 93 (1931), involved an action for an injunction requiring defendants to remove a foundation and wall from plaintiff's land: "[L]egal processes are inadequate to permit relief where the invasion consists of an overlapping foundation or wall. It is not reasonable to ask a sheriff to remove the invading portion of that wall or foundation, as he is guilty of trespass if in doing so he invades by a hairline the property of the defendants. The proceeding is as delicate and impracticable as the taking of the pound of flesh. The responsibility of removing the wall should, in justice, be left to the party who built it, and this the remedy of mandatory injunction does. If the plaintiff be left to his or her remedy in ejectment, that remedy must prove wholly inadequate. If it be said that the invasion is one of continuing trespass, a multiplicity of suits will follow. Either of these considerations is abundantly sufficient to support the jurisdiction of a court of equity."

LUMLEY v. WAGNER

Court of Chancery, 1852.
1 De Gex, Macnaghten & Gordon, 604.

[Defendants appealed from an order of the Vice–Chancellor, estraining defendant Wagner from singing at any but plaintiff's theatre and defendant Gye from employing her during the term of her contract with plaintiff.]

The Lord Chancellor. . . . The question which I have to decide in the present case arises out of a very simple contract, the effect of which is, that the Defendant Johanna Wagner should sing at her Majesty's Theatre for a certain number of nights, and that she should not sing elsewhere (for that is the true construction) during that period. As I understand the points taken by the Defendants' counsel in support of this appeal they in effect come to this, namely, that a Court of Equity ought not to grant an injunction except in cases connected with specific performance, or where the injunction being to compel a party to forbear from committing an act (and not to perform an act), that injunction will complete the whole of the agreement remaining unexecuted.

*   *   *

It was also contended that the Plaintiff's remedy, if any, was at law; but it is no objection to the exercise of the jurisdiction by injunction, that the Plaintiff may have a legal remedy. . . .

The present is a mixed case, consisting not of two correlative acts to be done, one by the Plaintiff and the other by the Defendants, which state of facts may have and in some cases has introduced a very important difference,—but of an act to be done by J. Wagner alone, to which is superadded a negative stipulation on her part to abstain from the commission of any act which will break in upon her affirmative covenant—the one being ancillary to, concurrent and operating together with the other. The agreement to sing for the Plaintiff during three months at his theatre, and during that time not to sing for anybody else, is not a correlative contract, it is in effect one contract; and though beyond all doubt this Court could not interfere to enforce the specific performance of the whole of this contract, yet in all sound construction, and according to the true spirit of the agreement, the engagement to perform for three months at one theatre must necessarily exclude the right to perform at the same time at another theatre. It was clearly intended that J. Wagner was to exert her vocal abilities to the utmost to aid the theatre to which she agreed to attach herself. I am of opinion, that if she had attempted, even in the absence of any negative stipulation, to perform at another theatre, she would have broken the spirit and true meaning of the contract as much as she would now do with reference to the contract into which she has actually entered.

Wherever this Court has not proper jurisdiction to enforce specific performance, it operates to bind men's consciences, as far as they can be bound, to a true and literal performance of their agreements; and it will not suffer them to depart from their contracts at their pleasure, leaving the party with whom they have contracted to the mere chance of any damages which a jury may give. The exercise of this jurisdiction has, I believe, had a wholesome tendency towards the maintenance of that good faith which exists in this country to a much greater degree perhaps than in any other; and although the jurisdiction is not to be extended, yet a Judge would desert his duty who did not act up to what his predecessors have handed down as the rule for his guidance in the administration of such an equity.

It was objected that the operation of the injunction in the present case was mischievous, excluding the Defendant J. Wagner from performing at any other theatre while this Court had no power to compel her to perform at her Majesty's Theatre. It is true, that I have not the means of compelling her to sing, but she has no cause of complaint, if I compel her to abstain from the commission of an act which she has bound herself not to do, and thus possibly cause her to fulfil her engagement. The jurisdiction which I now exercise is wholly within the power of the Court, and being of opinion that it is a proper case for interfering, I shall leave nothing unsatisfied by the judgment I pronounce. The effect, too, of the injunction, in restraining J. Wagner from singing elsewhere may, in the event of an action being brought against her by the Plaintiff, prevent any such amount of vindictive damages being given against her as a jury might probably be inclined to give if she had carried her talents and exercised them at the rival theatre: the injunction may also, as I have said, tend to the fulfilment of her engagement; though, in continuing the injunction, I disclaim doing indirectly what I cannot do directly. . . .

NOTES

(1) Paramount Pictures Corp. v. Holden, 166 F.Supp. 684 (S.D.Cal.1958): The plaintiff applied for an interlocutory injunction to prohibit the defendant, a motion picture actor, from performing in a movie called "The Horse Soldiers," relying upon a California statute which allows specific enforcement of written contracts for personal services where the minimum compensation "is at the rate of not less than six thousand dollars per annum, and where the promised service is of a special, unique, unusual, extraordinary or intellectual character which gives it peculiar value the loss of which cannot be reasonably or adequately compensated in damages in an action at law." In denying the injunction the court declared that the power to issue an injunction is discretionary and should not be exercised except when the right to it is "clear" and "free from doubt," irreparable injury threatens the plaintiff, for which damages will not compensate him, and when on "balancing of equities" the plaintiff's position is stronger.

(2) For a more recent example of a *Lumley v. Wagner* type of injunction, see New England Patriots Football Club, Inc. v. University of Colorado, 592 F.2d 1196 (1st Cir.1979), affirming the grant of an injunction enjoining defendants from employing the plaintiff's football coach contractually bound to the plaintiff.

(3) For an excellent discussion of the problems in balancing equities and the effect of availability of the remedy of specific performance on employment relationships, see Blake, Problem of Employee Agreements Not to Compete, 73 Harv.L.Rev. 625 (1960).

NOTE ON EQUITABLE RELIEF

1. *Its Subsidiary Nature.* Historically, equitable relief is not granted unless legal relief is unavailable or inadequate. This continues to be the rule today, although courts more readily find legal relief to be inadequate when equitable relief appears more appropriate. Now that law and equity have merged and the unitary action prevails, should the rule be jettisoned? Surely, its historical justification is no longer adequate. If there are other reasons for adhering to the rule, what are they? In civil law systems, the right to affirm specific performance is not conditioned upon the unavailability or inadequacy of other relief. See, e.g., Cappelletti & Perillo, Civil Procedure in Italy 148 (Smit ed. 1965); Herzog & Weser, Civil Procedure in France 556 (Smit ed. 1967); Bader Ginsburg & Bruzelius, Civil Procedure in Sweden 145 (Smit ed. 1965). The Restatement (Second) of Contracts § 361 (1981) provides:

> "In determining the adequacy of the remedy in damages, as to contracts other than for the transfer of an interest in land, the following factors are influential and may singly or in combination justify specific enforcement:

"(a) the degree of difficulty and uncertainty in making an accurate valuation of the subject matter involved, in determining the effect of a breach, and in estimating the plaintiff's harm;

"(b) the existence of sentimental associations and esthetic interests, not measurable in money, that would be affected by a breach;

"(c) the difficulty, inconvenience, or impossibility of obtaining a duplicate or substantial equivalent of the promised performance by means of money awarded as damages;

"(d) the degree of probability that damages awarded cannot in fact be collected;

"(e) the probability that full compensation cannot be had without multiple litigation."

Is this an appropriate approach or would it be better to follow the civil law example?

2. *Mutuality.* Courts have frequently ruled that equitable relief may be directed only if the opponent could have been given equitable relief for the enforcement of his rights. This rule has been significantly eroded. Epstein v. Gluckin, 233 N.Y. 490, 493, 135 N.E. 861, 862 (1922) (Cardozo, J.): "If ever there was a rule that mutuality of remedy existing, not merely at the time of a decree, but at the time of the formation of the contract, is a condition of equitable relief, it has been so qualified by exceptions that, viewed as a precept of general validity, it has ceased to be a rule today. [Citations omitted.] What equity exacts today as a condition of relief is the assurance that the decree, if rendered, will operate without injustice or oppression either to the plaintiff or to the defendant."

Should specific performance be granted if the plaintiff is not obligated to perform all of his obligations at the same time or earlier? The Restatement (Second) of Contracts § 363 (1981) provides:

"Specific performance or an injunction may be refused if a substantial part of the agreed exchange for the performance to be compelled is unperformed and its performance is not secured to the satisfaction of the court."

3. *Injunctions Against Criminal Proceedings.* Courts, for reasons readily perceived, generally refuse to enjoin criminal proceedings. See Broaddus, Enjoining Criminal Prosecutions, 37 Calif.L.Rev. 685 (1949). But, in egregious cases, the rule may give way. See, e.g., Murray v. Vaughn, 300 F.Supp. 688 (D.R.I.1969) (enjoining the U.S. attorney from prosecuting, for failure to report for induction into the armed forces, a Peace Corps volunteer who had been dismissed from the Peace Corps and drafted for having criticized U.S. involvement in Vietnam).

4. *Federal System Problems.* May state courts enjoin federal officers? See Arnold, The Power of State Courts to Enjoin Federal Officers, 73 Yale L.J. 1385 (1964). May federal courts enjoin state

officers or judicial proceedings? See, e.g., Younger v. Harris, 401 U.S. 37, 91 S.Ct. 746, 27 L.Ed.2d 669 (1971) (only in exceptional cases).

5. *Unclean Hands.* The doctrine of unclean hands may provide an equitable defense in an action brought by a plaintiff whose claim is based on objectionable conduct. See, e.g., Lowe v. Quinn, 27 N.Y.2d 397, 318 N.Y.S.2d 467, 267 N.E.2d 251 (1971) (plaintiff, a married man, may not recover an engagement ring given to the defendant who broke the engagement a month after she received the ring, even though plaintiff had lived apart from his wife for several years and he and his wife contemplated a divorce.) But see Friedman v. Geller, 82 Misc.2d 291, 368 N.Y.S.2d 980 (Civ.Ct., Kings County 1975) (criticizing the *Lowe* decision as anachronistic). On the clean hands doctrine generally, see Chafee, Coming Into Equity with Clean Hands, 47 Mich.L.Rev. 877, 1065 (1949); Snell, Principles of Equity (28th ed. 1982).

6. *Laches.* Another equitable defense is laches, the essence of which is an unreasonable delay in the assertion of one's rights. Although laches thus serves as an equitable counterpart to statutes of limitation it does not, as do the latter, depend upon legislative specification of fixed periods of time allowed for particular categories of actions. Uncertainty exists as to whether mere passage of time may be a proper basis for the defense or whether it is required in addition that the party invoking the defense has changed its position in reliance on the appearance of the absence of rights created by the party who delayed their assertion. Cf. Clark, Equity § 31 (1954); McClintock, Equity § 28 (2d ed. 1948); Walsh, Equity § 102 (1930). See also Note, Passage of Time as Laches, 61 W.Va.L.Rev. 126, 127 (1959).

7. *Continuing Judicial Supervision.* It is not uncommon for an injunction to contain at the foot of the decree a provision noting that "The cause will be retained for further action and either party may apply hereafter for appropriate relief." Georgia v. Tennessee Copper Co., 237 U.S. 474, 478, 35 S.Ct. 631, 632, 59 L.Ed. 1054 (1915). When there is a claim of violation, the court, instead of adjudging a party in contempt or modifying a decree may, by its opinion, "clarify" its meaning as a warning to the parties. See Wyoming v. Colorado, 309 U.S. 572, 582, 60 S.Ct. 765, 769, 84 L.Ed. 954 (1940), 298 U.S. 573, 56 S.Ct. 912, 80 L.Ed. 1339 (1936), 286 U.S. 494, 52 S.Ct. 621, 76 L.Ed. 1245 (1932), 260 U.S. 1, 43 S.Ct. 2, 66 L.Ed. 1026 (1922), 259 U.S. 419, 496, 42 S.Ct. 552, 594, 66 L.Ed. 999 (1922). In a particularly complex case, the court may even appoint a master to supervise its enforcement. See the decree in Georgia v. Tennessee Copper Co., supra, set out at 237 U.S. 678, 35 S.Ct. 752, 59 L.Ed. 1173.

E. DECLARATORY JUDGMENT

The remedies thus far examined have been concerned largely with past wrongs. The act had already been committed or the omission perpetrated, or so plaintiff alleged. Defendant had breached his contractual obligation or inflicted harm on plaintiff's person, converted his goods, encroached on his land; or not. The court was called upon to decide and award appropriate redress if any were due.

But many legal disputes take time to develop and cast warning shadows before. Often, if the parties could be assured of their rights or apprised of their duties, the threatened damage would not be done. Must all assurance come solely from counsel or may the courts be approached before the dispute has gone full course?

How far can this use of the judicial process be carried? How early in a developing controversy may a party obtain the court's determination of disputed legal interests? Where is the line between a controversy that has become "actual" and one that is too "hypothetical" or too unripe? Is there, indeed, a line or is there only a mist?

PUGH, THE FEDERAL DECLARATORY REMEDY: JUSTICIABILITY, JURISDICTION AND RELATED PROBLEMS

6 Vand.L.Rev. 79–83 (1952).*

BACKGROUND OF THE FEDERAL DECLARATORY REMEDY

The roots of the federal declaratory action run deep. It may be traced from its origins in Roman law and the law of the Middle Ages to Scotland, and in the nineteenth century from Scotland to England and thereafter to this country. Although it is quite true that from time immemorial Anglo–American courts of equity had afforded what amounted to declaratory relief in narrowly restricted areas (such as the action to quiet title), there was no concept, even in equity, of a *general* declaratory action. Perhaps equity's failure to provide general declaratory relief is to be attributed to the realization that such a procedure would subvert the right to jury trial. But, whatever the reason, the fact remains that until comparatively recently general declaratory relief was unknown to the Anglo–American system.

Thus despite the existence of real and actual controversy between vehement adverse parties, judicial redress was oftentimes refused. Unless the action could be fitted into some tightly knit category (such as the action to quiet title) declaratory relief was denied. Contracting parties differing on the proper interpretation of their rights and obligations were forced to act at their peril. The client of the counsel who guessed wrong was mulcted in damages. To paraphrase Congressman Gilbert, a party had to take his step in the dark before he turned on the light. The answer to this procedural void may appear obvious, but the intelligent response was given only after a prolonged stutter.

* Footnotes omitted.

Lord Brougham is largely responsible for the English declaratory action. In a speech before the House of Commons in 1828, he called attention to the advantages of the declaratory action used in Scottish courts and thereafter made repeated attempts to secure the adoption of an English declaratory act. By 1883, the way had been paved in England for a wide application of the declaratory remedy.

Progress in this country came much later. In the latter part of the nineteenth century, Rhode Island and Maryland enacted statutes affording a limited form of declaratory relief; but it was New Jersey, in 1915, which enacted the first adequate declaratory act. The articles of Professors Sunderland and Borchard and other legal scholars heralded the advantages of the new procedure, and the statutory response was rewarding. In 1922, the Uniform Declaratory Judgment Act was proposed, and today only some four states ** fail to provide some form of declaratory remedy.

The late Professor Borchard, the architect of the American declaratory remedy, was the foremost authority in the field. He wrote numerous articles urging the merits of the new action, and criticizing those courts which had veered from its salutary aims. The first and second editions of his Declaratory Judgments are works of erudition and wisdom, and have been constantly referred to by the courts. His prodigious labors are largely responsible for the presence of the Federal Declaratory Judgment Act.

It was in the federal sphere that resistance was most severe. It is hallowed hornbook law that federal constitutional courts do not render advisory opinions, and many thought that advisory opinions and declaratory actions were practically synonymous. The years of reassuring state experience failed to allay their fears. In 1927, the Supreme Court indicated by dictum in Liberty Warehouse Co. v. Grannis [273 U.S. 70, 74, 47 S.Ct. 282, 71 L.Ed. 541 (1926)] that a declaratory judgment is in effect an advisory opinion. Despite this dictum, a bill authorizing the use of the declaratory action was passed by the House of Representatives on January 25, 1928. By May 18 of that year hearings on the bill were concluded by the Senate Committee on the Judiciary, but on May 21, 1928, the movement was dealt a death blow by the Supreme Court's decision in the famous case of Willing v. Chicago Auditorium Association [277 U.S. 274, 48 S.Ct. 507, 72 L.Ed. 880 (1928)].

* * *

Federal declaratory relief was delayed six years by the Willing dictum. When the Court was actually called upon to determine the constitutionality of declaratory relief, the answer was in the affirmative. Nashville, Chattanooga & St. Louis Ry. v. Wallace [288 U.S. 249, 53 S.Ct. 345, 77 L.Ed. 730 (1933)] came to the Supreme Court from the highest state court of Tennessee. The action had been brought under the provisions of the Uniform Declaratory Judgments Act, which had

** Three more states have adopted the remedy since 1952, and at this time only Mississippi is without a statute allowing declaratory relief.

been adopted by the Tennessee legislature. Unless the case presented a "case" or "controversy" within the meaning of the Constitution, the Supreme Court would have been powerless to review the Tennessee decision. The Court very properly found that the case presented a justiciable controversy and fell within the ambit of its constitutional and statutory appellate jurisdiction. . . .

[Nashville] laid a solid foundation for the Federal Declaratory Judgment Act, which became the law of the land in 1934, the year after the Nashville decision.

FEDERAL DECLARATORY JUDGMENT ACT

28 U.S.C.A.

§ 2201. Creation of remedy

In a case of actual controversy within its jurisdiction, except with respect to Federal taxes, any court of the United States and the District Court for the Territory of Alaska, upon the filing of an appropriate pleading, may declare the rights and other legal relations of any interested party seeking such declaration, whether or not further relief is or could be sought. Any such declaration shall have the force and effect of a final judgment or decree and shall be reviewable as such.

§ 2202. Further relief

Further necessary or proper relief based on a declaratory judgment or decree may be granted, after reasonable notice and hearing, against any adverse party whose rights have been determined by such judgment.

UNIFORM DECLARATORY JUDGMENTS ACT

§ 1. Scope.—Courts of record within their respective jurisdictions shall have power to declare rights, status, and other legal relations whether or not further relief is or could be claimed. No action or proceeding shall be open to objection on the ground that a declaratory judgment or decree is prayed for. The declaration may be either affirmative or negative in form and effect; and such declarations shall have the force and effect of a final judgment or decree.

NOTES

(1) As of 1989, the Uniform Declaratory Judgment Act had been adopted in 42 states, Puerto Rico, and the Virgin Islands. With the sections of the Act set out above, compare the provisions of the federal statute and of Fed.R.Civ.P. 57.

(2) Can the declaratory judgment device be used to obtain judicial declaration of the invalidity of a penal statute? In Colorado State Board of Optometric Examiners v. Dixon, 165 Colo. 488, 440 P.2d 287 (1968), the Colorado Supreme Court, overruling a prior decision, gave an affirmative answer. See also Developments in the Law, Declaratory Judgments, 62 Harv.L.Rev. 787, 870–72 (1949); Note, Testing the Constitutionality of a Statute, 33 Rocky Mt.L.Rev. 235

(1961). To what extent is such a declaratory judgment the equivalent of an injunction against a criminal proceeding (see p. 98 supra)?

(3) On the right to trial by jury and declaratory relief, see Comment, Right to Trial by Jury in Declaratory Judgment Actions, 3 Conn.L.Rev. 564 (1971).

AETNA LIFE INSURANCE CO. v. HAWORTH

Supreme Court of the United States, 1937.
300 U.S. 227, 57 S.Ct. 461, 81 L.Ed. 617.

MR. CHIEF JUSTICE HUGHES delivered the opinion of the Court.

The question presented is whether the District Court had jurisdiction of this suit under the Federal Declaratory Judgment Act. Act of June 14, 1934, 48 Stat. 955, Jud.Code § 274d, 28 U.S.C. § 400 (28 U.S. C.A. § 400 and note *).

The question arises upon the plaintiff's complaint which was dismissed by the District Court upon the ground that it did not set forth a "controversy" in the constitutional sense and hence did not come within the legitimate scope of the statute. 11 F.Supp. 1016. The decree of dismissal was affirmed by the Circuit Court of Appeals. 84 F.2d 695. We granted certiorari. November 16, 1936. 299 U.S. 536, 57 S.Ct. 190, 81 L.Ed. 617.

From the complaint it appears that plaintiff is an insurance company which had issued to the defendant Edwin P. Haworth five policies of insurance upon his life, the defendant Cora M. Haworth being named as beneficiary. The complaint set forth the terms of the policies. They contained various provisions which for the present purpose it is unnecessary fully to particularize. It is sufficient to observe that they all provided for certain benefits in the event that the insured became totally and permanently disabled. In one policy, for $10,000, issued in 1911, the company agreed, upon receiving the requisite proof of such disability and without further payment of premiums, to pay the sum insured, and dividend additions, in twenty annual installments, or a life annuity as specified, in full settlement. In four other policies issued in 1921, 1928, and 1929, respectively, for amounts aggregating $30,000, plaintiff agreed upon proof of such disability to waive further payment of premiums, promising in one of the policies to pay a specified amount monthly and in the other three to continue the life insurance in force. By these four policies the benefits to be payable at death, and the cash and loan values to be available, were to be the same whether the premiums were paid or were waived by reason of the described disability.

The complaint alleges that in 1930 and 1931 the insured ceased to pay premiums on the four policies last mentioned and claimed the disability benefits as stipulated. He continued to pay premiums on the

---

* Footnotes omitted. The Federal Declaratory Judgment Act is now 28 U.S.C.A. §§ 2201 and 2202, p. 102, supra.

first mentioned policy until 1934 and then claimed disability benefits. These claims, which were repeatedly renewed, were presented in the form of affidavits accompanied by certificates of physicians. A typical written claim on the four policies is annexed to the complaint. It states that while these policies were in force, the insured became totally and permanently disabled by disease and was "prevented from performing any work or conducting any business for compensation or profit"; that on October 7, 1930, he had made and delivered to the company a sworn statement "for the purpose of asserting and claiming his right to have these policies continued under the permanent and total disability provision contained in each of them"; that more than six months before that date he had become totally and permanently disabled and had furnished evidence of his disability within the stated time; that the annual premiums payable in the year 1930 or in subsequent years were waived by reason of the disability; and that he was entitled to have the policies continued in force without the payment of premiums so long as the disability should continue.

With respect to the policy first mentioned, it appears that the insured claimed that prior to June 1, 1934, when he ceased to pay premiums, he had become totally and permanently disabled; that he was without obligation to pay further premiums and was entitled to the stipulated disability benefits including the continued life of the policy.

Plaintiff alleges that consistently and at all times it has refused to recognize these claims of the insured and has insisted that all the policies had lapsed according to their terms by reason of the nonpayment of premiums, the insured not being totally and permanently disabled at any of the times to which his claims referred. Plaintiff further states that taking loans into consideration four of the policies have no value and the remaining policy (the one first mentioned) has a value of only $45 as extended insurance. If, however, the insured has been totally and permanently disabled as he claims, the five policies are in full force, the plaintiff is now obliged to pay the accrued installments of cash disability benefits for which two of the policies provide, and the insured has the right to claim at any time cash surrender values accumulating by reason of the provisions for waiver of premiums, or at his death, Cora M. Haworth, as beneficiary, will be entitled to receive the face of the policies less the loans thereon.

Plaintiff thus contends that there is an actual controversy with defendants as to the existence of the total and permanent disability of the insured and as to the continuance of the obligations asserted despite the non-payment of premiums. Defendants have not instituted any action wherein the plaintiff would have an opportunity to prove the absence of the alleged disability and plaintiff points to the danger that it may lose the benefit of evidence through disappearance, illness, or death of witnesses; and meanwhile, in the absence of a judicial decision with respect to the alleged disability, the plaintiff in relation to these policies will be compelled to maintain reserves in excess of $20,000.

The complaint asks for a decree that the four policies be declared to be null and void by reason of lapse for non-payment of premiums and that the obligation upon the remaining policy be held to consist solely in the duty to pay the sum of $45 upon the death of the insured, and for such further relief as the exigencies of the case may require.

First. The Constitution (article 3, § 2) limits the exercise of the judicial power to "cases" and "controversies." "The term 'controversies,' if distinguishable at all from 'cases,' is so in that it is less comprehensive than the latter, and includes only suits of a civil nature." [Citations omitted.] The Declaratory Judgment Act of 1934, in its limitation to "cases of actual controversy," manifestly has regard to the constitutional provision and is operative only in respect to controversies which are such in the constitutional sense. The word "actual" is one of emphasis rather than of definition. Thus the operation of the Declaratory Judgment Act is procedural only. In providing remedies and defining procedure in relation to cases and controversies in the constitutional sense the Congress is acting within its delegated power over the jurisdiction of the federal courts which the Congress is authorized to establish. Turner v. Bank of North America, 4 Dall. 8, 10, 1 L.Ed. 718; Stevenson v. Fain, 195 U.S. 165, 167, 25 S.Ct. 6, 49 L.Ed. 142; Kline v. Burke Construction Co., 260 U.S. 226, 234, 43 S.Ct. 79, 82, 67 L.Ed. 226, 24 A.L.R. 1077. Exercising this control of practice and procedure the Congress is not confined to traditional forms or traditional remedies. The judiciary clause of the Constitution "did not crystallize into changeless form the procedure of 1789 as the only possible means for presenting a case or controversy otherwise cognizable by the federal courts." Nashville, Chattanooga & St. Louis R. Co. v. Wallace, 288 U.S. 249, 264, 53 S.Ct. 345, 348, 77 L.Ed. 730, 87 A.L.R. 1191. In dealing with methods within its sphere of remedial action the Congress may create and improve as well as abolish or restrict. The Declaratory Judgment Act must be deemed to fall within this ambit of congressional power, so far as it authorizes relief which is consonant with the exercise of the judicial function in the determination of controversies to which under the Constitution the judicial power extends.

A "controversy" in this sense must be one that is appropriate for judicial determination. Osborn v. Bank of United States, 9 Wheat. 738, 819, 6 L.Ed. 204. A justiciable controversy is thus distinguished from a difference or dispute of a hypothetical or abstract character; from one that is academic or moot. . . . The controversy must be definite and concrete, touching the legal relations of parties having adverse legal interests. . . . It must be a real and substantial controversy admitting of specific relief through a decree of a conclusive character, as distinguished from an opinion advising what the law would be upon a hypothetical state of facts. . . . Where there is such a concrete case admitting of an immediate and definitive determination of the legal rights of the parties in an adversary proceeding upon the facts alleged, the judicial function may be appropriately exercised although the adjudication of the rights of the litigants may not require the award of process or the payment of damages. . . . And as it is not essential to the exercise of the judicial power that an injunction be sought, allegations that irreparable injury is threatened are not required. . . .

With these principles governing the application of the Declaratory Judgment Act, we turn to the nature of the controversy, the relation and interests of the parties, and the relief sought in the instant case.

Second. There is here a dispute between parties who face each other in an adversary proceeding. The dispute relates to legal rights and obligations arising from the contracts of insurance. The dispute is definite and concrete, not hypothetical or abstract. Prior to this suit, the parties had taken adverse positions with respect to their existing obligations. Their contentions concerned the disability benefits which were to be payable upon prescribed conditions. On the one side, the insured claimed that he had become totally and permanently disabled and hence was relieved of the obligation to continue the payment of premiums and was entitled to the stipulated disability benefits and to the continuance of the policies in force. The insured presented this claim formally, as required by the policies. It was a claim of a present, specific right. On the other side, the company made an equally definite claim that the alleged basic fact did not exist, that the insured was not totally and permanently disabled and had not been relieved of the duty to continue the payment of premiums, that in consequence the policies had lapsed, and that the company was thus freed from its obligation either to pay disability benefits or to continue the insurance in force. Such a dispute is manifestly susceptible of judicial determination. It calls, not for an advisory opinion upon a hypothetical basis, but for an adjudication of present right upon established facts.

That the dispute turns upon questions of fact does not withdraw it, as the respondent seems to contend, from judicial cognizance. The legal consequences flow from the facts and it is the province of the courts to ascertain and find the facts in order to determine the legal consequences. That is everyday practice. Equally unavailing is respondent's contention that the dispute relates to the existence of a "mutable fact" and a "changeable condition—the state of the insured's health." The insured asserted a total and permanent disability occurring prior to October, 1930, and continuing thereafter. Upon that ground he ceased to pay premiums. His condition at the time he stopped payment, whether he was then totally and permanently disabled so that the policies did not lapse, is not a "mutable" but a definite fact. . . .

We have no occasion to deal with questions that may arise in the progress of the cause, as the complaint has been dismissed in limine. Questions of burden of proof or mode of trial have not been considered by the courts below and are not before us.

Our conclusion is that the complaint presented a controversy to which the judicial power extends and that authority to hear and determine it has been conferred upon the District Court by the Declaratory Judgment Act. The decree is reversed and the cause is remanded for further proceedings in conformity with this opinion.

     Reversed.

AMERICAN MACHINE & METALS, INC. v. DE BOTHEZAT IMPELLER CO., INC.

Circuit Court of Appeals of the United States, Second Circuit, 1948.
166 F.2d 535.

SWAN, CIRCUIT JUDGE. This appeal presents a question under the Declaratory Judgments Act, 28 U.S.C.A. § 400, which authorizes the courts of the United States "in cases of actual controversy" to declare "rights and other legal relations of any interested party petitioning for such declaration," without regard to whether further relief is or could be sought. Before answering the complaint, the defendant moved pursuant to Rule 12(b) of the Federal Rules of Civil Procedure, 28 U.S.C.A. following section 723, for dismissal of the action on the ground that (a) the complaint fails to state a claim upon which relief can be granted, and (b) the court lacks jurisdiction because there is no matter in controversy between the parties. This motion was granted for the reason, as we read the district court's opinion, that the facts alleged in the complaint did not show the existence of an "actual controversy." From the judgment of dismissal the plaintiff has appealed.

     In summary the allegations of the complaint are the following:

     In 1934 the parties entered into a contract under which the defendant conveyed to the plaintiff certain patents and certain physical equipment for the making of fans and other products and the plaintiff agreed to pay the defendant license fees (not less than $5,000 annually) based on the "net sales" of its products. So long as the contract continued the fees were to be paid on "net sales" regardless of whether the plaintiff's products were covered by the patents or whether the patents had expired. The contract contained no expiration date but could be terminated at any time by the plaintiff on six months' notice. In the event of such termination the plaintiff was to transfer the patents back to the defendant and to cease using the name "De Bothezat," which it agreed to use in its literature and sales promotion while the contract continued. Since February 19, 1946, the plaintiff has neither manufactured nor sold any product for which possession of the patents is essential. The plaintiff "desires and intends" to exercise its right of termination under the contract and "desires and intends" to continue in the business of selling fans and ventilating equipment. The defendant at various times has made claims and assertions to the plaintiff and other persons to the effect that upon termination of the contract the plaintiff will no longer have the right to continue the manufacture of fans and ventilating equipment, and "has led plaintiff to believe" that upon termination of the contract defendant will sue plaintiff if it does not cease the manufacture and sale of fans and ventilating equipment. Said claims and assertions by defendant "are without basis and an actual controversy exists between the parties," and plaintiff seeks a declaration of the rights of the parties in order to avoid the possible accrual of avoidable damages. The prayer requests a declaration "particularly with respect to the proper interpretation and effect of the agreement" and that the court declare the right of plaintiff to continue to manufacture and sell fans and other noninfringing products after termination of the agreement and without the payment of further sums to defendant.

In concluding that no controversy exists the district judge noted that the plaintiff has not yet given notice of termination of the contract and may never do so; the opinion states [75 F.Supp. 421, 424]:

"In this case, if the court should decide that plaintiff might terminate and continue its manufacture and sale of products other than those covered by patents, plaintiff might and probably would terminate. If the court should decide otherwise, plaintiff would probably continue under the agreement until its termination and no controversy such as now claimed to exist might ever be present. In other words, plaintiff has not elected what it wishes to do and its action might and could render academic the very declaration which it seeks.

"The complaint is, therefore, dismissed because no justiciable controversy exists which would justify the maintenance of an action under the Declaratory Judgment Statute. The relief prayed for should not be granted at this time either as a matter of discretion or otherwise."

We think the Judge construed the statute too narrowly. As the Supreme Court said in Maryland Casualty Co. v. Pacific Coal & Oil Co., 312 U.S. 270, 273, 61 S.Ct. 510, 85 L.Ed. 826, the difference between an abstract question and a "controversy" is one of degree. If notice of termination had been given, the defendant apparently concedes that there might be an actual controversy, although even after termination it would still be optional with the plaintiff whether to continue the business and an adverse decision would probably induce him not to continue. Before termination, the controversy is one step further removed from actuality but not so far removed as to present only an abstract question, in our opinion. Once the notice of termination is given, it is beyond recall; the dispute between the parties concerns the right of the plaintiff to continue business if that contingency happens. Where there is an actual controversy over contingent rights, a declaratory judgment may nevertheless be granted. Pennsylvania Casualty Co. v. Upchurch, 5 Cir., 139 F.2d 892, 894; Franklin Life Ins. Co. v. Johnson, 10 Cir., 157 F.2d 653, 658; Sigal v. Wise, 114 Conn. 297, 158 A. 891, 892, 893; Borchard, Declaratory Judgments, pp. 422–3. In Sigal v. Wise, supra, the tenant of premises destroyed by fire sought a declaration of his right to use the premises if the landlord should rebuild. Although the right claimed was contingent, the court thought that "its present determination may well serve a very real practical need of the parties for guidance in their future conduct." There, it is true, the contingency was within the control of the defendant, not of the plaintiff as here, but that does not seem to be a material distinction. After bringing the contingency to pass it will be too late to avoid an action for damages if the plaintiff acts as he intends by continuing the business. The very purpose of the declaratory judgment procedure is to prevent the accrual of such avoidable damages. This procedure has long been recognized in the law of Scotland and we may well be guided by Lord Justice Dunedin's opinion in Russian C. & I. Bank v. British Bank, [1921] 2 A.C. 438, 448. There the British bank had obtained a loan from the Russian bank and pledged securities to protect the lender. In order to decide whether to exercise its privilege of redeeming the pledged securities, the British bank wanted to know whether the loan was repayable in rubles or sterling—a question on which the parties were in dispute. Lord Dunedin was of opinion that the case was an appropriate one for a declaratory judgment even though it was probable that if sterling was declared to be the required currency the British bank would not exercise its privilege of redemption. This seems indistinguishable from the case at bar. Also pertinent are Altvater v. Freeman, 319 U.S. 359, 63 S.Ct. 1115, 87 L.Ed. 1450, and Sola Electric Co. v. Jefferson Electric Co., 317 U.S. 173, 63 S.Ct. 172, 87 L.Ed. 165. In the latter case the Supreme Court permitted a patent licensee to seek a declaratory judgment as to the validity of certain patents without previously relinquishing its rights under the license.

Johnson v. Interstate Transit Lines, 10 Cir., 163 F.2d 125, and Perlberg v. Northwestern Mut. Life Ins. Co., E.D.Pa., 62 F.Supp. 76, relied upon by the appellee, did not involve such an irrevocable choice as the termination of the contract presents to the plaintiff in the case at bar. Failure to declare his seniority rights did not seriously affect the employee in the Johnson case, since he was not threatened with immediate loss of employment or status; and the insured in the Perlberg case, seeking a declaration as to the consequences of a default, would have been able even in the event of a default to reinstate his policy without penalty, or failing that to receive paid-up insurance or the cash surrender value. By the decision below the appellant here must "act on his own view of his rights" and risk an otherwise profitable business in order to present a justiciable "controversy." The Declaratory Judgments Act was designed to obviate just this sort of peril, and we believe its benefits should be available to one in the appellant's situation. S.Rep. No. 1005, 73d Cong., 2 Sess., pp. 2–3; Borchard, Declaratory Judgments, pp. 58, 930.

Judgment reversed and cause remanded for trial on the merits.

*   *   *

NOTES

(1) May a federal court, as a result of being presented with a dispute at an earlier stage, adjudicate a controversy that it could not have heard at a later stage? See Franchise Tax Board v. Construction Laborers Vacation Trust, 463 U.S. 1, 103 S.Ct. 2841, 77 L.Ed.2d 420 (1983); p. 189, note (1), infra.

(2) Both the federal and the Uniform Act leave the court discretion in determining whether to grant declaratory relief. In "Declaratory Judgments in the Federal Courts," 9 Ohio State L.J. 209, 223 (1948), Vanneman and Kutner give the following list of criteria most often used by federal courts in determining whether or not, within their discretion, to take jurisdiction of a given case. . . . "(1) that the declaratory judgment will or will not serve a useful purpose, either because another action is pending between the same parties and involving the same issues, or the declaration would only give a piecemeal determination of the issues, or there is really no actual controversy; (2) that there is involved in such a declaration an interpretation of or an interference with a state law; (3) that the considerations of 'convenience, expediency, need, desirability, public interest or policy' are frequently favorable to or against the declaration; (4) that injunctive relief is or is not available; (5) that another remedy is or is not more effective, under the circumstances, or a statutory remedy is provided and has not been exhausted; and (6) utility, rather than necessity, is the proper test." See Borchard, Discretion to Refuse Jurisdiction of Actions for Declaratory Judgments, 26 Minn.L.Rev. 677 (1942); Note, Availability of a Declaratory Judgment When Another Suit Is Pending, 51 Yale L.J. 511 (1942); Note, Declaratory Judgment and Matured Causes of Action, 53 Colum.L.Rev. 1130 (1953).

(3) The Federal Act provides that declaratory relief may be granted "whether or not further relief is or could be sought." The Uniform Act provides that the courts have power to grant declaratory relief, "whether or not further relief is or could be claimed." The great majority of courts hold that a declaratory judgment is an alternative remedy and that the availability of another adequate remedy does not preclude declaratory relief. See Borchard, Declaratory Judgments 295–296, 315 (1941); Anderson, Declaratory Judgments §§ 47–50 (1940); Note, May Declaratory and Coercive or Executory Relief Be Granted in Action Under Declaratory Judgment Act, 155 A.L.R. 501 (1945). But a number of state courts have refused to grant declaratory relief in cases in which coercive relief was found to be available and appropriate. See Mid–Centre County Authority v. Township of Boggs, 34 Pa.Cmwlth. 494, 384 A.2d 1008 (1978) ("The Act bars declaratory judgment proceedings if another available and appropriate remedy exists"); Volkswagenwerk, A.G. v. Watson, 181 Ind. App. 155, 390 N.E.2d 1082 (1979) (declaratory relief unnecessary when a full and adequate remedy is provided by another form of action); Maryland National Capital Park and Planning Commission v. Washington National Arena, 282 Md. 588, 386 A.2d 1216 (1978). In all of these cases the courts so ruled, even though the applicable statute contained the provision from the Uniform Act that declares declaratory relief to be available "whether or not further relief is or could be claimed."

Md.Code, Cts. & Jud.Proc., § 3–403; 42 Pa.Consl.Stat.Ann. § 7532; West's Ann.Ind.Code 34–4–10–1; West's Rev.Code Wash.Ann. § 7.24.010. Can these decisions be reconciled with the statutory language on the ground that the statute permits, but does not require, the court to grant declaratory relief when coercive relief is available and that, in cases in which coercive relief is both available and appropriate, the court may exercise its discretion to deny the declaratory relief?

(4) In German negligence cases, declaratory judgments on the liability issue alone are extensively used with these claimed advantages: "first, it interrupts the statute of limitations. Under German law, the limitation (which is considered as an institution of substantive and not of procedural law) with regard to tort actions runs in three years from the time at which the injured person receives knowledge of both the injury and the identity of the delinquent. . . . In those cases where it is possible that the effects of the accident may not be apparent for a period greater than the period of limitation of actions, this German device performs a just mission. Secondly, the use of this device avoids the problem of having to claim all of one's damages at one time, which judgment then becomes res adjudicata of the claim even though serious results manifest themselves later. The necessity of claiming all damages at one time frequently causes plaintiffs to claim for all possible contingencies. Thus, the use of the German device could be of advantage to defendants in that it would render their liability in damages less susceptible to speculation as to amount, and to plaintiffs in that the amounts recovered might bear a fairer relation to the injury suffered." Stone, Separate Trials, Declaratory Rulings and Installment Damages: A Comparative Study, 35 Tulane L.Rev. 597, 600 (1961). A further argument for using this procedure may be to minimize court costs, which are based upon the amount of damage granted. In this country, would there be any obstacle to the use of declaratory judgments in a similar manner, or do American practices such as the contingent fee and trial by jury pose insuperable difficulties? See Weinstein, Routine Bifurcation of Jury Negligence Trials: An Example of the Questionable Use of Rule Making Power, 14 Vand.L.Rev. 831 (1961).

F. ATTORNEYS' FEES

SERRANO v. PRIEST *

Supreme Court of California, 1977.
20 Cal.3d 25, 141 Cal.Rptr. 315, 569 P.2d 1303.

SULLIVAN, JUSTICE. In Serrano v. Priest (1976) 18 Cal.3d 728, 135 Cal.Rptr. 345, 557 P.2d 929 (hereafter cited as *Serrano II*) we affirmed a judgment of the Los Angeles County Superior Court, entered on September 3, 1974, which held essentially (1) that the then-existing California public school financing system was invalid as in violation of state constitutional provisions guaranteeing equal protection of the laws, and (2) that the said system must be brought into constitutional compliance within a period of six years from the date of entry of judgment, the trial court retaining jurisdiction for the purpose of granting any necessary future relief. That judgment is now final.

Within a month after the entry of the foregoing judgment and prior to the filing of defendants' appeals, plaintiffs' attorneys (Public

* Footnote omitted.

R., S. & D.–Cs.Civ.Proc. 5th Ed. UCB—7

Advocates, Inc. and Western Center on Law and Poverty) made separate motions for an award of reasonable attorneys fees "against defendants Priest [then the state Treasurer], Rules [then and presently the state Superintendent of Public Instruction] and Flournoy [then the state Controller] in their official capacities as officials of the State of California." The motions were not based upon statute but were instead addressed to the equitable powers of the court. Three theories, to be examined in detail by us below, were advanced in support of the award: the so-called "common fund" theory, the "substantial benefit" theory, and the "private attorney general" theory.

*   *   *

(a) *The Common Fund Theory*

"Although American courts, in contrast to those of England, have never awarded counsels' fees as a routine component of costs, at least one exception to this rule has become as well established as the rule itself: that one who expends attorneys' fees in winning a suit which creates a fund from which others derive benefits, may require those passive beneficiaries to bear a fair share of the litigation costs." (Quinn v. State of California (1975) 15 Cal.3d 162, 167, 124 Cal.Rptr. 1, 4, 539 P.2d 761, 764; fns. omitted.) This, the so-called "common fund" exception to the American rule regarding the award of attorneys fees (i.e., the rule set forth in section 1021 of our Code of Civil Procedure), is grounded in "the historic power of equity to permit the trustee of a fund or property, or a party preserving or recovering a fund for the benefit of others in addition to himself, to recover his costs, including his attorneys' fees, from the fund or property itself or directly from the other parties enjoying the benefit." (Alyeska Pipeline Co. v. Wilderness Society (1975) 421 U.S. 240, 257, 95 S.Ct. 1612, 1621, 44 L.Ed.2d 141; fn. omitted.)

*   *   *

. . . We hold that here, where plaintiffs' efforts have not effected the creation or preservation of an identifiable "fund" of money out of which they seek to recover their attorneys fees, the "common fund" exception is inapplicable. . . .

(b) *The Substantial Benefit Theory*

As we indicated in our opinion in D'Amico v. Board of Medical Examiners, supra, 11 Cal.3d 1, 25, 112 Cal.Rptr. 786, 520 P.2d 10, the courts have fashioned another nonstatutory exception to the general rule on the award of attorneys [sic] fees. This exception, which may be viewed as an outgrowth of the "common fund" doctrine, permits the award of fees when the litigant, proceeding in a representative capacity, obtains a decision resulting in the conferral of a "substantial benefit" of a pecuniary or nonpecuniary nature. In such circumstance, the court, in the exercise of its equitable discretion, thereupon may decree that under dictates of justice those receiving the benefit should contribute to the costs of its production. Although of fairly recent development in California, this exception to the general rule is now well established in our law.

* * *

. . . Common sense as well speaks in favor of the proposition that plaintiffs and their attorneys, as a result of the *Serrano* litigation, have rendered an enormous service to the state and all of its citizens by insuring that the state educational financing system shall be brought into conformity with the equal protection provisions of our state Constitution so that the degree of educational opportunity available to the school children of this state will no longer be dependent upon the taxable wealth of the district in which each student lives. We have concluded, however, that to award fees on the "substantial benefit" theory on the basis of considerations of this nature—separate and apart from any consideration of actual and concrete benefits bestowed— would be to extend that theory beyond its rational underpinnings. . . .

In D'Amico v. Board of Medical Examiners, supra, 11 Cal.3d 1, 112 Cal.Rptr. 786, 520 P.2d 10, plaintiffs had sought an award of fees not only on the "common fund" and "substantial benefit" theories but also on two additional theories, both of which were grounded largely on federal case law. The first of these, involving awards against an opponent who has maintained an unfounded action or defense " 'in bad faith, vexatiously, wantonly or for oppressive reasons' " (11 Cal.3d at p. 26, 112 Cal.Rptr. at p. 804, 520 P.2d at p. 28), is not involved in the instant case and we do not address ourselves to it. However, the second, the so-called "private attorney general" concept, was adopted by the trial court as the basis for its award, and we are now called upon to determine its applicability in this jurisdiction.

In addressing ourselves to the "private attorney general" theory in *D'Amico*, we said "This concept, as we understand it, seeks to encourage suits effectuating a strong congressional or national policy by awarding substantial attorney's fees, regardless of defendants' conduct, to those who successfully bring such suits and thereby bring about benefits to a broad class of citizens." (11 Cal.3d at p. 27, 112 Cal.Rptr. at p. 805, 520 P.2d at p. 29.) Noting, however, that such doctrine was then under examination by the United States Supreme Court, we thought it prudent to await "an announcement by the high court concerning its limits and contours on the federal level" (id.) before determining its possible applicability in this jurisdiction.

The announcement has now been made. In Alyeska Pipeline Co. v. Wilderness Society, supra, 421 U.S. 240, 95 S.Ct. 1612, 44 L.Ed.2d 141, a five to two opinion authored by Justice White, the Supreme Court held that the awarding of attorneys fees on a "private attorney general" theory, in the absence of express statutory authorization, did not lie within the equitable jurisdiction of the federal courts. Such awards, the court held, "would make major inroads on a policy matter that

Congress has reserved for itself." (421 U.S. at p. 269, 95 S.Ct. at p. 1627.)

The high court rested its conclusion on two bases. The first, involving the interpretation of an 1853 court costs act, need not long concern us here, for the act in question (presently 28 U.S.C. §§ 1920, 1923) bears little resemblance to the governing statute in this state, section 1021 of the Code of Civil Procedure. In any event the fashioning of equitable exceptions to the statutory rule to be applied in California is a matter within the sole competence of this court. The second basis on which the Supreme Court grounded its decision, however, dealing with the manageability and fairness of such awards in the absence of legislative guidance, goes directly to the heart of the determination here before us. The making of such awards in the absence of statutory authorization, the high court indicated, would leave the courts "free to fashion drastic new rules with respect to the allowance of attorneys' fees to the prevailing party . . . or to pick and choose among plaintiffs and the statutes under which they sue and to award fees in some cases but not in others, depending upon the courts' assessment of the importance of the public policies involved in particular cases." (421 U.S. at p. 269, 95 S.Ct. at p. 1627.) This, the court suggested, would represent an unacceptable and unwise intrusion of the judicial branch of government into the domain of the Legislature.

It is with this consideration foremost in mind that we must assess the arguments advanced by plaintiffs and amici curiae in support of our adoption of the "private attorney general" concept in our state. Those arguments may be briefly summarized as follows: In the complex society in which we live it frequently occurs that citizens in great numbers and across a broad spectrum have interests in common. These, while of enormous significance to the society as a whole, do not involve the fortunes of a single individual to the extent necessary to encourage their private vindication in the courts. Although there are within the executive branch of the government offices and institutions (exemplified by the Attorney General) whose function it is to represent the general public in such matters and to ensure proper enforcement, for various reasons the burden of enforcement is not always adequately carried by those offices and institutions, rendering some sort of private action imperative. Because the issues involved in such litigation are often extremely complex and their presentation time-consuming and costly, the availability of representation of such public interests by private attorneys acting *pro bono publico* is limited. Only through the appearance of "public interest" law firms funded by public and foundation monies, argue plaintiffs and amici, has it been possible to secure representation on any large scale. The firms in question, however, are not funded to the extent necessary for the representation of all such deserving interests, and as a result many worthy causes of this nature are without adequate representation under present circumstances. One solution, so the argument goes, within the equitable powers of the judiciary to provide, is the award of substantial attorneys fees to those public-interest litigants and their attorneys (whether private attorneys acting *pro bono publico* or members of "public interest" law firms) who are successful in such cases, to the end that support may be provided for the representation of interests of similar character in future litigation.

In the several cases in which the courts, persuaded by these and similar arguments, have granted fees on the "private attorney general" theory, various formulations of the rule have appeared. In spite of variations in emphasis, all of these formulations seem to suggest that there are three basic factors to be considered in awarding fees on this theory. These are in general: (1) the strength or societal importance of the public policy vindicated by the litigation, (2) the necessity for private enforcement and the magnitude of the resultant burden on the plaintiff, (3) the number of people standing to benefit from the decision. (See generally, Comment, Equal Access, 122 U.Pa.L.Rev. 636, 666–674.) Thus it seems to be contemplated that if a trial court, in ruling that [sic] a motion for fees upon this theory, determines that the litigation has resulted in the vindication of a strong or societally important public policy, that the necessary costs of securing this result transcend the individual plaintiff's pecuniary interest to an extent requiring subsidization, and that a substantial number of persons stand to benefit from the decision, the court may exercise its equitable powers to award attorney fees on this theory.

It is at once apparent that a consideration of the first factor may in instances present difficulties since it is couched in generic terms, contains no specific objective standards and nevertheless calls for a subjective evaluation by the judge hearing the motion as to whether the litigation before the court has vindicated a public policy sufficiently strong or important to warrant an award of fees. We are aware of the apprehension voiced in some critiques that trial courts, whose function it is to apply existing law, will be thrust into the role of making assessments of the relative strength or weakness of public policies furthered by their decisions and of determining at the same time which public policy should be encouraged by an award of fees, and which not—a role closely approaching that of the legislative function. (See generally, Comment, Equal Access, 122 U.Pa.L.Rev. 636, 670–671; Comment, The Supreme Court, 1974 Term (1975) 89 Harv.L.Rev. 1, 178–180.) Since generally speaking the enactment of a statute entails in a sense the declaration of a public policy, it is arguable that, where it contains no provision for the awarding of attorney fees, the Legislature was of the view that the public policy involved did not warrant such encouragement. A judicial evaluation, then, of the strength or importance of such statutorily based policy presents difficult and sensitive problems whose resolution by the courts may be of questionable propriety.

Such difficulties, however, are not present in the instant case. The trial court, in awarding fees to plaintiffs, found that the public policy advanced by this litigation was not one grounded in statute but one grounded in the *state Constitution*. Thus, the trial court concluded as a matter of law: "If as a result of the efforts of plaintiffs' attorneys rights created or protected by *the State Constitution* are protected to the benefit of a large number of people, plaintiffs' attorneys are entitled to reasonable attorney's fees from the defendants under the private attorney general equitable doctrine." (Italics added.) Its factual findings, which are not here challenged, establish that the interests here furthered were *constitutional* in stature. Those findings also make clear that the benefits flowing from this adjudication are to be widely enjoyed among the citizens of this state and that the nature of the litigation was such that subsidization of the plaintiffs is justified in the event of their victory. In these circumstances we conclude that an award of attorneys fees to plaintiffs and their attorneys was proper under the theory posited by the trial court.

So holding, we need not, and do not, address the question as to whether courts may award attorney fees under the "private attorney general" theory, where the litigation at hand has vindicated a public policy having a statutory, as opposed to, a constitutional basis. The resolution of this question must be left for an appropriate case.

In sum, we hold that in the light of the circumstance of the instant case, the trial court acted within the proper limits of its inherent equitable powers when it concluded that reasonable attorneys fees should be awarded to plaintiffs' attorneys on the "private attorney general" theory.

 . . . For the reasons above stated we believe that the motion for an award of attorneys' fees on appeal must also be granted on the "private attorney general" theory. The amount of a reasonable fee shall be determined by the trial court upon application made after filing of the remittitur herein. . . .

[Dissenting opinions of JUSTICES RICHARDSON and CLARK have been omitted.]

NOTES

(1) In response to the *Alyeska* decision, Congress has enacted two statutes. The first, the Civil Rights Attorney's Fees/Awards Act of 1976, 42 U.S.C.A. § 1988, provides for the recovery from the government by the prevailing party of attorney's fees in civil rights cases. The second, the Equal Access to Justice Act of 1981, 28 U.S.C.A. § 2412 authorizes the award of attorney's fees against the government in civil cases under specified conditions. On these statutes, see Note, Promoting the Vindication of Civil Rights through the Attorney's Fees Awards Act, 80 Colum.L.Rev. 346 (1980); Note, The Equal Access to Justice Act in the Federal Courts, 84 Colum.L.Rev. 1089 (1984).

(2) In Christiansburg Garment Co. v. EEOC, 434 U.S. 412, 98 S.Ct. 694, 54 L.Ed.2d 648 (1978), the Supreme Court construed a provision that in "any action or proceeding under this title [i.e., Title VII of the Civil Rights Act of 1964] the court, in its discretion, may allow the prevailing party . . . a reasonable attorney's fee" to mean that a successful private defendant could recover attorney's fees only if the action was "frivolous, unreasonable, or

without foundation." But cf. Carpenters Southern California Administrative Corp. v. Russell, 726 F.2d 1410, 1415 (9th Cir.1984), quoting Hummell v. S.E. Rykoff & Co., 634 F.2d 446, 453 (9th Cir.1980) (in establishing factors to be weighed in deciding whether to award attorney's fees to prevailing defendants in suits under the Employee Retirement Income Security Act of 1974, 29 U.S. C.A. § 1132, the court rejected the *Christianburg* approach in favor of "(1) the degree of the opposing parties' culpability or bad faith; (2) the ability of the opposing parties to satisfy an award of fees; (3) whether an award of fees against the opposing parties would deter others from acting in similar circumstances; (4) whether the parties requesting fees sought to benefit all participants and beneficiaries of an ERISA plan or to resolve a significant legal question regarding ERISA; and (5) the relative merits of the parties' positions").

(3) As a general rule, the victorious litigant is entitled to "interest" and "costs." The scope of the term "costs" depends on applicable statutory provisions and on court decisions. See generally Peck, Taxation of Costs in the United States District Courts, 42 Neb.L.Rev. 788 (1963); Distler, The Course of Costs of Course, 46 Corn.L.Q. 76 (1966); Note, Use of Taxable Costs to Regulate the Conduct of Litigants, 53 Colum.L.Rev. 78 (1953). Typically, however, costs do not include attorneys' fees.

(4) As the principal case confirms, in the United States the victorious litigant is normally not awarded attorneys' fees. The exactly contrary rule prevails in England and the countries of the civil law tradition. See, e.g., Herzog, Civil Procedure in France 12.09 (1967); Ginsburg & Bruzelius, Civil Procedure in Sweden 10.01 (1965); Cappelletti & Perillo, Civil Procedure in Italy, 9.10 (1965); Goodhart, Costs, 38 Yale L.J. 849 (1929). On the American tradition, see also Cheek, Attorneys' Fees: Where Shall the Ultimate Burden Lie?, 20 Vand.L.Rev. 1216 (1967); Ehrenzweig, Reimbursement of Counsel Fees and the Great Society, 54 Calif.L.Rev. 792 (1966). A principal argument in favor of the American rule is that the risk of being saddled with attorneys' fees may deter the plaintiff with a meritorious claim from pursuing it. A principal argument against it is that the victorious party should not be put in the position of having to pay frequently substantial attorneys' fees to obtain what is his due. Note, however, that the force of the latter argument is considerably weakened in cases in which the jury includes an amount for attorneys' fees in the general verdict it returns. This is believed by many to be a prevailing practice in personal injury and similar cases, which juries frequently assume to be handled on a contingency fee basis. Further, plaintiffs who must pay substantial amounts to hire lawyers to handle their cases may not be appreciably deterred by the additional risk of also having to pay (part of) the counsel fees of their opponents. Whatever the force of these considerations, there appears to be a growing trend to permit or prescribe an award of attorneys' fees to victorious litigants in particular situations. See, e.g., Fed.R.Civ.P. 37. In studying the various steps in the progress of a civil action, you should ask yourself whether the award of attorneys' fees might be an appropriate alternative to other consequences imposed by the law. For example, why should a litigant's failure to introduce a dispositive argument or item of proof reasonably preclude him from introducing it late if he can be ordered to compensate his opponent fully for the expenses, including counsel fees, incurred as a result of the lateness of its introduction?

On whether a pro se litigant can recover attorney's fees, see Note, Pro Se Can You Sue? Attorney's Fees for Pro Se Litigants, 34 Stan.L.Rev. 659 (1980).

(5) In litigation conducted by or against indigents the problem of attorneys' fees has special aspects. An impecunious litigant may not worry unduly about having to pay his opponent's attorneys' fees. This is also a factor to be taken into account in determining whether to grant impecunious litigants a right to counsel. See p. 56 supra. On the other hand, of course, an impecunious litigant may more readily find legal assistance if victory will assure his counsel of appropriate remuneration by the opponent. See also Nussbaum, Attorney's Fees in Public Interest Litigation, 48 N.Y.U.L.Rev. 303 (1973); Rowe, The Legal Theory of Attorney Fee Shifting, 1982 Duke L.J. 651.

(6) In Blanchard v. Bergeron, ___ U.S. ___, 109 S.Ct. 939, 103 L.Ed.2d 67 (1989), the Supreme Court ruled that an attorney's fee allowed under Title 42 U.S.C.A. § 1988, the Civil Rights Attorney's Fees Award Act, is not limited to the amount provided in a contingency fee agreement between plaintiff and his counsel.

(7) Award of attorney's fees under Title 42 U.S.C.A. § 1988 is proper even if the plaintiff fails to obtain a significant part of the relief sought. Texas State Teachers Ass'n v. Garland Independent School District, ___ U.S. ___, 109 S.Ct. 1486, 103 L.Ed.2d 866 (1989).

(8) In a civil rights case, may the defendant condition an offer of settlement on the plaintiff's counsel's waiving his or her right to the statutorily allowable attorney's fees? In Evans v. Jeff D., 475 U.S. 717, 106 S.Ct. 1531, 89 L.Ed.2d 747 (1986), the Supreme Court answered affirmatively. On this case, see Comment, Giving Substance to the Bad Faith Exception of Evans v. Jeff D., 136 U.Pa.L.Rev. 553 (1987).

(9) In determining reasonable attorney's fees, does the extent of risk the plaintiff assumed in bringing the action justify a corresponding increase in his attorney's fee? In Pennsylvania v. Delaware Valley Citizens' Council for Clean Air, 483 U.S. 711, 107 S.Ct. 3078, 97 L.Ed.2d 585 (1987), the Supreme Court ruled that the risk factor should not be taken into account.

(10) In Independent Federation of Flight Attendants v. Zipes, ___ U.S. ___, 109 S.Ct. 2732, 105 L.Ed.2d 639 (1989), the Court held that attorney's fees may be awarded against a losing intervenor in a Title VII action only if the intervention had been "frivolous, unreasonable, or without foundation."

Chapter Four

PROVISIONAL REMEDIES

SECTION 1. TYPES OF PROVISIONAL REMEDIES

"Provisional remedies" is the generic term used to refer to several kinds of relief that may be available to a plaintiff during the course of an action—sometimes even before the action has been formally commenced by service of a summons or a summons and complaint—and which have the common function of seeking to preserve and protect the value of the final relief granted the plaintiff if he is successful. For example, in actions seeking as final relief the recovery of a sum of money this might involve seizure of property of the defendant located in the forum state to assure that it is not removed or dissipated before it can be applied to satisfaction of the plaintiff's claim. The provisional remedy usually used for this purpose is *attachment,* although if the property is of a kind requiring continuing supervision and management, such as an ongoing business, the device of a *temporary receivership* may instead be favored as a means of allowing appointment of a qualified person to undertake those tasks. In some states, attachment is referred to as "sequestration". And if the defendant's property is in the hands of a third person, the term garnishment rather than attachment is usually used to signify its seizure; the third person is then called the "garnishee" and the plaintiff the "garnishor." Intangible property, such as a debt owed the defendant, can also be seized by service of appropriate process on the debtor-garnishee.

In actions seeking an injunction as final relief, it is often necessary to stay the defendant's hand during the course of the action lest irreparable injury be done or the *status quo* be upset in a way that would make the final judgment nugatory. The provisional remedy used for this purpose is usually called a *preliminary injunction* if granted after the defendant was given notice and an opportunity to oppose it, and a *temporary restraining order* (TRO) if it is granted *ex parte*—that is, entirely on the basis of plaintiff's application without notice to the defendant.

Another kind of provisional remedy, of lesser and continually decreasing importance, is *arrest* of the defendant. This draconian mode of keeping him from mischief pending final judgment is of course reminiscent of imprisonment for debt and is explicitly barred by some state constitutions. Elsewhere legislation has narrowed its scope or abolished it entirely, as New York did in 1979. See Morris & Wiener, Civil Arrest: A Medieval Anachronism, 43 Brooklyn L.Rev. 383 (1976).

Still another device commonly grouped with the provisional remedies is the *notice of pendency,* a modern counterpart of the common law *lis pendens.* This allows the plaintiff in an action which may affect interests in real property to place a record of institution of the action with the county clerk or other local repository of title records, which has the effect of assuring a successful plaintiff priority over the interests of any prospective purchaser or encumbrancer.

Pursuant to the mandate of Rule 64 of the Federal Rules of Civil Procedure, the federal courts, in granting provisional relief, generally follow the law of the state in which they are sitting. And under Rule 4(e)(2), attachment, garnishment, or similar seizure in accordance with state law may also provide a basis for the exercise of adjudicatory power in the federal courts.

These materials will focus mainly on attachment and the two kinds of interim injunctive relief, which are by far the most important of the provisional remedies.

SECTION 2.   ATTACHMENT AND GARNISHMENT

NEW YORK CIVIL PRACTICE LAW AND RULES

§ 6201.   Grounds for Attachment

An order of attachment may be granted in any action, except a matrimonial action, where the plaintiff has demanded and would be entitled, in whole or in part, or in the alternative, to a money judgment against one or more defendants, when:

1.   the defendant is a nondomiciliary residing without the state, or is a foreign corporation not qualified to do business in the state; or

2.   the defendant resides or is domiciled in the state and cannot be personally served despite diligent efforts to do so; or

3.   the defendant, with intent to defraud his creditors or frustrate the enforcement of a judgment that might be rendered in plaintiff's favor, has assigned, disposed of, encumbered or secreted property, or removed it from the state or is about to do any of these acts; or

4.   the cause of action is based on a judgment, decree or order of a court of the United States or of any other court which is entitled to full faith and credit in this state, or on a judgment which qualifies for recognition . . . [in this state].

State laws regulating attachment and garnishment vary greatly. Some New England states are quite liberal in permitting recourse to these remedies, but most states make them available only in special circumstances. Typical among these are the defendant's non-residence or probable fraudulent removal or concealment of personal property. See 7th Ann.Rep., N.Y. Judicial Council 391–449 (1941).

The subject of attachment and garnishment is complicated by the fact that it has long been used to serve a second purpose quite different from securing the effectiveness of the final judgment. The presence and seizure of a defendant's property in the forum state has traditionally served to permit its courts to adjudicate claims against him or her for money damages even if there is no other contact between that state and either the defendant or the transactions underlying the controversy, with any judgment recovered limited to and to be satisfied out of the proceeds of a judicial sale of the property. The scope for exercise of this kind of jurisdiction has in recent years been severely curtailed by the U.S. Supreme Court—a subject to be more closely examined in Chapter 6. However, in studying the materials that follow, the student should be alert to this dual function of attachment and to the confusion which can be generated when precedents involving one are applied to the other without taking note of the different policy considerations that may be pertinent.

NOTE

A party whose property is wrongfully seized by attachment process is entitled to damages as in an action for conversion, including interest on the value of the property. Subin v. United States Fidelity and Guaranty Co., 12 A.D.2d 49, 208 N.Y.S.2d 278 (1st Dep't 1960); Gray v. American Surety Co. of N.Y., 129 Cal.App.2d 471, 277 P.2d 436 (1954). The date of attachment fixes the value of the property and the beginning of interest. Koski v. Haskins, 236 Mass. 346, 128 N.E. 427 (1920). See 36 A.L.R.2d 337 (1954).

SNIADACH v. FAMILY FINANCE CORPORATION OF BAY VIEW

Supreme Court of the United States, 1969.
395 U.S. 337, 89 S.Ct. 1820, 23 L.Ed.2d 349.

Mr. Justice Douglas delivered the opinion of the Court.[*]

Respondent instituted a garnishment action against petitioner as defendant and Miller Harris Instrument Co., as her employer, as garnishee. The complaint alleged a claim of $420 on a promissory note. The garnishee filed its answer stating it had wages of $63.18 under its control earned by petitioner and unpaid, and that it would pay one-half to petitioner as a subsistence allowance [1] and hold the other half subject to the order of the court.

---

[*] Some footnotes omitted; others renumbered.

1. Wis.Stat. § 267.18(2)(a) provides:

"When wages or salary are the subject of garnishment action, the garnishee shall pay over to the principal defendant on the date when such wages or salary would nor-mally be payable a subsistence allowance, out of the wages or salary then owing in the sum of $25 in the case of an individual without dependents or $40 in the case of an individual with dependents; but in no event in excess of 50% of the wages or salary owing. Said subsistence allowance

Petitioner moved that the garnishment proceedings be dismissed for failure to satisfy the due process requirements of the Fourteenth Amendment. The Wisconsin Supreme Court sustained the lower state court in approving the procedure. 37 Wis.2d 168, 154 N.W.2d 259. The same is here on a petition for a writ of certiorari. 393 U.S. 1078, 89 S.Ct. 849, 21 L.Ed.2d 771.

The Wisconsin statute gives a plaintiff 10 days in which to serve the summons and complaint on the defendant after service on the garnishee. In this case petitioner was served the same day as the garnishee. She nonetheless claims that the Wisconsin garnishment procedure violates that due process required by the Fourteenth Amendment, in that notice and an opportunity to be heard are not given before the *in rem* seizure of the wages. What happens in Wisconsin is that the clerk of the court issues the summons at the request of the creditor's lawyer; and it is the latter who by serving the garnishee sets in motion the machinery whereby the wages are frozen.

They may, it is true, be unfrozen if the trial of the main suit is ever had and the wage earner wins on the merits. But in the interim the wage earner is deprived of his enjoyment of earned wages without any opportunity to be heard and to tender any defense he may have, whether it be fraud or otherwise.

Such summary procedure may well meet the requirements of due process in extraordinary situations. Cf. Fahey v. Mallonee, 332 U.S. 245, 253–254, 67 S.Ct. 1552, 1554–1556, 91 L.Ed. 2030; Ewing v. Mytinger & Casselberry, Inc., 339 U.S. 594, 598–600, 70 S.Ct. 870, 872–873, 94 L.Ed. 1088; Ownbey v. Morgan, 256 U.S. 94, 110–112, 41 S.Ct. 433, 437–438, 65 L.Ed. 837; Coffin Bros. v. Bennett, 277 U.S. 29, 31, 48 S.Ct. 422, 423, 72 L.Ed. 768. But in the present case no situation requiring special protection to a state or creditor interest is presented by the facts; nor is the Wisconsin statute narrowly drawn to meet any such unusual condition. Petitioner was a resident of this Wisconsin community and *in personam* jurisdiction was readily obtainable.

The question is not whether the Wisconsin law is a wise law or unwise law. Our concern is not what philosophy Wisconsin should or should not embrace. See Green v. Frazier, 253 U.S. 233, 40 S.Ct. 499, 64 L.Ed. 878. We do not sit as a super-legislative body. In this case the sole question is whether there has been a taking of property without that procedural due process that is required by the Fourteenth Amendment. We have dealt over and again with the question of what constitutes "the right to be heard" (Schroeder v. New York, 371 U.S. 208, 212, 83 S.Ct. 279, 282, 9 L.Ed.2d 255) within the meaning of procedural due process. See Mullane v. Central Hanover Bank & Trust Co., 339 U.S. 306, 314, 70 S.Ct. 652, 657, 94 L.Ed. 865. In the latter case we said that the right to be heard "has little reality or worth unless one is informed that the matter is pending and can choose for himself

shall be applied to the first wages or salary earned in the period subject to said garnishment action."

whether to appear or default, acquiesce or contest." 339 U.S., at 314, 70 S.Ct., at 657. In the context of this case the question is whether the interim freezing of the wages without a chance to be heard violates procedural due process.

A procedural rule that may satisfy due process for attachments in general, see McKay v. McInnes, 279 U.S. 820, 49 S.Ct. 344, 73 L.Ed. 975, does not necessarily satisfy procedural due process in every case. The fact that a procedure would pass muster under a feudal regime does not mean it gives necessary protection to all property in its modern forms. We deal here with wages—a specialized type of property presenting distinct problems in our economic system. We turn then to the nature of that property and problems of procedural due process.

A prejudgment garnishment of the Wisconsin type is a taking which may impose tremendous hardship on wage earners with families to support. Until a recent Act of Congress, § 304 of which forbids discharge of employees on the ground that their wages have been garnisheed, garnishment often meant the loss of a job. Over and beyond that was the great drain on family income. As stated by Congressman Reuss:

> "The idea of wage garnishment in advance of judgment, of trustee process, of wage attachment, or whatever it is called is a most inhuman doctrine. It compels the wage earner, trying to keep his family together, to be driven below the poverty level."

Recent investigations of the problem have discussed the grave injustices made possible by prejudgment garnishment whereby the sole opportunity to be heard comes after the taking. Congressman Sullivan, Chairman of the House Subcommittee on Consumer Affairs who held extensive hearings on this and related problems stated:

> "What we know from our study of this problem is that in a vast number of cases the debt is a fraudulent one saddled on a poor, ignorant person who is trapped in an easy credit nightmare in which he is charged double for something he could not pay for even if the proper price was called for, and then hounded into giving up his pound of flesh, and being fired besides." 114 Cong.Rec. p. H. 688 (1968).

The leverage of the creditor on the wage earner is enormous. The creditor tenders not only the original debt but the "collection fees" incurred by its attorneys in the garnishment proceedings:

> "The debtor whose wages are tied up by a writ of garnishment, and who is usually in need of money, is in no position to resist demands for collection fees. If the debt is small, the debtor will be under considerable pressure to pay the debt and collection charges in order to get his wages back. If the debt is large, he will often sign a new contract of 'payment schedule' which incorporates these additional charges."

Apart from these collateral consequences, it appears that in Wisconsin the statutory exemption granted the wage earner is "generally insufficient to support the debtor for any one week."

The result is that a prejudgment garnishment of the Wisconsin type may as a practical matter drive a wage-earning family to the wall.[2] Where the taking of one's property is so obvious, it needs no extended argument to conclude that absent notice and a prior hearing (cf. Coe v. Armour Fertilizer Works, 237 U.S. 413, 423, 35 S.Ct. 625, 628, 59 L.Ed. 1027) this prejudgment garnishment procedure violates the fundamental principles of due process.

Reversed.

MR. JUSTICE HARLAN, concurring.

Particularly in light of my Brother Black's dissent, I think it not amiss for me to make explicit the precise basis on which I join the Court's opinion. The "property" of which petitioner has been deprived is the *use* of the garnished portion of her wages during the interim period between the garnishment and the culmination of the main suit. Since this deprivation cannot be characterized as *de minimis,* she must be accorded the usual requisites of procedural due process: notice and a prior hearing.

* * *

MR. JUSTICE BLACK, dissenting.

The Court here holds unconstitutional a Wisconsin statute permitting garnishment before a judgment has been obtained against the principal debtor. The law, however, requires that notice be given to the principal debtor and authorizes him to present all of his legal defenses at the regular hearing and trial of the case. The Wisconsin law is said to violate the "fundamental principles of due process." Of course the Due Process Clause of the Fourteenth Amendment contains no words that indicate that this Court has power to play so fast and loose with state laws. The arguments the Court makes to reach what I consider to be its unconstitutional conclusion, however, shows why it strikes down this state law. It is because it considers a garnishment law of this kind to be bad state policy, a judgment I think the state legislature, not this Court, has power to make. . . .

NOTES

(1) The opinion in the principal case does not in terms distinguish between the two possible functions of attachment and garnishment—as security for payment of the final judgment and as a basis of adjudicatory authority. Does the Court's ruling apply in both of these situations?

2. "For a poor man—and whoever heard of the wage of the affluent being attached?—to lose part of his salary often means his family will go without the essentials. No man sits by while his family goes hungry or without heat. He either files for consumer bankruptcy, and tries to begin again, or just quits his job and goes on relief. Where is the equity, the common sense in such a process?" Congressman Gonzales, 114 Cong.Rec., p. H. 690 (1968). For the impact of garnishment on personal bankruptcies see H.R.Rep. No. 1040, 90th Cong., 1st Sess., pp. 20–21.

(2) *Sniadach's* emphasis on the single importance of wages suggests that it might be limited to that kind of garnishment alone or perhaps to attachment of other goods considered "necessary"; on the other hand, application of due process principles does not ordinarily depend on the type of property interest that is the subject of the deprivation.

(3) What implications may *Sniadach* hold for provisional remedies other than attachment and garnishment? Receivership involves a similar kind of deprivation, at least temporarily, of the use of property. A preliminary injunction or temporary restraining order (TRO) may deprive a person of even more highly valued First Amendment rights of speech and assembly until the occasion for effective exercise of those rights has passed. And even a notice of pendency, though ordinarily having considerably less impact on the enjoyment of property than attachment or a temporary receivership, may significantly decrease the attractiveness of the subject property to prospective purchasers or encumbrancers.

(4) Does *Sniadach* impose a uniform requirement of prior notice and an opportunity to be heard before attachment or whether a prompt post-seizure hearing and some combination of other procedural safeguards serve as a suitable alternative.

(5) And what exactly were the "extraordinary situations" for which "such summary procedure" as the court struck down in *Sniadach* might "well meet the requirements of due process"? Of the cases cited at this point in Justice Douglas's opinion, all but *Ownbey* involved neither the acquisition of jurisdiction nor provision of security in a dispute between private litigants but rather seizures by government officials in response to such threats to the general public as a bank failure or the misbanding of drugs.

(6) Even though, under federal standards, a taxpayer and member of a teachers' association lacked standing to attack the constitutionality of a state statute governing mineral leases on state lands which allegedly deprived the state's school trust funds of millions of dollars, the Supreme Court, in ASARCO, Inc. v. Kadish, ___ U.S. ___, 109 S.Ct. 2037, 104 L.Ed.2d 696 (1989), reviewed the decision of the court below holding the statute unconstitutional. The Court stressed the undesirable consequences of dismissing the case for lack of standing to petitioners whose leases had been invalidated by the court below.

Some light is shed on these matters by three major decisions that the Court has since rendered elaborating on Sniadach: Fuentes v. Shevin in 1972, Mitchell v. W.T. Grant Co. in 1974, and North Georgia Finishing, Inc. v. Di-Chem, Inc., in 1975.

FUENTES v. SHEVIN

Supreme Court of the United States, 1972.
407 U.S. 67, 92 S.Ct. 1983, 32 L.Ed.2d 556.

MR. JUSTICE STEWART delivered the opinion of the Court.*

We here review the decisions of two three-judge federal District Courts that upheld the constitutionality of Florida and Pennsylvania laws authorizing the summary seizure of goods or chattels in a person's

---

* Some footnotes omitted; others renumbered.

possession under a writ of replevin. Both statutes provide for the issuance of writs ordering state agents to seize a person's possessions, simply upon the *ex parte* application of any other person who claims a right to them and posts a security bond. Neither statute provides for notice to be given to the possessor of the property, and neither statute gives the possessor an opportunity to challenge the seizure at any kind of prior hearing. The question is whether these statutory procedures violate the Fourteenth Amendment's guarantee that no State shall deprive any person of property without due process of law.

I

The appellant in No. 5039, Margarita Fuentes, is a resident of Florida. She purchased a gas stove and service policy from the Firestone Tire and Rubber Co. (Firestone) under a conditional sales contract calling for monthly payments over a period of time. A few months later, she purchased a stereophonic phonograph from the same company under the same sort of contract. The total cost of the stove and stereo was about $500, plus an additional financing charge of over $100. Under the contracts, Firestone retained title to the merchandise, but Mrs. Fuentes was entitled to possession unless and until she should default on her installment payments.

For more than a year, Mrs. Fuentes made her installment payments. But then, with only about $200 remaining to be paid, a dispute developed between her and Firestone over the servicing of the stove. Firestone instituted an action in a small-claims court for repossession of both the stove and the stereo, claiming that Mrs. Fuentes had refused to make her remaining payments. Simultaneously with the filing of that action and before Mrs. Fuentes had even received a summons to answer its complaint, Firestone obtained a writ of replevin ordering a sheriff to seize the disputed goods at once.

In conformance with Florida procedure, Firestone had only to fill in the blanks on the appropriate form documents and submit them to the clerk of the small-claims court. The clerk signed and stamped the documents and issued a writ of replevin. Later the same day, a local deputy sheriff and an agent of Firestone went to Mrs. Fuentes' home and seized the stove and stereo.

Shortly thereafter, Mrs. Fuentes instituted the present action in a federal district court, challenging the constitutionality of the Florida prejudgment replevin procedures under the Due Process Clause of the Fourteenth Amendment. She sought declaratory and injunctive relief against continued enforcement of the procedural provisions of the state statutes that authorize prejudgment replevin.

The appellants in No. 5138 filed a very similar action in a federal district court in Pennsylvania, challenging the constitutionality of that State's prejudgment replevin process. Like Mrs. Fuentes, they had had possessions seized under writs of replevin. Three of the appellants had purchased personal property—a bed, a table, and other household goods—under installment sales contracts like the one signed by Mrs. Fuentes; and the sellers of the property had obtained and executed summary writs of replevin, claiming that the appellants had fallen behind in their installment payments. The experience of the fourth appellant, Rosa Washington, had been more bizarre. She had been divorced from a local deputy sheriff and was engaged in a dispute with him over the custody of their son. Her former husband, being familiar with the routine forms used in the replevin process, had obtained a writ that ordered the seizure of the boy's clothes, furniture, and toys.

In both No. 5039 and No. 5138, three-judge District Courts were convened to consider the appellants' challenges to the constitutional validity of the Florida and Pennsylvania statutes. The courts in both cases upheld the constitutionality of the statutes. . . .

II

Under the Florida statute challenged here, "[a]ny person whose goods or chattels are wrongfully detained by any other person . . . may have a writ of replevin to recover them . . . ." Fla.Stat.Ann. § 78.01 (Supp.1972–1973). There is no requirement that the applicant make a convincing showing before the seizure that the goods are, in fact, "wrongfully detained." Rather, Florida law automatically relies on the bare assertion of the party seeking the writ that he is entitled to one and allows a court clerk to issue the writ summarily. It requires only that the applicant file a complaint, initiating a court action for repossession and reciting in conclusory fashion that he is "lawfully entitled to the possession" of the property, and that he file a security bond.

> "in at least double the value of the property to be replevied conditioned that plaintiff will prosecute his action to effect and without delay and that if defendant recovers judgment against him in the action, he will return the property, if return thereof is adjudged, and will pay defendant all sums of money recovered against plaintiff by defendant in the action." Fla.Stat. Ann. § 78.07 (Supp.1972–1973).

On the sole basis of the complaint and bond, a writ is issued "command[ing] the officer to whom it may be directed to replevy the goods and chattels in possession of defendant . . . and to summon the defendant to answer the complaint." Fla.Stat.Ann. § 78.08 (Supp. 1972–1973). If the goods are "in any dwelling house or other building or enclosure," the officer is required to demand their delivery; but, if they are not delivered, "he shall cause such house, building or enclosure to be broken open and shall make replevin according to the writ . . . ." Fla.Stat.Ann. § 78.10 (Supp.1972–1973).

Thus, at the same moment that the defendant receives the complaint seeking repossession of property through court action, the property is seized from him. He is provided no prior notice and allowed no opportunity whatever to challenge the issuance of the writ. *After* the property has been seized, he will eventually have an opportunity for a hearing, as the defendant in the trial of the court action for repossession, which the plaintiff is required to pursue. And he is also not wholly without recourse in the meantime. For under the Florida statute, the officer who seizes the property must keep it for three days, and during that period the defendant may reclaim possession of the property by posting his own security bond in double its value. But if he does not post such a bond, the property is transferred to the party who sought the writ, pending a final judgment in the underlying action for repossession. Fla.Stat.Ann. § 78.13 (Supp.1972–1973).

The Pennsylvania law differs, though not in its essential nature, from that of Florida. As in Florida, a private party may obtain a prejudgment writ of replevin through a summary process of *ex parte* application to a prothonotary. As in Florida, the party seeking the writ may simply post with his application a bond in double the value of the property to be seized. Pa.Rule Civ.Proc. 1073(a). There is no opportunity for a prior hearing and no prior notice to the other party. On this basis, a sheriff is required to execute the writ by seizing the specified property. Unlike the Florida statute, however, the Pennsylvania law does not require that there *ever* be opportunity for a hearing on the merits of the conflicting claims to possession of the replevied property. The party seeking the writ is not obliged to initiate a court action for repossession. Indeed, he need not even formally allege that he is lawfully entitled to the property. The most that is required is that he file an "affidavit of the value of the property to be replevied." Pa.Rule Civ.Proc. 1073(a). If the party who loses property through replevin seizure is to get even a post-seizure hearing, he must initiate a lawsuit himself. He may also, as under Florida law, post his own counterbond within three days after the seizure to regain possession. Pa.Rule Civ.Proc. 1076.

   *   *   *

IV

   *   *   *

The primary question in the present cases is whether these state statutes are constitutionally defective in failing to provide for hearings "at a meaningful time." The Florida replevin process guarantees an opportunity for a hearing after the seizure of goods, and the Pennsylvania process allows a post-seizure hearing if the aggrieved party shoulders the burden of initiating one. But neither the Florida nor the Pennsylvania statute provides for notice or an opportunity to be heard *before* the seizure. The issue is whether procedural due process in the context of these cases requires an opportunity for a hearing *before* the State authorizes its agents to seize property in the possession of a person upon the application of another.

The constitutional right to be heard is a basic aspect of the duty of government to follow a fair process of decisionmaking when it acts to deprive a person of his possessions. The purpose of this requirement is not only to ensure abstract fair play to the individual. Its purpose, more particularly, is to protect his use and possession of property from arbitrary encroachment—to minimize substantively unfair or mistaken deprivations of property, a danger that is especially great when the State seizes goods simply upon the application of and for the benefit of a private party. So viewed, the prohibition against the deprivation of property without due process of law reflects the high value, embedded in our constitutional and political history, that we place on a person's right to enjoy what is his, free of governmental interference. See Lynch v. Household Finance Corp., 405 U.S. 538, 552, 92 S.Ct. 1113, 1122, 31 L.Ed.2d 424.

* * *

If the right to notice and a hearing is to serve its full purpose, then, it is clear that it must be granted at a time when the deprivation can still be prevented. At a later hearing, an individual's possessions can be returned to him if they were unfairly or mistakenly taken in the first place. Damages may even be awarded to him for the wrongful deprivation. But no later hearing and no damage award can undo the fact that the arbitrary taking that was subject to the right of procedural due process has already occurred. "This Court has not . . . embraced the general proposition that a wrong may be done if it can be undone." Stanley v. Illinois, 405 U.S. 645, 647, 92 S.Ct. 1208, 1210, 31 L.Ed.2d 551.

This is no new principle of constitutional law. The right to a prior hearing has long been recognized by this Court under the Fourteenth and Fifth Amendments. Although the Court has held that due process tolerates variances in the *form* of a hearing "appropriate to the nature of the case," Mullane v. Central Hanover Tr. Co., 339 U.S. 306, 313, 70 S.Ct. 652, 657, 94 L.Ed. 865, and "depending upon the importance of the interests involved and the nature of the subsequent proceedings [if any]," Boddie v. Connecticut, 401 U.S. 371, 378, 91 S.Ct. 780, 786, 28 L.Ed.2d 113, the Court has traditionally insisted that, whatever its form, opportunity for that hearing must be provided before the deprivation at issue takes effect. . . .

The Florida and Pennsylvania prejudgment replevin statutes fly in the face of this principle. To be sure, the requirements that a party seeking a writ must first post a bond, allege conclusorily that he is entitled to specific goods, and open himself to possible liability in damages if he is wrong, serve to deter wholly unfounded applications for a writ. But those requirements are hardly a substitute for a prior hearing, for they test no more than the strength of the applicant's own belief in his rights.[1]

---

1. They may not even test that much. For if an applicant for the writ knows that he is dealing with an uneducated, uninformed consumer with little access to legal help and little familiarity with legal proce- dures, there may be a substantial possibility that a summary seizure of property— however unwarranted—may go unchallenged, and the applicant may feel that he can act with impunity.

. . . While the existence of these other, less effective, safeguards may be among the considerations that affect the form of hearing demanded by due process, they are far from enough by themselves to obviate the right to a prior hearing of some kind.

V

The right to a prior hearing, of course, attaches only to the deprivation of an interest encompassed within the Fourteenth Amendment's protection. In the present cases, the Florida and Pennsylvania statutes were applied to replevy chattels in the appellants' possession. The replevin was not cast as a final judgment; most, if not all, of the appellants lacked full title to the chattels; and their claim even to continued possession was a matter in dispute. Moreover, the chattels at stake were nothing more than an assortment of household goods. Nonetheless, it is clear that the appellants were deprived of possessory interests in those chattels that were within the protection of the Fourteenth Amendment.

A

A deprivation of a person's possessions under a prejudgment writ of replevin, at least in theory, may be only temporary. The Florida and Pennsylvania statutes do not require a person to wait until a post-seizure hearing and final judgment to recover what has been replevied. Within three days after the seizure, the statutes allow him to recover the goods if he, in return, surrenders other property—a payment necessary to secure a bond in double the value of the goods seized from him.[2] But it is now well settled that a temporary, nonfinal deprivation of property is nonetheless a "deprivation" in the terms of the Fourteenth Amendment. Sniadach v. Family Finance Corp., 395 U.S. 337, 89 S.Ct. 1820, 23 L.Ed.2d 349; Bell v. Burson, 402 U.S. 535, 91 S.Ct. 1586, 29 L.Ed.2d 90. Both *Sniadach* and *Bell* involved takings of property pending a final judgment in an underlying dispute. In both cases, the challenged statutes included recovery provisions, allowing the defendants to post security to quickly regain the property taken from them.[3] Yet the Court firmly held that these were deprivations of property that had to be preceded by a fair hearing.

---

2. The appellants argue that this opportunity for quick recovery exists only in theory. They allege that very few people in their position are able to obtain a recovery bond, even if they know of the possibility. Appellant Fuentes says that in her case she was never told that she could recover the stove and stereo and that the deputy sheriff seizing them gave them at once to the Firestone agent, rather than holding them for three days. She further asserts that of 442 cases of prejudgment replevin in small-claims courts in Dade County, Florida, in 1969, there was not one case in which the defendant took advantage of the recovery provision.

3. Bell v. Burson, 402 U.S. 535, 536, 91 S.Ct. 1586, 1587, 29 L.Ed.2d 90. Although not mentioned in the *Sniadach* opinion, there clearly was a quick-recovery provision in the Wisconsin prejudgment garnishment statute at issue. Wis.Stat.Ann. § 267.21(1) (Supp.1970–1971). Family Finance Corp. v. Sniadach, 37 Wis.2d 163, 173–174, 154 N.W.2d 259, 265. Mr. Justice Harlan adverted to the recovery provision in his concurring opinion. 395 U.S. 337, at

The present cases are no different. When officials of Florida or Pennsylvania seize one piece of property from a person's possession and then agree to return it if he surrenders another, they deprive him of property whether or not he has the funds, the knowledge, and the time needed to take advantage of the recovery provision. The Fourteenth Amendment draws no bright lines around three-day, 10-day or 50-day deprivations of property. Any significant taking of property by the State is within the purview of the Due Process Clause. While the length and consequent severity of a deprivation may be another factor to weigh in determining the appropriate form of hearing, it is not decisive of the basic right to a prior hearing of some kind.

B

The appellants who signed conditional sales contracts lacked full legal title to the replevied goods. The Fourteenth Amendment's protection of "property," however, has never been interpreted to safeguard only the rights of undisputed ownership. Rather, it has been read broadly to extend protection to "any significant property interest," Boddie v. Connecticut, 401 U.S., at 379, 91 S.Ct., at 786, including statutory entitlements. See Bell v. Burson, 402 U.S., at 539, 91 S.Ct., at 1589; Goldberg v. Kelly, 397 U.S., at 262, 90 S.Ct., at 1017.

The appellants were deprived of such an interest in the replevied goods—the interest in continued possession and use of the goods. See Sniadach v. Family Finance Corp., 395 U.S., at 342, 89 S.Ct., at 1823 (Harlan, J., concurring). They had acquired this interest under the conditional sales contracts that entitled them to possession and use of the chattels before transfer of title. In exchange for immediate possession, the appellants had agreed to pay a major financing charge beyond the basic price of the merchandise. Moreover, by the time the goods were summarily repossessed, they had made substantial installment payments. Clearly, their possessory interest in the goods, dearly bought and protected by contract,[4] was sufficient to invoke the protection of the Due Process Clause.

Their ultimate right to continued possession was, of course, in dispute. If it were shown at a hearing that the appellants had defaulted on their contractual obligations, it might well be that the sellers of the goods would be entitled to repossession. But even assuming that the appellants had fallen behind in their installment payments, and that they had no other valid defenses,[5] that is immaterial here. The

343, 89 S.Ct. 1820, at 1823, 23 L.Ed.2d 349.
. . .

4. The possessory interest of Rosa Washington, an appellant in No. 5138, in her son's clothes, furniture, and toys was no less sufficient to invoke due process safeguards. Her interest was not protected by contract. Rather, it was protected by ordinary property law, there being a dispute between her and her estranged husband over which of them had a legal right not only to custody of the child but also to possession of the chattels.

5. Mrs. Fuentes argues that Florida law allows her to defend on the ground that Firestone breached its obligations under the sales contract by failing to repair serious defects in the stove it sold her. We need not consider this issue here. It is enough that the right to continued posses-

right to be heard does not depend upon an advance showing that one will surely prevail at the hearing. . . .

C

Nevertheless, the District Courts rejected the appellants' constitutional claim on the ground that the goods seized from them—a stove, a stereo, a table, a bed, and so forth—were not deserving of due process protection, since they were not absolute necessities of life. The courts based this holding on a very narrow reading of Sniadach v. Family Finance Corp., supra, and Goldberg v. Kelly, supra, in which this Court held that the Constitution requires a hearing before prejudgment wage garnishment and before the termination of certain welfare benefits. They reasoned that *Sniadach* and *Goldberg,* as a matter of constitutional principle, established no more than that a prior hearing is required with respect to the deprivation of such basically "necessary" items as wages and welfare benefits.

This reading of *Sniadach* and *Goldberg* reflects the premise that those cases marked a radical departure from established principles of procedural due process. They did not. Both decisions were in the mainstream of past cases, having little or nothing to do with the absolute "necessities" of life but establishing that due process requires an opportunity for a hearing before a deprivation of property takes effect. . . .

No doubt, there may be many gradations in the "importance" or "necessity" of various consumer goods. Stoves could be compared to television sets, or beds could be compared to tables. But if the root principle of procedural due process is to be applied with objectivity, it cannot rest on such distinctions. The Fourteenth Amendment speaks of "property" generally. And, under our free-enterprise system, an individual's choices in the marketplace are respected, however unwise they may seem to someone else. It is not the business of a court adjudicating due process rights to make its own critical evaluation of those choices and protect only the ones that, by its own lights, are "necessary." [6]

VI

There are "extraordinary situations" that justify postponing notice and opportunity for a hearing. Boddie v. Connecticut, 401 U.S., at 379, 91 S.Ct., at 786. These situations, however, must be truly unusual.

---

sion of the goods was open to *some* dispute at a hearing since the sellers of the goods had to show, at the least, that the appellants had defaulted in their payments.

6. The relative weight of liberty or property interests is relevant, of course, to the form of notice and hearing required by due process. See, e.g., Boddie v. Connecticut, 401 U.S. 371, 378, 91 S.Ct. 780, 786, 28 L.Ed.2d 113, and cases cited therein. But *some* form of notice and hearing—formal or informal—is required before deprivation of a property interest that "cannot be characterized as *de minimis.*" Sniadach v. Family Finance Corp., supra, 395 U.S., at 342, 89 S.Ct., at 1823 (Harlan, J., concurring).

Only in a few limited situations has this Court allowed outright seizure [7] without opportunity for a prior hearing. First, in each case, the seizure has been directly necessary to secure an important governmental or general public interest. Second, there has been a special need for very prompt action. Third, the State has kept strict control over its monopoly of legitimate force: the person initiating the seizure has been a government official responsible for determining, under the standards of a narrowly drawn statute, that it was necessary and justified in the particular instance. Thus, the Court has allowed summary seizure of property to collect the internal revenue of the United States,[8] to meet the needs of a national war effort,[9] to protect against the economic disaster of a bank failure,[10] and to protect the public from misbranded drugs [11] and contaminated food.[12]

The Florida and Pennsylvania prejudgment replevin statutes serve no such important governmental or general public interest. They allow summary seizure of a person's possessions when no more than private gain is directly at stake.[13] The replevin of chattels, as in the

7. Of course, outright seizure of property is not the only kind of deprivation that must be preceded by a prior hearing. See, e.g., Sniadach v. Family Finance Corp., supra. In three cases, the Court has allowed the attachment of property without a prior hearing. In one, the attachment was necessary to protect the public against the same sort of immediate harm involved in the seizure cases—a bank failure. Coffin Bros. & Co. v. Bennett, 277 U.S. 29, 48 S.Ct. 422, 72 L.Ed. 768. Another case involved attachment necessary to secure jurisdiction in state court—clearly a most basic and important public interest. Ownbey v. Morgan, 256 U.S. 94, 41 S.Ct. 433, 65 L.Ed. 837. It is much less clear what interests were involved in the third case, decided with an unexplicated per curiam opinion simply citing *Coffin Bros.* and *Ownbey.* McKay v. McInnes, 279 U.S. 820, 49 S.Ct. 344, 73 L.Ed. 975. As far as essential procedural due process doctrine goes, *McKay* cannot stand for any more than was established in the *Coffin Bros.* and *Ownbey* cases on which it relied completely. See Sniadach v. Family Finance Corp., supra, 395 U.S., at 340, 89 S.Ct., at 1822; id., at 344, 89 S.Ct. 1823 (Harlan, J., concurring).

In cases involving deprivation of other interests, such as government employment, the Court similarly has required an unusually important governmental need to outweigh the right to a prior hearing. See, e.g., Cafeteria and Restaurant Workers v. McElroy, 367 U.S. 886, 895–896, 81 S.Ct. 1743, 1748–1749, 6 L.Ed.2d 1230.

8. Phillips v. Commissioner of Internal Revenue, 283 U.S. 589, 51 S.Ct. 608, 75 L.Ed. 1289. The Court stated that "[d]elay in the judicial determination of property rights is not uncommon where it is *essential* that governmental needs be *immediately* satisfied." Id., at 597, 51 S.Ct., at 611 (emphasis supplied). The Court, then relied on "the need of the government promptly to secure its revenues." Id., at 596, 51 S.Ct., at 611.

9. Central Union Trust Co. v. Garvan, 254 U.S. 554, 566, 41 S.Ct. 214, 215, 65 L.Ed. 403; Stoehr v. Wallace, 255 U.S. 239, 245, 41 S.Ct. 293, 296, 65 L.Ed. 604; United States v. Pfitsch, 256 U.S. 547, 553, 41 S.Ct. 569, 571, 65 L.Ed. 1084.

10. Fahey v. Mallonee, 332 U.S. 245, 67 S.Ct. 1552, 91 L.Ed. 2030.

11. Ewing v. Mytinger & Casselberry, Inc., 339 U.S. 594, 70 S.Ct. 870, 94 L.Ed. 1088.

12. North American Storage Co. v. Chicago, 211 U.S. 306, 29 S.Ct. 101, 53 L.Ed. 195.

13. By allowing repossession without an opportunity for a prior hearing, the Florida and Pennsylvania statutes may be intended specifically to reduce the costs for the private party seeking to seize goods in another party's possession. Even if the private gain at stake in repossession actions were equal to the great public interests recognized in this Court's past decisions, see nn. 24–28, supra, the Court has made clear that the avoidance of the ordinary costs imposed by the opportunity for a hearing is not sufficient to override the constitutional right. . . .

In any event, the aggregate cost of an opportunity to be heard before repossession

present cases, may satisfy a debt or settle a score. But state intervention in a private dispute hardly compares to state action furthering a war effort or protecting the public health.

Nor do the broadly drawn Florida and Pennsylvania statutes limit the summary seizure of goods to special situations demanding prompt action. There may be cases in which a creditor could make a showing of immediate danger that a debtor will destroy or conceal disputed goods. But the statutes before us are not "narrowly drawn to meet any such unusual condition." Sniadach v. Family Finance Corp., supra, 395 U.S., at 339, 89 S.Ct., at 1821. And no such unusual situation is presented by the facts of these cases.

The statutes, moreover, abdicate effective state control over state power. Private parties, serving their own private advantage, may unilaterally invoke state power to replevy goods from another. No state official participates in the decision to seek a writ; no state official reviews the basis for the claim to repossession; and no state official evaluates the need for immediate seizure. There is not even a requirement that the plaintiff provide any information to the court on these matters. The State acts largely in the dark.

VII

Finally, we must consider the contention that the appellants who signed conditional sales contracts thereby waived their basic procedural due process rights. The contract signed by Mrs. Fuentes provided that "in the event of default of any payment or payments, Seller at its option may take back the merchandise . . . ." The contracts signed by the Pennsylvania appellants similarly provided that the seller "may retake" or "repossess" the merchandise in the event of a "default in any payment." These terms were parts of printed form contracts, appearing in relatively small type and unaccompanied by any explanations clarifying their meaning.

In D.H. Overmyer Co. v. Frick Co., 405 U.S. 174, 92 S.Ct. 775, 31 L.Ed.2d 124, the Court recently outlined the considerations relevant to determination of a contractual waiver of due process rights. Applying the standards governing waiver of constitutional rights in a criminal proceeding—although not holding that such standards must necessarily apply—the Court held that, on the particular facts of that case, the contractual waiver of due process rights was "voluntarily, intelligently, and knowingly" made. Id., at 187, 92 S.Ct., at 783. The contract in *Overmyer* was negotiated between two corporations; the waiver provision was specifically bargained for and drafted by their lawyers in the process of these negotiations. As the Court noted, it was "not a case of

should not be exaggerated. For we deal here only with the right to an *opportunity* to be heard. Since the issues and facts decisive of rights in repossession suits may very often be quite simple, there is a likelihood that many defendants would forgo their opportunity, sensing the futility of the exercise in the particular case. And, of course, no hearing need be held unless the defendant, having received notice of his opportunity, takes advantage of it.

unequal bargaining power or overreaching. The Overmyer-Frick agreement, from the start, was not a contract of adhesion." Id., at 186, 92 S.Ct., at 782. Both parties were "aware of the significance" of the waiver provision. Ibid.

The facts of the present cases are a far cry from those of *Overmyer.* There was no bargaining over contractual terms between the parties who, in any event, were far from equal in bargaining power. The purported waiver provision was a printed part of a form sales contract and a necessary condition of the sale. The appellees made no showing whatever that the appellants were actually aware or made aware of the significance of the fine print now relied upon as a waiver of constitutional rights.

The Court in *Overmyer* observed that "where the contract is one of adhesion, where there is great disparity in bargaining power, and where the debtor receives nothing for the [waiver] provision, other legal consequences may ensue." Id., at 188, 92 S.Ct., at 783. Yet, as in *Overmyer,* there is no need in the present cases to canvass those consequences fully. For a waiver of constitutional rights in any context must, at the very *least,* be clear. We need not concern ourselves with the involuntariness or unintelligence of a waiver when the contractual language relied upon does not, on its face, even amount to a waiver.

The conditional sales contracts here simply provided that upon a default the seller "may take back," "may retake" or "may repossess" merchandise. The contracts included nothing about the waiver of a prior hearing. They did not indicate *how* or *through what process*—a final judgment, self-help, prejudgment replevin with a prior hearing, or prejudgment replevin without a prior hearing—the seller could take back the goods. Rather, the purported waiver provisions here are no more than a statement of the seller's right to repossession upon occurrence of certain events. The appellees do not suggest that these provisions waived the appellants' right to a full post-seizure hearing to determine whether those events had, in fact, occurred and to consider any other available defenses. By the same token, the language of the purported waiver provisions did not waive the appellants' constitutional right to a preseizure hearing of some kind.

VIII

We hold that the Florida and Pennsylvania prejudgment replevin provisions work a deprivation of property without due process of law insofar as they deny the right to a prior opportunity to be heard before chattels are taken from their possessor. Our holding, however, is a narrow one. We do not question the power of a State to seize goods before a final judgment in order to protect the security interests of creditors so long as those creditors have tested their claim to the goods through the process of a fair prior hearing. The nature and form of such prior hearings, moreover, are legitimately open to many potential variations and are a subject, at this point, for legislation—not adjudication. Since the essential reason for the requirement of a prior hearing is to prevent unfair and mistaken deprivations of property, however, it is axiomatic that the hearing must provide a real test. "[D]ue process is afforded only by the kinds of 'notice' and 'hearing' that are aimed at establishing the validity, or at least the probable validity, of the underlying claim against the alleged debtor *before* he can be deprived of his property . . . ." Sniadach v. Family Finance Corp., supra, 395 U.S. at 343, 89 S.Ct. at 1823 (Harlan, J., concurring). See Bell v. Burson, supra, 402 U.S. at 540, 91 S.Ct. at 1589; Goldberg v. Kelly, supra, 397 U.S. at 267, 90 S.Ct. at 1020.

For the foregoing reasons, the judgments of the District Courts are vacated and these cases are remanded for further proceedings consistent with this opinion.

It is so ordered.

Mr. Justice Powell and Mr. Justice Rehnquist did not participate in the consideration or decision of these cases.

Mr. Justice White, with whom The Chief Justice and Mr. Justice Blackmun join, dissenting.

Because the Court's opinion and judgment improvidently, in my view, call into question important aspects of the statutes of almost all the States governing secured transactions and the procedure for repossessing personal property, I must dissent for the reasons that follow.

* * *

Second: It goes without saying that in the typical installment sale of personal property both seller and buyer have interests in the property until the purchase price is fully paid, the seller early in the transaction often having more at stake than the buyer. Nor is it disputed that the buyer's right to possession is conditioned upon his making the stipulated payments and that upon default the seller is entitled to possession. Finally, there is no question in these cases that if default is disputed by the buyer he has the opportunity for a full hearing, and that if he prevails he may have the property or its full value as damages.

The narrow issue, as the Court notes, is whether it comports with due process to permit the seller, pending final judgment, to take possession of the property through a writ of replevin served by the sheriff without affording the buyer opportunity to insist that the seller establish at a hearing that there is reasonable basis for his claim of default. The interests of the buyer and seller are obviously antagonistic during this interim period: the buyer wants the use of the property pending final judgment; the seller's interest is to prevent further use and deterioration of his security. By the Florida and Pennsylvania laws the property is to all intents and purposes placed in custody and immobilized during this time. The buyer loses use of the property temporarily but is protected against loss; the seller is protected against deterioration of the property but must undertake by bond to make the buyer whole in the event the latter prevails.

* * *

. . . Viewing the issue before us in this light, I would not construe the Due Process Clause to require the creditors to do more than they have done in these cases to secure possession pending final hearing. Certainly, I would not ignore, as the Court does, the creditor's interest in preventing further use and deterioration of the property in which he has substantial interest. Surely under the Court's own definition, the creditor has a "property" interest as deserving of protection as that of the debtor. At least the debtor, who is very likely uninterested in a speedy resolution that could terminate his use of the property, should be required to make those payments, into court or otherwise, upon which his right to possession is conditioned. Cf. Lindsey v. Normet, 405 U.S. 56, 92 S.Ct. 862, 31 L.Ed.2d 36 (1972).

Third: The Court's rhetoric is seductive, but in end analysis, the result it reaches will have little impact and represents no more than ideological tinkering with state law. It would appear that creditors could withstand attack under today's opinion simply by making clear in the controlling credit instruments that they may retake possession without a hearing, or, for that matter, without resort to judicial process at all. Alternatively, they need only give a few days' notice of a hearing, take possession if hearing is waived or if there is default; and if hearing is necessary merely establish probable cause for asserting that default has occurred. It is very doubtful in my mind that such a hearing would in fact result in protections for the debtor substantially different from those the present laws provide. On the contrary, the availability of credit may well be diminished or, in any event, the expense of securing it increased.

None of this seems worth the candle to me. The procedure that the Court strikes down is not some barbaric hangover from bygone days. The respective rights of the parties in secured transactions have undergone the most intensive analysis in recent years. The Uniform Commercial Code, which now so pervasively governs the subject matter with which it deals, provides in Art. 9, § 9–503, that:

> "Unless otherwise agreed a secured party has on default the right to take possession of the collateral. In taking possession a secured party may proceed without judicial process if this can be done without breach of the peace or may proceed by action. . . ."

Recent studies have suggested no changes in Art. 9 in this respect. See Permanent Editorial Board for the Uniform Commercial Code, Review Committee for Article 9 of the Uniform Commercial Code, Final Report, § 9–503 (April 25, 1971). I am content to rest on the judgment of those who have wrestled with these problems so long and often and upon the judgment of the legislatures that have considered and so recently adopted provisions that contemplate precisely what has happened in these cases.

NOTES

(1) *Fuentes* seems in terms to impose a uniform requirement of pre-seizure notice and opportunity to be heard except in "extraordinary situations", which must be "truly unusual." The opinion limits such situations to those involving "an important governmental or general public interest" and a "special need for very prompt action", but with the state keeping "strict control over its monopoly of legitimate force." Could any attachment designed solely to secure payment of the final judgment in a private civil controversy meet this test? Could an attachment designed to secure quasi-in-rem jurisdiction in a private civil controversy (to the extent that such jurisdiction remains viable after *Shaffer v. Heitner*)?

(2) Footnote 7 of Justice Stewart's opinion in *Fuentes* refers to the attachment "necessary to secure jurisdiction in a state court" in *Ownbey v. Morgan*, which was an ordinary private civil action, and "clearly a most basic and important public interest." For persuasive arguments that the kind of Due Process standards developed in the *Sniadach-Fuentes-Mitchell-Di-Chem* decisions are appropriate only to the security and not the jurisdictional function of attachment, see Moore, Procedural Due Process in Quasi In Rem Actions After Shaffer v. Heitner, 20 Wm. and Mary L.Rev. 157 (1978); Silberman, Shaffer v. Heitner: The End of an Era, 53 N.Y.U.L.Rev. 33, 53–62 (1978).

(3) In Calero-Toledo v. Pearson Yacht Leasing Co., 416 U.S. 663, 94 S.Ct. 2080, 40 L.Ed.2d 452 (1974), the Court upheld the constitutionality of a Puerto Rican statute that provided for forfeiture, without prior notice or hearing, of a vessel used for the transportation of a controlled substance. The lessees of the vessel, who had used it for transporting marijuana, were given notice after the service, but the innocent owner had received no notice whatsoever. The Court held that the case presented "extraordinary circumstances" and therefore came within the exceptions mentioned in *Sniadach* and *Fuentes*. It ruled:

> "The considerations that justified postponement of notice and hearing in those cases are present here. First, seizure under the Puerto Rican statutes serves significant governmental purposes: Seizure permits Puerto Rico to assert *in rem* jurisdiction over the property in order to conduct forfeiture proceedings, thereby fostering the public interest in preventing continued illicit use of the property and in enforcing criminal sanctions. Second, preseizure notice and hearing might frustrate the interests served by the statutes, since the property seized—as here, a yacht—will often be of a sort that could be removed to another jurisdiction, destroyed, or concealed, if advance warning of confiscation were given. And finally, unlike the situation in *Fuentes*, seizure is not initiated by self-interested private parties; rather, Commonwealth officials determine whether seizure is appropriate under the provisions of the Puerto Rican statutes. In these circumstances, we hold that this case presents an "extraordinary" situation in which postponement of notice and hearing until after seizure did not deny due process."

See also Hodel v. Virginia Surface Mining and Reclamation Association, 452 U.S. 264, 101 S.Ct. 2352, 69 L.Ed.2d 1 (1981), in which the Court upheld a provision directing the Secretary of the Interior to order immediate cessation of a surface mining operation when the operation creates an immediate danger to health, safety, or the environment.

(4) Is Justice White correct in asserting that creditors can avoid the impact of these decisions by contractual provisions allowing them to repossess goods after a default in payment without a hearing or without resort to judicial process at all? Does the majority opinion satisfactorily respond to this argument?

(5) What of statutory provisions such as U.C.C. § 9–503, quoted in Justice White's dissenting opinion, allowing repossession without resort to judicial process if this can be done without breach of the peace? Do such statutes violate Due Process? The United States Supreme Court has sustained a similar provision in § 7–210 of the UCC against such a challenge on the ground that since they allow repossession by private persons without official assistance or intervention they do not involve the "state action" necessary to invoke the 14th Amendment's Due Process clause. Flagg Brothers, Inc. v. Brooks, 436 U.S. 149, 98 S.Ct. 1729, 56 L.Ed.2d 185 (1978).

(6) The New York Court of Appeals has found § 7–210 of the U.C.C. violative of the Due Process Clause of the New York State Constitution, notwithstanding *Flagg.* Invoking its power to interpret the State Due Process Clause differently from its Federal counterpart, the New York Court disagreed with the Supreme Court's reasoning and found the requisite state action. Svendsen v. Smith's Moving & Trucking Co., 54 N.Y.2d 865, 444 N.Y.S.2d 904, 429 N.E.2d 411 (1981).

(7) An attempt to shield garnishment from evaluation under the 14th Amendment by contending that it involved insufficient state action was repulsed in Lugar v. Edmondson Oil Co., Inc. et al., 457 U.S. 922, 102 S.Ct. 2744, 73 L.Ed.2d 482 (1982). The Court held that the issuance of the writ of attachment by the clerk of the court and its execution by the county sheriff constituted sufficient state action.

NORTH GEORGIA FINISHING, INC. v. DI–CHEM, INC.

Supreme Court of the United States, 1975.
419 U.S. 601, 95 S.Ct. 719, 42 L.Ed.2d 751.

MR. JUSTICE WHITE delivered the opinion of the Court.*

Under the statutes of the State of Georgia, plaintiffs in pending suits are "entitled to the process of garnishment." Ga.Code Ann. § 46–101. To employ the process, plaintiff or his attorney must make an affidavit before "some officer authorized to issue an attachment, or the clerk of any court of record in which the said garnishment is being filed or in which the main case is filed, stating the amount claimed to be due in such action * * * and that he has reason to apprehend the loss of the same or some part thereof unless process of garnishment shall issue." § 46–102. To protect defendant against loss or damage in the event plaintiff fails to recover, that section also requires plaintiff to file a bond in a sum double the amount sworn to be due. Section 46–401 permits the defendant to dissolve the garnishment by filing a bond "conditioned for the payment of any judgment that shall be rendered on said garnishment." Whether these provisions satisfy the Due Pro-

* Most footnotes omitted.

cess Clause of the Fourteenth Amendment is the issue before us in this case.

On August 20, 1971, respondent filed suit against petitioner in the Superior Court of Whitfield County, Ga., alleging an indebtedness due and owing from petitioner for goods sold and delivered in the amount of $51,279.17. Simultaneously with the filing of the complaint and prior to its service on petitioner, respondent filed affidavit and bond for process of garnishment, naming the First National Bank of Dalton as garnishee. The affidavit asserted the debt and "reason to apprehend the loss of said sum or some part thereof unless process of Garnishment issues." The clerk of the Superior Court forthwith issued summons of garnishment to the bank, which was served that day. On August 23, petitioner filed a bond in the Superior Court conditioned to pay any final judgment in the main action up to the amount claimed, and the judge of that court thereupon discharged the bank as garnishee. On September 15, petitioner filed a motion to dismiss the writ of garnishment and to discharge its bond, asserting, among other things, that the statutory garnishment procedure was unconstitutional in that it violated "defendant's due process and equal protection rights guaranteed him by the Constitution of the United States and the Constitution of the State of Georgia." App. 11. The motion was heard and overruled on November 29. The Georgia Supreme Court, finding that the issue of the constitutionality of the statutory garnishment procedure was properly before it, sustained the statute and rejected petitioner's claims that the statute was invalid for failure to provide notice and hearing in connection with the issuance of the writ of garnishment. 231 Ga. 260, 201 S.E.2d 321 (1973). We granted certiorari. 417 U.S. 907, 94 S.Ct. 2601, 41 L.Ed.2d 210 (1974). We reverse.

The Georgia court recognized that *Sniadach v. Family Finance Corp.*, 395 U.S. 337, 89 S.Ct. 1820, 23 L.Ed.2d 349 (1969), had invalidated a statute permitting the garnishment of wages without notice and opportunity for hearing, but considered that case to have done nothing more than to carve out an exception, in favor of wage earners, "to the general rule of legality of garnishment statutes." 231 Ga., at 264, 201 S.E.2d, at 323. The garnishment of other assets or properties pending the outcome of the main action, although the effect was to " 'impound [them] in the hands of the garnishee,' " id., at 263, 201 S.E.2d, at 323, was apparently thought not to implicate the Due Process Clause.

This approach failed to take account of *Fuentes v. Shevin*, 407 U.S. 67, 92 S.Ct. 1983, 32 L.Ed.2d 556 (1972), a case decided by this Court more than a year prior to the Georgia court's decision. There the Court held invalid the Florida and Pennsylvania replevin statutes which permitted a secured installment seller to repossess the goods sold, without notice or hearing and without judicial order or supervision, but with the help of the sheriff operating under a writ issued by the clerk of the court at the behest of the seller. That the debtor was deprived of only the use and possession of the property, and perhaps only temporarily, did not put the seizure beyond scrutiny under the

Due Process Clause. "The Fourteenth Amendment draws no bright lines around three-day, 10-day, or 50-day deprivations of property. Any significant taking of property by the State is within the purview of the Due Process Clause." Id., at 86, 92 S.Ct., at 1997. Although the length or severity of a deprivation of use or possession would be another factor to weigh in determining the appropriate form of hearing, it was not deemed to be determinative of the right to a hearing of some sort. Because the official seizures had been carried out without notice and without opportunity for a hearing or other safeguard against mistaken repossession, they were held to be in violation of the Fourteenth Amendment.

The Georgia statute is vulnerable for the same reasons. Here, a bank account, surely a form of property, was impounded and, absent a bond, put totally beyond use during the pendency of the litigation on the alleged debt, all by a writ of garnishment issued by a court clerk without notice or opportunity for an early hearing and without participation by a judicial officer.

Nor is the statute saved by the more recent decision in Mitchell v. W.T. Grant Co., 416 U.S. 600, 94 S.Ct. 1895, 40 L.Ed.2d 406 (1974). That case upheld the Louisiana sequestration statute which permitted the seller-creditor holding a vendor's lien to secure a writ of sequestration and, having filed a bond, to cause the sheriff to take possession of the property at issue. The writ, however, was issuable only by a judge upon the filing of an affidavit going beyond mere conclusory allegations and clearly setting out the facts entitling the creditor to sequestration. The Louisiana law also expressly entitled the debtor to an immediate hearing after seizure and to dissolution of the writ absent proof by the creditor of the grounds on which the writ was issued.

The Georgia garnishment statute has none of the saving characteristics of the Louisiana statute. The writ of garnishment is issuable on the affidavit of the creditor or his attorney, and the latter need not have personal knowledge of the facts. § 46–103. The affidavit, like the one filed in this case, need contain only conclusory allegations. The writ is issuable, as this one was, by the court clerk, without participation by a judge. Upon service of the writ, the debtor is deprived of the use of the property in the hands of the garnishee. Here a sizable bank account was frozen, and the only method discernible on the face of the statute to dissolve the garnishment was to file a bond to protect the plaintiff creditor. There is no provision for an early hearing at which the creditor would be required to demonstrate at least probable cause for the garnishment. Indeed, it would appear that without the filing of a bond the defendant debtor's challenge to the garnishment will not be entertained, whatever the grounds may be.

Respondent also argues that neither *Fuentes* nor *Mitchell* is apposite here because each of those cases dealt with the application of due process protections to consumers who are victims of contracts of adhesion and who might be irreparably damaged by temporary deprivation of household necessities, whereas this case deals with its application in the commercial setting to a case involving parties of equal bargaining power. See also Sniadach v. Family Finance Corp., 395 U.S. 337, 89 S.Ct. 1820, 23 L.Ed.2d 349 (1969). It is asserted in addition that the double bond posted here gives assurance to petitioner that it will be made whole in the event the garnishment turns out to be unjustified. It may be that consumers deprived of household appliances will more likely suffer irreparably than corporations deprived of bank accounts, but the probability of irreparable injury in the latter case is sufficiently great so that some procedures are necessary to guard against the risk of initial error. We are no more inclined now than we have been in the past to distinguish among different kinds of property in applying the Due Process Clause. Fuentes v. Shevin, 407 U.S., at 89–90, 92 S.Ct., at 1998–1999.

Enough has been said, we think, to require the reversal of the judgment of the Georgia Supreme Court. The case is remanded to that court for further proceedings not inconsistent with this opinion.

So ordered.

MR. JUSTICE STEWART, concurring.

It is gratifying to note that my report of the demise of Fuentes v. Shevin, 407 U.S. 67, 92 S.Ct. 1983, 32 L.Ed.2d 556, see Mitchell v. W.T. Grant Co., 416 U.S. 600, 629–636, 94 S.Ct. 1895, 1910–1914, 40 L.Ed.2d 406 (dissenting opinion), seems to have been greatly exaggerated. Cf. S. Clemens, cable from Europe to the Associated Press, quoted in 2 A. Paine, Mark Twain: A Biography 1039 (1912).

MR. JUSTICE POWELL, concurring in the judgment.

I join in the Court's judgment, but I cannot concur in the opinion as I think it sweeps more broadly than is necessary and appears to resuscitate Fuentes v. Shevin, 407 U.S. 67, 92 S.Ct. 1983, 32 L.Ed.2d 556 (1972). Only last term in Mitchell v. W.T. Grant Co., 416 U.S. 600, 94 S.Ct. 1895, 40 L.Ed.2d 406 (1974), the Court significantly narrowed the precedential scope of *Fuentes*. In my concurrence in *Mitchell*, I noted:

> "The Court's decision today withdraws significantly from the full reach of [*Fuentes'*] principle, and to this extent I think it fair to say that the *Fuentes* opinion is overruled." 416 U.S., at 623, 94 S.Ct., at 1908 (Powell, J., concurring).

* * *

The Court's opinion in this case, relying substantially on *Fuentes*, suggests that that decision will again be read as calling into question much of the previously settled law governing commercial transactions. I continue to doubt whether *Fuentes* strikes a proper balance, especially in cases where the creditor's interest in the property may be as significant or even greater than that of the debtor. . . .

As we observed in *Mitchell*, the traditional view of procedural due process had been that " '[w]here only property rights are involved, mere postponement of the judicial enquiry is not a denial of due process, if the opportunity given for ultimate judicial determination of liability is adequate.'" Id., at 611, 94 S.Ct., at 1902, quoting Phillips v. Commissioner, 283 U.S. 589, 596–597, 51 S.Ct. 608, 611–612, 75 L.Ed. 1289 (1931). Consistent with this view, the Court in the past unanimously approved prejudgment attachment liens similar to those at issue in this case. McKay v. McInnes, 279 U.S. 820, 49 S.Ct. 344, 73 L.Ed. 975 (1929); Coffin Bros. v. Bennett, 277 U.S. 29, 48 S.Ct. 422, 72 L.Ed. 768 (1928); Ownbey v. Morgan, 256 U.S. 94, 41 S.Ct. 433, 65 L.Ed. 837 (1921). See generally *Mitchell,* supra, at 613–614, 94 S.Ct., at 1903. But the recent expansion of concepts of procedural due process requires a more careful assessment of the nature of the governmental function served by the challenged procedure and of the costs the procedure exacts of private interests. See, e.g., Goldberg v. Kelly, 397 U.S. 254, 263–266, 90 S.Ct. 1011, 1018–1019, 25 L.Ed.2d 287 (1970); Cafeteria Workers v. McElroy, 367 U.S. 886, 895, 81 S.Ct. 1743, 1748, 6 L.Ed.2d 1230 (1961). Under this analysis, the Georgia provisions cannot stand.

. . .

MR. JUSTICE BLACKMUN, with whom MR. JUSTICE REHNQUIST joins, dissenting.

The Court once again—for the third time in less than three years—struggles with what it regards as the due process aspects of a State's old and long-unattacked commercial statutes designed to afford a way for relief to a creditor against a delinquent debtor. On this third occasion, the Court, it seems to me, does little more than make very general and very sparse comparisons of the present case with Fuentes v. Shevin, 407 U.S. 67, 92 S.Ct. 1983, 32 L.Ed.2d 556 (1972), on the one hand, and with Mitchell v. W.T. Grant Co., 416 U.S. 600, 94 S.Ct. 1895, 40 L.Ed.2d 406 (1974), on the other; concludes that this case resembles *Fuentes* more than it does *Mitchell;* and then strikes down the Georgia statutory structure as offensive to due process. One gains the impression, particularly from the final paragraph of its opinion, that the Court is endeavoring to say as little as possible in explaining just why the Supreme Court of Georgia is being reversed. And, as a result, the corresponding commercial statutes of all other States, similar to but not exactly like those of Florida or Pennsylvania or Louisiana or Georgia, are left in questionable constitutional status, with little or no applicable standard by which to measure and determine their validity under the Fourteenth Amendment. This, it seems to me, is an undesirable state of affairs, and I dissent. I do so for a number of reasons . . .

5. Neither do I conclude that, because this is a garnishment case, rather than a lien or vendor-vendee case, it is automatically controlled by *Sniadach*. *Sniadach,* as has been noted, concerned and reeks of wages. North Georgia Finishing is no wage earner. It is a corporation engaged in business. It was protected (a) by the fact that the garnishment procedure may be instituted in Georgia only after the primary suit has been filed or judgment obtained by the creditor, thus placing on the creditor the obligation to initiate the proceedings and the burden of proof, and assuring a full hearing to the debtor; (b) by the respon-

dent's statutorily required and deposited double bond; and (c) by the requirement of the respondent's affidavit of apprehension of loss. It was in a position to dissolve the garnishment by the filing of a single bond. These are transactions of a day-to-day type in the commercial world. They are not situations involving contracts of adhesion or basic unfairness, imbalance, or inequality. See D.H. Overmyer Co. v. Frick Co., 405 U.S. 174, 92 S.Ct. 775, 31 L.Ed.2d 124 (1972); Swarb v. Lennox, 405 U.S. 191, 92 S.Ct. 767, 31 L.Ed.2d 138 (1972). The clerk-judge distinction, relied on by the Court, surely is of little significance so long as the court officer is not an agent of the creditor. The Georgia system, for me, affords commercial entities all the protection that is required by the Due Process Clause of the Fourteenth Amendment.

*   *   *

Mr. Chief Justice Burger dissents for the reasons stated in numbered paragraph 5 of the opinion of Mr. Justice Blackmun.

NOTES

(1) How would you formulate the constitutional standards governing attachment and garnishment as a provisional remedy after the *Fuentes, Mitchell* and *Di-Chem* decisions? It might be a useful exercise to try drafting a model statute that would strike the balance the Court seems to be searching for between the interests of creditors, both secured and unsecured, and debtors.

A number of states, recognizing infirmities in their prior attachment law under this line of Supreme Court decisions, have substantially revised those laws within the past few years. Thus California's attachment laws were drastically revised after the prior law was ruled unconstitutional by the state Supreme Court in Randone v. Appellate Department, 5 Cal.3d 536, 96 Cal.Rptr. 709, 488 P.2d 13 (1971), cert. denied 407 U.S. 924, 92 S.Ct. 2452, 32 L.Ed.2d 811 (1972). See Shadlow, California's New Attachment Law: Problems in Interpretation, 23 U.C.L.A.L.Rev. 792 (1976); Note, Randone Revisited: Due Process Protection for Commercial Necessities, 26 Stan.L.Rev. 673 (1974). A similar revision of New York's attachment law is discussed in 7A, Weinstein, Korn and Miller, New York Civil Practice paragraph 6201.04 and Kheel, New York's Amended Attachment Statute: A Prejudgment Remedy in Need of Further Revision, 44 Brooklyn L.Rev. 199 (1978). See also Comment, Constitutional Dimensions of the Amended Texas Sequestration Statute, 29 Sw.L.J. 884 (1975).

(2) How would you evaluate the relative importance of each of the following in determining whether a particular state's attachment and garnishment laws comport with the *Sniadach-Fuentes-Mitchell-Di-Chem* standards: (1) whether the relief is granted by a court or a ministerial officer; (2) whether the applicant must submit an affidavit showing either (a) the substantive merit of his claim or (b) satisfaction of the requirements of the state's laws governing attachment; (3) whether the state law provides a procedure for prompt dissolution of the attachment on application of the defendant, and upon what grounds; (4) whether the plaintiff is required to furnish a bond securing the defendant against loss if it turns out that the attachment was wrongfully granted; (5) the nature of the property attached; (6) whether that property is in any way related to the plaintiff's claim; (7) whether the plaintiff has a pre-existing interest in the property pursuant to a contract of conditional sale, as in *Fuentes* and *Mitchell* but not *Sniadach* or *Di-Chem*; (8) whether any such contract

between the parties is one of adhesion or the product of an arm's-length bargain; and (9) whether the attachment is sought for security or jurisdictional purposes or both?

(3) See generally, on *Sniadach* and its progeny, Abbott & Peters, Fuentes v. Shevin: A Narrative of Federal Test Litigation in the Legal Services Program, 57 Iowa L.Rev. 955 (1972); Countryman, The Bill of Rights and the Bill Collector, 15 Ariz.L.Rev. 521 (1973); Catz & Robinson, Due Process and Creditor's Remedies: From Sniadach and Fuentes to Mitchell, North Georgia and Beyond, 28 Rutgers L.Rev. 541 (1975); Recent Decisions, 14 Duq.L.Rev. 494 (1976); Kay and Lubin, Making Sense of Prejudgment Seizure Cases, 64 Ky.L.J. 705 (1976); Comment, A Confusing Course Made More Confusing: The Supreme Court, Due Process and Summary Creditor Remedies, 70 Nw.U.L.Rev. 331 (1975); Zaretsky, Attachment Without Seizure: A Proposal for a New Creditors' Remedy, 1978 U.Ill.L.F. 819.

SECTION 3. PROVISIONAL INJUNCTIVE RELIEF

Read Fed.Rule Civ.Proc. 65.

WALKER v. BIRMINGHAM, 388 U.S. 307, 87 S.Ct. 1824, 18 L.Ed. 2d 1210 (1967), rehearing denied 389 U.S. 894, 88 S.Ct. 12, 19 L.Ed.2d 202. Martin Luther King, Jr., and others who had engaged with him in parades on Good Friday and Easter Sunday of 1963 to publicize the civil rights cause had been convicted in the Alabama courts of contempt for violating an injunction prohibiting the parades. The injunction was based on an ordinance of the City of Birmingham broadly requiring that no public demonstration or parade be held on city streets or public ways without a permit from the Commission of Public Safety, which was authorized to grant such permits "unless in its judgment the public welfare, peace, safety, health, decency, good order, morals or convenience require that it be refused."

The injunction had been granted ex parte two days before Good Friday and the demonstrators, persuaded through informal negotiations with city officials that they would not be able to obtain a permit and that the injunction and the ordinance underlying it were both unconstitutional as a prior restraint on speech, decided to march in violation of the injunction. In the contempt proceedings in the state courts, they sought to raise the defense of unconstitutionality but the courts ruled that this defense could not be considered because the only proper way to raise it would have been by motion to vacate the injunction. The U.S. Supreme Court sustained this reading and affirmed.

The majority of the Supreme Court, in an opinion by Justice Stewart, conceded that "[t]he generality of the language contained in the Birmingham parade ordinance upon which the injunction was based" as well as "the breadth and vagueness of the injunction itself" would unquestionably raise substantial constitutional issues, and indeed the very same Birmingham ordinance was held unconstitutional by the Court two years later in Shuttlesworth v. City of Birmingham, 394 U.S. 147, 89 S.Ct. 935, 22 L.Ed.2d 162 (1969). But the Court agreed with the rule of state law which it had approved in Howat v. Kansas, (258 U.S. 181, 42 S.Ct. 277, 66 L.Ed. 550 (1922)), and was "consistent with the rule of law followed by the Federal courts" that:

> "An injunction duly issuing out of a court of general jurisdiction with equity powers upon pleadings properly invoking its action, and served upon persons made parties therein and within the jurisdiction, must be obeyed by them however erroneous the action of the court may be, even if the error be in the assumption of the validity of a seeming but void law going to the merits of the case. It is for the court of first instance to determine the question of the validity of the law, and until its decision is reversed for error by orderly review, either by itself or by a higher court, its orders based on its decision are to be respected, and disobedience of them is contempt of its lawful authority, to be punished." 258 U.S., at 189–190, 42 S.Ct., at 280–281.

The *Walker* rule plainly poses a dilemma for any person or group against whom an unlawful injunction is granted at the eleventh hour when time is of the essence—a problem which can arise not only in connection with political advocacy but also student protests, labor union activity, and innumerable other contexts. What is the lawyer's obligation in this situation? If you were Dr. King's lawyer and were asked whether he should go ahead with the demonstrations despite the injunction, what would your advice have been?

———

CARROLL v. PRESIDENT AND COMMISSIONERS OF PRINCESS ANNE

Supreme Court of the United States, 1968.
393 U.S. 175, 89 S.Ct. 347, 21 L.Ed.2d 325.

Mr. Justice Fortas delivered the opinion of the Court.*

Petitioners are identified with a "white supremacist" organization called the National States Rights Party. They held a public assembly or rally near the courthouse steps in the town of Princess Anne, the county seat of Somerset County, Maryland, in the evening of August 6, 1966. The authorities did not attempt to interfere with the rally. Because of the tense atmosphere which developed as the meeting progressed, about 60 state policemen were brought in, including some from a nearby county. They were held in readiness, but for tactical reasons only a few were in evidence at the scene of the rally.

* Most footnotes omitted.

Petitioners' speeches, amplified by a public address system so that they could be heard for several blocks, were aggressively and militantly racist. Their target was primarily Negroes and, secondarily, Jews. It is sufficient to observe with the court below, that the speakers engaged in deliberately derogatory, insulting, and threatening language, scarcely disguised by protestations of peaceful purposes; and that listeners might well have construed their words as both a provocation to the Negroes in the crowd and an incitement to the whites. The rally continued for something more than an hour, concluding at about 8:25 p.m. The crowd listening to the speeches increased from about 50 at the beginning to about 150, of whom 25% were Negroes.

In the course of the proceedings it was announced that the rally would be resumed the following night, August 7.[1]

On that day, the respondents, officials of Princess Anne and of Somerset County, applied for and obtained a restraining order from the Circuit Court for Somerset County. The proceedings were *ex parte,* no notice being given to petitioners and, so far as appears, no effort being made informally to communicate with them, although this is expressly contemplated under Maryland procedure. The order restrained petitioners for 10 days from holding rallies or meetings in the county "which will tend to disturb and endanger the citizens of the County." [2] As a result, the rally scheduled for August 7 was not held. After the trial which took place 10 days later, an injunction was issued by the Circuit Court on August 30, in effect extending the restraint for 10 additional months. The court had before it, in addition to the testimony of witnesses, tape recordings made by the police of the August 6 rally.

On appeal, the Maryland Court of Appeals affirmed the 10-day order, but reversed the 10-month order on the ground that "the period of time was unreasonable and that it was arbitrary to assume that a clear and present danger of civil disturbance and riot would persist for ten months."

Petitioners sought review by this Court, under 28 U.S.C. § 1257(3), asserting that the case is not moot and that the decision of the

1. Petitioner Norton said, "I want you to . . . be back here at the same place tomorrow night, bring every friend you have . . . . We're going to take it easy tonight . . . " and "You white folks bring your friends, come back tomorrow night. . . . Come on back tomorrow night, let's raise a little bit of hell for the white race."

2. The text of the Writ of Injunction is as follows:

"We command and strictly enjoin and prohibit you the said Joseph Carroll, Richard Norton, J.B. Stoner, Connie Lynch, Robert Lyons, William Brailsford and National States Rights Party from holding rallies or meetings in Somerset County which will tend to disturb and endanger the citizens of the County and to enjoin you, the said defendants, from using and operating or causing to be operated within the County any devices or apparatus for the application [*sic*] of the human voice or records from any radio, phonograph or other sound making or producing device thereby disturbing the tranquility of the populace of the County, until the matter can be heard and determined in equity, or for a period of ten days from the date hereof.

"Hereof, fail not, as you will act to the contrary at your peril."

Maryland Court of Appeals continues to have an adverse effect upon petitioners' rights. We granted certiorari.

We agree with petitioners that the case is not moot. Since 1966, petitioners have sought to continue their activities, including the holding of rallies in Princess Anne and Somerset County, and it appears that the decision of the Maryland Court of Appeals continues to play a substantial role in the response of officials to their activities. In these circumstances, our jurisdiction is not at an end. . . .

. . . The underlying question persists and is agitated by the continuing activities and program of petitioners: whether, by what processes, and to what extent the authorities of the local governments may restrict petitioners in their rallies and public meetings.

This conclusion—that the question is not moot and ought to be adjudicated by this Court—is particularly appropriate in view of this Court's decision in Walker v. Birmingham, 388 U.S. 307, 87 S.Ct. 1824, 18 L.Ed.2d 1210 (1967). In that case, the Court held that demonstrators who had proceeded with their protest march in face of the prohibition of an injunctive order against such a march, could not defend contempt charges by asserting the unconstitutionality of the injunction. The proper procedure, it was held, was to seek judicial review of the injunction and not to disobey it, no matter how well-founded their doubts might be as to its validity. Petitioners have here pursued the course indicated by *Walker;* and in view of the continuing vitality of petitioners' grievance, we cannot say that their case is moot.

Since the Maryland Court of Appeals reversed the 10-month injunction of August 30, 1966, we do not consider that order. We turn to the constitutional problems raised by the 10-day injunctive order.

The petitioners urge that the injunction constituted a prior restraint on speech and that it therefore violated the principles of the First Amendment which are applicable to the States by virtue of the Fourteenth Amendment. . . .

* * *

We need not decide the thorny problem of whether, on the facts of this case, an injunction against the announced rally could be justified. The 10-day order here must be set aside because of a basic infirmity in the procedure by which it was obtained. It was issued *ex parte,* without notice to petitioners and without any effort, however informal, to invite or permit their participation in the proceedings. There is a place in our jurisprudence for *ex parte* issuance, without notice, of temporary restraining orders of short duration; but there is no place within the area of basic freedoms guaranteed by the First Amendment for such orders where no showing is made that it is impossible to serve or to notify the opposing parties and to give them an opportunity to participate.

We do not here challenge the principle that there are special, limited circumstances in which speech is so interlaced with burgeoning violence that it is not protected by the broad guarantee of the First

Amendment. In Cantwell v. Connecticut, 310 U.S. 296, at 308, 60 S.Ct. 900, at 905, 84 L.Ed. 1213 (1940), this Court said that "[n]o one would have the hardihood to suggest that the principle of freedom of speech sanctions incitement to riot." See also Chaplinsky v. New Hampshire, 315 U.S. 568, 572, 62 S.Ct. 766, 769, 86 L.Ed. 1031 (1942); Milk Wagon Drivers Union v. Meadowmoor Dairies, 312 U.S. 287, 294, 61 S.Ct. 552, 555, 85 L.Ed. 836 (1941). Ordinarily, the State's constitutionally permissible interests are adequately served by criminal penalties imposed after freedom to speak has been so grossly abused that its immunity is breached. The impact and consequences of subsequent punishment for such abuse are materially different from those of prior restraint. Prior restraint upon speech suppresses the precise freedom which the First Amendment sought to protect against abridgment.

restrictions before the act

The Court has emphasized that "[a] system of prior restraints of expression comes to this Court bearing a heavy presumption against its constitutional validity." Bantam Books v. Sullivan, 372 U.S. 58, 70, 83 S.Ct. 631, 639, 9 L.Ed.2d 584 (1963); Freedman v. Maryland, 380 U.S. 51, 57, 85 S.Ct. 734, 738, 13 L.Ed.2d 649 (1965). And even where this presumption might otherwise be overcome, the Court has insisted upon careful procedural provisions, designed to assure the fullest presentation and consideration of the matter which the circumstances permit. . . .

. . . In the present case, the reasons for insisting upon an opportunity for hearing and notice, at least in the absence of a showing that reasonable efforts to notify the adverse parties were unsuccessful, are even more compelling than in cases involving allegedly obscene books. The present case involves a rally and "political" speech in which the element of timeliness may be important. . . .

. . . [T]he record discloses no reason why petitioners were not notified of the application for injunction. They were apparently present in Princess Anne. They had held a rally there on the night preceding the application for and issuance of the injunction. They were scheduled to have another rally on the very evening of the day when the injunction was issued. And some of them were actually served with the writ of injunction at 6:10 that evening. In these circumstances, there is no justification for the *ex parte* character of the proceedings in the sensitive area of First Amendment rights.

The value of a judicial proceeding, as against self-help by the police, is substantially diluted where the process is *ex parte,* because the Court does not have available the fundamental instrument for judicial judgment: an adversary proceeding in which both parties may participate. The facts in any case involving a public demonstration are difficult to ascertain and even more difficult to evaluate. Judgment as to whether the facts justify the use of the drastic power of injunction necessarily turns on subtle and controversial considerations and upon a delicate assessment of the particular situation in light of legal standards which are inescapably imprecise. In the absence of evidence and argument offered by both sides and of their participation in the formulation of value judgments, there is insufficient assurance of the balanced analysis and careful conclusions which are essential in the area of First Amendment adjudication.

The same is true of the fashioning of the order. An order issued in the area of First Amendment rights must be couched in the narrowest terms that will accomplish the pin-pointed objective permitted by constitutional mandate and the essential needs of the public order. . . . The participation of both sides is necessary for this purpose. . . .

Finally, respondents urge that the failure to give notice and an opportunity for hearing should not be considered to invalidate the order because, under Maryland procedure, petitioners might have obtained a hearing on not more than two days' notice. . . . But this procedural right does not overcome the infirmity in the absence of a showing of justification for the *ex parte* nature of the proceedings. The issuance of an injunction which aborts a scheduled rally or public meeting, even if the restraint is of short duration, is a matter of importance and consequence in view of the First Amendment's imperative. The denial of a basic procedural right in these circumstances is not excused by the availability of post-issuance procedure which could not possibly serve to rescue the August 7 meeting, but, at best, could have shortened the period in which petitioners were prevented from holding a rally.

We need not here decide that it is impossible for circumstances to arise in which the issuance of an *ex parte* restraining order for a minimum period could be justified because of the unavailability of the adverse parties or their counsel, or perhaps for other reasons. In the present case, it is clear that the failure to give notice, formal or informal, and to provide an opportunity for an adversary proceeding before the holding of the rally was restrained, is incompatible with the First Amendment. Because we reverse the judgment below on this basis, we need not and do not decide whether the facts in this case provided a constitutionally permissible basis for temporarily enjoining the holding of the August 7 rally.

Reversed.

MR. JUSTICE BLACK concurs in the result.

MR. JUSTICE DOUGLAS, while joining the opinion of the Court, adheres to his dissent in Kingsley Books, Inc. v. Brown, 354 U.S. 436, 446–447, 77 S.Ct. 1325, 1330–1331, 1 L.Ed.2d 1469, and to his concurring opinion in Freedman v. Maryland, 380 U.S. 51, 61–62, 85 S.Ct. 734, 740–741.

NOTES

(1) To what extent is the probability of eventual success relevant in granting a temporary restraining order and a preliminary injunction? See In re Arthur Treacher's Franchisee Litigation, 689 F.2d 1137 (3d Cir.1982); Hamilton Watch Co. v. Benrus Watch Co., 206 F.2d 738 (2d Cir.1953). See also Note,

Probability of Ultimate Success Held Unnecessary for Grant of Interlocutory Injunction, 71 Colum.L.Rev. 165 (1971); Leubsdorf, The Standards for Preliminary Injunction, 91 Harv.L.Rev. 525 (1978).

(2) When a temporary restraining order or preliminary injunction is dissolved or vacated on the ground that it was improperly granted, the party enjoined is entitled to compensation for the damages he suffered as a result of the restraint. These damages may include attorney's fees. In Kolin v. Leitch, 351 Ill.App. 66, 113 N.E.2d 806 (3d Div.1953), the court said: "The rule seems well settled that a defendant may recover as damages, on dissolution of an injunction, the solicitor's fees which he has paid or become obligated to pay for services rendered in obtaining the dissolution of the injunction but not for those rendered in the general defense of the suit."

(3) How far does the court's authority extend to make its injunction applicable to unknown persons? See 7A Weinstein, Korn & Miller § 6301.25: ". . . the fact that a person has knowledge of the existence of a preliminary injunction or even is named in the order itself is insufficient for him to be bound by the order and subject to the sanction of contempt if he was not a party, in privity with a party or acting in concert or for the benefit of a party". See also Fed.R.Civ.P. 65(d). See also Rendleman, Beyond Contempt: Obligors to Injunctions, 53 Tex.L.Rev. 873 (1975).

(4) Note that special provisions may control the granting of injunctions. See, e.g., as to labor disputes, 29 U.S.C.A. §§ 101–115; N.Y.Labor L. §§ 807–808; United States v. United Mine Workers of America, 330 U.S. 258, 267, 67 S.Ct. 677, 682, 91 L.Ed. 884, 898 (1947).

SECTION 4. NOTICE OF PENDENCY

At common law, a purchaser of property, which was the subject of litigation, was charged with knowledge of the suit. At least with respect to real property, this common law doctrine has largely been replaced by statutory provisions. These require the filing of a notice of pendency before the purchaser can be charged with notice of the suit. See, e.g., N.Y.—McKinney's CPLR § 6501. However, it may remain uncertain whether the common law doctrine continues to be effective with respect to personal property. And it may also be uncertain whether an action in a federal court has the same effect as an action commenced in a state court. Cf. N.Y.—McKinney's CPLR § 6501 (eliminating this uncertainty). See also 28 U.S.C.A. § 1964 providing that a notice filed in a federal court must meet the "requirements of the State law . . . in order to give constructive notice."

Questions have also been raised concerning the constitutionality of lis pendens provisions in the light of the *Sniadach* line of cases. See Comment, Does California's Statutory Lis Pendens Violate Procedural Due Process? 6 Pac.L.J. 62 (1975); Note, A Proposal for the Reformation of the Iowa Lis Pendens Statute, 67 Iowa L.Rev. 289 (1982). The courts have given different answers. In Kukanskis v. Griffith, 180 Conn. 501, 430 A.2d 21 (1980), the Connecticut statute was ruled unconstitutional. But in Debral Realty, Inc. v. DiChiara, 383 Mass.

559, 420 N.E.2d 343 (1981); George v. Oakhurst Realty, Inc., 414 A.2d 471 (1980); Batey v. Digirolamo, 418 F.Supp. 695 (D.Hawaii 1976) and Empfield v. Superior Court for Los Angeles County, 33 Cal.App.3d 105, 108 Cal.Rptr. 375 (1973), the relevant statutes were held constitutional. The Connecticut statute was amended after *Griffith*.　See 1981 Conn. Acts 81–8.

Part III

WHICH COURTS, LAW AND LITIGANTS?

Chapter Five

JUSTICIABILITY

SECTION 1. INTRODUCTION

No legal system provides for judicial resolution of all disputes. The reasons for declaring a dispute not justiciable may vary. It may be thought that the dispute does not lend itself to resolution by resort to reasonably definite legal standards, or that a different branch of the government is more suitable for the task of resolving it, or that the party submitting it for adjudication has an insufficient stake in the outcome of the litigation, or that it arises in an insufficiently adversarial context, or that it is not sufficiently important to warrant the expenditure of judicial efforts. The cases in this chapter all raise questions of justiciability. You should try to determine which of the reasons here enumerated, or any others you may discern, justify the results reached.

Whatever the reasons advanced, decisions on justiciability concern the more general question of whether the dispute can be adjudicated at all. Justiciability thus forms the threshold which each dispute must pass before the more specific question of which court may hear it can be addressed. The latter question is treated in Chapter **6**.

Although their underpinnings may derive from legislative measures, rules of justiciability are predominantly judge-made. To the extent they find their inspiration in constitutional principles, they can not be modified by statute. This renders it most important to determine the exact status of particular rules in the constitutional hierarchy of the legal system in which they apply.

SECTION 2. STANDING

EX–CELL–O CORPORATION v. CITY OF CHICAGO

United States Court of Appeals, Seventh Circuit, 1940.
115 F.2d 627.

LINDLEY, DISTRICT JUDGE. In 7237 plaintiff is a manufacturer of patented machines for the production of paper milk bottles. It licenses certain milk distributors in Chicago to make and sell such bottles and collects valuable license fees therefor dependent upon the number of bottles made and sold. In 7334, plaintiff is a manufacturer of similar bottles which it sells for profit to dairy companies in Chicago. In each complaint, plaintiff sought to obtain a declaratory judgment that the milk ordinance of the City of Chicago does not prohibit the use of paper milk containers, or if it does, that it is invalid. The District Court held that neither plaintiff had any such direct interest in the purpose of the suits as to enable it to maintain the action. From the resulting judgment dismissing the complaint, each plaintiff appeals.

The general rule controlling the decision in this cause is announced by the Supreme Court in Massachusetts v. Mellon, 262 U.S. 447, 43 S.Ct. 597, 601, 67 L.Ed. 1078, as follows: "The party who invokes the power must be able to show, not only that the statute is invalid, but that he has sustained or is immediately in danger of sustaining some direct injury as the result of its enforcement, and not merely that he suffers in some indefinite way in common with people generally."

The immediate question, therefore, is whether either plaintiff is sustaining or in danger of sustaining some direct injury. It is obvious that each plaintiff has an ultimate pecuniary interest in the practical results of the alleged invalid ordinance or the averred erroneous interpretation of the ordinance by the municipal authorities. Is that interest direct, growing out of direct injury within the meaning of the Supreme Court's announcement? As to this, the parties are in sad disagreement.

     *   *   *

In the present case the American Can Company is not engaged in the distribution of milk. It manufactures and sells paper bottles. The ordinance complained of or the administrative acts of defendants in interpretation and administration thereof, in no wise forbid such manufacture and sale. The act, as interpreted by defendants, is asserted by them to forbid the use of paper milk bottles in Chicago. [Plaintiff] is free to manufacture and to sell such bottles wherever it may desire, even in Chicago. Obviously, few, if any, persons will purchase them for use there, but that result we deem incidental, consequential and indirect. Were plaintiff forbidden to manufacture and sell paper milk bottles in Chicago, the effect upon its business would be direct and inevitable.

Thus it is apparent that inevitable financial pecuniary damage is not the test of the sufficiency of plaintiff's interest. Otherwise the right to sue might be extended indefinitely to parties far removed, such as workmen in plaintiff's factories whose wages are reduced or lost because of lack of realization of profits by their employer. Just as clearly, privity of contract is not essential, for defendants are liable for their torts which directly affect the plaintiff, and for breach of their legal duties in that respect, defendants are liable in damages. Rather the whole question is whether the damage claimed springs directly to plaintiff from defendants. If it is incidental, if it is indirect, defendants may not invoke the court's jurisdiction. . . .

In Sproles v. Binford, D.C., 52 F.2d 730, 733, a court of three judges was convened at the suit of the Wichita Falls Motor Company et al. to determine the validity of a state statute which limited the size and weight of motor vehicles operated on the public highways of the state. The Wichita Falls Company was engaged in the manufacture and sale of motor vehicles of the prohibited size. By the act their market in Texas was destroyed—an effect similar to that upon plaintiff in the present instance. The court said: "The Wichita Falls Motor Company is not using the highways. The basis of its complaint is that it is now, and has been for many years, engaged in the manufacture and sale (frequently on credit) of a certain type or certain types of vehicles (and yet has many on hand), which, under the act, it alleges cannot be used on the public highways of Texas, and it therefore cannot sell them, nor collect for those already sold, and that its business will be wrecked by the enforcement of this act. . . . We think the injury alleged by it is too remote . . .."

* * *

. . . In Buchanan v. Warley, 245 U.S. 60, 38 S.Ct. 16, 17, 62 L.Ed. 149, L.R.A.1918C, 210, Ann.Cas.1918A, 1201, plaintiff sold to a colored man real estate in a section where it was illegal for a colored person to occupy land, and, except for the ordinance, plaintiff was entitled to specific performance. The statute was a bar to the relief. He was directly interested in his right to sell property. The court said: "The right of the plaintiff in error to sell his property was directly involved and necessarily impaired because it was held in effect that he could not sell the lot to a person of color who was willing and ready to acquire the property, and had obligated himself to take it." . . .

. . . [In] Pierce v. Society of Sisters, 268 U.S. 510, 45 S.Ct. 571, 69 L.Ed. 1070, 39 A.L.R. 468, plaintiffs, proprietors of schools, sued to enjoin enforcement of a statute which compelled children to be sent to public schools. The court held that plaintiffs were invoking protection against arbitrary, unreasonable and unlawful interference with plaintiffs' business, resulting in eventual destruction of property rights.

. . . We agree with the District Court's conclusion that plaintiff was without right to sustain the action.

In 7237 Ex-Cell-O Corporation is even more remotely interested. It is one step further removed from the object of the legislation, for it is the manufacturer and licensor of machines built to manufacture paper milk bottles which it has leased to distributors in the City of Chicago. It follows that our conclusion with regard to the rights of the American Can Company must be the same as to those of the Ex-Cell-O Corporation.

The judgments of the District Court are affirmed.

UNITED STATES v. STUDENTS CHALLENGING REGULATORY AGENCY PROCEDURES (SCRAP)

Supreme Court of the United States, 1973.
412 U.S. 669, 93 S.Ct. 2405, 37 L.Ed.2d 254.

Mr. Justice Stewart delivered the opinion of the Court.*

[The plaintiffs alleged they were an unincorporated association of law students formed to enhance the quality of human environment. They charged that the Interstate Commerce Commission had violated the law in approving of a surcharge on railroad freight rates and sought injunctive relief. They alleged that the increase in freight rates had made it less economical to ship refuse to recycling plants, that as a result more refuse was discarded in Washington parks, and that their use and enjoyment of these parks was thus diminished.]

* * *

On July 10, 1972, the District Court filed an opinion, 346 F.Supp. 189, and entered an injunction forbidding the Commission "from permitting," and the railroads "from collecting" the 2.5% surcharge "insofar as that surcharge relates to goods being transported for purposes of recycling, pending further order of this court." . . .

II

The appellants challenge the appellees' standing to sue, arguing that the allegations in the pleadings as to standing were vague, unsubstantiated and insufficient under our recent decision in Sierra Club v. Morton, supra. The appellees respond that unlike the petitioner in *Sierra Club,* their pleadings sufficiently alleged that they were "adversely affected" or "aggrieved" within the meaning of § 10 of the Administrative Procedure Act (APA), 5 U.S.C. § 702,[1] and they point specifically to the allegations that their members used the forests, streams, mountains and other resources in the Washington Metropoli-

---

* Most footnotes omitted; those retained renumbered.

1. Like the petitioner in *Sierra Club,* the appellees here base their standing to sue upon § 10 of the Administrative Procedure Act (APA), 5 U.S.C. § 702, which provides:

"A person suffering legal wrong because of agency action, or adversely affected or aggrieved by agency action within the meaning of a relevant statute, is entitled to judicial review thereof."

tan Area for camping, hiking, fishing, and sightseeing, and that this use was disturbed by the adverse environmental impact caused by the nonuse of recyclable goods brought about by a rate increase on those commodities. The District Court found these allegations sufficient to withstand a motion to dismiss. We agree.

The petitioner in *Sierra Club*, "a large and long-established organization, with a historic commitment to the cause of protecting our Nation's natural heritage from man's depredations," 405 U.S., at 739, 92 S.Ct., at 1368, sought a declaratory judgment and an injunction to restrain federal officials from approving the creation of an extensive ski-resort development in the scenic Mineral King Valley of the Sequoia National Forest. The Sierra Club claimed standing to maintain its "public interest" lawsuit because it had "a special interest in the conservation and [the] sound maintenance of the national parks, game refuges and forests of the country. . . ." Id., at 730, 92 S.Ct. at 1364. We held those allegations insufficient.

Relying upon our prior decisions in Association of Data Processing Services v. Camp, 397 U.S. 150, 90 S.Ct. 827, 25 L.Ed.2d 184, and Barlow v. Collins, 397 U.S. 159, 90 S.Ct. 832, 25 L.Ed.2d 192, we held that § 10 of the APA conferred standing to obtain judicial review of agency action only upon those who could show "that the challenged action had caused them 'injury in fact,' and where the alleged injury was to an interest 'arguably within the zone of interests to be protected or regulated' by the statutes that the agencies were claimed to have violated." 405 U.S., at 733, 92 S.Ct., at 1365.[2]

In interpreting "injury in fact" we made it clear that standing was not confined to those who could show "economic harm," although both *Data Processing* and *Barlow* had involved that kind of injury. Nor, we said, could the fact that many persons shared the same injury be sufficient reason to disqualify from seeking review of an agency's action any person who had in fact suffered injury. Rather, we explained: "Aesthetic and environmental well-being, like economic well-being, are important ingredients of the quality of life in our society, and the fact that particular environmental interests are shared by the many rather than the few does not make them less deserving of legal protection through the judicial process." Id., at 734, 92 S.Ct., at 1366. Consequently, neither the fact that the appellees here claimed only a harm to their use and enjoyment of the natural resources of the Washington area, nor the fact that all those who use those resources suffered the same harm, deprives them of standing.

In *Sierra Club*, though, we went on to stress the importance of demonstrating that the party seeking review be himself among the

2. As in *Sierra Club*, it is unnecessary to reach any question concerning the scope of the "zone of interests" test or its application to this case. It is undisputed that the "environmental interest" that the appellees seek to protect is within the interests to be protected by NEPA, and it is unnecessary to consider the various allegations of economic harm on which the appellees also relied in their pleadings and which the Government contends are outside the intended purposes of NEPA.

injured, for it is this requirement that gives a litigant a direct stake in the controversy and prevents the judicial process from becoming no more than a vehicle for the vindication of the value interests of concerned bystanders. No such specific injury was alleged in *Sierra Club.* In that case the asserted harm "will be felt directly only by those who use Mineral King and Sequoia National Park, and for whom the aesthetic and recreational values of the area will be lessened by the highway and ski resort," id., at 735, 92 S.Ct., at 1366, yet "[t]he Sierra Club failed to allege that it or its members would be affected in any of their activities or pastimes by the . . . development." Ibid. Here, by contrast, the appellees claimed that the specific and allegedly illegal action of the Commission would directly harm them in their use of the natural resources of the Washington Metropolitan Area.

Unlike the specific and geographically limited federal action of which the petitioner complained in *Sierra Club,* the challenged agency action in this case is applicable to substantially all of the Nation's railroads, and thus allegedly has an adverse environmental impact on all the natural resources of the country. Rather than a limited group of persons who used a picturesque valley in California, all persons who utilize the scenic resources of the country, and indeed all who breathe its air, could claim harm similar to that alleged by the environmental groups here. But we have already made it clear that standing is not to be denied simply because many people suffer the same injury. Indeed some of the cases on which we relied in *Sierra Club* demonstrated the patent fact that persons across the Nation could be adversely affected by major governmental actions. See, e.g., Environmental Defense Fund v. Hardin, 138 U.S.App.D.C. 391, 428 F.2d 1093, 1097 (interests of consumers affected by decision of Secretary of Agriculture refusing to suspend registration of certain pesticides containing DDT); Reade v. Ewing, 205 F.2d 630, 631–632 (2d Cir.) (interests of consumers of oleomargarine in fair labeling of product regulated by Federal Security Administration). To deny standing to persons who are in fact injured simply because many others are also injured would mean that the most injurious and widespread Government actions could be questioned by nobody. We cannot accept that conclusion.

But the injury alleged here is also very different from that at issue in *Sierra Club* because here the alleged injury to the environment is far less direct and perceptible. The petitioner there complained about the construction of a specific project that would directly affect the Mineral King Valley. Here, the Court was asked to follow a far more attenuated line of causation to the eventual injury of which the appellees complained—a general rate increase would allegedly cause increased use of nonrecyclable commodities as compared to recyclable goods, thus resulting in the need to use more natural resources to produce such goods, some of which resources might be taken from the Washington area, and resulting in more refuse that might be discarded in national parks in the Washington area. The railroads protest that the appellees could never prove that a general increase in rates would have this effect, and they contend that these allegations were a ploy to avoid the need to show some injury in fact.

Of course, pleadings must be something more than an ingenious academic exercise in the conceivable. A plaintiff must allege that he has been or will in fact be perceptibly harmed by the challenged agency action, not that he can imagine circumstances in which he could be affected by the agency's action. And it is equally clear that the allegations must be true and capable of proof at trial. But we deal here simply with the pleadings in which the appellees alleged a specific and perceptible harm that distinguished them from other citizens who had not used the natural resources that were claimed to be affected.[3] If, as the railroads now assert, these allegations were in fact untrue, then the appellants should have moved for summary judgment on the standing issue and demonstrated to the District Court that the allegations were sham and raised no genuine issue of fact. We cannot say on these pleadings that the appellees could not prove their allegations which, if proved, would place them squarely among those persons injured in fact by the Commission's action, and entitled under the clear import of *Sierra Club* to seek review. The District Court was correct in denying the appellants' motion to dismiss the complaint for failure to allege sufficient standing to bring this lawsuit.

III

We need not reach the issue whether, under conventional standards of equity, the District Court was justified in issuing a preliminary injunction, because we have concluded that the Court lacked jurisdiction to enter an injunction in any event . . . . [The Court's reasons for this conclusion have been omitted.]

Accordingly, because the District Court granted a preliminary injunction suspending railroad rates when it lacked the power to do so, its judgment must be reversed and the case remanded to that court for further proceedings consistent with this opinion.

Reversed and remanded.

---

3. The Government urges us to limit standing to those who have been "significantly" affected by agency action. But, even if we could begin to define what such a test would mean, we think it fundamentally misconceived. "Injury in fact" reflects the statutory requirement that a person be "adversely affected" or "aggrieved," and it serves to distinguish a person with a direct stake in the outcome of a litigation—even though small—from a person with a mere interest in the problem. We have allowed important interests to be vindicated by plaintiffs with no more at stake in the outcome of an action than a fraction of a vote, see Baker v. Carr, 369 U.S. 186, 82 S.Ct. 691, 7 L.Ed.2d 663; a five dollar fine and costs, see McGowan v. Maryland, 366 U.S. 420, 81 S.Ct. 1101, 6 L.Ed.2d 393; and a $1.50 poll tax. Harper v. Virginia Bd. of Elections, 383 U.S. 663, 86 S.Ct. 1079, 16 L.Ed.2d 169. While these cases were not dealing specifically with § 10 of the APA, we see no reason to adopt a more restrictive interpretation of "adversely affected" or "aggrieved." As Professor Davis has put it: "The basic idea that comes out in numerous cases is that an identifiable trifle is enough for standing to fight out a question of principle; the trifle is the basis for standing and the principle supplies the motivation." Davis, Standing: Taxpayers and Others, 35 U.Chi.L.Rev. 601, 613. See also K. Davis, Administrative Law Treatise, §§ 22.09–5 to 22.09–6 (1970 Supplement).

MR. JUSTICE POWELL took no part in the consideration or decision of these cases.

MR. JUSTICE BLACKMUN, with whom MR. JUSTICE BRENNAN joins, concurring. [Omitted.]

MR. JUSTICE DOUGLAS, dissenting in part. [Omitted.]

NOTE

In Ex-Cell-O and SCRAP, what were the substantive law bases of the plaintiff's claims for relief? What is the relation between the problem of standing and that of whether the plaintiff has a valid claim for relief? See Eason v. General Motors Acceptance Corp., 490 F.2d 654, 657–658 (7th Cir. 1973), cert. denied 416 U.S. 960, 94 S.Ct. 1979, 40 L.Ed.2d 312 (1974), rehearing denied 420 U.S. 967, 95 S.Ct. 1364, 43 L.Ed.2d 447 (1975); Albert, Standing to Challenge Administrative Action: An Inadequate Surrogate for Claim for Relief, 83 Yale L.J. 425 (1974).

FLAST v. COHEN, 392 U.S. 83, 88 S.Ct. 1942, 20 L.Ed.2d 947 (1968): Plaintiffs, relying for standing on their status as federal taxpayers and their being parents of children in public schools, sued to enjoin expenditure of federal funds under the Elementary and Secondary Education Act of 1965 to finance instruction in religious schools, alleging that such expenditures of federal tax funds violate the First Amendment because " 'they constitute a law respecting an establishment of religion' and because 'they prohibit the free exercise of religion on the part of the [appellants] . . . by reason of the fact that they constitute compulsory taxation for religious purposes.' " Plaintiffs' main obstacle was Frothingham v. Mellon, 262 U.S. 447, 43 S.Ct. 597, 67 L.Ed. 1078 (1923), which the Court viewed in these terms:

"The taxpayer in *Frothingham* attacked as unconstitutional the Maternity Act of 1921, 42 Stat. 224, which established a federal program of grants to those States which would undertake programs to reduce maternal and infant mortality. The taxpayer alleged that Congress, in enacting the challenged statute, had exceeded the powers delegated to it under Article I of the Constitution and had invaded the legislative province reserved to the several States by the Tenth Amendment. The taxpayer complained that the result of the allegedly unconstitutional enactment would be to increase her future federal tax liability and "thereby take her property without due process of law." 262 U.S., at 486, 43 S.Ct., at 600. The Court noted that a federal taxpayer's "interest in the moneys of the Treasury . . . is comparatively minute and indeterminable" and that "the effect upon future taxation, of any payment out of the [Treasury's] funds, . . . [is] remote, fluctuating and uncertain." Id., at 487. As a result, the Court ruled that the taxpayer had failed to allege the type of "direct injury" necessary to confer standing. Id., at 488."

The Court held that *Frothingham* erected no absolute bar to suits by federal taxpayers challenging allegedly unconstitutional federal taxing and spending programs and that there was a sufficient "logical nexus" between the status asserted by plaintiffs and the nature of the challenged action to support their claim of standing:

> "The nexus demanded of federal taxpayers has two aspects to it. First, the taxpayer must establish a logical link between that status and the type of legislative enactment attacked. Thus, a taxpayer will be a proper party to allege the unconstitutionality only of exercises of congressional power under the taxing and spending clause of Art. I, § 8, of the Constitution. It will not be sufficient to allege an incidental expenditure of tax funds in the administration of an essentially regulatory statute. This requirement is consistent with the limitation imposed upon state-taxpayer standing in federal courts in Doremus v. Board of Education, 342 U.S. 429, 72 S.Ct. 394, 96 L.Ed. 475 (1952). Secondly, the taxpayer must establish a nexus between that status and the precise nature of the constitutional infringement alleged. Under this requirement, the taxpayer must show that the challenged enactment exceeds specific constitutional limitations imposed upon the exercise of the congressional taxing and spending power and not simply that the enactment is generally beyond the powers delegated to Congress by Art. I, § 8. When both nexuses are established, the litigant will have shown a taxpayer's stake in the outcome of the controversy and will be a proper and appropriate party to invoke a federal court's jurisdiction.

> "The taxpayer-appellants in this case have satisfied both nexuses to support their claim of standing under the test we announce today. Their constitutional challenge is made to an exercise by Congress of its power under Art. I, § 8, to spend for the general welfare, and the challenged program involves a substantial expenditure of federal tax funds. In addition, appellants have alleged that the challenged expenditures violate the Establishment and Free Exercise Clauses of the First Amendment. . . . The Establishment Clause was designed as a specific bulwark against such potential abuses of governmental power, and that clause of the First Amendment operates as a specific constitutional limitation upon the exercise by Congress of the taxing and spending power conferred by Art. I, § 8."

NOTES

(1) Note the various contexts in which the issue of standing may arise: the interest sought to be protected by the plaintiff may be that of a citizen, a taxpayer, a voter, a legislator, a government official, a competitor or a member of a group with special economic, social or political goals. For a case in which a legislator was held to have standing to seek relief barring state officials from

certifying that Kansas had ratified the Child Labor Amendment, see Coleman v. Miller, 307 U.S. 433, 59 S.Ct. 972, 83 L.Ed. 1385 (1939). Can a state sue on behalf of its citizens? See Hawaii v. Standard Oil Co. of Calif., 405 U.S. 251, 92 S.Ct. 885, 31 L.Ed.2d 184 (1972) (giving negative answer in treble damage antitrust action). But see Alfred L. Snapp & Son, Inc., v. Puerto Rico, 458 U.S. 592, 102 S.Ct. 3260, 73 L.Ed.2d 995 (1982) (Puerto Rico held to have standing as parens patriae to enjoin defendant's discrimination against Puerto Rican immigrant farmworkers because of its quasi-sovereign interest in the subject matter of the suit).

(2) In *Flast*, were the plaintiffs injured in fact and was the interest injured arguably within the zone of interests protected by the Constitutional provision assertedly violated? Or do the justifications for granting or denying standing differ depending on the nature of the parties and the dispute?

VALLEY FORGE CHRISTIAN COLLEGE v. AMERICANS UNITED FOR SEPARATION OF CHURCH AND STATE, INC., 454 U.S. 464, 102 S.Ct. 752, 70 L.Ed.2d 700 (1982). Plaintiffs sued to challenge the gratis conveyance of surplus U.S. property by the United States to the College, operated by a religious order. The Court held that the plaintiffs lacked standing, both as taxpayers and as citizens interested in governmental observance of the Establishment Clause. Writing for the 5–4 majority, Mr. Justice Rehnquist first addressed whether the concept of standing was bottomed in Article III of the Constitution:

"A recent line of decisions, however, has resolved that ambiguity, at least to the following extent: at an irreducible minimum, Art. III requires the party who invokes the court's authority to 'show that he personally has suffered some actual or threatened injury as a result of the putatively illegal conduct of the defendant,' Gladstone, Realtors v. Village of Bellwood, 441 U.S. 91, 99 (1979), and that the injury 'fairly can be traced to the challenged action' and 'is likely to be redressed by a favorable decision,' Simon v. Eastern Kentucky Welfare Rights Organization, 426 U.S. 26, 38, 41 (1976). In this manner does Art. III limit the federal judicial power 'to those disputes which confine federal courts to a role consistent with a system of separated powers and which are traditionally thought to be capable of resolution through the judicial process.' Flast v. Cohen, 392 U.S., at 97.

"The requirement of 'actual injury redressable by the court,' *Simon,* supra, at 39, serves several of the 'implicit policies embodied in Article III,' *Flast,* supra, at 96. It tends to assure that the legal questions presented to the court will be resolved, not in the rarified atmosphere of a debating society, but in a concrete factual context conducive to a realistic appreciation of the consequences of judicial action. The 'standing' requirement serves other purposes. Because it assures an actual factual setting in which the litigant asserts a claim of injury in fact, a court may decide the case with some confidence that its decision will not pave the way for lawsuits which have some, but not all, of the facts of the case actually decided by the court.

"The Art. III aspect of standing also reflects a due regard for the autonomy of those persons likely to be most directly affected by a judicial order. The federal courts have abjured appeals to their authority which would convert the judicial process into 'no more than a vehicle for the vindication of the value interests of concerned bystanders.' United States v. SCRAP, 412 U.S. 669, 687 (1973). Were the federal courts merely publicly funded forums for the ventilation of public grievances or the refinement of jurisprudential understanding, the concept of 'standing' would be quite unnecessary. But the 'cases and controversies' language of Art. III forecloses the conversion of courts of the United States into judicial versions of college debating forums. As we said in Sierra Club v. Morton, 405 U.S. 727, 740 (1972):

> 'The requirement that a party seeking review must allege facts showing that he is himself adversely affected * * * does serve as at least a rough attempt to put the decision as to whether review will be sought in the hands of those who have a direct stake in the outcome.'

The exercise of judicial power, which can so profoundly affect the lives, liberty, and property of those to whom it extends, is therefore restricted to litigants who can show 'injury in fact' resulting from the action which they seek to have the court adjudicate.

"Beyond the constitutional requirements, the federal judiciary has also adhered to a set of prudential principles that bear on the question of standing. Thus, this Court has held that 'the plaintiff generally must assert his own legal rights and interests, and cannot rest his claim to relief on the legal rights or interests of third parties.' Warth v. Seldin, 422 U.S., at 499. In addition, even when the plaintiff has alleged redressable injury sufficient to meet the requirements of Art. III, the Court has refrained from adjudicating 'abstract questions of wide public significance' which amount to 'generalized grievances,' pervasively shared and most appropriately addressed in the representative branches. Id., at 499–500. Finally, the Court has required that the plaintiff's complaint fall within 'the zone of interests to be protected or regulated by the statute or constitutional guarantee in question.' Association of Data Processing Service Organizations v. Camp, 397 U.S. 150, 153 (1970).

"Merely to articulate these principles is to demonstrate their close relationship to the policies reflected in the Art. III requirement of actual or threatened injury amenable to judicial remedy. But neither the counsels of prudence nor the policies implicit in the 'case or controversy' requirement should be mistaken for the rigorous Art. III requirements themselves. Satisfaction of the former cannot substitute for a demonstration of ' "distinct and palpable injury" . . . that is likely to be redressed if the requested relief is granted.' Gladstone, Realtors v. Village of Bellwood, 441 U.S., at 100 (quoting Warth v. Seldin, supra, at 501). That requirement states a limitation on judicial power, not merely a factor to be balanced in the weighing of so-called 'prudential' considerations.

"We need not mince words when we say that the concept of 'Art. III standing' has not been defined with complete consistency in all of the various cases decided by this Court which have discussed it, nor when we say that this very fact is probably proof that the concept cannot be reduced to a one-sentence or one-paragraph definition. But of one thing we may be sure: Those who do not possess Art. III standing may not litigate as suitors in the courts of the United States. Article III, which is every bit as important in its circumscription of the judicial power of the United States as in its granting of that power, is not merely a troublesome hurdle to be overcome if possible so as to reach the 'merits' of a lawsuit which a party desires to have adjudicated; it is a part of the basic charter promulgated by the Framers of the Constitution at Philadelphia in 1787, a charter which created a general government, provided for the interaction between that government and the governments of the several States, and was later amended so as to either enhance or limit its authority with respect to both States and individuals."

Justice Rehnquist then found that plaintiffs lacked standing as taxpayers. The *Flast* decision was distinguished on the ground that plaintiffs did not complain, as they did in *Flast,* of an improper use of the taxing power, nor of improper congressional action. Also rejected was the claim that plaintiffs had a special and personal constitutional right to a government that does not establish religion:

"To the extent the Court of Appeals relied on a view of standing under which the Art. III burdens diminish as the 'importance' of the claim on the merits increases, we reject that notion. The requirement of standing 'focuses on the party seeking to get his complaint before a federal court and not on the issues he wishes to have adjudicated.' Flast v. Cohen, supra, at 99. Moreover, we know of no principled basis on which to create a hierarchy of constitutional values or a complementary 'sliding scale' of standing which might permit respondents to invoke the judicial power of the United States. 'The proposition that all constitutional provisions are enforceable by any citizen simply because citizens are the ultimate beneficiaries of those provisions has no boundaries.' Schlesinger v. Reservists Committee to Stop the War, 418 U.S., at 227."

NOTES

(1) Is the decision in the principal cases reconcilable with that in *Flast*? Are the distinctions made by the majority meaningful? Is the subject matter of the action irrelevant? Does it make a difference if a constitutional provision rather than a statute or administrative regulation is allegedly violated?

(2) What difference does it make whether standing is a constitutional or, as the judges call it, a "prudential" [i.e., judge-made] concept? In Jenkins v. McKeithen, 395 U.S. 411, 89 S.Ct. 1843, 23 L.Ed.2d 404 (1969), rehearing denied 396 U.S. 869, 90 S.Ct. 35, 24 L.Ed.2d 123, in which the issue of standing had not been raised below, Justice Marshall said that "since the question of standing goes to this Court's jurisdiction . . . we must decide the issue." In Craig v. Boren, 429 U.S. 190, 97 S.Ct. 451, 50 L.Ed.2d 397 (1976), rehearing denied 429 U.S. 1124, 97 S.Ct. 1161, 51 L.Ed.2d 574 (1977), the Court found an adult licensed vendor of 3.2% beer to have standing to assert the invalidity of a gender-based differential in an Oklahoma drinking age statute. Justice Brennan, noting that the defendant never raised the standing issue below, stated that "our decisions have settled that limitations on a litigant's assertion of *jus tertii* are not constitutionally mandated, but rather stem from a salutory 'rule of self-restraint'". See also Note, Standing: Nuance or Necessity, 41 U.Pitt.L. Rev. 821 (1980); Note, Art. III Justiciability and Class Actions: Standing and Mootness, 59 Tex.L.Rev. 297 (1981).

(3) In his concurring opinion in United States v. Richardson, 418 U.S. 166, 94 S.Ct. 2940, 41 L.Ed.2d 678 (1974) (taxpayer has no standing to obtain a declaration of the unconstitutionality of the Central Intelligence Agency Act on the ground that the act violates the constitutional provision requiring a regular statement and account of public funds), Justice Powell stated: "Relaxation of standing requirements is directly related to the expansion of judicial power. It seems to me inescapable that allowing unrestricted taxpayer or citizen standing would significantly alter the allocation of power at the national level, with a shift away from a democratic form of government" (418 U.S. at 188).

DUKE POWER CO. v. CAROLINA ENVIRONMENTAL STUDY GROUP, INC.

Supreme Court of the United States, 1978.
438 U.S. 59, 98 S.Ct. 2620, 57 L.Ed.2d 595.

[In this case, the plaintiffs sought a declaratory judgment that the Price–Anderson Act, limiting liability in case of a nuclear disaster, was unconstitutional. The District Court ruled the Act unconstitutional. The Supreme Court, before reviewing the merits, addressed two threshold issues: (1) whether the plaintiffs had standing, and (2) whether the district court had subject matter adjudicatory authority. The Court's opinion on the second issue is excerpted below (p. 195). In finding that the plaintiffs had standing, the Supreme Court said:]

We turn first to consider the kinds of injuries the District Court found the appellees suffered. It discerned two categories of effects

which resulted from the operation of nuclear power plants in potentially dangerous proximity to appellees' living and working environment.
The immediate effects included: (a) the production of small quantities
of non-natural radiation which would invade the air and water; (b) a
"sharp increase" in the temperature of two lakes presently used for
recreational purposes resulting from the use of the lake waters to
produce steam and to cool the reactor; (c) interference with the normal
use of the waters of the Catawba River; (d) threatened reduction in
property values of land neighboring the power plants; (e) "objectively
reasonable" present fear and apprehension regarding the "effect of the
increased radioactivity in air, land and water upon [appellees] and their
property, and the genetic effects upon their descendants"; and (f) the
continual threat of "an accident resulting in uncontrolled release of
large or even small quantities of radioactive material" with no assurance of adequate compensation for the resultant damage. 431 F.Supp.
203, 209. Into a second category of potential effects were placed the
damages "which may result from a core melt or other major accident in
the operation of a reactor . . . ." Id., at 209.

For purposes of the present inquiry, we need not determine whether all the putative injuries identified by the District Court, particularly
those based on the possibility of a nuclear accident and the present
apprehension generated by this future uncertainty, are sufficiently
concrete to satisfy constitutional requirements. . . .

The more difficult step in the standing inquiry is establishing that
these injuries "fairly can be traced to the challenged action of the
defendant," Simon v. Eastern Ky. Welfare Rights Org., supra, 426 U.S.,
at 41, 96 S.Ct., at 1926, or put otherwise, that the exercise of the Court's
remedial powers would redress the claimed injuries. 426 U.S., at 43, 96
S.Ct., at 1926. The District Court discerned a "but for" causal connection between the Price-Anderson Act, which appellees challenged as
unconstitutional, "and the construction of the nuclear plants which the
[appellees] view as a threat to them." 431 F.Supp., at 219. Particular-
izing that causal link to the facts of the instant case, the District Court
concluded that "there is a substantial likelihood that Duke would not
be able to complete the construction and maintain the operation of the
McGuire and Catawba Nuclear Plants but for the protection provided
by the Price-Anderson Act." Id., at 220.

*   *   *

Considering the documentary evidence and the testimony in the
record, we cannot say we are left with "the definite and firm conviction
that" the finding by the trial court of a substantial likelihood that the
McGuire and Catawba nuclear power plants would be neither completed nor operated absent the Price-Anderson Act is clearly erroneous;
and, hence, we are bound to accept it. . . .

The second attack on the District Court's finding of a causal link
warrants only brief attention. Essentially the argument is, as we
understand it, that Price-Anderson, is not a "but for" cause of the

injuries appellees claim since, if Price-Anderson had not been passed, the Government would have undertaken development of nuclear power on its own and the same injuries would likely have accrued to appellees from such Government-operated plants as from privately operated ones. Whatever the ultimate accuracy of this speculation, it is not responsive to the simple proposition that private power companies now do in fact operate the nuclear-powered generating plants injuring appellees, and that their participation would not have occurred but for the enactment and implementation of the Price-Anderson Act. Nothing in our prior cases requires a party seeking to invoke federal jurisdiction to negate the kind of speculative and hypothetical possibilities suggested in order to demonstrate the likely effectiveness of judicial relief.

*   *   *

NOTES

(1) In Simon v. Eastern Kentucky Welfare Rights Organization et al., 426 U.S. 26, 96 S.Ct. 1917, 48 L.Ed.2d 450 (1976), indigents had brought suit against the Secretary of the Treasury alleging that an IRS ruling that granted favorable tax treatment to hospitals that did not offer hospital service to indigents to the extent of their financial ability violated the Internal Revenue Code. The Court ruled the plaintiffs had no standing. It held that plaintiffs had to establish that they stood to profit in some personal interest and that they had failed to do so, since it was only "speculative whether the exercise of the court's remedial powers in this suit would result in the availability to respondents" of the services sought. On the face of the complaint, the Court ruled, it was just as plausible that the hospitals would forego favorable tax treatment. In Warth v. Seldin, 422 U.S. 490, 95 S.Ct. 2197, 45 L.Ed.2d 343 (1975), plaintiffs claimed that the zoning ordinance of the town of Penfield, that allocated 98% of the land to single family detached housing, was discriminatory and invalid. The plaintiffs included property owners in a nearby city who asserted that they had to pay higher taxes because that city had to build low-income housing, persons who allegedly sought low-income housing in Penfield, present residents of Penfield who alleged that they were deprived of the benefits of living in an integrated community, and building companies who alleged that they were injured because the zoning ordinances precluded them from building low-income housing in Penfield. All, Justice Powell ruled for the 5–4 majority, lacked standing. But in Village of Arlington Heights v. Metropolitan Housing Developments Corp., 429 U.S. 252, 97 S.Ct. 555, 50 L.Ed.2d 450 (1977), Justice Powell, writing on this issue for the whole court, ruled that the developer who had contracted to buy the land and to build low-income housing if the zoning ordinance were invalidated, and a black, who worked in Arlington Heights, who had lived 20 miles away, and who had testified that he would probably move if the developer were to build, both had standing. See also Haven Realty Corp. v. Coleman, 455 U.S. 363, 102 S.Ct. 1114, 71 L.Ed.2d 214 (1982) (black applicant for integrated housing has standing, but white applicant does not). Are these decisions and that in the principal case reconcilable and, if so, how?

(2) The concept of standing continues to challenge the commentators. See, e.g., Jaffe, The Citizen as Litigant in Public Actions: The Non-Hohfeldian or Ideological Plaintiff, 116 U.Pa.L.Rev. 1033 (1968); Bittker, The Case of the Fictitious Taxpayer, 36 U.Chi.L.Rev. 364 (1969); Davis, The Case of the Real Taxpayer: A Reply to Professor Bittker, 36 U.Chi.L.Rev. 375 (1969); Davis, The Liberalized Law of Standing, 37 U.Chi.L.Rev. 450 (1970); Jaffee, Standing Again, 84 Harv.L.Rev. 633 (1971); Albert, Standing to Challenge Administrative Action, 83 Yale L.J. 425 (1974); Roberts, Fact Pleading, Notice Pleading, and Standing, 65 Cornell L.Rev. 390 (1980); Comment, Judicial Resolution of Inter-Agency Legal Disputes, 89 Yale L.J. 1595 (1980); Le Bel, Standing After Havens Realty: A Critique and an Alternative Framework for Analysis, 1982 Duke L.J. 1013 (1982); Fallon, Of Justiciability, Remedies, and Public Law Litigation. Notes on the Jurisprudence of Lyons, 59 N.Y.U.L.Rev. 1 (1984).

SECTION 3. POLITICAL AND ADMINISTRATIVE QUESTIONS

CUDAHY JUNIOR CHAMBER OF COMMERCE v. QUIRK

Supra, p. 5.

ORLANDO v. LAIRD

United States Court of Appeals, Second Circuit, 1971.
443 F.2d 1039, cert. denied 404 U.S. 869, 92 S.Ct. 94, 30 L.Ed.2d 113.

ANDERSON, CIRCUIT JUDGE * : Shortly after receiving orders to report for transfer to Vietnam, Pfc. Malcolm A. Berk and Sp. E5 Salvatore Orlando, enlistees in the United States Army, commenced separate actions in June, 1970, seeking to enjoin the Secretary of Defense, the Secretary of the Army and the commanding officers, who signed their deployment orders, from enforcing them. The plaintiffs-appellants contended that these executive officers exceeded their constitutional authority by ordering them to participate in a war not properly authorized by Congress.

* * *

. . . We held in the first *Berk* opinion that the constitutional delegation of the war-declaring power to the Congress contains a discoverable and manageable standard imposing on the Congress a duty of mutual participation in the prosecution of war. Judicial scrutiny of that duty, therefore, is not foreclosed by the political question doctrine. Baker v. Carr, [369 U.S. 186, 82 S.Ct. 691, 7 L.Ed.2d 663 (1962)]; Powell

* Footnotes omitted.

v. McCormack, [395 U.S. 486, 89 S.Ct. 1944, 23 L.Ed.2d 491 (1969)]. As we see it, the test is whether there is any action by the Congress sufficient to authorize or ratify the military activity in question. The evidentiary materials produced at the hearings in the district court clearly disclose that this test is satisfied.

The Congress and the Executive have taken mutual and joint action in the prosecution and support of military operations in Southeast Asia from the beginning of those operations. The Tonkin Gulf Resolution, enacted August 10, 1964 (repealed December 31, 1970) was passed at the request of President Johnson and, though occasioned by specific naval incidents in the Gulf of Tonkin, was expressed in broad language which clearly showed the state of mind of the Congress and its intention fully to implement and support the military and naval actions taken by and planned to be taken by the President at that time in Southeast Asia, and as might be required in the future "to prevent further aggression." Congress has ratified the executive's initiatives by appropriating billions of dollars to carry out military operations in Southeast Asia and by extending the Military Selective Service Act with full knowledge that persons conscripted under that Act had been, and would continue to be, sent to Vietnam. Moreover, it specifically conscripted manpower to fill "the substantial induction calls necessitated by the current Vietnam buildup."

There is, therefore, no lack of clear evidence to support a conclusion that there was an abundance of continuing mutual participation in the prosecution of the war. Both branches collaborated in the endeavor, and neither could long maintain such a war without the concurrence and cooperation of the other.

Although appellants do not contend that Congress can exercise its war-declaring power only through a formal declaration, they argue that congressional authorization cannot, as a matter of law, be inferred from military appropriations or other war-implementing legislation that does not contain an express and explicit authorization for the making of war by the President. . . .

                    *   *   *

. . . What has been said and done by both the President and the Congress in their collaborative conduct of the military operations in Vietnam implies a consensus on the advisability of *not* making a formal declaration of war because it would be contrary to the interests of the United States to do so. The making of a policy decision of that kind is clearly within the constitutional domain of those two branches and is just as clearly not within the competency or power of the judiciary.

Beyond determining that there has been *some* mutual participation between the Congress and the President, which unquestionably exists here, with action by the Congress sufficient to authorize or ratify the military activity at issue, it is clear that the constitutional propriety of the means by which Congress has chosen to ratify and approve the protracted military operations in Southeast Asia is a political question.

The form which congressional authorization should take is one of policy, committed to the discretion of the Congress and outside the power and competency of the judiciary, because there are no intelligible and objectively manageable standards by which to judge such actions. Baker v. Carr, supra, 369 U.S. at 217, 82 S.Ct. 691; Powell v. McCormack, supra, 395 U.S. at 518, 89 S.Ct. 1944.

The judgments of the district court are affirmed.

* * *

[handwritten: P's actions were non-justiciable — just a political, not a legal issue]

NOTES

(1) In the course of time, the Supreme Court has tended to limit the number of questions it considers political and therefore non-justiciable. See, e.g., Baker v. Carr, 369 U.S. 186, 82 S.Ct. 691, 7 L.Ed.2d 663 (1962). In this case, qualified voters in Tennessee alleged that the existing apportionment of the state legislature produced inequality of representation and therefore discriminated in violation of the constitutionally guaranteed equal protection of the laws. The district court had dismissed for want of a justiciable controversy, but the Supreme Court reversed (at 217):

"It is apparent that several formulations which vary slightly according to the settings in which the questions arise may describe a political question, although each has one or more elements which identify it as essentially a function of the separation of powers. Prominent on the surface of any case held to involve a political question is found a textually demonstrable constitutional commitment of the issue to a coordinate political department; or a lack of judicially discoverable and manageable standards for resolving it; or the impossibility of deciding without an initial policy determination of a kind clearly for nonjudicial discretion; or the impossibility of a court's undertaking independent resolution without expressing lack of the respect due coordinate branches of government; or an unusual need for unquestioning adherence to a political decision already made; or the potentiality of embarrassment from multifarious pronouncements by various departments on one question.

Unless one of these formulations is inextricable from the case at bar, there should be no dismissal for nonjusticiability on the ground of a political question's presence. The doctrine of which we treat is one of "political questions," not one of "political cases." The courts cannot reject as "no law suit" a bona fide controversy as to whether some action denominated "political" exceeds constitutional authority. The cases we have reviewed show the necessity for discriminating inquiry into the precise facts and posture of the particular case, and the impossibility of resolution by any semantic cataloguing."

Which of the various reasons stated by the Supreme Court, if any, moved the district court in the principal case?

(2) On the political question doctrine, see also Scharpf, Judicial Review and the Political Question: A Functional Analysis, 75 Yale L.J. 517 (1966); Note, Political Question Doctrine and Adam Clayton Powell, 31 Alb.L.Rev. 320 (1967); Yokota, Political Questions and Judicial Review: A Comparison, 43 Wash.L. Rev. 1031 (1968); Note, Political Questions—Classical or Discretionary Application of Judicial Review, 4 Suffolk U.L.Rev. 127 (1969); Note, The Political

Question Doctrine—O'Brien v. Brown and Keane v. National Democratic Party, 22 Depaul L.Rev. 887 (1973); Note, Political Question Doctrine: Where Does It Stand After Powell v. McCormack, O'Brien v. Brown and Gilligan v. Morgan?, 44 U.Colo.L.Rev. 477 (1973); Strum, The Supreme Court and "Political Questions": A Study in Judicial Evasion (1974); Leventhal, Courts and Political Thickets, 77 Colum.L.Rev. 345 (1977); Note, Article V: Political Questions and Sensible Answers, 57 Tex.L.Rev. 1259 (1979); Note, Whether the President May Terminate a Mutual Defense Treaty Without Congressional Approval Under the Constitution is a Non-Justiciable Political Question, 29 Drake L.Rev. 659 (1979–80); Recent Developments, Political Questions, 21 Harv.Int'l L.J. 567 (1980); Bernstine, Political Question Doctrine: A Perspective on Its Political Ramifications, 31 U. Kan.L.Rev. 115 (1982).

(3) For a discussion of Orlando v. Laird as well as other legal aspects of the Vietnam War, see Alstyne, Congress, the President and the Power to Declare War: A Requiem for Vietnam, 121 U.Pa.L.Rev. 1 (1972).

SECTION 4.　MOOT, HYPOTHETICAL, AND ABSTRACT QUESTIONS

MATTER OF STATE INDUSTRIAL COMMISSION
Court of Appeals of New York, 1918.
224 N.Y. 13, 119 N.E. 1027.

CARDOZO, J.　On July 2, 1917, one of the members of the state industrial commission proposed to that body a resolution that every mutual compensation insurance company and every self-insurer should pay into the state fund, under section 27 of the Workmen's Compensation Law, as amended by chapter 705 of the Laws of 1917, the present value of death benefits under every award against such insurance carriers for deaths occurring between July 1, 1914, and July 1, 1917, inclusive.

The resolution was neither adopted nor rejected. All that the commission did was to recite that there was doubt about its power, and to certify to the Appellate Division a question of law to be answered by that court. The following is the question certified: "Has the state industrial commission power and authority under the provisions of section 27 of the Workmen's Compensation Law, as amended by chapter 705 of the Laws of 1917, to require the payment into the state fund, in accordance with the provisions of said section, of the present value of unpaid death benefits in cases in which awards were made prior to July 1, 1917?"

At the Appellate Division the Self-Insurer's Association, an unincorporated body of insurers, was allowed to appear and file a brief. Like permission was granted to the New York Central Railroad Company. Till then the attorney-general stood before the court alone. Even afterwards there were no adverse parties. There were merely friends of the court striving to enlighten its judgment. The Appellate Division did not order anything to be done or forborne. It could not. It merely answered a question. Its order was that the question propounded be answered in the affirmative. It thereupon granted leave to the intervenors to appeal to this court. The same question that was certified to the Appellate Division has been certified to us.

The determination of such an appeal is not within our jurisdiction. The practice is said to be justified under section 23 of the act. That section authorizes an appeal to the Appellate Division from an award or decision of the commission. It then provides that "the commission may also, in its discretion, certify to such Appellate Division of the Supreme Court, questions of law involved in its decision". Appeals may be taken to this court subject to the same limitations as in civil actions (Matter of Harnett v. Steen Co., 216 N.Y. 101, 110 N.E. 170).

Nothing in these provisions sustains the practice followed. The commission made no decision. There was no case or controversy before it. No summons to attend a hearing had been given to the insurance carriers. No carrier had appeared. The members of the commission, debating their powers among themselves, asked and obtained the advisory opinion of a court. Without notice to the carriers to be affected by their action, they fortified themselves in advance by judicial instruction. In such circumstances the answer of the Appellate Division bound no one and settled nothing. We do not know that the commission will ever adopt the proposed resolution. If it does, and so notifies the carriers, the legality of its action will remain open for contest in the courts. No advice that may now be given in response to a request for light and guidance can prejudge the issue or control the outcome.

In that situation our duty is not doubtful. The function of the courts is to determine controversies between litigants (Interstate Commerce Commission v. Brimson, 154 U.S. 447, 475, 14 S.Ct. 1125, 38 L.Ed. 1047; Osborn v. Bank of U.S., 9 Wheat. 738, 819, 6 L.Ed. 204; Mills v. Green, 159 U.S. 651, 16 S.Ct. 132, 40 L.Ed. 293; Marye v. Parsons, 114 U.S. 325, 330, 5 S.Ct. 932, 29 L.Ed. 205; American Book Co. v. Kansas, 193 U.S. 49, 24 S.Ct. 394, 48 L.Ed. 613). They do not give advisory opinions. The giving of such opinions is not the exercise of the judicial function (Thayer, Cases on Constitutional Law, vol. 1, p. 175; American Doctrine of Const. Law, 7 Harvard Law Review, 153). It is true that in England the custom of the constitution makes the judges of the high court the assistants of the Lords, and requires them, upon the demand of the Lords, to give "consultative" opinions (Thayer, supra; Opinion of the Justices, 126 Mass. 557, 562). But that custom is a survival of the days when the judges were members of the great council of the realm (Thayer, supra; T.E. May, Parliamentary Practice (12th ed.), pp. 55, 56, 182; Anson, Law and Custom of the Constitution, pp. 45, 52, 449). In the United States no such duty attaches to the judicial office in the absence of express provision of the Constitution (Dinan v. Swig, 223 Mass. 516, 519, 112 N.E. 91; Opinion of Court, 62 N.H. 704, 706; Rice v. Austin, 19 Minn. 103). Even in those states, e.g., Massachusetts, Maine and New Hampshire, where such provisions are found, the opinions thus given have not the quality of judicial authority. The judges then act, "not as a court, but as the constitutional advisers of the other departments" (Opinion of Justices, 126 Mass. 557, 566; Laughlin v. City of Portland, 111 Me. 486, 497, 90 A. 318). In this state the legislature is without power to charge the courts with the performance of non-judicial duties (Matter of Davies, 168 N.Y. 89, 61 N.E. 118). It has not attempted to do so by this statute. The questions to be certified under section 23 of the act must be incidental to a pending controversy with adverse parties litigant. Those limitations apply to the Appellate Division. Even more explicit are the restrictions on this court. Our jurisdiction is to be exercised subject to the same limitations as in civil actions (Workmen's Comp. Act, § 23; Code Civ.Proc. § 190). The order under review is not one which finally determines a special proceeding (Matter of Droege, 197 N.Y. 44, 50, 90 N.E. 340; Matter of Jones, 181 N.Y. 389, 74 N.E. 226). It is not an intermediate order in a special proceeding. There has been no judicial proceeding at all. There has been a tender of advice which may be accepted or rejected.

The record now before us supplies a pointed illustration of the need that the judicial function be kept within its ancient bounds. Some of the arguments addressed to us in criticism of the resolution apply to all awards for death benefits; others to awards made before June, 1916; others to awards where one of the dependents is a widow. It is thus conceivable that the proposed resolution may be valid as to some carriers and invalid as to others. We are asked by an omnibus answer to an omnibus question to adjudge the rights of all. That is not the way in which a system of case law develops. We deal with the particular instance; and we wait till it arises.

The appeal must be dismissed without costs to either party.

HISCOCK, CH. J., COLLIN, CUDDEBACK, POUND, CRANE and ANDREWS, JJ., concur.

Appeal dismissed.

DE FUNIS v. ODEGAARD

Supreme Court of the United States, 1974.
416 U.S. 312, 94 S.Ct. 1704, 40 L.Ed.2d 164.

PER CURIAM.* In 1971 the petitioner Marco DeFunis, Jr., applied for admission as a first-year student at the University of Washington Law School, a state-operated institution. The size of the incoming first-year class was to be limited to 150 persons, and the Law School received some 1,600 applications for these 150 places. DeFunis was eventually notified that he had been denied admission. He thereupon commenced this suit in a Washington trial court, contending that the procedures and criteria employed by the Law School Admissions Committee invidi-

* Footnotes omitted.

ously discriminated against him on account of his race in violation of the Equal Protection Clause of the Fourteenth Amendment to the United States Constitution.

DeFunis brought the suit on behalf of himself alone, and not as the representative of any class, against the various respondents, who are officers, faculty members, and members of the Board of Regents of the University of Washington. He asked the trial court to issue a mandatory injunction commanding the respondents to admit him as a member of the first-year class entering in September 1971, on the ground that the Law School admissions policy had resulted in the unconstitutional denial of his application for admission. The trial court agreed with his claim and granted the requested relief. DeFunis was, accordingly, admitted to the Law School and began his legal studies there in the fall of 1971. On appeal, the Washington Supreme Court reversed the judgment of the trial court and held that the Law School admissions policy did not violate the Constitution. By this time DeFunis was in his second year at the Law School.

He then petitioned this Court for a writ of certiorari and Mr. Justice Douglas, as Circuit Justice, stayed the judgment of the Washington Supreme Court pending the "final disposition of the case by this Court." By virtue of this stay, DeFunis has remained in law school, and was in the first term of his third and final year when this Court first considered his certiorari petition in the fall of 1973. Because of our concern that DeFunis' third-year standing in the Law School might have rendered this case moot, we requested the parties to brief the question of mootness before we acted on the petition. In response, both sides contended that the case was not moot. The respondents indicated that, if the decision of the Washington Supreme Court were permitted to stand, the petitioner could complete the term for which he was then enrolled but would have to apply to the faculty for permission to continue in the school before he could register for another term.

We granted the petition for certiorari on November 19, 1973. 414 U.S. 1038. The case was in due course orally argued on February 26, 1974.

In response to questions raised from the bench during the oral argument, counsel for the petitioner has informed the Court that DeFunis has now registered "for his final quarter in law school." Counsel for the respondents have made clear that the Law School will not in any way seek to abrogate this registration. In light of DeFunis' recent registration for the last quarter of his final law school year, and the Law School's assurance that his registration is fully effective, the insistent question again arises whether this case is not moot, and to that question we now turn.

The starting point for analysis is the familiar proposition that "federal courts are without power to decide questions that cannot affect the rights of litigants in the case before them." North Carolina v. Rice, 404 U.S. 244, 246, 92 S.Ct. 402, 404, 30 L.Ed.2d 413 (1971). The inability of the federal judiciary "to review moot cases derives from the requirement of Art. III of the Constitution under which the exercise of judicial power depends upon the existence of a case or controversy." Liner v. Jafco, Inc., 375 U.S. 301, 306 n. 3, 84 S.Ct. 391, 394 n. 3, 11 L.Ed.2d 347 (1964); see also Powell v. McCormack, 395 U.S. 486, 496 n. 7, 89 S.Ct. 1944, 1950 n. 7, 23 L.Ed.2d 491 (1969); Sibron v. New York, 392 U.S. 40, 50 n. 8, 88 S.Ct. 1889, 1896 n. 8, 20 L.Ed.2d 917 (1968). Although as a matter of Washington state law it appears that this case would be saved from mootness by "the great public interest in the continuing issues raised by this appeal," 82 Wash.2d 11, 23 n. 6, 507 P.2d 1169, 1177 n. 6 (1973), the fact remains that under Art. III "[e]ven in cases arising in the state courts, the question of mootness is a federal one which a federal court must resolve before it assumes jurisdiction." North Carolina v. Rice, supra, at 246.

The respondents have represented that, without regard to the ultimate resolution of the issues in this case, DeFunis will remain a student in the Law School for the duration of any term in which he has already enrolled. Since he has now registered for his final term, it is evident that he will be given an opportunity to complete all academic and other requirements for graduation, and, if he does so, will receive his diploma regardless of any decision this Court might reach on the merits of this case. In short, all parties agree that DeFunis is now entitled to complete his legal studies at the University of Washington and to receive his degree from that institution. A determination by this Court of the legal issues tendered by the parties is no longer necessary to compel that result, and could not serve to prevent it. . . . The controversy between the parties has thus clearly ceased to be "definite and concrete" and no longer "touch[es] the legal relations of parties having adverse legal interests." Aetna Life Ins. Co. v. Haworth, 300 U.S. 227, 240–241, 57 S.Ct. 461, 463–464, 81 L.Ed. 617 (1937).

* * *

It might also be suggested that this case presents a question that is "capable of repetition, yet evading review," Southern Pacific Terminal Co. v. ICC, 219 U.S. 498, 515, 31 S.Ct. 279, 283, 55 L.Ed. 310 (1911); Roe v. Wade, 410 U.S. 113, 125 (1973), and is thus amenable to federal adjudication even though it might otherwise be considered moot. But DeFunis will never again be required to run the gantlet of the Law School's admission process, and so the question is certainly not "capable of repetition" so far as he is concerned. Moreover, just because this particular case did not reach the Court until the eve of the petitioner's graduation from law school, it hardly follows that the issue he raises will in the future evade review. If the admissions procedures of the Law School remain unchanged, there is no reason to suppose that a subsequent case attacking those procedures will not come with relative speed to this Court, now that the Supreme Court of Washington has spoken. . . .

Because the petitioner will complete his law school studies at the end of the term for which he has now registered regardless of any decision this Court might reach on the merits of this litigation, we conclude that the Court cannot, consistently with the limitations of Art. III of the Constitution, consider the substantive constitutional issues tendered by the parties. Accordingly, the judgment of the Supreme Court of Washington is vacated, and the cause is remanded for such proceedings as by that court may be deemed appropriate.

It is so ordered.

MR. JUSTICE DOUGLAS, dissenting. [Omitted.]

MR. JUSTICE BRENNAN, with whom MR. JUSTICE DOUGLAS, MR. JUSTICE WHITE, and MR. JUSTICE MARSHALL concur, dissenting.

*   *   *

NOTES

(1) In the principal case, would the decision have been different if the suit had been brought as a class action?

(2) In Roe v. Wade, 410 U.S. 113, 125, 93 S.Ct. 705, 35 L.Ed.2d 147 (1973), the Supreme Court said: "Pregnancy provides a classic justification for a conclusion of nonmootness. It truly could be 'capable of repetition, yet evading review.'"

(3) In Regents of the University of California v. Bakke, 438 U.S. 265, 98 S. Ct. 2733, 57 L.Ed.2d 750 (1978), Bakke had been denied provisional admission to medical school, and the dispute remained concrete until the Court decided that Bakke had improperly been denied admission.

(4) On mootness, see also Firefighters Local Union No. 1784 v. Stotts, 467 U.S. 561, 104 S.Ct. 2576, 81 L.Ed.2d 483 (1984), holding that a proceeding seeking an injunction against laying off white firemen with greater seniority ahead of black firemen with lesser seniority had not become moot even though all white firemen affected had been restored to their jobs.

AETNA LIFE INSURANCE CO. v. HAWORTH

Supra, p. 103.

NOTES

(1) Could the Supreme Court have upheld declaratory judgments without explicit statutory authorization? Many European courts do so. See, e.g., Cappelletti & Perillo, Civil Procedure in Italy 147 (1965) ("Despite the absence of general statutory authority, the prevailing view of Italian case law and doctrine is that a declaratory judgment may be rendered whenever the prerequisite of objective uncertainty resulting in the need for judicial protection is met"); Herzog, Civil Procedure in France 241–242 (1967). See also Clark, Code Pleading 33 n. 131 (2d ed. 1947) (stating that the American declaratory judgment is largely an import from the civil law).

(2) To what extent is the constitutional requirement of "case or controversy" relevant in determining whether the courts have power (a) to render declaratory judgments, (b) to render advisory opinions, (c) to decide feigned or moot cases, (d) to hold that a party lacks standing, and (e) to decide so-called

political questions? See generally Hart & Wechsler, The Federal Courts and the Federal System 75–217 (1953).

(3) In promulgating a rule of procedure pursuant to the Enabling Act does the Supreme Court in effect render an advisory opinion that it will find the rule constitutional in a suit raising the issue? See J.B. Weinstein, Reform of Federal Court Rule Making Procedures (1976); Hanna v. Plumer, 380 U.S. 460, 85 S.Ct. 1136, 14 L.Ed.2d 8 (1965), p. 371 infra.

Chapter Six

ADJUDICATORY AUTHORITY: BASES AND MEANS OF EXERCISE

SECTION 1. THE VARIOUS KINDS OF ADJUDICATORY AUTHORITY

The adjudicatory authority of a court is commonly called jurisdiction. Etymologically, jurisdiction signifies the power to speak the law, both in the sense of formulating laws of general application and in the sense of applying the law to particular cases. But frequently the term has a different meaning. For example, it quite often is simply a synonym for state or other political unit. And in many instances courts have been said to lack jurisdiction not because they lacked the requisite adjudicatory power over the subject matter or the parties, but because they failed to exercise their power in a proper manner. See, e.g., Johnson v. Zerbst, 304 U.S. 458, 58 S.Ct. 1019, 82 L.Ed. 1461 (1938) (when the accused has been deprived of his right to counsel, the court lacks jurisdiction); Restatement, Second, Conflict of Laws § 25 (1971) (failure to give the defendant adequate notice or opportunity to defend deprives the court of jurisdiction); Montana–Dakota Utility Co. v. Northwestern Public Service Co., 341 U.S. 246, 249, 71 S.Ct. 692, 95 L.Ed. 912 (1951) (when no claim for relief is stated, the court lacks jurisdiction); Bank of California v. Superior Court, 16 Cal.2d 516, 106 P.2d 879 (1940) (when absent parties are indispensable, the court lacks jurisdiction to proceed) (dictum).

In view of the indiscriminate use of the term jurisdiction, certain distinctions should be made. The etymological meaning of the term provides a proper starting point. Jurisdiction is the power to say the law—that is, the power to affect legal interests. As such, it encompasses not only judicial jurisdiction, but also legislative and executive or administrative jurisdiction. A state exercises its legislative jurisdiction when it formulates laws of general application, its executive or administrative jurisdiction when it executes the law through its officers (the apprehension of a fugitive by the sheriff is an example), and its judicial jurisdiction when it resolves disputes through its adjudicatory processes.

In the final analysis, all powers are exercised by the state. Other bodies may exercise legislative, judicial, or executive powers only if so authorized by the state. The distinction is meaningful, because the state may possess the requisite power, but not have granted it to the body that purports to exercise it. The term jurisdiction may be used to denote the state's power, and the term competence to denote the power

178

of the body to which the state has given its power. Cf. Restatement, Second, Judgments § 11 (1982). In this terminology, judicial jurisdiction is the power of the state to affect legal interests through its judicial processes, and judicial competence the authority given by the state to its courts or other organs to exercise this power.*

Adjudicatory power may be defined by reference to various criteria. Since all courts do not adjudicate all kinds of controversies, adjudicatory power must be defined by reference to the subject matter of the dispute. Rules providing such definition are called rules of subject matter jurisdiction or competence. Furthermore, since judgments normally bind persons, adjudicatory power must also be defined by reference to the parties who may be bound. Rules that define this power are called rules of in personam or personal jurisdiction or competence. In common law countries, courts may also render judgments against things rather than against persons. Such judgments may be sought when it is desirable to determine the interests in a thing or when the party who would normally be made the defendant is beyond the court's reach and only his or her property can be subjected to the court's processes. Rules that define the power to proceed against things are called rules of in rem or quasi-in-rem jurisdiction or competence.

In most civil law countries, the judicial jurisdiction of the state is usually solely a function of its own largesse—that is, the state may extend its civil adjudicatory powers as far as it wants. Specifically, international law imposes no limitations.** But in the United States, the judicial jurisdiction of the state is subject to constitutional limitations. As a result, in American courts a dual inquiry is ordinarily required: first, does the state have judicial jurisdiction; and second, has it bestowed the requisite power upon the court?

The judicial jurisdiction of the United States is defined by the United States Constitution. The judicial jurisdiction of a state of the United States may be defined by the United States Constitution, a federal statute, or the state constitution. Rules of competence may be found either in the common law or in legislative measures.

---

* This is the terminology to be used in this chapter. The term adjudicatory authority or power is used as a designation of either judicial jurisdiction or competence or both. Those who prefer more common, but less discriminating, terminology may substitute the term "jurisdiction" for adjudicatory authority or power as long as it is realized that jurisdiction then signifies either the state's or the court's power or both.

** Of course, the conflict of law rules of a state that is asked to recognize a judgment originating in another state may impose limitations. These limitations then define the judicial jurisdiction of the state that rendered the judgment under the conflict of laws rules of the state in which it is presented for recognition. Here, we are concerned principally with the internal rather than the interstate or international situation.

SECTION 2. ADJUDICATORY AUTHORITY OVER THE SUBJECT MATTER

A. INTRODUCTION

The adjudication of disputes is normally distributed among a number of courts. A variety of factors may explain why a particular dispute must be adjudicated by a special court or will be left for adjudication to a court of what is often called general jurisdiction. Among these are the desire to have an adjudicating body with special knowledge and expertise, the historical development of a special court for certain matters, the desire to relegate relatively minor matters to special courts with simplified proceedings, and, in our federal system, the necessity of distributing the judicial business among the federal and state courts. The latter distribution is based in important measure on a political judgment as to how far the federal influence should extend.

In the United States, adjudicatory power over the subject matter, both on the federal and on the state level, is subject to constitutional limitations. The pertinent constitutional provisions either circumscribe generally the matters that are susceptible of judicial cognizance or assign particular matters to particular courts. In studying constitutional provisions, you should consider to what extent these limitations are desirable.

The following materials will pay only scant attention to such specialized tribunals—also called courts of special jurisdiction—as the Claims Court, the Tax Court, and the Court of International Trade on the federal level, and to such special courts as Surrogate's Courts, Justices of the Peace, and Equity Courts or Courts of Chancery (where these still exist), on the state level. You should give thought, however, to the reasons that may justify their continued existence.

B. CONSTITUTIONAL AND STATUTORY RULES

There are 94 United States district courts (including Puerto Rico, Guam, and the Virgin Islands) 28 U.S.C.A. §§ 81–131; 48 U.S.C.A. §§ 1424, 1611 (West Supp.1984).

There are thirteen courts of appeals. In 1980, the former Fifth Circuit was split into the Fifth and Eleventh Circuits. Fifth Circuit Reorganization Act of 1980 Pub.L. No. 96–452, 94 Stat. 1994, 28 U.S. C.A. §§ 41, 44, 48 (West Supp.1984).

On October 1, 1984, a new United States Court of Appeals for the Federal Circuit entered into operation. Federal Courts Improvement Act of 1982, Pub.L. No. 97–164, 96 Stat. 25 (codified as amended in numerous sections scattered throughout the U.S.C.A.) This court hears appeals from specialized tribunals and from district courts in such special areas as patents and certain claims against the United States.

There are a number of specialized courts, including the United States Claims Court, 28 U.S.C.A. § 171 (West Supp.1984), the United States Tax Court, 26 U.S.C.A. § 7441 (West Supp.1984), the United States Court of International Trade, 28 U.S.C.A. § 251 (West Supp. 1984), and the Temporary Emergency Court of Appeals, 12 U.S.C.A. § 1904 Note 87 (West Supp.1984) (hearing appeals under the Economic Stabilization Act of 1970).

State constitutions regulating subject matter powers of state courts vary. Typically, the general courts of first instance are given "unlimited" or "general original jurisdiction", with frequent provision for exception by statute. See, e.g., McKinney's Const. Amend. 6 & 7 (N.Y.); S.H.A. Const. Art. 6, § 9 (Ill.) Other constitutions leave the definition of subject matter power completely to statute. See, e.g., Purdon's Penn. Const. art. 5, § 2. The subject matter powers of appellate courts may be defined with great specificity. See, e.g., McKinney's Const. Art. 6, § 3 (N.Y.) (enumerating in detail which cases may be heard on appeal). What considerations determine whether the specifics of subject matter power are regulated in the constitution or by statute?

1. DIVERSITY

STRAWBRIDGE v. CURTISS

Supreme Court of the United States, 1806.
7 U.S. (3 Cranch) 267, 2 L.Ed. 435.

This was an appeal from a decree of the Circuit Court for the district of Massachusetts, which dismissed the complainants' bill in chancery, for want of jurisdiction. Some of the complainants were alleged to be citizens of the state of Massachusetts. The defendants were also stated to be citizens of the same state, excepting Curtiss, who was averred to be a citizen of the state of Vermont, and upon whom the *subpoena* was served in that state.

The question of jurisdiction was submitted to the court, without argument. . . .

MARSHALL, CH. J., delivered the opinion of the court.—The court has considered this case, and is of opinion, that the jurisdiction cannot be supported.

The words of the act of congress are, "where an alien is a party, or the suit is between a citizen of a state where the suit is brought, and a citizen of another state." The court understands these expressions to mean, that each distinct interest should be represented by persons, all of whom are entitled to sue, or may be sued, in the federal courts. That is, that where the interest is joint, each of the persons concerned in that interest must be competent to sue, or liable to be sued, in those courts.

But the court does not mean to give an opinion in the case where several parties represent several distinct interests, and some of those parties are, and others are not, competent to sue, or liable to be sued, in the courts of the United States.

Decree affirmed.

NOTES

(1) Is the rule of "complete" diversity laid down in the principal case constitutionally required? See State Farm Fire & Casualty Co. v. Tashire, p. 213 infra. Is it a desirable rule in view of the purposes to be served by adjudicatory authority based on diversity? What doctrine may alleviate the problems attendant upon strict application of the rule? See Freeman v. Howe, 65 U.S. (24 Howard) 450, 16 L.Ed. 749 (1860); p. 215, infra.

(2) Why were the federal courts given adjudicatory authority based on diversity? The traditional explanation is that given by Marshall in Bank of the United States v. Deveaux, 9 U.S. (5 Cranch) 61, 87, 3 L.Ed. 38, 45 (1809):

> "However true the fact may be, that the tribunals of the states will administer justice as impartially as those of the nation, to parties of every description, it is not less true that the constitution itself either entertains apprehensions on this subject, or views with such indulgence the possible fears and apprehensions of suitors, that it has established national tribunals for the decisions of controversies between aliens and a citizen, or between citizens of different states."

See also Martin v. Hunter's Lessee, 14 U.S. (1 Wheat.) 304, 347, 4 L.Ed. 97, 108 (1816). On the historical justification for diversity adjudicatory power, see also Phillips & Christenson, The Historical and Legal Background of the Diversity Jurisdiction, 46 A.B.A.J. 959 (1960); Frank, Historical Bases of the Federal Judicial System, 13 Law & Contemp.Prob. 322 (1948).

(3) It is disputed whether historically the fear of prejudice on the part of the state courts was justified. Compare Friendly, The Historical Basis of Diversity Jurisdiction, 41 Harv.L.Rev. 483 (1928) (not justified) with Yntema and Jaffin, Preliminary Analysis of Concurrent Jurisdiction, 79 U.Pa.L.Rev. 869, 876 (1931) (". . . it is not demonstrated that . . . local prejudice [was] inconsequential"). If fear of prejudice in regard to non-residents is the explicatory rationale, should a resident plaintiff be permitted to initiate an action against a non-resident in the federal court if the amount in controversy exceeds $10,000? Under present law, he may bring such an action. According to 1964 statistics, 45.3% of all actions originally commenced in the federal courts on the basis of diversity of citizenship were commenced by resident plaintiffs. See American Law Institute, Study of the Division of Jurisdiction Between State and Federal Courts, 123–124, 466 (1967) (proposing to eliminate this possibility). Can you think of cases in which a resident plaintiff may wish to seek recourse in the federal courts because of fear of prejudice on the part of the state courts grounded in circumstances other than his residence? Should the federal courts be opened for this purpose?

(4) Is the fear of prejudice in regard to non-residents a proper justification for diversity adjudicatory power in present times? What other reasons justify the continued existence of this power? See generally Hart & Wechsler, The Federal Courts and the Federal System (Bator, Meltzer, Mishkin & Shapiro 3d ed. 1988); Friendly, Federal Jurisdiction: A General View (1973); American Law Institute,

Study of the Division of Jurisdiction Between State and Federal Courts, Appendix A, 458–464 (1969). Empirical studies cite a number of reasons which move parties to prefer federal courts for the adjudication of diversity cases. These reasons include more liberal discovery, more liberal third-party practice, geographical convenience, better judges, better juries, less congestion, and greater protection against local prejudice. See Summers, Analysis of Factors that Influence Choice of Forum in Diversity Cases, 47 Iowa L.Rev. 933, 937–38 (1962); Note, The Choice Between State and Federal Court in Diversity Cases in Virginia, 51 Va.L.Rev. 178, 179–80 (1965). As you continue your studies of procedure, try to determine the validity of these reasons.

(5) Proposals were introduced in the House and the Senate in the late seventies designed to preclude reliance on diversity competence by a resident of the forum or to preclude diversity competence altogether. H.R. 9622, 95th Cong., 2d Sess. (1978); S. 2094, 95th Cong., S. 2094, 95th Cong. 1st Sess. (1977); H.R. 2202, 96th Cong., 1st Sess. (1979); S. 679, 96th Cong., 1st Sess. (1979). All of these proposals died in committee. See also Shapiro, Federal Diversity Jurisdiction: A Survey and a Proposal, 91 Harv.L.Rev. 317 (1977); Rowe, Abolishing Diversity Jurisdiction: Positive Side Effects and Potential for Further Reforms, 92 Harv.L. Rev. 963 (1979). Instead, in 1988, Congress increased the requisite amount in controversy to exceed $50,000. It also declared an alien admitted for permanent residence a citizen of the state in which he is domiciled.

————

STATE FARM FIRE & CASUALTY CO. v. TASHIRE

Supreme Court of the United States, 1967.
386 U.S. 523, 87 S.Ct. 1199, 18 L.Ed.2d 270.

MR. JUSTICE FORTAS delivered the opinion of the Court.*

Early one September morning in 1964, a Greyhound bus proceeding northward through Shasta County, California, collided with a southbound pickup truck. Two of the passengers aboard the bus were killed. Thirty-three others were injured, as were the bus driver, the driver of the truck and its lone passenger. One of the dead and 10 of the injured passengers were Canadians; the rest of the individuals involved were citizens of five American States. The ensuing litigation led to the present case, which raises important questions concerning administration of the interpleader remedy in the federal courts.

The litigation began when four of the injured passengers filed suit in California state courts, seeking damages in excess of $1,000,000. Named as defendants were Greyhound Lines, Inc., a California corporation; Theron Nauta, the bus driver; Ellis Clark, who drove the truck; and Kenneth Glasgow, the passenger in the truck who was apparently its owner as well. Each of the individual defendants was a citizen and resident of Oregon. Before these cases could come to trial and before other suits were filed in California or elsewhere, petitioner State Farm Fire & Casualty Company, an Illinois corporation, brought this action in the nature of interpleader in the United States District Court for the District of Oregon.

* Footnotes omitted.

In its complaint State Farm asserted that at the time of the Shasta County collision it had in force an insurance policy with respect to Ellis Clark, driver of the truck, providing for bodily injury liability up to $10,000 per person and $20,000 per occurrence and for legal representation of Clark in actions covered by the policy. It asserted that actions already filed in California and others which it anticipated would be filed far exceeded in aggregate damages sought the amount of its maximum liability under the policy. Accordingly, it paid into court the sum of $20,000 and asked the court (1) to require all claimants to establish their claims against Clark and his insurer in this single proceeding and in no other, and (2) to discharge State Farm from all further obligations under its policy—including its duty to defend Clark in lawsuits arising from the accident. Alternatively, State Farm expressed its conviction that the policy issued to Clark excluded from coverage accidents resulting from his operation of a truck which belonged to another and was being used in the business of another. The complaint, therefore, requested that the court decree that the insurer owed no duty to Clark and was not liable on the policy, and it asked the court to refund the $20,000 deposit.

Joined as defendants were Clark, Glasgow, Nauta, Greyhound Lines, and each of the prospective claimants. Jurisdiction was predicated upon 28 U.S.C.A. § 1335, the federal interpleader statute, and upon general diversity of citizenship, there being diversity between two or more of the claimants to the fund and between State Farm and all of the named defendants.

An order issued, requiring the defendants to show cause why they should not be restrained from filing or prosecuting "any proceeding in any state or United States Court affecting the property or obligation involved in this interpleader action, and specifically against the plaintiff and the defendant Ellis D. Clark." Personal service was effected on each of the American defendants, and registered mail was employed to reach the 11 Canadian claimants. Defendants Nauta, Greyhound, and several of the injured passengers responded, contending that the policy did cover this accident and advancing various arguments for the position that interpleader was either impermissible or inappropriate in the present circumstances. Greyhound, however, soon switched sides and moved that the court broaden any injunction to include Nauta and Greyhound among those who could not be sued except within the confines of the interpleader proceeding.

When a temporary injunction along the lines sought by State Farm was issued by the United States District Court for the District of Oregon, the present respondents moved to dismiss the action and, in the alternative, for a change of venue—to the Northern District of California, in which district the collision had occurred. After a hearing, the court declined to dissolve the temporary injunction, but continued the motion for a change of venue. The injunction was later broadened to include the protection sought by Greyhound, but modified to permit the filing—although not the prosecution—of suits. The injunction, therefore, provided that all suits against Clark, State Farm, Greyhound, and Nauta be prosecuted in the interpleader proceeding.

On interlocutory appeal, the Court of Appeals for the Ninth Circuit reversed. . . .

Before considering the issues presented by the petition for certiorari, we find it necessary to dispose of a question neither raised by the parties nor passed upon by the courts below. Since the matter concerns our jurisdiction, we raise it on our own motion. Treinies v. Sunshine Mining Co., 308 U.S. 66, 70, 60 S.Ct. 44, 84 L.Ed. 85 (1939). The interpleader statute, 28 U.S.C.A. § 1335, applies where there are "Two or more adverse claimants, of diverse citizenship . . . ." This provision has been uniformly construed to require only "minimal diversity," that is, diversity of citizenship between two or more claimants, without regard to the circumstance that other rival claimants may be co-citizens. The language of the statute, the legislative purpose broadly to remedy the problems posed by multiple claimants to a single fund, and the consistent judicial interpretation tacitly accepted by Congress, persuade us that the statute requires no more. There remains, however, the question whether such a statutory construction is consistent with Article III of our Constitution, which extends the federal judicial power to "Controversies . . . between Citizens of different States . . . and between a State, or the Citizens thereof, and foreign States, Citizens or Subjects." In Strawbridge v. Curtiss, 7 U.S. (3 Cranch) 267, 2 L.Ed. 435 (1806), this Court held that the diversity of citizenship statute required "complete diversity": where co-citizens appeared on both sides of a dispute, jurisdiction was lost. But Chief Justice Marshall there purported to construe only "The words of the act of congress," not the Constitution itself. And in a variety of contexts this Court and the lower courts have concluded that Article III poses no obstacle to the legislative extension of federal jurisdiction, founded on diversity, so long as any two adverse parties are not co-citizens. Accordingly, we conclude that the present case is properly in the federal courts.

*   *   *

NOTES

(1) When both parties are content to have the court adjudicate their dispute, why should the court raise the issue of subject matter adjudicatory power on its own motion? See Fed.R.Civ.P. 12(h)(3). Does it make any difference whether the court lacked the requisite power under the constitution or under the applicable statute? For example, when the court lacks adjudicatory power over the subject matter because the amount in controversy is exactly $50,000 (28 U.S.C.A. § 1332, requires that the amount in controversy *exceed* $50,000), but the parties have failed to raise an objection on this ground, what policy is served by the court's dismissing for lack of the requisite adjudicatory power on its own motion? Or should distinctions be drawn depending on whether there is no case or controversy, no diversity (in the constitutional or the statutory sense), no action arising under federal law (in the constitutional or the statutory sense), or an insufficient amount in controversy? See also

Dobbs, Beyond Bootstrap: Foreclosing the Issue of Subject Matter Jurisdiction before Final Judgment, 51 Minn.L.Rev. 491 (1967).

(2) When the court rendered judgment although it lacked adjudicatory power over the subject matter, is its judgment subject to collateral attack, i.e., an attack made in a subsequent independent proceeding? On what factors may the answer depend? See Restatement, Second, Judgments § 12 (1982), listing the following as relevant:

(1) The subject matter of the action was so plainly beyond the court's jurisdiction that its entertaining the action was a manifest abuse of authority; or

(2) Allowing the judgment to stand would substantially infringe the authority of another tribunal or agency of government; or

(3) The judgment was rendered by a court lacking capability to make an adequately informed determination of a question concerning its own jurisdiction and as a matter of procedural fairness the party seeking to avoid the judgment should have opportunity belatedly to attack the court's subject matter jurisdiction.

Can you think of any other factors that might be relevant? Should it make a difference whether the attacker had a reasonable opportunity to raise the issue in the original proceedings or whether the defect is of a constitutional or statutory nature? Compare also Chicot County Drainage District v. Baxter State Bank, 308 U.S. 371, 60 S.Ct. 317, 84 L.Ed. 329 (1940), reh. denied 309 U.S. 695, 60 S.Ct. 581, 84 L.Ed. 1035 (precluding collateral attack) with Kalb v. Feuerstein, 308 U.S. 433, 60 S.Ct. 343, 84 L.Ed. 370 (1940), conf. to 234 Wis. 507, 291 N.W. 840 (decided the same day and permitting collateral attack). On these cases, see also Boskey & Braucher, Jurisdiction and Collateral Attack: October Term, 1939, 40 Colum.L.Rev. 1006 (1940). In Durfee v. Duke, 375 U.S. 106, 84 S.Ct. 242, 11 L.Ed.2d 186 (1963), the Supreme Court rejected a collateral attack on a Nebraska judgment quieting title to land on the boundary between Nebraska and Missouri. The subject matter adjudicatory authority of the Nebraska court depended on whether the land was situated within Nebraska. This question had been actually litigated and determined in the Nebraska action. To what extent should res judicata policies be effective in this area? See also Moore, Collateral Attack on Subject Matter Jurisdiction: A Critique of the Restatement (Second) of Judgments, 66 Cornell L.Rev. 534 (1981).

(3) May a third party challenge the court's subject matter adjudicatory authority? In United States Catholic Conference v. Abortion Rights Mobilization, Inc., 487 U.S. 72, 108 S.Ct. 2268, 101 L.Ed.2d 69 (1988), in which a third party had been fined for failure to comply with a discovery order, the Supreme Court said yes. See also Note, Non party Witness Challenge to Federal Court's Subject Matter Jurisdiction, 61 Temple L.Rev. 213 (1988); Note, Filling the Void: Judicial Power and Jurisdictional Attacks on Judgments, 89 Yale L.J. 164 (1977).

(4) State citizenship for diversity purposes has two elements: (1) United States citizenship or admission to permanent residence in the United States and (2) domicile in the state. See, e.g., Brown v. Keene, 33 U.S. (8 Pet.) 112, 8 L.Ed. 885 (1834). In actions based on diversity of citizenship, a mere allegation of residence is insufficient. Mantin v. Broadcast Music, Inc., 244 F.2d 204 (9th Cir.1957).

What if one of the parties is a United States citizen domiciled abroad? See Van Der Schelling v. United States News & World Report, Inc., 213 F.Supp. 756 (E.D.Pa.1963), affirmed 324 F.2d 956 (3d Cir.) (not a citizen of a State). Does this result make sense in the light of any justificatory rationale? What of persons who are nationals, but not citizens of the United States? See 8 U.S. C.A. § 1468. And what of actions between aliens, a foreign state and an alien, and between foreign states? See Hodgson v. Bowerbank, 9 U.S. (5 Cranch) 303, 3 L.Ed. 108 (1809). Should the federal courts have subject matter adjudicatory authority in these cases?

(5) Originally, a citizen of the District of Columbia or a territory was not a "citizen of a state" within the meaning of 28 U.S.C.A. § 1332. In 1940, Congress extended federal adjudicatory power to controversies "between citizens of different States, or citizens of the District of Columbia, the Territory of Hawaii, or Alaska, and any State or Territory." Act of April 20, 1940, ch. 117, 54 Stat. 143. This Act was upheld by the Supreme Court in National Mutual Insurance Co. v. Tidewater Transfer Co., 337 U.S. 582, 69 S.Ct. 1173, 93 L.Ed. 1556 (1949). Was this decision correct? A majority of the Court rejected the argument that a citizen of the District was a citizen of a state in the sense of Article III of the Constitution, and a different majority rejected the argument that the Act was valid legislation under Article I which gives Congress the power to legislate for the inhabitants of the District. Upon the revision of the Judicial Code in 1948, the definition of "States" was amended to include "the Territories and the District of Columbia". Act of June 25, 1948, ch. 646, § 1332, 62 Stat. 869, 930. In 1952, Puerto Rico acquired a new constitution which designated it as the "Commonwealth of Puerto Rico". Since this raised doubt whether Puerto Rico was still a territory under 28 U.S.C.A. § 1332, the latter provision was amended to include in the definition of "States" "the Territories, the District of Columbia, and the Commonwealth of Puerto Rico." Act of July 26, 1956, c. 740, 70 Stat. 658. Is this amendment constitutional?

(6) The provision in subsection (c) of 28 U.S.C.A. § 1332 that a corporation is a citizen of the state of its incorporation and of the state in which it has its principal place of business was added in 1958. Act of July 25, 1958, 72 Stat. 415. Is it constitutional? Traditionally, since the decision in Marshall v. Baltimore & Ohio Railroad Co., 57 U.S. (16 How.) 314, 14 L.Ed. 953 (1853), a corporation has been considered a citizen of the state in which it is incorporated. Where does a corporation have its principal place of business? See Kelly v. United States Steel Corp., 284 F.2d 850 (3d Cir.1960) (center of activities). Compare Anniston Soil Pipe Co. v. Central Foundry Co., 329 F.2d 313 (5th Cir. 1964) (place of bulk of corporate activities) with Scot Typewriter Co. v. Underwood Corp., 170 F.Supp. 862 (S.D.N.Y.1959) (home office). See also Wright, Federal Courts § 27, at 152–3 (4th ed. 1983) (suggesting the last named test if the first cannot be applied); Comment, A Corporation's Principal Place of Business for Federal Diversity Jurisdiction, 38 N.Y.U.L.Rev. 148 (1963); Note, Location of Corporation's Principal Place of Business, 47 Iowa L.Rev. 1151 (1962); Comment, New Federal Jurisdictional Statute Achieves Early Success in Reducing Number of District Court Case Filings But Presents Interpretive Difficulties, 58 Colum.L.Rev. 1287, 1294–99 (1958).

(7) Is a corporation that is incorporated in more than one state a citizen of every state in which it is incorporated? See Gavin v. Hudson & Manhattan Railroad Co., 90 F.Supp. 172 (D.N.J.1950), reversed 185 F.2d 104 (3d Cir.1950); Friedenthal, New Limitations on Federal Jurisdiction, 11 Stan.L.Rev. 213, 236–41 (1959).

(8) Unincorporated associations do not possess an independent citizenship for diversity purposes. How can an action involving such an association be brought in a federal court? See International Allied Printing Trades Associa-

tion v. Master Printers Union, 34 F.Supp. 178 (D.N.J.1940); American Law Institute, Study of the Division of Jurisdiction Between State and Federal Courts 10, 114–117 (1969); Comment, Diversity Jurisdiction for Unincorporated Associations, 75 Yale L.J. 138 (1965). But see Puerto Rico v. Russell & Co., 288 U.S. 476, 484, 53 S.Ct. 447, 77 L.Ed. 903 (1933) (Puerto Rican *sociedad en comandita* assimilated to corporation).

(9) Can diversity be created by assignment (see 28 U.S.C.A. § 1359), change of domicile (see Morris v. Gilmer, 129 U.S. 315, 9 S.Ct. 289, 32 L.Ed. 690 (1889)), reincorporation in another state (see Miller & Lux v. East Side Canal and Irrigation Co., 211 U.S. 293, 29 S.Ct. 111, 53 L.Ed. 189 (1908)), or the appointment of an administrator or other representative of a different citizenship (see Bullard v. City of Cisco, 290 U.S. 179, 54 S.Ct. 177, 78 L.Ed. 254 (1933))? Can it be defeated by any of these means? See Kramer v. Caribbean Mills, Inc., 394 U.S. 823, 89 S.Ct. 1487, 23 L.Ed.2d 9 (1969) (assignment for collection only and motivated by desire to create diversity is invalid under 28 U.S.C.A. § 1359). See further American Law Institute, Study of the Division of Jurisdiction Between State and Federal Courts 22–23, 156–161 (1969).

(10) In 1988, Congress added a provision to Section 1332(c) declaring the legal representative of the estate of a decedent, an infant or an incompetent to have the citizenship of the decedent, infant, or incompetent. This precludes attempts to create or defeat diversity by choosing a representative of the desired citizenship. For an example of such an attempt, see Mecom v. Fitzsimmons Drilling Co., 284 U.S. 183, 52 S.Ct. 84, 76 L.Ed. 233 (1931).

(11) Does the plaintiff control the alignment of the parties or should the court realign them if necessary so as to properly reflect interests that are genuinely adverse? It is reasonably settled that the court must align. See, e.g., Dawson v. Columbia Avenue Savings Fund, Safe Deposit, Title & Trust Co., 197 U.S. 178, 25 S.Ct. 420, 49 L.Ed. 713 (1905). If the court must realign, how is it to determine which interests are adverse? In Smith v. Sperling, 354 U.S. 91, 77 S.Ct. 1112, 1 L.Ed.2d 1205 (1957); Swanson v. Traer, 354 U.S. 91, 77 S.Ct. 1119, 1 L.Ed.2d 1205 (1957), the Supreme Court, by a 5–4 decision, reversed a dismissal by a lower court in a derivative stockholders action for lack of diversity resulting from a realignment made after a fifteen day hearing. The majority said (at 96–97):

> "It seems to us that the proper course [in realigning the parties] is not to try out the issues presented by the charges of wrongdoing but to determine the issue of antagonism on the face of the pleadings and by the virtue of the controversy. The bill and answer normally determine whether the management is antagonistic to the stockholder . . . ." Collusion to satisfy the jurisdictional requirements of the District Court may, of course, always be shown . . . ."

What is collusion in this context and how can it be shown? See Developments in the Law: Multiparty Litigation in the Federal Courts, 71 Harv.L.Rev. 874, 958–61 (1958). See also Reed v. Robilio, 376 F.2d 392 (6th Cir.1967), on remand 273 F.Supp. 954 (W.D.Tenn.), affirmed 400 F.2d 730 (6th Cir.1968); Standard Oil Co. of California v. Perkins, 347 F.2d 379 (9th Cir.1965).

(12) Is a stateless person a citizen or subject of a foreign state? See Shoemaker v. Malaxa, 241 F.2d 129 (2d Cir.1957); Blair Holdings Corp. v. Rubinstein, 133 F.Supp. 496 (S.D.N.Y.1955). Could and should 28 U.S.C.A. § 1332(a)(2) be amended to reject this result?

(13) Note that the Eleventh Amendment precludes suits by citizens of a State or a citizen or subject of a foreign State against a State of the United States. Recent decisions of the court have limited states' sovereign immunity. In Pennsylvania v. Union Gas Co., ___ U.S. ___, 109 S.Ct. 2273, 105 L.Ed.2d 1 (1989), the court held that a state could be sued for money damages under the Comprehensive Environmental Response, Compensation, and Liability Act of 1980 (CERCLA) as amended by the Super-fund Amendments and Reauthorization Act of 1986 (SARA). Other decisions indicate reluctance to abrogate states' sovereign immunity on the basis of expansive statutory readings. See Dellmuth v. Muth, ___ U.S. ___, 109 S.Ct. 2397, 105 L.Ed.2d 181 (1989), (Education of the Handicapped Act does not abrogate state's sovereign immunity under Eleventh Amendment); Will v. Michigan Dept. of State Police, ___ U.S. ___, 109 S.Ct. 2304, 105 L.Ed.2d 45 (1989) (a state and state officials acting in their official capacities cannot be sued under 42 U.S.C.A. § 1983 because they are not "persons" within the meaning of that statute); Hoffman v. Connecticut Department of Income Maintenance, ___ U.S. ___, 109 S.Ct. 2818, 106 L.Ed.2d 76 (1989) (waiver of sovereign immunity in section 106(c) of the Bankruptcy Code applies only to claims specified in sections 106(a) and (b)).

2. FEDERAL QUESTION

FRANCHISE TAX BOARD OF THE STATE OF CALIFORNIA v. CONSTRUCTION LABORERS VACATION TRUST FOR SOUTHERN CALIFORNIA

Supreme Court of the United States, 1983.
463 U.S. 1, 103 S.Ct. 2841, 77 L.Ed.2d 420.

JUSTICE BRENNAN delivered the opinion of the Court.*

Appellee Construction Laborers Vacation Trust for Southern California (CLVT) is a trust established by an agreement between four associations of employers active in the construction industry in Southern California and the Southern California District Council of Laborers, an arm of the District Council and affiliated locals of the Laborers' International Union of North America. The purpose of the agreement and trust was to establish a mechanism for administering the provisions of a collective bargaining agreement that grants construction workers a yearly paid vacation. The trust agreement expressly proscribes any assignment, pledge, or encumbrance of funds held in trust by CLVT. The plan that CLVT administers is unquestionably an "employee welfare benefit plan" within the meaning of § 3 of ERISA, 29 U.S.C. § 1002(1), and CLVT and its individual trustees are thereby subject to extensive regulation under titles I and III of ERISA.

Appellant Franchise Tax Board is a California agency charged with enforcement of that State's personal income tax law. California law authorizes appellant to require any person in possession of "credits or other personal property belonging to a taxpayer" "to withhold . . . the amount of any tax, interest, or penalties due from the taxpayer . . . and to transmit the amount withheld to the Franchise Tax

* Some footnotes omitted; others renumbered.

Board." Cal.Rev. & Tax Code Ann. § 18817 (West Supp.1982). Any person who, upon notice by the Franchise Tax Board, fails to comply with its request to withhold and to transmit funds becomes personally liable for the amounts identified in the notice. § 18818.

In June 1980, the Franchise Tax Board filed a complaint in state court against CLVT and its trustees. Under the heading "First Cause of Action," appellant alleged that CLVT had failed to comply with three levies issued under § 18817, concluding with the allegation that it had been "damaged in a sum . . . not to exceed $380.56 plus interest from June 1, 1980." App. 3–8. Under the heading "Second Cause of Action," appellant incorporated its previous allegations and added:

> "There was at the time of the levies alleged above and continues to be an actual controversy between the parties concerning their respective legal rights and duties. The Board [appellant] contends that defendants [CLVT] are obligated and required by law to pay over to the Board all amounts held . . . in favor of the Board's delinquent taxpayers. On the other hand, defendants contend that section 514 of ERISA preempts state law and that the trustees lack the power to honor the levies made upon them by the State of California.
>
> " . . . [D]efendants will continue to refuse to honor the Board's levies in this regard. Accordingly, a declaration by this court of the parties' respective rights is required to fully and finally resolve this controversy." Id., at 8–9.

In a prayer for relief, appellant requested damages for defendants' failure to honor the levies and a declaration that defendants are "legally obligated to honor all future levies by the Board." Id., at 9.

CLVT removed the case to the United States District Court for the Central District of California, and the court denied the Franchise Tax Board's motion for remand to the state court. On the merits, the District Court ruled that ERISA did not preempt the State's power to levy on funds held in trust by CLVT. CLVT appealed, and the Court of Appeals reversed. 679 F.2d 1307 (CA9 1982). . . . We now hold that this case was not within the removal jurisdiction conferred by 28 U.S.C. § 1441, and therefore we do not reach the merits of the preemption question.

Since the first version of § 1331 was enacted, Act of Mar. 3, 1875, ch. 137, § 1, 18 Stat. 470, the statutory phrase "arising under the Constitution, laws, or treaties of the United States" has resisted all attempts to frame a single, precise definition for determining which cases fall within, and which cases fall outside, the original jurisdiction of the district courts. Especially when considered in light of § 1441's removal jurisdiction, the phrase "arising under" masks a welter of issues regarding the interrelation of federal and state authority and the proper management of the federal judicial system.[1]

---

1. The statute's "arising under" language tracks similar language in art. III, § 2 of the Constitution, which has been construed as permitting Congress to extend

The most familiar definition of the statutory "arising under" limitation is Justice Holmes' statement, "A suit arises under the law that creates the cause of action." American Well Works Co. v. Layne & Bowler Co., 241 U.S. 257, 260, 36 S.Ct. 585, 586, 60 L.Ed. 987 (1916). However, it is well settled that Justice Holmes' test is more useful for describing the vast majority of cases that come within the district courts' original jurisdiction than it is for describing which cases are beyond district court jurisdiction. We have often held that a case "arose under" federal law where the vindication of a right under state law necessarily turned on some construction of federal law, see, e.g., Smith v. Kansas City Title & Trust Co., 255 U.S. 180, 41 S.Ct. 243, 65 L.Ed. 577 (1921); Hopkins v. Walker, 244 U.S. 486, 37 S.Ct. 711, 61 L.Ed. 1270 (1917), and even the most ardent proponent of the Holmes test has admitted that it has been rejected as an exclusionary principle, see Flournoy v. Wiener, 321 U.S. 253, 270–272, 64 S.Ct. 548, 556–557, 88 L.Ed. 708 (1944) (Frankfurter, J., dissenting). See also T.B. Harms Co. v. Eliscu, 339 F.2d 823, 827 (CA2 1964) (Friendly, J.). Leading commentators have suggested that for purposes of § 1331 an action "arises under" federal law "if in order for the plaintiff to secure the relief sought he will be obliged to establish both the correctness and the applicability to his case of a proposition of federal law." P. Bator, P. Mishkin, D. Shapiro & H. Wechsler, Hart & Wechsler's The Federal Courts and the Federal System 889 (2d ed. 1973) (hereinafter Hart & Wechsler); cf. *T.B. Harms Co.,* supra ("a case may 'arise under' a law of the United States if the complaint discloses a need for determining the meaning or application of such a law").

One powerful doctrine has emerged, however—the "well-pleaded complaint" rule—which as a practical matter severely limits the number of cases in which state law "creates the cause of action" that may be initiated in or removed to federal district court, thereby avoiding more-or-less automatically a number of potentially serious federal-state conflicts.

> "[W]hether a case is one arising under the Constitution or a law or treaty of the United States, in the sense of the jurisdictional statute, . . . must be determined from what necessarily appears in the plaintiff's statement of his own claim in the bill or declaration, unaided by anything alleged in anticipation of avoidance of defenses which it is thought the defendant may interpose." Taylor v. Anderson, 234 U.S. 74, 75–76, 34 S.Ct. 724, 58 L.Ed. 1218 (1914).

federal jurisdiction to any case of which federal law potentially "forms an ingredient," see Osborn v. Bank of the United States, 9 Wheat. 738, 823, 6 L.Ed. 204 (1824), and its limited legislative history suggests that the 44th Congress may have meant to "confer the whole power which the Constitution conferred," 2 Cong.Rec. 4986 (1874) (remarks of Sen. Carpenter). Nevertheless, we have only recently reaffirmed what has long been recognized—that "Article III 'arising under' jurisdiction is broader than federal question jurisdiction under § 1331." Verlinden B.V. v. Central Bank of Nigeria, 461 U.S. 480, 495, 103 S.Ct. 1962, 1972, 76 L.Ed.2d 811 (1983).

Thus, a federal court does not have original jurisdiction over a case in which the complaint presents a state-law cause of action, but also asserts that federal law deprives the defendant of a defense he may raise, *Taylor v. Anderson,* supra; Louisville & Nashville R. Co. v. Mottley, 211 U.S. 149, 29 S.Ct. 42, 53 L.Ed. 126 (1908), or that a federal defense the defendant may raise is not sufficient to defeat the claim, Tennessee v. Union & Planters' Bank, 152 U.S. 454, 14 S.Ct. 654, 38 L.Ed. 511 (1894). "Although such allegations show that very likely, in the course of the litigation, a question under the Constitution would arise, they do not show that the suit, that is, the plaintiff's original cause of action, arises under the Constitution." Louisville & Nashville R. Co. v. Mottley, supra, 211 U.S., at 152, 29 S.Ct., at 43. For better or worse, under the present statutory scheme as it has existed since 1887, a defendant may not remove a case to federal court unless the *plaintiff's* complaint establishes that the case "arises under" federal law.[2]

Simply to state these principles is not to apply them to the case at hand. Appellants' complaint sets forth two "causes of action," one of which expressly refers to ERISA; if either comes within the original jurisdiction of the federal courts, removal was proper as to the whole case.

* * *

. . . For appellant's first cause of action—to enforce its levy, under § 18818—a straight-forward application of the well-pleaded complaint rule precludes original federal court jurisdictions.

* * *

Appellant's declaratory judgment action poses a more difficult problem. Whereas the question of federal preemption is relevant to appellant's first cause of action only as a potential defense, it is a necessary element of the declaratory judgment claim. Under Cal.Civ. Proc.Code § 1060, a party with an interest in property may bring an action for a declaration of another party's legal rights and duties with

---

2. The well-pleaded complaint rule applies to the original jurisdiction of the district courts as well as to their removal jurisdiction. See Phillips Petroleum Co. v. Texaco, Inc., 415 U.S. 125, 127, 94 S.Ct. 1002, 1003–1004, 39 L.Ed.2d 209 (1974) (per curiam) (case brought originally in federal court); Pan American Petroleum Corp. v. Superior Court, 366 U.S. 656, 663, 81 S.Ct. 1303, 1307–1308, 6 L.Ed.2d 584 (1961) (attack on jurisdiction of state court).

It is possible to conceive of a rational jurisdictional system in which the answer as well as the complaint would be consulted before a determination was made whether the case "arose under" federal law, or in which original and removal jurisdiction were not co-extensive. Indeed, until the 1887 amendments to the 1875 Act, Act of Mar. 3, 1887, ch. 373, 24 Stat. 552, as amended by Act of Aug. 13, 1888,

ch. 866, 25 Stat. 433, the well-pleaded complaint rule was not applied in full force to cases removed from state court; the defendant's petition for removal could furnish the necessary guarantee that the case necessarily presented a substantial question of federal law. See Railroad Co. v. Mississippi, 102 U.S. 135, 140, 26 L.Ed. 96 (1880); Gold–Washing & Water Co. v. Keyes, 96 U.S. 199, 203–204, 24 L.Ed. 656 (1877). Commentators have repeatedly proposed that some mechanism be established to permit removal of cases in which a federal defense may be dispositive. See, e.g., American Law Institute, Study of the Division of Jurisdiction Between State and Federal Courts § 1312, at 188–194 (1969) (ALI Study); Wechsler, Federal Jurisdiction and the Revision of the Judicial Code, 13 Law & Contemp.Prob. 216, 233–234 (1948). But those proposals have not been adopted.

respect to that property upon showing that there is an "actual controversy relating to the respective rights and duties" of the parties. The only questions in dispute between the parties in this case concern the rights and duties of CLVT and its trustees under ERISA. Not only does appellant's request for a declaratory judgment under California law clearly encompass questions governed by ERISA, but appellant's complaint identifies no other questions as a subject of controversy between the parties. Such questions must be raised in a well-pleaded complaint for a declaratory judgment. Therefore, it is clear on the face of its well-pleaded complaint that appellant may not obtain the relief it seeks in its second cause of action ("[t]hat the court declare defendants legally obligated to honor all future levies by the Board upon [CLVT]," App. 9) without a construction of ERISA and/or an adjudication of its preemptive effect and constitutionality—all questions of federal law.

Appellant argues that original federal court jurisdiction over such a complaint is foreclosed by our decision in Skelly Oil Co. v. Phillips Petroleum Co., 339 U.S. 667, 70 S.Ct. 876, 94 L.Ed. 1194 (1950). As we shall see, however, *Skelly Oil* is not directly controlling.

* * *

Skelly Oil has come to stand for the proposition that "if, but for the availability of the declaratory judgment procedure, the federal claim would arise only as a defense to a state created action, jurisdiction is lacking." 10A C. Wright, A. Miller & M. Kane, Federal Practice and Procedure § 2767, at 744–745 (2d ed. 1983).

Our interpretation of the federal Declaratory Judgment Act in *Skelly Oil* does not apply of its own force to state declaratory judgment statutes, many of which antedate the federal statute, see Developments in the Law—Declaratory Judgments—1941–1949, 62 Harv.L.Rev. 787, 790–791 (1949). Cf. Nashville, C. & St. L.R. Co. v. Wallace, 288 U.S. 249, 264–265, 53 S.Ct. 345, 348–349, 77 L.Ed. 730 (1933) (Supreme Court appellate jurisdiction over federal questions in a state declaratory judgment).

Yet while *Skelly Oil* itself is limited to the federal Declaratory Judgment Act, fidelity to its spirit leads us to extend it to state declaratory judgment actions as well.

* * *

. . . Therefore we hold that under the jurisdictional statutes as they now stand federal courts do not have original jurisdiction, nor do they acquire jurisdiction on removal, when a federal question is presented by a complaint for a state declaratory judgment, but *Skelly Oil* would bar jurisdiction if the plaintiff had sought a federal declaratory judgment.

The question, then, is whether a federal district court could take jurisdiction of appellant's declaratory judgment claim had it been brought under 28 U.S.C. § 2201.

* * *

Our concern in this case is consistent application of a system of statutes conferring original federal court jurisdiction, as they have been interpreted by this Court over many years. Under our interpretations, Congress has given the lower federal courts jurisdiction to hear, originally or by removal from a state court, only those cases in which a well-pleaded complaint establishes either that federal law creates the cause of action or that the plaintiff's right to relief necessarily depends on resolution of a substantial question of federal law. We hold that a suit by state tax authorities both to enforce its levies against funds held in trust pursuant to an ERISA-covered employee benefit plan, and to declare the validity of the levies notwithstanding ERISA, is neither a creature of ERISA itself nor a suit of which the federal courts will take jurisdiction because it turns on a question of federal law. Accordingly, we vacate the judgment of the Court of Appeals and remand so that this case may be remanded to the Superior Court of the State of California for the County of Los Angeles.

NOTES

(1) Is the statutory definition of "federal question" adjudicatory power as embracive as the constitutional definition? See American Law Institute, Study of the Division of Jurisdiction Between State and Federal Courts 176–182 (1969).

(2) In the principal case, did the Court decide correctly that, under the well-pleaded complaint rule, the claim for a declaratory judgment was based on federal law?

(3) In Skelly Oil Co. v. Phillips Petroleum Co., 339 U.S. 667, 70 S.Ct. 876, 94 L.Ed. 1194 (1950), the plaintiff sought a declaratory judgment that certain contracts had not been properly terminated. Whether the attempted termination was proper depended on whether the Federal Power Commission had issued a certificate of public convenience and necessity under the federal Natural Gas Act. The court held that it had no competence under § 1331. Does this ruling support the proposition for which it is cited in the principal case? Did the well-pleaded complaint in this case raise an issue of federal law?

(4) In Merrell Dow Pharmaceuticals Inc. v. Thompson, 478 U.S. 804, 106 S.Ct. 3229, 92 L.Ed.2d 650 (1986), plaintiffs sought recovery for injuries suffered as a result of the use of one of defendant's drugs. Their complaint alleged breach of warranty, strict liability, negligence, gross negligence and fraud. It also alleged that the defendant has misbranded the drug in violation of the Federal Food, Drug and Cosmetics Act. Defendant sought to remove the case to the federal court. The Supreme Court ruled removal to be improper. Is this decision compatible with that in *Skelly,* Note (3) supra?

(5) Interposition of a defense or counterclaim based on federal law does not create federal question competence. See, for a recent decision, Oklahoma Tax Commission v. Graham, ___ U.S. ___, 109 S.Ct. 1519, 103 L.Ed.2d 924 (1989), holding that, in an action against an Indian tribe to recover state excise taxes on bingo games and cigarette sales, interposition of a defense of tribal sovereign immunity does not warrant removal to the federal court.

(6) On federal question competence, see also Doernberg, There's No Reason for It; It's Just Our Policy: Why the Well–Pleaded Complaint Rule Sabotages the Purposes of Federal Question Jurisdiction 38 Hastings L.J. 597 (1987).

(7) Note that neither the federal question competence of 28 U.S.C.A. § 1331 nor the diversity competence of 28 U.S.C.A. § 1332 is exclusive in the sense of making the federal courts the only tribunals competent to adjudicate the controversies defined in these sections. The general rule is that, in the absence of an express provision to the contrary, the adjudicatory power of the federal courts is concurrent with that of the state courts. However, a number of controversies are reserved for adjudication exclusively by the federal courts. See, e.g., 15 U.S.C.A. § 15 (antitrust laws); 15 U.S.C.A. § 78aa (Securities and Exchange Act); 28 U.S.C.A. § 1333(1) (admiralty); 28 U.S.C.A. § 1334 (bankruptcy); 28 U.S.C.A. § 1338 (patents and copyrights); 28 U.S.C.A. § 1351 (actions against foreign consuls and vice consuls); 28 U.S.C.A. § 1335 (actions to recover a penalty, fine, or forfeiture under federal law); 28 U.S.C.A. § 1350 (actions involving seizure under federal law on land or upon waters not within admiralty and maritime jurisdiction). See also Note, Exclusive Jurisdiction of the Federal Courts in Private Civil Actions, 70 Harv.L.Rev. 509 (1957). Which of the following considerations are relevant to the determination of whether federal adjudicatory power should be exclusive: the need for uniformity, the relative case loads in the state and federal courts, the special nature of the subject matter, the quality of the federal courts, or any other considerations you may think of?

NOTE ON THE IMPACT OF THE DECLARATORY JUDGMENT ACT

Three possible standards have been suggested for determining whether there is federal question adjudicatory authority in an action for a declaratory judgment: (1) the usual standard, (2) adjudicatory authority exists only if it would exist in an action for coercive relief brought by the plaintiff, and (3) adjudicatory authority exists only if it would exist in an action for coercive relief brought by either party. See Note, Developments in the Law—Declaratory Judgments—1941–1949, 62 Harv.L.Rev. 787, 802–803 (1949). See also Note, Federal Question Jurisdiction of Federal Courts and the Declaratory Judgment Act, 4 Vand.L.Rev. 827 (1951).

DUKE POWER CO. v. CAROLINA ENVIRONMENTAL STUDY GROUP, INC.

Supreme Court of the United States, 1978.
438 U.S. 59, 98 S.Ct. 2620, 57 L.Ed.2d 595.

In this case, Chief Justice Burger, writing for the majority, ruled that there was the requisite subject matter authority (at 68–71):

As a threshold matter, we must address the question of whether the District Court had subject-matter jurisdiction over appellees' claims, despite the fact that none of the parties raised this issue and the District Court did not consider it. See Liberty Mutual Insurance Co. v. Wetzel, 424 U.S. 737, 740, 96 S.Ct. 1202, 1204, 47 L.Ed.2d 435 (1976). Appellees' complaint alleges jurisdiction under 28 U.S.C.A. § 1337

(1976 ed.), which provides for original jurisdiction in the district courts over "any civil action or proceeding arising under any Act of Congress regulating commerce or protecting trade and commerce against restraints and monopolies." Our reading of the pleadings, however, indicates that appellees' claims do not "arise under" the Price–Anderson Act as that statutory language has been interpreted in prior decisions. See Peyton v. Railway Express Agency, 316 U.S. 350, 353, 62 S.Ct. 1171, 1172, 86 L.Ed. 1525 (1942).

Specifically, as we read the complaint, appellees are making two basic challenges to the Act—both of which find their moorings in the Fifth Amendment. First, appellees contend that the Due Process Clause protects them against arbitrary governmental action adversely affecting their property rights and that the Price–Anderson Act—which both creates the source of the underlying injury and limits the recovery therefor—constitutes such arbitrary action. And second, they are contending that in the event of a nuclear accident their property would be "taken" without any assurance of just compensation. The Price–Anderson Act is the instrument of the taking since on this record, without it, there would be no power plants and no possibility of an accident. Implicit in the complaint is also the assumption that there exists a cause of action directly under the Constitution to vindicate appellees' federal rights through a suit against the NRC, the executive agency charged with enforcement and administration of the allegedly unconstitutional statute. Appellees' right to relief thus depends not on the interpretation or construction of the Price–Anderson Act itself, but instead "upon the construction or application of the Constitution," Smith v. Kansas City Title & Trust Co., 255 U.S. 180, 199, 41 S.Ct. 243, 245, 65 L.Ed. 577 (1921). Hence, if there exists jurisdiction to hear appellees' claims at all, it must be derived from 28 U.S.C.A. § 1331(a) (1976 ed.), the general federal-question statute, rather than from § 1337—the jurisdictional base pleaded.

For purposes of determining whether jurisdiction exists under § 1331(a) to resolve appellees' claims, it is not necessary to decide whether appellees' alleged cause of action against the NRC based directly on the Constitution is in fact a cause of action "on which [appellees] could actually recover." Bell v. Hood, 327 U.S. 678, 682, 66 S.Ct. 773, 776, 90 L.Ed. 939 (1946). Instead, the test is whether " 'the cause of action alleged is *so patently without merit* as to justify . . . the court's dismissal for want of jurisdiction.' " Hagans v. Lavine, 415 U.S. 528, 542–543, 94 S.Ct. 1372, 1382, 39 L.Ed.2d 577 (1974), quoting Bell v. Hood, supra, at 683, 66 S.Ct., at 776. (Emphasis added.) See also Oneida Indian Nation v. County of Oneida, 414 U.S. 661, 666, 94 S.Ct. 772, 778, 39 L.Ed.2d 73 (1974) (test is whether right claimed is "so insubstantial, implausible, foreclosed by prior decisions of this Court, or otherwise completely devoid of merit as not to involve a federal controversy"). In light of prior decisions, for example, Bivens v. Six Unknown Federal Narcotics Agents, 403 U.S. 388, 91 S.Ct. 1999, 29 L.Ed.2d 619 (1971) and Hagans v. Lavine, supra, as well as the general admonition that "where federally protected rights have been invaded courts will be alert to adjust their remedies so as to grant the necessary relief," Bell v. Hood, supra, at 684, we conclude that appellees' allegations are sufficient to sustain jurisdiction under § 1331(a).

The further question of whether appellees' cause of action under the Constitution is one generally to be recognized need not be decided here. The question does not directly implicate our jurisdiction, see Bell v. Hood, supra, was not raised in the court below, was not briefed, and was not addressed during oral argument. As we noted last Term in a similar context, questions of this sort should not be resolved on such an inadequate record; leaving them unresolved is no bar to full consideration of the merits. See Mount Healthy City Board of Education v. Doyle, 429 U.S. 274, 278–279, 97 S.Ct. 568, 571–572, 50 L.Ed.2d 471 (1977). It is enough for present purposes that the claimed cause of action to vindicate appellees' constitutional rights is sufficiently substantial and colorable to sustain jurisdiction under § 1331(a).

[Justices Rehnquist and Stevens disagreed with this analysis:]

Giving the conclusory allegations of appellees' complaint the most liberal possible reading, they purport to establish only two grounds for the declaratory relief requested. First, they contend that the Price–Anderson Act deprives them of their property without due process of law in that it irrationally limits the tort recovery otherwise available in the North Carolina courts. Second, they contend that the Act works an unconstitutional taking of their property for public use without just compensation. They purport to base District Court jurisdiction upon 28 U.S.C.A. § 1337 (1976 ed.) which covers "any civil action or proceeding arising under any Act of Congress regulating commerce or protecting trade and commerce against restraints and monopolies."

I

It is apparent that appellees' first asserted basis for relief does not state a claim "arising under" the Price–Anderson Act. Their complaint alleges that the operation of the two power plants will cause immediate injury to property within their vicinity. App. 32, ¶ 21. The District Court explicitly found that these injuries "give rise to an immediate right of action for redress. Under the law of North Carolina a right of action arises as soon as a wrongful act has created 'any injury, however slight,' to the plaintiff." 431 F.Supp. 203, 221 (W.D. N.C.1977) (citations omitted). This right of action provided by state, not federal, law is the property of which the appellees contend the Act deprives them without due process. Thus, the constitutionality of the Act becomes relevant only if the appellant Duke Power Co. were to invoke the Act as a defense to appellees' suit for recovery under their North Carolina right of action.

It has long been established that the mere anticipation of a possible federal defense to a state cause of action is not sufficient to invoke the federal-question jurisdiction of the district courts.

*   *   *

Nor does the fact that appellees seek only declaratory relief under the Declaratory Judgment Act, 28 U.S.C.A. § 2201 (1976 ed.), support a different result. This Court has held that the well-pleaded complaint rule applied in *Mottley* is fully applicable in cases seeking only declaratory relief, because the Declaratory Judgment Act merely expands the remedies available in the district courts without expanding their jurisdiction. "It would turn into the federal courts a vast current of litigation indubitably arising under State law, in the sense that the right to be vindicated was State-created, if a suit for a declaration of rights could be brought into the federal courts merely because an anticipated defense derived from federal law." Skelly Oil Co. v. Phillips Petroleum Co., 339 U.S. 667, 673, 70 S.Ct. 876, 880, 94 L.Ed. 1194 (1950).

*   *   *

. . . The Court's theory is that the complaint alleges the existence of an implied right of action under the Fifth Amendment to obtain relief against arbitrary federal statutes. It can hardly be said that this theory of the case emerges with crystal clarity from either the complaint or the brief of the appellees.

More importantly, there is no allegation in this complaint that the Nuclear Regulatory Commission has taken or will take any unconstitutional action at all. The complaint alleges only that the Commission granted construction permits to Duke, and that it will enter into an agreement "to indemnify Duke for any nuclear incident exceeding the amount of $125,000,000 subject to a maximum liability of $560,000,000." App. 31, ¶ 13. Neither of these actions is alleged to be unconstitutional. . . .

It simply cannot be said that these allegations make out an actual controversy against the Commission. . . .

. . . In short, appellees' only conceivable controversy is with Duke, over whom the District Court had no jurisdiction.

II

As appellees themselves describe the second aspect of their complaint, "the central issue is whether in the circumstances of this case, the complete destruction of appellees' property by a nuclear accident, occurring at one of Duke's plants, would be a 'taking' by the United States, as that term is defined in the Fifth Amendment." Brief for Appellees 62. This statement makes clear that appellees' claim arises not under the Price–Anderson Act but under the Fifth Amendment itself. Jurisdiction under § 1337 extends only to actions vindicating rights created by an Act of Congress. . . .

The District Court does have jurisdiction to consider claims of taking under the Tucker Act, 28 U.S.C.A. § 1346(a)(2) (1976 ed.), where the amount in controversy does not exceed $10,000. "But the Act has long been construed as authorizing only actions for money judgments and not suits for equitable relief against the United States." Richardson v. Morris, 409 U.S. 464, 465, 93 S.Ct. 629, 631, 34 L.Ed.2d 647 (1973). It is incontrovertibly established that neither the Court of Claims nor the district courts have jurisdiction under the Tucker Act to issue the sort of declaratory relief granted here. Compare ibid., with United States v. King, 395 U.S. 1, 89 S.Ct. 1501, 23 L.Ed.2d 52 (1969). Thus, the record does not establish any jurisdictional basis upon which the District Court could grant declaratory relief on appellees' taking claim.

* * *

NOTES

(1) Was the claim that the building of the reactor would diminish property values and the plaintiffs' enjoyment of their property a good one under the applicable substantive law? If so, did it arise under federal law? Was the claim that, in case of a disaster, the Price–Anderson Act would unconstitutionally limit plaintiffs' recovery, premised on a contingency that had not occurred? If so, why did the Court find this hypothetical case justiciable? In any event, even if this claim was justiciable, under the well-pleaded complaint rule, did it arise under federal law or does the dissent have the better of the argument?

(2) Plaintiffs sought damages in a federal district court, alleging that the defendants, F.B.I. agents, had imprisoned and searched them in violation of their constitutional rights under the Fourth and Fifth Amendments. The district court dismissed on its own motion on the ground that the action was not one that "arises under the Constitution or laws of the United States." The Supreme Court reversed the affirmance of the district court's decision by the Ninth Circuit. Bell v. Hood, 327 U.S. 678, 681, 66 S.Ct. 773, 90 L.Ed. 939 (1946):

> "Whether or not the complaint as drafted states a common law action in trespass made actionable by state law, it is clear from the way it was drawn that petitioners seek recovery squarely on the ground that respondents violated the Fourth and Fifth Amendments . . . .. It cannot be doubted therefore that it was the pleaders' purpose to make violation of these Constitutional provisions the basis of this suit. Before deciding that there is no jurisdiction, the district court must look to the way the complaint is drawn to see if it is drawn so as to claim a right to recover under the Constitution and laws of the United States. To that extent, 'the party who brings a suit is master to decide what law he will rely upon, and . . . does determine whether he will bring a "suit arising under" the . . . [Constitution or laws] of the United States by his declaration or bill.' The Fair v. Kohler Die & Speciality Co., 228 U.S. 22, 25, 33 S.Ct. 410, 411."

For a similar statement, see Pan American Petroleum Corp. v. Superior Court of Delaware, 366 U.S. 656, 662–63, 81 S.Ct. 1303, 1307, 6 L.Ed.2d 584 (1961); Fountain v. Metropolitan Atlanta Rapid Transit Authority, 678 F.2d 1038, 1042 (11th Cir.1982). *Bell v. Hood* was followed in a Title VII employment discrimination suit. Fellows v. Universal Restaurants, Inc., 701 F.2d 447 (5th Cir.1983).

(3) In *Bell v. Hood*, was federal law a material element of the plaintiff's claim for relief? Upon remand by the Supreme Court, the district court in Bell v. Hood dismissed the complaint on the ground that it failed to state a claim for relief. 71 F.Supp. 813 (S.D.Cal.1947). Was this decision, which was not appealed, compatible with that of the Supreme Court? Does a claim for relief

arise under federal law simply because it is asserted that federal law supports it? In *Bell v. Hood*, the majority opinion also said that " . . . the right of the petitioners to recover under their complaint will be sustained if the Constitution and laws of the United States are given one construction and will be defeated if they are given another. For this reason the district court has jurisdiction" (327 U.S. at 685). In Bivens v. Six Unknown Named Agents of Federal Bureau of Narcotics, 403 U.S. 388, 91 S.Ct. 1999, 29 L.Ed.2d 619 (1971), the Supreme Court answered in the affirmative the question, said to have been reserved in *Bell v. Hood*, of "whether violation of that command [i.e., that of the Fourth Amendment] by a federal agent acting under color of his authority gives rise to a cause of action for damages consequent upon his unconstitutional conduct." Thus, in retrospect, the plaintiff's claim in *Bell v. Hood* was grounded in federal law after all. But the *Bell v. Hood* rule was followed in Wheeldin v. Wheeler, 373 U.S. 647, 83 S.Ct. 1441, 10 L.Ed.2d 605 (1963), even when there was no claim based on federal law. In this case, the Supreme Court upheld a dismissal for failure to state a claim for relief of an action allegedly based on the Fourth Amendment and other federal law, even though it noted its agreement with the holding of the Court of Appeals that "on the face of the complaint the federal court had jurisdiction."

3. AMOUNT IN CONTROVERSY

DEUTSCH v. HEWES STREET REALTY CORP.
United States Court of Appeals, Second Circuit, 1966.
359 F.2d 96.

WATERMAN, CIRCUIT JUDGE.* On November 24, 1961 Mariana Deutsch, while washing dishes, allegedly was injured when one leg of the kitchen sink in her apartment gave way and fell on her left foot. As a result of this mishap appellant claims she suffered a comminuted fracture of the distal phalanx of the first toe of her left foot with subungual hematoma, extrusion of the nail, swelling, pain, tenderness, and discoloration. She further alleges that for some time she was unable to bear weight on the toes of her left foot and that she has continued to suffer pain.

With a view toward opening a small beauty shop upon completion of the prescribed course, appellant claims she had been attending a school that trained beauticians. She alleges that as a consequence of the accident she was compelled to abandon her plans to become a beautician because that job requires that one stand for long periods of time. She also claims that for at least one month after the accident she was unable to earn a living as a knitwear mender, the employment she had engaged in prior to her short-lived career as a student beautician. She did, however, return to her job as a knitwear mender in January, 1962, and at present she earns $125 a week performing this work.

Alleging that appellee, Hewes Street Realty Corporation, was negligent in failing properly to maintain her apartment and sink, appellant, on June 28, 1962, commenced this action in the Southern District of

* Some footnotes omitted; others renumbered.

New York to recover $25,000 for her alleged personal injuries.[1] She also commenced suit for $25,000 on the same claim in the New York state courts. The complaint in the action she began in the federal court stated that the district court had jurisdiction under 28 U.S.C. § 1332(a). By its answer the appellee denied the existence of a controversy "in excess of $10,000," the minimum amount required to confer federal jurisdiction in diversity suits, and it submitted interrogatories designed to elicit from appellant information concerning the elements of damage for which she sought recovery and the valuation that she placed on those elements. In her replies to these interrogatories appellant claimed special damages totaling only $141.00.[2] Moreover, she indicated that she sought recovery for approximately one month's complete disability; a claim which viewed charitably could not possibly have totaled more than $1,500.[3] Finally, appellant's replies indicated, albeit vaguely, that the balance of the *ad damnum* comprised a claim for damages due to the impairment of appellant's future earning capacity.

Appellee moved to dismiss the action on the ground that appellant's claims fell short of the $10,000 jurisdictional requirement, and that the court therefore lacked jurisdiction over the subject matter of the controversy. The district judge considered this motion in connection with appellant's replies to the interrogatories and in a memorandum opinion granted appellee's motion and dismissed appellant's complaint, stating that the complaint had not been made in good faith because "the claimed injuries and the monetary loss allegedly sustained could not justify a recovery in excess of $10,000." The district judge also noted that appellant simultaneously had filed suit in the state courts, a move that he concluded was designed solely to protect against a jurisdictional dismissal in the federal proceeding. Amplifying his decision that appellant's claim could not justify a recovery in excess of $10,000, he further stated that "in the remote unlikely possibility that a jury would return a verdict in the amount of $10,000 or more, the court in good conscience would be required to set it aside." We reverse the dismissal of the action by the district court and remand for further proceedings.

*   *   *

. . . "The rule governing dismissal for want of jurisdiction in cases brought in the federal court is that, unless the law gives a

---

1. Appellant's husband, Abraham Deutsch, joined a claim for loss of services. But since his claim is distinct from that of appellant the two claims cannot be aggregated in order to exceed the required jurisdictional amount. See Del Sesto v. Trans World Airlines, Inc., 201 F.Supp. 879 (D.C. R.I.1963). Appellant's claim, standing alone, must satisfy this requirement.

2. Appellant claimed doctors' bills totaling seventy dollars; she also expended thirty-five dollars for a steel shoe strip, and thirty-six dollars for two pairs of special therapeutic shoes.

3. If we charitably assume that appellant could not work at all for nine weeks and that she might have earned $125 per week during this period had she been able-bodied, she could recover $1125. Perhaps appellant might have earned more as a beautician during this period, but there is no proof of this fact presently in the record.

different rule, the sum claimed by the plaintiff controls if the claim is apparently made in good faith. It must appear to a legal certainty that the claim is really for less than the jurisdictional amount to justify dismissal." St. Paul Mercury Indem. Co. v. Red Cab Co., 303 U.S. 283, 288–289, 58 S.Ct. 586, 590, 82 L.Ed. 845 (1938).

Taking the Court's opinion in St. Paul Mercury Indem. Co., supra, as a point of departure, it might seem that a district court has the power to dismiss diversity suits when the court can conclude either that the sum claimed was not claimed in good faith or that it appears to a legal certainty that the plaintiff cannot recover the amount demanded. The end of clarity will be furthered, however, if the first test is seen to be but a linguistic variant of the second, for, as one authority has noted, "unless it appears to a legal certainty that plaintiff cannot recover the sum for which he prays, how can it be held that his claim for that sum is not in good faith?" Wright, Federal Courts, 95 (1963).

The issue, then, is how best to delimit the rule that the sum claimed by the plaintiff controls unless it appears to a legal certainty that this amount cannot be recovered. We confine our examination of this issue to the present and cognate cases in which a plaintiff is suing for unliquidated damages for an alleged tort. Two rules suggest themselves; each finds support in the decided cases. Following Turner v. Wilson Line, 242 F.2d 414 (1st Cir.1957) at least one other federal court of appeals has held that the district courts have the power to value a plaintiff's claim seeking unliquidated damages and dismiss the plaintiff's case if it does not reasonably appear that the plaintiff can recover in excess of $10,000. See Leehans v. American Employers Ins. Co., 273 F.2d 72 (5th Cir.1959); Sansome v. Ocean Acc. & Guar. Corp., 228 F.Supp. 554, 558 (E.D.La.1964). In the Third Circuit, however, the rule appears to be that, when unliquidated damages are sought, the district court, except in flagrant cases, should permit the case to proceed rather than attempt to decide the jurisdictional issue in a way that may deprive the claimant of the ordinary incidents of a trial. Wade v. Rogala, 270 F.2d 280 (3d Cir.1959). At least one court has gone so far as to suggest that in actions at law where trial by jury is a matter of right under the Seventh Amendment the plaintiff is entitled to demand that the issue be submitted to the jury, certainly in cases like the present one in which the problem of evaluation is inextricably bound up with the merits of the case. Shaffer v. Coty, Inc., 183 F.Supp. 662, 666–667 (S.D.Cal.1960); . . . But see Sansone v. Ocean Acc. & Guar. Corp., supra, 228 F.Supp. at 558 n. 5. Although Arnold v. Trocoli, supra, 344 F.2d at 846, suggests that this Circuit follows the rule announced in Wade v. Rogala, supra, our court has not yet squarely chosen one approach rather than the other.

The approach represented by Wade v. Rogala, supra, seems preferable for several reasons. First, we are impressed by the argument that to allow a district court judge to value a plaintiff's claim in a case which involves a demand for unliquidated damages and in which the jurisdictional issue is inextricably bound up with the merits of the controversy is tantamount to depriving the plaintiff of his present statutory right to a jury trial. See also, Wright, Federal Courts 95 (1963). Second, it should be apparent that within the present statutory framework there can be no brightline solution to this problem. The choice is essentially between a rule on the one hand that allows some cases involving inflated claims for relief to be brought in a federal forum in order to insure access to that forum for all those cases that properly may be brought there, and, on the other hand, a rule that closes the doors to the federal forum in the face of some claims that properly could be brought there in order to insure the denial of the forum to cases involving inflated claims. The present statutory pattern requires that we choose between these alternatives,[4] we feel the wiser choice is to choose the former and more liberal rule, as typified by the decision in Wade v. Rogala, supra. If access to federal district courts is to be further limited it should be done by statute and not by court decisions that permit a district court judge to prejudge the monetary value of an unliquidated claim.

Of course district courts are not restricted by the rule adopted here from looking further than the plaintiff's complaint in deciding whether a controversy involves recoverable sums in excess of $10,000. For example, dismissal will be proper when, under applicable law, the damages claimed are not recoverable, Parmelee v. Ackerman, 252 F.2d 721 (6th Cir.1958), or when the damages claimed, even though recoverable, cannot as a matter of law exceed $10,000. See, e.g., Trail v. Green, 206 F.Supp. 896 (D.N.J.1962). Furthermore, flagrant cases may arise in which, even though the complaint demands unliquidated damages in excess of $10,000, dismissal is proper because the district court can justifiably conclude that the amount demanded was inflated solely in order to gain access to the federal courts. This is the purport of Arnold v. Troccoli, 344 F.2d 842 (2d Cir.1965). There a suit demanding $6,000 in damages was initially filed in what is now the Civil Court of New York City. Nine months after the state suit was filed the plaintiff successfully moved to discontinue that action on the stated ground that a speedier trial might be had in the federal courts. The plaintiff then commenced a suit in the Southern District of New York in which she demanded $15,000. In affirming Judge Levet's dismissal of the federal action our court stated that the dismissal:

> . . . was grounded on the solid fact that suit had originally been brought for only $6,000 and there was no showing of change of circumstances or developing injuries to explain the inflation of the claim which alone gave color of federal jurisdiction. [344 F.2d at 846.]

4. Alternatively, it might be argued that every case in which a plaintiff claims damages in excess of $10,000 ought to be allowed to proceed to trial, but that, after trial, any case in which the final award is less than the requisite jurisdictional amount should be dismissed. Although such an approach is possible, it is unlikely that it will be adopted, for it would result in many wasteful jurisdictional dismissals after full trials on the merits.

Of course such cases should be dismissed; not because the district judge can conclude that a recovery in excess of $10,000 would not be justified but because there is independent evidence in such cases tending to prove that the claim had been inflated solely to exceed the jurisdictional threshold. See Brown v. Bodak, 188 F.Supp. 532 (S.D.N.Y.1960). Dismissal in such cases poses no danger that the judge will pass on the merits of issues that properly should be passed upon by the jury.

In the present case there is no independent evidence tending to establish that appellant's claim was inflated solely in order to gain access to the federal courts.

     *   *   *

Here we have a rather uncomplicated tort case in which appellant seeks unliquidated damages for the alleged impairment of her earning capacity, and the amount she demands seems far in excess of any likely verdict she can obtain. Nevertheless, under applicable New York tort law it appears that one who seriously has been preparing oneself for a change from a present vocation to a more remunerative one may, if the injury has impaired or frustrated the likelihood of success in the new vocation, recover nonspeculative damages for this damage factor based upon the loss of future probabilities of earning capacity. See Grayson v. Irvmar Realty Corp., 7 A.D.2d 436, 184 N.Y.S.2d 33, 34 (1959); Thornton & McNiece, Torts and Workmen's Compensation, 1959 Survey of N.Y.Law, 34 N.Y.U.Law Review 1538 (1959).

Though it may seem unlikely that plaintiff will be able to substantiate that she should recover damages in excess of $10,000, on this record it is not clear to a legal certainty that she cannot do so; we ought not affirmatively decide more than that. Accordingly, we reverse the district court order dismissing the plaintiffs' actions and remand for further proceedings below.

[Concurring opinions of C.J. Moore and J. Tyler omitted.]

NOTES

(1) Plaintiff brought an action in a federal district court to set aside an award of $1,050 made by the Texas Industrial Accident Board. He alleged that defendant was claiming $14,035, but was not entitled to recover anything. In Horton v. Liberty Mutual Insurance Co., 367 U.S. 348, 81 S.Ct. 1570, 6 L.Ed.2d 890 (1961), the Supreme Court, in a 5–4 decision, upheld the district court's competence. Noting that "determination of the value of the matter in controversy for purposes of federal jurisdiction is a federal question to be decided under federal standards", the Court went on to say (at 353–354):

> "The claim before the Board was $14,035; the state court suit of petitioner asked that much; the conditional counterclaim in the federal court claims the same amount. Texas law under which this claim was created and has its being leaves the entire $14,035 claim open for adjudication in a *de novo* court trial, regardless of the award. Thus the record before us shows beyond a doubt that the award is challenged by both parties and is binding on neither . . . Unquestionably, therefore, the amount in controversy is in excess of $10,000."

(2) As Section 1332(b) of Title 28 of the U.S.C.A. indicates, a federal court does not necessarily lose its competence when it is finally established that the plaintiff is entitled to less than the requisite amount. Although these provisions do not preclude the court from dismissing for lack of competence at a later stage of the proceedings, its inclination to dismiss is likely to decrease as the proceedings progress. See Emland Builders, Inc. v. Shea, 359 F.2d 927 (10th Cir.1966) (rejecting challenge after jury returned verdict for less than the requisite amount). But cf. Lynn v. Smith, 193 F.Supp. 887 (D.C.Pa.1961) (action dismissed after verdict was returned for $2,100); City of Boulder v. Snyder, 396 F.2d 853 (10th Cir.1968), cert. denied 393 U.S. 1051, 89 S.Ct. 692, 21 L.Ed.2d 693 (1969) and Matthiesen v. Northwestern Mutual Insurance Co., 286 F.2d 775 (5th Cir.1961) (evidence requires a dismissal even after the case has been tried). See also Note, Federal Jurisdictional Amount: Determination of the Matter in Controversy, 73 Harv.L.Rev. 1369 (1960).

(3) In 1789, the requisite amount in controversy was fixed at in excess of $500 (Judiciary Act of 1789, 1 Stat. 73, 78); in 1887, it was raised to in excess of $2,000 (24 Stat. 552); in 1911, it was increased to $3,000 (36 Stat. 1087, 1091); in 1958, it was fixed at $10,000 (72 Stat. 415), and in 1988, it was increased to $50,000. There are apparently still plaintiffs who formulate claims in federal courts for the statutorily specified dollar amount rather than an amount exceeding that figure, as well as defendants who fail to notice that this is insufficient. In such cases, should the court dismiss sua sponte? See, e.g., Matherson v. Long Island State Park Commission, 442 F.2d 566 (2d Cir.1971).

(4) In 1986, the amount in controversy requirement was abolished in federal question cases.

(5) Special problems arise in cases of joinder of claims, joinder of parties, counterclaims, and crossclaims. What rules would you consider appropriate? See 1 Moore's Federal Practice ¶¶ 0.97–0.98. See, e.g., Johns–Manville Sales Corp. v. Chicago Title & Trust Co., 261 F.Supp. 905 (N.D.Ill.1966) (claim of properly joined co-plaintiff need not be in requisite amount as long as claim of other plaintiff meets the statutory standard). But see Rompe v. Yablon, 277 F.Supp. 662 (S.D.N.Y.1967) (to the contrary effect). See also Snyder v. Harris, 394 U.S. 332, 89 S.Ct. 1053, 22 L.Ed.2d 319 (1969), rehearing denied 394 U.S. 1025, 89 S.Ct. 1622, 23 L.Ed.2d 50 (1969) (aggregation in what were formerly called spurious class actions not allowed); Zahn v. International Paper Co., 414 U.S. 291, 94 S.Ct. 505, 38 L.Ed.2d 511 (1973) (aggregation in such class actions similarly improper even when named parties assert claims in excess of requisite amount).

(6) How is the amount in controversy to be determined when the plaintiff does not seek monetary relief, but an injunction recovery of property, specific performance, or other relief? See 1 Moore's Federal Practice ¶¶ 0.92[5]–0.96. See also Comment, Federal Jurisdiction—Amount in Controversy in Suits for Non–Monetary Remedies, 46 Calif.L.Rev. 601 (1958); Note, Federal Jurisdictional Amount: Determination of the Matter in Controversy, 73 Harv.L.Rev. 1369 (1960); Wright, Federal Courts § 34 (4th ed. 1983).

4. Pendent, Ancillary, and Protective Adjudicatory
Authority

FINLEY v. UNITED STATES

Supreme Court of the United States 1989.
___ U.S. ___, 109 S.Ct. 2003, 104 L.Ed.2d 593.

Justice Scalia delivered the opinion of the Court.*

On the night of November 11, 1983, a twin-engine plane carrying petitioner's husband and two of her children struck electric transmission lines during its approach to a San Diego, California, airfield. No one survived the resulting crash. Petitioner brought a tort action in state court, claiming that San Diego Gas and Electric Company had negligently positioned and inadequately illuminated the transmission lines, and that the city of San Diego's negligent maintenance of the airport's runway lights had rendered them inoperative the night of the crash. When she later discovered that the Federal Aviation Administration (FAA) was in fact the party responsible for the runway lights, petitioner filed the present action against the United States in the United States District Court for the Southern District of California. The complaint based jurisdiction upon the Federal Tort Claims Act (FTCA), 28 U.S.C. § 1346(b), alleging negligence in the FAA's operation and maintenance of the runway lights and performance of air traffic control functions. Almost a year later, she moved to amend the federal complaint to include claims against the original state-court defendants, as to which no independent basis for federal jurisdiction existed. The District Court granted petitioner's motion and asserted "pendent" jurisdiction under Mine Workers v. Gibbs, 383 U.S. 715, 86 S.Ct. 1130, 16 L.Ed.2d 218 (1966), finding it "clear" that "judicial economy and efficiency" favored trying the actions together, and concluding that they arose "from a common nucleus of operative facts." . . . The District Court certified an interlocutory appeal to the Court of Appeals for the Ninth Circuit under 28 U.S.C. § 1292(b). That court summarily reversed on the basis of its earlier opinion in Ayala v. United States, 550 F.2d 1196 (1977), cert. dism'd, 435 U.S. 982, 98 S.Ct. 1635, 56 L.Ed.2d 76 (1978), which had categorically rejected pendent-party jurisdiction under the FTCA. We granted certiorari, 488 U.S. ___, 109 S.Ct. 52, 102 L.Ed.2d 31 (1988), to resolve a split among the Circuits on whether the FTCA permits an assertion of pendent jurisdiction over additional parties. . . .

The FTCA provides that "the district courts . . . shall have exclusive jurisdiction of civil actions on claims against the United States" for certain torts of federal employees acting within the scope of their employment. 28 U.S.C. § 1346(b). Petitioner seeks to append her claims against the city and the utility to her FTCA action against the United States, even though this would require the District Court to extend its authority to additional parties for whom an independent jurisdictional base—such as diversity of citizenship, 28 U.S.C. § 1332(a)(1)—is lacking.

In 1807 Chief Justice Marshall wrote for the Court that "courts which are created by written law, and whose jurisdiction is defined by written law, cannot transcend that jurisdiction." . . .

Despite this principle, in a line of cases by now no less well established we have held, without specific examination of jurisdictional statutes, that federal courts have "pendent" claim jurisdiction—that is, jurisdiction over nonfederal claims between parties litigating other matters properly before the court—to the full extent permitted by the Constitution. Mine Workers v. Gibbs, 383 U.S. 715, 86 S.Ct. 1130, 16 L.Ed.2d 218 (1966); Hurn v. Oursler, 289 U.S. 238, 53 S.Ct. 586, 77 L.Ed. 1148 (1933); Siler v. Louisville & Nashville R. Co., 213 U.S. 175, 29 S.Ct. 451, 53 L.Ed. 753 (1909). *Gibbs,* which has come to stand for the principle in question, held that "[p]endent jurisdiction, in the sense of judicial *power,* exists whenever there is a claim 'arising under [the] Constitution, the Laws of the United States, and Treaties made, or which shall be made, under their Authority . . .,' U.S. Const., Art. III, § 2, and the relationship between that claim and the state claim permits the conclusion that the entire action before the court comprises but one constitutional 'case.'" 383 U.S., at 725, 86 S.Ct., at 1138 (emphasis in original). The requisite relationship exists, *Gibbs* said, when the federal and nonfederal claims "derive from a common nucleus of operative fact" and are such that a plaintiff "would ordinarily be expected to try them in one judicial proceeding." Ibid. Petitioner contends that the same criterion applies here, leading to the result that her state-law claims against San Diego Gas and Electric Company and the city of San Diego may be heard in conjunction with her FTCA action against the United States.

Analytically, petitioner's case is fundamentally different from *Gibbs* in that it brings into question what has become known as pendent-*party* jurisdiction, that is, jurisdiction over parties not named in any claim that is independently cognizable by the federal court. We may assume, without deciding, that the constitutional criterion for pendent-party jurisdiction is analogous to the constitutional criterion for pendent-claim jurisdiction, and that petitioner's state-law claims pass that test. Our cases show, however, that with respect to the addition of parties, as opposed to the addition of only claims, we will not assume that the full constitutional power has been congressionally authorized, and will not read jurisdictional statutes broadly. In Zahn v. International Paper Co., 414 U.S. 291, 301, 94 S.Ct. 505, 512, 38 L.Ed. 2d 511 (1973), we refused to allow a plaintiff pursuing a diversity action worth less than the jurisdictional minimum of $10,000 to append his claim to the jurisdictionally adequate diversity claims of other members of a plaintiff class—even though all of the *claims* would together have amounted to a single "case" under *Gibbs,* see Owen Equipment & Erection Co. v. Kroger, 437 U.S. 365, 372, 98 S.Ct. 2396, 2401, 57 L.Ed. 2d 274 (1978). We based this holding upon "the statutes defining the jurisdiction of the District Court," 414 U.S., at 292, 94 S.Ct., at 507, and did not so much as mention *Gibbs*.

Two years later, the nontransferability of *Gibbs* to pendent-party claims was made explicit. In Aldinger v. Howard, 427 U.S. 1, 96 S.Ct. 2413, 49 L.Ed.2d 276 (1976), the plaintiff brought federal claims under 42 U.S.C. § 1983 against individual defendants, and sought to append to them a related state claim against Spokane County, Washington. . . . We specifically disapproved application of the *Gibbs* mode of analysis, finding a "significant legal difference." 427 U.S., at 15, 96 S.Ct., at 2420. "[T]he addition of a completely new party," we said, "would run counter to the well-established principle that federal courts . . . are courts of limited jurisdiction marked out by Congress." Ibid.

We reaffirmed and further refined our approach to pendent-party jurisdiction in Owen Equipment & Erection Co. v. Kroger, supra, 437 U.S., at 372–375, 98 S.Ct., at 2401–2403—a case, like *Zahn*, involving the diversity statute, 28 U.S.C. § 1332(a)(1), but focusing on the requirement that the suit be "between . . . citizens of different states," rather than the requirement that it "excee[d] the sum or value of $10,000." . . . While in a narrow class of cases a federal court may assert authority over such a claim "ancillary" to jurisdiction otherwise properly vested—for example, when an additional party has a claim upon contested assets within the court's exclusive control, see, e.g., Krippendorf v. Hyde, 110 U.S. 276, 4 S.Ct. 27, 28 L.Ed. 145 (1884); Freeman v. Howe, 24 How. 450, 460, 16 L.Ed. 749 (1861), or when necessary to give effect to the court's judgment, see, e.g., Local Loan Co. v. Hunt, 292 U.S. 234, 239, 54 S.Ct. 695, 697, 78 L.Ed. 1230 (1934); Julian v. Central Trust Co., 193 U.S. 93, 112–114, 24 S.Ct. 399, 407–408, 48 L.Ed. 629 (1904)—we have never reached such a result solely on the basis that the *Gibbs* test has been met. And little more basis than that can be relied upon by petitioner here. As in *Kroger*, the relationship between petitioner's added claims and the original complaint is one of "mere factual similarity," which is of no consequence since "neither the convenience of the litigants nor considerations of judicial economy can suffice to justify extension of the doctrine of ancillary jurisdiction," 437 U.S., at 376–377, 98 S.Ct., at 2404. It is true that here, unlike in *Kroger*, see id., at 376, 98 S.Ct., at 2404, the party seeking to bring the added claims had little choice but to be in federal rather than state court, since the FTCA permits the Federal Government to be sued only there. But that alone is not enough, since we have held that suits against the United States under the Tucker Act, 24 Stat. 505 (which can of course be brought only in federal court, see 28 U.S.C. §§ 1346(a)(2), 1491(a)(1)) cannot include private defendants. United States v. Sherwood, 312 U.S. 584, 61 S.Ct. 767, 85 L.Ed. 1058 (1941).

The second factor invoked by *Kroger*, the text of the jurisdictional statute at issue, likewise fails to establish petitioner's case. The FTCA, § 1346(b), confers jurisdiction over "civil actions on claims against the United States." It does not say "civil actions on claims that include requested relief against the United States," nor "civil actions in which there is a claim against the United States"—formulations one might expect if the presence of a claim against the United States constituted merely a minimum jurisdictional requirement, rather than a definition of the permissible scope of FTCA actions. Just as the statutory provision "between . . . citizens of different States" has been held to mean citizens of different States and no one else, see *Kroger,* 437 U.S. 365, 98 S.Ct. 2396, 57 L.Ed.2d 274 (1978), so also here we conclude that "against the United States" means against the United States and no one else. "Due regard for the rightful independence of state governments . . . requires that [federal courts] scrupulously confine their own jurisdiction to the precise limits which the statute has defined." Healy v. Ratta, 292 U.S. 263, 270, 54 S.Ct. 700, 703, 78 L.Ed. 1248 (1934); accord, Executive Jet Aviation, Inc. v. Cleveland, 409 U.S. 249, 272–273, 93 S.Ct. 493, 506, 34 L.Ed.2d 454 (1972); Shamrock Oil & Gas Corp. v. Sheets, 313 U.S. 100, 108–109, 61 S.Ct. 868, 872, 85 L.Ed. 1214 (1941). The statute here defines jurisdiction in a manner that does not reach defendants other than the United States.

Petitioner contends, however, that an affirmative grant of pendent-party jurisdiction is suggested by changes made to the jurisdictional grant of the FTCA as part of the comprehensive 1948 revision of the Judicial Code. See Pub.L. 773, 62 Stat. 869. In its earlier form, the FTCA had conferred upon district courts "exclusive jurisdiction to hear, determine, and render judgment *on any claim* against the United States" for specified torts. 28 U.S.C. § 931 (1946 ed.) (emphasis added). In the 1948 revision, this provision was changed to "exclusive jurisdiction of *civil actions on claims* against the United States." 28 U.S.C. § 1346(b) (1952 ed.) (emphasis added). Petitioner argues that this broadened the scope of the statute, permitting the assertion of jurisdiction over any "civil action," so long as that action *includes* a claim against the United States. We disagree.

The change from "claim against the United States" to "civil actions on claims against the United States" would be a strange way to express the substantive revision asserted by the petitioner—but a perfectly understandable way to achieve another objective. The 1948 recodification came relatively soon after the adoption of the Federal Rules of Civil Procedure, which provide that "[t]here shall be one form of action to be known as 'civil action.'" Fed.Rule Civ.Proc. 2. Consistent with this new terminology, the 1948 revision inserted the expression "civil action" throughout the provisions governing district-court jurisdiction. See H.R.Rep. No. 308, 80th Cong., 1st Sess., App. A114–A125 (1947) (Reviser's Notes).

Reliance upon the 1948 recodification also ignores the fact that the concept of pendent-party jurisdiction was not considered remotely viable until Gibbs liberalized the concept of pendent-claim jurisdiction— nearly 20 years later. . . . It is inconceivable that the much more radical change of adopting pendent-party jurisdiction would have been effected by the minor and obscure change of wording at issue here— especially when that revision is more naturally understood as stylistic.

Because the FTCA permits the Government to be sued only in federal court, our holding that parties to related claims cannot necessarily be sued there means that the efficiency and convenience of a consolidated action will sometimes have to be forgone in favor of separate actions in state and federal courts. We acknowledged this potential consideration in Aldinger, 427 U.S., at 18, 96 S.Ct., at 2422, but now conclude that the present statute permits no other result.

*   *   *   *   *   *   *   *   *

For the foregoing reasons, the judgment of the Court of Appeals is

Affirmed.

JUSTICE BLACKMUN'S dissenting opinion is omitted.

NO PENDANT JURISP. [handwritten]

JUSTICE STEVENS, with whom JUSTICE BRENNAN and JUSTICE MARSHALL join, dissenting.

The Court's holding is not faithful to our precedents and casually dismisses the accumulated wisdom of our best judges. As we observed more than 16 years ago, "numerous decisions throughout the courts of appeals since [Mine Workers v. Gibbs, 383 U.S. 715, 86 S.Ct. 1130, 16 L.Ed.2d 218 (1966)] have recognized the existence of judicial power to hear pendent claims involving pendent parties where 'the entire action before the court comprises but one constitutional "case"' as defined in *Gibbs*." Moor v. County of Alameda, 411 U.S. 693, 713, 93 S.Ct. 1785, 1797, 36 L.Ed.2d 596 (1973).

NOTE

In Moor v. County of Alameda, 411 U.S. 693, 93 S.Ct. 1785, 36 L.Ed.2d 596, cert. denied 412 U.S. 963, 93 S.Ct. 2999, 37 L.Ed.2d 1012 (1973), plaintiff sought to join a federal civil rights action against municipal officers with actions grounded in state law based on a theory of vicarious liability against the municipality. The Court, noting that the rationale of *Gibbs* could well be extended to cover pendent jurisdiction over additional parties, stated that it did not wish to resolve the issue. Even if it was assumed the power existed, the Court ruled, the court below had discretion not to exercise it, and the exercise of this discretion the Court would not review.

OWEN EQUIPMENT & ERECTION CO. v. KROGER

Supreme Court of the United States, 1978.
437 U.S. 365, 98 S.Ct. 2396, 57 L.Ed.2d 274.

MR. JUSTICE STEWART delivered the opinion of the Court.*

In an action in which federal jurisdiction is based on diversity of citizenship, may the plaintiff assert a claim against a third-party defendant when there is no independent basis for federal jurisdiction over that claim? The Court of Appeals for the Eighth Circuit held in this case that such a claim is within the ancillary jurisdiction of the federal courts. We granted certiorari, 434 U.S. 1008, 98 S.Ct. 715, 54

---

* Most footnotes omitted; others renumbered.

L.Ed.2d 749, because this decision conflicts with several recent decisions of other Courts of Appeals.

I

On January 18, 1972, James Kroger was electrocuted when the boom of a steel crane next to which he was walking came too close to a high tension electric power line. The respondent (his widow, who is the administratrix of his estate) filed a wrongful death action in the United States District Court for the District of Nebraska against the Omaha Public Power District (OPPD). Her complaint alleged that OPPD's negligent construction, maintenance and operation of the power line had caused Kroger's death. Federal jurisdiction was based on diversity of citizenship, since the respondent was a citizen of Iowa and OPPD was a Nebraska corporation.

OPPD then filed a third-party complaint pursuant to Fed.Rule Civ. Proc. 14(a) against the petitioner, Owen Equipment and Erection Company (Owen), alleging that the crane was owned and operated by Owen, and that Owen's negligence had been the proximate cause of Kroger's death. OPPD later moved for summary judgment on the respondent's complaint against it. While this motion was pending, the respondent was granted leave to file an amended complaint naming Owen as an additional defendant. Thereafter, the District Court granted OPPD's motion for summary judgment in an unreported opinion. The case thus went to trial between the respondent and the petitioner alone.

The respondent's amended complaint alleged that Owen was "a Nebraska corporation with its principal place of business in Nebraska." Owen's answer admitted that it was "a corporation organized and existing under the Laws of the State of Nebraska," and denied every other allegation of the complaint. On the third day of trial, however, it was disclosed that the petitioner's principal place of business was in Iowa, not Nebraska, and that the petitioner and the respondent were thus both citizens of Iowa. The petitioner then moved to dismiss the complaint for lack of jurisdiction. The District Court reserved decision on the motion, and the jury thereafter returned a verdict in favor of the respondent. In an unreported opinion issued after the trial, the District Court denied the petitioner's motion to dismiss the complaint.

The judgment was affirmed on appeal. 558 F.2d 417. The Court of Appeals held that under this Court's decision in Mine Workers v. Gibbs, 383 U.S. 715, 86 S.Ct. 1130, 16 L.Ed.2d 218, the District Court had jurisdictional power, in its discretion, to adjudicate the respondent's claim against the petitioner because that claim arose from the "core of 'operative facts' giving rise to both [respondent's] claim against OPPD and OPPD's claim against Owen." 558 F.2d at 424. It further held that the District Court had properly exercised its discretion in proceeding to decide the case even after summary judgment had been granted to OPPD, because the petitioner had concealed its Iowa citizenship from the respondent. Rehearing en banc was denied by an equally divided court. 558 F.2d 417.

II

It is undisputed that there was no independent basis of federal jurisdiction over the respondent's state-law tort action against the petitioner, since both are citizens of Iowa. And although Fed.Rule Civ. Proc. 14(a) permits a plaintiff to assert a claim against a third-party defendant, . . ., it does not purport to say whether or not such a claim requires an independent basis of federal jurisdiction. Indeed, it could not determine that question, since it is axiomatic that the Federal Rules of Civil Procedure do not create or withdraw federal jurisdiction.[1]

In affirming the District Court's judgment, the Court of Appeals relied upon the doctrine of ancillary jurisdiction, whose contours it believed were defined by this Court's holding in Mine Workers v. Gibbs, supra. The *Gibbs* case differed from this one in that it involved pendent jurisdiction, which concerns the resolution of a plaintiff's federal and state law claims against a single defendant in one action. By contrast, in this case there was no claim based upon substantive federal law, but rather state-law tort claims against two different defendants. Nonetheless, the Court of Appeals was correct in perceiving that *Gibbs* and this case are two species of the same generic problem: Under what circumstances may a federal court hear and decide a state-law claim arising between citizens of the same State?[2] But we believe that the Court of Appeals failed to understand the scope of the doctrine of the *Gibbs* case.

. . . [A] finding that federal and nonfederal claims arise from a "common nucleus of operative fact," the test of Gibbs, does not end the inquiry into whether a federal court has power to hear the nonfederal claims along with the federal ones. Beyond this constitutional minimum, there must be an examination of the posture in which the nonfederal claim is asserted and of the specific statute that confers jurisdiction over the federal claim, in order to determine whether "Congress in [that statute] has . . . expressly or by implication negated" the exercise of jurisdiction over the particular nonfederal claim.

* * *

III

The relevant statute in this case, 28 U.S.C. § 1332(a)(1), confers upon federal courts jurisdiction over "civil actions where the matter in controversy exceeds the sum or value of $10,000 . . . and is between . . . citizens of different States." This statute and its predecessors

---

1. Fed.Rule Civ.Proc. 82; see Snyder v. Harris, 394 U.S. 332, 89 S.Ct. 1053, 22 L.Ed.2d 319; Sibbach v. Wilson & Co., 312 U.S. 1, 10, 61 S.Ct. 422, 424, 85 L.Ed. 479.

2. No more than in Aldinger v. Howard, 427 U.S. 1, 96 S.Ct. 2413, 49 L.Ed.2d 276, is it necessary to determine here "whether there are any 'principled' differences between pendent and ancillary jurisdiction; or, if there are, what effect Gibbs had on such differences." Id., at 13, 96 S.Ct., at 2420.

have consistently been held to require complete diversity of citizenship. That is, diversity jurisdiction does not exist unless each defendant is a citizen of a different State from each plaintiff. Over the years Congress has repeatedly re-enacted or amended the statute conferring diversity jurisdiction, leaving intact this rule of complete diversity. Whatever may have been the original purposes of diversity of citizenship jurisdiction, this subsequent history clearly demonstrates a congressional mandate that diversity jurisdiction is not to be available when any plaintiff is a citizen of the same State as any defendant. Cf. Snyder v. Harris, 394 U.S. 332, 338–339, 89 S.Ct. 1053, 1057–1058, 22 L.Ed.2d 319.

* * *

It is true, as the Court of Appeals noted, that the exercise of ancillary jurisdiction over nonfederal claims has often been upheld in situations involving impleader, cross-claims or counterclaims.[3] But in determining whether jurisdiction over a nonfederal claim exists, the context in which the nonfederal claim is asserted is crucial. See Aldinger v. Howard, 427 U.S., at 14, 96 S.Ct., at 2420. And the claim here arises in a setting quite different from the kinds of nonfederal claim that have been viewed in other cases as falling within the ancillary jurisdiction of the federal courts.

First, the nonfederal claim in this case was simply not ancillary to the federal one in the same sense that, for example, the impleader by a defendant of a third-party defendant always is. A third-party complaint depends at least in part upon the resolution of the primary lawsuit. . . . .. Its relation to the original complaint is thus not mere factual similarity but logical dependence. Cf. Moore v. New York Cotton Exchange, 270 U.S. 593, 610, 46 S.Ct. 367, 371, 70 L.Ed. 750. The respondent's claim against the petitioner, however, was entirely separate from her original claim against ●PPD, since the petitioner's liability to her depended not at all upon whether or not ●PPD was also liable. Far from being an ancillary and dependent claim, it was a new and independent one.

Second, the nonfederal claim here was asserted by the plaintiff, who voluntarily chose to bring suit upon a state-law claim in a federal court. By contrast, ancillary jurisdiction typically involves claims by a defending party haled into court against his will, or by another person whose rights might be irretrievably lost unless he could assert them in

---

3. The ancillary jurisdiction of the federal courts derives originally from wrses such as Freeman v. Howe, 24 How. 450, 16 L.Ed. 749, which held that when federal jurisdiction "effectively controls the property or fund under dispute, other claimants thereto should be allowed to intervene in order to protect their interests, without regard to jurisdiction." Aldinger v. Howard, 427 U.S., at 11, 96 S.Ct. at 2419. More recently, it has been said to include cases that involve multiparty practice, such as compulsory counterclaims, e.g., Moore v. New York Cotton Exchange, 270 U.S. 593, 46 S.Ct. 367, 70 L.Ed. 750; impleader, e.g., H.L. Peterson Co. v. Applewhite, 383 F.2d 430, 433 (C.A.5); Dery v. Wyer, 265 F.2d 804 (C.A.2); cross-claims, e.g., LASA Per L'Industria Del Marmo Soc. Per Azioni v. Alexander, 414 F.2d 143 (C.A.6); Scott v. Fancher, 369 F.2d 842, 844 (C.A.5); Glen Falls Indemnity Co. v. United States ex rel. Westinghouse Electric Supply Co., 229 F.2d 370, 373, 374 (C.A.9); or intervention as of right, e.g., Phelps v. Oaks, 117 U.S. 236, 241, 6 S.Ct. 714, 716, 29 L.Ed. 888; Smith Petroleum Service, Inc. v. Monsanto Chemical Co., 420 F.2d 1103, 1113, 1115 (C.A.5).

an ongoing action in a federal court. A plaintiff cannot complain if ancillary jurisdiction does not encompass all of his possible claims in a case such as this one, since it is he who has chosen the federal rather than the state forum and must thus accept its limitations. "[T]he efficiency plaintiff seeks so avidly is available without question in the state courts." Kenrose Mfg. Co. v. Fred Whitaker Co., 512 F.2d 890, 894 (CA4).

It is not unreasonable to assume that, in generally requiring complete diversity, Congress did not intend to confine the jurisdiction of federal courts so inflexibly that they are unable to protect legal rights or effectively to resolve an entire, logically entwined lawsuit. Those practical needs are the basis of the doctrine of ancillary jurisdiction. But neither the convenience of litigants nor considerations of judicial economy can suffice to justify extension of the doctrine of ancillary jurisdiction to a plaintiff's cause of action against a citizen of the same State in a diversity case. Congress has established the basic rule that diversity jurisdiction exists under 28 U.S.C. § 1332 only when there is complete diversity of citizenship. "The policy of the statute calls for its strict construction." . . . To allow the requirement of complete diversity to be circumvented as it was in this case would simply flout the congressional command.

Accordingly, the judgment of the Court of Appeals is reversed.

It is so ordered.

MR. JUSTICE WHITE, with whom MR. JUSTICE BRENNAN joins, dissenting.

The Court today states that "[i]t is not unreasonable to assume that, in generally requiring complete diversity, Congress did not intend to confine the jurisdiction of federal courts so inflexibly that they are unable . . . effectively to resolve an entire, logically entwined lawsuit." . . . In spite of this recognition, the majority goes on to hold that in diversity suits federal courts do not have the jurisdictional power to entertain a claim asserted by a plaintiff against a third-party defendant, no matter how entwined it is with the matter already before the court, unless there is an independent basis for jurisdiction over that claim. Because I find no support for such a requirement in either Art. III of the Constitution or in any statutory law, I dissent from the Court's "unnecessarily grudging" approach.

* * *

We have previously noted that "[s]ubsequent decisions of this Court indicate that *Strawbridge* is not to be given an expansive reading." State Farm Fire & Cas. Co. v. Tashire, 386 U.S. 523, 531 n. 6, 87 S.Ct. 1199, 1203, 18 L.Ed.2d 270 (1967). . . . I would hold that in a diversity case the District Court has power, both constitutional and statutory, to entertain all claims among the parties arising from the same nucleus of operative fact as the plaintiff's original, jurisdiction-conferring claim against the defendant. Accordingly, I dissent from the Court's disposition of the present case.

NOTE

May an appellate court dismiss a dispensable non-diverse party? In Newman–Green, Inc. v. Alfonzo–Larrain, ___ U.S. ___, 109 S.Ct. 2218, 104 L.Ed.2d 893 (1989), the Supreme Court, resolving a conflict among the circuits, ruled in the affirmative.

NOTE ON "ANCILLARY" AND "PENDENT JURISDICTION"

The terms "pendent" and "ancillary jurisdiction" are not always used discriminately. The term "pendent jurisdiction" was originally thought to describe only the authority to adjudicate a claim based on state law that was premised on the court's having authority to adjudicate a related claim involving the same parties based on federal law. The classic example was provided by the *Gibbs* case, in which the Supreme Court held that the federal court could adjudicate a non-diversity claim based on state tort law on the ground that it had authority to adjudicate a related claim under a federal statute, even though the plaintiff did not prevail on the federal claim.

Once the concept of "pendent jurisdiction" was accepted, there appeared to be no good reason for limiting it to cases in which the related claim was by the same plaintiff or against the same defendant. Moor v. County of Alameda, 411 U.S. 693, 93 S.Ct. 1785, 36 L.Ed.2d 596, rehearing denied 412 U.S. 963, 93 S.Ct. 2999, 37 L.Ed.2d 1012 (1973), indicated that "pendent jurisdiction" could also apply in cases involving joinder of federal with state law claims and multiple plaintiffs or defendants. See Note, p. 210, supra.

The obvious next step was to apply the "pendent jurisdiction" doctrine to cases in which the claim cognizable by the federal court to which the related claim had to be appended was a diversity rather than a federal question claim. Of course, it had long been held that a plaintiff in a diversity case could aggregate his claims against the defendant in order to reach the requisite amount in controversy. See Crawford v. Neal, 144 U.S. 585, 12 S.Ct. 759, 36 L.Ed. 552 (1892). The real problem therefore was whether "pendent jurisdiction" could be used to sustain the court's authority to adjudicate an otherwise noncognizable claim by a co-plaintiff or against a codefendant. The traditional rule has been that claims for and against multiple parties may not be aggregated (for ample references to the cases, see 7 Wright, Miller & Kane, Federal Practice and Procedure § 1659 (1986)). In addition, the Supreme Court has refused to apply the doctrine to a Rule 23(b)(3) class action case, in which the named plaintiffs had claims in excess of the requisite amount. Zahn v. International Paper Co., 414 U.S. 291, 94 S.Ct. 505, 38 L.Ed.2d 511 (1973). The *Finley* and *Owen* cases demonstrate the continued reluctance of the Supreme Court to apply a doctrine of ancillary or pendent jurisdiction in order to sustain adjudicatory authority over a claim not independently cognizable in a federal court by appending it to a claim cognizable on the basis of diversity. It may be that *Owen* should be limited to its precise facts—

that of a plaintiff who seeks to assert against a co-defendant a claim on which the plaintiff could not have sued him independently in a federal court. This, at least was done in Hyman–Michaels Co. v. Swiss Bank Corp., 496 F.Supp. 663 (N.D.Ill.1980), in which it was held that ancillary jurisdiction could be invoked to sustain a claim by a third-party defendant against the original plaintiff that had a close connection with the main action. This decision warrants the further question of whether *Owen* permits reliance on ancillary jurisdiction to sustain a counterclaim by the plaintiff after the co-defendant has asserted a claim against him. Would your answer depend on whether the counterclaim was compulsory? See p. 424, Note (5), infra.

As the originally rather limited contours of the doctrine of "pendent jurisdiction" expanded, the confusion with the doctrine of "ancillary jurisdiction" grew apace. The doctrine of "ancillary jurisdiction" had from the beginning been applied in cases, in which, in an already pending action, a new, but related, claim was asserted by or against a party to the original action. Typically, the doctrine of "ancillary jurisdiction" had been applied to sustain counterclaims, cross-claims, third-party claims and claims in intervention as to which there was no independent federal basis of adjudicatory authority. See p. 218, Note 7, infra. The distinction between this doctrine and that of "pendent jurisdiction" in its original form was reasonably clear. However, as the doctrine of "pendent jurisdiction" expanded to include cases of multiple plaintiffs or defendants and, in the view of some courts, also to include diversity cases, the courts and commentators have increasingly come to use the terms "ancillary" and "pendent jurisdiction" indiscriminately. This is quite understandable, since the reasons for applying both doctrines, as the Supreme Court noted in an early leading case, "in principle, cannot be distinguished." Hurn v. Oursler, 289 U.S. 238, 242, 53 S.Ct. 586, 588, 77 L.Ed. 1148 (1932).

For illuminating discussions, see also Bratton, Pendent Jurisdiction in Diversity Cases—Some Doubts, 11 San Diego L.Rev. 276 (1974); Sullivan, Pendent Jurisdiction: The Impact of Hagans and Moor, 7 Ind. L.Rev. 925 (1974).

NOTES

(1) On pendent and ancillary jurisdiction generally, see 13 Wright, Miller & Cooper, Federal Practice and Procedure: Jurisdiction and Related Matters § 3567 (1984); Note, A Closer Look at Pendent and Ancillary Jurisdiction: Toward a Theory of Incidental Jurisdiction, 95 Harv.L.Rev. 1935 (1982). *Owen* and related cases, see Comment, Aldinger v. Howard and Pendent Jurisdiction, 77 Colum.L.Rev. 127 (1977); Note, Supreme Court Says No to Pendent Parties At Least This Time, 38 U.Pitt.L.Rev. 395 (1977); Note, Federal Jurisdiction–Ancillary Jurisdiction, 62 Mar.L.Rev. 89 (1978); Note, Federal Courts–Diversity Jurisdiction–Ancillary Jurisdiction and Third Party Practice, 46 Tenn.L.Rev. 865 (1978); Garvey, The Limits of Ancillary Jurisdiction, 57 Tex.L.Rev. 697 (1979); Comment, Limiting Federal Ancillary and Pendent Jurisdiction in Diversity Cases, 64 Iowa L.Rev. 930 (1979); Note, Critique–Ancillary and Pendent Party Jurisdiction in the Aftermath of Owen Equipment and Erection

Co. v. Kroger, 28 Drake L.Rev. 758 (1979); Note, Ancillary Jurisdiction: The Kroger Approach and the Federal Rules, 28 Emory L.J. 463 (1979); Note, Federal Civil Procedure: Limiting Ancillary Jurisdiction, 31 U.Fla.L.Rev. 442 (1979); Berch, The Erection of a Barrier Against Assertion of Ancillary Claims: An Examination of Owen Equipment and Erection Company v. Kroger, 1979 Ariz.St.L.J. 253 (1979); Brill, Federal Rule of Civil Procedure 14 and Ancillary Jurisdiction, 59 Neb.L.Rev. 631 (1980).

(2) The ruling in *Owen* was given a narrow reading in Ortiz v. United States, 595 F.2d 65 (1st Cir.1979). In this case, Ortiz sued the United States under the Federal Tort Claims Act for injuries suffered in a Veterans' Hospital. The United States impleaded the hospital under 28 U.S.C.A. § 1345, and Ortiz thereupon sought to amend to assert a claim directly against the hospital for which there was no independent basis of competence. The Fifth Circuit ruled that, under the *Gibbs* standard, the court had the judicial power to entertain the claim of the plaintiff against the hospital. On this case, see also Note, Pendent and Ancillary Jurisdiction, 45 J.Air L. & Comm. 757 (1980).

(3) Pendent jurisdiction cannot be used to support a claim against a state barred by the Eleventh Amendment. Pennhurst State School & Hospital v. Halderman, 465 U.S. 89, 104 S.Ct. 900, 79 L.Ed.2d 67 (1984).

(4) What factors are to be taken into account in determining whether the relationship between the claims is sufficiently close for either of these doctrines to apply? The *Gibbs* test of "common nucleus of operative facts" is frequently cited. Does it indicate with reasonable precision how to determine which facts form the nucleus of the two claims? The American Law Institute's proposal includes a provision for pendent jurisdiction with respect to a claim brought by a claimant on his own behalf or of that of a family member living in the same household if it "arises out of the transaction or occurrence that is the subject matter of the action." American Law Institute, Study of the Division of Jurisdiction Between State and Federal Courts 1301(e) (1969). Would general application of this test be acceptable? In answering this question, try to formulate the policies underlying these doctrines. Does it make a difference whether the claim the court does have independent authority to hear is a claim based on constitutional, federal, or state law and whether the element lacking in the authority to hear the related claim is a constitutional or statutory prerequisite?

(5) The Supreme Court has repeatedly said that in order for the doctrine of "pendent jurisdiction" to apply, the federal claim must "have substance." U.M.W. v. Gibbs, 383 U.S. 715, 86 S.Ct. 1130, 16 L.Ed.2d 218 (1966). It has said the same in regard to federal claims generally. Rosado v. Wyman, 397 U.S. 397, 90 S.Ct. 1207, 25 L.Ed.2d 442 (1970), on remand 322 F.Supp. 1173 (E.D. N.Y.), affd. 437 F.2d 619 (2d Cir.), affirmed 402 U.S. 991, 91 S.Ct. 2169, 29 L.Ed. 2d 157 (1971). Must federal claims to which state claims are to be appended be more "substantial" than federal claims asserted by themselves? Cf. Hagans v. Lavine, 415 U.S. 528, 94 S.Ct. 1372, 39 L.Ed.2d 577 (1974).

(6) At what stage of the litigation must the federal claim appear to have sufficient substance to carry the ancillary claim with it? What if the complaint supports application of the doctrine, but the federal claim appears to lack factual substance at a later stage of the litigation? Compare Bell v. Hood, 71 F.Supp. 813, 819–20 (S.D.Cal.1947) (looking at the complaint) with Strachman v. Palmer, 177 F.2d 427 (1st Cir.1949) (denying to hear the ancillary claim when

the principal claim is dismissed on the pleadings). See also Note, Discretionary Federal Jurisdiction Over the Pendent Cause, 46 Ill.L.Rev. 646 (1951).

(7) Once it is determined that the court has power to adjudicate the related claim, may the court nevertheless refuse to exercise this power? If, as stated in *Gibbs*, "pendent jurisdiction is a doctrine of discretion", what is the legal basis for this discretion? Has a court in an ordinary federal question case discretion to refuse to exercise its adjudicatory power? Or does the court use the term discretion in the sense of leaving the lower court a large measure of freedom in determining whether the circumstances are such as to warrant the exercise of ancillary or pendent jurisdiction? On these doctrines generally, see Baker, Toward a Relaxed View of Federal Ancillary and Pendent Jurisdiction, 33 U.Pitt.L.Rev. 759 (1972); Frazer, Ancillary Jurisdiction and the Joinder of Claims in the Federal Courts, 62 F.R.D. 483 (1973); Shakman, The New Pendent Jurisdiction of Federal Courts, 20 Stan.L.Rev. 262 (1968); Comment, Pendent Jurisdiction in Diversity Cases, 30 U.Pitt.L.Rev. 607 (1969); Wright, Federal Courts § 9 (4th ed. 1983).

NOTE ON PROTECTIVE JURISDICTION

According to the doctrine of protective jurisdiction, Congress, under the federal question clause of Article III of the Constitution, may grant the federal courts power to adjudicate controversies arising in areas over which it has legislative jurisdiction, even though it has not exercised this legislative jurisdiction to formulate substantive rules to be applied by the federal courts. It was thought at first that Section 301(a) of the Labor Management Relations Act of 1947, 29 U.S.C.A. § 185 (1965), provided an example of the exercise of protective jurisdiction. This section provides that suits for violation of collective bargaining agreements in an industry affecting interstate or foreign commerce may be brought in the federal courts "without respect to the amount in controversy" and "without regard to the citizenship of the parties." However, in Textile Workers Union of America v. Lincoln Mills, 353 U.S. 448, 77 S.Ct. 912, 1 L.Ed.2d 972 (1957), the Supreme Court held that the law applied in such an action is federal law that, in the absence of statutory prescriptions, must be fashioned by the court. On this case, see also Bickel & Wellington, Legislative Purpose and the Judicial Process: The Lincoln Mills Case, 71 Harv.L.Rev. 1 (1957). On protective jurisdiction, see Mishkin, the Federal "Question" Jurisdiction of the District Courts, 53 Colum.L.Rev. 157, 184–96 (1953); Wechsler, Federal Jurisdiction and the Revision of the Judicial Code, 13 Law & Contemp. Prob. 216, 224–25 (1948).

The doctrine has gained renewed interest as a result of efforts to give the federal courts authority to adjudicate claims in the consumer protection and environmental fields. To what extent is it constitutionally possible to give the federal courts competence to adjudicate claims based exclusively upon state law? See Note, Protective Jurisdiction and Adoption as Alternative Techniques for Conferring Jurisdiction on Federal Courts in Consumer Class Actions, 69 Mich.L.Rev. 70 (1971). See generally Hart & Wechsler, The Federal Courts and the Federal System 1040–1051, Bator, Meltner, Mishkin & Shapiro (3d ed. 1988).

Protective jurisdiction was argued to be an appropriate basis for a federal court's entertaining a suit between an alien and a foreign government in Verlinden B.V. v. Central Bank of Nigeria, 461 U.S. 480, 103 S.Ct. 1962, 76 L.Ed.2d 81 (1983). See also Smit, Foreign Sovereign Immunity–American Style, in International Contracts 255 (1981). However, the Supreme Court held in that case that the suit was brought under the Foreign Sovereign Immunity Act of 1976, 28 U.S. C.A. § 1330 (West 1976) and therefore arose under federal law. Is this holding correct? In *Verlinden,* neither the plaintiff nor the sovereign defendant sought to rely on any of the provisions of the Act regulating the sovereign's substantive obligations.

5. REMOVAL

Read 28 U.S.C.A. § 1441.

NOTES

(1) In what respects is the competence of a federal court upon removal different from its original competence? May a non-resident plaintiff sue a resident defendant for more than $50,000 in a federal district court? When such a plaintiff brings his action in a state court, may the defendant remove? What justification is there for the difference? See further 1 Moore's Federal Practice ¶ 0.60[9] at 662. Some federal statutes forbid removal of actions brought under such statutes in state courts. See Federal Employers' Liability Act, 45 U.S.C.A. §§ 51–60; Jones Act, 46 U.S.C.A. § 688. Why did Congress provide for these exceptions? The FELA statute seeks to facilitate the recovery of damages from an employer by an injured railroad worker engaged in interstate commerce. To this end, it eliminates the applicability of the fellow servant rule and institutes a rule of comparative negligence. The Jones Act follows this pattern in regulating the rights of seamen against their employers. See also 28 U.S.C.A. § 1445(c) (forbidding removal of cases brought under state workmen's compensation statutes).

(2) The procedure for removal is detailed in 28 U.S.C.A. §§ 1446–50. Failure to seek removal promptly may lead to waiver of the right to obtain it.

(3) "The jurisdiction of the federal court on removal is, in a limited sense, a derivative jurisdiction. If the state court lacks jurisdiction of the subject-matter or of the parties, the federal court acquires none, although it might in a like suit originally brought there have had jurisdiction". Lambert Run Coal Co. v. Baltimore & Ohio Railroad Co., 258 U.S. 377, 382, 42 S.Ct. 349, 351, 66 L.Ed. 671 (1922). But cf. Freeman v. Bee Machine Co., Inc., 319 U.S. 448, 63 S.Ct. 1146, 87 L.Ed. 1509 (1943) (holding that, after removal based on diversity, the plaintiff could amend his complaint to add an antitrust claim within the exclusive cognizance of the federal courts).

(4) Can a plaintiff in a state court action remove to the federal district court on the ground that the defendant has interposed a counterclaim cognizable in the federal court? In Shamrock Oil & Gas Corp. v. Sheets, 313 U.S. 100, 61 S.Ct. 868, 85 L.Ed. 1214 (1941), the Supreme Court answered in the negative. May the defendant who has interposed a counterclaim remove? Should the answer depend on whether the counterclaim is compulsory or permissive? See Wright, Federal Courts § 37 (4th ed. 1983). The American Law Institute favors

removal in these situations. See Study of the Division of Jurisdiction Between State and Federal Courts §§ 1304(c), 1372(a)(3) (Official Draft 1969).

(5) To what extent may the court look beyond the four corners of the complaint to determine whether removal is proper? Compare IA Moore's Federal Practice ¶¶ 0.163[4–3], 0.168[3–4], 0.168[4–1] ("removability is dependent upon the course of pleading employed by the plaintiff") with 13 Wright, Miller & Couper, Federal Practice and Procedure § 3721 (1985).

In American Fire & Case Co. v. Finn, 341 U.S. 6, 71 S.Ct. 534, 95 L.Ed. 702 (1951), the plaintiff had brought an action in a state court against two foreign insurance companies and their Texas agent. The complaint alleged that one or the other of insurers had issued a policy covering plaintiff's loss and that, if neither had, the agent was liable for having failed to obtain appropriate insurance. The insurers, relying on 28 U.S.C.A. § 1441(c), removed the entire case to the federal court. After judgment had been entered against one of the insurers, that insurer moved to vacate the judgment on the ground that the action had been improperly removed. The Supreme Court ruled the motion well-founded. It held that the claims asserted against the insurers were not "independent" in the sense of Section 1441(c).

NOTES

(1) In the *Finn* case, did the Court take due account of the circumstance that the party asserting the lack of subject matter authority was the party that had successfully sought removal and had raised the objection only after judgment had been entered? Are there no limitations on the right of a party to rely on absence of subject matter adjudicatory authority "at any time"?

(2) Is 28 U.S.C.A. § 1441(c) constitutional? Under the "pendent jurisdiction" doctrine or because constitutionally complete diversity is not required? Cf. American Fire & Casualty Co. v. Finn, 341 U.S. 6, 71 S.Ct. 534, 95 L.Ed. 702 (1951). On this provision, see Cohen, Problems in the Removal of a "Separate and Independent Claim or Cause of Action," 46 Minn.L.Rev. 1 (1961); Moore & Van Dercreek, Multi-party, Multi-claim Removal Problems: The Separate and Independent Claim under Section 1441(c), 46 Iowa L.Rev. 489 (1961); Lewis, The Federal Courts' Hospital Back Door–Removal of "Separate and Independent" Non–Federal Cause of Action, 66 Harv.L.Rev. 423 (1953); Keefe, et al., Venue and Removal Jokers in the New Federal Judicial Code, 38 Va.L.Rev. 569, 598–612 (1952); Comment, Diversity Removal Where the Federal Court Would Not Have Original Jurisdiction: A Suggested Reform, 114 U.Pa.L.Rev. 709 (1966). For a case involving multiple claims against two defendants, see Twentieth Century–Fox Film Corp. v. Taylor, 239 F.Supp. 913 (S.D.N.Y.1965). But cf. New England Concrete Pipe Corp. v. D/C Systems, Etc., 658 F.2d 867, 873 (1st Cir.1981).

(3) In Thermtron Products, Inc. v. Hermansdorfer, 423 U.S. 336, 96 S.Ct. 584, 46 L.Ed.2d 542 (1976), the Supreme Court held mandamus to be the proper writ for obtaining appellate review of a remand order on grounds improper under 28 U.S.C.A. § 1441(c). But in In re Weaver, 610 F.2d 335 (5th Cir.1980), the Fifth Circuit ruled that mandamus was unavailable to review a remand not based on application of 28 U.S.C.A. § 1441(c).

NOTE ON PROBLEMS OF ADJUDICATORY AUTHORITY IN MULTIPARTY CASES

In 1988, a bill was introduced in the Congress containing, *inter alia,* the following provision (H.R. 4807, 100th Cong.2d Sess.)

Sec. 301: **Jurisdiction of District Courts.**

(a) *Basis of Jurisdiction*—Chapter 85 is amended by adding at the end the following new section:

§ 1367. **Multiparty, multiforum jurisdiction**

"(a) The district courts shall have original jurisdiction of any civil action involving minimal diversity between adverse parties that arises from a single event or occurrence, where it is alleged in good faith that any 25 persons have either died or incurred injury in the event or occurrence and that, in the case of injury, the injury has resulted in damages which exceed $50,000 per person, exclusive of interest and costs, if—

"(1) a defendant resides in a State and a substantial part of the event or occurrence took place in another State,

"(2) any two defendants reside in different States; or

"(3) substantial parts of the event or occurrence took place in different States.

"(b) For purposes of this section—

"(1) minimal diversity exists between adverse parties if any party is a citizen of a State and any adverse party is a citizen of another State, a citizen or subject of a foreign state, or a foreign state as defined in section 1603(a) of this title;

"(2) a corporation is deemed to be a citizen of any State, and a citizen or subject of any foreign state, in which it is incorporated or has its principal place of business, and is deemed to be a resident of any State in which it is incorporated or licensed to do business or is doing business; and

"(3) 'injury' means physical harm to a natural person and physical damage to or destruction of tangible property.

"(c) In any action in a district court under this section, any person with a claim arising from the event or occurrence described in subsection (a) shall be permitted to intervene as a party plaintiff in the action, even if that person could not have brought an action in a district court as an original matter.

"(d) A district court in which an action under this section is pending shall promptly notify the judicial panel on multidistrict litigation of the pendency of the action".

(b) *Conforming Amendment.*—The table of sections at the beginning of chapter 85 is amended by adding at the end the following new item:

"1851. Multiparty, multiforum jurisdiction".

Sec. 302. Venue

Section 1391 is amended by adding at the end the following:

"(g) A civil action in which jurisdiction of the district court is based upon section 1867 of this title may be brought in any district in which any defendant resides or in which a substantial part of the event or occurrence giving rise to the action took place."

What is the purpose of these provisions? Could you improve them so as to achieve this purpose more effectively? How?

6. THE LAW APPLIED IN THE FEDERAL COURTS

The existence of a dual court structure naturally raises the problem of what law is to be applied by the courts sitting in this dual structure. This problem, the answer to which is in significant measure determined by constitutional rules, becomes particularly acute when federal courts adjudicate diversity cases and when state courts adjudicate cases based on federal law. It is treated separately in Chapter 7, but is so pervasive that you should ask yourself with every case you study whether it, in some form, presents itself.

SECTION 3. ADJUDICATORY AUTHORITY OVER PERSONS

A. HISTORICAL BACKGROUND

PENNOYER v. NEFF

Supreme Court of the United States, 1877.
95 U.S. (5 Otto) 714, 24 L.Ed. 565.

This was an action brought in the Federal court to recover the possession of a tract of land, of the alleged value of $15,000, situated in the State of Oregon. The plaintiff asserted title to the premises by a patent of the United States issued to him in March 1866, under the act of Congress of Sept. 27, 1850, usually known as the Donation Law of Oregon. The defense was that the defendant had acquired the land under a sheriff's deed given in execution of a judgment for lawyer's fees of less than $300 which had been recovered against the plaintiff in an Oregon state court in February, 1866. The plaintiff, who was a nonresident of Oregon, had been served by publication in this action and judgment had been rendered against him by default. The Supreme Court had found for the plaintiff on the ground that the Oregon judgment was invalid. The Court, per Mr. Justice Field, in affirming, said that there are:

> ". . . two well established principles of public law respecting the jurisdiction of an independent State over persons and property. . . . One of these principles is, that every State possesses exclusive jurisdiction and sovereignty over persons and property within its territory. . . . The other principle of public law referred to follows from the one mentioned; that is, that no State can exercise direct jurisdiction and authority over persons or property without its territory. . . . The several States are of equal dignity and authority, and the independence of one implies the exclusion of power from all others. And so it is laid down by jurists, as an elementary principle, that the laws of one State have no operation outside of its territory, except so far as is allowed by comity; and that no tribunal established by it can extend its process beyond that territory so as to subject either persons or property to its decisions. . . .

> "Substituted service by publication, or in any other authorized form, may be sufficient to inform parties of the object of proceedings taken where property is once brought under the control of the court by seizure or some equivalent act. The law assumes that property is always in the possession of its owner, in person or by agent; and it proceeds upon the theory that its seizure will inform him, not only that it is taken into the custody of the court, but that he must look to any proceedings authorized by law upon such seizure for its condemnation and sale. Such service may also be sufficient in cases where the object of the action is to reach and dispose of property in the State, or of some interest therein, by enforcing a contract or a lien respecting the same, or to partition it among different owners, or, when the public is a party, to condemn and appropriate it for a public purpose. In other words, such service may answer in all actions which are substantially proceedings in rem. But where the entire object of the action is to determine the personal rights and obligations of the defendants, that is, where the suit is merely in personam, constructive service in this form upon a non-resident is ineffectual for any purpose. Process from the tribunals of one State cannot run into another State, and summon parties there domiciled to leave its territory and respond to proceedings against them. Publication of process or notice within the State where the tribunal sits cannot create any greater obligation upon the

non-resident to appear. Process sent to him out of the State, and process published within it, are equally unavailing in proceedings to establish his personal liability. . . .

"Except in cases affecting the personal status of the plaintiff, and cases in which that mode of service may be considered to have been assented to in advance, . . . the substituted service of process by publication, allowed by the law of Oregon and by similar laws in other States, where actions are brought against non-residents, is effectual only where, in connection with process against the person for commencing the action, property in the State is brought under the control of the court, and subjected to its disposition by process adapted to that purpose, or where the judgment is sought as a means of reaching such property or affecting some interest therein; in other words, where the action is in the nature of a proceeding in rem. . . ."

[The Oregon state judgment had been entered prior to the adoption of the Fourteenth Amendment. The Supreme Court stated, however, by way of dictum that the principles announced in its opinion were required by the due process clause.]

Mr. Justice Hunt dissenting.

I am compelled to dissent from the opinion and judgment of the court, and, deeming the question involved to be important, I take leave to record my views upon it. . . .

* * *

4. It belongs to the legislative power of the State to determine what shall be the modes and means proper to be adopted to give notice to an absent defendant of the commencement of a suit; and if they are such as are reasonably likely to communicate to him information of the proceeding against him, and are in good faith designed to give him such information, and an opportunity to defend is provided for him in the event of his appearance in the suit, it is not competent to the judiciary to declare that such proceeding is void as not being by due process of law.

* * *

NOTES

(1) Is the central problem in the principal case one of adequate notice or of adjudicatory power? In your further studies of the subject, try to determine to what extent, if any, Justice Field's opinion reflects currently prevailing law. For a discussion of the principal case in its historical perspective, see Hazard, A General Theory of State Court Jurisdiction, 1965 S.Ct.Rev. 241.

(2) At common law, the court's adjudicatory power over the person of the defendant was grounded on actual physical power: The court had power to proceed only if the defendant, pursuant to a writ of *capias ad respondendum*, had been physically brought before it by the sheriff. In the course of time, the

service of the writ on the defendant personally took the place of the seizure of his person. On historical developments, see also p. 63 supra.

B. PRESENCE

RESTATEMENT, SECOND, CONFLICT OF LAWS (1971)

§ 28. Presence

A state has power to exercise judicial jurisdiction over an individual who is present within its territory, whether permanently or temporarily.

NOTES

(1) Personal service within the court's territorial verge has traditionally been held a sufficient basis for the exercise of in personam power even in cases in which the defendant's presence was of very short duration. See, e.g., Peabody v. Hamilton, 106 Mass. 217 (1870). In this case, the non-resident defendant was served on board a British steamer in the Boston harbor before she was even moored. The Court said: "When the party is in the state, however transiently, and the summons is actually served upon him there, the jurisdiction of the court is complete, as to the person of the defendant." Other old but oft-cited cases upholding the principle of "transient jurisdiction" include Darrah v. Watson, 36 Iowa 116 (1872) (the non-resident defendant was in the state for only a few hours) and Fisher v. Fielding, 67 Conn. 91, 34 A. 714 (1895). The principle was given unusual extension in Grace v. MacArthur, 170 F.Supp. 442 (E.D.Ark.1959), in which a non-resident defendant was served personally on board an airplane that at the time of service was flying over Arkansas. The court upheld the service as creating in personam adjudicatory power in the Arkansas court.

(2) The rule of "transient jurisdiction" has been attacked with typical verve by Ehrenzweig. Ehrenzweig, Conflict of Laws 102–104 (1962); Ehrenzweig, Transient Rule of Personal Jurisdiction: The Power Myth and Forum Conveniens, 65 Yale L.J. 289 (1956). In 1960, Schlesinger wrote that the rule is so well-settled that "as yet no lawyer has been bold enough to risk his client's money in a frontal assault upon the rule." Schlesinger, Methods of Progress in Conflict of Laws—Some Comments on Ehrenzweig's Treatment of Transient Jurisdiction, 9 J.Pub.L. 313, 316 (1960). And in England, where lawyers are apparently less timid, a frontal assault upon the rule was repulsed summarily in Colt Industries, Inc. v. Sarlie, 1 All.Eng.L.R. 673 (Q.B.1966). At present, the status of "transient jurisdiction" is doubtful. The Supreme Court's decision in Shaffer v. Heitner, p. 298 infra, provides significant support for the view that it is unconstitutional. After considerable speculation by courts and commentators (see, e.g., Vernon, Single–Factor Bases of In Personam Jurisdiction—A Speculation on the Impact of Shaffer v. Heitner: Seminal or Minimal? 45 Brooklyn L.Rev. 519, 523 (1979); Clermont, Restating Territorial Jurisdiction and Venue for State and Federal Courts, 66 Cornell L.Rev. 411 (1981)), the Supreme Court attempted to answer the question in Burnham v. Superior Court, ___ U.S. ___, ___ S.Ct. ___, ___ L.Ed.2d ___ (1990), Appendix, p. 1136,

infra. The Court unanimously upheld service on the facts of the case, with a majority sustaining presence as generally sufficient.

(3) Does the rule that personal service within the state creates in personam power find its most regular application in cases of brief visits by non-residents?

(4) Does personal service within the state create both in personam jurisdiction and competence? Does Fed.R.Civ.P. 4(d) regulate only the modalities of service or does it also regulate the in personam competence of the federal courts? Cf. Mississippi Publishing Corp. v. Murphree, 326 U.S. 438, 66 S.Ct. 242, 90 L.Ed. 185 (1946); Fed.R.Civ.P. 4(f). See also Arrowsmith v. United Press International, 320 F.2d 219 (2d Cir.1963), p. 325 infra. Does the scope of in personam jurisdiction created by personal service differ depending on whether the service is made in federal or state court proceedings? Even in diversity litigation? See Fed.R.Civ.P. 4(f). Is this reasonable? Do similar questions arise in connection with other bases of adjudicatory power?

(5) The rule that personal service within the state creates in personam adjudicatory power is unknown in civil law countries. In these countries, the basic rule—expressed by the Latin phrase *actor sequitur forum rei*—is that the defendant must be sued before the court of his domicile. But when this is impossible, recourse is often open to rules similar to our long-arm statutes, about which more below, or to so-called extraordinary rules that give the requisite in personam power over the defendant to the court of the plaintiff's nationality (France), the plaintiff's domicile or residence (Holland), or the court where assets, even of such trivial nature as an umbrella, of a non-resident defendant can be found (in Sweden, this is called the umbrella rule). Are these extraordinary rules compatible with our notions of due process? On European rules of in personam adjudicatory power, see Herzog, Civil Procedure in France 170–231 (1967); Ginsburg & Bruzelius, Civil Procedure in Sweden 125–192 (1965); Cappelletti & Perillo, Civil Procedure in Italy 80–115 (1965); Weser, Bases of Judicial Jurisdiction in the Common Market Countries, 10 Am.J.Comp. L. 323 (1961); deVries & Lowenfeld, Jurisdiction in Personal Actions—A Comparison of Civil Law Views, 44 Iowa L.Rev. 306 (1959); Smit, The Terms Jurisdiction and Competence in Comparative Law, 10 Am.J.Comp.L. 164 (1961). Louisiana has abandoned French rules of adjudicatory power in favor of Anglo–American concepts because, among other reasons, the latter have "been superimposed on the procedural law of Louisiana . . . by federal constitutional requirements of full faith and credit and due process of law". McMahon, Jurisdiction Under the Louisiana Code of Civil Procedure, 35 Tul.L.Rev. 501, 502 (1961).

(6) Note that personal service within the state satisfies two constitutional requirements: (1) that the court have in personam power and (2) that the defendant be given adequate notice. On the latter requirement, see p. 330 infra. In studying the materials that follow, determine whether service creates adjudicatory power in any other situation.

COOPER v. WYMAN

Supreme Court of North Carolina, 1898.
122 N.C. 784, 29 S.E. 947.

CLARK, J.: The defendant is a non-resident of this State and was served with a summons in this action while attending Swain Superior

[handwritten marginalia: "out-of-state) was served while he appeared ... ct for another case"]

Court to prosecute an action, in which he was sued, as a witness in his own behalf, and the affidavit (which was taken as true, not being controverted) states that he was not in this State for any other purpose whatever.

The motion to dismiss the action was properly refused, but the point relied on . . . is that a summons or other civil process cannot be served upon a non-resident who comes into this State for the sole purpose of attending a litigation in our courts as suitor or witness. This is the well established rule of law and the very numerous cases to that effect are collected in some 18 pages of small type in the notes to Mullen v. Sanborn, 25 L.R.A. 721. They represent so universal and so uniform a holding upon the point that it is unnecessary to do more than refer to them. The rule is thus stated in Rorer Inter-state Law, 26: "It is the policy of the law to protect (non-resident) suitors and witnesses from service of process in civil actions, whether the process be such as requires their arrest or be merely in the nature of a summons. Service in such cases will be set aside as well upon general principles as upon positive law, if there is such." As stated in many of the cases, this settled rule is based upon high considerations of public policy, not upon statutory law, since it is the public interest that suitors and witnesses from other States who cannot be compelled to attend our courts, may not be deterred from voluntarily appearing by fear of being served with process in other actions, their presence, if obtainable, being calculated to enable the courts to more thoroughly educe the truth of the matters in litigation. Baldwin v. Emerson, 16 R.I. 304.

* * *

NOTES

(1) To what extent has the question addressed in the principal case lost significance, now that transient presence is a questionable basis for adjudicatory authority? See p. 225, Note (2), supra.

(2) In the principal case, did the court lack jurisdiction or competence? Cf. Eberlin v. Pennsylvania Railroad, 402 Pa. 520, 522, 167 A.2d 155, 156–57 (1961): "The privilege of exemption from service of process enjoyed by a nonresident suitor or witness in a civil action is not a privilege of the individual but of the court itself . . .. The privilege is only extended as judicial necessities require . . .." Restatement, Second, Conflict of Laws § 83 (1971).

(3) Which of the following non-residents coming into the state to attend litigation pending there should be granted immunity from service of process: the plaintiff, the defendant, a witness who comes voluntarily, a witness who comes under compulsion, or an attorney? Does it make any difference whether the process initiates an action related to the proceedings for which the non-resident enters the state? See Lamb v. Schmitt, 285 U.S. 222, 52 S.Ct. 317, 76 L.Ed. 720 (1932).

(4) Should an immunity from process rule be applied when there exists a basis for the exercise of adjudicatory power over the defendant other than personal service within the court's verge—for example, a basis created by a long-arm statute (see p. 250 infra)? See Keeffe & Roscia, Immunity and Sentimentality, 32 Cornell L.Q. 471 (1947).

(5) Immunity from process is also extended in varying degrees to foreign states and their emissaries. See generally Henkin, Pugh, Schachter & Smit, International Law 490 (1985). This immunity is either grounded in international law or premised on specific statutory provisions. For the latter, see, e.g., Foreign Sovereign Immunities Act of 1976, 28 U.S.C.A. §§ 1330 et seq. (West Supp.1984). What is the justification for this immunity?

WYMAN v. NEWHOUSE

United States Court of Appeals, Second Circuit, 1937.
93 F.2d 313, cert. denied 303 U.S. 664, 58 S.Ct. 831, 82 L.Ed. 1122 (1938).

MANTON, CIRCUIT JUDGE. This appeal is from a judgment entered dismissing the complaint on motion before trial. The action is on a judgment entered by default in a Florida state court, a jury having assessed the damages. The recovery there was for money loaned, money advanced for appellee, and for seduction under promise of marriage.

Appellee's answer pleads facts supporting his claim that he was fraudulently enticed into the Florida jurisdiction, appellant's state of residence, for the sole purpose of service of process. A motion by the plaintiff-appellant to strike out this defense and for summary judgment, pursuant to rule 113 of the New York Rules of Civil Practice, was denied. For the purpose of such a motion, the facts alleged in the answer are deemed to be true. Rules 109, 112. Affidavits were submitted in support of and in opposition to these motions, and thereupon appellee moved to dismiss the complaint. The motion was granted.

Appellant and appellee were both married, but before this suit appellant's husband died. They had known each other for some years and had engaged in meretricious relations.

The affidavits submitted by the appellee deemed to be true for the purpose of testing the alleged error of dismissing the complaint established that he was a resident of New York and never lived in Florida. On October 25, 1935, while appellee was in Salt Lake City, Utah, he received a telegram from the appellant, which read: "Account illness home planning leaving. Please come on way back. Must see you." Upon appellee's return to New York he received a letter from appellant stating that her mother was dying in Ireland; that she was leaving the United States for good to go to her mother; that she could not go without seeing the appellee once more; and that she wanted to discuss her affairs with him before she left. Shortly after the receipt of this letter, they spoke to each other on the telephone, whereupon the appellant repeated, in a hysterical and distressed voice, the substance of her letter. Appellee promised to go to Florida in a week or ten days and agreed to notify her when he would arrive. This he did, but before leaving New York by plane he received a letter couched in endearing terms and expressing love and affection for him, as well as her delight at his coming. Before leaving New York, appellee telegraphed appellant, suggesting arrangements for their accommodations together while in Miami, Fla. She telegraphed him at a hotel in Washington, D.C., where he was to stop en route, advising him that the arrangements requested had been made. Appellee arrived at 6 o'clock in the morning at the Miami Airport and saw the appellant standing with her sister some 75 feet distant. He was met by a deputy sheriff who, upon identifying appellee, served him with process in a suit for $500,000. A photographer was present who attempted to take his picture. Thereupon a stranger introduced himself and offered to take appellee to his home, stating that he knew a lawyer who was acquainted with the appellant's attorney. The attorney whom appellee was advised to consult came to the stranger's home and seemed to know about the case. The attorney invited appellee to his office, and upon his arrival he found one of the lawyers for the appellant there. Appellee did not retain the Florida attorney to represent him. He returned to New York by plane that evening and consulted his New York counsel, who advised him to ignore the summons served in Florida. He did so, and judgment was entered by default. Within a few days after the service of process, the appellant came to New York and sought an interview with the appellee. It resulted in their meeting at the home of the appellee's attorney. She was accompanied by her Florida counsel.

These facts and reasonable deductions therefrom convincingly establish that the appellee was induced to enter the jurisdiction of the state of Florida by a fraud perpetrated upon him by the appellant in falsely representing her mother's illness, her intention to leave the United States, and her love and affection for him, when her sole purpose and apparent thought was to induce him to come within the Florida jurisdiction so as to serve him in an action for damages. Appellant does not deny making these representations. All her statements of great and undying love were disproved entirely by her appearance at the airport and participation in the happenings there. She never went to Ireland to see her mother, if indeed the latter was sick at all.

* * *

This judgment is attacked for fraud perpetrated upon the appellee which goes to the jurisdiction of the Florida court over his person. A judgment procured fraudulently, as here, lacks jurisdiction and is null and void. Lucy v. Deas, 59 Fla. 552, 52 So. 515. Thompson v. Thompson, 226 U.S. 551, 33 S.Ct. 129, 57 L.Ed. 347. A fraud affecting the jurisdiction is equivalent to a lack of jurisdiction. Dunlap & Co. v. Cody, 31 Iowa 260, 7 Am.Rep. 129; Duringer v. Moschino, 93 Ind. 495, 498; Abercrombie v. Abercrombie, 64 Kan. 29, 67 P. 539. The appellee was not required to proceed against the judgment in Florida. His equitable defense in answer to a suit on the judgment is sufficient. A judgment recovered in a sister state, through the fraud of the party procuring the appearance of another, is not binding on the latter when an attempt is made to enforce such judgment in another state. Gray v.

Richmond Bicycle Co., 167 N.Y. 348, 355, 60 N.E. 663, 82 Am.St.Rep. 720. There is a dictum to the contrary in Capwell v. Sipe, 51 F. 667, 668 (C.C.N.D.Ohio), where the defendant was sued in the foreign court while within the jurisdiction attending another case. His objection to service of process was overruled. There is authority to like effect in Vastine v. Bast, 41 Mo. 493. But we think the weight of authority is against such view. In Jaster v. Currie, 198 U.S. 144, 25 S.Ct. 614, 49 L.Ed. 988, to which appellant refers, the court decided only that the defendant had not been enticed into the jurisdiction by fraud and, therefore, that case is not helpful. Smith v. Apple, F.2d 559 (8th Cir.) and Cragin v. Lovell, 109 U.S. 194, 3 S.Ct. 132, 27 L.Ed. 903, deal with irregularities in procedure not voiding the judgment.

The appellee was not required to make out a defense on the merits to the suit in Florida. We are not here concerned with such rule, applicable to alleged fraud in the proceedings after valid jurisdiction of the person and the subject matter has been obtained. Here the court did not duly acquire jurisdiction and no such defense to the merits need be shown. An error made in entering judgment against a party over whom the court had no jurisdiction permits a consideration of the jurisdictional question collaterally. The complaint was properly dismissed.

Judgment affirmed.

NOTES

(1) Did the Florida court lack jurisdiction or competence?

(2) Can a corporate defendant be lured into the "jurisdiction"?

C. APPEARANCE

HARKNESS v. HYDE

Supreme Court of the United States, 1878.
98 U.S. (8 Otto) 476, 25 L.Ed. 237.

Error to the Supreme Court of the Territory of Idaho.

MR. JUSTICE FIELD delivered the opinion of the court.

This was an action to recover damages for maliciously and without probable cause procuring the seizure and detention of property of the plaintiff under a writ of attachment. It was brought in September, 1873, in a district court of the Territory of Idaho for the county of Oneida. The summons, with a copy of the complaint, was soon afterwards served by the sheriff of the county on the defendant, at his place of residence, which was on the Indian reservation, known as the Shoshonee reservation.

The defendant thereupon appeared specially by counsel appointed for the purpose, and moved the court to dismiss the action on the ground that the service thus made upon him on the Indian reservation was outside of the bailiwick of the sheriff, and without the jurisdiction of the court. Upon stipulation of the parties, the motion was adjourned to the Supreme Court of the Territory, and was there overruled. To the decision an exception was taken. The case was then remanded to the District Court, and the defendant filed an answer to the complaint. Upon the trial which followed, the plaintiff obtained a verdict for $3,500. Upon a motion for a new trial, the amount was reduced to $2,500; for which judgment was entered. On appeal to the Supreme Court of the Territory, the judgment was affirmed. The defendant thereupon brought the case here, and now seeks a reversal of the judgment, for the alleged error of the court in refusing to dismiss the action for want of jurisdiction over him.

The act of Congress of March 3, 1863, organizing the Territory of Idaho, provides that it shall not embrace within its limits or jurisdiction any territory of an Indian tribe without the latter's assent, but that "all such territory shall be excepted out of the boundaries, and constitute no part of the Territory of Idaho," until the tribe shall signify its assent to the President to be included within the Territory. 12 Stat. 808. . . .

There can be no jurisdiction in a court of a Territory to render a personal judgment against any one upon service made outside its limits. Personal service within its limits, or the voluntary appearance of the defendants, is essential in such cases. . . .

The right of the defendant to insist upon the objection to the illegality of the service was not waived by the special appearance of counsel for him to move the dismissal of the action on that ground, or what we consider as intended, that the service be set aside; nor, when that motion was overruled, by their answering for him to the merits of the action. Illegality in a proceeding by which jurisdiction is to be obtained is in no case waived by the appearance of the defendant for the purpose of calling the attention of the court to such irregularity; nor is the objection waived when being urged it is overruled, and the defendant is thereby compelled to answer. He is not considered as abandoning his objection because he does not submit to further proceedings without contestation. It is only where he pleads to the merits in the first instance, without insisting upon the illegality, that the objection is deemed to be waived.

The judgment of the Supreme Court of the Territory, therefore, must be reversed, and the case remanded with directions to reverse the judgment of the District Court for Oneida County, and to direct that court to set aside the service made upon the defendant; and it is

So ordered.

NOTES

(1) The problem adjudicated in the principal case has been resolved in various ways. In state courts, the solution depends on the applicable state law. See Note, Developments in the Law—State Court Jurisdiction, 73 Harv.L.Rev. 909, 993 (1960). In some states, even an interlocutory appeal from an adverse ruling waives the objection. See 1 Beale, Conflict of Laws, sec. 827 (1935); Note, Developments in the Law—State Court Jurisdiction, supra note 510 at 993, 73 Harv.L.Rev. 909, 993 n. 510 (1960).

(2) Does the plaintiff subject himself to the in personam adjudicatory power of the court in which he brings his action? In Adam v. Saenger, 303 U.S. 59, 58 S.Ct. 454, 82 L.Ed. 649 (1938), the plaintiff sued the defendant in a California court. The defendant, in accordance with California procedure, brought a cross-action against the plaintiff. Judgment was rendered in the cross-action in favor of the defendant. When the defendant sued to enforce this judgment in Texas, the Texas court held the judgment null and void on the ground that California had not obtained in personam adjudicatory power over the plaintiff. The Supreme Court reversed (at 67–68):

> "There is nothing in the Fourteenth Amendment to prevent a state from adopting a procedure by which a judgment in personam may be rendered in a cross-action against a plaintiff in its courts, upon service of process or of appropriate pleading upon his attorney of record. The plaintiff having, by his voluntary act in demanding justice from the defendant, submitted himself to the jurisdiction of the court, there is nothing arbitrary or unreasonable in treating him as being there for all purposes for which justice to the defendant requires his presence. It is the price which the state may exact as the condition of opening its courts to the plaintiff."

(3) Does assertion of a counterclaim waive the defense of lack of in personam adjudicatory power and of improper venue? Does the answer depend on whether the counterclaim is permissive or compulsory? See Beaunit Mills, Inc. v. Industrias Reunidas F Matarazzo, 23 F.R.D. 654 (S.D.N.Y.1959). How can a counterclaimant avoid waiver?

(4) May a state exercise in personam jurisdiction over a person who appears specially for the purpose of objecting to its exercise? See York v. Texas, 137 U.S. 15, 11 S.Ct. 9, 34 L.Ed. 604 (1890).

D. CONSENT

NATIONAL EQUIPMENT RENTAL, LIMITED v. SZUKHENT

Supreme Court of the United States, 1964.
375 U.S. 311, 84 S.Ct. 411, 11 L.Ed.2d 354.

[The respondents, two farmers residing in Michigan, had defaulted under a farm equipment lease concluded with the petitioner. The lease provided that "the Lessee hereby designates Florence Weinberg, 47–21 Forty-first Street, Long Island City, N.Y., as agent for the purpose of accepting service of any process within the State of New York." The respondents did not know Mrs. Weinberg, who was the wife of one of the petitioner's officers.

Petitioner commenced suit in the federal court in New York, and the marshal served the process on Mrs. Weinberg. Although the lease agreement did not require it, Mrs. Weinberg mailed the summons and complaint the same day to respondents in Michigan. The petitioner also notified the respondents of the service by certified mail.

The District Court quashed the service, and the Court of Appeals affirmed. The Supreme Court granted certiorari.]

MR. JUSTICE STEWART delivered the opinion of the Court.

*   *   *

. . . The question presented here . . . is whether a party to a private contract may appoint an agent to receive service of process within the meaning of Federal Rule of Civil Procedure 4(d)(1), where the agent is not personally known to the party, and where the agent has not expressly undertaken to transmit notice to the party.

The purpose underlying the contractual provision here at issue seems clear. The clause was inserted by the petitioner and agreed to by the respondents in order to assure that any litigation under the lease should be conducted in the State of New York. The contract specifically provided that "This agreement shall be deemed to have been made in Nassau County, New York, regardless of the order in which the signatures of the parties shall be affixed hereto, and shall be interpreted, and the rights and liabilities of the parties here determined, in accordance with the laws of the State of New York." And it is settled, as the courts below recognized, that parties to a contract may agree in advance to submit to the jurisdiction of a given court, to permit notice to be served by the opposing party, or even to waive notice altogether. See, e.g., Kenny Construction Co. v. Allen, 248 F.2d 656 (C.A.D.C.Cir.1957); Bowles v. Schmitt & Co., Inc., 170 F.2d 617 (C.A.2d Cir.1948); Gilbert v. Burnstine, 255 N.Y. 348, 174 N.E. 706 (1931).

Under well-settled general principles of the law of agency, Florence Weinberg's prompt acceptance and transmittal to the respondents of the summons and complaint pursuant to the authorization was itself sufficient to validate the agency, even though there was no explicit previous promise on her part to do so. . . . 2 Williston on Contracts (3d ed. 1959), § 274.

We deal here with a Federal Rule, applicable to federal courts in all 50 States. But even if we were to assume that this uniform federal standard should give way to contrary local policies, there is no relevant concept of state law which would invalidate the agency here at issue.

. . .

It is argued, finally, that the agency sought to be created in this case was invalid because Florence Weinberg may have had a conflict of interest. This argument is based upon the fact that she was not personally known to the respondents at the time of her appointment and upon a suggestion in the record that she may be related to an officer of the petitioner corporation. But such a contention ignores the narrowly limited nature of the agency here involved. Florence Weinberg was appointed the respondents' agent for the single purpose of receiving service of process. An agent with authority so limited can in no meaningful sense be deemed to have had an interest antagonistic to the respondents, since both the petitioner and the respondents had an equal interest in assuring that, in the event of litigation, the latter be given that adequate and timely notice which is a prerequisite to a valid judgment.

A different case would be presented if Florence Weinberg had not given prompt notice to the respondents, for then the claim might well be made that her failure to do so had operated to invalidate the agency. We hold only that, prompt notice to the respondents having been given, Florence Weinberg was their "agent authorized by appointment" to receive process within the meaning of Federal Rule of Civil Procedure 4(d)(1).

The judgment of the Court of Appeals is reversed. . . .

* * *

NOTES

(1) Does the principal case concern merely the modalities of service or does it also sanction consent as a basis for adjudicatory authority? Should it make a difference whether consent is given in a contract the terms of which were in effect dictated by the economically more powerful party or in a contract that is the product of bargaining between parties of approximately equal strength? See Ehrenzweig, Adhesion Contracts in the Conflict of Laws, 53 Colum.L.Rev. 1072 (1953). Does your answer depend on state law concerning adhesion contracts?

(2) Is consent given without consideration sufficient to create in personam adjudicatory power or must it take the form of a regular contract? See Restatement, Second, Conflict of Laws § 32 (1971). If the consent is embodied in a contract, should its effectiveness be determined under the law governing the contract? See Egley v. T.B. Bennett & Co., 196 Ind. 50, 145 N.E. 830 (1924). Would your answer depend on whether the action is brought in a state or a federal court?

(3) Advance consent to being sued in a particular court may take the form of a cognovit note, in which the debtor authorizes his creditor or the latter's attorney to receive service and confess judgment on his behalf. Reliance on cognovit notes may be severely limited by state statute. According to a relatively recent survey, 15 states declare them illegal, 23 states condition their validity on the meeting of various requirements, only 7 states expressly allow them, and the remaining states do not regulate their use by statute. Hopson, Cognovit Judgments: An Ignored Problem of Due Process and Full Faith and Credit, 29 U.Chi.L.Rev. 111, 126 (1961). Must the federal courts apply state statutes regulating cognovit note practice?

Judgments based on cognovit notes do not necessarily offend due process. In D.H. Overmyer Co. v. Frick Co., 405 U.S. 174, 92 S.Ct. 775, 31 L.Ed.2d 124

(1972), the Supreme Court upheld such a judgment on the ground that the defendant, who was the debtor in an amount of more than $100,000, had "voluntarily and knowingly waived the rights it otherwise possessed to prejudgment notice and hearing." The Court stressed, however, that the parties were of equal bargaining power and that a different result might obtain "where there is great disparity in bargaining power, and where the debtor receives nothing for the cognovit provision . . . ." Acting upon this qualification, the Court, in Swarb v. Lennox, 405 U.S. 191, 92 S.Ct. 767, 31 L.Ed.2d 138 (1972), rehearing denied 405 U.S. 1049, 92 S.Ct. 1303, 31 L.Ed.2d 592 (1972), upheld on the same day a decision in a class action ruling unconstitutional the Pennsylvania confession of judgment procedure as applied to persons earning less than $10,000 per year, who had been found to have waived prejudgment notice and hearing "without adequate understanding." On cognovit notes, see also Note, 24 Hastings L.Rev. 1045 (1973).

(4) Is the rule that consent creates adjudicatory power one of common or statutory law?

(5) What would you have advised Mrs. Weinberg if she had consulted you on whether she should inform the Szukhents of the bringing of the action? What would have been your advice if you had concluded that she was not legally required to do so?

(6) Will the courts enforce an agreement not to sue except in a designated forum? See Lenhoff, The Parties' Choice of a Forum: Prorogation Agreements, 15 Rutgers L.Rev. 414 (1961).

In the Bremen v. Zapata Off–Shore Co., 407 U.S. 1, 92 S.Ct. 1907, 32 L.Ed. 2d 513 (1972), a case arising under federal law, the Supreme Court held that the Florida court had to heed a clause in the contract designating London as the exclusive forum and could not proceed with the adjudication of the dispute. It did so, even though it seemed clear that the English court would give effect to a clause that limited the defendant's liability and that was argued to be ineffective under American law. See also Scherk v. Alberto–Culver Co., 417 U.S. 506, 94 S.Ct. 2449, 41 L.Ed.2d 270 (1974), rehearing denied 419 U.S. 885, 95 S.Ct. 157, 42 L.Ed.2d 129 (1975), holding that a New York court could not adjudicate a dispute arising under a contract that provided for arbitration in Lichtenstein.

On the *Zapata* case, see also Juenger, Supreme Court Validation of Forum–Selection Clauses, 19 Wayne L.Rev. 49 (1972); Nadelmann, Choice-of-Court Clauses in the United States: The Road to Zapata, 21 Am.J.Comp.L. 124 (1973); Reese, The Supreme Court Supports Enforcement of Choice-of-Forum Clauses, 7 The International Lawyer 530 (1973).

E. DOMICILE AND NATIONALITY

MILLIKEN v. MEYER, ADMINISTRATRIX

Supreme Court of the United States, 1940.
311 U.S. 457, 61 S.Ct. 339, 85 L.Ed. 278.

[Milliken commenced an action against Meyer in a Wyoming court which resulted in a judgment in his favor. Thereafter, Meyer brought an action against Milliken in a Colorado court seeking a decree that the Wyoming judgment was "a nullity for want of jurisdiction". The lower

Colorado court found that Meyer was domiciled in Wyoming when the Wyoming suit was commenced, that service had properly been made in accordance with a Wyoming statute which provided for service by publication in "actions where the defendant, being a resident of the state, has departed from the county of his residence . . .", and that the Wyoming judgment was valid. The Colorado Supreme Court held the Wyoming decree void on its face "because of an irreconcilable contradiction between the findings and the decree." The Supreme Court granted certiorari.]

MR. JUSTICE DOUGLAS delivered the opinion of the Court.   . . .

Where a judgment rendered in one state is challenged in another, a want of jurisdiction over either the person or the subject matter is of course open to inquiry. Grover & Baker Sewing Machine Co. v. Radcliffe, 137 U.S. 287, 11 S.Ct. 92, 34 L.Ed. 670; Adam v. Saenger, 303 U.S. 59, 58 S.Ct. 454, 82 L.Ed. 649. But if the judgment on its face appears to be a "record of a court of general jurisdiction, such jurisdiction over the cause and the parties is to be presumed unless disproved by extrinsic evidence, or by the record itself." Adam v. Saenger, supra, 303 U.S. at page 62, 58 S.Ct. at page 456, 82 L.Ed. 649. In such case the full faith and credit clause of the Constitution precludes any inquiry into the merits of the cause of action, the logic or consistency of the decision, or the validity of the legal principles on which the judgment is based. Fauntleroy v. Lum, 210 U.S. 230, 28 S.Ct. 641, 52 L.Ed. 1039; Roche v. McDonald, 275 U.S. 449, 48 S.Ct. 142, 72 L.Ed. 365; Titus v. Wallick, 306 U.S. 282, 59 S.Ct. 557, 83 L.Ed. 653. Whatever mistakes of law may underlie the judgment (Cooper v. Reynolds, 10 Wall. 308, 19 L.Ed. 931) it is "conclusive as to all the *media concludendi.*" Fauntleroy v. Lum, supra, 210 U.S. at page 237, 28 S.Ct. at page 643, 52 L.Ed. 1039.

Accordingly, if the Wyoming court had jurisdiction over Meyer, the holding by the Colorado Supreme Court that the Wyoming judgment was void because of an inconsistency between the findings and the decree was not warranted.

On the findings of the Colorado trial court, not impaired by the Colorado Supreme Court, it is clear that Wyoming had jurisdiction over Meyer in the 1931 suit. Domicile in the state is alone sufficient to bring an absent defendant within the reach of the state's jurisdiction for purposes of a personal judgment by means of appropriate substituted service. Substituted service in such cases has been quite uniformly upheld where the absent defendant was served at his usual place of abode in the state (Huntley v. Baker, 33 Hun 578; Hurlbut v. Thomas, 55 Conn. 181, 10 A. 556; Harryman v. Roberts, 52 Md. 64) as well as where he was personally served without the state . . . Certainly then Meyer's domicile in Wyoming was a sufficient basis for that extraterritorial service. As in case of the authority of the United States over its absent citizens (Blackmer v. United States, 284 U.S. 421, 52 S.Ct. 252, 76 L.Ed. 375), the authority of a state over one of its citizens is not terminated by the mere fact of his absence from the state. The state which accords him privileges and affords protection to him and his property by virtue of his domicile may also exact reciprocal duties. "Enjoyment of the privileges of residence within the state, and the attendant right to invoke the protection of its laws, are inseparable" from the various incidences of state citizenship. See Lawrence v. State Tax Commission, 286 U.S. 276, 279, 52 S.Ct. 556, 557, 76 L.Ed. 1102; New York ex rel. Cohn v. Graves, 300 U.S. 308, 57 S.Ct. 466, 81 L.Ed. 666. The responsibilities of that citizenship arise out of the relationship to the state which domicile creates. That relationship is not dissolved by mere absence from the state. The attendant duties, like the rights and privileges incident to domicile, are not dependent on continuous presence in the state. One such incident of domicile is amenability to suit within the state even during sojourns without the state, where the state has provided and employed a reasonable method for apprising such an absent party of the proceedings against him. See Restatement, Conflict of Laws, §§ 47, 79; Dodd, Jurisdiction in Personal Actions, 23 Ill.L.Rev. 427. Here such a reasonable method was so provided and so employed.

Reversed.

NOTES

(1) Is residence also a proper basis of in personam adjudicatory power? Does the answer depend on the meaning of the term residence? See Reese & Green, That Elusive Word "Residence", 6 Vand.L.Rev. 561 (1953); Restatement (Second) of Conflict of Laws § 30 (1971). Under Order XI, Rule 1(c) of the English Rules of the Supreme Court of Judicature, the court may permit service "out of the jurisdiction" whenever relief is sought "against any person domiciled or ordinarily resident within the jurisdiction." Does this rule regulate merely extraterritorial service?

(2) After the Teapot Dome scandal broke, Blackmer, a United States citizen, fled to France. He was there served by the United States consul with two subpoenas requiring him to appear as a witness at a criminal trial in the United States. When he failed to appear, the court imposed two fines of $30,000 each, to be satisfied out of Blackmer's property seized in the United States. Before the Supreme Court, Blackmer challenged the constitutionality of the proceedings under the Fifth Amendment. The Supreme Court rejected the challenge. Blackmer v. United States, 284 U.S. 421, 52 S.Ct. 252, 76 L.Ed. 375 (1932). What types of jurisdiction were involved in this case? What was the basis for each type? See also Restatement, Second, Judgments § 5 (1982): "A court of the United States may acquire jurisdiction over a citizen of the United States although he is not domiciled within the United States." Is nationality as acceptable a basis as domicile or as presence? The statute, 28 U.S.C.A. §§ 1783–1784, that authorized the proceedings in the Blackmer case had been specifically enacted for the purpose. It was amended so as to extend its application to United States residents and also otherwise to liberalize its provisions, which generally regulate the service of subpoenas in the federal courts. See Fed.R.Civ.P. 45(e); Fed.R.Crim.P. 17(e)(2). On the history of the statute and its reform, see Smit, International Aspects of Federal Civil Proce-

dure, 61 Colum.L.Rev. 1031, 1044–1053 (1961); Smit, International Litigation Under the United States Code, 65 Colum.L.Rev. 1015, 1035–1040 (1965).

(3) May the court proceed in personam against a domiciliary, resident, or national of the forum even if there is no statute authorizing it to do so? Cf. Restatement, Second, Conflict of Laws § 29, Comment c (1971).

F. CLAIMS ARISING FROM LOCAL ACTS OR CONSEQUENCES

HESS v. PAWLOSKI

Supreme Court of the United States, 1927.
274 U.S. 352, 47 S.Ct. 632, 71 L.Ed. 1091.

MR. JUSTICE BUTLER delivered the opinion of the Court.

This action was brought by defendant in error to recover damages for personal injuries. The declaration alleged that plaintiff in error negligently and wantonly drove a motor vehicle on a public highway in Massachusetts and that by reason thereof the vehicle struck and injured defendant in error. Plaintiff in error is a resident of Pennsylvania. No personal service was made on him and no property belonging to him was attached. The service of process was made in compliance with c. 90, General Laws of Massachusetts, as amended by Stat.1923, c. 431, § 2, the material parts of which follow:

"The acceptance by a non-resident of the rights and privileges conferred by section three or four, as evidenced by his operating a motor vehicle thereunder, or the operation by a non-resident of a motor vehicle on a public way in the commonwealth other than under said sections, shall be deemed equivalent to an appointment by such non-resident of the registrar or his successor in office, to be his true and lawful attorney upon whom may be served all lawful processes in any action or proceeding against him, growing out of any accident or collision in which said non-resident may be involved while operating a motor vehicle on such a way, and said acceptance or operation shall be a signification of his agreement that any such process against him which is so served shall be of the same legal force and validity as if served on him personally. Service of such process shall be made by leaving a copy of the process with a fee of two dollars in the hands of the registrar, or in his office, and such service shall be sufficient service upon the said non-resident; provided, that notice of such service and a copy of the process are forthwith sent by registered mail by the plaintiff to the defendant, and the defendant's return receipt and the plaintiff's affidavit of compliance herewith are appended to the writ and entered with the declaration. The court in which the action is pending may order such continuances as may be necessary to afford the defendant reasonable opportunity to defend the action."

Plaintiff in error appeared specially for the purpose of contesting jurisdiction and filed an answer in abatement and moved to dismiss on the ground that the service of process, if sustained, would deprive him of his property without due process of law in violation of the Fourteenth Amendment. The court overruled the answer in abatement and denied the motion. The Supreme Judicial Court held the statute to be a valid exercise of the police power, and affirmed the order. 250 Mass. 22. At the trial the contention was renewed and again denied. Plaintiff in error excepted. The jury returned a verdict for defendant in error. The exceptions were overruled by the Supreme Judicial Court. 253 Mass. 478. Thereupon the Superior Court entered judgment. The writ of error was allowed by the chief justice of that court.

The question is whether the Massachusetts enactment contravenes the due process clause of the Fourteenth Amendment.

The process of a court of one State cannot run into another and summon a party there domiciled to respond to proceedings against him. Notice sent outside the State to a non-resident is unavailing to give jurisdiction in an action against him personally for money recovery. Pennoyer v. Neff, 95 U.S. 714, 24 L.Ed. 565. There must be actual service within the State of notice upon him or upon some one authorized to accept service for him. Goldey v. Morning News, 156 U.S. 518, 15 S.Ct. 559, 39 L.Ed. 517. A personal judgment rendered against a non-resident who has neither been served with process nor appeared in the suit is without validity. McDonald v. Mabee, 243 U.S. 90, 37 S.Ct. 343, 61 L.Ed. 608. The mere transaction of business in a State by non-resident natural persons does not imply consent to be bound by the process of its courts. Flexner v. Farson, 248 U.S. 289, 39 S.Ct. 97, 63 L.Ed. 250. The power of a State to exclude foreign corporations, although not absolute but qualified, is the ground on which such an implication is supported as to them. Pennsylvania Fire Insurance Co. v. Gold Issue Mining Co., 243 U.S. 93, 96, 37 S.Ct. 344, 61 L.Ed. 610. But a State may not withhold from non-resident individuals the right of doing business therein. The privileges and immunities clause of the Constitution, § 2, Art. IV, safeguards to the citizens of one State the right "to pass through, or to reside in any other state for purposes of trade, agriculture, professional pursuits, or otherwise." And it prohibits state legislation discriminating against citizens of other States, Corfield v. Coryell, 4 Wash.C.C. 371, 381; Ward v. Maryland, 12 Wall. 418, 430, 20 L.Ed. 449; Paul v. Virginia, 8 Wall. 168, 180, 19 L.Ed. 357.

Motor vehicles are dangerous machines; and even when skillfully and carefully operated, their use is attended by serious dangers to persons and property. In the public interest the State may make and enforce regulations reasonably calculated to promote care on the part of all, residents and non-residents alike, who use its highways. The measure in question operates to require a non-resident to answer for his conduct in the State where arise causes of action alleged against him, as well as to provide for a claimant a convenient method by which he may sue to enforce his rights. Under the statute the implied consent is limited to proceedings growing out of accidents or collisions on a highway in which the non-resident may be involved. It is required that he shall actually receive and receipt for notice of the service and a copy of the process. And it contemplates such continuances as may be found necessary to give reasonable time and opportunity for defense. It makes no hostile discrimination against non-residents but tends to put them on the same footing as residents. Literal and precise equality in respect of this matter is not attainable; it is not required. Canadian Northern Ry. Co. v. Eggen, 252 U.S. 553, 561–562, 40 S.Ct. 402, 64 L.Ed. 713. The State's power to regulate the use of its highways extends to their use by non-residents as well as by residents. Hendrick v. Maryland, 235 U.S. 610, 622, 35 S.Ct. 140, 59 L.Ed. 385. And, in advance of the operation of a motor vehicle on its highway by a non-resident, the State may require him to appoint one of its officials as his agent on whom process may be served in proceedings growing out of such use. Kane v. New Jersey, 242 U.S. 160, 167, 37 S.Ct. 30, 61 L.Ed. 222. That case recognizes power of the State to exclude a non-resident until the formal appointment is made. And, having the power so to exclude, the State may declare that the use of the highway by the non-resident is the equivalent of the appointment of the registrar as agent on whom process may be served. Cf. Pennsylvania Fire Insurance Co. v. Gold Issue Mining Co., supra, 96 (37 S.Ct. 344); Lafayette Ins. Co. v. French, 18 How. 404, 407, 408, 15 L.Ed. 451. The difference between the formal and implied appointment is not substantial so far as concerns the application of the due process clause of the Fourteenth Amendment.

Judgment affirmed.

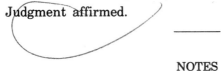

NOTES

(1) In Wuchter v. Pizzutti, 276 U.S. 13, 48 S.Ct. 259, 72 L.Ed. 446 (1928), service was made under a New Jersey non-resident motorists statute by leaving the process with the New Jersey Secretary of State. Although the statute did not require it, notice was served personally on the defendant outside the state. The Court held that the due process clause had been violated: "But it is said that the defendant here had actual notice by service out of New Jersey in Pennsylvania. He did not, however, appear in the cause and such notice was not required by the statute. Not having been directed by the statute, it can not, therefore, supply constitutional validity to the statute or to service under it." Is this holding compatible with the implied consent analysis?

(2) The fiction of implied consent has proved to be of hardy stock. Long after the International Shoe case, a plaintiff in a non-resident motorist case sought to argue that the defendant, by consenting to be sued in the state, also waived his objection to improper venue in the federal court. Olberding v. Illinois Central Railroad Co., 346 U.S. 338, 74 S.Ct. 83, 98 L.Ed. 39 (1953). Justice Frankfurter met the attempt with some frank talk (at 340–341):

"This is a horse soon curried. . . . It is true that in order to ease the process by which new decisions are fitted into pre-existing modes of analysis there has been some fictive talk to the effect that the reason why a non-resident can be subjected to a state's jurisdiction is that the non-resident has 'impliedly' consented to be sued there. In point of fact, however, jurisdiction in these cases does not rest on consent at all

. . . .. The defendant may protest to high heaven his unwillingness to be sued and it avails him not."

(3) Does a state's long arm also reach the owner of the car? Does this depend on whether it was driven within the state with the owner's consent?

INTERNATIONAL SHOE CO. v. WASHINGTON

Supreme Court of the United States, 1945.
326 U.S. 310, 66 S.Ct. 154, 90 L.Ed. 95.

MR. CHIEF JUSTICE STONE delivered the opinion of the Court.

The questions for decision are (1) whether, within the limitations of the due process clause of the Fourteenth Amendment, appellant, a Delaware corporation, has by its activities in the State of Washington rendered itself amenable to proceedings in the courts of that state to recover unpaid contributions to the state unemployment compensation fund exacted by state statutes, Washington Unemployment Compensation Act, Washington Revised Statutes, § 9998–103a through § 9998–123a, 1941 Supp., and (2) whether the state can exact those contributions consistently with the due process clause of the Fourteenth Amendment.

The statutes in question set up a comprehensive scheme of unemployment compensation, the costs of which are defrayed by contributions required to be made by employers to a state unemployment compensation fund. The contributions are a specified percentage of the wages payable annually by each employer for his employees' services in the state. The assessment and collection of the contributions and the fund are administered by appellees. Section 14(c) of the Act (Wash. Rev.Stat., 1941 Supp., § 9998–114c) authorizes appellee Commissioner to issue an order and notice of assessment of delinquent contributions upon prescribed personal service of the notice upon the employer if found within the state, or, if not so found, by mailing the notice to the employer by registered mail at his last known address. That section also authorizes the Commissioner to collect the assessment by distraint if it is not paid within ten days after service of the notice. . . .

In this case notice of assessment for the years in question was personally served upon a sales solicitor employed by appellant in the State of Washington, and a copy of the notice was mailed by registered mail to appellant at its address in St. Louis, Missouri. Appellant appeared specially before the office of unemployment and moved to set aside the order and notice of assessment on the ground that the service upon appellant's salesman was not proper service upon appellant; that appellant was not a corporation of the State of Washington and was not doing business within the state; that it had no agent within the state upon whom service could be made; and that appellant is not an employer and does not furnish employment within the meaning of the statute.

The motion was heard on evidence and a stipulation of facts by the appeal tribunal which denied the motion and ruled that appellee Commissioner was entitled to recover the unpaid contributions. That action was affirmed by the Commissioner; both the Superior Court and the Supreme Court affirmed. 22 Wash.2d 146, 154 P.2d 801. Appellant in each of these courts assailed the statute as applied, as a violation of the due process clause of the Fourteenth Amendment, and as imposing a constitutionally prohibited burden on interstate commerce. The cause comes here on appeal under § 237(a) of the Judicial Code, 28 U.S.C.A. § 344(a), appellant assigning as error that the challenged statutes as applied infringe the due process clause of the Fourteenth Amendment and the commerce clause.

The facts as found by the appeal tribunal and accepted by the state Superior Court and Supreme Court, are not in dispute. Appellant is a Delaware corporation, having its principal place of business in St. Louis, Missouri, and is engaged in the manufacture and sale of shoes and other footwear. It maintains places of business in several states, other than Washington, at which its manufacturing is carried on and from which its merchandise is distributed interstate through several sales units or branches located outside the State of Washington.

Appellant has no office in Washington and makes no contracts either for sale or purchase of merchandise there. It maintains no stock of merchandise in that state and makes there no deliveries of goods in intrastate commerce. During the years from 1937 to 1940, now in question, appellant employed eleven to thirteen salesmen under direct supervision and control of sales managers located in St. Louis. These salesmen resided in Washington; their principal activities were confined to that state; and they were compensated by commissions based upon the amount of their sales. The commissions for each year totaled more than $31,000. Appellant supplies its salesmen with a line of samples, each consisting of one shoe of a pair, which they display to prospective purchasers. On occasion they rent permanent sample rooms, for exhibiting samples, in business buildings, or rent rooms in hotels or business buildings temporarily for that purpose. The cost of such rentals is reimbursed by appellant.

The authority of the salesmen is limited to exhibiting their samples and soliciting orders from prospective buyers, at prices and on terms fixed by appellant. The salesmen transmit the orders to appellant's office in St. Louis for acceptance or rejection, and when accepted the merchandise for filling the orders is shipped f.o.b. from points outside Washington to the purchasers within the state. All the merchandise shipped into Washington is invoiced at the place of shipment from which collections are made. No salesman has authority to enter into contracts or to make collections.

The Supreme Court of Washington was of opinion that the regular and systematic solicitation of orders in the state by appellant's salesmen, resulting in a continuous flow of appellant's product into the state, was sufficient to constitute doing business in the state so as to make appellant amenable to suit in its courts. But it was also of opinion that there were sufficient additional activities shown to bring the case within the rule frequently stated, that solicitation within a state by the agents of a foreign corporation plus some additional activities there are sufficient to render the corporation amenable to suit brought in the courts of the state to enforce an obligation arising out of its activities there. International Harvester Co. v. Kentucky, 234 U.S. 579, 587, 34 S.Ct. 944, 946, 58 L.Ed. 1479; People's Tobacco Co. v. American Tobacco Co., 246 U.S. 79, 87, 38 S.Ct. 233, 235, 62 L.Ed. 587; Frene v. Louisville Cement Co., 77 U.S.App.D.C. 129, 134 F.2d 511, 516. The court found such additional activities in the salesmen's display of samples sometimes in permanent display rooms, and the salesmen's residence within the state, continued over a period of years, all resulting in a substantial volume of merchandise regularly shipped by appellant to purchasers within the state. The court also held that the statute as applied did not invade the constitutional power of Congress to regulate interstate commerce and did not impose a prohibited burden on such commerce.

Appellant's argument, renewed here, that the statute imposes an unconstitutional burden on interstate commerce need not detain us. . . .

Appellant also insists that its activities within the state were not sufficient to manifest its "presence" there and that in its absence the state courts were without jurisdiction, that consequently it was a denial of due process for the state to subject appellant to suit. It refers to those cases in which it was said that the mere solicitation of orders for the purchase of goods within a state, to be accepted without the state and filled by shipment of the purchased goods interstate, does not render the corporation seller amenable to suit within the state. See Green v. Chicago, B. & Q. R. Co., 205 U.S. 530, 533, 27 S.Ct. 595, 596, 51 L.Ed. 916; International Harvester Co. v. Kentucky, supra, 586–587; Philadelphia & Reading R. Co. v. McKibbin, 243 U.S. 264, 268, 37 S.Ct. 280, 61 L.Ed. 710; People's Tobacco Co. v. American Tobacco Co., supra, 246 U.S. 87, 38 S.Ct. 235, 62 L.Ed. 587, Ann.Cas.1918C, 537. And appellant further argues that since it was not present within the state, it is a denial of due process to subject it to taxation or other money exaction. It thus denies the power of the state to lay the tax or to subject appellant to a suit for its collection.

Historically the jurisdiction of courts to render judgment in personam is grounded on their de facto power over the defendant's person. Hence his presence within the territorial jurisdiction of a court was prerequisite to its rendition of a judgment personally binding him. Pennoyer v. Neff, 95 U.S. 714, 733, 24 L.Ed. 565. But now that the capias ad respondendum has given way to personal service of summons or other form of notice, due process requires only that in order to subject a defendant to a judgment in personam, if he be not present within the territory of the forum, he have certain minimum contacts with it such that the maintenance of the suit does not offend "traditional notions of fair play and substantial justice." Milliken v. Meyer, 311 U.S. 457, 463, 61 S.Ct. 339, 85 L.Ed. 278. See Holmes, J., in McDonald v. Mabee, 243 U.S. 90, 91, 37 S.Ct. 343, 61 L.Ed. 608. Compare Hoopeston Canning Co. v. Cullen, 318 U.S. 313, 316, 319, 63 S.Ct. 602, 604, 87 L.Ed. 1722. See Blackmer v. United States, 284 U.S. 421, 52 S.Ct. 252, 76 L.Ed. 375; Hess v. Pawloski, 274 U.S. 352, 47 S.Ct. 632, 71 L.Ed. 1091; Young v. Masci, 289 U.S. 253, 53 S.Ct. 599, 77 L.Ed. 1158.

Since the corporate personality is a fiction, although a fiction intended to be acted upon as though it were a fact, Klein v. Board of Supervisors, 282 U.S. 19, 24, 51 S.Ct. 15, 16, 75 L.Ed. 140, it is clear that unlike an individual its "presence" without, as well as within, the state of its origin can be manifested only by activities carried on in its behalf by those who are authorized to act for it. To say that the corporation is so far "present" there as to satisfy due process requirements, for purposes of taxation or the maintenance of suits against it in the courts of the state, is to beg the question to be decided. For the terms "present" or "presence" are used merely to symbolize those activities of the corporation's agent within the state which courts will deem to be sufficient to satisfy the demands of due process. L. Hand, J., in Hutchinson v. Chase & Gilbert, 45 F.2d 139, 141. Those demands may be met by such contacts of the corporation with the state of the forum as make it reasonable, in the context of our federal system of government, to require the corporation to defend the particular suit which is brought there. An "estimate of the inconveniences" which would result to the corporation from a trial away from its "home" or principal place of business is relevant in this connection. Hutchinson v. Chase & Gilbert, supra, 141.

"Presence" in the state in this sense has never been doubted when the activities of the corporation there have not only been continuous and systematic, but also give rise to the liabilities sued on, even though no consent to be sued or authorization to an agent to accept service of process has been given. St. Clair v. Cox, 106 U.S. 350, 355, 1 S.Ct. 354, 359, 27 L.Ed. 222; Connecticut Mutual Co. v. Spratley, 172 U.S. 602, 610–611, 19 S.Ct. 308, 311, 43 L.Ed. 569; Pennsylvania Lumbermen's Ins. Co. v. Meyer, 197 U.S. 407, 414–415, 25 S.Ct. 483, 484, 49 L.Ed. 810; Commercial Mutual Co. v. Davis, 213 U.S. 245, 255–256, 29 S.Ct. 445, 53 L.Ed. 782; International Harvester Co. v. Kentucky, supra; cf. St. Louis S.W.R. Co. v. Alexander, 227 U.S. 218, 33 S.Ct. 245, 57 L.Ed. 486. Conversely it has been generally recognized that the casual presence of the corporate agent or even his conduct of single or isolated items of activities in a state in the corporation's behalf are not enough to subject it to suit on causes of action unconnected with the activities there. St. Clair v. Cox, supra, 359, 360; Old Wayne Life Assn. v. McDonough, 204 U.S. 8, 21, 27 S.Ct. 236, 240, 51 L.Ed. 345; Frene v. Louisville Cement Co., supra, 515, and cases cited. To require the corporation in such circumstances to defend the suit away from its home or other jurisdiction where it carries on more substantial activities has been thought to lay too great and unreasonable a burden on the corporation to comport with due process.

While it has been held, in cases on which appellant relies, that continuous activity of some sorts within a state is not enough to support the demand that the corporation be amenable to suits unrelated to that activity, Old Wayne Life Assn. v. McDonough, supra; Green v. Chicago, B. & Q.R. Co., supra; Simon v. Southern R. Co., 236 U.S. 115, 35 S.Ct. 255, 59 L.Ed. 492; People's Tobacco Co. v. American Tobacco Co., supra; cf. Davis v. Farmers Co-operative Co., 262 U.S. 312, 317, 43 S.Ct. 556, 558, 67 L.Ed. 996, there have been instances in which the continuous corporate operations within a state were thought so substantial and of such a nature as to justify suit against it on causes of action arising from dealings entirely distinct from those activities. See Missouri, K. & T.R. Co. v. Reynolds, 255 U.S. 565, 41 S.Ct. 446, 65 L.Ed. 788; Tauza v. Susquehanna Coal Co., 220 N.Y. 259, 115 N.E. 915; cf. St. Louis S.W.R. Co. v. Alexander, supra.

Finally, although the commission of some single or occasional acts of the corporate agent in a state sufficient to impose an obligation or liability on the corporation has not been thought to confer upon the state authority to enforce it, Rosenberg Bros. & Co. v. Curtis Brown Co., 260 U.S. 516, 43 S.Ct. 170, 67 L.Ed. 372, other such acts, because of their nature and quality and the circumstances of their commission, may be deemed sufficient to render the corporation liable to suit. Cf. Kane v. New Jersey, 242 U.S. 160, 37 S.Ct. 30, 61 L.Ed. 222; Hess v. Pawloski, supra; Young v. Masci, supra. True, some of the decisions holding the corporation amenable to suit have been supported by resort to the legal fiction that it has given its consent to service and suit, consent being implied from its presence in the state through the acts of its authorized agents. Lafayette Insurance Co. v. French, 18 How. 404, 407, 15 L.Ed. 451; St. Clair v. Cox, supra, 356; Commercial Mutual Co. v. Davis, supra, 213 U.S. 254, 29 S.Ct. 447, 53 L.Ed. 782; Washington v. Superior Court, 289 U.S. 361, 364–365, 53 S.Ct. 624, 626, 77 L.Ed. 1256. But more realistically it may be said that those authorized acts were of such a nature as to justify the fiction. Smolik v. Philadelphia & Reading Co., 222 F. 148, 151. Henderson, The Position of Foreign Corporations in American Constitutional Law, 94–95.

It is evident that the criteria by which we mark the boundary line between those activities which justify the subjection of a corporation to suit, and those which do not, cannot be simply mechanical or quantitative. The test is not merely, as has sometimes been suggested, whether the activity, which the corporation has seen fit to procure through its agents in another state, is a little more or a little less. St. Louis S.W.R. Co. v. Alexander, supra, 227 U.S. 228, 33 S.Ct. 248, 57 L.Ed. 486, Ann. Cas.1915B, 77; International Harvester Co. v. Kentucky, supra, 587. Whether due process is satisfied must depend rather upon the quality and nature of the activity in relation to the fair and orderly administration of the laws which it was the purpose of the due process clause to insure. That clause does not contemplate that a state may make binding a judgment in personam against an individual or corporate defendant with which the state has no contacts, ties, or relations. Cf. Pennoyer v. Neff, supra; Minnesota Commerical Assn. v. Benn, 261 U.S. 140, 43 S.Ct. 293, 67 L.Ed. 573.

But to the extent that a corporation exercises the privilege of conducting activities within a state, it enjoys the benefits and protection of the laws of that state. The exercise of that privilege may give rise to obligations, and, so far as those obligations arise out of or are connected with the activities within the state, a procedure which requires the corporation to respond to a suit brought to enforce them can, in most instances, hardly be said to be undue. Compare International Harvester Co. v. Kentucky, supra, with Green v. Chicago, B. & Q.R. Co., supra, and People's Tobacco Co. v. American Tobacco Co., supra. Compare Connecticut Mutual Co. v. Spratley, supra, 172 U.S. 619, 620, 19 S.Ct. 314, 315, 43 L.Ed. 569 and Commercial Mutual Co. v. Davis, supra, with Old Wayne Life Assn. v. McDonough, supra. See 29 Columbia Law Review, 187–195.

Applying these standards, the activities carried on in behalf of appellant in the State of Washington were neither irregular nor casual. They were systematic and continuous throughout the years in question. They resulted in a large volume of interstate business, in the course of which appellant received the benefits and protection of the laws of the state, including the right to resort to the courts for the enforcement of its rights. The obligation which is here sued upon arose out of those very activities. It is evident that these operations establish sufficient contacts or ties with the state of the forum to make it reasonable and just, according to our traditional conception of fair play and substantial justice, to permit the state to enforce the obligations which appellant has incurred there. Hence we cannot say that the maintenance of the present suit in the State of Washington involves an unreasonable or undue procedure.

We are likewise unable to conclude that the service of the process within the state upon an agent whose activities establish appellant's "presence" there was not sufficient notice of the suit, or that the suit was so unrelated to those activities as to make the agent an inappropriate vehicle for communicating the notice. It is enough that appellant has established such contacts with the state that the particular form of substituted service adopted there gives reasonable assurance that the notice will be actual. Connecticut Mutual Co. v. Spratley, supra, 172 U.S. 618, 619, 19 S.Ct. 314, 315, 43 L.Ed. 569; Board of Trade v. Hammond Elevator Co., 198 U.S. 424, 437–438, 25 S.Ct. 740, 744, 49 L.Ed. 1111; Commercial Mutual Co. v. Davis, supra, 213 U.S. 254–255, 29 S.Ct. 447, 448, 53 L.Ed. 782. Cf. Riverside Mills v. Menefee, 237 U.S. 189, 194, 195, 35 S.Ct. 579, 580, 59 L.Ed. 910; see Knowles v. Gaslight & Coke Co., 19 Wall. 58, 61, 22 L.Ed. 70; McDonald v. Mabee, supra; Milliken v. Meyer, supra. Nor can we say that the mailing of the notice of suit to appellant by registered mail at its home office was not reasonably calculated to apprise appellant of the suit. Compare Hess v.

Pawloski, supra, with McDonald v. Mabee, supra, 92, and Wuchter v. Pizzutti, 276 U.S. 13, 19, 24, 48 S.Ct. 259, 260, 72 L.Ed. 446; cf. Becquet v. MacCarthy, 2 B. & Ad. 951; Maubourquet v. Wyse, 1 Ir.Rep.C.L. 471. See Washington v. Superior Court, supra, 365.

Only a word need be said of appellant's liability for the demanded contributions to the state unemployment fund. The Supreme Court of Washington, construing and applying the statute, has held that it imposes a tax on the privilege of employing appellant's salesmen within the state measured by a percentage of the wages, here the commissions payable to the salesmen. This construction we accept for purposes of determining the constitutional validity of the statute. The right to employ labor has been deemed an appropriate subject of taxation in this country and England, both before and since the adoption of the Constitution. Steward Machine Co. v. Davis, 301 U.S. 548, 579 et seq., 57 S.Ct. 883, 887, 81 L.Ed. 1279. And such a tax imposed upon the employer for unemployment benefits is within the constitutional power of the states. Carmichael v. Southern Coal Co., 301 U.S. 495, 508 et seq., 57 S.Ct. 868, 871, 81 L.Ed. 1245.

Appellant having rendered itself amenable to suit upon obligations arising out of the activities of its salesmen in Washington, the state may maintain the present suit *in personam* to collect the tax laid upon the exercise of the privilege of employing appellant's salesmen within the state. For Washington has made one of those activities, which taken together establish appellant's "presence" there for purposes of suit, the taxable event by which the state brings appellant within the reach of its taxing power. The state thus has constitutional power to lay the tax and to subject appellant to a suit to recover it. The activities which establish its "presence" subject it alike to taxation by the state and to suit to recover the tax. Equitable Life Society v. Pennsylvania, 238 U.S. 143, 146, 35 S.Ct. 829, 830, 59 L.Ed. 1239; cf. International Harvester Co. v. Department of Taxation, 322 U.S. 435, 442, et seq., 64 S.Ct. 1060, 1064, 88 L.Ed. 1373; Hoopeston Canning Co. v. Cullen, supra, 318 U.S. 316–319, 63 S.Ct. 604–606, 87 L.Ed. 1722, 145 A.L.R. 1113; see General Trading Co. v. Tax Com., 322 U.S. 335, 64 S.Ct. 1028, 88 L.Ed. 1309.

Affirmed.

* * *

MR. JUSTICE BLACK delivered the following opinion.

I believe that the Federal Constitution leaves to each State, without any "ifs" or "buts," a power to tax and to open the doors of its courts for its citizens to sue corporations whose agents do business in those States. Believing that the Constitution gave the States that power, I think it a judicial deprivation to condition its exercise upon this Court's notion of "fair play," however appealing that term may be. Nor can I stretch the meaning of due process so far as to authorize this Court to deprive a State of the right to afford judicial protection to its citizens on the ground that it would be more "convenient" for the corporation to be sued somewhere else.

There is a strong emotional appeal in the words "fair play," "justice," and "reasonableness." But they were not chosen by those who wrote the original Constitution or the Fourteenth Amendment as a measuring rod for this Court to use in invalidating State or Federal laws passed by elected legislative representatives. No one, not even those who most feared a democratic government, ever formally proposed that courts should be given power to invalidate legislation under any such elastic standards. Express prohibitions against certain types of legislation are found in the Constitution, and under the long-settled practice, courts invalidate laws found to conflict with them. This requires interpretation, and interpretation, it is true, may result in extension of the Constitution's purpose. But that is no reason for reading the due process clause so as to restrict a State's power to tax and sue those whose activities affect persons and businesses within the State, provided proper service can be had. . . .

NOTES

(1) Since the decision in the principal case, does in personam jurisdiction based on acts done, or consequences caused, within the state depend on whether the defendant is a corporation or an individual? Can a corporation be served personally? Cf. Riverside & Dan River Cotton Mills v. Menefee, 237 U.S. 189, 35 S.Ct. 579, 59 L.Ed. 910 (1915) (personal service on a director does not create in personam adjudicatory power over the corporation).

(2) Is the fiction of presence based on business done within the state definitively dead? Do courts have in personam competence based on continuous and systematic business done within the state, irrespective of whether a legislative measure grants it? Cf. N.Y. CPLR § 301; Gelfand v. Tanner Motor Tours, Limited, 385 F.2d 116 (2d Cir.1967), cert. denied 390 U.S. 996, 88 S.Ct. 1198, 20 L.Ed.2d 95 (1968), p. 288, Note (2), infra.

(3) The decision in the principal case cleared the way for adoption of so-called long-arm statutes.

McGEE v. INTERNATIONAL LIFE INSURANCE CO.

Supreme Court of the United States, 1957.
355 U.S. 220, 78 S.Ct. 199, 2 L.Ed.2d 223.

Opinion of the Court by MR. JUSTICE BLACK, announced by MR. JUSTICE DOUGLAS.*

Petitioner, Lulu B. McGee, recovered a judgment in a California state court against respondent, International Life Insurance Company, on a contract of insurance. Respondent was not served with process in California but by registered mail at its principal place of business in Texas. The California court based its jurisdiction on a state statute which subjects foreign corporations to suit in California on insurance

---

* Footnotes omitted.

contracts with residents of that State even though such corporations cannot be served with process within its borders.

Unable to collect the judgment in California petitioner went to Texas where she filed suit on the judgment in a Texas court. But the Texas courts refused to enforce her judgment holding it was void under the Fourteenth Amendment because service of process outside California could not give the courts of that State jurisdiction over respondent. 288 S.W.2d 579. Since the case raised important questions, not only to California but to other States which have similar laws, we granted certiorari. 352 U.S. 924, 77 S.Ct. 239, 1 L.Ed.2d 160. It is not controverted that if the California court properly exercised jurisdiction over respondent the Texas courts erred in refusing to give its judgment full faith and credit. 28 U.S.C.A. § 1738.

The material facts are relatively simple. In 1944, Lowell Franklin, a resident of California, purchased a life insurance policy from the Empire Mutual Insurance Company, an Arizona corporation. In 1948 the respondent agreed with Empire Mutual to assume its insurance obligations. Respondent then mailed a reinsurance certificate to Franklin in California offering to insure him in accordance with the terms of the policy he held with Empire Mutual. He accepted this offer and from that time until his death in 1950 paid premiums by mail from his California home to respondent's Texas office. Petitioner, Franklin's mother, was the beneficiary under the policy. She sent proofs of his death to the respondent but it refused to pay claiming that he had committed suicide. It appears that neither Empire Mutual nor respondent has ever had any office or agent in California. And so far as the record before us shows, respondent has never solicited or done any insurance business in California apart from the policy involved here.

      *   *   *

. . . we think it apparent that the Due Process Clause did not preclude the California court from entering a judgment binding on respondent. It is sufficient for purposes of due process that the suit was based on a contract which had substantial connection with that State. . . . The contract was delivered in California, the premiums were mailed from there and the insured was a resident of that State when he died. It cannot be denied that California has a manifest interest in providing effective means of redress for its residents when their insurers refuse to pay claims. These residents would be at a severe disadvantage if they were forced to follow the insurance company to a distant State in order to hold it legally accountable. When claims were small or moderate individual claimants frequently could not afford the cost of bringing an action in a foreign forum—thus in effect making the company judgment proof. Often the crucial witnesses—as here on the company's defense of suicide—will be found in the insured's locality. Of course there may be inconvenience to the insurer if it is held amenable to suit in California where it had this contract but certainly nothing which amounts to a denial of due process. Cf. Travelers Health Assn. v. Virginia ex rel. State Corporation Comm'n,

339 U.S. 643, 70 S.Ct. 927, 94 L.Ed. 1154. There is no contention that respondent did not have adequate notice of the suit or sufficient time to prepare its defenses and appear.

The judgment is reversed . . ..

NOTE

Is the holding in the principal case limited to insurance claims? If the plaintiff in the principal case, after having received the insurance certificate, had moved to another state from where he mailed the premiums to defendant, would the court of the latter state have had in personam adjudicatory power over the defendant in an action on the policy? Cf. Schutt v. Commercial Travelers Mutual Accident Association, 229 F.2d 158 (2d Cir.1956), cert. denied 351 U.S. 940, 76 S.Ct. 836, 100 L.Ed. 1466 (1956). Would the result in the principal case have been different if the insured or the beneficiary had not been residents of California?

ILLINOIS PRACTICE ACT AND RULES SMITH–HURD
ILL.ANN.STAT. c. 110

§ 17. Act Submitting to Jurisdiction—Process

(1) Any person whether or not a citizen or resident of this State, who in person or through an agent does any of the acts hereinafter enumerated, thereby submits such person, and, if an individual, his personal representative to the jurisdiction of the courts of this State as to any cause of action arising from the doing of any such acts:

(a) The transaction of any business within this State;

(b) The commission of a tortious act within this State;

(c) The ownership, use, or possession of any real estate situated in this State;

(d) Contracting to insure any person, property or risk located within this State at the time of contracting;

(e) With respect to actions of divorce and separate maintenance, the maintenance in this State of a matrimonial domicile at the time the cause of action arose or the commission in this State of any act giving rise to the cause of action.

(2) Service of process upon any person who is subject to the jurisdiction of the courts of this State, as provided in this Section, may be made by personally serving the summons upon the defendant outside this State, as provided in this Act, with the same force and effect as though summons had been personally served within this State.

(3) Only causes of action arising from acts enumerated herein may be asserted against a defendant in an action in which jurisdiction over him is based upon this Section.

(4) Nothing herein contained limits or affects the right to serve any process in any other manner now or hereafter provided by law.

NOTES

(1) For the legislative history of the Illinois statute, see Historical and Practice Notes, Ill.Ann.Stat., Chapter 110, at pp. 163–71 (Smith–Hurd 1956); Note, Section 17(1)(a) of the Illinois C.P.A. and the Limits of Due Process, 55 Nw.U.L.Rev. 238 (1960).

(2) When the court's adjudicatory power is allegedly based on the commission of a tortious act within the state, must the court find all the elements of substantive liability before it can proceed? Nelson v. Miller, 11 Ill.2d 378, 391–95, 143 N.E.2d 673, 680–82 (1957), gives a negative answer:

> "An act or omission within the State, in person or by an agent, is a sufficient basis for the exercise of jurisdiction to determine whether or not the act or omission gives rise to liability in tort. . . .

> "Since ultimate liability in tort is not a jurisdictional fact under section 17(1)(b), it follows that there is no substance in the contention that the non-resident defendant is discriminated against by the assignment of the burden of proof on that issue. Moreover, to the extent that issues common to the merits and the jurisdictional question may be determined preliminarily by the court for purposes of a motion to quash, the determination will of course not be conclusive on the merits."

Under *Nelson v. Miller*, could the defendant default in Illinois and then force a trial on the question of liability in his home state by collaterally attacking the Illinois Court's adjudicatory power?

(3) After the defendant has filed an appearance in an action based on a long-arm statute, may the plaintiff assert additional claims for which there exists no basis of adjudicatory power other than appearance? See N.Y. CPLR § 302(b): "Where personal jurisdiction is based solely upon this section, an appearance does not confer such jurisdiction with respect to causes of action not arising from an act enumerated in this section."

(4) Other states quickly followed the Illinois example. See the Appendix to the summary by Reese, in 1959 N.Y.L.Rev.Com.Rep. 69, 131 (1959). Indeed, the efforts of the states to expand their judicial reach to the fullest extent permitted by due process developed into somewhat of a race. Rhode Island did all it could to make sure it would at least end up in a tie for first place.

RHODE ISLAND GENERAL LAWS

§ 9–5–33. Jurisdiction Over Foreign Corporations and Over Nonresident Individuals, Partnerships, or Associations

Every foreign corporation, every individual not a resident of this state or his executor or administrator, and every partnership or association, composed of any person or persons, not such residents, that shall have the necessary minimum contacts with the state of Rhode Island, shall be subject to the jurisdiction of the state of Rhode Island, and the courts of this state shall hold such foreign corporations and such nonresident individuals or their executors or administrators, and such partnerships or associations amenable to suit in Rhode Island in every case not contrary to the provisions of the constitution or laws of the United States.

Service of process may be made on any such foreign corporation, nonresident individual or his executor or administrator, and such partnership or association within or without the state in the manner provided by any applicable procedural rule or in the manner prescribed by order of the court in which such action is brought.

Nothing herein shall limit or affect the right to serve process upon such nonresident individual or his executor or administrator, or such partnership or association, or a foreign corporation within this state or without this state in any manner now or hereafter permitted by law.

NOTES

(1) The Rhode Island example has found ready emulators. On June 1, 1970, the following provision became effective in California:

"A Court of this state may exercise jurisdiction on any basis not inconsistent with the Constitution of this state or of the United States." West's Ann.Cal.Civ.Code § 410.10.

On the California developments, see also Garfinkel & Levine, Long–Arm Jurisdiction in California under New Section 410.10 of the Code of Civil Procedure, 21 Hast.L.J. 1163 (1970). Note, The Development of In Personam Jurisdiction over Individuals and Corporations in California: 1849–1970, 21 Hast.L.J. 1105, 1155 (1970).

A similar provision has been adopted in New Jersey. N.J.R.R. 4:4–4 (1972). In Cooke v. Yarrington, 62 N.J. 123, 299 A.2d 400 (1973), the New Jersey Supreme Court held that a Pennsylvania resident, who injured a New Jersey plaintiff in an automobile accident in Pennsylvania, was subject to suit in New Jersey under the New Jersey long-arm statute on the grounds that, at the time of the accident, he was a resident of New Jersey, that he was driving his father's New Jersey-registered vehicle under a driver's license issued by New Jersey, and that he had regularly visited New Jersey since the time of the accident. For a comment on this decision, see 6 Rutgers Camden L.J. 144 (1974).

(2) Are these provisions unconstitutional because they fail to lay down sufficiently specific rules for the guidance of the citizen? Is it desirable as a matter of policy for a state to extend its competence as far as it can? Do these provisions extend in personam, and in rem and quasi-in-rem, competence to the outer limits?

(3) In an effort to achieve a reasonable accommodation of competing interests, the Commissioners on Uniform State Laws requested the Columbia University Project on International Procedure to draft a long-arm statute for inclusion in a more comprehensive uniform statute on interstate and international litigation. Professors Willis L.M. Reese and Jack B. Weinstein were the principal draftsmen.

UNIFORM INTERSTATE AND INTERNATIONAL PROCEDURE ACT

§ 1.03. "[Personal Jurisdiction Based upon Conduct]

(a) A court may exercise personal jurisdiction over a person, who acts directly or by an agent, as to a [cause of action] [claim for relief] arising from the person's

(1) transacting any business in this state;

(2) contracting to supply services or things in this state;

(3) causing tortious injury by an act or omission in this state;

(4) causing tortious injury in this state by an act or omission outside this state if he regularly does or solicits business, or engages in any other persistent course of conduct, or derives substantial revenue from goods used or consumed or services rendered, in this state; [or]

(5) having an interest in, using, or possessing real property in this state [; or

(6) contracting to insure any person, property, or risk located within this state at the time of contracting.]"

NOTES

(1) The Uniform Act, approved by the Commissioners on Uniform State Laws in 1962 and by the American Bar Association in 1963, deals, in addition, with making service outside of the state, taking depositions outside of the state, determination of foreign law, and proof of official records. Its provisions, with the exception of the long-arm rules, parallel those of federal legislative measures enacted around the same time. See generally Smit, International Co-Operation in Litigation: Europe 1–15 (1965). Within a few years the Act was adopted in Arkansas (without Article III), Oklahoma, and the Virgin Islands. Its adoption was then recommended in Massachusetts, Michigan, and New York. See Smit, Report of the Administrative Board of the Judicial Conference of the State of New York 131, 132 (1966).

(2) Compare the provisions of the Uniform Act with the Illinois statute, supra, and the New York Civil Practice Law and Rules, infra.

(3) For a list of the states that have adopted the Uniform Act either in whole or in part, see Sutton, Today's Long–Arm and Products Liability: A Plea for a Contemporary Notion of Fair Play and Substantial Justice, 41 Ins.C.J. 85 (1974).

NEW YORK CIVIL PRACTICE LAW AND RULES

§ 302. Personal jurisdiction by acts of non-domiciliaries

(a) Acts which are the basis of jurisdiction. A court may exercise personal jurisdiction over any non-domiciliary or his executor or administrator, as to a cause of action arising from any of the acts enumerated in this section, in the same manner as if he were a domiciliary of the state, if, in person or through an agent, he:

1. transacts any business within the state or contracts anywhere to supply goods or services in the state; or

2. commits a tortious act within the state, except as to a cause of action for defamation of character arising from the act; or

3. commits a tortious act without the state causing injury to person or property within the state, except as to a cause of action for defamation of character arising from the act, if he

(i) regularly does or solicits business, or engages in any other persistent course of conduct, or derives substantial revenue from goods used or consumed or services rendered, in the state, or

(ii) expects or should reasonably expect the act to have consequences in the state and derives substantial revenue from interstate or international commerce; or

4. owns, uses or possesses any real property situated within the state.

(b) Personal jurisdiction over non-resident defendant. A court in any matrimonial action or family court proceeding involving a demand for support or alimony may exercise personal jurisdiction over the respondent or defendant notwithstanding the fact that he or she no longer is a resident or domiciliary of this state, or over his or her executor or administrator, if the party seeking support is a resident of or domiciled in this state at the time such demand is made, provided that this state was the matrimonial domicile of the parties before their separation, or the defendant abandoned the plaintiff in this state, or the obligation to pay support or alimony or alimony accrued under the laws of this state or under an agreement executed in this state.

(c) Effect of appearance. Where personal jurisdiction is based solely upon this section, an appearance does not confer such jurisdiction with respect to causes of action not arising from an act enumerated in this section.

NOTES

(1) For applications of the New York statute, see Homburger & Laufer, Expanding Jurisdiction over Foreign Torts: The 1966 Amendments of New York's Long–Arm Statute, 16 Buffalo L.Rev. 67 (1966); Reese, A Study of CPLR 302 In Light of Recent Judicial Decisions, in N.Y. Judicial Conference, Eleventh Annual Report 132 (1966).

(2) May a long-arm statute be given retroactive effect to support the exercise of adjudicatory power after enactment of the statute based on acts performed before the enactment? For an affirmative answer, see Simonson v. International Bank, 14 N.Y.2d 281, 251 N.Y.S.2d 433, 200 N.E.2d 427 (1964).

(3) The constitutionality of the New York long arm statute was challenged in Rosenblatt v. American Cyanamid. The Supreme Court dismissed the appeal for want of a substantial federal question. 382 U.S. 110, 86 S.Ct. 256, 15 L.Ed.2d 192 (1965).

(4) How long-fingered is the New York long-arm statute? In Parke–Bernet Galleries, Inc. v. Franklyn, 26 N.Y.2d 13, 308 N.Y.S.2d 337, 256 N.E.2d 506

(1970), the Court of Appeals held that the defendant, who had bid by telephone from California at an auction held in New York, transacted business in New York within the sense of N.Y. CPLR § 302(a)(1). The Second Circuit relied on this ruling in American Eutectic Welding Alloys Sales Co. v. Dytron Alloys Corp., 439 F.2d 428 (2d Cir.1971), in holding subject to suit in New York under N.Y. CPLR § 302(a)(1) non-resident former employees who, by luring away customers in other states, had allegedly breached contracts concluded with the New York plaintiff in New York. However, in the same case, the Second Circuit refused to uphold adjudicatory authority over the non-resident new employer, who allegedly had competed unfairly by inducing plaintiff's former employees to breach their obligations. It held that this conduct did not "cause injury" to the plaintiff "within the state," as required by N.Y. CPLR § 302(a)(3). As to where injury is suffered in unfair competition cases, see also Spectacular Promotions, Inc. v. Radio Station WING, 272 F.Supp. 734 (E.D.N.Y.1967) (place where plaintiff lost business).

(5) Does a cause of action based upon a theory of strict manufacturer's liability arise from "a tortious act" within the meaning of N.Y. CPLR § 302(a) (2) and (3)? A New York resident purchases and takes thalidomide pills in Italy manufactured by a German manufacturer. A deformed child is born to her in New York. Does New York have adjudicatory authority over the German manufacturer? Cf. Harvey v. Chemie Grunenthal, 354 F.2d 428 (2d Cir.1965), cert. denied 384 U.S. 1001, 86 S.Ct. 1923, 16 L.Ed.2d 1015 (1966).

(6) For a survey of the various types of long-arm statutes, see Sutton, Today's Long–Arm And Products Liability: A Plea For a Contemporary Notion of Fair Play And Substantial Justice, 41 Ins.C.J. 85 (1974). Long-arm provisions similar to N.Y. CPLR § 302(b) have been adopted by a number of states. See Note, Long–Arm Jurisdiction in Alimony and Custody Cases, 73 Colum.L. Rev. 289 (1973).

G. THE SPECIAL PROBLEMS OF ADJUDICATORY AUTHORITY OVER CORPORATE AND OTHER ASSOCIATIONS—FROM FICTIONS TO REALITY

Incorporation has traditionally been a proper basis for the exercise of in personam adjudicatory power, even in cases in which the corporation has engaged in no activities within the state other than those necessary to continue its legal existence. Indeed, originally, it was thought that this basis, which continues to be recognized today, was exclusive in the sense that a corporation could not be sued in personam outside the state of its incorporation. This notion was based on the premise that a corporation owed its existence to the law that permitted its creation and therefore could not exist beyond the realm of that law's effectiveness. As Chief Justice Taney stated in Bank of Augusta v. Earle, 38 U.S. (13 Pet.) 519, 588, 10 L.Ed. 274 (1839): "It is very true that a corporation can have no legal existence out of the bundaries [sic] of the sovereignty by which it is created . . . It must dwell in the place of its creation, and cannot migrate to another sovereignty."

Although consistent application of this approach would preclude a corporation from engaging in any activities outside of the state of its incorporation—a conclusion that was generally rejected and that would preclude even a consenting corporation from being sued outside of that state—, this conceptual approach persisted in exercising its influence even when the pressures for developing additional bases of in personam adjudicatory power became irresistible.

At first, in response to these pressures, the rule that consent creates in personam adjudicatory power was called in aid. It had long been held that a state could preclude a foreign corporation from engaging in local, as distinguished from interstate, business. For an early case to this effect, see Paul v. Virginia, 75 U.S. (8 Wall.) 168, 19 L.Ed. 357 (1868). The next step was obvious. When a state could prevent a foreign corporation from engaging in local business, it could also permit the foreign corporation to engage in local business on the condition that the corporation consent to being sued within the state. Lafayette Insurance Co. v. French, 59 U.S. (18 How.) 404, 15 L.Ed. 451 (1855). Consent so given created in personam jurisdiction over the foreign corporation to the fullest extent, including the power to render personal judgments on obligations not arising from business done within the state or arising from interstate business. Whether it also created in personam competence to the fullest extent or whether it limited in personam competence to actions on claims arising from the business done locally depended on the applicable state law.

This use of an old rule to meet the exigencies of new developments produced the desired result if the foreign corporation did in fact give its consent, usually by filing the appropriate form with the secretary of state or some other local official. But what if the corporation failed to do so? Now fiction came to the rescue. The courts upheld the construction that, by engaging in business within the state, a foreign corporation gave its implied consent to being sued there. It remained unclear whether implied consent could also form the basis for in personam adjudicatory power in actions on claims not arising from the business done within the state. Compare St. Clair v. Cox, 106 U.S. 350, 1 S.Ct. 354, 27 L.Ed. 222 (1882), Old Wayne Mut. Life Ins. Ass'n v. McDonough, 204 U.S. 8, 27 S.Ct. 236, 51 L.Ed. 345 (1907), and Simon v. Southern Ry. Co., 236 U.S. 115, 35 S.Ct. 255, 59 L.Ed. 492 (1915) with Tauza v. Susquehanna Coal Co., 220 N.Y. 259, 115 N.E. 915 (1917). But the implied consent construction was upheld even when the foreign corporation engaged in interstate business and could therefore not be excluded from the state.

Clearly, this latter result could not be reconciled with the consent rationale. Efforts were therefore made to justify the exercise of in personam adjudicatory power over foreign corporations on another traditionally recognized basis. This time it was presence that was called in aid. Of course, reliance on presence necessarily implied rejection of the thesis of Bank of Augusta, supra, that a corporation could legally exist only within the state of its incorporation. On the contrary, this approach to the problem sought to equate activities of a foreign corporation within the state with its presence there. As Justice

Brandeis stated in Philadelphia & Reading R.R. v. McKibbin, 243 U.S. 264, 37 S.Ct. 280, 61 L.Ed. 710 (1917): "A foreign corporation is amenable to process to enforce a personal liability in the absence of consent, only if it is doing business within the State in such manner and to such extent as to warrant the inference that it is present there" (at 265). Under this analysis, the crucial question became what the nature and frequency of the corporation's activities within the state had to be before it could be found present there. This question, unanswerable upon purely conceptual grounds, caused the courts serious problems, especially since under the traditional rule a person, and therefore also a foreign corporation, when found present within the state, could be sued there on all claims, whether or not they arose from the business done within the state. It need cause no wonder that the courts, to escape the straightjacket of this rule, were more readily inclined to find presence when the claim pursued arose out of the activities that were alleged to render the corporation present within the state.

These had been the developments when, after a vigorous attack upon the fictional presence approach by a leading appellate court (see Hutchinson v. Chase & Gilbert, 45 F.2d 139 (2d Cir.1930)), the Supreme Court squarely faced the problem in International Shoe Co. v. Washington, p. 241 supra.

H. PARTNERSHIPS

RESTATEMENT (SECOND) OF CONFLICT OF LAWS (1971)

§ 40. Partnerships or Other Unincorporated Associations

(1) A state in which a partnership or other unincorporated association is subject to suit in the firm or common name has power to exercise judicial jurisdiction over the partnership or association if under the circumstances it could exercise judicial jurisdiction over an individual on one or more of the bases set forth in §§ 32–39.

(2) A valid judgment rendered against a partnership or association is a binding adjudication as to the liability of the partnership or association with respect to its assets in every state.

NOTES

(1) Does in personam adjudicatory power over a partner create power to bind partnership property without the state? In Sugg v. Thornton, 132 U.S. 524, 10 S.Ct. 163, 33 L.Ed. 447 (1889), personal service was made on one of the partners outside the state. Judgment was rendered against the partner personally served as well as against "the partnership as a distinct legal entity." The Supreme Court upheld the judgment over due process objections, stating that the judgment did not bind the partner served outside the state personally, but only with respect to the firm assets.

(2) In what circumstances may a court render an in personam judgment against other partners, not otherwise subject to the court's in personam power, for claims against the partnership?

(3) Do questions posed in the preceding notes become less significant as the bases of in personam adjudicatory power are liberalized? On this subject generally, see Kaplan, Suits Against Unincorporated Associations under the Federal Rules of Associations under the Federal Rules of Civil Procedure, 53 Mich.L.Rev. 945 (1955); Magruder & Fister, Jurisdiction over Partnerships, 37 Harv.L.Rev. 793 (1924).

I. CLAIMS BASED ON OWNERSHIP OF PROPERTY WITHIN THE STATE

DUBIN v. CITY OF PHILADELPHIA, 34 Pa.D. & C. 61 (1938): A resident of New Jersey was made a third party defendant in an action against the City for damages to plaintiff when she fell on a broken sidewalk abutting property mortgaged to the third party defendant. Jurisdiction was based on a statute which provided that any "nonresident * * * owner, tenant, or user, of real estate" should be amenable to suit in Pennsylvania courts on actions arising out of injury involving such real estate. The court upheld the statute against attack on due process grounds. "This creates another exception to the rule of personal service in personal actions. Modern life is breaking down State barriers, and as it becomes easier to travel, or to do business, or to own property in other States, one must also expect the obligations arising out of such activities to follow more easily. It is just as important that nonresident owners of Philadelphia real estate should keep their property in such shape as not to injure our citizens as it is that nonresident owners of cars should drive about our streets with equal care. It is only a short step beyond this to assert that defendants in both classes of cases should be answerable in this forum. If it be argued that it would be unfair to make Philadelphians chase car owners to distant States in order to sue them, whereas Philadelphians who fall on streets can stay here and sue the city, the answer is that they are interested as taxpayers in preventing the expense incident upon the city's bringing suit against foreign property owners in foreign forums."

NOTE

In what respects does the basis of adjudicatory power found in the principal case differ from in rem or quasi-in-rem adjudicatory power? See also Uniform Interstate and the International Procedure Act § 1.03(a)(b).

J. OUTER LIMITS

HANSON v. DENCKLA

Supreme Court of the United States, 1958.
357 U.S. 235, 78 S.Ct. 1228, 2 L.Ed.2d 1283.

MR. CHIEF JUSTICE WARREN delivered the opinion of the Court.*

This controversy concerns the right to $400,000, part of the corpus of a trust established in Delaware by a settlor who later became domiciled in Florida. One group of claimants, "legatees," urge that this property passed under the residuary clause of the settlor's will, which was admitted to probate in Florida. The Florida courts have sustained this position. . . . Other claimants, "appointees" and "beneficiaries," contend that the property passed pursuant to the settlor's exercise of the *inter vivos* power of appointment created in the deed of trust. The Delaware courts adopted this position and refused to accord full faith and credit to the Florida determination because the Florida court had not acquired jurisdiction over an indispensable party, the Delaware trustee. . . .

[The following excerpts relate only to whether the Florida court could exercise in personam adjudicatory power over the Delaware trustee].

Appellees' stronger argument is for *in personam* jurisdiction over the Delaware trustee. They urge that the circumstances of this case amount to sufficient affiliation with the State of Florida to empower its courts to exercise personal jurisdiction over this nonresident defendant. Principal reliance is placed upon McGee v. International Life Ins. Co., 355 U.S. 220, 78 S.Ct. 199, 2 L.Ed.2d 223. In *McGee* the Court noted the trend of expanding personal jurisdiction over nonresidents. As technological progress has increased the flow of commerce between States, the need for jurisdiction over nonresidents has undergone a similar increase. At the same time, progress in communications and transportation has made the defense of a suit in a foreign tribunal less burdensome. In response to these changes, the requirements for personal jurisdiction over nonresidents have evolved from the rigid rule of Pennoyer v. Neff, 95 U.S. 714, 24 L.Ed. 565 to the flexible standard of International Shoe Co. v. Washington, 326 U.S. 310, 66 S.Ct. 154, 90 L.Ed. 95. But it is a mistake to assume that this trend heralds the eventual demise of all restrictions on the personal jurisdiction of state courts. See Vanderbilt v. Vanderbilt, 354 U.S. 416, 418, 77 S.Ct. 1360, 1362, 1 L.Ed.2d 1456. Those restrictions are more than a guarantee of immunity from inconvenient or distant litigation. They are a consequence of territorial limitations on the power of the respective States. However minimal the burden of defending in a foreign tribunal, a defendant may not be called upon to do so unless he has had the "minimal contacts" with that State that are a prerequisite to its

---

* Footnotes omitted.

exercise of power over him. See International Shoe Co. v. Washington, 326 U.S. 310, 319, 66 S.Ct. 154, 159, 90 L.Ed. 95.

We fail to find such contacts in the circumstances of this case. The defendant trust company has no office in Florida, and transacts no business there. None of the trust assets has ever been held or administered in Florida, and the record discloses no solicitation of business in that State either in person or by mail. Cf. International Shoe Co. v. Washington, 326 U.S. 310, 66 S.Ct. 154, 90 L.Ed. 95; McGee v. International Life Ins. Co., 355 U.S. 220, 78 S.Ct. 199, 2 L.Ed.2d 223; Travelers Health Assn. v. Virginia, 339 U.S. 643, 70 S.Ct. 927, 94 L.Ed. 1154.

The cause of action in this case is not one that arises out of an act done or transaction consummated in the forum State. In that respect, it differs from McGee v. International Life Ins. Co., 355 U.S. 220, 78 S.Ct. 199, 201, 2 L.Ed.2d 223, and the cases there cited. . . . The agreement was executed in Delaware by a trust company incorporated in that State and a settlor domiciled in Pennsylvania. The first relationship Florida had to the agreement was years later when the settlor became domiciled there, and the trustee remitted the trust income to her in that State. From Florida Mrs. Donner carried on several bits of trust administration that may be compared to the mailing of premiums in *McGee*. But the record discloses no instance in which the *trustee* performed any acts in Florida that bear the same relationship to the agreement as the solicitation in *McGee*. Consequently, this suit cannot be said to be one to enforce an obligation that arose from a privilege the defendant exercised in Florida. Cf. International Shoe Co. v. Washington, 326 U.S. 310, 319, 66 S.Ct. 154, 159, 90 L.Ed. 95. This case is also different from *McGee* in that there the State had enacted special legislation (Unauthorized Insurers Process Act) to exercise what *McGee* called its "manifest interest" in providing effective redress for citizens who had been injured by nonresidents engaged in an activity that the State treats as exceptional and subjects to special regulation. Cf. Travelers Health Assn. v. Virginia, 339 U.S. 643, 647–649, 70 S.Ct. 927, 929–930, 94 L.Ed. 1154; Doherty & Co. v. Goodman, 294 U.S. 623, 627, 55 S.Ct. 553, 554, 79 L.Ed. 1097; Hess v. Pawloski, 274 U.S. 352, 47 S.Ct. 632, 71 L.Ed. 1091.

The execution in Florida of the powers of appointment under which the beneficiaries and appointees claim does not give Florida a substantial connection with the contract on which this suit is based. . . . The unilateral activity of those who claim some relationship with a nonresident defendant cannot satisfy the requirement of contact with the forum State. The application of that rule will vary with the quality and nature of the defendant's activity, but it is essential in each case that there be some act by which the defendant purposefully avails itself of the privilege of conducting activities within the forum State, thus invoking the benefits and protections of its laws. International Shoe Co. v. Washington, 326 U.S. 310, 319, 66 S.Ct. 154, 159, 90 L.Ed. 95. The settlor's execution in Florida of her power of appointment cannot remedy the absence of such an act in this case.

It is urged that because the settlor and most of the appointees and beneficiaries were domiciled in Florida the courts of that State should be able to exercise personal jurisdiction over the nonresident trustees. This is a non sequitur. With personal jurisdiction over the executor, legatees, and appointees, there is nothing in federal law to prevent Florida from adjudicating concerning the respective rights and liabilities of those parties. But Florida has not chosen to do so. . . .

. . . the judgment of the Florida Supreme Court is reversed and the cause is remanded for proceedings not inconsistent with this opinion.

It is so ordered.

MR. JUSTICE BLACK, whom MR. JUSTICE BURTON and MR. JUSTICE BRENNAN join, dissenting. [Omitted.]

*   *   *

NOTES

(1) In determining whether the exercise of jurisdiction is reasonable, should the court look only to the defendant's contacts with the state or also consider the plaintiff's interest in obtaining an adjudication in a convenient forum and the public interest of disposing of all the ramifications of a dispute in one adjudication? See also Davis v. St. Paul–Mercury Indemnity Co., 294 F.2d 641, 647 (4th Cir.1961):

> "The meaning of due process in this area can be determined only by weighing the competing interests. Therefore, what is required is an analysis and weighing of the interests of a defendant in not being called upon to defend in the forum, of the plaintiff in being able to acquire jurisdiction over a defendant in the place where the cause of action arose, and of a state in being able to open its courts to the particular lawsuit."

(2) A gas station owner in a little village in California sells a tire to the vacationing owner of a car with North Carolina license plates. After the owner of the car returns to North Carolina, the tire blows causing personal injuries and property damage. May the gas station owner be sued in North Carolina under the North Carolina long-arm statute? Cf. Erlanger Mills Inc. v. Cohoes Fibre Mills, 239 F.2d 502 (4th Cir.1956). What would be the answer if the owner of the car were a New Yorker and sought to bring suit in New York under the N.Y. CPLR?

WORLD–WIDE VOLKSWAGEN CORP. v. WOODSON

Supreme Court of the United States, 1980.
444 U.S. 286, 100 S.Ct. 559, 62 L.Ed.2d 490.

MR. JUSTICE WHITE delivered the opinion of the Court.*

The issue before us is whether, consistently with the Due Process Clause of the Fourteenth Amendment, an Oklahoma court may exercise

---

* Most footnotes omitted; others renumbered.

in personam jurisdiction over a nonresident automobile retailer and its wholesale distributor in a products liability action, when the defendants' only connection with Oklahoma is the fact that an automobile sold in New York to New York residents became involved in an accident in Oklahoma.

I

Respondents Harry and Kay Robinson purchased a new Audi automobile from petitioner Seaway Volkswagen, Inc. (Seaway) in Massena, N.Y., in 1976. The following year the Robinson family, who resided in New York, left that State for a new home in Arizona. As they passed through the State of Oklahoma, another car struck their Audi in the rear, causing a fire which severely burned Kay Robinson and her two children.

The Robinsons subsequently brought a products liability action in the District Court for Creek County, Okla., claiming that their injuries resulted from defective design and placement of the Audi's gas tank and fuel system. They joined as defendants the automobile's manufacturer, Audi NSU Auto Union Aktiengesellschaft (Audi); its importer Volkswagen of America, Inc. (Volkswagen); its regional distributor, petitioner World–Wide Volkswagen Corporation (World–Wide); and its retail dealer, petitioner Seaway. Seaway and World–Wide entered special appearances, claiming that Oklahoma's exercise of jurisdiction over them would offend the limitations on the State's jurisdiction imposed by the Due Process Clause of the Fourteenth Amendment.

The facts presented to the District Court showed that World–Wide is incorporated and has its business office in New York. It distributes vehicles, parts and accessories, under contract with Volkswagen, to retail dealers in New York, New Jersey, and Connecticut. Seaway, one of these retail dealers, is incorporated and has its place of business in New York. Insofar as the record reveals, Seaway and World–Wide are fully independent corporations whose relations with each other and with Volkswagen and Audi are contractual only. Respondents adduced no evidence that either World–Wide or Seaway does any business in Oklahoma, ships or sells any products to or in that State, has an agent to receive process there, or purchases advertisements in any media calculated to reach Oklahoma. In fact, as respondents' counsel conceded at oral argument, . . . there was no showing that any automobile sold by World–Wide or Seaway has ever entered Oklahoma with the single exception of the vehicle involved in the present case.

Despite the apparent paucity of contacts between petitioners and Oklahoma, the District Court rejected their constitutional claim 'and reaffirmed that ruling in denying petitioners' motion for reconsideration. Petitioners then sought a writ of prohibition in the Supreme Court of Oklahoma to restrain the District Judge, respondent Charles S. Woodson, from exercising *in personam* jurisdiction over them. They renewed their contention that because they had no "minimal contacts,"

App. 32, with the State of Oklahoma, the actions of the District Judge were in violation of their rights under the Due Process Clause.

The Supreme Court of Oklahoma denied the writ, 585 P.2d 351 (1978), holding that personal jurisdiction over petitioners was authorized by Oklahoma's "Long–Arm" Statute Okla.Stat., Tit. 12, § 1701.03(a) (4) (1971).[1] Although the Court noted that the proper approach was to test jurisdiction against both statutory and constitutional standards, its analysis did not distinguish these questions, probably because § 1701.03(a)(4) has been interpreted as conferring jurisdiction to the limits permitted by the United States Constitution. . . .

We granted certiorari, 440 U.S. 907, 99 S.Ct. 1212, 59 L.Ed.2d 453 (1979), to consider an important constitutional question with respect to state-court jurisdiction and to resolve a conflict between the Supreme Court of Oklahoma and the highest courts of at least four other States. We reverse.

* * *

As has long been settled, and as we reaffirm today, a state court may exercise personal jurisdiction over a nonresident defendant only so long as there exist "minimum contacts" between the defendant and the forum State. International Shoe Co. v. Washington, supra, at 316, 66 S.Ct., at 158. The concept of minimum contacts, in turn, can be seen to perform two related, but distinguishable, functions. It protects the defendant against the burdens of litigating in a distant or inconvenient forum. And it acts to ensure that the States through their courts, do not reach out beyond the limits imposed on them by their status as coequal sovereigns in a federal system.

* * *

The limits imposed on state jurisdiction by the Due Process Clause, in its role as a guarantor against inconvenient litigation, have been substantially relaxed over the years.

* * *

Nevertheless, we have never accepted the proposition that state lines are irrelevant for jurisdictional purposes, nor could we and remain faithful to the principles of interstate federalism embodied in the Constitution. . . . The sovereignty of each State, in turn, implied a limitation on the sovereignty of all of its sister States—a limitation express or implicit in both the original scheme of the Constitution and the Fourteenth Amendment.

1. This subsection provides:

"A court may exercise personal jurisdiction over a person, who acts directly or by an agent, as to a cause of action or claim for relief arising from the person's . . . causing tortious injury in this state by an act or omission outside this state if he regularly does or solicits business or engages in any other persistent course of conduct, or derives substantial revenue from goods used or consumed or services rendered, in this state . . . .."

The State Supreme Court rejected jurisdiction based on § 1701.03(a)(3), which authorizes jurisdiction over any person "causing tortious injury in this state by an act or omission in this state." Something in addition to the infliction of tortious injury was required.

Hence, even while abandoning the shibboleth that "[t]he authority of every tribunal is necessarily restricted by the territorial limits of the State in which it is established," Pennoyer v. Neff, supra, 95 U.S., at 720, we emphasized that the reasonableness of asserting jurisdiction over the defendant must be assessed "in the context of our federal system of government," International Shoe Co. v. Washington, supra, 326 U.S., at 317, 66 S.Ct., at 158, and stressed that the Due Process Clause ensures, not only fairness, but also the "orderly administration of the laws," id., at 319, 66 S.Ct., at 159. . . .

*   *   *

III

Applying these principles to the case at hand, we find in the record before us a total absence of those affiliating circumstances that are a necessary predicate to any exercise of state-court jurisdiction. Petitioners carry on no activity whatsoever in Oklahoma. They close no sales and perform no services there. They avail themselves of none of the privileges and benefits of Oklahoma law. They solicit no business there either through salespersons or through advertising reasonably calculated to reach the State. Nor does the record show that they regularly sell cars at wholesale or retail to Oklahoma customers or residents or that they indirectly, through others, serve or seek to serve the Oklahoma market. In short, respondents seek to base jurisdiction on one, isolated occurrence and whatever inferences can be drawn therefrom: the fortuitous circumstance that a single Audi automobile, sold in New York to New York residents, happened to suffer an accident while passing through Oklahoma.

It is argued, however, that because an automobile is mobile by its very design and purpose it was "foreseeable" that the Robinsons' Audi would cause injury in Oklahoma. Yet "foreseeability" alone has never been a sufficient benchmark for personal jurisdiction under the Due Process Clause. . . .

*   *   *

This is not to say, of course, that foreseeability is wholly irrelevant. But the foreseeability that is critical to due process analysis is not the mere likelihood that a product will find its way into the forum State. Rather, it is that the defendant's conduct and connection with the forum State are such that he should reasonably anticipate being hauled into court there. . . .

When a corporation "purposefully avails itself of the privilege of conducting activities within the forum State," Hanson v. Denckla, supra, 357 U.S., at 253, 78 S.Ct., at 1240, it has clear notice that it is subject to suit there, and can act to alleviate the risk of burdensome litigation by procuring insurance, passing the expected costs on to customers, or, if the risks are too great, severing its connection with the State. Hence if the sale of a product of a manufacturer or distributor such as Audi or Volkswagen is not simply an isolated occurrence, but arises from the efforts of the manufacturer or distributor to serve directly or indirectly, the market for its product in other States, it is not unreasonable to subject it to suit in one of those States if its allegedly defective merchandise has there been the source of injury to its owner or to others. . . .

But there is no such or similar basis for Oklahoma jurisdiction over World–Wide or Seaway in this case. Seaway's sales are made in Massena, N.Y. World–Wide's market, although substantially larger, is limited to dealers in New York, New Jersey, and Connecticut. There is no evidence of record that any automobiles distributed by World–Wide are sold to retail customers outside this tri-State area. It is foreseeable that the purchasers of automobiles sold by World–Wide and Seaway may take them to Oklahoma. But the mere "unilateral activity of those who claim some relationship with a nonresident defendant cannot satisfy the requirement of contact with the forum State." Hanson v. Denckla, supra, at 253, 78 S.Ct., at 1239–1240.

*   *   *

Because we find that petitioners have no "contacts, ties, or relations" with the State of Oklahoma, International Shoe Co. v. Washington, supra, 326 U.S., at 319, 66 S.Ct., at 159, the judgment of the Supreme Court of Oklahoma is

Reversed.

MR. JUSTICE MARSHALL, with whom MR. JUSTICE BLACKMUN joins, dissenting.

*   *   *

The majority apparently acknowledges that if a product is purchased in the forum State by a consumer, that State may assert jurisdiction over everyone in the chain of distribution. See ante, at 567. With this I agree. But I cannot agree that jurisdiction is necessarily lacking if the product enters the State not through the channels of distribution but in the course of its intended use by the consumer.

*   *   *

Of course, the Constitution forbids the exercise of jurisdiction if the defendant had no judicially cognizable contacts with the forum. But as the majority acknowledges, if such contacts are present the jurisdictional inquiry requires a balancing of various interests and policies. . . . I believe such contacts are to be found here and that, considering all of the interests and policies at stake, requiring petitioners to defend this action in Oklahoma is not beyond the bounds of the Constitution. Accordingly, I dissent.

MR. JUSTICE BLACKMUN, dissenting.

I confess that I am somewhat puzzled why the plaintiffs in this litigation are so insistent that the regional distributor and the retail dealer, the petitioners here, who handled the ill-fated Audi automobile involved in this litigation, be named defendants.* It would appear that the manufacturer and the importer, whose subjectability to Oklahoma jurisdiction is not challenged before this Court, ought not to be judgment-proof. It may, of course, ultimately amount to a contest between insurance companies that, once begun, is not easily brought to a termination. Having made this much of an observation, I pursue it no further.

For me, a critical factor in the disposition of the litigation is the nature of the instrumentality under consideration. It has been said that we are a Nation on wheels. . . .

It therefore seems to me not unreasonable—and certainly not unconstitutional and beyond the reach of the principles laid down in International Shoe Co. v. Washington, 326 U.S. 310, 66 S.Ct. 154, 90 L.Ed. 95 (1945), and its progeny—to uphold Oklahoma jurisdiction over this New York distributor and this New York dealer when the accident happened in Oklahoma. . . .

* * *

KULKO v. SUPERIOR COURT OF CALIFORNIA, 436 U.S. 84, 98 S.Ct. 1690, 56 L.Ed.2d 132 (1978). A mother, domiciled in California, sued her former husband, domiciled in New York, for custody of, and support for, the couple's two children. The action was brought in a California state court under California's long-arm statute (see p. 283 supra). The father had agreed that the daughter would move to California to live with her mother and had paid for her travel there. The son had moved to California without the father's consent. The father did not contest the application for custody. In a 6–3 decision, the Supreme Court ruled that California lacked in personam jurisdiction over the father sufficient to sustain the claims for support. The Court held that the father's contacts with California were too attenuated to meet the test of International Shoe. Stressing basic consideration of fairness, the Court noted that California's interest in ensuring the support of the children was adequately served by the Uniform Reciprocal Enforcement of Support Act of 1968, under which the mother could have filed her petition for support in California in order to obtain a decision by a New York Court.

NOTES

(1) On the principal cases, see Note, Unified Jurisdictional Test Applied to In Personam Jurisdiction, 1978 Wash.U.L.Q. 797; Note, "Doing Business": Defining State Control over Foreign Corporations, 32 Vand.L.Rev. 1105 (1979); Note, The Long Arm Reach of the Courts Under the Effect Test After Kulko v. Superior Court, 65 Va.L.Rev. 175 (1979); Note, Kulko v. California Superior Court: Has the Long Arm Extended Too Far?, 1979 Det.C.L.Rev. 159; Comment, Federalism, Due Process and Minimum Contacts: World–Wide Volks-

---

* Does their presence in the action defeat diversity? Eds.

wagen v. Woodson, 80 Colum.L.Rev. 1341 (1980); Redish, Due Process, Federalism, and Personal Jurisdiction: A Theoretical Evaluation, 75 Nw.U.L.Rev. 1112 (1981); Clermont, Restating Territorial Jurisdiction and Venue for State and Federal Courts, 66 Cornell L.Rev. 411 (1981).

(2) Insurance Corp. v. Compagnie des Bauxites de Guinee, 456 U.S. 694, 102 S.Ct. 2099, 72 L.Ed.2d 492 (1982). In this case, when the defendants raised the defense of lack of in personam jurisdiction, the district court permitted discovery as to this defense. When the defendants failed to comply with the discovery orders, the district court ruled the defense waived. The Supreme Court upheld this ruling. Justice White indicated that the waiver rationale necessarily implied rejection of the notion that concepts of federalism were an independent consideration in limiting personal jurisdiction (456 U.S. at 702, n. 10):

> "That [i.e., the Due Process] Clause is the only source of the personal jurisdiction requirement and the clause itself makes no mention of federation concerns. Furthermore, if the federalism concept operated as an independent restriction on the sovereign powers of the court, it would not be possible to waive their personal jurisdiction requirement. Individual actions cannot change the powers of sovereignty . . .."

Is Justice White's analysis correct?

CALDER v. JONES, 465 U.S. 783, 104 S.Ct. 1482, 79 L.Ed.2d 804 (1984). Jones sued in a California court the president and editor of the National Enquirer and the author of an allegedly defamatory article published in the National Enquirer. The Supreme Court reversed the lower court's ruling that California lacked personal jurisdiction over the defendants. It ruled that the defendants "Knew that the brunt of that injury [i.e., the injury caused by the libel] would be felt by Respondent in the state in which he lives and works and in which the *National Enquirer* has its circulation" and could therefore reasonably have expected to be haled into a California court. The Court also stated that "we reject the suggestions that First Amendment concerns into the jurisdictional analysis." The First Amendment concerns, it ruled, were already reflected in the constitutional limitations on the substantive law of libel.

BURGER KING CORPORATION v. RUDZEWICZ

Supreme Court of the United States, 1985.
471 U.S. 462, 105 S.Ct. 2174, 85 L.Ed.2d 528.

JUSTICE BRENNAN delivered the opinion of the Court.*

The State of Florida's long-arm statute extends jurisdiction to "[a]ny person, whether or not a citizen or resident of this state," who, *inter alia*, "[b]reach[es] a contract in this state by failing to perform acts required by the contract to be performed in this state," so long as the cause of action arises from the alleged contractual breach. Fla.

---

* Some footnotes omitted; others renumbered.

Stat. § 48.193(1)(g) (Supp.1984). The United States District Court for the Southern District of Florida, sitting in diversity, relied on this provision in exercising personal jurisdiction over a Michigan resident who allegedly had breached a franchise agreement with a Florida corporation by failing to make required payments in Florida. The question presented is whether this exercise of long-arm jurisdiction offended "traditional conception[s] of fair play and substantial justice" embodied in the Due Process Clause of the Fourteenth Amendment. International Shoe Co. v. Washington, 326 U.S. 310, 320, 66 S.Ct. 154, 160, 90 L.Ed. 95 (1945).

I

A

Burger King Corporation is a Florida corporation whose principal offices are in Miami. It is one of the world's largest restaurant organizations, with over 3,000 outlets in the 50 States, the Commonwealth of Puerto Rico, and 8 foreign nations. Burger King conducts approximately 80% of its business through a franchise operation that the company styles the "Burger King System"—"a comprehensive restaurant format and operating system for the sale of uniform and quality food products." . . . Burger King licenses its franchisees to use its trademarks and service marks for a period of 20 years and leases standardized restaurant facilities to them for the same term. In addition, franchisees acquire a variety of proprietary information concerning the "standards, specifications, procedures and methods for operating a Burger King Restaurant." . . . They also receive market research and advertising assistance; ongoing training in restaurant management; and accounting, cost-control, and inventory-control guidance. By permitting franchisees to tap into Burger King's established national reputation and to benefit from proven procedures for dispensing standardized fare, this system enables them to go into the restaurant business with significantly lowered barriers to entry.

In exchange for these benefits, franchisees pay Burger King an initial $40,000 franchise fee and commit themselves to payment of monthly royalties, advertising and sales promotion fees, and rent computed in part from monthly gross sales. Franchisees also agree to submit to the national organization's exacting regulation of virtually every conceivable aspect of their operations. Burger King imposes these standards and undertakes its rigid regulation out of conviction that "[u]niformity of service, appearance, and quality of product is essential to the preservation of the Burger King image and the benefits accruing therefrom to both Franchisee and Franchisor." . . .

Burger King oversees its franchise system through a two-tiered administrative structure. The governing contracts provide that the franchise relationship is established in Miami and governed by Florida law, and call for payment of all required fees and forwarding of all relevant notices to the Miami headquarters. The Miami headquarters sets policy and works directly with its franchisees in attempting to resolve major problems. . . . Day-to-day monitoring of franchisees, however, is conducted through a network of 10 district offices which in turn report to the Miami headquarters.

The instant litigation grows out of Burger King's termination of one of its franchisees, and is aptly described by the franchisee as "a divorce proceeding among commercial partners." . . . The appellee John Rudzewicz, a Michigan citizen and resident, is the senior partner in a Detroit accounting firm. In 1978, he was approached by Brian MacShara, the son of a business acquaintance, who suggested that they jointly apply to Burger King for a franchise in the Detroit area. . . .

Rudzewicz and MacShara jointly applied for a franchise to Burger King's Birmingham, Michigan district office in the autumn of 1978. Their application was forwarded to Burger King's Miami headquarters, which entered into a preliminary agreement with them in February 1979. During the ensuing four months it was agreed that Rudzewicz and MacShara would assume operation of an existing facility in Drayton Plains, Michigan. MacShara attended the prescribed management courses in Miami during this period, . . . and the franchisees purchased $165,000 worth of restaurant equipment from Burger King's Davmor Industries division in Miami. Even before the final agreements were signed, however, the parties began to disagree over site-development fees, building design, computation of monthly rent, and whether the franchisees would be able to assign their liabilities to a corporation they had formed. During these disputes Rudzewicz and MacShara negotiated both with the Birmingham district office and with the Miami headquarters. With some misgivings, Rudzewicz and Mac-Shara finally obtained limited concessions from the Miami headquarters, signed the final agreements, and commenced operations in June 1979. By signing the final agreements, Rudzewicz obligated himself personally to payments exceeding $1 million over the 20–year franchise relationship.

The Drayton Plains facility apparently enjoyed steady business during the summer of 1979, but patronage declined after a recession began later that year. Rudzewicz and MacShara soon fell far behind in their monthly payments to Miami. Headquarters sent notices of default, and an extended period of negotiations began among the franchisees, the Birmingham district office, and the Miami headquarters. After several Burger King officials in Miami had engaged in prolonged but ultimately unsuccessful negotiations with the franchisees by mail and by telephone,[1] headquarters terminated the franchise and ordered

1. Miami's policy was to "deal directly" with franchisees when they began to encounter financial difficulties, and to involve district office personnel only when necessary. 5 id., at 95. In the instant case, for example, the Miami office handled all credit problems, ordered cost-cutting measures, negotiated for a partial refinancing of the franchisees' debts, communicated directly with the franchisees in attempting to resolve the dispute, and was responsible for all termination matters. See 2 id., at 59–69; 5 id., at 84–89, 94–95, 97–98, 100–103, 116–128, 151–152, 158, 163; 6 id., at 395–397, 436–438, 510–511, 524–525.

Rudzewicz and MacShara to vacate the premises. They refused and continued to occupy and operate the facility as a Burger King restaurant.

B

Burger King commenced the instant action in the United States District for the Southern District of Florida in May 1981, invoking that court's diversity jurisdiction pursuant to 28 U.S.C. § 1332(a) and its original jurisdiction over federal trademark disputes pursuant to § 1338(a). Rudzewicz and MacShara entered special appearances and argued, *inter alia*, that because they were Michigan residents and because Burger King's claim did not "arise" within the Southern District of Florida, the District Court lacked personal jurisdiction over them. The District Court denied their motions after a hearing, holding that, pursuant to Florida's long-arm statute, "a nonresident Burger King franchisee is subject to the personal jurisdiction of this Court in actions arising out of its franchise agreements." . . . Rudzewicz and MacShara then filed an answer and a counterclaim seeking damages for alleged violations by Burger King of Michigan's Franchise Investment Law, Mich.Comp.Laws § 445.1501 *et seq.* (1979).

After a 3-day bench trial, the court again concluded that it had "jurisdiction over the subject matter and the parties to this cause." . . . Finding that Rudzewicz and MacShara had breached their franchise agreements with Burger King and had infringed Burger King's trademarks and service marks, the court entered judgment against them, jointly and severally, for $228,875 in contract damages. The court also ordered them "to immediately close Burger King Restaurant Number 775 from continued operation or to immediately give the keys and possession of said restaurant to Burger King Corporation," . . . found that they had failed to prove any of the required elements of their counterclaim, and awarded costs and attorney's fees to Burger King.

Rudzewicz appealed to the Court of Appeals for the Eleventh Circuit.[2] A divided panel of that Circuit reversed the judgment, concluding that the District Court could not properly exercise personal jurisdiction over Rudzewicz pursuant to Fla.Stat. § 48.193(1)(g) (Supp. 1984) because "the circumstances of the Drayton Plains franchise and the negotiations which led to it left Rudzewicz bereft of reasonable notice and financially unprepared for the prospect of franchise litiga-

---

2. MacShara did not appeal his judgment. See Burger King Corp. v. MacShara, 724 F.2d 1505, 1506, n. 1 (CA11 1984). In addition, Rudzewicz entered into a compromise with Burger King and waived his right to appeal the District Court's finding of trademark infringement and its entry of injunctive relief. See 4 Record 804–816. Accordingly, we need not address the extent to which the tortious act provisions of Florida's long-arm statute, see Fla.Stat. § 48.193(1)(b) (Supp.1984), may constitutionally extend to out-of-state trademark infringement. Compare Calder v. Jones, 465 U.S. 783, 788–789, 104 S.Ct. 1482, 1486–1487, 79 L.Ed.2d 804 (1984) (tortious out-of-state conduct); Keeton v. Hustler Magazine, Inc., 465 U.S. 770, 776, 104 S.Ct. 1473, 1479, 79 L.Ed.2d 790 (1984) (same).

tion in Florida." Burger King Corp. v. MacShara, 724 F.2d 1505, 1513 (1984). Accordingly, the panel majority concluded that "[j]urisdiction under these circumstances would offend the fundamental fairness which is the touchstone of due process." Ibid.

Burger King appealed the Eleventh Circuit's judgment to this Court . . . [which treated the appeal as if it were properly before the Court on a writ of certiorari].

II

A

The Due Process Clause protects an individual's liberty interest in not being subject to the binding judgments of a forum with which he has established no meaningful "contacts, ties, or relations." International Shoe Co. v. Washington, 326 U.S. at 319, 66 S.Ct., at 160.[3] By requiring that individuals have "fair warning that a particular activity may subject [them] to the jurisdiction of a foreign sovereign," Shaffer v. Heitner, 433 U.S. 186, 218, 97 S.Ct. 2569, 2587, 53 L.Ed.2d 683 (1977) (Stevens, J., concurring in judgment), the Due Process Clause "gives a degree of predictability to the legal system that allows potential defendants to structure their primary conduct with some minimum assurance as to where that conduct will and will not render them liable to suit," World–Wide Volkswagen Corp. v. Woodson, 444 U.S. 286, 297, 100 S.Ct. 559, 567, 62 L.Ed.2d 490 (1980).

Where a forum seeks to assert specific jurisdiction over an out-of-state defendant who has not consented to suit there, this "fair warning" requirement is satisfied if the defendant has "purposefully directed" his activities at residents of the forum, Keeton v. Hustler Magazine, Inc., 465 U.S. 770, 774, 104 S.Ct. 1473, 1478, 79 L.Ed.2d 790 (1984), and the litigation results from alleged injuries that "arise out of or relate to" those activities, Helicopteros Nacionales de Colombia, S.A. v. Hall, 466 U.S. 408, 414, 104 S.Ct. 1868, 1872, 80 L.Ed.2d 404 (1984). . . .

Once it has been decided that a defendant purposefully established minimum contacts within the forum State, these contacts may be considered in light of other factors to determine whether the assertion of personal jurisdiction would comport with "fair play and substantial justice." International Shoe Co. v. Washington, 326 U.S., at 320, 66 S.Ct., at 160. Thus courts in "appropriate case[s]" may evaluate "the burden on the defendant," "the forum State's interest in adjudicating the dispute," "the plaintiff's interest in obtaining convenient and effective relief," "the interstate judicial system's interest in obtaining the most efficient resolution of controversies," and the "shared interest of the several States in furthering fundamental substantive social poli-

3. Although this protection operates to restrict state power, it "must be seen as ultimately a function of the individual liberty interest preserved by the Due Process Clause" rather than as a function "of fed- eralism concerns." Insurance Corp. of Ireland, Ltd. v. Compagnie des Bauxites de Guinee, 456 U.S. 694, 702–703, n. 10, 102 S.Ct. 2099, 2104–2105, n. 10, 72 L.Ed.2d 492 (1982).

cies." World–Wide Volkswagen Corp. v. Woodson, supra, 444 U.S., at 292, 100 S.Ct., at 564. These considerations sometimes serve to establish the reasonableness of jurisdiction upon a lesser showing of minimum contacts than would otherwise be required. [Citations omitted.] On the other hand, where a defendant who purposefully has directed his activities at forum residents seeks to defeat jurisdiction, he must present a compelling case that the presence of some other considerations would render jurisdiction unreasonable. Most such considerations usually may be accommodated through means short of finding jurisdiction unconstitutional. For example, the potential clash of the forum's law with the "fundamental substantive social policies" of another State may be accommodated through application of the forum's choice-of-law rules. Similarly, a defendant claiming substantial inconvenience may seek a change of venue. Nevertheless, minimum requirements inherent in the concept of "fair play and substantial justice" may defeat the reasonableness of jurisdiction even if the defendant has purposefully engaged in forum activities. World–Wide Volkswagen Corp. v. Woodson, 444 U.S., at 292, 100 S.Ct., at 564; see also Restatement (Second) of Conflict of Laws §§ 36–37 (1971). As we previously have noted, jurisdictional rules may not be employed in such a way as to make litigation "so gravely difficult and inconvenient" that a party unfairly is at a "severe disadvantage" in comparison to his opponent. The Bremen v. Zapata Off–Shore Co., 407 U.S. 1, 18, 92 S.Ct. 1907, 1917, 32 L.Ed.2d 513 (1972) (*re* forum-selection provisions); McGee v. International Life Insurance Co., supra, 355 U.S., at 223–224, 78 S.Ct., at 201–202.

B

(1)

Applying these principles to the case at hand, we believe there is substantial record evidence supporting the District Court's conclusion that the assertion of personal jurisdiction over Rudzewicz in Florida for the alleged breach of his franchise agreement did not offend due process. At the outset, we note a continued division among lower courts respecting whether and to what extent a contract can constitute a "contact" for purposes of due process analysis. If the question is whether an individual's contract with an out-of-state party *alone* can automatically establish sufficient minimum contacts in the other party's home forum, we believe the answer clearly is that it cannot. The Court long ago rejected the notion that personal jurisdiction might turn on "mechanical" tests . . . or on "conceptualistic . . . theories of the place of contracting or of performance," . . . . Instead, we have emphasized the need for a "highly realistic" approach that recognizes that a "contract" is "ordinarily but an intermediate step serving to tie up prior business negotiations with future consequences which themselves are the real object of the business transaction." . . . It is these factors—prior negotiations and contemplated future consequences, along with the terms of the contract and the parties' actual course of dealing—that must be evaluated in determining whether the defendant purposefully established minimum contacts within the forum.

In this case, no physical ties to Florida can be attributed to Rudzewicz other than MacShara's brief training course in Miami. Rudzewicz did not maintain offices in Florida and, for all that appears from the record, has never even visited there. Yet this franchise dispute grew directly out of "a contract which had a *substantial* connection with that State." McGee v. International Life Insurance Co., 355 U.S., at 223, 78 S.Ct., at 201 (emphasis added). Eschewing the option of operating an independent local enterprise, Rudzewicz deliberately "reach[ed] out beyond" Michigan and negotiated with a Florida corporation for the purchase of a long-term franchise and the manifold benefits that would derive from affiliation with a nationwide organization. Travelers Health Assn. v. Virginia, 339 U.S., at 647, 70 S.Ct., at 929. Upon approval, he entered into a carefully structured 20–year relationship that envisioned continuing and wide-reaching contacts with Burger King in Florida. In light of Rudzewicz's voluntary acceptance of the long-term and exacting regulation of his business from Burger King's Miami headquarters, the "quality and nature" of his relationship to the company in Florida can in no sense be viewed as "random," "fortuitous," or "attenuated." Hanson v. Denckla, 357 U.S., at 253, 78 S.Ct., at 1239; Keeton v. Hustler Magazine, Inc., 465 U.S., at 774, 104 S.Ct., at 1478; World–Wide Volkswagen Corp. v. Woodson, 444 U.S., at 299, 100 S.Ct., at 568. Rudzewicz's refusal to make the contractually required payments in Miami, and his continued use of Burger King's trademarks and confidential business information after his termination, caused foreseeable injuries to the corporation in Florida. For these reasons it was, at the very least, presumptively reasonable for Rudzewicz to be called to account there for such injuries.

* * *

Moreover, we believe the Court of Appeals gave insufficient weight to provisions in the various franchise documents providing that all disputes would be governed by Florida law. The franchise agreement, for example, stated:

> "This Agreement shall become valid when executed and accepted by BKC at Miami, Florida; it shall be deemed made and entered into in the State of Florida and shall be governed and construed under and in accordance with the laws of the State of Florida. The choice of law designation does not require that all suits concerning this Agreement be filed in Florida."

* * *

The Court of Appeals reasoned that choice-of-law provisions are irrelevant to the question of personal jurisdiction, relying on Hanson v. Denckla for the proposition that "the center of gravity for choice-of-law purposes does not necessarily confer the sovereign prerogative to assert jurisdiction." 724 F.2d, at 1511–1512, n. 10, citing 357 U.S., at 254, 78

S.Ct., at 1240. This reasoning misperceives the import of the quoted proposition. The Court in *Hanson* and subsequent cases has emphasized that choice-of-law *analysis*—which focuses on all elements of a transaction, and not simply on the defendant's conduct—is distinct from minimum-contacts jurisdictional analysis—which focuses at the threshold solely on the defendant's purposeful connection to the forum. Nothing in our cases, however, suggests that a choice-of-law *provision* should be ignored in considering whether a defendant has "purposefully invoked the benefits and protections of a State's laws" for jurisdictional purposes. Although such a provision standing alone would be insufficient to confer jurisdiction, we believe that, when combined with the 20–year interdependent relationship Rudzewicz established with Burger King's Miami headquarters, it reinforced his deliberate affiliation with the forum State and the reasonable foreseeability of possible litigation there. As Judge Johnson argued in his dissent below, Rudzewicz "purposefully availed himself of the benefits and protections of Florida's laws" by entering into contracts expressly providing that those laws would govern franchise disputes. 724 F.2d, at 1513.

(2)

Nor has Rudzewicz pointed to other factors that can be said persuasively to outweigh the considerations discussed above and to establish the *unconstitutionality* of Florida's assertion of jurisdiction. We cannot conclude that Florida had no "legitimate interest in holding [Rudzewicz] answerable on a claim related to" the contacts he had established in that State. . . .

The Court of Appeals also concluded, however, that the parties dealings involved "a characteristic disparity of bargaining power" and "elements of surprise," and that Rudzewicz "lacked fair notice" of the potential for litigation in Florida because the contractual provisions suggesting to the contrary were merely "boilerplate declarations in a lengthy printed contract." 724 F.2d, at 1511–1512, and n. 10. . . . After a 3–day bench trial, the District Court found that Burger King had made no misrepresentations, that Rudzewicz and MacShara "were and are experienced and sophisticated businessmen," and that "at no time" did they "ac[t] under economic duress or disadvantage imposed by" Burger King. . . .

III

[T]he Court of Appeals apparently believed that it was necessary to reject jurisdiction in this case as a prophylactic measure, reasoning that an affirmance of the District Court's judgment would result in the exercise of jurisdiction over "out-of-state consumers to collect payments due on modest personal purchases" and would "sow the seeds of default judgments against franchisees owing smaller debts." . . . We share the Court of Appeals' broader concerns and therefore reject any talismanic jurisdictional formulas; "the facts of each case must [always] be weighed" in determining whether personal jurisdiction would comport with "fair play and substantial justice." Kulko v. California Superior Court, 436 U.S., at 92, 98 S.Ct., at 1696–1697.[4] The "quality and nature" of an interstate transaction may sometimes be so "random," "fortuitous," or "attenuated" that it cannot fairly be said that the potential defendant "should reasonably anticipate being haled into court" in another jurisdiction. World–Wide Volkswagen Corp. v. Woodson, 444 U.S., at 297, 100 S.Ct., at 567; . . . We also have emphasized that jurisdiction may not be grounded on a contract whose terms have been obtained through "fraud, undue influence, or over-weening bargaining power" and whose application would render litigation "so gravely difficult and inconvenient that [a party] will for all practical purposes be deprived of his day in court." Because Rudzewicz established a substantial and continuing relationship with Burger King's Miami headquarters, received fair notice from the contract documents and the course of dealing that he might be subject to suit in Florida, and has failed to demonstrate how jurisdiction in that forum would otherwise be fundamentally unfair, we conclude that the District Court's exercise of jurisdiction pursuant to Florida Stat. § 48.193(1)(g) (Supp.1984) did not offend due process. The judgment of the Court of Appeals is accordingly reversed, and the case is remanded for further proceedings consistent with this opinion.

It is so ordered.

JUSTICE POWELL took no part in the consideration or decision of this case.

JUSTICE STEVENS, with whom JUSTICE WHITE joins, dissenting.

In my opinion there is a significant element of unfairness in requiring a franchisee to defend a case of this kind in the forum chosen by the franchisor. It is undisputed that respondent maintained no place of business in Florida, that he had no employees in that State, and that he was not licensed to do business there. Respondent did not prepare his french fries, shakes, and hamburgers in Michigan, and then deliver them into the stream of commerce "with the expectation that they [would] be purchased by consumers in" Florida. . . . To the contrary, respondent did business only in Michigan, his business, property, and payroll taxes were payable in that state, and he sold all of his products there.

Throughout the business relationship, respondent's principal contacts with petitioner were with its Michigan office. Notwithstanding its disclaimer, . . . the Court seems ultimately to rely on nothing more than standard boilerplate language contained in various documents, . . . to establish that respondent " 'purposefully availed himself of the benefits and protections of Florida's laws.' " . . . Such

---

4. This approach does, of course, preclude clear-cut jurisdictional rules. But any inquiry into "fair play and substantial justice" necessarily requires determinations "in which few answers will be written 'in black and white. The greys are dominant and even among them the shades are innumberable.' " Kulko v. California Superior Court, 436 U.S., at 92, 98 S.Ct. at 1697.

superficial analysis creates a potential for unfairness not only in negotiations between franchisors and their franchisees but, more signif- icantly, in the resolution of the disputes that inevitably arise from time to time in such relationships.

   *   *   *

Accordingly, I respectfully dissent.

NOTES

(1) To what extent does a choice-of-law clause imply a choice of forum? And to what extent does a choice-of-forum clause imply a choice of law?

(2) Could Burger King have saved itself the cost of the litigation that led to its ultimate victory in the Supreme Court by inclusion of a choice-of-forum clause in the franchise agreement? See p. 235 supra. Would Burger King have a claim for this cost upon its lawyer for having failed to include such a clause?

(3) To what extent does the principal case warrant the conclusion that a party to a contract may constitutionally be sued for breach of contract in the forum of his contract partner?

(4) Are judicial and legislative jurisdiction as separate as the Court indi- cates? What differences are there in the bases for legislative, as distinguished from judicial, jurisdiction? Cf. Silberman, Shaffer v. Heitner, The End of an Era, 53 N.Y.U.L.Rev. 33 (1978) (If legislative jurisdiction exists, judicial jurisdic- tion should exist.); Martin, Personal Jurisdiction and Choice of Law, 78 Mich.L. Rev. 872 (1980); Peterson, Proposals of Marriage Between Jurisdiction and Choice of Law, 14 U.C.D.L.Rev. 869 (1981). On legislative jurisdiction general- ly, see Reese, Legislative Jurisdiction, 78 Colum.L.Rev. 1587 (1978).

(5) Is the notion that federalism concerns can play no independent role in limiting personal jurisdiction, since concededly personal jurisdiction can be created by consent, analytically correct? Do federalism concerns play any role, when the defendant consents to be sued within the state?

(6) In *World–Wide Volkswagen,* if the German manufacturer had objected to the exercise of jurisdiction, would the plea have been successful? In Poyner v. Erma Werke GmbH, 618 F.2d 1186 (6th Cir.1980), the court, in upholding jurisdiction over the German manufacturer who sold in the United States only through an independent distributor, indicated that lesser contacts may be required in the case of an alien defendant: "While minimum contacts also serve the related function of checking the judicial reach of coequal sovereigns in a Federal system, the impact of such a purpose is minimized in an interna- tional setting as opposed to interstate operations" (617 F.2d at 1192).

(7) In Curtis Publishing Co. v. Birdsong, 360 F.2d 344 (5th Cir.1966), citizens of Mississippi brought a libel action against the defendant in Alabama. Stressing that the plaintiffs were non-residents of Alabama and that Alabama had an attenuated interest in the suit, the Fifth Circuit held there was no judicial jurisdiction over the defendant. What is the present status of this decision? Cf. also Smit, Common and Civil Law Rules of In Personam Adjudi- catory Authority: An Analysis of Underlying Policies, 21 Int. & Comp.L.Q. 335 (1972).

(8) Can in personam judicial powers be extended through interstate com- pacts? See Note, Interstate Jurisdictional Compacts: A New Theory of Person- al Jurisdiction, 49 Fordham L.Rev. 1097 (1981).

ASAHI METAL INDUSTRY CO., LTD. v. SUPERIOR COURT OF CALIFORNIA, SOLANO COUNTY

Supreme Court of the United States, 1987.
480 U.S. 102, 107 S.Ct. 1026, 94 L.Ed.2d 92.

JUSTICE O'CONNOR announced the judgment of the Court and delivered the unanimous opinion of the Court with respect to Part I, the opinion of the Court with respect to Part II–B, in which The Chief Justice, Justice Brennan, Justice White, Justice Marshall, Justice Blackmun, Justice Powell, and Justice Stevens join, and an opinion with respect to Parts II–A and III, in which The Chief Justice, Justice Powell, and Justice Scalia join.

This case presents the question whether the mere awareness on the part of a foreign defendant that the components it manufactured, sold, and delivered outside the United States would reach the forum state in the stream of commerce constitutes "minimum contacts" between the defendant and the forum state such that the exercise of jurisdiction "does not offend 'traditional notions of fair play and substantial justice.' "　. . .

I

On September 23, 1978, on Interstate Highway 80 in Solano County, California, Gary Zurcher lost control of his Honda motorcycle and collided with a tractor. Zurcher was severely injured, and his passenger and wife, Ruth Ann Moreno, was killed. In September 1979, Zurcher filed a product liability action in the Superior Court of the State of California in and for the County of Solano. Zurcher alleged that the 1978 accident was caused by a sudden loss of air and an explosion in the rear tire of the motorcycle, and alleged that the motorcycle tire, tube, and sealant were defective. Zurcher's complaint named, *inter alia,* Cheng Shin Rubber Industrial Co., Ltd. (Cheng Shin), the Taiwanese manufacturer of the tube. Cheng Shin in turn filed a cross-complaint seeking indemnification from its codefendants and from petitioner, Asahi Metal Industry Co., Ltd. (Asahi), the manufacturer of the tube's valve assembly. Zurcher's claims against Cheng Shin and the other defendants were eventually settled and dismissed, leaving only Cheng Shin's indemnity action against Asahi.

California's long-arm statute authorizes the exercise of jurisdiction "on any basis not inconsistent with the Constitution of this state or of the United States." Cal.Code Civ.Proc.Ann. § 410.10 (West 1973). Asahi moved to quash Cheng Shin's service of summons arguing the State could not exert jurisdiction over it consistent with the Due Process Clause of the Fourteenth Amendment.

In relation to the motion, the following information was submitted by Asahi and Cheng Shin. Asahi is a Japanese corporation. It manufactures tire valve assemblies in Japan and sells the assemblies to Cheng Shin, and to several other tire manufacturers, for use as components in finished tire tubes. Asahi's sales to Cheng Shin took place in

Taiwan. The shipments from Asahi to Cheng Shin were sent from Japan to Taiwan. Cheng Shin bought and incorporated into its tire tubes 150,000 Asahi valve assemblies in 1978; 500,000 in 1979; 500,000 in 1980; 100,000 in 1981; and 100,000 in 1982. Sales to Cheng Shin accounted for 1.24 percent of Asahi's income in 1981 and 0.44 percent in 1982. Cheng Shin alleged that approximately 20 percent of its sales in the United States are in California. Cheng Shin purchases valve assemblies from other suppliers as well, and sells finished tubes throughout the world.

In 1983 an attorney for Cheng Shin conducted an informal examination of the valve stems of the tire tubes sold in one cyclery in Solano County. The attorney declared that of the approximately 115 tire tubes in the store, 97 were purportedly manufactured in Japan or Taiwan, and of those 97, 21 valve stems were marked with the circled letter "A", apparently Asahi's trademark. Of the 21 Asahi valve stems, 12 were incorporated into Cheng Shin tire tubes. The store contained 41 other Cheng Shin tubes that incorporated the valve assemblies of other manufacturers. . . .

Primarily on the basis of the above information, the Superior Court denied the motion to quash summons, stating that "Asahi obviously does business on an international scale. It is not unreasonable that they defend claims of defect in their product on an international scale." . . .

The Court of Appeal of the State of California issued a peremptory writ of mandate commanding the Superior Court to quash service of summons. The court concluded that "it would be unreasonable to require Asahi to respond in California solely on the basis of ultimately realized foreseeability that the product into which its component was embodied would be sold all over the world including California." . . .

The Supreme Court of the State of California reversed and discharged the writ issued by the Court of Appeal. . . . The court observed that "Asahi has no offices, property or agents in California. It solicits no business in California and has made no direct sales [in California]." . . . Moreover, "Asahi did not design or control the system of distribution that carried its valve assemblies into California." . . . Nevertheless, the court found the exercise of jurisdiction over Asahi to be consistent with the Due Process Clause. . . . The court considered Asahi's intentional act of placing its components into the stream of commerce—that is, by delivering the components to Cheng Shin in Taiwan—coupled with Asahi's awareness that some of the components would eventually find their way into California, sufficient to form the basis for state court jurisdiction under the Due Process Clause.

    *   *   *

II

A

The Due Process Clause of the Fourteenth Amendment limits the power of a state court to exert personal jurisdiction over a nonresident defendant. "[T]he constitutional touchstone" of the determination whether an exercise of personal jurisdiction comports with due process "remains whether the defendant purposefully established 'minimum contacts' in the forum State." Burger King Corp. v. Rudzewicz, 471 U.S. 462, 474, 105 S.Ct. 2174, 2183, 85 L.Ed.2d 528 (1985) . . .

Applying the principle that minimum contacts must be based on an act of the defendant, the Court in World–Wide Volkswagen Corp. v. Woodson, 444 U.S. 286, 100 S.Ct. 559, 62 L.Ed.2d 490 (1980), rejected the assertion that a *consumer's* unilateral act of bringing the defendant's product into the forum State was a sufficient constitutional basis for personal jurisdiction over the defendant. . . .

. . . The placement of a product into the stream of commerce, without more, is not an act of the defendant purposefully directed toward the forum State. Additional conduct of the defendant may indicate an intent or purpose to serve the market in the forum State, for example, designing the product for the market in the forum State, advertising in the forum State, establishing channels for providing regular advice to customers in the forum State, or marketing the product through a distributor who has agreed to serve as the sales agent in the forum State. But a defendant's awareness that the stream of commerce may or will sweep the product into the forum State does not convert the mere act of placing the product into the stream into an act purposefully directed toward the forum State.

Assuming, *arguendo,* that respondents have established Asahi's awareness that some of the valves sold to Cheng Shin would be incorporated into tire tubes sold in California, respondents have not demonstrated any action by Asahi to purposefully avail itself of the California market. Asahi does not do business in California. It has no office, agents, employees, or property in California. It does not advertise or otherwise solicit business in California. It did not create, control, or employ the distribution system that brought its valves to California.

On the basis of these facts, the exertion of personal jurisdiction over Asahi by the Superior Court of California * exceeds the limits of Due Process.

---

* We have no occasion here to determine whether Congress could, consistent with the due Process Clause of the Fifth Amendment, authorize federal court personal jurisdiction over alien defendants based on the aggregate of *national* contacts, rather than on the contacts between the defendant and the State in which the federal court sits. See Max Daetwyler Corp. v. R. Meyer, 762 F.2d 290, 293–295 (CA3 1985); DeJames v. Magnificence Carriers, Inc., 654 F.2d 280, 283 (CA3 1981): see also Born, Reflections on Judicial Jurisdiction in International Cases, to be published in 17 Ga.J.Int'l & Comp.L. 1 (1987); Lilly, Jurisdiction Over Domestic and Alien Defendants, 69 Va.L.Rev. 85, 127–145 (1983).

B

*   *   *

We have previously explained that the determination of the reasonableness of the exercise of jurisdiction in each case will depend on an evaluation of several factors. A court must consider the burden on the defendant, the interests of the forum state, and the plaintiff's interest in obtaining relief. It must also weigh in its determination "the interstate judicial system's interest in obtaining the most efficient resolution of controversies; and the shared interest of the several States in furthering fundamental substantive social policies." World–Wide Volkswagen, 444 U.S., at 292, 100 S.Ct., at 564 (citations omitted).

A consideration of these factors in the present case clearly reveals the unreasonableness of the assertion of jurisdiction over Asahi, even apart from the question of the placement of goods in the stream of commerce.

Certainly the burden on the defendant in this case is severe. Asahi has been commanded by the Supreme Court of California not only to traverse the distance between Asahi's headquarters in Japan and the Superior Court of California in and for the County of Solano, but also to submit its dispute with Cheng Shin to a foreign nation's judicial system. The unique burdens placed upon one who must defend oneself in a foreign legal system should have significant weight in assessing the reasonableness of stretching the long arm of personal jurisdiction over national borders.

When minimum contacts have been established, often the interests of the plaintiff and the forum in the exercise of jurisdiction will justify even the serious burdens placed on the alien defendant. In the present case, however, the interests of the plaintiff and the forum in California's assertion of jurisdiction over Asahi are slight. All that remains is a claim for indemnification asserted by Cheng Shin, a Tawainese corporation, against Asahi. The transaction on which the indemnification claim is based took place in Taiwan; Asahi's components were shipped from Japan to Taiwan. Cheng Shin has not demonstrated that it is more convenient for it to litigate its indemnification claim against Asahi in California rather than in Taiwan or Japan.

Because the plaintiff is not a California resident, California's legitimate interests in the dispute have considerably diminished. The Supreme Court of California argued that the State had an interest in "protecting its consumers by ensuring that foreign manufacturers comply with the state's safety standards."

. . . The State Supreme Court's definition of California's interest, however, was overly broad. The dispute between Cheng Shin and Asahi is primarily about indemnification rather than safety standards. Moreover, it is not at all clear at this point that California law should govern the question whether a Japanese corporation should indemnify a Taiwanese corporation on the basis of a sale made in Taiwan and a shipment of goods from Japan to Taiwan.

. . . . The possibility of being haled into a California court as a result of an accident involving Asahi's components undoubtedly creates an additional deterrent to the manufacture of unsafe components; however, similar pressures will be placed on Asahi by the purchasers of its components as long as those who use Asahi components in their final products, and sell those products in California, are subject to the application of California tort law.

World–Wide Volkswagen also admonished courts to take into consideration the interests of the "several States," in addition to the forum state, in the efficient judicial resolution of the dispute and the advancement of substantive policies. In the present case, this advice calls for a court to consider the procedural and substantive policies of other *nations* whose interests are affected by the assertion of jurisdiction by the California court. The procedural and substantive interests of other nations in a state court's assertion of jurisdiction over an alien defendant will differ from case to case. In every case, however, those interests, as well as the Federal interest in its foreign relations policies, will be best served by a careful inquiry into the reasonableness of the assertion of jurisdiction in the particular case, and an unwillingness to find the serious burdens on an alien defendant outweighed by minimal interests on the part of the plaintiff or the forum State. . . .

Considering the international context, the heavy burden on the alien defendant, and the slight interests of the plaintiff and the forum State, the exercise of personal jurisdiction by a California court over Asahi in this instance would be unreasonable and unfair.

III

Because the facts of this case do not establish minimum contacts such that the exercise of personal jurisdiction is consistent with fair play and substantial justice, the judgment of Supreme Court of California is reversed, and the case is remanded for further proceedings not inconsistent with this opinion.

It is so ordered.

JUSTICE BRENNAN, with whom JUSTICE WHITE, JUSTICE MARSHALL, and JUSTICE BLACKMUN join, concurring in part and in the judgment.

I do not agree with the plurality's interpretation of the stream-of-commerce theory, nor with its conclusion that Asahi did not "purposely avail itself of the California market," . . .—I do agree, however, with the Court's conclusion in Part II–B that the exercise of personal jurisdiction over Asahi in this case would not comport with "fair play and substantial justice," International Shoe Co. v. Washington, 326 U.S. 310, 320, 66 S.Ct. 154, 160, 90 L.Ed. 95 (1945). This is one of those rare cases in which "minimum requirements inherent in the concept of 'fair play and substantial justice' . . . defeat the reasonableness of jurisdiction even [though] the defendant has purposefully engaged in forum activities." Burger King Corp. v. Rudzewicz, 471 U.S. 462, 477–478, 105 S.Ct. 2174, 2184–2185, 85 L.Ed.2d 528 (1985). I therefore join Parts I and II–B of the Court's opinion, and write separately to explain my disagreement with Part II–A.

The plurality states that "a defendant's awareness that the stream of commerce may or will sweep the product into the forum State does not convert the mere act of placing the product into the stream into an act purposefully directed toward the forum State." . . . The plurality would therefore require a plaintiff to show "[a]dditional conduct" directed toward the forum before finding the exercise of jurisdiction over the defendant to be consistent with the Due Process Clause. . . . I see no need for such a showing, however.

JUSTICE STEVENS, with whom JUSTICE WHITE and JUSTICE BLACKMUN join, concurring in part and concurring in the judgment.

The judgment of the Supreme Court of California should be reversed for the reasons stated in Part II–B of the Court's opinion. While I join Parts I and II–B, I do not join Part II–A for two reasons. First, it is not necessary to the Court's decision. An examination of minimum contacts is not always necessary to determine whether a state court's assertion of personal jurisdiction is constitutional . . .. Part II–B establishes, after considering the factors set forth in World–Wide Volkswagen Corp. v. Woodson, 444 U.S. 286, 292, 100 S.Ct. 559, 564, 62 L.Ed. 2d 490 (1980), that California's exercise of jurisdiction over Asahi in this case would be "unreasonable and unfair." . . . This finding alone requires reversal; this case fits within the rule that "minimum requirements inherent in the concept of 'fair play and substantial justice' may defeat the reasonableness of jurisdiction even if the defendant has purposefully engaged in forum activities." . . . Accordingly, I see no reason in this case for the Court to articulate "purposeful direction" or any other test as the nexus between an act of a defendant and the forum State that is necessary to establish minimum contacts.

Second, even assuming that the test ought to be formulated here, Part II–A misapplies it to the facts of this case. The Court seems to assume that an unwavering line can be drawn between "mere awareness" that a component will find its way into the forum State and "purposeful availment" of the forum's market. . . . Over the course of its dealings with Cheng Shin, Asahi has arguably engaged in a higher quantum of conduct than "[t]he placement of a product into the stream of commerce, without more. . . ." Whether or not this conduct rises to the level of purposeful availment requires a constitutional determination that is affected by the volume, the value, and the hazardous character of the components. In most circumstances I would be inclined to conclude that a regular course of dealing that results in deliveries of over 100,000 units annually over a period of several years would constitute "purposeful availment" even though the item delivered to the forum State was a standard product marketed throughout the world.

NOTES

(1) Would the Supreme Court have ruled the same way against the manufacturer of the motorcycle or the manufacturer of the tire, even if these had sold the motorcycles and tires only in Japan and Taiwan?

(2) Would the result in the principal case have been different if the plaintiff had been a resident of California?

(3) Do federal considerations play any role when the defendant is an alien? Does the decision in the principal case mark a departure from those in *Bauxites*? See p. 267, supra.

(4) In Nelson v. Park Industries, Inc., 717 F.2d 1120 (7th Cir.1983), cert. denied 465 U.S. 1024, 104 S.Ct. 1277, 79 L.Ed.2d 682 (1984), a Hong Kong manufacturer produced all flannel shirts sold by Woolworth in the United States. Woolworth purchased the shirts from another Hong Kong corporation, a buying agent, f.o.b. Hong Kong. One of the shirts caught fire and injured the plaintiff in Wisconsin. Distinguishing the case from *World–Wide,* the Seventh Circuit ruled that the Hong Kong manufacturer was subject to in personam jurisdiction in Wisconsin.

(5) The decisions in *World–Wide* and *Asahi* have focussed attention on the extent to which a person who puts a product into the stream of commerce becomes subject to the judicial jurisdiction of the place where the product causes damage or injury. For a discussion of the stream of commerce approach, see Hay, Refining Personal Jurisdiction in United States Conflicts Law, 35 Int'l & Comp.L.Cf. 32 (1986); Hay, Judicial Jurisdiction over Foreign Country Corporate Defendants—Comments on Recent Case Law, 63 Oregon L.Rev. 431 (1984). See also Hay, Judicial Jurisdiction and Choice of Law: Constitutional Limitations, 59 Colo.L.Rev. 9 (1988).

(6) It has been argued that the crucial question in determining specific jurisdiction is whether the local contacts are substantively relevant to the plaintiff's claim. On this approach, see Brilmayer, How Contacts Count: Due Process Limitations on State Court Jurisdiction, 1980 Sup.Ct.Rev. 77; Twitchell, The Myth of General Jurisdiction, 101 Harv.L.Rev. 610 (1988); Brilmayer, Related Contacts and Personal Jurisdiction, 101 Harv.L.Rev. 1444 (1988); Twitchell, A Rejoinder to Professor Brilmayer, 101 Harv.L.Rev. 1465 (1988).

(7) Is there a trend away from the purposeful availment and benefits test exemplified by *Hanson v. Denckla* to the circumstances affiliating the defendant with the forum and the foreseeability of litigation at that forum? See Stewart, A New Litany of Personal Jurisdiction, 60 U.Colo.L.Rev. 5 (1989); Weber, Purposeful Availment, 39 S.C.L.Rev. 815 (1988).

STATUTORY LIMITATIONS ON STATE JURISDICTION

Federal statutes may limit the judicial jurisdiction of the states. They do so when they limit the subject matter jurisdiction of the states, such as in patent cases. See p. 195, supra. But they may also limit the in personam and in rem jurisdiction of the states. For an example, see Spiegel, Inc. v. The Federal Trade Commission, 540 F.2d 287 (7th Cir. 1976), upholding an FTC order restraining a mail order house from suing customers in a state other than the customer's domicile or the place where the contract was made. Could Congress, under the due process clause, validly enact a statute prohibiting franchisers from suing franchisees at places other than the franchiser's domicile or place of business. Cf. Burger King Corp. v. Rudzewicz, 471 U.S. 462, 105 S.Ct. 2174, 85 L.Ed.2d 528 (1985), p. 267 supra.

K. BUSINESS DONE IN THE STATE—UNRELATED CLAIMS

HELICOPTEROS NACIONALES DE COLOMBIA S.A. v. HALL

Supreme Court of the United States, 1984.
466 U.S. 408, 104 S.Ct. 1868, 80 L.Ed.2d 404.

JUSTICE BLACKMUN delivered the opinion of the Court.*

We granted certiorari in this case, 460 U.S. 1021, 103 S.Ct. 1270, 75 L.Ed.2d 493 (1983), to decide whether the Supreme Court of Texas correctly ruled that the contacts of a foreign corporation with the State of Texas were sufficient to allow a Texas state court to assert jurisdiction over the corporation in a cause of action not arising out of or related to the corporation's activities within the State.

I

Petitioner Helicopteros Nacionales de Columbia, S.A., (Helicol) is a Colombian corporation with its principal place of business in the city of Bogota in that country. It is engaged in the business of providing helicopter transportation for oil and construction companies in South America. On January 26, 1976, a helicopter owned by Helicol crashed in Peru. Four United States citizens were among those who lost their lives in the accident. Respondents are the survivors and representatives of the four decedents.

At the time of the crash, respondents' decedents were employed by Consorcio, a Peruvian consortium, and were working on a pipeline in Peru. Consorcio is the alter-ego of a joint venture named Williams–Sedco–Horn (WSH). The venture had its headquarters in Houston, Tex. Consorcio had been formed to enable the venturers to enter into a contract with Petro Peru, the Peruvian state-owned oil company. Consorcio was to construct a pipeline for Petro Peru running from the interior of Peru westward to the Pacific Ocean. Peruvian law forbade construction of the pipeline by any non-Peruvian entity.

Consorcio/WSH needed helicopters to move personnel, materials, and equipment into and out of the construction area. In 1974, upon request of Consorcio/WSH, the chief executive officer of Helicol, Francisco Restrepo, flew to the United States and conferred in Houston with representatives of the three joint venturers. At that meeting, there was a discussion of prices, availability, working conditions, fuel, sup-

---

* Some footnotes omitted; others renumbered.

plies, and housing. Restrepo represented that Helicol could have the first helicopter on the job in 15 days. The Consorcio/WSH representatives decided to accept the contract proposed by Restrepo. Helicol began performing before the agreement was formally signed in Peru on November 11, 1974. The contract was written in Spanish on official government stationery and provided that the residence of all the parties would be Lima, Peru. It further stated that controversies arising out of the contract would be submitted to the jurisdiction of Peruvian courts. In addition, it provided that Consorcio/WSH would make payments to Helicol's account with the Bank of America in New York City. . . .

Aside from the negotiation session in Houston between Restrepo and the representatives of Consorcio/WSH, Helicol had other contacts with Texas. During the years 1970–1977, it purchased helicopters (approximately 80% of its fleet), spare parts, and accessories for more than $4,000,000 from Bell Helicopter Company in Fort Worth. In that period, Helicol sent prospective pilots to Fort Worth for training and to ferry the aircraft to South America. It also sent management and maintenance personnel to visit Bell Helicopter in Fort Worth during the same period in order to receive "plant familiarization" and for technical consultation. Helicol received into its New York City and Panama City, Fla., bank accounts over $5,000,000 in payments from Consorcio/WSH drawn upon First City National Bank of Houston.

Beyond the foregoing, there have been no other business contacts between Helicol and the State of Texas. Helicol never has been authorized to do business in Texas and never has had an agent for the service of process within the State. It never has performed helicopter operations in Texas or sold any product that reached Texas, never solicited business in Texas, never signed any contract in Texas, never had any employee based there, and never recruited an employee in Texas. In addition, Helicol never has owned real or personal property in Texas and never has maintained an office or establishment there. Helicol has maintained no records in Texas and has no shareholders in that State. None of the respondents or their decedents were domiciled in Texas,[1] . . . but all of the decedents were hired in Houston by Consorcio/WSH to work on the Petro Peru pipeline project.

Respondents instituted wrongful death actions in the District Court of Harris County, Tex., against Consorcio/WSH, Bell Helicopter Company, and Helicol. Helicol filed special appearances and moved to dismiss the actions for lack of *in personam* jurisdiction over it. The motion was denied. After a consolidated jury trial, judgment was entered against Helicol on a jury verdict of $1,141,200 in favor of respondents. . . .

---

1. Respondents' lack of residential or other contacts with Texas of itself does not defeat otherwise proper jurisdiction. Keeton v. Hustler Magazine, Inc., ante, . . . 104 S.Ct. 1473 at 1481 . . . Calder v. Jones, . . . 104 S.Ct. 1482 at 1486 . . .. We mention respondents' lack of contacts merely to show that nothing in the nature of the relationship between respondents and Helicol could possibly enhance Helicol's contacts with Texas. The harm suffered by respondents did not occur in Texas. Nor is it alleged that any negligence on the part of Helicol took place in Texas.

The Texas Court of Civil Appeals, Houston, First District, reversed the judgment of the District Court, holding that *in personam* jurisdiction over Helicol was lacking. 616 S.W.2d 247 (Tex.1981). The Supreme Court of Texas, with three Justices dissenting, initially affirmed the judgment of the Court of Civil Appeals. App. to Pet. for Cert. 46a–62a. Seven months later, however, on motion for rehearing, the court withdrew its prior opinions and, again with three Justices dissenting, reversed the judgment of the intermediate court. 638 S.W.2d 870 (Tex. 1982). In ruling that the Texas courts had *in personam* jurisdiction, the Texas Supreme Court first held that the State's long-arm statute reaches as far as the Due Process Clause of the Fourteenth Amendment permits . . . the only question remaining for the court to decide was whether it was consistent with the Due Process Clause for Texas courts to assert *in personam* jurisdiction over Helicol. Ibid.

II

The Due Process Clause of the Fourteenth Amendment operates to limit the power of a State to assert *in personam* jurisdiction over a nonresident defendant. Pennoyer v. Neff, 95 U.S. 714, 24 L.Ed. 565 (1877). Due process requirements are satisfied when *in personam* jurisdiction is asserted over a nonresident corporate defendant that has "certain minimum contacts with [the forum] such that the maintenance of the suit does not offend 'traditional notions of fair play and substantial justice.'" International Shoe Co. v. Washington, 326 U.S. 310, 316, 66 S.Ct. 154, 158, 90 L.Ed. 95 (1945), quoting Milliken v. Meyer, 311 U.S. 457, 463, 61 S.Ct. 339, 342, 85 L.Ed. 278 (1940). . . .

Even when the cause of action does not arise out of or relate to the foreign corporation's activities in the forum State, due process is not offended by a State's subjecting the corporation to its *in personam* jurisdiction when there are sufficient contacts between the State and the foreign corporation. Perkins v. Benguet Consolidated Mining Co., 342 U.S. 437, 72 S.Ct. 413, 96 L.Ed. 485 (1952); see Keeton v. Hustler Magazine, Inc., 465 U.S. 770, 779–780, 104 S.Ct. at 1473, 1480–1481, 79 L.Ed.2d 780 (1984).

All parties to the present case concede that respondents' claims against Helicol did not "arise out of," and are not related to, Helicol's activities within Texas. We thus must explore the nature of Helicol's contacts with the State of Texas to determine whether they constitute the kind of continuous and systematic general business contacts the Court found to exist in *Perkins*. We hold that they do not.

It is undisputed that Helicol does not have a place of business in Texas and never has been licensed to do business in the State. Basically, Helicol's contacts with Texas consisted of sending its chief executive officer to Houston for a contract-negotiation session; accepting into its New York bank account checks drawn on a Houston bank; purchasing helicopters, equipment, and training services from Bell Helicopter for substantial sums; and sending personnel to Bell's facilities in Fort Worth for training.

The one trip to Houston by Helicol's chief executive officer for the purpose of negotiating the transportation-services contract with Consorcio/WSH cannot be described or regarded as a contact of a "continuous and systematic" nature, as *Perkins* described it, see also International Shoe Co. v. Washington, 326 U.S., at 320, 66 S.Ct., at 160, and thus cannot support an assertion of *in personam* jurisdiction over Helicol by a Texas court. Similarly, Helicol's acceptance from Consorcio/WSH of checks drawn on a Texas bank is of negligible significance for purposes of determining whether Helicol had sufficient contacts in Texas. There is no indication that Helicol ever requested that the checks be drawn on a Texas bank or that there was any negotiation between Helicol and Consorcio/WSH with respect to the location or identity of the bank on which checks would be drawn. Common sense and everyday experience suggest that, absent unusual circumstances, the bank on which a check is drawn is generally of little consequence to the payee and is a matter left to the discretion of the drawer. Such unilateral activity of another party or a third person is not an appropriate consideration when determining whether a defendant has sufficient contacts with a forum State to justify an assertion of jurisdiction.

* * *

III

We hold that Helicol's contacts with the State of Texas were insufficient to satisfy the requirements of the Due Process Clause of the Fourteenth Amendment. Accordingly, we reverse the judgment of the Supreme Court of Texas.

It is so ordered.

JUSTICE BRENNAN, dissenting.

* * *

Based on essentially undisputed facts, the Court concludes that petitioner Helicol's contacts with the State of Texas were insufficient to allow the Texas state courts constitutionally to assert "general jurisdiction" over all claims filed against this foreign corporation. Although my independent weighing of the facts leads me to a different conclusion, . . . the Court's holding on this issue is neither implausible nor unexpected.

What is troubling about the Court's opinion, however, are the implications that might be drawn from the way in which the Court approaches the constitutional issue it addresses. First, the Court limits its discussion to an assertion of general jurisdiction of the Texas courts because, in its view, the underlying cause of action does "not aris[e] out of or relat[e] to the corporation's activities within the State."

* * *

In contrast, I believe that the undisputed contacts in this case between petitioner Helicol and the State of Texas are sufficiently important, and sufficiently related to the underlying cause of action, to make it fair and reasonable for the State to assert personal jurisdiction over Helicol for the wrongful death actions filed by the respondents.

NOTES

(1) The Paris edition of the New York Herald Tribune frequently carried the following advertisement:

> "WE ACT AS YOUR NEW YORK OFFICE 5th Ave address, phone and lobby listing. Messages & orders taken, mail forwarded . . . Fifth Ave . . ., New York City, U.S.A."

What would you advise your foreign client who wished to avail himself of this opportunity?

(2) Can a non-resident avoid the danger that local activities will be found to have created a constitutionally and statutorily sufficient basis of adjudicatory power by acting through an independent legal entity, such as a subsidiary or an independent contractor? In Gelfand v. Tanner Motor Tours, Limited, 385 F.2d 116 (2d Cir.1967), a New York resident brought suit against non-resident defendants for injuries suffered in Arizona when a wheel broke off a Gray Line bus in which they were riding. The defendants themselves did no business in New York, but had entered into an agreement with a New York representative, Herbert J. DeGraff. . . . Noting that the court below had found that the New York representative was an independent contractor, the court nevertheless found the requisite constitutional power (at 121): "We conclude that Tanner's reliance upon DeGraff Associated for three-sevenths of its business on the Grand Canyon tour, generating $120,000 a year in bookings confirmed in New York is sufficient contact with New York to satisfy the due process requirements . . . ."

(3) The New York Court of Appeals has balked at extending the *Gelfand* approach too far. In Delagi v. Volkswagenwerk, A.G., 29 N.Y.2d 426, 328 N.Y.S.2d 653, 278 N.E.2d 895 (1972), it held that the mere sale of the defendant's products in New York by an independent distributor was insufficient to create in personam adjudicatory authority with respect to a claim arising from an accident in Germany. But cf. Regie Nationale Des Usines Renault v. Superior Court, 208 Cal.App.2d 702, 25 Cal.Rptr. 530 (1962), upholding, in an action on a claim arising from an accident in California, the California court's adjudicatory authority over the French defendant, who sold cars through a "chain of sales" involving a wholly-owned American subsidiary and independently-owned distributorships and dealerships.

(4) The classical rule is that mere ownership of all of the stock of a local subsidiary does not render the foreign parent corporation subject to suit in the local courts. Cannon Manufacturing Co. v. Cudahy Packing Co., 267 U.S. 333, 45 S.Ct. 250, 69 L.Ed. 634 (1925). But the modern tendency is away from this rule and to stress activities of the subsidiary on behalf of the parent as proof of the subsidiary's being a "mere agent" or "merely the instrumentality" of the parent. See, e.g., Bialek v. Racal–Milgo, Inc., 545 F.Supp. 25, 32 (S.D.N.Y.1982); Finance Co. of America v. BankAmerica Corp., 493 F.Supp. 895, 905 (D.Md. 1980); Roorda v. Volkswagenwerk, A.G., 481 F.Supp. 868, 879 (D.S.C.1979); Energy Reserves Group, Inc. v. Superior Oil Company, 460 F.Supp. 483, 490 (D.Kan.1978); Mas v. Orange Crush Co., 99 F.2d 675 (4th Cir.1938); State of Maryland v. Capital Airlines, Inc., 199 F.Supp. 335 (S.D.N.Y.1961); Comment, Jurisdiction over Parent Corporations, 51 Cal.L.Rev. 574 (1963). But see Blount

v. Peerless Chemicals (PR) Inc., 316 F.2d 695 (2d Cir.1963). See also North Car. Gen.Stat. § 55–145(b) (1965):

> "Whenever a foreign parent corporation is subject to liability for any obligations of a subsidiary corporation that is subject to suit in this State, the parent corporation is itself so subject in any action to enforce the said liability. In any such action against a foreign corporation, service may be made on any person who could be served in an action against such subsidiary corporation."

A foreign subsidiary has even been held subject to suit on the basis of its parent's local activities. United States v. Watchmakers of Switzerland Information Center, Inc., 133 F.Supp. 40 (S.D.N.Y.1955). Should a finding of agency for substantive law purposes always imply a finding of agency for purposes of in personam adjudicatory power?

SECTION 4.　ADJUDICATORY AUTHORITY OVER THINGS

The Restatement, Second, Conflict of Laws, C. 3, Introductory Note, defines jurisdiction in rem as jurisdiction to affect the interest of all persons in a thing. A common example is the jurisdiction exercised in a proceeding in admiralty to determine the interests of all persons in a vessel. The Restatement defines jurisdiction quasi in rem as the authority to affect the interests of particular, rather than all, persons in a thing. Jurisdiction quasi in rem is said to be exercised in two types of proceedings: in the first, the plaintiff seeks to establish or to deny the existence of a pre-existing interest in the thing; in the second, the plaintiff does not seek to assert a pre-existing interest in a thing but to enforce a personal claim by applying the thing to the satisfaction of the claim. An example of the first type of proceeding is an action to partition land or to foreclose a mortgage; an example of the second is an action for damages in which jurisdiction is exercised by attachment of a thing owned by the tortfeasor.

A more appropriate terminology reserves the term jurisdiction in rem for all proceedings aimed at determining the interests of all persons or of only particular persons in a thing. In that terminology, quasi in rem jurisdiction is exercised only in proceedings aimed at applying a thing concededly owned by the debtor to the satisfaction of a personal claim.

In rem type proceedings are usually commenced by an attachment or seizure of the thing. This seizure may serve the additional function of providing security for the satisfaction of the judgment sought. However, the function of creating a basis of adjudicatory authority should be distinguished from that of creating security. On whether the thing may properly be seized without prior notice, see Chapter 3 on Provisional Remedies.

COMBS v. COMBS

Supreme Court of Kentucky, 1933.
249 Ky. 155, 60 S.W.2d 368.

OPINION OF THE COURT BY JUDGE THOMAS—Affirming.

The appellant, A.T. Combs, who was one of the defendants below, became indebted to the appellees and plaintiffs below, in a considerable sum. A lien to secure it was created on a tract of land in Washington county, Ark. Plaintiffs were and are residents of Kentucky and of other states, and all of them were and are nonresidents of the state of Arkansas. Appellant's brother, who was a joint defendant with him, is a resident of this commonwealth, and this action was filed by plaintiffs in the Breathitt circuit court against appellant and his brother to obtain a personal judgment against them for the amount of the debt. Personal process could not and was not served on appellant for a considerable time after he was proceeded against and made a defendant in the action. During that time he filed an equity action in the chancery court of Washington county, Ark., in which the land in lien was situated, against the plaintiffs in this action, and proceeded against them exclusively by constructive process in accordance with the prescribed practice of the Arkansas forum. In his petition in that court he set forth the facts creating the indebtedness, as well as the lien on his land to secure it, and stated that he had paid part of the debt, leaving a named sum as the balance due,* and that the lien to secure it was a cloud on the title to his land which he desired released, and he asked that court to enter judgment fixing the amount of the balance due by him to plaintiffs in this action (but defendants in that one) and to permit him to pay that amount into that court to be followed by a decree canceling the lien on his land. The Arkansas practice for that kind of procedure was followed, and upon submission, without any of the defendants therein entering their appearance in any manner, that court adjudged that plaintiff therein, appellant herein, was indebted to the defendants in that action (plaintiffs herein) in the sum admitted in his petition, and ordered him to pay it to the master commissioner of that court which he did, and, when done, that the lien on his land should be released. Appellant then procured a copy of that proceeding and filed his answer in this action relying upon the Arkansas judgment in bar of a recovery herein. The court disallowed that defense and rendered judgment against appellant for the amount it found to be due plaintiffs, and to reverse it defendant prosecutes this appeal.

The only argument made, and the only possible one that could be made, against the propriety of the judgment appealed from is that the Arkansas judgment, under the provisions of section 1 of article 4 of the Federal Constitution, is entitled to full faith and credit in this state the same as if it had been rendered by a court of competent jurisdiction in

---

* The lien was to secure a balance due of $1,000, according to the debtor. The credi-tors' suit was for $5,000, which they claimed to be the balance due.

this state, and that, since it is argued that the Arkansas court had jurisdiction to render the judgment relied on as a defense herein, it is binding on plaintiffs, and that they may not impeach it in this collateral attack. In making that argument, counsel assumes the correctness of the crucial point in this case, and we think erroneously so. It is, that the Arkansas court had jurisdiction, upon constructive process alone, to finally and conclusively adjudge the amount of plaintiff's debt owed to them by defendant, and then to assume to collect it through its master commissioner, or, more appropriately, to direct plaintiff in the Arkansas judgment to discharge it by paying the amount found to be due to the court's master commissioner, and to thereby completely discharge defendant from all further liability to plaintiffs. The error in the assumption of counsel for defendant lies in their failure to appraise and comprehend the nature of the relief granted by the Arkansas judgment and relied on as a defense in this case; confusing it with the power and jurisdiction of that court to deal with and adjudicate concerning the res within its jurisdiction, which in this case was the land in lien for plaintiff's debt.

[The Court first questioned "whether the Arkansas court had jurisdiction even of the res".] But, since that question is not presented by this record, we will pursue its discussion no farther, and will devote the remainder of the opinion to a discussion of the in personam portion of the Arkansas judgment which is questioned in this case.

* * *

. . . In such [i.e., quasi-in-rem] cases it is thoroughly settled that the personal rights of the defendant in and to the res within the custody of the court may be dealt with and adjudicated in so far as it adjudicates the status of the particular res, including the title thereto; and such an adjudication, if the defendant were properly proceeded against even by constructive process, would be binding and obligatory on defendant in any court of any state.

Hence, in this case, conceding that there was no doubt of the proper cloud upon defendant's title to his Arkansas land so as to authorize the action in that state to remove it, the judgment rendered by the Arkansas court would be obligatory on plaintiffs herein in so far as it released their lien upon the land in that state. But, when the court undertook to grant additional relief strictly in personam, it transgressed its jurisdiction so as to render such unauthorized additional relief of no force and effect whatever. That relief in this case was the adjudication that defendant herein had paid to plaintiffs herein any part of his debt and thereby discharged a part of his obligation to them, and that the court could and did fix the amount due from him to plaintiffs herein and directed its payment to the commissioner of that court. The rights so attempted to be adjudicated were and are strictly personal. It may be that the Arkansas court was vested with authority to lift the lien from the land involved, and for that purpose to incidentally determine the amount of the lien, and whether or not it had been paid, but the only binding effect of such adjudications would be that of releasing the lien as an incumbrance upon the title to the res. Such adjudications in so far as they affected the personal obligations and rights of the parties were and are not binding upon plaintiffs herein, nor do they operate as a res adjudicata estoppel in any future action.

    *   *   *

    Wherefore the judgment is affirmed.

NOTES

(1) Plaintiff seeks specific performance in a New York court of a contract to convey real estate in New York. The defendant is served personally in Connecticut where he resides. Can the court grant relief? If so, what is the form of relief it can grant? See Garfein v. McInnis, 248 N.Y. 261, 162 N.E. 73 (1928); See also Rozan v. Rozan, 49 Cal.2d 322, 317 P.2d 11 (1957).

(2) Plaintiff seeks enforcement in a South Carolina court of a contract whereby he agreed to sell local real estate. The non-resident defendant is personally served in North Carolina. What relief, if any, will the court grant? See Prudential Insurance Co. v. Berry, 153 S.C. 496, 151 S.E. 63 (1930). Would the state's having a long arm statute have any bearing on your answer? See Carmichael v. Snyder, 209 Va. 451, 164 S.E.2d 703 (1968).

(3) In a Kentucky court, the plaintiff, a citizen of Virginia, seeks to compel the Kentucky defendant to convey land located in Ohio. Will the court grant the relief demanded? See Massie v. Watts, 10 U.S. (6 Cranch) 148, 31 L.Ed. 181 (1810). If the defendant disobeyed the court's decree, could the court authorize the sheriff or some other official to transfer title? Would the courts of the state where the land is situated give full faith and credit to the court's decree? See McElreath v. McElreath, 162 Tex. 190, 345 S.W.2d 722 (1961). Would the court foreclose a mortgage upon out-of-state land if it had in personam power over the defendant? See Beach v. Youngblood, 215 Iowa 979, 247 N.W. 545 (1933).

(4) On these problems, see Currie, Full Faith and Credit to Foreign Land Decrees, 21 U.Chi.L.Rev. 620 (1959).

———

RESTATEMENT, SECOND, CONFLICT OF LAWS (1971)

§ 60. Judicial Jurisdiction Over Chattel

    A state has power to exercise judicial jurisdiction to affect interests in a chattel in the state, which is not in the course of transit in interstate or foreign commerce, although a person owning or claiming an interest in the chattel is not personally subject to the judicial jurisdiction of the state.

NOTES

(1) Is attachment or an equivalent measure a prerequisite to the proper exercise of in rem or quasi-in-rem adjudicatory power over a chattel? See Martin v. Better Taste Popcorn Co., 89 F.Supp. 754 (S.D.Iowa 1950) (giving a negative answer). Cf. also Pennoyer v. Neff, p. 222 supra; Note, Quasi-in-Rem Jurisdiction Without Attachment, 39 U.M.K.C.L.Rev. 103 (1970).

(2) Can the problems discussed on pp. 226–230 supra also arise in regard to chattels? Should they be resolved the same ways?

(3) May the court exercise adjudicatory power over a chattel that is usually situated within the state even though it was temporarily absent from the state at the time of the commencement of the action? See North Carolina Land & Lumber Co. v. Boyer, 191 Fed. 552 (6th Cir.1911). May the court exercise adjudicatory power over a chattel that is fraudulently enticed into the state? See Sea–Gate Tire & Rubber Co. v. Moseley, 161 Okl. 256, 18 P.2d 276 (1933). See generally Note, The Power of a State to Affect Title in a Chattel Atypically Removed to It, 47 Colum.L.Rev. 767 (1947); Note, Jurisdiction of Person and Property for Purpose of Attachment, 7 N.C.L. Rev. 294 (1929).

(4) In civil law countries, in rem and quasi-in-rem jurisdiction are unknown concepts. But in some civil law countries the presence of property of a non-resident within state provides a basis of in personam adjudicatory power even as to claims wholly unrelated to the property and even if the property is not subject to enforcement measures. See Rosenberg, Lehrbuch des Deutschen Zivilprozessrechts 141–142 (8th ed. 1960). See also Ginsburg & Bruzelius, Civil Procedure in Sweden 159–161 (1965). However, property fraudulently brought into the state does not meet the requirements of the rule. Rosenberg, loc. cit. supra.

HARRIS v. BALK

Supreme Court of the United States, 1905.
198 U.S. 215, 25 S.Ct. 625, 49 L.Ed. 1023.

Statement by MR. JUSTICE PECKHAM. The plaintiff in error brings the case here in order to review the judgment of the supreme court of North Carolina, affirming a judgment of a lower court against him for $180, with interest, as stated therein. . . .

The facts are as follows: The plaintiff in error, Harris, was a resident of North Carolina at the time of the commencement of this action, in 1896, and prior to that time was indebted to the defendant in error, Balk, also a resident of North Carolina, in the sum of $180, for money borrowed from Balk by Harris during the year 1896, which Harris verbally promised to repay, but there was no written evidence of the obligation. During the year above mentioned one Jacob Epstein, a resident of Baltimore, in the state of Maryland, asserted that Balk was indebted to him in the sum of over $300. In August, 1896, Harris visited Baltimore for the purpose of purchasing merchandise, and while he was in that city temporarily on August 6, 1896, Epstein caused to be issued out of a proper court in Baltimore a foreign or nonresident writ of attachment against Balk, attaching the debt due Balk from Harris, which writ the sheriff at Baltimore laid in the hands of Harris, with a summons to appear in the court at a day named. With that attachment, a writ of summons and a short declaration against Balk (as provided by the Maryland statute) were also delivered to the sheriff, and by him set up at the courthouse door, as required by the law of Maryland. Before the return day of the attachment writ Harris left Baltimore, and returned to his home in North Carolina. He did not contest the garnishee process, which was issued to garnish the debt which Harris owed Balk. After his return Harris made an affidavit on August 11, 1896, that he owed Balk $180, and stated that the amount had been attached by Epstein, of Baltimore, and by his counsel in the Maryland proceeding Harris consented therein to an order of condemnation against him as such garnishee for $180, the amount of his debt to Balk. Judgment was thereafter entered against the garnishee, and in favor of the plaintiff, Epstein, for $180. After the entry of the garnishee judgment, condemning the $180 in the hands of the garnishee, Harris paid the amount of the judgment to one Warren, an attorney of Epstein, residing in North Carolina. On August 11, 1896, Balk commenced an action against Harris before a justice of the peace in North Carolina, to recover the $180 which he averred Harris owed him. The plaintiff in error, by way of answer to the suit, pleaded in bar the recovery of the Maryland judgment and his payment thereof, and contended that it was conclusive against the defendant in error in this action, because that judgment was a valid judgment in Maryland, and was therefore entitled to full faith and credit in the courts of North Carolina. This contention was not allowed by the trial court, and judgment was accordingly entered against Harris for the amount of his indebtedness to Balk, and that judgment was affirmed by the supreme court of North Carolina. The ground of such judgment was that the Maryland court obtained no jurisdiction to attach or garnish the debt due from Harris to Balk, because Harris was but temporarily in the state, and the situs of the debt was in North Carolina.

* * *

MR. JUSTICE PECKHAM, after making the foregoing statement, delivered the opinion of the court:

* * *

. . . Attachment is the creature of the local law; that is, unless there is a law of the state providing for and permitting the attachment, it cannot be levied there. If there be a law of the state providing for the attachment of the debt, then, if the garnishee be found in that state, and process be personally served upon him therein, we think the court thereby acquires jurisdiction over him, and can garnish the debt due from him to the debtor of the plaintiff, and condemn it, provided the garnishee could himself be sued by his creditor in that state. We do not see how the question of jurisdiction vel non can properly be made to depend upon the so-called original situs of the debt, or upon the character of the stay of the garnishee, whether temporary or permanent, in the state where the attachment is issued. Power over the person of the garnishee confers jurisdiction on the courts of the state where the writ issues. Blackstone v. Miller, 188 U.S. 189–206, 23 S.Ct. 277, 47 L.Ed. 439–445. If, while temporarily there, his creditor might sue him there and recover the debt, then he is liable to process of garnishment, no matter where the situs of the debt was originally. We do not see the materiality of the expression "situs of the debt," when used in connection with attachment proceedings. If by situs is meant the place of the creation of the debt, that fact is immaterial. If it be meant that the obligation to pay the debt can only be enforced at the situs thus fixed, we think it plainly untrue. The obligation of the debtor to pay his debt clings to and accompanies him wherever he goes. He is as much bound to pay his debt in a foreign state when therein sued upon his obligation by his creditor, as he was in the state where the debt was contracted. We speak of ordinary debts, such as the one in this case. It would be no defense to such suit for the debtor to plead that he was only in the foreign state casually or temporarily. His obligation to pay would be the same whether he was there in that way or with an intention to remain. It is nothing but the obligation to pay which is garnished or attached. This obligation can be enforced by the courts of the foreign state after personal service of process therein, just as well as by the courts of the domicil of the debtor. If the debtor leave the foreign state without appearing, a judgment by default may be entered, upon which execution may issue, or the judgment may be sued upon in any other state where the debtor might be found. In such case the situs is unimportant. It is not a question of possession in the foreign state, for possession cannot be taken of a debt or of the obligation to pay it, as tangible property might be taken possession of. Notice to the debtor (garnishee) of the commencement of the suit, and notice not to pay to his creditor, is all that can be given, whether the garnishee be a mere casual and temporary comer, or a resident of the state where the attachment is laid. His obligation to pay to his creditor is thereby arrested, and a lien created upon the debt itself. Cahoon v. Morgan, 38 Vt. 236; National F. Ins. Co. v. Chambers, 53 N.J.Eq. 468, 483, 32 A. 663. We can see no reason why the attachment could not be thus laid, provided the creditor of the garnishee could himself sue in that state, and its laws permitted the attachment.

    *   *   *

It seems to us, therefore, that the judgment against Harris in Maryland, condemning the $180 which he owed to Balk, was a valid judgment, because the court had jurisdiction over the garnishee by personal service of process within the state of Maryland.

It ought to be and it is the object of courts to prevent the payment of any debt twice over. Thus, if Harris, owing a debt to Balk, paid it under a valid judgment against him, to Epstein, he certainly ought not to be compelled to pay it a second time, but should have the right to plead his payment under the Maryland judgment.

But most rights may be lost by negligence, and if the garnishee were guilty of negligence in the attachment proceeding, to the damage of Balk, he ought not to be permitted to set up the judgment as a defense. Thus it is recognized as the duty of the garnishee to give notice to his own creditor, if he would protect himself, so that the creditor may have the opportunity to defend himself against the claim of the person suing out the attachment. . . . This notification by the garnishee is for the purpose of making sure that his creditor shall have an opportunity to defend the claim made against him in the attachment suit. Fair dealing requires this at the hands of the garnishee.

. . . The defendant in error, Balk, had notice of this attachment, certainly within a few days after the issuing thereof and the entry of judgment thereon, because he sued the plaintiff in error to recover his debt within a few days after his (Harris') return to North Carolina, in which suit the judgment in Maryland was set up by Harris as a plea in bar to Balk's claim. . . .

The judgment of the Supreme Court of North Carolina must be reversed, and the cause remanded for further proceedings not inconsistent with the opinion of this court.

Reversed.

MR. JUSTICE HARLAN and MR. JUSTICE DAY dissented.

NOTE

If Epstein had sued Balk in North Carolina, could he have invoked as res judicata a finding by the Maryland court that Balk owed him $300? In an in personam action, could Balk have recovered from Epstein the $180 recovered in the Maryland action on the ground that Balk did not owe Epstein anything? If the Maryland court had found against Epstein on the ground that Epstein had no claim on Balk, would the latter finding have been res judicata in an action in personam by Epstein against Balk? And if Harris had denied his indebtedness to Balk in the Maryland action and the court had decided against Epstein on that ground, could Harris have invoked that finding as res judicata in an action in personam by Balk against Harris?

NEW YORK LIFE INSURANCE CO. v. DUNLEVY

Supreme Court of the United States, 1916.
241 U.S. 518, 36 S.Ct. 613, 60 L.Ed. 1140.

[A judgment creditor of Mrs. Dunlevy, by proper garnishment proceedings in a Pennsylvania court, sought to satisfy his claim out of money due under an insurance policy issued by the New York Life Insurance Co. The insurance company appeared, admitted its indebtedness under the policy, and set up conflicting claims to the fund by Mrs. Dunlevy and by Gould, her father. Notice was given to Mrs. Dunlevy in California, but she did not appear. The Pennsylvania court found in favor of Gould. Mrs. Dunlevy then brought suit against the insurance company in California to recover the surrender value of the policy. The insurance company pleaded the Pennsylvania judgment in bar. The California courts rejected the plea.]

MR. JUSTICE MCREYNOLDS delivered the opinion of the Court.

* * *

Beyond doubt, without the necessity of further personal service of process upon Mrs. Dunlevy, the court of common pleas of Pittsburgh had ample power through garnishment proceedings to inquire whether she held a valid claim against the insurance company, and, if found to exist, then to condemn and appropriate it so far as necessary to discharge the original judgment. Although herself outside the limits of the state, such disposition of the property would have been binding on her. . . . But the interpleader initiated by the company was an altogether different matter. This was an attempt to bring about a final and conclusive adjudication of her personal rights, not merely to discover property and apply it to debts. And unless in contemplation of law she was before the court, and required to respond to that issue, its orders and judgments in respect thereto were not binding on her. . . .

Counsel maintain that having been duly summoned in the original suit instituted by Boggs & Buhl in 1907, and notwithstanding entry of final judgment therein, "Mrs. Dunlevy was in the Pennsylvania court and was bound by every order that court made, whether she remained within the jurisdiction of that court after it got jurisdiction over her person or not;" and hence, the argument is, "When the company paid the money into court where she was, it was just the same in legal effect as if it had paid it to her." This position is supposed to be supported by our opinion in Michigan Trust Co. v. Ferry, 228 U.S. 346, 57 L.Ed. 867, 33 Sup.Ct.Rep. 550 . . . The judgment under consideration was fairly within the reasonable anticipation of the executor when he submitted himself to the probate court. But a wholly different and intolerable condition would result from acceptance of the theory that, after final judgment, a defendant remains in court and subject to whatsoever orders may be entered under title of the cause. . . . The interpleader proceedings were not essential concomitants of the original action by Boggs & Buhl against Dunlevy, but plainly collateral; and, when summoned to respond in that action, she was not required to anticipate them. . . .

It has been affirmatively held in Pennsylvania that a judgment debtor is not a party to a garnishment proceeding to condemn a claim due him from a third person, and is not bound by a judgment discharging the garnishee (Ruff v. Ruff, 85 Pa. 333); and this is the generally accepted doctrine. . . .

We are of opinion that the proceedings in the Pennsylvania court constituted no bar to the action in California, and the judgment below is accordingly affirmed.

　　　*　　*　　*

Affirmed.

NOTES

(1) Would there have been in personam jurisdiction over Mrs. Dunlevy if the action had been brought in a federal court? If Pennsylvania had enacted a California-type long-arm statute, would a federal court in Pennsylvania sitting today have in personam adjudicatory authority over Mrs. Dunlevy? See Note 1, p. 324 infra.

(2) The holding in this case added impetus to demands for an interpleader statute. See p. 480 infra.

───────

SHAFFER v. HEITNER

Supreme Court of the United States, 1977.
433 U.S. 186, 97 S.Ct. 2569, 53 L.Ed.2d 683.

MR. JUSTICE MARSHALL delivered the opinion of the Court.*

The controversy in this case concerns the constitutionality of a Delaware statute that allows a court of that State to take jurisdiction of a lawsuit by sequestering any property of the defendant that happens to be located in Delaware. . . .

I

Appellee Heitner, a nonresident of Delaware, is the owner of one share of stock in the Greyhound Corporation, a business incorporated under the laws of Delaware with its principal place of business in Phoenix, Ariz. On May 22, 1974, he filed a shareholder's derivative suit in the Court of Chancery for New Castle County, Del., in which he named as defendants Greyhound, its wholly owned subsidiary Greyhound Lines, Inc.,[1] and 28 present or former officers or directors of one or both of the corporations. In essence, Heitner alleged that the individual defendants had violated their duties to Greyhound by causing it and its subsidiary to engage in actions that resulted in the corporations being held liable for substantial damages in a private antitrust suit and a large fine in a criminal contempt action. The activities which led to these penalties took place in Oregon.

Simultaneously with his complaint, Heitner filed a motion for an order of sequestration of the Delaware property of the individual defendants pursuant to 10 Del.C. § 366. . . . The requested sequestration order was signed the day the motion was filed. Pursuant to that order, the sequestrator "seized" approximately 82,000 shares of Greyhound common stock belonging to 19 of the defendants, and options belonging to another two defendants. . . . So far as the record shows, none of the certificates representing the seized property was physically present in Delaware. The stock was considered to be in Delaware, and so subject to seizure, by virtue of 8 Del.C. § 169, which makes Delaware the situs of ownership of all stock in Delaware corporations.

All 28 defendants were notified of the initiation of the suit by certified mail directed to their last known addresses and by publication in a New Castle County newspaper. The 21 defendants whose property was seized (hereafter referred to as appellants) responded by entering a special appearance [asserting] that under the rule of International Shoe Co. v. Washington, 326 U.S. 310, 66 S.Ct. 154, 90 L.Ed. 95 (1945), they

---

* Some footnotes omitted; others renumbered.

1. Greyhound Lines, Inc., is incorporated in California and has its principal place of business in Phoenix, Arizona.

did not have sufficient contacts with Delaware to sustain the jurisdiction of that State's court.

*   *   *

II

The Delaware courts rejected appellants' jurisdictional challenge by noting that this suit was brought as a *quasi in rem* proceeding. Since *quasi in rem* jurisdiction is traditionally based on attachment or seizure of property present in the jurisdiction, not on contacts between the defendant and the State, the courts considered appellants' claimed lack of contacts with Delaware to be unimportant. This categorical analysis assumes the continued soundness of the conceptual structure founded on the century-old case of Pennoyer v. Neff, 95 U.S. 714, 24 L.Ed. 565 (1877).

[Justice Marshall here discussed the *Pennoyer* case and noted that it based authority to adjudicate . . . on the State's power over either persons or property. He stated that with respect to judicial jurisdiction over persons the *Pennoyer* rule has been supplanted by the rule of *International Shoe.* He continued:]

No equally dramatic change has occurred in the law governing jurisdiction *in rem.* There have, however, been intimations that the collapse of the *in personam* wing of *Pennoyer* has not left that decision unweakened as a foundation for *in rem* jurisdiction. Well-reasoned lower court opinions have questioned the proposition that the presence of property in a State gives that State jurisdiction to adjudicate rights to the property regardless of the relationship of the underlying dispute and the property owner to the forum. . . . The overwhelming majority of commentators have also rejected *Pennoyer's* premise that a proceeding "against" property is not a proceeding against the owners of that property. Accordingly, they urge that the "traditional notions of fair play and substantial justice" that govern a State's power to adjudicate *in personam* should also govern its power to adjudicate personal rights to property located in the State. See, e.g., . . . Von Mehren & Trautman, Jurisdiction to Adjudicate: A Suggested Analysis, 79 Harv.L.Rev. 1121 (1966); Traynor, Is This Conflict Really Necessary?, 37 Tex.L.Rev. 657 (1959); Ehrenzweig, The Transient Rule of Personal Jurisdiction: The 'Power' Myth and Forum Conveniens, 65 Yale L.J. 289 (1956) . . .

Although this Court has not addressed this argument directly, we have held that property cannot be subjected to a court's judgment unless reasonable and appropriate efforts have been made to give the property owners actual notice of the action. Schroeder v. City of New York, 371 U.S. 208, 83 S.Ct. 279, 9 L.Ed.2d 255 (1962); Walker v. City of Hutchinson, 352 U.S. 112, 77 S.Ct. 200, 1 L.Ed.2d 178 (1956); Mullane v. Central Hanover Bank & Trust Co., 339 U.S. 306, 70 S.Ct. 652, 94 L.Ed. 865 (1950). This conclusion recognizes, contrary to *Pennoyer,* that an adverse judgment *in rem* directly affects the property owner by divesting him of his rights in the property before the court. . . .

III

The case for applying to jurisdiction *in rem* the same test of "fair play and substantial justice" as governs assertions of jurisdiction *in personam* is simple and straightforward. It is premised on recognition that "[t]he phrase, 'judicial jurisdiction over a thing, is a customary elliptical way of referring to jurisdiction over the interests of persons in a thing.' " Restatement (Second) of Conflict of Laws § 56, introductory note. This recognition leads to the conclusion that in order to justify an exercise of jurisdiction *in rem,* the basis for jurisdiction must be sufficient to justify exercising "jurisdiction over the interests of persons in a thing." The standard for determining whether an exercise of jurisdiction over the interests of persons is consistent with the Due Process Clause is the minimum contacts standard elucidated in *International Shoe.*

This argument, of course, does not ignore the fact that the presence of property in a State may bear on the existence of jurisdiction by providing contacts among the forum State, the defendant, and the litigation. For example, when claims to the property itself are the source of the underlying controversy between the plaintiff and the defendant, it would be unusual for the State where the property is located not to have jurisdiction. In such cases, the defendant's claim to property located in the State would normally indicate that he expected to benefit from the State's protection of his interest. The State's strong interests in assuring the marketability of property within its borders and in providing a procedure for peaceful resolution of disputes about the possession of that property would also support jurisdiction, as would the likelihood that important records and witnesses will be found in the State.[2] The presence of property may also favor jurisdiction in cases, such as suits for injury suffered on the land of an absentee owner, where the defendant's ownership of the property is conceded but the cause of action is otherwise related to rights and duties growing out of that ownership.

It appears, therefore, that jurisdiction over many types of actions which now are or might be brought *in rem* would not be affected by a holding that any assertion of state court jurisdiction must satisfy the *International Shoe* standard.[3] For the type of *quasi in rem* action typified by *Harris v. Balk* [page 293, supra] and the present case, however, accepting the proposed analysis would result in significant change. These are cases where the property which now serves as the

---

2. We do not suggest that these illustrations include all the factors that may affect the decision, nor that the factors we have mentioned are necessarily decisive.

3. Cf. Smit, The Enduring Utility of In Rem Rules: A Lasting Legacy of Pennoyer v. Neff, 48 Brooklyn L.Rev. 600 (1977). We do not suggest that jurisdictional doctrines other than those discussed in text, such as the particularized rules governing adjudications of status, are inconsistent with the standard of fairness. . . .

basis for state court jurisdiction is completely unrelated to the plaintiff's cause of action. Thus, although the presence of the defendant's property in a State might suggest the existence of other ties among the defendant, the State, and the litigation, the presence of the property alone would not support the State's jurisdiction. If those other ties did not exist, cases over which the State is now thought to have jurisdiction could not be brought in that forum.

Since acceptance of the *International Shoe* test would most affect this class of cases, we examine the arguments against adopting that standard as they relate to this category of litigation.[4] Before doing so, however, we note that this type of case also presents the clearest illustration of the argument in favor of assessing assertions of jurisdiction by a single standard. For in cases such as *Harris* and this one, the only role played by the property is to provide the basis for bringing the defendant into court. Indeed, the express purpose of the Delaware sequestration procedure is to compel the defendant to enter a personal appearance. In such cases, if a direct assertion of personal jurisdiction over the defendant would violate the Constitution, it would seem that an indirect assertion of that jurisdiction should be equally impermissible.

The primary rationale for treating the presence of property as a sufficient basis for jurisdiction to adjudicate claims over which the State would not have jurisdiction if *International Shoe* applied is that a wrongdoer "should not be able to avoid payment of his obligations by the expedient of removing his assets to a place where he is not subject to an in personam suit." Restatement (Second) of Conflicts § 66, comment a. . . .

This justification, however, does not explain why jurisdiction should be recognized without regard to whether the property is present in the State because of an effort to avoid the owner's obligations. Nor does it support jurisdiction to adjudicate the underlying claim. At most, it suggests that a State in which property is located should have jurisdiction to attach that property, by use of proper procedures, as security for a judgment being sought in a forum where the litigation can be maintained consistently with *International Shoe*. . . . Moreover, we know of nothing to justify the assumption that a debtor can avoid paying his obligations by removing his property to a State in which his creditor cannot obtain personal jurisdiction over him. The Full Faith and Credit Clause, after all, makes the valid *in personam* judgment of one State enforceable in all other States.

It might also be suggested that allowing *in rem* jurisdiction avoids the uncertainty inherent in the *International Shoe* standard and as-

---

4. Concentrating on this category of cases is also appropriate because in the other categories to the extent that presence of property in the State indicates the existence of sufficient contacts under *International Shoe,* there is no need to rely on the property as justifying jurisdiction regardless of the existence of those contacts.

sures a plaintiff of a forum.[5] . . . We believe, however, that the fairness standard of *International Shoe* can be easily applied in the vast majority of cases. Moreover, when the existence of jurisdiction in a particular forum under *International Shoe* is unclear, the cost of simplifying the litigation by avoiding the jurisdictional question may be the sacrifice of "fair play and substantial justice." That cost is too high. . . .

We are left, then, to consider the significance of the long history of jurisdiction based solely on the presence of property in a State. Although the theory that territorial power is both essential to and sufficient for jurisdiction has been undermined, we have never held that the presence of property in a State does not automatically confer jurisdiction over the owner's interest in that property. This history must be considered as supporting the proposition that jurisdiction based solely on the presence of property satisfies the demands of due process, . . . but it is not decisive. . . . The fiction that an assertion of jurisdiction over property is anything but an assertion of jurisdiction over the owner of the property supports an ancient form without substantial modern justification. Its continued acceptance would serve only to allow state court jurisdiction that is fundamentally unfair to the defendant.

We therefore conclude that all assertions of state court jurisdiction must be evaluated according to the standards set forth in *International Shoe* and its progeny.[6]

IV

The Delaware courts based their assertion of jurisdiction in this case solely on the statutory presence of apellants' property in Delaware. Yet that property is not the subject matter of this litigation, nor is the underlying cause of action related to the property. Appellants' holdings in Greyhound do not, therefore, provide contacts with Delaware sufficient to support the jurisdiction of that State's courts over appellants. If it exists, that jurisdiction must have some other foundation.

Appellee Heitner did not allege and does not now claim that appellants have ever set foot in Delaware. Nor does he identify any act related to his cause of action as having taken place in Delaware. Nevertheless, he contends that appellants' positions as directors and officers of a corporation chartered in Delaware provide sufficient "contacts, ties, or relations," *International Shoe Co. v. Washington,* supra, at 319, with that State to give its courts jurisdiction over appellants in this

---

5. This case does not raise, and we therefore do not consider, the question whether the presence of a defendant's property in a State is a sufficient basis for jurisdiction when no other forum is available to the plaintiff.

6. It would not be fruitful for us to reexamine the facts of cases decided on the rationales of *Pennoyer* and *Harris* to determine whether jurisdiction might have been sustained under the standard we adopt today. To the extent that prior decisions are inconsistent with this standard, they are overruled.

stockholder's derivative action. This argument is based primarily on what Heitner asserts to be the strong interest of Delaware in supervising the management of a Delaware corporation. That interest is said to derive from the role of Delaware law in establishing the corporation and defining the obligations owed to it by its officers and directors. In order to protect this interest, appellee concludes, Delaware's courts must have jurisdiction over corporate fiduciaries such as appellants.

This argument is undercut by the failure of the Delaware Legislature to assert the state interest appellee finds so compelling. Delaware law bases jurisdiction not on appellants' status as corporate fiduciaries, but rather on the presence of their property in the State. Although the sequestration procedure used here may be most frequently used in derivative suits against officers and directors, . . . the authorizing statute evinces no specific concern with such actions. Sequestration can be used in any suit against a nonresident, . . ., and reaches corporate fiduciaries only if they happen to own interests in a Delaware corporation, or other property in the State. But as Heitner's failure to secure jurisdiction over seven of the defendants named in his complaint demonstrates, there is no necessary relationship between holding a position as a corporate fiduciary and owning stock or other interests in the corporation. If Delaware perceived its interest in securing jurisdiction over corporate fiduciaries to be as great as Heitner suggests, we would expect it to have enacted a statute more clearly designed to protect that interest.

Moreover, even if Heitner's assessment of the importance of Delaware's interest is accepted, his argument fails to demonstrate that Delaware is a fair forum for this litigation. The interest appellee has identified may support the application of Delaware law to resolve any controversy over appellants' actions in their capacities as officers and directors. But [in Hanson v. Denckla, page 259, supra] we . . . rejected the argument that if a State's law can properly be applied to a dispute, its courts necessarily have jurisdiction over the parties to that dispute. . . .

Appellee suggests that by accepting positions as officers or directors of a Delaware corporation, appellants performed the acts required by *Hanson v. Denckla.* He notes that Delaware law provides substantial benefits to corporate officers and directors, and that these benefits were at least in part the incentive for appellants to assume their positions. It is, he says, "only fair and just" to require appellants, in return for these benefits, to respond in the State of Delaware when they are accused of misusing their powers.

*   *   *

But like Heitner's first argument, this line of reasoning establishes only that it is appropriate for Delaware law to govern the obligations of appellants to Greyhound and its stockholders. It does not demonstrate that appellants have "purposefully avail[ed themselves] of the privilege of conducting activities within the forum State," *Hanson v. Denckla,* supra, . . . in a way that would justify bringing them before a Delaware tribunal. Appellants have simply had nothing to do with the State of Delaware. Moreover, appellants had no reason to expect to be haled before a Delaware court. Delaware, unlike some States, has not enacted a statute that treats acceptance of a directorship as consent to jurisdiction in the State. . . . Appellants, who were not required to acquire interests in Greyhound in order to hold their positions, did not by acquiring those interests surrender their right to be brought to judgment only in States with which they had had "minimum contacts."

. . .

. . . The judgment of the Delaware Supreme Court must, therefore, be reversed.

MR. JUSTICE REHNQUIST took no part in the consideration or decision of this case.

MR. JUSTICE POWELL, concurring.

I agree that the principles of International Shoe Co. v. Washington, 326 U.S. 310, 66 S.Ct. 154, 90 L.Ed. 95 (1945), should be extended to govern assertions of *in rem* as well as *in personam* jurisdiction in state court. I also agree that neither the statutory presence of appellants' stock in Delaware nor their positions as directors and officers of a Delaware corporation can provide sufficient contacts to support the Delaware courts' assertion of jurisdiction in this case.

I would explicitly reserve judgment, however, on whether the ownership of some forms of property whose situs is indisputably and permanently located within a State may, without more, provide the contacts necessary to subject a defendant to jurisdiction within the State to the extent of the value of the property. In the case of real property, in particular, preservation of the common law concept of *quasi in rem* jurisdiction arguably would avoid the uncertainty of the general *International Shoe* standard without significant cost to " 'traditional notions of fair play and substantial justice.' " . . .

Subject to that reservation, I join the opinion of the Court.

MR. JUSTICE STEVENS, concurring in the judgment.

. . . I . . . agree with the Court that on the record before us no adequate basis for jurisdiction exists and that the Delaware statute is unconstitutional on its face.

How the Court's opinion may be applied in other contexts is not entirely clear to me. I agree with Mr. Justice Powell that it should not be read to invalidate *in rem* jurisdiction where real estate is involved. . . . My uncertainty as to the reach of the opinion, and my fear that it purports to decide a great deal more than is necessary to dispose of this case, persuade me merely to concur in the judgment.

MR. JUSTICE BRENNAN, concurring and dissenting.

I join Parts I–III of the Court's opinion. I fully agree that the minimum-contacts analysis developed in International Shoe Co. v. Washington, 326 U.S. 310, 66 S.Ct. 154, 90 L.Ed. 95 (1945), represents a far more sensible construct for the exercise of state court jurisdiction than the patchwork of legal and factual fictions that has been generated from the decision in Pennoyer v. Neff, 95 U.S. 714, 24 L.Ed. 565 (1877). It is precisely because the inquiry into minimum contacts is now of such overriding importance, however, that I must respectfully dissent from Part IV of the Court's opinion.

*   *   *

. . . I am convinced that as a general rule a state forum has jurisdiction to adjudicate a shareholder derivative action centering on the conduct and policies of the directors and officers of a corporation chartered by that State. Unlike the Court, I therefore would not foreclose Delaware from asserting jurisdiction over appellants were it persuaded to do so on the basis of minimum contacts.

*   *   *

NOTES

(1) For a treatment of the issues exposed by the principal case, see Smit, The Continuing Utility of In Rem Rules: A Lasting Legacy of Pennoyer v. Neff, 43 Brooklyn L.Rev. 600 (1977). On the principal case, see also Silberman, Shaffer v. Heitner: The End of an Era, 53 N.Y.U.L.Rev. 33 (1978); Casad, Shaffer v. Heitner: An End to Ambivalence in Jurisdictional Theory?, 26 Kan. L.Rev. 61 (1977); Younger, Quasi In Rem Defaults After Shaffer v. Heitner: Some Unanswered Questions, 45 Brooklyn L.Rev. 675 (1979); Riesenfeld, Shaffer v. Heitner: Holding, Implications, Forebodings, 30 Hastings L.J. 1183 (1979).

(2) In which circumstances can the exercise of in rem or quasi-in-rem jurisdiction be regarded as meeting the standards of *International Shoe?* Does the answer depend on whether the res within the state is an immovable, a movable, or an intangible? Note that, originally, attachment of a debt could be laid only at the debtor's domicile.

(3) In determining whether the due process test is met, must the court look at the facts presented in the case, or decide on the basis of the facts the applicable statute declares determinative? Cf. Wuchter v. Pizzutti, 276 U.S. 13, 48 S.Ct. 259, 72 L.Ed. 446 (1928).

(4) Is it reasonable for Delaware to hold accountable in that state directors and officers of a Delaware corporation accused of having breached their fiduciary obligations, when recovery is limited to the value of their stock in the corporation? Could Delaware constitutionally adopt a long-arm statute authorizing in personam suits for alleged breach of fiduciary obligations by nonresident officers or directors of Delaware corporations? After the decision in the principal case, Delaware enacted a statute creating competence over directors and officers of Delaware corporations in actions concerning their corporate activities Del.Code Ann. tit. 10, § 3114 (1982). The Delaware Supreme Court upheld this statute in Armstrong v. Pomerance, 423 A.2d 174 (Del.1980). Is this decision correct? If so, is the decision in the principal case wrong?

(5) Should any weight be placed on the fact that some defendants were officers or directors of a wholly-owned California subsidiary of the Delaware corporation and that the subsidiary's principal place of business was in Arizona?

(6) There has been vigorous debate about the impact of the principal case on transient personal jurisdiction. See Burnham v. Superior Court, ___ U.S. ___, ___ S.Ct. ___, ___ L.Ed.2d ___ (1990), **Appendix, p. 1136, infra.**

(7) Compare Grand Bahama Petroleum Co., Limited v. Canadian Transportation Agencies, Limited, 450 F.Supp. 447 (W.D.Wash.1978), suggesting that Rule B(1) of the Supplemental Rules for Certain Admiralty and Maritime Claims of the Federal Rules of Civil Procedure is not unconstitutional when applied to obtain a maritime attachment, because the history of admiralty jurisprudence indicates that the common law principles of *Shaffer* do not apply. But cf. Karl Senner, Inc. v. M/V Acadian Valor, 485 F.Supp. 287 (E.D.La.1980), holding unconstitutional an in rem proceeding, commenced by service of a vessel without notice, under Rule C of the Federal Admiralty Rules. See also Note, At Sea with Shaffer v. Heitner, 4 N.C.J. Int'l L. & Com.Reg. 311 (1979); Note, Attachment Jurisdiction after Shaffer v. Heitner, 32 Stan.L.Rev. 167 (1979).

RUSH v. SAVCHUK

Supreme Court of the United States, 1980.
444 U.S. 320, 100 S.Ct. 571, 62 L.Ed.2d 516.

MR. JUSTICE MARSHALL delivered the opinion of the Court.*

This appeal presents the question whether a State may constitutionally exercise *quasi in rem* jurisdiction over a defendant who has no forum contacts by attaching the contractual obligation of an insurer licensed to do business in the State to defend and indemnify him in connection with the suit.

I

On January 13, 1972, two Indiana residents were involved in a single-car accident in Elkhart, Ind. Appellee Savchuk, who was a passenger in the car driven by appellant Rush, was injured. The car, owned by Rush's father, was insured by appellant State Farm Mutual Automobile Insurance Co. (State Farm) under a liability insurance policy issued in Indiana. Indiana's guest statute would have barred a claim by Savchuk. Ind.Stat. § 9–3–31.

Savchuk moved with his parents to Minnesota in June 1973. On May 28, 1974, he commenced an action against Rush in the Minnesota state courts. As Rush had no contacts with Minnesota that would support *in personam* jurisdiction, Savchuk attempted to obtain *quasi in rem* jurisdiction by garnishing State Farm's obligation under the insurance policy to defend and indemnify Rush in connection with such a suit. State Farm does business in Minnesota. Rush was personally served in Indiana. The complaint alleged negligence and sought $125,000 in damages.

. . . Rush and State Farm moved to dismiss the complaint for lack of jurisdiction over the defendant. The trial court denied the

---

* Footnotes omitted.

motion to dismiss and granted the motion for leave to file the supplemental complaint.

On appeal, the Minnesota Supreme Court affirmed the trial court's decision. 311 Minn. 480, 245 N.W.2d 624 (1976) (*Savchuk I*). It held, first, that the obligation of an insurance company to defend and indemnify a nonresident insured under an automobile liability insurance policy is a garnishable res in Minnesota for the purpose of obtaining *quasi in rem* jurisdiction when the incident giving rise to the action occurs outside Minnesota but the plaintiff is a Minnesota resident when the suit is filed. Second, the court held that the assertion of jurisdiction over Rush was constitutional because he had notice of the suit and an opportunity to defend, his liability was limited to the amount of the policy, and the garnishment procedure may be used only by Minnesota residents. The court expressly recognized that Rush had engaged in no voluntary activity that would justify the exercise of *in personam* jurisdiction. The court found, however, that considerations of fairness supported the exercise of *quasi in rem* jurisdiction because in accident litigation the insurer controls the defense of the case, State Farm does business in and is regulated by the State, and the State has an interest in protecting its residents and providing them with a forum in which to litigate their claims.

Rush appealed to this Court. We vacated the judgment and remanded the cause for further consideration in light of Shaffer v. Heitner, 433 U.S. 186, 97 S.Ct. 2569, 53 L.Ed.2d 683 (1977).

On remand, the Minnesota Supreme Court held that the assertion of *quasi in rem* jurisdiction through garnishment of an insurer's obligation to an insured complied with the due process standards enunciated in *Shaffer*. 272 N.W.2d 888 (Minn.1978) (*Savchuk II*). The court found that the garnishment statute differed from the Delaware stock sequestration procedure held unconstitutional in *Shaffer* because the garnished property was intimately related to the litigation and the garnishment procedure paralleled the asserted state interest in "facilitating recoveries for resident plaintiffs." Id., at 891. This appeal followed.

II

The Minnesota Supreme Court held that the Minnesota garnishment statute embodies the rule stated in Seider v. Roth, 17 N.Y.2d 111, 269 N.Y.S.2d 99, 216 N.E.2d 312 (1966), that the contractual obligation of an insurance company to its insured under a liability insurance policy is a debt subject to attachment under state law if the insurer does business in the State. *Seider* jurisdiction was upheld against a due process challenge in Simpson v. Loehmann, 21 N.Y.2d 305, 287 N.Y.S.2d 633, 234 N.E.2d 669 (1967), rearg. denied, 21 N.Y.2d 990, 290 N.Y.S.2d 914, 238 N.E.2d 319 (1968).   . . .

* * *

New York has continued to adhere to *Seider*. New Hampshire follows *Seider* if the defendant resides in a *Seider* jurisdiction, but not in other cases. Minnesota is the only other State that has adopted *Seider*-type jurisdiction. The Second Circuit recently reaffirmed its conclusion that *Seider* does not violate due process after reconsidering the doctrine in light of Shaffer v. Heitner. O'Connor v. Lee–Hy Paving Corp., 579 F.2d 194 (CA2), cert. denied, 439 U.S. 1034, 99 S.Ct. 638, 58 L.Ed.2d 696 (1978).

III

In Shaffer v. Heitner we held that "all assertions of state-court jurisdiction must be evaluated according to the standards set forth in *International Shoe* and its progeny." 433 U.S., at 212, 97 S.Ct., at 2584. . . . In determining whether a particular exercise of state-court jurisdiction is consistent with due process, the inquiry must focus on "the relationship among the defendant, the forum, and the litigation." Shaffer v. Heitner, supra, 433 U.S., at 204, 97 S.Ct., at 2580.

It is conceded that Rush has never had any contacts with Minnesota, and that the auto accident that is the subject of this action occurred in Indiana and also had no connection to Minnesota. The only affiliating circumstance offered to show a relationship among Rush, Minnesota, and this lawsuit is that Rush's insurance company does business in the State. . . .

We held in *Shaffer* that the mere presence of property in a State does not establish a sufficient relationship between the owner of the property and the State to support the exercise of jurisdiction over an unrelated cause of action. The ownership of property in the State is a contact between the defendant and the forum, and it may suggest the presence of other ties. 433 U.S., at 209, 97 S.Ct., at 2582. Jurisdiction is lacking, however, unless there are sufficient contacts to satisfy the fairness standard of *International Shoe*.

Here, the fact that the defendant's insurer does business in the forum State suggests no further contacts between the defendant and the forum, and the record supplies no evidence of 'any. State Farm's decision to do business in Minnesota was completely adventitious as far as Rush was concerned. He had no control over that decision, and it is unlikely that he would have expected that by buying insurance in Indiana he had subjected himself to suit in any State to which a potential future plaintiff might decide to move. In short, it cannot be said that the *defendant* engaged in any purposeful activity related to the forum that would make the exercise of jurisdiction fair, just, or reasonable, see Kulko v. California Superior Court, 436 U.S. 84, 93–94, 98 S.Ct. 1690, 1697–98, 56 L.Ed.2d 132 (1978); Hanson v. Denckla, 357 U.S. 235, 253, 78 S.Ct. 1228, 1239, 2 L.Ed.2d 1283 (1952), merely because his insurer does business there.

      *   *   *

An alternative approach for finding minimum contacts in *Seider* - type cases, referred to with approval by the Minnesota Supreme Court, is to attribute the insurer's forum contacts to the defendant by treating the attachment procedure as the functional equivalent of a direct action against the insurer. This approach views *Seider* jurisdiction as fair both to the insurer, whose forum contacts would support *in personam* jurisdiction even for an unrelated cause of action, and to the "nominal defendant." Because liability is limited to the policy amount, the defendant incurs no personal liability, and the judgment is satisfied from the policy proceeds which are not available to the insured for any purpose other than paying accident claims, the insured is said to have such a slight stake in the litigation as a practical matter that it is not unfair to make him a "nominal defendant" in order to obtain jurisdiction over the insurance company.

Seider actions are not equivalent to direct actions, however. The State's ability to exert its power over the "nominal defendant" is analytically prerequisite to the insurer's entry into the case as a garnishee. If the Constitution forbids the assertion of jurisdiction over the insured based on the policy, then there is no conceptual basis for bringing the "garnishee" into the action. Because the party with forum contacts can only be reached through the out of state party, the question of jurisdiction over the nonresident cannot be ignored. Moreover, the assumption that the defendant has no real stake in the litigation is far from self-evident.

* * *

The justifications offered in support of *Seider* jurisdiction share a common characteristic: they shift the focus of the inquiry from the relationship among the defendant, the forum, and the litigation to that among the plaintiff, the forum, the insurer, and the litigation. The insurer's contacts with the forum are attributed to the defendant because the policy was taken out in anticipation of such litigation. The State's interests in providing a forum for its residents and in regulating the activities of insurance companies are substituted for its contacts with the defendant and the cause of action. This subtle shift in focus from the defendant to the plaintiff is most evident in the decisions limiting *Seider* jurisdiction to actions by forum residents on the ground that permitting nonresidents to avail themselves of the procedure would be unconstitutional. In other words, the plaintiff's contacts with the forum are decisive in determining whether the defendant's due process rights are violated.

Such an approach is forbidden by *International Shoe* and its progeny. . . .

The judgment of the Minnesota Supreme Court is, therefore,

Reversed.

MR. JUSTICE STEVENS, dissenting.

As the Court notes, appellant had no contact with Minnesota that would support personal jurisdiction over him in that State. *Ante*, at

574. Moreover, Shaffer v. Heitner, 433 U.S. 186, 97 S.Ct. 2569, 53 L.Ed. 2d 683, precludes the assertion of *quasi-in-rem* jurisdiction over his property in that forum if the intangible property attached is unrelated to the action. It does not follow, however, that the plaintiff may not obtain *quasi-in-rem* jurisdiction over appellant's insurance policy, since his carrier does business in Minnesota and since it has also specifically contracted in the policy attached to defend the very litigation that plaintiff has instituted in Minnesota.

In this kind of case, the Minnesota statute authorizing jurisdiction is correctly characterized as the "functional equivalent" of a so-called direct action statute. The impact of the judgment is against the insurer. I believe such a direct action statute is valid as applied to a suit brought by a forum resident, see Watson v. Employers Liability Corp., 348 U.S. 66, 72, 75 S.Ct. 166, 169, 99 L.Ed. 74, even if the accident giving rise to the action did not occur in the forum State, see Minichiello v. Rosenberg, 410 F.2d 106 (CA2 1968), cert. denied, 396 U.S. 844, 90 S.Ct. 69, 24 L.Ed.2d 94, so long as it is understood that the forum may exercise no power whatsoever over the individual defendant. As so understood it makes no difference whether the insurance company is sued in its own name or, as Minnesota law provides, in the guise of a suit against the individual defendant.

In this case, although appellant may have a contractual obligation to his insurer to appear in court to testify and generally to cooperate in the defense of the lawsuit, it is my understanding that Minnesota law does not compel him to do so through the contempt power or otherwise. Moreover, any judgment formally entered against the individual defendant may only be executed against the proceeds of his insurance policy. In my opinion, it would violate the Due Process Clause to make any use of such a judgment against that individual—for example, by giving the judgment collateral estoppel effect in a later action against him arising from the same accident. Accord, Minichiello v. Rosenberg, supra, 410 F.2d, at 112; Note, The Constitutionality of Seider v. Roth after Shaffer v. Heitner, 78 Colum.L.Rev. 409, 418–419 (1978). But we are not now faced with any problem concerning use of a *quasi-in-rem* judgment against an individual defendant personally. I am therefore led to the conclusion that the Federal Constitution does not require the Minnesota courts to dismiss this action.

NOTES

(1) In civil law countries, the distinction between in personam and in rem or quasi in rem adjudicatory power is not made. Adjudicatory power, even if based merely on the presence of assets within the state, acts in personam. See, e.g., Ginsburg & Bruzelius, Civil Procedure in Sweden 159–60 (1965). Furthermore, in many civil law countries in personam adjudicatory power over the defendant may be premised on the plaintiff's being a national or resident of the forum. See Herzog, Civil Procedure in France 176–88 (1967) (the French courts may proceed if either the plaintiff or the defendant is a French national); Weser, Bases of Judicial Jurisdiction in Common Market Countries, 10 Am.J.

Comp.L. 323, 325–26 (1961) (under Belgian law, a foreigner may be sued before the court of the plaintiff's domicile or residence), 327 (under Dutch law, a defendant without a domicile or residence in The Netherlands may be sued before the court of the plaintiff's domicile). Are these civil law rules unreasonable? European countries generally refuse to recognize judgments based on the exercise of so-called exorbitant bases of jurisdiction. The 1968 Brussels convention on Jurisdiction and the Recognition of Judgments in Civil and Commercial Matters, in effect in most of the EEC countries, requires for recognition specific contacts between the defendant and the forum, with an exception made for defendants from non-member states. Is this form of discrimination justifiable? The 1988 Lugano Convention between members of the EEC and the European Free Trade Association follows the same pattern. See Juenger, Judicial Jurisdiction in the United States and the European Communities: A Comparison, 82 Mich.L.Rev. 1195 (1984).

(2) On in rem and quasi-in-rem adjudicatory authority after the *Shaffer* and *Rush* decisions, see Smit, The Importance of Shaffer v. Heitner: Seminal or Minimal?, 45 Brooklyn L.Rev. 519 (1979); Note, Attachment Jurisdiction after Shaffer v. Heitner, 32 Stan.L.Rev. 167 (1979).

(3) In the principal case, could the Minnesota court have applied Minnesota law to the merits of the dispute without violating the due process clause? Cf. Allstate Insurance Co. v. Hague, 449 U.S. 302, 101 S.Ct. 633, 66 L.Ed.2d 521 (1981); Reese, Legislative Jurisdiction, 78 Colum.L.Rev. 1587 (1978).

NOTE ON THE DIMINISHING DISTINCTIONS BETWEEN IN PERSONAM AND QUASI IN REM JURISDICTION

The *Shaffer v. Heitner* and *Rush v. Savchuk* decisions have given added impetus to the notion that concepts of quasi in rem and even in rem jurisdiction may have no continuing utility. On this subject, see Smit, The Enduring Utility of In Rem Rules: A Lasting Legacy of Pennoyer v. Neff, 43 Brooklyn L.Rev. 600 (1977); Smit, The Importance of Shaffer v. Heitner: Seminal or Minimal, 45 Brooklyn L.Rev. 519 (1979). In *Shaffer v. Heitner,* Mr. Justice Marshall, writing for the majority, was careful to point out that the Court did not automatically condemn all exercises of in rem jurisdiction. But *Rush v. Savchuk* makes clear that quasi in rem jurisdiction in regard to intangibles may have been dealt a mortal blow. If it survives at all, in what situations may it do so? The cases that follow may provide some answers. However, they predate more recent Supreme Court decisions, and their present status may therefore be uncertain. You should also consider to what extent quasi in rem and in rem jurisdiction over tangible res, both movable and immovable, are affected by the more recent Supreme Court pronouncements.

MULLANE v. CENTRAL HANOVER BANK & TRUST CO.

Supreme Court of the United States, 1950.
339 U.S. 306, 70 S.Ct. 652, 94 L.Ed. 865.

MR. JUSTICE JACKSON delivered the opinion of the Court.*

This controversy questions the constitutional sufficiency of notice to beneficiaries on judicial settlement of accounts by the trustee of a common trust fund established under the New York Banking Law. The New York Court of Appeals considered and overruled objections that the statutory notice contravenes requirements of the Fourteenth Amendment and that by allowance of the account beneficiaries were deprived of property without due process of law. 299 N.Y. 697, 87 N.E.2d 73. The case is here on appeal under 28 U.S.C. § 1257.

Common trust fund legislation is addressed to a problem appropriate for state action. Mounting overheads have made administration of small trusts undesirable to corporate trustees. In order that donors and testators of moderately sized trusts may not be denied the service of corporate fiduciaries, the District of Columbia and some thirty states other than New York have permitted pooling small trust estates into one fund for investment administration. The income, capital gains, losses and expenses of the collective trust are shared by the constituent trusts in proportion to their contribution. By this plan diversification of risk and economy of management can be extended to those whose capital standing alone would not obtain such advantage.

Statutory authorization for the establishment of such common trust funds is provided in the New York Banking Law, § 100–c (c. 687, L.1937, as amended by c. 602, L.1943 and c. 158, L.1944). Under this Act a trust company may, with approval of the State Banking Board, establish a common fund and, within prescribed limits, invest therein the assets of an unlimited number of estates, trusts or other funds of which it is trustee. Each participating trust shares ratably in the common fund, but exclusive management and control is in the trust company as trustee, and neither a fiduciary nor any beneficiary of a participating trust is deemed to have ownership in any particular asset or investment of this common fund. The trust company must keep fund assets separate from its own, and in its fiduciary capacity may not deal with itself or any affiliate. Provisions are made for accountings twelve to fifteen months after the establishment of a fund and triennially thereafter. The decree in each such judicial settlement of accounts is made binding and conclusive as to any matter set forth in the account upon everyone having any interest in the common fund or in any participating estate, trust or fund.

In January, 1946, Central Hanover Bank and Trust Company established a common trust fund in accordance with these provisions, and in March, 1947, it petitioned the Surrogate's Court for settlement of its first account as common trustee. During the accounting period a

* Footnotes omitted.

total of 113 trusts, approximately half *inter vivos* and half testamentary, participated in the common trust fund, the gross capital of which was nearly three million dollars. The record does not show the number or residence of the beneficiaries, but they were many and it is clear that some of them were not residents of the State of New York.

The only notice given beneficiaries of this specific application was by publication in a local newspaper in strict compliance with the minimum requirements of N.Y.Banking Law § 100–c(12): "After filing such petition [for judicial settlement of its account] the petitioner shall cause to be issued by the court in which the petition is filed and shall publish not less than once in each week for four successive weeks in a newspaper to be designated by the court a notice or citation addressed generally without naming them to all parties interested in such common trust fund and in such estates, trusts or funds mentioned in the petition, all of which may be described in the notice or citation only in the manner set forth in said petition and without setting forth the residence of any such decedent or donor of any such estate, trust or fund." Thus the only notice required, and the only one given, was by newspaper publication setting forth merely the name and address of the trust company, the name and the date of establishment of the common trust fund, and a list of all participating estates, trusts or funds.

At the time the first investment in the common fund was made on behalf of each participating estate, however, the trust company, pursuant to the requirements of § 100–c(9), had notified by mail each person of full age and sound mind whose name and address were then known to it and who was "entitled to share in the income therefrom . . . [or] . . . who would be entitled to share in the principal if the event upon which such estate, trust or fund will become distributable should have occurred at the time of sending such notice." Included in the notice was a copy of those provisions of the Act relating to the sending of the notice itself and to the judicial settlement of common trust fund accounts.

Upon the filing of the petition for the settlement of accounts, appellant was, by order of the court pursuant to § 100–c(12), appointed special guardian and attorney for all persons known or unknown not otherwise appearing who had or might thereafter have any interest in the income of the common trust fund; and appellee Vaughan was appointed to represent those similarly interested in the principal. There were no other appearances on behalf of any one interested in either interest or principal.

Appellant appeared specially, objecting that notice and the statutory provisions for notice to beneficiaries were inadequate to afford due process under the Fourteenth Amendment, and therefore that the court was without jurisdiction to render a final and binding decree. Appellant's objections were entertained and overruled, the Surrogate holding that the notice required and given was sufficient. 75 N.Y.S.2d 397. A final decree accepting the accounts has been entered, affirmed by the Appellate Division of the Supreme Court, 275 App.Div. 769, 88 N.Y.S.2d 907, and by the Court of Appeals of the State of New York, 299 N.Y. 697, 87 N.E.2d 73.

The effect of this decree, as held below, is to settle "all questions respecting the management of the common fund." We understand that every right which beneficiaries would otherwise have against the trust company, either as trustee of the common fund or as trustee of any individual trust, for improper management of the common trust fund during the period covered by the accounting is sealed and wholly terminated by the decree. [Citations omitted.]

We are met at the outset with a challenge to the power of the State—the right of its courts to adjudicate at all as against those beneficiaries who reside without the State of New York. It is contended that the proceeding is one *in personam* in that the decree affects neither title to nor possession of any *res*, but adjudges only personal rights of the beneficiaries to surcharge their trustee for negligence or breach of trust. Accordingly, it is said, under the strict doctrine of Pennoyer v. Neff, 95 U.S. 714, the Surrogate is without jurisdiction as to nonresidents upon whom personal service of process was not made.

Distinctions between actions *in rem* and those *in personam* are ancient and originally expressed in procedural terms what seems really to have been a distinction in the substantive law of property under a system quite unlike our own. Buckland and McNair, Roman Law and Common Law, 66; Burdick, Principles of Roman Law and Their Relation to Modern Law, 298. The legal recognition and rise in economic importance of incorporeal or intangible forms of property have upset the ancient simplicity of property law and the clarity of its distinctions, while new forms of proceedings have confused the old procedural classification. American courts have sometimes classed certain actions as *in rem* because personal service of process was not required, and at other times have held personal service of process not required because the action was *in rem*. See cases collected in Freeman on Judgments, §§ 1517 et seq. (5th ed.).

Judicial proceedings to settle fiduciary accounts have been sometimes termed *in rem*, or more indefinitely *quasi in rem*, or more vaguely still, "in the nature of a proceeding *in rem*." It is not readily apparent how the courts of New York did or would classify the present proceeding, which has some characteristics and is wanting in some features of proceedings both *in rem* and *in personam*. But in any event we think that the requirements of the Fourteenth Amendment to the Federal Constitution do not depend upon a classification for which the standards are so elusive and confused generally and which, being primarily for state courts to define, may and do vary from state to state. Without disparaging the usefulness of distinctions between actions *in rem* and those *in personam* in many branches of law, or on other issues, or the reasoning which underlies them, we do not rest the power of the State to resort to constructive service in this proceeding upon how its courts or this Court may regard this historic antithesis. It is sufficient to observe that, whatever the technical definition of its chosen procedure, the interest of each state in providing means to close trusts that exist by the grace of its laws and are administered under the supervision of its courts is so insistent and rooted in custom as to establish beyond doubt the right of its courts to determine the interests of all claimants, resident or nonresident, provided its procedure accords full opportunity to appear and be heard.

Quite different from the question of a state's power to discharge trustees is that of the opportunity it must give beneficiaries to contest. Many controversies have raged about the cryptic and abstract words of the Due Process Clause but there can be no doubt that at a minimum they require that deprivation of life, liberty or property by adjudication be preceded by notice and opportunity for hearing appropriate to the nature of the case.

In two ways this proceeding does or may deprive beneficiaries of property. It may cut off their rights to have the trustee answer for negligent or illegal impairments of their interests. Also, their interests are presumably subject to diminution in the proceeding by allowance of fees and expenses to one who, in their names but without their knowledge, may conduct a fruitless or uncompensatory contest. Certainly the proceeding is one in which they may be deprived of property rights and hence notice and hearing must measure up to the standards of due process.

Personal service of written notice within the jurisdiction is the classic form of notice always adequate in any type of proceeding. But the vital interest of the State in bringing any issues as to its fiduciaries to a final settlement can be served only if interests or claims of individuals who are outside of the State can somehow be determined. A construction of the Due Process Clause which would place impossible or impractical obstacles in the way could not be justified.

Against this interest of the State we must balance the individual interest sought to be protected by the Fourteenth Amendment. This is defined by our holding that "The fundamental requisite of due process of law is the opportunity to be heard." Grannis v. Ordean, 234 U.S. 385, 394, 34 S.Ct. 779, 783, 58 L.Ed. 1563. This right to be heard has little reality or worth unless one is informed that the matter is pending and can choose for himself whether to appear or default, acquiesce or contest.

The Court has not committed itself to any formula achieving a balance between these interests in a particular proceeding or determining when constructive notice may be utilized or what test it must meet. Personal service has not in all circumstances been regarded as indispensable to the process due to residents, and it has more often been held unnecessary as to nonresidents. We disturb none of the established rules on these subjects. No decision constitutes a controlling or even a very illuminating precedent for the case before us. But a few general principles stand out in the books.

An elementary and fundamental requirement of due process in any proceeding which is to be accorded finality is notice reasonably calculated, under all the circumstances, to apprise interested parties of the pendency of the action and afford them an opportunity to present their objections. Milliken v. Meyer, 311 U.S. 457; Grannis v. Ordean, 234 U.S. 385, 34 S.Ct. 779, 58 L.Ed. 1563; Priest v. Las Vegas, 232 U.S. 604, 34 S.Ct. 443, 58 L.Ed. 751; Roller v. Holly, 176 U.S. 398, 20 S.Ct. 410, 44 L.Ed. 520. The notice must be of such nature as reasonably to convey the required information, Grannis v. Ordean, supra, and it must afford a reasonable time for those interested to make their appearance, Roller v. Holly, supra, and cf. Goodrich v. Ferris, 214 U.S. 71, 29 S.Ct. 580, 53 L.Ed. 914. But if with due regard for the practicalities and peculiarities of the case these conditions are reasonably met, the constitutional requirements are satisfied. "The criterion is not the possibility of conceivable injury but the just and reasonable character of the requirements, having reference to the subject with which the statute deals." American Land Co. v. Zeiss, 219 U.S. 47, 67, 31 S.Ct. 200, 207, 55 L.Ed. 82; and see Blinn v. Nelson, 222 U.S. 1, 7, 32 S.Ct. 1, 2, 56 L.Ed. 65.

But when notice is a person's due, process which is a mere gesture is not due process. The means employed must be such as one desirous of actually informing the absentee might reasonably adopt to accomplish it. The reasonableness and hence the constitutional validity of any chosen method may be defended on the ground that it is in itself reasonably certain to inform those affected, compare Hess v. Pawloski, 274 U.S. 352, 47 S.Ct. 632, 71 L.Ed. 1091, with Wuchter v. Pizzutti, 276 U.S. 13, 48 S.Ct. 259, 72 L.Ed. 446, or, where conditions do not reasonably permit such notice, that the form chosen is not substantially less likely to bring home notice than other of the feasible and customary substitutes.

It would be idle to pretend that publication alone, as prescribed here, is a reliable means of acquainting interested parties of the fact that their rights are before the courts. It is not an accident that the greater number of cases reaching this Court on the question of adequacy of notice have been concerned with actions founded on process constructively served through local newspapers. Chance alone brings to the attention of even a local resident an advertisement in small type inserted in the back pages of a newspaper, and if he makes his home outside the area of the newspaper's normal circulation the odds that the information will never reach him are large indeed. The chance of actual notice is further reduced when, as here, the notice required does not even name those whose attention it is supposed to attract, and does not inform acquaintances who might call it to attention. In weighing its sufficiency on the basis of equivalence with actual notice, we are unable to regard this as more than a feint.

Nor is publication here reinforced by steps likely to attract the parties' attention to the proceeding. It is true that publication traditionally has been acceptable as notification supplemental to other action which in itself may reasonably be expected to convey a warning. The ways of an owner with tangible property are such that he usually arranges means to learn of any direct attack upon his possessory or proprietary rights. Hence, libel of a ship, attachment of a chattel or entry upon real estate in the name of law may reasonably be expected to come promptly to the owner's attention. When the state within which the owner has located such property seizes it for some reason, publication or posting affords an additional measure of notification. A state may indulge the assumption that one who has left tangible property in the state either has abandoned it, in which case proceedings against it deprive him of nothing, cf. Anderson National Bank v. Luckett, 321 U.S. 233, 64 S.Ct. 599, 88 L.Ed. 692; Security Savings Bank v. California, 263 U.S. 282, 44 S.Ct. 108, 68 L.Ed. 301, or that he has left some caretaker under a duty to let him know that it is being jeopardized. Ballard v. Hunter, 204 U.S. 241, 27 S.Ct. 261, 51 L.Ed. 461; Huling v. Kaw Valley R. Co., 130 U.S. 559, 9 S.Ct. 603, 32 L.Ed. 1045. As phrased long ago by Chief Justice Marshall in The Mary, 9 Cranch 126, 144, "It is the part of common prudence for all those who may have any interest in [a thing], to guard that interest by persons who are in a situation to protect it."

In the case before us there is, of course, no abandonment. On the other hand these beneficiaries do have a resident fiduciary as caretaker of their interest in this property. But it is their caretaker who in the accounting becomes their adversary. Their trustee is released from giving notice of jeopardy, and no one else is expected to do so. Not even the special guardian is required or apparently expected to communicate with his ward and client, and, of course, if such a duty were merely transferred from the trustee to the guardian, economy would not be served and more likely the cost would be increased.

This Court has not hesitated to approve of resort to publication as a customary substitute in another class of cases where it is not reasonably possible or practicable to give more adequate warning. Thus it has been recognized that, in the case of persons missing or unknown, employment of an indirect and even a probably futile means of notification is all that the situation permits and creates no constitutional bar to a final decree foreclosing their rights. Cunnius v. Reading School District, 198 U.S. 458, 25 S.Ct. 721, 49 L.Ed. 1125; Blinn v. Nelson, 222 U.S. 1, 32 S.Ct. 1, 56 L.Ed. 65; and see Jacob v. Roberts, 223 U.S. 261, 32 S.Ct. 303, 56 L.Ed. 429.

Those beneficiaries represented by appellant whose interests or whereabouts could not with due diligence be ascertained come clearly within this category. As to them the statutory notice is sufficient. However great the odds that publication will never reach the eyes of such unknown parties, it is not in the typical case much more likely to fail than any of the choices open to legislators endeavoring to prescribe the best notice practicable.

Nor do we consider it unreasonable for the State to dispense with more certain notice to those beneficiaries whose interests are either conjectural or future or, although they could be discovered upon investigation, do not in due course of business come to knowledge of the common trustee. Whatever searches might be required in another situation under ordinary standards of diligence, in view of the character of the proceedings and the nature of the interests here involved we think them unnecessary. We recognize the practical difficulties and costs that would be attendant on frequent investigations into the status of great numbers of beneficiaries, many of whose interests in the common fund are so remote as to be ephemeral; and we have no doubt that such impracticable and extended searches are not required in the name of due process. The expense of keeping informed from day to day of substitutions among even current income beneficiaries and presumptive remaindermen, to say nothing of the far greater number of contingent beneficiaries, would impose a severe burden on the plan, and would likely dissipate its advantages. These are practical matters in which we should be reluctant to disturb the judgment of the state authorities.

Accordingly we overrule appellant's constitutional objections to published notice insofar as they are urged on behalf of any beneficiaries whose interests or addresses are unknown to the trustee.

As to known present beneficiaries of known place of residence, however, notice by publication stands on a different footing. Exceptions in the name of necessity do not sweep away the rule that within the limits of practicability notice must be such as is reasonably calculated to reach interested parties. Where the names and post office addresses of those affected by a proceeding are at hand, the reasons disappear for resort to means less likely than the mails to apprise them of its pendency.

The trustee has on its books the names and addresses of the income beneficiaries represented by appellant, and we find no tenable ground for dispensing with a serious effort to inform them personally of the accounting, at least by ordinary mail to the record addresses. Cf. Wuchter v. Pizzutti, supra. Certainly sending them a copy of the statute months and perhaps years in advance does not answer this purpose. The trustee periodically remits their income to them, and we think that they might reasonably expect that with or apart from their remittances word might come to them personally that steps were being taken affecting their interests.

We need not weigh contentions that a requirement of personal service of citation on even the large number of known resident or nonresident beneficiaries would, by reasons of delay if not of expense, seriously interfere with the proper administration of the fund. Of course personal service even without the jurisdiction of the issuing

authority serves the end of actual and personal notice, whatever power of compulsion it might lack. However, no such service is required under the circumstances. This type of trust presupposes a large number of small interests. The individual interest does not stand alone but is identical with that of a class. The rights of each in the integrity of the fund and the fidelity of the trustee are shared by many other beneficiaries. Therefore notice reasonably certain to reach most of those interested in objecting is likely to safeguard the interests of all, since any objection sustained would inure to the benefit of all. We think that under such circumstances reasonable risks that notice might not actually reach every beneficiary are justifiable. "Now and then an extraordinary case may turn up, but constitutional law like other mortal contrivances has to take some chances, and in the great majority of instances no doubt justice will be done." Blinn v. Nelson, supra, 7.

The statutory notice to known beneficiaries is inadequate, not because in fact it fails to reach everyone, but because under the circumstances it is not reasonably calculated to reach those who could easily be informed by other names at hand. However it may have been in former times, the mails today are recognized as an efficient and inexpensive means of communication. Moreover, the fact that the trust company has been able to give mailed notice to known beneficiaries at the time the common trust fund was established is persuasive that postal notification at the time of accounting would not seriously burden the plan.

In some situations the law requires greater precautions in its proceedings than the business world accepts for its own purposes. In few, if any, will it be satisfied with less. Certainly it is instructive, in determining the reasonableness of the impersonal broadcast notification here used, to ask whether it would satisfy a prudent man of business, counting his pennies but finding it in his interest to convey information to many persons whose names and addresses are in his files. We are not satisfied that it would. Publication may theoretically be available for all the world to see, but it is too much in our day to suppose that each or any individual beneficiary does or could examine all that is published to see if something may be tucked away in it that affects his property interests. We have before indicated in reference to notice by publication that, "Great caution should be used not to let fiction deny the fair play that can be secured only by a pretty close adhesion to fact." McDonald v. Mabee, 243 U.S. 90, 91, 37 S.Ct. 343, 61 L.Ed. 608.

We hold that the notice of judicial settlement of accounts required by the New York Banking Law § 100–c(12) is incompatible with the requirements of the Fourteenth Amendment as a basis for adjudication depriving known persons whose whereabouts are also known of substantial property rights. Accordingly the judgment is reversed and the

cause remanded for further proceedings not inconsistent with this opinion.

* * *

NOTES

(1) New York Banking Law § 100–c was amended to conform to the decision in the principal case. Chap. 778, §§ 3, 4, Laws of 1951.

(2) In the principal case, did the Court exercise in personam adjudicatory power over non-residents? If so, on what basis did it do so? What is the impact of *Hanson v. Denckla,* p. 258 supra, *Shaffer v. Heitner,* p. 298 supra, and *Calder v. Jones,* p. 267 supra, on the decision in the principal case? To what extent, in the principal case, does the reasonableness of the exercise of jurisdiction depend on the interests of the plaintiffs and those of the state?

(3) In civil law countries, a court that has in personam adjudicatory authority over one of the defendants generally has, by virtue of that circumstance, in personam authority over all other defendants if the claims asserted are the same or closely related. See, e.g., Herzog, Civil Procedure in France 193–94 (1967); Hattori & Henderson, Civil Procedure in Japan § 405(5) (1983). Is there room in our law for a concept of pendent party in personam jurisdiction? Cf. Bodine's, Inc. v. Sunny–O Inc., 494 F.Supp. 1279 (N.D.Ill.1980) (finding in personam power over defendant in regard to contract claim that was not within Illinois long-arm statute, but that was related to fraud claim within the statute).

ATKINSON v. SUPERIOR COURT OF LOS ANGELES COUNTY

Supreme Court of California, 1957.
49 Cal.2d 338, 316 P.2d 960.

TRAYNOR, J. Separate class actions were brought by two groups of musicians attacking the validity of collective bargaining contracts between their employers and the American Federation of Musicians and certain trust agreements related thereto. One action is on behalf of the employees of various motion picture companies and the other is on behalf of the employees of various phonograph record companies. The gist of plaintiffs' complaints is that in violation of its duty as their collective bargaining agent and in fraud of their rights the federation contracted with the employers that certain royalty payments and payments for reuse of motion pictures on television should be paid to a trustee for specified trust purposes instead of to the employees.

Plaintiffs allege that these payments constitute wages earned by the employees and that their diversion to the trust is violative of their rights; that the purpose of the trust is to contribute to the public knowledge and appreciation of music throughout the United States and Canada, and the trustee is authorized and directed to expend the trust funds in presenting personal performances by instrumental musicians to which the public is admitted without charge; that the trust arrangement diverts wages earned by California employees, members of Local

Number 47, for the benefit of federation members elsewhere without corresponding benefit to plaintiffs from the operation of similar arrangements made elsewhere; that the employers are willing to make the payments to their employees, but for their agreements with the federation to make the payments to the trustee; and that the national executive officers of the federation insisted on this arrangement for the selfish purpose of perpetuating themselves in office and of maintaining their hold and control over the affairs of the federation and used the trust fund to win the support of officials of the federation's locals and member musicians throughout the United States and Canada, who vastly outnumber plaintiffs and are not employed by the employers here involved.

In each action, the federation, the trustee, and the respective employers are named as defendants. Plaintiffs seek a declaration of the invalidity of the collective bargaining agreement and their right to the payments either as beneficiaries of a constructive trust or on the ground that the payments constitute wages withheld in violation of sections 222 and 224 of the Labor Code. They also seek damages against the federation for breach of its duty to them. At the commencement of the actions they moved for the appointment of a receiver to collect the payments and preliminary injunctions to prevent the employers from making the payments to the trustee. The employers have been personally served with process in this state, and personal jurisdiction has been obtained over the federation. The trustee was served pursuant to court order by delivery of summonses and complaints and motion papers within the State of New York, but he has not appeared.

The trial court held that insofar as plaintiffs sought to intercept the delivery of payments to the trustee by the appointment of a receiver and temporary injunctions, the trustee was an indispensable party and that the court had no jurisdiction to grant plaintiffs' motions for provisional relief without personal jurisdiction over the trustee. It was careful to point out that its ruling was based solely on lack of jurisdiction and stated that "if the court had jurisdiction to do so, the exercise of a sound discretion would probably require the granting of a preliminary injunction and perhaps the appointment of a receiver. . . ."

. . . We have concluded that personal service upon the trustee in New York was sufficient to give the court jurisdiction to adjudicate his right to receive payments under the contracts here involved. Code of Civil Procedure, section 412, provides: "Where the person on whom service is to be made resides out of the State . . . and it . . . appears . . . that it is an action which relates to or the subject of which is real or personal property in this State, in which such person defendant . . . has or claims a lien or interest, actual or contingent, therein, or in which the relief demanded consist wholly or in part in excluding such person . . . from any interest therein, such court, or judge, may make an order that the service be made by the publication of the summons." Section 413 provides that personal service outside the state is equivalent to publication. Plaintiffs claim that the employers' obligation to make the payments involved is one owing to them instead of to the trustee. That obligation is a chose in action and is therefore personal property within the meaning of the statutory provisions. (Code Civ.Proc., § 17, subd. 3.) Being an intangible, it has no situs in fact.

"An intangible, unlike real or tangible personal property, has no physical characteristics that would serve as a basis for assigning it to a particular locality. The location assigned to it depends on what action is to be taken with reference to it." (Estate of Waits, 23 Cal.2d 676, 680, 146 P.2d 5.) The question presented, therefore, is whether the chose in action in question may be treated as being within this state within the meaning of section 412 for purposes of exercising in rem or quasi in rem jurisdiction over it in these actions.

Plaintiffs rely on cases holding that having jurisdiction over the obligor, the state has power to enforce the obligation and cut off the right, if any, of a nonresident claimant thereto without personal jurisdiction over the nonresident.

. . . Defendants contend, however, that in the case of ordinary choses in action such power is limited to situations in which the local claimant admits the validity of the local debtor's obligation to the nonresident and seeks to reach the interest he admits is the property of the nonresident. . . .

In their view it is immaterial in an action to adjudicate conflicting claims to an obligation, whether the action is commenced by the obligor, where only one of the claimants can be served, or is commenced by one of the claimants, where he can secure personal jurisdiction over the obligor but not over the rival claimant.

. . . In the absence of a settled rule governing the situation before us, and in light of the fact that an intangible may be subjected to the jurisdiction of the court without personal jurisdiction over all of the parties involved for some purposes but not for others, we conclude that the solution must be sought in the general principles governing jurisdiction over persons and property rather than in an attempt to assign a fictional situs to intangibles.

It is significant that with respect to jurisdiction to tax intangibles (Curry v. McCanless, 307 U.S. 357, 373–374, 59 S.Ct. 900, 83 L.Ed. 1339, 123 A.L.R. 162), jurisdiction over foreign corporations (International Shoe Co. v. Washington, 326 U.S. 310, 316, 66 S.Ct. 154, 90 L.Ed. 95, 161 A.L.R. 1057; Perkins v. Benguet Min. Co., 342 U.S. 437, 445, 72 S.Ct. 413, 96 L.Ed. 485), and jurisdiction to adjudicate trust obligations (Mullane v. Central Hanover Bank & Trust Co., 339 U.S. 306, 311–313, 70 S.Ct. 652, 94 L.Ed. 865), emphasis is no longer placed on actual or physical presence but on the bearing that local contacts have to the question of over-all fair play and substantial justice. A similar change in emphasis has been taking place with respect to personal jurisdiction over individuals.

. . . In the present case, since the trustee is not and has not been a resident of California, section 417 of the Code of Civil Procedure precludes the entry of a personal judgment against him, and it is therefore unnecessary to determine whether his activities as trustee have sufficient connection with this state constitutionally to justify an assumption of personal jurisdiction without service of process here. The relevant contacts with this state are significant, however, in deciding whether due process permits exercising a more limited or quasi in rem jurisdiction to determine his and plaintiffs' interests in the intangibles in question.

We find no relevance in the distinction defendants seek to make between jurisdiction to take over a nonresident's claim to a chose in action admittedly his and jurisdiction to establish that it was never his. In both situations the nonresident can protect his interest in the property only by submitting to the jurisdiction of the court. It is true that in the former situation he must litigate a controversy solely between himself and his creditor unrelated to preexisting rights in the obligation garnished, whereas in the latter situation preexisting conflicting rights to the obligation itself are involved; but this distinction alone has no bearing on the fairness of making him appear.

. . . The present case is not one in which an obligor has invoked the jurisdiction of a court remote from the obligee solely for the purpose of terminating his obligation or sought to compel conflicting claimants to adjudicate their rights in a forum of his own choice. The obligation plaintiffs seek to enforce grows out of their employment by defendants here. The payments involved are alleged to be consideration for work performed in this state. The federation defendant is before the court. Under these circumstances, fairness to plaintiffs demands that they be able to reach the fruits of their labors before they are removed from the state. Moreover, fairness to the defendants who are personally before the court also demands that the conflicting claims of the trustee be subject to final adjudication. Even if we were to hold that his absence prevents the granting of the provisional remedies here sought, plaintiffs would not be foreclosed thereby from asserting that payment to him did not discharge the employers' obligation to them and that the federation was independently liable for damages for breach of its fiduciary duty. The evil of exposing the obligor to actions to enforce the same obligation in two jurisdictions with the attendant risk of double liability would not be obviated. It was just such double liability that was sustained in the Dunlevy case [New York Life Ins. Co. v. Dunlevy, 241 U.S. 518, 36 S.Ct. 613, 60 L.Ed.2d 1140 (1916)] and gave impetus to the passage of federal interpleader legislation. (See Chafee, Interstate Interpleader, 33 Yale L.J. 685, 711.) It is doubtful whether today the United States Supreme Court would deny to a state court the interstate interpleader jurisdiction that federal courts may exercise. A remedy that a federal court may provide without violating due process of law does not become unfair or unjust because it is sought in a state court instead. To sustain jurisdiction in these cases, however, we are not required to forecast the overruling of the Dunlevy case and to act on that basis. For the reasons stated above, this case is clearly distinguishable from the Dunlevy case, and the multiple contacts with this state fully sustain the jurisdiction of the superior court to exercise quasi in rem jurisdiction over the intangibles in question.

Let the writ of mandate issue in each case commanding respondent superior court to assume and exercise jurisdiction over petitioners' application for a preliminary injunction and the appointment of a receiver as prayed herein.

GIBSON, C.J., SHENK, J., CARTER, J., SCHAUER, J., SPENCE, J., and McCOMB, J., concurred.

NOTES

(1) In the principal case, under the California long-arm statute (Note 1, p. 252 supra), could the Court have bound the trustee personally? Cf. Traynor, Is this Conflict Really Necessary, 37 Tex.L.Rev. 657 (1959), who, in commenting on this case, states (at 662–663):

> ". . . It seemed as irrational to resolve the problem by assigning a fictional situs to intangibles as it would to pin a tail blindfolded to a nonexistent donkey. Instead it was identified as a problem of jurisdiction over persons and property. . . .

> "The case graphically illustrates how local statutes can limit the jurisdiction of courts available under the due process clause. The statute precluding a personal judgment unless the defendant was a resident at the time of suit ruled out the possibility of a judgment against the trustee that would hold him liable for an alleged breach of trust or compel him to make an accounting. At most the court could determine only his interest in the trust res under another statute authorizing the determination of a nonresident's interest in property in the state. Clearly the Legislature did not regard a judgment under this statute as a personal judgment such as was precluded by the other statute. Yet it would affect the rights of persons as any judgment does, and the jurisdictional question is not solved simply by regarding the proceeding as in rem. The case made clear that realistic tests to determine jurisdiction to grant the specific relief sought must be applied regardless of labels. Justice is ill-served by mechanical ones.

> "It is time we had done with mechanical distinctions between in rem and in personam, high time now in a mobile society where property increasingly becomes intangible and the fictional res becomes stranger and stranger. Insofar as courts remain given to asking 'Res, res—who's got the res?,' they cripple their evaluation of the real factors that should determine jurisdiction. They cannot evaluate the real factors squarely until they give up the ghost of the res. As they do so, the gap will narrow between the tests of jurisdiction and the tests of *forum non conveniens*."

Does Justice Traynor suggest that the distinction between in personam and in rem jurisdiction should be discarded? Cf. also Simpson v. Loehmann, 21 N.Y.2d

305, 311, 287 N.Y.S.2d 633, 637, 234 N.E.2d 669, 672 (1967): "The historical limitations on both in personam and in rem jurisdiction, with their rigid tests, are giving way to a more realistic and reasonable evaluation of the respective rights of plaintiffs, defendants, and the State in terms of fairness". See also Note, Jurisdiction in New York: A Proposed Reform, 69 Colum.L.Rev. 1412 (1969).

(2) What is the impact of more recent Supreme Court decisions on the holding in the principal case? See p. 305, Note (2), supra.

NOTE ON LIMITED APPEARANCES

If a defendant appears in an in rem or quasi in rem proceeding to protect his interest in the thing, does he subject himself to the court's personal adjudicatory authority? In this context again, the distinction between jurisdiction and competence is useful. The Supreme Court's decision in York v. Texas, p. 232, Note (4), supra, supports the conclusion that a state acquires in personam jurisdiction by such an appearance. Nevertheless, in at least some instances, especially in cases involving quasi in rem proceedings in regard to intangibles, to the extent these survive at all, it may be constitutionally required to afford the defendant an opportunity to defend his interest in the thing without exposing himself, by his mere appearance, to the court's in personam power. This was held constitutionally required in a *Seider* type of proceedings before the Supreme Court ruled the exercise of quasi in rem authority in such a proceeding unconstitutional in *Rush v. Savchuk,* p. 306, supra.

Another question is whether a state should reasonably adjust or construe its rules of competence in order to permit a limited appearance. Many states have answered this question in the negative, although the more recent tendency is to permit limited appearances. The Federal Rules contain no provision addressing this problem specifically. However, Rule 12, which provides that no defense or objection is waived by being joined with any other defense or objection, would appear to permit a defendant who appears to defend his interest in an in rem type proceeding to object to the court's exercising in personam competence over him. But in United States v. Balanovski, 236 F.2d 298, 303 (2d Cir.1956), the Second Circuit ruled, per Clark, C.J., that Rule 12 should not be "tortuously construed in circumstances like the present to promote unnecessary litigations" and to permit a limited appearance.

SECTION 5. FEDERAL BASES

ARROWSMITH v. UNITED PRESS INTERNATIONAL, 320 F.2d 219 (2d Cir.1963). Plaintiff brought a libel action in the District Court in Vermont against UPI, a New York corporation. The District Court dismissed the action on the ground that the complaint failed to state a claim for relief. The Second Circuit reversed on the ground that the District Court should have considered themotion to dismiss for want of in personam competence first. It then addressed the question of whether the action could be maintained on a federal basis of competence. Rejecting the ruling in Jaftex Corporation v. Randolph Mills, Inc., 282 F.2d 508 (2d Cir.1960) (per Clark, C.J.), that, in a diversity case, a federal court could proceed on a federal basis of competence grounded on the doing of business, the Second Circuit, per Friendly, ruled that there is no such independent basis of federal competence.

COLEMAN v. AMERICAN EXPORT ISBRANDTSEN LINES, INC.

United States Court of Appeals, Second Circuit, 1968.
405 F.2d 250.

FRIENDLY, CIRCUIT JUDGE.* Plaintiff Coleman, a longshoreman employed by John McGrath Corporation, brought this action in the District Court for the Southern District of New York to recover for injuries sustained aboard the S.S. Exchequer, a vessel owned and operated by defendant American Export Isbrandtsen Lines, Inc., while the ship was in Hoboken, N.J. American Export filed a third-party complaint under F.R.Civ.P. 14(a) against Atlantic & Gulf Stevedores, Inc., claiming that any liability to Coleman on its part would be due to the negligence of Atlantic & Gulf in having failed properly to secure a hatch when the Exchequer was in Philadelphia, Pa. before sailing to Hoboken. Atlantic & Gulf is a Pennsylvania corporation, having its principal office in Philadelphia and engaged in stevedoring at that port but assertedly not doing business in New York. The summons and complaint were served by a United States marshal on Atlantic & Gulf at its Philadelphia office, avowedly pursuant to the second sentence of F.R.Civ.P. 4(f).
. . . .

Atlantic & Gulf moved to dismiss the third party complaint for lack of jurisdiction. The court granted its motion. See to the same effect Karlsen v. Hanff v. Manchonoc Trawler Corp., 278 F.Supp. 864 (S.D. N.Y.1967); contra, Sevits v. McKiernan–Terry Corporation (New Jersey), 270 F.Supp. 887, 891 (S.D.N.Y.1967). American Export has appealed; we disagree and reverse.

The service of process here appears to fit the language of the Rule snugly enough. Atlantic & Gulf was brought in as a party pursuant to Rule 14. It was served in the manner provided in Rule 4(d)(3). And the place of service was not more than 100 miles from the Federal Courthouse in the Southern District of New York.

Atlantic & Gulf contends that the new provision of Rule 4(f) simply allowed service outside the state where the court is sitting with respect to persons already subject to the jurisdiction of that state. For exam-

* Footnotes omitted.

ple, if Atlantic & Gulf had been doing business in New York but had no office there, the amendment would permit personal service to be made on it in Philadelphia pursuant to Rule 4(d)(3). If the amendment had done no more than that, it would have accomplished little. Most states have statutes, like New York CPLR § 313, providing for out-of-state service on persons subject to the jurisdiction of their courts, and Rule 4(d)(7) was amended in 1963 to overcome whatever doubts had previously existed as to the ability of a federal court to utilize these. See Griffin v. Ensign, 234 F.2d 307, 311 (3d Cir.1956); Deveny v. Rheem Mfg. Co., 319 F.2d 124 (2d Cir.1963) (Clark, J.); and Wolfe v. Doucette, 348 F.2d 635 (9th Cir.1965), upholding out-of-state service under the less clear language of Rule 4(d)(7) prior to the amendment. The Notes of the Advisory Committee . . . show that the purpose of the amendment was not simply to provide a second way of serving persons already subject to the state long-arm statutes, but rather to allow complicated controversies to be ended by a single lawsuit if all the necessary third parties could be found within 100 miles of the courthouse. See 2 Moore, Federal Practice ¶ 4.42[2] (2d ed. 1967). Since Congress has power "to provide that the process of every District Court shall run into every part of the United States," Robertson v. Railroad Labor Board, 268 U.S. 618, 622, 45 S.Ct. 621, 622, 69 L.Ed. 1119 (1925), the Supreme Court as its delegate can provide that process shall be effective if served within 100 miles of the courthouse even if a state line intervenes, and we are convinced that Rule 4(f) exercised this power. To be sure, process can be validly served in another state within the "bulge" created by Rule 4(f) only on persons over whom that state has jurisdiction and, very likely, only on persons within that class over whom it has chosen to exercise it. While in Arrowsmith v. United Press International, 320 F.2d 219, 228 n. 9 (2d Cir.1963), decided shortly before amended Rule 4(f) became effective, we noted that some problems on the latter score might arise, nothing in that opinion, cited by the district judge, suggested the result here reached. See 2 Moore, supra, at 1293–36. There can be no doubt whatever that Pennsylvania can and does provide that a Pennsylvania corporation with its principal office in Pennsylvania and doing business there can be validly served at its headquarters in Philadelphia, 12 P.S.App.R.C.P. §§ 2179 and 2180.

The district judge rested his decision primarily on a sentence in this court's opinion in Petrol Shipping Corp. v. Kingdom of Greece, 360 F.2d 103, 109, certiorari denied 385 U.S. 931, 87 S.Ct. 291, 17 L.Ed.2d 213 (1966):

> "We do not equate 'presence,' or amenability to suit, with service of process . . . and we regard Rule 4 as speaking to service alone, and not both service and amenability."

This was said in support of the position that where a party—in that instance a foreign government—was amenable to suit within the state, the lack of a provision in Rule 4 as to how service could be effected in this *casus omissus* would not prevent a court from fashioning one. Quite plainly we were not focusing on the particular problem raised by the second sentence of amended Rule 4(f). Apart from that, however, we see nothing in the statement in *Petrol* inconsistent with upholding the service of process here. What we meant, as the reference to *Arrowsmith* in *Petrol* makes clear, is that, although Rule 4 fixes the manner and scope of service, it does not say when the person served is subject to the jurisdiction of the court that served him. Similarly, although Rule 4(f) provides for out-of-state service on certain defendants, such service will not be valid unless they have enough contacts with the state of service to be subject to suit there.

The order dismissing the third party complaint for lack of jurisdiction is reversed.

NOTES

(1) Does the Fifth Amendment permit the exercise of in personam jurisdiction by a federal court over any person outside of the state in which it is sitting, but within the United States? May the Federal Rules specifically grant such in personam power to a federal court? Does Rule 4(f) do so to a limited extent? In cases in which Rule 4(f) applies, should state or federal standards govern the suability of the defendant in the state of service?

(2) In Sprow v. Hartford Insurance Co., 594 F.2d 412 (5th Cir.1979), the Court stated that Rule 4(f) applied when the party served "has minimum contacts with the forum state *or* the bulge area." It held the bulge area to be measured by the "as the crow flies" method. The court cited with approval Judge Friendly's opinion in the *Coleman* case. Is its analysis different from that of Judge Friendly? See also Note, Bulge Service Amenability: A Federal Standard, 41 U.Pitt.L.Rev. 801 (1980); Note, Fifth Amendment Due Process Limitations on Nationwide Federal Jurisdiction, 61 B.U.L.Rev. 403 (1981).

———

OMNI CAPITAL INTERNATIONAL v. WOLFF & CO., 479 U.S. 1063, 107 S.Ct. 946, 93 L.Ed.2d 995 (1987). In an action brought in the United States District Court for the Eastern District of Louisiana, the plaintiffs asserted a claim against the defendants under the federal Commodity Exchange Act. The defendants moved to dismiss for lack of in personam adjudicatory authority. The District Court initially ruled that the defendants had sufficient contacts with the United States to justify the exercise of in personam jurisdiction and that, in the absence of a specific provision in the controlling federal act, the court could and should fashion an appropriate basis of competence. However, following a contrary ruling by the Fifth Circuit in a different case, the District Court reconsidered its earlier ruling and granted the motion to dismiss. This ruling was upheld by the Fifth Circuit, ruling *en banc*. The Supreme Court affirmed unanimously. It ruled that, in the absence of a provision for a basis of competence by Louisiana law, the federal statute under which the claim was asserted, or the Federal Rules of Civil Procedure, the federal courts should not fashion a rule of nationwide competence in the absence of congressional authorization.

NOTE

The Louisiana long-arm statute in effect when this issue was decided was patterned on the provisions of the Uniform Interstate and International Procedure Act, Art. 1, p. 284 supra. Would the Supreme Court have reached the same conclusion if Louisiana had had the California or New Jersey long-arm statute?

See also Comment, Alien Corporations and Aggregate Contacts, 95 Harv.L. Rev. 470 (1981). May such contacts be aggregated for the purpose of determining competence? De James v. Magnificence Carriers, Inc., 654 F.2d 280 (3d Cir. 1981) (ruling, in a federal question case, that only the contacts with the State, rather than aggregated national contacts, should be considered). Could this approach be of service in the state courts? See also Comment, "Doing Business," Defining State Control over Foreign Corporations, 32 Vand.L.Rev. 1105 (1979).

NOTE ON 1989 PROPOSED AMENDMENTS TO THE FEDERAL RULES

Amendments to the Federal Rules proposed on September 15, 1989, would, if adopted, substantially change existing law in a number of respects. Preliminary Draft of Proposed Amendments to the Federal Rules of Appellate Procedure and the Federal Rules of Civil Procedure published by the Committee on Rules of Practice and Procedure of the United States (September 1989). One of the proposed changes would greatly enlarge the in personam competence of federal courts in federal question cases. Proposed Rule 4(1), (2) provides that service of a summons or filing of a waiver of service is effective to establish competence over the person of any defendant against whom is asserted a claim arising under federal law unless the Constitution or an applicable federal statute requires otherwise. Proposed Rule 4(3)(i) and (ii) and (f) provide that service upon an individual may be made in any district of the United States or in a foreign country and proposed Rule 4(h) provides for similar service upon a corporation or an association. As stated in the Advisory Committee's Note to proposed Rule 4(b), the combined effect of the two proposed Rules is to extend the federal reach in cases arising under federal law to the full extent allowed by the Fifth Amendment and any applicable federal enactment.

In diversity cases governed by state law, the existing territorial limits continue to apply. The proposed amendments therefore do not propose to resolve the *Coleman* problem. Nor do they make the bulge rule available in Rule 22 interpleader.

SECTION 6. ADEQUATE NOTICE AND OPPORTUNITY TO BE HEARD

MULLANE v. CENTRAL HANOVER BANK & TRUST CO.
Supra, p. 312.

NOTES

(1) Must the notice actually given or that prescribed by the applicable statute or rule meet the due process test? See Wuchter v. Pizzutti, 276 U.S. 13, 48 S.Ct. 259, 72 L.Ed. 446 (1928), p. 240 supra. What impact on this holding has the *Szukhent* case, p. 232 supra? Under Austrian law, any notice that actually reaches the addressee is sufficient, regardless of whether it complies with the otherwise applicable rules. See International Co–Operation in Litigation: Europe 18 (Smit ed. 1965). Is the Austrian rule preferable? If not, what rule would you prefer?

(2) In in rem or quasi-in-rem cases, is service by publication always constitutionally sufficient? See Walker v. City of Hutchinson, 352 U.S. 112, 77 S.Ct. 200, 1 L.Ed.2d 178 (1956), holding unconstitutional service by publication in a condemnation proceeding. The Court said (at 116): "Measured by the principles stated in the *Mullane* case, we think that the notice by publication here falls short of the requirements of due process . . . Appellant's name was known to the city and was on the official records. Even a letter would have apprised him that his property was about to be taken and that he must appear if he wanted to be heard as to its value." To the same effect, see Schroeder v. City of New York, 371 U.S. 208, 83 S.Ct. 279, 9 L.Ed.2d 255 (1962).

(3) In in personam cases, is service by publication ever sufficient? Cf. Wis. Stat.Ann. § 262.06(c) (if with reasonable diligence the defendant cannot be served personally or by leaving the document at his usual place of abode within the state with a competent member of his family of at least 14 years of age, the summons may be served by publication and mailing). See also Sellars v. Raye, 25 A.D.2d 757, 269 N.Y.S.2d 7 (2d Dep't 1966), affirmed 18 N.Y.2d 782, 275 N.Y.S.2d 266, 221 N.E.2d 808 (1966); Smit, 1967 Report of the Administrative Board of the Judicial Conference of the State of New York 153–54 (1967).

(4) Is service by mail, or by certified mail, or by registered mail, return receipt requested, always constitutionally sufficient? Cf. Durfee v. Durfee, 293 Mass. 472, 200 N.E. 395 (1936). Does it make any difference whether the addressee is in a foreign country?

(5) In Greene v. Lindsey, 456 U.S. 444, 102 S.Ct. 1874, 72 L.Ed.2d 249 (1982), the Court held constitutionally deficient the posting of a copy of an eviction notice on the door of the defendant's apartment, but intimated that service by mail would have been sufficient. In Feinstein v. Bergner, 48 N.Y.2d 234, 422 N.Y.S.2d 356, 397 N.E.2d 1161 (1979), "nail and mail" service of process was held ineffective, even though defendant had received the mailed copy, because the process had not been affixed to defendant's residence.

(6) In order to avoid the *Wuchter* v. *Pizzuti* problem, Note (1) supra, and to ensure that all possible methods of service are made available, would you recommend enactment of a statute permitting service to be made "by all constitutionally permissible methods"? Cf. the Rhode Island long-arm statute,

p. 252 supra. In what other way can the necessary flexibility be achieved? Cf. Fed.R.Civ.P. 4(i)(1).

(7) Is notice in the prescribed form constitutionally sufficient, even if the party requesting the service knows that the addressee is illiterate or knows only a foreign language?

(8) Can the notice requirement be waived before the commencement of the action? Cf. D.H. Overmeyer v. Frick; Swarb v. Lennox, p. 234, Note (3) supra. See also Isbell v. County of Sonoma, 21 Cal.3d 61, 145 Cal.Rptr. 368, 577 P.2d 188 (1978).

———

TULSA PROFESSIONAL COLLECTION SERVICES, INC. v. POPE, 485 U.S. 478, 108 S.Ct. 1340, 99 L.Ed.2d 565 (1988), held unconstitutional an Oklahoma statute that barred claims against an estate not presented within two months after notice to creditors by publication of the commencement of probate proceedings. The Court rejected the argument that the Oklahoma provision was in the nature of a self-executing statute of limitations which had been upheld as compatible with the Due Process Clause in Texaco, Inc. v. Short, 454 U.S. 516, 102 S.Ct. 781, 70 L.Ed.2d 738 (1982).

———

A. SERVICE IN A FOREIGN COUNTRY

VOLKSWAGENWERK AKTIENGESELLSCHAFT v. SCHLUNK

Supreme Court of the United States, 1988.
486 U.S. 694, 108 S.Ct. 2104, 100 L.Ed.2d 722.

JUSTICE O'CONNOR delivered the opinion of the Court.*

This case involves an attempt to serve process on a foreign corporation by serving its domestic subsidiary which, under state law, is the foreign corporation's involuntary agent for service of process. We must decide whether such service is compatible with the Convention on Service Abroad of Judicial and Extrajudicial Documents in Civil and Commercial Matters, Nov. 15, 1965 (Hague Service Convention), [1969] 20 U.S.T. 361, T.I.A.S. No. 6638.

I

The parents of respondent Herwig Schlunk were killed in an automobile accident in 1983. Schlunk filed a wrongful death action on their behalf in the Circuit Court of Cook County, Illinois. Schlunk alleged that Volkswagen of America, Inc. (VWoA) had designed and sold the automobile that his parents were driving, and that defects in the automobile caused or contributed to their deaths.

* * *

Schlunk successfully served his complaint on VWoA, and VWoA filed an answer denying that it had designed or assembled the automo-

---

* Footnotes omitted.

bile in question. Schlunk then amended the complaint to add as a defendant Volkswagen Aktiengesellschaft (VWAG), which is the petitioner here. VWAG, a corporation established under the laws of the Federal Republic of Germany, has its place of business in that country. VWoA is a wholly owned subsidiary of VWAG. Schlunk attempted to serve his amended complaint on VWAG by serving VWoA as VWAG's agent.

VWAG filed a special and limited appearance for the purpose of quashing service. VWAG asserted that it could be served only in accordance with the Hague Service Convention, and that Schlunk had not complied with the Convention's requirements. The Circuit Court denied VWAG's motion. . . . The court relied on the facts that VWoA is a wholly-owned subsidiary of VWAG, that a majority of the members of the board of directors of VWoA are members of the board of VWAG, and that VWoA is by contract the exclusive importer and distributor of VWAG products sold in the United States. The court concluded that, because service was accomplished within the United States, the Hague Service Convention did not apply.

The Circuit Court certified two questions to the Appellate Court of Illinois. The Appellate Court determined that VWoA is VWAG's agent for service of process under Illinois law, and that the service of process in this case did not violate the Hague Service Convention. . . . We granted certiorari to address this issue, 484 U.S. ___, 108 S.Ct. 226, 98 L.Ed.2d 185 (1987), which has given rise to disagreement among the lower courts. . . .

II

The Hague Service Convention is a multilateral treaty that was formulated in 1964 by the Tenth Session of the Hague Conference of Private International Law. The Convention revised parts of the Hague Conventions on Civil Procedure of 1905 and 1954. The revision was intended to provide a simpler way to serve process abroad, to assure that defendants sued in foreign jurisdictions would receive actual and timely notice of suit, and to facilitate proof of service abroad. 3 1964 Conférence de la Haye de Droit International Privé, Actes et Documents de la Dixième Session (Notification) 75–77, 363 (1965) (3 Actes et Documents); 1 B. Ristau, International Judicial Assistance (Civil and Commercial) § 4–1 (1984 and 1 Supp.1986) (1 Ristau). Representatives of all 23 countries that were members of the Conference approved the Convention without reservation. Thirty-two countries, including the United States and the Federal Republic of Germany, have ratified or acceded to the Convention. Brief for United States as *Amicus Curiae* 2, n. 2 (filed Sep. 12, 1987).

The primary innovation of the Convention is that it requires each state to establish a central authority to receive requests for service of documents from other countries. 20 U.S.T. 362, T.I.A.S. 6638, Art. 2. Once a central authority receives a request in the proper form, it must serve the documents by a method prescribed by the internal law of the receiving state or by a method designated by the requester and compatible with that law. Art. 5. The central authority must then provide a certificate of service that conforms to a specified model. Art. 6. A state also may consent to methods of service within its boundaries other than a request to its central authority. Arts. 8–11, 19. The remaining provisions of the Convention that are relevant here limit the circumstances in which a default judgment may be entered against a defendant who had to be served abroad and did not appear, and provide some means for relief from such a judgment. Arts. 15, 16.

Article 1 defines the scope of the Convention, which is the subject of controversy in this case. It says: "The present Convention shall apply in all cases, in civil or commercial matters, where there is occasion to transmit a judicial or extrajudicial document for service abroad." 20 U.S.T., at 362. The equally authentic French version says, "La présente Convention est applicable, en matière civile ou commerciale, dans tous les cas où un acte judiciaire ou extrajudiciaire doit être transmis à l'étranger pour y être signifié ou notifié." Ibid. This language is mandatory, as we acknowledged last Term in Société Nationale Industrielle Aerospaciale v. United States District Court, 482 U.S. ___, ___, n. 15, 107 S.Ct. 2542, 2550, n. 15, 96 L.Ed.2d 461 (1987). By virtue of the Supremacy Clause, U.S. Const., Art. VI, the Convention pre-empts inconsistent methods of service prescribed by state law in all cases to which it applies. Schlunk does not purport to have served his complaint on VWAG in accordance with the Convention. Therefore, if service of process in this case falls within Article I of the Convention, the trial court should have granted VWAG's motion to quash. . . . The Convention does not specify the circumstances in which there is "occasion to transmit" a complaint "for service abroad." But at least the term "service of process" has a well-established technical meaning. Service of process refers to a formal delivery of documents that is legally sufficient to charge the defendant with notice of a pending action. 1 Ristau § 4–5(2), p. 123 (interpreting the Convention); Black's Law Dictionary 1227 (5th ed. 1979); see 4 C. Wright & A. Miller, Federal Practice and Procedure § 1063, p. 225 (2d ed. 1987). The legal sufficiency of a formal delivery of documents must be measured against some standard. The Convention does not prescribe a standard, so we almost necessarily must refer to the internal law of the forum state. If the internal law of the forum state defines the applicable method of serving process as requiring the transmittal of documents abroad, then the Hague Service Convention applies.

The negotiating history supports our view that Article I refers to service of process in the technical sense. . . .

The negotiating history of the Convention also indicates that whether there is service abroad must be determined by reference to the law of the forum state.

*　*　*

Nor are we persuaded that the general purposes of the Convention require a different conclusion.

*　*　*

Furthermore, nothing that we say today prevents compliance with the Convention even when the internal law of the forum does not so require. The Convention provides simple and certain means by which to serve process on a foreign national. Those who eschew its procedures risk discovering that the forum's internal law required transmittal of documents for service abroad, and that the Convention therefore provided the exclusive means of valid service. In addition, parties that comply with the Convention ultimately may find it easier to enforce their judgments abroad. See Westin, Enforcing Foreign Commercial Judgments and Arbitral Awards in the United States, West Germany, and England, Law & Policy Int'l Bus. 325, 340–341 (1987). For these reasons, we anticipate that parties may resort to the Convention voluntarily, even in cases that fall outside the scope of its mandatory application.

III

In this case, the Illinois long-arm statute authorized Schlunk to serve VWAG by substituted service on VWoA, without sending documents to Germany. See Ill.Rev.Stat., ch. 110, ¶ 2–209(a)(1) (1985). VWAG has not petitioned for review of the Illinois Appellate Court's holding that service was proper as a matter of Illinois law. VWAG contends, however, that service on VWAG was not complete until VWoA transmitted the complaint to VWAG in Germany. According to VWAG, this transmission constituted service abroad under the Hague Service Convention.

VWAG explains that, as a practical matter, VWoA was certain to transmit the complaint to Germany to notify VWAG of the litigation. Indeed, as a legal matter, the Due Process Clause requires every method of service to provide "notice reasonably calculated, under all the circumstances, to apprise interested parties of the pendency of the action and afford them an opportunity to present their objections." Mullane v. Central Hanover Bank & Trust Co., 339 U.S. 306, 314, 70 S.Ct. 652, 657, 94 L.Ed. 865 (1950). VWAG argues that, because of this notice requirement, every case involving service on a foreign national will present an "occasion to transmit a judicial . . . document for service abroad" within the meaning of Article 1. Tr. of Oral Arg. 8. VWAG emphasizes that in this case, the Appellate Court upheld service only after determining that "the relationship between VWAG and VWoA is so close that it is certain that VWAG 'was fully apprised of the pendency of the action' by delivery of the summons to VWoA." 145 Ill.App.3d 594, 606, 105 Ill.Dec. 39, 47, 503 N.E.2d 1045, 1053 (1986) (quoting Maunder v. DeHavilland Aircraft of Canada, Ltd., 102 Ill.2d 342, 353, 80 Ill.Dec. 765, 771, 466 N.E.2d 217, 223, cert. denied, 469 U.S. 1036, 105 S.Ct. 511, 83 L.Ed.2d 401 (1984).

We reject this argument. Where service on a domestic agent is valid and complete under both state law and the Due Process Clause, our inquiry ends and the Convention has no further implications. Whatever internal, private communications take place between the agent and a foreign principal are beyond the concerns of this case. The only transmittal to which the Convention applies is a transmittal abroad that is required as a necessary part of service. And, contrary to VWAG's assertion, the Due Process Clause does not require an official transmittal of documents abroad every time there is service on a foreign national. Applying this analysis, we conclude that this case does not present an occasion to transmit a judicial document for service abroad within the meaning of Article 1. Therefore the Hague Service Convention does not apply, and service was proper. The judgment of the Appellate Court is

Affirmed.

JUSTICE BRENNAN, with whom JUSTICE MARSHALL and JUSTICE BLACKMUN join, concurring in the judgment.

NOTE

Is the text of the Convention as mandatory as the Supreme Court finds? Would a ruling that the Convention is not exclusive have afforded greater flexibility? See also Société Nationale Industrielle Aérospatiale v. U.S. District Court of Southern District, Iowa, 482 U.S. 522, 107 S.Ct. 2542, 96 L.Ed.2d 461 (1987), p. 744, infra.

NOTE ON PROPOSED 1989 AMENDMENTS TO THE FEDERAL RULES

The 1989 Proposed Amendments, p. 329 supra, would also change the provisions relating to service on a person in a foreign country. Apart from codifying the result reached in *Schlunk,* they would impose on the methods of service now permitted by Rule 4(i) the requirements that the service be reasonably calculated to give notice and that service by personal delivery, by registered mail, return receipt requested, or by a diplomatic or consular officer not be prohibited by foreign law. Are these requirements desirable? The United States Commission on International Rules of Judicial Procedure, which developed Rule 4(i), rejected proposals to impose these requirements. Why?

SECTION 7. VENUE AND FORUM NON CONVENIENS

Read 28 U.S.C.A. §§ 1391–92

NOTES

(1) Once the court has adjudicatory power over the subject matter and the parties or the thing, why should it also have to meet the requirements of venue? Do venue rules serve the same purpose within the state—namely, to identify the proper place of adjudication—that in personam and in rem rules of adjudicatory power serve within the interstate or international arena? If so, why are these rules not the same? Note particularly that both the federal and the New York venue rules permit venue to be laid in the court of the plaintiff's

residence. Note also that there are many special rules that permit venue to be laid in additional places. See, e.g., 15 U.S.C.A. § 77 (1963) (in actions under the securities laws, venue may be laid in any district wherein the defendant is found or is an inhabitant or transacts business, or in the district where the offer or sale took place); 15 U.S.C.A. § 22 (1963) (in actions against a corporation under the antitrust laws, "in the judicial district whereof it is an inhabitant, but also in any district wherein it may be found or transacts business") 28 U.S.C.A. § 1400(a) (1962) (in copyright actions, where the defendant resides or may be found). See also ALI, Study of the Division of Jurisdiction Between State and Federal Courts, Appendix F, at 498–501 (1969); Barrett, Venue and Service of Process in the Federal Courts—Suggestion for Reform, 7 Vand.L.Rev. 608 (1954).

(2) State venue rules also show a great variety. Stevens, Venue Statutes: Diagnosis and Proposed Cure, 49 Mich.L.Rev. 307 (1951) lists "some thirteen different fact situations upon which venue statutes are predicated": "A. Where the subject of action or part thereof is situated . . . B. Where the cause of action, or part thereof arose or accrued . . . C. Where some fact is present or happened . . . D. Where the defendant resides . . . E. Where the defendant is doing business . . . F. Where the defendant has an office or place of business, or an agent, or representative, or where an agent or officer of defendant resides . . . G. Where the plaintiff resides . . . H. Where the plaintiff is doing business . . . I. Where the defendant may be found . . . J. Where the defendant may be summoned or served . . . K. In the county designated in the plaintiff's complaint . . . L. In any county . . . M. Where the seat of government is located . . . " Which of these criteria make sense? See also, Venue Statutes in the Forty–Eight States, First Preliminary Report, Advisory Committee on Practice and Procedure, N.Y.Leg.Doc. No. 6(b), at 497 (1957).

(3) On problems of construction of venue provisions, see Comment, Federal Venue: Locating the Place Where the Claim Arose, 54 Tex.L.Rev. 392 (1976); Sunstein, Participation, Public Law and Venue Reform, 49 U.Chi.L.Rev. 976 (1982).

PIPER AIRCRAFT COMPANY v. REYNO

Supreme Court of the United States, 1981.
454 U.S. 235, 102 S.Ct. 252, 70 L.Ed.2d 419.

JUSTICE MARSHALL delivered the opinion of the court.*

These cases arise out of an air crash that took place in Scotland. Respondent, acting as representative of the estates of several Scottish citizens killed in the accident, brought wrongful death actions against petitioners in the United States District Court for the Middle District of Pennsylvania. Petitioners moved to dismiss on the ground of *forum non conveniens*. After noting that an alternative forum existed in Scotland, the District Court granted their motions. Reyno v. Piper

* Most footnotes omitted; those remaining renumbered.

Aircraft Co., 479 F.Supp. 727 (MD Pa.1979). The United States Court of Appeals for the Third Circuit reversed. Reyno v. Piper Aircraft Co., 630 F.2d 149 (CA3 1980). The Court of Appeals based its decision, at least in part, on the ground that dismissal is automatically barred where the law of the alternative forum is less favorable to the plaintiff than the law of the forum chosen by the plaintiff. Because we conclude that the possibility of an unfavorable change in law should not, by itself, bar dismissal, and because we conclude that the District Court did not otherwise abuse its discretion, we reverse.

I

A

In July 1976, a small commercial aircraft crashed in the Scottish highlands during the course of a charter flight from Blackpool to Perth. The pilot and five passengers were killed instantly. The decedents were all Scottish subjects and residents, as are their heirs and next of kin. There were no eyewitnesses to the accident. At the time of the crash the plane was subject to Scottish air traffic control.

The aircraft, a twin engine Piper Aztec, was manufactured in Pennsylvania by petitioner Piper Aircraft Company ("Piper"). The propellers were manufactured in Ohio by petitioner Hartzell Propeller, Inc. ("Hartzell"). At the time of the crash the aircraft was registered in Great Britain and was owned and maintained by Air Navigation and Trading Co., Ltd. ("Air Navigation"). It was operated by McDonald Aviation, Ltd. ("McDonald"), a Scottish air taxi service. Both Air Navigation and McDonald were organized in the United Kingdom. The wreckage of the plane is now in a hangar in Farnsborough, England.

The British Department of Trade investigated the accident several months after it occurred. . . .

The Review Board found no evidence of defective equipment and indicated that pilot error may have contributed to the accident. The pilot, who had obtained his commercial pilot's license only three months earlier, was flying over high ground at an altitude considerably lower than the minimum height required by his company's operations manual.

In July 1977, a California probate court appointed respondent Gaynell Reyno administratrix of the estates of the five passengers. Reyno is not related to and does not know any of the decedents or their survivors; she was a legal secretary to the attorney who filed this lawsuit. Several days after her appointment, Reyno commenced separate wrongful death actions against Piper and Hartzell in the Superior Court of California, claiming negligence and strict liability. Air Navigation, McDonald, and the estate of the pilot are not parties to this litigation. The survivors of the five passengers whose estates are represented by Reyno filed a separate action in the United Kingdom against Air Navigation, McDonald, and the pilot's estate. Reyno candidly admits that the action against Piper and Hartzell was filed in the United States because its laws regarding liability, capacity to sue, and damages are more favorable to her position than are those of Scotland. Scottish law does not recognize strict liability in tort. Moreover, it permits wrongful death actions only when brought by a decedent's relatives. The relatives may sue only for "loss of support and society."

On petitioners' motion, the suit was removed to the United States District Court for the Central District of California. Piper then moved for transfer to the United States District Court for the Middle District of Pennsylvania, pursuant to 28 U.S.C. § 1404(a). Hartzell moved to dismiss for lack of personal jurisdiction, or in the alternative, to transfer. In December 1977, the District Court quashed service on Hartzell and transferred the case to the Middle District of Pennsylvania. Respondent then properly served process on Hartzell.

B

In May 1978, after the suit had been transferred, both Hartzell and Piper moved to dismiss the action on the ground of *forum non conveniens*. The District Court granted these motions in October 1979. It relied on the balancing test set forth by this Court in Gulf Oil Corporation v. Gilbert, 330 U.S. 501, 67 S.Ct. 839, 91 L.Ed. 1055 (1947) and its companion case, Koster v. Lumbermen's Mut. Cas. Co., 330 U.S. 518, 67 S.Ct. 828, 91 L.Ed. 1067 (1947). . . .

After describing our decisions in *Gilbert* and *Koster,* the District Court analyzed the facts of this case. It began by observing that an alternative forum existed in Scotland; Piper and Hartzell had agreed to submit to the jurisdiction of the Scottish courts and to waive any statute of limitations defense that might be available. It then stated that plaintiff's choice of forum was entitled to little weight. The court recognized that a plaintiff's choice ordinarily deserves substantial deference. It noted, however, that Reyno "is a representative of foreign citizens and residents seeking a forum in the United States because of the more liberal rules concerning products liability law," and that "the courts have been less solicitous when the plaintiff is not an American citizen or resident, and particularly, when the foreign citizens seek to benefit from the more liberal tort rules provided for the protection of citizens and residents of the United States." Reyno v. Piper Aircraft Co., 479 F.Supp. 727, 731 (MD Pa.1979).

The District Court next examined several factors relating to the private interests of the litigants, and determined that these factors strongly pointed towards Scotland as the appropriate forum. Although evidence concerning the design, manufacture, and testing of the plane and propeller is located in the United States, the connections with Scotland are otherwise "overwhelming." Id., at 732. The real parties in interest are citizens of Scotland, as were all the decedents. Witnesses who could testify regarding the maintenance of the aircraft, the training of the pilot, and the investigation of the accident—all essential to the defense—are in Great Britain. Moreover, all witnesses to damages are located in Scotland. Trial would be aided by familiarity with Scottish topography, and by easy access to the wreckage.

The District Court reasoned that because crucial witnesses and evidence were beyond the reach of compulsory process, and because the defendants would not be able to implead potential Scottish third-party defendants, it would be "unfair to make Piper and Hartzell proceed to trial in this forum." Id., at 733. The survivors had brought separate actions in Scotland against the pilot, McDonald, and Air Navigation. "[I]t would be fairer to all parties and less costly if the entire case was presented to one jury with available testimony from all relevant witnesses." Ibid. Although the court recognized that if trial were held in the United States, Piper and Hartzell could file indemnity or contribution actions against the Scottish defendants, it believed that there was a significant risk of inconsistent verdicts.

The District Court concluded that the relevant public interests also pointed strongly towards dismissal. The court determined that Pennsylvania law would apply to Piper and Scottish law to Hartzell if the case were tried in the Middle District of Pennsylvania. As a result, "trial in this forum would be hopelessly complex and confusing for a jury." Id., at 734. In addition, the court noted that it was unfamiliar with Scottish law and thus would have to rely upon experts from that country. The court also found that the trial would be enormously costly and time-consuming; that it would be unfair to burden citizens with jury duty when the Middle District of Pennsylvania has little connection with the controversy; and that Scotland has a substantial interest in the outcome of the litigation.

In opposing the motions to dismiss, respondent contended that dismissal would be unfair because Scottish law was less favorable. The District Court explicitly rejected this claim. It reasoned that the possibility that dismissal might lead to an unfavorable change in the law did not deserve significant weight; any deficiency in the foreign law was a "matter to be dealt with in the foreign forum." Id., at 738.

C

On appeal, the United States Court of Appeals for the Third Circuit reversed and remanded for trial. The decision to reverse appears to be based on two alternative grounds. First, the Court held that the District Court abused its discretion in conducting the *Gilbert* analysis. Second, the Court held that dismissal is never appropriate where the law of the alternative forum is less favorable to the plaintiff.

* * *

We granted certiorari in these cases to consider the questions they raise concerning the proper application of the doctrine of *forum non conveniens*. 450 U.S. 909, 101 S.Ct. 1346, 67 L.Ed.2d 333 (1981).

II

The Court of Appeals erred in holding that plaintiffs may defeat a motion to dismiss on the ground of *forum non conveniens* merely by showing that the substantive law that would be applied in the alternative forum is less favorable to the plaintiffs than that of the present forum. The possibility of a change in substantive law should ordinarily not be given conclusive or even substantial weight in the *forum non conveniens* inquiry.

*   *   *

It is true that *Canada Malting* was decided before *Gilbert,* and that the doctrine of *forum non conveniens* was not fully crystallized until our decision in that case.[1] However, *Gilbert* in no way affects the validity of *Canada Malting.* Indeed, by holding that the central focus of the *forum non conveniens* inquiry is convenience, *Gilbert* implicitly recognized that dismissal may not be barred solely because of the possibility of an unfavorable change in law. Under *Gilbert,* dismissal will ordinarily be appropriate where trial in the plaintiff's chosen forum imposes a heavy burden on the defendant or the court, and where the plaintiff is unable to offer any specific reasons of convenience supporting his choice. If substantial weight were given to the possibility of an unfavorable change in law, however, dismissal might be barred even where trial in the chosen forum was plainly inconvenient.

The Court of Appeals' decision is inconsistent with this Court's earlier *forum non conveniens* decisions in another respect. Those decisions have repeatedly emphasized the need to retain flexibility. In *Gilbert,* the Court refused to identify specific circumstances "which will justify or require either grant or denial of remedy." *Gilbert,* supra, 330 U.S. at 508, 67 S.Ct., at 843. Similarly, in *Koster,* the Court rejected the contention that where a trial would involve inquiry into the internal affairs of a foreign corporation, dismissal was always appropriate. "That is one, but only one, factor which may show convenience." *Koster,* supra, 330 U.S. at 527, 67 S.Ct., at 833. And in Williams v. Green Bay & Western R., 326 U.S. 549, 557, 66 S.Ct. 284, 288, 90 L.Ed. 311 (1946), we stated that we would "not lay down a rigid rule to govern

1. The doctrine of *forum non conveniens* has a long history. It originated in Scotland, see Braucher, The Inconvenient Federal Forum, 60 Harv.L.Rev. 908, 909–911 (1947), and became part of the common law of many states, see id., at 911–912; Blair, The Doctrine of Forum Non Conveniens in Anglo–American Law, 29 Colum.L.Rev. 1 (1929). The doctrine was also frequently applied in federal admiralty actions. See, e.g., Canada Malting Co. v. Paterson Steamships, Ltd., 285 U.S. 413, 52 S.Ct. 413, 76 L.Ed. 837 (1932); see also Bickel, The Doctrine of Forum Non Conveniens As Applied in the Federal Courts in Matters of Admiralty, 35 Cornell L.Q. 12 (1949). In Williams v. Green Bay & Western R., 326 U.S. 549, 66 S.Ct. 284, 90 L.Ed. 311 (1946), the Court first indicated that motions to dismiss on grounds of *forum non conveniens* could be made in federal diversity actions. The doctrine became firmly established when *Gilbert* and *Koster* were decided one year later.

In previous *forum non conveniens* decisions, the Court has left unresolved the question whether under Erie R. v. Tompkins, 304 U.S. 64, 58 S.Ct. 817, 82 L.Ed. 118 (1938), state or federal law of *forum non conveniens* applies in a diversity case. *Gilbert,* supra, 330 U.S. at 509, 67 S.Ct., at 843; *Koster,* supra, 330 U.S. at 529, 67 S.Ct., at 834; Williams v. Green Bay & Western R., supra, 326 U.S. at 551, 558–559, 66 S.Ct., at 288–89 (1946). The Court did not decide this issue because the same result would have been reached in each case under federal or state law. The lower courts in this case reached the same conclusion: Pennsylvania and California law on *forum non conveniens* dismissals are virtually identical to federal law. See Reyno v. Piper Aircraft Co., 630 F.2d 149, 158 (CA3 1980). This, here also, we need not resolve the *Erie* question.

discretion," and that "each case turns on its facts." If central emphasis were placed on any one factor, the *forum non conveniens* doctrine would lose much of the very flexibility that makes it so valuable.

In fact, if conclusive or substantial weight were given to the possibility of a change in law, the *forum non conveniens* doctrine would become virtually useless. Jurisdiction and venue requirements are often easily satisfied. As a result, many plaintiffs are able to choose from among several forums. Ordinarily, these plaintiffs will select that forum whose choice of law rules are most advantageous. Thus, if the possibility of an unfavorable change in substantive law is given substantial weight in the *forum non conveniens* inquiry, dismissal would rarely be proper.

Except for the court below, every federal court of appeals that has considered this question after *Gilbert* has held that dismissal on grounds of *forum non conveniens* may be granted even though the law applicable in the alternative forum is less favorable to the plaintiff's chance of recovery. See, e.g., Pain v. United Technologies Corp., 205 U.S.App.D.C. 229, 248–249, 637 F.2d 775, 794–795 (CADC 1980); . . .

The Court of Appeals' approach is not only inconsistent with the purpose of the *forum non conveniens* doctrine, but also poses substantial practical problems. If the possibility of a change in law were given substantial weight, deciding motions to dismiss on the ground of *forum non conveniens* would become quite difficult. Choice-of-law analysis would become extremely important, and the courts would frequently be required to interpret the law of foreign jurisdictions. First, the trial court would have to determine what law would apply if the case were tried in the chosen forum, and what law would apply if the case were tried in the alternative forum. It would then have to compare the rights, remedies, and procedures available under the law that would be applied in each forum. Dismissal would be appropriate only if the court concluded that the law applied by the alternative forum is as favorable to the plaintiff as that of the chosen forum. The doctrine of *forum non conveniens,* however, is designed in part to help courts avoid conducting complex exercises in comparative law. As we stated in *Gilbert,* the public interest factors point towards dismissal where the court would be required to "untangle problems in conflict of laws, and in law foreign to itself." *Gilbert,* supra, 330 U.S. at 509, 67 S.Ct., at 843.

Upholding the decision of the Court of Appeals would result in other practical problems. At least where the foreign plaintiff named an American manufacturer as defendant, a court could not dismiss the case on grounds of *forum non conveniens* where dismissal might lead to an unfavorable change in law. The American courts, which are already extremely attractive to foreign plaintiffs,[2] would become even

---

2. First, all but six of the 50 American states—Delaware, Massachusetts, Michigan, North Carolina, Virginia, and Wyoming—offer strict liability. 1 CCH Prod. Liab.Rep. § 4016. Rules roughly equivalent to American strict liability are effective in France, Belgium, and Luxembourg. West Germany and Japan have a strict liability statute for pharmaceuticals. However, strict liability remains primarily an American innovation. Second, the tort plaintiff may choose, at least potentially,

more attractive. The flow of litigation into the United States would
increase and further congest already crowded courts.[3]

* * *

We do not hold that the possibility of an unfavorable change in law
should *never* be a relevant consideration in a *forum non conveniens*
inquiry. Of course, if the remedy provided by the alternative forum is
so clearly inadequate or unsatisfactory that it is no remedy at all, the
unfavorable change in law may be given substantial weight; the
district court may conclude that dismissal would not be in the interests
of justice.[4] In this case, however, the remedies that would be provided
by the Scottish courts do not fall within this category. Although the
relatives of the decedents may not be able to rely on a strict liability
theory, and although their potential damage award may be smaller,
there is no danger that they will be deprived of any remedy or treated
unfairly.

from among 50 jurisdictions if he decides
to file suit in the United States. Each of
these jurisdictions applies its own set of
malleable choice-of-law rules. Third, jury
trials are almost always available in the
United States, while they are never provided in civil law jurisdictions. G. Gloss,
Comparative Law 12 (1979); J. Merryman,
The Civil Law Tradition 121 (1969). Even
in the United Kingdom, most civil actions
are not tried before a jury. W. Keeton,
The United Kingdom: The Development of
its Laws and Constitution 309 (1955).
Fourth, unlike most foreign jurisdictions,
American courts allow contingent attorney's fees, and do not tax losing parties
with their opponents' attorney's fees. R.
Schlesinger, Comparative Law: Cases,
Text, Materials 275–277 (3d ed. 1970); Or-
ban, supra, at 393. Fifth, discovery is
more extensive in American than in foreign courts. R. Schlesinger, supra, at 307,
310 and n. 33.

3. In holding that the possibility of a
change in law unfavorable to the plaintiff
should not be given substantial weight, we
also necessarily hold that the possibility of
a change in law favorable to defendant
should not be considered. Respondent suggests that Piper and Hartzell filed the motion to dismiss, not simply because trial in
the United States would be inconvenient,
but also because they believe the laws of
Scotland are more favorable. She argues
that this should be taken into account in
the analysis of the private interests. We
recognize, of course, that Piper and Hartzell may be engaged in reverse forum-shopping. However, this possibility ordinarily
should not enter into a trial court's analy-

sis of the private interests. If the defendant is able to overcome the presumption
in favor of plaintiff by showing that trial in
the chosen forum would be unnecessarily
burdensome, dismissal is appropriate—regardless of the fact that defendant may
also be motivated by a desire to obtain a
more favorable forum. Cf. Klockener
Reederei and Kohlenhandel v. A/S
Hakedal, 210 F.2d 754, 757 (C.A.2), cert.
dismissed by stipulation, 348 U.S. 801, 75
S.Ct. 17, 99 L.Ed. 633 (1954) (defendant not
entitled to dismissal on grounds of forum
non conveniens solely because the law of
the original forum is less favorable to him
than the law of the alternative forum).

4. At the outset of any *forum non conveniens* inquiry, the court must determine
whether there exists an alternative forum.
Ordinarily, this requirement will be satisfied when the defendant is "amenable to
process" in the other jurisdiction. *Gilbert,*
supra 330 U.S. at 506–507, 67 S.Ct., at 842.
In rare circumstances, however, where the
remedy offered by the other forum is clearly unsatisfactory, the other forum may not
be an adequate alternative, and the initial
requirement may not be satisfied. Thus,
for example, dismissal would not be appropriate where the alternative forum does
not permit litigation of the subject matter
of the dispute. Cf. Phoenix Canada Oil Co.
Ltd. v. Texaco, Inc., 78 F.R.D. 445 (DC Del.
1978) (court refuses to dismiss, where alternative forum is Ecuador, it is unclear
whether Ecuadorian tribunal will hear the
case, and there is no generally codified
Ecuadorian legal remedy for the unjust
enrichment and tort claims asserted).

III

The Court of Appeals also erred in rejecting the District Court's *Gilbert* analysis. The Court of Appeals stated that more weight should have been given to the plaintiff's choice of forum, and criticized the District Court's analysis of the private and public interests. However, the District Court's decision regarding the deference due plaintiff's choice of forum was appropriate. Furthermore, we do not believe that the District Court abused its discretion in weighing the private and public interests.

A

The District Court acknowledged that there is ordinarily a strong presumption in favor of the plaintiff's choice of forum, which may be overcome only when the private and public interest factors clearly point towards trial in the alternative forum. It held, however, that the presumption applies with less force when the plaintiff or real parties in interest are foreign.

The District Court's distinction between resident or citizen plaintiffs and foreign plaintiffs is fully justified. . . .

B

The *forum non conveniens* determination is committed to the sound discretion of the trial court. It may be reversed only when there has been a clear abuse of discretion; where the court has considered all relevant public and private interest factors, and where its balancing of these factors is reasonable, its decision deserves substantial deference. . . . In examining the District Court's analysis of the public and private interests, however, the Court of Appeals seems to have lost sight of this rule, and substituted its own judgment for that of the District Court.

 . . . the District Court did not act unreasonably in concluding that fewer evidentiary problems would be posed if the trial were held in Scotland. A large proportion of the relevant evidence is located in Great Britian.

* * *

The Court of Appeals found that the problems of proof could not be given any weight because Piper and Hartzell failed to describe with specificity the evidence they would not be able to obtain if trial were held in the United States. . . . Such detail is not necessary.

 . . . Our examination of the record convinces us that sufficient information was provided here. Both Piper and Hartzell submitted affidavits describing the evidentiary problems they would face if the trial were held in the United States.

The District Court correctly concluded that the problems posed by the inability to implead potential third party defendants clearly supported holding the trial in Scotland. Joinder of the pilot's estate, Air Navigation, and McDonald is crucial to the presentation of petitioners' defense. . . . The Court of Appeals rejected this argument. Forcing petitioners to rely on actions for indemnity or contributions would be "burdensome" but not "unfair." Reyno v. Piper Aircraft Co., 630 F.2d 149, 162 (CA3 1980). Finding that trial in the plaintiff's chosen forum would be burdensome, however, is sufficient to support dismissal on grounds of *forum non conveniens.*

(2)

The District Court's review of the factors relating to the public interest was also reasonable. . . .

. . . The American interest in this accident is simply not sufficient to justify the enormous commitment of judicial time and resources that would inevitably be required if the case were to be tried here.

IV

The Court of Appeals erred in holding that the possibility of an unfavorable change in law bars dismissal on the ground of *forum non conveniens.* It also erred in rejecting the District Court's *Gilbert* analysis. The District Court properly decided that the presumption in favor of the respondent's forum choice applied with less than maximum force because the real parties in interest are foreign. It did not act unreasonably in deciding that the private interests pointed towards trial in Scotland. Nor did it act unreasonably in deciding that the public interests favored trial in Scotland. Thus, the judgment of the Court of Appeals is

Reversed.

JUSTICE POWELL took no part in the decision of this case.

JUSTICE O'CONNOR took no part in the consideration or decision of this case.

JUSTICE WHITE, concurring in part and dissenting in part.

I join Parts I and II of the Court's opinion. However, like Justice Brennan and Justice Stevens, I would not proceed to deal with the issues addressed in Part III. To that extent, I am in dissent.

JUSTICE STEVENS, with whom JUSTICE BRENNAN joins, dissenting.

In No. 80–848, only one question is presented for review to this Court:

> "Whether, in an action in federal district court brought by foreign plaintiffs against American defendants, the plaintiffs may defeat a motion to dismiss on the ground of *forum non conveniens* merely by showing that the substantive law that would be applied if the case were litigated in the district court is more favorable to them than the law that would be applied by the courts of their own nation." Pet. for Cert. in No. 80–848, p. i.

In No. 80 883, the Court limited its grant of certiorari, see 450 U.S. 909, 101 S.Ct. 1346, 67 L.Ed.2d 33, to the same question:

"Must a motion to dismiss on grounds of *forum non conveniens* be denied whenever the law of the alternate forum is less favorable to recovery than that which would be applied by the district court?" Pet. for Cert. in No. 80–883, p. i.

I agree that this question should be answered in the negative. Having decided that question, I would simply remand the case to the Court of Appeals for further consideration of the question whether the District Court correctly decided that Pennsylvania was not a convenient forum in which to litigate a claim against a Pennsylvania company that a plan was defectively designed and manufactured in Pennsylvania.

NOTES

(1) Is the forum in which the plaintiff or defendant is domiciled necessarily convenient? In Silver v. Great American Insurance Co., 29 N.Y.2d 356, 328 N.Y.S.2d 398, 278 N.E.2d 619 (1972), the New York Court of Appeals, rejecting contrary lower court decisions, ruled that the plaintiff's domicile in New York did not necessarily render New York a convenient forum. This decision followed upon a recommendation to the New York legislature, which was not adopted, that the CPLR be amended to provide that neither the plaintiff's nor the defendant's domicile in New York is necessarily decisive. Smit, 1967 Report of the Administrative Board of the New York Judicial Conference 136–38.

(2) In Islamic Republic of Iran v. Pahlavi, 62 N.Y.2d 474, 478 N.Y.S.2d 597, 467 N.E.2d 245 (1984), the New York Court of Appeals dismissed an action brought by Iran against the former Shah to recover 35 billion dollars for alleged misappropriation, embezzlement, and conversion, despite the fact that, as asserted by plaintiff, there was no alternate forum in which the action could be brought.

(3) Are the recent expansions of bases of adjudicatory power likely to increase application of the forum non conveniens doctrine? Compare Smit, 1967 Report of the Administrative Board of the New York Judicial Conference 130, 139 (1967) with Morley, Forum Non Conveniens: Restraining Long–Arm Jurisdiction, 68 Nw.U.L.Rev. 24 (1973).

(4) Rather than dismiss, the court may elect to stay the local proceedings in order to permit the parties to go forward in another forum. See, e.g., Wis.Stat. Ann. Tit. 25, § 262.19:

     *   *   *

(5) May the more convenient forum be in the same place as the inconvenient forum? In Mottolese v. Kaufman, 176 F.2d 301 (2d Cir.1949), the federal court stayed a derivative stockholders' action in order to permit the parties to proceed in the state court first. The order was conditioned upon the defendants' consent to permit as full pre-trial discovery in the state court as would be available in the federal court. See also P. Beiersdorf & Co. v. McGohey, 187 F.2d 14 (2d Cir.1951); Note, Advisability of Withholding Decision in Federal Court Pending State Court's Interpretation of Unsettled State Law, 25 Ind.L.J. 316 (1950). See also P. Beiersdorf & Co. v. McGohey, 187 F.2d 14 (2d Cir.1951). But cf. England v. Louisiana State Board of Medical Examiners, 375 U.S. 411, 430 n. 2, 84 S.Ct. 461, 472 n. 2, 11 L.Ed.2d 440 (1964) (Douglas, J. concurring) ("Some federal courts have used the doctrine to shuttle over to state courts cases properly in the federal court yet not involving constitutional issues dependent on the meaning of state law (citing *Mottolese* and *Beiersdorf*)—

decisions which baldly deny a suitor the remedy granted by Congress because it is not convenient to the district judge to decide the case.")

(6) May the more convenient court enjoin a party from proceeding in the inconvenient forum? See, e.g., Delaware L. & W.R. v. Ashelman, 300 Pa. 291, 150 A. 475 (1930) (injunction denied, since there was no showing that the defendants were prompted by fraud or by the desire to embarrass or oppress or to evade the local laws). See generally Note, State Injunction of Proceedings in Federal Courts, 75 Yale L.J. 150 (1965); Comment, Forum Non Conveniens, Injunctions Against Suit and Full Faith and Credit, 29 U.Chi.L.Rev. 740 (1962); Comment, Injunctions Against Suits in Foreign Jurisdictions, 10 La.L.Rev. 302 (1950). What is the position of the parties if the inconvenient forum, on a different balancing of the conveniences, issues a counterinjunction? See James v. Grand Trunk Western Railway Co., 14 Ill.2d 356, 152 N.E.2d 858 (1958).

(7) In the federal courts, the inconvenient forum may transfer the proceedings directly to the more convenient forum. See 28 U.S.C.A. § 1404(a).

(8) Restatement (Second) of Conflict of Laws § 84, Comment d, at 252 (1971) states:

> "*Internal affairs of foreign corporation.* At one time, it was customary for the courts to evince strong reluctance to interfere with the 'internal affairs' of a corporation that had been incorporated in another state. On this basis, stockholders' suits against foreign corporations were frequently dismissed in situations where the alleged wrong affected plaintiff solely in his capacity as a member of the corporation. This doctrine enjoys less force at the present time. The fact that the suit involves the internal affairs of a foreign corporation is held by the courts today to be but one of the factors to be considered in determining whether the forum selected is an appropriate one for the suit."

(9) On the problem addressed in the *Piper Aircraft* case, see also Comment, Forum Non Conveniens and American Plaintiffs in the Federal Courts, 47 U.Chi.L.Rev. 373 (1980).

IN RE UNION CARBIDE CORPORATION GAS PLANT DISASTER AT BHOPAL, INDIA IN DECEMBER, 1984

United States Court of Appeals, Second Circuit, 1987.
809 F.2d 195.

[In December, 1984, lethal gas escaped from a chemical plant operated by Union Carbide India Limited (UCIL). More than 2,000 persons were killed and hundreds of thousands injured. Shortly thereafter, some 145 actions were commenced by victims of the disaster in United States district courts against Union Carbide Corporation (UCC), a Connecticut corporation. A few months later, the Union of India (UOI) enacted the Bhopal Gas Leak Disaster (Processing of Claims) Act, which gave the Indian government the exclusive right to represent the victims. The Indian government then commenced an action on behalf of all of the victims in the United States District Court for the Southern District of New York. Under multi-district procedures, that court was designated the court for resolution of all the federal actions.

UCC moved to dismiss the complaints of the individual Indian plaintiffs as well as UOI on the ground of *forum non conveniens.*

The district judge, after settlement negotiations had failed because of UOI's refusal to endorse the settlement tentatively reached with the individual plaintiffs, granted the motion on the condition that UCC (1) consent to the adjudicatory authority of India and waive defenses based on statutes of limitation, (2) agree to satisfy any judgment by the Indian courts in final instance, provided that judgment would "comport with minimal requirements of due process", and (3) make itself subject to discovery under the U.S. Federal Rules of Civil Procedure.

The Second Circuit affirmed the dismissal, but modified the latter two conditions.]

MANSFIELD, CIRCUIT JUDGE.

In requiring that UCC consent to enforceability of an Indian judgment against it, the district court proceeded at least in part on the erroneous assumption that, absent such a requirement, the plaintiffs, if they should succeed in obtaining an Indian judgment against UCC, might not be able to enforce it against UCC in the United States. The law, however, is to the contrary. . . .

UCC contends that Indian courts, while providing an adequate alternative forum, do not observe due process standards that would be required as a matter of course in this country. As evidence of this apprehension it points to the haste with which the Indian court in Bhopal issued a temporary order freezing its assets throughout the world and the possibility of serious prejudice to it if the UOI is permitted to have the double and conflicting status of both plaintiff and co-defendant in the Indian court proceedings. It argues that we should protect it against such denial of due process by authorizing Judge Keenan to retain the authority, after *forum non conveniens* dismissal of the cases here, to monitor the Indian court proceedings and be available on call to rectify in some undefined way any abuses of UCC's right to due process as they might occur in India.

UCC's proposed remedy is not only impractical but evidences an abysmal ignorance of basic jurisdiction principles, so much that it borders on the frivolous. The district court's jurisdiction is limited to proceedings before it in this country. Once it dismisses those proceedings on grounds of *forum non conveniens* it ceases to have any further jurisdiction over the matter unless and until a proceeding may some day be brought to enforce here a final and conclusive Indian money judgment. . . . Any denial by the Indian courts of due process can be raised by UCC as a defense to the plaintiffs' later attempt to enforce a resulting judgment against UCC in this country.

We are concerned, however, that as it is written the district court's requirement that UCC consent to the enforcement of a final Indian judgment, which was imposed on the erroneous assumption that such a judgment might not otherwise be enforceable in the United States, may create misunderstandings and problems of construction. Although the order's provision that the judgment "comport with *minimal* requirements of due process" (emphasis supplied) probably is intended to refer to "due process" as used in the New York Foreign Country Money Judgments Law and others like it, there is the risk that it may also be interpreted as providing for a lesser standard than we would otherwise require. Since the court's condition with respect to enforceability of any final Indian judgment is predicated on an erroneous legal assumption and its "due process" language is ambiguous, and since the district court's purpose is fully served by New York's statute providing for recognition of foreign-country money judgments, it was error to impose this condition upon the parties.

We also believe that the district court erred in requiring UCC to consent (which UCC did under protest and subject to its right of appeal) to broad discovery of it by the plaintiffs under the Federal Rules of Civil Procedure when UCC is confined to the more limited discovery authorized under Indian law. We recognize that under some circumstances, such as when a moving defendant unconditionally consents thereto or no undiscovered evidence of consequence is believed to be under the control of a plaintiff or co-defendant, it may be appropriate to condition a *forum non conveniens* dismissal on the moving defendant's submission to discovery under the Federal Rules without requiring reciprocal discovery by it of the plaintiff. See, e.g., Piper Aircraft v. Reyno, supra, 454 U.S. at 257 n. 25, 102 S.Ct. at 267 n. 25 (suggesting that district courts can condition dismissal upon a defendant's agreeing to provide all relevant records); Ali v. Offshore Co., 753 F.2d 1327, 1334 n. 16 (5th Cir.1985) (same); Boskoff v. Transportes Aereos Portugueses, 17 Av.Cas. (CCH) 18,613, at 18,616 (N.D.Ill.1983) (accepting defendant's voluntary commitment to provide discovery in foreign forum according to Federal Rules). Basic justice dictates that both sides be treated equally, with each having equal access to the evidence in the possession or under the control of the other. Application of this fundamental principle in the present case is especially appropriate since the UOI, as the sovereign government of India, is expected to be a party to the Indian litigation, possibly on both sides.

For these reasons we direct that the condition with respect to the discovery of UCC under the Federal Rules of Civil Procedure be deleted without prejudice to the right of the parties to have reciprocal discovery of each other on equal terms under the Federal Rules, subject to such approval as may be required of the Indian court in which the cases will be pending. If, for instance, Indian authorities will permit mutual discovery pursuant to the Federal Rules, the district court's order, as modified in accordance with this opinion, should not be construed to bar such procedure. In the absence of such a court-sanctioned agreement, however, the parties will be limited by the applicable discovery rules of the Indian court in which the claims will be pending.

NOTES

(1) Should UCC have been required to pay costs and attorneys fees for having proposed a remedy evidencing "abysmal ignorance" and bordering "on

the frivolous"? What could have been the legal basis for imposing such a sanction?

(2) In the proceedings against UCC brought by UOI in the Indian court, after a number of decisions had been rendered on preliminary matters, the Indian judge assigned to the case was removed when it was disclosed that he was one of the plaintiffs. What influence, if any, would this occurrence have had on the recognition of an eventual Indian judgment in the United States? The Indian proceedings have resulted in a court-approved settlement.

(3) To what extent should an American court, in determining whether the American forum is convenient, take into account that the plaintiff has the benefit of a contingency fee agreement, a jury, and a more favorable law, all of which would be unavailable in the place where the claim arose?

(4) Is a federal court's decision denying a motion to dismiss on forum non conveniens grounds immediately appealable? The Second Circuit has said no (Carlenstolpe v. Merck & Co., Inc., 819 F.2d 33 (2d Cir.1987)). The Supreme Court has agreed. Van Cauwenberghe v. Biard, 486 U.S. 517, 108 S.Ct. 1945, 100 L.Ed.2d 517 (1988). Should the same answer be given if the motion to dismiss is based on a contractual forum selection clause? The Supreme Court has said yes (Lauro Lines S.R.L. v. Chasser, ___ U.S. ___, 109 S.Ct. 1976, 104 L.Ed.2d 548 (1989).

(5) In a diversity action in a federal court, is the enforceability of an exclusive forum selection clause to be determined under federal or state law? In Stewart Organization, Inc. v. Ricoh Corp., 810 F.2d 1066 (11th Cir.1987) (en banc), an Alabama dealer sought to sue a nationwide manufacturer in Alabama notwithstanding a provision in their contract that provided for "exclusive jurisdiction" of "the courts in New York City, borough of Manhattan." When the defendant invoked this provision, the plaintiff asserted that the provision was against Alabama's public policy. The Eleventh Circuit, stressing that the Alabama rule sought to protect the jurisdiction of the state courts rather than the state's citizens, ruled that federal law controlled and rendered the provision enforceable. Would it have reached the same result if it had concluded that the purpose of the Alabama rule was to protect Alabama dealers against their principals?

Read 28 U.S.C.A. § 1404

NOTES

(1) This provision was enacted shortly after the decision in Gulf Oil Corp. v. Gilbert, p. 338 supra. Can the plaintiff obtain a transfer under Section 1404(a)? See Philip Carey Manufacturing Co. v. Taylor, 286 F.2d 782 (6th Cir.1961), cert. denied 366 U.S. 948, 81 S.Ct. 1903, 6 L.Ed.2d 1242 (1961); Korbel, The Law of Federal Venue and Choice of the Most Convenient Forum, 15 Rutgers L.Rev. 607 (1961).

(2) In Hoffman v. Blaski, 363 U.S. 335, 80 S.Ct. 1084, 4 L.Ed.2d 1254 (1960), the Supreme Court, stressing the statutory words "where it might have been brought," held that transfer pursuant to Title 28, U.S.C.A. § 1404, was appropriate only if the transferee court was a court of proper venue and could properly have exercised adjudicatory power over the defendant at the time of commencement of the action in the transferor court. Subsequent waiver of the objection to improper venue in the transferee court and consent by the defendant to being sued there were held ineffective to satisfy the requirement that

the action "might have been brought" in the transferee forum. See also Comment, The Requirement of Personal Jurisdiction When Transferring an Action Under Section 1404(a), 57 Nw.U.L.Rev. 456 (1962).

(3) In Goldlawr, Inc. v. Heiman, 369 U.S. 463, 82 S.Ct. 913, 8 L.Ed.2d 39 (1962), the Supreme Court held that transfer could properly be ordered to a transferee court of proper adjudicatory power and venue by a transferor court of improper venue that lacked personal power. See also Note, Change of Venue In Absence of Personal Jurisdiction Under 28 U.S.C.A. 1404(a) and 1406(a), 30 U.Chi.L.Rev. 735 (1963); Comment, Personal Jurisdiction Requirements Under Federal Change of Venue Statutes, 1962 Wis.L.Rev. 342 (1962). This ruling was confirmed by statutes. 28 U.S.C.A. § 1631 (West Supp.1984), enacted in 1982, authorizes transfer "to cure want of jurisdiction."

(4) In Van Dusen v. Barrack, 376 U.S. 612, 84 S.Ct. 805, 11 L.Ed.2d 945 (1964), defendants in wrongful death actions sought transfer from a Pennsylvania to a Massachusetts district court. The plaintiffs, Pennsylvania fiduciaries representing the estates of Pennsylvania decedents, opposed the transfer on the ground that they were not qualified to act as fiduciaries in Massachusetts and that, consequently, their actions could not have been brought in Massachusetts. The Supreme Court held that the "might have been brought" language of Section 1404(a) referred only to venue and adjudicatory power. Accordingly, a possible lack by the Pennsylvania representatives of standing to sue in Massachusetts could not justify the conclusion that the actions might not have been brought in Massachusetts within the meaning of Section 1404(a). The plaintiffs also argued that under Rule 17(b) of the Federal Rules of Civil Procedure their standing to sue had to be determined "by the law of the state in which the district court is held", that this was the law of Massachusetts, that under that law they lacked standing to sue and that transfer, which would introduce them into a court in which they lacked capacity to act, would therefore not be "in the interest of justice." The Supreme Court held that this argument had to be considered within the framework of the broader question of what law had to be applied by the transferee court generally. It concluded that "in cases such as the present, where the defendants seek transfer, the transferee court must be obligated to apply the state law that would have been applied if there had been no change of venue" (at 639). This principle was held to require interpretation of Rule 17(b) as prescribing a similar reference to the law of the transferor state for the purpose of determining the plaintiff's standing to sue. Since the Court of Appeals had held otherwise both as to Section 1404(a) and as to Rule 17(b), its judgment was reversed.

Chapter Seven

AT THE INTERSECTION OF STATE AND FEDERAL LAW

SECTION 1. IDENTIFYING THE APPLICABLE LAW

After a court is found that has authority to entertain the dispute and possesses power over the parties, the next question that must be resolved is, what law should this court apply? To see why this is sometimes a problem, consider the following set of facts:

RULE 6.10 Any League may elect to use the Designated Hitter Rule.

* * *

(b) The Rule provides as follows: A hitter may be designated to bat for the starting pitcher and all subsequent pitchers in any game without otherwise affecting the status of the pitcher(s) in the game. A Designated Hitter for a pitcher must be selected prior to the game and must be included in the line up cards presented to the Umpire in Chief.

Official Baseball Rules (1988).

In their December 1975 meeting, the American League adopted the designated hitter as a permanent official rule. The National League decided against adopting the designated hitter rule for its use.

The Baseball Encyclopedia 2873 (7th ed. 1988).

So long as American League teams play only against each other, and National League teams do the same, the difference between the National and American League rules is of no significance. But what happens in the World Series, when the winners of the league championships compete against one another? If the National League rule is used during the Series, the American League team is disadvantaged because its pitchers have not had to bat all season. On the other hand, if the American League rule were adopted, the National League team would likely suffer because its roster is chosen for combined hitting and fielding proficiency while the American League team has members chosen solely for hitting ability. This situation raises a conflict of laws issue: two entities with the same level of legislative authority have promulgated contradictory rules to regulate the same behavior. Whichever rule is applied, one team will be disadvantaged and disappointed.

In the legal context, similar predicaments occur. Say, for example, someone dies in Florida without a will and the heirs reside in New

351

Jersey and Massachusetts. If the states have inconsistent rules of intestate succession, and use of one or the other will produce significantly different results for the parties, the court charged with distributing the estate will have to choose which state's rules to apply. Similarly, a court entertaining a tort action between a New Yorker whose car collided in Michigan with a car driven by a Californian must decide whether the significance of contributory negligence should be determined by the differing law of New York, Michigan, or California.

To resolve such disputes, the states—and major league baseball officials—usually need *choice of law* rules. These are provisions that determine which law applies when parties from different states (or leagues) interact and their relevant decisional norms are inconsistent. Baseball, for example, adopted what choice-of-law specialists call a *lex fori* rule. It provides:

> RULE 6.10(a) In the event of inter-league competition between clubs of Leagues using the Designated Hitter Rule and clubs of Leagues not using the Designated Hitter Rule, the rule will be used as follows:
>
> 1. In World Series or exhibition games, the rule will be used or not used as is the practice of the home team. . . .

Official Baseball Rules (1988).

Other traditional choice of law rules include *lex domicilii,* which is often used in estate cases, and *lex loci delicti,* which is sometimes invoked in torts cases. Some judicial systems have, however, moved away from these rigid provisions and have favored a more flexible approach that looks at the extent to which the dispute and its resolution affect the legitimate interests of the states involved. A vast body of doctrine has accumulated on these questions, and although a few cases in this chapter refer to it, this subject is treated in a separate course, usually called "Conflict of Laws."

Note that all the examples given above are similar in one important respect: the bodies promulgating the conflicting rules—the American and National Leagues on the one hand; Florida, New Jersey, Massachusetts, New York, Michigan, and California, on the other—have the same level of authority. Because of this hierarchical equivalence, these choice-of-law questions are regarded as "horizontal" conflicts. But another sort of choice-of-law issue also arises. This question, which is the primary subject of this chapter, involves the choice between state and federal law. It is called a "vertical" problem because the states and the federal government are not hierarchically equivalent. Whenever Congress enacts valid legislation, the Supremacy Clause, Article VI of the Constitution, decrees that this legislation overrides inconsistent state laws. Thus, in some respects, federal law is of higher authority than state law. At the same time, however, the Constitution created a federal government of limited power. Except for the national powers enumerated in the Constitution, the exercise of governmental authority is reserved to the states. Accordingly, in many respects, state law is of greater authority than federal law.

Congress has long recognized the need for vertical choice-of-law rules for cases litigated in federal courts. Prior to 1938, two sets of such rules had been enacted, one dealing with substantive law and the other with procedure. On the procedural side, these rules were found in the Conformity Acts, the Equity Rules of 1912, and the Admiralty Rules. As embodied in 28 U.S.C.A. § 724, the Conformity Act provided:

> The practice, pleading and forms and modes of proceedings in civil causes . . . in the district courts, shall conform, as near as may be, to the practice, pleadings, and forms and modes of proceedings existing at the time in like causes in the courts of record of State within which such district courts are held . . . ."

In other words, the federal courts were directed to imitate the procedural rules of the states in which they were located. In contrast, the substantive choice-of-law rule, found in the Rules of Decision Act, now at 28 U.S.C.A. § 1652, provided:

> The laws of the several States, except where the Constitution, treaties or statutes of the United States shall otherwise require or provide shall be regarded as rules of decision in trials at common law in the courts of the United States in cases where they apply.

This provision was first interpreted by the Supreme Court in Swift v. Tyson, 41 U.S. (16 Pet.) 1, 10 L.Ed. 865 (1842), which involved a transaction that occurred in New York. The issue in the case was whether an endorsee of a bill of exchange became a holder in due course when the bill was given in payment for a pre-existing debt. The Circuit Court of New York, applying general principles of New York commercial law, found the payment had sufficient "value" to make Swift a bona fide purchaser for value, and therefore, a holder in due course. The Supreme Court reversed. Justice Story interpreted the "laws of the several States" to mean only "enactments" (i.e., statutes) and "long established local customs." Decisional law was, "at most, only evidence of what the laws are." Accordingly, federal judges were not, in Story's view, bound to follow local decisions and could apply their own general federal common law to decide the case. Since federal common law did not regard payment of preexisting debts as value, Swift was held not to be a holder in due course.

In 1938, all this was changed. The questions of how judicial machinery functions and how court processes are administered were recognized as primarily of interest to the forum. In 1934, Congress enacted the Rules Enabling Act, the current version of which is 28 U.S. C.A. § 2072. It empowered the Supreme Court to "prescribe by general rules, the forms of process, writs, pleadings, and motions, and the practice and procedure of the district courts and courts of appeals in the United States in civil actions . . . ." The Federal Rules of Civil

Procedure, produced pursuant to this authority, were promulgated four years later.

In that same year, the following case, which revisited the substantive choice-of-law question at issue in *Swift,* was decided.

SECTION 2.   THE ERIE DECISION

ERIE RAILROAD CO. v. TOMPKINS
Supreme Court of the United States, 1938.
304 U.S. 64, 58 S.Ct. 817, 82 L.Ed. 1188, 114 A.L.R. 1487.

Certiorari to the United States Circuit Court of Appeals for the Second Circuit.

Mr. Justice Brandeis delivered the opinion of the Court.

The question for decision is whether the oft-challenged doctrine of Swift v. Tyson shall now be disapproved.

Tompkins, a citizen of Pennsylvania, was injured on a dark night by a passing freight train of the Erie Railroad Company while walking along its right of way at Hughestown in that state. He claimed that the accident occurred through negligence in the operation, or maintenance, of the train; that he was rightfully on the premises as licensee because on a commonly used beaten footpath which ran for a short distance alongside the tracks; and that he was struck by something which looked like a door projecting from one of the moving cars. To enforce that claim he brought an action in the federal court for Southern New York, which had jurisdiction because the company is a corporation of that state. It denied liability; and the case was tried by a jury.

The Erie insisted that its duty to Tompkins was no greater than that owed to a trespasser. It contended, among other things, that its duty to Tompkins, and hence its liability, should be determined in accordance with the Pennsylvania law; that under the law of Pennsylvania, as declared by its highest court, persons who use pathways along the railroad right of way—that is, a longitudinal pathway as distinguished from a crossing—are to be deemed trespassers; and that the railroad is not liable for injuries to undiscovered trespassers resulting from its negligence, unless it be wanton or willful. Tompkins denied that any such rule had been established by the decisions of the Pennsylvania courts; and contended that, since there was no statute of the state on the subject, the railroad's duty and liability is to be determined in federal courts as a matter of general law.

The trial judge refused to rule that the applicable law precluded recovery. The jury brought in a verdict of $30,000; and the judgment entered thereon was affirmed by the Circuit Court of Appeals, which held (2 Cir., 90 F.2d 603, 604), that it was unnecessary to consider whether the law of Pennsylvania was as contended, because the question was one not of local, but of general, law, and that "upon questions of general law the federal courts are free, in absence of a local statute, to exercise their independent judgment as to what the law is. . . ."

Because of the importance of the question whether the federal court was free to disregard the alleged rule of the Pennsylvania common law, we granted certiorari. 302 U.S. 671 . . . .

First. Swift v. Tyson, 16 Pet. 1, 18, 10 L.Ed. 865, held that federal courts exercising jurisdiction on the ground of diversity of citizenship need not, in matters of general jurisprudence, apply the unwritten law of the state as declared by its highest court; that they are free to exercise an independent judgment as to what the common law of the state is—or should be; and that, as there stated by Mr. Justice Story, "the true interpretation of the 34th section * limited its application to state laws, strictly local, that is to say, to the positive statutes of the state, and the construction thereof adopted by the local tribunals, and to rights and titles to things having a permanent locality, such as the rights and titles to real estate, and other matters immovable and intraterritorial in their nature and character. It never has been supposed by us, that the section did apply, or was designed to apply, to questions of a more general nature, not at all dependent upon local statutes or local usages of a fixed and permanent operation, as, for example, to the construction of ordinary contracts or other written instruments, and especially to questions of general commercial law, where the state tribunals are called upon to perform the like functions as ourselves, that is, to ascertain, upon general reasoning and legal analogies, what is the true exposition of the contract or instrument, or what is the just rule furnished by the principles of commercial law to govern the case."

The federal courts assumed, in the broad field of "general law," the power to declare rules of decision which Congress was confessedly without power to enact as statutes. Doubt was repeatedly expressed as to the correctness of the construction given section 34, and as to the soundness of the rule which it introduced. But it was the more recent research of a competent scholar, who examined the original document, which established that the construction given to it by the Court was erroneous; and that the purpose of the section was merely to make certain that, in all matters except those in which some federal law is controlling, the federal courts exercising jurisdiction in diversity of citizenship cases would apply as their rules of decision the law of the state, unwritten as well as written.[1]   . . .

* "The laws of the several States, except where the Constitution, treaties or statutes of the United States shall otherwise require or provide shall be regarded as rules of decision in trials at common law in the courts of the United States in cases where they apply." (Federal Judiciary Act of 1789, sec. 34, 28 U.S.C.A. § 725.) [In the 1948 revision, the phrase "civil actions" was substituted for "trials at common law." See 28 U.S.C.A. § 1652.]

1. Charles Warren, New Light on the History of the Federal Judiciary Act of

. . .

Second. Experience in applying the doctrine of Swift v. Tyson had revealed its defects, political and social; and the benefits expected to flow from the rule did not accrue. Persistence of state courts in their own opinions on questions of common law prevented uniformity; and the impossibility of discovering a satisfactory line of demarcation between the province of general law and that of local law developed a new well of uncertainties.

On the other hand, the mischievous results of the doctrine had become apparent. Diversity of citizenship jurisdiction was conferred in order to prevent apprehended discrimination in state courts against those not citizens of the state. Swift v. Tyson introduced grave discrimination by noncitizens against citizens. It made rights enjoyed under the unwritten "general law" vary according to whether enforcement was sought in the state or in the federal court; and the privilege of selecting the court in which the right should be determined was conferred upon the noncitizen. Thus, the doctrine rendered impossible equal protection of the law. In attempting to promote uniformity of law throughout the United States, the doctrine had prevented uniformity in the administration of the law of the state.

The discrimination resulting became in practice far-reaching. This resulted in part from the broad province accorded to the so-called "general law" as to which federal courts exercised an independent judgment. . . .

The injustice and confusion incident to the doctrine of Swift v. Tyson have been repeatedly urged as reasons for abolishing or limiting diversity of citizenship jurisdiction. Other legislative relief has been proposed. If only a question of statutory construction were involved, we should not be prepared to abandon a doctrine so widely applied throughout nearly a century. But the unconstitutionality of the course pursued has now been made clear, and compels us to do so.

Third. Except in matters governed by the Federal Constitution or by acts of Congress, the law to be applied in any case is the law of the state. And whether the law of the state shall be declared by its Legislature in a statute or by its highest court in a decision is not a matter of federal concern. There is no federal general common law. Congress has no power to declare substantive rules of common law applicable in a state whether they be local in their nature or "general," be they commercial law or a part of the law of torts. And no clause in the Constitution purports to confer such a power upon the federal courts. . . .

The fallacy underlying the rule declared in Swift v. Tyson is made clear by Mr. Justice Holmes. The doctrine rests upon the assumption that there is "a transcendental body of law outside of any particular State but obligatory within it unless and until changed by statute," that

1789 (1923) 37 Harv.L.Rev. 49, 51–52, 81–
88, 108. [Other footnotes omitted.]

federal courts have the power to use their judgment as to what the rules of common law are; and that in the federal courts "the parties are entitled to an independent judgment on matters of general law":

"but law in the sense in which courts speak of it today does not exist without some definite authority behind it. The common law so far as it is enforced in a State, whether called common law or not, is not the common law generally but the law of that State existing by the authority of that State. . . ."

Thus, the doctrine of Swift v. Tyson is, as Mr. Justice Holmes said, "an unconstitutional assumption of powers by the Courts of the United States which no lapse of time or respectable array of opinion should make us hesitate to correct." In disapproving that doctrine we do not hold unconstitutional section 34 of the Federal Judiciary Act of 1789 or any other act of Congress. We merely declare that in applying the doctrine this Court and the lower courts have invaded rights which in our opinion are reserved by the Constitution to the several states.

Fourth. The defendant contended that by the common law of Pennsylvania as declared by its highest court in Falchetti v. Pennsylvania R. Co., 307 Pa. 203, 160 A. 859, the only duty owed to the plaintiff was to refrain from wilful or wanton injury. The plaintiff denied that such is the Pennsylvania law. In support of their respective contentions the parties discussed and cited many decisions of the Supreme Court of the State. The Circuit Court of Appeals ruled that the question of liability is one of general law; and on that ground declined to decide the issue of state law. As we hold this was error, the judgment is reversed and the case remanded to it for further proceedings in conformity with our opinion.

Reversed.

MR. JUSTICE CARDOZO took no part in the consideration or decision of this case.

[MR. JUSTICE BUTLER dissented, with MR. JUSTICE MCREYNOLDS concurring. Besides arguing for adherence to Swift v. Tyson, the dissent urged that the case be set down for reargument, since counsel on both sides had assumed that Swift v. Tyson was valid. It declared that such an important question, especially with asserted constitutional overtones, should not be decided without argument.]

[MR. JUSTICE REED concurred in the result but thought overruling Swift v. Tyson did not require declaring that the "course pursued" was "unconstitutional." He believed it enough merely to say that the term "the laws" in Section 34 included decisional laws as well as statutory. He said: "If the opinion commits this Court to the position that the Congress is without power to declare what rules of substantive law shall govern the federal courts, that conclusion also seems questionable. The line between procedural and substantive law is hazy but no one doubts federal power over procedure."]

NOTES

(1) The principal case has produced enough legal commentary to sink it without a trace. Some of the writers would be pleased to do so, including the fearsome foursome of Keeffe, Gilhooley, Bailey and Day, authors of Weary Erie, 34 Corn.L.Q. 494 (1949). *But cf.* Friendly, In Praise of Erie—and of the New Federal Common Law, 19 Record of N.Y.C.B.A. 64, 65 (1964): "Mr. Justice Brandeis not only reached the right result but reached it for the only right reason, and . . . by uprooting the spurious uniformity of Swift v. Tyson and insisting that federal courts defer to the states on matters outside the states' grant of power to the nation, he cleared the way for the truly uniform federal common law on issues of national concern . . . ." See also, Clark, State Law in the Federal Courts: The Brooding Omnipresence of Erie v. Tompkins, 55 Yale L.J. 267 (1946). Excellent discussions are Hill, The Erie Doctrine and the Constitution, 53 Nw.U.L.Rev. 427 (1958), and Hart, The Relations Between State and Federal Law, 54 Colum.L.Rev. 489 (1954). See also Younger, What Happened in Erie, 56 Tex.L.Rev. 1011 (1978), who notes that the *Erie* decision was so poorly understood that it went unreported until Justice Brandeis wrote a letter to Arthur Krock of the New York Times calling his attention to "the most important opinion since I have been on the court." (A nice photo of the *loci delicti* is included in the law review article).

(2) Interestingly, neither the lawyer who argued the case for the Erie Railroad, nor Tompkin's lawyer urged that *Swift* be overruled. Nor did the Supreme Court set the case for reargument, as it normally does when it wishes to decide an issue that the parties have not briefed. (For an example of such a procedure, see *Patterson v. McLean Credit Union,* p. 955, infra). Why did the Court act in this dramatic fashion? In order to comply with the latest in scholarly research? Because it saw what was best for America? To correct a newly discerned constitutional problem? Or because it had fundamentally changed its perception of the authority underlying the rule of law?

(3) Was *Swift v. Tyson* such a bad decision? For multistate actors, such as railroads, uniform treatment across the United States is important, for otherwise, they must tailor their behavior to the demands of each state in which they are subject to personal jurisdiction. When the laws of the states are in conflict, this can be an impossible task. Given that *Erie* remains good law but the number of multistate actors has grown, this issue is even more critical today. What other methods exist for creating national law?

(4) Was *Erie v. Tompkins* such a good decision? As it happens, the Pennsylvania courts had apparently considered the substantive point at issue in *Erie.* But what if this question had never been raised before in Pennsylvania? What if the issue had been addressed, but not in the state's highest court? What if the issue was addressed a long time ago, and circumstances or legal philosophy changed, so that the state court was likely to overrule its prior decision? In Garland v. Herrin, 724 F.2d 16 (2d Cir.1983), parents sued a Yale student who had bludgeoned to death their daughter, his former girl friend, in their home in Westchester County, New York, claiming negligent infliction of emotional distress. Based on a 1974 New York case holding such claims nonactionable, the Second Circuit ordered the complaint dismissed. Ten weeks later, the New York Court of Appeals announced it was joining the trend to recognize this tort, Bovsun v. Sanperi, 61 N.Y.2d 219, 473 N.Y.S.2d 357, 461 N.E.2d 843 (1984). The Garlands' case was, of course, res judicata.

Can a litigant interested in application of an arguably outmoded law maneuver the case into federal court to avoid state court reconsideration of the issue? If so, is this kind of forum shopping any better than "mischievous results" contemplated by Justice Brandeis?

(5) To avoid results like *Garland*, many states have authorized their courts to answer unsettled questions of state law arising in federal court actions upon certification of such questions to them by the federal court, with the federal court meanwhile retaining jurisdiction of the case for eventual disposition in accordance with the state court's answer. The United States Supreme Court looked favorably on this procedure in Clay v. Sun Insurance Office Limited, 363 U.S. 207, 80 S.Ct. 1222, 4 L.Ed.2d 1170 (1960), and gave it another boost in 1974 by instructing the Second Circuit to reconsider whether it should certify a question to the Florida Supreme Court in Lehman Brothers v. Schein, 416 U.S. 386, 94 S.Ct. 1741, 40 L.Ed.2d 215 (1974). For an interesting case demonstrating that this procedure is not foolproof, see Redgrave v. Boston Symphony Orchestra, 855 F.2d 888 (1st Cir. 1988).

(6) The perception in *Erie* that Congress lacked power to regulate the conduct at issue is based on reasoning that also applies to pendent state law questions arising in federal cases.

THE HORIZONTAL CHOICE QUESTION

Examine the disposition in Erie. Once Justice Brandeis had decided that federal law was not applicable, he immediately turned to the rulings of Pennsylvania courts. But the case was tried in New York and the defendant was a New York corporation: why was not New York's law the appropriate choice?

There are two ways to arrive at Justice Brandeis' decision to apply the law of Pennsylvania rather than that of New York. The first is to say that like the duty-of-care issue discussed in the opinion, Justice Brandeis considered the horizontal choice-of-law question to be governed by the law of the state in which the federal court sat, and that the Justice had consulted New York law. Since this *sub silentio* consultation revealed that *New York* had adopted *lex loci delicti* as its choice-of-law rule, and the locus of the accident was Pennsylvania, the law of that state governed. Indeed, it was this view that was adopted by the Supreme Court in Klaxon Co. v. Stentor Electric Manufacturing Co., 313 U.S. 487, 61 S.Ct. 1020, 85 L.Ed. 1477 (1941), the Court stating:

> "We are of opinion that the prohibition declared in Erie Railroad Co. v. Tompkins, 304 U.S. 64, 58 S.Ct. 817, 82 L.Ed. 1188, 114 A.L.R. 1487, against such independent determinations by the federal courts, extends to the field of conflict of laws. The conflict of laws rules to be applied by the federal court in Delaware must conform to those prevailing in Delaware's state courts. Otherwise, the accident of diversity of citizenship would constantly disturb equal administration of justice in coordinate state and federal courts sitting side by side. See Erie Railroad Co. v. Tompkins, supra, 304 U.S. at 74–

77, 58 S.Ct. at 820–822, 82 L.Ed. 1188, 114 A.L.R. 1487. Any other ruling would do violence to the principle of uniformity within a state, upon which the *Tompkins* decision is based. Whatever lack of uniformity this may produce between federal courts in different states is attributable to our federal system, which leaves to a state, within the limits permitted by the Constitution, the right to pursue local policies diverging from those of its neighbors. It is not for the federal courts to thwart such local policies by enforcing an independent "general law" of conflict of laws. Subject only to review by this Court on any federal question that may arise, Delaware is free to determine whether a given matter is to be governed by the law of the forum or some other law. . . . This Court's views are not the decisive factor in determining the applicable conflicts rule. . . . And the proper function of the Delaware federal court is to ascertain what the state law is, not what it ought to be . . . ."

See also Sampson v. Channell, 110 F.2d 754 (1st Cir.1940), cert. denied 310 U.S. 650, 60 S.Ct. 1099, 84 L.Ed. 1415; McCoid, Hanna v. Plumer: The Erie Doctrine Changes Shape, 51 Va.L.Rev. 884, 908–912 (1965).

NOTES

What effect does the rule of the *Klaxon* case have on Erie's purported "twin aims" of "discouragement of forum-shopping and avoidance of inequitable administration of the laws." Hanna v. Plumer, p. 371, infra. How is the answer to this question affected by each of the following:

(a) the recently expanding bases for in personam jurisdiction over defendants;

(b) the propensities of courts applying modern approaches to horizontal choice of law in the wake of the recent "choice of law revolution" for applying their own law rather than that dictated by traditional rules of choice, and the failure of the United States Supreme Court in Allstate Insurance Co. v. Hague, p. 311 supra, to impose any significant limitation on these propensities (on this subject, and on the relations between judicial jurisdiction, legislative jurisdiction, and choice of law generally, see Korn, The Choice of Law Revolution: A Critique, 83 Colum.L.Rev. 772, 778–799 (1983);

(c) the rule of *Van Dusen v. Barrack* (p. 350, supra) that after a forum non conveniens transfer under 28 U.S.C.A. § 1404, the transferee court must apply the law of the same state that would have been applied by the courts of the inconvenient forum state in which the plaintiff commenced his action;

(d) the applicability of the principle, in horizontal as well as in vertical choice of law contexts, that the forum is free to apply its own procedural laws irrespective of the source of the properly governing substantive laws.

———

Note, however, that there is another way in which the disposition in *Erie* could have been achieved. It could be argued that although the substantive question as to the duty the Erie Railroad owed Tompkins is not the proper subject of federal law, the choice-of-law rule for deciding between New York and Pennsylvania law *does* raise a federal question, either because it is a procedural matter or because the Constitution empowers the national government to regulate such choices. Under this reasoning, Justice Brandeis adopted *lex loci delicti* as a matter of federal, not New York state, law.

In view of the problems raised by *Klaxon,* would not this be the wiser view? Recently, the Supreme Court has indicated that the Full Faith and Credit Clause does limit the horizontal choices of law that the states can make, Phillips Petroleum Co. v. Shutts, p. 513, infra. However, these limitations are not as strict as those laid down by *Erie* for the vertical context. Thus, in *Phillips,* the Supreme Court held that the Constitution prohibited Kansas from applying its own law to interpret obligations under land leases that had no connection with Kansas. But in a related case, Sun Oil Co. v. Wortman, 486 U.S. 717, 108 S.Ct. 2117, 100 L.Ed.2d 743 (1988), Kansas was permitted to apply its own statute of limitations to claims under these same leases. In the latter case, the Supreme Court stated:

". . . [W]e have held that statutes of limitation are substantive, see Guaranty Trust Co. v. York, 326 U.S. 99, 65 S.Ct. 1464, 89 L.Ed. 2079 (1945).

. . . *Guaranty Trust* itself rejects the notion that there is an equivalence between what is substantive under the *Erie* doctrine and what is substantive for purposes of conflict of laws. Id., at 108, 65 S.Ct., at 1469. Except at the extremes, the terms 'substance' and 'procedure' precisely describe very little except a dichotomy, and what they mean in a particular context is largely determined by the purposes for which the dichotomy is drawn. In the context of our *Erie* jurisprudence, see Erie R. Co. v. Tompkins, 304 U.S. 64, 58 S.Ct. 817, 82 L.Ed. 1188 (1938), that purpose is to establish (within the limits of applicable federal law, including the prescribed Rules of Federal Procedure) substantial uniformity of predictable outcome between cases tried in a federal court and cases tried in the courts of the State in which the federal court sits. See Guaranty Trust, supra, 326 U.S. at 109, 65 S.Ct., at 1469; Hanna v. Plumer, 380 U.S. 460, 467, 471–474, 85 S.Ct. 1136, 1141, 1143–45, 14 L.Ed.2d 8 (1965). The purpose of the substance-procedure dichotomy in the context of the Full Faith and Credit Clause, by contrast, is not to establish uniformity but to delimit spheres of state legislative competence. How different the two purposes (and hence the appropriate meanings) are is suggested by this: It is never the case under *Erie* that either federal *or* state law—if the two differ—can properly be applied to a particular issue, cf. *Erie,* supra, 304 U.S., at 72–73, 58 S.Ct. at 819; but since the legislative jurisdictions of the States overlap, it is frequently the case under the Full Faith and Credit Clause that a court can lawfully apply either the law of

one State or the contrary law of another, see *Shutts III,* 472
U.S., at 823, 105 S.Ct., at 2981 ('in many situations a state
court may be free to apply one of several choices of law').
Today, for example, we do not hold that Kansas must apply its
own statute of limitations to a claim governed in its substance
by another State's law, but only that it may."

NOTE

See also Miller & Crump, Jurisdiction and choice of law in Multistate Class
Actions After Phillips Petroleum Co. v. Shutts, 96 Yale L.J. 1 (1986).

SECTION 3. "SUBSTANCE" AND "PROCEDURE" FROM GUARANTY TRUST v. YORK TO HANNA v. PLUMER

Compare the majority opinion in *Erie* with Justice Reed's concurrence. Did Justice Brandeis disagree with the statement that "no one
doubts federal power over procedure"? As noted above, at the time
that *Erie* was under consideration by the Supreme Court, the Federal
Rules of Civil Procedure were being promulgated to displace state
procedural law in federal courts. Because it was always contemplated
that these rules (and by extension, other federal procedural rules)
would be applicable even in diversity, *Erie* has required the courts to
decide what issues are "substantive" and which are "procedural" for
vertical choice-of-law purposes.

GUARANTY TRUST CO. v. YORK

Supreme Court of the United States, 1945.
326 U.S. 99, 65 S.Ct. 1464, 89 L.Ed. 2079.

[In 1942 York filed a class suit in a Federal district court in New
York, charging defendant with breach of trust in connection with
transactions in 1931. Defendant obtained a summary judgment on the
ground the suit was time-barred under the New York rule, but this was
reversed, the Court of Appeals ruling that in a diversity action brought
on its equity side the district court was not bound to apply the statute
of limitations as it would have been applied by a New York court. The
Supreme Court granted certiorari.]

MR. JUSTICE FRANKFURTER delivered the opinion of the Court. . . .

Our starting point must be the policy of federal jurisdiction which
Erie R. Co. v. Tompkins, 304 U.S. 64, 58 S.Ct. 817, 82 L.Ed. 1188, 114
A.L.R. 1487, embodies. . . . [and which] was promptly applied to a
suit in equity. Ruhlin v. New York Life Ins. Co., 304 U.S. 202, 58 S.Ct.
860, 82 L.Ed. 1290.

. . . this case reduces itself to the narrow question whether, when
no recovery could be had in a State court because the action is barred
by the statute of limitations, a federal court in equity can take cognizance of the suit because there is diversity of citizenship between the

parties. Is the outlawry, according to State law, of a claim created by the States a matter of "substantive rights" to be respected by a federal court of equity when that court's jurisdiction is dependent on the fact that there is a State-created right, or is such statute of "a mere remedial character" . . . which a federal court may disregard?

Matters of "substance" and matters of "procedure" are much talked about in the books as though they defined a great divide cutting across the whole domain of law. But, of course, "substance" and "procedure" are the same key-words to very different problems. Neither "substance" nor "procedure" represents the same invariants. Each implies different variables depending upon the particular problem for which it is used. See Home Ins. Co. v. Dick, 281 U.S. 397, 409, 50 S.Ct. 338, 341, 74 L.Ed. 926, 74 A.L.R. 701. And the different problems are only distantly related at best, for the terms are in common use in connection with situations turning on such different considerations as those that are relevant to questions pertaining to ex post facto legislation, the impairment of the obligations of contract, the enforcement of federal rights in the State courts and the multitudinous phases of the conflict of laws.

Here we are dealing with a right to recover derived not from the United States but from one of the States. When, because the plaintiff happens to be a non-resident, such a right is enforceable in a federal as well as in a State court, the forms and mode of enforcing the right may at times, naturally enough, vary because the two judicial systems are not identic. But since a federal court adjudicating a state-created right solely because of the diversity of citizenship of the parties is for that purpose, in effect, only another court of the State, it cannot afford recovery if the right to recover is made unavailable by the State nor can it substantially affect the enforcement of the right as given by the State.

And so the question is not whether a statute of limitations is deemed a matter of "procedure" in some sense. The question is whether such a statute concerns merely the manner and the means by which a right to recover, as recognized by the State, is enforced, or whether such statutory limitation is a matter of substance in the aspect that alone is relevant to our problem, namely does it significantly affect the result of a litigation for a federal court to disregard a law of a State that would be controlling in an action upon the same claim by the same parties in a State court?

It is therefore immaterial whether statutes of limitation are characterized either as "substantive" or "procedural" in State court opinions in any use of those terms unrelated to the specific issue before us. Erie R. Co. v. Tompkins was not an endeavor to formulate scientific legal terminology. It expressed a policy that touches vitally the proper distribution of judicial power between State and federal courts. In essence, the intent of that decision was to insure that, in all cases where a federal court is exercising jurisdiction solely because of the diversity of citizenship of the parties, the outcome of the litigation in the federal court should be substantially the same, so far as legal rules determine the outcome of a litigation, as it would be if tried in a State court. The nub of the policy that underlies Erie R. Co. v. Tompkins is that for the same transaction the accident of a suit by a nonresident litigant in a federal court instead of in a State court a block away, should not lead to a substantially different result. And so, putting to one side abstractions regarding "substance" and "procedure", we have held that in diversity cases the federal courts must follow the law of the State as to burden of proof, Cities Service Oil Co. v. Dunlap, 308 U.S. 208, 60 S.Ct. 201, 84 L.Ed. 196, as to conflict of laws, Klaxon Co. v. Stentor Co., 313 U.S. 487, 61 S.Ct. 1020, 85 L.Ed. 1477, as to contributory negligence, Palmer v. Hoffman, 318 U.S. 109, 117. And see Sampson v. Channell, 1 Cir., 110 F.2d 754, 128 A.L.R. 394. Erie R. Co. v. Tompkins has been applied with an eye alert to essentials in avoiding disregard of State law in diversity cases in the federal courts. A policy so important to our federalism must be kept free from entanglements with analytical or terminological niceties.

Plainly enough, a statute that would completely bar recovery in a suit if brought in a State court bears on a State-created right vitally and not merely formally or negligibly. As to consequences that so intimately affect recovery or nonrecovery a federal court in a diversity case should follow State law. See Morgan, Choice of Law Governing Proof (1944) 58 Harv.L.Rev. 153, 155–158. . . .

Diversity jurisdiction is founded on assurance to non-resident litigants of courts free from susceptibility to potential local bias. The Framers of the Constitution, according to Marshall, entertained "apprehensions" lest distant suitors be subjected to local bias in State courts, or, at least, viewed with "indulgence the possible fears and apprehensions" of such suitors. Bank of the United States v. Deveaux, 5 Cranch 61, 87. And so Congress afforded out-of-State litigants another tribunal, not another body of law. The operation of a double system of conflicting laws in the same State is plainly hostile to the reign of law. Certainly, the fortuitous circumstance of residence out of a State of one of the parties to a litigation ought not to give rise to a discrimination against others equally concerned but locally resident. The source of substantive rights enforced by a federal court under diversity jurisdiction, it cannot be said too often, is the law of the States. Whenever that law is authoritatively declared by a State, whether its voice be the legislature or its highest court, such law ought to govern in litigation founded on that law, whether the forum of application is a State or a federal court and whether the remedies be sought at law or may be had in equity. . . .

The judgment is reversed and the case is remanded for proceedings not inconsistent with this opinion. . . .

[Mr. Justice Rutledge, joined by Mr. Justice Murphy, dissented, contending that the case arose from "interstate transactions" involving rights of security holders throughout the country and that national law was involved.]

THE "OUTCOME TEST" IN ACTION

Judge Charles E. Clark complained that rigorous application of the standard laid down in Guaranty Trust v. York tended to make the federal courts "ventriloquists' dummies" in cases resting on state law. His point was that almost any variation in procedure might "significantly affect the outcome" of the case in given circumstances. Yet in the same year the Guaranty Trust decision was handed down, the Supreme Court firmly put its standard into practice in three other diversity cases.*

In Woods v. Interstate Realty Co., 337 U.S. 535, 69 S.Ct. 1235, 93 L.Ed. 1524 (1949), a foreign corporation which was qualified under federal law to bring suit was held to be barred from suing in a federal court because of state law. The corporation did business locally but had failed to designate an agent for service of process. A state statute closed state courts to it under those facts, so federal court doors must also close.

In Ragan v. Merchants Transfer and Warehouse Co., 337 U.S. 530, 69 S.Ct. 1233, 93 L.Ed. 1520 (1949), a state rule again defeated a federal rule that would have permitted suit. In a personal injury action, the suit was timely begun according to Rule 3, which measured "commencement" of the action by the date of filing the complaint. Nevertheless, the action was held to be barred by limitations because the complaint had not been served until months after filing and state law made the date of service the critical one for limitations purposes.

In Cohen v. Beneficial Industrial Loan Corp., 337 U.S. 541, 69 S.Ct. 1221, 93 L.Ed. 1528 (1949), plaintiff's complaint in a stockholders derivative action was dismissed for failure to comply with a state requirement of security for costs. Rule 23, under which the action was brought in the federal court, did not require any security to be posted.

Over the next several years, the outcome test threatened to submerge many federal rules governing conduct of diversity litigation as they came into collision with state rules. The tide crested in Bernhardt v. Polygraphic Co. of America, 350 U.S. 198, 76 S.Ct. 273, 100 L.Ed. 199 (1956), where the United States District Court for Vermont refused to stay an action pending arbitration because state law was thought to control and it did not order arbitration agreements enforced. This view prevailed in the Supreme Court. The majority held that under the Erie doctrine a constitutional problem would arise if federal courts in ordinary contract actions enforced arbitration in accordance with the United States Arbitration Act and contrary to applicable state law.

---

* The *Ragan* and *Cohen* cases are discussed in the concurring opinion of Mr. Justice Harlan in Hanna v. Plumer, p. 371 infra.

But in 1958 the following decision of the United States Supreme Court seemed to herald a change in the direction of the Erie doctrine.

BYRD v. BLUE RIDGE RURAL ELECTRIC COOPERATIVE, INC.

Supreme Court of the United States, 1958.
356 U.S. 525, 78 S.Ct. 893, 2 L.Ed.2d 953.

MR. JUSTICE BRENNAN delivered the opinion of the Court.*

This case was brought in the District Court for the Western District of South Carolina. Jurisdiction was based on diversity of citizenship. 28 U.S.C. § 1332. The petitioner, a resident of North Carolina, sued respondent, a South Carolina corporation, for damages for injuries allegedly caused by the respondent's negligence. He had judgment on a jury verdict. The Court of Appeals for the Fourth Circuit reversed and directed the entry of judgment for the respondent. 238 F.2d 346. We granted certiorari, 352 U.S. 999, 77 S.Ct. 557, 1 L.Ed.2d 554, and subsequently ordered reargument, 355 U.S. 950, 78 S.Ct. 530, 2 L.Ed.2d 527.

The respondent is in the business of selling electric power to subscribers in rural sections of South Carolina. The petitioner was employed as a lineman in the construction crew of a construction contractor. The contractor, R.H. Bouligny, Inc., held a contract with the respondent in the amount of $334,300 for the building of some 24 miles of new power lines, the reconversion to higher capacities of about 88 miles of existing lines, and the construction of 2 new substations and a breaker station. The petitioner was injured while connecting power lines to one of the new substations.

One of respondent's affirmative defenses was that, under the South Carolina Workmen's Compensation Act, the petitioner—because the work contracted to be done by his employer was work of the kind also done by the respondent's own construction and maintenance crews—had the status of a statutory employee of the respondent and was therefore barred from suing the respondent at law because obliged to accept statutory compensation benefits as the exclusive remedy for his injuries. Two questions concerning this defense are before us: (1) whether the Court of Appeals erred in directing judgment for respondent without a remand to give petitioner an opportunity to introduce further evidence; and (2) whether petitioner, state practice notwithstanding, is entitled to a jury determination of the factual issues raised by this defense.

[On the first question, the Supreme Court held that the Court of Appeals had erred and the case had to be remanded for the taking of

---

* Some footnotes omitted; others renumbered.

such further evidence and trial on the issue whether respondent was a statutory employer within the South Carolina Act.]

* * *

II.

A question is also presented as to whether on remand the factual issue is to be decided by the judge or by the jury. The respondent argues on the basis of the decision of the Supreme Court of South Carolina in Adams v. Davison-Paxon Co., 230 S.C. 532, 96 S.E.2d 566,[1] that the issue of immunity should be decided by the judge and not by the jury. That was a negligence action brought in the state trial court against a store owner by an employee of an independent contractor who operated the store's millinery department. The trial judge denied the store owner's motion for a directed verdict made upon the ground that § 72–111 barred the plaintiff's action. The jury returned a verdict for the plaintiff. The South Carolina Supreme Court reversed, holding that it was for the judge and not the jury to decide on the evidence whether the owner was a statutory employer, and that the store owner had sustained his defense. The court rested its holding on decisions, listed in footnote 3 [in original] infra, involving judicial review of the Industrial Commission and said:

> "Thus the trial court should have in this case resolved the conflicts in the evidence and determined the fact of whether . . . [the independent contractor was performing a part of the 'trade, business or occupation' of the department store-appellant and, therefore, whether . . . [the employee's] remedy is exclusively under the Workmen's Compensation Law." 230 S.C. at page 543, 96 S.E.2d at page 572.

The respondent argues that this state-court decision governs the present diversity case and "divests the jury of its normal function" to decide the disputed fact question of the respondent's immunity under § 72–111. This is to contend that the federal court is bound under Erie R. Co. v. Tompkins, 304 U.S. 64, to follow the state court's holding to secure uniform enforcement of the immunity created by the State.[2]

First. It was decided in Erie R. Co. v. Tompkins that the federal courts in diversity cases must respect the definition of state-created rights and obligations by the state courts. We must, therefore, first examine the rule in Adams v. Davison-Paxon Co. to determine whether

1. The decision came down several months after the Court of Appeals decided this case.

2. See Cities Service Oil Co. v. Dunlap, 308 U.S. 208, 60 S.Ct. 201, 84 L.Ed. 196; West v. American Tel. & Tel. Co., 311 U.S. 223, 61 S.Ct. 179, 85 L.Ed. 139; Klaxon Co. v. Stentor Co., 313 U.S. 487, 61 S.Ct. 1020, 85 L.Ed. 1477; Guaranty Trust Co. v. York, 326 U.S. 99, 65 S.Ct. 1464, 89 L.Ed. 2079; Angel v. Bullington, 330 U.S. 183, 67 S.Ct. 657, 91 L.Ed. 832; Ragan v. Merchants Transfer Co., 337 U.S. 530, 69 S.Ct. 1233, 93 L.Ed. 1520; Woods v. Interstate Realty Co., 337 U.S. 535, 69 S.Ct. 1235, 93 L.Ed. 1524; Cohen v. Beneficial Loan Corp., 337 U.S. 541, 69 S.Ct. 1221, 93 L.Ed. 1528; Bernhardt v. Polygraphic Co., 350 U.S. 198, 76 S.Ct. 273, 100 L.Ed. 199; Sampson v. Channell, 1 Cir., 110 F.2d 754, 128 A.L.R. 394.

it is bound up with these rights and obligations in such a way that its application in the federal court is required. Cities Service Oil Co. v. Dunlap, 308 U.S. 208, 60 S.Ct. 201, 84 L.Ed. 196.

The Workmen's Compensation Act is administered in South Carolina by its Industrial Commission. The South Carolina courts hold that, on judicial review of actions of the Commission under § 72–111, the question whether the claim of an injured workman is within the Commission's jurisdiction is a matter of law for decision by the court, which makes its own findings of fact relating to that jurisdiction.[3] The South Carolina Supreme Court states no reasons in Adams v. Davison-Paxon Co. why, although the jury decides all other factual issues raised by the cause of action and defenses, the jury is displaced as to the factual issue raised by the affirmative defense under § 72–111. The decisions cited to support the holding are those listed in footnote 8, which are concerned solely with defining the scope and method of judicial review of the Industrial Commission. A State may, of course, distribute the functions of its judicial machinery as it sees fit. The decisions relied upon, however, furnish no reason for selecting the judge rather than the jury to decide this single affirmative defense in the negligence action. They simply reflect a policy, cf. Crowell v. Benson, 285 U.S. 22, 52 S.Ct. 285, 76 L.Ed. 598, that administrative determination of "jurisdictional facts" should not be final but subject to judicial review. The conclusion is inescapable that the *Adams* holding is grounded in the practical consideration that the question had theretofore come before the South Carolina courts from the Industrial Commission and the courts had become accustomed to deciding the factual issue of immunity without the aid of juries. We find nothing to suggest that this rule was announced as an integral part of the special relationship created by the statute. Thus the requirement appears to be merely a form and mode of enforcing the immunity, Guaranty Trust Co. v. York, 326 U.S. 99, 108, 65 S.Ct. 1464, 1469, 89 L.Ed. 2079, and not a rule intended to be bound up with the definition of the rights and obligations of the parties. The situation is therefore not analogous to that in Dice v. Akron, C. & Y.R. Co., 342 U.S. 359, 72 S.Ct. 312, 96 L.Ed. 398, where this Court held that the right to trial by jury is so substantial a part of the cause of action created by the Federal Employers' Liability Act that the Ohio courts could not apply, in an action under that statute, the Ohio rule that the question of fraudulent release was for determination by a judge rather than by a jury.

Second. But cases following *Erie* have evinced a broader policy to the effect that the federal courts should conform as near as may be—in

---

3. Knight v. Shepherd, 191 S.C. 452, 4 S.E.2d 906; Tedars v. Savannah River Veneer Co., 202 S.C. 363, 25 S.E.2d 235, 14 A.L.R. 914; McDowell v. Stilley Plywood Co., 210 S.C. 173, 41 S.E.2d 872; Miles v. West Virginia Pulp & Paper Co., 212 S.C. 424, 48 S.E.2d 26; Watson v. Wannamaker & Wells, Inc., 212 S.C. 506, 48 S.E.2d 447; Gordon v. Hollywood-Beaufort Package Corp., 213 S.C. 438, 49 S.E.2d 718; Holland v. Georgia Hardwood Lumber Co., 214 S.C. 195, 51, S.E.2d 744; Younginer v. Jones Construction Co., 215 S.C. 135, 54 S.E.2d 545; Horton v. Baruch, 217 S.C. 48, 59 S.E. 2d 545.

the absence of other considerations—to state rules even of form and mode where the state rules may bear substantially on the question whether the litigation would come out one way in the federal court and another way in the state court if the federal court failed to apply a particular local rule. E.g., Guaranty Trust Co. v. York, supra; Bernhardt v. Polygraphic Co., 350 U.S. 198, 76 S.Ct. 273, 100 L.Ed. 199. Concededly the nature of the tribunal which tries issues may be important in the enforcement of the parcel of rights making up a cause of action or defense, and bear significantly upon achievement of uniform enforcement of the right. It may well be that in the instant personal-injury case the outcome would be substantially affected by whether the issue of immunity is decided by a judge or a jury. Therefore, were "outcome" the only consideration, a strong case might appear for saying that the federal court should follow the state practice.

But there are affirmative countervailing considerations at work here. The federal system is an independent system for administering justice to litigants who properly invoke its jurisdiction. An essential characteristic of that system is the manner in which, in civil common-law actions, it distributes trial functions between judge and jury and, under the influence—if not the command [4]—of the Seventh Amendment, assigns the decisions of disputed questions of fact to the jury. Jacob v. New York, 315 U.S. 752, 62 S.Ct. 854, 86 L.Ed. 1166. The policy of uniform enforcement of state-created rights and obligations, see, e.g., Guaranty Trust Co. v. York, supra, cannot in every case exact compliance with a state rule [5]—not bound up with rights and obligations—which disrupts the federal system of allocating functions between judge and jury. Herron v. Southern Pacific Co., 283 U.S. 91, 51 S.Ct. 383, 75 L.Ed. 857. Thus the inquiry here is whether the federal policy favoring jury decisions of disputed fact questions should yield to the state rule in the interest of furthering the objective that the litigation should not come out one way in the federal court and another way in the state court.

We think that in the circumstances of this case the federal court should not follow the state rule. It cannot be gainsaid that there is a strong federal policy against allowing state rules to disrupt the judge-jury relationship in the federal courts. In Herron v. Southern Pacific Co., supra, the trial judge in a personal-injury negligence action brought in the District Court for Arizona on diversity grounds directed a verdict for the defendant when it appeared as a matter of law that the plaintiff was guilty of contributory negligence. The federal judge refused to be bound by a provision of the Arizona Constitution which made the jury the sole arbiter of the question of contributory negli-

---

4. Our conclusion makes unnecessary the consideration of—and we intimate no view upon—the constitutional question whether the right of jury trial protected in federal courts by the Seventh Amendment embraces the factual issue of statutory immunity when asserted, as here, as an affirmative defense in a common-law negligence action.

5. This Court held in Sibbach v. Wilson & Co., 312 U.S. 1, 655, 61 S.Ct. 422, 85 L.Ed. 479, that Federal Rules of Civil Procedure 35 should prevail over a contrary state rule.

gence. This Court sustained the action of the trial judge, holding that "state laws cannot alter the essential character or function of a federal court" because that function "is not in any sense a local matter, and state statutes which would interfere with the appropriate performance of that function are not binding upon the federal court under either the Conformity Act or the 'rules of decision' Act." Id., 283 U.S. at page 94, 51 S.Ct. at page 384. Perhaps even more clearly in light of the influence of the Seventh Amendment, the function assigned to the jury "is an essential factor in the process for which the Federal Constitution provides." Id., 283 U.S. at page 95, 51 S.Ct. at page 384. Concededly the *Herron* case was decided before Erie R. Co. v. Tompkins, but even when Swift v. Tyson, 16 Pet. 1, 10 L.Ed. 865, was governing law and allowed federal courts sitting in diversity cases to disregard state decisional law, it was never thought that state statutes or constitutions were similarly to be disregarded. Green v. Neal's Lessee, 6 Pet. 291, 8 L.Ed. 402. Yet *Herron* held that state statutes and constitutional provisions could not disrupt or alter the essential character or function of a federal court.[6]

Third. We have discussed the problem upon the assumption that the outcome of the litigation may be substantially affected by whether the issue of immunity is decided by a judge or a jury. But clearly there is not present here the certainty that a different result would follow, cf. Guaranty Trust Co. v. York, supra, or even the strong possibility that this would be the case, cf. Bernhardt v. Polygraphic Co., supra. There are factors present here which might reduce that possibility. The trial judge in the federal system has powers denied the judges of many States to comment on the weight of evidence and credibility of witnesses, and discretion to grant a new trial if the verdict appears to him to be against the weight of the evidence. We do not think the likelihood of a different result is so strong as to require the federal practice of jury determination of disputed factual issues to yield to the state rule in the interest of uniformity of outcome.[7]

The Court of Appeals did not consider other grounds of appeal raised by the respondent because the ground taken disposed of the case. We accordingly remand the case to the Court of Appeals for the decision of the other questions, with instructions that, if not made unnecessary by the decision of such questions, the Court of Appeals

6. Diederich v. American News Co., 10 Cir., 128 F.2d 144, decided after Erie R. Co. v. Tompkins, held that an almost identical provision of the Oklahoma Constitution was not binding on a federal judge in a diversity case.

7. Stoner v. New York Life Ins. Co., 311 U.S. 464, 61 S.Ct. 336, 85 L.Ed. 284, 311 U.S. 464, is not contrary. It was there held that the federal court should follow the state rule defining the evidence sufficient to raise a jury question whether the state-created right was established. But the state rule did not have the effect of nullifying the function of the federal judge to control a jury submission as did the Arizona constitutional provision which was denied effect in *Herron*. The South Carolina rule here involved affects the jury function as the Arizona provision affected the function of the judge: The rule entirely displaces the jury without regard to the sufficiency of the evidence to support a jury finding of immunity.

shall remand the case to the District Court for a new trial of such issues as the Court of Appeals may direct.

Reversed and remanded.

[Concurring and dissenting opinions omitted.]

NOTE

The "balancing" approach employed in *Byrd* was soon reflected in decisions of the lower Federal courts. An outstanding example was Iovino v. Waterson, 274 F.2d 41 (2d Cir.1959), cert. denied sub nom. Carlin v. Iovino, 362 U.S. 949, 80 S.Ct. 860, 4 L.Ed.2d 867 (1960), in which the court allowed substitution of a deceased defendant's administratrix under Fed.R.Civ.P. 25(a)(1) though the relevant state law contained no provision for such substitution. Judge Friendly's opinion neatly summarized the balancing process that underlay the decision as follows:

> "This is an area where the positive inference from Article III and the 'necessary and proper' clause outweighs the negative inference from the limited grant of legislative power in Article I, § 8, and the Tenth Amendment that must have afforded the basis for the constitutional precept of Erie."

The Supreme Court's next major pronouncement on the problem, however, in the 1965 case of Hanna v. Plumer, took yet another turn.

HANNA v. PLUMER

Supreme Court of the United States, 1965.
380 U.S. 460, 85 S.Ct. 1136, 14 L.Ed.2d 8.

MR. CHIEF JUSTICE WARREN delivered the opinion of the Court.*

The question to be decided is whether, in a civil action where the jurisdiction of the United States district court is based upon diversity of citizenship between the parties, service of process shall be made in the manner prescribed by state law or that set forth in Rule 4(d)(1) of the Federal Rules of Civil Procedure.

On February 6, 1963, petitioner, a citizen of Ohio, filed her complaint in the District Court for the District of Massachusetts, claiming damages in excess of $10,000 for personal injuries resulting from an automobile accident in South Carolina, allegedly caused by the negligence of one Louise Plumer Osgood, a Massachusetts citizen deceased at the time of the filing of the complaint. Respondent, Mrs. Osgood's executor and also a Massachusetts citizen, was named as defendant. On February 8, service was made by leaving copies of the summons and the complaint with respondent's wife at his residence, concededly in compliance with Rule 4(d)(1). . . . Respondent filed his answer on February 26, alleging, inter alia, that the action could not be maintained because it had been brought "contrary to and in violation of the

----

* All footnotes but one omitted.

provisions of Massachusetts General Laws (Ter.Ed.) Chapter 197, Section 9." That section provides:

> "Except as provided in this chapter, an executor or administrator shall not be held to answer to an action by a creditor of the deceased which is not commenced within one year from the time of his giving bond for the performance of his trust, or to such an action which is commenced within said year unless before the expiration thereof the writ in such action has been served by delivery in hand upon such executor or administrator or service thereof accepted by him or a notice stating the name of the estate, the name and address of the creditor, the amount of the claim and the court in which the action has been brought has been filed in the proper registry of probate. . . . ." Mass.Gen.Laws Ann., c. 197, § 9 (1958).

On October 17, 1963, the District Court granted respondent's motion for summary judgment, citing Ragan v. Merchants Transfer & Warehouse Co., 337 U.S. 530, 69 S.Ct. 1233, 93 L.Ed. 1520, and Guaranty Trust Co. of New York v. York, 326 U.S. 99, 65 S.Ct. 1464, 89 L.Ed. 2079, in support of its conclusion that the adequacy of the service was to be measured by § 9, with which, the court held, petitioner had not complied. On appeal, petitioner admitted noncompliance with § 9, but argued that Rule 4(d)(1) defines the method by which service of process is to be effected in diversity actions. The Court of Appeals for the First Circuit, finding that "[r]elatively recent amendments [to § 9] evince a clear legislative purpose to require personal notification within the year," [1] concluded that the conflict of state and federal rules was over "a substantive rather than a procedural matter," and unanimously affirmed. 331 F.2d 157. Because of the threat to the goal of uniformity of federal procedure posed by the decision below, we granted certiorari, 379 U.S. 813, 85 S.Ct. 52, 14 L.Ed.2d 8 (1964).

---

1. Section 9 is in part a statute of limitations, providing that an executor need not "answer to an action . . . which is not commenced within one year from the time of his giving bond . . . ." This part of the statute, the purpose of which is to speed the settlement of estates, Spaulding v. McConnell, 307 Mass. 144, 146, 29 N.E.2d 713, 715 (1940); Doyle v. Moylan, 141 F.Supp. 95 (D.C.D.Mass.1956), is not involved in this case, since the action clearly was timely commenced. (Respondent filed bond on March 1, 1962; the complaint was filed February 6, 1963; and the service—the propriety of which if in dispute—was made on February 8, 1963.) 331 F.2d, at 159. Cf. Guaranty Trust Co. v. York, supra; Ragan v. Merchants Transfer Co., supra.

Section 9 also provides for the manner of service. Generally, service of process must be made by "delivery in hand," although there are two alternatives: acceptance of service by the executor, or filing of a notice of claim, the components of which are set out in the statute, in the appropriate probate court. The purpose of this part of the statute, which *is* involved here, is, as the court below noted, to insure that executors will receive actual notice of claims. Parker v. Rich, 297 Mass. 111, 113–114, 8 N.E.2d 345, 347 (1937). Actual notice is of course also the goal of Rule 4(d)(1); however, the Federal Rule reflects a determination that this goal can be achieved by a method less cumbersome than that prescribed in § 9. In this case the goal seems to have been achieved; although the affidavit filed by respondent in the District Court asserts that he had not been served in hand nor had he accepted service, it does not allege lack of actual notice.

We conclude that the adoption of Rule 4(d)(1), designed to control service of process in diversity actions, neither exceeded the congressional mandate embodied in the Rules Enabling Act nor transgressed constitutional bounds, and that the Rule is therefore the standard against which the District Court should have measured the adequacy of the service.   Accordingly, we reverse the decision of the Court of Appeals.

. . . Under the cases construing the scope of the Enabling Act, Rule 4(d)(1) clearly passes muster.   Prescribing the manner in which a defendant is to be notified that a suit has been instituted against him, it relates to the "practice and procedure of the district courts."   Cf. Insurance Co. v. Bangs, 103 U.S. 435, 439, 26 L.Ed. 580.

> "The test must be whether a rule really regulates procedure,— the judicial process for enforcing rights and duties recognized by substantive law and for justly administering remedy and redress for disregard or infraction of them."   Sibbach v. Wilson & Co., 312 U.S. 1, 14, 61 S.Ct. 422, 426, 85 L.Ed. 479.

In Mississippi Pub. Corp. v. Murphree, 326 U.S. 438, 66 S.Ct. 242, 90 L.Ed. 185, this Court upheld Rule 4(f), which permits service of a summons anywhere within the State (and not merely the district) in which a district court sits:

> "We think that Rule 4(f) is in harmony with the Enabling Act . . . .. Undoubtedly most alterations of the rules of practice and procedure may and often do affect the rights of litigants.   Congress' prohibition of any alteration of substantive rights of litigants was obviously not addressed to such incidental effects as necessarily attend the adoption of the prescribed new rules of procedure upon the rights of litigants who, agreeably to rules of practice and procedure, have been brought before a court authorized to determine their rights. Sibbach v. Wilson & Co., 312 U.S. 1, 11–14, 61 S.Ct. 422, 425– 427, 85 L.Ed. 479.   The fact that the application of Rule 4(f) will operate to subject petitioner's rights to adjudication by the district court for northern Mississippi will undoubtedly affect those rights.   But it does not operate to abridge, enlarge or modify the rules of decision by which that court will adjudicate its rights."   Id., at 445–446, 66 S.Ct. at 246.

Thus were there no conflicting state procedure, Rule 4(d)(1) would clearly control.   National Rental v. Szukhent, 375 U.S. 311, 316, 84 S.Ct. 411, 414, 11 L.Ed.2d 354.   However, respondent, focusing on the contrary Massachusetts rule, calls to the Court's attention another line of cases, a line which—like the Federal Rules—had its birth in 1938. Erie R. Co. v. Tompkins, 304 U.S. 64, 58 S.Ct. 817, 82 L.Ed. 1188, overruling Swift v. Tyson, 16 Pet. 1, held that federal courts sitting in diversity cases, when deciding questions of "substantive" law, are bound by state court decisions as well as state statutes.   The broad command of Erie was therefore identical to that of the Enabling Act:

federal courts are to apply state substantive law and federal procedural law. However, as subsequent cases sharpened the distinction between substance and procedure, the line of cases following Erie diverged markedly from the line construing the Enabling Act. Guaranty Trust Co. v. York, 326 U.S. 99, 65 S.Ct. 1464, 89 L.Ed. 2079, made it clear that Erie-type problems were not to be solved by reference to any traditional or common-sense substance-procedure distinction. . . .

Respondent, by placing primary reliance on York and Ragan, suggests that the Erie doctrine acts as a check on the Federal Rules of Civil Procedure, that despite the clear command of Rule 4(d)(1), Erie and its progeny demand the application of the Massachusetts rule. Reduced to essentials, the argument is: (1) Erie, as refined in York, demands that federal courts apply state law whenever application of federal law in its stead will alter the outcome of the case. (2) In this case a determination that the Massachusetts service requirements obtain will result in immediate victory for respondent. If, on the other hand, it should be held that Rule 4(d)(1) is applicable, the litigation will continue, with possible victory for petitioner. (3) Therefore, Erie demands application of the Massachusetts rule. The syllogism possesses an appealing simplicity, but is for several reasons invalid.

In the first place, it is doubtful that, even if there were no Federal Rule making it clear that in-hand service is not required in diversity actions, the Erie rule would have obligated the District Court to follow the Massachusetts procedure. "Outcome-determination" analysis was never intended to serve as a talisman. Byrd v. Blue Ridge Cooperative, 356 U.S. 525, 537, 78 S.Ct. 893, 900, 2 L.Ed.2d 953. Indeed, the message of York itself is that choices between state and federal law are to be made not by application of any automatic, "litmus paper" criterion, but rather by reference to the policies underlying the Erie rule. . . .

The Erie rule is rooted in part in a realization that it would be unfair for the character or result of a litigation materially to differ because the suit had been brought in a federal court. . . . The decision was also in part a reaction to the practice of "forum-shopping" which had grown up in response to the rule of Swift v. Tyson. . . . That the York test was an attempt to effectuate these policies is demonstrated by the fact that the opinion framed the inquiry in terms of "substantial" variations between state and federal litigation. . . . Not only are nonsubstantial, or trivial, variations not likely to raise the sort of equal protection problems which troubled the Court in Erie; they are also unlikely to influence the choice of a forum. The "outcome-determination" test therefore cannot be read without reference to the twin aims of the Erie rule: discouragement of forum-shopping and avoidance of inequitable administration of the laws.

The difference between the conclusion that the Massachusetts rule is applicable, and the conclusion that it is not, is of course at this point "outcome-determinative" in the sense that if we hold the state rule to apply, respondent prevails, whereas if we hold that Rule 4(d)(1) governs, the litigation will continue. But in this sense *every* procedural variation is "outcome-determinative." For example, having brought suit in a federal court, a plaintiff cannot then insist on the right to file subsequent pleadings in accord with the time limits applicable in state courts, even though enforcement of the federal timetable will, if he continues to insist that he must meet only the state time limit, result in determination of the controversy against him. So it is here. Though choice of the federal or state rule will at this point have a marked effect upon the outcome of the litigation, the difference between the two rules would be of scant, if any, relevance to the choice of a forum. Petitioner, in choosing her forum, was not presented with a situation where application of the state rule would wholly bar recovery; rather, adherence to the state rule would have resulted only in altering the way in which process was served. Moreover, it is difficult to argue that permitting service of defendant's wife to take the place of in-hand service of defendant himself alters the mode of enforcement of state-created rights in a fashion sufficiently "substantial" to raise the sort of equal protection problems to which the Erie opinion alluded.

There is, however, a more fundamental flaw in respondent's syllogism: the incorrect assumption that the rule of Erie R. Co. v. Tompkins constitutes the appropriate test of the validity and therefore the applicability of a Federal Rule of Civil Procedure. The Erie rule has never been invoked to void a Federal Rule. It is true that there have been cases where this Court has held applicable a state rule in the face of an argument that the situation was governed by one of the Federal Rules. But the holding of each such case was not that Erie commanded displacement of a Federal Rule by an inconsistent state rule, but rather that the scope of the Federal Rule was not as broad as the losing party urged, and therefore, there being no Federal Rule which covered the point in dispute, Erie commanded the enforcement of state law. * * * (Here, of course, the clash is unavoidable; Rule 4(d)(1) says—implicitly, but with unmistakable clarity—that in-hand service is not required in federal courts.) At the same time, in cases adjudicating the validity of Federal Rules, we have not applied the York rule or other refinements of Erie, but have to this day continued to decide questions concerning the scope of the Enabling Act and the constitutionality of specific Federal Rules in light of the distinction set forth in Sibbach. E.g., Schlagenhauf v. Holder, 379 U.S. 104, 85 S.Ct. 234, 13 L.Ed.2d 152.

Nor has the development of two separate lines of cases been inadvertent. The line between "substance" and "procedure" shifts as the legal context changes. "Each implies different variables depending upon the particular problem for which it is used." Guaranty Trust Co. v. York, supra, 326 U.S. at 108, 65 S.Ct. at 1469; Cook, The Logical and Legal Bases of the Conflict of Laws, pp. 154–183 (1942). It is true that both the Enabling Act and the Erie rule say, roughly, that federal courts are to apply state "substantive" law and federal "procedural" law, but from that it need not follow that the tests are identical. For they were designed to control very different sorts of decisions. When a situation is covered by one of the Federal Rules, the question facing the court is a far cry from the typical, relatively unguided Erie choice: the court has been instructed to apply the Federal Rule, and can refuse to do so only if the Advisory Committee, this Court, and Congress erred in their prima facie judgment that the Rule in question transgresses neither the terms of the Enabling Act nor constitutional restrictions.

We are reminded by the Erie opinion that neither Congress nor the federal courts can, under the guise of formulating rules of decision for federal courts, fashion rules which are not supported by a grant of federal authority contained in Article I or some other section of the Constitution; in such areas state law must govern because there can be no other law. But the opinion in Erie, which involved no Federal Rule and dealt with a question which was "substantive" in every traditional sense (whether the railroad owed a duty of care to Tompkins as a trespasser or a licensee), surely neither said nor implied that measures like Rule 4(d)(1) are unconstitutional. For the constitutional provision for a federal court system (augmented by the Necessary and Proper Clause) carries with it congressional power to make rules governing the practice and pleading in those courts, which in turn includes a power to regulate matters which, though falling within the uncertain area between substance and procedure, are rationally capable of classification as either. Cf. M'Culloch v. Maryland, 4 Wheat. 316, 421, 4 L.Ed. 579. Neither York nor the cases following it ever suggested that the rule there laid down for coping with situations where no Federal Rule applies is coextensive with the limitation on Congress to which Erie had adverted. Although this Court has never before been confronted with a case where the applicable Federal Rule is in direct collision with the law of the relevant State, courts of appeals faced with such clashes have rightly discerned the implications of our decisions.

> "One of the shaping purposes of the Federal Rules is to bring about uniformity in the federal courts by getting away from local rules. This is especially true of matters which relate to the administration of legal proceedings, an area in which federal courts have traditionally exerted strong inherent power, completely aside from the powers Congress expressly conferred in the Rules. The purpose of the Erie doctrine, even as extended in York and Ragan, was never to bottle up federal courts with 'outcome-determinative' and 'integral-relations' stoppers—when there are 'affirmative countervailing [federal] considerations' and when there is a Congressional mandate (the Rules) supported by constitutional authority." Lumbermen's Mutual Casualty Co. v. Wright, 322 F.2d 759, 764 (C.A.5th Cir.1963).

Erie and its offspring cast no doubt on the long-recognized power of Congress to prescribe housekeeping rules for federal courts even though some of those rules will inevitably differ from comparable state rules. . . . Thus, though a court, in measuring a Federal Rule against the standards contained in the Enabling Act and the Constitution, need not wholly blind itself to the degree to which the Rule makes the character and result of the federal litigation stray from the course it would follow in state courts, Sibbach v. Wilson & Co., supra, 312 U.S. at 13–14, 61 S.Ct. at 426–427, it cannot be forgotten that the Erie rule, and the guidelines suggested in York, were created to serve another purpose altogether. To hold that a Federal Rule of Civil Procedure must cease to function whenever it alters the mode of enforcing state-created rights would be to disembowel either the Constitution's grant of power over federal procedure or Congress' attempt to exercise that power in the Enabling Act. Rule 4(d)(1) is valid and controls the instant case.

Reversed.

MR. JUSTICE BLACK concurs in the result.

MR. JUSTICE HARLAN, concurring.

It is unquestionably true that up to now Erie and the cases following it have not succeeded in articulating a workable doctrine governing choice of law in diversity actions. I respect the Court's effort to clarify the situation in today's opinion. However, in doing so I think it has misconceived the constitutional premises of Erie and has failed to deal adequately with those past decisions upon which the courts below relied.

Erie was something more than an opinion which worried about "forum-shopping and avoidance of inequitable administration of the laws," . . . although to be sure these were important elements of the decision. I have always regarded that decision as one of the modern cornerstones of our federalism, expressing policies that profoundly touch the allocation of judicial power between the state and federal systems. Erie recognized that there should not be two conflicting systems of law controlling the primary activity of citizens, for such alternative governing authority must necessarily give rise to a debilitating uncertainty in the planning of everyday affairs. And it recognized that the scheme of our Constitution envisions an allocation of law-making functions between state and federal legislative processes which is undercut if the federal judiciary can make substantive law affecting state affairs beyond the bounds of congressional legislative powers in this regard. Thus, in diversity cases Erie commands that it be the state law governing primary private activity which prevails.

The shorthand formulations which have appeared in some past decisions are prone to carry untoward results that frequently arise from oversimplification. The Court is quite right in stating that the "outcome-determinative" test of Guaranty Trust Co. of New York v. York, 326 U.S. 99, 65 S.Ct. 1464, 89 L.Ed. 2079, if taken literally, proves too much, for any rule, no matter how clearly "procedural," can affect the outcome of litigation if it is not obeyed. In turning from the "outcome" test of York back to the unadorned forum-shopping rationale of Erie, however, the Court falls prey to like oversimplification, for a simple forum-shopping rule also proves too much; litigants often choose a federal forum merely to obtain what they consider the advantages of the Federal Rules of Civil Procedure or to try their cases before a supposedly more favorable judge. To my mind the proper line of approach in determining whether to apply a state or a federal rule, whether "substantive" or "procedural," is to stay close to basic principles by inquiring if the choice of rule would substantially affect those primary decisions respecting human conduct which our constitutional system leaves to state regulation. If so, Erie and the Constitution require that the state rule prevail, even in the face of a conflicting federal rule.

The Court weakens, if indeed it does not submerge, this basic principle by finding, in effect, a grant of substantive legislative power in the constitutional provision for a federal court system . . ., and through it, setting up the Federal Rules as a body of law inviolate. . . . So long as a reasonable man could characterize any duly adopted federal rule as "procedural," the Court, unless I misapprehend what is said, would have it apply no matter how seriously it frustrated a State's substantive regulation of the primary conduct and affairs of its citizens. Since the members of the Advisory Committee, the Judicial Conference, and this Court who formulated the Federal Rules are presumably reasonable men, it follows that the integrity of the Federal Rules is absolute. Whereas the unadulterated outcome and forum-shopping tests may err too far toward honoring state rules, I submit that the Court's "arguably procedural, *ergo* constitutional" test moves too fast and far in the other direction.

The courts below relied upon this Court's decisions in Ragan v. Merchants Transfer & Warehouse Co., 337 U.S. 530, 69 S.Ct. 1233, 93 L.Ed. 1520, and Cohen v. Beneficial Indus. Loan Corp., 337 U.S. 541, 69 S.Ct. 1221, 93 L.Ed. 1528. Those cases deserve more attention than this Court has given them, particularly Ragan which, if still good law, would in my opinion call for affirmance of the result reached by the Court of Appeals. Further, a discussion of these two cases will serve to illuminate the "diversity" thesis I am advocating.

. . . I think that [Ragan] was wrong. At most, application of the Federal Rule would have meant that potential Kansas tort defendants would have to defer for a few days the satisfaction of knowing that they had not been sued within the limitations period. The choice of the Federal Rule would have had no effect on the primary stages of private activity from which torts arise, and only the most minimal effect on behavior following the commission of the tort. In such circumstances the interest of the federal system in proceeding under its own rules should have prevailed.

Cohen v. Beneficial Indus. Loan Corp. held that a federal diversity court must apply a state statute requiring a small stockholder in a stockholder derivative suit to post a bond securing payment of defense costs as a condition to prosecuting an action. Such a statute is not "outcome determinative"; the plaintiff can win with or without it. . . . The proper view of Cohen is in my opinion, that the statute was meant to inhibit small stockholders from instituting "strike suits," and thus it was designed and could be expected to have a substantial impact on private primary activity. Anyone who was at the trial bar during the period when Cohen arose can appreciate the strong state policy reflected in the statute. I think it wholly legitimate to view Federal Rule 23 as not purporting to deal with the problem. But even had the Federal Rules purported to do so, and in so doing provided a substantially less effective deterrent to strike suits, I think the state rule should still have prevailed. That is where I believe the Court's view differs from mine; for the Court attributes such overriding force to the Federal Rules that it is hard to think of a case where a conflicting state rule would be allowed to operate, even though the state rule reflected policy considerations which, under Erie, would lie within the realm of state legislative authority.

It remains to apply what has been said to the present case. The Massachusetts rule provides that an executor need not answer suits unless in-hand service was made upon him or notice of the action was filed in the proper registry of probate within one year of his giving bond. The evident intent of this statute is to permit an executor to distribute the estate which he is administering without fear that further liabilities may be outstanding for which he could be held personally liable. If the Federal District Court in Massachusetts applies Rule 4(d)(1) of the Federal Rules of Civil Procedure instead of the Massachusetts service rule, what effect would that have on the speed and assurance with which estates are distributed? As I see it, the effect would not be substantial. It would mean simply that an executor would have to check at his own house or the federal courthouse as well as the registry of probate before he could distribute the estate with impunity. As this does not seem enough to give rise to any real impingement on the vitality of the state policy which the Massachusetts rule is intended to serve, I concur in the judgment of the Court.

NOTES

(1) Is *Hanna* a pathway to an "unfair" federal forum? "The case for unfairness would seem strongest when a citizen of State A and a citizen of State B sue another citizen of State B in separate actions arising out of the same tort. Both states might have the same restrictive rules of discovery which would prevent the plaintiffs from discovering the evidence needed to win. The more lenient Federal Rules, on the other hand, would enable a plaintiff to discover this evidence. Because the citizen of State A can bring suit in federal court, he wins, while his counterpart across the state line loses." See Comment, Choice of Procedure in Diversity Cases, 75 Yale L.J. 477, 481 (1966), a thoughtful discussion which approves the hypothetical case as consistent with the responsibility of federal courts to provide proper and fair rules of procedure.

(2) Is Harlan, J., correct in asserting that the majority's test of "arguably procedural, *ergo* constitutional" moves too fast and too far from the *Guaranty Trust* same-outcome test? Does he have the key to the *Erie* puzzle in his contention that the purpose of the substance-procedure distinction should be to avoid causing uncertainty in citizens' day-to-day primary activity by assuring

that they not be subject to two conflicting sets of laws? Would his view lead to a different decision in *Guaranty Trust*? Is he right about *Ragan* and *Cohen*? How would he analyze Woods? Cf. Angel v. Bullington, 330 U.S. 183, 67 S.Ct. 657, 91 L.Ed. 832 (1947).

(3) Does it make sense to call upon the same body, the United States Supreme Court, both to approve the adoption of Federal Rules of Civil Procedure and to be ultimate arbiter of their validity if later challenged in a lawsuit? Does the Court's initial approval of such rules amount in effect to an advisory opinion on their validity? What effect should it be given when the Court rules on the subsequent challenge? Do these apparent incongruities suggest that the rulemaking function under the Enabling Act should be transferred to a different body? See generally Weinstein, Reform of Federal Court Rule Making Procedures (1976); Carrington, "Substance" and "Procedure" in the Rules Enabling Act, 1989 Duke L.Rev. 281.

(4) For an historical account of the adoption of the Rules Enabling Act and its relationship to *Erie*, see Burbank, The Rules Enabling Act of 1934, 130 U.Pa. L.Rev. 1015 (1982). In honor of the 50th birthday of the Federal Rules of Civil Procedure, several symposia were held. For a sampling of the festivities, see Weinstein, The Ghost of Process Past: The Fiftieth Anniversary of the Federal Rules of Civil Procedure and Erie, 54 Brooklyn L.Rev. 1 (1988), and the other articles appearing in this volume; Symposium: The 50th Anniversary of the Federal Rules of Civil Procedure, 1938–1988, 137 U.Pa.L.Rev. 1901 (1989).

SECTION 4. THE AFTERMATH OF HANNA

A. WHEN THERE IS A FEDERAL RULE DIRECTLY IN POINT

1. FEDERAL RULES OF CIVIL PROCEDURE

The part of the *Hanna* opinion dealing with the validity of Federal Rules promulgated under the Enabling Act has, not surprisingly, produced a marked increase in the proportion of decisions applying federal rather than state law in situations falling within its terms. As of 1972, for example, a review of such decisions by the First Circuit in Johnson Chemical Co. v. Condado Center, Inc. (453 F.2d 1044, 1046–47 (1st Cir. 1972)), included Sylvestri v. Warner & Swasey Co., 398 F.2d 598 (2 Cir. 1968) (commencement of action governed by Federal Rules); Szantay v. Beech Aircraft Corp., 349 F.2d 60, 66 (4 Cir. 1965) (federal policy favoring convenient forums outweighs state doorclosing statute); Atkins v. Schmutz Mfg. Co., 435 F.2d 527 (4 Cir. 1970) (tolling effect of pendency of identical suit in another federal court determined by federal law); Wratchford v. S.J. Groves & Sons Co., 405 F.2d 1061 (4 Cir. 1969) (sufficiency of evidence to go to jury determined by federal law); Har-Pen Truck Lines, Inc. v. Mills, 378 F.2d 705 (5 Cir. 1967) (joinder of claims governed by federal rules); Fidelity & Casualty Co. of N.Y. v. Funel, 383 F.2d 42 (5 Cir. 1967) (Federal Rule 43(a) governs admissibility of evidence); Eyerly Aircraft Co. v. Killian, 414 F.2d 591 (5 Cir. 1969) (federal rules of pleading govern in federal court); Ransom v. Brennan, 437 F.2d 513 (5 Cir. 1971) (manner of substitution of executor governed by federal rules); Crowder v. Gordons Transports, Inc., 387 F.2d 413 (8 Cir. 1967) (relation back of amended complaint governed by federal rules).

2. THE FEDERAL RULES OF EVIDENCE

At the time the *Hanna* decision appeared, the Advisory Committee charged with drafting the Federal Rules of Evidence was well into its task. Since Evidence is considered a branch of the law of Procedure and the Federal Evidence codification had been undertaken under the general authority of the same Rules Enabling Act as the Federal Rules of Civil Procedure, it was generally understood that the portion of the *Hanna* opinion governing the validity of such rules rather than that relating to the "relatively unguided Erie choice" would apply. This would significantly diminish the hazard that some rules of evidence, such as those governing privilege for confidential communications between attorney and client, doctor and patient, etcetera, might be held invalid.

Thus as to privileges, the Evidence Advisory Committee noted that

"Regardless of what might once have been thought to be the command of Erie Railroad Co. v. Tompkins, . . . as to observance of state created privileges in diversity cases, Hanna v. Plumer, . . . is believed to locate the problem in the area of choice rather than necessity."

Not all commentators were equally sanguine.

Compare Green, Highlights of the Proposed Federal Rules of Evidence, 4 Ga.L.Rev. 1, 14–17 (1969) *with* Korn, Continuing Effect of State Rules of Evidence in the Federal Courts, 48 F.R.D. 65 (1969) and Weinstein, the Uniformity-Conformity Dilemma Facing Draftsmen of Federal Rules of Evidence, 69 Colum.L.Rev. 353 (1969).

And in the end the *Hanna* philosophy proved no obstacle to congressional alteration of the rules proposed by the Committee and approved by the Court relating to presumptions and the competency of witnesses as well as the confidential communication privileges, requiring the Federal courts to apply state law on these matters in actions otherwise governed by state substantive law. The Congressional thinking is clearly articulated in the pertinent legislative documents, of which the following excerpts from the House Report are fairly representative (House Rep. No. 93–650 [Comm. on the Judiciary], U.S.Code Cong. & Ad.News, 93d Cong., 2d Sess., No. 12A, pp. 72–73 [Jan. 15, 1975]):

Article V

* * *

The Committee amended Article V to eliminate all of the Court's specific Rules on privileges. . . . The Committee also included in its amendment a proviso . . . designed to require the application of State privilege law in civil actions and proceedings governed by Erie Railroad Co. v. Tompkins, 304 U.S. 64 (1938), a result in accord with current federal court decisions. See Republic Gear Co. v. Borg-Warner Corp., 381 F.2d 551, 555–556 n. 2 (2nd Cir.1967). The Committee deemed the proviso to be necessary in the light of the Advisory Committee's view (see its note to Court Rule 501) that this result is not mandated under *Erie*.

The rationale underlying the proviso is that federal law should not supersede that of the States in substantive areas such as privilege absent a compelling reason. The Committee believes that in civil cases the federal courts where an element of a claim or defense is not grounded upon a federal question, there is no federal interest strong enough to justify departure from State policy. In addition, the Committee considered that the Court's proposed Article V would have promoted forum shopping in some civil actions, depending upon differences in the privilege law applied as among the State and federal courts. The Committee's proviso, on the other hand, under which the federal courts are bound to apply the State's privilege law in actions founded upon a State-created right or defense, removes the incentive to "shop".

Rule 601

Rule 601 as submitted to the Congress provided that "Every person is competent to be a witness except as otherwise provided in these rules." One effect of the Rule as proposed would have been to abolish age, mental capacity, and other grounds recognized in some State jurisdictions as making a person incompetent as a witness. The greatest controversy centered around the Rule's rendering inapplicable in the federal courts the so-called Dead Man's Statutes which exist in some States. Acknowledging that there is substantial disagreement as to the merit of Dead Man's Statutes, the Committee nevertheless believed that where such statutes have been enacted they represent State policy which should not be overturned in the absence of a compelling federal interest. The Committee therefore amended the Rule to make competency in civil actions determinable in accordance with State law with respect to elements of claims or defenses as to which State law supplies the rule of decision. Cf. Courtland v. Walston & Co., Inc., 340 F.Supp. 1076, 1087–1092 (S.D.N.Y.1972).

B. THE "RELATIVELY UNGUIDED ERIE CHOICE"

The latter part of the *Hanna* opinion propounded a test for rules promulgated under the Rules Enabling Act, and this test has led to a relatively consistent pattern of results. But the same cannot be said when other procedural rules have been at issue. For one, *Hanna* offers no test for cases such as *Byrd,* which involve federal rules not enacted under the authority of the Rules Enabling Act. Some commentators have argued that *Hanna* overruled *Byrd,* leaving the courts bereft of a rule for deciding the vertical choice-of-law question outside the Rules Enabling Act context. Some courts have continued to apply *Byrd* in those situations; others use *York.* Compare, for example, Masino v. Outboard Marine Corp., 652 F.2d 330 (3d Cir.1981), cert. denied 454 U.S. 1055, 102 S.Ct. 601, 70 L.Ed.2d 591 (1981) (choosing federal requirement for a unanimous jury verdict over state rule requiring only five-sixths vote) with Edelson v. Soricelli, 610 F.2d 131 (3d Cir.1979) (upholding federal court's use of a state law that requires parties to submit medical malpractice claims to arbitration before they can litigate them in court). But see Justice Scalia's dissent in Stewart Organization, Inc. v. Ricoh Corp., discussed p. 388, Note (3), infra.

The second set of cases that are problematic after *Hanna* are those in which it is plausible to deny that there is a direct conflict between state law and a federal rule enacted under the Rules Enabling Act. This issue was created by the *Hanna* decision itself. The majority had made the statement that *Erie* had never led to the "displacement of a Federal Rule by an inconsistent state rule," but, in fact, *Ragan, Woods,* and *Cohen,* p. 365, supra, had all favored state law over ostensibly inconsistent federal provisions (Rules 3, 17(b), and what is now 23.1 respectively).

In his concurrence, Justice Harlan had tried to spare the federal courts the very difficult task of deciding which cases presented genuine conflicts and which did not by suggesting that *Ragan* was not good law after *Hanna.* Unfortunately, however, his view was rejected in Walker v. Armco Steel Corp., 446 U.S. 740, 100 S.Ct. 1978, 64 L.Ed.2d 659 (1980). The facts of that diversity case were virtually identical to *Ragan:* the complaint was filed before the statute of limitations had run, but process was not served on the defendant's authorized agent until after the limitations period had expired. As in *Ragan,* the state had a statute providing that actions commence for statute of limitations purposes at the date on which the summons was served, and the plaintiff argued that Rule 3 displaced this provision by defining commencement in federal court as the day on which the action was filed. By affirming dismissal of the action under the authority of *Ragan,* and arguing that "there is no direct conflict between the federal rule and the state law," the *Walker* Court invited further litigation on the question of when federal and state laws are in sufficiently direct conflict to invoke the *Hanna* test.

BURLINGTON NORTHERN RAILROAD CO. v. WOODS

Supreme Court of the United States, 1987.
480 U.S. 1, 107 S.Ct. 967, 94 L.Ed.2d 1.*

JUSTICE MARSHALL delivered the opinion of the Court.

This case presents the issue whether, in diversity actions, federal courts must apply a state statute that imposes a fixed penalty on appellants who obtain stays of judgment pending unsuccessful appeals.

* * *

[In this personal injury action, brought in the Alabama state court and removed to the federal district court, a judgment on a jury verdict for the plaintiff had been affirmed on appeal without modification. The Court of Appeals then assessed the penalty prescribed by an Alabama statute.]

The Alabama statute provides in relevant part:

"When a judgment or decree is entered or rendered for money, whether debt or damages, and the same has been stayed on appeal by the execution of bond, with surety, if the appellate court affirms the judgment of the court below, it must also enter judgment against all or any of the obligors on the bond for the amount of the affirmed judgment, 10 percent damages thereon and the costs of the appellate court . . . ." Ala.Code § 12–22–72 (1986). . . .

Petitioner contends that the statute's underlying purposes and mandatory mode of operation conflict with the purposes and operation of Rule 38 of the Federal Rules of Appellate Procedure, and therefore that the statute should not be applied by federal courts sitting in diversity. Entitled "Damages for delay," Rule 38 provides: "If the court of appeals shall determine that an appeal is frivolous, it may award just damages and single or double costs to the appellee." See also 28 U.S.C. § 1912. Under this Rule, "damages are awarded by the court in its discretion in the case of a frivolous appeal as a matter of justice to the appellee and as a penalty against the appellant." Advisory Committee's Notes on Fed.Rule App.Proc. 38, 28 U.S.C.App., p. 492.

In Hanna v. Plumer, 380 U.S. 460, 85 S.Ct. 1136, 14 L.Ed.2d 8 (1965), we set forth the appropriate test for resolving conflicts between state law and the Federal Rules. The initial step is to determine whether, when fairly construed, the scope of Federal Rule 38 is "sufficiently broad" to cause a "direct collision" with the state law or, implicitly, to "control the issue" before the court, thereby leaving no room for the operation of that law. Walker v. Armco Steel Corp., 446 U.S. 740, 749–750, and n. 9, 100 S.Ct. 1978, 1984–85, and n. 9, 64 L.Ed. 2d 659 (1980); *Hanna*, supra, 380 U.S., at 471–472, 85 S.Ct., at 1143–44. The Rule must then be applied if it represents a valid exercise of Congress' rule-making authority, which originates in the Constitution

---

* Footnotes omitted.

and has been bestowed on this Court by the Rules Enabling Act, 28 U.S.C. § 2072. *Hanna,* 380 U.S., at 471–474, 85 S.Ct., at 1143–45.

The constitutional constraints on the exercise of this rulemaking authority define a test of reasonableness. Rules regulating matters indisputably procedural are *a priori* constitutional. Rules regulating matters "which, though falling within the uncertain area between substance and procedure, are rationally capable of classification as either," also satisfy this constitutional standard. . . .

The Rules Enabling Act, however, contains an additional requirement. The Federal Rule must not "abridge, enlarge or modify any substantive right . . .." 28 U.S.C. § 2072. The cardinal purpose of Congress in authorizing the development of a uniform and consistent system of rules governing federal practice and procedure suggests that Rules which incidentally affect litigants' substantive rights do not violate this provision if reasonably necessary to maintain the integrity of that system of rules.

. . . Moreover, the study and approval given each proposed Rule by the Advisory Committee, the Judicial Conference, and this Court, and the statutory requirement that the Rule be reported to Congress for a period of review before taking effect, see 28 U.S.C. § 2072, give the Rules presumptive validity under both the constitutional and statutory constraints. See *Hanna,* supra, at 471, 85 S.Ct., at 1144.

Applying the *Hanna* analysis to an analogous Mississippi statute which provides for a mandatory affirmance penalty, the United States Court of Appeals for the Fifth Circuit concluded in Affholder, Inc. v. Southern Rock, Inc., 746 F.2d 305 (1984), that the statute conflicted with Rule 38 and thus was not applicable in federal diversity actions. The Fifth Circuit discussed two aspects of the conflict: (1) the discretionary mode of operation of the Federal Rule, compared to the mandatory operation of the Mississippi statute, and (2) the limited effect of the Rule in penalizing only frivolous appeals or appeals interposed for purposes of delay, compared to the effect of the Mississippi statute in penalizing every unsuccessful appeal regardless of merit. Id., at 308–309.

We find the Fifth Circuit's analysis persuasive. Rule 38 affords a Court of Appeals plenary discretion to assess "just damages" in order to penalize an appellant who takes a frivolous appeal and to compensate the injured appellee for the delay and added expense of defending the District Court's judgment. Thus, the Rule's discretionary mode of operation unmistakably conflicts with the mandatory provision of Alabama's affirmance penalty statute. Moreover, the purposes underlying the Rule are sufficiently co-extensive with the asserted purposes of the Alabama statute to indicate that the Rule occupies the statute's field of operation so as to preclude its application in federal diversity actions.

Petitioner nevertheless argues that, because Alabama has a similar Appellate Rule which may be applied in state court alongside the affirmance penalty statute, see Ala.Rule App.Proc. 38; McAnnally v.

Levco, Inc., 456 So.2d 66, 67 (Ala.1984), a federal court sitting in diversity could impose the mandatory penalty and likewise remain free to exercise its discretionary authority under Federal Rule 38. This argument, however, ignores the significant possibility that a Court of Appeals may, in any given case, find a limited justification for imposing penalties in an amount *less than* 10% of the lower court's judgment. Federal Rule 38 adopts a case-by-case approach to identifying and deterring frivolous appeals; the Alabama statute precludes any exercise of discretion within its scope of operation. Whatever circumscriptive effect the mandatory affirmance penalty statute may have on the state court's exercise of discretion under Alabama's Rule 38, that Rule provides no authority for defining the scope of discretion allowed under Federal Rule 38.

Federal Rule 38 regulates matters which can reasonably be classified as procedural, thereby satisfying the constitutional standard for validity. Its displacement of the Alabama statute also satisfies the statutory constraints of the Rules Enabling Act. The choice made by the drafters of the Federal Rules in favor of a discretionary procedure affects only the process of enforcing litigants' rights and not the rights themselves.

We therefore hold that the Alabama mandatory affirmance penalty statute has no application to judgments entered by federal courts sitting in diversity.

Reversed.

NOTES

(1) For a decision upholding the constitutionality of a similar penalty, see Bankers Life and Casualty v. Crenshaw, 486 U.S. 71, 108 S.Ct. 1645, 100 L.Ed.2d 62 (1988).

(2) Is there really a "direct" collision in *Burlington*? The federal rule gives the court authority to impose costs for frivolous appeals; it does not by its terms address the question of who bears the cost of nonfrivolous appeals. Thus, it could be argued that the collision is no greater than that involved in Cohen v. Beneficial Industrial Loan Corp., p. 365, supra, where state law mandated that a bond be posted to secure costs in stockholder derivative actions while federal law was silent on this issue. Might it be that the strict collision mandated by the *Hanna* majority and by *Walker* applies only to federal rules whose applicability in diversity had been adjudicated prior to *Hanna?*

NOTE ON OTHER FEDERAL STATUTES

What analysis should be used to decide the applicability in diversity of federal statutes *not* enacted under the authority of the Rules Enabling Act? In Stewart Organization, Inc. v. Ricoh Corp., 487 U.S. 22, 108 S.Ct. 2239, 101 L.Ed.2d 22 (1988), the issue was "whether a federal court sitting in diversity should apply state or federal law in adjudicating a motion to transfer a case to a venue provided in a contractual forum-selection clause." Alabama law would not have honored the clause, which provided that "the Borough of Manhattan,

New York City, New York, shall have exclusive jurisdiction over any case or controversy arising under or in connection with this Agreement," but the transfer may have been possible under 28 U.S.C.A. § 1404(a) or through a dismissal pursuant to 28 U.S.C.A. § 1406. In directing the district court to entertain the § 1404(a) motion, the Court stated (footnotes omitted):

> "A District Court's decision whether to apply a federal statute such as § 1404(a) in a diversity action, however, involves a considerably less intricate analysis than that which governs the 'relatively unguided Erie choice.' Hanna v. Plumer, 380 U.S. 460, 471, 85 S.Ct. 1136, 1144, 14 L.Ed.2d 8 (1965) (referring to Erie R. Co. v. Tompkins, 304 U.S. 64, 58 S.Ct. 817, 82 L.Ed. 1188 (1938)). Our cases indicate that when the federal law sought to be applied is a congressional statute, the first and chief question for the District Court's determination is whether the statute is 'sufficiently broad to control the issue before the Court.' Walker v. Armco Steel Corp., 446 U.S. 740, 749–750, 100 S.Ct. 1978, 1985, 64 L.Ed.2d 659 (1980); Burlington Northern R. Co. v. Woods, 480 U.S. 1, ___, 107 S.Ct. 967, ___, 94 L.Ed.2d 1 (1987). This question involves a straightforward exercise in statutory interpretation to determine if the statute covers the point in dispute. See Walker v. Armco Steel Corp., supra, at 750, and n. 9. See also Burlington Northern R. Co. v. Woods, supra (identifying inquiry as whether the Federal Rule 'occupies [a state rule's] field of operation'). If the District Court determines that a federal statute covers the point in dispute, it proceeds to inquire whether the statute represents a valid exercise of Congress' authority under the Constitution. See Hanna v. Plumer, supra, 380 U.S., at 471, 85 S.Ct., at 1144 (citing Erie R. Co. v. Tompkins, 304 U.S. 64, 77–79, 58 S.Ct. 817, 822–23, 82 L.Ed. 1188 (1938)). If Congress intended to reach the issue before the District Court, and if it enacted its intention into law in a manner that abides with the Constitution, that is the end of the matter; '[f]ederal courts are bound to apply rules enacted by Congress with respect to matters . . . over which it has legislative power.' Prima Paint Corp. v. Flood & Conklin Mfg. Co., 388 U.S. 395, 406, 87 S.Ct. 1801, 1807, 18 L.Ed.2d 1270 (1967) . . . . Thus, a District Court sitting in diversity must apply a federal statute that controls the issue before the court and that represents a valid exercise of Congress' constitutional powers."

In applying this test, the Court stated:

> "The constitutional authority of Congress to enact section 1404(a) is not subject to serious question. As the Court made plain in Hanna, 'the constitutional provision for a federal court system . . . carries with it congressional power to make rules governing the practice and pleading in those courts, which in turn includes a power to regulate matters which, though fall-

ing within the uncertain area between substance and procedure, are rationally capable of classification as either.' 380
U.S., at 472, 85 S.Ct., at 1144. . . . Section 1404(a) is doubtless capable of classification as a procedural rule, and indeed,
we have so classified it in holding that a transfer pursuant to
§ 1404(a) does not carry with it a change in the applicable law.
See Van Dusen v. Barrack, supra, 376 U.S., at 636–637, 84
S.Ct., at 819–820 ('[B]oth the history and purposes of § 1404(a)
indicate that it should be regarded as a federal judicial housekeeping measure'). It therefore falls comfortably within Congress's powers under Article III as augmented by the Necessary and Proper Clause."

NOTES

(1) See also Budinich v. Becton Dickinson & Co., p. 1050, infra, finding the
federal rules on appealability applicable in diversity.

(2) Note that as in *Burlington,* the federal and state laws at issue in *Ricoh*
were not in the direct collision seemingly required by *Hanna.* Thus, in dissent,
Justice Scalia argued:

> In this case, the Court must determine whether the scope of § 1404(a)
> is sufficiently broad to cause a direct collision with state law or
> implicitly to control the issue before the Court, i.e., validity between
> the parties of the forum-selection clause, thereby leaving no room for
> the operation of state law. . . . I conclude that it is not.

On this point, the majority had dropped the following footnote:

> n. 4. Our cases at times have referred to the question at this stage of
> the analysis as an inquiry into whether there is a "direct collision"
> between state and federal law. See, e.g., Walker v. Armco Steel Corp.,
> 446 U.S., at 749; Hanna v. Plumer, 380 U.S. 460, 472 (1965). Logic
> indicates, however, and a careful reading of the relevant passages
> confirms, that this language is not meant to mandate that federal law
> and state law be perfectly coextensive and equally applicable to the
> issue at hand; rather, the "direct collision" language, at least where
> the applicability of a federal statute is at issue, expresses the require-
> ment that the federal statute be sufficiently broad to cover the point in
> dispute. See Hanna v. Plumer, supra, at 470. It would make no sense
> for the supremacy of federal law to wane precisely because there is no
> state law directly on point.

Again: does the strict collision envisioned by *Hanna* and *Walker* remain good
law?

(3) Upon finding the *Hanna* test inapplicable to the § 1404(a) issue, Justice
Scalia was faced with the task, alluded to earlier, of proposing an analysis for
the "relatively unguided Erie choice." Interestingly, he went back to *York,* p.
362, supra, finding that "it has been common ground in this Court since Erie
. . . that when a federal procedural statute or Rule of Procedure is not on
point, substantial uniformity of predictable outcome between federal and state
courts in adjudicating claims should be striven for." Thus, Justice Scalia would
have applied Alabama law and refused to enforce the forum selection clause.

(4) Would a better way to avoid "the mischievous results" identified in *Erie* be to abolish diversity jurisdiction? Why did the Framers create this jurisdiction? Are their concerns valid today? See Friendly, The Historic Basis of Diversity Jurisdiction, 41 Harv.L.Rev. 483 (1928); H. Friendly, Federal Jurisdiction: A General View 139–52 (1973) (advocating abolition of most of this jurisdiction).

SECTION 5. FEDERAL COMMON LAW

Return once again to *Erie*. In his discussion of the constitutionality of *Swift*, Justice Brandeis said: "There is no federal general common law." Does this mean there is no federal common law at all? We have seen that "no one doubts federal power over procedure," and have explained that principle on the ground that the forum court should apply rules regulating that conduct which is of unique concern to it. Might it not be that there are other issues of such significant national interest that federal judge-made law displaces contrary state provisions? In fact, several such spheres have been identified and are discussed in greater detail in courses such as Federal Courts. Briefly, these include:

1. *Controversies between the states.* The lead case here is Hinderlider State Engineer v. La Plata River & Cherry Creek Ditch Co., 304 U.S. 92 (1938), which was decided the same day as *Erie* and also authored by Justice Brandeis. The underlying substantive issue was the allocation of water rights between Colorado and New Mexico, but before that question could be addressed, the choice-of-law issue had to be resolved. Not unsurprisingly, Colorado law would have led to an allocation favoring the Colorado claimants, while the case would have been resolved for the New Mexicans had their law governed. Instead, the Supreme Court announced that when boundary questions arise between the states, they are governed by "federal common law."

2. *Proprietary interests of the United States.* Clearfield Trust Co. v. United States, 318 U.S. 363, 63 S.Ct. 573, 87 L.Ed. 838 (1943), is an example. The United States had issued a check which was stolen, forged, and cashed at J.C. Penney Co. Upon honoring the presentation of the check by Penney's bank, the United States' account was debited. Although a bank is liable for debiting the drawer's account when it mistakenly honors a forged check, state laws do require the drawer to notify the bank of the forgery within a specified period of time. The United States had not complied with the time limit, and so state law would have barred a suit to recover the proceeds. The Supreme Court, however, allowed the Government to recover. It found that application of state law to the commercial transactions of the United States "would subject the rights and duties of the United States to exceptional uncertainties." Accordingly, the Court fashioned its own—federal—law to govern the transaction.

3. *International affairs.* In Banco Nacional de Cuba v. Sabbatino, 376 U.S. 398, 84 S.Ct. 923, 11 L.Ed.2d 804 (1964), a diversity case, the

issue involved ownership of a sugar shipment that had been expropriated by the Cuban government. The original recipient claimed rights to the sugar under New York and international law, but the Supreme Court held that federal law applied and then announced that this law barred judicial examination of expropriations. The Court reasoned that international relations involved problems that "are uniquely federal in nature." Admiralty claims are decided under federal law for similar reasons.

4. *Implied rights of action.* Review note (2) on page 199. From time to time, litigants have successfully argued that although a particular federal enactment does not expressly provide a private right of action for the people it protects, the court should imply that such a right exists in order to effectuate fully the goals of the law. When such a claim is recognized, the right that is created is, of course, federal common law. An example of such a claim is discussed in footnote 9 of the next case.

The following decision is the first of several on the product liability case between veterans of the war in Vietnam and chemical companies that supplied the United States with the defoliant, Agent Orange. To gain a deeper perspective on the case, which raises many interesting procedural issues and larger questions on the role of courts, P. Schuck, Agent Orange on Trial (1986), is highly recommended.

IN RE "AGENT ORANGE" PRODUCT LIABILITY LITIGATION

United States Court of Appeals, Second Circuit, 1980.
635 F.2d 987.

KEARSE, CIRCUIT JUDGE *: This appeal presents the question whether claims asserted by veterans of the United States armed forces against companies which supplied the United States government with chemicals that are alleged to have been contaminated and to have injured the veterans and their families, are governed by federal common law. Defendants-appellants Diamond Shamrock Corporation, Monsanto Company, Thompson–Hayward Chemical Company, Hercules Incorporated and the Dow Chemical Company were the manufacturers of various herbicides including "Agent Orange" for use by the military as defoliants in the Vietnam War. The plaintiffs, veterans of that war and their families, allege that they have sustained various physical injuries by reason of the veterans' exposure to Agent Orange. Plaintiffs seek redress of those injuries under federal common law, and have invoked the "federal question" jurisdiction of the district court. 28 U.S.C. § 1331(a) (1976). Defendants contest the existence of a federal common law cause of action, and moved below to dismiss for lack of subject matter jurisdiction. . . .

* Some footnotes omitted.

I

* * *

Plaintiffs argue that federal common law should be applied to their claims principally because of the unique federal nature of the relationship between the soldier and his government. . . . They contend that this interest brings the case within the doctrine of Clearfield Trust Co. v. United States, 318 U.S. 363, 366 (1943), which held that, in order to ensure uniformity and certainty, "[the] rights and duties of the United States on commercial paper which it issues are governed by federal rather than local law." Plaintiffs argue that the government similarly has an interest in having all of its veterans compensated by government contractors who manufactured or marketed Agent Orange, and that application of the respective state laws would impede recovery on a uniform basis.

The district court rejected the contention that Clearfield Trust stated the controlling principle, recognizing that the United States, a party to Clearfield Trust, is not party to the plaintiffs' claims here. Rather, . . . the district court applied a three-factor test to determine whether federal common law governs plaintiffs' claims:

> (1) the existence of a substantial federal interest in the outcome of a litigation; (2) the effect on this federal interest should state law be applied; and (3) the effect on state interests should state law be displaced by federal common law.

[After analyzing these factors, the district court decided the case for the plaintiffs and certified this appeal pursuant to 28 U.S.C. § 1292(b) (1976) [9].]

9. The district court correctly determined that there is no private right of action under [the Federal Insecticide, Fungicide, and Rodenticide Act], 7 U.S.C. § 135 et seq. (1976). The four factors to be considered [in deciding whether there is a right of action] under Cort v. Ash are (1) whether the plaintiff is "one of the class for whose especial benefit the statute was enacted," (2) whether there is "any indication of legislative intent, explicit or implicit, either to create such a remedy or to deny one," (3) whether a right of action would be "consistent with the underlying purposes of the legislative scheme," and (4) whether the cause of action is "one traditionally relegated to state law, in an area basically the concern of the States, so that it would be inappropriate to infer a cause of action based solely on federal law."

First, there is no indication that the bill was enacted for the especial benefit of military men. It is clear that Congress's intent was to protect the public in general, with perhaps some special consideration for "agricultural producers and other users" of pesticides and rodenticides. FIFRA makes no special mention of soldiers. As to the second of the Cort factors, we see no clear indication of legislative intent to create a private remedy. Plaintiffs have cited no legislative history on this point, nor have they presented any detailed statutory analysis. The Act itself is primarily concerned with establishing an administrative scheme of labeling, registration and enforcement; there are indications that Congress expected that scheme to be the exclusive means of enforcement. The third Cort factor is of little assistance here. While a private right of action might enhance enforcement of the Act's substantive provisions to some extent, it would also increase the burden on manufacturers (without commensurately increasing protection of injured persons who can recover damages under state product liability law), something which the administrative scheme of registration was specifically intended to avoid. Finally, the fourth Cort factor cuts strongly against the plaintiffs. The area of product liability

II

Both plaintiffs and defendants accept the three-part test that the district court applied to the federal common law issue, and for purposes of discussion we accept that framework. But, focusing our consideration chiefly on the first factor of the test, i.e., "the existence of a substantial federal interest in the outcome of the litigation," we disagree with the district court's analysis and conclude that the court gave insufficient weight to the Supreme Court's repeated admonition that

> [in] deciding whether rules of federal common law should be fashioned, normally the guiding principle is that *a significant conflict between some federal policy or interest and the use of state law in the premises must first be specifically shown.*
>
> * * *

Wallis v. Pan American Petroleum Corp., 384 U.S. [63, 68, 86 S.Ct. 1301, 1304, 53 L.Ed.2d 369 (1966)], quoted with emphasis in Miree v. DeKalb County, [433 U.S. 25, 97 S.Ct. 2490, 53 L.Ed.2d 557 (1977)]. . . . Principally we reject the district court's conclusion that there is an identifiable federal policy at stake in this litigation that warrants the creation of federal common law rules.

In considering plaintiffs' contentions, it is essential to delineate precisely the relation of the United States to the claims here at issue. These claims are brought by former servicemen and their families against private manufacturers; they are not asserted by or against the United States, and they do not directly implicate the rights and duties of the United States. They are thus unlike the claims in . . . Clearfield Trust Co. v. United States, supra, in which the government brought suit to enforce its rights in commercial paper issued by it. In [that case] analysis reveals two federal concerns . . . . First, the government has an interest in having uniform rules govern its rights and obligations. Second, the government has a substantive interest in the contents of those uniform rules. . . .

The present litigation is fundamentally different . . . . Since this litigation is between private parties and no substantial rights or duties of the government hinge on its outcome, there is no federal interest in uniformity for its own sake. . . . The fact that application of state law may produce a variety of results is of no moment. It is in the nature of a federal system that different states will apply different rules of law, based on their individual perceptions of what is in the best interests of their citizens. That alone is not grounds in private litigation for judicially creating an overriding federal law. . . .

has been "traditionally relegated to state law," and this is no less true of the products regulated by the FIFRA. See, e.g., Muncy v. Magnolia Chemical Co., 437 S.W.2d 15 (Tex.Civ.App.1968). Thus, we conclude that the district court was correct in ruling that there is no private right of action under the original FIFRA. [A similar result was obtained from the court's analysis of the 1972 amendments to FIFRA].

The second fundamental difference between the present litigation and the Clearfield Trust type of case is that in the latter, the government's substantive interest in the litigation is essentially monothetic, in that it is concerned only with preserving the federal fisc, whereas here the government has two interests; and here the two interests have been placed in sharp contrast with one another. Thus, the government has an interest in the welfare of its veterans; they have given of themselves in the most fundamental way possible in the national interest. But the government also has an interest in the suppliers of its materiel; imposition, for example, of strict liability as contended for by plaintiffs would affect the government's ability to procure materiel without the exaction of significantly higher prices, or the attachment of onerous conditions, or the demand of indemnification or the like. . . .

The extent to which either group *should* be favored, and its welfare deemed "paramount" (see dissent of Chief Judge Feinberg, *post*), is preeminently a policy determination of the sort reserved in the first instance for Congress. The welfare of veterans and that of military suppliers are clearly federal concerns which Congress should appropriately consider in setting policy for the governance of the nation, and it is properly left to Congress in the first instance to strike the balance between the conflicting interests of the veterans and the contractors, and thereby identify federal policy. Although Congress has turned its attention to the Agent Orange problem, it has not determined what the federal policy is with respect to the reconciliation of these two competing interests. . . .

We conclude, therefore, that the district court erred in ruling that plaintiffs' claims were governed by federal common law. The order denying defendants' motion to dismiss for lack of subject matter jurisdiction is accordingly reversed.

FEINBERG, CHIEF JUDGE (dissenting):

. . . I agree with District Judge Pratt that this case should be tried in federal court under rules of federal common law. I therefore dissent from the opinion of the majority.

That the present case is sui generis, and national in its proportions, is evident from the complaint itself. The defendants in this action are five of the largest chemical companies in the nation, all of which admittedly manufactured "Agent Orange," a defoliant, for use by our nation's armed forces in Vietnam between 1962 and 1971. . . . [T]he complaint identifies fifteen groups of plaintiffs, totalling over 800 plaintiffs who, we are told, have filed complaints in 25 judicial districts all across the country. By this time it is probable that 30 to 40 districts are affected, since additional plaintiffs appear daily; plaintiffs' counsel assures us that many more complaints would already have been filed, but for the request of Judge Pratt not to do so until the question of class certification has been resolved. How many plaintiffs will ultimately come forward is unclear. Present plaintiffs assert that as many as 2,400,000 men and women who served in the armed forces could be eligible to sue defendants—not to mention their parents, dependents, and dead or stillborn children. . . . The plaintiffs in these cases complain of injuries sustained as the result of service in our nation's military, in a national endeavor in a foreign land. To the non-legal mind, it would be an odd proposition indeed that this litigation, so patently of national scope and concern, should not be tried in federal court.

As for the legal mind, all involved in this case—the parties, Judge Pratt, and the panel on appeal—appear to agree that federal question jurisdiction depends upon whether a federal common law rule of product liability should be applied.

* * *

The majority concludes that on the facts of this case "there is no federal interest in uniformity for its own sake," and that there is no federal "substantive interest in the content of the rules to be applied." I disagree on both counts. As to uniformity of treatment, this court noted in Owens [v. Haas, 601 F.2d 1242 (2d Cir.), cert. denied, 444 U.S. 980, 100 S.Ct. 483, 62 L.Ed.2d 407 (1979)] that "[because] there is a federal regulatory scheme, there is a federal interest in assuring uniform treatment of federal prisoners." 601 F.2d at 1249. It is anomalous for this court to hold, on the one hand, that the federal government has an interest in "uniform treatment" of its *prisoners* sufficient to warrant the use of a federal rule of recovery, and, on the other hand, that the federal government has no such interest in "uniform treatment" of its *soldiers*. . . .

The majority also concludes that because the government has arguably conflicting substantive interests in the outcome of the litigation, "the federal policy is not yet identifiable." The allegedly conflicting federal interests are in the welfare of veterans and in the welfare of suppliers of war material. But that the plaintiff veterans and the defendant contractors have opposing interests in this litigation hardly means that the paramount federal interest is somehow divided or self-contradictory. The United States has a clear interest in the protection of its soldiers from harm caused by defective war materiel. What other interests does the United States arguably have that might conflict with this clear interest? One such interest might be in seeing that defendants, as suppliers of war materiel, are treated fairly. But that interest cannot be said to conflict with the government's interest in the safety of its soldiers. . . .

Having discerned a significant federal interest, we are next required to determine whether or not a "significant conflict" exists between that interest and the application of state law. This factor is not reached by the majority. But that such a conflict does exist in the present case can hardly be disputed. Given the "distinctively federal" character of the relationship between the federal government and its soldiers, there is an inherent federal interest in the uniform definition of the aspects of that relationship involved in this case. . . .

The third and last factor involves the extent to which state interests would be affected, if state law were to be "displaced" by federal common law in the present case. . . . [T]he states' product liability law is in flux; with respect to a case as novel as the one before us, a consistent and established body of state law is even less discernible. Accordingly, I think that Judge Pratt was correct in holding that the application of federal common law to the case before us would not "displace" state law, because there is no substantial body of state law on this point to be displaced. I thus conclude that all three factors, accepted by the majority as the proper analytical framework, point to the use of a federal common law rule in the present case, giving rise to federal question jurisdiction.

*   *   *

NOTES

(1) Since the plaintiffs and defendants came from so many states, why were the veterans interested in establishing federal question jurisdiction? In fact, the case remained in federal court as a diversity case.

(2) Once the court had decided the vertical choice-of-law question in favor of applying state law, how should it resolve the horizontal issue, namely, which state law applies to claims arising between citizens of the 50 states and defendants from several different states? Or more precisely in light of *Klaxon*, p. 359, supra, which state's choice-law-rule should apply? In a later stage of the proceedings, see p. 486, infra, Judge Weinstein (who took over the case when Judge Pratt was elevated to the Second Circuit) announced that there was no horizontal problem as he perceived "a consensus among the states with respect to the rules of conflicts and applicable substantive law that provides, in effect, a national substantive rule governing the main issues in the case." Is Judge Weinstein correct that there is a national consensus? Did Judge Feinberg win this in the end?

SECTION 6.   "REVERSE" ERIE

So far, the focus has been on the vertical choice-of-law questions occurring in federal courts, issues that arise because the subject matter jurisdiction is broad enough to encompass some cases and issues that do not raise federal questions. But since state courts have concurrent jurisdiction with federal courts on many federal questions, it is also possible for state courts to hear cases that do not raise state questions. In those situations, the same vertical choice-of-law issue is presented, but in reverse.

DICE v. AKRON, CANTON & YOUNGSTOWN RAILROAD CO.

Supreme Court of the United States, 1952.
342 U.S. 359, 72 S.Ct. 312, 96 L.Ed. 398.

MR. JUSTICE BLACK *:

Petitioner, a railroad fireman, was seriously injured when an engine in which he was riding jumped the track. Alleging that his injuries were due to respondent's negligence, he brought this action for damages under the Federal Employers' Liability Act, 35 Stat. 65, 45 U.S.C.A. § 51 et seq., in an Ohio court of common pleas. Respondent's defenses were (1) a denial of negligence and (2) a written document signed by petitioner purporting to release respondent in full for $924.63. Petitioner admitted that he had signed several receipts for payments made him in connection with his injuries but denied that he had made a full and complete settlement of all his claims. He alleged that the purported release was void because he had signed it relying on respondent's deliberately false statement that the document was nothing more than a mere receipt for back wages.

[After a jury decided for the petitioner, the trial judge entered judgment notwithstanding the verdict, reasoning that the validity of the release was governed by Ohio law, and that Ohio law required the judge, not the jury, to decide it. This view was ultimately sustained by the Ohio Supreme Court, one justice dissenting.] We granted certiorari because the decision of the Supreme Court of Ohio appeared to deviate from previous decisions of this Court that federal law governs cases arising under the Federal Employers' Liability Act.

First. We agree with the dissenting judge in the Ohio Supreme Court and hold that validity of releases under the Federal Employers' Liability Act raises a federal question to be determined by federal rather than state law. Congress in § 1 of the Act granted petitioner a right to recover against his employer for damages negligently inflicted. State laws are not controlling in determining what the incidents of this federal right shall be.

    *   *   *

Second. In effect the Supreme Court of Ohio held that an employee trusts his employer at his peril, and that the negligence of an innocent worker is sufficient to enable his employer to benefit by its deliberate fraud. Application of so harsh a rule to defeat a railroad employee's claim is wholly incongruous with the general policy of the Act to give railroad employees a right to recover just compensation for injuries negligently inflicted by their employers. . . . We hold that the correct federal rule is that a release of rights under the Act is void when the employee is induced to sign it by the deliberately false and material statements of the railroad's authorized representatives made to deceive the employee as to the contents of the release. . . .

---

* Footnotes omitted.

Third. Ohio provides and has here accorded petitioner the usual jury trial of factual issues relating to negligence. But Ohio treats factual questions of fraudulent releases differently. It permits the judge trying a negligence case to resolve all factual questions of fraud "other than fraud in the factum." The factual issue of fraud is thus split into fragments, some to be determined by the judge, others by the jury.

It is contended that since a state may consistently with the Federal Constitution provide for trial of cases under the Act by a nonunanimous verdict, Minneapolis & St. Louis R. Co. v. Bombolis, 241 U.S. 211, 36 S.Ct. 595, 60 L.Ed. 961, Ohio may lawfully eliminate trial by jury as to one phase of fraud while allowing jury trial as to all other issues raised. The Bombolis case might be more in point had Ohio abolished trial by jury in all negligence cases including those arising under the federal Act. But Ohio has not done this. It has provided jury trials for cases arising under the federal Act but seeks to single out one phase of the question of fraudulent releases for determination by a judge rather than by a jury. Compare Testa v. Katt, 330 U.S. 386, 67 S.Ct. 810, 9 L.Ed. 967.

We have previously held that "The right to trial by jury is 'a basic and fundamental feature of our system of federal jurisprudence'" and that it is "part and parcel of the remedy afforded railroad workers under the Employers Liability Act." Bailey v. Central Vermont R. Co., 319 U.S. 350, 354, 63 S.Ct. 1062, 1064, 87 L.Ed. 1444. We also recognized in that case that to deprive railroad workers of the benefit of a jury trial where there is evidence to support negligence "is to take away a goodly portion of the relief which Congress has afforded them." It follows that the right to trial by jury is too substantial a part of the rights accorded by the Act to permit it to be classified as a mere "local rule of procedure" for denial in the manner that Ohio has here used. Brown v. Western R. Co., 338 U.S. 294, 70 S.Ct. 105, 94 L.Ed. 100.

The trial judge and the Ohio Supreme Court erred in holding that petitioner's rights were to be determined by Ohio law and in taking away petitioner's verdict when the issues of fraud had been submitted to the jury on conflicting evidence and determined in petitioner's favor. The cause is reversed and remanded to the Supreme Court of Ohio for further action not inconsistent with this opinion.

MR. JUSTICE FRANKFURTER, whom MR. JUSTICE REED, MR. JUSTICE JACKSON and MR. JUSTICE BURTON join, concurring for reversal but dissenting from the Court's opinion. [Omitted.]

NOTES

This case raised two vertical choice issues: (1) whether federal or state law applies to the question of the validity of the release and (2) which law applies to the question whether a judge or a jury should decide the issue of fraud. The first question is clearly substantive, so it should come as no surprise that the Court decided that federal law (even federal common law) should apply.

But what about the judge versus jury question? This Court stated that "the right to trial by jury is too substantial a part of the rights accorded by the Act to permit it to be classified as a mere 'local rule of procedure,'" and so required the application of federal law. Review *Byrd*, p. 366, supra. Does *Byrd* overrule *Dice?* Is *Dice* just another example of balancing? If so, why does the balance tip in opposite directions in two cases raising the same issue? Would *Dice* have come out differently had Ohio abolished the civil jury entirely?

Chapter Eight

THE SCOPE OF THE LAWSUIT

ESSENTIAL DISTINCTIONS

This Chapter deals with the last question that must be resolved before litigation can begin in earnest. The three issues discussed, real party in interest, capacity to sue and be sued, and joinder, define the ultimate scope of the case by determining what claims and parties should or may be involved. Like the standing requirement encountered earlier, real-party-in-interest rules focus on the litigants' stake in the lawsuit. In standing law, the question is whether the judicial system is well served by having claims presented to it by a litigant with that particular slant on the proceedings. Here, in contrast, the focus is mainly on the opponent: is his objective to see the controversy ended served by requiring him to defend himself against this particular litigant. Capacity rules also focus on the parties; they are intended to make sure that the participants in the suit are adequately represented in the proceedings.

The joinder rules occupy most of the Chapter. These encompass a variety of devices which enable, and sometimes require, the parties to expand the initial lawsuit to include more claims and parties. These rules protect the judicial system, the litigants, and sometimes even strangers to the suit. With each rule, the following questions should be considered: (1) what interests are protected by the rule, (2) who can invoke its benefits, (3) how does the rule differ from other joinder devices, and (4) how does the rule deal with the general requirements for adjudication, such as personal and subject matter jurisdiction?

In many cases, failure to observe these rules is evident only after the lawsuit has terminated. If so, the rules are tested not in the course of the first trial, but rather, in later litigation. For example, a party may bring a second suit to assert a claim that existed at the time of the first case but had not been pressed, or a later suit may be brought by or against parties who were not present the first time around. In those instances, the opponent may make the argument that the earlier omission is fatal to the later case; that the new suit is precluded under the laws of res judicata. Because of the close alignment between the material presented here and res judicata, the interaction between this Chapter and Chapter Sixteen bears careful scrutiny.

[handwritten margin notes: "Substitute for insured as a party in a suit against US?", "Can this", "Substituted", "S. 3477", "You", "Can it substitute a party or agency suit against fields"]

SECTION 1. REAL PARTY IN INTEREST

UNITED STATES v. AETNA CASUALTY & SURETY CO.

Supreme Court of the United States, 1949.
338 U.S. 366, 70 S.Ct. 207, 94 L.Ed. 171.

MR. CHIEF JUSTICE VINSON delivered the opinion of the Court.*

These cases, here on certiorari, present this important question under the Federal Tort Claims Act: May an insurance company bring suit in its own name against the United States upon a claim to which it has become subrogated by payment to an insured who would have been able to bring such an action? That question, in turn, requires our consideration of R.S. 3477, the "anti-assignment" statute.

* * *

It is the Government's position that R.S. 3477, which in terms makes "All transfers and assignments . . . of any claim upon the United States, or of any part or share thereof, or interest therein . . . absolutely null and void . . . " except for assignments made after payment of the claim and in accordance with certain prescribed safeguards, includes assignments by operation of law and prohibits suit by the subrogee in its own name.

* * *

Only in brief and argument here was it suggested that the insurance carrier could recover if suit was brought in the name of the insured to the use of the insurer . . . .. It is for that reason that the opinions below were focused upon whether R.S. 3477 is an absolute bar to recovery by the subrogee rather than merely a bar to recovery in the name of the subrogee. We think, however, that even this limited, and somewhat anomalous, reliance upon R.S. 3477 is untenable, first, because of the uniform interpretation given that statute by this Court for the past 75 years, and, second, because of many affirmative indications of congressional intent that subrogation claims should not be excluded from suit in the name of the subrogee under the Tort Claims Act.

. . .

If, then, R.S. 3477 is inapplicable, the Government must defend suits by subrogees as if it were a private person. Rule 17(a) of the Federal Rules of Civil Procedure, which were specifically made applicable to Tort Claims litigation, provides that "Every action shall be prosecuted in the name of the real party in interest," and of course an insurer-subrogee, who has substantive equitable rights, qualifies as such. If the subrogee has paid an entire loss suffered by the insured, it is the only real party in interest and must sue in its own name. 3 Moore Federal Practice (2d ed.) p. 1339. If it has paid only part of the loss, both the insured and insurer (and other insurers, if any, who have

_____
* Footnotes omitted.

also paid portions of the loss) have substantive rights against the tortfeasor which qualify them as real parties in interest.

In cases of partial subrogation the question arises whether suit may be brought by the insurer alone, whether suit must be brought in the name of the insured for his own use and for the use of the insurance company, or whether all parties in interest must join in the action. Under the common-law practice rights acquired by subrogation could be enforced in an action at law only in the name of the insured to the insurer's use, Hall & Long v. Railroad Companies, 13 Wall. 367, 20 L.Ed. 594 (1872); United States v. American Tobacco Co., supra, as was also true of suits on assignments, Glenn v. Marbury, 145 U.S. 499, 12 S.Ct. 914, 36 L.Ed. 790 (1892). Mr. Justice Stone characterized this rule as "a vestige of the common law's reluctance to admit that a chose in action may be assigned, [which] is today but a formality which has been widely abolished by legislation." Aetna Life Ins. Co. v. Moses, 287 U.S. 530, 540, 53 S.Ct. 231, 233, 77 L.Ed. 477 (1933). Under the Federal Rules, the "use" practice is obviously unnecessary, as has long been true in equity, Garrison v. Memphis Insurance Co., 19 How. 312 (1857), and admiralty, Liverpool & Great Western Steam Co. v. Phenix Insurance Co., 129 U.S. 397, 462, 9 S.Ct. 469, 479, 32 L.Ed. 788 (1889). Rule 17(a) was taken almost verbatim from Equity Rule 37. No reason appears why such a practice should now be required in cases of partial subrogation, since both insured and insurer "own" portions of the substantive right and should appear in the litigation in their own names.

Although either party may sue, the United States, upon timely motion, may compel their joinder. Delaware County v. Diebold Safe & Lock Co., 133 U.S. 473, 488, 10 S.Ct. 399, 403, 33 L.Ed. 674 (1890) (applying a state code under the Conformity Act.) 3 Moore, Federal Practice (2d ed.) p. 1348. Both are "necessary" parties. Rule 19(b), Federal Rules of Civil Procedure. The pleadings should be made to reveal and assert the actual interest of the plaintiff, and to indicate the interests of any others in the claim. Additional parties may be added at any stage of the proceedings, on motion of the United States, upon such terms as may be just. Rule 21.

It is true that under this rationale, there will be cases in which all parties cannot be joined because one or more are outside the jurisdiction, and the court may nevertheless proceed in the action under Rule 19(b). In such cases the United States, like other tortfeasors, may have to defend two or more actions on the same tort and may be unable to assert counterclaims and offsets against the original claimant upon unrelated transactions.

If R.S. 3477 is inapplicable, as we think is clearly the case, these objections have no legal foundation upon which to rest. . . .

Affirmed.

MR. JUSTICE BLACK dissents.

MR. JUSTICE DOUGLAS took no part in the consideration or decision of this case.

NOTE ON THE HISTORY OF THE REAL PARTY IN INTEREST RULE

The real party in interest rule must be studied in historical perspective. Originally at common law, an assignee or subrogee was not recognized as having acquired the rights of his assignor or subrogor. Only equity recognized and enforced his rights as holder of the "beneficial" (in contrast to "legal") interest. In the course of time, the common law courts modified their original stance and permitted an assignee or subrogee to sue by allowing him to resort to the fiction that he sued in the assignor's or subrogor's name. When this led to difficulties in cases in which the assignor or subrogor had in some way compromised the assignee's or subrogee's rights—for example, by giving a release—, the courts disregarded the fiction by declaring the assignee or subrogee, the holder of the beneficial interest, to be the "real party in interest." This doctrine was incorporated into the Field Code and eventually into Rule 17(a) of the Federal Rules of Civil Procedure. Lest statement of the rule might lead to the unwarranted conclusion that (*only*) the party with the beneficial interest could sue, it was followed by an enumeration, such as now appears in the second sentence of Rule 17(a), of certain persons who continued to be able to sue in their own names though they hold non-beneficial interests. The enumeration was confusingly worded, however, in the form of an exception or qualification of the "real party in interest" doctrine, and it was thereafter mistakenly taken to be exclusive rather than merely illustrative. Federal Rule 17(a) was amended in 1966 to eliminate these ambiguities, and its counterpart in the New York CPLR now omits any mention of the real party in interest doctrine. CPLR 1004; see 2 Weinstein, Korn and Miller, New York Civil Practice ¶ 1004.01. Also suggesting that it be abolished is Kennedy, Federal Rule 17(a): Will the Real Party in Interest Please Stand?, 51 Minn.L.Rev. 675 (1967).

NOTES

(1) Virginia Electric and Power Co. v. Westinghouse Electric Corp., 485 F.2d 78, 84–85 (4th Cir.1973):

> Under the common-law practice, a subrogee or assignee could enforce his rights only in the name of his subrogor or assignor. The original purpose of Rule 17 was to liberalize party rules, *i.e.*, to allow an assignee or subrogee to enforce his rights in his own name. The permissive function of Rule 17 has been accomplished, and Rule 17 now serves primarily a negative function. It is to enable a defendant to present defenses he has against the real party in interest, to protect the defendant against a subsequent action by the party actually entitled to relief, and to ensure that the judgment will have proper res judicata effect. . . .

As noted, the modern function of Rule 17 is to prevent the defendant from being subjected to subsequent suits. In Provident Tradesmens Bank & Trust Co. v. Patterson, 390 U.S. 102, 88 S.Ct. 733, 19 L.Ed.2d 936 (1968), the Court stated that one of the primary considerations under Rule 19 in whether to allow a suit to continue where a party cannot be joined is the protection of a defendant from multiple litigation, or inconsistent relief. 390 U.S. at 10, 88 S.Ct. 733. In view of this overlap between Rule 17 and Rule 19, we think the emphasis in a case such as this should be on whether under Rule 19 the action should be allowed to continue without joinder of the absent party. That an absent person who cannot be joined is a real party in interest does not conclude the matter—the court must determine whether, in equity and good conscience, the action should proceed without the person.

(2) In some cases, the real-party-in-interest rule also protects the jurisdictional limitations of the federal courts, for it prevents parties from having surrogates litigate their cases in order to create diversity jurisdiction. Cf. Comment, 55 Calif.L.Rev. 1452 (1967). In this connection, note that 28 U.S.C.A. § 1359 provides that: "A district court shall not have jurisdiction of a civil action in which any party, by assignment or otherwise, has been improperly or collusively made or joined to invoke the jurisdiction of such court." For an application of this provision, see Kramer v. Caribbean Mills, Inc., 394 U.S. 823, 89 S.Ct. 1487, 23 L.Ed.2d 9 (1969).

Note that the provision speaks only to the question of *creating* adjudicatory power: should courts also disregard assignments when they are made for the purpose of *defeating* jurisdiction? See Mecom v. Fitzsimmons Drilling Co., 284 U.S. 183, 52 S.Ct. 84, 76 L.Ed. 233 (1931); American Law Institute, Study of the Division of Jurisdiction Between State and Federal Courts 22–23, 160–161 (1969).

TYLER v. DOWELL, INC.

United States Court of Appeals, Tenth Circuit, 1960.
274 F.2d 890, cert. denied 363 U.S. 812, 80 S.Ct. 1248, 4 L.Ed.2d 1153.

MURRAH, CHIEF JUDGE. This is an appeal from a judgment of the District Court of New Mexico on a jury verdict in a tort action by appellants against appellee Dowell, Inc., for loss or damage to its oil well drilling equipment caused by fire.

The basic facts are these. Tyler and King, doing business as King Drilling Company, contracted with Phillips Petroleum Company to drill and complete an oil well in New Mexico for a stipulated amount per vertical foot, and another agreed amount for work performed on a daily basis when not actually engaged in drilling operations. After the well had been drilled to the producing formation and virtually completed, and while the contractor was standing by on a day basis, Phillips arranged with appellee, Dowell, to sand frack the producing formation to increase productivity. This operation involved the injection of a mixture or blend of crude oil and sand into the producing formation under high pressure by means of pressure pumps, followed by injections of rubberized nylon balls to seal off the fractured formation . . .

In our case, the fracking operation had been completed and the well hole was being washed under pressure with clean oil, when one of the nipples on the frack head failed, causing oil to spray in a radius of approximately 100 feet in about a 45 degree arc, within which area was located the pressure pumps about 80 feet distant from the well head, and the nylon-ball pumping truck approximately 60 feet. The spraying oil caught fire, causing the asserted loss. The contractor, King Drilling Co., sued Dowell, charging negligent conduct in the fracking operation. Dowell denied negligence and pleaded contributory negligence and assumption of risk, and by a third party action against Phillips, invoked an indemnity agreement, whereby Phillips agreed to "secure Dowell against loss or damage not expressly accepted by Dowell." Phillips thereupon counterclaimed against the contractor, pleading an assumption of risk and hold-harmless agreement with the contractor.

Before trial, Phillips and Dowell composed their differences and the trial court sustained Dowell's motion to make the contractor's insurance carrier a party plaintiff, apparently on the grounds that it had paid part of the loss and was therefore a necessary or real party in interest. The case went to the jury on the issues drawn between the contractor and its insurance carrier on the one hand, and Dowell and Phillips on the other. The contractor objected to making the insurance company party plaintiff on the grounds that it had not actually paid any of the loss, but rather had merely entered into a loan agreement with the contractor by which it had advanced the contractor a stipulated sum of money to be repaid from the proceeds of this litigation.

The question under both New Mexico and federal law is whether by this transaction with its insured, the insurance company became a real party in interest, i.e., whether it is the owner or part owner of the right sought to be enforced. Sellman v. Haddock, 62 N.M. 391, 310 P.2d 1045 . . . Courts have generally sanctioned agreements between the insured and insurer, whereby the insurer advances a sum of money to its insured, to be repaid from the proceeds of an action against a tortfeasor. . . . And, there is authority for saying that the insurer does not thereby become the owner of the right of action so as to make it the real party in interest.

* * *

The question is whether by the terms of the loan receipt in this case, the insurer actually became the subrogee of the insured, hence the real party in interest to the extent of the "loan." The insured agreed to promptly present the claim, and if necessary prosecute a suit against the parties whose negligence or other fault caused the loss "with all due diligence in their own name." And, the insurer was furthermore given complete control of the litigation "with irrevocable power to collect any such claim or claims, and to begin, prosecute, compromise or withdraw . . . [in the name of the insured] any and all legal proceedings that the said company may deem necessary to enforce such claim or claims, and to execute in the name of the insured any documents that may be necessary to carry the same into effect for the purpose of this agreement." The nature of the "loan receipt" in Sellman v. Haddock, supra [62 N.M. 391, 310 P.2d 1045], was not disclosed. But, there was testimony to the effect that it gave the insurer authority to "collect from who ever caused the damage if they could determine that." The New Mexico court construed this authority as giving the insurer an interest in the litigation which made it a necessary, even indispensable, party to the action against the tort-feasor. Evidently the trial court was of the view that what was in form a loan was in fact a payment of the loss and a subrogation of the claim to the extent thereof. Involving as it does a mixed question of state and federal procedural law, we adopt the decision of the trial court thereon.

[Reversed on other grounds].

NOTES

(1) Notice that there are two questions at issue in *Tyler:* first, whether a certain interest *entitles* a party to join in the lawsuit; second, whether a party with that interest *must* be joined. In some states, such as California, partial assignees and subrogees are considered indispensable parties and must be joined. Bank of the Orient v. Superior Court, 67 Cal.App.3d 588, 136 Cal.Rptr. 741 (Ct. of Appeal, 1st Dist., Div. 2, 1977). See also Note, Compulsory Joinder of Partial Subrogees: Implications of the Alaska Rule, 1 Alaska L.Rev. 171 (1984). In federal courts, the second question is controlled by Fed.R.Civ.P. 19, which is discussed in Section 7, infra.

(2) In a case in which the insurer is held to be the real party in interest, may he be substituted as a party plaintiff even after the statute of limitations has run? See Link Aviation, Inc. v. Downs, 325 F.2d 613 (D.C.Cir.1963), and the last sentence added to Rule 17(a) by the 1966 Amendments. How is the insurer to be substituted? By a motion to substitute under Fed.R.Civ.P. 25(c) or by a motion to amend under Fed.R.Civ.P. 15(c)(2)?

(3) Fed.R.Civ.P. 25 on substitution of parties was amended in 1963 and 1966 to eliminate most of the problems that had arisen under its original version. On the still existing problems, see 7C Wright, Miller & Kane, Federal Practice and Procedure: Civil §§ 1951–1962 (1986).

(4) In the federal courts, does state law determine whether the insurer who has taken a loan receipt is the proper party in interest? Cf. Condor Investment Co. v. Pacific Coca-Cola Bottling Co., 211 F.Supp. 671 (D.Or.1962) (even though he conceded to be bound by Oregon decisions upholding the validity of loan receipt agreements, the judge, a former counsel of insurance companies, upon analysis of the facts, found that the parties intended payment rather than loan and held the insurer to be a real party in interest). See also McNeil Construction Co. v. Livingston State Bank, 300 F.2d 88 (9th Cir.1962).

SECTION 2. CAPACITY TO SUE AND TO BE SUED

OSKOIAN v. CANUEL

United States Court of Appeals, First Circuit, 1959.
269 F.2d 311.

MAGRUDER, CIRCUIT JUDGE (Retired).*

This appeal was prosecuted by leave of this court granted in order to resolve a basic and difficult problem of practice, 264 F.2d 591. The case was begun by a complaint filed in the United States District Court for the District of Rhode Island, containing five counts sounding in tort. It alleges that in 1956 the Independent Bakery Workers Union won an election conducted by the National Labor Relations Board among the employees of a certain bakery of The Great Atlantic & Pacific Tea Company, that Local 184 of the Bakery and Confectionery Workers International Union of America was rejected by the employees at that election, and that the Independent Union was then duly certified by the NLRB as the collective bargaining agent for the employees at that bakery. Thereafter the International Union "maliciously and unlawfully interfered with the employment contract and rights" of the members of the Independent Union (Count 1), conspired with the A. & P. so to interfere (Count 2), "intentionally and maliciously induced and persuaded" the A. & P. to sever such employment (Count 3), conspired with the A. & P. to commit such inducement (Count 4), and conspired with the A. & P. to deprive the members of the Independent Union of their rights under the National Labor Relations Act, 29 U.S.C.A. § 151 et seq. (Count 5).

The plaintiffs are three individuals alleged to have been members of the Independent Union (which is now defunct) and to be Massachusetts citizens. They purport to sue on behalf of themselves and others similarly situated, but the district court ruled that they constituted a so-called "spurious" class under Rule 23(a)(3) of the Federal Rules of Civil Procedure, 28 U.S.C.A., and that the rights of absent members of the plaintiff class would not be adjudicated. The thirteen named defendants, said to be Rhode Island citizens and members of the International Union, are sued as members and representatives of that Union, an unincorporated labor organization having in excess of 50,000 members. Plaintiffs claim that defendant Oskoian is an "international representative" of the International Union and that defendants Kavanaugh and Boudreau are officers of Local 184; assuming these allegations to be true, the district court found that the named defendants adequately represent the defendant class.

The defendants filed timely motions to dismiss for sundry reasons and various motions for other relief, all of which were denied. . . .

* * *

* Some footnotes omitted.

. . . . One ground of the motions to dismiss was in essence that the named defendants lacked the capacity to be sued as representatives of the International Union; the motions affirmatively stated that no named defendant was an officer of the International Union and that the officers of that Union were known to the plaintiffs. The court below held that the propriety of an action against the defendant class was a question of procedural law governed only by F.R.Civ.P. 23(a), and that neither the rule of Erie R. Co. v. Tompkins, 1938, 304 U.S. 64, 58 S.Ct. 817, 82 L.Ed. 1188, nor F.R.Civ.P. 17(b) required compliance with state law; the court also certified that its order denying the motion to dismiss involved a controlling question of law as to which there was substantial ground for difference of opinion and that immediate appeal therefrom might materially advance the ultimate termination of the litigation. On the defendants' motion we then granted leave to appeal under 28 U.S.C. § 1292(b) because we thought the question of capacity of the defendant class to be sued presented the "exceptional case" that justified invocation of the new interlocutory appeal procedure. 1 Cir., 1959, 264 F.2d 591. Our permission to appeal was limited to this one issue; although the district court's decisions on other related matters are accepted as premises for our decision of this question, nothing in this opinion should be construed as a review of those matters.

As our opinion granting leave to appeal intimated, our inquiry must start with Rule 17(b) F.R.Civ.P., which provides in pertinent part:

> "[C]apacity to sue or be sued shall be determined by the law of the state in which the district court is held, except (1) that a partnership or other unincorporated association, which has no such capacity by the law of such state, may sue or be sued in its common name for the purpose of enforcing for or against it a substantive right existing under the Constitution or laws of the United States . . . ."

We went on to say that, "It is apparent that the present case is not one for enforcing against an unincorporated association a substantive right 'existing under the Constitution or laws of the United States'. Therefore, since the exception has no application, the general rule becomes operative, that capacity to be sued must be governed by the law of the state in which the district court is held, in this case by the law of Rhode Island." 264 F.2d at page 593. . . .

One method of suit against an unincorporated labor union under the law of the state is defined by §§ 9–2–10 through 9–2–15 of the General Laws of Rhode Island. In particular, § 9–2–12 provides:

> "Actions against unincorporated associations.—Any action or other proceeding at law may be maintained to recover any property, or upon any cause of action for or upon which the plaintiff may maintain such an action or proceeding at law against all the associates, by reason of their interest or ownership, or claim of ownership therein, against the president and secretary of such association, or the officers or members exer-

cising substantially the duties, respectively, of president and secretary, or if there be no such officer, or officers or members exercising such duties, or either of them, then against any other two (2) officers of such association, or if there be but one (1) officer, then against such single officer, or if there be no officer known to the plaintiff, then against any member of such association, describing such officer or officers, member or members, as the representative or representatives of such association."

Section 9–2–14 prohibits execution of the judgment in such an action against the person or property of members or officers of the association, and authorizes execution out of property of the association instead.

If the plaintiffs had complied with this procedure, the suit would have been properly brought under Rule 17(b) against the Union as an entity. Compare Van Sant v. American Express Co., 3 Cir., 1948, 169 F.2d 355, 372. It is clear, however, that plaintiffs have failed either to join the president and secretary of the International Union or more than one alleged officer thereof, or to allege that such other officers do not exist or are unknown to them. On the contrary, they apparently admit that they know the identity of the statutorily designated officers, and they claim that, since those officers are located outside Rhode Island, failure to join them is justified. This excuse is completely without support in the statutory language, which is unambiguous. Furthermore, it seems quite reasonable that the Rhode Island legislature might demand the presence of the principal officers of a union within the state as a prerequisite to the assertion of jurisdiction over that union as an entity. We must construe the plain words of § 9–2–12 to require that the Union be sued through service on the specified officers. . . .

Still, it does not follow that the action should have been dismissed. Although the substantive allegations of the complaint plead tortious conduct of the International Union, the individual defendants may have been named as representatives not of the Union but rather of a class comprising its members. Compare Lowry v. International Brotherhood of Boilermakers, etc., 5 Cir., 1958, 259 F.2d 568; Fennell v. Bache, 1941, 74 App.D.C. 247, 123 F.2d 905, certiorari denied 1941, 314 U.S. 689, 62 S.Ct. 359, 86 L.Ed. 551. It appears that the law of Rhode Island recognizes one other remedy for the torts of an unincorporated association, that is, a suit against all the members of the union. This was the established method at common law, United Mine Workers v. Coronado Coal Co., 1922, 259 U.S. 344, 42 S.Ct. 570, 66 L.Ed. 975; Local Union No. 1, Textile Workers v. Barrett, 1896, 19 R.I. 663, 36 A. 5, and there is no reason to believe that it was abolished by the statute. That a suit against all the members may be maintained despite the statute is indicated by the permissive phraseology of § 9–2–12, and by the express terms of § 9–2–15 barring suits against the members while an action under the statute is pending. The defendants concede in their brief that an action against all the members may yet be brought. To have complied with Rule 17(b), as plaintiffs were clearly obliged to do, they must have brought suit by one of these two state-created methods—against the International Union as an entity or against all of its members. Conversely, such compliance fully satisfies Rule 17(b).

Whereas Rhode Island law recognizes two procedures, the Pennsylvania statute, to which reference was required by Rule 17(b) in the cases the defendants rely upon, is exclusive and mandatory in its terms, eliminating all other methods of enforcing the liability of an unincorporated association. See Underwood v. Maloney, 3 Cir., 1958, 256 F.2d 334, 337 note 3, 342; Lloyd A. Fry Roofing Co. v. Textile Workers Union of America, AFL–CIO, D.C.E.D.Pa.1957, 149 F.Supp. 695; D.C. E.D.Pa.1957, 152 F.Supp. 19. These cases are therefore no authority for our decision. The present litigation may be maintained, consistently with both Rule 17(b) and the law of Rhode Island pertaining to capacity to be sued, if, and only if, by the terms of Rule 23(a)(1) a class action such as the present one may be used as a procedural device in the federal court to effect a suit against all the members of the International Union, and to obtain a binding judgment against all of them.[2]

Rule 23(a) F.R.Civ.P., in so far as here relevant, reads:

"(a) Representation. If persons constituting a class are so numerous as to make it impracticable to bring them all before the court, such of them, one or more, as will fairly insure the adequate representation of all may, on behalf of all, sue or be sued, when the character of the right sought to be enforced for or against the class is

"(1) joint, or common, or secondary in the sense that the owner of a primary right refuses to enforce that right and a member of the class thereby becomes entitled to enforce it;

     *   *   *

"(3) several, and there is a common question of law or fact affecting the several rights and a common relief is sought."

As a matter of federal law, then, all the members of a union may be sued and bound by a "true" class action under Rule 23(a)(1). See 3 Moore's Federal Practice, par. 23.08 (2d ed. 1948).

The state courts in Rhode Island will entertain a nonbinding class suit of a "spurious" nature (cf. Rule 23(a)(3)), e.g., Vernon v. Reynolds, 1898, 20 R.I. 552, 40 A. 419, but a binding class suit, such as this one would have to be (under Rule 23(a)(1)), is forbidden in those state courts by Equity Rule 67, which has the force of a statute, see Letendre v. Rhode Island Hospital Trust Co., 1948, 74 R.I. 276, 60 A.2d 471. The defendants contend that by the rule of Erie R. Co. v. Tompkins, supra,

---

2. If the defendants were only a "spurious" class under Rule 23(a)(3) F.R.Civ.P., we would be constrained to agree with their contentions on appeal, since the only Rhode Island alternative to the statutory procedure is a suit against *all* the members and an action against only thirteen of them is not authorized by the state substantive law. This distinction is crucial.

304 U.S. 64, 58 S.Ct. 817, 82 L.Ed. 1188, and Guaranty Trust Co. of New York v. York, 1945, 326 U.S. 99, 65 S.Ct. 1464, 89 L.Ed. 2079, this prohibition and/or the specific definition of representatives in a virtual representation suit found in § 9–2–12, are binding on the federal court.

* * *

Of course, the rule of Guaranty Trust Co. of New York v. York, supra, 326 U.S. at page 109, 65 S.Ct. at page 1470, that "the outcome of the litigation in the federal court should be substantially the same, so far as legal rules determine the outcome of a litigation, as it would be if tried in a State court", cannot be read so literally as to mean that no recovery may be had from a federal court that might not have been obtained from a state court. The same opinion recognizes (326 U.S. at page 105, 65 S.Ct. at page 1468) that "[t]his does not mean that whatever equitable remedy is available in a State court must be available in a diversity suit in a federal court, or conversely, that a federal court may not afford an equitable remedy not available in a State court." The fact that a federal court can offer a procedure different from that available in the state court does not preclude the application of the state substantive law so that the result will be the same as it would be in such an action brought in the state court. See Griffin v. McCoach, 1941, 313 U.S. 498, 61 S.Ct. 1023, 85 L.Ed. 1481 (interpleader); D'Onofrio Construction Co., Inc. v. Recon Co., Inc., 1 Cir., 1958, 255 F.2d 904 (third-party claim). In the present case the result in the federal court—binding all the International Union's members—will be the same as that in a state court common law action against the membership, and the plaintiffs must make out a good cause of action under Rhode Island law against all members of the defendant class. Only in the manner of conducting this litigation does any deviation occur.

Undeniably a class action involving members of an unincorporated association is a venerable device of equity. See Mr. Justice Story in West v. Randall, C.C.D.R.I.1820, 29 Fed.Cas. at page 722, No. 17,424. It is equally certain that there are many procedural problems raised by a suit such as this one, for example, determining the liability of the individual members of the class because of their participation in, ratification of, or authorization of the tortious conduct, cf. Martin v. Curran, 1951, 303 N.Y. 276, 101 N.E.2d 683; Browne v. Hibbets, 1943, 290 N.Y. 459, 49 N.E.2d 713; Torres v. Lacey, 1957, 5 Misc.2d 11, 159 N.Y.S.2d 411, ascertaining the share of the plaintiffs' recovery, if any, to be borne by each member of the defendant class, and assuring that the absent members are afforded due process, cf. Hansberry v. Lee, 1940, 311 U.S. 32, 61 S.Ct. 115, 85 L.Ed. 22. But these are merely procedural problems of the federal court in applying the controlling state substantive law, and their resolution must be judged by the guaranties of the Federal Bill of Rights. Such difficulties alone cannot justify a rule elevating the state procedural law to a supreme position. The district court would be faced with many other (probably insurmountable) procedural problems if there had to be over 50,000 parties defendant.

Thus we are clear that Rule 23(a)(1) is a valid "procedural" device, as applied to avoid the necessity of having more than 50,000 parties defendant in the United States District Court for the District of Rhode Island. The present class action under that rule is a proper exercise of the Rhode Island law allowing an action for the tort of a labor union to be brought against all the members thereof, which will require the same result as would be reached if all the International Union's members were sued in the state court. The fact, if it is a fact, that as a practical matter only under Rule 23(a) in the federal court might an action be brought against the members of the International Union is certainly not to be condemned as unseemly, mischievous, discriminatory, or unconstitutional, any more than the jurisdictional advantages of the Federal Interpleader Act, 28 U.S.C.A. §§ 1335, 1397, 2361, invalidate that Act. It follows that the adequacy of representation assured the defendant class by the presence of the named parties defendant, as found by the district court, is a corollary federal question and is not prejudged by R.I.Gen.L. § 9–2–12. The decision of the district court on the issue which is the subject of this appeal was correct.

* * *

NOTES

(1) When subject matter jurisdiction is based on diversity, capacity considerations often complicate matters. If jurisdiction in the principal case had been based on diversity, whose domicile should be considered, the named representatives or every member of the association? The current state of the law seems to be that if the suit is brought against the entity, the domicile of each member counts, but if the association is sued as a class, an action which would now be maintained under Fed.R.Civ.P. 23.2, only the domicile of the named representatives will be considered. See also C.T. Carden v. Arkoma Associates, ___ U.S. ___, 110 S.Ct. 1015, 108 L.Ed.2d 157 (1990) (domicile of limited partners in a limited partnership counts in determining diversity).

(2) Most states appear to treat labor unions as entities for purposes of suit. See Forkosch, The Legal Status and Suability of Labor Organizations, 28 Temp. L.Q. 1 (1954). But the capacity to sue or be sued of other unincorporated associations frequently continues to be uncertain. See Kaplan, Suits Against Unincorporated Associations Under the Federal Rules of Civil Procedure, 53 Mich.L.Rev. 945 (1955); Sturges, Unincorporated Associations as Parties to Actions, 33 Yale L.J. 383 (1924); Note, 76 Harv.L.Rev. 983 (1963); Comment, 42 Calif.L.Rev. 812 (1954).

NOTE ON THE CAPACITY TO SUE AND TO BE SUED OF NATURAL PERSONS AND CORPORATIONS

Problems of capacity to sue or to be sued may also arise in regard to natural persons and corporations. See generally James and Hazard, Civil Procedure §§ 10.1–10.9 (3d ed. 1985); Kennedy, Federal Civil Rule 17(b) and (c): Qualifying to Litigate in Federal Court, 43 Notre Dame L.Rev. 273 (1968).

a. *Natural persons.* A minor must be represented in litigation by either his guardian or a specially appointed guardian ad litem. The same is true of incompetents. The common law disabilities of married women and convicts have been long since removed by statute in most states. An individual acting in a representative capacity may sue and be sued in his capacity in the state of his appointment. Originally, he could neither sue nor be sued outside of this state, but this rule is the subject of rapid change. See Currie, The Multiple Personality of the Dead: Executors, Administrators, and the Conflict of Laws, 33 U.Chi.L. Rev. 429 (1966).

b. *Corporations.* Originally, uncertainty as to the exact nature of a corporation created uncertainty as to how it should be treated procedurally. But by the end of the 19th century it had become settled that a domestic corporation could sue and be sued as an entity in its own name. The situation in regard to foreign corporations is less simple. Bank of Augusta v. Earle, 13 Pet. (38 U.S.) 519, 589 (1839) stated that "Every power . . ., which a corporation exercises in another state, depends for its validity upon the laws of the sovereignty in which it is exercised." This premise has provided the foundation for the many state statutes that condition access to the local court upon the foreign corporation's having obtained a license to engage in business in the state. For an example of such a statute, see Eli Lilly & Co. v. Sav-On-Drugs, Inc., 366 U.S. 276, 81 S.Ct. 1316, 6 L.Ed.2d 288 (1961); Note, 110 U.Pa.L.Rev. 241 (1961). Statutes of this kind continue to impose limitations upon the capacity to sue (but not of being sued) of foreign corporations.

In 1989, 28 U.S.C.A. § 1332 was revised to make clear whose citizenship counts for diversity purposes when a minor, incompetent, or estate sues or is sued through its legal representative, see § 1332(c)(2).

SECTION 3. JOINDER OF CLAIMS

HARRIS v. AVERY

Supreme Court of Kansas, 1869.
5 Kan. 146.

BY THE COURT, VALENTINE, J. This action was brought in the court below by Avery, as plaintiff. The petition states two causes of action—false imprisonment and slander—and alleges that both arose out of the same transaction. Harris demurred to this petition, on the ground "that it appears on the face of the petition, that several causes of action are improperly joined." The district court overruled the demurrer, and this ruling is assigned as error.

The petition shows that the two causes of action are founded upon the following facts. Harris met Avery in the city of Fort Scott, and in the presence of several other persons called Avery a thief; said he had a stolen horse; took the horse from Avery, and kept the horse four or five days; arrested Avery and confined him in the county jail with felons four or five days.

We think these facts as detailed in the petition constitute *only one transaction*, [Brewer v. Temple, 15 Howard Pr.R. 286] ; and whether they constitute more than one cause of action, under our code practice, may be questionable. Under the authority we have referred to they would not. But as we have not been asked to decide the latter question, we will pass it over and treat the case as though the facts stated constitute two causes of action.

Section 89 of the code [Comp.Laws, 138,] provides "that the plaintiff may unite several causes of action in the same petition, whether they be such as have heretofore been denominated legal or equitable, or both, when they are included in either one of the following classes: First, *the same transaction* or transactions connected with the same subject of action."

This differs in many respects from the common law rule. At common law "where the same form of action may be adopted for several distinct injuries, the plaintiff may, in general, proceed for all in one action, though the several rights effected were derived from different titles," [1 Chitty's Pl., 201; Tidd's Pr., 11,] and different forms of action may be united "where the same plea may be pleaded and the same judgment given on all the counts of the declaration, or whenever the counts are of the same nature, and the same judgment is to be given on them although the pleas be different." 1 Chitty's Pl., 200.

In the action at bar if Harris had arrested Avery on a warrant, which Harris had maliciously and without probable cause obtained from a court of competent jurisdiction, and had also converted the horse to his own use, then at common law, Avery would have had three distinct causes of action, which he could unite in one suit—first, an action for the false imprisonment or malicious prosecution; second, an action of slander for the words spoken, and third, an action of trover for the conversion of the horse. These may all be united in an action on the case [1 Chitty's Pl., 133, 134, 146; 1 Tidd's Pr., 5]; trover being a species of case. Avery might, also, at common law, unite with these causes of action as many other causes of action as he might have, for malicious prosecution, slander, trover, criminal conversation, nuisance, and other causes of action which may be sued in an action on the case, and although they each may have arisen out of a different transaction, and at a different time, and in a different place.

But if Harris arrested Avery without any process—which was the fact in this case—and in an entirely irregular manner, then the two causes of action for false imprisonment and slander could not at common law be united, as the first would have to be sued in an action of trespass and the second in an action on the case, and it would make no difference whether they both arose out of the same transaction or not.

Our code has abolished all the common law forms of action, and has established a system for the joinder of actions,—more philosophical, and complete within itself. It follows the rules of equity more closely than it does those of the common law, one object seeming to be to avoid the multiplicity of suits, and to settle in one action, as equity did, as far as practicable, the whole subject matter of a controversy. Hence the common law on this question is no criterion. It is probably true that the two causes of action for false imprisonment and slander cannot, under our code, be united, unless both arise out of the same transaction, one being an injury to the person and the other being an injury to the character; but we do not know of any reason why they should not be united when both do arise out of the same transaction. . . .

The order of the district court overruling the demurrer to the petition is affirmed.

All the justices concurring.

BLUME, FREE JOINDER OF PARTIES, CLAIMS AND COUNTERCLAIMS

American Bar Association Special Committee on Improving the Administration
of Justice, the Judicial Administration Monographs, Series A
(Collected) 41, 46–48 (1942).

JOINDER OF CLAIMS

(a) *Under the codes.* The original Field Code provided:

"The plaintiff may unite several causes of action in the same complaint where they all arise out of,

"1. Contract, express or implied; or,

"2. Injuries by force, to person or property; or,

"3. Injuries without force to person or property; or,

"4. Injuries to character; or,

"5. Claims to recover real property; with or without damages for the withholding thereof; or,

"6. Claims to recover personal property, with or without damages for the withholding thereof; or,

"7. Claims against a trustee by virtue of a contract or by operation of law."

The code further provided that causes of actions united must belong to one only of these classes, must *equally* affect all the parties to the action, and not require different places of trial. In 1851 the word "equally" was dropped out. In 1852 a new class was added: Causes may be joined "where they all arise out of the same transaction or transactions connected with the same subject of the action."

As originally written, the code provision for the joinder of claims offered little or no improvement over the common-law scheme and made no allowance for joinder in equity. The arbitrary classes were merely substitutes for the forms of action which were abolished by the code. The common-questions principle and the principle of convenience were entirely ignored.

The amendment of 1852, which was adopted in practically all of the code states, was intended to introduce the equity principle of trial convenience, but was poorly worded for this purpose. Where claims arise out of the same transaction, it is probable, but by no means certain, they will present a common question of law or fact. If they do not involve a common question, the fact that they "arise out of the same transaction or transactions connected with the same subject of the action" is of no significance. If they do involve a common question, the other feature seems unimportant.

At least one state which adopted the New York code refused to take the provisions for joinder. In rejecting the arbitrary classifications, the Iowa code commissioners of 1860 said:

"Hence the only question of joinder with us rests upon policy. This chiefly concerns the plaintiff, and he should be left to his own sense, in guiding him either to unite a slander suit with a promissory note, or keep them distinct. The court can, if it likes, order cases, the joinder of which it doesn't favor, to be disunited and tried separately. The English Commissioners on this subject, say that the good sense of the plaintiff will be a better guide than can any rule, to determine what causes should be united."

Other code states (Kansas, Wisconsin, and New York) have repealed the original joinder section and have substituted provisions which allow complete freedom of joinder in cases which do not involve the joinder of parties.

Some non-code states (New Jersey, Michigan, and Illinois) allow similar freedom in the joinder of claims.

(b) *Under the English rules.* Under the English rules the only limitation on the joinder of claims (not involving the joinder of parties) is a prohibition against joining with an action for recovery of land other actions not relating to the land, unless by leave of the court. In Ontario even this restriction has been abolished. The advances made in the United States toward free joinder, as noted above, were made under the influence of the English reform.

(c) *Under the federal rules.* Section a of Rule 18 provides: *

"The plaintiff in his complaint . . . may join either as independent or as alternate claims as many claims either legal or equitable or

---

* Rule 18(a) was amended in 1966 to cover all claims to relief, whether by way or original claim, counterclaim, cross-claim or third-party claim. [Eds.].

both as he may have against an opposing party. There may be a like joinder of claims when there are multiple parties if the requirements of Rules 19, 20, and 22 are satisfied . . . "

The report of the Advisory Committee points out that "recent development, both in code and common law states, has been toward unlimited joinder of actions."

Cases which involve the joinder of parties usually involve the joinder of claims. In these cases under the codes it is necessary to satisfy both sets of joinder provisions. A joinder may meet one test but not the other. Under the federal rule this situation is greatly simplified. If multiple parties are involved and their joinder is authorized by the rules governing joinder of parties, the road to joinder is clear, as there is no obstacle of any kind in the rule which governs the joinder of claims. If a joinder of parties is not involved, the joinder of claims is entirely free.

(d) *Further reform.* When it is recognized that complete freedom, subject to direction by the court, should be allowed in the joinder of claims, a question arises as to whether joinder should not be encouraged and perhaps compelled in some situations. Where a plaintiff has two or more claims which involve a common question of law or fact, should he be permitted to maintain a separate action on each claim? If the parties will be the same in each action, the doctrine of estoppel may save the court the necessity of deciding the question more than once. If the parties will not be the same, yet joinder is permitted, required joinder will avoid repeated decisions of the common question. Even where the parties will not be the same, required joinder will effect some saving of time and expense, e.g., the empaneling of separate juries, and this is true regardless of whether a common question will be involved.

While the possibilities of encouraging or requiring joinder should not be overlooked, the great need at the present time is provision for free joinder of claims in those states which have not made this advance. The language of the federal rule is well suited for this purpose. If the language of the federal rule is not used, great care should be exercised to make the joinder of claims entirely free so that the provisions for joinder of parties can operate without restriction.

NOTES

(1) In an action against a tortfeasor, does Federal Rule 18(b) permit the plaintiff to join the liability insurer as defendant? Should federal courts be influenced by state policy on this matter? See, e.g., Pitcairn v. Rumsey, 32 F.Supp. 146 (W.D.Mich.1940); Annot., Construction, application, and effect of Federal Civil Procedure Rule 18(b) and like state rules or statutes pertaining to joinder in a single action of two claims although one was previously cognizable only after the other had been prosecuted to a conclusion, 61 A.L.R.2d 688, 701–705 (1958).

(2) Despite the fact that the joinder-of-claim rule appears to be permissive, a plaintiff may find herself precluded from pursuing further ligitation based upon claims that could have been joined in the first suit. This segment of res

judicata, called "claim preclusion," is discussed in Chapter 16. See also Blume, Required Joinder of Claims, 45 Mich.L.Rev. 797 (1947). For an example of statutorily required joinder of claims, see Michigan General Court Rule 2.203(A); Meisenholder, The New Michigan Pre-Trial Procedural Rules—Models for Other States?, 61 Mich.L.Rev. 1389, 1417 (1963). What is the significance in this context of the compulsory counterclaim rule? See Fed.R.Civ.P. 13(a). What practical considerations may force a party to join his claims? In an action arising from an airplane crash, may the court direct that notice be given to other potential claimants? See Pan American World Airways, Inc. v. United States District Court, 523 F.2d 1073 (9th Cir.1975).

(3) What problems may arise upon the joint adjudication of several claims? What procedural devices are available to mitigate these problems? See Fed.R. Civ.P. 42(b).

(4) Could parties be joined if claims could not be joined? On the relationship between joinder of claims and joinder of parties, see pp. 427–431, infra.

SECTION 4. COUNTERCLAIMS

MULCAHY v. DUGGAN

Supreme Court of Montana, 1923.
67 Mont. 9, 214 P. 1106.

MR. COMMISSIONER BENNETT prepared the opinion for the court.

This action was instituted by the plaintiff, J.B. Mulcahy, against the defendant, Lawrence Duggan, to recover actual and exemplary damages alleged to have resulted from a physical encounter between the parties, which took place on May 17, 1920, at the city of Butte. Plaintiff alleged that "the defendant violently, wantonly and maliciously did assault the plaintiff, . . . " and defendant answered admitting that he "did strike the plaintiff several blows and did knock him down." In addition to the admissions and denials, defendant set up counterclaim for a libel published by plaintiff of and concerning the defendant on May 8, 1920. He also alleged that the altercation between himself and plaintiff was the result of plaintiff's publication of the article charged to be libelous. Plaintiff demurred to the counterclaim on the grounds "that the counterclaim set up in defendant's answer is not of the character specified in section 6541 of the Revised Codes [1907] of the State of Montana." . . . The demurrer was overruled and plaintiff replied. The action came on for trial before a jury. After plaintiff had closed, and shortly after the defense proceeded, the court ruled, in effect, that the matter set out in the counterclaim was not properly before the court as such, but that it might be proper in mitigation of damages. The record discloses that it was the trial court's theory that the counterclaim was not properly triable in the action before it, but to negative and rebut the element of malice, which was pleaded by plaintiff for the purpose of enabling him to recover exemplary damages, it was permissible for defendant to show that as a reasonable man he was so provoked by the publication of the libel that he assaulted the plaintiff without malice. Upon a ruling to this effect the defendant asked for and was granted leave to file an amendment to his answer. The amendment as filed set up the facts as an affirmative defense by way of justification and as a partial defense in mitigation of damages. The court, however, held to the theory that the matter relied on was not a justification of the assault, but that it was proper to be considered in mitigation of exemplary damages. The trial resulted in a verdict for plaintiff. After a motion for a new trial was made and overruled, the defendant appealed from the judgment.

* * *

3. The Provisions of . . . section [9138], with which we are here concerned, are: "The counterclaim . . . must be . . . a cause of action arising out of the . . . transaction, set forth in the complaint, as the foundation of the plaintiff's claim . . . ."

* * *

The purpose of this statute is to enable and require parties to adjust in one action the various differences which grow out of any given transaction.

. . . . [T]he counterclaim was properly interposed. Webster's Dictionary defines "transaction" as "the doing or performing any affair." "Affair" is defined as "that which is done or to be done." The plaintiff commenced the "affair" by his publication of the article complained of by the defendant. As a result the defendant assaulted the plaintiff. This "combination of acts and events" resulted in the two rights of action set out in the pleadings, both arising out of the transaction commenced by the publication of the libelous article.

We recognize that there are cases from other jurisdictions which hold contrary to our conclusions. We do not, however, agree with the reasoning in those cases. For instance, on the authority of Macdougall v. Maguire, 35 Cal. 274, 95 Am.Dec. 98, the supreme court of California held in the case of Earl v. Times-Mirror Co., 185 Cal. 165, 196 P. 57, that an action for a libel caused by the publication of a libel could not be set up as a counterclaim in an action for damages against the defendant for publication of the second libel. In deciding that case the court says: "A cause of action for libel on one day could not be set up as a counterclaim to a cause of action for libel arising the next day, even though the second libel was the result of the first. . . . Though connected in the sense that one is the result of the other, they are, in contemplation of law, entirely separate." . . .

We cannot approve a rule which arbitrarily uses the element of time in determining whether or not various causes of action arise out of the same "transaction." If, as a matter of fact, there is such a connection that the acts complained of were the result of complainant's own acts, we think all causes of action arising therefrom must be litigated in one action.

We might add, in passing, that the rule which permits the showing of acts of provocation in mitigation of exemplary damages is of itself a recognition that there is a connection between certain slanders, certain libels, and between certain slanders, libels, and other tortious acts and assaults. Wherever such connection exists they are parts of the same transaction.

*   *   *

We are therefore of the opinion that the trial court erred in excluding from the consideration of the jury the counterclaim as set out in defendant's answer, and we recommend that the judgment be reversed, and the cause remanded to the district court, with directions to grant a new trial, permitting the defendant to proceed with his proof of the allegations of his counterclaim.

*   *   *

Reversed and remanded.

NOTES

(1) Distinguish between counterclaims that are permissible—i.e. are allowed to be asserted, from those that are compulsory—i.e. are barred unless they are asserted. In federal practice, Rule 13(b) states that in general, claims that a defendant has against the plaintiff are permissible (or, in federal nomenclature, permissive). But claims that are transactionally related to the main claim are, with certain exceptions, compulsory per 13(a). Contrast this rule with Rule 18, which leaves it to res judicata law to determine which of the plaintiff's claims are lost if they are not asserted.

(2) States have widely divergent rules with respect to when counterclaims are compulsory. Thus, in Montana, at the time of Duggan, the transaction test was used to determine whether a claim was compulsory, see 3 Revised Code of Montana §§ 9138, 9144 (1921). In other states, defendants are barred from bringing separate actions by res judicata rules, see, e.g., Meyer v. S.S. Vance, 406 P.2d 996 (Okl.1965). However, there are states that never require defendants to assert their claims; in some of these states, the transaction test is used to decide whether defendants' claims are permissible.

(3) Why would a jurisdiction choose to require the assertion of claims? Why would a jurisdiction consider it fair to require plaintiffs to assert their transactionally related claims, but allow defendants to wait, and bring claims bearing an equivalent relation to the lawsuit in a subsequent action?

(4) Suppose that the defendant had bought goods, part of which proved defective. When the seller sued for the price, there would be obvious economy of effort if in the same action the defendant could assert his claim for breach of warranty. What if the goods had arrived in proper order, but in his zeal to collect the price the seller had assaulted the buyer and then brought suit for the price? Would the same argument of economy prevail? See Lyric Piano Co. v. Purvis, 194 Ky. 826, 241 S.W. 69 (1922). If the plaintiff were defamed in the defendant's newspaper and, before suing, took the trouble to punch the defendant's nose, should the defendant be allowed to urge a claim for assault and battery in the libel action? Should he be compelled to do so at the peril of losing his right of action?

(5) From rather early times the common law—as well as Roman and modern civil law—permitted the defendant to diminish plaintiff's recovery by

way of "recoupment." This required showing facts arising out of the same transaction or subject matter that would have been sufficient basis for a separate action. The defendant's claim need not have been liquidated or of the same form of action (e.g., contract or tort).

Following the lead of the equity courts, which allowed "set-off" of unrelated claims, England by statutes in 1705 and 1729 (4 Anne, c. 17, § 11; 2 Geo. 2, c. 22, § 13) permitted set-off at law of unrelated liquidated claims. Under neither recoupment nor set-off was an affirmative recovery to defendant allowed.

In the 1852 amendments to New York's Field code, the "counterclaim" emerged *eo nomine*. While retaining certain restrictions that endured into this century, the code provision broadened both earlier devices by permitting the defendant to recover a judgment from the plaintiff if the counterclaim warranted.

An excellent discussion of the genesis of the contemporary counterclaim appears in Clark, Code Pleading 633–66 (2d ed. 1947). See also Lowry, Counterclaims (or Cross-Petitions) in Ohio Practice, 19 U.Cinc.L.Rev. 311 (1950); 20 id. 1 (1951). The present New York statute provides (C.P.L.R. § 3019(a)):

> "Subject of counterclaims. A counterclaim may be any cause of action in favor of one or more defendants or a person whom a defendant represents against one or more plaintiffs, a person whom a plaintiff represents or a plaintiff and other persons alleged to be liable."

ROSENTHAL v. FOWLER

District Court of the United States, Southern District of New York, 1952.
12 F.R.D. 388.

IRVING R. KAUFMAN, DISTRICT JUDGE. Plaintiff moves this Court for an order pursuant to Rule 12(b) of the Federal Rules of Civil Procedure, 28 U.S.C.A., dismissing the counterclaims pleaded in the answer to the complaint in the instant action on the ground that the Court lacks jurisdiction of the subject matter, and, in the event that said motion is denied for an order pursuant to Rule 12(b) of the Federal Rules of Civil Procedure dismissing the second counterclaim and the second portion of the demand for judgment pleaded in said answer on the ground that they fail to state a claim upon which relief can be granted, or, in the alternative, for an order, pursuant to Rule 56 of the Federal Rules of Civil Procedure, granting summary judgment in favor of plaintiff and against defendant as to the second counterclaim and the second portion of the demand for relief pleaded in said answer.

Two causes of action are alleged in the complaint. In the first, plaintiff seeks to recover treble damages for rent paid by him pursuant to leases entered into between him and defendant, which allegedly exceeded the maximum rent prescribed by the Housing and Rent Act of 1947, 50 U.S.C.A. Appendix, § 1881 et seq. In the second, plaintiff alleges that defendant failed to provide certain essential services which, pursuant to the lease in effect on the maximum rent date of July 1, 1942 defendant was obligated to furnish, and that as a result of the absence of those services, plaintiff is entitled to treble damages of $4,500.

Two counterclaims were interposed by defendant in her answer. The first is based on the allegation that the essential services were, under the language of the lease, required to be furnished by plaintiff, and that as a result of his failure to do so, defendant suffered damages to her property of $2,000.

The second counterclaim is grounded on the allegation that plaintiff "induced or caused" a real estate appraiser to alter his appraisal of defendant's premises by reducing his estimate of the fair rental value of the premises from $450 per month to $375 per month, as a result of which defendant allegedly suffered damages of $7,200.

The initial prayer in plaintiff's motion is for an order pursuant to Rule 12(b) of the Federal Rules of Civil Procedure dismissing the counterclaims on the ground that the Court lacks jurisdiction of their subject matter.

Plaintiff's claim for treble damages is based on the Housing and Rent Act of 1947, as amended, 50 U.S.C.A. Appendix, § 1891 et seq. Jurisdiction is thus founded on the presence of a federal question in the action. In order to decide the issue of jurisdiction over the subject matter of the counterclaims, this Court must first resolve the question of whether one or both of them are compulsory or permissive.

Rule 13(a) of the Federal Rules of Civil Procedure provides in its here relevant portion:

> "(a) *Compulsory Counterclaims.* A pleading shall state as a counterclaim any claim which at the time of serving the pleading the pleader has against any opposing party, if it arises out of the transaction or occurrence that is the subject matter of the opposing party's claim and does not require for its adjudication the presence of third parties of whom the court cannot acquire jurisdiction . . .."

If a counterclaim is compulsory, the same jurisdiction which supports the main claim will also support the counterclaim. United States to Use and for Benefit of Foster Wheeler Corporation v. American Surety Co. of New York, D.C.E.D.N.Y.1938, 25 F.Supp. 700. Allegations of such counterclaims are to be considered in a spirit consonant with the liberal and realistic policy of the Federal Rules of Civil Procedure. Professor Moore, in 3 Moore's Federal Practice (2nd ed.) Par. 13.13 wisely suggests:

> "An all-embracing definition [of 13(a)] cannot be given, nor is one desirable. The same flexibility and same empirical treatment is necessary in connection with 'transaction or occurrence' that has been advocated and discussed in connection with 'cause of action'. [2 Moore's Federal Practice (2nd ed.) Par. 2.06.] . . . [C]ourts should give the phrase 'transaction or occurrence that is the subject matter' of the suit a broad

realistic interpretation in the interest of avoiding a multiplicity of suits. Subject to the exceptions, [not instantly relevant] any claim that is logically related to another claim that is being sued on is properly the basis for a compulsory counterclaim; only claims that are unrelated or are related, but within the exceptions, need not be pleaded."

If there be one compelling test of compulsoriness, it seems clearly to be that of the logical relationship of all claims in any given litigation. [Citations omitted.] If that logical relationship exists between a counterclaim and the main claim, then the counterclaim is compulsory and need not have independent jurisdiction to support it. Such jurisdiction is necessary only if the counterclaim is permissive as provided for in Rule 13(b), Federal Rules of Civil Procedure. [Citations omitted.]

Do one or both of the instant counterclaims have the logical relationship which is the *sine qua non* of compulsoriness?

The nub of the controversy before me is that defendant urges the counterclaims do have the logical connection adverted to, while plaintiff insists that they are completely unrelated to the main claim. I find that defendant's first counterclaim, which sounds in waste or the failure of plaintiff to provide essential services as allegedly required by the terms of the leases, is logically related to the second cause of action pleaded by plaintiff, namely, that it was defendant who failed to provide those services as allegedly required by the Housing and Rent Act of 1947, as amended, supra.[1] However, the leases or the applicable provisions of the Act may ultimately be construed, it is clear that these adverse claims have grown from the disintegration of the services for which each party claims the other is liable. No such contention appears in Marks v. Spitz, D.C.D.Mass.1945, 4 F.R.D. 348, hence I believe it is factually and therefore legally distinguishable from the instant case.

Moore v. New York Cotton Exchange, supra, although involving facts very different from the instant ones, nonetheless stands for a proposition of judicial construction which was further strengthened by the promulgation of rule 13(a)[2] and which is applicable to the case before me. That case applies logic as the test, and not legal technicalities or rigidly similar circumstances as between claim and counterclaim. What was sought in the Moore case is also sought here: the avoidance of law suits whose multiplicity lends nothing to the cause of fair and expeditious judicial administration.

1. Specifically, Controlled Housing Rent Regulations, sec. 825.3, as recodified in sec. 76 of the Recodification of Regulations.

2. The Moore case was decided under Equity Rule 30. "The decision in the Moore case and the opinion are authority under Rule 13, since 13(a) is broader in scope than Equity Rule 30, for whereas Equity Rule 30 required a counterclaim 'arising out of the transaction which is the subject matter of the suit,' Rule 13(a) requires a counterclaim 'arising out of the transaction *or occurrence* that is the subject matter' of the suit." 3 Moore's Federal Practice (2nd ed.) Par. 13.13 and n. 4 thereto.

I find that the Court has jurisdiction of the subject matter of defendant's first counterclaim by virtue of the compulsory nature of that counterclaim.

Defendant's second counterclaim does not meet the test by which a compulsory counterclaim is established. The counterclaim, if meritorious, can at best be permissive which leads to the conclusion that jurisdiction of its subject matter must be supported independently of the main claim. That counterclaim makes no allegation of jurisdiction as required by Rule 8(a), Federal Rules of Civil Procedure. The second counterclaim is dismissed for lack of an allegation showing jurisdiction of the subject matter, with leave to defendant to amend the answer as to the jurisdiction supporting the second counterclaim within five days after service of a copy of the order to be entered hereon. Plaintiff's application for summary judgment addressed to the second counterclaim thus becomes academic.

Settle order.

BAKER v. GOLD SEAL LIQUORS, INC., 417 U.S. 467, 469, 94 S.Ct. 2504, 2506, 41 L.Ed.2d 243, 247 n. 1 (1974): "[Federal] Rule 13(a), the compulsory counterclaim rule, requires a defendant to plead any counterclaim which 'arises out of the transaction or occurrence that is the subject matter of the opposing party's claim and does not require for its adjudication the presence of third parties of whom the court cannot acquire jurisdiction.' The claim is not compulsory if it was the subject of another pending action at the time the action was commenced, or if the opposing party brought his suit by attachment or other process not resulting in personal jurisdiction but only *in rem* or *quasi in rem* jurisdiction. A counterclaim which is compulsory but is not brought is thereafter barred, e.g., Mesker Brothers Iron Company v. Donata Corp., 401 F.2d 275, 279.

" . . . Under 13(a)'s predecessor this Court held that 'transaction' is a word of flexible meaning which may comprehend a series of occurrences if they have logical connection, Moore v. New York Cotton Exchange, 270 U.S. 593, [46 S.Ct. 367, 70 L.Ed. 750 (1926)] and this is the rule generally followed by the lower courts in construing Rule 13(a) . . .."

Rule 13(b) permits as counterclaims, although not compulsory, "any claim against an opposing party not arising out of the transaction or occurrence that is the subject matter of the opposing party's claim." Thus the court may dispose of all claims between the parties in one proceeding whether or not they arose in the "same transaction."

NOTES

(1) Does the test of logical relationship applied in the principal case indicate with reasonable clarity the considerations that should determine whether a counteraction is compulsory? Did its application in the principal case lead to the correct result? Because res judicata law has similar goals to

compulsory joinder rules, the test used there to determine when claims are precluded is also relevant here. See pp. 959–964, infra.

(2) "Transaction" is a much-used word in procedural contexts, appearing not only in counterclaim provisions, but also, for example, in rules respecting amendment of pleadings, joinder of causes of action, pendent and ancillary jurisdiction. Should the meaning of "transaction" for one of these purposes determine its meaning for another, such as the necessity of counterclaiming or losing the right?

(3) A defendant may wish to counterclaim for a sum higher than the jurisdictional limit of the court in which plaintiff has brought the action. Some states permit him to counterclaim and then remove the cause to a court of higher jurisdiction; in some other states, he may bring a separate suit in the court of higher jurisdiction and consolidate the actions. See Clark, Code Pleading 652–53, 490–93 (2d ed. 1947).

(4) Does a lender, sued for the statutory penalty under the [Federal Truth in Lending Act,] have a compulsory counterclaim for the amount lent? Compare Whigham v. Beneficial Finance Co., 599 F.2d 1322 (4th Cir.1979) (no) with Plant v. Blazer Financial Services, Inc., 598 F.2d 1357 (5th Cir.1979) (yes).

(5) *Baker* noted one exception to the compulsoriness of counterclaims, namely that claims are not compulsory (even if transactionally related) if they require the presence of third parties over whom the court cannot acquire jurisdiction. What is the justification for this exception? As noted, Rule 13(a) contains several other exceptions as well:

a. Claims that are the subject of pending litigation need not be asserted. Let us say that A sues B on claim 1 in a state court and then B sues A in a federal court on claim 2. Both claims arise out of the same occurrence. Must A interpose claim 1 as a counterclaim in the federal action? If the counterclaim is interposed, should the state court stay the action pending before it? See Admiral Corp. v. Reines Distributors, Inc., 9 A.D.2d 410, 194 N.Y.S.2d 932 (3d Dep't 1959), affirmed 8 N.Y.2d 773, 201 N.Y.S.2d 784, 168 N.E.2d 118 (1960).

b. Claims are not compulsory when the court lacks personal jurisdiction over the defendant. This exception was added in 1963. The change was explained by the Committee on Rules of Practice and Procedure of the Judicial Conference of the United States, as follows: "When a defendant, if he desires to defend his interest in property, is obliged to come in and litigate in a court to whose jurisdiction he could not ordinarily be subjected, fairness suggests that he should not be required to assert counterclaims, but should rather be permitted to do so at his election. If, however, he does elect to assert a counterclaim, it seems fair to require him to assert any other which is compulsory within the meaning of Rule 13(a). . . . It will apply to various cases described in Rule 4(e), as amended, where service is effected through attachment or other process by which the court does not acquire jurisdiction to render a personal judgment against the defendant. Clause (2) will also apply to actions commenced in State courts jurisdictionally grounded on attachment or the like, and removed to the Federal courts."

The importance of this exception has been significantly decreased by the U.S. Supreme Court's decision in Shaffer v. Heitner, p. 298 supra.

(6) The Supreme Court created another exception to the compulsory counterclaim rule in Southern Construction Co. v. Pickard, 371 U.S. 57, 83 S.Ct. 108, 9 L.Ed.2d 31 (1962). In that case, substantive federal law required the plaintiff to institute two separate lawsuits. The defendant asserted its counterclaim in

only one of these actions. After the action in which the claim was not asserted went to judgment, the plaintiff moved in the remaining action to have the counterclaim dismissed on the ground that it had been compulsory, and since it had not been asserted in the action that went to judgment, it was lost. The Court denied the motion, holding that the compulsory counterclaim rule is designed to streamline litigation. Where two lawsuits are unavoidable, that goal is unattainable. Consequently, there is no point in holding the defendant to the rule.

(7) Some states that have adopted the Federal Rules have included additional provisions designed to protect against unduly harsh applications of the compulsory counterclaim rule. The Alabama rule contains two additional exceptions. See Hoff, Joinder of Claims and Parties Under the Alabama Rules of Civil Procedure, 25 Ala.L.Rev. 663, 673–674 (1973) (footnotes omitted):

> "The third and fourth exceptions stated by Alabama Rule 13(a) have no counterparts in the federal rules. Under the third exception, the claims of a defendant will not be compulsory if the plaintiff's claim for damage is covered by a liability insurance policy under which the insurer has the right or the obligation to conduct the defense. This exception was copied from the Vermont Rules of Civil Procedure. If insurance counsel are conducting the defense, it seems clear that they will be less than wholeheartedly enthusiastic about presenting the insured's counterclaims. This exception thus permits the defendant to retain his own counsel to press these claims in separate litigation. The exception literally applies whenever the insurer has the right to conduct the defense, even if it is not in fact conducting it. In this respect it is suggested that modification of the Rule is in order since the exception seems to serve no function if the defendant's own attorney is conducting the defense without supervision by the insurance company or its attorneys. Under the fourth exception the counterclaim need not be pleaded if it 'exceeds the jurisdictional amount of an inferior court having direct appeal to the Supreme Court or Court of Civil Appeals.'"

(8) If forced to interpose his counterclaim, a defendant faces the dilemma that by doing so he may waive an otherwise valid objection to the court's adjudicatory authority. Cognizant of the problem, Ohio held that the filing of a counterclaim does not waive the right to contest the court's jurisdiction. Bennett v. Radlick, 104 Ohio App. 265, 145 N.E.2d 334 (1957). Cf. Johnson v. Fire Association of Philadelphia, 240 Mo.App. 1187, 225 S.W.2d 370 (1949); Buckley v. John, 314 Mass. 719, 51 N.E.2d 317 (1943). But see Merchants' Heat and Light Co. v. Clow, 205 U.S. 286, 27 S.Ct. 285, 51 L.Ed. 488 (1907).

CONSEQUENCES OF FAILURE TO INTERPOSE COMPULSORY COUNTERCLAIM

Although it is fairly clear that unasserted compulsory counterclaims are lost, the technical basis for precluding later litigation is obscure. Some courts rely entirely on the compulsory counterclaim rule, some on a theory of waiver, others on res judicata. *Compare* Wright, Estoppel by Rule: The Compulsory Counterclaim under Modern Pleading, 38 Minn.L.Rev. 423 (1954) *with* Scott, Collateral Estoppel by Judgment, 56 Harv.L.Rev. 1 (1942). Does it make any difference which is recognized to be the proper basis?

Equally complicated is the effect of successive actions in different judicial systems. Consider what happens, for example, if the first action was brought in a federal court, where the defendant's compulsory counterclaim was not asserted. Later, the defendant brings an action on this claim in the court of a state that does not deem counterclaims compulsory. Is the state required to follow the federal law and dismiss the action, or can it favor its own policy of allowing defendants the benefit of becoming plaintiffs? Conversely, if the first action was brought in a state that lacks a compulsory counterclaim rule, and the second action is brought in a federal court, should the federal court dismiss? Are these *Erie* (or reverse-*Erie*) problems? The topic of intersystem preclusion is discussed in Chapter 16, pp. 1021–1030 infra.

SECTION 5. PERMISSIVE JOINDER OF PARTIES

HISTORICAL NOTE

In the common law courts, compulsory joinder of parties was a more familiar phenomenon than the permissive kind, largely owing to the view that joinder was a function of substantive relationships rather than procedural convenience. Persons who under the substantive law possessed a "joint" right were required to join as plaintiffs in an action to enforce that right. Typical examples were the case of a single debt owed to a partnership or a single trespass committed against property owned jointly by several persons. Upon failure of all the parties or all the joint tenants to combine in suing at law, the action was vulnerable to a plea in abatement or other defensive maneuvers.

When the joint interest was defensive, such as that of joint obligors on a promissory note, the plaintiff was required to sue all the obligors. This meant that valid claims might frequently fail if one obligor could not be served with process or was otherwise immune to suit. In time, meliorating exceptions developed. Joint tortfeasors were considered to be severally as well as jointly liable in most circumstances and a plaintiff was accorded the option of suing them singly or together.

In short, where no "joint" right or liability existed by substantive standards, the common law did not permit the joinder of multiple plaintiffs or defendants, except in certain instances where the interest could be classified as "joint and several".

In the equity courts, on the other hand, the practice was more flexible, having as its touchstones the objectives of trial convenience and complete justice to the parties concerned. Equity permitted (but did not require) joinder of plaintiffs if they were interested in the subject of the action and in obtaining the relief demanded. It has been said that this requirement was in practice alternative rather than conjunctive. See generally James & Hazard, Civil Procedure § 9.2 (3d ed. 1985).

CHAMBERLAIN v. WHITE AND GOODWIN
King's Bench, 1622.
79 Eng.Rep. 558.

Action for words. For that they two spake these words of the plaintiff: "Thou hast the plate of J.S. and we will charge thee with that felony." After verdict, upon not guilty, and found for the plaintiff, it was moved in arrest of judgment, that the action lies not jointly against them; for the speaking of the one is not the speaking of the other: wherefore they ought to have been severally charged.—And it was thereupon adjudged for the defendants.

NOTE

A more modern case holding that an action for slander may not be maintained against two or more persons jointly where the complaint charges distinct causes of action against the several defendants is Stansberry v. McKenzie, 192 Tenn. 638, 241 S.W.2d 600 (1951); Annot., 34 A.L.R. 345. In that case the declaration alleged that "the said accusations were made by the defendants in the presence of each other, by common design or previously formed conspiracy, and jointly each aiding and abetting the other in such false and slanderous accusations". What should be the ruling on defendants' demurrer for misjoinder? See also Schoedler v. Motometer Gauge & Equipment Corp., 134 Ohio St. 78, 15 N.E.2d 958 (1938).

Do these decisions take into account proper policy considerations? What are the considerations that should determine whether joinder of parties is permissible? In what respects, if any, are they different from the considerations that determine the permissibility of joinder of claims? Note that Fed.R. Civ.P. 20(a) imposes stricter requirements than Fed.R.Civ.P. 18. Should it?

AKELY v. KINNICUTT
Court of Appeals of New York, 1924.
238 N.Y. 466, 144 N.E. 682.

*   *   *

HISCOCK, CH. J. This case involves the interpretation of a new and rather revolutionary provision of the Civil Practice Act.

The action is brought by 193 plaintiffs, each one claiming to have an individual, separate and independent cause of action against the defendants for damages caused by the fraud of the latter. The substance of each cause of action is that the defendants, with others, conspired to organize a corporation and then to float its stock at much more than its actual value; that in pursuance of this conspiracy they caused to be prepared a prospectus which was widely circulated throughout the country and which was intended to induce those who read it or learned of its contents to buy the stock at a price much higher than its actual value, and that this prospectus thus issued was intentionally false and fraudulent and misrepresented the value of the stock; that the plaintiff (in each cause of action) either seeing and relying upon the truthfulness of the prospectus or relying upon the advice of some one who had seen and believed it was induced to buy at a given date a certain number of shares of the stock in question at a price far in excess of its actual value and each alleged cause of action seeks to recover from defendants the damages thus suffered.

These many causes of action being separate and distinct can be joined in one complaint if at all only by virtue of section 209 of the Civil Practice Act, which provides:

"§ 209.   Joinder of plaintiffs generally.   All persons may be joined in one action as plaintiffs, in whom any right to relief in respect of or arising out of the same transaction or series of transactions is alleged to exist whether jointly, severally or in the alternative, where if such persons brought separate actions any common question of law or fact would arise;   provided that if upon the application of any party it shall appear that such joinder may embarrass or delay the trial of the action, the court may order separate trials or make such other order as may be expedient, and judgment may be given for such one or more of the plaintiffs as may be found to be entitled to relief, for the relief to which he or they may be entitled."

* * *

The statute before us is substantially a copy of a provision in the English Practice Act and of course its purpose is to lessen the delay and expense of litigation by permitting the claims of different plaintiffs to be decided in one action instead of many when, although legally separate and distinct, they nevertheless so involve common questions and spring out of identical or related transactions that their common trial may be had with fairness to the different parties.   The statute is a remedial one in promotion of the purpose in these times so insistent and widespread that the delays and expenses of litigation shall be lessened where possible and as such it is to be liberally construed.

We shall consider first the question certified and earnestly argued by counsel whether the causes of action which have been joined in this complaint do involve such a common question of law or fact as justifies the court in permitting them to be united in one complaint.   It is necessarily admitted by the defendants that they do involve some common questions of law and fact but it is insisted that these common questions when compared with all of the questions which must be determined in each case are not of such comparative weight or importance as to justify the union which is being attempted.   We are not able to agree with this view.   We do not need to hold that the presence in each cause of action of some common but inconsequential or theoretical issue would be a sufficient reason for assembling in one complaint nearly two hundred causes of action. We shall assume in this case that such common questions must be of substantial importance as compared with all of the issues and that the question of the comparative weight and importance of common and separate issues involved in each cause of action is quite largely a matter of judgment. But even on that theory we do not think that it can be said by us as a matter of law in this case that there are not present in each cause of action common issues which amply satisfy the test of the statute. The common issues are basic and would seem to be the ones around which must revolve the greatest struggle and to which must be directed the greatest amount of evidence. These are in the ones in substance whether the defendants conspired to organize a corporation and float its stock at much more than its real value and whether in pursuance of this conspiracy they fraudulently issued a prospectus showing the stock to be much more valuable than it really was, and whether they did this with the deliberate intent to cheat and defraud the public into buying the stock at an unconscionable value. These questions are common to every cause of action. The separate issues which must be tried in each instance will be in the main whether the plaintiff saw the prospectus or learned of its representations, was influenced thereby and at a certain date bought a certain amount of stock at a certain price in advance of its real value in reliance thereon. While these latter may equal in number the common ones it seems from the face of the complaint, by which we must decide the question, that the majority of them cannot involve much evidence or lengthy dispute, but that the trial of them will yield in contentious importance and difficulty to the questions which have been first suggested and that, therefore, this is a case which comes well within the meaning of the statute so far as relates to common questions.

Then it is urged by appellants that there is lacking that feature, essential to the collection in one complaint of all of these causes of action, that they should be "in respect of or arising out of the same transaction or series of transactions." We do not find any basis for this claim. Each cause of action is based upon a purchase of stock at a fictitious value in reliance upon representations, as alleged, of defendants in respect of the value of that stock which were untrue and fraudulent and made for the purpose of inducing the public including plaintiff to make such purchases. The transaction in respect of or out of which the cause of action arises is the purchase by plaintiff of his stock under such circumstances, and such purchases conducted by one plaintiff after another respectively plainly constitute a series of transactions within the meaning of the statute. The purchase by a plaintiff of his stock is not robbed of its character as a "transaction" because, as appellants seem to suggest, the transaction was not a dual one occurring between the plaintiff and the defendants, and the many purchases by plaintiffs respectively do not lose their character as a series of transactions because they occurred at different places and times extending through many months.

* * *

NOTES

(1) Contrast with the principal case Taylor v. Brown, 92 Ohio St. 287, 110 N.E. 739 (1915), in which Brown and others sued Taylor for fraud and deceit for inducing them to invest in a joint venture involving purchase of land in Long Island. Each plaintiff had bought a definite share in the venture. The court sustained the defendant's demurrer for misjoinder of parties plaintiff:

"Section 11254, General Code, provides that:

" 'All persons having an interest in the subject of the action, and in obtaining the relief demanded, may be joined as plaintiffs except as otherwise provided.'

"Neither of the plaintiffs in this action had any interest in the 'subject of the action' of the other. The action being one at law, the subject of the action in each case was the particular damages that each plaintiff had suffered because of the tortious act of the defendant. It is possible that some of the plaintiffs might be able to establish their case and the others lose. The gist of the action was deceit, and the testimony offered to support the case of one of the plaintiffs might not legally affect the case of another. The jury must determine whether each plaintiff relied upon the false representations made to him individually, or whether reliance was had upon investigations independent of the representations made, if such are proven. Baker v. Jewell, 6 Mass. 460, 4 Am.Dec. 162. It is difficult to perceive how in such a case the parties could be joined."

(2) For a discussion of the factors to be considered by the joining defendants, see Friedenthal, Whom to Sue—Multiple Defendants, 5 Am.Jur.Trials 1–25 (1966).

(3) How can the defendant insure that the plaintiffs adjudicate their claims against other defendants simultaneously? See Ryan, Effect of Calendar Control on the Disposition of Litigation, 28 F.R.D. 37, 73 (1961): "We have found that an airplane accident in Maryland gave rise to 13 suits, all of which were filed in the Southern District of New York; another similar disaster at Riker's Island, close to LaGuardia Airport in New York, was followed with 18 civil suits; and still another at Nantucket Island in Massachusetts, was followed with 19 civil suits. These cases have been identified and assigned in groups to a single Judge. A marine disaster, of which many are litigated in the Southern District of New York, is followed not only with one or more limitation proceedings in the Admiralty but with a number of individual civil and admiralty Jones Act, 46 U.S.C.A. § 688, passenger, cargo and hull damage suits. These, too, we are attempting to identify at an early date and to assign each grouping to a single Judge."

(4) When the requirement of a common question of law or fact is met, what purpose is served by the additional requirement that the claims arise out of the same transaction or series of transactions? Note that for consolidation Fed.R. Civ.P. 42(a) requires only a common question of law or fact. Can this difference be justified?

(5) If the principal case had been brought in a federal court, what would have been the requirements of (a) diversity of citizenship and (b) amount in controversy? Could the court's competence have been sustained by reliance on the doctrine of "ancillary jurisdiction"? Cf. Finley v. United States, ___ U.S. ___, 109 S.Ct. 2003, 104 L.Ed.2d 593 (1989), p. 206, supra. Could the various claims have been aggregated to reach the requisite amount in controversy? See Phillips Petroleum v. Taylor, 115 F.2d 726 (5th Cir.1940), cert. denied 313 U.S. 565, 61 S.Ct. 941, 85 L.Ed. 1524 (1941). Cf. Snyder v. Harris, 394 U.S. 332, 89 S.Ct. 1053, 22 L.Ed.2d 319 (1969), and Zahn v. International Paper Co., 414 U.S. 291, 94 S.Ct. 505, 38 L.Ed.2d 511 (1973), p. 512, infra.

TANBRO FABRICS CORP. v. BEAUNIT MILLS, INC.

Supreme Court of New York, Appellate Division, First Department, 1957.
4 A.D.2d 519, 167 N.Y.S.2d 387.

BREITEL, J. Stripped of procedural details, the question here is whether a buyer of textile goods may obtain a single trial against the seller and the processor of the goods, either by joinder in a single action, or by consolidation of actions, to determine whether the goods are defective, and if so, whether the defect is the consequence of breach by the seller, or the processor, or both of them. Special Term held that such joinder or consolidation is not available. A contrary view is reached here. It is held that the buyer is entitled to have such a common trial, either by joinder in a single action or by a consolidation of actions.

The underlying business dispute spawned three lawsuits. In the first action . . ., the seller, Beaunit, sought to recover the purchase price of goods sold and delivered to Tanbro. The buyer, Tanbro, counterclaimed for breach of warranty for improper manufacture, as a result of which the goods were subject to "yarn slippage". The seller replied to the counterclaim by denying that the slippage was due to improper manufacture. A portion of the goods still being in the hands of the processor, Tanbro initiated another action . . ., in replevin, to recover these goods. The processor, Amity, counterclaimed for its charges and asserted its claim to the goods under an artisan's lien. In the exchanges that preceded and attended the bringing of these lawsuits, the buyer Tanbro received Beaunit's assertion that the yarn slippage was caused by the processor's improper handling, while with equal force the processor charged the same defect to Beaunit as a consequence of its improper manufacture.

At this juncture, Tanbro, the buyer, brought the third lawsuit . . . against Beaunit and Amity, charging the goods were defective because of yarn slippage and that such slippage was caused by either the seller, Beaunit, or alternatively the processor, Amity, or both. This is the main action before the court.

At Special Term, the buyer Tanbro moved to consolidate the three actions. Beaunit and Amity separately cross-moved to dismiss the complaint in the buyer's main action on the ground that there were prior actions pending between the parties with respect to the same cause of action. The motion to consolidate was denied and Beaunit's cross motion to dismiss the complaint as against it was granted.

The order should be modified by granting the consolidation, denying the cross motion of the seller Beaunit to dismiss the complaint as to it in the buyer's main action and otherwise affirming the order.

Both the seller and the processor resist consolidation. They do so on the ground that each had a separate and different relationship to the buyer, and that each was involved in a separate and independent contract. Therefore, they say, there is not involved the "same transaction or occurrence", nor any common question of law or fact to sustain either a joinder of parties or a consolidation of the actions.[1] . . .

The controlling statute is section 212 of the Civil Practice Act. That section is a product of a codification revision in 1949 (L.1949, ch. 147; Fifteenth Annual Report of N.Y. Judicial Council, 1949, p. 211 et seq.). The portion pertinent to the joinder of defendants reads as follows: "2. All persons may be joined in one action as defendants if there is asserted against them jointly, severally, or in the alternative, any right to relief in respect of or arising out of the same transaction, occurrence, or series of transactions or occurrences and if any question of law or fact common to all of them would arise in the action. Judgment may be given according to their respective liabilities, against one or more defendants as may be found to be liable upon all of the evidence, without regard to the party by whom it has been introduced."

. . .

*   *   *

. . . In the instant case the common questions are: Were the goods defective, and if so, by whom was the defect caused?

The emphasis in the legislative and decisional history is that the joinder statute is to be accorded broad liberality and interpretation in order to avoid multiplicity of suits and inconsistencies in determination. Moreover, the philosophy of broad joinder of parties has been followed in many jurisdictions.

. . . It should be beyond argument, by now, that it is no longer a bar to joinder, and, by parallel reasoning, a fortiori, to consolidation, that there is not an identity of duty or contract upon which to assert alternative liability. It is still necessary, of course, that there be a finding that the alternative liability arises out of a common transaction or occurrence involving common questions of fact and law. But this is

---

1. Both at Special Term and by the argument of the parties in this court it has been assumed that if a joinder of parties were permissible, then a consolidation of the actions was likewise authorized. As a matter of fact the statute authorizing consolidation is a much broader one than that permitting joinder of parties (see Civ.Prac. Act, § 96). It is true, however, that on occasion tests justifying joinder have been used in determining whether consolidation was proper. (See 2 Carmody-Wait on New York Practice, 466 et seq., esp. 474–475.) Such an assumed identity of test is not justified by the statutes. Nevertheless, for the purposes of this case, if the parties may be joined, a fortiori, the actions may be consolidated.

if separately both of could be found
not
liable:
injustice
to
p

not a rigid test. It is to be applied with judgment and discretion, in the balancing of convenience and justice between the parties involved . . . .. Indeed, the buyer's situation prompted Special Term to comment that the buyer, Tanbro, "is in the unenviable position of not knowing possibly which of its contracting parties is responsible and in separate actions may find itself confronted with defeat in each event though the product as finally delivered may be defective."

On the other hand, the view taken here does not mean that the buyer is not obliged to make out a prima facie case. Of course, it must. Its situation would be, as the Judicial Council foresaw in its Fifteenth Annual Report (supra, p. 220); "Similarly, when a party is in doubt as to the person from whom he is entitled to relief, the pleading of necessity will assert a right in the alternative; for only by asserting facts which in the alternative fasten liability either upon one or the other defendant can the plaintiff make out a cause of action and, by proving such facts, establish a prima facie case."

* * *

In the light of this reasoning, the cross motion dismissing the complaint in the buyer's main action against the seller, Beaunit, on the ground of prior action pending, should have been determined otherwise. It is in that action and under that complaint that both defendants are charged with alternative liability. While consolidation would bring all of the parties and their respective claims and cross claims together, there would actually be no pleading which asserts alternative liability under section 212. There is no reason why the issue should not be presented by a forthright pleading, although, concededly, so long as consolidation is granted the matter is not of the greatest moment.

The right of joinder and the privilege to obtain consolidation is always counterbalanced, of course, by the power of the court to grant a severance, or to deny a consolidation, if prejudice or injustice appear. In this case, the danger of separate trials, leading, perhaps, to an unjust and illogical result, is a possibility well worth avoiding. The buyer is entitled to a less hazardous adjudication of his dispute, so long as he is able to make out a prima facie case of alternative liability.

Accordingly, the order of Special Term insofar as it granted the cross motion to dismiss the complaint in the first-described action as against the defendant Beaunit and denied the buyer Tanbro's motion to consolidate the three actions should be modified to deny the cross motion and to grant the motion to consolidate, and otherwise should be affirmed, on the law and in the exercise of discretion of the court, with costs to the appellant-respondent against the respondents-appellants.

NOTES

(1) How much substance does the principal case leave to the requirement that the claims arise from the same transaction or series of transactions? See p. 430, Note (4), supra. See also Note, Procedure: Consolidation of Actions Against Multiple Parties in New York, 43 Cornell L.Q. 709 (1958).

(2) If multiple claims are asserted in an action with multiple parties, must all claims arise from the same transaction or series of transactions and raise a question of law or fact common to all parties? See Federal Housing Administrator v. Christianson, 26 F.Supp. 419 (D.Conn.1939), overruled by the 1966 Amendment to Fed.R.Civ.P. 20.

(3) What is the relationship between Fed.R.Civ.P. 20(b), 21, and 42?

(4) Weinstein, Revision of Procedure: Some Problems in Class Actions, 9 Buffalo L.Rev. 433, 444–46 (1960): *

"Stays are a useful device to avoid parallel litigation involving the same questions of fact or law . . . where consolidation [is] impracticable. New York courts have stayed their own proceedings in deference to actions pending in federal courts, courts of sister states, and other New York courts. They have even stayed actions pending in other New York courts of comparable authority. The test is necessarily imprecise; 'considerations of comity and orderly procedure,' as Judge Fuld noted, offer the guiding principles when one court is asked to defer to another.

"Courts should make every endeavor during pre-trial hearings and preliminary motions to induce the parties to handle related litigation in one forum. Where the parties cannot agree, the court might even go so far as to communicate with other courts, in or outside the jurisdiction, to decide where the matter would best be handled. Stays should then be utilized to force the parties into one court where the dispute can be adjudicated at one time through intervention, consolidation or joint trials."

(5) For an intermediate form of consolidation of actions brought in different districts, see 28 U.S.C.A. § 1407:

"**Multidistrict litigation.** (a) When civil actions involving one or more common questions of fact are pending in different districts, such actions may be transferred to any district for coordinated or consolidated pretrial proceedings. Such transfers shall be made by the judicial panel on multidistrict litigation authorized by this section upon its determination that transfers for such proceedings will be for the convenience of parties and witnesses and will promote the just and efficient conduct of such actions. Each action so transferred shall be remanded by the panel at or before the conclusion of such pretrial proceedings to the district from which it was transferred unless it shall have been previously terminated: *Provided, however,* That the panel may separate any claim, cross-claim, counter-claim, or third-party claim and remand any of such claims before the remainder of the action is remanded."

On Section 1407, see Comment, A Survey of Federal Multidistrict Litigation, 28 U.S.C.A. § 1407, 15 Vill.L.Rev. 916 (1970). See Manual for Complex Litigation: including Rules of Procedure of the Judicial Panel on Multidistrict Litigation (1982). See also, Martin, Multidistrict Litigation—A Panacea or a Blight, 10 Forum 853 (1975).

---

* Footnotes omitted.

SECTION 6. CROSS–CLAIMS

Cross claims differ from counterclaims in that they are asserted against coparties rather than opponents. In addition, the standards for their interposition are often divergent. Thus, in the federal system, Rules 18, 13(a) and 13(b) permit parties to assert any claim against opponents, and may require the assertion of transactionally related claims, but Rule 13(g) never requires parties to assert cross claims. Indeed, parties are allowed to state only those cross claims that are transactionally related to the main claim. What is the logic of treating cross claims differently from counterclaims?

Should the test for transactional relationship be the same in Rule 13(g) as it is in 13(a)? Although most authorities favor application of the same standards, some courts have applied a stricter test to cross-claims. See generally 6 Wright & Miller, Federal Practice and Procedure: Civil § 1432 (1971); see also Liebhauser v. Milwaukee Electric Railway & Light Co., 180 Wis. 468, 193 N.W. 522, 43 A.L.R. 870 (1923). For an excellent formulation of the relevant considerations, see Jefferson Standard Insurance Co. v. Craven, 365 F.Supp. 861 (M.D.Pa.1973):

> "A cross-claim is logically related to the original claim and is permissible when separate trials on each of the respective claims would involve a substantial duplication of effort and time by the parties and the court and when the claims involve many of the same factual or legal issues or when they are offshoots of the same basic controversy between the parties."

What arguments favor application of a narrower test? Note that a proper cross-claim "may", but need not, be interposed.

The reference "to any property that is the subject matter of the original action" was inserted in Rule 13(g) by the 1946 Amendments. This was done, as the Advisory Committee's Note advises, to include "a situation such as where a second mortgage is made defendant in a foreclosure proceeding and wishes to file a cross-complaint against the mortgagor in order to secure a personal judgment for the indebtedness and foreclose his lien."

Cross-claims may be asserted only "against a co-party." The last sentence of Rule 13(g) makes clear that they may also assert a contingent liability. See, e.g., Providential Development Co. v. United States Steel Co., 236 F.2d 277 (10th Cir.1956). However, at least one court, in the teeth of Rule 13(g)'s explicit language, has dismissed a cross-claim asserted against a co-plaintiff. Danner v. Anskis, 256 F.2d 123 (3d Cir. 1958).

Rule 13(g) sets no time limit for the assertion of a cross-claim. The courts have generally been most lenient in granting leave to file a cross-claim. See, e.g., Lyons v. Marrud, Inc., 46 F.R.D. 451 (S.D.N.Y. 1968) (two years after institution of main action). Does a properly interposed cross-claim relate back to the time of commencement of the principal action against the defendant on the cross-claim?

Courts generally use the concepts of ancillary jurisdiction and ancillary venue to permit the assertion of cross claims that lack an independent basis of federal jurisdiction. See, e.g., LASA Per L'Industria Del Marmo Societa Per Azioni v. Alexander, 414 F.2d 143 (6th Cir. 1969). Since cross claims can be asserted only if they are transactionally related to the main claim, this usually means that a cross claim that is permissible will support ancillary jurisdiction. But what if the main claim is dismissed? In Fairview Park Excavating Co. v. Al Monzo Construction Co., 560 F.2d 1122 (3d Cir.1977), the court concluded that dismissal of the principal claim between plaintiff township and the diverse defendant on nonjurisdictional (i.e., state substantive) grounds did not divest the Federal court of ancillary subject matter jurisdiction over a cross claim between the two non-diverse defendants. "The basis for the distinction," the court wrote (id. at 1125):

> between jurisdictional and nonjurisdictional dismissals is readily apparent. If a federal court dismisses a plaintiff's claim for lack of subject matter jurisdiction, any cross-claims dependent upon ancillary jurisdiction must necessarily fall as well, because it is the plaintiff's claim—to which the cross-claim is ancillary—that provides the derivative source of jurisdiction for the cross-claim. Deviation from this rule would work an impermissible expansion of federal subject matter jurisdiction. Yet by the same token, once a district court judge has properly permitted a cross-claim under F.R.Civ.P. 13(g), as was the case here, the ancillary jurisdiction that results should not be defeated by a decision on the merits adverse to the plaintiff on the plaintiff's primary claim. As Judge Aldrich has stated:
>
> > [i]f [a defendant] had a proper cross-claim against its co-defendants this gave the court ancillary jurisdiction even though all the parties to the cross-claim were citizens of the same state. The termination of the original claim would not affect this. This is but one illustration of the elementary principle that jurisdiction which has once attached is not lost by subsequent events.
>
> Atlantic Corp. v. United States, 311 F.2d 907, 910 (1st Cir.1963) (citations omitted); see Parris v. St. Johnsbury Trucking Co., 395 F.2d 543, 544 (2d Cir.1968) (reviewing decision on cross-claim between co-citizen defendants although plaintiff's diversity claim had been settled during trial); Barker v. Louisiana & Arkansas Railway Co., 57 F.R.D. 489, 491 (W.D.La.1972). The contrary rule, which the Township urges here, would operate to make subject matter jurisdiction over every ancillary cross-claim dependent upon that claim's being resolved *prior to* the plaintiff's primary action. (Otherwise a judgment on the merits adverse to the plaintiff would drain the cross-claim of jurisdiction in every instance, a completely indefensible result.) Given that cross-claims necessarily involve co-defen-

dants, Danner v. Anskis, 256 F.2d 123, 124 (3d Cir.1958), a rule which would restrict the duration of federal court jurisdiction over cross-claims to the pendency of plaintiff's primary claim would be untenable: in many cases, cross-claims need not be heard until plaintiff has obtained a judgment on the merits. To permit the raising of a threat of a dismissal for want of jurisdiction at that point would destroy cross-claims otherwise properly maintainable by virtue of ancillary jurisdiction.

NOTES

(1) Are cases like *Fairview*, which permit the court to entertain the claims of nondiverse parties, good law after Finley v. United States, ___ U.S. ___, 109 S.Ct. 2003, 104 L.Ed.2d 593 (1989), p. 206, supra?

(2) What is the relationship between cross claims and counterclaims? Consider A v. B + C. Once B asserts a cross claim against C, may C consider himself an opponent of B and use 13(b) to assert any claim that he has against B? Must he assert transactionally related claims pursuant to 13(a)?

SECTION 7. COMPULSORY JOINDER OF PARTIES

SHIELDS v. BARROW

Supreme Court of the United States, 1854.
58 U.S. (17 How.) 130, 15 L.Ed. 158.

[Barrow had sold property to Shields for a sum payable in installments, the unpaid balance being secured by negotiable papers endorsed by six guarantors, four of whom were citizens of Louisiana and two of Mississippi. After a default, an agreement of compromise was executed. The compromise provided that Barrow would retain ownership of the property sold and of certain payments already made, and that he would receive specified payments from Shields and each endorser (each of whom executed a new note for the amount he agreed to pay) in full satisfaction of all claims against the original purchaser and the endorsers of the latter's note. The purchaser and all six endorsers were parties to the agreement, but in the rescission suit the only defendants were the two endorsers resident in Mississippi.]

The bill further alleges, that though the notes were given, and the complainant went into possession under the agreement of compromise, the agreement ought to be rescinded, and the complainant restored to his original rights under the contract of sale; and it alleges various reasons therefor, which it is not necessary in this connection to state. It concludes with a prayer that the act of compromise may be declared to have been improperly procured, and may be annulled and set aside, and that the defendants may be decreed to pay such of the notes, bearing their indorsement, as may fall due during the progress of the suit, and for general relief.

Such being the scope of this bill and its parties, it is perfectly clear that the circuit court of the United States for Louisiana, could not make any decree thereon. The contract of compromise was one entire subject, and from its nature could not be rescinded, so far as respected two of the parties to it, and allowed to stand as to the others. Thomas R. Shields, the principal, and four out of six of his indorsers, being citizens of Louisiana, could not be made defendants in this suit; yet each of them was an indispensable party to a bill for the rescission of the contract. Neither the act of congress of February 28, 1839 (5 Stat. at Large, 321, sec. 1,) nor the 47th rule for the equity practice of the circuit courts of the United States, enables a circuit court to make a decree in equity, in the absence of an indispensable party, whose rights must necessarily be affected by such decree. . . .

[There are] three classes of parties to a bill in equity. They are: (1. Formal parties. (2.) Persons having an interest in the controversy, and who ought to be made parties, in order that the court may act on that rule which requires it to decide on, and finally determine the entire controversy, and do complete justice, by adjusting all the rights involved in it. These persons are commonly termed necessary parties; but if their interests are separable from those of the parties before the court, so that the court can proceed to a decree, and do complete and final justice, without affecting other persons not before the court, the latter are not indispensable parties. (3. Persons who not only have an interest in the controversy, but an interest of such a nature that a final decree cannot be made without either affecting that interest, or leaving the controversy in such a condition that its final termination may be wholly inconsistent with equity and good conscience.

A bill to rescind a contract affords an example of this kind. For, if only a part of those interested in the contract are before the court, a decree of rescission must either destroy the rights of those who are absent, or leave the contract in full force as respects them; while it is set aside, and the contracting parties restored to their former condition, as to the others. We do not say that no case can arise in which this may be done; but it must be a case in which the rights of those before the court are completely separable from the rights of those absent, otherwise the latter are indispensable parties. . . .

This court regrets that a litigation, which has now lasted upwards of thirteen years, should have proved wholly fruitless; but it is under the necessity of reversing the decree of the circuit court, ordering the clause to be remanded, and the original and cross-bills dismissed.

NOTES

(1) Would any judgment rendered by the court on the merits have bound absent parties to the contract? If not, how could it have destroyed their rights? In the principal case, if the court had adjudicated the merits in the absence of

the other parties interested in the contract, what decrees could it have rendered? Would the result have been the same if Barrow had asked for different relief, such as damages?

(2) Could Barrow have sued all interested parties in any other federal court or in a state court? Should impossibility of joinder in any court have a bearing on whether joinder should be held mandatory?

(3) Apart from the interest of the absent parties not to have the adjudication on the merits proceed without them, what other interests should be considered in determining whether joinder should be mandatory? What about the interest of the plaintiff in having an adjudication in a convenient forum, the interest of the defendant in not being involved in multiple litigation, and the public interest in disposing efficiently of disputes involving multiple parties and in avoiding inconsistent judgments? Can an evaluation of these interests be generalized or must it be made in each individual case? See First Preliminary Report of the New York Advisory Committee on Practice and Procedure, N.Y.Leg.Doc. No. 6(b), pages 248–51 (1957).

(4) Reed, Compulsory Joinder of Parties in Civil Actions, 55 Mich.L.Rev. 327 (1957) traces the history of the indispensable party rule in this country from the time of Shields v. Barrow. Hazard, Indispensable Party: The Historical Origin of a Procedural Phantom, 61 Colum.L.Rev. 1254 (1961), analyzes the period between "the emergence of 'modern equity' in the latter part of the seventeenth century and the reception . . . by American courts in the early nineteenth century." Id. at 1255. Both are critical of the doctrine.

KEENE v. CHAMBERS

Court of Appeals of New York, 1936.
271 N.Y. 326, 3 N.E.2d 443.

CRANE, CH. J. This is an action for rent, taxes and other sums due under a lease of certain premises situate in Chicago, Ill. . . .

For the purposes of this appeal we find that the plaintiffs are the owners of a joint life estate in an undivided one-half interest in the leased premises. Bertha Kline Baker is vested with a life estate in the remaining half. All her interest in the rents under the lease and income therefrom she has transferred to the Chicago Title and Trust Company. At the beginning of this action, therefore, the plaintiffs and the Chicago Title and Trust Company were in effect the lessors, entitled to the rents under the lease and all the rights for the enforcement of taxes and other amounts due.

The Chicago Title and Trust Company is an Illinois corporation over which the State of New York has no jurisdiction. The defendants are residents of New York State, over whom the courts of Illinois have no jurisdiction. The plaintiffs have brought this action for the rent and taxes, with interest thereon, but have not joined either as plaintiff or defendant the Chicago Title and Trust Company. The plaintiffs requested this company to join with them in this action but the request was refused. The defendants made a motion to compel the plaintiffs to join the Chicago Title and Trust Company as a party, which motion was denied. The Appellate Division affirmed the order, certifying, however, to this court the following two questions:

"1. Is Chicago Title and Trust Company a necessary party to this action?

"2. Should plaintiffs be required to join Chicago Title and Trust Company as a party defendant, although it is without the jurisdiction of the Supreme Court of the State of New York and refuses to join?"

We answer both these questions in the negative.

* * *

The plaintiffs cannot sue in Illinois, where the real property is, as the defendants are not residents of that State. The State of New York has no jurisdiction over the Chicago Title and Trust Company, and an order to bring it in and make it a party in this action would be futile and meaningless. It is apparent, therefore, that this section of the Civil Practice Act has limitations and must be interpreted so as to direct an enforceable act. To command a party to be brought in where there is no process to bring him in and no jurisdiction over him lacks sense. Parties who are united in interest must be joined as plaintiffs or be brought into the action as defendants, pursuant to this section 194 of the Civil Practice Act, where they are within the jurisdiction of the court, so that the judgment may effectually bind them. Where any of such parties are without the State, and cannot be served or brought into the action effectually, they need not be parties, and an order would be improperly granted which directed that they be made parties. This is the interpretation which the courts have given to this section and which we approve. [Citations omitted.] The law has been stated in Ruling Case Law, Vol. 7, § 110, p. 910, as follows: "Likewise, one tenant in common of personal property may separately maintain an action for a wrong done to it, if his cotenants refuse to join with him as plaintiffs, and they are nonresidents of and are without the state."

If the plaintiffs collect the entire rent they must of course account to their cotenant for the latter's share. [Citations omitted.]

The order appealed from should be affirmed, with costs, and the questions certified answered in the negative.

NOTES

(1) When there exists no obstacle to the joinder of the additional parties interested in the premises of the litigation, should their joinder be held mandatory? See N.Y.C.P.L.R. § 1001. See also Kamhi v. Cohen, 512 F.2d 1051 (2d Cir.1975) (since wife is subject to suit and her presence would not defeat diversity, she must be joined in action by husband to set aside sequestrations of his assets effectuated to secure claims for alimony and support).

(2) Once it has been decided that the joinder of absent parties is mandatory, could it be argued that the court, by virtue of that determination, has in personam adjudicatory power over them? Cf. Mullane v. Central Hanover Bank & Trust Co., p. 312, supra; Atkinson v. Superior Court, p. 320, supra, and Fed.R.Civ.P. 4(f). In civil law countries, adjudicatory power over one defendant

generally creates adjudicatory power over all other defendants interested in the dispute before the court. See p. 310, Note (1), supra.

(3) Would it be desirable to adopt rules extending nationwide the competence of the federal courts over indispensable parties? Has this been done in regard to officers or employees of the United States by 28 U.S.C.A. § 1391(e), providing that in an action against such a public official in his official capacity service "may be made by certified mail beyond the territorial limits of the district in which the action is brought"?

(4) What other procedural device might permit a litigant to avoid the problem of lack of adjudicatory power over absent interested parties? See p. 482, Note (5), infra.

PROVIDENT TRADESMENS BANK & TRUST CO. v. PATTERSON

Supreme Court of the United States, 1968.
390 U.S. 102, 88 S.Ct. 733, 19 L.Ed.2d 936.

MR. JUSTICE HARLAN delivered the opinion of the Court.*

This controversy, involving in its present posture the dismissal of a declaratory judgment action for nonjoinder of an "indispensable" party, began nearly 10 years ago with a traffic accident. An automobile owned by Edward Dutcher, who was not present when the accident occurred, was being driven by Donald Cionci, to whom Dutcher had given the keys. John Lynch and John Harris were passengers. The automobile crossed the median strip of the highway and collided with a truck being driven by Thomas Smith. Cionci, Lynch, and Smith were killed and Harris was severely injured.

Three tort actions were brought. Provident Tradesmens Bank, the administrator of the estate of passenger Lynch and petitioner here, sued the estate of the driver, Cionci, in a diversity action. Smith's administratrix, and Harris in person, each brought a state-court action against the estate of Cionci, Dutcher the owner, and the estate of Lynch. These Smith and Harris actions, for unknown reasons, have never gone to trial and are still pending. The Lynch action against Cionci's estate was settled for $50,000, which the estate of Cionci, being penniless, has never paid.

Dutcher, the owner of the automobile and a defendant in the as yet untried tort actions, had an automobile liability insurance policy with Lumbermens Mutual Casualty Company, a respondent here. That policy had an upper limit of $100,000 for all claims arising out of a single accident. This fund was potentially subject to two different sorts of claims by the tort plaintiffs. First, Dutcher himself might be held vicariously liable as Cionci's "principal"; the likelihood of such a judgment against Dutcher is a matter of considerable doubt and dispute. Second, the policy by its terms covered the direct liability of any person driving Dutcher's car with Dutcher's "permission."

---

* Footnotes omitted.

The insurance company had declined, after notice, to defend in the tort action brought by Lynch's estate against the estate of Cionci, believing that Cionci had not had permission and hence was not covered by the policy. The facts allegedly were that Dutcher had entrusted his car to Cionci, but that Cionci had made a detour from the errand for which Dutcher allowed his car to be taken. The estate of Lynch, armed with its $50,000 liquidated claim against the estate of Cionci, brought the present diversity action for a declaration that Cionci's use of the car had been "with permission" of Dutcher. The only named defendants were the company and the estate of Cionci. The other two tort plaintiffs were joined as plaintiffs. Dutcher, a resident of the State of Pennsylvania as were all the plaintiffs, was not joined either as plaintiff or defendant. The failure to join him was not adverted to at the trial level.

The major question of law contested at trial was a state-law question. The District Court had ruled that, as a matter of the applicable (Pennsylvania) law, the driver of an automobile is presumed to have the permission of the owner. Hence, unless contrary evidence could be introduced, the tort plaintiffs, now declaratory judgment plaintiffs, would be entitled to a directed verdict against the insurance company. The only possible contrary evidence was testimony by Dutcher as to restrictions he had imposed on Cionci's use of the automobile. The two estate plaintiffs claimed, however, that under the Pennsylvania "Dead Man Rule" Dutcher was incompetent to testify on this matter as against them. The District Court upheld this claim. . . . The District Court, therefore, directed verdicts in favor of the two estates. Dutcher was, however, allowed to testify as against the live plaintiff, Harris. The jury, nonetheless, found that Cionci had had permission, and hence awarded a verdict to Harris also.

Lumbermens appealed the judgment to the Court of Appeals for the Third Circuit, raising various state-law questions. The Court of Appeals did not reach any of these issues. Instead, after reargument *en banc*, it decided, 5–2, to reverse on two alternative grounds neither of which had been raised in the District Court or by the appellant.

The first of these grounds was that Dutcher was an indispensable party. The court held that the "adverse interests" that had rendered Dutcher incompetent to testify under the Pennsylvania Dead Man Rule also required him to be made a party. The court did not consider whether the fact that a verdict had already been rendered, without objection to the nonjoinder of Dutcher, affected the matter. Nor did it follow the provision of Rule 19 of the Federal Rules of Civil Procedure that findings of "indispensability" must be based on stated pragmatic considerations. It held, to the contrary, that the right of a person who "may be affected" by the judgment to be joined is a "substantive" right, unaffected by the federal rules; that a trial court "may not proceed" in the absence of such a person; and that since Dutcher could not be joined as a defendant without destroying diversity jurisdiction the action had to be dismissed.

Since this ruling presented a serious challenge to the scope of the newly amended Rule 19, we granted certiorari. 386 U.S. 940, 87 S.Ct. 972, 17 L.Ed.2d 872. Concluding that the inflexible approach adopted by the Court of Appeals in this case exemplifies the kind of reasoning that the Rule was designed to avoid, we reverse.

I.

We may assume, at the outset, that Dutcher falls within the category of persons who, under § 19(a), should be "joined if feasible." The action was for an adjudication of the validity of certain claims against a fund. Dutcher, faced with the possibility of judgments against him, had an interest in having the fund preserved to cover that potential liability. Hence there existed, when this case went to trial, at least the possibility that a judgment might impede Dutcher's ability to protect his interest, or lead to later relitigation by him.

The optimum solution, an adjudication of the permission question that would be binding on all interested persons, was not "feasible," however, for Dutcher could not be made a defendant without destroying diversity. Hence the problem was the one to which Rule 19(b) appears to address itself: in the absence of a person who "should be joined if feasible," should the court dismiss the action or proceed without him? Since this problem emerged for the first time in the Court of Appeals, there were also two subsidiary questions. First, what was the effect, if any, of the failure of the defendants to raise the matter in the District Court? Second, what was the importance, if any, of the fact that a judgment, binding on the parties although not binding on Dutcher, had already been reached after extensive litigation? The three questions prove, on examination, to be interwoven.

We conclude, upon consideration of the record and applying the "equity and good conscience" test of Rule 19(b), that the Court of Appeals erred in not allowing the judgment to stand.

Rule 19(b) suggests four "interests" that must be examined in each case to determine whether, in equity and good conscience, the court should proceed without a party whose absence from the litigation is compelled. Each of these interests must, in this case, be viewed entirely from an appellate perspective since the matter of joinder was not considered in the trial court. First, the plaintiff has an interest in having a forum. Before the trial, the strength of this interest obviously depends upon whether a satisfactory alternative forum exists. On appeal, if the plaintiff has won, he has a strong additional interest in preserving his judgment. Second, the defendant may properly wish to avoid multiple litigation, or inconsistent relief, or sole responsibility for a liability he shares with another. After trial, however, if the defendant has failed to assert this interest, it is quite proper to consider it foreclosed.

Third, there is the interest of the outsider whom it would have been desirable to join. Of course, since the outsider is not before the

444 WHICH COURTS, LAW & LITIGANTS Pt. 3

court, he cannot be bound by the judgment rendered. This means, however, only that a judgment is not *res judicata* as to, or legally enforceable against, a nonparty. It obviously does not mean either (a) that a court may never issue a judgment that, in practice, affects a nonparty or (b) that (to the contrary) a court may always proceed without considering the potential effect on nonparties simply because they are not "bound" in the technical sense. Instead, as Rule 19(a) expresses it, the court must consider the extent to which the judgment may "as a practical matter impair or impede his ability to protect" his interest in the subject matter. When a case has reached the appeal stage the matter is more complex. The judgment appealed from may not in fact affect the interest of any outsider even though there existed, before trial, a possibility that a judgment affecting his interest would be rendered. When necessary, however, a court of appeals should, on its own initiative, take steps to protect the absent party, who of course had no opportunity to plead and prove his interest below.

Fourth, there remains the interest of the courts and the public in complete, consistent, and efficient settlement of controversies. We read the Rule's third criterion, whether the judgment issued in the absence of the nonjoined person will be "adequate," to refer to this public stake in settling disputes by wholes, whenever possible, for clearly the plaintiff, who himself chose both the forum and the parties defendant, will not be heard to complain about the sufficiency of the relief obtainable against them. After trial, considerations of efficiency of course include the fact that the time and expense of a trial have already been spent.

Rule 19(b) also directs a district court to consider the possibility of shaping relief to accommodate these four interests. Commentators had argued that greater attention should be paid to this potential solution to a joinder stymie, and the Rule now makes it explicit that a court should consider modification of a judgment as an alternative to dismissal. Needless to say, a court of appeals may also properly require suitable modification as a condition of affirmance.

Had the Court of Appeals applied Rule 19's criteria to the facts of the present case, it could hardly have reached the conclusion it did. We begin with the plaintiffs' viewpoint. It is difficult to decide at this stage whether they would have had an "adequate" remedy had the action been dismissed before trial for non-joinder: we cannot here determine whether the plaintiffs could have brought the same action, against the same parties plus Dutcher, in a state court. After trial, however, the "adequacy" of this hypothetical alternative, from the plaintiffs' point of view, was obviously greatly diminished. Their interest in preserving a fully litigated judgment should be overborne only by rather greater opposing considerations than would be required at an earlier stage when the plaintiffs' only concern was for a federal rather than a state forum.

Opposing considerations in this case are hard to find. The defendants had no stake, either asserted or real, in the joinder of Dutcher.

They showed no interest in joinder until the Court of Appeals took the matter into its own hands. This properly forecloses any interest of theirs, but for purposes of clarity we note that the insurance company, whose liability was limited to $100,000, had or will have full opportunity to litigate each claim on that fund against the claimant involved. Its only concern with the absence of Dutcher was and is to obtain a windfall escape from its defeat at trial.

The interest of the outsider, Dutcher, is more difficult to reckon. The Court of Appeals, concluding that it should not follow Rule 19's command to determine whether, as a practical matter, the judgment impaired the nonparty's ability to protect his rights, simply quoted the District Court's reasoning on the Dead Man issue as proof that Dutcher had a "right" to be joined. . . . There is a logical error in the Court of Appeals' appropriation of this reasoning for its own quite different purposes: Dutcher had an "adverse" interest (sufficient to invoke the Dead Man Rule) because he would have been *benefited* by a ruling *in favor of* the insurance company; the question before the Court of Appeals, however, was whether Dutcher was *harmed* by the judgment *against* the insurance company.

The two questions are not the same. If the three plaintiffs had lost to the insurance company on the permission issue, that loss would have ended the matter favorably to Dutcher. If, as has happened, the three plaintiffs obtain a judgment against the insurance company on the permission issue, Dutcher may still claim that as a nonparty he is not estopped by that judgment from relitigating the issue. At that point it might be argued that Dutcher should be bound by the previous decision because, although technically a nonparty, he had purposely bypassed an adequate opportunity to intervene. We do not now decide whether such an argument would be correct under the circumstances of this case. If, however, Dutcher is properly foreclosed by his failure to intervene in the present litigation, then the joinder issue considered in the Court of Appeals vanishes, for any rights of Dutcher's have been lost by his own inaction.

If Dutcher is not foreclosed by his failure to intervene below, then he is not "bound" by the judgment against the insurance company and, in theory, he has not been harmed. There remains, however, the practical question whether Dutcher is likely to have any need, and if so will have any opportunity, to relitigate. The only possible threat to him is that if the fund is used to pay judgments against Cionci the money may in fact have disappeared before Dutcher has an opportunity to assert his interest. Upon examination, we find this supposed threat neither large nor unavoidable.

The state-court actions against Dutcher had lain dormant for years at the pleading stage by the time the Court of Appeals acted. Petitioner asserts here that under the applicable Pennsylvania vicarious liability law there is virtually no chance of recovery against Dutcher. We do not accept this assertion as fact, but the matter could have been explored below. Furthermore, even in the event of tort judgments against Dutcher, it is unlikely that he will be prejudiced by the outcome here. The potential claimants against Dutcher himself are identical with the potential claimants against Cionci's estate. Should the claimants seek to collect from Dutcher personally, he may be able to raise the permission issue defensively, making it irrelevant that the actual monies paid from the fund may have disappeared: Dutcher can assert that Cionci did not have his permission and that therefore the payments made on Cionci's behalf out of Dutcher's insurance policy should properly be credited against Dutcher's own liability. Of course, when Dutcher raises this defense he may lose, either on the merits of the permission issue or on the ground that the issue is foreclosed by Dutcher's failure to intervene in the present case, but Dutcher will not have been prejudiced by the failure of the District Court here to order him joined.

If the Court of Appeals was unconvinced that the threat to Dutcher was trivial, it could nevertheless have avoided all difficulties by proper phrasing of the decree. The District Court, for unspecified reasons, had refused to order immediate payment on the Cionci judgment. Payment could have been withheld pending the suits against Dutcher and relitigation (if that became necessary) by him. In this Court, furthermore, counsel for petitioner represented orally that the tort plaintiffs would accept a limitation of all claims to the amount of the insurance policy. Obviously such a compromise could have been reached below had the Court of Appeals been willing to abandon its rigid approach and seek ways to preserve what was, as to the parties, subject to the appellant's other contentions, a perfectly valid judgment.

The suggestion of potential relitigation of the question of "permission" raises the fourth "interest" at stake in joinder cases—efficiency. It might have been preferable, at the trial level, if there were a forum available in which both the company and Dutcher could have been made defendants, to dismiss the action and force the plaintiffs to go elsewhere. Even this preference would have been highly problematical, however, for the actual threat of relitigation by Dutcher depended on there being judgments against him and on the amount of the fund, which was not revealed to the District Court. By the time the case reached the Court of Appeals, however, the problematical preference on efficiency grounds had entirely disappeared: there was no reason then to throw away a valid judgment just because it did not theoretically settle the whole controversy.

II.

Application of Rule 19(b)'s "equity and good conscience" test for determining whether to proceed or dismiss would doubtless have led to a contrary result below. The Court of Appeals' reasons for disregarding the Rule remain to be examined. The majority of the court concluded that the Rule was inapplicable because "substantive" rights are involved, and substantive rights are not affected by the Federal Rules. . . .

The Court of Appeals concluded, although it was the first court to hold, that the 19th century joinder cases in this Court created a federal, common-law, substantive right in a certain class of persons to be joined in the corresponding lawsuits. . . .

[The part of the Court's opinion rejecting this conclusion has been omitted].

Reversed.

SCHUTTEN v. SHELL OIL CO.
United States Court of Appeals, Fifth Circuit, 1970.
421 F.2d 869.

CARSWELL, CIRCUIT JUDGE.* Appellants filed suit in the District Court seeking to evict the appellee, Shell Oil Company, and seeking an accounting for the removal of oil, gas, and other minerals from land in Plaquemines Parish, Louisiana. Appellants, who are not in possession, claim ownership of the land and demand an accounting from Shell because of its failure to deal with appellants in removing the minerals.

Appellee filed a Motion to Dismiss on the ground that its lessor, the Board of Commissioners of the Orleans Levee District, who also claims title to the land in question, is an "indispensable party" who cannot be joined since such action would destroy the District Court's diversity jurisdiction. The District Court granted the appellee's motion and dismissed the case.

Both parties agree that if the Levee Board is indispensable to the action the suit would have to be dismissed since both appellants and the Levee Board are citizens of Louisiana and diversity jurisdiction under 28 U.S.C. § 1332 would not be obtainable. Thus the sole issue before this Court is that of the indispensability of the Levee Board.

In deciding this issue it is clear that the provisions of Rule 19 of the Federal Rules of Civil Procedure control. . . .

*   *   *

As pointed out by the Advisory Committee, . . . the term "indispensable" as utilized in the present Rule 19 is not "definitive" but "conclusionary". The term simply denotes a conclusion reached upon due consideration that the person is one who should be joined but whose joinder is impossible and that it is preferable to dismiss the case than to proceed without him. It is to be stressed that the criteria set forth in Rule 19 are not to be applied mechanically nor are they to be used to override compelling substantive interests. . . .

*   *   *

Considering the present case in the light afforded by Rule 19 we cannot say that the district court erred in dismissing the action and declaring the Levee Board an "indispensable" party.

* Footnotes omitted.

Under subdivision (a) the Levee Board is clearly a party "to be joined if feasible." Its joinder is impossible, however, since it would destroy the District Court's diversity jurisdiction. Appellants argue that under Louisiana substantive law their action is merely personal against Shell for trespass and that the Levee Board has no "interest" in the action. As pointed out above, the concept of substantive severability is no longer the guiding star of the joinder problem. Nevertheless, a review of the relevant statutory provisions and their interpretation by the Louisiana courts leads us to reject the appellants' argument that the interests of the lessor and lessee of mineral rights are "severable" under Louisiana law. See Le Sage v. Union Producing Co., 249 La. 42, 184 So.2d 727 (1966). It cannot be denied that appellants' action in trespass is based upon its claim of ownership of the land overlying the mineral deposits. This claim is directly opposed to the Levee Board's claim of ownership which is "backed up" by its possession in fact. This question of actual ownership must necessarily be adjudicated before the trespass and accounting issues are reached. There is no doubt that the Levee Board has an interest in this litigation and is a "party to be joined if feasible." Since it is not feasible to join the Levee Board we must now consider what alternatives are available under the "equity and good conscience" standard. To do this we must apply the pragmatic criteria of subdivision (b) of Rule 19.

The first factor that must be considered is the extent to which a judgment might prejudice the unjoined Levee Board or those already parties. Appellants argue that the Levee Board would not be prejudiced because it would not be bound, in the res judicata sense, by any judgment which might be rendered. Nor would the Board be precluded from asserting its rights in another action presumably in Louisiana state courts. We decline to accept the appellants' narrow and technical view of what would constitute prejudice to the Levee Board. It is clear that courts should not proceed simply because the unjoined party is not "bound" in the technical sense. Provident Tradesmens Bank & Trust Co. v. Patterson, supra 390 U.S. at 110, 88 S.Ct. 733. Furthermore, one of the purposes, though not the sole purpose, of Rule 19 is the avoidance of multiple litigation of essentially the same issues.

The possibility of prejudice to the Levee Board is most certainly not superficial. First, if Shell is ousted the Levee Board's royalty interest would cease in practically the same manner as if the court had decreed a cancellation of the lease. This would happen despite the fact that the Levee Board's claim of ownership would be technically unimpaired by the judgment in the sense that it would not be bound by the judgment.

Second, though not technically bound a judgment would most assuredly create a cloud on the Levee Board's title and greatly diminish the value of the property. This result would be adverse to both appellants and the Board and would require yet more litigation. A judgment in favor of the appellants would in effect adjudicate the Levee Board's claim of ownership without giving them the right to present their defense and assert their own claim on its merits. While Shell does have a substantial interest in the Levee Board's claim this "interest" would not justify placing the burden of proving the Levee Board's ownership on Shell.

Third, a judgment might result in inconsistent obligations for the defendant Shell Oil Company. Furthermore, a judgment in appellant's favor might render the Levee Board liable to Shell for loss or damage for the peaceable possession of mineral rights. See La.Civ.Code Arts. 2692, 2696. Again all of this could come about without affording the Levee Board the opportunity to defend its interests even though the Board would not be bound by the judgment.

A conclusion that as a practical matter the Levee Board would be prejudiced by a judgment rendered in their absence leads us to consider the second and third "factors" of Rule 19: "the extent to which, by protective provisions in the judgment, by the shaping of relief, or other measures, the prejudice can be lessened or avoided", and whether a judgment rendered in the Levee Board's absence will be adequate. Appellants have suggested no way in which these objectives could be accomplished and we are unable to discover any ourselves. Since the litigation revolved around the conflicting claims of ownership, we are unable to envision a decree which would effectively settle any controversy between the appellants and the present defendant, Shell, without doing substantial practical injury to the Levee Board's unassertable claims. Any attempt to fashion a judgment which would lessen this harm would result in a meaningless decree.

A judgment rendered at this time and without the Levee Board would simply result in additional costly litigation no matter how such judgment was formulated. This fact leads us to consider the fourth and final criteria of Rule 19: whether the appellant has an adequate remedy elsewhere. The answer to this question is that appellants will by no means be prejudiced themselves if forced to pursue their remedy in the courts of the State of Louisiana. Both the Levee Board and Shell are amenable to process in Louisiana. This litigation concerns land situated in Louisiana, is governed by Louisiana law and involves a claim of ownership asserted by an agency of the State of Louisiana. Appellants cannot be heard to complain about the competence of the courts of Louisiana in such matters. There is, however, an even more compelling reason for appellants to seek relief in the Louisiana courts. Even if the district court below could fashion a judgment which was adequate while at the same time protective of unassertable rights, additional litigation would most assuredly develop later in the Louisiana courts. By dismissing the case now and directing the appellants to proceed in the Louisiana courts, most if not all issues can be settled in one bout of litigation. As noted above, the expeditious and effective disposition of litigation is desirable if not always obtainable. In the present case it is not only desirable but obtainable and is indeed made necessary under the circumstances.

We therefore conclude that under Rule 19, Federal Rules of Civil Procedure, the present case in all "equity and good conscience" should not proceed without joinder of the Orleans Levee Board. Moreover, this decision is made easier by the knowledge that the courts of the State of Louisiana offer a forum in which a complete adjudication of all interests can be obtained without fear of needless multiple litigation.

The order of the District Court dismissing the complaint for non-joinder of the Orleans Levee Board is

Affirmed.

NOTES

(1) Suppose that A, a citizen of New York and a member of a partnership, sues C, a citizen of New Jersey, in a federal court on a debt owed to the partnership. B, A's partner and also a citizen of New York, refuses to join in the action, and because his presence is mandatory he is joined as a defendant by A. Mechanically viewed, the requisite diversity of citizenship to sustain federal jurisdiction does not appear to exist. But the rule is that the court will look to the real interests of the parties in determining whether there is diversity. See Niles-Bement-Pond Co. v. Iron Moulders Union, 254 U.S. 77, 41 S.Ct. 39, 65 L.Ed. 145 (1920). From one standpoint, since any recovery by A will inure to the benefit of the partnership, B has a plaintiff's interest. On the other hand, B has shown antagonism and hostility toward A and therefore has an adverse interest. This question arises frequently with respect to the corporation whose right is supposedly being championed in a stockholder's derivative action. Should the court realign the corporation (which appears formally as a defendant) to sustain or defeat jurisdiction? See, e.g., Smith v. Sperling, 354 U.S. 91, 77 S.Ct. 1112, 1 L.Ed.2d 1205 (1957); Gratz v. Murchison, 130 F.Supp. 709 (D.Del.1955).

(2) The logic of Rule 19 is that the doctrine of ancillary jurisdiction cannot be used to expand the court's authority to reach the claims of indispensable parties. Since the claims of these parties are (by definition) completely enmeshed in the case before the court, is not this result surprising? After all, the doctrines of pendent and ancillary jurisdiction are premised on the notion that a constitutional court has power to do justice between the parties before it. If another party is required to dispense justice, should not the court have the authority to entertain the entire case? Perhaps the anomaly can be explained by noting that courts traditionally viewed the joinder of an indispensable party as essential to their jurisdiction, see, e.g., Calcote v. Texas Pacific Coal & Oil Co., 157 F.2d 216 (5th Cir.1946), cert. denied 329 U.S. 782, 67 S.Ct. 205, 91 L.Ed. 671 (1947). In other words, the court has no power until all necessary parties appeared before it. Without primary power, there is nothing to be "pendent" or "ancillary" to. See Hazard, Indispensable Party: The Historical Origin of a Procedural Phantom, 61 Colum.L.Rev. 1254 (1961).

But is this analysis correct? Compare Fed.R.Civ.P. 12(h)(2) with 12(h)(3). Under 12(h)(3), a case can be dismissed whenever it appears that the court lacks subject matter jurisdiction, but 12(h)(2) limits the power to dismiss a case for failure to join an indispensable party to the trial on the merits. Doesn't this imply that even without the indispensable party, the court has authority to decide the case? Does the result in *Provident Tradesmen* make sense under any other interpretation?

It is sometimes argued that if ancillary jurisdiction applied to indispensable parties, the subject matter limitations on federal jurisdiction could be evaded by artful pleading (by, for example, "neglecting" to sue the indispensable party that would spoil jurisdiction). Could that problem be handled by analogy to 28 U.S.C.A. § 1359 by dismissing cases in which deliberate circumvention of jurisdictional limitations was attempted?

(3) What is the significance of the Court's suggestion that "it might be argued that Dutcher should be bound by the previous decision because, although technically a nonparty, he had purposely bypassed an adequate opportunity to intervene"? Litigants and courts have been intrigued by the possibility of using this language to bind nonparties. However, in Martin v. Wilks, ___ U.S. ___, 109 S.Ct. 2180, 104 L.Ed.2d 835 (1989), p. 971, infra, the Supreme Court reconsidered this sentence, and rejected its implications. The Court held that the parties who are present in an action have an obligation to use Rule 19 to join those whom they wish to be bound by the judgment. Those who were never joined cannot be affected by the judgment. After reading this case, consider whether, in addition to repudiating this sentence in *Provident Tradesmen*, the *Martin* Court contemplated expanding the tests for deciding which parties are indispensable and which should be joined if feasible.

(4) What action should be taken when a party who destroys federal jurisdiction has been joined, but is found dispensable? Fed.R.Civ.P. 21 permits the district court to dismiss the party. The Supreme Court has authorized the court of appeals to exercise similar authority when the problem is first recognized at the appellate stage, Newman-Green, Inc. v. Alejandro Alfonzo-Larrain, ___ U.S. ___, 109 S.Ct. 2218, 104 L.Ed.2d 893 (1989).

CAREY v. KLUTZNICK, 653 F.2d 732 (2d Cir.1981) *. This was an action alleging undercounts of the population of the State and City of New York in the 1980 Census. The lower court's judgment had ordered the Census Bureau to adjust population figures for the State and City "in a reasonable and scientific manner" and to report to the court within thirty days the Bureau's plan to effectuate the court's ruling.

Though reversal and a new trial would in any event have been required by error and prejudice resulting from the District court's discovery orders and sanctions imposed in that connection, the Second Circuit panel also found all fifty states fall within Rule 19(a) category of persons who should be joined in the action if feasible and, since this was not feasible, "pragmatic equitable alternatives should have been considered": The court wrote:

> The House of Representatives has 435 members, and this number must be apportioned among the fifty States. If one State gains a member, another must lose one. Following the 1960 census, seven States each gained one seat, one State gained four, and one gained eight. As a result, twelve States each lost one seat, three States each lost two seats, and one State lost three seats. Following the 1970 census, three States each gained one seat, one gained three, and one gained five. Seven States each lost one seat, and two States each lost two seats. In

---

* Most footnotes omitted.

effect, House membership is a fund in which fifty States have an interest. No State's share can be increased without adversely affecting at least one other State. The question presented by litigation such as the one now before us is whether one State can be granted such an increase without full consideration having been given to its effect on other States.

Persons "who not only have an interest in the controversy but an interest of such a nature that a final decree cannot be made without either affecting that interest, or leaving the controversy in such a condition that its final termination may be wholly inconsistent with equity and good conscience" are traditionally considered to be indispensable parties. Equity suggests that a person be brought into the litigation if the case cannot be decided on its merits without prejudicing his rights. This not only prevents possible injury to the absent person; it avoids multiplicity of suits and the danger of inconsistent decisions.[17]

We think it clear beyond cavil that a statistically formulated increase in the population of only one State, such as New York, will have an adverse effect on other States which are entitled to, but do not receive, the benefit of a similar adjustment. Even if the increase is insufficient to change House membership, it will nonetheless increase New York's share in the numerous revenue sharing plans that are tied into the census. The adversely affected States therefore fall within the category of parties who should be joined in the instant litigation if feasible. Because compulsory joinder of all fifty States was not feasible in the district court, pragmatic equitable alternatives should have been considered.

The first alternative, which the prior panel of this Court has already rejected, would have been to substitute Bureau and congressional review for that of the court.[23] This is the recommendation of the Association of the Bar's Special Committee on Empirical Data in Legal Decision Making which concludes its report with the following observation:

> The path to a better census is more likely to be found in scrutiny of Bureau procedures by the Bureau itself, Con-

---

17. See Ward v. Louisiana Wildlife & Fisheries Commission, 224 F.Supp. 252, 256 (E.D.La.1963), aff'd, 347 F.2d 234 (5th Cir.1965). Because the financial and political effects of population apportionment make it a competitive process, the proper method of determining disproportionate undercount would seem to be on a State vs. State basis, rather than that of State vs. national average. If statistical adjustments are to be made, they should be made in all States where needed and in a uniformly fair manner. This is not apt to occur when claims of disproportionate undercount are made in fifty separate cases, particularly when there is no consensus among the experts as to feasible and accurate methods of adjusting undercounts.

23. The existence of half-a-hundred separately-sued legal challenges to the 1980 census, see note 10, supra, indicates that there may be a basic defect in the procedure for census review. If the courts cannot correct this situation, it may be wise for Congress to do so.

gress, other federal agencies, and interested professional groups than in litigation to compel adjustment.

A second alternative would have been to require that notice of suit be given to all of the States, with permission to intervene given any State which felt that its interests were imperiled. Apparently, no notice was given anyone; only the County of Suffolk sought intervention, and its application was denied.

A third alternative would have been to seek multidistrict coordinated or consolidated pretrial proceedings pursuant to 28 U.S.C. § 1407. It appears that thirty-one of the above listed actions have been transferred to the District of Maryland for coordinated or consolidated proceedings. The wisdom vel non of adopting a uniform nationwide method of making statistical adjustments might perhaps be fully explored if complete multidistrict joinder were agreed upon.

As a fourth alternative, the district court could have stayed the operation of its judgment pending a definitive appellate ruling as to whether the Census Bureau's conduct of the 1980 census could properly be challenged in fifty separate and unrelated actions and whether the requirements imposed on the Bureau by the district court in this action were proper.

SECTION 8. IMPLEADER

The impleader device permits nonplaintiff parties to introduce into the lawsuit litigants who have no relationship to the plaintiff in the case. Because the new participants are there as opponents of parties other than the plaintiff, impleader is called "third-party practice;" the newly introduced party is the "third-party defendant," and the party who brought him into the action is the "third-party plaintiff." Impleader is traceable to the "vouching to warranty" procedure at common law. A person whose title to land came under attack could "vouch in" his grantor because the latter had warranted the title. Whether the grantor thereafter took part in the action or not, he would be bound by its determination if he were later sued by the grantee. See 3 Moore's Federal Practice ¶ 14.02 (2d ed. 1948); 37 Cornell L.Q. 721–22 (1952). Vouching to warranty is still available but it is rarely used because it requires two suits. Courts have tended to construe strictly this common law procedure partly because the cases "demonstrate the 'vexations inherent in the practice' of vouching in, and provoke 'controversy as to the adequacy of notice and opportunity to defend.'" Glens Falls Insurance Co. v. Wood, 8 N.Y.2d 409, 413, 208 N.Y.S.2d 978, 980, 171 N.E.2d 321, 322 (1960). See Comment, Due Process Constraints on Vouching as a Device to Bind Non-Parties, 14 Colum.J.L. & Soc. Problems 189 (1978). As does its common law ancestor, the impleader device aims to resolve common questions of fact and law in a single litigation, without duplication, delay and the danger of inconsistent results.

UNITED STATES v. De HAVEN

United States District Court, Western District of Michigan, 1953.
13 F.R.D. 435.

STARR, DISTRICT JUDGE. The plaintiff brings this action to recover on a certain promissory note executed by defendants April 9, 1947, payable to Vander Broek Bros. Roofing Co. in the amount of $979.61, which note was endorsed and negotiated "without recourse" by the roofing company to the Commercial Credit Corporation. This note was given by defendants in payment for certain repairs and improvements made upon their home by the Vander Broek company, and after default in payment of certain monthly instalments, the Commercial Credit Corporation on December 4, 1947, assigned the note to the plaintiff, which had insured its payment by its agency, the Federal Housing Administration. 12 U.S.C.A. § 1702 et seq. In their answer filed January 3, 1950, defendants denied liability on the grounds that there was no consideration for their execution of the note; that the plaintiff had knowledge of the failure of consideration; and that plaintiff is not a holder of the note in due course. In their answer defendants alleged in substance that the roofing company breached its contract in that it failed to make the repairs and improvements to their home in a proper and workmanlike manner and that they have a claim against that company for damages.

On January 11, 1950, the defendants filed a motion, in pursuance of Rule 14(a) of the Federal Rules of Civil Procedure as amended, 28 U.S.C.A., for leave as third-parties plaintiff to implead Gilbert J. and Kenneth E. Vander Broek, copartners doing business as the Vander Broek Bros. Roofing Co., as third-parties defendant, on the ground that the Vander Broeks will be liable to them for all or part of the plaintiff's claim on the promissory note in question and also for additional damages. The plaintiff opposes this motion on the ground that under the facts and circumstances shown by the pleadings and the affidavit of defendant Floyd De Haven, this is not a proper case for the impleading of third-parties defendant under Rule 14(a), and that as a matter of judicial discretion the court should deny the motion. . . .

The plaintiff's claim in this action is on the promissory note executed by the defendants for money loaned to them. The defendants' asserted claim against the Vander Broeks is for damages for their alleged breach of contract in connection with the repairing and improving of defendants' home. The defendants' claim for breach of contract is separate and distinct from the plaintiff's claim on their note, and defendants' claim is not dependent upon the outcome of the present suit. Furthermore, as the Vander Broeks endorsed and negotiated the defendants' note to the Commercial Credit Corporation "without re-course," they could not be held liable for all or any part of the plaintiff's claim against the defendants. Although the Vander Broeks might be liable to the defendants for breach of contract, it is clear that they would not be liable to defendants for all or part of the plaintiff's claim on defendants' note. Therefore, to allow the impleading of the Vander Broeks as third-parties defendant would be to introduce a new and separate controversy into the present case. In Woods v. Batchel-der, D.C., 8 F.R.D. 194, 195, the court said:

> "The underlying policy for Rule 14 is the avoidance of multiplicity of litigation. However, the third-party procedure is not designed as a vehicle for the trying together of separate and distinct causes of action. . . .

> "The trial of the third-party complaint would involve a determination of issues wholly unrelated to the issues involved in the trial of the original complaint."

* * *

The court accordingly holds that the defendants are not entitled under Rule 14 to implead the Vander Broeks as third-parties defendant in the present case.

Furthermore, it has repeatedly been held that the question as to whether a third party should be impleaded on the motion of a defendant is a matter for the exercise of judicial discretion. [Citations omitted.]

* * *

In the present case the issues of fact and law in connection with plaintiff's claim on defendants' promissory note are entirely different from the issues of fact and law which would be involved in connection with the defendants' claim against the Vander Broeks for breach of contract. The plaintiff was not a party to the contract between the defendants and the Vander Broeks for the repairing and improving of the defendants' home. The principal issue in the plaintiff's present action against the defendants is whether the plaintiff is a holder of defendants' promissory note in due course. The defendants' claim against the Vander Broeks for damages is in no way ancillary to the plaintiff's suit on the note in question. The third-party procedure provided by Rule 14 was not designed as a vehicle for the trying together of separate and distinct causes of action. Furthermore, in actions by the government to recover money loaned to home owners for the repair of their homes, the Federal courts should not be burdened with disputes and litigation between the home owners and the contrac-tors or builders who made the repairs. The court is convinced that under the facts and circumstances in the present case defendants' motion to implead the Vander Broeks should be denied.

For the reasons herein stated, defendants' motion for leave as third-parties plaintiff, to serve a summons and complaint upon the Vander Broeks as third-parties defendant, is denied and an order will be entered accordingly. No costs will be allowed in connection with this motion.

NOTES

(1) In Tanbro Fabrics Corp. v. Beaunit Mills, Inc., p. 431 supra, if the plaintiff had sued only the seller, could the latter have impleaded the processor? Should the defendant be given the right to introduce into the action, and to force the plaintiff to litigate with, any additional defendant the plaintiff would have been permitted to sue? As originally promulgated, Fed.R.Civ.P. 14 allowed a defendant to bring in a third party "who is or may be liable to him *or to the plaintiff.*" The italicized words were dropped in 1946 as being inefficacious either to force the plaintiff to accept the third party as a defendant or to overcome problems of subject matter competence—for example, in a diversity case, if the third party were a co-citizen of the plaintiff. Should the rulemakers have forced the plaintiff to litigate against the third-party defendant and have declared minimal diversity sufficient? See also Fed.R.Civ.P. 82. If the rulemakers had not dealt with the subject matter competence problem, could the courts have overcome it?

(2) The second portion of Fed.R.Civ.P. 14 controls the claims the third-party defendant can assert in the litigation. As a general matter, the third-party plaintiff and third-party defendant are treated much as ordinary plaintiffs and defendants with respect to the claims they can and must assert against each other. The principal (initial) plaintiff and the third-party defendant are not, however, adversaries; the Rule treats them in a manner close to the way that Rule 13(g) handles coparties, but in addition, permits the third-party defendant to assert against the plaintiff any defenses the principal defendant could have asserted.

Rule 14 also permits the third-party defendant to assert claims against "other third-party defendants." Let us say that A sues B and C, and that B impleads B' and B" while C impleads C'. Does this provision allow B' to assert claims against both B" and C', or just against B"? See 6 Wright and Miller § 1456.

(3) Third-party practice raises several thorny subject matter jurisdiction problems. First, with respect to the claims that arise between the third-party defendant and the principal plaintiff, must there be an independent basis for federal jurisdiction? In a carefully written opinion, the Fifth Circuit held that there is no need for an independent basis of adjudicatory authority for claims asserted by the third-party defendant against the plaintiff, Revere Copper & Brass Inc. v. Aetna Casualty & Surety Co., 426 F.2d 709 (5th Cir.1970). However, in Owen Equipment & Erection Co. v. Kroger, p. 210, supra, which was decided after *Revere Copper,* the Supreme Court held that there must be an independent basis for jurisdiction over claims asserted by the plaintiff against the third-party defendant. Reread *Owen Equipment.* Is *Revere Copper* still good law? How would the Court have treated a claim of Owen Equipment against Kroger?

Until recently, it has been assumed that, by analogy to compulsory counterclaims, ancillary jurisdiction (and venue) applied to the claims between the third-party plaintiff and the third-party defendant. But see Hartford Accident and Indemnity Co. v. Sullivan, 846 F.2d 377 (7th Cir.1988) (reasoning that since res judicata does not block subsequent litigation of third-party complaints, the analogy between compulsory counterclaims and impleader claims is imperfect, thus there is no ancillary jurisdiction over impleader claims), cert. denied ___ U.S. ___, 109 S.Ct. 2428, 104 L.Ed.2d 985 (1989).

(4) As to in personam adjudicatory authority, it has been held consistently that an independent basis for power over the third-party defendant must be found. See, e.g., Coleman v. American Export Isbrandtsen Lines, Inc., p. 326, supra. Rule 4(f) permits the federal courts to reach 100 miles from the court house, and it has been argued that Congress should extend the power to the constitutional limit. What is that limit? In this connection, recall that the jurisdiction problem in Asahi Metal Industry Co. v. Superior Court, p. 277, supra, arose when Asahi was impleaded. Is it likely the Court would have thought differently about the personal jurisdiction question had Zurcher's claims remained in the case?

(5) Is the third-party defendant entitled to a jury trial on the legal issues arising between the principal plaintiff and defendant, the determination of which may be binding upon him, even if the principal parties desire a bench trial? See Bevemet Metais, Ltda. v. Gallie Corp., 3 F.R.D. 352 (S.D.N.Y.1942).

(6) On third-party practice in the states that have not adopted the federal rule, see Friedenthal, The Expansion of Joinder in Cross-Complaints by the Erroneous Interpretation of Section 442 of the California Code of Civil Procedure, 51 Calif.L.Rev. 494 (1963).

NOTE ON IMPLEADING INSURERS

The words "may be liable" in impleader rules raise the question whether and when the third party's liability to the defendant may be "accelerated." In a traffic accident case A sues B (who is insured by C) for "loss" arising out of negligent operation of B's vehicle. Does the fact that under the policy C's liability is specifically made contingent upon B's first satisfying A's judgment prevent impleader? See Glens Falls Indemnity Co. v. Atlanta Building Corp., 199 F.2d 60 (4th Cir. 1952); Schultze v. Ocean Accident & Guarantee Corp., Limited, 239 App.Div. 309, 267 N.Y.S. 284 (1st Dep't.1933). Some insurance policies contain a provision that "no action" may be brought on the policy until the amount has been fixed by a final judgment against the insured or by an agreement between the insured and the carrier. Do such clauses prevent impleader? See Jordan v. Stephens, 7 F.R.D. 140 (W.D.Mo. 1945); Koerner, Modern Third-Party Practice—Substantive or Procedural, 3 N.Y.L.F. 158 (1957). May the availability of impleader affect the substantive law position of the third-party defendant by indirectly exposing him to liability for injuries to a plaintiff to whom he was not directly answerable? How?

What becomes of the stern rule against disclosing the presence of liability insurance in an accident case when impleader of the insurance carrier is allowed? The courts divide sharply on the question. Compare American Zinc Co. of Illinois v. H.H. Hall Construction Co., 21 F.R.D. 190 (E.D.Ill.1957) with Rosalis v. Universal Distributors, Inc., 21 F.R.D. 169 (D.Conn.1957). Should it make any difference if a jury trial has been waived? Cf. Koolery v. Lindemann, 91 N.Y.S.2d 505 (Sup.

1949), Remch v. Grabow, 193 Misc. 731, 70 N.Y.S.2d 462 (1947). Can an insurance or other company write an enforceable provision against impleader into its contract? Is there an *Erie* problem in failing to enforce a state-based contract right or a state policy that prevents insurance companies from being impleaded?

————

NOTE ON IMPLEADER FOR TACTICAL REASONS

A defendant may wish to implead a third-party defendant, even though he does not intend to enforce the judgment he might obtain. For example, an employer may seek to implead his employee in the hope that the jury will favor the employee and be forced to render a verdict absolving both the employer and the employee. Is it compatible with professional ethics for the defendant's attorney to seek to implead the third-party defendant in such circumstances? If he does attempt impleader, will his attempt be successful? See Goodhart v. United States Lines Co., 26 F.R.D. 163, 164 (S.D.N.Y.1960):

> "Defendant's proposed third party complaint is against the operator of the hi-lo and is based on the operator's duty to indemnify defendant if defendant is held liable because of the primary or active negligence of the operator.

> "I feel safe in taking judicial notice of the fact that the operator of a hi-lo will not be financially able to indemnify defendant to any substantial extent. Defendant must have some other reason or reasons for seeking impleader. One of those reasons is that jurors will likely render a smaller verdict if they are required to find that an individual employee of defendant is ultimately responsible for its payment. Another is that the interest of the hi-lo operator in a verdict for his employer will be heightened. . . .

> "In seeking the first result defendant, in effect, asks me to give it the advantage of the chance that the jury will proceed upon a false supposition that the hi-lo operator will pay the judgment. In seeking the second result defendant, in effect, asks me to help him threaten the hi-lo operator with the necessity of going through bankruptcy unless he testifies favorably to defendant. Neither of these pleas recommends itself to the court as a subject for exercise of the court's discretion. . . ."

How did the court know what the defendant's motives were? How did it know that the third-party defendant could not indemnify the defendant to any substantial extent? Could resort to Fed.R.Civ.P. 42(b) provide a solution?

————

SECTION 9. INTERVENTION

NEW YORK JUDICIAL COUNCIL, RECOMMENDATIONS RELATING TO THE EXTENSION OF THE REMEDY OF INTERVENTION

1946 Annual Report 218–225.

"Intervention may be defined as the procedural device whereby a stranger can present a claim or defense in a pending action or in a proceeding incidental thereto, and become a party for the purpose of the claim or defense presented." [1] . . .

The chief utility of intervention lies in affording to the vast and undefined group of non-parties the means of protecting their interests which may be affected by a particular law suit.

* * *

"The practice of allowing a stranger to intervene was first developed in the civil, the ecclesiastical, and the admiralty courts. Apparently, intervention practice in Roman law was rather extensive, although intervention seems to have taken place only at the appeal stage and then on the theory that the losing party might refuse to appeal or might not be vigilant in prosecuting the appeal and the petitioner's interest thus be inadequately protected." [2]

"Indigenous to the old common law and tending to restrict the extension of rights of intervention, was an unusual concern that the plaintiff be enabled by the courts to control his action; the modern common law theories of joinder and intervention of parties, however, brings us toward a rapprochment with the theories of the civil law." [3]

The practice of intervention developed slowly in the English and American law, but by the middle of the nineteenth century was permitted in equity by a device known as an examination *pro interesse suo* and at law by an analogous but more limited practice.

New York's present intervention statute, subdivision 4 of section 193 of the Civil Practice Act, became part of the New York Code of Procedure in 1851.[4] . . .

* * *

1. 2 Moore's Fed.Prac. (1938) 2307 (cited hereafter as "Moore"). The treatment of "intervention" by Moore represents a definitive and comprehensive review of the remedy of intervention. [Some footnotes omitted; others renumbered or moved.]

2. Id. at 2310.

3. Id. at 2311.

4. . . . Subdivision 4 of section 193 now reads as follows: "4. Where a person not a party to the action has an interest in the subject thereof, or in real property the title to which may in any manner be affected by the judgment, or in real property for injury to which the complaint demands relief, and makes application to the court to be made a party, it must direct him to be brought in by the proper amendment."

. . .

The statutes and rules of courts governing intervention in other jurisdictions may be characterized briefly as the "broad" and the "narrow" types. The "broad" type is exemplified by the California provision [5] which permits intervention by "any person, who has an interest in the matter in litigation, or in the success of either of the parties, or an interest against both." The "narrow" type is exemplified by . . . the New York [provision].

Rule 24 of the Federal Rules of Civil Procedure is a comprehensive and liberal provision for intervention which embodies features of both the "narrow" and the "broad" types of intervention statutes. Unlike either the California or New York provisions, however, Rule 24 of the Federal Rules differentiates between situations wherein intervention is a matter of right and those in which it rests in the discretion of the court. The New York provision is framed in mandatory terms, while the California provision uses words of permission.

* * *

The most unusual intervention provision found in an examination of the law in other jurisdictions is the Texas provision [6] which permits *anyone* to intervene in a pending action, subject to being stricken out by the court, simply by filing a pleading in the cause. This is intervention "as of course" and should be distinguished from intervention "as of right" which is provided in Federal Rule 24(a). The present New York, California and Federal provisions do not permit intervention as of course, since, as has been seen, they require an application to the court for an order permitting intervention in the first instance. Because of the possibility of abuse of the remedy by a stranger to the action, the present requirement of an application to the court for an order of intervention is proposed to be retained in New York.

ATLANTIS DEVELOPMENT CORP., LIMITED v. UNITED STATES

United States Court of Appeals, Fifth Circuit, 1967.
379 F.2d 818.

JOHN R. BROWN, CIRCUIT JUDGE.* This case involves a little bit of nearly everything—a little bit of oceanography, a little bit of marine biology, a little bit of the tidelands oil controversy, a little bit of international law, a little bit of latter day Marco Polo exploration. But these do not command our resolution since the little bits are here controlled by the less exciting bigger, if not big, problem of intervention. The District Court declined to permit mandatory intervention as a matter of right or to allow intervention as permissive. As is so often true, a ruling made to avoid delay, complications, or expense turns out

---

5. Cal.Code of Civ.Proc. (Deering, 1941) § 387.

6. Tex.Rules of Civ.Proc. (Vernon, 1942) Rule 60. See also Minn.Stat. (Henderson,

et al., 1941) sec. 54.113. Cf. N.Y.C.P.A. § 1151; Gen.Mun.Law, § 25.

* Some footnotes omitted; others renumbered.

to have generated more of its own. With the main case being stayed by the District Court pending this appeal, it is pretty safe to assume that the case would long have been decided on its merits (or lack of them) had intervention of either kind been allowed. . . . Adding to the problem, or perhaps more accurately, aiding in the solution of it, are the mid-1966 amendments to the Federal Rules of Civil Procedure including specifically those relating to intervention. We reverse.

What the jousting is all about is the ownership in, or right to control the use, development of and building on a number of coral reefs or islands comprising Pacific Reef, Ajax Reef, Long Reef, an unnamed reef and Triumph Reef which the intervenor has called the "Atlantis Group" because of the name given them by Anderson, its predecessor in interest and the supposed discoverer. . . .

Just how or in what manner these reefs were "discovered" is so far unrevealed. Some time in 1962 William T. Anderson discovered the reefs apparently by conceiving the idea of occupying them through the construction of facilities for fishing club, marina, skin diving club, a hotel, and perhaps as the chief lure, a gambling casino. Anderson made some sort of claim to it and with facilities unavailable to the adventurous explorers of the long past, he gave public notice of this in the United States and in England by newspaper advertisements in late 1962 and early 1963. These "rights" were acquired by Atlantis Development Corporation, Ltd., the proposed intervenor. Reflecting the desire manifested now by the persistent efforts to intervene to have legal rights ascertained in a peaceful fashion through established tribunals and not by self-help or the initiation of physical activities which would precipitate counter moves, physical or legal, or both, Atlantis (and predecessors) patiently sought permission from all governmental agencies, state and federal—just short of the United Nations—but to no avail. . . .." Subsequently, Atlantis spent approximately $50,000 for surveys and the construction of four prefabricated buildings, three of which were destroyed by a hurricane in September 1963. Thereafter upon learning that the United States Corps of Engineers was asserting that permission was needed to erect certain structures on two of the reefs, Triumph and Long Reef, Atlantis commenced its long, but unrewarding, efforts either to convince the Corps of Engineers, the United States Attorney General, or both, that the island reefs were beyond the jurisdiction of United States control or to initiate litigation which would allow a judicial, peaceful resolution. The Engineers ultimately reaffirmed the earlier decision to require permits. In December 1964 on learning that the defendants in the main case had formally sought a permit from the Engineers, Atlantis notified the Government of its claim to ownership of the islands and the threatened unauthorized actions by the defendants. This precipitated further communications with the Department of Justice with Atlantis importuning, apparently successfully, the Government to initiate the present action.

It was against this background that the litigation commenced. The suit is brought by the United States against the main defendants. The complaint was in two counts seeking injunctive relief. In the first the Government asserted that Triumph and Long Reefs are part of the bed of the Atlantic Ocean included in the Outer Continental Shelf subject to the jurisdiction, control and power of disposition of the United States. The action of the defendants . . . in the erection of caissons on the reefs, the dredging of material from the seabed, and the depositing of the dredged material within the caissons without authorization was charged as constituting a trespass on government property. In the second count the Government alleged that the defendants were engaged in the erection of an artificial island or fixed structure on the Outer Continental Shelf in the vicinity of the reefs without a permit from the Secretary of the Army in violation of the Outer Continental Shelf Lands Act, 43 U.S.C.A. § 1333(f) and 33 U.S.C.A. § 403. Denying that the complaint stated a claim, F.R.Civ.P. 12(b), the defendants besides interposing general denial asserted that the Secretary of the Army lacks jurisdiction to require a permit for construction on the Outer Continental Shelf and that the District Court lacks jurisdiction since the reefs and the defendants' actions thereon are outside the territorial limits of the United States. As thus framed, the issues in the main case are whether (1) the District Court has jurisdiction of subject matter, (2) the defendants are engaged in acts which constitute a trespass against government property, and (3) the defendants' construction activities without a permit violate 43 U.S.C.A. § 1333(f) and 33 U.S.C.A. § 403.

Atlantis seeking intervention by proposed answer and cross-claim against the defendants admitted the jurisdiction of the District Court. It asserted that the United States has no territorial jurisdiction, dominion or ownership in or over the reefs and cannot therefore maintain the action for an injunction, and that conversely Atlantis has title to the property by discovery and occupation. In the cross-claim, Atlantis charged the defendants as trespassers against it. Appropriate relief was sought by the prayer.

The District Court without opinion declared in the order that intervenor "does not have such an interest in this cause as will justify its intervention, either as a matter of right or permissively." Leave was granted to appear amicus curiae.

We think without a doubt that under former F.R.Civ.P. 24(a), intervention as a matter of right was not compelled under (a)(2).[1] The

---

1. F.R.Civ.P. 24. Intervention

"(a) Intervention of Right. Upon timely application anyone shall be permitted to intervene in an action: (1) when a statute of the United States confers an unconditional right to intervene; or (2) when the representation of the applicant's interest by existing parties is or may be inadequate and the applicant is or may be bound by a judgment in the action; or (3) when the applicant is so situated as to be adversely affected by a distribution or other disposition of property which is in the custody or subject to the control or disposition of the court or an officer thereof.

"(b) Permissive Intervention. Upon timely application anyone may be permitted to intervene in an action: (1) when a

situation did not present one in which the intervenor "is or may be bound" by a decree rendered in his absence in the sense articulated most recently in *Sam Fox* in terms of res judicata. Although not quite so clear, we also think it did not measure up to the notions loosely reflected in a case-by-case development under which, although res judicata was technically lacking, the decree is considered "binding" since in a very practical sense it would have an immediate operative effect upon the intervenor. In none of these cases was it suggested that if the only effect of the decree in intervenor's absence would be to raise the hurdle of stare decisis, this would amount to the absentee being bound as a practical matter.

This brings us squarely to the effect of the 1966 Amendments and the new F.R.Civ.P. 24(a). Before examining its intrinsic meaning and purpose, the question arises, of course, whether in testing action taken in June 1965, amendments effective July 1, 1966, should be invoked. The order of the Supreme Court approving the Rules affords the guide. As we did most recently with amended F.R.Civ.P. 23 on class actions, Alvarez v. Pan American Life Ins. Co., 5 Cir., 375 F.2d 992 [No. 22761, Mar. 27, 1967], and more significant, as did the Supreme Court in *El Paso I* we think it appropriate that to the maximum extent possible, the amended Rules should be given retroactive application.

Certainly that should be true here. For here no possible intrinsic prejudice can occur. Nothing has happened in this case since the filing of the pleadings. The further action has been stayed pending determination of whether intervention should be permitted in the case yet to be tried. Except for the irrelevant circumstance that this apparently puts the trial Judge in error by subsequent events for a decision which presumably was correct at the time made, there is no reason why we ought not to judge this question in the light of today's standards. Certainly that is the general aim of the Rules that they "shall be construed to secure the just, speedy and inexpensive determination of every action." F.R.Civ.P. 1.

In assaying the new Rule, several things stand out. The first, as the Government acknowledges, is that this amounts to a legislative repeal of the rigid *Sam Fox* . . . res judicata rule. But more important, the revision was a coordinated one to tie more closely together the related situations of joinder, F.R.Civ.P. 19, and class actions, F.R.Civ.P. 23.

As the Advisory Committee's notes reflect, there are competing interests at work in this area. On the one hand, there is the private suitor's interests in having his own lawsuit subject to no one else's direction or meddling. On the other hand, however, is the great public interest, especially in these explosive days of ever-increasing dockets, of

statute of the United States confers a conditional right to intervene; or (2) when an applicant's claim or defense and the main action have a question of law or fact in common. . . . In exercising its discretion the court shall consider whether the intervention will unduly delay or prejudice the adjudication of the rights of the original parties."

having a disposition at a single time of as much of the controversy to as many of the parties as is fairly possible consistent with due process.

In these three Rules the Advisory Committee, unsatisfied with the former Rules which too frequently defined application in terms of rigid legal concepts such as joint, common ownership, res judicata, or the like, as well as court efforts in applying them, deliberately set out on a more pragmatic course. For the purposes of our problem, this course is reflected in the almost, if not quite, uniform language concerning a party who claims an interest relating to the subject of the action and is so situated that the disposition of the action may as a practical matter impair or impede his ability to protect that interest . . . .

Although this is question-begging and is therefore not a real test, this approach shows that the question of whether an intervention as a matter of right exists often turns on the unstated question of whether joinder of the intervenor was called for under new Rule 19. Were this the controlling inquiry, we find ample basis here to answer it in the affirmative. Atlantis—having formally informed the Government in detail of its claim of ownership to the very reefs in suit, that the defendants were trespassing against it, and having successfully urged the Government to institute suit against the defendants—seems clearly to occupy the position of a party who ought to have been joined as a defendant under new Rule 19(a)(2)(i). . . .

This interim conclusion is, of course, a rejection of the Government's approach made for this day, case, and time only that all new Rule 24(a) was to do was to abandon the rigidity of *Sam Fox* and codify the ameliorative exceptions (see note 10, supra) to escape the unfortunate consequences of a rule expressed in terms of the party being "bound," i.e., res judicata. Any such narrow approach is to deprecate the painstaking work of the Advisory Committee especially the deliberate efforts to dovetail F.R.Civ.P. 19, 24 and 23 together with two of them being radically rewritten.

When approached in this light, we think that both from the terms of new Rule 24(a) and its adoption of 19(a)(2)(i) intervention of right is called for here. Of course F.R.Civ.P. 24(a)(2) requires both the existence of an interest which may be impaired as a practical matter and an absence of adequate representation of the intervenor's interest by existing parties. There can be no difficulty here about the lack of representation. On the basis of the pleadings, see Kozak v. Wells, 8 Cir., 1960, 278 F.2d 104, 109, 84 A.L.R.2d 1400; cf. Stadin v. Union Electric Co., 8 Cir., 1962, 309 F.2d 912, 917, certiorari denied 1963, 373 U.S. 915, 83 S.Ct. 1298, 10 L.Ed.2d 415, Atlantis is without a friend in this litigation. The Government turns on the defendants and takes the same view both administratively and in its brief here toward Atlantis. The defendants, on the other hand, are claiming ownership in and the right to develop the very islands claimed by Atlantis.

Nor can there be any doubt that Atlantis "claims an interest relating to the property or transaction which is the subject of the action." The object of the suit is to assert the sovereign's exclusive dominion and control over two out of a group of islands publicly claimed by Atlantis. This identity with the very property at stake in the main case and with the particular transaction therein involved (the right to build structures with or without permission of the Corps of Engineers) is of exceptional importance. For 24(a)(2) is in the conjunctive requiring both an interest relating to the property or transaction and the practical harm if the party is absent. This sharply reduces the area in which stare decisis may, as we later discuss, supply the element of practical harm.

This brings us then to the question whether these papers reflect that in the absence of Atlantis, a disposition of the main suit may as a practical matter impair or impede its ability to protect that interest— its claim to ownership and the right to control, use and develop without hindrance from the Government, the Department of Defense, or other agencies. Certain things are clear. Foremost, of course, is the plain proposition that the judgment itself as between Government and defendants cannot have any direct, immediate effect upon the rights of Atlantis, not a party to it.

But in a very real and practical sense is not the trial of this lawsuit the trial of Atlantis' suit as well? Quite apart from the contest of Atlantis' claim of sovereignty vis-a-vis the Government resulting from its "discovery" and occupation of the reefs, there are at least two basic substantial legal questions directly at issue, but not yet resolved in any Court at any time between the Government and the defendants which are inescapably present in the claim of Atlantis against the Government. One is whether these coral reefs built up by accretion of marine biology are "submerged lands" under the Outer Continental Shelf Lands Act, 43 U.S.C.A. § 1331 et seq. The second basic question is whether, assuming both from the standpoint of geographical location and their nature they constitute "lands," does the sovereignty of the United States extend to them with respect to any purposes not included in or done for the protection of the "exploring for, developing, removing, and transporting . . . " natural resources therefrom, 43 U.S.C.A. § 1333(a)(1). Another, closely related, is whether the authority of the Secretary of the Army to prevent obstruction of navigation extended by § 1333(f) to "artificial islands and fixed structures," includes structures other than those "erected thereon for the purpose of exploring for, developing, removing, and transporting" mineral resources therefrom. . . .

The Government would avoid all of these problems by urging us to rule as a matter of law on the face of the moving papers that the intervenors could not possibly win on the trial of the intervention and consequently intervention should be denied. In support it asserts that the claim that the reefs are beyond the jurisdiction of the United States is self-defeating, and under the plain meaning of the Outer Continental Shelf Lands Act and the facts revealed from the Coast and Geodetic

Chart of which we must take judicial knowledge as proof of all facts shown. . . .

If in its claim against the defendants in the main suit these questions are answered favorably to the Government's position, the claim of Atlantis for all practical purposes is worthless. That statement assumes, of course, that such holding is either approved or made by this Court after an appeal to it and thereafter it is either affirmed, or not taken for review, on certiorari. It also assumes that in the subsequent separate trial of the claim of Atlantis against the Government the prior decision would be followed as a matter of stare decisis. Do these assumptions have a realistic basis? Anyone familiar with the history of the Fifth Circuit could have but a single answer to that query. This Court, unlike some of our sister Circuit Courts who occasionally follow a different course, has long tried earnestly to follow the practice in which a decision announced by one panel of the Court is followed by all others until such time as it is reversed, either outright or by intervening decisions of the Supreme Court, or by the Court itself en banc. That means that if the defendants in the main action do not prevail upon these basic contentions which are part and parcel of the claim of Atlantis, the only way by which Atlantis can win is to secure a rehearing en banc with a successful overruling of the prior decision or, failing in either one or both of those efforts, a reversal of the earlier decision by the Supreme Court on certiorari. With the necessarily limited number of en banc hearings in this Circuit and with the small percentage of cases meriting certiorari, it is an understatement to characterize these prospects as formidable.

That is but a way of saying in a very graphic way that the failure to allow Atlantis an opportunity to advance its own theories both of law and fact in the trial (and appeal) of the pending case will if the disposition is favorable to the Government "as a practical matter impair or impede [its] ability to protect [its] interest." That is, to be sure, a determination by us that in the new language of 24(a)(2) stare decisis may now—unlike the former days under 24(a)(2)—supply that practical disadvantage which warrants intervention of right. It bears repeating, however, that this holding does not presage one requiring intervention of right in every conceivable circumstance where under the operation of the Circuit's stare decisis practice, the formidable nature of an en banc rehearing or the successful grant of a writ of certiorari, an earlier decision might afford a substantial obstacle. We are dealing here with a conjunction of a claim to and interest in the very property and the very transaction which is the subject of the main action. When those coincide, the Court before whom the potential parties in the second suit must come must itself take the intellectually straight forward, realistic view that the first decision will in all likelihood be the second and the third and the last one. Even the possibility that the decision might be overturned by en banc ruling or reversal on certiorari does not overcome its practical effect, not just as an obstacle, but as the forerunner of the actual outcome. In the face of that, it is "as a practical matter" a certainty that an absent party seeking a right to enter the fray to advance his interest against all or some of the parties as to matters upon which he is for all practical purposes shortly to be foreclosed knows the disposition in his absence will "impair or impede his ability to protect that interest, ..."

Reversed.

NOTES

(1) The *Atlantis* principle that stare decisis, in contrast to res judicata, "might be sufficient to satisfy the requirement of practical impairment" was followed in Natural Resources Defense Council, Inc. v. United States Nuclear Regulatory Commission, 578 F.2d 1341, 1345 (10th Cir.1978) in support of the decision allowing the American Mining Congress and Kerr-McGee Nuclear Corporation to intervene as of right in an action instituted by the Natural Resources Defense Council and others to enjoin alleged circumvention by the U.S. Nuclear Regulatory Commission of the Federal requirement of an environmental impact statement by entering into agreements with states allowing them to issue bonds for the operation of uranium mills within the state. See also Smith v. Pangilinan, 651 F.2d 1320, 1325 (9th Cir.1981) (principle applied in holding Attorney General of the U.S. entitled to intervene as of right and by permission in a class action brought to compel issuance to the class of 140 Filipinos of certificates of identity under certificate of Identity Act adopted by Northern Marianas Commonwealth Legislature).

Do these decisions broaden the principle that *Atlantis* appears to have laid down?

(2) Prior to its amendment in 1966, Fed.R.Civ.P. 24(a)(2) provided for intervention as of right if the intervenor "is or may be bound" by the judgment. The prevailing view was that an intervenor could be bound by a judgment only if it could be invoked against him as res judicata. See Sam Fox Publishing Co. v. United States, 366 U.S. 683, 81 S.Ct. 1309, 6 L.Ed.2d 604 (1961); Ar-Tik Systems, Inc. v. Dairy Queen, Inc., 22 F.R.D. 122 (E.D.Pa.1958). But see Kozak v. Wells, 278 F.2d 104 (8th Cir.1960). This put the proposed intervenor in a predicament. In order to be entitled to intervention as of right, he had to establish not only that he would be bound by the judgment, but also that the representation of his interests would be inadequate. If the latter were the case, however, due process precluded his being bound by the judgment; and if interests were adequately represented, he failed to meet the other of the two conditions of Rule 24(a)(2). The 1966 Amendments to the Rule eliminate this impasse by concentrating on the practical rather than the legal effects of the judgment on the proposed intervenor's interests in the subject of the action.

(3) Under Fed.R.Civ.P. 24(b)(2), permissive intervention is proper "when an applicant's claim or defense and the main action have a question of law or fact in common." Should joinder of parties by the plaintiff and impleader also be permitted upon satisfaction of this requirement, subject to the court's ordering severance in appropriate cases? Upon what ground can the single requirement of Fed.R.Civ.P. 24(b)(2), as distinguished from the dual requirements of Fed.R. Civ.P. 20(a), be justified?

(4) In case of intervention, what are the requirements of subject matter adjudicatory power and of venue? Does it make any difference whether the intervention is as of right? *Compare* Kozak v. Wells, 278 F.2d 104 (8th Cir.

1960) (when intervention is as of right, no independent requirements of subject matter adjudicatory power need be met) *with* Hunt Tool Co. v. Moore, Inc., 212 F.2d 685 (5th Cir.1954) (in case of permissive intervention, independent grounds of subject matter adjudicatory power must exist). See generally Fraser, Ancillary Jurisdiction of Federal Courts of Persons Whose Interest May Be Impaired If Not Joined, 62 F.R.D. 483; Ancillary Jurisdiction and the Joinder of Claims in the Federal Courts, 33 F.R.D. 27, 43–45 (1963); Developments in the Law—Multiparty Litigation in the Federal Courts, 71 Harv.L.Rev. 874, 905–906 (1958). If the action in intervention arises from the same transaction or occurrence as the principal action, even though intervention is not as of right, should the concept of "ancillary jurisdiction" be applied? Cf. Rosenthal v. Fowler, 12 F.R.D. 388 (S.D.N.Y.1952), p. 420, supra (compulsory counterclaim needs no independent basis of subject matter adjudicatory power). Cf. generally 3B Moore's Federal Practice ¶ 24.18[1].

(5) Must independent bases of subject matter adjudicatory power and venue exist, when the intervenor is a party whose joinder is required by Fed.R. Civ.P. 19(a)? See Johnson v. Middleton, 175 F.2d 535 (7th Cir.1949) (requiring independent basis of subject matter power). Does this ruling make sense? *Compare* the standard for intervention as of right stated in Fed.R.Civ.P. 24(a)(2) *with* the criterion stated in Fed.R.Civ.P. 19(a)(2).

(6) There is substantial disagreement about what claims a successful intervenor can assert. At one extreme are courts that align the intervenor and then treat her like any other party, see, e.g., Dickinson v. Burnham, 197 F.2d 973 (2d Cir.), cert. denied 344 U.S. 875, 73 S.Ct. 169, 97 L.Ed. 678 (1952); at the other, are courts that hold that the intervenor should not disrupt the original litigation any more than necessary, and so refuse to permit her to interpose anything new into the litigation, see, e.g., Northern Ins. Co. v. Grone, 126 F.Supp. 457 (M.D.Pa.1954). Most courts will, however, allow an intervenor-as-of-right to assert transactionally related counterclaims, see, e.g., United States v. Martin, 267 F.2d 764 (10th Cir.1959). See generally, 7C Wright, Miller & Kane, Federal Practice and Procedure Civ. § 1921 (1986).

(7) For the right to appeal orders granting and denying applications to intervene, see J.B. Stringfellow, Jr. v. Concerned Neighbors in Action, p. 1068, infra.

(8) Intervention presents special problems in cases where the resolution will likely have considerable impact on parties other than the named plaintiffs and defendants. For example, in New Orleans Public Service, Inc. v. United Gas Pipe Line Co., 690 F.2d 1203 (5th Cir.1982), the mayor of New Orleans, members of its City Council, and consumers attempted to intervene in a rate dispute between the New Orleans Public Service, Inc. (NOPSI), which held the franchise to supply gas to the Parish of Orleans, and NOPSI's supplier, United Gas Pipe Line Co. The Fifth Circuit agreed with the lower court that the consumers had no right to intervene, but found that the city officials had a right pursuant to Fed.R.Civ.P. 24(a), and also that the district court's failure to permit intervention under 24(b) was an abuse of discretion. The court reasoned that the consumers were adequately represented by NOPSI, and that if NOPSI failed to conduct the litigation adequately and fully, the city officials would protect their interest. See also Bustop v. Superior Court, 69 Cal.App.3d 66, 137 Cal.Rptr. 793 (1977), criticized by Yeazell, Intervention and the Idea of Litigation: A Commentary on the Los Angeles School Case, 25 U.C.L.A.L.Rev. 244 (1977); Natural Resources Defense Council, Inc. v. United States Nuclear Regulatory Commission, 578 F.2d 1341 (10th Cir.1978); Planned Parenthood v.

Citizens for Community Action, 558 F.2d 861 (8th Cir.1977); New Orleans Public Service, Inc. v. United Gas Pipe Line Co., 690 F.2d 1203 (5th Cir.1982) (city official, but not consumer, allowed to intervene). On this problem generally, see Symposium, Problems of Intervention in Public Law Litigation, 13 U.Cal. Davis L.Rev. 211 (1980).

(9) Can there be intervention of right in an action brought by the United States? See Cascade Natural Gas Corp. v. El Paso Natural Gas Co., 386 U.S. 129, 87 S.Ct. 932, 17 L.Ed.2d 814 (1967), on remand 291 F.Supp. 3 (1968), vacated Utah Public Service Commission v. El Paso Natural Gas Co., 395 U.S. 464, 89 S.Ct. 1860, 23 L.Ed.2d 474 (1969) (recognizing the right of California to intervene in an antitrust proceeding seeking dissolution of a merger of two gas pipeline companies). See also Note, Private Participation in Department of Justice Antitrust Proceedings, 39 U.Chi.L.Rev. 143 (1971).

(10) Does the distinction between intervention as of right and permissive intervention serve a useful function or would it be better to permit intervention as of right, subject to exclusion by the court, or intervention only by leave of the court? Cf. Shreve, Questioning Intervention of Right: Toward A New Methodology of Decisionmaking, 74 Nw.U.L.Rev. 894 (1980). Does the requirement of timeliness turn every form of intervention into the permissive kind? See Comment, Timeliness Threat to Interventions of Right, 59 Yale L.J. 586 (1980); Comment, Preclusion of Absent Disputants to Compel Intervention, 79 Colum.L.Rev. 1551 (1979).

(11) Should a party that intervenes with respect to some facets of a lawsuit have the independent right to appeal every aspect of the judgment? Should the right to appeal depend on whether the intervenor came in as-of-right or permissively? See Federal Trade Commission v. Owens–Corning Fiberglas Corp., 853 F.2d 458 (6th Cir.1988), cert. denied ___ U.S. ___, 109 S.Ct. 1128, 103 L.Ed.2d 190 (1989).

(12) When intervenors lose, should they be liable under fee-shifting statutes such as 42 U.S.C.A. § 2000e–5(k), which gives federal courts discretion to "allow the prevailing party [in certain civil rights actions] a reasonable attorney's fee?" Reasoning that liability for attorneys' fees would discourage intervention and foster more litigation, the Supreme Court held that good-faith intervenors should not be assessed their opponents' fees. Independent Federation of Flight Attendants v. Zipes, ___ U.S. ___, 109 S.Ct. 2732, 105 L.Ed.2d 639 (1989).

SECTION 10. INTERPLEADER

A. THE EMERGENCE OF THE MODERN INSTITUTION

Although rooted in the common law, interpleader was developed principally by equity to permit a person confronted by conflicting claims to involve all claimants in one proceeding.

The equitable bill of interpleader has traditionally been said to encompass four essential elements: (1) the same thing, debt, or duty had to be claimed by both or all the parties against whom the relief is demanded; (2) all of the adverse title or claims had to be dependent, or derived from a common source; (3) the one seeking the relief could neither have nor claim any interest in the subject matter; and (4) he could have incurred no independent liability to either of the claimants.

If the stakeholder was not disinterested, equity further permitted him to proceed by way of a petition in the nature of a bill of interpleader rather than by a strict bill of interpleader, but only if he sought affirmative relief independent of the conflicting claims of the defendants. See 4 Pomeroy's Equity Jurisprudence §§ 1322, 1481 (5th ed. 1941).

In Texas v. Florida, 306 U.S. 398, 59 S.Ct. 563, 83 L.Ed. 817 (1939), the Supreme Court explained the difference as follows (306 U.S. 406–407, 59 S.Ct. 567–568):

> "The peculiarity of the strict bill of interpleader was that the plaintiff asserted no interest in the debt or fund, the amount of which he placed at the disposal of the court and asked that the rival claimants be required to settle in the equity suit the ownership of the claim among themselves. But as the sole ground for equitable relief is the danger of injury because of the risk of multiple suits when the liability is single, . . . and as plaintiffs who are not mere stakeholders may be exposed to that risk, equity extended its jurisdiction to such cases by the bill in the nature of interpleader. The essential of the bill in the nature of interpleader is that it calls upon the court to exercise its jurisdiction to guard against the risks of loss from the prosecution in independent suits of rival claims where the plaintiff himself claims an interest in the property or fund which is subjected to the risk. The object and ground of the jurisdiction are to guard against the consequent depletion of the fund at the expense of the plaintiff's interest in it and to protect him and the other parties to the suit from the jeopardy resulting from the prosecution of numerous demands, to only one of which the fund is subject. While in point of law or fact only one party is entitled to succeed, there is danger that recovery may be allowed in more than one suit. Equity avoids the danger by requiring the rival claimants to litigate before it the decisive issue, and will not withhold its aid where the plaintiff's interest is either not denied or he does not assert any claim adverse to that of the other parties, other than the single claim, determination of which is decisive of the rights of all. . . . ."

In 1917, following the Supreme Court's decision in New York Life Insurance Co. v. Dunlevy, p. 296 supra, the Congress, in response to pressures from insurance companies, passed the first interpleader statute. Subsequently, at the urgings of Professor Zechariah Chafee, the principal proponent of the institution, the language of the statute was broadened by successive amendments to make interpleader more generally available. These amendments culminated in the Federal Interpleader Act of 1936, as modified by the Judicial Code Revision Act of 1948.

A second form of interpleader is also available, see Fed.R.Civ.P. 22. In reading these materials, compare the Statutory Interpleader available under the Act with the Rule Interpleader provided by the Federal Rules of Civil Procedure. Like the other joinder devices, Rule Interpleader relies upon the general personal jurisdiction, venue, and subject matter provisions encountered earlier. Statutory Interpleader, however, has its own procedural rules, § 1335 (subject matter jurisdiction), 1397 (venue) and 2361 (process and procedure), and these differ from the general rules in several important respects. See 7 Wright & Miller, Federal Practice and Procedure: Civil §§ 1703, 1710, 1717 (1986).

Both interpleader devices are best thought of as remedies—solutions to the problem of conflicting demands for the same thing, debt, or duty—rather than as simply procedural tools. Thus, just as parties in, say, a contract dispute often ask for more than one form of relief, expecting that at trial, the court will determine the remedy to which they are entitled, parties subject to multiple claims often invoke both Statutory and Rule Interpleader, expecting that facts uncovered during discovery will decide which remedy is the appropriate one.

Interpleader actions usually have two stages. In the first, the court determines whether the remedy is available. If it is, then in the second stage, the stakeholder deposits the res, withdraws from the proceedings, and the claimants are left to carry out the lawsuit that the stakeholder has instigated. Under modern procedures, a stakeholder who is also a claimant remains in the suit in that capacity.

On interpleader and its historical evolution, see Chafee, Modernizing Interpleader, 30 Yale L.J. 814 (1921); Interstate Interpleader, 33 Yale L.J. 685 (1924); Federal Interpleader Since the Act of 1936, 49 Yale L.J. 377 (1940); Broadening the Second Stage of Interpleader, 56 Harv.L.Rev. 541, 929 (1943); Ilsen & Sardell, Interpleader in the Federal Courts, 35 St. John's L.Rev. 1 (1960); Hazard & Moskovitz, An Historical and Critical Analysis of Interpleader, 52 Calif.L.Rev. 706 (1964).

Read 28 U.S.C.A. § 1335 in the Supplement.

INDIANAPOLIS COLTS v. MAYOR OF BALTIMORE

United States Court of Appeals, Seventh Circuit, 1984.
741 F.2d 954.

BAUER, Circuit Judge.*

* * *

* Footnotes omitted.

I.

Through the 1983 season, the Colts played their home games in Baltimore Memorial Stadium. In February 1984, the Colts and the stadium managers began negotiating a renewal of the Memorial Stadium lease. At the same time, the Colts negotiated with the Capital Improvement Board of Managers of Marion County, Indiana [CIB] regarding the possibility of moving the team to the Hoosier Dome.

On March 27, 1984, Colts owner Robert Irsay learned that the Maryland Senate passed a bill granting the City of Baltimore the power to acquire the Colts by eminent domain. Irsay decided to move the team to Indianapolis and promptly executed a lease with the CIB. The Colts fled Baltimore under the cloak of darkness; eight moving vans full of Colts equipment arrived in Indianapolis on March 29.

On March 29, Maryland's governor signed into law the bill authorizing Baltimore to acquire the Colts by condemnation. Baltimore filed a condemnation petition against the Colts on March 30 in Maryland state court. The state court restrained the Colts from transferring any element of the team from Baltimore.

After learning about the condemnation suit by telegram, the Colts took two actions. First, on April 2, the Colts caused removal of the state court condemnation proceeding to federal district court in Maryland. Second, on April 5, the Colts filed this action in the United States District Court for the Southern District of Indiana, claiming that their obligations under the lease with the CIB conflicted with Baltimore's attempts to acquire the team through eminent domain. [Finding that interpleader was appropriate, the district court granted orders restraining Baltimore from having the Colts condemned and having a Maryland state court enjoin them from moving. This appeal followed.]

II.

Our review of this case extends to the question of whether the interpleader was proper. Allstate Insurance Co. v. McNeill, 382 F.2d 84 (4th Cir.1967), cert. denied, 392 U.S. 931, 88 S.Ct. 2290, 20 L.Ed.2d 1390 (1968). This question is an issue of law entitled to full appellate review.

We hold that the Colts have not successfully satisfied the pleading requirements of 28 U.S.C. § 1335. Despite the Colts' argument that it is unfair for the City of Indianapolis to lose the team by another city's condemnation suit, we find that the CIB and Baltimore do not have conflicting claims over a single stake. Additionally, even assuming the CIB and Baltimore have claims over the same stake, the Colts do not face a reasonable danger of multiple liability or vexatious, conflicting claims from the claimants, and thus interpleader is not justified here.

A.

A basic jurisdictional requirement of statutory interpleader is that there be adverse claimants to a particular fund. See Libby, McNeill & Libby v. City National Bank, 592 F.2d 504 (9th Cir.1978). The CIB and Baltimore are not claimants to the same stake. Baltimore seeks ownership of the Colts franchise, whereas the CIB has no claim to ownership of the franchise. Instead, the CIB has a lease with the Colts that requires the team to play its games in the Hoosier Dome and imposes other obligations to ensure the success of the enterprises.

The Colts argue in part that clause 11 of their lease with the CIB raises an interest in the CIB which conflicts with Baltimore's attempt to obtain the franchise. Clause 11 grants the CIB the first chance to find purchasers for the team if Irsay decides to sell his controlling interest. This right of first refusal is the CIB's contractual guarantee either that Irsay always will control the team or that the CIB will have the right to choose his successor. Yet this provision does not give the CIB a present right to buy the Colts, and thus does not raise a claim against the franchise conflicting with Baltimore's claim.

A successful eminent domain action obviously will defeat the CIB's interests in keeping the Colts in Indianapolis. Nevertheless, interpleader is not designed to aid every plaintiff confronted by one claim which, if successful, would defeat a second claim because the plaintiff has lost the ability to pay damages. Such an interpretation would twist interpleader into protection for defendants from losing the opportunity to recover damages because the plaintiff's resources already have been depleted. Interpleader is warranted only to protect the plaintiff-stakeholder from conflicting liability to the stake.

Interpleader is proper in cases such as a surety confronted by claims of subcontractors and materialmen which exceed the surety's contractual liability, conflicting claims of entitlement to the proceeds of a life insurance policy, or automobile insurers surrendering the maximum sum of their liability to the court for disposition to plaintiffs in an accident case. The issue of whether the interpleaded defendants' claims are adverse does not arise often. The Colts' argument here that the "bottom line" of this case is which city "gets" the Colts clouds the issue of adversity. Only reasonable legal claims can form the adversity to the plaintiff necessary to justify interpleader. The CIB has no reasonable legal claim to ownership of the franchise sought by Baltimore. For the Colts, losing their franchise to Baltimore may lead to breach of the lease claims by the CIB, but this is not a situation for which interpleader was designed. See Texas v. Florida, 306 U.S. 398, 405–08, 59 S.Ct. 563, 567–568, 83 L.Ed. 817 (1939); Indianapolis Colts, 733 F.2d at 487.

B.

Interpleader is a suit in equity. See Champlin Petroleum Co. v. Ingram, 560 F.2d 994 (10th Cir.1977), cert. denied, 436 U.S. 958, 98 S.Ct. 3072, 57 L.Ed.2d 1123 (1978); see also First National Bank v. United States, 633 F.2d 1168 (5th Cir.1981); United States v. Major Oil Corp., 583 F.2d 1152 (10th Cir.1978). Because the sole basis for equitable relief to the stakeholder is the danger of exposure to double liability or the vexation of conflicting claims, Texas v. Florida, 306 U.S. at 406, the stakeholder must have a real and reasonable fear of double liability or vexations, conflicting claims to justify interpleader. . . . Even assuming that Baltimore and the CIB are fighting over the same stake, the Colts do not have a reasonable fear of double liability or vexations claims here. The Colts and the CIB foresaw the likelihood of legal obstacles to prevent the Colts from leaving Baltimore, among which was an eminent domain action. The Colts and the CIB thus specifically contracted that the lease obligations will terminate at the Colts' option if the Colts' franchise is acquired by eminent domain. Clause 21.6 of the lease states in part:

> 21.6 *Club Option.* 21.6(a) Actions. The parties acknowledge and recognize that at the present time there are pending various lawsuits in the state and federal courts dealing with the issues of the provisions of the Constitution and By–Laws of the League, the Constitution of the United States, and various State Constitutions, state and federal antitrust laws, and state and federal laws of eminent domain and other state and federal laws which may . . . impact on the provisions of this Agreement. In acknowledgement and contemplation of those lawsuits and of the fact: that certain parties may institute lawsuits of a similar or dissimilar nature, including without limitation those described in the preceding sentence and those seeking injunctive relief to prevent the Club from keeping, observing and/or performing any of this Agreement . . ., the parties agree that:
>
> . . .
>
> (iii) If Club is ordered by a final order of such court of final appellate jurisdiction to play other than at the Stadium or the Franchise is acquired by eminent domain, this Agreement shall terminate at Club's option, and the parties shall have no further obligations hereunder except as stated in this Paragraph [dealing with a few final financial affairs].

This "escape" clause renders unreasonable the Colts' claim that they will face a second suit over the same stake if Baltimore ultimately succeeds in its eminent domain action. The Colts' characterization of the CIB's claim does not meet a "minimal threshold level of substantiality." 7 C. Wright & A. Miller, Federal Practice and Procedure § 1704,

370–71 (1972); Frances I. duPont & Co., 365 F.2d at 143 (cited in Wright & Miller).

*   *   *

Because the Colts cannot assert a reasonable fear of multiple liability or vexatious, conflicting claims, interpleader jurisdiction was not proper. There is no other basis for federal jurisdiction in the federal district court in Indiana to hear the Colts' action and thus this suit must be dismissed.

*   *   *

COFFEY, CIRCUIT JUDGE, dissenting.

*   *   *

The majority asserts that even if there is a common, identifiable stake, the claims of the CIB and Baltimore are not adverse and vexatious. The majority supports its position with reference to section 21.6(a)(iii) of the Lease. . . . According to the majority, this " 'escape' clause renders unreasonable the Colts' claim that they will face a second lawsuit over the same stake if Baltimore ultimately succeeds in its eminent domain action." The majority erroneously assumes that nothing will prevent the Colts from performing their obligations under the Lease except the successful eminent domain proceeding by Baltimore. The majority completely overlooks the fact that the Colts may be prevented from performing their obligations under the Lease before a final unappealable order of eminent domain is entered.

The Lease clearly provides that the Colts may terminate the Lease only if a *final order of a court of final appellate jurisdiction* is issued allowing Baltimore to acquire the Colts by eminent domain. The record reveals that in the eminent domain proceeding of April 5, 1984, the Maryland state court issued a restraining order enjoining the Colts from "selling, removing, transferring, encumbering or otherwise affecting the franchise and contractual rights related thereto which is being condemned in these proceedings." It is probable, indeed likely, that during the course of an eminent domain proceeding in the Maryland district court, Baltimore will again seek to enjoin the Colts from playing any games in Indianapolis to prevent the Colts from becoming further entrenched in the Indianapolis market. There is absolutely nothing in the record before this court to suggest that a new injunction similar to the one previously issued by the Maryland state court will not be entered when the Colts' interpleader action is dismissed. Such an injunction would prevent the Colts from preparing for the upcoming season and preclude the franchise from fulfilling its obligation to play all pre-season and home games in the Indianapolis Hoosier Dome. The Colts' hands would be tied under the terms of the contract for they would not be able to terminate the Lease because no final unappealable order of eminent domain would have been entered. Thus, the CIB would be fully justified in suing the Colts for breach of their contractual duties. The Colts would unnecessarily be presented with simultaneous, adverse, and vexatious claims from both the CIB and the Baltimore City Council.

The City of Baltimore has fought, and will continue to fight, as is its right, the CIB's interest in the Colts. Thus, the above scenario is certainly sufficient to satisfy the language of 28 U.S.C. § 1335 that two adverse claimants "may claim to be entitled" to the same stake. See, e.g., State Farm Fire & Cas. Co. v. Tashire, 386 U.S. at 534, 87 S.Ct. at 1205; United States v. Major Oil Corp., 583 F.2d 1152, 1157 (10th Cir. 1978). In light of the liberal construction to be accorded the Federal interpleader statute to protect the stakeholder from the expense and risk of double litigation, I am convinced that the Colts satisfy the jurisdictional requirement of 28 U.S.C. § 1335.

NOTE

As the principal case assumes, the traditional requirement that adverse claims be derived from a common source has not survived modern developments. Nor is it generally required that the stakeholder deny a claim to the subject matter. This is in keeping with the trend to make procedural rules more flexible, despite the greater complexity that this introduces into the lawsuit. At the same time, however, the core of interpleader is that a remedy is needed when a stakeholder faces the risk of double vexation for a single liability. Thus, the essential requirement is now that of conflicting claims. See also Alton & Peters v. Merritt, 145 Minn. 426, 177 N.W. 770 (1920).

STATE FARM FIRE & CASUALTY CO. v. TASHIRE

Supreme Court of the United States, 1967.
386 U.S. 523, 87 S.Ct. 1199, 18 L.Ed.2d 270.

Mr. Justice Fortas delivered the opinion of the Court.*

[For a statement of the facts of the case and the Court's holding on the diversity problem, see p. 212 supra.]

On interlocutory appeal,[1] the Court of Appeals for the Ninth Circuit reversed. 363 F.2d 7. The court found it unnecessary to reach respondents' contentions relating to service of process and the scope of the injunction, for it concluded that interpleader was not available in the circumstances of this case. It held that in States like Oregon which do not permit "direct action" suits against insurance companies until

---

* Some footnotes omitted; others renumbered.

1. We need not pass upon the Court of Appeals' conclusions with respect to the interpretation of interpleader under Rule 22, which provides that "(1) Persons having claims against the plaintiff may be joined as defendants and required to interplead when their claims are such that the plaintiff is or may be exposed to double or multiple liability. . . ." First, as we indicate today, this action was properly brought under § 1335. Second, State Farm did not purport to invoke Rule 22. Third, State Farm could not have invoked it in light of venue and service of process limitations. Whereas statutory interpleader may be brought in the district where any claimant resides (28 U.S.C.A. § 1397), Rule interpleader based upon diversity of citizenship may be brought only in the district where all plaintiffs or all defendants reside (28 U.S.C.A. § 1391(a)). And whereas statutory interpleader enables a plaintiff to employ nationwide service of process (28 U.S.C.A. § 2361), service of process under Rule 22 is confined to that provided in Rule 4. See generally 3 Moore, Federal Practice ¶ 22.04.

judgments are obtained against the insured, the insurance companies may not invoke federal interpleader until the claims against the insured, the alleged tortfeasor, have been reduced to judgment. Until that is done, said the court, claimants with unliquidated tort claims are not "claimants" within the meaning of § 1335, nor are they "persons having claims against the plaintiff" within the meaning of Rule 22 of the Federal Rules of Civil Procedure. Id., at 10. In accord with that view, it directed dissolution of the temporary injunction and dismissal of the action. Because the Court of Appeals' decision on this point conflicts with those of other federal courts, and concerns a matter of significance to the administration of federal interpleader, we granted certiorari. 385 U.S. 811, 87 S.Ct. 90, 17 L.Ed.2d 52 (1966). Although we reverse the decision of the Court of Appeals upon the jurisdictional question, we direct a substantial modification of the District Court's injunction for reasons which will appear.

     *   *   *

We do not agree with the Court of Appeals that, in the absence of a state law or contractual provision for "direct action" suits against the insurance company, the company must wait until persons asserting claims against its insured have reduced those claims to judgment before seeking to invoke the benefits of federal interpleader. That may have been a tenable position under the 1926[2] and 1936 interpleader statutes.[3] These statutes did not carry forward the language in the 1917 Act authorizing interpleader where adverse claimants "may claim" benefits as well as where they "are claiming" them.[4] In 1948, however, in the revision of the Judicial Code, the "may claim" language was restored.[5] Until the decision below, every court confronted by the question has concluded that the 1948 revision removed whatever requirement there might previously have been that the insurance company wait until at least two claimants reduced their claims to judgments. The commentators are in accord.

Considerations of judicial administration demonstrate the soundness of this view which, in any event, seems compelled by the language

---

2. 44 Stat. 416 (1926), which added casualty companies to the enumerated categories of plaintiffs able to bring interpleader, and provided for the enjoining of proceedings in other courts.

3. 49 Stat. 1096 (1936), which authorized "bills in the nature of interpleader," meaning those in which the plaintiff is not wholly disinterested with respect to the fund he has deposited in court. See Chafee, The Federal Interpleader Act of 1936: I, 45 Yale L.J. 963 (1936).

4. 39 Stat. 929 (1917). See Klaber v. Maryland Casualty Co., 69 F.2d 934, 938–939 (C.A. 8th Cir.1934), which held that the omission in the 1926 Act of the earlier statute's "may claim" language required the denial of interpleader in the face of unliquidated claims (alternative holding).

5. Although the Reviser's Note did not refer to the statutory change or its purpose, we have it on good authority that it was the omission in the Note rather than the statutory change which was inadvertent. See 3 Moore, Federal Practice ¶ 22.08, at 3025–3026, n. 13. And it was widely assumed that restoration of the "may claim" language would have the effect of overruling the holding in Klaber, supra, that one may not invoke interpleader to protect against unliquidated claims. See, e.g., Chafee, 45 Yale L.J., at 1163–1167; Chafee, Federal Interpleader Since the Act of 1936, 49 Yale L.J. 377, 418–420 (1940). In circumstances like these, the 1948 revision of the Judicial Code worked substantive changes. Ex parte Collett, 337 U.S. 55, 69 S.Ct. 944, 93 L.Ed. 1207 (1949).

of the present statute, which is remedial and to be liberally construed. Were an insurance company required to await reduction of claims to judgment, the first claimant to obtain such a judgment or to negotiate a settlement might appropriate all or a disproportionate slice of the fund before his fellow claimants were able to establish their claims. The difficulties such a race to judgment pose for the insurer, and the unfairness which may result to some claimants, were among the principal evils the interpleader device was intended to remedy.

    * * *

The fact that State Farm had properly invoked the interpleader jurisdiction under § 1335 did not, however, entitle it to an order both enjoining prosecution of suits against it outside the confines of the interpleader proceeding and also extending such protection to its insured, the alleged tortfeasor. Still less was Greyhound Lines entitled to have that order expanded so as to protect itself and its driver, also alleged to be tortfeasors, from suits brought by its passengers in various state or federal courts. Here, the scope of the litigation, in terms of parties and claims, was vastly more extensive than the confines of the "fund," the deposited proceeds of the insurance policy. In these circumstances, the mere existence of such a fund cannot, by use of interpleader, be employed to accomplish purposes that exceed the needs of orderly contest with respect to the fund.

There are situations, of a type not present here, where the effect of interpleader is to confine the total litigation to a single forum and proceeding. One such case is where a stakeholder, faced with rival claims to the fund itself, acknowledges—or denies—his liability to one or the other of the claimants. In this situation, the fund itself is the target of the claimants. It marks the outer limits of the controversy. It is, therefore, reasonable and sensible that interpleader, in discharge of its office to protect the fund, should also protect the stakeholder from vexatious and multiple litigation. In this context, the suits sought to be enjoined are squarely within the language of 28 U.S.C.A. § 2361 . . .

But the present case is another matter. Here, an accident has happened. Thirty-five passengers or their representatives have claims which they wish to press against a variety of defendants: the bus company, its driver, the owner of the truck, and the truck driver. The circumstance that one of the prospective defendants happens to have an insurance policy is a fortuitous event which should not of itself shape the nature of the ensuing litigation. For example, a resident of California, injured in California aboard a bus owned by a California corporation should not be forced to sue that corporation anywhere but in California simply because another prospective defendant carried an insurance policy. And an insurance company whose maximum interest in the case cannot exceed $20,000 and who in fact asserts that it has no interest at all, should not be allowed to determine that dozens of tort plaintiffs must be compelled to press their claims—even those claims which are not against the insured and which in no event could be satisfied out of the meager insurance fund—in a single forum of the insurance company's choosing. There is nothing in the statutory scheme, and very little in the judicial and academic commentary upon that scheme, which requires that the tail be allowed to wag the dog in this fashion.

State Farm's interest in this case, which is the fulcrum of the interpleader procedure, is confined to its $20,000 fund. That interest receives full vindication when the court restrains claimants from seeking to enforce against the insurance company any judgment obtained against its insured, except in the interpleader proceeding itself. To the extent that the District Court sought to control claimants' lawsuits against the insured and other alleged tortfeasors, it exceeded the powers granted to it by the statutory scheme.

We recognize, of course, that our view of interpleader means that it cannot be used to solve all the vexing problems of multiparty litigation arising out of a mass tort. But interpleader was never intended to perform such a function, to be an all-purpose "bill of peace." Had it been so intended, careful provision would necessarily have been made to insure that a party with little or no interest in the outcome of a complex controversy should not strip truly interested parties of substantial rights—such as the right to choose the forum in which to establish their claims, subject to generally applicable rules of jurisdiction, venue, service of process, removal, and change of venue. None of the legislative and academic sponsors of a modern federal interpleader device viewed their accomplishment as a "bill of peace," capable of sweeping dozens of lawsuits out of the various state and federal courts in which they were brought and into a single interpleader proceeding. And only in two reported instances has a federal interpleader court sought to control the underlying litigation against alleged tortfeasors as opposed to the allocation of a fund among successful tort plaintiffs. See Commercial Union Insurance Co. of New York v. Adams, 231 F.Supp. 860 (D.C.S.D.Ind.1964) (where there was virtually no objection and where all of the basic tort suits would in any event have been prosecuted in the forum state), and Pan American Fire & Casualty Co. v. Revere, 188 F.Supp. 474 (D.C.E.D.La.1960). Another district court, on the other hand, has recently held that it lacked statutory authority to enjoin suits against the alleged tortfeasor as opposed to proceedings against the fund itself. Travelers Indemnity Co. v. Greyhound Lines, Inc., 260 F.Supp. 530 (D.C.W.D.La.1966).

In light of the evidence that federal interpleader was not intended to serve the function of a "bill of peace" in the context of multiparty litigation arising out of a mass tort, of the anomalous power which such a construction of the statute would give the stakeholder, and of the thrust of the statute and the purpose it was intended to serve, we hold that the interpleader statute did not authorize the injunction entered in the present case. Upon remand, the injunction is to be modified consistently with this opinion.[6]

MR. JUSTICE DOUGLAS, dissenting in part. . . .

6. We find it unnecessary to pass upon respondents' contention, raised in the courts below but not passed upon by the Court of Appeals, that interpleader should

NOTES

(1) Where else do the Rules use "accelerating language?" See Fed.R.Civ.P. 13(g) and 14(a). May an insurer in a tort case interplead both the insured and the victim? Should the insurer's liability be accelerated for this purpose, even if he denies liability? See also N.Y.—McKinney's CPLR 1006(a): "A stakeholder is a person who is or may be exposed to multiple liability as a result of adverse claims."

(2) Is it within the court's discretion to award the stakeholder costs, including reasonable attorney's fees, out of the deposited fund? See Travelers Indemnity Co. v. Israel, 354 F.2d 488 (2d Cir.1965).

B. PROBLEMS OF ADJUDICATORY AUTHORITY

NEW YORK LIFE INSURANCE CO. v. DUNLEVY
P. 296, supra.

Read 28 U.S.C.A. §§ 1397 and 2361 in the Supplement.

NOTES

(1) Why was the Pennsylvania court's determination of the interest of Mrs. Dunlevy in the res before the court—i.e., the $2,479.70 paid into court—not binding upon her in California?

(2) In St. Louis Southwestern Railway Co. v. Meyer, 364 Mo. 1057, 272 S.W.2d 249 (1954), appeal dismissed 349 U.S. 942, 75 S.Ct. 871, 99 L.Ed. 1269 (1955), rehearing denied 350 U.S. 856, 76 S.Ct. 38, 100 L.Ed. 761, the railroad had declared a dividend of $370,648. Because of doubt as to whether preferred stockholders could participate in this dividend, the railroad deposited this amount into a special bank account and sought to interplead all stockholders, both common and preferred. Service on non-resident stockholders was made by publication pursuant to a statute permitting such service "in all cases affecting a fund, . . . specific property, or any interest therein, or any res or status within the jurisdiction of the court." The Supreme Court of Missouri rejected the contention that the service was invalid, because there was no res within the state. It held that the amount, "set apart by resolution from the company's assets" was a "fund," "specific property," or a "res within the jurisdiction of the

have been dismissed on the ground that the 11 Canadian claimants are "indispensable parties" who have not been properly served. The argument is that 28 U.S.C.A. § 2361 provides the exclusive mode of effecting service of process in statutory interpleader, and that § 2361—which authorizes a district court to "issue its process for all claimants" but subsequently refers to service of "such process" by marshals "for the respective districts where the claimants reside or may be found"—does not permit service of process beyond the Nation's borders. Since our decision will require basic reconsideration of the litigation by the parties as well as the lower courts, there appears neither need nor necessity to determine this question at this time. We intimate no view as to the exclusivity of § 2361, whether it authorizes service of process in foreign lands, whether in light of the limitations we have imposed on the interpleader court's injunctive powers the Canadian claimants are in fact "indispensable parties" to the interpleader proceeding itself, or whether they render themselves amenable to service of process under § 2361 when they come into an American jurisdiction to establish their rights with respect either to the alleged tortfeasors or to the insurance fund. See 2 Moore, Federal Practice ¶ 4.20, at 1091–1105.

court." Was this decision correct? Is it reconcilable with that reached in *Dunlevy*? Is *Dunlevy* still good law today?

(3) How can a state court obtain in personam adjudicatory power over a non-resident claimant? Would the state's interest in avoiding multiple litigation and conflicting judgments and in effectively disposing of multiparty disputes be a sufficient basis of in personam adjudicatory power? And what about the stakeholder's interest in being protected against multiple liability? Cf. Western Union Telegraph Co. v. Pennsylvania, 368 U.S. 71, 82 S.Ct. 199, 7 L.Ed. 2d 139 (1961). In this case, Pennsylvania sought to escheat undisbursed money held by Western Union arising out of money orders bought in Pennsylvania offices to be transmitted to parties in Pennsylvania and other states. In holding that Pennsylvania had no power to escheat the money, the Court stated (at 74–75):

> "We find it unnecessary to decide any of Western Union's contentions as to the adequacy of notice to and validity of service on the individual claimants by publication. For as we view these proceedings, there is a far more important question raised by this record—whether Pennsylvania had power at all to render a judgment of escheat which would bar New York or any other State from escheating this same property.

> "Pennsylvania does not claim and could not claim that the same debts or demands could be escheated by two States. See Standard Oil Co. v. New Jersey, 341 U.S. 428, 443, 71 S.Ct. 822, 831, 95 L.Ed. 1078. And our prior opinions have recognized that when a state court's jurisdiction purports to be based, as here, on the presence of property within the State, the holder of such property is deprived of due process of law if he is compelled to relinquish it without assurance that he will not be held liable again in another jurisdiction or in a suit brought by a claimant who is not bound by the first judgment. Anderson National Bank v. Luckett, 321 U.S. 233, 242–243, 64 S.Ct. 599, 604, 88 L.Ed. 692; Security Savings Bank v. California, 263 U.S. 282, 286–290, 44 S.Ct. 108, 110–111, 68 L.Ed. 301. Applying that principle, there can be no doubt that Western Union has been denied due process by the Pennsylvania judgment here unless the Pennsylvania courts had power to protect Western Union from any other claim, including the claim of the State of New York that these obligations are property 'within' New York and are therefore subject to escheat under its laws. But New York was not a party to this proceeding and could not have been made a party, and, of course, New York's claims could not be cut off where New York was not heard as a party. Moreover, the potential multistate claims to the 'property' which is the subject of this escheat make it not unlikely that various States will claim *in rem* jurisdiction over it. Therefore, Western Union was not protected by the Pennsylvania judgment, for a state court judgment need not be given full faith and credit by other States as to parties or property not subject to the jurisdiction of the court that rendered it."

Can long-arm statutes serve a useful function in this context? See von Mehren & Trautman, Jurisdiction to Adjudicate: A Suggested Analysis, 79 Harv.L.Rev. 1121, 1156–59 (1966); Developments in the Law—Multiparty Litigation in the Federal Courts, 71 Harv.L.Rev. 874, 914–18 (1958). Can the stakeholder deposit the stake in the court and thus create a basis for in rem adjudicatory power? See N.Y.CPLR § 1006(g):

"Deposit of money as basis for jurisdiction. Where a stakeholder is otherwise entitled to proceed under this section for the determination of a right to, interest in or lien upon a sum of money, whether or not liquidated in amount, payable in the state pursuant to a contract or claimed as damages for unlawful retention of specific real or personal property in the state, he may move, either before or after an action has been commenced against him, for an order permitting him to pay the sum of money or part of it into court or to a designated person or to retain it to the credit of the action. Upon compliance with a court order permitting such deposit or retention, the sum of money shall be deemed specific property within the state within the meaning of paragraph two of section 314."

In view of New York Life Insurance Co. v. Dunlevy, p. 296 supra, is this a wholly effective solution? See also Cordner v. Metropolitan Life Insurance Co., 234 F.Supp. 765 (S.D.N.Y.1964); St. Louis Southwestern Railway Co. v. Meyer, p. 480, Note (2), supra.

(4) Can the state enter into a compact with another state to acquire adjudicatory power over non-residents? Five states have adopted such a compact, but it has not been approved by the United States. Its key provision reads: "Service of process sufficient to acquire personal jurisdiction may be made within a state party to this compact, by a person who institutes an interpleader proceeding or interpleader part of a proceeding in another state, party to the compact". On the interpleader compact, see Zimmermann, Wendell & Heller, Effective Interpleader via Interstate Compacts, 55 Colum.L.Rev. 56 (1955); Note, 58 Mich.L.Rev. 612 (1960).

(5) Can a state protect the stakeholder against conflicting claims by non-residents in a way other than by asserting in personam adjudicatory power over them? See N.Y.—McKinney's CPLR 216 which provides that the stakeholder may move the court for leave to give notice of the pending action to any adverse claimant who is not subject to the court's adjudicatory power. If the leave is given, the proceeding is stayed for a year after the giving of the notice to permit the non-resident to join the proceedings. If he fails to do so within this period, his claim is barred. What are the problems created by this approach? Does its effectiveness depend on whether other states will "borrow" the New York provision? Is it constitutional? See Kuerschner & Rauchwarefabrik v. New York Trust Co., 126 F.Supp. 684 (S.D.N.Y.1954).

(6) Can state limitations upon recourse to interpleader play a role in the federal courts? See Fed.R.Civ.P. 22.

C. CONFLICT OF LAWS RULES IN FEDERAL INTERPLEADER ACTIONS

In Griffin v. McCoach, 313 U.S. 498, 61 S.Ct. 1023, 85 L.Ed. 1481 (1941), the Supreme Court held that, in an interpleader action based on diversity, a federal court must apply the conflict of law rules of the state in which it sits. It thus extended to interpleader cases the same rule it had laid down on the same day for ordinary diversity cases in Klaxon Co. v. Stentor Electric Manufacturing Co., 313 U.S. 487, 61 S.Ct. 1020, 85 L.Ed. 1477 (1941). How can a federal court determine what state rules would be when it is clear that a state court, because of limitations on the state's judicial jurisdiction, could not have heard the case? The ALI Study on the Division of Jurisdiction Between State and Federal Courts 87 (1969) has proposed the following provision: "Whenever State law supplies the rule of decision on an issue, the district court may make its own determination as to which state rule of decision is applicable." Is this provision constitutional? Does it provide the most appropriate solution? For criticism of the *Griffin* decision, see Cook, The Federal Court and the Conflict of Laws, 36 Ill.L.Rev. 493 (1942).

SECTION 11. CLASS ACTIONS

A. HISTORICAL DEVELOPMENT

Like interpleader, the class action has undergone considerable expansion over time. It developed initially as the equitable bill of peace, which was designed to aid a defendant who was threatened by multiple similar actions or a plaintiff who had separate, but similar, grievances against multiple defendants. Because joinder of parties and claims was most limited at common law, equity permitted resort to a bill that would put these multiple claims at peace. See Chafee, Bills of Peace With Multiple Parties, 45 Harv.L.Rev. 1297 (1932). The bill of peace led naturally to the class suit, in which multiple plaintiffs or defendants were represented rather than present. See Story, Equity Pleadings § 97 (3d ed. 1844).

The Field Code sought to delineate the cases in which resort to the class action was proper by providing that "when the question in dispute is one of a common or general interest of many persons or when the parties are numerous and it is impracticable to bring them all before the court, one or more may sue or defend for the benefit of all." See Clark, Code Pleading 63 (2d ed. 1947). Although the Field Code used the disjunctive "or," several states required that both conditions be met before a class action was proper. See Daar v. Yellow Cab Co., p. 551 infra. When, in 1912, Federal Equity Rule 38 replaced former Federal Equity Rule 48, which had been in effect since 1842, it also combined the two requirements into one brief provision: "When the question is one of common or general interest to many persons constituting a class so numerous as to make it impracticable to bring them all before the court, one or more may sue or defend for the whole."

By the time the Federal Rules were adopted, a considerable body of class action law had already come into existence. Building upon and going beyond this, the rule makers attempted to formulate in old Federal Rule 23 the various categories of cases in which class actions would be appropriate. However, they did so by using highly conceptual language that attempted to define the various categories of cases in which class actions could be brought by characterizing the right sought to be enforced. In time, the three categories so distinguished became known as the "true," "hybrid," and "spurious" class actions. In the "true" category belonged actions involving joint, common, or secondary rights. The "hybrid" category embraced all actions involving several rights related to specific property. And the "spurious" category comprehended actions involving several rights affected by a common question or related to common relief. However, considerable difficulties were encountered in determining the precise scope of these categories. The seriousness of this problem was aggravated by the fact that the legal consequences, and particularly the reach of the judgment, differed considerably, depending on the category in which the class action was placed.

Specifically, judgments in "true" class actions bound all members of the class, judgments in "hybrid" actions also bound all members of the class, but only with respect to the specific property involved, while judgments rendered in "spurious" class actions bound only the named parties or those who had intervened. It was not surprising that the courts appeared ready to juggle the labels, depending on the effect they wish to grant to the judgment rendered.

In addition, old Federal Rule 23 failed to regulate the various procedural steps, including the giving of notice to absent class members, that were likely to occur in a class action. The only provision of this nature it contained related to dismissal or compromise.

When, in the 1960's, the rule makers, within the context of their overall review of the Rules, addressed their attention to the class action, they naturally sought to cope with the problems that had arisen. They did so by seeking to describe the cases in which class actions were permitted in functional, rather than conceptual, language, and by specifying the practical considerations to be taken into account. They also decided to regulate in detail the various procedural steps to be taken in a class action. Because derivative stockholders' actions and actions by or against unincorporated associations have special distinctive aspects, they were dealt with in separate rules.

While substitution of functional insight for abstract classification was an important contribution, the Rule has continued to present a host of problems to the legal system. Its new text has needed substantial interpretation. Furthermore, courts have questioned the extent to which litigation using this device can be allowed to depart from core principles of adjudication: that each plaintiff is master of whether, where, when, etc. to enforce his rights, that no judgment is binding against a person who has not had her day in court, and that notice is a prerequisite to adjudicatory authority.

More fundamentally, however, is the fact that the popularity of the class action has made it an almost reflexive response to social ills. In addition to fulfilling the goals the rulemakers intended to perform—

such as providing a simple and efficient way for processing numerous interrelated claims, meeting the problem of unknown or unlocatable persons, and overcoming the obstacle on the indispensable party who is unamenable to service or destroys diversity—the device is used to vindicate economically impracticable claims, to augment governmental regulation, and as a substitute for political action. Civil rights, consumer, antitrust, and securities laws (to take a few examples) may be more vigorously enforced because of class actions, but the student should consider throughout this section whether such suits are manageable enough to assure that justice is done. To what extent are the functions of class actions performed alternatively, and perhaps preferably, by the government, the political system, and through such legal doctrines, institutions, and procedures as res judicata, test cases, and public interest litigation by organizations championing particular agenda, such as the NAACP, the ACLU, the Sierra Club, or the U.S. Chamber of Commerce?

The decisions presented below cannot alone convey a sense of the awesome task of bringing and litigating a class action. A good picture is presented by P. Schuck, Agent Orange on Trial (1986). For the point of view of one who was later to preside over that case, see Weinstein, Some Reflections on the "Abusiveness" of Class Actions, 58 F.R.D. 299 (1973). See also Kaplan, Continuing Work of the Civil Committee: 1966 Amendments of the Federal Rules of Civil Procedure (I), 81 Harv. L.Rev. 356 (1967); Frankel, Amended Rule 23 From A Judge's Point of View, 32 Antitrust L.J. 295 (1966).

B. REQUIREMENTS FOR CLASS ACTIONS

Because the federal rulemakers were at the forefront of developing the class action device, states that have been attracted to the procedure have for the most part adopted the federal rules, with a few modifications. Thus, except for restrictions that flow from constitutional limitations on federal jurisdiction, the requirements in state and federal court are similar. There are three sets of conditions: general prerequisites, which are set out in 23(a) and are common to all class actions; the special requirements of 23(b), which vary according to where within the three functional classifications a case falls; and the usual requirements for adjudication, such as subject matter and personal jurisdiction, notice and venue.

THE REQUIREMENTS OF RULE 23

IN RE "AGENT ORANGE" PRODUCT LIABILITY LITIGATION

United States District Court, Eastern District of New York, 1983.
100 F.R.D. 718.

MEMORANDUM AND PRETRIAL ORDER

WEINSTEIN, CHIEF JUDGE:*

Plaintiffs, Vietnam War veterans and members of their families, claim to have suffered damages as a result of the veterans' exposure to herbicides in Vietnam. Defendants allegedly produced these herbicides.

Some years ago this court ruled that the litigation would proceed as a class action pursuant to Rule 23(b)(3) of the Federal Rules of Civil Procedure. In re Agent Orange Product Liability Litigation, 506 F.Supp. 762, 787 ff. (E.D.N.Y.1980). No certification order was, however, entered. The court noted that later stages of this litigation, especially those concerned with individual causation and damages, "may require reconsideration" of the certification. Id. at 790. Those later stages have now been reached.

The questions to be decided are whether the class should be certified, which of the types of classes described by Rule 23 should be utilized, how the class should be described, and for what issues. For the reasons indicated below, the class is certified for all issues under 23(b)(3), and on the issue of punitive damages under 23(b)(1)(B). This certification requires a number of decisions on the mechanics of notice described in the following discussion.

INTRODUCTION

Plaintiffs have increasingly sought to use class actions to redress injuries caused by a single product manufactured for widespread use. A number of courts have seen the class action as the only alternative "to trying . . . virtually identical lawsuits, one-by-one," resulting in the "bankruptcy of both the state and federal court systems." Williams, Mass Tort Class Actions, 98 F.R.D. 323, 324 (1983). Three factors in the instant litigation make the desirability of class certification even greater than it would be in most mass tort litigation.

The first is size. The potential size of plaintiffs' class in this litigation numbers in the tens of thousands. If the claims are dealt with individually, the result might "result in a tedium of repetition lasting well into the next century." In re No. Dist. of Cal. "Dalkon Shield" IUD Product Liability Litigation, 526 F.Supp. 887 (N.D.Cal.), rev'd, 693 F.2d 847 (9th Cir.1982), cert. denied sub nom. A.H. Robins v. Abed, 459 U.S. 1171, 103 S.Ct. 817, 74 L.Ed.2d 1015 (1983). By way of contrast, there were only several hundred plaintiffs in the class certi-

* Footnotes omitted.

fied by the district court in In re Federal Skywalk Cases, 93 F.R.D. 415 (W.D.Mo.), vacated, 680 F.2d 1175 (8th Cir.1982), cert. denied sub nom. Johnson v. Stover, 459 U.S. 988, 103 S.Ct. 342, 74 L.Ed.2d 383 (1983) and less than 4,000 in the *"Dalkon Shield"* litigation.

2. Second is the need to assure that the financial burden will ultimately fall on the party which, it may be found, should as a matter of fairness bear it. As this court pointed out:

> Overarching the entire dispute is a feeling on both sides that whatever existing law and procedures may technically require, fairness, justice and equity in this unprecedented controversy demand that the government assume responsibility for the harm caused our soldiers and their families by its use of Agent Orange in Southeast Asia.

In re Agent Orange Product Liability Litigation, 506 F.Supp. 762, 784 (E.D.N.Y.1980). A class action is the best vehicle for achieving that end. A single class-wide determination on the issue of causation will focus the attention of Congress, the Executive branch and the Veterans Administration on their responsibility, if any, in this case. By contrast, possibly conflicting determinations made over many years by different juries make it less likely that appropriate authorities and the parties will arrive at a fair allocation of the financial burden, if any.

3. Third, certification may encourage settlement of the litigation. In a situation where there are potentially tens of thousands of plaintiffs, the defendants may naturally be reluctant to settle with individual claimants on a piecemeal basis.

LAW

Rule 23(a) contains four prerequisites to the maintenance of a class action. They are:

> (1) the class is so numerous that joinder of all members is impracticable, (2) there are questions of law or fact common to the class, (3) the claims . . . of the representative parties are typical of the claims of the class, and (4) the representative parties will fairly and adequately protect the interests of the class.

The four prerequisites as they applied to this litigation have already been carefully analyzed by the court and found to exist. See In re "Agent Orange" Product Liability Litigation, 506 F.Supp. 762, 787 (E.D.N.Y.1980). [In that phase of the litigation, the court examined the general requirements set out in R. 23(a). It found that the class of veterans, their spouses, parents and children was large enough to meet the numerosity requirement, that there were enough common questions of law and fact in their claims to meet the commonality requirement, that it would be possible to designate plaintiffs such that the typicality requirement would be satisfied, and that the adequacy requirement could be met by choosing named representatives who have a substantial stake in the outcome, lack antagonism, conflict, or eccentric motivation and by making sure that counsel is experienced, capable, and willing to undertake the commitment of vigorous prosecution, id. at 787–88.] Present as well as prior counsel for plaintiffs appear adequate to their complex task. The only matter on which further elaboration is needed is the second prerequisite, the requirement that there be "questions of law or fact common to the class." Discussion of this point will be combined with a discussion of Rule 23(b)(3).

D argues if they contracted for govt, then they should be immune.

Rule 23(b)(3)

Rule 23(b)(3) states that if the four prerequisites of 23(a) are met, the class will be certified if, in addition, the court finds that the questions of law or fact common to the members of the class predominate over any questions affecting only individual members, and that a class action is superior to other available methods for the fair and efficient adjudication of the controversy. Thus, the issues to be decided are (1) do questions of law or fact common to the class predominate over any questions affecting only individual members, and (2) is a class action the best method for resolution of the litigation.

This court's prior finding that the government contract defense and the affirmative defense of misuse are common to the class is not contested by the parties. Defendants strongly contend, however, that the heart of any product liability claim, causation, can never be common to the class since each veteran, spouse and offspring who has instituted a lawsuit claiming direct or derivative injuries from the veteran's exposure to Agent Orange brings to this case a unique history upon which his or her claim for damages is predicated. Each veteran was exposed, if at all, at different times, at different places and under different circumstances. Therefore, the argument continues, a determination on the issue of causation, whether made as a finding of general causation or as a result of a finding in "test" cases, can never be dispositive of the claims of the other class members and as a result common questions do not "predominate."

Defendants support their argument by citing the Advisory Committee's Notes on Rule 23 and a number of recent cases that have denied (b)(3) certification in mass tort cases. See, e.g., In re No. Dist. of Cal. "Dalkon Shield" IUD Product Liability Litigation, 693 F.2d 847 (9th Cir.1982), cert. denied sub nom. A.H. Robins v. Abed, 459 U.S. 1171, 103 S.Ct. 817, 74 L.Ed.2d 1015 (1983); Payton v. Abbott Labs, 100 F.R.D. 336 (D.Mass.1983) (DES Claims); Boring v. Medusa Portland Cement Co., 63 F.R.D. 78 (M.D.Pa.1974) (county residents seeking damages for air pollution); Yandle v. PPG Industries, Inc., 65 F.R.D. 566 (E.D.Tex.1974) (employees of asbestos plant).

Without setting forth the details and analysis of each case, it is fair to say that the reasoning of all of the cases they rely upon is the same as that of the Advisory Committee and is supportive of defendants' reasoning. The drafters' notes state:

[handwritten top margin: 2 types of (mass) tort cases:]
[handwritten: ① a mass accident (plane crash) v.]

> A 'mass accident' resulting in injuries to numerous persons is
> ordinarily not appropriate for a class certification because of
> the likelihood that significant questions not only of damages
> but of liability and defenses to liability, would be present,
> affecting the individuals in different ways. In these circum-
> stances an action nominally conducted as a class action would
> degenerate in practice into multiple lawsuits separately tried.

[handwritten right margin: ② separate cases of same injury (defective toothpaste)]

Advisory Committee Notes to Proposed Rules of Civil Procedure, 39
F.R.D. 69, 103 (1966). The defendants insist that the Agent Orange
situation is even worse in that the focus of the litigation is not a "mass
accident," but a mass products liability based upon a series of discrete
events.

Following defendants' analysis, the District Court in Texas, in
denying certification of a (b)(3) class consisting of all former employees
and survivors of former employees of the defendant's asbestos plant,
stated that the litigation

> is very different from the single mass accident cases that have
> in the past allowed a class action to proceed on the liability
> issues. Those cases have normally involved a single tragic
> happening which caused physical harm or property damage to
> a group of people, and affirmative defenses are absent. Usual-
> ly, one set of operative facts will establish liability . . . The
> Court is in agreement with the defendant that there is not a
> single act of negligence or proximate cause which would apply
> to each potential class member and each defendant in this
> case.

Yandle v. PPG Industries, Inc., 65 F.R.D. 566, 571 (E.D.Tex.1974).
Similarly, the District Court of New Hampshire denied (b)(3) certification to a class consisting of all New Hampshire women claiming injury
from DES. Plaintiffs sought a blanket determination that DES causes
injury *in utero*. The court stated that "such a determination [would] do
nothing to advance the cause of class members as a group." Mertens v.
Abbott Laboratories, 99 F.R.D. 38 at 41 (D.N.H.1983). If the class is
certified, defendants suggest that the certification and class trial should
be limited to the only issue which they see as common to the entire
class, that is, the government contract defense. *[handwritten: Common causation is]*

The force of the defense contention is substantial since commonali- *[handwritten: critical]*
ty is critical to certification. Nevertheless, it is not conclusive. In
deciding whether common questions predominate, a pragmatic evalua- *[handwritten: but not]*
tion of the interest of the class members is given great weight. As
Professors Wright and Miller put it: *[handwritten: conclusive]*

> "In general, a Rule 23(b)(3) action is appropriate whenever the
> actual interests of the parties can be served best by a single
> action. * * * [T]he proper standard under Rule 23(b)(3) is a
> pragmatic one, which is in keeping with the basic objectives of
> the Rule 23(b)(3) class action. Thus, when common questions
> represent a significant aspect of the case and they can be

[handwritten bottom margin: We must try this in one single suit.]

resolved for all members of the class in a single adjudication, there is a clear justification for handling the dispute on a representative rather than on an individual basis."

7A C. Wright & A. Miller, Federal Practice and Procedure §§ 1777, 1778 (1972). See also id. at § 1783; Wright & Colussi, The Successful Use of the Class Action Device in the Management of the *Skywalk* Mass Tort Litigation,—Univ. of Missouri-Kansas City L.Rev.—(1984) (forthcoming) (noting the successful use of a 23(b)(3) class in the *Skywalk* litigation); Note, Federal Mass Tort Class Action: A Step Toward Equity and Efficiency, 47 Albany L.Rev. 1180 (1983). Litigation economies are also relevant. One commentator has gone so far as to suggest that "the chief purpose of the predomination inquiry is not to measure the compatibility of class action procedures with substantive law but to determine whether a class action will in fact realize any litigation economies." Note, Developments in the Law—Class Actions, 89 Harv. L.Rev. 1318, 1505 (1976).

Unlike litigations such as those involving DES, Dalkon Shield and asbestos, the trial is likely to emphasize critical common defenses applicable to the plaintiffs' class as a whole. They will include such matters as that the substances manufactured could not have caused the injuries claimed; that if any injuries were caused by defendants' product it was because of the particular use and misuse made by the government; and that the government, not the manufacturers were wholly responsible because the former knew of all possible dangers and assumed full responsibility for any damage. No "defenses to liability [are] present affecting the individuals in different ways." Advisory Committee Notes, 39 F.R.D. at 103. It is anticipated that a very substantial portion of a prospective four-month trial will be devoted to just those defenses. Certification would be justified if only to prevent relitigating those defenses over and over again in individual cases.

Defendants' proposal to limit the class trial to the issue of the government contract defense is not a workable one. As this court has already noted, the issue of the government contract defense is inextricably interwoven with the issue of causation. In re Agent Orange Product Liability Litigation, 565 F.Supp. 1263, 1275–76 (E.D.N.Y.1983). It would be impossible to try the former without litigating and reaching conclusions as to the latter.

Even more persuasive is the extraordinary size of plaintiffs' class and the posture of the dispute. Unlike a case such as *Mertens* or *"Dalkon Shield"*, a determination on the issue of causation would do much to resolve the individual claims of the class members. The plaintiffs have indicated that there are a number of types of injuries which Agent Orange allegedly caused. The court has, therefore, ordered that, for purposes of the causation issue, plaintiffs' counsel will choose representative claimants for each type of injury alleged. A determination adverse to the plaintiffs in all categories could resolve the litigation and save considerable judicial and lawyers' time. Even if there is a finding of no causation as to less than all of the types of damage alleged, that determination alone would be likely to resolve tens of thousands of individual claims. Cf. In re Antibiotic Antitrust Actions, 333 F.Supp. 278, 281, modified, 333 F.Supp. 291; 333 F.Supp. 299 (S.D.N.Y.1971).

Were there a finding of causation favorable to the plaintiffs across the board, that, too, will help resolve the individual claims of the class members. Unlike the asbestos, *DES, Dalkon Shield,* and *Federal Skywalk* cases, defendants contest liability not just as to individual members of the class, but as to any members of the class. Thus, unlike other mass product liability cases, a determination of general causation will serve both the interests of judicial economy and assist in the speedy and less expensive resolution of individual class member's claims. Cf. Thompson v. Proctor & Gamble Co., No. C–80–3711 EFL (N.D.Cal. December 7, 1982), slip op. at 4; Mertens v. Abbott Laboratories, at 42–43. See also Note, Class Actions in a Products Liability Context—The Predomination Requirement and Cause-In-Fact, 7 Hofstra L.Rev. 859 (1979).

Finally, the court may not ignore the real world of dispute resolution. As already noted, a classwide finding of causation may serve to resolve the claims of individual members, in a way that determinations in individual cases would not, by enhancing the possibility of settlement among the parties and with the federal government.

The considerations already described make it clear why effective case management would not be possible were the court to pursue the alternative of allowing individual plaintiffs to intervene in a single case. A verdict in such a case either as to the affirmative defenses or causation might not be binding on the tens of thousands of plaintiffs not parties to the suit. A class action is, therefore, "superior to other available methods for the fair and efficient adjudication of the controversy."

Defendants further object that even if the litigation is otherwise suited for (b)(3) certification, the need to apply the law of dozens of different states would preclude certification or at least require different subclasses for each state. In most cases, this argument would have considerable force. As this court's opinions dealing with the choice-of-law problem in diversity cases and the law applicable to manufacturers' liability will show, it is of relatively little significance in this litigation. There is, as will be demonstrated, a consensus among the states with respect to the rules of conflicts and applicable substantive law that provides, in effect, a national substantive rule governing the main issues in this case. Since, in the main, one law applies to all the claims, certification of one class is appropriate. Cf. In re No. Dist. of Calif. "Dalkon Shield" IUD Product Liability Litigation, 693 F.2d 847, 850 (9th Cir.1982), cert. denied sub nom. A.H. Robins v. Abed, 459 U.S. 1171, 103 S.Ct. 817, 74 L.Ed.2d 1015 (1983).

A national substantive law governs, b/t [?]

Should there subsequently develop a need for creation of subclasses as the litigation develops and applicable substantive or procedural law requires application of individual states' laws, further subclasses can be created. See, e.g., Halderman v. Pennhurst State School & Hospital, 612 F.2d 84, 110 (3d Cir.1979), rev'd on other grounds, 451 U.S. 1, 101 S.Ct. 1531, 67 L.Ed.2d 694 (1981); Kaufman v. Dreyfus Fund, Inc., 434 F.2d 727, 737 (3d Cir.1970); Eisen v. Carlisle & Jacquelin, 391 F.2d 555, 566 (2d Cir.1968); In re Caesars Palace Securities Litigation, 360 F.Supp. 366, 398 (S.D.N.Y.1973).

The last objection the defendants have to (b)(3) certification is that a class-wide trial on causation violates their right to have a single jury rule on the question of the defendants' liability to each Agent Orange plaintiff. Issues may not be bifurcated for trial, they point out, unless it appears that the issues are "so distinct and separable" that they may be tried separately "without prejudice." Gasoline Products Co. v. Champlin Refining Co., 283 U.S. 494, 500, 501, 51 S.Ct. 513, 515, 75 L.Ed. 1188 (1931); Franchi Construction Co. v. Combined Ins. Co., 580 F.2d 1, 8 (1st Cir.1978). If the issues are so interwoven that separate trials would cause confusion and uncertainty, a litigant is denied his right of fair trial. As applied to the *Agent Orange* litigation, defendants contend that advising a jury in a subsequent trial on "specific" causation that there has already been a "general" determination that Agent Orange could cause plaintiff's illness would unfairly prejudice the jury in plaintiff's favor. Defendants' argument is not persuasive. It is common in product liability suits for there to be a tacit admission that the defendant's product *could* have caused the injury alleged with the question for the jury being whether it actually did cause it. Juries often distinguish between general and specific causation.

In sum, the court finds (1) that the affirmative defenses and the question of general causation are common to the class, (2) that those questions predominate over any questions affecting individual members, and (3) given the enormous potential size of plaintiffs' case and the judicial economies that would result from a class trial, a class action is superior to all other methods for a "fair and efficient adjudication of the controversy."

Rule 23(b)(1)(A)

Certification is sought pursuant to Rule 23(b)(1)(A). The rule requires a risk of — *only a possibility*

> (A) inconsistent or varying adjudications with respect to individual members of the class which would establish incompatible standards of conduct for the party opposing the class.

The court has already stated that "Rule 23(b)(1)(A) is not meant to apply . . . . where the risk of inconsistent results in individual actions is merely the possibility that the defendants will prevail in some cases and not in others, thereby paying damages to some claimants and not others." 506 F.Supp. at 789 (citations omitted). If the risk of paying money damages to some and not others were sufficient for (b)(1)(A) certification, almost every class action could be certified under (b)(1)(A). See McDonnell Douglas Corporation v. United States District Court, Central District of California, 523 F.2d 1083, 1086 (9th Cir.1975), cert. denied sub nom. Flanagan v. McDonnell Douglas Corporation, 425 U.S. 911, 96 S.Ct. 1506, 47 L.Ed.2d 761 (1976); see also A. Miller, An Overview of Federal Class Actions: Past, Present and Future 43 (1973).

* * *

Rule 23(b)(1)(B)

[handwritten: — $0 that P's can control litigation —no one can opt out.]

Plaintiffs also seek certification of a mandatory class under Rule 23(b)(1)(B). Under that section, when the four prerequisites of 23(a) are met, the class will be certified if, in addition, as a practical matter, individual adjudications would prevent or greatly impede the ability of other members to protect their interests. It reads in part:

> adjudications with respect to individual members of the class . . . would as a practical matter be dispositive of the interests of the other members not parties to the adjudications or substantially impair or impede their ability to protect their interests . . ..

The rationale for using (b)(1)(B) in mass tort litigation is that of the "limited fund." As Professor Miller put the matter:

> The paradigm Rule 23(b)(1)(B) case is one in which there are multiple claimants to a limited fund . . . and there is a risk that if litigants are allowed to proceed on an individual basis those who sue first will deplete the fund and leave nothing for latecomers.

A. Miller, An Overview of Federal Class Actions: Past, Present and Future 45 (1977). *[handwritten: we don't want P to sue first + grab all of D's money.]*

As applied to mass tort litigation, the "limited fund" is generally construed to be the assets of the defendants as extended by insurance coverage and the assets of the insurers. The "fund" may also have a more limited bearing, as where the first judgments may take all of a limited punitive damage award. If earlier claimants proceed on an individual basis, it is urged, they will deplete the defendants' assets and leave nothing for later claimants. See, e.g., Note, Mechanical and Constitutional Problems in the Certification of Mandatory Multistate Mass Tort Class Actions under Rule 23, 49 Brooklyn L.Rev. 517 (1983); Note, Class Actions for Punitive Damages, 81 Mich.L.Rev. 1787 (1983); Note, Class Certification in Mass Accident Cases Under Rule 23(b)(1), 96 Harv.L.Rev. 1143 (1981).

Before determining whether to certify the plaintiffs' class under (b)(1)(B), two threshold questions must be addressed. The first is whether (b)(1)(B) should ever be applied in mass tort litigation. The second, assuming that it should, is what standard to use in determining whether there is a risk that earlier litigants will deplete the fund and leave nothing for latecomers.

23B: ① general damages + ② people can opt out
③ nobody can opt out for punitive damages
494   ③ no WHICH COURTS, LAW & LITIGANTS   Pt. 3

Although the matter is not free from doubt, most courts that have considered the issue have concluded that, in the proper circumstances, Rule (b)(1)(B) may be used in mass tort cases. See, e.g., Green v. Occidental Petroleum Corp., 541 F.2d 1335, 1340 n. 9 (9th Cir.1976); Coburn v. 4–R Corp., 77 F.R.D. 43 (E.D.Ky.1977), petition for mandamus denied sub nom. Union Light, Heat & Power Co. v. United States Dist. Court, 588 F.2d 543 (6th Cir.1978), cert. dismissed, 443 U.S. 913, 99 S.Ct. 3103, 61 L.Ed.2d 877 (1979); Hernandez v. Motor Vessel Skyward, 61 F.R.D. 558 (S.D.Fla.1973). See also, Seltzer, Punitive Damages in Mass Tort Litigation: Addressing the Problems of Fairness, Efficiency and Control, 52 Fordham L.Rev. 37 (1983); Note, Federal Mass Tort Class Action: A Step Toward Equity and Efficiency, 47 Albany L.Rev. 1180 (1983).

Two recent circuit courts reversed after certifications of a Rule (b)(1)(B) class in mass tort litigation. See "Dalkon Shield," 693 F.2d 847 (9th Cir.1982); Federal Skywalk Cases, 680 F.2d 1175 (8th Cir.1982). Both courts recognized the applicability of (b)(1)(B) certification in mass tort cases. In "Dalkon Shield," the court stated that "[we] are not necessarily ruling out the class action tool as a means for expediting multi-party product liability actions in appropriate cases." 693 F.2d at 851. The court's decision was based largely on the fact that no plaintiff or defendant supported class certification. In In re Federal Skywalk cases, the court's decision was expressly based on the narrow grounds that the district court's certification violated the Anti-Injunction Act. 680 F.2d at 1183. Neither of these considerations apply here.

Courts that have considered the issue disagree over how to determine when the danger of fund exhaustion is great enough to justify certification. All conclude that "without more, numerous plaintiffs and a large ad damnum clause should not guarantee (b)(1)(B) certification." Payton v. Abbott Labs, 83 F.R.D. 382, 389 (D.Mass.1979). The Ninth Circuit has held that (b)(1)(B) certification is proper only when "separate punitive damage claims necessarily will affect later claims." "Dalkon Shield," 693 F.2d at 852 (emphasis supplied). Strict adherence to the Ninth Circuit certainty standard would mean either the elimination of (b)(1)(B) certification in mass tort actions (which is the position at least one court has taken (see Payton, 83 F.R.D. 382, 389)), or require a pretrial determination on the merits, which the Supreme Court has frowned on in another class action context. See Eisen v. Carlisle & Jacquelin, 417 U.S. 156, 177–78, 94 S.Ct. 2140, 2152–53, 40 L.Ed.2d 732 (1974); cf. Dolgow v. Anderson, 438 F.2d 825 (2d Cir.1970) (no mini-trial on the merits). This strict Ninth Circuit standard flies in the face of the language of Rule 23, which requires only that there be a "risk" of impairment, not that there be a conclusive determination of impairment. See Note, Class Certification in Mass Accident Cases Under Rule 23(b)(1), 96 Harv.L.Rev. 1143, 1158 (1983).

In Coburn, 77 F.R.D. at 46, one of three unreversed mass tort cases where (b)(1)(B) certification was actually granted, the court did not articulate what standard it was using, stating merely that it found a "risk" of impairment. Given the speculative nature of many of the rulings that must be made at the time of a class certification when the facts have not been fully developed, such as typicality of representative claims and adequacy of representation, the probable risk standard appears most useful.

*   *   *

Plaintiffs contend that the limited fund can be found here in one of two ways. First, they contend that compensatory damages will exceed the net worth of the defendants. Second, they contend that even if the compensatory damages do not satisfy (b)(1), punitive damages will.

As to their first contention, the information elicited at the hearing and in appearances before this court indicates that sufficient assets are and will be available to respond to any probable judgments. Without the aid of a full trial, on the basis of facts presently available, it cannot be said that there is a substantial probability that if plaintiffs' claims are successful, the compensatory recovery will exceed defendants' assets.

Based on information thus far supplied to the court, it also cannot be found, as a preliminary matter, that there is a substantial probability that punitive damages, if allowed will, when added to compensatory damages, exceed defendants' assets. . . .

*   *   *

Nevertheless, there is a substantial probability that limited punitive damages may be allowed. If they are, it would be equitable to share this portion of the possible award among all plaintiffs who ultimately recover compensatory damages. Yet, if no class is certified under Rule (b)(1)(B), nonclass members who opt out under Rule 23(b)(3) would conceivably receive all of the punitive damages or, if their cases, are not completed first, none at all.

. . . Accordingly, a class of all those described as members of the (b)(3) class are also certified under (b)(1)(B). The (b)(1)(B) certification is for the award of punitive damages.

*   *   *

CLASS DEFINITION AND NOTICE

There remain the questions of defining the class and notice to the class. The defendants' contention that the class as the court has defined it is unworkable because it is subjective ("all veterans who were injured . . . by exposure to Agent Orange") is a *non sequitur*. Subjectiveness does not affect the applicability of the class trial's findings to members of the class and it does not prejudice the defendants in any way. The class is, therefore, adequately defined and clearly ascertainable. See Ihrke v. Northern States Power Company, 459 F.2d 566 (8th Cir.1972).

Federal Rule 23(c)(2) provides that, in a class action maintained under Rule 23(b)(3), the court shall direct to the members of the class the best notice practicable under the circumstances, including individual notice to all members who can be identified through reasonable effort.

When members of the class can be identified through reasonable effort, individual notice is required; the expense of giving the notice must be paid by plaintiffs. See Eisen v. Carlisle & Jacquelin, 417 U.S. 156, 94 S.Ct. 2140, 40 L.Ed.2d 732 (1974); Abrams v. Interco, Inc., 719 F.2d 23 at 30 (2d Cir.1983).

What is "the best notice practicable under the circumstances" and what constitutes "reasonable effort" is a determination of fact to be made in the individual litigation. In re Franklin National Bank Securities Litigation, 599 F.2d 1109 (2d Cir.1978); see also In re Nissan Motor Corp. Antitrust Litigation, 552 F.2d 1088, 1098 n. 11 (5th Cir. 1977) (and cases cited therein); C. Wright & A. Miller, Federal Practice & Procedure, at § 1786; Manual for Complex Litigation, § 1.45 (1982).

Accordingly, it is ORDERED:

1. Certification of this matter as a class action under Federal Rule of Civil Procedure 23(b)(3) is granted. Judge Pratt's decision certifying the class action status of this litigation under Rule 23(b)(3) is modified and confirmed. Plaintiffs' motion seeking certification under Rule 23(b)(1)(B) is granted only with respect to the claim for punitive damages.

2. The plaintiff class is defined as those persons who were in the United States, New Zealand or Australian Armed Forces at any time from 1961 to 1972 who were injured while in or near Vietnam by exposure to Agent Orange or other phenoxy herbicides, including those composed in whole or in part of 2, 4, 5-trichlorophenoxyacetic acid or containing some amount of 2, 3, 7, 8-tetrachlorodibenzo-p-dioxin. The class also includes spouses, parents, and children of the veterans born before January 1, 1984, directly or derivatively injured as a result of the exposure.

The definition does not imply a conclusion that anyone within the class was injured as a result of exposure to any herbicide.

3. Notice to the members of the class shall be provided as follows:

(a) Plaintiffs' counsel, at their own expense, shall cause a copy of the written notice, attached as Exhibit A, to be mailed by first class United States mail to all persons who have filed actions as plaintiffs in the District Courts of the United States, or filed actions in state courts later removed to a federal court, which are pending in or have been transferred to this court for consolidated proceedings by the Panel on Multi-District Litigation, together with all persons who have moved to intervene or are intervenors, and each class member presently represented by counsel associated with plaintiffs' management committee who has not yet commenced an action or sought intervention. Mailing of the notice shall take place within 30 days of this Order.

(b) Plaintiffs' counsel, at their own expense, shall cause to be mailed a copy of the written notice to all persons who are currently listed on the United States Government's Veteran's Administration "Agent Orange Registry." This mailing shall take place within 50 days of this Order.

* * *

(e) Plaintiffs' counsel, at their own expense, shall serve a radio and television announcement notice in the form of Exhibit B on the nationwide networks of the American Broadcasting Company, the Columbia Broadcasting System, the Mutual Broadcasting System, the National Broadcasting Company, and the Public Broadcasting and Television Networks and on radio stations with a combined coverage of at least 50 percent of the listener audience in each of the top one hundred radio markets in the United States within 50 days of this Order.

* * *

(f) Plaintiffs' counsel, at their own expense, shall publish in the following newspapers and magazines an announcement in two successive weeks (but if publication is monthly, only once) in the form of Exhibit C: the nationwide edition of *The New York Times, U.S.A. Today, Time Magazine,* the *American Legion Magazine, VFW Magazine, Air Force Times, Army Times, Navy Times,* and the *Leatherneck;* the ten largest circulation newspapers in Australia, including *The Australian;* and the five largest daily circulation newspapers in New Zealand, including *The Dominion.* Publication shall be completed as soon as practicable, but no later than March 1, 1984. The size of the notice shall be not less than one-eighth, nor more than one-third, of the newspaper or magazine page.

(g) Plaintiffs' counsel shall, at their own expense, obtain a toll-free "800" telephone number in the name of the Clerk of the Court. . . .

Exhibit A

LEGAL NOTICE TO CLASS MEMBERS OF PENDENCY OF CLASS ACTION

This notice is given to you pursuant to an Order of the United States District Court for the Eastern District of New York and Rule 23(c)(2) of the Federal Rules of Civil Procedure. It is to inform you of the pendency of a class action in which you may be a member of the class, and of how to request exclusion from the class if you do not wish to be a class member. None of the claims described below have been proven. It is contemplated that a trial by court and jury will take place in this court beginning in May, 1984.

1. There are now pending in the United States District Court for the Eastern District of New York claims brought by individuals who were in the United States, New Zealand, or Australian Armed Forces assigned to or near Vietnam at any time from 1961 to 1972, who allege personal injury from exposure to "Agent Orange" or other phenoxy herbicides, including those composed in whole or in part of 2, 4, 5-

trichlorophenoxyacetic acid or containing some amount of 2, 3, 7, 8-tetrachlorodibenzo-p-dioxin (collectively referred to as "Agent Orange").

2. The plaintiffs include spouses, parents, and children born before January 1, 1984, of the servicepersons who claim direct or derivative injury as a result of exposure. Plaintiffs include children asserting claims in their own right for genetic injury and birth defects caused by their parents' exposure to "Agent Orange" and other phenoxy herbicides. Wives of veterans exposed to "Agent Orange" in Vietnam seek to recover in their own right for miscarriages. Plaintiffs' theories of liability include negligence, strict products liability, breach of warranty, intentional tort and nuisance. Damage claims of family members include pecuniary loss for wrongful death, loss of society, comfort, companionship, services, consortium, guidance and support. In addition, plaintiffs seek punitive damages for defendants' alleged misconduct in furnishing herbicides to the United States Government.

3. The defendants, who are alleged to have manufactured or sold "Agent Orange" to the United States Government, are Dow Chemical Company, Monsanto Company, T.H. Agriculture & Nutrition Company, Inc., Diamond Shamrock Chemicals Company, Uniroyal, Inc., Hercules Incorporated, and Thompson Chemical Corporation. All the defendants deny that the plaintiffs' alleged injuries were in any way caused by "Agent Orange." They assert that injury, if any, was not caused by a product produced by them. The defendants have challenged these suits on various other grounds including plaintiffs' lack of standing to sue, lack of jurisdiction, statutes of limitation, insufficiency in law, plaintiffs' contributory negligence, and plaintiffs' assumption of known risks. Each has also asserted such affirmative defenses as the "government contract defense" and the Government's misuse of its product. In third-party complaints, the defendants asserted claims against the United States of America seeking indemnification or contribution in the event the defendants are held liable to the plaintiffs. The Government has asserted its power to prevent anyone from suing it.

4. This court has certified a class action in this proceeding under Rule 23(b)(3) of the Federal Rules of Civil Procedure. The plaintiff class consists of those persons who were in the United States, New Zealand, or Australian Armed Forces assigned to Vietnam at any time from 1961 to 1972 who were injured while in or near Vietnam by exposure to "Agent Orange" or other phenoxy herbicides including those composed in whole or in part of 2, 4, 5-trichlorophenoxyacetic acid or containing some amount of 2, 3, 7, 8-tetrachlorodibenzo-p-dioxin. The class also includes spouses, parents, and children born before January 1, 1984, directly or derivatively injured as a result of the exposure.

The court may reconsider this decision, by decertifying, modifying the definition of the class, or creating subclasses in the light of future developments in the case. The definition does not imply a conclusion that anyone within the class was injured as a result of exposure to any herbicide.

5. The court has also certified a Rule 23(b)(1)(B) class limited to claims for punitive damages. The class includes the same persons as are in the Rule 23(b)(3) class. The court has decided not to permit members of the class to seek exclusion on the issue of punitive damages. You will therefore be bound by the court's rulings on punitive damages whether or not you seek exclusion on the issue of compensatory damages.

6. Trial of the representative plaintiffs' claims is scheduled to commence before Jack B. Weinstein, Chief Judge of the United States District Court for the Eastern District of New York, and a jury on May 7, 1984.

7. If you are a member of the plaintiff class you will be deemed a party to this action for all purposes unless you request exclusion from the Rule 23(b)(3) class action covering compensatory damages.

8. If you do not request exclusion from the class by May 1, 1984, you will be considered one of the plaintiffs of this class action for all purposes. You may enter an appearance through counsel of your own choice. You will be represented by counsel for the class representatives unless you choose to enter an appearance through your own legal counsel.

9. Class members who do not request exclusion will receive the benefit of, and will be bound by, any settlement or judgment favorable to the class covering compensatory damages. The class representatives' attorneys fees and costs will be paid out of any recovery of compensatory and other damages obtained by the class members. You will not be charged with costs or expenses whether or not you remain a member of the class. However, if you choose to enter an appearance through your own legal counsel, you will be liable for the legal fees of your personal counsel.

10. Class members who do not request exclusion will be bound by any judgment adverse to the class, and will not have the right to maintain a separate action even if they have already filed their own action.

11. If you wish to remain a member of the class for all purposes, you need do nothing at this stage of the proceedings.

12. *If you wish to be excluded from the class for compensatory damages, you must submit a written request for exclusion.* For your convenience, the request for exclusion may be submitted on the attached form, entitled "Request for Exclusion." If you received this notice by mail, a Request for Exclusion form should have accompanied it. If you did not receive a Request for Exclusion form, you may obtain a copy by writing to the Clerk of the Court, P.O. Box ___, Smithtown, New York 11787. A written Request for Exclusion may be submitted without using the Request for Exclusion form, but it must refer to the

litigation as "In re 'Agent Orange' Product Liability Litigation, MDL No. 381"; include your name and address in your statement requesting exclusion. Any request for exclusion must be received on or before May 1, 1984 by the Clerk of the United States District Court for the Eastern District of New York at Post Office Box ___, Smithtown, New York, 11787 or at a federal courthouse in the Eastern District of New York.

13.   Under the court's Order, all potential plaintiffs are deemed to be members of a Rule 23(b)(1)(B) class on the issue of punitive damages. At the time of trial the court will determine whether the facts presented warrant the submission of a punitive damage claim to the jury. In the event that there is a recovery for punitive damages, it will be shared by those plaintiffs who are successful in prosecuting their claims in this or other suits on an appropriate basis to be determined by the court. If you choose to exclude yourself from this class action on the issue of compensatory damages, you may do so without necessarily losing your right to share in any punitive damages.

14.   The plaintiffs in this class action are represented by a group of attorneys who have been tentatively approved by the Court as the Agent Orange Plaintiffs' Management Committee. Members of this committee include: [List of names and addresses omitted]   . . .

15.   *Examination of pleadings and papers.* This notice is not all inclusive. References to pleadings and other papers and proceedings are only summaries. For full details concerning the class action and the claims and defenses which have been asserted by the parties, you or your counsel may review the pleadings and other papers filed at the office of the Clerk of the United States District Court for the Eastern District of New York, 225 Cadman Plaza East, Brooklyn, New York 11201, on any business day from 9:00 a.m. to 5:00 p.m.

16.   *Interpretation of this Notice.* Except as indicated in the orders and decisions of the United States District Court for the Eastern District of New York, no court has yet ruled on the merits of any of the claims or defenses asserted by the parties in this class action. This notice is not an expression of an opinion by the court as to the merits of any claims or defenses. This notice is being sent to you solely to inform you of the nature of the litigation, your rights and obligations as a class member, the steps required should you desire to be excluded from the class, the court's certification of the class, and the forthcoming trial.

Robert C. Heinemann

Clerk, United States District

Court for the Eastern District of New York

DATED: Brooklyn, New York

January 12, 1984

EXCLUSION REQUEST FORM

Clerk
United States District Court for
the Eastern District of New York
P.O. Box ___
Smithtown, New York 11787

    Re: In re "Agent Orange" Product Liability Litigation MDL No. 381

    I hereby request to be excluded from the class action in the above-captioned matter.

                             _____

                             (Signature)

                             Name (print): _____

                             Address: _____

If not a member of the armed forces who served in or near Vietnam, how are you related to such a serviceperson? _____

Armed forces unit of serviceperson_____
Armed forces identifying number of serviceperson_____
Period of service in or near Vietnam_____

I learned about this suit by_____

Exhibit B (Radio and Television Communication)

SPECIAL ANNOUNCEMENT

    Were you or anyone in your family on military duty in or near Vietnam at any time from 1961 to 1972? If so, listen carefully to this important message about a pending "Agent Orange" lawsuit that may affect your rights.

    If you or anyone in your family claim injury, illness, disease, death, or birth defect as a result of exposure to "Agent Orange," or any other herbicide in or near Vietnam at any time from 1961 to 1972, you are now a member of a class in an action brought on your behalf in the United States District Court for the Eastern District of New York, unless you take steps to exclude yourself. The class is limited to those who were injured by exposure to Agent Orange or any other herbicide while serving in the armed forces in or near Vietnam at any time from

1961 to 1972. The class also includes members of families who claim derivative injuries such as those to spouses and children.

The court expresses no opinion as to the merit or lack of merit of the lawsuit. It has ordered that this message be transmitted to give as many persons as is practicable notice of this suit.

For details about your rights in this "Agent Orange" class action lawsuit, call 1–800–___, or write to the Clerk of the United States District Court, Box ___, Smithtown, New York 11787. That address again is Clerk of the United States District Court, P.O. Box ___, Smithtown, New York 11787, or call 1–800–___.

Exhibit C (Newspaper and Magazine Notice)

TO ALL PERSONS WHO SERVED IN OR NEAR VIETNAM AS MEMBERS OF THE ARMED FORCES OF THE UNITED STATES, AUSTRALIA AND NEW ZEALAND FROM 1961–1972

If you or anyone in your family can claim injury, illness, disease, death or birth defect as a result of exposure to "Agent Orange" or any other herbicide while assigned in or near Vietnam at any time from 1961 to 1972, you are a member of a class in an action brought on your behalf in the United States District Court for the Eastern District of New York unless you take steps to exclude yourself from the class. The class is limited to those who were injured by exposure to "Agent Orange" or any other herbicide while serving in the armed forces in or near Vietnam at any time during 1961–1972. The class also includes members of families who claim derivative injuries such as those to spouses and children.

The court expresses no opinion as to the merit or lack of merit of the lawsuit.

For details about your rights in this "Agent Orange" class action lawsuit, call 1–800–___, or write to Clerk of the Court, Box ___, Smithtown, New York 11787.

       Robert C. Heinemann

       Clerk, United States District

       Court for the Eastern

       District of New York

DATED: Brooklyn, New York

       December ___, 1983

NOTES

(1) What are the lower limits of the requirement of numerousness? Compare Atwood v. National Bank of Lima, 115 F.2d 861 (6th Cir.1940) (requirement not met in case of approximately thirty-nine beneficiaries of a trust fund)

with Citizens Banking Co. v. Monticello State Bank, 143 F.2d 261 (8th Cir.1944) (forty holders of collateral trust notes numerous enough).

(2) Must the interest of the named representative be coextensive with the interests of the other members of the class? See Dolgow v. Anderson, 43 F.R.D. 472, 491–92 (E.D.N.Y.1968) (plaintiffs can represent only those shareholders who purchased their stock in the same manner and in the same periods in which plaintiffs obtained theirs). But see Green v. Wolf Corp., 406 F.2d 291, 299 (2d Cir.1968) (plaintiff in an SEC Rule 10b–5 action who purchased after issuance of third prospectus, since faulted misstatements appear in all three prospectuses, may represent all purchasers, at least with respect to the common misrepresentations). Does Fed.R.Civ.P. 23(a)(3) seek to ensure merely that the members of the class be represented adequately? Can the named representative's claim be typical if it does not raise questions of fact or law common to the class? What happens if the defendant satisfies the claims of the named plaintiffs?

(3) In a class action that does not meet the requirements of Fed.R.Civ.P. 23(b)(3), must the common questions predominate? Can the named representative's claim be typical if they do not?

(4) What is the meaning of "predominate"? Does the term refer to the quantity or the quality of the common issues or to both? See Dolgow v. Anderson, 43 F.R.D. 472, 490 (E.D.N.Y.1968): "The common issues need not be dispositive of the entire litigation. The fact that questions peculiar to each individual member of the class may remain after the common questions have been resolved does not dictate the conclusion that a class action is not permissible." Was Judge Weinstein's tactic of creating a predominance of common questions for Rule 23(b)(3) purposes persuasive? Review the Second Circuit's opinion at an earlier phase of the proceedings, p. 390, supra.

(5) What other available methods for the fair and efficient adjudication of the controversy must be considered in determining whether a class action of the kind referred to in subdivision (b)(3) is superior? What are the advantages and disadvantages of a test case, intervention, consolidation, and joinder of parties, as compared with those of a class action? Consider in this context also 28 U.S. C.A. § 1407(a), quoted Note 5, p. 434, supra. Some defendants have also tried to resolve the claims of a large number of claimants by joining them all as creditors in a bankruptcy proceeding, see, e.g., Roberts v. Johns-Manville Corp. (In re Johns-Manville Corp.), 45 Bankr. 823 (D.C.N.Y.1984) (pooling the claims of asbestos victims); Kennedy, Creative Bankruptcy? Use and Abuse of the Bankruptcy Law—Reflection on Some Recent Cases, 71 Iowa L.Rev. 199 (1985). See also A.H. Robins Co., Inc. v. Piccinin, 788 F.2d 994 (4th Cir.1986) and Breland v. Aetna Casualty & Surety, 85 Bankr. 373 (D.C.Va.1988) (after tentative certification, defendant, manufacturer of the Dalkon Shield, declared bankruptcy and women who claimed injury became creditors of the estate).

(6) May a class member who opted out of a Rule 23(b)(3) class action invoke the judgment rendered in favor of a class as conclusively establishing the defendant's liability in an action brought subsequently against the same defendant? In Premier Electrical Construction Co. v. National Electrical Contractors Ass'n, Inc., 814 F.2d 358 (7th Cir.1987), the Seventh Circuit said no, but ruled that the prior judgment by the Fourth Circuit on the issue for which preclusive effect was claimed was entitled to persuasive effect, and should be followed. Is the Court's reliance on stare decisis as supporting this result appropriate?

THE GENERAL REQUIREMENTS FOR ADJUDICATION

1. NOTICE

How effective was the notice provided by Judge Weinstein? Does it comport with the requirements of Mullane v. Central Hanover Bank & Trust Co., p. 312, supra? In Eisen v. Carlisle & Jacquelin, 417 U.S. 156, 94 S.Ct. 2140, 40 L.Ed.2d 732 (1974), the Supreme Court considered the notice question in connection with a class action brought on behalf of securities traders who claimed that the cost of making odd-lot trades (i.e. trades in amounts of less than 100 shares) was too high and violated the securities and antitrust laws. Since there were over 2,250,000 such traders, the cost of individual notice far exceeded the $70 or so that the named representative stood to collect. Accordingly, the district court found that publication was the best notice practicable within the meaning of Rule 23(c)(2). The Supreme Court reversed, holding that:

"[I]ndividual notice to identifiable class members is not a discretionary consideration to be waived in a particular case. It is, rather, an unambiguous requirement of Rule 23 . . . Accordingly, each class member who can be identified through reasonable effort must be notified that he may request exclusion from the action and thereby preserve his opportunity to press his claim separately or that he may remain in the class and perhaps participate in the management of the action. There is nothing in Rule 23 to suggest that the notice requirements can be tailored to fit the pocketbooks of particular plaintiffs."

Did Judge Weinstein comply with *Eisen?* Was the notice requirement mandated in *Eisen* constitutionally required? By the text of Rule 23?

The district court in *Eisen* also tried to ease the cost of notice by shifting part of it to the defendants. It held a preliminary hearing and after finding that the plaintiff's class was likely to prevail on the merits, it entered an order imposing 90% of the notice costs on the defendants. The Supreme Court reversed here as well, finding it directly contrary to the command of 23(c)(1), and contrary to the "usual rule . . . that a plaintiff must initially bear the cost of notice." Eisen v. Carlisle & Jacquelin, 417 U.S. 156, 94 S.Ct. 2140, 40 L.Ed.2d 732 (1974).

Oppenheimer Fund, Inc. v. Sanders, 437 U.S. 340, 98 S.Ct. 2380, 57 L.Ed.2d 253 (1978), another securities case, represented yet another attempt to reduce the cost of notice to the plaintiff. The lower courts used the discovery rules to order defendants, securities brokers, to compile a list of their customers. Because these customers were the members of the class, the order effectively shifted a portion of the notice costs to the defendants. Again the Supreme Court reversed, holding that so long as the defendants made their records available to the plaintiffs, the cost of converting the records into a list of class members ($16,000) was equivalent for both sides. Since the federal rules impose these costs on plaintiffs, they must be borne by plaintiffs. Note that the *Oppenheimer* Court stressed the relative cost of notifying class members. Does this mean that if, for some reason, the cost of notice were lower for the defendant than the plaintiff, it might be permissible to shift the burden?

---

2. OPPORTUNITY TO BE HEARD

HANSBERRY v. LEE

Supreme Court of the United States, 1940.
311 U.S. 32, 61 S.Ct. 115, 85 L.Ed. 22.

MR. JUSTICE STONE delivered the opinion of the Court.

The question is whether the Supreme Court of Illinois, by its adjudication that petitioners in this case are bound by a judgment rendered in an earlier litigation to which they were not parties, has deprived them of the due process of law guaranteed by the Fourteenth Amendment.

Respondents brought this suit in the Circuit Court of Cook County, Illinois, to enjoin the breach by petitioners of an agreement restricting the use of land within a described area of the City of Chicago, which was alleged to have been entered into by some five hundred of the landowners. The agreement stipulated that for a specified period no part of the land should be "sold, leased to or permitted to be occupied by any person of the colored race," and provided that it should not be effective unless signed by the "owners of 95 per centum of the frontage" within the described area. The bill of complaint set up that the owners of 95 per cent of the frontage had signed; that respondents are owners of land within the restricted area who have either signed the agreement or acquired their land from others who did sign; and that petitioners Hansberry, who are Negroes, have, with the alleged aid of the other petitioners and with knowledge of the agreement, acquired and are occupying land in the restricted area formerly belonging to an owner who had signed the agreement.

To the defense that the agreement had never become effective because owners of 95 per cent of the frontage had not signed it, respondents pleaded that that issue was *res judicata* by the decree in an earlier suit. Burke v. Kleiman, 277 Ill.App. 519. To this petitioners pleaded, by way of rejoinder, that they were not parties to that suit or bound by its decree, and that denial of their right to litigate, in the present suit, the issue of performance of the condition precedent to the validity of the agreement would be a denial of due process of law guaranteed by the Fourteenth Amendment. It does not appear, nor is it contended that any of petitioners is the successor in interest to or in privity with any of the parties in the earlier suit.

The circuit court, after a trial on the merits, found that owners of only about 54 per cent of the frontage had signed the agreement, and that the only support of the judgment in the Burke case was a false and fraudulent stipulation of the parties that owners of 95 per cent had signed.   But it ruled that the issue of performance of the condition precedent to the validity of the agreement was *res judicata* as alleged and entered a decree for respondents.   The Supreme Court of Illinois affirmed.   372 Ill. 369, 24 N.E.2d 37.   We granted certiorari to resolve the constitutional question.   309 U.S. 652.

The Supreme Court of Illinois, upon an examination of the record in Burke v. Kleiman, supra, found that that suit, in the Superior Court of Cook County, was brought by a landowner in the restricted area to enforce the agreement, which had been signed by her predecessor in title, in behalf of herself and other property owners in like situation, against four named individuals, who had acquired or asserted an interest in a plot of land formerly owned by another signer of the agreement; that, upon stipulation of the parties in that suit that the agreement had been signed by owners of 95 per cent of all the frontage, the court had adjudged that the agreement was in force, that it was a covenant running with the land and binding all the land within the described area in the hands of the parties to the agreement and those claiming under them, including defendants, and had entered its decree restraining the breach of the agreement by the defendants and those claiming under them, and that the appellate court had affirmed the decree.   It found that the stipulation was untrue but held, contrary to the trial court, that it was not fraudulent or collusive.   It also appears from the record in Burke v. Kleiman that the case was tried on an agreed statement of facts which raised only a single issue, whether by reason of changes in the restricted area, the agreement had ceased to be enforcible in equity.

From this the Supreme Court of Illinois concluded in the present case that Burke v. Kleiman was a "class" or "representative" suit, and that in such a suit, "where the remedy is pursued by a plaintiff who has the right to represent the class to which he belongs, other members of the class are bound by the results in the case unless it is reversed or set aside on direct proceedings"; that petitioners in the present suit were members of the class represented by the plaintiffs in the earlier suit and consequently were bound by its decree, which had rendered the issue of performance of the condition precedent to the restrictive agreement *res judicata,* so far as petitioners are concerned.   The court thought that the circumstance that the stipulation in the earlier suit that owners of 95 per cent of the frontage had signed the agreement was contrary to the fact, as found in the present suit, did not militate against this conclusion, since the court in the earlier suit had jurisdiction to determine the fact as between the parties before it, and that its determination, because of the representative character of the suit, even though erroneous, was binding on petitioners until set aside by a direct attack on the first judgment.

State courts are free to attach such descriptive labels to litigations before them as they may choose and to attribute to them such consequences as they think appropriate under state constitutions and laws, subject only to the requirements of the Constitution of the United States. But when the judgment of a state court, ascribing to the judgment of another court the binding force and effect of *res judicata,* is challenged for want of due process it becomes the duty of this Court to examine the course of procedure in both litigations to ascertain whether the litigant whose rights have thus been adjudicated has been afforded such notice and opportunity to be heard as are requisite to the due process which the Constitution prescribes. Western Life Indemnity Co. v. Rupp, 235 U.S. 261, 273, 35 S.Ct. 37.

It is a principle of general application in Anglo-American jurisprudence that one is not bound by a judgment *in personam* in a litigation in which he is not designated as a party or to which he has not been made a party by service of process. Pennoyer v. Neff, 95 U.S. 714; 1 Freeman on Judgments (5th ed.), § 407. A judgment rendered in such circumstances is not entitled to the full faith and credit which the Constitution and statute of the United States, R.S. § 905, 28 U.S.C. § 687, prescribe, Pennoyer v. Neff, supra; Lafayette Ins. Co. v. French, 18 How. 404; Hall v. Lanning, 91 U.S. 160; Baker v. Baker, Eccles & Co., 242 U.S. 394, 37 S.Ct. 152; and judicial action enforcing it against the person or property of the absent party is not that due process which the Fifth and Fourteenth Amendments require. Postal Telegraph Cable Co. v. Newport, 247 U.S. 464, 38 S.Ct. 566; Old Wayne Mutual Life Ass'n v. McDonough, 204 U.S. 8, 27 S.Ct. 236.

To these general rules there is a recognized exception that, to an extent not precisely defined by judicial opinion, the judgment in a "class" or "representative" suit, to which some members of the class are parties, may bind members of the class or those represented who were not made parties to it. Smith v. Swormstedt, 16 How. 288; Royal Arcanum v. Green, 237 U.S. 531; Hartford Life Ins. Co. v. Ibs, 237 U.S. 662, 35 S.Ct. 692; Hartford Life Ins. Co. v. Barber, 245 U.S. 146, 38 S.Ct. 54; Supreme Tribe of Ben-Hur v. Cauble, 255 U.S. 356, 41 S.Ct. 338; cf. Christopher v. Brusselback, 302 U.S. 500, 58 S.Ct. 350.

The class suit was an invention of equity to enable it to proceed to a decree in suits where the number of those interested in the subject of litigation is so great that their joinder as parties in conformity to the usual rules of procedure is impracticable. Courts are not infrequently called upon to proceed with causes in which the number of those interested in the litigation is so great as to make difficult or impossible the joinder of all because some are not within the jurisdiction or because their whereabouts is unknown or where if all were made parties to the suit its continued abatement by the death of some would prevent or unduly delay a decree. In such cases where the interests of those not joined are of the same class as the interests of those who are, and where it is considered that the latter fairly represent the former in the prosecution of the litigation of the issues in which all have a common interest, the court will proceed to a decree. Brown v. Vermuden, Ch.Cas. 272; City of London v. Richmond, 2 Vern. 421;

Cockburn v. Thompson, 16 Ves.Jr. 321; West v. Randall, Fed.Cas. No. 17,424; 2 Mason 181; Beatty v. Kurtz, 2 Pet. 566; Smith v. Swormstedt, supra; Supreme Tribe of Ben-Hur v. Cauble, supra; Story, Equity Pleading (2d ed.) § 98.

It is evident that the considerations which may induce a court thus to proceed, despite a technical defect of parties, may differ from those which must be taken into account in determining whether the absent parties are bound by the decree or, if it is adjudged that they are, in ascertaining whether such an adjudication satisfies the requirements of due process and of full faith and credit. Nevertheless, there is scope within the framework of the Constitution for holding in appropriate cases that a judgment rendered in a class suit is *res judicata* as to members of the class who are not formal parties to the suit. Here, as elsewhere, the Fourteenth Amendment does not compel state courts or legislatures to adopt any particular rule for establishing the conclusiveness of judgments in class suits; cf. Brown v. New Jersey, 175 U.S. 172, 20 S.Ct. 77; Brown v. Mississippi, 297 U.S. 278, 56 S.Ct. 461; United Gas Public Service Co. v. Texas, 303 U.S. 123; Avery v. Alabama, 308 U.S. 444, 446, 447, 60 S.Ct. 321, nor does it compel the adoption of the particular rules thought by this Court to be appropriate for the federal courts. With a proper regard for divergent local institutions and interests, cf. Jackson County v. United States, 308 U.S. 343, 60 S.Ct. 285, 351, this Court is justified in saying that there has been a failure of due process only in those cases where it cannot be said that the procedure adopted, fairly insures the protection of the interests of absent parties who are to be bound by it. Chicago, B. & Q.R. Co. v. Chicago, 166 U.S. 226, 235, 17 S.Ct. 581.

It is familiar doctrine of the federal courts that members of a class not present as parties to the litigation may be bound by the judgment where they are in fact adequately represented by parties who are present, or where they actually participate in the conduct of the litigation in which members of the class are present as parties, Plumb v. Goodnow's Administrator, 123 U.S. 560, 8 S.Ct. 216; Confectioners' Machinery Co. v. Racine Engine & Mach. Co., 163 F. 914, 170 F. 1021; Bryant Electric Co. v. Marshall, 169 F. 426, or where the interest of the members of the class, some of whom are present as parties, is joint, or where for any other reason the relationship between the parties present and those who are absent is such as legally to entitle the former to stand in judgment for the latter. Smith v. Swormstedt, supra; cf. Christopher v. Brusselback, supra, 302 U.S. 503, 504, 58 S.Ct. 350, and cases cited.

In all such cases, so far as it can be said that the members of the class who are present are, by generally recognized rules of law, entitled to stand in judgment for those who are not, we may assume for present purposes that such procedure affords a protection to the parties who are represented, though absent, which would satisfy the requirements of due process and full faith and credit. See Bernheimer v. Converse, 206 U.S. 516, 27 S.Ct. 755; Marin v. Augedahl, 247 U.S. 142, 38 S.Ct.

452; Chandler v. Peketz, 297 U.S. 609, 56 S.Ct. 602. Nor do we find it necessary for the decision of this case to say that, when the only circumstance defining the class is that the determination of the rights of its members turns upon a single issue of fact or law, a state could not constitutionally adopt a procedure whereby some of the members of the class could stand in judgment for all, provided that the procedure were so devised and applied as to insure that those present are of the same class as those absent and that the litigation is so conducted as to insure the full and fair consideration of the common issue. Compare New England Divisions Case, 261 U.S. 184, 197, 43 S.Ct. 270; Taggart v. Bremner, 236 F. 544. We decide only that the procedure and the course of litigation sustained here by the plea of res judicata do not satisfy these requirements.

The restrictive agreement did not purport to create a joint obligation or liability. If valid and effective its promises were the several obligations of the signers and those claiming under them. The promises ran severally to every other signer. It is plain that in such circumstances all those alleged to be bound by the agreement would not constitute a single class in any litigation brought to enforce it. Those who sought to secure its benefits by enforcing it could not be said to be in the same class with or represent those whose interest was in resisting performance, for the agreement by its terms imposes obligations and confers rights on the owner of each plot of land who signs it. If those who thus seek to secure the benefits of the agreement were rightly regarded by the state Supreme Court as constituting a class, it is evident that those signers of their successors who are interested in challenging the validity of the agreement and resisting its performance are not of the same class in the sense that their interests are identical so that any group who had elected to enforce rights conferred by the agreement could be said to be acting in the interest of any others who were free to deny its obligation.

Because of the dual and potentially conflicting interests of those who are putative parties to the agreement in compelling or resisting its performance, it is impossible to say, solely because they are parties to it, that any two of them are of the same class. Nor without more, and with the due regard for the protection of the rights of absent parties which due process exacts, can some be permitted to stand in judgment for all.

It is one thing to say that some members of a class may represent other members in a litigation where the sole and common interest of the class in the litigation, is either to assert a common right or to challenge an asserted obligation. Smith v. Swormstedt, supra; Supreme Tribe of Ben-Hur v. Cauble, supra; Groves v. Farmers State Bank, 368 Ill. 35, 12 N.E.2d 618. It is quite another to hold that all those who are free alternatively either to assert rights or to challenge them are of a single class, so that any group, merely because it is of the class so constituted, may be deemed adequately to represent any others of the class in litigating their interests in either alternative. Such a selection of representatives for purposes of litigation, whose substantial interests are not necessarily or even probably the same as those whom they are deemed to represent, does not afford that protection to absent parties which due process requires. The doctrine of representation of absent parties in a class suit has not hitherto been thought to go so far. See Terry v. Bank of Cape Fear, 20 F. 777, 781; Weidenfeld v. Northern Pacific Ry. Co., 129 F. 305, 310; McQuillen v. National Cash Register Co., 22 F.Supp. 867, 873, aff'd 112 F.2d 877, 882; Brenner v. Title Guarantee & Trust Co., 276 N.Y. 230, 11 N.E.2d 890; cf. Wabash R. Co. v. Adelbert College, 208 U.S. 38, 28 S.Ct. 182; Coe v. Armour Fertilizer Works, 237 U.S. 413, 35 S.Ct. 625. Apart from the opportunities it would afford for the fraudulent and collusive sacrifice of the rights of absent parties, we think that the representation in this case no more satisfies the requirements of due process than a trial by a judicial officer who is in such situation that he may have an interest in the outcome of the litigation in conflict with that of the litigants. Tumey v. Ohio, 273 U.S. 510, 47 S.Ct. 437.

The plaintiffs in the Burke case sought to compel performance of the agreement in behalf of themselves and all others similarly situated. They did not designate the defendants in the suit as a class or seek any injunction or other relief against others than the named defendants, and the decree which was entered did not purport to bind others. In seeking to enforce the agreement the plaintiffs in that suit were not representing the petitioners here whose substantial interest is in resisting performance. The defendants in the first suit were not treated by the pleadings or decree as representing others or as foreclosing by their defense the rights of others; and, even though nominal defendants, it does not appear that their interest in defeating the contract outweighed their interest in establishing its validity. For a court in this situation to ascribe to either the plaintiffs or defendants the performance of such functions on behalf of petitioners here, is to attribute to them a power that it cannot be said that they had assumed to exercise, and a responsibility which, in view of their dual interests it does not appear that they could rightly discharge.

Reversed.

NOTES

(1) Were all the members of the class as defined in the principal case equally enthusiastic about enforcing their rights? If not, should this bar use of the class action device? Cf. Ackert v. Union Pacific Railroad Co., 4 A.D.2d 819, 165 N.Y.S.2d 330 (4th Dep't 1957) (small shareholders might not wish to see contract annulled by class action but representatives of majority permitted to bring class action; the point was not decisive because the contract was not severable and all shareholders would have to be treated in the same way).

(2) Would the result in the principal case have been the same if the plaintiffs in the first action had sued the defendants as representing the class of all individuals who had acquired or asserted an interest in a plot of land formerly owned by another signer of the restrictive agreement? To what

extent can a member of the class who opposes the position taken by the named members be bound by a judgment against the class? May it depend on the nature of the subject matter of the suit? See Weinstein, Revision of Procedure: Some Problems in Class Actions, 9 Buffalo L.Rev. 433, 460–469 (1960); Note, Class Actions: Defining the Typical and Representative Plaintiff Under Subsections (a)(3) and (4) of Federal Rule 23, 53 B.U.L.Rev. 406 (1973).

(3) To what extent was the collusive stipulation in the first action the reason for rejecting the conclusive effect of the first judgment?

(4) One way judges try to avoid entertaining collusive class actions is by utilizing their power under Fed.R.Civ.P. 53 to appoint special masters, who go into the community to speak to those upon whom the suit is likely to have an impact. For an illuminating discussion of how this procedure works, see Berger, Away From the Court and Into the Field: The Odyssey of a Special Master, 78 Colum.L.Rev. 707 (1978).

(5) In class actions that go to trial, the judge's presence provides some assurance that the proceedings are fair to unrepresented parties. However, many class actions settle before trial. To assure the fairness of the settlement, Rule 23(e) requires that to be valid, dismissals or compromises of the case must be judicially approved. Often, the court holds a fairness hearing, at which dissatisfied class members can seek to persuade the court to withhold approval.

The Agent Orange litigation is an example of a class action that settled, with the vigorous help and encouragement of the judge and his Special Master. See In re Agent Orange Product Liability Litigation, 597 F.Supp. 740 (E.D.N.Y. 1984) (Weinstein, J.), affirmed, 821 F.2d 139 (2d Cir.1987). Does it make sense for the same judge who oversaw the negotiations approve the settlement?

(6) Are there other avenues for unnamed parties to attack the resolution of a class action? Several courts have held that they cannot appeal a disposition with which the named representatives are satisfied, Walker v. Mesquite, 858 F.2d 1071 (5th Cir.1988); Guthrie v. Evans, 815 F.2d 626 (11th Cir.1987). Should dissatisfied class members be allowed to intervene as parties? See Section 9, supra; cf. Marino v. Ortiz, 484 U.S. 301, 108 S.Ct. 586, 98 L.Ed.2d 629 (1988) (per curiam).

(7) The systemic sort of relief achieved in class actions has the potential to affect strangers to the lawsuit. In Martin v. Wilks, ___ U.S. ___, 109 S.Ct. 2180, 104 L.Ed.2d 835 (1989), p. 971, infra, white firefighters brought a separate proceeding to challenge a consent decree entered in a lawsuit brought on behalf of black applicants for firefighter positions against the City of Birmingham, Alabama and the Jefferson County Personnel Board, alleging discriminatory hiring and promotion practices in various public service jobs in violation of the civil rights laws. The Supreme Court rejected claims that the white firefighters had a duty to intervene in the first suit and were therefore barred by res judicata from challenging the decree. Does that decision render the class device ineffective when unrepresented parties can stay out of the action and later attack it collaterally?

3. SUBJECT MATTER JURISDICTION

Diversity-based class actions raise special problems regarding the amount-in-controversy requirement. For example, in a Federal Rule 23(b)(3) action, may the claims of the individual members of the class be aggregated for the purpose of determining whether the requisite amount is in controversy? Under old Federal Rule 23, a negative answer had been held appropriate on the ground that it was well settled that separate and distinct claims of multiple parties could not be aggregated for this purpose and that a spurious class action was in essence a permissive joinder device. See Clark v. Paul Gray, Inc., 306 U.S. 583, 59 S.Ct. 744, 83 L.Ed. 1001 (1939). In Snyder v. Harris, 394 U.S. 332, 89 S.Ct. 1053, 22 L.Ed.2d 319 (1969), rehearing denied 394 U.S. 1025, 89 S.Ct. 1622, 23 L.Ed.2d 50, the Supreme Court held that the old doctrine continued to apply under new Federal Rule 23. It said: "Nothing in the amended Rule 23 changes this doctrine . . . .. Any change in the Rules that did purport to effect a change in the definition of 'matter in controversy' would clearly conflict with the demand of Rule 82 . . . .." Do you agree? In what respects, relevant in this context, does the new Rule differ from the old? See also Note, 27 U.Miami L.Rev. 243 (1972).

The decision in Snyder v. Harris, which seriously limits access to a class action in the federal courts, did not seem to preclude the possibility of entertaining claims under the requisite amount, as long as one or more of the representative members of the class alleged claims that did satisfy the amount in controversy requirement. However, in Zahn v. International Paper Co., 414 U.S. 291, 94 S.Ct. 505, 38 L.Ed.2d 511 (1973), the Supreme Court ruled also this avenue foreclosed. Should it have applied the doctrine of "pendent jurisdiction?" Would Fed.R.Civ.P. 82 have stood in the way? On the Zahn case, see also Note, 35 Ohio St.L.J. 190 (1974); Note, 62 Ill.B.J. 516 (1974); Note, 28 Sw.L.J. 815 (1974).

NOTES

(1) Is the Supreme Court's decision in *Zahn* consistent with its decisions allowing ancillary jurisdiction in cases of incomplete diversity? Cf. Oskoian v. Canuel, p. 406, supra.

(2) The availability of a class action may be crucial in affording any relief when the claims of the individual members of the class are too small to warrant individual actions. This aspect is stressed in many decisions. Cf. Daar v. Yellow Cab Co., p. 541, infra. It has been said that the "historic mission" of the class action has been to take "care of the smaller guy." See Frankel, Amended Rule 23 From a Judge's Point of View, 32 Antitrust L.J. 295, 299 (1966) (quoting Professor Benjamin Kaplan).

(3) One class of cases in which individual suits are less likely because of the small amounts involved are consumer cases. The increased attention to the interests of the consumer have added to the pressures for increased availability of the class action for the vindication of these interests. These, in turn, have led to efforts to preclude it. *Compare* Dole, Consumer Class Actions Under Recent Consumer Credit Legislation, 44 N.Y.U.L.Rev. 80 (1969), Eckhardt, Consumer Class Actions, 45 Notre Dame Law. 663 (1970) (favoring the consumer class action), and Starrs, The Consumer Class Action, 49 B.U.L.Rev. 209, 407 (1969) *with* Handler, The Shift From Substantive to Procedural Innovations in Anti-Trust Suits, 71 Colum.L.Rev. 1 (1971) ("legalized blackmail") and Kirkpatrick, Consumer Class Litigation, 50 Ore.L.Rev. 21 (1971). See also Class Action Bibliography, 26 Record Ass'n Bar City N.Y. 412 (1971); Consumer Class Action

Under Federal Rule 23: Consumer Protection Causes of Action Under Federal Statutes, 25 So.Car.L.Rev. 239 (1973).

(4) The severe curtailment of availability of the class action in the Federal courts owing to the Supreme Court's decision in *Eisen, Oppenheimer Fund, Snyder* and *Zahn* has resulted in litigants' increasingly looking to the analogous procedural devices provided for in state courts.

Federal Rules 23 through 23.2 are in effect, either in unchanged or in modified form, in all states that have made the Federal Rules part of their procedural law, but since state courts are free to put their own constructions on their provisions and are not limited by federal rules circumscribing subject matter competence (see p. 179, supra), conclusions reached by federal courts as to the propriety of class actions do not automatically apply in state courts. In states that have not borrowed their class action provisions from the Federal Rules, either the Field Code provisions or newer enactments apply.

4. PERSONAL JURISDICTION

PHILLIPS PETROLEUM CO. v. SHUTTS

Supreme Court of the United States, 1985.
472 U.S. 797, 105 S.Ct. 2965, 86 L.Ed.2d 628.*

JUSTICE REHNQUIST delivered the opinion of the Court.

[Respondents had brought a class action in a Kansas state court on behalf of some 28,000 owners of rights to leases of land located in 11 different states from which petitioner produced gas, seeking the payment of interest on royalty payments that had been delayed. The trial court granted recovery of interest on the basis of Kansas law. The Kansas Supreme Court affirmed. In the Supreme Court, petitioner argued that Kansas had no jurisdiction over members of the class who did not have sufficient contacts with Kansas. It also argued that Kansas could not constitutionally apply Kansas law to all claims, since over 99% of the gas leases and some 97% of the plaintiffs had no connection with Kansas. The Court first ruled that petitioner could properly rely on the asserted denial of due process to the lease owners who had insufficient contacts with Kansas. Petitioner had the requisite interest to advance this objection, the Court ruled in Part I, since it could be exposed to multiple claims by the royalty owners if Kansas lacked jurisdiction over them. The Court then addressed the two objections advanced.]

II

Reduced to its essentials, petitioner's argument is that unless out-of-state plaintiffs affirmatively consent, the Kansas courts may not exert jurisdiction over their claims. Petitioner claims that failure to execute and return the "request for exclusion" provided with the class notice cannot constitute consent of the out-of-state plaintiffs; thus Kansas courts may exercise jurisdiction over these plaintiffs only if the

* Some footnotes renumbered; others omitted.

plaintiffs possess the sufficient "minimum contacts" with Kansas as that term is used in cases involving personal jurisdiction over out-of-state defendants. E.g., International Shoe Co. v. Washington, 326 U.S. 310, 66 S.Ct. 154, 90 L.Ed. 95 (1945); Shaffer v. Heitner, 433 U.S. 186, 97 S.Ct. 2569, 53 L.Ed.2d 683 (1977); World-wide Volkswagen Corp. v. Woodson, 444 U.S. 286, 100 S.Ct. 559, 62 L.Ed.2d 490 (1980). Since Kansas had no prelitigation contact with many of the plaintiffs and leases involved, petitioner claims that Kansas has exceeded its jurisdictional reach and thereby violated the due process rights of the absent plaintiffs.

* * *

Although the cases like *Shaffer* and *Woodson* which petitioner relies on for a minimum contacts requirement all dealt with out-of-state defendants or parties in the procedural posture of a defendant, cf. New York Life Ins. Co. v. Dunlevy, 241 U.S. 518, 36 S.Ct. 613, 60 L.Ed. 1140 (1916); Estin v. Estin, 334 U.S. 541, 68 S.Ct. 1213, 92 L.Ed. 1561 (1948), petitioner claims that the same analysis must apply to absent class-action plaintiffs. In this regard petitioner correctly points out that a chose in action is a constitutionally recognized property interest possessed by each of the plaintiffs. Mullane v. Central Hanover Bank & Trust Co., 339 U.S. 306, 70 S.Ct. 652, 94 L.Ed. 865 (1950). An adverse judgment by Kansas courts in this case may extinguish the chose in action forever through res judicata. Such an adverse judgment, petitioner claims, would be every bit as onerous to an absent plaintiff as an adverse judgment on the merits would be to a defendant. Thus, the same due process protections should apply to absent plaintiffs: Kansas should not be able to exert jurisdiction over the plaintiff's claims unless the plaintiffs have sufficient minimum contacts with Kansas.

We think petitioner's premise is in error. The burdens placed by a State upon an absent class-action plaintiff are not of the same order or magnitude as those it places upon an absent defendant. An out-of-state defendant summoned by a plaintiff is faced with the full powers of the forum State to render judgment *against* it. The defendant must generally hire counsel and travel to the forum to defend itself from the plaintiff's claim, or suffer a default judgment. The defendant may be forced to participate in extended and often costly discovery, and will be forced to respond in damages or to comply with some other form of remedy imposed by the court should it lose the suit. The defendant may also face liability for court costs and attorney's fees. These burdens are substantial, and the minimum contacts requirement of the Due Process Clause prevents the forum State from unfairly imposing them upon the defendant.

A class-action plaintiff, however, is in quite a different posture. The Court noted this difference in Hansberry v. Lee, 311 U.S. 32, 40–41, 61 S.Ct. 115, 117–118, 85 L.Ed. 22 (1940), which explained that a "class" or "representative" suit was an exception to the rule that one could not be bound by judgment *in personam* unless one was made fully a party in the traditional sense. Ibid., citing Pennoyer v. Neff, 95 U.S. (5 Otto)

714, 24 L.Ed. 565 (1878). As the Court pointed out in *Hansberry,* the class action was an invention of equity to enable it to proceed to a decree in suits where the number of those interested in the litigation was too great to permit joinder. The absent parties would be bound by the decree so long as the named parties adequately represented the absent class and the prosecution of the litigation was within the common interest.[1]   311 U.S., at 41, 61 S.Ct., at 117.

Modern plaintiff class actions follow the same goals, permitting litigation of a suit involving common questions when there are too many plaintiffs for proper joinder. Class actions also may permit the plaintiffs to pool claims which would be uneconomical to litigate individually. For example, this lawsuit involves claims averaging about $100 per plaintiff; most of the plaintiffs would have no realistic day in court if a class action were not available.

In sharp contrast to the predicament of a defendant haled into an out-of-state forum, the plaintiffs in this suit were not haled anywhere to defend themselves upon pain of a default judgment. As commentators have noted, from the plaintiffs' point of view a class action resembles a "quasi-administrative proceeding, conducted by the judge." 3B J. Moore & J. Kennedy, Moore's Federal Practice ¶ 23.45[4.–5] (1984); Kaplan, Continuing Work of the Civil Committee: 1966 Amendments to the Federal Rules of Civil Procedure (I), 81 Harv.L.Rev. 356, 398 (1967).

A plaintiff class in Kansas and numerous other jurisdictions cannot first be certified unless the judge, with the aid of the named plaintiffs and defendant, conducts an inquiry into the common nature of the named plaintiff's and the absent plaintiffs' claims, the adequacy of representation, the jurisdiction possessed over the class, and any other matters that will bear upon proper representation of the absent plaintiffs' interest. See, e.g., Kan.Stat.Ann. § 60–223 (1983); Fed.Rule Civ. Proc. 23. Unlike a defendant in a civil suit, a class-action plaintiff is not required to fend for himself. See Kan.Stat.Ann. § 60–223(d) (1983). The court and named plaintiffs protect his interests. Indeed, the class-action defendant itself has a great interest in ensuring that the absent plaintiff's claims are properly before the forum. In this case, for example, the defendant sought to avoid class certification by alleging that the absent plaintiffs would not be adequately represented and were not amenable to jurisdiction. See Phillips Petroleum v. Duckworth, No. 82–54608 (Kan., June 28, 1982).

The concern of the typical class-action rules for the absent plaintiffs is manifested in other ways. Most jurisdictions, including Kansas, require that a class action, once certified, may not be dismissed or compromised without the approval of the court. In many jurisdictions

---

1. The holding in *Hansberry,* of course, was that petitioners in that case had not a sufficient common interest with the parties to a prior lawsuit such that a decree against those parties in the prior suit would bind the petitioners. But in the present case there is no question that the named plaintiffs adequately represent the class, and that all members of the class have the same interest in enforcing their claims against the defendant.

such as Kansas the court may amend the pleadings to ensure that all sections of the class are represented adequately. Kan.Stat.Ann. § 60–223(d) (1983); see also e.g., Fed.Rule Civ.Proc. 23(d).

Besides this continuing solicitude for their rights, absent plaintiff class members are not subject to other burdens imposed upon defendants. They need not hire counsel or appear. They are almost never subject to counterclaims or cross-claims, or liability for fees or costs.[2] Absent plaintiff class members are not subject to coercive or punitive remedies. Nor will an adverse judgment typically bind an absent plaintiff for any damages, although a valid adverse judgment may extinguish any of the plaintiff's claim which was litigated.

Unlike a defendant in a normal civil suit, an absent class-action plaintiff is not required to do anything. He may sit back and allow the litigation to run its course, content in knowing that there are safeguards provided for his protection. In most class actions an absent plaintiff is provided at least with an opportunity to "opt out" of the class, and if he takes advantage of that opportunity he is removed from the litigation entirely. This was true of the Kansas proceedings in this case. The Kansas procedure provided for the mailing of a notice to each class member by first-class mail. The notice, as we have previously indicated, described the action and informed the class member that he could appear in person or by counsel, in default of which he would be represented by the named plaintiffs and their attorneys. The notice further stated that class members would be included in the class and bound by the judgment unless they "opted out" by executing and returning a "request for exclusion" that was included in the notice.

Petitioner contends, however, that the "opt out" procedure provided by Kansas is not good enough, and that an "opt in" procedure is required to satisfy the Due Process Clause of the Fourteenth Amendment. Insofar as plaintiffs who have no minimum contacts with the forum State are concerned, an "opt in" provision would require that each class member affirmatively consent to his inclusion within the class.

Because States place fewer burdens upon absent class plaintiffs than they do upon absent defendants in nonclass suits, the Due Process Clause need not and does not afford the former as much protection from state-court jurisdiction as it does the latter. The Fourteenth Amendment does protect "persons," not "defendants," however, so absent plaintiffs as well as absent defendants are entitled to some protection from the jurisdiction of a forum State which seeks to adjudicate their claims. In this case we hold that a forum State may exercise jurisdiction over the claim of an absent class-action plaintiff, even

2. Petitioner places emphasis on the fact that absent class members might be subject to discovery, counterclaims, cross-claims or court costs. Petitioner cites no cases involving any such imposition upon plaintiffs, however. We are convinced that such burdens are rarely imposed upon plaintiff class members, and that the disposition of these issues is best left to a case which presents them in a more concrete way.

though that plaintiff may not possess the minimum contacts with the forum which would support personal jurisdiction over a defendant. If the forum State wishes to bind an absent plaintiff concerning a claim for money damages or similar relief at law,[3] it must provide minimal procedural due process protection. The plaintiff must receive notice plus an opportunity to be heard and participate in the litigation, whether in person or through counsel. The notice must be the best practicable, "reasonably calculated, under all the circumstances, to apprise interested parties of the pendency of the action and afford them an opportunity to present their objections." Mullane, 399 U.S., at 314–315, 70 S.Ct., at 657; cf. Eisen v. Carlisle & Jacquelin, 417 U.S. 156, 174–175, 94 S.Ct. 2140, 2151, 40 L.Ed.2d 732 (1974). The notice should describe the action and the plaintiffs' rights in it. Additionally, we hold that due process requires at a minimum that an absent plaintiff be provided with an opportunity to remove himself from the class by executing and returning an "opt out" or "request for exclusion" form to the court. Finally, the Due Process Clause of course requires that the named plaintiff at all times adequately represent the interests of the absent class members. Hansberry, 311 U.S., at 42–43, 45, 61 S.Ct., at 118–119, 120.

We reject petitioner's contention that the Due Process Clause of the Fourteenth Amendment requires that absent plaintiffs affirmatively "opt in" to the class, rather than be deemed members of the class if they do not "opt out." We think that such a contention is supported by little, if any precedent, and that it ignores the differences between class action plaintiffs, on the one hand, and defendants in non-class civil suits on the other. Any plaintiff may consent to jurisdiction. Keeton v. Hustler Magazine, Inc., 465 U.S. 770, 104 S.Ct. 1473, 79 L.Ed.2d 790 (1984). The essential question, then, is how stringent the requirement for a showing of consent will be.

We think that the procedure followed by Kansas, where a fully descriptive notice is sent first-class mail to each class member, with an explanation of the right to "opt out," satisfies due process. Requiring a plaintiff to affirmatively request inclusion would probably impede the prosecution of those class actions involving an aggregation of small individual claims, where a large number of claims are required to make it economical to bring suit. See, e.g., Eisen, supra, 417 U.S., at 161, 94 S.Ct., at 2144. The plaintiff's claim may be so small, or the plaintiff so unfamiliar with the law, that he would not file suit individually, nor would he affirmatively request inclusion in the class if such a request were required by the Constitution.[4] If, on the other hand, the plain-

---

3. Our holding today is limited to those class actions which seek to bind known plaintiffs concerning claims wholly or predominantly for money judgments. We intimate no view concerning other types of class action lawsuits, such as those seeking equitable relief. Nor, of course, does our discussion of personal jurisdiction address class actions where the jurisdiction is asserted against a *defendant* class.

4. In this regard the Reporter for the 1966 amendments to the Federal Rules of Civil Procedure stated,

"[R]equiring the individuals affirmatively to request inclusion in the lawsuit

tiff's claim is sufficiently large or important that he wishes to litigate it on his own, he will likely have retained an attorney or have thought about filing suit, and should be fully capable of exercising his right to "opt out."

In this case over 3,400 members of the potential class did "opt out," which belies the contention that "opt out" procedures result in guaranteed jurisdiction by inertia. Another 1,500 were excluded because the notice and "opt out" form was undeliverable. We think that such results show that the "opt out" procedure provided by Kansas is by no means *pro forma*, and that the Constitution does not require more to protect what must be the somewhat rare species of class member who is unwilling to execute an "opt out" form, but whose claim is nonetheless so important that he cannot be presumed to consent to being a member of the class by his failure to do so. Petitioner's "opt in" requirement would require the invalidation of scores of state statutes and of the class-action provision of the Federal Rules of Civil Procedure,[5] and for the reasons stated we do not think that the Constitution requires the State to sacrifice the obvious advantages in judicial efficiency resulting from the "opt out" approach for the protection of the *rara avis* portrayed by petitioner.

We therefore hold that the protection afforded the plaintiff class members by the Kansas statute satisfies the Due Process Clause. The interests of the absent plaintiffs are sufficiently protected by the forum State when those plaintiffs are provided with a request for exclusion that can be returned within a reasonable time to the court. See Insurance Corp. of Ireland, 456 U.S., at 702–703, and n. 10, 102 S.Ct., at 2104–2105, and n. 10. Both the Kansas trial court and the Supreme Court of Kansas held that the class received adequate representation, and no party disputes that conclusion here. We conclude that the Kansas court properly asserted personal jurisdiction over the absent plaintiffs and their claims against petitioner.

---

would result in freezing out the claims of people—especially small claims held by small people—who for one reason or another, ignorance, timidity, unfamiliarity with business or legal matters, will simply not take the affirmative step." Kaplan, Continuing Work of the Civil Committee: 1966 Amendments of the Federal Rules of Civil Procedure (1), 81 Harv.L.Rev. 356, 397–398 (1967).

5. The following statutes permit "opt out" notice in some types of class actions.

Fed.Rule Civ.Proc. 23(c)(2)(A); Ala.Rule Civ.Proc. 23(c)(2)(A); Alaska Rule Civ.Proc. 23(c)(2)(A); Ariz.Rule Civ.Proc. 23(c)(2)(A); Cal.Civ.Code Ann. § 1781(e)(1) (West 1973) (consumer class action); Colo.Rule Civ. Proc. 23(c)(2)(A); Del.Ch.Ct.Rule 23(c)(2)(A); D.C.Super.Ct.Rule Civ.Proc. 23(c)(2)(A); Fla.Rule Civ.Proc. 1.220(d)(2)(A); Idaho Rule Civ.Proc. 23(c)(2)(A); Ind.Rule Trial Proc. 23(C)(2)(a); Iowa Rule Civ.Proc. 42.1–8(b); Kan.Stat.Ann. § 60–223(c)(2) (1983); Ky.Rule Civ.Proc. 23.–03(2)(a); Me.Rule Civ.Proc. 23(c)(2)(A); Md.Rule Civ.Proc. 2–231(3)(1); Mich.Ct.Rule 3.501(C)(5)(b); Minn.Rule Civ.Proc. 23.03(2)(A); Mo.Rule Civ.Proc. 52.08; Mont.Rule Civ.Proc. 23(c)(2)(A); Nev.Rule Civ.Proc. 23(c)(2)(A); N.J. Civ.Prac.Rule 4:32–2; N.Y.Civ.Prac.Law § 904 (McKinney 1976); N.D.Rule Civ. Proc. 23(g)(2)(B); Ohio Rule Civ.Proc. 23(C)(2)(a); Okla.Stat., Tit. 12, § 2023(C)(2)(a) (Supp.1984–1985); Ore.Rule Civ.Proc. 32F(1)(b)(ii); Pa.Rule Civ.Proc. 1711(a); Tenn.Rule Civ.Proc. 23.03(2)(a); Vt.Rule Civ.Proc. 23(c)(2)(A); Wash.Ct.Rule 23(c)(2)(i); Wyo.Rule Civ.Proc. 23(c)(2)(A).

III

The Kansas courts applied Kansas contract and Kansas equity law to every claim in this case, notwithstanding that over 99% of the gas leases and some 97% of the plaintiffs in the case had no apparent connection to the State of Kansas except for this lawsuit. Petitioner protested that the Kansas courts should apply the laws of the States where the leases were located, or at least apply Texas and Oklahoma law because so many of the leases came from those States. The Kansas courts disregarded this contention and found petitioner liable for interest on the suspended royalties as a matter of Kansas law, and set the interest rates under Kansas equity principles. . . .

Kansas must have a "significant contact or aggregation of contacts" to the claims asserted by each member of the plaintiff class, contacts "creating state interests" in order to ensure that the choice of Kansas law is not arbitrary or unfair. . . . [Allstate Ins. Co. v. Hague, 449 U.S. 302, 312–13, 101 S.Ct. 633, 639–40 (1981).] Given Kansas' lack of "interest" in claims unrelated to that State, and the substantive conflict with jurisdictions such as Texas, we conclude that application of Kansas law to every claim in this case is sufficiently arbitrary and unfair as to exceed constitutional limits.

* * *

Here the Supreme Court of Kansas took the view that in a nationwide class action where procedural due process guarantees of notice and adequate representation were met, "the laws of the forum should be applied unless compelling reasons exist for applying a different law." 235 Kan. at 221, 679 P.2d at 1181. Whatever practical reasons may have commended this rule to the Supreme Court of Kansas, for the reasons already stated we do not believe that it is consistent with the decisions of this Court. We make no effort to determine for ourselves which law must apply to the various transactions involved in this lawsuit, and we reaffirm our observation in *Allstate* that in many situations a state court may be free to apply one of several choices of law. But the constitutional limitations laid down in cases such as Allstate and Home Insurance Co. v. Dick, [281 U.S. 397, 50 S.Ct. 338, 74 L.Ed. 926 (1930)], must be respected even in a nationwide class action.

We therefore affirm the judgment of the Supreme Court of Kansas insofar as it upheld the jurisdiction of the Kansas courts over the plaintiff class members in this case, and reverse its judgment insofar as it held that Kansas law was applicable to all of the transactions which it sought to adjudicate. We remand the case to that Court for further proceedings not inconsistent with this opinion.

It is so ordered.

JUSTICE POWELL took no part in the decision of this case.

[JUSTICE STEVENS concurred in Parts I and II but dissented from Part III of the Court's opinion on the ground that there were insufficient dissimilarities between the laws of Kansas and the other interested states to invoke either Due Process or Full Faith and Credit as a bar to the Kansas forum's application of its own law to all the claims. His opinion is omitted here.]

NOTES

(1) There have been a few attempts to certify a defendant class action. Would the logic of *Phillips Petroleum,* which relies in part on the notion that adequate representation is a substitute for personal jurisdiction, apply to such a class? Should such classes be certified? See, e.g., Henson v. East Lincoln Township, 814 F.2d 410 (7th Cir.), cert. granted, 484 U.S. 923, 108 S.Ct. 283, 98 L.Ed.2d 244 (1987); La Mar v. H & B Novelty & Loan Co., 489 F.2d 461 (9th Cir. 1973); Comment, Defendant Class Actions and Federal Civil Rights Litigation, 33 U.C.L.A. L.Rev. 283 (1985); Note, Certification of Defendant Classes Under Rule 23(b)(2), 84 Colum.L.Rev. 1371 (1985). See also Breland v. Aetna Casualty & Surety, 85 Bankr. 373 (D.C.Va.1988), discussed in p. 503, Note (5) supra, where an impleaded party (the defendant's insurer) attempted to have a class of plaintiffs involuntarily certified.

(2) To what extent is the result in the principal case dependent on the ability of the plaintiffs to opt out? Does the result apply to cases in which notice is not required by either the statute or the court? To actions where opting out is not possible? See In re Real Estate Title and Settlement Services Antitrust Litigation, 869 F.2d 760 (3d Cir.1989). That case also raises the question whether the personal jurisdiction considerations that apply to state courts also apply to federal courts. Should Rule 23 be read as supplying a basis for the court's in personam adjudicatory authority over absent class members? Could Congress constitutionally provide for national adjudicatory authority in class actions? See Fullerton, Constitutional Limits on Nationwide Personal Jurisdiction in the Federal Courts, 79 Nw.L.Rev. 1 (1984).

(3) In what other areas are class actions seeking monetary relief likely to be attractive? In mass accident cases? See Weinstein, Revision of Procedure: Some Problems in Class Actions, 9 Buff.L.Rev. 433, 469 (1960):

"Theoretically, the rule proposed . . . for New York, . . . could be utilized in negligence cases. There are, however, serious objections to using class actions where an accident has resulted in injury to many persons. The economics of the contingent fee in tort litigation—and settlement practices of public insurers and self-insurers—today insures effective legal service for any injured person who wants a lawyer. Permitting a class action would create an unseemly rush to bring the first case and provide, through notice to all injured persons, a kind of legalized ambulance chasing. As a matter of practice, disasters usually do not result in a large number of separate trials. Cases are referred to specialist attorneys who represent a number of the parties, actions are consolidated, and settlement negotiations dispose of most claims. Where insurance coverage and assets of the defendant are less than prospective recoveries, the pressure to cooperate in settlement negotiations is too great to resist. Both the plaintiff's bar and defendant's bar in the negligence field are so closely knit that, as a practical matter, they can informally provide most of the advantages of class actions. Our courts are certainly aware of the realities of negligence litigation today. As in other kinds of actions, some assurance may be placed on their not permitting unnecessary use of class actions."

In cases involving franchise operations? See Siegel v. Chicken Delight, Inc., 271 F.Supp. 722 (N.D.Cal.1967). In civil rights cases?

5. VENUE

The venue issue in class actions has been noncontroversial and easy to apply, for courts have tested venue by looking only to the residence of the named representatives, not the entire class. See 7A Wright, Miller & Kane, Federal Practice and Procedure: Civ. § 1757 (1986).

C. SPECIAL PROBLEMS IN CLASS ACTIONS

1. STATUTE OF LIMITATIONS

AMERICAN PIPE & CONSTRUCTION CO. v. UTAH, 414 U.S. 538, 552–53, 94 S.Ct. 756, 765–66, 38 L.Ed.2d 713 (1974): In this case, a suit under federal antitrust laws had been commenced as a class action before, but denied class action status after, the running of the statute of limitations. Members of the potential class thereupon sought intervention. To the plea that the statute of limitations had run, the Court held "that in this posture, at least where class action status has been denied solely because of failure to demonstrate that 'the class is so numerous that joinder of all members is impracticable,' the commencement of the original class suit tolls the running of the statute for all purported members of the class who make timely motions to intervene after the court has found the suit inappropriate for class action status.

. . .

"A contrary rule allowing participation only by those potential members of the class who had earlier filed motions to intervene in the suit would deprive Rule 23 class actions of the efficiency and economy of litigation which is a principal purpose of the procedure. Potential class members would be induced to file protective motions to intervene or to join in the event that a class was later found unsuitable."

NOTE

In Crown, Cork & Seal Co., Inc. v. Parker, 462 U.S. 345, 103 S.Ct. 2392, 76 L.Ed.2d 628 (1983), the Court held that the rule of *American Pipe* was not limited to intervenors and tolls the statute of limitations also for putative class members who file actions of their own after the denial of class action status. See also Chardon v. Soto, 462 U.S. 650, 103 S.Ct. 2611, 77 L.Ed.2d 74 (1983) (under federal law "borrowing" state statute of limitations, question whether running of the limitations period is merely suspended or begins to run anew after denial of class action status is also governed by state law).

As to the timeliness of intervention by a putative class member in order to appeal the denial of class certification, see United Airlines, Inc. v. McDonald, 432 U.S. 385, 97 S.Ct. 2464, 53 L.Ed.2d 423 (1977).

2. Mootness

UNITED STATES PAROLE COMMISSION v. GERAGHTY

Supreme Court of the United States, 1980.
445 U.S. 388, 100 S.Ct. 1202, 63 L.Ed.2d 479.

MR. JUSTICE BLACKMUN delivered the opinion of the Court.*

This case raises the question whether a trial court's denial of a motion for certification of a class may be reviewed on appeal after the named plaintiff's personal claim has become "moot." The United States Court of Appeals for the Third Circuit held that a named plaintiff, respondent here, who brought a class action challenging the validity of the United States Parole Commission's Parole Release Guidelines, could continue his appeal of a ruling denying class certification even though he had been released from prison while the appeal was pending. We granted certiorari, 440 U.S. 945, 99 S.Ct. 1420, 59 L.Ed.2d 632 (1979), to consider this issue of substantial significance, under Art. III of the Constitution, to class-action litigation, and to resolve the conflict in approach among the Courts of Appeals.

In 1973, the United States Parole Board adopted explicit Parole Release Guidelines for adult prisoners. These guidelines establish a "customary range" of confinement for various classes of offenders. The guidelines utilize a matrix, which combines a "parole prognosis" score (based on the prisoner's age at first conviction, employment background, and other personal factors) and an "offense severity" rating, to yield the "customary" time to be served in prison.

Subsequently, in 1976, Congress enacted the Parole Commission and Reorganization Act (PCRA), Pub.L. 94–233, 90 Stat. 219, 18 U.S.C. §§ 4201–4218. This Act provided the first legislative authorization for parole release guidelines. It required the newly created Parole Commission to "promulgate rules and regulations establishing guidelines for the powe[r] . . . to grant or deny an application or recommendation to parole any eligible prisoner." § 4203. Before releasing a prisoner on parole, the Commission must find, "upon consideration of the nature and circumstances of the offense and the history and characteristics of the prisoner," that release "would not depreciate the seriousness of his offense or promote disrespect for the law" and that it "would not jeopardize the public welfare." § 4206(a).

Respondent John M. Geraghty was convicted in the United States District Court for the Northern District of Illinois of conspiracy to commit extortion, in violation of 18 U.S.C. § 1951, and of making false material declarations to a grand jury, in violation of 18 U.S.C. § 1623 (1976 ed. and Supp. II). On January 25, 1974, two months after initial

* Footnotes omitted.

promulgation of the release guidelines, respondent was sentenced to concurrent prison terms of four years on the conspiracy count and one year on the false declarations count. . . .

Geraghty later, pursuant to a motion under Federal Rule of Criminal Procedure 35, obtained from the District Court a reduction of his sentence to 30 months. The court granted the motion because, in the court's view, application of the guidelines would frustrate the sentencing judge's intent with respect to the length of time Geraghty would serve in prison. . . .

Geraghty then applied for release on parole. His first application was denied in January 1976 with the following explanation:

> "Your offense behavior has been rated as very high severity. You have a salient factor score of 11. You have been in custody for a total of 4 months. Guidelines established by the Board for adult cases which consider the above factors indicate a range of 26–36 months to be served before release for cases with good institutional program performance and adjustment. After review of all relevant factors and information presented, it is found that a decision at this consideration outside the guidelines does not appear warranted." App. 5.

If the customary release date applicable to respondent under the guidelines were adhered to, he would not be paroled before serving his entire sentence minus good-time credits. Geraghty applied for parole again in June 1976; that application was denied for the same reasons. He then instituted this civil suit as a class action in the United States District Court for the District of Columbia, challenging the guidelines as inconsistent with the PCRA and the Constitution, and questioning the procedures by which the guidelines were applied to his case.

Respondent sought certification of a class of "all federal prisoners who are or will become eligible for release on parole." . . .

The District Court . . . denied Geraghty's request for class certification . . . It found class certification inappropriate because Geraghty raised certain individual issues and, inasmuch as some prisoners might be benefited by the guidelines, because his claims were not typical of the entire proposed class. 429 F.Supp., at 740–741. . . .

Respondent, individually "and on behalf of a class," appealed to the United States Court of Appeals for the Third Circuit. App. 29. . . .

On June 30, 1977, before any brief had been filed in the Court of Appeals, Geraghty was mandatorily released from prison; he had served 22 months of his sentence, and had earned good-time credits for the rest. Petitioners then moved to dismiss the appeals as moot. . . .

The Court of Appeals, concluding that the litigation was not moot, reversed the judgment of the District Court and remanded the case for further proceedings. 579 F.2d 238 (CA3 1978). If a class had been certified by the District Court, mootness of respondent Geraghty's personal claim would not have rendered the controversy moot. See e.g., Sosna v. Iowa, 419 U.S. 393, 95 S.Ct. 553, 42 L.Ed.2d 532 (1975). The Court of Appeals reasoned that an erroneous *denial* of a class certification should not lead to the opposite result. 579 F.2d, at 248–252. Rather, certification of a "certifiable" class, that erroneously had been denied, relates back to the original denial and thus preserves jurisdiction. Ibid.

On the question whether certification erroneously had been denied . . . the Court of Appeals reversed the denial of class certification and remanded the case to the District Court for an initial evaluation of the proper subclasses. . . .

      *   *   *

Article III of the Constitution limits federal "Judicial Power," that is, federal-court jurisdiction, to "Cases" and "Controversies." This case-or-controversy limitation serves "two complementary" purposes. Flast v. Cohen, 392 U.S. 83, 95, 88 S.Ct. 1942, 1949, 20 L.Ed.2d 947 (1968). It limits the business of federal courts to "questions presented in an adversary context and in a form historically viewed as capable of resolution through the judicial process," and it defines the "role assigned to the judiciary in a tripartite allocation of power to assure that the federal courts will not intrude into areas committed to the other branches of government." Ibid. Likewise, mootness has two aspects: "when the issues presented are no longer 'live' or the parties lack a legally cognizable interest in the outcome." Powell v. McCormack, 395 U.S. 486, 496, 89 S.Ct. 1944, 1951, 23 L.Ed.2d 491 (1969).

It is clear that the controversy over the validity of the Parole Release Guidelines is still a "live" one between petitioners and at least some members of the class respondent seeks to represent. This is demonstrated by the fact that prisoners currently affected by the guidelines have moved to be substituted, or to intervene, as "named" respondents in this Court. We therefore are concerned here with the second aspect of mootness, that is, the parties' interest in the litigation. The Court has referred to this concept as the "personal stake" requirement. . . .

      *   *   *

On several occasions the Court has considered the application of the "personal stake" requirement in the class-action context. In Sosna v. Iowa, 419 U.S. 393, 95 S.Ct. 553, 42 L.Ed.2d 532 (1975), it held that mootness of the named plaintiff's individual claim *after* a class has been duly certified does not render the action moot. It reasoned that "even though appellees . . . might not again enforce the Iowa durational residency requirement against [the class representative], it is clear that they will enforce it against those persons in the class that appellant sought to represent and that the District Court certified." Id., at 400, 95 S.Ct., at 557, 558. The Court stated specifically that an Art. III case or controversy "may exist . . . between a named defendant and a member of the class represented by the named plaintiff, even though the claim of the named plaintiff has become moot." Id., at 402, 95 S.Ct., at 559.

Although one might argue that *Sosna* contains at least an implication that the critical factor for Art. III purposes is the timing of class certification, other cases, applying a "relation back" approach, clearly demonstrate that timing is not crucial. When the claim on the merits is "capable of repetition, yet evading review," the named plaintiff may litigate the class certification issue despite loss of his personal stake in the outcome of the litigation. E.g., Gerstein v. Pugh, 420 U.S. 103, 110, n. 11, 95 S.Ct. 854, 861, n. 11, 43 L.Ed.2d 54 (1975). . . .

. . . Some claims are so inherently transitory that the trial court will not have even enough time to rule on a motion for class certification before the proposed representative's individual interest expires. The Court considered this possibility in Gerstein v. Pugh, 420 U.S., at 110, n. 11, 95 S.Ct., at 861 n. 11. *Gerstein* was an action challenging pretrial detention conditions. The Court assumed that the named plaintiffs were no longer in custody awaiting trial at the time the trial court certified a class of pretrial detainees. There was no indication that the particular named plaintiffs might again be subject to pretrial detention. Nonetheless, the case was held not to be moot because:

> "The length of pretrial custody cannot be ascertained at the outset, and it may be ended at any time by release on recognizance, dismissal of the charges, or a guilty plea, as well as by acquittal or conviction after trial. It is by no means certain that any given individual, named as plaintiff, would be in pretrial custody long enough for a district judge to certify the class. Moreover, in this case the constant existence of a class of persons suffering the deprivation is certain. The attorney representing the named respondents is a public defender, and we can safely assume that he has other clients with a continuing live interest in the case." Ibid.

See also Sosna v. Iowa, 419 U.S., at 402, n. 11, 95 S.Ct., at 861, n. 11.

In two different contexts the Court has stated that the proposed class representative who proceeds to a judgment on the merits may appeal *denial* of class certification. First, this assumption was "an important ingredient," Deposit Guaranty Nat. Bank v. Roper, 445 U.S., at 338, 100 S.Ct., at 1173, in the rejection of interlocutory appeals, "as of right," of class certification denials. Coopers & Lybrand v. Livesay, 437 U.S. 463, 469, 470, n. 15, 98 S.Ct. 2454, 2459 n. 15, 57 L.Ed.2d 351 (1978). The Court reasoned that denial of class status will not necessarily be the "death knell" of a small-claimant action, since there still remains "the prospect of prevailing on the merits and reversing an order denying class certification." Ibid.

Second, in United Airlines, Inc. v. McDonald, 432 U.S. 385, 393–395, 97 S.Ct. 2464, 2469–2471, 53 L.Ed.2d 423 (1977), the Court held that a putative class member may intervene, for the purpose of appealing the denial of a class certification motion, after the named plaintiffs' claims have been satisfied and judgment entered in their favor. Underlying that decision was the view that "refusal to certify was subject to appellate review after final judgment at the behest of the named plaintiffs." Id., at 393, 97 S.Ct., at 2469. And today, the Court holds that named plaintiffs whose claims are satisfied through entry of judgment over their objections may appeal the denial of a class certification ruling. Deposit Guaranty Nat. Bank v. Roper, 445 U.S. 326, 100 S.Ct. 1166, 63 L.Ed.2d 427.

Gerstein, McDonald, and *Roper* are all examples of cases found not to be moot, despite the loss of a "personal stake" in the merits of the litigation by the proposed class representative. The interest of the named plaintiffs in *Gerstein* was precisely the same as that of Geraghty here. Similarly, after judgment had been entered in their favor, the named plaintiffs in *McDonald* had no continuing narrow personal stake in the outcome of the class claims. And in *Roper* the Court points out that an individual controversy is rendered moot, in the strict Art. III sense, by payment and satisfaction of a final judgment. 445 U.S., at 333, 100 S.Ct., at 1171.

These cases demonstrate the flexible character of the Art. III mootness doctrine. . . .

* * *

. . . [T]he fact that a named plaintiff's substantive claims are mooted due to an occurrence other than a judgment on the merits does not mean that all the other issues in the case are mooted. A plaintiff who brings a class action presents two separate issues for judicial resolution. One is the claim on the merits; the other is the claim that he is entitled to represent a class. "The denial of class certification stands as an adjudication of one of the issues litigated," *Roper,* 445 U.S., at 336, 100 S.Ct., at 1172. We think that in determining whether the plaintiff may continue to press the class certification claim, after the claim on the merits "expires," we must look to the nature of the "personal stake" in the class certification claim. Determining Art. III's "uncertain and shifting contours," see Flast v. Cohen, 392 U.S., at 97, 88 S.Ct., at 1951, with respect to nontraditional forms of litigation, such as the class action, requires reference to the purposes of the case-or-controversy requirement.

Application of the personal-stake requirement to a procedural claim, such as the right to represent a class, is not automatic or readily resolved. A "legally cognizable interest," as the Court described it in Powell v. McCormack, 395 U.S., at 496, 89 S.Ct., at 1950, in the traditional sense rarely ever exists with respect to the class certification claim. The justifications that led to the development of the class action include the protection of the defendant from inconsistent obligations, the protection of the interests of absentees, the provision of a convenient and economical means for disposing of similar lawsuits, and the facilitation of the spreading of litigation costs among numerous litigants with similar claims. See, e.g., Advisory Committee Notes on Fed.Rule Civ.Proc. 23, 28 U.S.C.App., pp. 427–429; Note, Developments in the Law, Class Actions, 89 Harv.L.Rev. 1318, 1321–1323, 1329–1330

(1976). Although the named representative receives certain benefits from the class nature of the action, some of which are regarded as desirable and others as less so, these benefits generally are byproducts of the class-action device. In order to achieve the primary benefits of class suits, the Federal Rules of Civil Procedure give the proposed class representative the right to have a class certified if the requirements of the Rules are met. This "right" is more analogous to the private attorney general concept than to the type of interest traditionally thought to satisfy the "personal stake" requirement. See *Roper*, 445 U.S., at 338, 100 S.Ct., at 1173–1174.

As noted above, the purpose of the "personal stake" requirement is to assure that the case is in a form capable of judicial resolution. The imperatives of a dispute capable of judicial resolution are sharply presented issues in a concrete factual setting and self-interested parties vigorously advocating opposing positions. Franks v. Bowman Transportation Co., 424 U.S., at 753–756, 96 S.Ct., at 1253–1260; Baker v. Carr, 369 U.S., at 204, 82 S.Ct., at 703; Poe v. Ullman, 367 U.S., at 503, 81 S.Ct., at 1755 (plurality opinion). We conclude that these elements can exist with respect to the class certification issue notwithstanding the fact that the named plaintiff's claim on the merits has expired. The question whether class certification is appropriate remains as a concrete, sharply presented issue. In Sosna v. Iowa it was recognized that a named plaintiff whose claim on the merits expires *after* class certification may still adequately represent the class. Implicit in that decision was the determination that vigorous advocacy can be assured through means other than the traditional requirement of a "personal stake in the outcome." Respondent here continues vigorously to advocate his right to have a class certified.

We therefore hold that an action brought on behalf of a class does not become moot upon expiration of the named plaintiff's substantive claim, even though class certification has been denied. The proposed representative retains a "personal stake" in obtaining class certification sufficient to assure that Art. III values are not undermined. If the appeal results in reversal of the class certification denial, and a class subsequently is properly certified, the merits of the class claim then may be adjudicated pursuant to the holding in *Sosna*.

Our holding is limited to the appeal of the denial of the class certification motion. A named plaintiff whose claim expires may not continue to press the appeal on the merits until a class has been properly certified. See *Roper*, 445 U.S., at 336–337, 100 S.Ct., at 1173. If, on appeal, it is determined that class certification properly was denied, the claim on the merits must be dismissed as moot.

Our conclusion that the controversy here is not moot does not automatically establish that the named plaintiff is entitled to continue litigating the interests of the class. "[I]t does shift the focus of examination from the elements of justiciability to the ability of the named representative to 'fairly and adequately protect the interests of the class.' Rule 23(a)." Sosna v. Iowa, 419 U.S., at 403, 95 S.Ct., at 559. We hold only that a case or controversy still exists. The question of who is to represent the class is a separate issue.

We need not decide here whether Geraghty is a proper representative for the purpose of representing the class on the merits. No class as yet has been certified. Upon remand, the District Court can determine whether Geraghty may continue to press the class claims or whether another representative would be appropriate. We decide only that Geraghty was a proper representative for the purpose of appealing the ruling denying certification of the class that he initially defined. . . .

The judgment of the Court of Appeals is vacated, and the case is remanded for further proceedings consistent with this opinion.

[Dissenting opinion omitted]

NOTE

As to the appealability in general of orders granting or denying class action status, see Chapter 17.

3. ETHICAL PROBLEMS

May named parties and their counsel freely seek to communicate with other members of the class they represent? To what extent is their freedom in this regard constitutionally protected? See United Mine Workers v. State Bar of Illinois, p. 58, supra. The Board of Editors For the Manual for Complex and Multidistrict Litigation, in Bulletin No. 12 (1970), has recommended adoption of the following local rule:

> "In every potential and actual class action under Rule 23, F.R.Civ.P., all parties hereto and their counsel are hereby forbidden, directly or indirectly, orally or in writing, to communicate concerning such action with any potential or actual class member not a formal party to the action without the consent of and approval of the communication by order of the Court. Any such proposed communication shall be presented to the Court in writing with a designation of or description of all addresses and with a motion and proposed order for prior approval by the Court of the proposed communication and proposed addresses. The communications forbidden by this rule, include, but are not limited to, (a) solicitation directly or indirectly of legal representation of potential and actual class members who are not formal parties to the class action; (b) solicitation of fees and expenses and agreements to pay fees and expenses, from potential and actual class members who are not formal parties to the class action; (c) solicitation by formal parties to the class action of requests by class members to opt out in class actions under subparagraph (b)(3) of Rule 23, F.R.Civ.P.; and (d) communications from counsel or a party which may tend to misrepresent the status, purposes and

effects of the action, and of actual or potential Court orders therein, which may create impressions tending, without cause, to reflect adversely on any party, any counsel, the Court, or the administration of justice. The obligations and prohibitions of this rule are not exclusive. All other ethical, legal and equitable obligations are unaffected by this rule."

However, in Gulf Oil Co. v. Bernard, 452 U.S. 89, 101 S.Ct. 2193, 68 L.Ed.2d 693 (1981), the United States Supreme Court found a so-called "gag" order patterned on the one in the Manual for Complex Litigation to be an unconstitutional prior restraint on expression. The record failed to reveal any grounds on which the lower court's action was based and the order interfered with the class representatives' efforts to inform potential class members of the suit's existence and to obtain information about the merits of the case from the persons they sought to represent.

4. ATTORNEYS' FEES

LINDY BROTHERS BUILDERS, INC. OF PHILADELPHIA v. AMERICAN RADIATOR & STANDARD SANITARY CORP.

United States Court of Appeals, Third Circuit, 1973.
487 F.2d 161, opinion after remand 382 F.Supp. 999 (1974).

SEITZ, CHIEF JUDGE.* These appeals concern the award of attorneys' fees following the settlement of a class action. Two members of the class here involved, Friendswood Development Company and Humble Oil and Refining Company, appeal from the award of fees to attorneys Kohn and Berger and members of their law firms. Also before us is an appeal by attorneys of the firm of Thoma, Schoenthal, Davis, Hockenberg and Wine, who were denied fees. Kohn and Berger are attorneys for Lindy Bros. Builders and the Philadelphia Housing Authority, appellees in both appeals. We will deal first with the appeal of Friendswood and Humble.

Following the indictment of plumbing fixture manufacturers and their trade association for price-fixing violations of the antitrust laws, numerous civil suits were filed on behalf of several classes of plaintiffs seeking treble damages. One such class action was filed by appellees on behalf of builders and owners shortly after the indictments were returned. The various class actions were consolidated for pretrial proceedings and transferred to the Eastern District of Pennsylvania. Several years of procedural maneuvering followed between plaintiffs and defendants, who wanted the civil suits stayed or enjoined pending resolution of the criminal actions. During the stay proceedings, in which the plaintiffs eventually prevailed, the criminal action proceeded, and on May 2, 1969, a jury verdict was returned against those defendants who had pleaded not guilty. The schedule of depositions in

---

* Some footnotes omitted; others renumbered.

the civil suit was filed in June 1969, and the taking of depositions was to have begun in the fall of 1969.

In October 1969, settlement negotiations were undertaken, primarily by attorneys Kohn and Berger and their firms. The first settlement agreement involving the builder-owner class was reached early in 1970. As a result of the settlement agreement a single fund was created to satisfy the claims of all builder-owners, those who had not filed suit ("unrepresented" claimants) as well as those who had.[1] The district court gave preliminary approval to the settlement plan in May 1971, after the Supreme Court denied defendants' petition for certiorari to review this Court's affirmance of the criminal convictions. In its order preliminarily approving the settlement the district court appointed appellees as Class Representatives. The settlement was given final approval by the district court in April 1972.

At the time the district court gave final approval to the settlement, numerous attorneys petitioned for award of fees. Among these was a petition by Kohn and Berger as attorneys for the Class Representatives. Kohn and Berger had private fee agreements with the appellees and also with many other builder-owners who made claims against the fund. In their fee petition, Kohn and Berger asked for an award to be given to them directly in addition to the amounts to be received pursuant to contracts with individual claimants. For purposes of their petition, Kohn and Berger divided the class into four categories. The first category was composed of claimants who had contractual fee arrangements with Kohn and Berger. Kohn and Berger were to receive over $800,000 from these claimants. The second category included claimants who had filed suit and whose attorneys Kohn and Berger felt had contributed to the creation of the settlement fund. Kohn and Berger were to receive no fees from these claimants and sought none. Other claimants who had joined in the suits but whose attorneys Kohn and Berger concluded had not contributed to the creation of the settlement fund comprised the third category. From these claimants, who had contracted to pay varying fees to other attorneys, Kohn and Berger sought a fee award equal to one-sixth of the claimants' share of the settlement fund.[2] The final category was made up of builder-owners who filed claims against the fund, but who had not joined in the suit and, therefore, had not contracted with any attorney participating in the settlement negotiations or other related proceedings. Kohn and Berger asked the court to award them one-third of the amounts to be recovered by these last claimants.[3] The

1. At the time the court below ruled on petitions for attorneys' fees, the fund plus interest amounted to approximately $26 million.

2. At the time of the district court ruling on the fee petitions, the fees sought by Kohn and Berger from this category of claimants amounted to $745,733.

3. The fees Kohn and Berger asked of unrepresented claimants totalled nearly $2.3 million at the time of their fee petition, bringing the amount requested from the third and fourth categories to over $3 million.

petition was opposed by unrepresented claimants Friendswood Development Company and Humble Oil and Refining Company.

The district court, 341 F.Supp. 1077, denied Kohn and Berger's petition for fees from the third category of claimants and granted fees from the last category equal to 20% of the amount of the fund apportioned to the unrepresented claimants. Kohn and Berger have not appealed the denial of fees from claimants in category three nor the award of fees from unrepresented claimants in an amount less than requested.

Friendswood and Humble appeal from the award of fees out of the settlement apportioned to them and other unrepresented claimants.

Basis for Fee Awards

The first contention advanced by Friendswood and Humble is that the court below lacked authority to award any fees to Kohn and Berger. We assume that appellants are correct in stating that Section 4 of the Clayton Act, 15 U.S.C. § 15 (1970), does not authorize award of attorneys' fees to a plaintiff who has settled his antitrust action, rather than pursue it to successful judgment. Cf. Milgram v. Loew's, Inc., 192 F.2d 579 (3d Cir.1951), cert. den. 343 U.S. 929, 72 S.Ct. 762, 96 L.Ed. 1339 (1952); Decorative Stone Co. v. Building Trades Council, 23 F.2d 426 (2d Cir.), cert. den. 277 U.S. 594, 48 S.Ct. 530, 72 L.Ed. 1005 (1928). There is, however, authority for the award of fees under the general equitable powers of the court. E.g., Trustees v. Greenough, 105 U.S. 527, 26 L.Ed. 1157 (1882). These equitable powers may, under the equitable fund doctrine, be used to compensate individuals whose actions in commencing, pursuing or settling litigation, even if taken solely in their own name and for their own interest, benefit a class of persons not participating in the litigation. See Sprague v. Ticonic National Bank, 307 U.S. 161, 59 S.Ct. 777, 83 L.Ed. 1184 (1939).

     *   *   *

Standards Governing Fee Awards

In awarding attorneys' fees, the district judge is empowered to exercise his informed discretion, and any successful challenge to his determination must show that the judge abused that discretion. Tranberg v. Tranberg, 456 F.2d 173, 175 (3d Cir.1972). Appellants contend that, by failing to observe appropriate standards and procedures, the judge below did abuse his discretion in awarding fees to Kohn and Berger. Friendswood and Humble are correct in arguing that failure to adhere to proper standards and to follow appropriate procedures would constitute abuse of the district court's discretion to award attorneys' fees. We proceed, therefore, to an examination of appellants' claim that the standards applied below in awarding fees to Kohn and Berger were improper.

The district judge listed four factors that he considered in his award of fees to Kohn and Berger. These were: the percentage of a claimant's recovery awarded as attorneys' fees in other cases, the amount of the recovery from which fees were being awarded, the amount the attorneys received from their clients under private agreements, and the time spent by Kohn and Berger "in connection with this litigation." 341 F.Supp. 1077, 1089–1090 (E.D.Pa.1972). The court below elaborated on these considerations by noting that the percentage of a recovery awarded as attorneys' fees should decline as the amount of the recovery increased and that the time spent by the attorneys was not so important here as in most cases. The judge did not indicate why time was less important here, nor did he explain what use was made of his knowledge of Kohn and Berger's private fee agreements.

The mere listing of four factors for consideration by the court makes meaningful review difficult and gives little guidance to attorneys and claimants. In detailing the standards that should guide the award of fees to attorneys successfully concluding class suits, by judgment or settlement, we must start from the purpose of the award: to compensate the attorney for the reasonable value of services benefiting the unrepresented claimant. Before the value of the attorney's services can be determined, the district court must ascertain just what were those services. To this end the first inquiry of the court should be into the hours spent by the attorneys—how many hours were spent in what manner by which attorneys. It is not necessary to know the exact number of minutes spent nor the precise activity to which each hour was devoted nor the specific attainments of each attorney. But without some fairly definite information as to the hours devoted to various general activities, e.g., pretrial discovery, settlement negotiations, and the hours spent by various classes of attorneys, e.g., senior partners, junior partners, associates, the court cannot know the nature of the services for which compensation is sought.

Ascertaining, within appropriately specific categories, the time spent is only the first step the district court should follow in determining the proper attorneys' fees to be awarded. In light of the comments of the judge below, however, we wish to make clear its importance. In this case, partly as a result of the procedures employed by the district court, the only information furnished to the district judge regarding the time spent by Kohn, Berger and their associates was that they had spent "in excess of 6,000 hours in connection with this litigation." 341 F.Supp. at 1090. This information was insufficient to support the award of fees to Kohn and Berger.

After determining, as above, the services performed by the attorneys, the district court must attempt to value those services. In some cases it may be possible to identify the hours spent as having benefited the individual client, the unrepresented claimants, or both. Where this is feasible, the district judge may want to assess directly the value of the attorneys' services to the unrepresented claimants without first determining the overall value of the attorneys' services in the case. Here, it would seem artificial to segregate the attorneys' efforts into categories as aiding clients, unrepresented claimants or the entire class.

A single fund was created after negotiations on behalf of all claimants. Absent some contrary showing, we presume that all the attorneys' time contributed to the recoveries of each claimant. Where all of an attorney's services benefit the whole class, it seems simplest to determine the value of his services to the class and then to assess the extent to which the unrepresented claimants benefited from these services as compared with the rest of the class.

The value of an attorney's time generally is reflected in his normal billing rate. A logical beginning in valuing an attorney's services is to fix a reasonable hourly rate for his time—taking account of the attorney's legal reputation and status (partner, associate). Where several attorneys file a joint petition for fees, the court may find it necessary to use several different rates for the different attorneys. Similarly, the court may find that the reasonable rate of compensation differs for different activities.

Finding the reasonable hourly rate for each attorney does not end the court's inquiry into the value of the attorney's services. The court cannot properly fix attorneys' fees merely by multiplying the hourly rate for each attorney times the number of hours he worked on the case. Before discussing the other factors to be considered in fixing fees, we stress, however, the importance of deciding, in each case, the amount to which attorneys would be entitled on the basis of an hourly rate of compensation applied to the hours worked. This figure provides the only reasonably objective basis for valuing an attorney's services. As Judge Wyzanski observed a decade ago in a case similar to this:

> No one expects a lawyer to give his services at bargain rates in a civil matter on behalf of a client who is not impecunious. No one expects a lawyer whose compensation is contingent upon his success to charge, when successful, as little as he would charge a client who in advance had agreed to pay for his services, regardless of success. Nor, particularly in complicated cases producing large recoveries, is it just to make a fee depend solely on the reasonable amount of time expended. Yet unless time spent and skill displayed be used as a constant check on applications for fees there is a grave danger that the bar and bench will be brought into disrepute, and that there will be prejudice to those whose substantive interests are at stake and who are unrepresented except by the very lawyers who are seeking compensation. Cherner v. Transitron Electronic Corp., 221 F.Supp. 55, 61 (D.Mass.1963).

While the amount thus found to constitute reasonable compensation should be the lodestar of the court's fee determination, there are at least two other factors that must be taken into account in computing the value of attorneys' services. The first of these is the contingent nature of success; this factor is of special significance where, as here, the attorney has no private agreement that guarantees payment even if no recovery is obtained. In assessing the extent to which the attorneys' compensation should be increased to reflect the unlikelihood of success, the district court should consider any information that may help to establish the probability of success. The most important such information in a civil antitrust suit may be the progress of any criminal action brought against the defendants. Here, the United States had obtained indictments against all the defendants before the civil suits were filed; the defendants who pleaded not guilty had been convicted before serious settlement negotiations were begun; and those convictions were affirmed before the court gave final approval to the settlement. The court may find that the contingency was so slight or the amount found to constitute reasonable compensation for the hours worked was so large a proportion of the total recovery that an increased allowance for the contingent nature of the fee would be minimal.

The second additional factor the district court must consider is the extent, if any, to which the quality of an attorney's work mandates increasing or decreasing the amount to which the court has found the attorney reasonably entitled. In evaluating the quality of an attorney's work in a case, the district court should consider the complexity and novelty of the issues presented, the quality of the work that the judge has been able to observe, and the amount of the recovery obtained. This last factor may be the only means by which the quality of an attorney's performance can be judged where a suit is settled before any significant in-court proceedings. In making allowance for the quality of work, the court must keep in mind that the attorney will receive an otherwise reasonable compensation for his time under the figure arrived at from the hourly rate. Any increase or decrease in fees to adjust for the quality of work is designed to take account of an unusual degree of skill, be it unusually poor or unusually good. If the district judge determines that particular work was of a typical quality, he should, in increasing or decreasing the fee, be cognizant of the amount of time devoted to that given activity. Further, in increasing or decreasing an attorney's compensation, the district judge should set forth as specifically as possible the facts that support his conclusion, particularly where, as in this case, the judge determining the fees to be awarded did not sit in the case throughout the entire proceeding. The value to be placed on these additional factors will, of course, vary from . case to case. Often, however, their value will bear a reasonable relationship to the aggregate hourly compensation.

After determining the total reasonable value of an attorney's services in securing recovery of a fund for the class, the district court must determine what portion of the amount arrived at should be paid by the unrepresented claimants. Absent extraordinary circumstances, the unrepresented claimants should pay for the attorneys' services in proportion to their benefit from them—that is, the unrepresented claimants should pay a percentage of the reasonable value of the attorneys' services to the class equal to their percentage of the class' recovery. We reiterate that we are not here called upon to decide whether his private clients can require that all or part of the fees recovered by the attorney be applied against the fees charged those clients.

Procedure—Requirement of a Hearing

Friendswood and Humble contend that the district judge erred in failing to grant the requested evidentiary hearing before awarding fees. Had the district court been guided by the proper standards for setting attorneys' fees, the necessity of an evidentiary hearing would have been apparent. In determining the amount of time spent by various attorneys on different activities, the standard billing rate appropriate for each attorney, the extent of the contingency, and the degree to which an attorney's efforts advanced the interests of claimants from whom he seeks fees, the district judge must possess a great deal of information not presented below. Much of the evidence on which the judge will base his award or denial of fees may be disputed; the evidence presented by an attorney petitioning for fees may be incomplete. The denial of fees obviously harms the petitioning attorney. Just as obviously, award of attorneys' fees harms the unrepresented claimant by reducing his net recovery. These opposing interests should be afforded a hearing to provide an evidentiary basis for resolution of disputed factual matters and to allow the parties to supplement possibly incomplete statements of opposing parties.

* * *

We conclude that the failure of the district court to hold an evidentiary hearing and its failure to follow proper standards in awarding fees to attorneys Kohn and Berger were inconsistent with the sound exercise of discretion.

The Thoma Petition

Of the attorneys whose petitions for fees were denied, only one group has appealed. These attorneys are members of the firm of Thoma, Schoenthal, Davis, Hockenberg and Wine (hereinafter "Thoma"). In denying the Thoma petition, which asked for $17,646, the district court did not hold an evidentiary hearing nor was it guided by the standards set forth above. We hold that the denial of the Thoma petition was inconsistent with the sound exercise of discretion.

The orders granting attorneys' fees to Kohn and Berger and denying fees to the Thoma attorneys are vacated and the matters remanded to the district court for further proceedings consistent with this opinion.

NOTE

(1) See also Boeing Co. v. Van Gemert, 444 U.S. 472, 100 S.Ct. 745, 62 L.Ed. 2d 676 (1980); Comment, Attorneys' Fees in Individual and Class Action Antitrust Litigation, 60 Calif.L.Rev. 1656 (1972). On the award of attorneys' fees generally, see Chapters 2 and 3. See also 7B Wright, Miller & Kane, Federal Practice and Procedure: Civil § 1803 (1986).

(2) In class actions that settle for money damages, the allocation of the fund between class members and their attorneys raises conflict-of-interest problems. See Kornhauser, Control of Conflicts of Interest in Class–Action Suits, 41 Pub.Choice 145 (1983).

5. DISTRIBUTION OF THE RECOVERY

IN RE "AGENT ORANGE" PRODUCT LIABILITY LITIGATION

United States District Court, Eastern District of New York, 1988.
689 F.Supp. 1250.

MEMORANDUM AND ORDER ON DISTRIBUTION ON REMAND

WEINSTEIN, DISTRICT JUDGE.*

* * *

After three and a half years of appeals, the distribution of the settlement fund is at hand. The court regrets any inconvenience or harm suffered by members of the class as a result of the delays caused by the legal process. Detailed consideration of the issues raised by the lawyers for plaintiffs on appeal was necessary to ensure fairness to members of the class and to their attorneys, and to guarantee compliance with the law in unique and highly complex circumstances.

* * *

I. PROCEDURAL HISTORY

[In the first part of the opinion, the court reviews the extensive history of this litigation, including the decision to certify the class, the order settling the action, and the granting of summary judgment against claimants who opted out. These decisions were appealed and affirmed (with some modifications) by the Second Circuit, and certiorari was denied by the Supreme Court. The court continues as follows:]

The original total settlement was $180 million. Since that time, the funds have been held by the Clerk of the Court for the Eastern District of New York, and additional interest has been earned, bringing the total to approximately $240 million on June 30, 1988.

* * *

Following the April 1987 opinions of the court of appeals, this court held a public hearing on distribution on May 26, 1987. Members of the bar, individual class members, representatives of veterans' organizations, and others participated.

Beginning in September of 1987, the court convened a representative Class Assistance Advisory Board to advise the court on the best ways to allocate the monies originally designated for the Foundation. . . . In addition, a second group of veterans met repeatedly over a

* Footnotes omitted. This opinion has been vigorously edited and is included to give you a sense of the magnitude of the task of administering the Agent Orange recovery.

number of years with Special Masters Kenneth Feinberg and Richard Davis to consider the details of the Payment Program. [The court names the members of the Boards and provides short biographies].

. . .

This order is based upon the court's hearings, on its oral consultations with the assembled Advisory Boards, and on the communications it has received in writing. It sets out the manner in which the settlement fund is to be allocated. The court urges all those in a position to do so to assist it in expediting payments to members of the class.

II. SUMMARY OF ALLOCATION OF FUNDS

General principles and specific suggestions for distribution were put forward at the 1984 Fairness Hearings. . . . The court held an additional hearing on distribution on May 26, 1987, shortly after the court of appeals' nine decisions were announced. The court has convened the two Advisory Boards composed of veterans mentioned above, and has worked with those boards, with the Special Masters, and with numerous advisors to design a distribution plan that will simultaneously meet the needs of the class and comport with legal policy as determined by the court of appeals.

A. Original and Revised Payment Program

In May of 1985 the court issued an order directing distribution of approximately three-quarters of the fund (approximately $130 million of the original $180 million total) to a Payment Program which would compensate individual veterans and their family members in the form of disability benefits to 100% disabled veterans and payments of death benefits to the families of deceased veterans. See In re "Agent Orange" Product Liability Litigation, 611 F.Supp. 1396 (E.D.N.Y.1985), aff'd in part, rev'd in part, 818 F.2d 179 (2d Cir.1987). The Payment Program was designed to run for ten years, beginning January 1, 1985 and ending December 31, 1994.

The Payment Program was intended to provide annual payments to veterans for past and future continuous disabilities. Vietnam veterans exposed to Agent Orange who suffered total (100%) disabilities arising from non-traumatic, non-accidental and non-self-inflicted causes would be eligible for payments. See id., 611 F.Supp. at 1412. The definition of total disability was taken from the Social Security Act, and Social Security Administration determinations of disability would be taken as evidence of disability for the Agent Orange Payment Program. Independent determinations of disability would be made for veterans who had not obtained a Social Security ruling. See id. at 1412–13. Variation in the award would be based on age at the onset of disability, duration of disability, and the year of occurrence. Extension of the Payment program over a ten year period, beginning January 1, 1985, would permit the inclusion of veterans not disabled at the time the program began and would maximize the amount available for payment.

See id. at 1417–1422, aff'd in relevant part, 818 F.2d 179, 183–84 (2d Cir.1987). . . . The court estimated that the maximum disability award, for a veteran disabled in 1970 and continuously disabled through 1995, would be a total of $12,790.00, distributed over the ten years of the program. . . .

In addition, death benefits were to be paid in a lump sum to the surviving spouses or dependent children of veterans who died before the Payment Program began and, in lesser amounts, to survivors of veterans who die during the years of operation of the Payment Program. See id. at 611 F.Supp. 1420–22, aff'd in relevant part, 818 F.2d 179, 183–84 (2d Cir.1987). . . . In its 1985 order, the court estimated that the maximum death benefit, for families of veterans who died before 1985, would be approximately $3,400.00, paid in one lump sum. . . .

The court orders that the Payment Program now created will operate along the same standards for eligibility and methods of computing benefits as the program originally proposed [, as augmented by the interest earned in the interim.] . . .

B. Australian and New Zealand Class Members

The distribution plan allocated two percent of the fund (now approximately $240,000,000) for class members from Australia (1.8%) and New Zealand (0.2%). The percentage allocated to these veterans reflects the percent of exposed Vietnam veterans from the Australian and New Zealand armed forces. Australian members of the class will receive $4,500,000 U.S. and New Zealand veterans $500,000 U.S. These figures are rounded off to the next highest half million. [The Court set up trust funds to administer this plan.]

* * *

C. Class Assistance Program

The remainder of the fund, originally $45 million, was directed to the endowment of a Class Assistance Foundation "to fund projects and services that will benefit the entire class." In re "Agent Orange" Product Liability Litigation, 611 F.Supp. 1396, 1432 (E.D.N.Y.1985). The class includes all Vietnam veterans who may have been exposed to "Agent Orange" and related phenoxy herbicides in Vietnam, and the family members of such veterans. The class is therefore significantly larger than the group of people who have filed claims as part of the Payment Program. The Payment Program and the Foundation were designed in tandem to maximize the benefit to the class of a multimillion dollar fund that might otherwise degenerate into some quarter of a million small awards incapable of providing any real aid to any class member (amounting to only about $80 each).

* * *

A sum of $40 million plus interest earned from this date is immediately allocated to [this] portion of the program . . . [which is] devoted to service programs for the benefit of the entire class [including those who do not meet the eligibility requirements for other awards, children with birth defects born to class member veterans, and other members of the class who remain outside the mainstream of society.] This "Class Assistance Program" will be administered and monitored by the court. . . .

In addition, a fund of $10 million must, in accordance with the settlement agreement, be placed in reserve for a period of twenty-five years from the date of the settlement. The court will retain discretion over this reserve fund. Under the terms of the Settlement Agreement, this reserve will be used to cover possible claims in state courts. It will be available to compensate injured Vietnam veterans exposed to Agent Orange, should future evidence indicate a legally cognizable link between Agent Orange exposure and specific ailments. . . .

D. Attorneys' Fees and Expenses

The original total of allowed attorneys' fees and expenses was $10,767,443.63 plus interest accrued since the final judgment on June 18, 1985. . . .

The appeals have not appreciably increased the total fees awarded. Because of the elimination of the offset against Ashcraft & Gerel, the grand total of attorneys' fees and expenses is now $10,906,331.63, plus interest from June 18, 1985. The average rate of interest earned on the Agent Orange Settlement Fund is over 6.9%. To simplify computations, the clerk, in making payments to attorneys, shall add interest of 7% from June 18, 1985 (the date attorneys' fees were finally ordered) until July 1, 1988. See 611 F.Supp. 1329, 1346. The total payable as attorneys fees and expenses with interest will therefore be approximately $13,225,000.00. Even at the time of determination of the attorney fee awards in 1985, the settlement fund had already earned over $15,000,000.00 in interest—more than enough to pay the total fees and expenses allowed without impairing the original fund of $180,000,000.00. See 611 F.Supp. 1296, 1301.

Pursuant to the court's order, any counsel receiving a fee is deemed to waive any private contractual right to a fee; if such a private fee was received it must be returned to the client before payment is sought. See 611 F.Supp. 1318. If the client cannot be located, compliance by paying the fee into the court for the Agent Orange Fund or deducting the fee from the request for payment from the clerk will suffice.

* * *

E. Division of Funds

Summarizing these decisions, present funds are allocated as follows (rounded to the nearest million):

Purpose	Amounts
Death & Permanent Disability	$170,000,000
Class Assistance Program	52,000,000
Australian and New Zealand Trusts	5,000,000
Attorneys' Fees & Expenses with Interest	13,000,000
Total	$240,000,000

III. PAYMENT PROGRAM

A. INCLUSION OF OPT–OUT CLAIMANTS AND LATE CLAIMANTS

Under the terms of the court of appeals' affirmances, those plaintiffs who opted out of the class on the advice of counsel would be entitled to no recovery. . . . As of May 7, 1984, the date of the settlement, 2,440 requests for exclusion from the class had been received by the Clerk of the Court. See In re "Agent Orange" Product Liability Litigation, 597 F.Supp. 740, 756 (E.D.N.Y.1984). This is almost precisely one percent of the 244,162 timely filed claims.

* * *

In view of the special obligation of the court to veterans and their families, the court inquired of class members present at the May 26, 1987 hearing on implementation whether those who opted out should now "be permitted to opt in so they (or their families) can share equally with those who were their comrades-in-arms?" See Memorandum and Order dated April 23, 1987, No. MDL–381 (E.D.N.Y.1987). Unanimously, veterans, representatives of veterans' organizations, and the veterans' attorneys have answered this question in the affirmative. [The court goes on to make arrangements for notifying opt outs of the right to opt back in.]

* * *

Late claims filed before January 1, 1989 will also be accepted for inclusion within the class of claimants against the settlement fund. The equities with regard to late claims compellingly favor inclusion. The late claimants are class members who were eligible to file their claims but did not do so until after this court's May 28, 1985 order on distribution of the fund. . . .

The filing deadline for veterans who later learn of adverse health effects previously unknown to them remains 120 days from the date of discovery of the disability. See, e.g., In re "Agent Orange" Product Liability Litigation, 611 F.Supp. 1396, 1401 (E.D.N.Y.1985), aff'd in relevant part, 818 F.2d 179 (2d Cir.1987). Similarly, the deadline for claims filed by the survivors of veterans who later die is 120 days from the date of death. See id., 611 F.Supp. at 1417. Thus the cutoff date for filing a claim will be January 1, 1989, or 120 days after death or discovery of disability, whichever is later.

[In the remainder of the opinion, the court discusses administrative issues. It sets forth methods for determining who was exposed to Agent Orange (and is thus a member of the class), sets a 10 year time limit on the payment program, appoints a Claims Administrator and a Special Master for Appeals, and makes orders relative to other implementation problems, such as tax implications. The Court more fully describes the Assistance Program, to be administered by the court with the advice of the veterans Class Assistance Advisory Board, an Executive Director, staff, and consultants. Among the projects discussed are services to benefit the children and families of Vietnam veterans, an information-referral network, aid to homeless veterans, genetic counseling, legal aid, social work and counseling, employment assistance, substance abuse treatment, post-traumatic stress disorder treatment, and diverse local community assistance grants. Finally, the court makes detailed arrangements for financial management of the fund during the distribution process.]

NOTES

(1) State courts have also experimented with distribution methods. In Daar v. Yellow Cab Co., 67 Cal.2d 695, 63 Cal.Rptr. 724, 433 P.2d 732 (1967), a class action was brought to recover overcharges allegedly made to all users of defendant's taxi cabs during the four years preceding commencement of the action. The overcharges were alleged to result from an adjustment of the meters that caused them to register rates in excess of lawful amounts. Upon a finding of liability, the court determined that direct reimbursement to past users of the defendant's cabs would not be possible. Instead, the defendant was ordered to lower its rates for a specified period in the future. Was this "fluid recovery" a proper form of relief? Would this judgment preclude subsequent recovery by a member of the class who proved a greater overcharge?

For other procedures, see West Virginia v. Chas. Pfizer & Co., 440 F.2d 1079 (2d Cir.1971). See also Miller, Problems in Administering Judicial Relief in Class Actions Under Federal Rule 23(b)(3), 54 F.R.D. 501 (1972). What happens if individual claimants from various non-forum states do not come forward to claim their due? Do their claims escheat to the state and, if so, to which state? See Western Union Tel. Co. v. Commonwealth of Pennsylvania, 368 U.S. 71, 82 S.Ct. 199, 7 L.Ed.2d 139 (1961), Note 2, p. 500, supra; Texas v. New Jersey, 379 U.S. 674, 85 S.Ct. 626, 13 L.Ed.2d 596 (1965), supplemented 380 U.S. 518, 85 S.Ct. 1136, 14 L.Ed.2d 49, motion denied 381 U.S. 931, 85 S.Ct. 1762, 14 L.Ed.2d 698, motion denied 381 U.S. 948, 85 S.Ct. 1795, 14 L.Ed.2d 723.

(2) What about Judge Weinstein's willingness to allow veterans who opted out to enjoy the fruits of the settlement? Note that, under old Federal Rule 23, a member of a spurious class could intervene after judgment. Intervention after judgment was attractive, because a judgment in a spurious class action bound only the parties present in the action. By waiting until judgment, the class member could therefore have the best of two worlds: if the judgment was unfavorable, he was not bound; and if it was favorable, he could obtain its benefits by intervening after it had been rendered. See Union Carbide & Carbon Corp. v. Nisley, 300 F.2d 561 (10th Cir.1961). This form of one-way intervention came to an end when new Federal Rule 23 became effective. But what happens if a member of the class who was not properly notified seeks to intervene after judgment to participate in its benefits? Compare Pasquier v. Tarr, 318 F.Supp. 1350 (E.D.La.1970), affirmed 444 F.2d 116 (1971) with Schrader v. Selective Service System Local Board No. 76 of Wisconsin, 329 F.Supp. 966 (W.D.Wis.1971).

Given this history was it appropriate to allow the opt–outs back in?

(3) If an action is brought against the defendants in the principal case on behalf of a Vietnam veteran's handicapped child or grandchild, born after 1988, will the claim that the injury was caused by exposure to Agent Orange be barred by res judicata? Cf. Martin v. Wilks, ___ U.S. ___, 109 S.Ct. 2180, 104 L.Ed.2d 835 (1989), p. 971, infra.

(4) Distribution of monetary damages is not the only problem facing courts entertaining class actions. Class actions have been used to challenge the constitutionality of conditions in schools, hospitals, mental institutions, and prisons. When successful, these actions have resulted in federal courts taking over administrative responsibilities, sometimes for years. The courts appoint administrators, oversee placement, treatment and management of students, patients, and inmates, supervise employees, and in many cases, spend state funds. Is this the best use of judicial resources? Are the institutions thus administered better off managed by judges than by professional educators, doctors, and penologists? Is the class action a viable device for curing social problems? See Horowitz, Decreeing Organizational Change: Judicial Supervision of Public Institutions, 1983 Duke L.J. 1265; Chayes, The Role of the Judge in Public Law Litigation, 89 Harv.L.Rev. 1281 (1976).

6. DERIVATIVE ACTIONS

Derivative actions evolved in order to permit beneficiaries to safeguard their rights when the fiduciaries charged with the representation of their interests failed to do so. The most common example of such actions is a stockholders' derivative action. This is an unusual form of class action, since the rights of the stockholders in a derivative action are secondary and the recovery in such an action accrues to the benefit of the corporation. Under old Federal Rule 23, derivative actions were treated as part of the "true" class actions. Because of the different nature and distinctive aspects of these actions, the rule makers, when revising Federal Rule 23, decided to treat them in a separate rule, Fed. R.Civ.P. 23.1.

Many states permit a stockholder to bring a derivative action even though he purchased his shares after the transaction of which he complains. See Stevens, Corporation 812 (2d ed. 1949). In these states, must a federal court in a diversity case follow the state rule or Fed.R. Civ.P. 23.1? See Hanna v. Plumer, p. 371, supra. When state law imposes more exacting requirements, does satisfaction of the requirements of Fed.R.Civ.P. 23.1 nevertheless suffice? See Cohen v. Beneficial Industrial Loan Corp., 337 U.S. 541, 69 S.Ct. 1221, 93 L.Ed. 1528 (1949) (state law requirement that plaintiff in a derivative action post bond must be met in federal court).

7. ACTIONS RELATING TO UNINCORPORATED ASSOCIATIONS

As appears from Oskoian v. Canuel, p. 406 supra, the class action device has been used by the courts to treat as an entity an unincorporated association that could otherwise not sue or be sued. Because in that situation the representative parties must properly protect the interests of the association and therefore satisfaction of the normal class action rules is not necessarily sufficient, it was also thought desirable to treat this form of class action in a separate rule, Fed.R.Civ. P. 23.2.

Part IV

PRELIMINARIES TO THE TRIAL

Chapter Nine

PLEADING

SECTION 1. NATURE AND FUNCTIONS OF PLEADINGS

A. GENERAL OBJECTIVES

The law's attitudes towards pleading requirements mirror the general procedural revolutions which have occurred since informal oral presentation of the parties' positions in the early common law writ proceedings before the fifteenth century, gradually to be replaced by written statements of claim and defense. Written pleadings became the keystone of the procedural system; they were often accorded a quasi-jurisdictional significance, since a good complaint was regarded as essential to a valid judgment * and any variance between allegation and proof was fatal to the pleader's cause. "The plaintiff," it was said, "must recover upon the facts stated in the complaint, or not at all." Walrath v. Hanover Fire Insurance Co., 216 N.Y. 220, 225, 110 N.E. 426, 427 (1915).

The formal and technical requirements, both as to pleadings and to measures challenging their sufficiency, became intricate and abstruse

---

* A 20th century example is Rhodes v. Sewell, 21 Ala.App. 441, 109 So. 179 (1926). Plaintiff filed an attachment affidavit and bond which alleged that defendant owed him $189.63 and one-fourth of the cotton and one-third of all corn raised in 1921. No complaint was filed. After answer by the defendant and trial, judgment was rendered for the plaintiff. The Alabama Court of Appeals dismissed the appeal from this judgment, holding that "[T]he attachment and the suit are distinctive matters", "that a complaint that does not show a cause of action is insufficient to support a judgment and a judgment thereon is ordinarily void", and that therefore "the court below had no jurisdiction to render a judgment against the defendant".

Modern procedural codes may provide for actions without some or all of the usual pleadings. Thus, in some types of actions in New York, the plaintiff may elect to serve a motion for summary judgment in lieu of a complaint. See N.Y. CPLR § 3213. New York practice also permits the parties to join in submitting one document stating their respective claims and defenses (N.Y. CPLR § 3031); they are even permitted to submit a single document stipulating all propositions of fact believed to be necessary predicates for a decision the controversy, and to request the court to make a decision thereon. In the latter case, the court is authorized to draw from the stated facts the inferences it deems appropriate. N.Y. CPLR § 3222.

to an extent equalled today, perhaps, only by the Internal Revenue Code. A single misstep by counsel ordinarily led to forfeiture of the litigant's claim or defense—a circumstance surely contributing to the low repute in which courts were held in the times when Charles Dickens wrote.

Today, the written words of the pleadings no longer control the admissibility of evidence to the extent they formerly did. To a large degree, pleadings may be amended (or sometimes even totally disregarded) in light of the actual proof. So too, the technicality of pleading standards and sudden-death rigor of their enforcement has largely given way to the contemporary disfavor of pre-trial skirmishing unrelated to the merits and disposition of cases on procedural points. But that difficulties and disagreements still attend the subject is attested to by the variety of general approaches to pleadings found in contemporary procedural codes as well as the frequent disparities of result found in the continuing though somewhat diminished flow of judicial opinions deciding particular pleading points.

At the heart of the differences in general approach toward pleading standards and their enforcement are large questions concerning the proper role and function of pleading in relation to other aspects of procedure before trial. The main objectives that pleadings have generally been thought to serve are to:

(1) narrow the issues to be tried; (2) give notice to the parties in order to avoid surprise at the trial; (3) give notice to the court of the nature of the case; (4) serve as a permanent record and as a basis for res judicata; and (5) dispose of cases without trial when the pleadings revealed there were no real issues of fact to be tried.

Green, Basic Civil Procedure 108–109 (2d ed. 1979) (footnotes omitted).

To a large extent, of course, the formulation of a state's general pleading rules will depend upon its views regarding the relative importance to be attached to, and the efficacy of the pleadings as a means of pursuing each of these objectives.

There is considerable room for disagreement, for example, about the impact of the modern policy favoring liberal amendment on both the fourth and fifth items in the foregoing enumeration. Amendments to conform to proof during or after trial, and sometime entertainment of issues raised by the proof without formally recorded amendment at all, may often require that an inquiry into the *res judicata* effects of a judgment go well beyond the pleadings; * and the routine granting of

---

* See, e.g., Cardozo, J., in People ex rel. Village of Chateaugay v. Public Service Commission, 255 N.Y. 232, 238–39, 174 N.E. 637, 639–40 (1931):

"The burden is on a litigant who claims the benefit of a former judgment as *res judicata* to prove that the *res* to be thus established by estoppel was either involved by implication or actually determined in the former litigation [citations omitted]. If, adhering to that presumption, we look to the pleadings in the former litigation, we find that a franchise distinct altogether from the one to Smith and his assigns was the subject of the controversy. The test of the pleadings and their implications, how-

leave to amend after successful challenge to a pleading's sufficiency has seriously undercut the efficacy of such challenges as a means of quickly disposing of cases that turn entirely on questions of law. In addition, even as to the first three of the listed objectives—generally accepted as important today—whatever advantages inhere in strict pleading standards rigorously enforced must be balanced against an attendant disservice to the interests of expedition and economy as a result of opening the door to extensive dilatory pretrial motion practice, accompanied in some states by a series of piecemeal interlocutory appeals.

The problems posed are compounded by the fact that the traditional tasks of the pleadings are increasingly met by other more recently developed procedural devices—the notice and issue-spotting functions, by liberal discovery procedures and the pre-trial conference, and the dispositive function, by motions for summary judgment. Hence the efficacy of pleadings in serving their traditionally asserted objectives must be balanced against not only the attendant cost but also against the relative efficacy and cost of these more modern alternatives.

These problems recur throughout the materials in this chapter. The remainder of this section offers first a historical survey of their impact on the evolution of pleading standards and then an illustration of the relation of pleading to other aspects of procedure before trial in a sophisticated modern procedural system.

NOTE

For further discussion of the aims of American pleading, see e.g., James and Hazard, Civil Procedure § 3.1 (3rd ed. 1985); Blume, Theory of Pleading, 47 Mich.L.Rev. 297 (1949); Cleary, The Uses of Pleading, 40 Ky.L.J. 46 (1951); Simpson, A Possible Solution of the Pleading Problem, 53 Harv.L.Rev. 169 (1950); Morgan, Some Problems of Proof Under the Anglo-American System of Litigation 1 (1956); Epstein, Pleading and Presumptions, 40 U.Chi.L.Rev. 565 (1973).

---

ever, is not final and exclusive. The course of the trial or the form of the decision may show that the pleadings were abandoned, and that controversies beyond them were determined after trial . . .. This extension of the pleadings is not to be presumed. The burden of proving it is on the party asserting the estoppel."

Sometimes it is necessary to go beyond not only the pleadings but the entire written record of the case below. See Berkowitz v. Equitable Life Assurance Society of United States, 21 N.Y.S.2d 206, 208 (App.T.1940):

"If the issue previously tried can be determined from the record alone, without extrinsic evidence it is a question of law for the court. When it is necessary to show the matter tried and determined in the prior action by extrinsic evidence,

it becomes a question of fact for the jury. If the record is silent or ambiguous as to the points at issue and determined by the judgment, parol evidence is competent to identify same and necessary to insure the effect of the judgment as an estoppel."

The earlier common law view, advanced in Campbell v. Butts, 3 N.Y. 173, 174–75 (1849), was that the record "imports incontrovertible verity", and that parol evidence is not admissible to show that, in an earlier action between the parties, matter outside the issues formed by the pleadings was litigated. The court declared that to admit such evidence "would be to contradict the record, which shows the issue, and the verdict and judgment upon that issue, to the exclusion of all other matters whatsoever."

B. PLEADING STANDARDS IN HISTORICAL PERSPECTIVE

WEINSTEIN AND DISTLER, DRAFTING PLEADING RULES *
57 Colum.L.Rev. 518 (1957).

I. THE DRAFTER'S DILEMMA

Written pleadings are virtually unique among the writings required by our procedure. Communication of information alone and compliance with simple formalities are not enough. The theory, at least of the codes, is that pleadings erect a structure upon which will depend the trial or other disposition of the case as well as the record to be preserved. The heart of a pleading, so the theory goes, is the description of occurrences in the form of a recitation of "material" or "ultimate" facts asserted in the context of the substantive law and in a manner that will define and isolate disputes about questions of fact and law. It follows that only those particulars of the occurrences which are "material" under the substantive law should be stated, and that they should be described in a form permitting distillation of a limited number of definite yes-or-no propositions from two inconsistent descriptions.

A specific and precise rule designed to elicit pleadings that meet these qualifications is difficult to draft because of large differences in the substantive law applicable to individual cases. But even if it were possible by rule to dictate the exact contents and structure of pleadings in all cases, there remains serious doubt of the efficacy of a strict rule. Even a competent draftsman may find it a formidable task to walk the fact-pleading tight-rope between "conclusion" and "evidence" in truthfully describing an occurrence which implies a complete and valid rule of substantive law, and a strict rule requires that he do this without anticipating defenses while separately stating and numbering his definite and certain allegations.

Moreover, enforcement of high and strict standards of pleading has been demonstrated to be a practical impossibility. Adept pleaders are reluctant to reveal their position in too precise a form early in the litigation—often because it is not then clear what evidence will be produced at the trial—and inept pleaders may be unable to do so. It is generally conceded that the outcome of a case ought not to depend upon technical deficiencies in draftsmanship, whether or not intended. Thus, amendments are freely granted and leave to replead has become the routine disposition of motions to compel pleadings to measure up to rigid standards. Such repeated motions do little more than waste the efforts of both the court and the litigants. As a practical matter the moving party is usually well aware of the substance of the amendment that will result from a motion. Since a motion will serve to educate his

* Footnotes omitted. Following the article there is a bibliographical note referring to selected writings in the field. See 57 Colum.L.Rev. 518, 524–25 (1957).

opponent, when courts do not penalize merely technical deficiency, a prudent attorney will only attack a pleading to gain delay or to test his belief that his opponent's technical deficiency reflects a substantive lack that will dispose of the case. The former motive cannot be condoned; the latter is a disguised attack on the merits and creates an artificial distinction in procedure between pleading an essential, but untrue, allegation and wholly failing to plead it.

If a strict rule of pleading is thus unworkable, a flexible rule has equally serious objections. Since flexible pleadings—in the sense both of general rules and of non-technical enforcement—cannot precisely define and limit issues, other pre-trial procedures must be relied upon. Yet, flexibility itself creates problems in the utilization of such procedures. For example, free discovery may be unnecessarily costly—indeed, it is subject to abuse as an instrument of harassment and bad faith—unless the court is able to determine the relevancy of proposed inquiry. The minimal standard for pleadings would seem to be determined by this limitation and by considerations of fairness in facilitating preparation for trial or serious settlement negotiations by the parties to the dispute.

In short, the draftsman of a rule of pleading is faced with a dilemma. On the one hand, a rule which sets strict standards, emphasizing the importance of pleadings, does not achieve the expected results and is difficult to enforce and wasteful of court energy. On the other hand, a rule which provides flexible standards, minimizing written pleadings, places burdens upon pre-trial procedures but may inadequately control them and is wasteful of litigants' energy in preparation for trial. Neither extreme represents an acceptable solution, although each has advantages. A reexamination of the pleading problem, made in historical perspective, indicates that each new reform to a large extent reflects a shift from one horn of the dilemma to the other.

II.   PLEADING IN HISTORICAL PERSPECTIVE

A.   *The Common Law*

Written pleadings as we know them today were evolved through resort to both logic and experience. Issues were originally formulated at an oral and informal consultation so that they could be tried at nisi prius where they involved an issue of fact or en banc at London where they turned on an issue of law. The logic of the common law and the pressure on the judges' time gave rise to a system of using successive stages of written pleadings to boil down a controversy to a single issue of law or fact. The forms of action were limited and rigid, and controversies that would not easily fit into the molds were forced into them. This necessitated legal fictions and artificial devices and led to use of noninformative multiple and common counts and the general issue. The results were pleadings that conformed to the rules but frustrated their functions.

Pressure for change culminated in such reforms as the Hilary Rules of 1834 which required extensive detail and strict standards. Thereafter, none but the special pleaders had the skill to draft pleadings which conformed to the new requirements. The Hilary Rules were intended to revitalize common law pleading, to return to issues easily formulated and expeditiously resolved. Their effect was nothing short of disastrous: as a result of the technicality of the Rules an intolerable burden of procedural litigation clogged the courts. The conclusion of the common law experience was clear—it was neither possible nor wise to utilize written pleadings to reduce an entire controversy to one defined issue.

B. *Code Pleading*

The theory persisted that pleadings should, and could, effectively isolate and precisely formulate the issues. In 1848 David Dudley Field and his fellow reformers tried a different approach. Their New York Code . . . sought only simple truthful statements of the facts showing that there was a cause of action. The number of pleadings was severely curtailed. It was hoped that all issues of fact in an action could be thus quickly and simultaneously developed so that they could be tried together. The Field Code was widely adopted as a step in the direction of flexibility, but strict enforcement soon hampered its implementation. For, in order to formulate precise factual issues, a pleader had to state "facts," not "conclusions"; and in order that the issues be material according to the substantive law, the stating of "evidence" was condemned.

Although giving lip-service to the code requirements, courts soon developed exceptions and characterizations to avoid either technical dispositions regardless of merits or virtually impossible drafting standards. "Evidence" was not only permitted, it was sometimes required in order to give adequate notice of the pleader's intentions. On the other hand, "conclusions" were permitted to avoid unnecessary prolixity. Special pleading rules were promulgated for the pleading of particular matters and for certain types of actions. In some, general allegations are expressly permitted in exception to the rule prohibiting conclusions. In others, specific details are required, details which otherwise would be considered "evidence." Thus, there developed by statutory and judicial pronouncement a gradual whittling away of the theoretical requirements of pleading.

But the trend away from a strict enforcement of the code requirement was costly. When particular language was judicially tagged acceptable in particular situations as the allegation of a material fact, the procedural litigation shifted to other language. Requirements of pleading were strict in one area, flexible in another, and undefined in a third. Lengthy disputes were had over the meaning of such phrases as "facts constituting a cause of action." The procedural structure was again overly technical and complex, and pleadings were still not effectively isolating and formulating issues. Some measure of relief was effected by discovery devices, developed to take over these functions, and by liberal interpretation clauses and provisions for free amendment and joinder.

C. *The English Experience Under the Judicature Acts*

A procedural revolution came about in England as a result of the Judicature Acts of 1873–75. Although the first years of the unfamiliar procedure were marked by confusion and expense, the broad powers in the courts to draft rules soon brought forth bold and imaginative suggestions for reform.

Among the proposals seriously considered was one for the total abolition of written pleadings. It had become apparent that in limited classes of action, pleadings were wholly unnecessary, for the issues were always the same and were simple and well understood. Moreover, the "summons for directions," and concomitant transfer of control of the litigation from the parties to a master, were more effective at issue formulation and isolation than pleadings had ever been. The proposal for abolition of pleadings was widely debated, and, although it was adopted only in limited areas, the value and function of pleading were brought into sharp focus. The result was an approach to pleading that has helped stamp English procedure as a modern prototype for about three-quarters of a century.

The English solution to the rule-drafting problem was not astonishing: it comprised a general admonition to pleaders in much the same language as the codes combined with illustrative forms of greatly simplified pleading. Although the strict pleaders protested and critics assailed the forms as not complying with the rule (as indeed was the case), the curious formula was successful. As a result, it has been a powerful influence on subsequent pleading reform, most notably in the federal rules, adopted in 1938.

Of course, not all of the credit for the English success belongs to the use of illustrative forms. The "summons for directions," the consolidation of objections to a pleading and their reservation until a later stage, the supervision of the master, all were large factors in de-emphasizing the technicalities of English pleading; the forms were only a small part of the structure. The existence of a specialized English bar of trial lawyers also undoubtedly played a part in the success of these reforms. Nevertheless, it seems worthwhile to point out that the Connecticut Practice Book, in existence for as long as the new English practice, contains a multitude of simple forms and has contributed largely to the lack of technicality of pleading in that state.

D. *The Federal Rules*

[Draftsmen of] the Federal Rules of Civil Procedure were faced with thousands of decisions construing the code requirements of pleading which were phrased in terms of "ultimate facts," "material facts," and "cause of action." A study of these decisions led to the conclusion that the terms had acquired shades of meaning—and of obscurity—wholly unwarranted by the purposes of the rules in which they were contained. Consequently, a new terminology was adopted and these code terms were entirely abandoned. This change swept away all of the interpretations that had caused so much difficulty. A complaint under the new federal rules was only required to contain "a short and plain statement of the claim showing that the pleader is entitled to relief." Illustrative forms indicated the simplicity of the new requirement.

Despite the hostility that the new terminology engendered, this de-emphasis of pleading discouraged procedural hair-splitting. The terminology and forms have been adopted with apparent success in many jurisdictions. Others, in adopting the federal rules generally, have altered the federal formulation of the pleading requirement to include the terms "facts" or "cause of action," while retaining the identical forms. Proposals for similar amendment of the federal rule itself, however, have been rejected.

III. THE NEW YORK PROBLEM

To some extent, the multitude of procedural decisions in New York have determined the present scope of the pleading requirement. A rephrasing of the present formulation, or the abandonment of its terms, may provoke more litigation as interpretations and constructions are sought for unusual situations. The compromise must be made on two levels: between loose and strict pleading requirements and between the practical virtues of the known and the theoretical perfection of the unknown.

Further, the inertia of habit must be considered. Attorneys will undoubtedly continue to plead for some time in their accustomed ways—the experience after each pleading reform. If rules are to be made more flexible, a pleading formerly sufficient should still be so; only the fringe areas, where unnecessary procedural litigation is engendered, need be affected.

It seems apparent that no perfect solution exists; no formulation of pleading requirements can accomplish the classical objectives of issue formulation, notice, and recordation in every case. The most practical solution seems to be a recognition that specificity is the real criterion with a resulting general requirement that pleadings be sufficiently detailed to give the parties and court notice of the particular transactions relied upon and of the rule of law being invoked. Stated in another way, the allegations made must indicate some probability that the transaction, if it occurred as stated, supports a right to legal relief. The interstitial areas can then be provided for by special rules for pleading in certain types of cases. An appendix of forms can be utilized to clarify the rules and to illustrate the specificity and simplicity desired.

The success of any pleading requirement will depend on other procedures. The rules relating to how and when objections to pleadings may be made, the rules for pre-trial conferences, for discovery, and for judgment without trial must each contribute to decisions made swiftly, economically, and on the merits.

SECTION 2. RELATION OF PLEADING RULES TO SUBSTANTIVE LAW

A. ILLUSTRATIVE STATUTES

MARYLAND RULES OF PROCEDURE

Rule 301b. Necessary Facts Only

A pleading shall . . . contain . . . such statements of fact as may be necessary to constitute a cause of action or ground of defense . . . ..

CALIFORNIA CODE OF CIVIL PROCEDURE

425.10 Statement of facts; demand for judgment. A complaint or cross-complaint shall contain both of the following:

(a) A statement of the facts constituting the cause of action, in ordinary and concise language.

(b) A demand for judgment for the relief to which the pleader claims he is entitled. . . .

Read and compare Rule 8 of the Federal Rules of Civil Procedure. What is the practical effect of the requirement that "facts" to be pleaded rather than a "statement of the claim showing that the pleader is entitled to relief"? Would Forms 5, 9 and 11 in the Appendix of Forms annexed to the Federal Rules appear to satisfy Maryland's Rule 301b and West's Ann. California's C.C.P. § 425.10?

B. NATURE OF THE LEGAL SYLLOGISM

MICHAEL, THE BASIC RULES OF PLEADING
5 Record of N.Y.C.B.A. 175, 181, 184–85 (1950).

* * *

[W]hat does it mean to say that the facts stated shall be sufficient to constitute a cause of action or a defense? Well, now, there are two things of which one can be perfectly certain: First, that in every legal controversy the plaintiff is seeking to obtain—and the defendant is seeking to avoid—the award of a legal remedy. (I use "remedy" in this context to mean some mode of righting a legal wrong, for example, compensatory damages.) Second, that every legal controversy is regulated by a rule of substantive law. We can therefore define a cause of action as a prima facie right to a remedy, and a defense as a right to avoid a remedy. Every statement of a cause of action or of a defense is structurally a syllogism, an inference consisting of a major premise, a minor premise and a conclusion, which are the elements of every syllogism. The minor premise of a pleading, whether a complaint or an answer, is always explicitly stated in the pleading. It consists of the propositions about matters of fact which the pleading alleges. The conclusion of a pleading is usually made explicit. The conclusion of the statement of a cause of action is that the defendant's conduct was wrongful and the plaintiff is entitled to a remedy. The conclusion of a statement of a defense is either that the defendant's conduct was not wrongful or, although it was wrongful, the plaintiff nevertheless is not entitled to a remedy. You will see that that marks the distinction between negative and affirmative defenses. The major premise of a syllogism, of a proof or an inference, is always implicit in the minor premise and the conclusion; and this is true of the minor premise and the conclusion of a pleading. Implicit in every pleading is what the pleader contends to be a valid rule of substantive law. If this implied rule of substantive law, this implied major premise of the pleading, is a valid rule of substantive law, the pleading, if a complaint, states facts sufficient to constitute a cause of action, and, if an answer, facts sufficient to constitute a defense.

. . . I think that it will now be apparent to you that, as *transmuted* by the procedural rules regulating the burden of pleading, the substantive hypothesis of a legal controversy is always of the form "If X1 *and* if X2 *and* if X3 . . ., then the actor's conduct is wrongful and the person wronged is entitled to an appropriate remedy, unless X11 *or* X12 *or* X13 . . .." The non-verbal symbols, the numbered X's, necessarily represent ideas in the legal order, since what is being represented is a rule of substantive law, but they are kinds of things and events of each of which there can be an indefinite number of singular instances. That is to say that, as we have seen, legal ideas are ultimately defined, either wholly or partly, in factual terms. Consequently, rules of substantive law can be viewed as specifying the factual conditions of obtaining and of avoiding remedies. The conditions of obtaining a remedy are those introduced by "if"; the conditions of avoiding a remedy are those introduced by "unless." That is to say that the conditions introduced by "unless" are those traditionally referred to as "new matter," such as fraud, a release, illegality, and so on.

A proposition is material to the statement of a cause of action if it reports a specific instance of one of the conditions introduced by "if . . .."

A defense, I repeat, is the right to avoid a remedy, but a defendant has the right to avoid a remedy either if one or more of the factual conditions of the remedy are *not* satisfied or if one or more of the factual conditions of avoiding the remedy *are* satisfied. This marks the distinction between negative and affirmative defenses. A negative defense is interposed by denying one or more of the propositions which are material to the statement of the cause of action. If we let "P" represent any such proposition, then its contradictory, "not-P," is material to the statement of a negative defense. But, logically, to deny P is to allege not-P. P and not-P are related as contradictories in the sense that if one of those propositions is true the other must be false and one of them must be true. Thus, the allegation and denial of a material proposition will create a material issue, an issue which is legally significant in the sense that upon its resolution legal consequences depend.

     *   *   *

CLEARY, PRESUMING AND PLEADING: AN ESSAY ON JURISTIC IMMATURITY *

12 Stan.L.Rev. 1, 5–8 (1959).

. . . [A] preliminary look at the nature of substantive law, as viewed procedurally, is appropriate.

Every dog, said the common law, is entitled to one bite. This result was reached from reasoning that man's best friend was not in general dangerous, and hence the owner should not be liable when the dog departed from his normally peaceable pursuits and inflicted injury. Liability should follow only when the owner had reason to know of the dangerous proclivities of his dog, and the one bite afforded notice of those proclivities. So the formula for holding a dog owner liable at common law is: + *ownership* + *notice of dangerous character* + *biting.*

This rule of law becomes monotonous to postmen. Hence the postmen caused to be introduced in the legislature a bill making owners of dogs absolutely liable, *i.e.,* eliminating notice from the formula for liability. At the hearing on the bill, however, the dog lovers appear and, while admitting the justness of the postmen's complaint, point out that a dog ought at least to be entitled to defend himself against human aggression. Then the home owners' lobby points out the usefulness of dogs in guarding premises against prowlers. Balancing these factors, there emerges a statute making dog owners liable for bites inflicted except upon persons tormenting the dog or unlawfully on the owner's premises. The formula for liability now becomes: + *ownership* + *biting* – *being tormented* – *unlawful presence on the premises.*

So in any given situation, the law recognizes certain elements as material to the case, and the presence or absence of each of them is properly to be considered in deciding the case. Or, to rephrase in somewhat more involved language, rules of substantive law are "statements of the specific factual conditions upon which specific legal

---

* Some footnotes omitted; others renumbered.

consequences depend. . . . Rules of substantive law are conditional imperatives, having the form: *If* such and such *and* so and so, *etc.* is the case, *and unless* such and such *or unless* so and so, *etc.* is the case *then* the defendant is liable. . . . Now obviously the weighing and balancing required to determine what elements ought to be considered material cannot be accomplished by any of the methodologies of procedure. The result is purely a matter of substantive law, to be decided according to those imponderables which travel under the name of jurisprudence.

This view of the substantive law may seem unduly Euclidean, yet some system of analysis and classification is necessary if the law is to possess a measure of continuity and to be accessible and usable.

PRIMA FACIE CASE AND DEFENSE

Under our adversary method of litigation a trial is essentially not an inquest or investigation but rather a demonstration conducted by the parties.

Since plaintiff is the party seeking to disturb the existing situation by inducing the court to take some measure in his favor, it seems reasonable to require him to demonstrate his right to relief. How extensive must this demonstration be? Should it include every substantive element, which either by its existence or nonexistence may condition his right to relief? If the answer is "yes," then plaintiff under our dog statute would be required to demonstrate each of the elements in the formula: $+$ *ownership* $+$ *biting* $-$ *tormenting* $-$ *illegal presence on the premises.*

In the ordinary dog case this would not be unduly burdensome, but if the suit is on a contract and we require plaintiff to establish the existence or nonexistence, as may be appropriate, of every concept treated in Corbin and Williston, then the responsibility of plaintiff becomes burdensome indeed and the lawsuit itself may include a large amount of unnecessary territory. Actually, of course, the responsibility for dealing with every element is not placed on plaintiff. Instead we settle for a "prima facie case" or "cause of action," consisting of certain selected elements which are regarded as sufficient to entitle plaintiff to recover, *if* he proves them and *unless* defendant in turn establishes other elements which would offset them. Thus in a simple contract case, by establishing $+$ *offer* $+$ *acceptance* $+$ *consideration* $+$ *breach,* plaintiff is entitled to recover, unless defendant establishes $+$ *accord and satisfaction* or $+$ *failure of consideration* or $+$ *illegality* or $-$ *capacity to contract,* and so on.

Observe that the plus and minus signs change, in accord with proper mathematical rules, when we shift elements to the defendant's side of the equation as "defenses." For example, if plaintiff were required to deal with capacity to contract, it would become $+$ *capacity to contract* as a part of his case, rather than the $-$ *capacity to contract* of defendant's case.

Defenses, too, may be prima facie only and subject to being offset by further matters produced by plaintiff, as in the case of the defense of release, offset by the further fact of fraud in the inducement for the release. The entire process is the familiar confessing and avoiding of the common law.

C. ALLOCATING THE BURDEN OF PLEADING

It must be clear by this point that the substantive law does not, in and of itself, pre-ordain which party shall have the burden of pleading a particular material proposition. It should be equally evident that one adversary or the other must be saddled with this burden, for only rarely is a proposition one which the court will notice on its own motion, without requiring a pleading. (On judicial notice, see pp. 599–602, infra.) Thus, without an allocation of the pleading burden to one of the adversaries, stalemate would result and pleadings would lose what little shape they possess in modern procedural systems.

Compare Federal Rule of Civil Procedure 8(c) *with* the following statute:

NEW YORK CIVIL PRACTICE LAW AND RULES

§ 3018(b). **Affirmative Defenses**

A party shall plead all matters which if not pleaded would be likely to take the adverse party by surprise or would raise issues of fact not appearing on the face of a prior pleading such as arbitration and award, collateral estoppel, culpable conduct claimed in diminution of damages as set forth in Article fourteen-A, discharge in bankruptcy, facts showing illegality either by statute or common law, fraud, infancy or other disability of the party defending, payment, release, res judicata, statute of frauds, or statute of limitation. The application of this subdivision shall not be confined to the instances enumerated.

Apart from the practical, common-sense considerations cited at the outset of the New York statute, it is not easy to identify and articulate generally serviceable principles for determining whether one party or the other should be required to raise any particular matter material to the controversy in his or her pleading. Usually, though not always, the burdens of pleading a material proposition and of proving it at the trial go together; and since important reasons of fairness and practicality are more readily apparent for assigning the burden of proof than the burden of pleading to one party or the other, efforts of legal commentators to develop a rationale for dealing with either aspect of the allocation problem tend to focus mainly on evidentiary rather than pleading considerations.

See the discussion of burdens of proof at pp. 842–845, infra. At the pleading level, some concrete guidance is available from the Official Pleading Forms in jurisdictions that have them and from local statutes or rules, such as those quoted at p. 558 infra, concerned with pleading particular matters or in particular kinds of actions.

The reported decisions allocating the burden of pleading do not often provide helpful reasoning. Consider, for instance, Gomez v. Toledo, 446 U.S. 635, 100 S.Ct. 1920, 64 L.Ed.2d 572 (1980), an action under 42 U.S.C.A. § 1983 against the Superintendent of Police of the Commonwealth of Puerto Rico by Gomez, who had been discharged without a hearing from his police job. After winning reinstatement, Gomez sued the Superintendent for damages. His complaint was dismissed by the lower courts for failure to state a cause of action in that he had failed to overcome the defendant's qualified immunity by alleging he had acted in bad faith. The Supreme Court reversed:

> Nothing in the language or legislative history of § 1983, . . . suggests that in an action brought against a public official whose position might entitle him to immunity if he acted in good faith, a plaintiff must allege bad faith in order to state a claim for relief. By the plain terms of § 1983, two— and only two—allegations are required in order to state a cause of action under that statute. First, the plaintiff must allege that some person has deprived him of a federal right. Second, he must allege that the person who has deprived him of the right acted under color of state or territorial law. See *Monroe v. Pape,* 365 U.S. 167, 171, 81 S.Ct. 473, 475, 5 L.Ed.2d 492 (1961). Petitioner has made both of the required allegations. He alleged that his discharge by respondent violated his right to procedural due process, see *Board of Regents v. Roth,* 408 U.S. 564, 92 S.Ct. 2701, 33 L.Ed.2d 548 (1972), and that respondent acted under color of Puerto Rican law. . . .

> Moreover, this Court has never indicated that qualified immunity is relevant to the existence of the plaintiff's cause of action; instead we have described it as a defense available to the official in question. . . . Since qualified immunity is a defense, the burden of pleading it rests with the defendant. See Fed.Rule Civ.Proc. 8(c). . . . It is for the official to claim that his conduct was justified by an objectively reasonable belief that it was lawful. We see no basis for imposing on the plaintiff an obligation to anticipate such a defense by stating in his complaint that the defendant acted in bad faith.

> Our conclusion as to the allocation of the burden of pleading is supported by the nature of the qualified immunity defense. As our decisions make clear, whether such immunity has been established depends on facts peculiarly within the

knowledge and control of the defendant. . . . The existence of a subjective belief will frequently turn on facts which a plaintiff cannot reasonably be expected to know. For example, the official's belief may be based on state or local law, advice of counsel, administrative practice, or some other factor of which the official alone is aware. To impose the pleading burden on the plaintiff would ignore this elementary fact and be contrary to the established practice in analogous areas of the law.

. . . The decision of the Court of Appeals is reversed, and the case is remanded to that court for further proceedings consistent with this opinion.

SECTION 3. SEQUENCE OF PLEADINGS AND CHALLENGES TO THE PLEADINGS

A. ILLUSTRATIVE STATUTES

With Federal Rules of Civil Procedure 7, 8 and 12 compare the following provisions:

NEW YORK CIVIL PRACTICE LAW AND RULES

§ 3018. Responsive Pleadings

(a) Denials. A party shall deny those statements known or believed by him to be untrue. He shall specify those statements as to the truth of which he lacks knowledge or information sufficient to form a belief and this shall have the effect of a denial. All other statements of a pleading are deemed admitted, except that where no responsive pleading is permitted they are deemed denied or avoided.

(b) Affirmative defenses. [See p. 555 supra.]

R 3024. Motion to Correct Pleadings

(a) Vague or ambiguous pleadings. If a pleading is so vague or ambiguous that a party cannot reasonably be required to frame a response he may move for a more definite statement.

(b) Scandalous or prejudicial matter. A party may move to strike any scandalous or prejudicial matter unnecessarily inserted in a pleading.

R 3211. **Motion to Dismiss**

(a) Motion to dismiss cause of action. A party may move for judgment dismissing one or more causes of action asserted against him on the ground that:

1. a defense is founded upon documentary evidence; or

2. the court has not jurisdiction of the subject matter of the cause of action; or

3. the party asserting the cause of action has not legal capacity to sue; or

4. there is another action pending between the same parties for the same cause of action in a court of any state or the United States; the court need not dismiss upon this ground but may make such order as justice requires; or

5. the cause of action may not be maintained because of arbitration and award, collateral estoppel, discharge in bankruptcy, infancy or other disability of the moving party, payment, release, res judicata, statute of limitations, or statute of frauds; or

6. with respect to a counterclaim, it may not properly be interposed in the action; or

7. the pleading fails to state a cause of action; or

8. the court has not jurisdiction of the person of the defendant; or

9. the court has not jurisdiction in an action where service was made under section 314 or 315; or

10. the court should not proceed in the absence of a person who should be a party.

(b) Motion to dismiss defense. A party may move for judgment dismissing one or more defenses, on the ground that a defense is not stated or has no merit.

(c) Evidence permitted; immediate trial; motion treated as one for summary judgment. Upon the hearing of a motion made under subdivision (a) or (b), either party may submit any evidence that could properly be considered on a motion for summary judgment. Whether or not issue has been joined, the court, after adequate notice to the parties, may treat the motion as a motion for summary judgment.

*   *   *

ARKANSAS STATUTES, CIVIL PROCEDURE (1962)

§ 27–1115. **Demurrer to Complaint—Grounds**

The defendant may demur to the complaint where it appears on its face, either:

First. That the court has no jurisdiction of the person of the defendant, or the subject of the action; or,

Second. That the plaintiff has not legal capacity to sue; or

Third. That there is another action pending between the same parties for the same cause; or,

Fourth. That there is a defect of parties, plaintiff or defendant; or,

Fifth. That the complaint does not state facts sufficient to constitute a cause of action.

§ 27–1116. Demurrer to Specify Objection

The demurrer shall distinctly specify the grounds of objection to the complaint; unless it does so, it shall be regarded as objecting only that the complaint does not state facts sufficient to constitute a cause of action.

§ 27–1119. Defects Not Appearing on Face of Complaint—Objection by Answer—Waiver by Failure to Object

When any of the matters enumerated in . . . [§ 27–1115] do not appear upon the face of the complaint, the objection may be taken by answer. If no such objection is taken, either by demurrer or answer, the defendant shall be deemed to have waived the same, except only the objection to the jurisdiction of the court over the subject of the action, and the objection that the complaint does not state facts sufficient to constitute a cause of action.

§ 27–1120. Demurrer to Part and Answer to Part of Complaint

The defendant may demur to one or more of the several causes of action alleged in the complaint, and answer as to the residue.

———

OHIO RULES OF CIVIL PROCEDURE

Rule 12(F)   Motion to Strike

Upon motion made by a party before responding to a pleading or, if no responsive pleading is permitted by these rules, upon motion made by a party within twenty-eight days after the service of the pleading upon him or upon the court's own initiative at any time, the court may order stricken from any pleading any insufficient claim or defense or any redundant, immaterial, impertinent or scandalous matter.

———

B. COMMON LAW AND CONTEMPORARY DEVICES

A useful way to examine the range of pre-trial litigative activity at the pleading stage is to survey the relevant procedural institutions and devices at common law and their contemporary counterparts. Whatever the faults of the common law system, its internal logic and consisten-

cy make it a still-useful tool of analysis, and its terminology remains in any event an inescapably familiar part of present-day judicial parlance.

The initial pleading in a lawsuit is today usually called the "complaint", although the common law term "declaration" is retained in some states and it is also referred to sometimes as the "bill" (a legacy from chancery proceedings) or, in some kinds of special or summary judicial proceedings, as the "petition". All of these expressions refer to a complainant's opening pleading and as such must be distinguished from a "motion," which is an application to the court by either party concerning some matter arising in the course of the action or proceeding.

The defendant's response to the complaint (assuming a default at this point) depends upon the type of resistance the defendant plans to mount.

Challenges Directed to Matters Other Than the Merits

At common law, objections to pleadings based on matters other than the substantive merits of the controversy were raised either by *special demurrer* or *dilatory plea*. The special demurrer tested whether the pleading's allegations complied with various formal and technical requirements regarding such matters as clarity and specificity. Its closest counterparts today are the motions for a more definite statement and to strike specified types of objectionable matter from the pleading (e.g., Fed.R.Civ.P. 12(e), (f)). Dilatory pleas consisted of *pleas to the jurisdiction* and *pleas in abatement*, the latter embracing such matters as a party's lack of capacity, the pendency of another action, and nonjoinder or misjoinder of parties. Insofar as the defects raised by dilatory pleas were transitory or curable, dismissal on such a plea did not bar a later suit on the same claim once the impediment was removed. Such defects are now raised either by motion or in defendant's responsive pleading, the answer (e.g., Fed.R.Civ.P. 12(b)(1)–(5), (7).)

Challenges to the Merits

Here it is helpful to employ the syllogistic analysis propounded in the materials by Professors Michael and Cleary set forth above at pp. 551, 557. We will utilize X_1, X_2, X_3, etc. to refer to the elements of plaintiff's prima facie case; Y_1, Y_2, etc., to affirmative defenses (e.g., release of a contract obligation); and Z_1, Z_2, etc., to matters that defeat the affirmative defense (e.g., that the release was procured through fraud). Assume that the complaint alleges specific instances of conditions X_1, X_2 and X_3. Defendant may be able to challenge its merits in one or more of three ways:

1. *Demurrer.* This motion attacks the major premise of the legal syllogism implicit in the complaint by challenging the validity of the rule of law on which plaintiff relies. The defendant would be well advised to do this if, for example, in plaintiff's contract case, X_1 were an

invitation to dinner, or if the rule relied upon actually requires the existence of an additional condition, X_4—e.g., privity, reliance, proximate cause. The appropriate device at common law was the "general demurrer"—which is what is usually meant when the term "demurrer" is used alone. Its present analogues in most states are the motions to dismiss for failure to state a "cause of action" (the Field Code formulation) or "claim upon which relief can be granted", and the same kind of objection may be assertable alternatively in the answer (e.g., Fed.R.Civ. P. 12(b)) and after answer by a motion for judgment on the pleadings (Fed.R.Civ.P. 12(c)) the term remains in common use. Even where the common law device is formally abolished as a convenient shorthand for challenges to what is often called the pleading's legal sufficiency. Such a challenge, however raised or denominated, says in effect that, assuming (arguendo) plaintiff's allegations of specific instances of X_1 and X_2 and X_3 are true and even absent either Y_1 or Y_2, the law does not entitle the plaintiff to any relief.

2. *Traverse.* The other two ways of challenging a pleading on the merits were called *peremptory* (as opposed to dilatory) *pleas* at common law. One, the *traverse,* challenged the minor premise of the plaintiff's syllogism by denying the truth of one or more of the allegations of specific instances of X_1, X_2 and X_3. Like its contemporary analogue, the denial, it could be either general or specific and was raised in defendant's responsive pleading.

3. *Confession and Avoidance.* The other kind of peremptory plea at common law was the *confession and avoidance.* It asserted in effect that, assuming (again arguendo) plaintiff's allegations are all true and make out a prima facie right to relief under a valid rule of law, additional circumstances exist which invoke a qualification to that rule and thus defeat the prima facie claim. In our hypothetical case this would involve the assertion of say, Y_1, which today would usually be done in the answer though some affirmative defenses may in some states be raised alternatively by a motion to dismiss—e.g., release and payment under New York—McKinney's CPLR 3211(a)(5).

Joinder of Issue

If the hypothetical defendant mounts the first type of challenge against the complaint, the demurrer, the result will be to join issue with the plaintiff on a question of law. If defendant chooses the traverse, joinder of issue will occur on a question of fact. The third type of challenge, however, produces no joinder of issue at all. Instead, it requires, the plaintiff again to take up the challenge and respond to the allegation of X_1 if the claim is to be kept alive. This the plaintiff can do in one or more of the same three ways in which the allegations of the complaint were previously subject to challenge. The plaintiff could demur or challenge the legal sufficiency of Y_1—i.e., assert in effect that it does not under the applicable rule of substantive law

actually defeat the prima facie claim, thus producing an issue of law.*
Or the plaintiff could deny the truth of Y_1 and raise an issue of fact;
confess and avoid Y_1 (say, a release) by alleging in a responsive
pleading, Z_1 (that the release was procured through fraud). The latter
procedure again joins no issue but rather casts upon the opponent (now
the defendant again) the burden of challenging Z_1 in one or more of the
three ways. If Z_1 is also itself subject to confession and avoidance, the
process could continue for another round—indeed, theoretically could
continue indefinitely until the single issue of fact or law sought by the
common law system of pleading was produced. Apparently, it sometimes continued long enough to leave us common law names for five
rounds of responsive pleadings after the defendant's plea—plaintiff's
replication, then defendant's *rejoinder,* and then successively a *surrender, rebutter* and *surrebutter.*

The term *confession and avoidance* is still in familiar use today; it
has the advantage of not being limited, as is *affirmative defense,* to
allegations of new matter (another synonymous term) in the defendant's first responsive pleading. But most modern procedural systems
cut off the pleadings at either the answer or the pleading responding to
it, now called the reply. When an answer alleges new matter and no
reply is allowed, the new matter is automatically deemed either denied
or itself avoided (F.R.Civ.P. 8(d)) for the purpose of allowing the plaintiff to introduce evidence of its untruth or of matter avoiding it at the
trial.

Prompt decision by the court of an issue of law resulting from a
demurrer or one of its contemporary analogues will often dispose of a
case without the delay and expense incident to a trial. Issues of fact
raised by denials, in contrast, will require a trial unless they can be
exposed as spurious or groundless issues through the use of affidavits,
depositions and the other forms of documentary evidence available on a
motion for summary judgment. (Chapter X infra).

NOTE

"A demurrer which sets up a ground dehors the record or which, to be
sustained, requires reference to facts not appearing upon the face of the
pleading is a speaking demurrer. . . . A demurrer is proper when a defect
appears upon the face of a complaint. . . . Otherwise, such defects ordinarily
are to be raised by answer. . . . Speaking demurrers are not to be considered
. . . ." Hoggard & Sons Enterprises v. Russell Burial Association of Piggott,
225 Ark. 576, 501 S.W.2d 613 (1973). The equivalent of a speaking demurrer is
allowed under the provisions in Federal Rule 12 and McKinney's New York
CPLR 3211 authorizing submission of any evidence that could properly be
considered on a motion for summary judgment.

---

* Under the Federal Rules, this would be
done by a Rule 12(f) motion to strike "any
insufficient defense."

SECTION 4. HONESTY IN PLEADING

A. NATURE OF THE PROBLEM

If the parties to a lawsuit could be motivated, to agree on and fully and accurately state the facts underlying their controversy in the pleadings, there would be no need for trials; only issues of law would arise and these could be promptly decided through demurrer-type motions. Procedural systems have, however, at least until relatively modern times, reflected less concern with the bona fides than with the artfulness of the pleader. Fictions, indeed, occupy a venerable and esteemed position in the history of the common law; and it was not until the gradual introduction of summary judgment procedures in the first half of this century that any effective technique existed for testing at the pre-trial stage whether an allegation was supportable by proof.

How vigorously and in what manner should procedural systems pursue the goal of honesty in pleading? The question has many facets. To what extent is "the truth" about the facts knowable at the pre-trial stage, or ever? What do litigants stand to gain by postponing the day of reckoning when they know the facts actually to be otherwise than as alleged in their pleadings? Do plaintiffs and defendants differ in this respect? And to what extent should the attorney be held responsible for investigating and endorsing the bona fides of his client's position? This question implicates issues regarding the attorney-client privilege and professional ethics.

Contemporary efforts to grapple with this subject take one or another, or some combination of, two routes: verification by oath of the party and certification by the attorney's signature. The following materials illustrate the difficulties attending each route.

B. VERIFICATION

CALIFORNIA CODE OF CIVIL PROCEDURE

§ 446. Subscription; necessity of verification; contents of affidavit; persons who may verify; answer by state, political subdivision, etc.; verification under penalty of perjury

Every pleading shall be subscribed by the party or his attorney. When the state, any county thereof, city, school district, district, public agency, or public corporation, or any officer of the state, or of any county thereof, city, school district, district, public agency, or public corporation, in his or her official capacity, is plaintiff, the answer shall be verified, unless an admission of the truth of the complaint might subject the party to a criminal prosecution, or, unless a county thereof, city, school district, district, public agency, or public corporation, or an officer of the state, or of any county, city, school district, district, public agency, or public corporation, in his or her official capacity, is defendant. When the complaint is verified, the answer shall be verified. In all cases of a verification of a . . . pleading, the affidavit of the party shall state that the same is true of his own knowledge, except as to the matters which are therein stated on his or her information or belief, and as to those matters that he or she believes it to be true; and where a pleading is verified, it shall be by the affidavit of a party, unless the parties are absent from the county where the attorney has his or her office, or from some cause unable to verify it, or the facts are within the knowledge of his or her attorney or other person verifying the same. When the pleading is verified by the attorney, or any other person except one of the parties, he or she shall set forth in the affidavit the reasons why it is not made by one of the parties.

When a corporation is a party, the verification may be made by any officer thereof.   . . .

---

3 WEINSTEIN, KORN AND MILLER, NEW YORK CIVIL PRACTICE *:

¶ 3020.01. History of Verification

Verification made its initial appearance in New York in the 1848 Code of Procedure. The Code required every pleading to be verified by the party or his agent or attorney, except when the party would be privileged from testifying to the matter in the pleading. The need for verification was expressed by the draftsmen of the Code in the following passage written in 1848:

> By the verification of pleadings in the qualified manner here proposed, several important advantages are gained. The system of pleading heretofore in use, has encouraged, if it has not absolutely required, fictitious statements, until men otherwise scrupulous, have lost sight of all limits of veracity in the character of their allegations in pleading. It is designed to bring back to legal allegations, made in solemn form in writing, at least the same regard to truth, that prevails between members of society, in their daily communications to one another. It is not required of a party, that he state absolutely, that the matters pleaded are true, inasmuch as his knowledge may not extend to the whole case; but it is intended to put him upon his veracity, and to require him to state nothing, that he does not believe to be true.

Verification was also expected to serve "as a means of preventing groundless suits and defences, and of compeling [sic] the parties respectively to admit the undisputed facts.   . . ."

* Footnotes omitted.

Shortly thereafter the Commissioners on Practice and Pleadings recommended that the original provision be changed to compel the party to make the affidavit and allow the attorney to verify only in certain enumerated instances. This change was adopted. . . .

In 1849 the Legislature on its own motion revised the verification requirement to make verification optional. Any pleadings subsequent to a verified pleading, however, were required to be sworn.

* * *

¶ 3020.02. Verification in Other Jurisdictions

* * *

Every state in the United States appears to have some verification or certification requirement. These requirements fall into four broad categories. Some states have provisions similar to federal rule 11, which provide for certification by the attorney of all pleadings and no verification except in special instances provided for by rule or statute. The special matters for which verification is required often include ex parte applications for preliminary injunctions, proceedings for the appointment of receivers, complaints in an action involving a note, account, or other written instrument, petitions for writs of habeas corpus, proceedings in which a litigant sues or defends as a poor person, and motions for a continuance in a civil action.

Another group of states adopts the English approach. In these states there is no comprehensive requirement either of verification or certification but there are verification requirements for certain enumerated actions, proceedings, motions, or specified pleadings. Typically, the verification requirements in these states are similar to those enumerated for the group of states following the federal practice. In addition, verification is often required for dilatory pleas, pleas in abatement of the action, or pleas to the jurisdiction.

A third group of states follows the New York practice under the former Civil Practice Act and Rules of Civil Practice, which was the same as the practice under the CPLR, see ¶¶ 3020.06, 3020.08, of allowing verification at the option of the pleader, and requiring verification for all subsequent pleadings with some exceptions. These states also usually require verification in the same situations in which it is required by the states in the second group.

The fourth group of states requires verification of all pleadings, with certain exceptions. These exceptions generally are also found in the statutes of those states that follow the New York plan. Among them are pleadings by an infant through his guardian *ad litem,* by an incompetent through his committee, by an imprisoned pleader, and pleadings that might tend to incriminate.

¶ 3020.03. Objections to Verification

Doubts as to the efficacy of any form of verification requirement have been expressed in many quarters. In disposing of a proposed revision of the working of the verification requirement, the Commission on the Administration of Justice concluded that "[i]t is doubtful whether any change in the mere form of verification can accomplish very much by way of discouraging unmeritorious complaints or fictitious answers."

Ineffective enforcement by means of perjury prosecutions and disciplinary proceedings undoubtedly has been one of the major objections to verification of pleadings. See ¶¶ 3020.04, 3020.05. There are other objections, however. As Professor Millar has stated,

> it tends to reduce the oath to a mere matter of convention and to favor the unscrupulous litigant at the expense of his conscientious opponent; furthermore, it offers an unnecessary obstacle to the presentation of inconsistent defenses, for which, by the consensus of enlightened opinion, opportunity should always be afforded.

Finally, verification by a party ignores the fact that it is the attorney, and not the client, who drafts pleadings, and that it is the attorney, and not his client, who owes a professional obligation to the courts.

* * *

C. CERTIFICATION

In 1983 Federal Rule of Civil Procedure 11, the prototype of most of the modern provisions that rely mainly on lawyer certification rather than party verification, was extensively revised with a view to eliminating deficiencies perceived in its previous operation. These deficiencies and the attempted correctives may be gleaned from the changes made in the text of Rule 11 and the explanatory Advisory Committee Note.

In substance, the 1983 revision aimed to increase the litigating bar's responsibility for the reasonableness of assertions made and positions taken in court papers. The amended rule was given a deterrent orientation. In signing the pleading or other paper the lawyer certifies that the factual and legal positions asserted are based on reasonable inquiry, are well founded if fact, or plausible if law; and are not interposed for any improper purpose. If the rule is violated, the court *shall* impose a sanction. In practice the sanction has usually been a payment to the other side of a sum of money for attorneys' fees.

A vast industry sprang up overnight, revealing widespread excesses in claiming, defending and making motions—for instance, that the income tax laws are unconstitutional; that wages are not taxable income; that federal notes are not legal tender, etc. Even though other sanctions for irresponsible actions in litigation are on the books, post–1983 Rule 11 has far eclipsed them all.

ZALDIVAR v. CITY OF LOS ANGELES

United States Court of Appeals, Ninth Circuit, 1986.
780 F.2d 823.

[In a political dispute over an effort to recall a councilman, plain-tiffs sued the city of Los Angeles and its clerk to block the recall election, claiming violation of the Federal Voting Rights Act. The district court granted summary judgment against them and imposed sanctions under Rule 11 on plaintiffs and their attorneys. The test applied was whether the plaintiffs' action was so lacking in factual and legal foundation it could be considered frivolous or unreasonable.]

Standard of Review

Appellate review of orders imposing sanctions under Rule 11 may require a number of separate inquiries. If the facts relied upon by the district court to establish a violation of the Rule are disputed on appeal, we review the factual determinations of the district court under a clearly erroneous standard. If the legal conclusion of the district court that the facts constitute a violation of the Rule is disputed, we review that legal conclusion *de novo*. Finally, if the appropriateness of the sanction imposed is challenged, we review the sanction under an abuse of discretion standard.

Here, we focus upon the legal conclusion of the district court that the signature of plaintiffs' attorney to a complaint alleging a Voting Rights Act violation under the circumstances therein stated violated the attorney's Rule 11 certification. Our review is thus *de novo*.

The Legal Standard

At the outset we must adopt a standard against which alleged violations of Rule 11 are to be tested. This court has not done so since the Rule was amended.

First, we consider whether a finding of subjective bad faith by the signing attorney is necessary to the imposition of sanctions under the Rule. We hold that it is not and, therefore, reject plaintiffs' argument that sanctions are inappropriate here because the district court did not find counsel's actions to be taken in bad faith.

Prior to the 1983 amendments, Rule 11 was interpreted to require subjective bad faith by the signing attorney to warrant the imposition of sanctions. See, e.g., Badillo v. Central Steel & Wire Co., 717 F.2d 1160, 1166 (7th Cir.1983); Nemeroff v. Abelson, 620 F.2d 339, 350 (2nd Cir.1980). This interpretation was compelled because the text of the former Rule was plainly subjective in its focus: "The signature of an attorney constitutes a certificate by him that he has read the pleading; that to the best of *his knowledge, information, and belief,* there is good ground to support it. . . ." Fed.R.Civ.P. 11 (1982) (emphasis added). Moreover, under the former Rule, sanctions against the signing attor-ney were reserved for a "willful violation of this rule. . . ." Id.

The new text represents an intentional abandonment of the subjective focus of the Rule in favor of an objective one. The certificate now tests the knowledge of the signing attorney by a "reasonableness" standard. The former requirement of willfulness has been deleted. "The [new] standard is one of reasonableness under the circumstances. This standard is more stringent than the original good-faith formula and thus it is expected that a greater range of circumstances will trigger its violation." Fed.R.Civ.P. 11 advisory committee note.

The Advisory Committee Notes make clear that Rule 11, as amended, is intended to be applied by district courts vigorously to curb widely acknowledged abuse from the filing of frivolous pleadings, and other papers. Id.[1] It is apparent that district courts have heeded the admonition of the drafters of the rules. The large number of reported opinions from those courts can only be a fraction of the number of instances in which sanctions have been imposed under the authority of recent rule amendments.

Our conclusion that subjective bad faith is not an element to be proved under present Rule 11 is consistent with the advisory committee's purpose to revitalize the Rule by encouraging the use of sanctions where appropriate. This conclusion is also supported by recent opinions in other circuits addressing the same question. See, e.g., Eastway Construction Corp. v. City of New York, 762 F.2d 243, 253 (2nd Cir. 1985) ("Simply put, subjective good faith no longer provides the safe harbor it once did"). See also Schwarzer, Sanctions Under the New Federal Rule 11—A Closer Look, 104 F.R.D. 181, 187 (1985) ("There is no room for a pure heart, empty head defense under Rule 11").

We next consider the kind of conduct or neglect by counsel which may appropriately trigger sanctions under the Rule.

Rule 11 is not a panacea intended to remedy all manner of attorney misconduct occurring before or during the trial of civil cases. It does not repeal or modify existing authority of federal courts to deal with abuses of counsel under 28 U.S.C.A. § 1927 (1982) (an attorney who, in bad faith, "so multiplies the proceedings in any case" may be assessed excess costs, expenses, and attorneys fees) or under the court's inherent power to discipline attorney misconduct. See Roadway Express, Inc. v. Piper, 447 U.S. 752, 764–67, 100 S.Ct. 2455, 2463–65, 65 L.Ed.2d 488 (1980). Nor is it properly used to sanction the inappropriate filing of papers where other rules more directly apply. For example, excessive discovery requests should be dealt with under Rule 26(g) rather than Rule 11, and the filing of inappropriate affidavits in support of, or in opposition to, motions for summary judgment should be considered

---

1. The amendments to Rule 11 must be viewed as only a part of a recent general effort by the Courts and the Congress to encourage the use of sanctions as a means of addressing delay and expense in civil proceedings caused by various inappropriate litigation tactics. Rule 16 was amended to authorize sanctions for delay caused by lack of preparedness at scheduling and pretrial conferences. Fed.R.Civ.P. 16(f). Delay and expense caused by excessive discovery practices, was addressed by a certification procedure similar to that found in Rule 11. Fed.R.Civ.P. 26(g). [Footnote renumbered; other footnotes omitted. Eds.]

under Rule 56(g), rather than Rule 11. To apply Rule 11 literally to all papers filed in the case, including those which are the subject of special rules, would risk the denial of the protection afforded by those special rules. See Chipanno v. Champion International Corp., 702 F.2d 827, 831 (9th Cir.1983).

Rule 11 applies to the filing of a "pleading, motion, and other paper" in a civil action. The Rule requires that such a paper be signed. If it is not signed, the paper "shall be stricken unless it is signed promptly after the omission is called to the attention of the pleader or movant." The purpose of the signature, of course, is to fix responsibility upon a specific person for those matters that are the subject of the certificate.

The certificate is addressed to two separate problems, both of which have been identified as major sources of unnecessary litigation delay and expense: first, the problem of frivolous filings; and second, the problem of misusing judicial procedures as a weapon for personal or economic harassment.

In its opinion imposing sanctions here, the district court characterized plaintiffs' complaint as "totally frivolous." The court also noted that "plaintiffs appear to be ready and willing parties in an effort to stall the recall petition process initiated by Intervenors. Every attempt in state court to derail the recall process failed and plaintiffs made a last ditch effort in this court." *Zaldivar,* 590 F.Supp. at 857. The district court thus relied to some extent upon both prongs of the Rule 11 certificate, the frivolousness clause and the improper purpose clause. We consider briefly the essential elements of each.

1. The "Frivolousness" Clause

As we have observed, the subjective intent of the pleader or movant to file a meritorious document is of no moment. The standard is reasonableness. The "reasonable man" against which conduct is tested is a competent attorney admitted to practice before the district court.

The Rule admits of no exceptions to the requirement that all reasonable attorneys will read a document before filing it in court. In practical effect, an obviously meritorious paper will go unchallenged, whether read or not. The force of the rule is to eliminate the defense of personal ignorance of defects in a paper challenged as unmeritorious.

The signing attorney also certifies that to the best of his knowledge, information, and belief formed after reasonable inquiry, the signed document is well grounded in fact and is warranted by existing law or a good faith argument for the extension, modification, or reversal of existing law. In the present case, no serious claim is made that the complaint is not supported by a foundation of facts. The certificate fails, if at all, under this prong of the rule because of counsel's certification that the facts gave rise to a legal right in the plaintiffs under "existing law" or a "good faith argument for the extension, modification, or reversal of existing law."

It is obvious from the text of the Rule that the pleader need not be correct in his view of the law. Thus the granting of a motion to dismiss the complaint for failure to state a claim, or the granting of a summary judgment against the pleader is not dispositive of the issue of sanctions. The pleader, at a minimum, must have a "good faith argument" for his or her view of what the law is, or should be. A good faith belief in the merit of a legal argument is an objective condition which a competent attorney attains only after "reasonable inquiry." Such inquiry is that amount of examination into the facts and legal research which is reasonable under the circumstances of the case. Of course, the conclusion drawn from the research undertaken must itself be defensible. Extended research alone will not save a claim that is without legal or factual merit from the penalty of sanctions.

Courts have grappled in other contexts with the proper formulation of words that characterize an indefensible, meritless legal argument. We believe the district court correctly adopted and applied for purposes of Rule 11 sanctions the standard applicable for the award of fees to prevailing defendants in litigation under the civil rights acts. See Christiansburg Garment Co. v. EEOC, 434 U.S. 412, 421–2, 98 S.Ct. 694, 700–01, 54 L.Ed.2d 648 (1977). Thus, we affirm that Rule 11 sanctions shall be assessed if the paper filed in district court and signed by an attorney or an unrepresented party is frivolous, legally unreasonable, or without factual foundation, even though the paper was not filed in subjective bad faith.[2]

We accept this formulation fully aware that no combination of abstract words may correctly apply to every case. However, the rule for the payment of fees to prevailing defendants in litigation under the civil rights acts is well known to the federal courts and to the bar. We believe an acceptable degree of certainty over a subject matter which is inherently uncertain will be best achieved by applying the same test in Rule 11 sanctions cases.

2. *The "Improper Purpose" Clause*

The second prong of the Rule 11 certification is that the signer represents that the paper filed "is not interposed for any improper purpose, such as to harass or to cause unnecessary delay or needless increase in the cost of litigation."

We view this prong as an extension of existing law found in 28 U.S. C.A. § 1927 (1982). That statute is burdened with several limitations. Sanctions under section 1927 may be imposed only against attorneys, and not parties; the conduct of the attorney must be in bad faith, thus excusing the blissfully ignorant filing of frivolous documents; and the *multiplication* of proceedings is punished, thus placing *initial* pleadings beyond its reach.

2. Elsewhere in this opinion, we use the single term "frivolous" as a short hand means of describing the rule which we state here.

The improper purpose clause of Rule 11 is more comprehensive. A violation of this clause justifies sanctions against parties, as well as counsel; as we have shown, it reaches improper purposes based upon an objective standard; and finally, it can be invoked if an *initial* pleading is signed for an improper purpose.

Because an element of harassment was detected by the district court in this case and may have accounted in part for its imposition of sanctions against plaintiffs and their counsel, it is necessary to examine the meaning of "harass" as used in Rule 11.

We believe the conduct forming the basis of the charge of harassment must do more than in fact bother, annoy or vex the complaining party. Harassment under Rule 11 focuses upon the improper purpose of the signer, objectively tested, rather than the consequences of the signer's act, subjectively viewed by the signer's opponent. In the present case, the district court noted that the issue raised by the plaintiffs in federal court had been rejected in a different case filed in state court. Without question, successive complaints based upon propositions of law previously rejected may constitute harassment under Rule 11.

A more difficult question of interpretation exists as to whether a pleading or other paper which is well grounded in fact and in law as required by the Rule may ever be the subject of a sanction because it is signed and filed for an improper purpose. In short, may an attorney be sanctioned for doing what the law allows, if the attorney's motive for doing so is improper? The Rule itself does not provide a clear answer to this question. The "well grounded in fact and warranted by existing law" clause is coupled with the "improper purpose" clause by the conjunction "and." By signing the pleading or other paper, the attorney certifies to both, thus suggesting that the two clauses are to be viewed independently.

For purposes of deciding this case, it is unnecessary to answer this difficult question in other situations.[3] We deal here with the signing of a complaint that initiates the action. We hold that a defendant cannot be harassed under Rule 11 because a plaintiff files a complaint against that defendant which complies with the "well grounded in fact and warranted by existing law" clause of the Rule.

[After a close review of the applicability of the Voting Rights Act to the recall election materials the court concluded the plaintiffs' argument was not frivolous for Rule 11 purposes and that plaintiffs' action was not brought for an improper purpose. The court reversed the sanctions award.]

3. The filing of excessive motions, for example, even if each is well grounded in fact and law, may under particular circumstances be "harassment" under Rule 11 or sanctionable under some other provision of law, a question we need not decide here.

NOTES

(1) The Ninth Circuit is alone in applying the trifurcated approach of *Zaldivar* to review of Rule 11 determinations. In Mars Steel Corp. v. Continental Bank N.A., 880 F.2d 928 (7th Cir.1989), the Seventh Circuit (en banc) opted for a "uniformly deferential standard"—abuse of discretion (880 F.2d at 933). In doing so it became the seventh circuit to announce for the abuse-of-discretion standard. In three other circuits a so-called "de novo" standard is used to review questions of law in Rule 11 proceedings. A ruling from the Supreme Court to settle the question appears likely.

(2) In its first ruling on post–1983 Rule 11, the Supreme Court held that even when the attorney signing the pleading or other paper subscribes on behalf of his whole law firm, sanctions run only against the signer, not the firm. Responding to the argument that holding the firm liable would promote "internal monitoring" and fewer baseless claims, the Court said that while such an interpretation might better guarantee reimbursing the victimized party because of the firm's greater assets, the "purpose of the provision in question . . . is not reimbursement but 'sanction.'" Pavelic & Leflore v. Marvel Entertainment Group, __ U.S. __, 110 S.Ct. 456, 107 L.Ed.2d 438 (1989).

(3) Post–1983 Rule 11 has produced a flood of lower court opinions and a vast literature, including a number of empirical studies of the impact in the amended rule and the legal profession's evaluation of its desirability. Among them are: *Report of the Third Circuit Task Force on Federal Rule of Civil Procedure 11* (1989); Willging, *The Rule 11 Sanctioning Process* (1988); *Standards and Guidelines for Practice Under Rule 11 of the Federal Rules of Civil Procedure*, 121 F.R.D. 101–30 (1988); *Report of the Committee on Federal Court Sanctions and Attorneys' Fees* (1987); Kassin, *An Empirical Study of Rule 11 Sanctions* (1985).

(4) The main complaints about Rule 11 are that it has spawned legions of unpleasant satellite proceedings; that it is applied inconsistently and unpredictably from court to court and even from judge to judge; that it chills creative and adventurous legal theories, particularly in the civil rights field; that it is used abusively by many lawyers, who bring or threaten Rule 11 proceedings for illicit reasons; and that it stirs distrust between lawyer and client and creates animosity between adversary attorneys. However, generally speaking, the empirical surveys have recorded a high level of satisfaction with the general themes of the rule and have not confirmed the complaints about chilling effects or bad blood.

(5) Of the deluge of books and articles, the following comprise a fairly representative sampling: Joseph, Sanctions: The Federal Law of Litigation Abuse (1989); American Bar Association, Federal Procedure Committee, Sanctions: Rule 11 and Other Powers (2d ed. 1988); Nelken, Sanctions Under Amended Federal Rule 11—Some "Chilling" Problems in the Struggle Between Compensation and Punishments, 74 Geo.L.J. 1313 (1986); Schwarzer, Sanctions Under the New Rule 11—A Closer Look, 104 F.R.D. 181 (1985); Schwarzer, Rule 11 Revisited, 101 Harv.L.Rev. 1013 (1988); Untereiner, A Uniform Approach to Rule 11 Sanctions, 97 Yale L.J. 901 (1988); Vairo, Rule 11: A Critical Analysis, 118 F.R.D. 189 (1988).

D. INCONSISTENT, ALTERNATIVE, AND HYPOTHETICAL PLEADING

Rule 8(e)(2) of the Federal Rules of Civil Procedure includes the usual provision freeing the pleadings from concern over self-contradictions: "A party may . . . state as many claims or defenses as the party has regardless of consistency. . . ."

The objection to such pleadings is sometimes put on the ground of untruthfulness though their lack of candor may be more apparent than real. In some cases, indeed, the asserted inconsistency may involve nothing more than a trick of semantics or logic, as when a defendant both denies his own negligence and pleads an affirmative defense of plaintiff's contributory negligence. E.g., compare Crabbe v. Mammoth Channel Gold Mining Co., 168 Cal. 500, 143 P. 714 (1914) with Mardesich v. C.J. Hendry Co., 51 Cal.App.2d 567, 125 P.2d 595 (1942).

Professors Field, Kaplan and Clermont pose a more challenging kind of inconsistency in Materials on Civil Procedure 38 (5th ed. 1984): "There is in the folklore of the common law the famous Case of the Kettle. The plaintiff claimed damages for a kettle that assertedly the defendant had borrowed and had allowed to become cracked while in his possession. The defendant is supposed to have pleaded (1) that he did not borrow the kettle, (2) that it was never cracked, and (3) that it was cracked when he borrowed it. Would this pleading be permissible today under the Federal Rules?" *

Even the famous Case of the Kettle, however, was cut down to size in Rudd v. Dewey, 121 Iowa 454, 96 N.W. 973 (1903), an action for defendant's alienation of the affection of plaintiff's wife, in which the defendant pleaded both a general denial and that "whatever relations he had with plaintiff's wife, were with the knowledge, acquiescence, and consent of the plaintiff." Said the Iowa court in Rudd (Id. at 458–459, 96 N.W. at 975):

> "Absurd as it may seem at first blush to allow defendant, charged with having negligently broken a borrowed kettle, to answer that he never borrowed the kettle, that it was broken when he borrowed it, and that it was sound when returned, nevertheless, when it is reflected that the controversy may be about a kettle borrowed by defendant's servant, as to which defendant had no knowledge whatever, and that, the servant having disappeared, defendant will be entirely dependent on such casual evidence as he may be able to scrape up in the neighborhood, the rule is not by any means unreasonable or without support in public policy. The defendant may not know what set of facts he will be able to establish. He is absolutely dependent upon the testimony of witnesses as to matters not

---

* To the effect that "the folklore of the common law" enjoys no monopoly on enjoyment of the famous "Case of the Kettle" see Sigmund Freud, The Interpretation of Dreams, Chap. II, pp. 152–153 (Avon Paperback ed.).

within his personal knowledge, and he ought not to be defeated if on the trial any legitimate defense which he has pleaded is established by the evidence. Bell v. Brown, 22 Cal. 671 (1863); Buhne v. Corbett, 43 Cal. 264 (1872). The case before us illustrates the policy of this rule, for defendant, in his testimony, absolutely denied sexual intercourse with plaintiff's wife, and also testified as to a proposition made by the husband, which, if truly related, would have justified defendant in believing that such intercourse would not be objectionable to the husband. Whatever doubts the jury might have entertained with reference to the credibility of this testimony, defendant had the right to have it considered by them, as judges of the facts."

NOTES

(1) Are there additional reasons for sustaining inconsistent, alternative, or hypothetical pleading besides those cited by the Iowa court in Rudd v. Dewey?

(2) Should there be any limitations at all on the allowance of inconsistent, alternative, or hypothetical allegations in pleadings? If so, what should they be? One commonly asserted litmus test for impermissibly inconsistent allegations is "whether proof of one necessarily disproves the other." E.g., Shuffelberger v. Hopkins, 177 Kan. 513, 280 P.2d 933 (1955). Is this a satisfactory formulation?

(3) How should the following cases be treated:

(a) Plaintiff alleges in one count of a complaint that she will be "sick, sore, lame and disordered for the rest of her life" and in another count that she has "regained her health"? Cf. Church v. Adler, 350 Ill. App. 471, 483, 113 N.E.2d 327, 332 (1953).

(b) Allegations by the plaintiff, who had obtained a decree of divorce against the defendant in an earlier action in a Florida court, (1) that the Florida divorce decree is valid and that she is therefore entitled to alimony as a divorcee, and (2) that the Florida decree is invalid because procured on fraudulent allegations of Florida domicile, that the parties are still married and that she is entitled now to a divorce and alimony. See Chirelstein v. Chirelstein, 8 N.J.Super. 504, 73 A.2d 628 (1950).

In the *Chirelstein* case the court said (id. at 511, 73 A.2d at 632):

"I see no basis for requiring an election. Where the interplay of the facts and the law is such that the legal soundness of the respective legal positions is debatable, alternative or hypothetical claims should be permitted. I can perceive no reason for requiring a litigant in these circumstances to make a conclusive anticipation of the views of the court. . . . Where the judicial treatment of the facts is in doubt, justice demands that the litigant be permitted to assert alternative positions which depend upon the successive determinations of the issues raised by the facts."

SECTION 5. THE COMPLAINT

A. FORMAL REQUIREMENTS

1. IN GENERAL

See Fed.Rule Civ.Proc. 8(a), California Code of Civil Procedure § 425.10 at p. 551, supra; and Ohio Rule Civ.Proc. 12(F) at p. 559 supra, and compare the following provisions:

MARYLAND RULES OF PROCEDURE

Rule 301b. Necessary Facts Only . . .

A pleading shall be brief and concise and contain only such statements of fact as may be necessary to constitute a cause of action or ground of defense, except as may otherwise be necessary for purposes of demurrers and motions. It shall not include (a) argument; (b) inference; (c) matter of law or evidence; (d) matter of which the court may take notice *ex officio;* (e) unnecessary recitals of documents; or (f) any impertinent scandalous or irrelevant matter.

NEW YORK CIVIL PRACTICE LAW AND RULES

§ 3013. Particularity of Statements Generally

Statements in a pleading shall be sufficiently particular to give the court and parties notice of the transactions, occurrences, or series of transactions or occurrences, intended to be proved and the material elements of each cause of action or defense.

A complaint ordinarily consists of (1) a caption identifying the court in which the action is brought and stating its title and the name, address and telephone number of counsel; (2) allegations of the particular circumstances (transactions, events, conditions, relationships, etc.) thought by the pleader to call for judicial relief—i.e., in terms of the analysis set forth above, the minor premise of the legal syllogism on which the pleader relies: this is the body of the complaint, on which its legal sufficiency depends; and (3) a prayer or demand for relief—the conclusion of the syllogism. Often in courts of specified jurisdiction (notably, in the federal courts) the complaint will also be required to allege the grounds of the court's adjudicatory authority.

The form that the allegations in the body of the complaint should take depends on both the relevant substantive law and the pleading rules and standards of the particular jurisdiction. Contemporary American procedural systems fall into three groups in terms of their general approach to such pleading standards: (1) a small minority in which common law pleading rules retain the dominant role; (2) a somewhat larger number which remain patterned after the New York Field Code of 1848 ("code states"); and (3) those, constituting the largest group, that are in main part adapted from the Federal Rules of Civil Procedure.

In some jurisdictions—e.g., New York and Connecticut and under the Federal Rules—officially prepared and approved forms of complaint in common types of actions are provided for the guidance of the practitioner. Elsewhere reliance is chiefly on commercially prepared formbooks. The latter need not be slavishly followed. Since they are based in turn on actual pleadings drawn from the files of litigated cases they tend to exert a conservative influence, often preserving archaic phraseology which, however colorful, has become meaningless. Compare, for example, the following common law complaint sounding in trespass with the one prescribed for similar actions by Form 9 ("Complaint for Negligence") in the APPENDIX OF FORMS to the Federal Rules of Civil Procedure.

GREGORY'S COMMON LAW FORMS
1927, pp. 77–78.

No. 55.   Declaration in Trespass, for Running Against Plaintiff's Automobile and Injuring Plaintiff

In the _____ Court of _____:

C. _____ C. _____,
                           v.   } Declaration
D. _____ D. _____

C.C. complains of D.D. of a plea of trespass, for this, to-wit: that heretofore, to-wit, on the _____ day of _____, 19__, the said defendant, with force and arms, drove a certain automobile, to-wit, a _____, which the said defendant was then driving along the public highway, with great force and violence against a certain other automobile, to-wit, a _____ of the said plaintiff, of great value, to-wit, of the value of _____ dollars, and in which said automobile the said plaintiff was then riding in and along the said highway, and thereby greatly broke to pieces, damaged, and spoiled the said automobile of the said plaintiff. And by means of the premises, the said plaintiff was then thrown with great force and violence out of his said automobile to the ground, and by means of the premises, the said plaintiff was afterwards, to-wit, on the day, month, and year aforesaid, obliged to lay out and expend, and did necessarily lay out and expend, a large sum of money, to-wit, the sum of _____ dollars, in and about the repairing and amending the damage so done to the said automobile as aforesaid; and also, by means of the premises, the plaintiff's leg was broken and the said plaintiff then became and was greatly bruised, hurt, and wounded, and sick, sore, lame, and disordered, and so remained and continued for a long space of time, to-wit, for the space of _____ weeks next following, and during all that time suffered and underwent great pain, and was hindered from transacting his lawful business by him during that time to be done, performed and transacted; and was also thereby obliged to pay and expend, and did necessarily pay and expend, divers sums of money, in the whole amounting to a large sum of money, to-wit, the sum of _____ dollars, in and about endeavoring to be cured of the sickness, soreness, lameness and disorder aforesaid, occasioned aforesaid.

And other wrongs to the said plaintiff, the said defendant then and there did to the damage of the said plaintiff of _____ dollars. And therefore he institutes this action of trespass.

W.G.D., p.q.

2. CLARITY AND SPECIFICITY

STROMILLO v. MERRILL LYNCH, PIERCE, FENNER & SMITH, INC.

United States District Court, Eastern District of New York, 1971.
54 F.R.D. 396.

WEINSTEIN, DISTRICT JUDGE. Defendants move, pursuant to Rules 9(b), 9(g) and 12(e) of the Federal Rules of Civil Procedure, to require plaintiff to more definitely state the various claims in the complaint. The motion must be denied.

I.

The complaint alleges in essence that the defendants wrongfully "churned" her account, i.e., engaged in excessive stock transactions on her behalf principally to generate brokerage commissions for their own gain. Jurisdiction is premised upon the Securities and Exchange Act of 1934 and Rule 10b–5. 15 U.S.C.A. §§ 78f, 78j, 78s and 78aa; 17 C.F.R. 240.10b–5.

In considerable detail covering ten legal size pages, plaintiff states her grievances. She was a widow with cash in a savings bank and a dormant brokerage account consisting primarily of American Telephone and Telegraph stocks acquired over the years as an employee of that company. A short while ago the individual defendant, as an agent of his employee, the defendant Merrill Lynch, began, she avers, to churn her stocks. Despite the fact that he knew she was about to retire and was interested primarily in security and income, he induced her to withdraw substantially all of her accumulated savings and then engaged on her account in a series of transactions resulting in high brokerage fees and the loss of a large part of her capital.

Many of the trades are set out in detail and the damages sought are justified by specific figures. For example, the first claim for relief states that there were excess brokerage commissions in the amount of $10,924.50, unjustified margin loans and interest of $15,129.98 and dividend losses in the amount of $13,171.34. In the second claim for relief specific transactions are described showing losses in value due to changes in investment of \$26,118.26.

II.

A motion for a more definite statement is available only if "a pleading . . . is so vague or ambiguous that a party cannot reasonably be required to frame a responsive pleading." Fed.R.Civ.P. 12(e). This complaint is quite definite and is unambiguous. An adequate answer should provide no challenge to defendants' attorneys.

Rule 9(b) requires "averments of fraud . . . [to] be stated with particularity." The statements in the complaint are particularized to the point that details of individual purchases and sales are described. Practically nothing is left to the imagination; the level of abstraction is as low as it is possible to get without erring on the side of verbosity. Moreover, the defendants have in their own records a complete statement of all trades in connection with the plaintiff's account giving further color to her allegations.

When "items of special damage are claimed, they shall be specifically stated," according to Rule 9(g). But it seems unlikely that plaintiff's are the kinds of special damages referred to in the Rules. See, e.g., 2A Moore's Federal Practice ¶ 9.08; Wright and Miller, Federal Practice and Procedure § 1310 (1969). In any event, the complaint is sufficiently specific with respect to the computation of damages. Wright & Miller, Federal Practice and Procedure: Civil §§ 1311–1312 (1969).

The tendency under the Federal Rules is to discourage motions to compel more definite complaints and to encourage the use of discovery procedures to apprise the parties of the basis for the claims made in the pleadings. [Citations omitted.] As the bench and bar were told some time ago,

> "Particularization of the issues is indeed the first order of business. But the Rules do not contemplate their definition by paper pleadings. They are to be ascertained and articulated by the free use of controlled pretrial discovery under the guiding hand of the judge who has the responsibility for the trial of the case." New Home Appliance Center v. Thompson, 250 F.2d 881, 883–884 (10th Cir.1957).

Apparently defendants are making no claim that a complaint based upon unnecessary trading by a broker fails to state a claim for relief. * * *

III.

Particularly in view of the fact that the individual calendar system—providing for the assignment for all purposes to a specific judge of a case immediately after filing the complaint—is utilized in this District, generalized motions of this kind should be discouraged. . . .

The court stands ready to aid the parties in the prompt resolution of the merits of the claim. In accordance with standard practice, as soon as the answer is filed a conference will be scheduled to discuss discovery, motions, settlement, and, if possible, to set a specific date for trial. If there are, in the interim, any difficulties in connection with discovery or if the court's assistance is needed for any other reason, a telephone or face-to-face conference can be arranged by telephoning the court.

We note that this motion has, without any useful purpose, expanded several times the thickness of an otherwise slim file with motion papers, memoranda of law and affidavits. Litigants should avoid burdening the courts, themselves and their adversaries with excess paperwork where cheaper and more flexible means exist to accomplish the same objectives. Here a telephone call from one attorney to the other, with or without the court's intervention, probably would have resulted in supplying the defendants with any particular detail they really needed to investigate and file an answer. We add to the file with this opinion with the hope that it will alert the bar to some of the advantages of the more informal procedures now available under the individual calendar system.

The motion is denied with costs.

So ordered.

---

3. "Facts", "Evidence", and "Conclusions"

One consequence of the typical Code formulation requiring the pleader to state "facts constituting a cause of action" (or defense) was to spawn fruitless and time-consuming objections to allegations in pleadings as constituting merely "evidence" whereby the "facts" are to be proved or "conclusions," either of fact or of law, rather than "material (or "ultimate" or "operative") facts". A major reason for dropping the word "facts" from the formulations adopted in Federal Rule 8 and New York—McKinney's CPLR 3013 was to eliminate pre-trial skirmishing of this kind. The extent to which the Federal Rule formulation has succeeded in this purpose will be examined at pp. 589–596 infra. The following Notes are illustrative of the problem as it exists under Code formulations.

NOTES

(1) Prudential Insurance Co. v. Moore, 197 Ind. 50, 52, 149 N.E. 718, 719 (1925): Action by the beneficiary upon a life insurance policy. One of the questions was the sufficiency of plaintiff's allegations that on a certain date the insured "absented himself from his usual place of residence and went to parts unknown, and has absented himself from said place of residence ever since said time, and for a space of more than five years, and that he has not been heard of or seen by any one since said time." Holding these allegations to be insufficient, the court said: "It might be true, as alleged, that at the time the

complaint was filed, the insured had been absent continuously for many years during which he was not heard from, and yet he might be alive and might appear on the day of the trial, to testify as a witness. Plaintiff's right to recover depended on the ultimate fact that the insured was dead. And by what ever means that fact was to be established, whether direct testimony or proof of circumstances or presumptions, the complaint, either directly or indirectly, must allege the ultimate fact relied on, or it will not withstand a demurrer. A complaint which alleges only rebuttable presumptions or evidence tending to establish a fact on which the right of recovery depends, instead of alleging the fact itself, is not sufficient to withstand a demurrer, if all that is alleged might be true, just as stated, notwithstanding the non-existence of the fact or facts on which plaintiff's right to recover depends." Id. at 61–62, 149 N.E. at 722.

(2) Thayer v. Gile, 42 Hun 268, 269–70 (N.Y., App.Div., 1886): Plaintiff alleged that as tenant in common with defendant he was in possession of certain hay which defendant converted to his own use to plaintiff's damage, etc. Judgment sustaining a demurrer to the complaint reversed. (i) "It is still good pleading to state facts according to their legal effect unless the pleader so narrates the facts as to show that he has mistaken their legal effect. . . . Thus, it was not necessary for the plaintiff to allege the details from which her tenancy in common, or possession, or the conversion by the defendant would follow as their legal effect. These details are rather in the nature of the evidence, to be adduced upon the trial to support these three allegations." (ii) "By using the word 'converted' the plaintiff has concisely condensed in a single word the notice to the defendant that whatever it may be necessary to prove she intends to prove it." (iii) "A converted B's hay is a fact; A's liability to B, the law." The statement of the conversion "is the statement of a fact, ascertained by the rules of law."

(3) Desautel v. North Dakota Workmen's Compensation Bureau, 72 N.D. 35, 36–37, 4 N.W.2d 581, 582 (1942): "The demurrer admits the truth of well pleaded facts and those presumed or reasonably or necessarily inferred from the facts alleged in the complaint. [Citations omitted.] Conclusions of law in the absence of allegations of fact to support them are not admitted by demurrer. [Citations omitted.] The statement in the complaint that the accident occurred in the course of plaintiff's employment is a conclusion that is not admitted by the demurrer. It is the point in controversy upon which the sufficiency of the complaint must be determined. If facts pleaded are sufficient to show that the plaintiff was injured in the course of her employment, the complaint states a cause of action. If such facts are not stated, the complaint is fatally defective. An injury to be compensable under the North Dakota Workmen's Compensation Law, chapter 286, Session Laws N.D.1935, must arise in the course of employment."

(4) Southern Railway Co. v. King, 217 U.S. 524, 534–36, 30 S.Ct. 594, 596–97, 54 L.Ed. 868 (1910): Plaintiff contended that defendant was negligent in failing to comply with a statute which required railroads to install a post on each side of, and at a distance of 400 feet from, each grade crossing, and which also required an engineer, upon arriving at such a post, to blow the locomotive's whistle and to check and keep checking its speed so as to be able to stop in time if any person or thing were using the crossing. Defendant contended that the statute placed such a burden upon interstate commerce as to violate the commerce clause of the Federal Constitution, and in that connection alleged that "it is impossible to observe said statute and carry the mails as defendant is required to carry them under the contract it has with the Government; and it

is likewise impossible to do an interstate business, and at the same time comply with the terms of said statute." The court held that "these averments are mere conclusions," setting forth no facts which would make the operation of the statute unconstitutional. Dissenting, Mr. Justice Holmes said: "These are pure allegations of fact. They mean on their face that the requirement that the engineer at every grade crossing should have his train under such control as to be able to stop if necessary to avoid running down a man or wagon crossing the track requires such delays as to prevent or seriously to interfere with commerce among the States. They refer to physical conditions and to physical facts; they can refer to nothing else. I think it obvious that they mean that the crossings are so numerous as to make the requirement impracticable, since I can think of nothing but the number of them that would have that effect.

"The statement may be called a conclusion, but it is a conclusion of fact, just as the statement that a certain liquid was beer is a conclusion of fact from certain impressions of taste, smell and sight. If the objection to the pleading had been that more particulars were wanted, although, for my part, I think it would have been unnecessarily detailed and prolix pleading to set forth what and where the crossings were, the pleading should not have been rejected, but the details should have been required." Id. at 538, 30 S.Ct. at 598.

(5) "We think the allegations that the corporations were so organized, controlled and managed that they were the instrumentalities, agents, and adjuncts of each other and were, in fact, one unit, coupled with the averments of common ownership, directorship, control, management and operation at one location and that the licensed corporation was uncollectible, while involving expressions of legal conclusions, constitute, at the same time, sufficient pleading of facts to admit of offers of proofs of such agency, particularly when knowledge of the facts relating thereto is peculiarly within the possession of defendants rather than plaintiff." Pfaffenberger v. Pavilion Restaurant Co., 352 Mich. 1, 7, 88 N.W.2d 488, 492 (1958).

(6) Kelley v. Kelley, 74 Ohio App. 225, 226–27, 57 N.E.2d 791, 792 (1944). Plaintiff pleaded, using statutory operative words, only that the defendant has been guilty of "gross neglect of duty" and of "extreme cruelty" toward plaintiff. The appellate court affirmed a refusal to sustain a demurrer on the grounds that the petition did not state a cause of action, and that it merely stated conclusions, but noted: "We have frequently had before us these abbreviated petitions for divorce, wherein counsel for plaintiff merely pleads the ground set up in the statute, without giving any details which, if proved, would sustain the allegations. We wish to register our condemnation of such forms of pleading. The defendant is entitled to know the facts upon which the action is based, other than the naked statement that he is guilty of extreme cruelty or other statutory offenses. This form of pleading saves no time in that it gives rise to the contention upon the part of the defendant, either that the petition is demurrable, or subject to a motion to make definite and certain. If the pleader would state the facts which he claims constitute his cause of action, the matter could proceed without the delay incident to this abbreviated and inartistic form of the pleading."

4. PARTICULAR ACTIONS AND ALLEGATIONS

Negligence actions present an especially troublesome aspect of the evidence—fact—conclusion continuum. Even states that are receptive in general to the type of pleading reform represented by Federal Rule 8(a) may not be content with the limited information provided by the accompanying Federal Official Form of "Complaint for Negligence" (Form 9, Appendix of Forms to Federal Rules of Civil Procedure). Thus New York combines a similar Official Form of Complaint with provision for obtaining supplementary details through a "bill of particulars":

NEW YORK CPLR APPENDIX OF OFFICIAL FORMS (1968)

Official Form 12

Complaint for Negligence in an Automobile Accident Case

SUPREME COURT OF THE STATE OF NEW YORK
COUNTY OF NEW YORK

A.B., Plaintiff, —against— C.D. and E.F., Defendants	Complaint Index No.

1. On June 1, 1966, in a public highway called Broadway in New York City, defendant C.D. negligently drove a motor vehicle against plaintiff who was then crossing the highway.

2. That motor vehicle was then owned by defendant E.F. and driven by defendant C.D. with defendant E.F.'s permission.

3. Solely as a result of defendant C.D.'s negligence, plaintiff was personally injured, lost earnings and incurred expenses for [e.g., care and treatment].

Wherefore plaintiff demands judgment against C.D. and E.F. for the sum of twenty thousand dollars, and costs and disbursements.

[Print Name]

Attorney for Plaintiff
Address:
Telephone Number:

NEW YORK CIVIL PRACTICE LAW AND RULES

R. 3041. Bill of Particulars in Any Case

Any party may require any other party to give a bill of particulars of his claim . . ..

R. 3043. Bill of Particulars in Personal Injury Actions

(a) Specified particulars. In actions to recover for personal injuries the following particulars may be required:

(1) The date and approximate time of day of the occurrence;

(2) Its approximate location;

(3) General statement of the acts or omissions constituting the negligence claimed;

(4) Where notice of a condition is a prerequisite, whether actual or constructive notice is claimed;

(5) If actual notice is claimed, a statement of when and to whom it was given;

(6) Statement of the injuries and description of those claimed to be permanent, and in an action designated in subdivision one of section six hundred seventy-three of the insurance law, for personal injuries arising out of negligence in the use or operation of a motor vehicle in this state, in what respect plaintiff has sustained a serious injury, as defined in subdivision four of section six hundred seventy-one of the insurance law, or economic loss greater than basic economic loss, as defined in subdivision one of section six-hundred seventy-one of the insurance law;

(7) Length of time confined to bed and to house;

(8) Length of time incapacitated from employment; and

(9) Total amounts claimed as special damages for physicians' services and medical supplies; loss of earnings, with name and address of the employer; hospital expenses; nurses' services.

* * *

(c) Discretion of court. Nothing contained in the foregoing shall be deemed to limit the court in denying in a proper case, any one or more of the foregoing particulars, or in a proper case, in granting other, further or different particulars.

The functions of a bill of particulars are to amplify the pleadings, limit proof, and to assist in preparing for and avoiding surprise at the trial. See 3 Weinstein, Korn and Miller ¶ 3041.03. Formerly a more popular procedural device available in most types of actions, it has come to be increasingly criticized as of limited value in a modern procedural system. Judge Charles E. Clark, for example, wrote in his treatise on Code Pleading that:

"[A]t best it is an inadequate method of discovery, since it does not seek directly the parties' own stories, but attacks only the formal allegations of their lawyers. Consequently it operates more as a means of perfecting the paper pleadings, with all the shadowboxing and Fabian tactics thus rendered profitable, than as a direct road to the merits of the litigation. In a system adequately supplied with modern devices for reaching the heart of a case—discovery, pre-trial conference, summary judgment—the motion for a bill of particulars becomes just a nuisance, as the history of the federal provision has quickly demonstrated."

And although the Federal Rules of Civil Procedure as originally promulgated provided for bills of particulars, they were eliminated as part of the 1946 amendments to Rule 12, which one court explained as follows:

> "The 1946 amendment to Rule 12 of the Federal Rules of Civil Procedure ('FRCP') in deleting the reference to a bill of particulars and in changing the language of the rule from 'a party may move for a more definite statement or for a bill of particulars of any matter which is not covered with sufficient definiteness or particularity to enable him properly to prepare his responsive pleading or to prepare for trial' to 'If a pleading . . . is so vague or ambiguous that a party cannot reasonably be required to frame a responsive pleading, he may move for a more definite statement' makes it plain that the rule is designed to strike at unintelligibility rather than want of detail. If the pleading meets the requirements of Rule 8 FRCP and fairly notifies the opposing party of the nature of the claim, a motion for a more definite statement should not be granted. . . . The deletion of the phrase 'or to prepare for trial' makes it clear that a motion for a more definite statement should not be granted to require evidentiary detail which is normally the subject of discovery under Rules 26 through 36 of the FRCP."

Wishnick v. One Stop Food & Liquor Store, Inc., 60 F.R.D. 496 (N.D.Ill. 1973). See also Hodgson v. Virginia Baptist Hospital, Inc., 482 F.2d 821 (4th Cir.1973).

In negligence and other actions for personal injuries, however, the type of information called for in the nine subcategories of New York CPLR 3043 is so routinely sought and needed to facilitate planning and settlement negotiations early in the controversy that a simple procedural technique for securing it seems less objectionable. Indeed, even though the Advisory Committee that drafted New York's CPLR proposed to eliminate bills of particulars (they were later reinstated by the Legislature), it would have required that precisely the same information be included directly in the complaint in such actions. (See 3 Weinstein, Korn and Miller ¶ 3041.01). The following two cases illustrate disparate judicial reactions to additional problems concerning the level of specificity to be required of pleadings in negligence actions.

RANNARD v. LOCKHEED AIRCRAFT CORP.

Supreme Court of California, 1945.
26 Cal.2d 149, 157 P.2d 1.

SPENCE, JUSTICE. Plaintiffs, who are husband and wife, have appealed from a judgment on the pleadings which was rendered in response to a motion made by defendant Lockheed Aircraft Corporation at the commencement of the trial after an objection to plaintiffs' introduction of any evidence had been sustained. . . .

In considering whether the judgment on the pleadings was properly granted, it is but necessary to determine the sufficiency of the complaint upon the same principle as though it had been attacked by general demurrer. In other words, it is only where there is an entire absence of some essential allegation that a motion for judgment on the pleadings may be properly granted [citations omitted].

The action is for damages for the alleged malpractice of one Z.P. King, a physician and surgeon, who, it is averred, was in the employ of defendant Lockheed Aircraft Corporation for the purpose of giving physical examinations to persons who applied to said corporation for employment and of rendering certain other professional services. . . .

Under the authorities, it is sufficient to allege that an act was negligently done by defendant, and that it caused damage to plaintiff.
. . .

The same rule permitting the pleading of negligence in general terms has been applied in malpractice cases. Dunn v. Dufficy, 194 Cal. 383, 228 P. 1029; Ragin v. Zimmerman, 206 Cal. 723, 276 P. 107; McGehee v. Schiffman, 4 Cal.App. 50, 87 P. 290. That in such instances, in addition to general allegations of negligence, the complaint may include a recital of certain related particulars does not deflect from the force of the general rule that "it is sufficient in cases of this class to plead that the thing done was negligently done." Ragin v. Zimmerman, supra, 206 Cal. at page 725, 276 P. at page 108; cf. Blakeslee v. Tannlund, 25 Cal.App.2d 32, 76 P.2d 216. While the statement of other facts auxiliary to the main fact—"the fact which caused the injury" (McGehee v. Schiffman, supra, 4 Cal.App. at page 53, 87 P. at page 291)—might tend to provide a clearer conception of the principal act, it has been the settled rule in this state since the decision of Stephenson v. Southern Pacific Co., supra, that "negligence and proximate cause may be simply set forth." . . .

Tested by the requirements of the established rule for negligence pleading, the complaint in the present case must be held sufficient. Negligence is expressly alleged with respect to three successive stages in the medical services rendered to plaintiff H.H. Rannard: the diagnosis, the operation, and the subsequent treatment. In relation to this premise of negligence, the complaint further alleges that "as a direct and proximate consequence and result" thereof various items of damage had been sustained by plaintiffs, thus satisfying the requirement of pleading "a causal connection between the act and the injury." 19 Cal. Jur., "Negligence," § 101, pp. 677, 678. While the complaint is couched in very general language, "All that is required of a plaintiff, as a matter of pleading, even as against a special demurrer, is that his complaint set forth the essential facts of the case with reasonable precision and with sufficient particularity to acquaint the defendant with the nature, source, and extent of his cause of action." Dunn v. Dufficy, supra, 194 Cal. at page 391, 228 P. at page 1032.

This the complaint here does and it should be no more necessary, after the general charge of negligence in the diagnosis, the operation and the subsequent treatment, to detail the specific act or omission upon which plaintiffs rely than it is incumbent upon a plaintiff in an automobile collision case to specify the particular in which the vehicle was negligently operated, such as driving on the wrong side of the road, driving at an excessive speed, or failure to give proper traffic signals. These are matters of evidence which may be shown under the scope of the general negligence charge. Taylor v. Oakland Scavenger Co., 12 Cal.2d 310, 316, 317, 83 P.2d 948.

The standard of pleading in negligence cases rests upon considerations of fairness and convenience in view of the situation of the opposing parties, and the rule permitting the pleading of negligence in general terms finds justification in the fact that the person charged with negligence may ordinarily be assumed to possess at least equal, if not superior, knowledge of the affair to that possessed by the injured party. Stephenson v. Southern Pacific Co., supra. . . .

It follows from the above observations that the complaint here is a sufficient pleading of a cause of action against defendant Lockheed Aircraft Corporation.

The judgment is reversed.

———

LUBLINER v. RUGE

Supreme Court of Washington, 1944.
21 Wn.2d 881, 153 P.2d 694.

GRADY, J. This action was brought by Carl Lubliner against Edward S. Ruge and Edwin T. Kinerk and wife to recover damages for injuries sustained as the result of an automobile driven by Ruge coming in contact with him as he was traveling across a street intersection. The case was tried before the court and a jury, and a verdict for the defendants was returned. Plaintiff has taken an appeal from the judgment entered dismissing his action. Mr. Ruge will be referred to as though he were the only respondent.

     *   *   *

The defense is based upon the alleged contributory negligence of appellant, in that he entered the intersection against the red light and otherwise failed to exercise reasonable care for his own safety.

The appellant assigns as error that the court refused to permit him to refer in his opening statement to the jury and to prove that respondent had been drinking intoxicating liquor prior to the happening of the accident. The respondent contends that the proof of such fact was not admissible because it was not pleaded in the complaint, and appellant meets this by asserting that the condition of respondent arising out of the consumption of an intoxicant was evidentiary, and it was not necessary to plead it.

The cases cited by appellant support the rule for which he contends; namely, that if it appeared from the evidence that respondent was under the influence of intoxicating liquor at the time of the accident, such condition in and of itself would not constitute negligence, but could be considered by the jury as evidence bearing upon the question whether respondent was or was not guilty of one of the acts of negligence charged in the complaint, but in none of them does it appear that the question of pleading we now have before us was raised or decided.

In deciding the question of pleading, we must take into consideration the foregoing rule; Rem.Rev.Stat., Vol. 7A, § 6360–119 [P.C. § 2696–877], making it unlawful to operate any vehicle upon a public highway while under the influence of or affected by the use of intoxicating liquor; the general rule that a pleading should allege ultimate facts, and not contain evidentiary matter; and that the adverse party should be apprised of that with which he is charged as a basis of liability with sufficient certainty so as to enable him to prepare for and meet it at the trial of the action. A violation of a statute is negligence as a matter of law. When the violation of a statute is relied upon as a basis of negligence, such statute need not be set forth in the pleading, but the facts making the statute applicable must be alleged. Anderson v. Pantages Theatre Co., 114 Wash. 24, 194 P. 813. Evidence of being under the influence of or affected by the use of intoxicating liquor while driving an automobile or while doing any other act likely to do harm, is very damaging to one charged with negligence, and he should be informed of such charge so as to be able to gather and submit proof to the contrary. We, therefore, state the rule to be that, when a party to an action contemplates submitting affirmative proof that, by reason of the use of intoxicating liquor, there was thereby a contribution to some act or omission which it is alleged constituted negligence, such fact must be pleaded by such party. This was the ruling of the trial judge, and he was correct in such action.

[For errors in the trial court's instructions to the jury, the judgment was reversed and a new trial ordered.]

B. ILLUSTRATIVE STATUTORY TREATMENT

NEW YORK CIVIL PRACTICE LAW AND RULES

Rule 3015. Particularity as to Specific Matters

(a) Conditions precedent. The performance or occurrence of a condition precedent in a contract need not be pleaded. A denial of performance or occurrence shall be made specifically and with particularity. In case of such denial, the party relying upon the performance or occurrence shall be required to prove on the trial only such performance or occurrence as shall have been so specified.

(b) Corporate status. Where any party is a corporation, the complaint shall so state and, where known, it shall specify the state, country or government by or under whose laws the party was created.

. . .

Rule 3016. Particularity in Specific Actions

(a) Libel or slander. In an action for libel or slander, the particular words complained of shall be set forth in the complaint, but their application to the plaintiff may be stated generally.

(b) Fraud or mistake. Where a cause of action or defense is based upon misrepresentation, fraud, mistake, wilful default, breach of trust or undue influence, the circumstances constituting the wrong shall be stated in detail.

(c) Separation or divorce. In an action for separation or divorce, the nature and circumstances of a party's alleged misconduct, if any, and the time and place of each act complained of, if any, shall be specified in the complaint or counterclaim as the case may be.

(d) Judgment. In an action on a judgment, the complaint shall state the extent to which any judgment recovered by the plaintiff against the defendant, or against a person jointly liable with the defendant, on the same cause of action has been satisfied.

(e) Law of foreign country. Where a cause of action or defense is based upon the law of a foreign country or its political subdivision, the substance of the foreign law relied upon shall be stated.

(f) Sale and delivery of goods or performing of labor or services. In an action involving the sale and delivery of goods, or the performing of labor or services, or the furnishing of materials, the plaintiff may set forth and number in his verified complaint the items of his claim and the reasonable value or agreed price of each. Thereupon the defendant by his verified answer shall indicate specifically those items he disputes and whether in respect of delivery or performance, reasonable value or agreed price. . . .

Compare F.R.Civ.P. 9.

C. SUBSTANTIVE LEGAL SUFFICIENCY

1. IN GENERAL

NOTE ON INFLUENCE OF FORMAL REQUIREMENTS ON DETERMINATION OF CHALLENGES TO SUBSTANTIVE LEGAL SUFFICIENCY

The separate treatment in this section of the formal and substantive aspects of the complaint's sufficiency is convenient but somewhat artificial. The interdependence of the two topics is reflected most clearly in the venerable doctrine that the demurrer and its code successors admit (arguendo) only the "well-pleaded" allegations of the challenged pleading. E.g., Desautel v. North Dakota Workmen's Compensation Bureau, p. 580, Note (3), supra. For this means that in determining whether the complaint alleges all the elements of a prima facie case under the applicable rule of substantive law, the court will ignore any allegations it considers not "well-pleaded"—i.e., it will read the complaint as not containing them at all. Hence, the result of departures from formal requirements may be to effectively delete an essential allegation or otherwise so riddle the body of the complaint that the remainder becomes insufficient in point of substantive law. It is because of this process, coupled with liberal allowance of amendment and the inability of the traditional common law and Code demurrers to probe the verity of the challenged pleading's allegations, that the demurrer is sometimes said to operate more as a device for polishing the pleadings than as one for disposing of cases summarily on their substantive merits in law.

GARCIA v. HILTON HOTELS INTERNATIONAL, INC.

District Court of the United States, District of Puerto Rico, 1951.
97 F.Supp. 5.

ROBERTS, DISTRICT JUDGE. The action here is for damages for defamation brought by plaintiff, a citizen and resident of Puerto Rico, against defendant, a Delaware corporation, in the District Court of Puerto Rico and removed to this Court by defendant corporation. The complaint sets forth two causes of action and the paragraphs considered herein are identical in each cause. Defendant has moved to dismiss the complaint for failure to state a claim upon which relief can be granted and, in the alternative, to strike Paragraphs 5, 6, 7 and 8 and for a more definite statement.

In support of its motion to dismiss, defendant contends that no publication of the alleged slanderous statement is alleged and that the complaint, therefore, fails to state a cause of action. This contention will be considered first with respect to Paragraph 4 of the complaint, which reads as follows: "4. On August 22, 1950, the plaintiff was violently discharged by the defendant, being falsely and slanderously accused of being engaged in bringing women from outside the Hotel and introducing them into the rooms thereof for the purpose of developing prostitution in the Hotel and that such women brought by him from outside the Hotel and introduced therein carried on acts of prostitution in said Hotel."

The motion to dismiss contemplated in Fed.Rules Civ.Proc. rule 12(b)(6), 28 U.S.C.A., is not concerned with failure of the pleader to state a cause of action, but only with failure to state a claim upon which relief can be granted. There is an obvious distinction between stating a cause of action and stating a claim upon which relief can be granted. It is clear from the terms of rule 8(a) that a pleader is required to set forth only "a short plain statement of the claim showing that the pleader is entitled to relief," and there is no *pleading* requirement that the pleader state a cause of action upon peril of having his complaint dismissed. "If a claim is stated which shows that the pleader is entitled to relief, it is enough to require the service of a responsive pleading; whether a cause of action can be and has been established is for the determination of the trial judge." Van Kirk v. Campbell, 7 F.R.D. 231, 232 (D.C.). . . .

The controlling question here, with respect to the motion to dismiss, is whether the allegations of Paragraph 4 of the complaint, state a claim upon which relief can be granted. An examination of the authorities is persuasive that it does. It is settled, with respect to motions to dismiss for insufficiency of statement, that the complaint is to be construed in the light most favorable to the plaintiff with all doubts resolved in his favor and the allegations accepted as true. If, when a complaint is so considered, it reasonably may be anticipated that plaintiff, on the basis of what has been alleged, could make out a case at trial entitling him to some relief, the complaint should not be dismissed. Asher v. Ruppa, 7 Cir., 173 F.2d 10, 12. This view of the law is supported in Manosky v. Bethlehem-Hingham Shipyard, Inc., 177 F.2d 529, at page 531, where the Court of Appeals of the First Circuit said, ". . . It is true, the complaint did not in so many words allege that Manosky and Sheppard were engaged in the production of goods for interstate commerce. But this is not fatal. Castaing v. Puerto Rican American Sugar Refinery, Inc., 1 Cir., 1944, 145 F.2d 403. As stated in 2 Moore's Federal Practice (2d Ed.) par. 8.13, p. 1653, 'the courts have ruled time and again that a motion to dismiss for failure to state a claim should not be granted unless it appears to a certainty that the plaintiff would be entitled to no relief under any state of facts which could be proved in support of his claim. If, within the framework of the complaint, evidence may be introduced which will sustain a grant of relief to the plaintiff, the complaint is sufficient.' "

Further, it has been a long recognized and generally accepted policy of the courts to look with disfavor upon the practice of terminating litigation, believed to be without merit, by dismissing the complaint for insufficiency of statement. See, Tyler Fixture Corporation v. Dun & Bradstreet, Inc., D.C., 3 F.R.D. 258, citing Winget v. Rockwood, 8 Cir.,

69 F.2d 326 and Leimer v. State Mutual Life Assurance Co., 8 Cir., 108 F.2d 302. In that case, the District Court quoted with approval from Winget v. Rockwood, supra, [69 F.2d 329] as follows: ". . . To warrant such dismissal, it should appear from the allegations that a cause of action does not exist, rather than that a cause of action has been defectively stated. . . .

"That rule of procedure should be followed which will be most likely to result in justice between the parties, and, generally speaking, that result is more likely to be attained by leaving the merits of the cause to be disposed of after answer and the submission of proof, than by attempting to deal with the merits on motion to dismiss the bill."

In the instant case, it is true that Paragraph 4, of the complaint, fails to state, in so many words, that there was a publication of the alleged slanderous utterance and, to that extent, the cause of action is defectively stated. However, it does not follow that the allegations do not state a claim upon which relief can be granted. It is alleged that plaintiff was "violently discharged" and was "falsely and slanderously accused" of procuring for prostitution. While in a technical sense, this language states a conclusion, it is clear that plaintiff used it intending to charge publication of the slanderous utterance and it would be unrealistic for defendant to claim that it does not so understand the allegations. See, Edelman v. Locker, D.C., 6 F.R.D. 272, 274. Clearly, under such allegations it reasonably may be conceived that plaintiff, upon trial, could adduce evidence tending to prove a publication. If the provisions of rule 8(a) are not to be negatived by recourse to rule 12(b), the statement in Paragraph 4 of the complaint must be deemed sufficient.

. . . However, the allegations suffer from vagueness with respect to the utterance alleged to have been slanderously made and the facts relied upon to establish a publication of the utterance. It is concluded that the defendant here is entitled to a more definite statement setting forth substantially the words alleged to have been slanderously uttered and the facts relied upon to establish a publication thereof.

* * *

ALBANY WELFARE RIGHTS ORGANIZATION DAY CARE CENTER, INC. v. SCHRECK

United States Court of Appeals, Second Circuit, 1972.
463 F.2d 620, cert. denied 410 U.S. 944, 93 S.Ct. 1393, 35 L.Ed.2d 611.

HAYS, CIRCUIT JUDGE. Plaintiffs commenced this action for damages and injunctive and declaratory relief on the ground that defendants have improperly denied Albany Welfare Rights Organization Day Care Center, Inc., the right to provide day care services for children of recipients of public assistance. The Executive Director of A.W.R.O. Day Care Center, Catherine Boddie, is one of the named plaintiffs; the other named plaintiffs, mothers of children eligible to receive day care services, sue on behalf of their children and all others similarly situated. The controversy stems from the refusal of appellees Schreck and Jay, the Commissioner and Deputy Commissioner of the Albany County Department of Social Services, to refer eligible children to the Center. The plaintiffs sought to invoke the jurisdiction of the district court under 28 U.S.C.A. §§ 1331, 1343 (1970). They set forth twelve "federal" claims for relief and four "pendent" claims based on appellees' alleged violations of state law. We affirm the district court's dismissal of the complaint on the ground that it fails to allege facts sufficient to state claims upon which relief can be granted.

I

The Albany County Department of Social Services purchases day care services for children eligible to receive such care and pays for the services with funds provided by federal, state, and local agencies. The complaint alleges that Albany County appropriated sufficient funds for the purchase from the Center of day care services for 33 children for the calendar year 1972, subject to the approval of the Center by the New York State Department of Social Services. The New York State Board of Social Welfare issued the Center a certificate authorizing it to operate a day care center and the New York State Department of Social Services issued it a permit to operate a day care center for 20 children. The complaint alleges that thereafter on several occasions plaintiff Boddie and staff members of the Center met with officials of the Albany County Welfare Department and demanded that the Department refer 20 children to the Center for day care. The complaint goes on to state that, although there was a waiting list of over 300 children in Albany County eligible to receive day care services who have not been placed because of the lack of adequate facilities, appellees Schreck and Jay have refused to purchase day care services from the Center as long as plaintiff Boddie is its Executive Director. According to the complaint appellee Schreck told both the temporary Chairman of the Board of Directors of the Center and plaintiff Boddie that he did not believe plaintiff Boddie to be qualified to direct the operations of a day care center and that no children would be referred to the Center as long as plaintiff Boddie remained as Executive Director. The complaint then alleges:

> "14. Upon information and belief, the actions of defendants SCHRECK and JAY as aforesaid are in retaliation for plaintiff Boddie's activities in organizing the Albany Welfare Rights Organization, in asserting the claims of its members and in promoting the interests of the Albany Welfare Rights Organization through speech."

The Center, predicating federal jurisdiction on 28 U.S.C.A. §§ 1331, 1343(3) (1970), alleged that the refusal of appellee Schreck and Jay to refer children to the Center and the refusal of appellee Wyman to direct appellees Schreck and Jay to refer children, inhibited the

Center's constitutional right to associate with Boddie, and violated its constitutional rights to due process and equal protection of the laws, as well as federal and state statutory rights. Plaintiff Boddie, relying for federal jurisdiction on § 1343(3), alleged that the refusal to refer children violated her right to free speech under the First and Fourteenth Amendments. Plaintiffs Shoultz and Milner, suing on behalf of children eligible to receive day care services, predicated jurisdiction on § 1343(3), and alleged that the actions of Schreck and Jay violated rights secured by the First and Fourteenth Amendments and federal statutes, and added pendent claims against appellees Schreck and Jay and appellee Wyman for violations of state law.

II

The basic constitutional claim raised by plaintiff Boddie is that the refusal of Schreck and Jay to refer children to the Center was in retaliation for her activities in organizing the Albany Welfare Rights Organization and her advocacy of the interests of its members, activities which Boddie claims are protected from state interference by the First and Fourteenth Amendments. The Center maintains that appellees' retaliatory refusal inhibits its right to associate with plaintiff Boddie, and the plaintiffs representing the class of eligible children argue that the refusal "chills" the right to associate with plaintiff Boddie, thus depriving them of rights guaranteed them by the First and Fourteenth Amendments. The Center and plaintiff Boddie also assert Fourteenth Amendment due process and equal protection claims.

The facts alleged in the complaint are insufficient as a matter of law to state a claim for relief under 42 U.S.C.A. § 1983 and 28 U.S.C.A. § 1343(3) (1970), and the district court properly dismissed the complaint. Mere conclusory allegations do not provide an adequate basis for the assertion of a claim for violation of these sections. Birnbaum v. Trussell, 347 F.2d 86, 89–90 (2d Cir.1965); Powell v. Workmen's Compensation Board, 327 F.2d 131, 136 (2d Cir.1964). See also Brooke v. Family Court of The State of New York, 420 F.2d 296, 297 (2d Cir.1969), certiorari denied 397 U.S. 1000, 90 S.Ct. 1148, 25 L.Ed.2d 411 (1970). This court has recently held that conclusory allegations of politically motivated discrimination are insufficient as a matter of law to state a claim for relief. Avins v. Mangum, 450 F.2d 932 (2d Cir.1971).

The complaint in the instant action presents no facts to support the allegation that the refusal to refer children was in retaliation for Boddie's organizing activities. It appears from the complaint that Boddie "is Chairwoman of the Upstate Welfare Rights Organization and is Treasurer of the Albany Welfare Rights Organization." However the complaint does not suggest any reason to believe that there was any connection between Boddie's official position in the welfare rights groups and appellees' refusal to refer children to the Center. In fact, according to the complaint, appellee Schreck told plaintiff Boddie and the Chairman of the Board of the Center that the reason children would not be referred was because Schreck did not believe Boddie to be qualified to direct a day care center.

The allegation that the refusal to refer children to the Center was a retaliatory measure designed to prevent or to inhibit plaintiff Boddie from exercising First Amendment rights is wholly conclusory. No facts were alleged which would provide any ground for believing that the refusal was politically motivated or which would tend to explain why appellees Schreck and Jay should want to retaliate against Boddie. The complaint was thus properly dismissed as insufficient as a matter of law.

* * *

The order dismissing the complaint is affirmed.

FEINBERG, CIRCUIT JUDGE (dissenting). This case raises the issue whether Albany County officials can arbitrarily refuse to obtain sorely needed day care for children of welfare recipients because the officials do not like the well-known, aggressive political and legal activities of the Executive Director of a day care center. Beneath all the papers and briefs with which we have been favored, that is what this litigation is all about. In view of the uncontradicted assertion of plaintiffs that there are no other day care facilities available in the entire county for the children of the two plaintiff welfare mothers, the issue is a grave one.

If the complaint in this action offered nothing more than the bald assertion that upon information and belief defendants Schreck and Jay have refused to refer children to the Albany Welfare Rights Organization Day Care Center, Inc. because they disapprove of Director Boddie's political and litigious activities on behalf of welfare recipients, I would agree that dismissal for failure to state a claim for relief would be proper under Avins v. Mangum, 450 F.2d 932 (2d Cir.1971). But the complaint before us does not consist solely of such a conclusory allegation unsupported by any factual basis. In fact, the complaint is the antithesis of the typically sparse, bare bones, conclusory pleading that might justify dismissal. The "factual allegations" are contained in 20 separately numbered paragraphs, full of evidentiary detail. In them, plaintiffs trace the events leading up to this controversy and assert, with supporting documents, that the Day Care Center has been duly approved by the State Board of Social Welfare and licensed by the State Department of Social Services. As to the action of the latter agency, the complaint further states that the Department issued a permit to the Center only after it specifically determined that a definite need exists in the Albany area for day care services and that the Center's staff members, including plaintiff Boddie as its Executive Director, meet all requirements under the law for their positions. Indeed, the district judge below noted that "[a]fter an affidavit was filed as to the [un]fitness of Mrs. Boddie by Commissioner Schreck, the State reinvestigated her background and let the revocable permit . . . issued to AWRO Day Care Center . . . stand unchanged." [1]

Thus, the allegations in the complaint, which of course we must accept as true for purposes of testing its sufficiency, show at the very least that plaintiffs have a factual foundation upon which they may be able to establish at trial that defendants Schreck and Jay have refused to deal with the Center because of Boddie's welfare rights advocacy and not because she is unqualified. Obviously, plaintiffs have not yet proved retaliation, but they have sufficiently alleged it. The complaint must be upheld unless

> it appears to a certainty that the plaintiff would be entitled to no relief under any state of facts which could be proved in support of his claim. If, within the framework of the complaint, evidence may be introduced which will sustain a grant of relief to the plaintiff, the complaint is sufficient. [Footnotes omitted.]

2A Moore, Federal Practice, ¶ 8.13 at 1705–06 (2d ed. 1968). See also Conley v. Gibson, 355 U.S. 41, 47–48, 78 S.Ct. 99, 2 L.Ed.2d 80 (1957); Escalera v. New York City Housing Authority, 425 F.2d 853, 857 (2d Cir.), certiorari denied 400 U.S. 853, 91 S.Ct. 54, 27 L.Ed.2d 91 (1970). In my view, the complaint in this action clearly meets that test of sufficiency.

Accordingly, I dissent. Plaintiffs are entitled to their day in court on their serious charge of arbitrary and unconstitutional action by defendants. At the very least, we should follow the procedure used in Avins v. Mangum, supra, and give plaintiffs an opportunity to amend their complaint before dismissing the action. See also 3 Moore, Federal Practice, ¶ 15.10 (2d ed. 1968).

NOTES

(1) Do you agree with the court in *Garcia* that "There is an obvious distinction between stating a cause of action and stating a claim upon which relief can be granted"? Does the *Garcia* opinion adequately explain the nature

1. [One footnote omitted; this footnote renumbered.] The majority opinion refuses to accept plaintiffs' allegation that the Department found Boddie qualified to serve as Executive Director. The majority justifies its abandonment of the usual rule that such allegations must be accepted as true by arguing that the complaint is internally inconsistent in that the Department's approval of Boddie is alleged to have occurred on December 31, 1971, while elsewhere in the complaint it is stated that Boddie has been employed as director since January 3, 1972. Quite frankly, I am unable to see any inconsistency between the two statements. The statement that Boddie has been Director since January 3, 1972 is included in a paragraph which follows the allegation that "at all times since January 3, 1972, defendants Schreck and Jay have failed or refused to place children in the A.W.R.O. Day Care Center. . . ." Obviously, the reference to Boddie's employment as of January 3, 1972 is intended to show only that she was Director when Schreck and Jay began refusing to cooperate with the Center and cannot be read as negatively implying that she was never associated with the Center before that date or that the State Department of Social Services, when it issued a permit to the Center, did not know that Boddie would serve as Director when the Center opened three days later.

of this distinction?   Are the *Garcia* and *Albany Welfare Rights decisions* reconcilable?

(2) The permissive formulations relied upon by both the *Garcia* court and Judge Feinberg's dissenting opinion in the *Schreck* case of what suffices to withstand demurrer-type attacks under the Federal Rules rest on impressive authority: in Conley v. Gibson, 355 U.S. 41, 45–46, 78 S.Ct. 99, 102, 2 L.Ed.2d 80 (1957), the United States Supreme Court said that the pleading should be held sufficient unless "it appears beyond doubt that the plaintiff can prove no set of facts in support of his claim which would entitle him to relief."   Does that mean that a complaint for breach of contract will be upheld even though it fails to allege a material element such as consideration or breach?   If not, why not?

2.   BUILT–IN DEFENSES

PENTON v. CANNING
Supreme Court of Wyoming, 1941.
57 Wyo. 390, 118 P.2d 1002.

RINER, CHIEF JUSTICE.   [This was an action for the malicious prosecution of plaintiff by defendant for the theft of a heifer calf.   Plaintiff's amended petition alleged in substance that "without probable cause therefor" defendant maliciously made complaint to a Justice of the Peace that plaintiff had stolen the calf from defendant; that plaintiff pleaded not guilty to the charge but that upon the preliminary hearing the Justice of the Peace, "in utter disregard of the testimony of the parties and witnesses" and without sufficient evidence, "found that a crime had been committed and that there was probable cause to believe the defendant guilty of the offense," and ordered plaintiff to appear at the next term of the District Court to answer the complaint; that thereafter defendant brought an action of replevin against plaintiff before another Justice of the Peace to recover possession of the calf and that after a trial of that action the Justice of the Peace rendered judgment for plaintiff which was affirmed on appeal to the District Court; and that for that reason the criminal proceeding against plaintiff was thereafter dismissed on motion of the Prosecuting Attorney.

Defendant demurred to the petition on the ground that it failed to state facts sufficient to constitute a cause of action, but her demurrer was overruled.   She then answered, denying the allegations of the petition, and, after a trial, judgment for $1,000 was rendered in plaintiff's favor, from which defendant appealed, assigning, among other errors, the overruling of her demurrer.]

The attitude of the courts and authorities generally toward the action of malicious prosecution has been well stated by Mr. Newell in his text dealing with that subject.   The author says in section 13, at page 21: "Actions for malicious prosecutions are regarded by the law with jealousy.   Lord Holt said more than two hundred years ago that they 'ought not to be favored but managed with great caution'.   Their tendency is to discourage prosecution for crime, as they expose the prosecutors to civil suits, and the love of justice may not always be strong enough to induce individuals to commence prosecutions, when, if they fail, they may be subjected to the expense of litigation, if they be not mulcted in damages."

*   *   *

Under the authorities [cited above] the action, not being a favored one, should require at the very least a careful examination of the pleadings and proofs appearing in the case. At the very least also these matters, i.e., pleadings and proof, should be consistent with sound logic and elementary principles.

An inspection of the allegations of plaintiff's pleading quoted above discloses that he has set forth the fact that the result of the preliminary examination before the Justice of the Peace Dobler was unfavorable to the plaintiff in this, the malicious prosecution action, on account of the action of the Justice of the Peace in binding plaintiff over to respond in the District Court to the charge of theft of the calf in question. To avoid the effect of this allegation plaintiff states, as we have seen, that the officer acted "in utter disregard of the testimony of the parties and witnesses and wholly without any adequate, sufficient or competent evidence upon which to base any judgment or find against the plaintiff".

*   *   *

This court has heretofore in McIntosh et al. v. Wales, 21 Wyo. 397, 134 P. 274, 276, Ann.Cas.1916C, 273, pointed out that: "The essential elements necessary to be shown by the petition and evidence in an action for malicious prosecution are (1) the institution of the proceedings; (2) without probable cause; (3) with malice; (4) that the proceedings have terminated and in plaintiff's favor; (5) damage to plaintiff."

The question then presents itself whether the allegations quoted above are in this case affected by these rules. A careful examination of the authorities we have been able to find would indicate that an affirmative answer be given to this query. . . . 38 C.J. 411, § 45 . . . says that: "While there is some authority to the contrary, it has been generally held that, where the result of the preliminary examination before a magistrate is unfavorable to accused and he is held or committed by the magistrate, this is prima facie but not conclusive evidence of probable cause. This prima facie case may be overcome by evidence that the action of the magistrate was obtained by false testimony or other improper means; but unless it is overthrown by testimony of that character, it becomes conclusive and must prevent plaintiff from prevailing."

*   *   *

Viewing in their entirety the authorities examined, as above set forth, we are obliged to conclude that the amended petition in the case at bar quite fails to measure up to the standard set by them and accordingly fails to state a cause of action. As we have seen, that pleading avers that the Justice of the Peace Dobler, found that "a crime had been committed and that there was probable cause to believe the defendant guilty of the offense" and ordered the plaintiff to be bound over to answer the charge in the district court of Fremont County. This was an allegation of prima facie probable cause for instituting the prosecution.

In order to avoid the effect of this statement, the pleading alleges merely that the action of the Justice was taken "in utter disregard of the testimony of the parties and witnesses and wholly without any adequate, sufficient or competent evidence upon which to base any judgment or finding against the plaintiff". Surveyed in the light of the foregoing authorities, this is not such an allegation as will avoid a prima facie averment of probable cause made as aforesaid.

It must not be overlooked that the case at bar is an asserted malicious prosecution of the plaintiff, Penton, by the appellant and defendant, Mrs. Gertrude C. Boyd Canning, and by no one else. What connection did this woman have with the conduct of the officer in acting as he did? According to plaintiff's pleading, absolutely none. On the contrary, that pleading expressly asserts that the Justice disregarded her testimony, as well as that of Penton, and the testimony of all the witnesses given on the preliminary hearing. That is all. The pleading would even appear to attack the testimony of plaintiff himself by its allegation that the officer acted "without any adequate, sufficient or competent evidence". However, this is but the pleading of a legal conclusion. Is Mrs. Canning to be held responsible for the error of the official when neither plaintiff's pleading nor his proofs aver or establish that she was? We hardly think that can be the law. Otherwise she could have told the Justice of the Peace in her testimony given on the preliminary hearing—and what she said we do not know—that she was in good faith in error concerning the charge made against Penton, and because the Justice wrongfully disregarded her testimony, she should nevertheless be held responsible for his action in finding that there was probable cause to believe the defendant, Penton, guilty of the offense charged. This can hardly be so. There is nothing alleged or proven to impeach the independent action of the Justice of the Peace in the matter with which Mrs. Canning was concerned, according to the allegations of plaintiff's pleading. She employed no fraud or other improper means to influence the officer's conduct.

* * *

Reversed.

NOTE

In Leggett v. Montgomery Ward & Co., 178 F.2d 436 (10th Cir.1949), the federal court, following Penton v. Canning, held a malicious prosecution complaint insufficient under Wyoming law, stating:

> "It is the general rule of pleading that where a complaint alleges facts constituting a cause of action and also alleges facts which constitute a valid defense, unless it alleges further facts avoiding such defense, it may be attacked by demurrer or motion to dismiss."

Does *Penton v. Canning* furnish the correct test of the sufficiency of the complaint in a federal court action such as *Leggett*? Suppose *Penton v. Canning* itself had arisen in a federal rather than a Wyoming state court. How should a federal court then have decided it? How would the *Garcia* court have decided it?

3. JUDICIAL NOTICE

HANCOCK v. BURNS, 158 Cal.App.2d 785, 323 P.2d 456 (Dist.Ct. of Appeals, First District, 1958: . . . Although it is often stated that in considering a demurrer a court is bound to accept the truth of the allegations thereof, this statement may, in certain instances, be modified where, by the nature of the pleading, the court is apprised of the existence of a fact or facts of which it is bound to take judicial notice under the laws of this state. In 39 Cal.Jur.2d, § 22, under the title "Facts Judicially Noticed" it is said: ". . . In determining the sufficiency of a pleading, it may be read as though it included all such facts, though not pleaded, and even when the pleading contains an express allegation to the contrary. But the general rule of pleading that a demurrer admits the facts pleaded has no application to facts of which the court may take judicial notice. Allegations contrary to facts which the court may judicially notice are not admitted by demurrer, but must be disregarded and treated as a nullity." . . .

NOTES

(1) In Clough v. Goggins, 40 Iowa 325 (1875), the court sustained defendant's demurrer to plaintiff's petition in an action upon two promissory notes alleged to have been made on October 1, 1871, declaring that courts "will judicially take notice of the coincidence of days of the week with days of the month" and that the date in question was a Sunday; hence, the contracts sued upon were void.

(2) In an action against a meat retailer for breach of warranty in selling fresh pork which, when eaten after proper cooking, caused plaintiffs to contract trichinosis, defendant's motion to dismiss the complaint was granted. The appellate court held that the trial court properly took judicial notice of the scientific fact that proper cooking of fresh pork kills the trichinae which cause the disease. Nicketta v. National Tea Co., 338 Ill.App. 159, 87 N.E.2d 30 (1949), followed in Golaris v. Jewel Tea Co., 22 F.R.D. 16 (N.D.Ill.1958). The court said:

> "If the matter falls within the domain of judicial knowledge, it is beyond the realm of dispute; therefore, evidence is unnecessary. It is the judge's function to decide whether a matter is a subject of evidence or of judicial notice. The judge should be free to make for himself such investigation as he desires, but he should also be able to call upon the parties for assistance. . . . A trial court will take judicial notice of many things, such as the statutes of the United States and the States, well established and well known historical and scientific facts and matters of common knowledge which it would be senseless to make a litigant prove or to permit him to prove. The courts will take judicial notice of scientific facts which have been well established by authorita-

tive scientists and are generally accepted as irrefutable by living scientists.

THE FEDERAL RULES OF EVIDENCE

Rule 201. Judicial Notice of Adjudicative Facts

(a) **Scope of Rule.** This rule governs only judicial notice of adjudicative facts.

(b) **Kinds of Facts.** A judicially noticed fact must be one not subject to reasonable dispute in that it is either (1) generally known within the territorial jurisdiction of the trial court or (2) capable of accurate and ready determination by resort to sources whose accuracy cannot reasonably be questioned.

(c) **When Discretionary.** A court may take judicial notice, whether requested or not.

(d) **When Mandatory.** A court shall take judicial notice if requested by a party and supplied with the necessary information.

(e) **Opportunity to Be Heard.** A party is entitled upon timely request to an opportunity to be heard as to the propriety of taking judicial notice and the tenor of the matter noticed. In the absence of prior notification, the request may be made after judicial notice has been taken.

(f) **Time of Taking Notice.** Judicial notice may be taken at any stage of the proceeding.

(g) **Instructing Jury.** In a civil action or proceeding, the court shall instruct the jury to accept as conclusive any fact judicially noticed. In a criminal case, the court shall instruct the jury that it may, but is not required to, accept as conclusive any fact judicially noticed.

NOTES

(1) When the court takes judicial notice of adjudicative facts it is ordinarily dealing with scientific findings that affect the interests of the immediate parties to the litigation, but not the interests of other persons or their cases. Another type of judicially noticed finding may provide the factual basis for the way the court formulates a rule of law of general applicability and is called a "legislative fact." The courts' methods of noticing legislative facts is haphazard and unreliable. Recent proposals would provide institutional means and regular procedures to assist the courts in taking judicial notice of non-record data, such as social science findings on questions of significance to the law. See Rosenberg, Improving the Courts' Ability to Absorb Scientific Information in Golden, Science and Technology Advice to the President, Congress and the Judiciary, 480–83 (1988).

(2) The concept of judicial notice is also invoked as the basis for American courts' ascertaining for themselves—thus avoiding any need for either pleading or proof—the statutory and case law of sister states and the United States when

such "foreign" law is applicable to a case before them. Not so, however, when the properly applicable law is that of a foreign country, which may entail difficulties of access as well as of language.

4. FOREIGN LAW

Most recent enactments relating to the pleading and proof of the law of a foreign country substitute a notice requirement for a mandatory pleading requirement. See Federal Civil Rule 44.1, which became effective in 1966, and Section 4.01 of the Uniform Interstate and International Procedure Act. As the draftsmen's comment to Section 4.01 of the Uniform Interstate and International Procedure Act points out:

> "Although a pleading requirement may be justified as a notice device, pleading is neither the only nor always the most desirable method of giving notice of the presence of an issue of foreign law. The shift in focus in many modern procedural systems from the pleading stage to other phases of pre-trial was intended to eliminate much of the hyper-technicality of pleading and time-consuming and sterile motion practice that may polish the pleadings, but rarely disposes of the case on the merits. A requirement that notice of intent to rely on foreign law be given in the pleading only perpetuates prior notions and invites dilatory motions and amendments.

> Further, to force a party to set forth the substance of the foreign law at the pleading stage may be an onerous burden in view of the frequent lack of command over the operative facts at that embryonic stage. In some states, this is partially ameliorated by liberal provisions for amendment of pleadings and for hypothetical and alternative pleadings. Even so, no reason exists for requiring counsel to examine extensively the complexities of foreign law or, for that matter, to engender reliance on the part of his opponent, before it is apparent what law will control. If notice to court and adversary is the goal, there is ample opportunity prior to trial or, if necessary, at trial for informal notification of an intent to rely on foreign law."

NOTES

(1) Many states continue to insist that the law of foreign countries be pleaded. See, e.g., N.Y.—McKinney's CPLR § 3016(e). The exact manner in which this is to be done depends upon the particular state involved. See the excellent treatment in Schlesinger, Baade, Damaska & Herzog, Comparative Law 108–109 (5th ed. 1988).

(2) For a criticism of the New York rules, see Smit, Report of the Adm. Board of the N.Y.Jud.Conf. 170–181 (1967). The most comprehensive discussion of the federal rule is in Miller, Federal Rule 44.1 and the "Fact" Approach to

Determining Foreign Law: Death Knell for a Die-Hard Doctrine, 65 Mich.L. Rev. 613 (1965).

––––––––

D. DEMAND FOR RELIEF

––––––––

RIGGS, FERRIS & GEER v. LILLIBRIDGE

United States Court of Appeals, Second Circuit, 1963.
316 F.2d 60.

CLARK, CIRCUIT JUDGE. Plaintiff, a firm of lawyers practicing in New York City, brought this action in the court's diversity jurisdiction to recover the fair and reasonable value of legal services rendered to defendant by Trafford a senior partner in the plaintiff firm. Liability was conceded, the only issue being the value of the services. Plaintiff's final bill was for $35,000, although it made a written offer to settle for $25,000. When this was refused, plaintiff filed suit, demanding $35,000. At the pretrial conference, plaintiff amended its complaint, increasing its demand to $50,000. The jury returned a verdict of $56,000 which, as defendant points out on this appeal, is $21,000, or 60 per cent, more than plaintiff's final bill.

* * *

Since we reject out of hand defendant's contention that the $56,000 verdict was excessive, only one further point need detain us. Defendant urges that it was improper for the jury to award an amount in excess of that claimed in the amended ad damnum clause, relying on New York law as controlling in this diversity case and citing for authority Michalowski v. Ey, 7 N.Y.2d 71, 75, 195 N.Y.S.2d 633, 163 N.E.2d 863. Even were we to accept New York law as overriding the federal rules on this purely procedural issue, we should still find difficulty, in the light of code history explaining N.Y.C.P.A. § 479, in holding the suggested limitation applicable here, where the defendant had *answered* and the parties were at issue. . . . But we are quite clear that this is a matter of procedure, governed entirely by F.R. 54(c), as many cases have held. [Citations omitted.] Any other conclusion would upset, in diversity actions, the entire plan of federal procedure, with its lessened emphasis upon the formal pleadings, its greater stress on depositions and discovery and on pretrial, its use of amendments conforming to the evidence [even if not formally made, see F.R. 15(b)], and so on. In no proper sense can these interwoven and useful devices of modern litigation be held to affect the "outcome" of the litigation except as they lead more directly to a correct decision on the merits, which even the state rule must envisage. Here the plaintiff could easily have amended, as it did once, except that we have said that to be unnecessary and even undesirable. Wendy v. McLean Trucking Co., supra. So we turn to F.R. 54(c) as here controlling.

. . . it is made expressly clear there that only as to a party against whom a judgment is entered *by default* is recovery limited to that prayed for in the demand for judgment. Where defendant has appeared and the parties are at issue, the final judgment shall grant the relief to which the party in whose favor it is rendered is entitled, even if not demanded. [Citations omitted.]

Affirmed.

NOTES

(1) Section 3215 of N.Y.—McKinney's CPLR, in limiting a default judgment to the relief demanded in the complaint, states the usual rule. If the summons contains a notice that in the event of default, judgment in the sum of $49,600 will be taken against the defendant and defendant enters a general appearance, may the complaint then ask for relief exceeding $400,000? Everitt v. Everitt, 4 N.Y.2d 13, 171 N.Y.S.2d 836, 148 N.E.2d 891 (1958), answers this question in the affirmative.

(2) Permitting amendment of the "ad damnum" clause before the close of the trial is within the trial judge's discretion. See, e.g., Robichaud v. St. Cyr, 150 Me. 168, 107 A.2d 540 (1954). But cf. Wyman v. Morone, 33 A.D.2d 168, 306 N.Y.S.2d 115 (3d Dep't 1969) (majority construes N.Y. CPLR § 3017(a) authorizing the court to "grant any type of relief within its jurisdiction appropriate to the proof whether or not demanded," as not authorizing increase of ad damnum clause at the trial to conform to the proof).

In Bail v. Cunningham Brothers, Inc., 452 F.2d 182 (7th Cir.1971), the court allowed a $135,000 damage award, although only $100,000 had been requested in the complaint.

(3) Ellis v. Crockett, 51 Hawaii 45, 451 P.2d 814 (1969): "The law divides damages into two broad categories—*general* and *special.* General damages are said to encompass all the damages which naturally and necessarily result from a legal wrong done. . . . Such damages follow by implication of law upon proof of a wrong. On the other hand, special damages are considered to be the natural but not the necessary result of an alleged wrong. . . . *[S]pecial damages* are those damages which are of a relatively unusual kind and which, without specific notice to the adversary, may not be understood to be part of the claim."

See Fed.R.Civ.P. 9(g). For a discussion of what items constitute special damages and what degree of detail is required in pleading them see Note, The Definition and Pleading of Special Damage Under the Federal Rules of Civil Procedure, 55 Va.L.Rev. 542 (1969).

SECTION 6. RESPONSIVE PLEADINGS

A. DENIALS AND DEFENSES

DAVID v. CROMPTON & KNOWLES CORP.
District Court of the United States, Eastern District of Pennsylvania, 1973.
58 F.R.D. 444.

MEMORANDUM

HUYETT, DISTRICT JUDGE. The present case is a products liability action involving a serious personal injury. Defendant, Crompton & Knowles Corporation (Crompton), seeks to amend its answer to paragraph 5 of the complaint which alleges that Crompton designed, manufactured and sold a shredding machine, 600 AAZ Series 11, to Crown Products Corporation (Crown).[1] In its answer to the complaint Crompton averred that it was without sufficient knowledge or information to admit or deny the allegation and demanded proof. It now seeks to deny that it designed, manufactured and sold the machine in question.[2]

Crompton bases its proffered denial upon information which it claims it discovered during 1972. It alleges that the machine was designed, manufactured and sold by James Hunter Corporation (Hunter) prior to its purchase of Hunter, and that it did not assume liabilities for the negligent design, manufacture or sale of machines by Hunter prior to its purchase of Hunter's assets in 1961.

An answer to an averment in a complaint which states that the party lacks sufficient information or knowledge to admit or deny the averments is permitted by Fed.R.Civ.P. 8(b) and it has the effect of a denial. A party, however, may not deny sufficient information or knowledge with impunity, but is subject to the requirements of honesty in pleading. See, 2A J. Moore, Federal Practice ¶ 8.22 (1968). An averment will be deemed admitted when the matter is obviously one as to which defendant has knowledge or information. Mesirow v. Duggan, 240 F.2d 751 (8 Cir.), cert. denied sub nom. Duggan v. Green, 355 U.S. 864, 78 S.Ct. 93, 2 L.Ed.2d 70 (1957). Crompton claims that it only recently discovered the information which it now uses as a basis to deny the allegations of Paragraph 5. Plaintiff contends that

1. Crompton filed a third-party complaint against Crown, which in turn filed a third-party complaint against George Young Company, which installed the machine on Crown's premises.

2. The shredding machine denominated in the complaint is not the correct machine. The proper machine was a Model F–4000 Garnett machine which Crompton referred to in answers to interrogatories filed October 1, 1971. This machine was sold by Hunter to Crown as was the shredding machine mentioned in the complaint.

Crompton's denial of knowledge or information was patently false and should be treated as an admission.

The request for leave to amend assumes significance if Crompton's original answer to Paragraph 5 is deemed an admission. If it is considered an admission, then it is necessary to decide whether an amendment which might greatly affect plaintiff's right to recovery should be allowed, but if it is not deemed admitted and is considered denied in the original answer, then the amendment will only serve as a clarification.

The machine which was involved in the accident was designed, manufactured and sold by Hunter to Crown in 1961. Crompton admits that it was aware that the machine was a Hunter product at the time it answered the complaint or very shortly thereafter.[3] Nevertheless, in answers to interrogatories and in a third-party complaint Crompton indicated that it was responsible for the design, manufacture and sale of the machine which was made prior to its purchase of Hunter. Crompton relies entirely on its claim that it has only recently discovered that the contract by which it purchased Hunter did not make it responsible for liabilities of this kind.

In Mesirow v. Duggan, supra, the court held that if the matter alleged in the averment was a matter of record peculiarly within the control and knowledge of the defendant, an answer that defendant was without knowledge or information sufficient to form a belief did not constitute a denial under Fed.R.Civ.P. 8(b). See also, American Photocopy Equipment Co. v. Rovico, Inc., 359 F.2d 745 (7 Cir.1966); Harvey Aluminum, Inc. v. N.L.R.B., 335 F.2d 749 (9 Cir.1964); Squire v. Levan, 32 F.Supp. 437 (E.D.Pa.1940); 2A J. Moore, Federal Practice ¶ 8.22 (1968). In the present case Crompton admits knowledge of Hunter's role in the design, manufacture and sale of the machine. Its assertion of lack of knowledge or information, therefore, must have been in relation to responsibility which it assumed for such a claim. Any responsibility, of course, arises from the agreement of sale between Crompton and Hunter. The terms of this agreement are certainly peculiarly within the control and knowledge of Crompton, one of the parties to the agreement. It does not seem too burdensome to hold Crompton to knowledge of the terms of its purchase agreement and their effect on its rights and liabilities more than nine years after the sale of Hunter was completed. The averment of lack of knowledge or information sufficient to admit or deny the allegations of Paragraph 5 is not proper under these circumstances and plaintiff's allegation should be deemed admitted.

---

3. In answers to interrogatories Crompton asserted that it learned of the action from Hunter, which is now a division of Crompton.

SINCLAIR REFINING CO. v. HOWELL

Court of Appeals of the United States, Fifth Circuit, 1955.
222 F.2d 637.

RIVES, CIRCUIT JUDGE.* A father suing under the Alabama statute for the wrongful death of his nineteen year old son, secured a verdict and judgment for damages in the amount of $30,000 from which this appeal is prosecuted. Three questions are presented for decision. The first and most important is whether, within the issues tried, the deceased was subject to the Workmen's Compensation Act of Alabama and whether, for that reason, the district court erred in denying the defendant's motions for a directed verdict and for judgment non obstante veredicto. . . .

Hayward Howell, the brother of the deceased minor, John Arthur Howell, was in the process of opening a general store and gasoline filling station on U.S. Highway 231 in Montgomery County, Alabama, on the 17th day of November, 1951. John Arthur Howell was "in the general employ" of Hayward Howell on this date. One A.O. Hall, an employee of appellant as a maintenance mechanic, whose duties were to supervise and assist in the installation of equipment at various filling stations, was engaged in supervising and assisting in the installation of a pole at Hayward Howell's filling station. . . . The top of the pole came in contact with the high voltage line and John Arthur Howell was electrocuted.

The general verdict for the plaintiff was based upon two counts, one charging the defendant with negligence, and the other charging it with wanton misconduct. Under the rulings of the court, the plaintiff was required to amend his complaint so as to aver ". . . that the said John Arthur Howell . . . was not subject to the Workmen's Compensation Laws of Alabama . . .." There was no express denial of this averment in the defendant's answer, and the only way that it was even impliedly denied was by the concluding sentence of the answer: "Defendant denies that the plaintiff is entitled to recover any damages in this cause." Rule 8(b) of the Federal Rules of Civil Procedure, 28 U.S.C.A., provides: "A party shall state in short and plain terms his defenses to each claim asserted and shall admit or deny the averments upon which the adverse party relies." Rule 8(d) provides: "Averments in a pleading to which a responsive pleading is required, other than those as to the amount of damage, are admitted when not denied in the responsive pleading." The effect of the defendant's answer was to admit the averment that the deceased was not subject to the Workmen's Compensation Law of Alabama. If the issue of applicability of the Workmen's Compensation Act had been clearly drawn, as required by the rule, the appellee would have had the opportunity of developing that the deceased's "working for" his brother was at most a "casual" employment excluded from the terms of the Act, or that the Act did not apply

* Footnotes omitted.

because his brother regularly employed less than eight employees. Such possibilities illustrate the wisdom of the rule in requiring issues to be clearly drawn.

* * *

Affirmed.

FUENTES v. TUCKER

Supreme Court of California, 1947.
31 Cal.2d 1, 187 P.2d 752.

GIBSON, C.J. The minor sons of the respective plaintiffs were killed by an automobile operated by defendant. The two actions were consolidated for trial, and in each case the verdict of the jury awarded the plaintiffs $7,500. Defendant appealed from the judgments claiming the trial court erred in permitting plaintiffs to present evidence of facts outside the issues framed by the pleadings.

On the day of the trial defendant filed an amended answer in each case which admitted "that he was and is liable for the death of the deceased . . . and the damages directly and proximately caused thereby." Plaintiffs were nevertheless permitted to prove the circumstances of the accident, including the facts that defendant was intoxicated and that the children were thrown 80 feet by the force of the impact.

It is defendant's position that the introduction of evidence as to the circumstances of the accident was error because it was not relevant or material to the amount of the damages, which was the only issue to be determined by the jury. Plaintiffs contend that defendant could not, by acknowledging legal responsibility for the deaths of the children deprive them of the right to show the circumstances surrounding the accident, and that therefore it was not error to admit evidence of such facts. They do not claim, however, that the evidence was material to any of the facts in dispute under the pleadings as they stood at the commencement of the trial.

It is a doctrine too long established to be open to dispute that the proof must be confined to the issues in the case and that the time of the court should not be wasted, and the jury should not be confused, by the introduction of evidence which is not relevant or material to the matters to be adjudicated. This is merely one aspect of the larger problem of delay in the conduct of litigation. Every court has a responsibility to the public to see that justice is administered efficiently and expeditiously and that the facilities of the court are made available at the first possible moment to those whose cases are awaiting trial. It would be an unwarranted waste of public funds, and a manifest injustice to the many litigants seeking an early trial date, to allow counsel in a particular case to occupy substantial periods of time in the useless presentation of evidence on matters not in controversy; and we know of no well-considered opinion which asserts such a right.

One of the functions of pleadings is to limit the issues and narrow the proofs. If facts alleged in the complaint are not controverted by the answer, they are not in issue, and no evidence need be offered to prove their existence. (Travelers Ins. Co. v. Byers, 123 Cal.App. 473, 482 [11 P.2d 444]; Code Civ.Proc., §§ 462, 588, 1868, 1870 subds. (1), (15); see 1 Wigmore on Evidence [3d ed. 1940], p. 9, § 2.)

Evidence which is not pertinent to the issues raised by the pleadings is immaterial, and it is error to allow the introduction of such evidence. [Citations omitted.]

It follows, therefore, if an issue has been removed from a case by an admission in the answer, that it is error to receive evidence which is material solely to the excluded matter. This, of course, does not mean that an admission of liability precludes a plaintiff from showing how an accident happened if such evidence is material to the issue of damages. In an action for personal injuries, where liability is admitted and the only issue to be tried is the amount of damage, the force of the impact and the surrounding circumstances may be relevant and material to indicate the extent of plaintiff's injuries. (Johnson v. McRee, 66 Cal. App.2d 524, 527 [152 P.2d 526]; Martin v. Miqueu, 37 Cal.App.2d 133, 137 [98 P.2d 816] .) Such evidence is admissible because it is relevant and material to an issue remaining in the case.

The defendant here by an unqualified statement in his answer admitted liability for the deaths of the children, and the sole remaining question in issue was the amount of damages suffered by the parents. In an action for wrongful death of a minor child the damages consist of the pecuniary loss to the parents in being deprived of the services, earnings, society, comfort and protection of the child. (Bond v. United Railroads, 159 Cal. 270, 285 [113 P. 366, Ann.Cas.1912C 50, 48 L.R.A.,N.S. 687].) The manner in which the accident occurred, the force of the impact, or defendant's intoxication could have no bearing on these elements of damage. The evidence, therefore, was not material to any issue before the jury, and its admission was error.

* * *

The introduction of evidence of admitted facts is permissible in cases where the admission is ambiguous in form or limited in scope or where, during the trial of a case, a party seeks to deprive his opponent of the legitimate force and effect of material evidence by the bald admission of a probative fact. [Citations omitted.]

. . . The boys involved in this accident were approximately 12 years old when they were killed. Certainly the sum of $7,500, which was awarded by the jury in each case, cannot be said to be an unreasonable amount to allow for the wrongful death of a child of that age, and the verdict are not so large as to indicate that the jury was unduly influenced by the admission of the immaterial testimony in question. It does not appear, therefore, that the error resulted in a miscarriage of justice.

* * *

The judgments are affirmed.

* * *

CARTER, J. [concurring] . . .

The effect of the majority holding in this case is to deny to an injured person the benefit of presenting to the trier of fact the entire factual situation surrounding the accident out of which the injury arose. It cannot be denied that either a jury or a trial judge is more disposed to award a substantial amount of damages in a case where the defendant is shown to have been guilty of gross negligence and his conduct was such as to indicate a reckless disregard for the safety of others, than where the negligence amounted to only an error in judgment. The present holding will make it possible for a defendant who has been guilty of the most heinous kind of reckless and wanton conduct, including intoxication, to conceal from the trier of fact the extent of his culpability, and thereby gain any advantage which might flow from the absence of such disclosure. Theoretically and technically, and judged by academic standards, this practice may be justified, but when gauged by actual experience in the administration of justice it favors the worst offenders by permitting them to escape from a larger award of damages which the trier of fact might feel justified in awarding if the entire picture were presented. This does not mean that a person injured as the result of the negligence of another should receive more damages because his tortfeasor was grossly and wantonly negligent than another with like injuries whose tortfeasor was only slightly negligent. But it simply recognizes the human tendency to weigh liability against culpability. Since the law must be administered by human beings, the effect of this tendency must be considered as incidental to its administration. To argue to the contrary requires a denial of the obvious. . . .

NOTES

(1) Is Justice Carter right that the trial court should have power to admit evidence relevant to a proposition whose truth has been admitted?

(2) Suppose a plaintiff sues to recover the amount of a promissory note. One of the elements of the cause of action, which must be alleged, is non-payment of the note by the defendant. If the defendant denied this allegation the parties would seemingly be at issue on the question of payment. However, payment is regarded as an affirmative defense that must be pleaded by the defendant. Illogical as this may seem, it may be justified on the pragmatic ground that it is easier to prove a positive fact than a negative one. Green, Basic Civil Procedure 93 (1972).

NOTE ON THE SUFFICIENCY OF PLEADINGS SUBSEQUENT TO THE COMPLAINT

Responsive pleadings are of course subject to challenge for departure from required standards of either formal or substantive sufficiency comparable to those encountered in studying the complaint. Thus, the substantive sufficiency of affirmative defenses may be reached by demurrer-type motions—"speaking" ones under Federal Rule 12(f) and N.Y.—McKinney's CPLR 3211(b) (p. 558 supra)—and, as in the case of similar challenges to the complaint, the determination of such motions may be influenced by defects of form (see p. 588 supra). In addition, denials at common law were subject to various kinds of often highly technical requirements of form, most of which have since fallen by the wayside of procedural reform. One type that survives, albeit much diminished in vigor, is by the so-called "negative pregnant," illustrated by the following Notes.

NOTES

(1) In Ex parte Wall, 107 U.S. 265, 275, 2 S.Ct. 569, 577–78, 27 L.Ed. 552 (1882), the petitioner had been disbarred for participating in a lynching. In refusing to grant him a writ of mandamus to compel the court below to vacate the disbarment order, the Supreme Court noted:

> As . . . much stress is laid upon the fact that the petitioner, by his answer, denied the charge . . . it is proper to notice the manner in which this denial was made. The charge, as we have seen, was specific and particular: "That J.B. Wall, an attorney of this court, did, on the sixth day of this present month, engage in and with an unlawful, tumultuous, and riotous gathering, he advising and encouraging thereto, take from the jail of Hillsborough County and hang by the neck until he was dead, one John, otherwise unknown, thereby showing an utter disregard and contempt for the law and its provisions," &c. The denial of this charge was a mere negative pregnant, amounting only to a denial of the attending circumstances and legal consequences ascribed to the act. The respondent denied "counselling, advising, encouraging, or assisting an unlawful, tumultuous, and riotous gathering or mob in taking one John from the jail of Hillsborough County and causing his death by hanging, in contempt and defiance of the law." He was not required to answer under oath, and did not do so. Yet, free from this restriction, he did not come out fully and fairly and deny that he was engaged in the transaction at all; but only that he did not engage in it with the attendant circumstances and legal consequences set out in the charge. Even the name of the victim is made a material part of the traverse.

> Upon such a special plea as this, we think the court was justified in regarding the denial as unsatisfactory. It was really equivalent to an admission of the substantial matter of the charge.

(2) ". . . Negatives pregnant come in two varieties. One is the literal denial. If the complaint alleges that the defendant was driving his car at 75 miles an hour and the defendant denies that he was driving his car at 75 miles an hour, this would be an admission that he may have been driving it at any other speed, i.e., 74 or 76 miles per hour. The other type of negative pregnant is the conjunctive denial. If the complaint alleges that the defendant was careless and negligent and reckless and the defendant denies that he was careless and negligent and reckless this would constitute an admission that he was guilty of any combination less than all three. To avoid this the defendant should have denied the facts in the disjunctive, i.e., denied that he was careless *or* negligent *or* reckless. Another type of denial which has been held bad is the argumentative denial which consists of making a contradictory statement

rather than a categorical denial. For example, if the complaint alleges that the defendant was in Chicago on a certain date and the answer alleges that on said date he was in New York, this might be held bad as an argumentative denial. In each of these situations, if the court holds the denial is insufficient, then the allegation is deemed admitted. The only sound reason for these highly technical rules is that such denials are evasive. In view of the modern trend towards liberality in pleading and the availability of pretrial discovery to avoid surprise, it is believed that technical rules such as these will fall into disuse. The best way to avoid all such pitfalls is to carefully select those allegations in the complaint which are true, admit them, and then deny each and every other allegation in said complaint." Green, Basic Civil Procedure 103–104 (1972).

B. WAIVER OF DEFENSES AND OBJECTIONS

We have seen in the preceding materials several ways in which valid objections to a claim may be foreclosed or "waived," pursuant to long-standing general pleading principles preserved in all modern procedural systems, by failure to raise them at the right time and in the proper manner. Thus, allegations in the complaint are deemed admitted if not denied in the answer and affirmative defenses are said to be lost if not raised either in the answer or by one of the various motions to dismiss which are alternatively provided for some of them in many states. Is loss of a lawsuit through forfeitures of this kind ever justifiable? What kinds of considerations might support them?

Provisions such as Federal Rule 12(g) and (h) seek to discourage dilatory motion practice directed to the pleadings by requiring consolidation of all motions raising enumerated types of defenses and objections, in addition to providing for waiver or forfeiture of those not raised by answer or motion in the prescribed manner. Both the Federal and New York rules reflect prevailing views in exempting from ordinary standards of preclusion the "favored" objections of failure to state a cause of action or claim to relief, lack of subject matter jurisdiction and absence of an indispensable party. Why are these objections accorded this special treatment? How long does it continue? Can they be raised after the trial? After final judgment?

It is important to remember that the waivers we speak of are not final and irrevocable in all cases. Relief from them may be available by amendment of the pleadings, which is treated in the next section, and these two subjects are therefore closely related. Cf. 4 Weinstein, Korn and Miller ¶¶ 3211.04, 3211.05.

BLACK, SIVALLS & BRYSON v. SHONDELL

United States Court of Appeals, Eighth Circuit, 1949.
174 F.2d 587.

WOODROUGH, CIRCUIT JUDGE. This action was brought in a Missouri state court and came within the federal jurisdiction on removal because there was diversity of citizenship and requisite amount involved. The plaintiffs sued for damages for breach of express and implied warranty in the sale of five oil storage tanks manufactured by defendant and sold to plaintiffs [by Midwest Equipment Company, a retailer] and upon the jury trial plaintiffs obtained a verdict and judgment against defendant in the sum of $9,332 from which the defendant appeals.

*   *   *

It was alleged in the petition that . . . in ordering the tanks from defendant Midwest advised defendant that the tanks were to be manufactured for the special purpose of underground storage of oil and oil products at Shondell's distributing station in Kansas City, Kansas.

. . .

*   *   *

The defendant demanded a jury and the case went to jury trial on the petition, answer and evidence. Defendant did not move against the petition for failure to state a claim and at the conclusion of the evidence it did not move for directed verdict. On the trial the court instructed the jury in effect that if it found that Shondell ordered the tanks in the course of and as the result of negotiations carried on orally at a certain interview at the Midwest Equipment Company's office, between plaintiff Shondell, a Mr. Williams, managing officer of Midwest, and one Traylor, a sales agent of defendant, and that defendant through its agent Traylor was fully informed of the particular use for which Shondell was buying the tanks and to which he intended to put them, namely, to set them three feet under ground and store oil products in them, and that Traylor stated that defendant would manufacture them in its own way with certain reenforcement described by him and that they would be strong enough and fit for such use and that Shondell believed and relied on what Traylor said and in reliance thereon installed the tanks three feet underground and that they were in fact unfit and of no value for such use and soon collapsed under the pressure and that as a direct result plaintiff suffered the losses shown, then plaintiff would be entitled to a recovery. Defendant took no exception to the instructions given by the court. It preserved exceptions to oral testimony received over its objections during the trial and made timely request to the court to give certain instructions which were refused, and it excepted to each refusal. After the verdict had been returned and judgment entered thereon it moved for judgment notwithstanding the verdict or in the alternative for new trial and the motion was denied.

It is contended on this appeal that the plaintiffs' petition did not state a cause of action and that when the facts alleged in it are considered in the light of the evidence it affirmatively appears that no right of recovery against the defendant existed. The contention is grounded upon the assertion that under the law of Missouri the right to maintain an action ex contractu for breach of warranty depends upon privity of contract and that a sub-purchaser who is not in privity with the seller cannot maintain an action for the seller's breach of warranty.

It is contended that as plaintiff assumed no obligation to the defendant manufacturer but bought the tanks from and agreed to and did pay the independent dealer Midwest therefor, and Midwest ordered them from and agreed to and did pay defendant for them, there was no privity of contract between plaintiff and defendant and that Missouri law denies plaintiff any right to recover from defendant manufacturer for breach of any warranty it may have made in respect to the tanks. [Citations omitted.] The plaintiffs concede that their action is an action ex contractu for breach of warranty but insist that the Missouri courts would hold that in the exceptional case where the manufacturer of an article itself enters into the negotiations for the sale thereof to an intending purchaser as defendant did through its agent Traylor in this instance, and, to get the business and induce the sale, makes a warranty respecting the article and its fitness for a certain purpose as alleged and shown here, then and in that case the action for breach of the warranty may be maintained by such purchaser against the manufacturer. [Citations omitted.]

It is clear that Missouri law is controlling in this case because the warranty and transactions involved, including the delivery of the tanks, occurred in Missouri, but it does not appear that said question now sought to be raised has been properly brought here for review. Under Rule 12, Rules of Civil Procedure, 28 U.S.C.A., a defendant waives all defenses and objections which he does not present either by motion or in his answer except that the defense of failure to state a claim upon which relief may be granted may also be made by a later pleading if one is permitted or by motion for judgment on the pleadings or at the trial on the merits. The record shows no such defense presented by defendant in a motion or answer and it must be deemed to have waived the defense that the petition did not state a claim upon which relief may be granted. The motion which defendant made for judgment notwithstanding the verdict was on the grounds that "the plaintiff's petition and the evidence discloses that there was no privity of contract between the plaintiff and the defendant" and that "it is uncontroverted in the evidence that the five tanks delivered by defendant complied with the terms specified in the [written] order" given by Midwest to defendant. It was made after the trial and not on the trial and did not preserve the defense of failure of the petition to state a claim. The defendant is therefore in the position of having waived that defense and may not urge it here.

[The court's discussion of other alleged errors is omitted.]

No error has been found in any of the matters properly preserved for review. The judgment is affirmed.

NOTES

(1) Compare Watson v. Lee County, 244 N.C. 508, 31 S.E.2d 535 (1944), applying the North Carolina rule that a demurrer for failure to state a cause of action may be interposed at any time in either the trial or appellate court:

"The reason of the rule is that if the basis of the action, the statement of the cause of action in the complaint, is defective in substance and insufficient, the action itself must fail, and when this is brought to the attention of the Court it will so declare. . . ."

A California position more hospitable to aider by verdict is explained in O'Neil v. Spillane, 45 Cal.App.3d 147, 119 Cal.Rptr. 245 (1975). "It is a general proposition that the objection that a complaint does not state facts sufficient to constitute a cause of action is not waived by failure to demur, but may be raised for the first time on appeal. However, if objection is interposed for the first time on appeal, the pleading will be liberally construed and will be upheld if the necessary facts in the complaint appear by implication or as a conclusion of law." Accord, In re Reller's Trust, 193 Neb. 54, 225 N.W.2d 397 (1975).

(2) As to aider through interjection of an issue by an opposing party, see Overseas Motors, Inc. v. Import Motors Limited, Inc., 375 F.Supp. 499, 512–513 (E.D.Mich.1974): "An affirmative defense is not waived, even though not specifically pleaded, where it is based upon the opposing party's own proofs or pleadings, where there was no opportunity to raise it in the pleadings, or where it is tried by express or implied consent of the opposing party."

(3) For a state court implying an amendment to conform the pleadings to the proof, see Dacus v. Burns, 206 Ark. 810, 177 S.W.2d 748 (1944): "In the instant case, while appellee did not specifically allege in his complaint that he was a licensed real estate dealer, however, without objection, he testified that he was a licensed dealer at the time the sale in question was made and had been so licensed since 1929. . . .   Had appellant made timely objection by demurrer to the complaint or otherwise, the complaint could have been amended at that time. The amendment did not change substantially the claim of appellee and the trial court properly treated the complaint as amended to conform to the proof." Cf. Rule 15(b) and Topic D, p. 619, infra; Wallin v. Fuller, p. 823 infra.

SECTION 7.   AMENDMENT

A.   AT COMMON LAW

PHILADELPHIA, BALTIMORE & WASHINGTON RAILROAD v. GATTA, 27 Del. 38, 44–45, 85 A. 721, 724–25 (1913): "The methods by which actions at law are instituted in those American jurisdictions that derive their jurisprudence from the common law, have as their original the method of commencing actions at common law. The common-law mode of commencing an action at law was originally by petition to the king and later, to him, through his Court of Chancery, praying for leave to bring an action in one of his courts of law upon a cause of action specifically stated in the petition. When the prayer of the petition was allowed, there issued an original writ, which in form was a mandate issuing out of the Court of Chancery, in the King's name, directed to the sheriff of the county wherein the injury was committed or the wrong was done, containing a statement of the cause of complaint, and requiring him to demand the defendant either to satisfy the claim and do justice to the complainant, or else appear in one of the superior courts of law and answer the accusations made against him.

"The principal object of the original writ was to confer jurisdiction upon a court of law to hear the matter in controversy, for at common law no action could be maintained in any superior court without the sanction of the king's original writ. Its other object was to compel the appearance of the defendant. As this writ issued out of one court for the purpose of conferring jurisdiction upon another, obviously the writ could not be amended in the latter court. As the jurisdiction conferred by the writ upon the law court was limited to the trial of the specific cause of action stated in it, any subsequent statement of a cause of action different from the one stated in the writ was in excess of the jurisdiction conferred by the writ, and constituted a departure, and of course would not be allowed by amendment. Amendments of pleadings subsequent to the declaration at common law were liberally allowed both in point of character and time (2 Burr. 756), but an amendment to a declaration was restricted to one that did not depart from the action stated in the writ and then only when asked for before the end of the second term, for after that term the amendment was considered 'a new declaration' and would not be allowed, 1 Wilf. 149, 223; Say.R. 234."

NOTE

To what extent is the right to amend "when defects exist in the original complaint which can be cured" one required by due process? Cf. Lathrop v. Donohue, 367 U.S. 820, 869, 81 S.Ct. 1826, 1851, 6 L.Ed.2d 1191 (1961) (dissenting op.).

B. DIMENSIONS OF THE AMENDMENT PROBLEM

To the extent that courts are free in granting leave to amend pleadings, they lessen incentive to obey pleading rules. If there were no restraints on amendment, pleadings would become practically useless. On the other hand, it is contrary to the spirit of the modern procedural philosophy of reaching the merits of the controversy to foreclose valid claims or defenses for pleaders' errors. What other considerations should play a role in the decision to grant or withhold permission to amend?

It is hardly surprising that during the period before trial, the earlier leave to amend is sought the more freely it is allowed. Indeed, leave of court is not required at all during the portion of the pleading stage for which Federal Rule 15(a) and similar statutes provide for one amendment as of course; and the routine grant of leave to amend that ordinarily accompanies orders sustaining challenges to a pleading has been noted in an earlier section of the chapter. As the case progresses on the calendar toward a trial date, the court's exercise of discretion to permit or deny amendment comes increasingly to involve a more complex and subtle balancing process, but one which does not change in essential character until trial. At the point of commencement of the trial, however, an entirely new set of considerations is injected by the fact that the court thenceforth deals with actual evidence of the facts supporting the parties' respective claims and defenses rather than words on a piece of paper. It is for this reason that Federal Rule 15(b) makes special provision for amendments during and after trial and that we focus separately on the periods before and after the commencement of trial in the succeeding materials. Another crucial point requiring a major shift in the balance of pertinent considerations comes when the statute of limitations runs on a claim or defense which the proponent means to assert in the amended pleading. This accounts for the further subdivision of our topic reserving treatment of cases in which the statute has run mainly to subsection e.

NOTE

As to supplemental pleadings, see Federal Rule 15(d).

"Supplemental pleadings have frequently been regarded much the same as amended pleadings although, unlike an amended pleading which supersedes the original, a supplemental pleading adds to the original some matter occurring after the beginning of the action or after a responsive pleading has been filed. . . . Rule 15(a) of Federal Rules of Civil Procedure, which governs amendment of pleadings by permission of the court provides that leave to amend 'shall be freely given when justice so requires' and, by universally accepted principles, this provision too invokes the sound discretion of the court where amendments are pressed after ordinary pleading time has passed." Garrison v. Baltimore & Ohio Railroad Co., 20 F.R.D. 190 (W.D.Pa.1957).

C. LEAVE TO AMEND BEFORE TRIAL

FRIEDMAN v. TRANSAMERICA CORP.

District Court of the United States, District of Delaware, 1946.
5 F.R.D. 115.

[Class action by Jack Friedman and others against the Transamerica Corporation. On plaintiffs' motion to amend their complaint.]

LEAHY, DISTRICT JUDGE.* Plaintiffs ask leave to amend their complaint. It has been amended three times before and this is their fourth attempt to state their cause of action. The proposed amendments include (a) an allegation "that defendant furnished to Axton-Fisher the necessary funds to enable it to call the Class A stocks" and (b) the addition of a new count which charges that defendant was under a fiduciary obligation to the minority Class A stockholders to disclose the increase in value of the Axton-Fisher tobacco leaf inventory and defendant's intention to dissolve Axton-Fisher. In substance, the first count is based on the assumption that plaintiffs would not have converted

* Footnote omitted.

their Class A stock into Class B stock if they had known all the facts concerning defendant's interest in Axton-Fisher; and the second count is bottomed on the assumption that plaintiffs would have converted their Class A shares if they had been aware of all the facts and on the further assumption that the redemption or call of the Class A stock was legal. Without pausing to determine whether the first and second counts are so inconsistent as not to come within the inconsistency of claims allowed by Rule 8(e) of the Federal Rules of Civil Procedure, 28 U.S.C.A., following section 723c, the present application to amend may be determined on other grounds.

The matter of defendant's controlling ownership in Axton-Fisher has been the subject of much litigation in this court. See Geller v. Transamerica, D.C., 53 F.Supp. 625, affirmed 3 Cir., 151 F.2d 534; Geller v. Transamerica, D.C., 63 F.Supp. 248; Zahn v. Transamerica, D.C., 63 F.Supp. 243; and Speed v. Transamerica, D.C., 5 F.R.D. 56. A reading of these cases will show that the redemption of the Class A stock of Axton-Fisher, that company's final dissolution and defendant's activities as majority stockholder have all been subject to attack and critical examination. Nothing is contained in the proposed amendments to the complaint which was not known to plaintiffs or at least to plaintiffs' counsel four months ago because the new matter sought to be added was already contained in some of the complaints filed in the cases supra.

Rule 15(a) provides that leave to amend "shall be freely given when justice so requires." The word "freely" was used with deliberate intention to obviate technical restrictions on amendment. Moore, Federal Practice, p. 806. But, this does not mean that leave to amend is to be granted without limit; otherwise, the right to amend would be absolute and not rest in the discretion of the court. The interests of both parties should be considered when an application to amend is made. Opportunity should be given to a plaintiff to present his alleged grievance; yet equal attention should be given to the proposition that there must be an end finally to a particular litigation.

It has been held that four unsuccessful attempts, each time by way of amendment, to set out a cause of action, would support a ruling that no further amendments should be allowed. Laughlin v. Garnett, 78 U.S.App.D.C. 194, 138 F.2d 931. So, too, an order of a district court dismissing, without further leave to amend, a complaint which had been twice amended was sustained. C.E. Stevens Co. v. Foster & Kleiser Co., 9 Cir., 109 F.2d 764. Failure on the part of the party seeking the amendment to show that his delay in tendering the amendment was due to excusable oversight will support a refusal to allow the amendment. Frank Adam Electric Co. v. Westinghouse Elec. Mfg. Co., 8 Cir., 146 F.2d 165. In short, the matter of giving leave to amend is one in the sound discretion of the nisi prius court. I agree with Judge Rifkind that "Rule 15(a) prescribes a liberal policy in granting leave to amend." But "a liberal policy does not mean the absence of all restraint. Were that the intention, leave of court would not be required. The requirement of judicial approval suggests that there are instances where leave should not be granted." Here, I believe we have such an instance. This is plaintiffs' fourth attempt to state their cause of action and their third request to amend, more than sixteen months after the complaint was filed. The subject matter of the amendment was known four months ago and the "new" matter sought to be incorporated into the complaint was once included in the original and first amended complaint and later was abandoned or deleted when plaintiffs filed their second amended complaint. Moreover, the present motion to amend was not filed until after the date was fixed for argument on defendant's motion to dismiss the complaint and after briefs had been exchanged and filed.

The motion to amend falls into the category of those instances where such leave should be denied. An order may be submitted denying plaintiffs' motion to amend; defendant's pending motion to dismiss the complaint in its present form should be placed on the argument list.

NOTES

(1) *Compare* the statement in the principal case, "Failure on the part of the party seeking the amendment to show that his delay in tendering the amendment was due to excusable oversight will support a refusal to allow the amendment," *with* Ozark Air Lines, Inc. v. Delta Air Lines, Inc., 63 F.R.D. 69 (N.D.Ill.1974): ". . . it is well established that delay itself, excusable or inexcusable, is not sufficient to warrant denial of a motion to amend pleadings. It must be shown that to allow the amendment would result in substantial prejudice to the opposite party." Accord, Middle Atlantic Utilities Co. v. SMW Development Corp., 392 F.2d 380, 384 (2d Cir.1968); Hageman v. Signal L.P. Gas, Inc., 486 F.2d 479, 484 (6th Cir.1973).

California follows a stricter rule. "The law is also clear that even if a good amendment is proposed in proper form, unwarranted delay in presenting it may—of itself—be a valid reason for denial." Roemer v. Retail Credit Co., 44 Cal.App.3d 926, 119 Cal.Rptr. 82, 90 (1975). Cf. Hayden v. Ford Motor Co., 497 F.2d 1292 (6th Cir.1974) (defendant's delay for some 30 months in making motion and plaintiff's dismissal of pending state action mandates allowance of amendment relating back to avoid statute of limitations); Zenith Radio Corp. v. Hazeltine Research, Inc., 401 U.S. 321, 91 S.Ct. 795, 28 L.Ed.2d 77 (1971) (delay precluded amendment to plead limitation and release).

(2) How would you define the type of "prejudice" that will persuade a court to deny leave to amend a pleading? In Bowman v. De Peyster, 2 Daly 203, 206 (N.Y.C.P.1867), the court said: "A plaintiff cannot be said to have a right to deprive a defendant of the privilege of setting up a defense which, from any excusable cause, he has neglected to do, or has done in such a manner as to make it unavailable; and where a judge, in the exercise of his discretion, grants to a defendant this privilege, he does not thereby affect any substantial right of the plaintiff. It deprives him of nothing. The only effect of it is, that he is compelled to meet a defense which he would have been compelled to meet in the first instance, had the defendant set it up. It may put him to inconvenience, or delay the trial of the cause, but this is a matter for the consideration

of the judge, in the exercise of his discretion to refuse the application, or in imposing the conditions upon which the amendment will be allowed."

(3) Does a defendant stand differently from a plaintiff in respect to amendment of the pleading? In the *Bowman* case, Note (2) supra, the court further said, id. at p. 208: "At common law, a plaintiff was not allowed to add additional counts after two terms had elapsed; but a defendant, upon proper conditions being imposed, if it were in furtherance of justice, would be allowed to amend, by setting up an additional defense, at any time before judgment (Tidd's Practice, 708, 9th London ed.). The reason for this distinction was, that the plaintiff, if he had another cause of action, could sue upon it afterward; while a defendant had to avail himself of his defense in the action brought against him, or he might lose the benefit of it (Waters v. Boville, 1 Wills. 223; Dryden v. Langley, Barnes' Notes, 22; Skitt v. Woodward, 1 H.Bl. 238)."

(4) Are amendments more liberally granted in some types of litigation than in others? For an affirmative answer, see Penn Galvanizing Co. v. Lukens Steel Co., 65 F.R.D. 80 (E.D.Pa.1974).

> Where antitrust litigation is involved, allowance of amendments to complaints is perhaps especially proper for at least two reasons. First, antitrust litigation often involves complex legal issues and voluminous facts, most of which are usually in the possession of the defendant. As a result, it is not unusual that plaintiff in such a case should find it necessary to adjust his position and contentions as the case and its discovery proceed. Second. . . . Congress has determined that private litigation serves a useful and valuable role in the antitrust field, and the courts if at all possible should not impair this role of private litigation by placing unnecessarily strict pleading requirements on the parties involved."

(5) A motion to dismiss is not by itself a "responsive pleading" within the meaning of Rule 15(a); hence, after such a motion is granted, plaintiff retains the right to amend his complaint as a matter of course. Nolen v. Fitzharris, 450 F.2d 958 (9th Cir.1971).

D. AMENDMENT DURING AND AFTER TRIAL

MANNING v. LOEW

Supreme Judicial Court of Massachusetts, 1943.
313 Mass. 252, 46 N.E.2d 1022.

LUMMUS, J. In this action of contract the plaintiff was the only witness on the question of liability. Her testimony tended to prove the following facts. The defendant lives in Boston, but the parties met in January, 1941, in a restaurant in Miami, Florida, where the plaintiff was employed as a waitress. The defendant owned a chain of moving picture theatres in New England, and also had such a theatre in Miami, where he gave the plaintiff employment. Later, at the invitation of the defendant, the plaintiff came to Boston, where the defendant met her. She later went to New York, but returned to Boston on request of the defendant.

When the plaintiff got back to Boston, the defendant met her, and told her, to use her words, that "if I would stay here in Boston, and not go back to New York, and be like a daughter to him, accompany him to his home and on trips and see him any time that he wanted to see me, and be a companion and daughter to him, that he would then put me in the movies; he would get me a screen test. He would see that I got this screen test; if I couldn't that he would produce a picture himself, he would star me in it." It could be found that the plaintiff accepted this offer and agreed to perform its terms.

Subsequently the plaintiff accompanied the defendant to his house, to eating places, to New York and other cities, and on a yachting trip. The defendant was living apart from his wife. In December, 1941, the defendant told the plaintiff that he was through with her and that he was not serious about the alleged agreement. The plaintiff then consulted a lawyer, and this action was begun. At the trial a verdict was directed for the defendant, subject to the plaintiff's exception.

The declaration set forth as the consideration for the defendant's promise that the plaintiff agreed "that she would devote herself at all times required by him [the defendant] to the companionship and service of the defendant and to accompany him to such places as he should designate." Nothing was said in the declaration about being a daughter, or like a daughter, to him, though that was an essential part of the contract according to the plaintiff's testimony, by which she is bound. There was therefore a variance between the declaration and the proof. The action of the judge in directing a verdict for the defendant was not error, even though there was no express statement that the ruling was made with the pleadings in mind. Ferris v. Boston & Maine Railroad, 291 Mass. 529, 533.

But if we consider the merits without regard to the pleadings, the direction of a verdict for the defendant was not error. Not only did the plaintiff admit that she had sexual intercourse at various times with the defendant (French v. Boston Safe Deposit & Trust Co., 282 Mass. 600, 607), but she also admitted that she had been in bed with another man and had had her picture taken in bed with him, and had gone to resorts with that man after the defendant had left her at her hotel for the night, as he thought. Her admitted conduct was not consistent with her promise to act as a daughter to the defendant.

Exceptions overruled.

NOTES

(1) Would the result in *Manning* have been the same under Federal Rule 15(b)? Compare N.Y.—McKinney's CPLR 3025(c): "Amendment to conform to the evidence. The court may permit pleadings to be amended before or after judgment to conform them to the evidence, upon such terms as may be just including the granting of costs and disbursements."

(2) "To require a finding for the adverse party, a variance must be material or substantial, requiring different kinds and degrees of proof and the applica-

tion of different rules of law." Cantara v. Massachusetts Bay Transportation Authority, 3 Mass.App.Ct. 81, 323 N.E.2d 759 (1975), which held that a complaint alleging that an accident occurred on Nov. 22 at Wood Island Station and proof that it occurred on Nov. 26 just outside the station was not a material variance.

MANGUM v. SURLES

Supreme Court of North Carolina, 1972.
281 N.C. 91, 187 S.E.2d 697.

SHARP, JUSTICE. . . . In addition to her lack of mental capacity, plaintiff alleged that the manner and circumstances by which defendants obtained her signature to the challenged deed "constituted a fraudulent act." She did not, as required by G.S. § 1A–1, Rule 9(b), state "with particularity" the circumstances constituting the alleged fraud. Rule 9(b) codifies the requirement previously existing in our State practice that the facts relied upon to establish fraud, duress or mistake must be alleged.

Prior to 1 January 1970, the effective date of the Rules of Civil Procedure, absent *allegations* of fact which would constitute fraud if true, evidence of fraud—no matter how complete and convincing—could not be submitted to the jury. Proof without allegation was as ineffective as allegation without proof. . . .

Under the former procedure, because of plaintiff's failure to allege fraud with particularity, Judge Hall's refusal to permit the amendment tendered at the close of the evidence and to submit the issue of fraud would have been unassailable. However, to eliminate the waste, delay, and the injustice which sometimes resulted from belated confrontations between insufficient allegations and plenary proof, Rule 15(b) was enacted. . . .

[W]here no objection is made to evidence on the ground that it is outside the issues raised by the pleadings, the issue raised by the evidence is nevertheless before the trial court for determination. The pleadings are regarded as amended to conform to the proof even though the defaulting pleader made no formal motion to amend. Failure to make the amendment will not jeopardize a verdict or judgment based upon competent evidence. If an amendment to conform the pleadings to the proof should have been made in order to support the judgment, the Appellate Court will presume it to have been made. However, amendments should always be freely allowed unless some material prejudice is demonstrated, for it is the essence of the Rules of Civil Procedure that decisions be had on the merits and not avoided on the basis of mere technicalities. . . .

Reversed.

NOTES

(1) Why should Rule 15(b) trump Rule 9(b)? Is the implication correct that Rule 9(b) will be enforced only when the party claiming fraud feels like pleading it specifically? See Sovern, Reconsidering Rule 9(b): Do We Need Particularized Pleading Requirements in Fraud Cases? 104 F.R.D. 143 (1985); Richman, Lively & Mell, The Pleading of Fraud: Rhymes Without Reason, 60 S.Cal.L.Rev. 959 (1987).

(2) To what extent may pleadings be amended in the appellate court? See Purofied Down Products Corp. v. Travelers Fire Insurance Co., 278 F.2d 439 (2d Cir.1960) (no counterclaim asserted but in view of trial of issue, appellate court deemed pleadings amended and credited defendant with unpaid premiums); Diemer v. Diemer, 8 N.Y.2d 206, 203 N.Y.S.2d 829, 168 N.E.2d 654 (1960), in which the New York Court of Appeals, repudiating the "theory of the pleadings" doctrine, granted a decree of separation on the ground of abandonment, though the complaint relied, and the case had been tried and separation denied in the courts below, on the theory of cruel and inhuman treatment.

E. STATUTE OF LIMITATIONS AND "RELATION BACK"

HUMPHRIES v. GOING

District Court of the United States, Eastern District of North Carolina, 1973.
59 F.R.D. 583.

MEMORANDUM OPINION AND ORDER

LARKINS, DISTRICT JUDGE: This cause is before this Court on Defendant Colonial Flooring's motion to dismiss the Plaintiffs' Amendment to the Amended Complaint, or in the alternative to grant summary judgment for Defendant Colonial Flooring on this issue.

On or about July 4, 1968, the Plaintiffs, Virginia residents, and Defendant Going, a North Carolina resident, were involved in an automobile accident on U.S. Route 158 about .5 miles south of Grandy, North Carolina. The Complaints were filed on October 29, 1969. On May 11, 1970, Plaintiffs filed an Amended Complaint alleging that the vehicle driven by Going was registered to Colonial and that Going was operating said vehicle with the consent of Colonial and in the furtherance of Colonial's business.

On March 12, 1973, the Plaintiffs filed an Amendment to the Amended Complaint alleging that prior to the time of the accident Defendant Going had been treated on numerous occasions for alcoholism, that Going was in fact an alcoholic, that he drove a motor vehicle while intoxicated, and at the time of the accident he was in an intoxicated condition. Plaintiffs further allege that Defendant Colonial had full knowledge of the said alcoholic condition of Going, that Colonial nevertheless allowed Going to use their vehicle, and that Colonial was negligent in entrusting said vehicle to Going.

The Defendants allege that the Plaintiffs' Amendment to the Amended Complaint sets forth a new, separate, and distinct claim for relief and that such claim is barred by the three year statute of limitations in North Carolina governing the time for the commencement of personal injury actions. In support of their position, Colonial contends that under Rule 15(c) of the Federal Rules of Civil Procedure an amended complaint which states a new claim will not relate back to the time of filing of the original complaint so as to defeat the statute of limitations. First, Colonial argues that the Amendment charges a violation of a different obligation in that the Amended Complaint is predicated on the negligent acts of Going and the imputation of this negligence to Colonial whereas the Amendment alleges negligent entrustment of the vehicle to Going. Secondly, Colonial contends that the negligence in question does not arise out of the same transaction in that the negligence alleged in the Amended Complaint would arise out of the accident whereas any negligence alleged in the Amendment would have arisen prior to the accident in relation to Going's alcoholism.

It is true that if the Plaintiffs' Amendment to the Amended Complaint is such that if it cannot be held to relate back to the date of the original Complaint, it is barred by the three year statute of limitations. Therefore the issue for determination at this time is whether or not such Amendment relates back to the date of the original Complaint.

* * *

In both theories the facts surrounding the accident are the same. Both theories are predicated on Colonial's letting Going use their vehicle. And Going's alcoholism, the basis of the Amendment, could also be a factor in the negligence at the time of the accident. In fact, the depositions and interrogatories show that the Plaintiffs considered this avenue of approach long before the Amendment was filed but had good cause to delay in such filing, and the Defendants certainly had notice that alcoholism could be a factor in the suit. . . .

The Defendants contend that it would be burdensome to now bring in evidence of alcoholism prior to the accident, and this makes the instant Amendment an unfair and different cause of action. Of course, this Court recognizes that certain rights of the Defendants must be protected, namely notice, possible prejudice, and the range of facts in the Defendants' knowledge.

It was held in Williams v. United States [405 F.2d 234, 236 (5th Cir. 1968)] that notice clearly is the critical element involved in Rule 15(c) determinations. And Jackson v. Airways Parking, supra, 297 F.Supp. at 1382 held:

"The point of Rule 15(c) is that it is fair to have an amended complaint relate back if the initial complaint put the defendant on notice that a certain range of matters was in controversy and the amended complaint falls within that range."

* * *

It appears to this Court that although the Plaintiffs' Amendment came after the three year statute of limitations had run, in all probability it was the Defendants' fault and not the Plaintiffs' that the Amendment was delayed. The Plaintiff requested the medical records of Going in January, 1971. It was not until this Court ordered that Defendants give Plaintiffs those records on October 2, 1972, that such was done. The Amendment in question is most likely a result of those records. It is also pointed out that in the deposition of Going dated November 16, 1970 and the interrogatories to Going filed January 13, 1971, although Plaintiffs inquired as to Going's alcoholism, no answers were given which would have led Plaintiffs to Amend at an earlier time. In fact, Going stated that he had not been treated for alcoholism by a doctor or at a hospital prior to the accident (dep. of Going, p. 38).

It appears to this Court that Defendants had notice of this case and all possible claims regarding the accident, including the alleged alcoholism of Going. Had the Defendants produced Going's medical records when requested, which was within the three year statute of limitation period, this problem would not be an issue now. Therefore, this Amendment would not be prejudicial or unfair to the Defendants as they had facts in their knowledge regarding the claims in the Amended Complaint and the Amendment to the Amended Complaint.

It being the conclusion of this Court (1) that the Amendment does not create a new cause of action and is so closely related to the facts and circumstances surrounding the conduct, transactions, and occurrences alleged in the Complaint and the Amended Complaint that it should relate back to the date of the original Complaint and (2) that the Defendants are not prejudiced nor deprived of notice or any other rights in this action, it is adjudged that the Amendment to the Amended Complaint should be allowed.

Nor will a continuance be granted to the Defendants in the instant case. It was stated in Heay v. Phillips, supra, 201 F.2d at 222,

> "While it is true that any substantial amendment which operates as a surprise to the opposite party may constitute a basis for granting a continuance, the granting of a continuance is not a matter of right, but is always within the discretion of the court."

In the case at bar, the Defendants cannot be said to be surprised at the allegations in the Amendment.

NOTES

(1) In Tiller v. Atlantic Coast Line Railroad, 323 U.S. 574, 65 S.Ct. 421, 89 L.Ed. 465 (1945), the Supreme Court allowed a widow to amend her complaint to charge that the defendant railroad violated the Federal Boiler Inspection Act, in addition to an original charge that the railroad negligently caused her husband's death. The court explained, "The amended complaint charged the failure to have the locomotive properly lighted. Both of them related to the same general conduct, transaction and occurrence which involved the death of

the deceased. . . . The cause of action . . . is the same—it is a suit to recover damages for the alleged wrongful death of the deceased. . . . There is no reason to apply a statute of limitations when, as here, the respondent has had notice from the beginning that petitioner was trying to enforce a claim against it because of the events leading up to the death. . . ."

(2) In 1963, the present second sentence permitting a supplementary pleading even if the original pleading is defective was added to Rule 15(d) of the Federal Rules of Civil Procedure. In its notes the Advisory Committee declared that "the amendment does not attempt to deal with such questions as the relation of the statute of limitations to supplemental pleadings."

SCHIAVONE v. FORTUNE

Supreme Court of the United States, 1986.
477 U.S. 21, 106 S.Ct. 2379, 91 L.Ed.2d 18.

[Near the expiration of the applicable New Jersey statute of limitations the plaintiffs filed diversity libel actions misnaming "Fortune" as the defendant. After the statute had run plaintiffs served amended complaints on "Fortune, also known as Time, Incorporated." The lower courts dismissed the actions, rejecting plaintiffs' contention that the amendment should relate back to the timely filing date. The Supreme Court affirmed.]

JUSTICE BLACKMUN delivered the opinion of the Court.

* * *

Central to the resolution of this issue is the language of Rule 15(c). . . . Relation back is dependent upon four factors, all of which must be satisfied: (1) the basic claim must have arisen out of the conduct set forth in the original pleading; (2) the party to be brought in must have received such notice that it will not be prejudiced in maintaining its defense; (3) that party must or should have known that, but for a mistake concerning identity, the action would have been brought against it; and (4) the second and third requirements must have been fulfilled within the prescribed limitations period. We are not concerned here with the first factor, but we are concerned with the satisfaction of the remaining three.

The first intimation that Time had of the institution and maintenance of the three suits took place after . . ., the date the Court of Appeals said the statute ran. . . .

It seems to us inevitably to follow that notice to Time and the necessary knowledge did not come into being "within the period provided by law for commencing the action against" Time, as is so clearly required by Rule 15(c). That occurred only after the expiration of the applicable 1–year period. This is fatal, then, to petitioners' litigation.

We do not have before us a choice between a "liberal" approach toward Rule 15(c), on the one hand, and a "technical" interpretation of the Rule, on the other hand. The choice, instead, is between recognizing or ignoring what the Rule provides in plain language. We accept the Rule as meaning what it says.

We are not inclined, either, to temper the plain meaning of the language by engrafting upon it an extension of the limitations period equal to the asserted reasonable time, inferred from Rule 4, for the service of a timely filed complaint. Rule 4 deals only with process. Rule 3 concerns the "commencement" of a civil action. Under Rule 15(c), the emphasis is upon "the period provided by law for commencing the action against" the defendant. An action is commenced by the filing of a complaint and, so far as Time is concerned, no complaint against it was filed on or prior to May 19, 1983.

Any possible doubt about this should have been dispelled 20 years ago by the Advisory Committee's 1966 Note about Rule 15(c). The Note specifically states that the Rule's phrase "within the period provided by law for commencing the action" means "within the applicable limitations period". . . . Although the Advisory Committee's comments do not foreclose judicial consideration of the Rule's validity and meaning, the construction given by the Committee is "of weight." Mississippi Publishing Corp. v. Murphree, 326 U.S. 438, 444 (1946). . . .

The linchpin is notice, and notice within the limitations period. Of course, there is an element of arbitrariness here, but that is a characteristic of any limitations period. And it is an arbitrariness imposed by the legislature and not by the judicial process. . . .

NOTES

(1) The *Schiavone* decision has drawn criticism from the commentators. See Brussack, Outrageous Fortune: The Case for Amending Rule 15(c) Again, 61 S.Cal.L.Rev. 671 (1988); Lewis, The Excessive History of Federal Rule 15(c) and Its Lessons for Civil Rules Revision; 85 Mich.L.Rev. 1507 (1987). Compare Metropolitan Paving Co. v. International Union of Operating Engineers, 439 F.2d 300, 306 (10th Cir.1971) (plaintiff was allowed to amend his complaint to substitute three individual corporations for a joint venture originally sued, and the amended complaint related back to the original pleadings; "clear from the outset that the three corporations were the real party in interest").

(2) Should amendments seeking to change a party plaintiff and those seeking to change a party defendant be treated the same way? Cf. Perez v. Sudakoff, 50 F.R.D. 1 (S.D.N.Y.1970), in which the court found sufficient prejudice to refuse plaintiff leave to add a claim for breach of warranty against a subcontractor floor installer, because by the time leave was sought the statute of limitations had run against any claim over by the subcontractor against the flooring manufacturer (the party primarily at fault) through impleader or independent suit.

(3) May a plaintiff who cannot herself maintain a cause of action amend her complaint after the statute of limitations has run to substitute one who can? See Yorden v. Flaste, 374 F.Supp. 516 (D.Del.1974), allowing relation back of an amendment substituting lawful widow for alleged common law wife in wrongful death action.

F. "RELATION BACK" OF COUNTERCLAIMS

AZADA v. CARSON

United States District Court, District of Hawaii, 1966.
252 F.Supp. 988.

TAVARES, DISTRICT JUDGE. On October 12, 1963, plaintiff Mariano Azada was driving a car which collided with a car driven by defendant Roger Carson. Plaintiff and his wife filed suit for personal injuries three days before the running of the two-year statute of limitations.

Defendant was not served with process until nearly three months after the complaint was filed; thus the counterclaim later filed by the defendant was filed more than two years following the date of the collision. Plaintiffs move to dismiss the counterclaim on the ground that it was filed after the statute of limitations had become a bar.

Jurisdiction here is based upon diversity of citizenship, and therefore this Court must apply Hawaii law. However, no Hawaii statute nor reported decision had been found that disposes of the question here.

Authorities outside of Hawaii are divided on the question. C.J.S. Limitations of Actions § 285, pp. 342–343, reports:

> "There is a conflict of opinion as to when a claim interposed as a setoff or counterclaim becomes barred by the statute of limitations. The weight of authority supports the rule, said to be the better rule, that, where defendant's claim, asserted in a set-off or counterclaim, was an existing debt not barred by the statute of limitations at the time plaintiff's action was begun, it will be a valid set-off or counterclaim, although the statutory period may have elapsed before the filing of the answer setting it up, provided, under some of the statutes, the counterclaim arose out of the same transaction as gave rise to the main action."

Plaintiff argues that most of the cases allowing a counterclaim, if it was not barred at the time the action was begun, involved contracts and not torts. But there seems to be no logical reason for making such a distinction. The same considerations of fair play and justice apply, whether the action is based upon contract or tort.

Statutes of limitation are statutes of repose—they are designed to bar stale claims. Where, as in this case, the counterclaim arises from the same incident as the complaint, the counterclaim is no more stale than the complaint.

Simple justice dictates that if the plaintiffs are given an opportunity to present a claim for relief based upon a particular automobile collision, the defendant should not be prevented from doing so by a mere technicality.

Without meaning to suggest in any way that the instant suit involves frivolous claims, the rule adopted by this Court will also have the beneficial effect of tending to discourage the filing of frivolous claims just before the running of the statute of limitations.

Therefore plaintiffs' motion to dismiss the counterclaim is hereby denied.

STONER v. TERRANELLA
United States Court of Appeals, Sixth Circuit, 1967.
372 F.2d 89.

JOHN W. PECK, CIRCUIT JUDGE. On June 29, 1964, a head-on collision occurred in Nelson County, Kentucky, between a tractor-trailer driven by appellant Terranella (hereinafter "appellant"), and owned by defendant Glenos, and an automobile driven by James Crowe. Crowe was killed, substantial damage was done to the tractor-trailer, and appellant was injured. Stoner, as administrator of Crowe's estate, appellee herein, filed a complaint against both Terranella and Glenos. Both defendants filed answers and defendant Glenos filed a counter-claim for property damage to the truck. At that time no counterclaim was filed by appellant and on July 17, 1965, the Kentucky statute of limitations expired, barring personal injury claims against the decedent's estate. Subsequently, on September 13, 1965, appellant filed a motion for leave to file an amended answer and a counterclaim for his personal injuries. The district judge sustained the motion for leave to file an amended answer, but overruled the motion with respect to the counterclaim for personal injuries, holding that it was barred by limitations. After defendant Glenos received a $3,000 judgment on his counterclaim for property damage, based on a jury verdict, appellant sought review of the order barring his counterclaim. Jurisdiction is based on diversity of citizenship.

In his original answer appellant alleged that the accident in question resulted solely from the negligence of Crowe, or in the alternative, that Crowe's negligence contributed thereto. Appellant thus contends that since the claim asserted by way of counterclaim in the amended pleading, based on Crowe's negligence, arose out of the "conduct, transaction, or occurrence" set forth in the original answer, his counterclaim relates back to the date of the original pleading pursuant to Rule 15(c), Federal Rules of Civil Procedure. The district judge implicitly held that the counterclaim did not relate back to the date of the original pleading in light of his ruling that the counterclaim was barred, and it is this question which is before us here.

. . . the . . . question narrows to an inquiry of whether Rule 15(c) applies to the amended pleading tendered by appellant.

Although neither party cited or relied upon Rule 13(f), Federal Rules of Civil Procedure, and although there is no indication that this Rule was considered at the trial level, comment concerning it seems appropriate. Rule 13(f) provides:

"**Omitted Counterclaims.** When a pleader fails to set up a counterclaim through oversight, inadvertence or excusable neglect, or when justice requires, he may by leave of court set up the counterclaim by amendment."

With respect to the scope of this Rule, it is clear that it provides a remedy for setting up omitted counterclaims which is separate and apart from the remedy provided in Rule 15(a) dealing with pleading amendments in general. While Rule 13(f) provides that an omitted counterclaim may be set up only by leave of court, under Rule 15 a pleading may be amended at any time within 20 days after it is served "if the pleading is one to which no responsive pleading is permitted [e.g., an answer only, without a counterclaim] . . .." Thus, the courts which have passed upon motions for leave to file amended pleadings embracing previously omitted counterclaims have generally considered only Rule 13(f), and not Rule 15. [Citations omitted.] We conclude that the remedies provided by the two rules are mutually exclusive in the sense that an amendment asserting a previously omitted counterclaim, such as was attempted in the instant case, is made pursuant to Rule 13(f) and not Rule 15(a). Consequently, since Rule 15(c) is applicable only to amendments made pursuant to Rule 15(a) (1A Barron & Holtzoff, op. cit. supra at § 448, pp. 757, 760), amendments made pursuant to Rule 13(f) do not relate back to the original pleadings.

Appellant here does not claim that his tendered amendment relates back under Kentucky law. Indeed, although no case factually similar to the one at bar has been cited to or found by the court, it appears that Kentucky would not permit an amended pleading to relate back in this situation as Kentucky takes a very narrow view of amendments which properly relate back. Totten v. Loventhal, 373 S.W.2d 421 (Ky.1963). In addition, under Kentucky law counterclaims seeking affirmative relief are treated as original petitions for purposes of statutes of limitations, and the limitations statutes are not tolled by the filing of the original petition. Winkle v. Jones, 265 S.W.2d 792 (Ky. 1954); Harvey Coal Corp. v. Smith, et al., 268 S.W.2d 634 (Ky.1954). Accordingly, no error was committed by the District Court in refusing to grant leave to file the counterclaim proffered by appellant and the judgment of the District Court is affirmed.

Chapter Ten

DISPOSITION WITHOUT FULL TRIAL

SECTION 1. IN GENERAL

Since trial calendars are chronically overcrowded and trials often costly and time-consuming, it serves the interests of both the litigants and the judicial system in expedition and economy to dispose of cases or at least significant issues without the necessity for a trial. In fact, the vast majority of actions formally instituted by service or filing of summonses and complaints—estimates range roughly between 85 and 97 per cent—never do reach the stage of a completed trial. Most of these are terminated by compromise and settlement. Of those that are not, some expire because of the plaintiff's failure to move the case through its various stages from commencement to final judgment. Some simply languish and are forgotten because the motivation that led to their commencement has since disappeared; others are formally stricken from the calendar on defendant's motion to dismiss for want of prosecution, based on a lack of due diligence by the plaintiff in not moving the case along to the next stage. See Fed.R.Civ.P. 41(b).

Sometimes, the plaintiff wishes to terminate a pending action and begin again in a different court or at a more propitious time. This may be accomplished, if the defendant is agreeable, by stipulation of the parties; otherwise, the plaintiff, unless he discontinues at an early stage, must move for an order of discontinuance or dismissal. As might be expected, the later the stage of the proceedings, the smaller is the likelihood of his obtaining such a dismissal without prejudice to a new action on the same claim—particularly after the trial has begun and the plaintiff's only reason for seeking it is that the evidence is going against him. See Fed.R.Civ.P. 41(a).

Another way in which actions may terminate without full trial and without any adjudication of the merits is through forfeiture of a claim or defense because of a litigant's failure to comply with some procedural requirement, as, for example, under Fed.R.Civ.P. 37, for non-compliance with the rules regarding pre-trial discovery.

But the most common type of disposition of this kind is of course the default judgment decreed, typically, for defendant's failure to appear in response to the summons or to answer the complaint or appear at the trial. This is governed by Fed.R.Civ.P. 55 and analogous state statutes and rules. As to the res judicata effect of all such dispositions without full trial and not "on the merits", in the sense that they are not based on determination of any of the material issues of fact or substantive law, see Chapter 15, infra.

Dispositions without full trial that *are* on the merits in the sense indicated are the main concern of this chapter. We have already considered the termination of cases presenting only issues of law on the pleadings through the demurrer and its modern counterpart motions to dismiss for failure to state a cause of action or claim to relief. We turn now to the more recently developed and more effective procedural device that has taken away from these traditional ones the dominant role in pre-trial disposition of cases on the merits—the motion for summary judgment.

SECTION 2. SUMMARY JUDGMENT

A. FUNCTIONS

While demurrers and analogous motions challenge the legal suffi- ciency of a complaint, they rarely end litigation because the usual result of a well-taken motion attacking a pleading for substantive insufficiency is [judicial permission] to amend it. The temptation is for the challenged pleader to modify the allegations in the manner neces- sary to cure the deficiency—not necessarily mendaciously, but at times by stretching the truth. This creates the need for a procedural device short of a full trial whereby the opponent may pierce the outwardly sufficient assertions of an amended pleading to expose their untenabili- ty in fact.

A similar need also arises in the case of an original pleading, adroitly drawn to avoid both dismissal and outright untruthfulness, but resting on probably unprovable factual averments. The problem is aggravated to the extent modern systems patterned after the Federal Rules allow even pleadings which omit material factual allegations— such as that of publication in the *Garcia* case, p. 589, supra—to survive motions to dismiss. Still another common problem not reached by demurrer-type motions is the presence of a potentially dispositive issue of law which the pleadings fail to reveal. Assume that a defendant intends to rely on a defense of res judicata based on a former adjudica- tion which the plaintiff will contend does not as a matter of law preclude his present action. In this situation the complaint may well simply omit any mention of the earlier litigation; the defendant then would need, in order to raise the issue of law, a vehicle capable of conveying to the court the pertinent additional facts concerning that litigation. The summary judgment motion, permitting affidavits and exhibits, provides such a vehicle.

Since a motion for summary judgment is a speaking motion, it discloses, and solicits disclosure of, evidence and other information, by affidavits and briefs, in support of the contentions of the parties. To the extent it does, the motion, and the answering papers, serve a discovery function. Lawyers do, in fact, use summary judgment motions as a form of omnibus discovery device. As such, the motion for summary judgment may be less effective than other discovery devices, because it will tend to produce primarily information sufficient to show that genuine issues exist. However, since it may be difficult to predict what showing the court will judge sufficient, the speaking papers are likely to disclose more than necessary for this purpose. In addition, while a motion for summary judgment may result in significant disclosure, its denial does tend to settle that the case presents triable issues. This is a consequence the movant must be prepared to accept.

NOTES

(1) A summary judgment avoids a trial and is distinct from a "summary procedure" designed to bring on a trial quickly. See, e.g., N.J.Rules of Civil Procedure, Rule 4.46, Summary Judgment; McMahon, Summary Procedure: A Comparative Study, 31 Tul.L.Rev. 573 (1957).

(2) Can the court on its own motion grant summary judgment for the non-moving party? District courts have generally answered affirmatively. Lemon v. Zelker, 358 F.Supp. 554, 555 (S.D.N.Y.1972); International Distributing Co., Inc. v. American District Telegraph Co., 385 F.Supp. 871, 874 (D.D.C.1974). Some states expressly provide that judgments may be granted to the opponent as well as the proponent of the motion. See Annot., 48 A.L.R.2d 1188 (1956).

(3) Although a grant of full summary judgment is everywhere appealable, not so denials or grants of partial summary judgment, which are usually not considered ripe for appeal under the "final decision" rule, 28 U.S.C.A. § 1291. The situation is otherwise when appeal from intermediate or interlocutory orders is allowed.

B. HISTORICAL DEVELOPMENT

In its beginnings, the summary judgment motion was primarily designed as a plaintiff's weapon, particularly in actions on bills of exchange and promissory notes. "Before the Hilary Rules of 1834 the English common law system tolerated to a considerable extent the wholly indefensible practice of pleading, for the purpose of delay, pleas which were altogether unfounded in fact, so-called 'sham pleas.' Favorite types of plea used in this end were those of judgment recovered or accord and satisfaction. Certain cases of sham pleas, however, fell outside the toleration. Such were pleas made 'the subject of indecorous justing' or otherwise absurd on their face, as where there was pleaded a judgment recovered in the Court of Piepoudre at Bartholomew's Fair; and these could be treated as nullities without much ado. . . . In this case, if the court had reason to believe that the plea was not interposed in good faith, it would proceed summarily to set it aside on affidavit of its untruth and allow judgment to go forthwith for the plaintiff. There was no real question of interference with the normal trial of facts, for if the plea were actually sham the traditions of the bar naturally forbade any insistence by counsel upon carrying the dishonesty further." Millar, Civil Procedure of the Trial Court in Historical Perspective 237 (1952).

NOTES

(1) An excellent historical tracing appears in Bauman, Evolution of the Summary Judgment Procedure, 31 Ind.L.J. 329 (1956). Among the leading American cases on striking sham pleadings are Walter v. Walker & Smith, 35 N.J.L. 262 (1871) and Wayland v. Tysen, 45 N.Y. 281 (1871).

(2) The first American summary judgment statutes were based upon English developments. They were limited to certain types of actions, notably for breach of contract. Following Federal Rule 56, many states have made the summary judgment procedure applicable in all types of civil actions, including those formerly designated equitable. A few other states limit the procedure to actions on a liquidated demand arising on a negotiable instrument or contract. States with the most restrictive rules permit summary judgment only in actions against specified officers for certain defaults—for example, against sheriffs, coroners, tax collectors and attorneys for failure to pay over money collected. See, e.g., Booth v. Barber Transportation Co., 256 F.2d 927 (8th Cir.1958). A few states allow only the plaintiff to move for summary judgment.

C. RELATION TO MODERN "SPEAKING DEMURRERS" AND TO THE MOTION FOR JUDGMENT ON THE PLEADINGS

The motions to dismiss for legal insufficiency that are the analogues of the demurrer in Federal Rule 12 and the state provisions patterned after it, as well as under N.Y.—McKinney's CPLR 3211, reject the common law and traditional code state view that such a challenge must be determined on the basis of the face of the pleading alone; instead they authorize the submission on such a motion of the same types of extrinsic evidence that are allowed on a motion for summary judgment. When such evidence is received, the motion becomes in effect one for summary judgment; the label given the motion is then of no consequence.

Another traditional device for pre-trial disposition of cases on the merits is the motion for judgment on the pleadings. At common law and in contemporary but traditional code systems, this motion raises the same questions as the demurrer and is similarly to be decided without reference to any extrinsic evidence; it differs from the demurrer and analogous motions to dismiss only in that it can not be made until after a responsive pleading is served. Federal Rule 12 retains the motion for judgment on the pleadings but treats it, as it does the motion under 12(b)(6), as one for summary judgment if extrinsic proof is presented to and not excluded by the court. Under New York's CPLR, since a motion for summary judgment cannot in any event be made until after issue is joined (CPLR 3212), provision for a separate motion for judgment on the pleadings was omitted as superfluous.

NOTES

(1) See Clark, The Summary Judgment, 36 Minn.L.Rev. 567, 573 (1952) (footnotes omitted):

"It is true that the writer, as Reporter to the Advisory Committee, originally recommended what he hoped would be a simpler procedure whereby the motion for summary judgment would swallow all other motions and become the one single form for making all objections in advance of the answer. But the Advisory Committee decided otherwise, a decision of policy with which he has no serious quarrel. For it is often true that accepting as a procedural principle what seems on the surface to be broad, flexible and simple actually defeats its own end as it leaves the bench and bar without apparent guide. Then procedural inhibitions of the past come into play to make only the ancient practice seem the sure and safe way. Consequently the sharply marked course, however narrow, may be the one most used."

(2) The assertions in the affidavits used on a motion for summary judgment must be based on the personal knowledge of the affiant and meet all other general requirements of the law of Evidence. Thus, "Affidavits replete with hearsay, conclusions and personal opinion" will not be considered. Maltby v. Shook, 131 Cal.App.2d 349, 280 P.2d 541 (1955).

(3) An attorney's affidavit is frequently helpful on a summary judgment motion to convey to the court material passages from depositions and documents even though the attorney lacks personal knowledge of the underlying facts. Not at all helpful is the quite common practice of filing memoranda of law in affidavit form. Taylor v. The African Methodist Episcopal Church, 265 App.Div. 858, 37 N.Y.S.2d 675 (2d Dep't 1942).

D. DETERMINING THE MOTION

The moment litigants begin disputing the genuineness of issues of fact or the factual inferences to be drawn from admitted basic facts, the court faces the problem of whether it may abort a trial by deciding the issues. This is the heart of the problem of summary judgment and it is a particularly acute difficulty in the light of the prevalent guaranty of trial by jury. Thus Federal Rule 56(c), in language similar to that used generally, limits granting a summary judgment to cases in which there is "no genuine issue as to any material fact" and in which the moving party is "entitled to a judgment as a matter of law." But what constitutes a genuine issue of material fact, and what the moving party must show to sustain the burden of demonstrating that there is no such issue, are apt to be most perplexing questions.

In studying the materials in the remainder of this chapter, consider the possible significance of each of the following factors in determining whether or not a motion for summary judgment should be granted:

(1) Whether the moving party is the plaintiff or the defendant.

(2) Whether the movant or the opponent would have the burden of proof on the issue whose genuineness is disputed if the case were to go

to trial; and perhaps the reasons, in light of the materials on pp. 555–557, supra, why the burden of proof would be thus allocated.

(3) Which party has greater access to evidence on the issue.

(4) Whether or not either party has made use of available pretrial discovery procedures; and perhaps the potential cost of such discovery in relation to the "worth" of the case (in the sense of the monetary value of any judgment reasonably to be expected).

(5) Whether the issue would be tried by the court or a jury.

(6) Whether the issue is one purely of so-called "historical fact"—e.g., did defendant go through the red light?—or involves instead the drawing of inferences from such facts or the application to them of a legal standard—e.g., did defendant's conduct tend to create a "monopoly"? Was it a "proximate cause" of the plaintiff's injury?

(7) Whether the evidence bearing on the issue is primarily testimonial or circumstantial and, if it is testimonial, whether the witness or witnesses it comes from are disinterested or not.

Even if the court decides that there are one or more genuine issues of material fact, should it grant partial summary judgment as to these facts as to which it finds that no genuine issues exist? *Compare* Fed.R. Civ.P. 56(d) *with* N.Y.—McKinney's CPLR 3212(g) (providing that the court must grant partial summary judgment as to these issues).

———

ARNSTEIN v. PORTER

United States Court of Appeals, Second Circuit, 1946.
154 F.2d 464.

Plaintiff, a citizen and resident of New York, brought this suit, charging infringement by defendant, a citizen and resident of New York, of plaintiff's copyrights to several musical compositions, infringement of his rights to other uncopyrighted musical compositions, and wrongful use of the titles of others. Plaintiff, when filing his complaint, demanded a jury trial. Plaintiff took the deposition of defendant, and defendant, the deposition of plaintiff. Defendant then moved for an order striking out plaintiff's jury demand, and for summary judgment. Attached to defendant's motion papers were the depositions, phonograph records of piano renditions of the plaintiff's compositions and defendant's alleged infringing compositions, and the court records of five previous copyright infringement suits brought by plaintiff in the court below against other persons, in which judgments had been entered, after trials, against plaintiff. Defendant also moved for dismissal of the action on the ground of "vexatiousness."

Plaintiff alleged that defendant's "Begin the Beguine" is a plagiarism from plaintiff's "The Lord Is My Shepherd" and "A Mother's Prayer." Plaintiff testified, on deposition, that "The Lord Is My Shepherd" had been published and about 2,000 copies sold, that "A Mother's Prayer" had been published, over a million copies having been sold. In his depositions, he gave no direct evidence that defendant saw or heard these compositions. He also alleged that defendant's "My Heart Belongs to Daddy" had been plagiarized from plaintiff's "A Mother's Prayer."

Plaintiff also alleged that defendant's "I Love You" is a plagiarism from plaintiff's composition "La Priere," stating in his deposition that the latter composition had been sold. He gave no direct proof that plaintiff knew of this composition.

He also alleged that defendant's song "Night and Day" is a plagiarism of plaintiff's song "I Love You Madly," which he testified had not been published but had once been publicly performed over the radio, copies having been sent to divers radio stations but none to defendant; a copy of this song, plaintiff testified, had been stolen from his room. He also alleged that "I Love You Madly" was in part plagiarized from "La Priere." He further alleged that defendant's "You'd Be So Nice To Come Home To" is plagiarized from plaintiff's "Sadness Overwhelms My Soul." He testified that this song had never been published or publicly performed but that copies had been sent to a movie producer and to several publishers. He also alleged that defendant's "Don't Fence Me In" is a plagiarism of plaintiff's song "A Modern Messiah" which has not been published or publicly performed; in his deposition he said that about a hundred copies had been sent to divers radio stations and band leaders but that he sent no copy to defendant. Plaintiff said that defendant "had stooges right along to follow me, watch me, and live in the same apartment with me," and that plaintiff's room had been ransacked on several occasions. Asked how he knew that defendant had anything to do with any of these "burglaries," plaintiff said, "I don't know that he had to do with it, but I only know that he could have." He also said " . . . many of my compositions had been published. No one had to break in to steal them. They were sung publicly."

Defendant in his deposition categorically denied that he had ever seen or heard any of plaintiff's compositions or had had any acquaintance with any persons said to have stolen any of them.

The prayer of plaintiff's original complaint asked "at least one million dollars out of the millions the defendant has earned and is earning out of all the plagiarism." In his amended complaint the prayer is "for judgment against the defendant in the sum of $1,000,000 as damages sustained by the plagiarism of all the compositions named in the complaint." Plaintiff, not a lawyer, appeared pro se below and on this appeal.

FRANK, CIRCUIT JUDGE. . . . The principal question on this appeal is whether the lower court, under Rule 56, properly deprived plaintiff of a trial of his copyright infringement action. The answer depends on whether "there is the slightest doubt as to the facts." Doehler Metal Furniture Co. v. United States, 2 Cir., 149 F.2d 130, 135; Sartor v. Arkansas Natural Gas Corp., 321 U.S. 620, 64 S.Ct. 724, 88 L.Ed. 967;

Arenas v. United States, 322 U.S. 419, 434, 64 S.Ct. 1090, 88 L.Ed. 1363; Associated Press v. United States, 326 U.S. 1, 6, 7, 65 S.Ct. 1416; . . ..
In applying that standard here, it is important to avoid confusing two separate elements essential to a plaintiff's case in such a suit: (a) that defendant copied from plaintiff's copyrighted work and (b) that the copying (assuming it to be proved) went so far as to constitute improper appropriation. . . .

Each of these two issues—copying and improper appropriation—is an issue of fact. If there is a trial, the conclusions on those issues of the trier of the facts—of the judge if he sat without a jury, or of the jury if there was a jury trial—bind this court on appeal, provided the evidence supports those findings, regardless of whether we would ourselves have reached the same conclusions. . . .

We turn first to the issue of copying. After listening to the compositions as played in the phonograph recordings submitted by defendant, we find similarities; but we hold that unquestionably, standing alone, they do not compel the conclusion, or permit the inference, that defendant copied. The similarities, however, are sufficient so that, if there is enough evidence of access to permit the case to go to the jury, the jury may properly infer that the similarities did not result from coincidence.

Summary judgment was, then, proper if indubitably defendant did not have access to plaintiff's compositions. Plainly that presents an issue of fact. On that issue, the district judge, who heard no oral testimony, had before him the depositions of plaintiff and defendant. The judge characterized plaintiff's story as "fantastic"; and, in the light of the references in his opinion to defendant's deposition, the judge obviously accepted defendant's denial of access and copying. Although part of plaintiff's testimony on deposition (as to "stooges" and the like) does seem "fantastic," yet plaintiff's credibility, even as to those improbabilities, should be left to the jury. If evidence is "of a kind that greatly taxes the credulity of the judge, he can say so, or, if he totally disbelieves it, he may announce that fact, leaving the jury free to believe it or not." If, said Winslow, J., "evidence is to be always disbelieved because the story told seems remarkable or impossible, then a party whose rights depend on the proof of some facts out of the usual course of events will always be denied justice simply because his story is improbable." We should not overlook the shrewd proverbial admonition that sometimes truth is stranger than fiction.

But even if we were to disregard the improbable aspects of plaintiff's story, there remain parts by no means "fantastic." On the record now before us, more than a million copies of one of his compositions were sold; copies of others were sold in smaller quantities or distributed to radio stations or band leaders or publishers, or the pieces were publicly performed. If, after hearing both parties testify, the jury disbelieves defendant's denials, it can, from such facts, reasonably infer access. It follows that, as credibility is unavoidably involved, a genuine issue of material fact presents itself. With credibility a vital factor, plaintiff is entitled to a trial where the jury can observe the witnesses while testifying. Plaintiff must not be deprived of the invaluable privilege of cross-examining the defendant—the "crucial test of credibility"—in the presence of the jury. Plaintiff, or a lawyer on his behalf, on such examination may elicit damaging admissions from defendant; more important, plaintiff may persuade the jury, observing defendant's manner when testifying, that defendant is unworthy of belief.

To be sure, plaintiff examined defendant on deposition. But the right to use depositions for discovery, or for limited purposes at a trial, of course does not mean that they are to supplant the right to call and examine the adverse party, if he is available, before the jury. For the demeanor of witnesses is recognized as a highly useful, even if not an infallible, method of ascertaining the truth and accuracy of their narratives.   . . .

With all that in mind, we cannot now say—as we think we must say to sustain a summary judgment—that at the close of a trial the judge could properly direct a verdict.

We agree that there are cases in which a trial would be farcical. . . . But where, as here, credibility, including that of the defendant, is crucial, summary judgment becomes improper and a trial indispensable.

      *   *   *

Assuming that adequate proof is made of copying, that is not enough; for there can be "permissible copying," copying which is not illicit. Whether (if he copied) defendant unlawfully appropriated presents, too, an issue of fact. The proper criterion on that issue is not an analytic or other comparison of the respective musical compositions as they appear on paper or in the judgment of trained musicians. The plaintiff's legally protected interest is not, as such, his reputation as a musician but his interest in the potential financial returns from his compositions which derive from the lay public's approbation of his efforts. The question, therefore, is whether defendant took from plaintiff's works so much of what is pleasing to the ears of lay listeners, who comprise the audience for whom such popular music is composed, that defendant wrongfully appropriated something which belongs to the plaintiff.

Surely, then, we have an issue of fact which a jury is peculiarly fitted to determine. Indeed, even if there were to be a trial before a judge, it would be desirable (although not necessary) for him to summon an advisory jury on this question.

      *   *   *

At the trial, plaintiff may play, or cause to be played, the pieces in such manner that they may seem to a jury to be inexcusably alike, in terms of the way in which lay listeners of such music would be likely to react. The plaintiff may call witnesses whose testimony may aid the jury in reaching its conclusion as to the responses of such audiences.

Expert testimony of musicians may also be received, but it will in no way be controlling on the issue of illicit copying, and should be utilized only to assist in determining the reactions of lay auditors. The impression made on the refined ears of musical experts or their views as to the musical excellence of plaintiff's or defendant's works are utterly immaterial on the issue of misappropriation; for the views of such persons are caviar to the general—and plaintiff's and defendant's compositions are not caviar. . . .

CLARK, CIRCUIT JUDGE (dissenting). While the procedure followed below seems to me generally simple and appropriate, the defendant did make one fatal tactical error. In an endeavor to assist us, he caused to be prepared records of all the musical pieces here involved, and presented these transcriptions through the medium of the affidavit of his pianist. Though he himself did not stress these records and properly met plaintiff's claims as to the written music with his own analysis, yet the tinny tintinnabulations of the music thus canned resounded through the United States Courthouse to the exclusion of all else, including the real issues in the case. Of course, sound is important in a case of this kind, but it is not so important as to falsify what the eye reports and the mind teaches. Otherwise plagiarism would be suggested by the mere drumming of repetitious sound from our usual popular music, as it issues from a piano, orchestra, or hurdy-gurdy—particularly when ears may be dulled by long usage, possibly artistic repugnance or boredom, or mere distance which causes all sounds to merge. And the judicial eardrum may be peculiarly insensitive after long years of listening to the "beat, beat, beat" (I find myself plagiarizing from defendant and thus in danger of my brothers' doom) of sound upon it, though perhaps no more so than the ordinary citizen juror—even if tone deafness is made a disqualification for jury service, as advocated.

Pointing to the adscititious fortuity inherent in the stated standard is, it seems to me, the fact that after repeated hearings of the records, I could not find therein what my brothers found. The only thing definitely mentioned seemed to be the repetitive use of the note e in certain places by both plaintiff and defendant, surely too simple and ordinary a device of composition to be significant. In our former musical plagiarism cases we have, naturally, relied on what seemed the total sound effect; but we have also analyzed the music enough to make sure of an intelligible and intellectual decision. . . .

Consequently, I do not think we should abolish the use of the intellect here even if we could. When, however, we start with an examination of the written and printed material supplied by the plaintiff in his complaint and exhibits, we find at once that he does not and cannot claim extensive copying, measure by measure, of his compositions. . . .

But of course as the record now stands, the case is still stronger, for it appears that access must rest only upon a showing of similarities in the compositions. Under the procedure employed, the parties were entitled to require discovery of the case relied on by the other. . . . This they did by each taking the deposition of the other, resulting in a categorical denial by defendant of having ever seen or heard plaintiff's compositions and no showing by plaintiff of any evidence of access worthy of submission to any trier of fact.[1] And I take it as conceded that these trifling bits of similarities will not permit of the inference of copying. My brothers, in a trusting belief in the virtues of cross-examination, rely upon a trial to develop more. But cross-examination can hardly construct a whole case without some factual basis on which to start. And they overlook, too, the operation of F.R. 26(d)(3)2, as to the use of depositions, under which the defendant, if elsewhere on business, need not return for trial, but may rely upon his already clear deposition, and the plaintiff may not have the luxury of another futile cross-examination. Further, my brothers reject as "utterly immaterial" the help of musical experts as to the music itself (as distinguished from what lay auditors may think of it, where, for my part, I should think their competence least), contrary to what I had supposed was universal practice, . . . thereby adding a final proof of the anti-intellectual and book-burning nature of their decision. Thus it seems quite likely that the record at trial will be the one now before us.

NOTES

(1) A fascinating account of the in-fighting between Judges Frank and Clark in this and other cases that found them divided appears in Schick, Judicial Relations on the Second Circuit, 1941–1951, 44 N.Y.U.L.Rev. 939 (1969). An example: In his first memorandum Judge Frank said of the musical works in controversy:

> "I have listened to them. I am relatively unversed in this field. But I think that (1) Porter's Begin the Beguine has some marked resemblances to (2) Arnstein's Duet from his Song of David, his Lord is my Shepherd, and his A Mother's Prayer. Ditto as to (1) Porter's I Love You and (2) Arnstein's La Priere. So too does my secretary who improvises music. . . ." (quoted id. at p. 944)

For his part, Judge Clark studied, listened, and concluded there was no possibility of plagiarism, a judgment "concurred in by my secretary and my law clerk, both of whom have studied music somewhat as I have." Clark also called upon his friend, Professor Luther Noss, who was the Yale organist, and reported that after having played and sung all the music in issue, Noss concluded that the claim of copying was fantastic. (Ibid.)

(2) After trial, the verdict was for the defendant. It was affirmed *per curiam*, Arnstein v. Porter, 158 F.2d 795 (2d Cir.1946).

(3) For an illustration of the difficulties in establishing plagiarism even in a "clear case" see the description of "The case of the plagiarized song 'Rum and

---

1. Even his vague and reckless charge of burglary of his various rooming places—a repeated feature of his plagiarism cases, see, e.g., Arnstein v. American Soc. of Composers, Authors and Publishers, D.C.S.D. N.Y., 29 F.Supp. 388, 391, 392; Arnstein v. Twentieth Century Fox Film Corp., D.C. S.D.N.Y., 52 F.Supp. 114—upon cross-examination dissolved into nothing so far as this defendant is concerned. [Some footnotes have been omitted; others have been renumbered. Eds.]

Coca-Cola,' " Nizer, My Life in Court 233 (1961). Are there classes of cases in which, in fact, summary judgment is relatively more difficult to obtain?

DYER v. MACDOUGALL, 201 F.2d 265 (2d Cir.1952): P's complaint alleged that defendant slandered him in plaintiff's absence, but in the presence of two witnesses. D's motion for summary judgment was supported by his own affidavit and those of the alleged witnesses, all denying that the slander had been committed. Plaintiff's affidavit presented no evidence but merely urged the possibility of cross-examining the defendant or his witnesses.* The trial judge summarily dismissed the complaint and the Court of Appeals affirmed. Judge Hand recognized that the jury might rationally be convinced by the demeanor of the defendant on the witness stand that the truth was the opposite of what he said it was. Nevertheless, he voted to affirm: "This is owing to the fact that otherwise in such cases there could not be an effective appeal from the judge's disposition of a motion for a directed verdict. He, who has seen and heard the 'demeanor' evidence, may have been right or wrong in thinking that it gave rational support to a verdict; yet, since that evidence has disappeared, it will be impossible for an appellate court to say which he was."

Judge Frank disagreed with Judge Hand's reasoning, although he voted to affirm on other grounds. First, he pointed out that the problem bothering Judge Hand is equally pressing in any case in which oral testimony plays a significant role; then, Judge Frank disposed of the issue by noting that on a motion for a directed verdict the trial judge does not weigh the evidence, including the credibility of witnesses, but assumes that the jury will believe all the evidence, including demeanor evidence, favorable to the adverse party. "The rule that a trial judge . . . may not legitimately consider demeanor in considering directed verdict motions means that his orders on such motions are readily reviewable." See NLRB v. Walton Manufacturing Co., 369 U.S. 404, 408, 417–21, 82 S.Ct. 853, 855, 860–62, 7 L.Ed.2d 829 (1962), for a sharp difference among the members of the Court as to practical significance and application of the principles put forward in Dyer v. MacDougall.

NOTES

(1) On summary judgment generally, see Bogart, Summary Judgment—A Comparative and Critical Analysis, 19 Osgoode L.J. 552 (1981); Symposium, Summary Judgment, Default Judgment, 9 Mem.St.U.L.Rev. 481 (1979); Damsel, Summary Judgment: Obsolete or Useful Tool, 51, Fla. B.J. 535 (1977); Sheehan, Summary Judgment: Let the Movant Beware, 8 St. Mary's L.J. 253 (1976).

(2) In Heyman v. Commerce and Industry Insurance Co., 524 F.2d 1317 (2d Cir.1975), the Court, although noting that the reluctance "to approve summary

---

* If plaintiff were to call the two alleged witnesses, he would have to cope with the rule against impeaching one's own witness.

judgment in any but the most extraordinary circumstances", as exemplified by Arnstein v. Porter, has long been "jettisoned in favor of an approach more in keeping with the spirit of Rule 56", reversed the summary judgment rendered by the court below to the effect that the terms of a settlement agreement between the insured and insurance company required judgment for the insured.

(3) On the relation between the summary judgment and directed verdict standards, see Currie, Thoughts on Directed Verdicts and Summary Judgments, 45 U.Chi.L.Rev. 72 (1977).

(4) May summary judgment be denied because a case involves significant and unsettled constitutional issues? United States v. St. Thomas Beach Resorts, Inc., 386 F.Supp. 769, 771 (D. Virgin Islands 1974), states that summary judgment is no less appropriate, assuming there is no genuine issue as to any material fact, because "constitutional or other questions of large public import are raised." But cf. Waldie v. Schlesinger, 509 F.2d 508 (D.C.Cir.1974), reversing the lower court's grant of summary judgment for defendants in a sex-based discrimination case and stressing that "this area of constitutional law is still evolving and is often highly dependent on the facts of each case. Accordingly, a full development of the facts of these cases is essential to any meaningful assessment of appellants' claim against the rapidly changing, and variously interpreted, case law." See also Chitwood v. Feaster, 468 F.2d 359 (4th Cir. 1972), reversing district court's grant of summary judgment against plaintiffs (non-tenured college teachers), who claimed they were discharged because they engaged in constitutionally protected activity (attending protest demonstrations).

(5) Adequacy of proof for summary judgment in diversity actions in the federal courts is determined by federal law. Lloyd v. Lawrence, 472 F.2d 313, 316 (5th Cir.1973), on remand 60 F.R.D. 116 (1973); Ando v. Great Western Sugar Co., 475 F.2d 531, 534 (10th Cir.1973).

E. RECENT FEDERAL DEVELOPMENTS

In 1986, the Supreme Court of the United States rendered three decisions that had the apparent purposes of bringing greater clarity to summary judgment standards and procedures. In Matsushita Electrical Industrial Co., Ltd. v. Zenith Radio Corp., 475 U.S. 574, 106 S.Ct. 1348, 89 L.Ed.2d 538 (1986), the Court upheld the grant of summary judgment in a case involving the defendant's state of mind, traditionally a difficult issue on which to rest a motion for summary judgment. That the defendant's state of mind was involved (conspiratorial motive in an anti-trust case) was held not to be a bar to summary judgment when the opponent failed to come forward with specific facts showing that there was a genuine issue for trial. The majority ruled that the Court of Appeals had not given due weight to the absence of any evidence of plausible motive by defendant to engage in the conduct charged.

In Anderson v. Liberty Lobby, Inc., 477 U.S. 242, 106 S.Ct. 2505, 91 L.Ed.2d 202 (1986), the plaintiff charged the defendants with defamation. As a public figure, the plaintiff had the burden of showing that the defendant acted with "actual malice" which had to be proved by "clear and convincing evidence." The district court had granted summary judgment because on the evidence there was no basis for a finding of actual malice with convincing clarity. The Court of Appeals reversed, holding that the requirement that actual malice be proved by clear and convincing evidence, rather than by a preponderance, was irrelevant on the motion for summary judgment. However, the Supreme Court ruled that the substantive evidentiary burden had to be taken into account on the motion for summary judgment. The Court defined a "material" fact in Rule 56 as relating to disputes of fact that might affect the outcome of the suit and a "genuine issue" as one as to which the evidence would allow a reasonable jury to return a verdict for the opponent of the motion. The test for summary judgment was said to mirror the directed verdict standard at trial and to vary according to the standard of proof applicable to the issue involved.

Finally, in Celotex Corp. v. Catrett, 477 U.S. 317, 106 S.Ct. 2548, 91 L.Ed.2d 265 (1986), the Supreme Court again reinstated a summary judgment granted by the district court and reversed on appeal. The case involved a wrongful death action based on the decedent's alleged exposure to asbestos products made by the defendants. Some of the defendants moved for summary judgment on the ground that there was no evidence connecting them to any asbestos to which the decedent had been exposed. The appellate court reversed the lower court's grant of summary judgment because the motion was not supported by any evidence in the form of affidavits or otherwise to show the decedent had not come in contact with any of the movants' products. The Supreme Court held, despite that lack, that Celotex was entitled to judgment as a matter of law because the plaintiff had failed to make a sufficient showing on an essential element of her case with respect to which she had the burden of proof.

The message sent in these decisions has not escaped the attention of the lower courts. In Knight v. United States Fire Insurance Co., 804 F.2d 9 (2d Cir.1986), Chief Judge Feinberg, quoting from *Celotex,* emphasized the availability of summary judgment. He noted the "perception that this court is unsympathetic" to summary judgment motions and stated that "[w]hatever may have been the accuracy of this view in years gone by, it is decidedly inaccurate at the present time, 804 F.2d at 12." The court then went on to affirm the grant of summary judgment in an action to recover on an insurance policy. The motion was based on the ground that the insured had failed to disclose in his application for the insurance a material fact, namely the cancellation of prior insurance on the same risk. The court affirmed the lower court's holding that the information not disclosed would have been material, rejecting the argument that its materiality should have been determined by a jury. It also made the independent determination (which the district court had failed to make) that the evidence adduced by the insured that the movant had knowledge from other sources of the information not disclosed was insufficient to create a genuine issue of fact. The evidence relied on by the insured was that the reinsurers on the policy were the primary insurers on the cancelled policy and that two of the defendants were subsidiaries or affiliates of the underwriters of the cancelled policy. Was that information sufficient to create a genuine issue as to the insurers' actual or constructive knowledge? If not, should the insured have been afforded an opportunity to obtain additional information on this point by pre-trial discovery?

NOTE

On recent summary judgment practice, see Sayler, Rule 56: Proposals for an Underused Rule, in *ADR and the Courts: A Manual for Judges and Lawyers* 313 (1987); Collins, Summary Judgment and Circumstantial Evidence, 40 Stan. L.Rev. 491 (1988); Fiedenthal, Cases on Summary Judgment: Has There Been a Material Change in Standards, 63 Notre Dame L.Rev. 770 (1988); Stempel, A Distorted Mirror: The Supreme Court's Shimmering View of Summary Judgment, Directed Verdict and the Adjudication Process, 49 Ohio St.L.J. 95 (1988); Kennedy, Federal Summary Judgment: Reconciling Celotex v. Catrett with Adickes v. Kress and the Evidentiary Problems Under Rule 56, 6 Rev. of Litigation 227 (1987); Mullenix, Summary Judgment: Taming the Beast of Burdens, 10 American J.Tr. Advocacy 433 (1987).

Proposed Amendment to Rule 56

Proposed amendments to the Federal Rules of Civil Procedure approved by the Advisory Committee on Civil Rules on April 29, 1989, if approved, would substantially recast Rule 56. The revised Rule would authorize not only summary judgment, but also summary establishment of fact or law when expedition and economy may be achieved by such summary establishment. It thus seeks to enable a court to eliminate from the issues to be tried those that can be established without a trial even in cases in which the decision on such issues does not warrant the granting of summary judgment on all or part of a party's claim. The proposal liberalizes and expands the provisions of present Rule 56(d). What are the advantages and disadvantages of the proposed change?

DI SABATO v. SOFFES

Supreme Court of New York, Appellate Division, First Department, 1959.
9 A.D.2d 297, 193 N.Y.S.2d 184.

M.M. FRANK, JUSTICE. In this action for personal injuries, the plaintiffs appeal from an order denying their motion, made pursuant to Rule 113 of the Rules of Civil Practice, for summary judgment striking out the defendants' answer and directing an assessment of damages.

At the outset it should be stated that there is no claim that the plaintiffs were contributorily negligent. Nor could there be such a claim on the facts in the case.

The plaintiffs were employed as counter girls in a drug store which was located at the corner of two intersecting streets. At the time of the accident they were stationed between the counter and a glass and brick wall which formed the outer shell of the building.

It is not disputed that a 1957 Chrysler owned by the defendant, Soffes, and in charge of his brother-in-law, the defendant Grubetz, careened under its own power from a point diagonally across the street from the store and 50 or 60 feet distant therefrom, while Grubetz was out of the car and not at its wheel. The car traveled through the intersection with such speed and force that, after hitting a parking meter stanchion, it mounted the sidewalk and crashed into and partially through the outer wall of the store. It demolished a section of the wall and dislodged coffee urns and window cases. This equipment, in turn, felled the plaintiffs, who were rendered unconscious and removed to the hospital in that condition.

We are enjoined by the Rule to grant the motion, "if upon all the papers and proof submitted, the action or claim . . . shall be established sufficiently to warrant the court as a matter of law in directing judgment, interlocutory or final".

The recent amendment to Rule 113 extended it to include actions grounded in negligence. However, the change was not intended to vary the basic principles which have evolved since the inception of the Rules of Civil Practice in 1921.

One of the recognized purposes of summary judgment is to expedite the disposition of civil cases where no issue of material fact is presented to justify a trial. While the courts are cautioned to exercise the power to summarily direct judgment with full recognition that a party with a just claim or a valid defense is entitled to his day in court, timidity in exercising the power in favor of a legitimate claim and against an unmerited one, not alone defeats the ends of justice in a specific case, but contributes to calendar congestion which, in turn, denies to other suitors their rights to prompt determination of their litigation.

On a motion such as this, the Court is called upon to determine whether a bona fide issue exists. If the plaintiff's pleadings and other papers disclose no real defense and if the defendant fails to controvert such proof and establish by affidavits or other evidence the existence of a genuine defense, the Court may find that no triable issue exists and grant summary judgment. . . .

With these principles in mind, we turn to the case at hand. The defendants have failed to submit a single affidavit, by anyone having knowledge of the facts, to controvert the prima facie showing of negligence which flows from the occurrence together with the examination. . . .

. . . An opposing affidavit by an attorney without personal knowledge of the facts has no probative value and should be disregarded. . . .

The plaintiffs rely upon the undisputed physical facts of the accident and the examination before trial of the defendant Grubetz. [After reviewing the circumstances, as disclosed in Grubetz' deposition, the opinion concluded that defendants had failed to establish a triable issue of fact with regard to their liability and awarded plaintiffs summary judgment.]

Order denying motion to strike the answer of the defendants and for an assessment of damages reversed on the law, with $20 costs and disbursements to appellants and motion granted with $10 costs. Settle order.

All concur except BOTEIN, P.J., and BREITEL, J., who dissent and vote to affirm in dissenting opinion by BREITEL, J.

BREITEL, JUSTICE (dissenting). The issue is whether plaintiffs are entitled to summary judgment in this negligence action. A driverless automobile under power rolled across the street, crashed a building, and caused injuries to the infant plaintiffs. The facts, as they are known on this record, were developed on the examination of the defendant driver in a deposition taken before trial at the behest of plaintiffs.

Defendant driver brought his automobile to a stop in order to let off his mother, a passenger. He put the vehicle into neutral, he says; set his parking brake, but did not turn off the ignition. He stepped out of the vehicle on the left side to assist his mother. He walked to the other side but the right hand door did not open. His four-year-old nephew, who was also sitting in the front seat, climbed into the back; he and then the driver told the mother to get out on the left side of the car. As she moved over, across the front seat, the driver heard the engine race and told her to get her foot off the gas. The mother continued to the left and, as she did, her hand hit the gear push buttons on the dashboard.

At first the automobile started to move slowly. The driver attempted to get in, but the vehicle picked up such momentum that he could not do so and was dragged across the intersection. The vehicle jumped the opposite curb, struck the building and thus caused the injuries to infant plaintiffs.

Defendant driver inferred, as anyone must, if he had told the truth, that the mother must have inadvertently stepped on the accelerator pedal. Because the police officer at the scene is quoted as having said the parking brake was not set after the accident, one could infer that the mother somehow disengaged the brake, or that the impact of the accident did so. Or one could, of course, infer that the driver never set the hand brake, although he testified he had.

These are the key facts of the accident. From these facts negligence may not be concluded as a matter of law, which is what is required, if summary judgment is to be granted.

Whether an automobile operator should turn off his engine when he leaves the driver's seat momentarily is a question of fact depending upon the circumstances, namely: type of engine; idling speed of engine; grade of street; condition and type of brakes; persons remaining in the vehicle; character, age, driving skill, and propensities of the persons remaining in the vehicle; the location of such persons in the vehicle; and the general character of the area in which the vehicle is standing.

Whether the driver in fact set his parking brake is a manifest and disputed question of fact.

The findings to be drawn from the vehicle setting into motion, despite the driver's testimony on deposition that he put the engine into neutral and set his parking brake, involve questions of fact from which contradictory inferences could undoubtedly be drawn by the fact-finders.

Whether this particular automobile could move, although the parking brake was set, is a question of fact.

Whether the parking brake in this automobile was constructed to have as effective a braking force as the main brakes is a question of fact.

Whether the policeman's quoted extrajudicial statement that the parking brake was found not set after the accident, uncritically accepted by the driver when testifying on deposition, is to be believed is a question of fact.

The inferences to be drawn from the policeman's quoted statement, if accepted as true, namely, whether the driver did not set his brake, or that the brake lever was sprung by the impact of the accident are questions of fact.

Whether the driver, as a careful operator, should have permitted his mother to move across the front seat, is a question of fact.

Whether the driver should have foreseen that the mother in moving across the front seat, might step on the accelerator pedal, or push the gear push buttons, is a compound question of fact.

Whether the mother not only pressed the accelerator pedal but continued to press on it, as if it were a brake, is a question of fact, on which the record is unenlightening. But whether she did so is not, at this stage of the case, determinative, for one of the prime questions in the case is whether the driver was bound to foresee what she would do and did. It is for that reason that the absence of an affidavit by the mother is of no consequence on this motion.

Whether the driver could have done anything more than he did to stop his mother's actions or the motion of the vehicle, once the accident had started, is a question of fact.

Yet, in order for plaintiffs to recover, as a matter of law without trial, on a motion for summary judgment, each one of these questions of fact must be viewed as questions answerable in law, and in law alone.

Much is made that no affidavit by either defendant was submitted. Of course, testimony by deposition, taken by plaintiffs is a higher order of proof than an affidavit. An affidavit, usually prepared by a lawyer, and signed by the affiant, is hardly the equivalent in value of a deposition by question and answer, especially when the questioning is done by the adverse attorney. So, the contention that defendants have supplied less than they should have, is difficult to understand. Indeed, plaintiffs annexed the deposition, and from it the issues of fact appear to be present. The trouble is that plaintiffs not only presented a prima facie case in their affidavits but at the same time presented the facts which establish the elements of a defense and require a jury determination.

The jury's function in a trial is not only to find as between contradicted facts, which are true, but also to find as between contradictory inferences, which are true. Indeed, even the drawing of reasonable inferences is exclusively the province of the fact finders. It is only inferences which *must* be drawn from evidentiary facts that are the stuff of what is referred to as "matter of law."

On this record, ultimately, defendants may not be held liable on a motion for summary judgment unless it is held, as a matter of law, that when a driver gets out of an automobile, not for parking but for a momentary stop, without turning off the motor, he must have foreseen that another in moving across the front seat might inadvertently set the automobile in motion.　.　.　.

NOTES

(1) Does the *Di Sabato* case stand for any more than the proposition of law summarized by Judge Breitel in his dissent? Does it have a helpful impact upon plaintiffs' prospects for recovery of maximum damages to establish liability by motion for summary judgment?

(2) In personal injury actions the issues of negligence and contributory negligence are generally not resolved by a summary judgment. They ordinarily evoke conflicting testimony and the "reasonableness" of the actor's conduct, both of which are traditionally for the jury to determine. See David, The Summary Judgment in California: The Case for Judicial Reform, 25 Hast.L.J. 119, 139 (1973), for a discussion of summary judgment in negligence cases in that state.

(3) In Tancredi v. Mannino, 75 A.D.2d 579, 426 N.Y.S.2d 577 (1980), involving an action upon a promissory note in which the defendant's only defense was an alleged oral discharge by the plaintiff's deceased predecessor in interest, the lower court had granted summary judgment on the ground that testimony as to the alleged discharge would, upon objection, be inadmissible at trial under the Dead Man's Statute. The appellate court reversed on the ground that the court should not apply the Statute "in anticipation of the objection". Is the result acceptable if the plaintiff invoked the Statute in the moving papers?

(4) Does a party in a negligence case lose anything besides the motion by moving for summary judgment and eliciting a decision that a genuine issue exists as to the main disputed matter?

————

PRUSINKI v. HOLLAND, 228 F.Supp. 959, 960–61 (E.D.Wis.1964): P, while a guest at D's resort, jumped off the end of a pier into shallow water and injured his foot on a "foreign object" he never saw. To recover under the Wisconsin statute governing resorts, P had to prove that D had notice of the alleged hazardous condition and an opportunity to correct it. D filed an affidavit swearing he and his son checked daily for the presence of foreign objects and removed any they found. D was granted a summary judgment.

"Plaintiff does not know what the 'foreign object' was other than his belief that it was a bottle. He never saw the object himself nor asked anyone to look for it. The presence of such a bottle was apparently an afterthought to the plaintiff since he did not allege its presence in his original complaint. A jury would be forced to speculate as to whether there was in fact a bottle or any object there.

 * * *

"Additionally, plaintiff has not produced a shred of evidence which raises a fact question as to whether or not defendant had either actual or constructive notice of the alleged hazardous condition. . . .

". . . Nor has he shown this Court any reason to believe that an attack on defendant's credibility would be the least bit successful. Had plaintiff chosen to avail himself of the various pretrial discovery procedures provided for in the Federal Rules, he might then have been in a position to show this Court that he has more than mere speculation that the defendant will contradict himself. He has not advanced any reason for failing to seek pretrial discovery."

————

STREETER v. ERIE RAILROAD CO., 25 F.R.D. 272 (S.D.N.Y.1960): A train conductor sued under the Federal Employers Liability Act for injuries sustained in a train collision while he was riding to work on a free pass. The pass was accepted on the plaintiff's agreement that it was a gratuity and he assumed "all risks of accidents, death, or personal injury," but he claimed he did paper work in preparation for his regular duties and was therefore "employed" for purposes of the F.E.L.A. Plaintiff moved for summary judgment and defendant cross-moved to dismiss. The court denied the motions, holding that the question of whether the plaintiff was "employed" at the time of injury was one of fact (p. 273):

"Even where there is no dispute as to the facts of the event, the determination calls for an inference or a conclusion of fact, and this— like questions of fault or causation—must be left to a jury unless 'reasonable men could not reach differing conclusions.' Cf. Baker v.

Texas & P.R. Co., 1959, 359 U.S. 227, 79 S.Ct. 664, 665, 3 L.Ed.2d 756;
. . .

"Given the undisputed facts of this case, reasonable men may reach differing conclusions as to whether plaintiff was 'employed' (within the statutory meaning) at the time of the accident."

The court noted that in two similar cases (Sassaman v. Pennsylvania Railroad, 144 F.2d 950 (3d Cir.1944); Metropolitan Coal Co. v. Johnson, 265 F.2d 173 (1st Cir.1959), the question of employment status was decided as a matter of law.

SECTION 3. VOLUNTARY DISMISSAL

A plaintiff's lawyer sometimes finds himself faced with sure defeat and wishing he had not commenced his action when or where or on quite the grounds he chose. A voluntary nonsuit would present no problem if he could abandon his action and sue again without prejudice or penalty. To give such a privilege to the plaintiff would accord with the law's policy of not compelling a party to sue against his will, but it is open to abuse, for example, as a tool of oppression or as a trick to learn the defendant's secrets. Without an empowering statute or rule, has a court power to refuse or condition plaintiff's voluntary discontinuance of his action?

LITTMAN v. BACHE & CO.
United States Court of Appeals, Second Circuit, 1958.
252 F.2d 479.

WATERMAN, CIRCUIT JUDGE. The question presented by this appeal is whether the plaintiff-appellant had an unconditional right to dismiss this action before service by the defendant of an answer or of a motion for summary judgment. The answer lies in construction of Rule 41(a) Fed.Rules Civ.Proc., 28 U.S.C., which rule we previously have construed in Harvey Aluminum, Inc., v. American Cyanamid Co., 2 Cir., 1953, 203 F.2d 105, cert. den. 345 U.S. 964, 73 S.Ct. 949, 97 L.Ed. 1383.

Appellant commenced this action by the filing of a complaint on March 18, 1957, served upon the defendant on the following day. The District Court granted a three-week extension of time, or until April 29, within which the defendant might answer or otherwise move with respect to the complaint. Within this extended time, by motion dated April 26 the defendant obtained an order directing plaintiff to show cause why the action should not be transferred to the Southern District of Florida pursuant to 28 U.S.C.A. § 1404(a). On May 7 the District Court granted the motion despite plaintiff's objections, and directed that the transfer order be settled upon two days' notice. The following day plaintiff obtained an order returnable May 14 directing the defendant to show cause why the motion to transfer should not be reargued, and, upon reargument, denied. The date for the settlement of the transfer order was therefore set over until May 14. On May 13 the plaintiff filed a notice of voluntary dismissal. Defendant moved to vacate the dismissal and after hearing argument, the District Court, on May 16, entered an order directing that the action be transferred to the Southern District of Florida, and that the plaintiff's notice of dismissal, be vacated. The plaintiff appealed from these orders. Upon motion of the defendant to dismiss the appeal we held, 2 Cir., 246 F.2d 490, that the § 1404(a) order was not appealable, but that an appeal would lie from the order vacating plaintiff's notice of dismissal.

Voluntary dismissal of actions commenced in the District Court is governed by Rule 41(a) which, insofar as pertinent, provides that "an action may be dismissed by the plaintiff without order of the court (1) by filing a notice of dismissal at any time before service by the adverse party of an answer or of a motion for summary judgment, whichever first occurs . . . ." The Rule was intended to limit the right of dismissal to an early stage of the proceedings, thereby curbing the abuse of the right which had previously been possible. See 5 Moore's Federal Practice 1007 (2d Ed.1951). In furtherance of the purpose underlying the Rule, we held in Harvey Aluminum, Inc., v. American Cyanamid Co., supra [203 F.2d 108] that under the circumstances of that case the notice of dismissal filed by the plaintiff was properly vacated even though no "paper labeled 'answer' or 'motion for summary judgment' " had been served by the defendant. There the dismissal had been attempted by the plaintiff after an adverse ruling on its motion for an injunction *pendente lite*. The injunction had been denied after several days of argument and testimony before the District Court. We noted that the merits of the controversy were squarely raised and the district court in part based its denial of the injunction on its conclusion that the plaintiffs' chance of success was "remote, if not completely nil." 203 F.2d 105, 107. Cf. Butler v. Denton, 10 Cir., 1945, 150 F.2d 687; Love v. Silas Mason Co., D.C.W.D.La.1946, 66 F.Supp. 753. These decisions rest on the ground that prior to filing of the voluntary dismissal the parties had joined issue on the merits of the controversy, irrespective of the status of the formal pleadings. Where, on the other hand, issue has not been joined prior to notice of dismissal, the courts have held that the dismissal may not be vacated. Kilpatrick v. Texas & P. Ry. Co., 2 Cir., 1948, 166 F.2d 788; Wilson & Co. v. Fremont Cake & Meal Co., D.C.D.Neb.1949, 83 F.Supp. 900; cf. Pennsylvania R. Co. v. Daoust Construction Co., 7 Cir., 1952, 193 F.2d 659.

The present case is akin to the latter group of decisions. The only issue that was raised before the District Court was whether to grant defendant's motion to transfer the action to the Southern District of Florida. The merits of the controversy were never before the court. To be sure, both parties were familiar with the subject matter of the litigation, but this was clearly insufficient to deprive plaintiff of his right to a voluntary dismissal. We hold that the District Court erred in vacating the dismissal. See White v. Thompson, D.C.N.D.Ill.1948, 80 F.Supp. 411; Toulmin v. Industrial Metal Protectives, D.C.D.Del.1955, 135 F.Supp. 925.

Reversed.

LUMBARD, CIRCUIT JUDGE (dissenting). I would affirm. I agree with the majority that the issues had not been joined on the merits so as to allow the District Court to treat the stage of the proceedings as equivalent to an answer or motion for summary judgment. If Harvey Aluminum, Inc., v. American Cyanamid Co., 2 Cir., 1953, 203 F.2d 105, cert. den. 345 U.S. 964, 73 S.Ct. 949, 97 L.Ed. 1383 and the other cases cited by Judge Herlands stand only for that proposition and if that is the sole exception to the literal language of Rule 41(a)(1), the decision should be reversed. I believe, however, that Harvey means that we need not allow the literal language of the Rules to defeat the interests of justice and sound judicial administration. Cf. Hormel v. Helvering, 1941, 312 U.S. 552, 557, 61 S.Ct. 719, 85 L.Ed. 1037; Bucy v. Nevada Const. Co., 9 Cir., 1942, 125 F.2d 213, 216.

The facts set out by Judge Herlands show, and the thrust of his opinion is, that the plaintiff presumed upon the Court in an attempt to shift his forum. The plaintiff filed the notice of dismissal after he had been defeated on the motion to transfer and after he had expressly requested and received a delay in transfer for the purpose of reargument. On the same day that he dismissed he initiated an action in the New York courts. The District Court has an area of discretion to prevent trifling tactics of this nature. The action of the majority seems to me to lose sight of the larger objective in the process of embracing a technicality.

It seems apparent that the plaintiff, not having achieved the result for which he hoped on the motion to transfer the action to Florida, has now changed his tune as to his citizenship and has started an action in the Supreme Court of New York County on the theory that he is a New York citizen. Thus the merry-go-round goes around again and under the removal statute the parties may be knocking on the door of the Federal Courthouse once more.

Rule 1 of the Federal Rules of Civil Procedure enjoins us to construe the rules "to secure the just, speedy, and inexpensive determination of every action." I think the injunction applies to this kind of forum shopping which multiplies expense and delay. The District Court had the power to vacate the voluntary dismissal under such circumstances as took place here. Exercising this power in such a proper case was not an abuse of discretion and I would affirm.

NOTES

(1) At common law, the plaintiff had an unfettered right to a nonsuit. "The plaintiff had a right to be nonsuited at any stage of the proceedings he might prefer, and thereby reserve to himself the power of bringing a fresh action for the same subject matter; and this right continued to the last moment

of the trial, even till after verdict rendered, or, where the case was tried by the court without the intervention of a jury, until the judge had pronounced his judgment. [Citation omitted.] Consequently, if he was not satisfied with the damages given by the jury, he might become nonsuit." Washburn v. Allen, 77 Me. 344, 346 (1885); see also Head, The History and Development of Nonsuit, 27 W.Va.L.Q. 20 (1920).

(2) In most states, the right to a voluntary nonsuit is now governed by statute or court rule. "The problem confronting the legislators in drafting their nonsuit statutes has been to decide at which point the plaintiff's right to halt the proceedings without prejudice should cease; or rather, at which point the defendant should have his right to final litigation protected by the discretion of the trial judge. There are, obviously, numerous places in the proceedings of a trial which the legislature could conveniently choose. And, for the most part, the various jurisdictions have shown their individuality by striking variations in the time limit imposed upon the plaintiff—one state denying the right only after verdict is entered, others more stringent, to the most strict of all where the plaintiff's right is limited to the time before receipt of the defendant's answer." Note, The Right of a Plaintiff to Take a Voluntary Nonsuit or to Dismiss His Action Without Prejudice, 37 Va.L.Rev. 969, 970–71 (1951). See also Annot., Time when Voluntary Nonsuit or Dismissal May be Taken as of Right under Statute Authorizing at Any Time Before "Trial," "Commencement of Trial," "Trial of the Facts," or the Like, 1 A.L.R.3d 711 (1965).

For a tabulation of the various cut-off points adopted in the United States, see Note, Exercise of Discretion in Permitting Dismissal Without Prejudice Under Federal Rule 41(a), 54 Colum.L.Rev. 616 (1954); see also 19 N.Y.Jud. Council Rep. 206 (1956); Annot., 126 A.L.R. 284 (1940).

(3) Where plaintiff has an absolute right to dismissal without prejudice, what is to prevent him from repeatedly bringing new actions and dismissing them voluntarily for the purpose of harassing the defendant? See Renfroe v. Johnson, 142 Tex. 251, 177 S.W.2d 600 (1944). Is this a problem under Federal Rule 41?

(4) Does a dismissal on the merits which would bar the bringing of another action also bar asserting the same cause of action in a subsequent counterclaim? In Headley v. Noto, 22 N.Y.2d 1, 290 N.Y.S.2d 726, 237 N.E.2d 871 (1968), the Court stated:

> "While as a general rule a plaintiff whose action has been dismissed 'on the merits' for such want of prosecution as appears here should be barred from again bringing an action or asserting a counterclaim on the same claim, he should not be precluded from asserting the same facts *defensively* in an action brought against him involving the same subject matter or arising out of the same transaction. This is consonant with the philosophy underlying CPLR 203(c) which provides that a defense or counterclaim ordinarily barred by the Statute of Limitations can be asserted as a set-off if it arose out of the transaction upon which the affirmative claim is asserted."

Due to the peculiar facts of the *Headley* case, however (the suit involved title to real property), the Court allowed the counterclaim to stand so that the title question could be finally resolved. A dissent argued that the counterclaim should not have been assertible despite the title dispute, since the principles of *res judicata* should have been held to have barred any use of defendant's claim of title.

SECTION 4. INVOLUNTARY DISMISSALS

Rule 41(b) of the Federal Rules of Civil Procedure provides for involuntary dismissal of an action or claim for failure of the plaintiff to prosecute or to comply with these rules or any order of court. Unless the court specifies otherwise, such a dismissal "operates as an adjudication on the merits."

REPUBLIC OF THE PHILIPPINES v. MARCOS et al.
United States Court of Appeals, Second Circuit, 1989.
888 F.2d 954.

OAKES, CHIEF JUDGE:

This appeal arises from the dismissal of Canadian Land Company of America, N.V. v. Bernstein, No. 86 Civ. 9087, ordered by Judge Pierre N. Leval, United States District Court for the Southern District of New York, as a sanction for the disobedience by Adnan Khashoggi and Sami Fadel Barakat ("Fadel") of repeated orders to appear in New York for deposition as managing agents of the corporate plaintiffs. Arguing that Khashoggi and Fadel are not managing agents of plaintiff corporations, that Khashoggi and Fadel had compelling personal reasons for avoiding appearance in New York, and that measures less drastic than dismissal should have been pursued, plaintiffs-appellants seek reversal of the district court order. Because the sanction in this case is well within the discretion of the trial judge, we affirm dismissal, with modification of the district court order as noted below.

FACTS

Canadian Land is one aspect of the three-sided contest among the Republic of the Philippines ("the Philippines"), Joseph and Ralph Bernstein and their affiliated corporations ("the Bernsteins"), and Adnan Khashoggi to establish ownership of four valuable Manhattan properties. In the principal action, Republic of the Philippines v. Marcos, the Philippines claimed that the late Philippine President Ferdinand Marcos purchased the properties with illegally acquired wealth and then used a complicated structure of shell corporations to cover up his interest in the properties. In that action, the Philippines obtained a preliminary injunction prohibiting Marcos, the Bernsteins, the four corporations holding legal title to the properties ("the Owner Corporations"), and others from directly or indirectly transferring the properties or the Owner Corporations. See New York Land Co. v. Republic of Philippines, 634 F.Supp. 279 (S.D.N.Y.), aff'd sub nom. Republic of Philippines v. Marcos, 806 F.2d 344 (2d Cir.1986), cert. denied, 481 U.S. 1048, 107 S.Ct. 2178, 95 L.Ed.2d 835 (1987). In the part of the action still pending, see No. 86 Civ. 2294, the Republic of the Philippines is contesting both the Bernsteins' and Khashoggi's claims to have purchased the Owner Corporations from Marcos before the injunction issued.

In *Canadian Land,* Karl Peterson brought suit on behalf of three of the four Owner Corporations against the Bernsteins for their alleged breaches of fiduciary duty in managing the properties from 1983 to 1986. Peterson claimed authority to bring suit by producing documents that allegedly named him managing director or attorney-in-fact of the three plaintiff corporations. The Bernsteins challenged his authority, arguing that Peterson acted under the control of Khashoggi, and that his alleged authority was the result of Khashoggi's fraudulent scheme of backdating documents in order to present himself, and not Marcos, as the true beneficial owner of the properties since well before issuance of the *Philippines* injunction. During Peterson's thirty-one day deposition by the Bernsteins, Peterson admitted that many of his actions with regard to the properties were directed by Khashoggi, and that he had little knowledge of when and how Khashoggi acquired ownership over the properties.

Judge Leval found that Khashoggi was a managing agent of all of the plaintiff corporations and that Fadel, who ran a Swiss Khashoggi corporation called Management & Control, was an additional managing agent of one of the plaintiff corporations. Judge Leval ordered both Khashoggi and Fadel to appear in New York for deposition and refused to allow the depositions to occur in Canada or Switzerland. When Khashoggi and Fadel disregarded numerous orders to appear for deposition to avoid being served with process on other matters while in the United States, Judge Leval dismissed the action pursuant to Fed.R.Civ. P. 37.

DISCUSSION

Rule 37 of the Federal Rules of Civil Procedure provides for sanctions where "a party or . . . managing agent of a party or a person designated under Rule 30(b)(6) . . . to testify on behalf of a party fails to obey an order to provide or permit discovery." Fed.R.Civ. P. 37(b)(2). Although dismissal of an action or proceeding is the most severe of appropriate sanctions, see National Hockey League v. Metropolitan Hockey Club, Inc., 427 U.S. 639, 642–43, 96 S.Ct. 2778, 2780–81, 49 L.Ed.2d 747 (1976) (per curiam), the " 'element of willfulness or conscious disregard' for the discovery process . . . justifies the sanction of dismissal." Founding Church of Scientology, Inc. v. Webster, 802 F.2d 1448, 1458 (D.C.Cir.1986) (citation omitted), cert. denied, 484 U.S. 871, 108 S.Ct. 199, 98 L.Ed.2d 150 (1987).

On the basis of the record before us, we cannot conclude that Judge Leval abused his discretion in holding that Khashoggi's and Fadel's testimony were so important to this action that their failure to appear for deposition prejudiced the defendants greatly. Much of Peterson's testimony suggests that his authority derives from Khashoggi's alleged ownership of the properties, and that Khashoggi and Fadel alone can clarify how and when the transfer of ownership took place. Because Peterson alleged that Khashoggi is the actual beneficial owner of the properties, the district court had ample reason to hold that Khashoggi's interests were so closely intertwined with the plaintiff corporations in commencing this action that he could be considered their alter ego.

Judge Leval also acted within his discretion by not allowing the depositions to take place abroad. Even if plaintiffs-appellants had *promptly* offered the alternative of a feasible foreign location, the burden that such an alternative would impose on defendants' counsel is unwarranted in this case, where the persons seeking to avoid deposition are central to the plaintiffs', rather than defendants', case. As Judge Leval properly concluded, it would be fundamentally unfair to allow Khashoggi to invoke the authority of this court and at the same time to withhold information vital to the Bernsteins' defense. We therefore affirm the district court's order of dismissal.

Nevertheless, we take judicial cognizance of Khashoggi's extradition to the United States. In light of Khashoggi's current United States presence, appellants are free to move the district court to vacate its judgment upon tendering him for deposition.

Furthermore, we note that dismissal of the claims against the Bernsteins in this case does not preclude litigation of similar claims against the Bernsteins in the *Philippines* action. The district court did not expressly decide the merits of appellants' claims. We have not considered the merits, and we do not think that the dismissal in this action should in any way have preclusive effect in the *Philippines* case. Accordingly, we direct the district court to modify its order by adding the following:

> This order is not intended to pass upon the merits of the Republic of the Philippines' claims against the defendants in No. 86 Civ. 2294 now pending in this court or in Civil Case No. 0001 PCGG No. 2 brought by the Republic of the Philippines in Sandiganbayan, Third Division, Manila; and dismissal of the complaint in No. 86 Civ. 9087 is without prejudice to the two said actions brought by the Republic of the Philippines. This dismissal shall have no binding effect on principles of res judicata or otherwise in those actions.

We further direct the district court to delete that portion of footnote 1 in its order that declares the Philippines' motion for sanctions moot.

The district court order is thus affirmed as modified.

NOTES

(1) Under Rule 41(b), Judge Leval's order operated as an adjudication on the merits. On what grounds did the Second Circuit modify this order? Did it have the authority to do this?

(2) If Khashoggi, although now available for deposition in the United States, not only declined to appear for a deposition in the United States, but refused to testify in defiance of a renewed order, would the district court have the authority to dismiss the complaint with prejudice? Would or should the Second Circuit modify such an order?

(3) On involuntary dismissal as a sanction for failure to comply with a pretrial discovery generally, see Chapter 11, Section 9.

(4) Does an order of involuntary dismissal that operates as an adjudication on the merits have the same effect as a default judgment? May it be entered without complying with the requirements for default judgments? See Fed.R. Civ.P. 54(b)(2) and compare Wilver v. Fisher, 387 F.2d 66 (10th Cir.1967) with Vitale v. Elliott, 120 R.I. 328, 387 A.2d 1379 (1978).

SECTION 5. DEFAULT JUDGMENTS

Rule 55 of the Federal Rules of Civil Procedure provides for a default judgment against a party that has failed to plead or otherwise defend. Under Rule 55(a), the clerk enters that party's default when the relevant failure has been "made to appear by affidavit or otherwise." Rule 55(c) provides that an entry of default by the clerk may be set aside "[F]or good cause shown." Judgment by default may be entered by the clerk when the plaintiff's claim is for a definite sum. In other cases the court may enter judgment on compliance with Rule 55(b). When a default judgment has been entered, it may be set aside only upon compliance with the more exacting requirements of Rule 60(b). As might be expected, however, courts are generally more ready to set aside default judgments than judgments rendered after a contest on the merits.

NOTES

(1) May a court refuse to enter a default judgment on the ground that the complaint fails to state a proper claim for relief? See C & H Transportation Co. v. Wright, 396 S.W.2d 443 (Tex.Civ.App.1965) (complaint dismissed on appeal). See also Hughes Tool Co. v. TWA, 409 U.S. 363, 93 S.Ct. 647, 34 L.Ed.2d 577 (1973) (dismissing complaint on certiorari from a default judgment for failure to appear at a deposition).

(2) May a party seeking to set aside a default judgment be required to show that it has a meritorious defense? Does it make a difference if the defaulting party was not given constitutionally required notice? In Peralta v. Heights Medical Center, 485 U.S. 80, 108 S.Ct. 896, 99 L.Ed.2d 75 (1988), the Supreme Court reversed a lower Texas court's ruling that, in order to have the default judgment set aside, the defaulting party must show that it has a meritorious defense.

Chapter Eleven

OBTAINING INFORMATION BEFORE TRIAL

SECTION 1. BACKGROUND AND PERSPECTIVES

An insistent theme in modern American civil procedure is that the process go forward in a way that assures that law suits will be disposed of on their merits. If this is to occur, the merits of the case must somehow come to light by formal or informal exchanges of information. In other legal systems the exchange is sometimes accomplished by requiring the pleadings to contain material that modern American procedure does not regard as suitable in the statements of claims or defenses. Since pleadings are not expected to expose the merits and since motions rarely reveal anything about the merits, the work of uncovering the essential validity of most claims or defenses must in the main be done by other procedural tools. Today, the task falls very largely to the pretrial discovery devices.

Litigants and lawyers are naturally interested in acquiring information about their own and their adversaries' cases. Efforts to enlarge their private avenues of investigating the facts of the case by providing formal procedures for discovery are not new to the law. Old chancery practice allowed discovery of a limited kind. Procedural reforms in the 19th and early 20th centuries in the United States substantially expanded the litigants' opportunities for pretrial discovery. But many limitations remained. Typically a discovering party could obtain evidence only if it supported that party's own side of the case rather than the other side's positions. The target of the discovery generally was restricted to admissible evidence, not mere clues or leads to potential evidence. See G. Ragland, Discovery Before Trial (1932).

Of all the significant changes introduced by the Federal Rules of Civil Procedure in 1938 the most far reaching was the major expansion of pretrial discovery procedures. The Federal Rules discarded many of the old restrictions on the availability, scope and use of discovery. Discovery was to serve broad and significant ends: to obtain leads or clues to evidence as well as admissible proof; and to uncover ammunition for cross-examination as well as evidence-in-chief. They permitted as a matter of course and without need to obtain leave of court oral examinations before trial of ordinary witnesses simply by showing that the latter had relevant information that was not blocked by a claim of privilege. Non-party witnesses were to be as readily subject to discovery by deposition as the parties themselves. However, parties were also open to discovery by means of written interrogatories that had to be answered under oath and for which, again, no special court permission was required. The lawyer had merely to draw up questions that were proper in scope and form and send them to the responding party's lawyer.

Under the rules effective in 1938 a court order for discovery was necessary only when a party sought to compel production of documents for inspection and copying, to gain access to things, or to enter upon land or to subject a person to a physical or mental examination. Courts also became involved when a dispute broke out over the scope of discovery or the way it was being conducted.

As late as 1982 one of the premises of the rules was that in discovery practice redundancy and duplication were not improper. Rule 26(a) flatly stated that unless a court saw fit to order otherwise for substantial reasons, "the frequency of use of these methods is not limited."

A second premise was that discovery ordinarily should not and would not require judicial attention. The theory was that the lawyers would practice under a rule of reason reinforced by their mutual self-interest in avoiding the waste of their own time and their client's money. That waste would result if unnecessary pursuit or resistance occurred during discovery proceedings. Prompted by self-interest the lawyers could be counted upon to conduct discovery without judicial oversight except in the rare situations when the lawyers found themselves unable to resolve differences on their own.

For more than 20 years the rulemakers, the courts and the profession appeared to be satisfied with the basic premises and overall impact of the discovery procedures. But by 1960 problems were perceived in several aspects of the process. The Advisory Committee on Rules of Civil Procedure thought it necessary to go beyond the reported cases and the commentary to learn how discovery was actually working. With the support of Chief Justice Earl Warren, the Committee requested the Project for Effective Justice at Columbia Law School to make a field survey of discovery practice. In an introduction to proposed amendments in 1970, the Committee explained why:

> "Despite widespread acceptance of discovery as an essential part of litigation, disputes have inevitably arisen concerning the values claimed for discovery and abuses alleged to exist. Many disputes about discovery relate to particular rule provisions or court decisions and can be studied in traditional fashion with a view to specific amendment. Since discovery is in large measure extrajudicial, however, even these disputes may be enlightened by a study of discovery 'in the field.' And some of the larger questions concerning discovery can be pursued only by a study of its operation at the law office level and in unreported cases."

Advisory Committee's Explanatory Statement Concerning Amendments to the Discovery Rules, 48 F.R.D. 487, 489 (1970).

The Columbia Project for Effective Justice during the years 1960–1964 completed a nationwide survey, in which social scientists participated. In 1965 the Columbia group submitted its report, entitled *Field Survey of Federal Pretrial Discovery,* to the Advisory Committee on Civil Rules. Its main conclusion was:

> . . . Federal discovery is on the whole working well and doing the main work it was intended to do. It is improving the quality of the trial process and very probably the quality of the settlement process, according to the heavily preponderant weight of the evidence from the field survey.

Rosenberg, Changes Ahead in Federal Pretrial Discovery, 45 F.R.D. 479, 488 (1968).

A few years after the curative amendments of 1970 took effect a sharp change in the profession's view of the discovery rules surfaced. By the late 1970's the perception that discovery was often abusive and excessive had gathered wide support. The Advisory Committee's response was the introduction into the rules of limits on the scope of discovery and restrictions on how the lawyers practiced discovery. In addition, the amendments that became effective in 1980 and 1983 encouraged judges to take a more active part in enforcing the restrictions. This is not to suggest that there has been a radical cutback in the parties' ability to obtain evidence and leads to evidence in the pretrial stages. It is merely to say that the tide that had been flowing strongly in favor of a more expanded discovery practice had ebbed. The next decade or so will reveal whether a major reversal has occurred or whether the tide merely crested.

* * * * *

DODSON v. PERSELL
Supreme Court of Florida, 1980.
390 So.2d 704.

OVERTON, JUSTICE.

* * *

Petitioner Dodson's complaint alleges that respondent Persell negligently collided his automobile with the automobile of Dodson, causing Dodson serious injury. The record reflects that the petitioner, as plaintiff in the trial court, propounded interrogatories to discover whether surveillance of the petitioner had taken place, whether photographs or movies were taken, and, if so, the time and place taken, the substance of what the films purported to show, and the qualifications of the photographer. Additionally, petitioner properly requested production of any such photographs or films. [The defendant's objection on "work product" grounds was upheld by the trial court.]

At trial, the respondent did in fact present both the testimony of its private investigator and surveillance materials which the court, over objection, admitted into evidence. The jury subsequently rendered its verdict for respondent, and the trial court entered judgment accordingly. On appeal, the Third District affirmed, holding that surveillance films may constitute work product and may be excluded from discovery on that basis. 365 So.2d at 413. We disagree and expressly disapprove this holding.

Petitioner contends that the existence and contents of surveillance films need to be disclosed prior to trial and must be treated like any other evidence in order to avoid misuse of the film. Petitioner cites Snead v. American Export-Isbrandtsen Lines, Inc., 59 F.R.D. 148 (E.D. Pa.1973), in which the court stated:

> [T]he camera may be an instrument of deception. It can be misused. Distances may be minimized or exaggerated. Lighting, focal lengths, and camera angles all make a difference. Action may be slowed down or speeded up. The editing and splicing of films may change the chronology of events. An emergency situation may be made to appear commonplace. That which has occurred once, can be described as an example of an event which recurs frequently. We are all familiar with Hollywood techniques which involve stuntmen and doubles. Thus, that which purports to be a means to reach the truth may be distorted, misleading, and false.

Id. at 150. Petitioner further asserts that if pretrial disclosure of surveillance films is not required, plaintiffs will be without means to effectively challenge or prepare rebuttal evidence against surveillance materials, citing the following statement by the Supreme Court of New Jersey in Jenkins v. Rainner, 69 N.J. 50, 350 A.2d 473 (1976):

> The surprise which results from distortion or misidentification is plainly unfair. If it is unleashed at the time of trial, the opportunity for an adversary to protect against its damaging inference by attacking the integrity of the film and developing counter-evidence is gone or at least greatly diminished.

Id. at 57, 350 A.2d at 477. In short, the petitioner urges that we should side with the weight of authority by holding that surveillance movies must be treated as any other evidence which will be presented at trial.[1]

Rosenberg, Smit & Korn, Elements of Civil Procedure, 4th Edition (1985). . . . The respondents assert that if a plaintiff is informed of the existence of surveillance materials and views the contents before trial, he will tailor his testimony to reconcile any possible inconsistencies. In respondents' view, allowing discovery would severely limit the impact that surveillance materials would have upon the jury and would

---

1. See Martin v. Long Island RR., 63 F.R.D. 53 (E.D.N.Y.1974); Blyther v. Northern Lines, Inc., 61 F.R.D. 610 (E.D. Pa.1973); Snead v. American Export-Isbrandtsen Lines, Inc., 59 F.R.D. 148 (E.D. Pa.1973); Zimmerman v. Superior Court, 98 Ariz. 85, 402 P.2d 212 (1965); Crist v. Goody, 31 Colo.App. 496, 507 P.2d 478 (1972); Olszewski v. Howell, 253 A.2d 77 (Del.Super.1969); Boldt v. Sanders, 261 Minn. 160, 111 N.W.2d 225 (1961); Jenkins v. Rainner, 69 N.J. 50, 350 A.2d 473 (1976). Cf. Hughes v. Groves, 47 F.R.D. 52 (W.D. Mo.1969) (addresses photographs generally). [Other footnotes omitted. Eds.]

practically eliminate surveillance as a means to prevent overstated and fraudulent claims. Respondents further contend that discovery of surveillance films is not necessary to eliminate surprise because the surveillance film involves facts more readily known by the plaintiff than the defendant and consequently there is no surprise. In summary, the respondents assert that we should . . . hold that surveillance films which are to be used for impeachment purposes constitute work product and may be excluded from discovery.

This Court, as most jurisdictions, adopted discovery as part of our procedural rules to improve our system of justice. It is a tool intended (1) to identify at early stages of a proceeding the real issues to be resolved; (2) to provide each party with all available sources of proof as early as possible to facilitate trial preparation; and (3) to abolish the tactical element of surprise in our adversary trial process. In Surf Drugs, Inc. v. Vermette, 236 So.2d 108 (Fla.1970), we stated that the primary purpose of our rules:

> is to prevent the use of surprise, trickery, bluff and legal gymnastics. Revelation through discovery procedures of the strength and weaknesses of each side before trial encourages settlement of cases and avoids costly litigation. Each side can make an intelligent evaluation of the entire case and may better anticipate the ultimate results.

Id. at 111. . . .

A search for truth and justice can be accomplished only when all relevant facts are before the judicial tribunal. Those relevant facts should be the determining factor rather than gamesmanship, surprise, or superior trial tactics. We caution that discovery was never intended to be used and should not be allowed as a tactic to harass, intimidate, or cause litigation delay and excessive costs.

First, adhering to the philosophy expressed in *Surf* and in accordance with the majority view, we hold that upon request a party must reveal the existence of any surveillance information he possesses whether or not it is intended to be presented at trial. What we require is that a party must disclose the existence of material which is or may be relevant to the issues in the cause whether as substantive, corroborative, or impeachment evidence. Relevant evidence cannot be allowed to remain hidden in a party's or an attorney's files. Knowledge of its existence is necessary before a judicial determination can be made as to whether the contents are privileged.

Second, we hold the contents of surveillance films and materials are subject to discovery in every instance where they are intended to be presented at trial either for substantive, corroborative, or impeachment purposes. . . . [I]f the materials are only to aid counsel in trying the case, they are work product. But, if they will be used as evidence, the materials, including films, cease to be work product and become subject to an adversary's discovery.

Third, in limited instances, the contents of surveillance materials that are not intended to be submitted as evidence are subject to discovery if they are unique and otherwise unavailable, and materially relevant to the cause's issues. An example is a photograph of a scene which has been changed or cannot be reproduced. . . .

Fourth, with reference to our holding that a party is entitled to discover the existence and contents of surveillance information which will be used as evidence, it necessarily follows that the seeking party must be afforded a reasonable opportunity to view the surveillance information before trial. The surveilling party's failure to comply with such a discovery request will bar the information's use as evidence in the cause unless the trial court finds that the failure to disclose was not willful and either that no prejudice will result or that any existing prejudice may be overcome by allowing a continuance of discovery during a trial recess.

Fifth, we recognize that there is some merit in respondent's contention that surveillance can prevent fraudulent and overstated claims. In this regard, fairness requires that we allow the use of surveillance materials to establish any inconsistency in a claim by allowing the surveilling party to depose the party surveilled after the movies have been taken or evidence acquired but before their contents are presented for the adversary's pretrial examination. We note that under present procedural time constraints, the surveilling party in a personal injury action ordinarily has the opportunity to take discovery in this manner without any court order. In our view, the trial court's discretion to allow the discovery deposition before disclosure is an appropriate middle road to ensure that all relevant evidence reaches the trier of fact in a fair and accurate fashion. See Jenkins v. Rainner, 69 N.J. 50, 350 A.2d 473 (1976).

For the reasons expressed, we quash the instant decision of the Third District Court of Appeal and disapprove its decision in Collier v. McKesson, 121 So.2d 673 (Fla.3d DCA 1960), and remand the cause with directions to grant a new trial. . . .

NOTE

What if the surveillance film lends no support to the defense and the defendant therefore does not plan to introduce it into evidence, or to use it in any other way? May the plaintiff (a) ask whether a film exists and (b) on receiving an affirmative answer, compel its disclosure? Then, since precluding defendant from using the film in evidence would not be an effective sanction, what kind of remedy should the court impose if defendant fails to obey a court order to produce the film?

GLASER, W.A., PRETRIAL DISCOVERY AND THE ADVERSARY SYSTEM

58–63 (1968).

PURPOSES OF DISCOVERY

The lawyer's discovery goals depend on whether he represents a plaintiff or a defendant and whether the issues involve personal injuries or commercial disputes.

When attorneys discover, what are their intentions? They are revealed in part by a question in the interview, asking lawyers to describe their intentions during their first step. A list of possible purposes was given, and Table 3 shows the proportions of discovering attorneys who rated each purpose "very important" in their first step.

Discovery was planned to be a system for getting evidence and information, and lawyers seem motivated in the expected way. More say they discovered with evidentiary aims than with tactical aims—that is, the percentages in the upper half of Table 3 exceed those in the lower half. Gaining evidence about liability is rated a "very important" or "important" purpose by nearly all lawyers.

* * *

TABLE 3. PURPOSES OF DISCOVERY, TYPE OF CASE, AND PARTIES

Percentages Answering "Very Important"

Purposes of First Discovery Step	Plaintiffs		Defendants		Totals		Totals		
	Personal Injury	Commercial	Personal Injury	Commercial	Personal Injury	Commercial	Plaintiffs	Defendants	All
Obtaining information:									
1. Obtain evidence bearing on liability	82%	75%	78%	79%	80%	77%	79%	79%	79%
2. Learn more about adversary's factual contentions	54	48	69	67	63	57	51	68	60
3. Ascertain damages	31	28	75	26	56	27	30	56	44
4. Learn names of new witnesses	54	14	49	22	51	18	36	39	37
5. Get clues to new lines of inquiry	39	14	40	30	39	22	28	36	32
6. Make sure I saw all the issues	39	22	32	26	35	24	32	30	31
7. Learn more about adversary's legal theory	20	17	14	19	17	18	19	16	17
8. Nothing specific, just get any information I could	6	1	6	8	6	5	4	7	5
Making use of information:									
9. Confirm accuracy of reports already in our possession	45	36	34	32	39	34	41	33	37
10. Put known evidence into admissible form	31	25	13	20	21	23	29	16	22
11. Perpetuate testimony	16	12	10	12	13	12	14	11	13
Tactical aims:									
12. Freeze adversary's story	28	38	65	56	49	47	32	62	48

| Purposes of First Discovery Step | Plaintiffs | | Defendants | | Totals | | Totals | | |
	Per-sonal Injury	Com-mercial	Per-sonal Injury	Com-mercial	Per-sonal Injury	Com-mercial	Plain-tiffs	Defen-dants	All
13. Develop weaknesses for cross-examination	29%	22%	50%	43%	41%	33%	26%	48%	38%
14. Show adversary I meant to fight this case	11	9	8	28	9	18	10	15	13
15. Size up adversary	6	6	17	17	12	11	6	17	12
16. Get worst on record to show client our problems	2	2	4	2	3	2	2	3	3
17. Show client I was fighting this case	4	1	3	5	3	3	3	4	3
18. Gain time	1	0	1	3	1	1	0+	2	1
Number of lawyers	(177)	(145)	(227)	(140)	(404)	(285)	(322)	(367)	(689)

Source: Interviews. Every respondent was asked "Could you think back to what you were after at the time [of your first discovery step]? As you thought about it then, how would you characterize the relative importance in your own mind of each of the several possible purposes listed on this chart?" The list is quoted along the left-hand margin of this table. Each respondent rated each purpose as "very important," "important but not primary," "of minor importance," and "didn't think of it, does not apply." The table presents the proportions answering "very important," but the pattern of variations by party and case would be the same if the proportions saying "important" were added.

NOTES

(1) Compare the purposes for discovery disclosed by the Columbia Project field study, reported above, with the purposes of discovery mentioned in the Dodson case, supra, and with the purposes disclosed in the Federal Rules. Which, if any, of the lawyers' purposes are inconsistent with the rules?

(2) What are the main differences in the "Very Important" discovery aims of plaintiffs and defendants in personal injury and commercial cases?

In the materials that follow, attention is directed first to the *scope* of permissible discovery. Then the various *devices* are examined for the special problems some of them raise; the *use* of discovered materials at trial is considered; and then the problems of *enforcement* are examined.

SECTION 2. SCOPE: RELEVANCE

RULE 401, FEDERAL RULES OF EVIDENCE

"Relevant evidence" means evidence having any tendency to make the existence of any fact that is of consequence to the determination of the action more probable or less probable than it would be without the evidence.

O'DONNELL v. BREUNINGER

District Court of the United States, District of Columbia, 1949.
9 F.R.D. 245.

KEECH, DISTRICT JUDGE.* This matter is before the Court on a motion by the defendant under Rule 37(a), Federal Rules of Civil Procedure, 28 U.S.C.A., for an order to compel plaintiff to answer questions upon a discovery deposition, and a motion by plaintiff under Rule 30(b) for an order that certain matters shall not be inquired into by defendant, of plaintiff, upon the discovery deposition.

This is an action for alienation of affections and loss of consortium brought by a husband. Count 1 of the complaint alleges, in part, that during the summer of 1943 and continuing up to and including March 28, 1947, and subsequent thereto, the defendant, "by various and divers means, acts, and devices, and by continuous association and illicit conduct, influenced and persuaded plaintiff's wife to permanently desert and abandon the plaintiff and take up a residence separate and apart from the plaintiff * * *." Count 2 alleges, in part, under the same dates, that "the defendant * * * in divers ways, and by using various means and devices, by association and a continuous course of illicit conduct, wickedly, maliciously and intentionally enticed, allured and persuaded plaintiff's wife to permanently desert and abandon plaintiff * * *."

In the course of taking the deposition of plaintiff, the following question was put to him:

"Q. Mr. O'Donnell, have you any information regarding the question as to Mr. Breuninger and your wife have [sic] registered at the same hotel in Washington, or out of Washington, at any time, from the date of your marriage until today? A. I have information, yes.

"Q. What is that information? A. Through my attorneys. They investigated it."

Subsequently, the plaintiff stated, "The only information I have was through my attorneys in that regard." There was no further answer by the plaintiff, the deposition was suspended, and the motions here under consideration were filed.

* * *

Under Rule 8 a complaint may withstand a motion to dismiss even though it alleges conclusions of fact, the only requirements being that it contain "a short and plain statement of the claim showing that the pleader is entitled to relief" and that each averment be "simple, concise, and direct." The opposing party, however, has the right, under Rule 12(e), to file a motion for a more definite statement if the pleading is so vague or ambiguous that he cannot reasonably be required to frame a responsive pleading.

* Footnotes omitted.

Under Rule 26 either party has the right to take the testimony of any person, including a party, by deposition for the purpose of discovery or for use as evidence in the action, or for both purposes. * * * Thus, each party is entitled to such facts as will permit him at the time of trial to be prepared to meet such evidence, and will prevent, so far as possible, his being taken by surprise with the possible necessity of requesting a continuance in order that he may fortify his position and get the true facts before the court. Proper application of the discovery procedure is important not only to the parties, but to the orderly and expeditious disposition of the court's business.

The allegations of the complaint, quoted above, that the alienation and loss of consortium were caused by "illicit conduct" of the defendant, indicate an intent to prove at the trial immoral acts by the defendant and plaintiff's wife, and are sufficiently broad to permit such evidence. In order for the defendant to be accorded a fair trial, it is necessary that he be apprised beforehand of the particulars of the charge which he is expected to meet. It is my view, therefore, that the defendant is entitled to know whether, and, if so, where and when, plaintiff intends to prove the defendant and plaintiff's wife did register at the same hotel in Washington or elsewhere, as the facts underlying plaintiff's conclusion of "illicit conduct."

Prior to the new rules the course which could have been properly pursued in this case would have been a motion for a bill of particulars, to which defendant would have been entitled. Under the present rules, "Except where the pleadings are so vague or ambiguous as to preclude a fair understanding of the nature of the claims asserted or the relief sought, parties should resort to the methods provided by Rules 26 and 37 for securing detailed or particular information in regard to claims asserted against them, rather than the more cumbersome procedure under Rule 12(e)." Slusher v. Jones, et al., D.C., 3 F.R.D. 168, 169. [Citation omitted.]

Plaintiff argues "if defendant was at any hotel with plaintiff's wife, or if he was in another city, or other place with plaintiff's wife, then such information is peculiarly within the knowledge of the defendant, and there is no need or reason to permit defendant to ask the plaintiff what information the plaintiff has on those points." This contention is without merit. "The mere circumstance that the facts sought to be elicited are within the knowledge of the examining party does not constitute any reason to deny the privilege of taking depositions." Holtzoff, "New Federal Procedure and the Courts," p. 73–74.

The only limitations on the scope of examination on a discovery deposition are, first, that it must deal with a topic which is relevant to the subject matter involved in the pending action, and, second, that the deponent may not be examined regarding any privileged matter. The question here involved is certainly relevant to the issue of "illicit conduct", and clearly falls outside the scope of attorney-client privilege. Even if the information sought could be considered part of the so-called "work product of the lawyer," necessity is shown for requiring plaintiff to respond to the question put.

The motion of the defendant to compel plaintiff to answer is granted, and the motion of plaintiff for an order that certain matters shall not be inquired into by defendant, of plaintiff, upon discovery deposition is denied. Counsel will present appropriate order.

NOTES

(1) What good purpose does it serve to allow discovery here? Is there any relationship between this and the issue of discovery of surveillance movies in the *Dodson* case, supra?

(2) As to attorney-client privilege, see pp. 689–692 infra. It is clear that the information O'Donnell's lawyer gave him does not fall within the privilege? Why?

(3) When *O'Donnell* was decided the "scope" provision of Rule 26 expressly mentioned the relevance and not-privileged requirements, but said nothing about work product. What is the source in federal law for the "work-product" objection raised by Mr. O'Donnell? See Hickman v. Taylor, p. 692 infra.

OPPENHEIMER FUND, INC. v. SANDERS

Supreme Court of the United States, 1978.
437 U.S. 340, 98 S.Ct. 2380, 57 L.Ed.2d 253.

[The main issue in this class action against the investment fund, its management corporation and a brokerage firm was whether the defendants (petitioners) could be required to help compile a list of names and addresses of members of the plaintiff class at a cost of $16,000. The Second Circuit affirmed the District Court ruling that the discovery rules authorized the order. Justice Powell wrote for the Court in reversing, holding that it was Rule 23(d), not the discovery rules, that applied and that "although the District Court has some discretion in allocating the cost of complying with such an order, that discretion was abused in this case" (p. 342). With regard to the scope and effect of the discovery rules, Justice Powell quoted Rule 26(b)(1) and then continued (pp. 351–353):]

* * * The key phrase in this definition—"relevant to the subject matter involved in the pending action"—has been construed broadly to encompass any matter that bears on, or that reasonably could lead to other matter that could bear on, any issue that is or may be in the case. See Hickman v. Taylor, 329 U.S. 495, 501, 67 S.Ct. 385, 388, 91 L.Ed. 451 (1947). Consistently with the notice-pleading system established by the Rules, discovery is not limited to issues raised by the pleadings, for discovery itself is designed to help define and clarify the issues. Id., at 500–501, 67 S.Ct. at 388. Nor is discovery limited to the merits of a case, for a variety of fact-oriented issues may arise during litigation that are not related to the merits.

At the same time, "discovery, like all matters of procedure, has ultimate and necessary boundaries." Id., at 507, 67 S.Ct., at 392. Discovery of matter not "reasonably calculated to lead to the discovery of admissible evidence" is not within the scope of Rule 26(b)(1).

Thus, it is proper to deny discovery of matter that is relevant only to claims or defenses that have been stricken, or to events that occurred before an applicable limitations period, unless the information sought is otherwise relevant to issues in the case. For the same reason, an amendment to Rule 26(b) was required to bring within the scope of discovery the existence and contents of insurance agreements under which an insurer may be liable to satisfy a judgment against a defendant, for that information ordinarily cannot be considered, and would not lead to information that could be considered, by a court or jury in deciding any issues.

Respondents' attempt to obtain the class members' names and addresses cannot be forced into the concept of "relevancy" described above. The difficulty is that respondents do not seek this information for any bearing that it might have on issues in the case. See 558 F.2d, at 653 (en banc dissent). If respondents had sought the information because of its relevance to the issues, they would not have been willing, as they were, to abandon their request if the District Court would accept their proposed redefinition of the class and method of sending notice. Respondents argued to the District Court that they desired this information to enable them to send the class notice, and not for any other purpose. Taking them at their word, it would appear that respondents' request is not within the scope of Rule 26(b)(1).

RELEVANCE AND REMOTENESS

If, as Justice Powell said, "discovery is not limited to issues raised by the pleadings," yet has "boundaries" of relevance, what defines the boundaries?

In revising the discovery rules in the 1960's, the Advisory Committee on Civil Rules was unable to devise an encompassing and helpful definition of "relevant." It recommended "a flexible treatment of relevance." (See 48 F.R.D. 487, 498 (1970)). What is the correct definition of relevance for discovery purposes? Consider these examples:

(1) Judge Edward Weinfeld said in Kaiser-Frazer Corp. v. Otis & Co., 11 F.R.D. 50, 53–54 (S.D.N.Y.1951):

" 'Relevant' as used in Section 26(b) of the Federal Rules of Civil Procedure, 28 U.S.C.A., is not to be equated with 'relevant' as ordinarily used in determining admissibility of evidence upon a trial. This is clear from the very rule which [makes] . . . relevancy to the subject matter . . . the test

and subject matter is broader than the precise issues presented
by the pleadings.

* * *

"It may well eventuate that evidence secured as a result of
the depositions will be inadmissible upon the trial, or, perhaps,
defendant will find the testimony disappointing, of little or no
value in its defense or resistance to plaintiff's claim. On the
other hand, the information may be of aid in preparing the
defense or anticipating the testimony of Werntz and other
witnesses called by the plaintiff or in cross-examining them, or
there is a possible use of the deposition under Rule 26(d)(3).

(2) While deposing W, a witness in an automobile collision case, the
plaintiff's lawyer asks how fast W estimates D's car was traveling at a
point five miles before the crash. Assume that evidence of speeding so
far from the collision site would be excluded at the trial as too remote
to be relevant. On any test of relevance could the question be allowed
at W's pretrial examination?

(3) Defendant in an employment discrimination suit resisted discovery of records for years prior to the effective date of the statute on
which the suit was based, arguing lack of relevance. The court overruled the objection:

. . . The fact that the statute did not become operative
until July 1965 does not render evidence of prior conduct
irrelevant. While the law may be prospective, as argued by
the defendants, it is prospective only in the sense that conduct
prior to the effective date cannot constitute a violation of the
Act. But, in considering whether defendants have violated the
statute, evidence of prior courses of conduct is clearly relevant.

See United States v. Building & Construction Trades Council of St.
Louis, Missouri, AFL–CIO, 271 F.Supp. 454, 459 (E.D.Mo.1966).

RELEVANCE OF ADVERSARY'S WEALTH OR ASSETS

Rule 26(b)(2) permits discovery of liability or indemnity insurance
policies, but does not thereby make the information admissible in
evidence at the trial. The Advisory Committee note justified that
approach as aiding settlement prospects. In what way will knowing
the defendant's insurance coverage and limits induce settlement?

Should a defendant's net worth be discoverable? Courts answer in
the affirmative when plaintiff claims punitive damages. See Marsee v.
United States Tobacco Co., 639 F.Supp. 466, 471 (W.D.Okl.1986). Holli-
man v. Redman Development Corp., 61 F.R.D. 488, 491 (D.S.C.1973). To
warrant discovery the punitive damage claim must be a plausible one,
not merely a pretext. Chenoweth v. Schaaf, 98 F.R.D. 587, 589 (W.D.
Pa.1983).

Defendants have been allowed to discover the plaintiff's assets in limited circumstances. In a class action the court allowed discovery against the plaintiff, declaring:

"Inquiry into plaintiff's financial status and fee arrangement is relevant to the question of plaintiff's ability to protect the interests of potential class members by adequate funding of the lawsuit." Klein v. Miller, 82 F.R.D. 6 (N.D.Tex.1978). See also P.D.Q. Inc. of Miami v. Nissan Motor Corp. in U.S.A., 61 F.R.D. 372 (S.D.Fla.1973); Ralston v. Volkswagenwerk, A.G., 61 F.R.D. 427 (W.D.Mo.1973); compare Sanderson v. Winner, 507 F.2d 477 (10th Cir.1974)."

SECTION 3. OPINIONS AND CONTENTIONS

LEUMI FINANCIAL CORP. v. HARTFORD ACCIDENT & INDEMNITY CO.

United States District Court, Southern District of New York, 1969.
295 F.Supp. 539.

CROAKE, DISTRICT JUDGE. [Between December 1965 and July 1966 the plaintiff insured suffered losses as the result of unspecified conduct of an assistant vice-president. Defendant contends plaintiff discovered the losses in May 1966 but failed to give prompt written notice of loss and proof of claim as required by the insurer's bond. Plaintiff notified defendant of possible losses in October 1966 and filed proof of claim in November, with supplements in December and then in August 1967.]

The defendant insurance company has objected to certain interrogatories propounded by the plaintiff in this action to recover on a Brokers' Blanket Bond issued by the defendant. The bond was to recover "[a]ny loss through any dishonest, fraudulent or criminal act of any of the Employees . . ." of the plaintiff.[1] The plaintiff claims that it has suffered such a loss.

I.

Defendant has objected to Interrogatories 14 and 19 which, respectively, ask the defendant corporation to define "dishonest act" and "fraudulent act," and to state if certain specific acts are dishonest and fraudulent.[2] The basic objection to each of these interrogatories is that

1. More fully "(A) Any loss through any dishonest, fraudulent or criminal act of any of the Employees, committed anywhere and whether committed alone or in collusion with others, including loss of Property through any such act of any of the Employees." The bond had a $150,000 limit. [Some footnotes renumbered;

others omitted. Quotations marks as in original report.]

2. "14. If the answer to question "12" is No, how does the defendant define a) a dishonest act; b) a fraudulent act?"

"19. State whether defendant considers the following acts (if proven) dishonest,

legal opinions are sought. Since the view of the courts toward this objection is changing, some discussion is warranted.

A strict construction of Rule 30 would make objectionable most interrogatories requiring opinions or conclusions as answers since they would neither be relevant nor lead to the discovery of admissible evidence. This approach was initially adopted by the courts which rigidly sustained objections to interrogatories asking for opinions. Today, however, factual conclusions are regularly considered proper objects of interrogation and interrogatories requiring legal opinions as answers are met with a flexible approach. The latter will be permitted if

> ". . . the court is convinced that by requiring responses thereto the lawsuits could be expedited, the information obtained could lead to relevant evidence, the issues could be narrowed, unnecessary testimony and wasteful preparation could be avoided, or any other substantial purpose sanctioned by the discovery provisions of the Federal Rules could be served." [3]

Under this approach interrogatories requiring various degrees of factual conclusion and legal opinion have been approved. Defendants in antitrust cases may require the United States to define the relevant market and line of commerce. In patent cases—where opinion-seeking interrogatories have most frequently been approved—questions requiring an interpretation of the patent in suit and asking for the manner and extent of infringement have withstood objections. A defendant employer has been required to say whether its employee was acting within the scope of his authority when a tort was committed. Courts frequently and readily require parties to state the facts underlying their claim or defense.

These examples show that any attempt to draw a fine line between interrogatories seeking legal opinions and those asking for factual conclusions is destined to fail. A question asking for facts underlying a claim raises issues of legal relevancy at least, and an abstractly-framed question, such as Interrogatory 19 in this case, will inevitably be keyed to the facts in controversy. A distinction can be drawn based on the

---

fraudulent, or neither dishonest or fraudulent?

(a) The actions of the principal in issuing guarantees of payment in the name of his employer without the employer's authority.

(b) The actions of the principal in issuing guarantees of payment in the name of his employer without the employer's authority, and contrary to the employer's explicit instructions.

(c) The action of the principal in secreting from his employer the letters of guarantee issued by him, and notices received as to the amounts being guaranteed.

(d) The actions of the principal in representing to the employer that he had examined shipping receipts when, in fact, no such shipping receipts were examined by him, knowing that the employer would rely on such a representation and advance money thereon.

(e) The actions of the principal in failing to report to his employers his knowledge that his employer was lending money against accounts receivable which did not exist, or were duplicate billings."

3. Empire Scientific Corp. v. Pickering & Co., 44 F.R.D. 5, 6 (E.D.N.Y.1968).

primary goal of interrogatories; the term "opinion-seeking interrogatories" will be used here to designate interrogatories primarily intended to obtain legal opinions rather than to elicit factual conclusions.

The value of opinion-seeking interrogatories is that they may narrow the legal issues in a case and thus lessen the preparation needed. Particularly in complex litigation such as patent and antitrust actions, discovery is necessarily extensive. The time of counsel and the funds of clients are sometimes consumed by searches for hidden legal problems that the opposition is not concerned with or in painstaking documentation of some point that will not be seriously opposed. In spite of the fruitlessness of such discovery, the courts may be called upon to supervise it. In the process, justice is delayed for the parties directly involved as well as for other litigants in the court. Pretrial hearings and orders serve to narrow legal issues for trial; the administration of justice would be improved if a means to this end were available in the proper cases during discovery.

The only vehicle for narrowing issues during discovery is discovery itself. The goal of the federal rules, "to secure the just, speedy, and inexpensive determination of every action," will be fostered by permitting opinion-seeking interrogatories to be used in proper cases.

Objections to opinion-seeking interrogatories have occasionally been sustained on the technical theory that it is the party rather than the attorney to whom interrogatories are directed and a party should not be asked for, and cannot swear to, a legal opinion. Particularly in complex cases where opinion-seeking interrogatories would be useful, it is unrealistic to suppose that a party draws answers to interrogatories himself.[4]

The value of opinion-seeking interrogatories may sometimes be outweighed by the possibility that the interrogated party may be prejudiced by his answer. An interrogatory may, for example, require the party to select his legal theory before he is ready; subsequently, discovered facts may render his answer damaging.[5] In order to calculate the possibility of prejudice, the court should weigh the nature of the case, the knowledge of the answering party, the amount of discovery to be completed, and the proximity of the issue to be narrowed to the central issues in the case. Only if the economy to be achieved is greater than the possible prejudice to the answering party may the court compel an answer to an opinion-seeking interrogatory.

The present case does not appear to be one of great complexity. Its resolution will require an interpretation of "dishonest, fraudulent, or

---

4. Particularly in patent cases, the party rather than the attorney may have the expertise necessary to answer the interrogatory. See Microtron Corp. v. Minnesota Mining & Mfg. Co., 269 F.Supp. 22 (D.N.J.1967); Meese v. Eaton Mfg. Co., 35 F.R.D. 162 (N.D.Ohio 1964). Where the party has such expertise (as is true in this case), the argument that the opinion sought is the attorney's work-product carries little weight even if a "pure" legal opinion is sought.

5. Strictly speaking, a party would not be bound by his answer since he could amend it. The value of opinion-seeking interrogatories would be lost, however, if the answer given were not fairly firm.

criminal act," an application of that interpretation to the acts of the employee, and a determination of the timeliness of the notice of claim. Requiring the defendant to define the critical language of the bond would eliminate the need for some discovery; since, however, the interrogatories ask the defendant to resolve a central issue of the case, the possibility of the answer prejudicing the defendant is great. Under the standards set out above, this court finds that the possibility of prejudice outweighs the advantages narrowing this issue would yield to the plaintiff and to the court; the objections to Interrogatories 14 and 19 are therefore sustained.

II.

Interrogatories 15, 16, 17 and 18 seek information on the way the defendant handled claims on bonds similar to plaintiff's from the time the bond was issued to plaintiff to about five months after the last transaction for which recovery is sought. The defendant objects to these interrogatories, set out below, as irrelevant and burdensome.

"15. Between August, 1965 and December, 1966, how many policies of the type which is the subject of this action did plaintiff [sic] have in force?

"16. During the period August, 1965 to December, 1966, how many reports of losses through claimed a) dishonest acts; b) fraudulent acts, did the defendant receive?

"17. On what types or categories of a) dishonest acts; b) fraudulent acts, did the defendant make payment under its policies?

"18. On how many of the claims set forth in interrogatory "16" did the defendant receive sworn proofs of loss within 90 days of discovery of same?"

Full consideration of the objections to these interrogatories requires knowledge of facts underlying the litigation. Unfortunately, neither the full text of the bond in question nor a detailed account of the allegedly dishonest and/or fraudulent acts of the employee of the plaintiff have been given to the court. . . .

The burden of proof is generally on the party that objects to an interrogatory. The objection of burdensomeness will therefore not be considered without some indication of why the interrogatory is difficult to answer. Since the defendants have made no effort to explain why the particular questions asked would be difficult to answer the objection cannot be sustained on the ground of burdensomeness alone. The plaintiff has been just as lax, however, in showing that the interrogatories it propounded were within the scope of permissible interrogation. Plaintiff's affidavit and memorandum say that the information sought will be of great value to it but only briefly suggest two possible theories for sustaining the interrogatories.

Plaintiff seems to contend that the defendant is estopped from defending on the ground that the notice of loss and proof of claim were untimely because payments were made under similar policies after similar delays. This theory seems to underlie Interrogatories 15, 16 and 18. Where it is clear from the face of an interrogatory that a considerable amount of effort would be necessary to answer it, and the purpose of the interrogatory is not to determine the existence of an issue but to obtain evidence to buttress a position on an issue, then the interrogating party should come forward with some evidence to show that the issue is in fact in the case. With no evidence of an estoppel before it, this court is loath to compel the defendant to search through its files to compile what may prove to be useless information.

The second theory appears to support Interrogatory 17. Where an insurance policy, or other contract, is ambiguous on its face, the practical construction of that language by the parties is evidence of the intended meaning. The circumstances under which the defendant has paid other bondholders may be of some help to a court in construing the words "dishonest" and "fraudulent." Since, however, this court does not know just what the employee of the plaintiff is alleged to have done, it has no way of determining whether all the information sought in Interrogatory 17 will be useful to the plaintiff. Since answering the interrogatory would require an analysis of all the claims paid during the period in question and many of the claims may be dissimilar to this one, we are unwilling to compel an answer to the interrogatory as now framed.

Ordinarily where interrogatories appear too broad, although some of the information sought may be within the scope of permissible interrogation, the court will assist the parties in limiting the question. Because of the paucity of information before this court, that is impossible.

For the reasons stated, the objections to Interrogatories 15, 16, 17 and 18 are sustained at this time.

So ordered.

NOTES

(1) Skillful phrasing is often the make-or-break characteristic of interrogatories that seek to uncover the other side's opinions, theories and conclusions. With the inartful language of Leumi's interrogatories compare the ones propounded in Atlanta Coca-Cola Bottling Co. v. Transamerica Insurance Co., 61 F.R.D. 115, 118–19 (N.D.Ga.1972). The suit was to recover insurance for losses sustained when employees took money from vending machines they serviced. The court ordered defendant to answer plaintiff's Interrogatory 40 which read:

"If defendant contends that the loss and damage to plaintiff described in the complaint is excluded from coverage under Section 2(b) of the 'Exclusions' contained in the policy, please state with particularity:

"(a) Each item, type of item, product and type of product which constitute 'inventory' of plaintiff in defendant's application of Section 2(b) to the facts shown by plaintiff's claim.

"(b) Identify and describe each document and type of document utilized by plaintiff to prove its covered loss, or the amount thereof which constitutes an 'inventory computation' in defendant's application of Section 2(b) to the facts shown by plaintiff's claim.

"(c) Each 'profit and loss computation' which defendant contends was made by plaintiff in its claim.

"(d) Identify and describe each document and type of document utilized by plaintiff to prove its covered loss, or the amount thereof, which constitutes a 'profit and loss computation' in defendant's application of Section 2(b) to the facts shown by plaintiff's claim."

What is the key difference between the preceding interrogatory and those numbered 14 and 19 in the *Leumi* case?

(2) Would it be useful for the Federal Rules to provide a mechanism to smoke out the other side's legal and factual theories? Originally they did so by allowing requests for "bills of particulars," but were amended in 1948 to eliminate the device. Is there danger the contention-seeking interrogatories will prematurely freeze a litigant's strategy by fastening on an untenable or unduly weak theory? See James, The Revival of Bills of Particulars Under the Federal Rules, 71 Harv.L.Rev. 1473 (1958).

(3) New York provides a mechanism for probing the other side's pleadings by bills of particulars. N.Y. CPLR 3041 (McKinney 1983) provides:

"Any party may require any other party to give a bill of particulars of his claim, or copy of the items of the account alleged in the pleading."

Rule 3043 specifies the particulars that may be called for in an action for personal injury. They include the date and approximate time of the occurrence; its location; the acts or omissions constituting the negligence claim; type and details of notice; the injuries, with a description of those claimed to be permanent; length of time plaintiff was confined to bed and incapacitated; and the amount of special damages claimed for particular items.

O'BRIEN v. INTERNATIONAL BROTHERHOOD OF ELECTRICAL WORKERS

United States District Court, Northern District of Georgia, 1977.
443 F.Supp. 1182.

EDENFIELD, DISTRICT JUDGE.

This action was brought pursuant to the Labor Management Reporting and Disclosure Act, 29 U.S.C. §§ 401, et seq., against a local union and its parent international union. The complaint alleges, in part, that plaintiff has been restrained in the exercise of his rights of free speech and assembly. The action is now before the court on defendant International Brotherhood of Electrical Workers' (IBEW's) motion for summary judgment and on various discovery motions.

Plaintiff was charged by a fellow union member with violating certain sections of the IBEW constitution when he distributed certain information which was allegedly detrimental to the union. Local 613's executive board heard the charges on January 27, 1976 and found plaintiff guilty, fining him $2,725.00 and temporarily suspending him from local union activities. The decision of Local 613 was rescinded when it was discovered that defendant IBEW, not Local 613, had jurisdiction over the charges pursuant to the IBEW constitution. On March 15, 1976 plaintiff was notified of a new hearing to be held before the International Executive Council of IBEW on May 6, 1976. At this hearing, plaintiff was found guilty and fined $100. Thereafter, plaintiff filed this action.

Plaintiff has alleged that the charges, trials and disciplinary measures violated plaintiff's rights of free speech and assembly as guaranteed by the LMRDA in 29 U.S.C. § 411(a)(2).* . . .

. . . Plaintiff's interrogatories, filed May 18, 1977, seek to have defendants explain why they found plaintiff guilty of the union charges.

. . .

Interrogatory numbers 1(a) and (b) ask for the specific statements allegedly made by plaintiff for which he was tried. The court sees no reason why defendant should not be required to set out these statements, despite the fact that plaintiff might be able to cull this information from the hearing transcript. The same may be said with respect to interrogatory number 2, wherein plaintiff asks that defendant Local 613 state which provisions of the IBEW constitution were violated by which statements.

Interrogatory number 3 seeks an explanation as to why these statements violated these constitutional provisions. While defendant Local 613 argues that this question seeks a legal theory which is not discoverable, when the constitutional provisions presumably involved are examined, the interrogatory appears to be one that Local 613 should answer. All but one of the provisions proscribe false statements. Plaintiff is entitled to know the facts which render his utterances untrue. One constitutional provision deals with conduct which causes dissension and dissatisfaction among union members. Plaintiff is entitled to know the facts which, in Local 613's view, constituted dissension caused by plaintiff's statements.

Interrogatory number 4 provides as follows:

In respect to each act and/or utterance listed in response to Interrogatory 1. above, explain the manner in which each said

---

* Section 411(a)(2) of Title 29, U.S.C., provides:

"Every member of any labor organization shall have the right to meet and assemble freely with other members; and to express any views, arguments, or opinions; and to express at meetings of the labor organization his views, upon candidates in an election of the labor organization or upon any business properly before the meeting, subject to the organization's established and reasonable rules pertaining to the conduct of meetings: *Provided,* That nothing herein shall be construed to impair the right of a labor organization to adopt and enforce reasonable rules as to the responsibility of every member toward the organization as an institution and to his refraining from conduct that would interfere with its performance of its legal or contractual obligations."

act and/or utterance (a) violated plaintiff's responsibility toward Local 613, IBEW and IBEW as institutions, and (b)
interfered with Local 613, IBEW's, and IBEW's performance of
their respective legal or contractual obligations. (If any of said
acts/utterances violated neither standard, please indicate
which did not.)

Clearly this question seeks to discover defendant's legal theory based on
the facts elicited from the other interrogatories. Interrogatory number
4 is based on the exceptions in the free speech section of the LMRDA
. . . 29 U.S.C. § 411(a)(2). Anticipating that defendant will rely on
this language as a defense to this action, plaintiff asks defendant to
explain its application to the communications made by the plaintiff.

Rule 33(b), Fed.R.Civ.P., makes clear that such discovery is in fact
permissible. . . . This rule cuts against many older cases which
imposed a strict rule against opinions, contentions and conclusions.
The Advisory Committee Note only excludes those interrogatories
which "extend to issues of 'pure law,' i.e., legal issues unrelated to the
facts of the case." Note to 1970 Amendment of Rule 33(b), 48 F.R.D.
485, 524 (1970), see Wright & Miller, Federal Practice and Procedure,
§ 2167 at 513. Interrogatory number 4 seeks an application of law to
the central facts of the case, and accordingly is permissible under Rule
33(b). Since the discovery period is nearly complete, there is no danger
of tying defendant to a legal theory before he has had an opportunity to
fully explore the case, see Wright & Miller, supra, at 514.

Interrogatory number 6 reads as follows:

In respect to each and every constitutional provision listed
in response to Interrogatory 2., state and explain the reasons
why each provision is *not* deprived of force and effect by
operation of 29 U.S.C. § 411(b) in respect to plaintiff and the
acts and utterances listed in response to Interrogatory 1.

In contrast to the interrogatory previously discussed, this question
seeks pure legal conclusions which are related not to the facts, but to
the law of the case. While the line demarcating permissible discovery
under Rule 33(b) may be obscure, the court concludes that this interrogatory exceeds the bounds of permissible discovery under the rule.

For these reasons, plaintiff's motion to compel discovery is DE-
NIED as to interrogatories numbered 1(c) and (d), 2(2), 5 and 6, but is
GRANTED as to the balance of the interrogatories in dispute. The
court further concludes that each party should bear the cost incurred in
bringing and opposing these discovery motions.

NOTE

In an action for personal injuries that resulted when materials allegedly
fell upon plaintiff while she was along side defendant's property, one of her
interrogatories read: "Why did the material fall from or above defendant's
property onto North Street on December 3, 1970." The court held the interrogatory would be proper if rephrased: "How, if you know, did the material fall

from or above Defendant's property onto North Street on December 3, 1970?" Goodman v. International Business Machs. Corp., 59 F.R.D. 278, 279 (N.D.Ill. 1973). The court ordered stricken as irrelevant another interrogatory asking: "Has any person or entity made a claim against you or your insurer arising from the falling of material onto State Street on December 3, 1970?" Were the rulings sound? Why?

<hr>

SECTION 4. SCOPE: PRIVILEGE

<hr>

PAYNE v. HOWARD

United States District Court, District of Columbia, 1977.
75 F.R.D. 465.

SIRICA, DISTRICT JUDGE.

* * *

This is a bitterly contested malpractice action in which plaintiff, Kay Stanton Payne, seeks to recover damages from Dr. Daniel M. Howard and Greater Southeast Community Hospital. The complaint basically alleges that Dr. Howard performed a sagittal split osteotomy on plaintiff in a negligent manner and without her informed consent. The complaint also alleges that the Hospital was negligent by failing to provide sterile facilities and capable personnel to care for plaintiff after the surgery was performed. Both defendants deny any wrongdoing in connection with the professional care and treatment plaintiff received.

. . . This dispute arose when plaintiff took the deposition of defendant Howard on November 1, 1976. In the notice of deposition, defendant was requested to produce a number of documents relating to his dental practice as well as to his private affairs. Defendant Howard did produce, or agreed to produce, for inspection and copying, much of the requested information. But he refused to produce other requested documents and to answer certain questions on the grounds that the information being sought was either irrelevant or privileged, or both.

These refusals prompted plaintiff to move the Court for an order entering a default judgment against defendant, or in the alternative, compelling him to make the requested discovery and imposing costs pursuant to F.R.Civ.P. 37(a)(4). Defendant Howard opposed this motion and cross-moved for an award of costs on the grounds that plaintiff's motion to compel was not substantially justified within the meaning of Rule 37(a)(4). In addition, defendant Howard moved for an order striking parts of plaintiff's motion as immaterial, impertinent and scandalous. In this tangled posture, the case awaits judicial intervention. For the reasons that follow, the Court holds (A) that defendant Howard is entitled to an order striking certain portions of plaintiff's motion, (B) that plaintiff's motion to compel discovery should be granted in part and denied in part and (C) that neither party is entitled to an award of costs; nor is plaintiff entitled to entry of a default judgment.

* * *

Throughout the papers filed in support of her motion to compel discovery, plaintiff repeatedly likens defendant Howard to a notorious medical practitioner whose malpractice is chronicled in an article from *New Times* magazine entitled, "Meet Dr. Nork, America's Leading Malpractitioner." A copy of this article was attached to plaintiff's motion. In it, Dr. Nork is described as "perhaps the worst physician ever to practice medicine in the United States." Dr. Nork's professional misconduct is detailed as having run the gamut from self-prescribing amphetamines, to performing wholly unnecessary surgical procedures, to falsifying medical records. According to the article, Dr. Nork's practice has spawned a virtual industry of malpractice claims in the California community where he resided, producing judgments against him amounting to many millions of dollars.

Plaintiff has attempted to justify the attachment of this article to the record of the instant case by asserting that the article about Dr. Nork points out how a malpractitioner can escape detection until after he has proved to be a menace to society. Plaintiff zealously insinuates that the professional misconduct of defendant Howard has similarly escaped detection in this community. In the Court's view, however, this attempt to draw parallels misconstrues the purpose of this lawsuit. Plaintiff is a private litigant seeking to recover damages on account of injuries she allegedly sustained during and after she underwent surgery in 1974. She is not a prosecutor duly charged with bringing persons to task for alleged misdeeds. . . . It belabors the obvious to say that . . . references [to the article for the purpose of drawing comparisons between defendant Howard and Dr. Nork] qualify as "indecent" and "scandalous" within the meaning of F.R.Civ.P. 11, and for this reason, they must be stricken.

* * *

In the notice of deposition, plaintiff requested defendant Howard to produce copies of pleadings filed in malpractice suits in which he is a party defendant. On the advice of counsel, defendant Howard refused to produce the requested items, but nevertheless provided plaintiff with the caption and docket number of the single case where he is named a defendant. Plaintiff contends that this response was inadequate.

The threshold question here is relevance.[1] Although relevance in the context of discovery is decidedly broader than in the context of admissible evidence, it is not without limits. Parties to a lawsuit are only entitled to discover information that "appears reasonably calculated to lead to the discovery of admissible evidence." F.R.Civ.P. 26(b)(1).

---

1. In addition to relevancy, the request for copies of pleadings also raises a question concerning the discoverability *vel non* of public documents to which the requesting party has equal access. But because decision of the relevancy issue disposes of the request in question, the Court need not address this second issue. [Some footnotes have been omitted; others renumbered. Eds.]

Whether pleadings in one suit are "reasonably calculated" to lead to admissible evidence in another suit is far from clear. F.R.Evid. 401, 406. In the Court's view, discovery of this type of information typically will *not* lead to admissible evidence. Id. But that determination depends on the nature of the claims, the time when the critical events in each case took place, and the precise involvement of the parties, among other considerations. To date, there has been no inquiry into how—let alone a showing that—the pleadings sought by plaintiff are related to any of the issues raised in the instant case. Given that fact, and given also the unlikelihood that an adequate proffer could be made, the Court must conclude that the items sought are not "reasonably calculated" to lead to the discovery of admissible evidence. Of course, this situation would have been different if plaintiff had preceded her request with discovery that furnished a basis for believing that the pleadings in other suits against defendant Howard were related to matters involved in the present suit. But no foundation of this kind has yet been laid. Until it is, discovery should not be permitted along these lines.

*   *   *

In addition to the pleadings in cases where he was named a party defendant, defendant Howard refused to produce his federal income tax returns for the years 1972–1974. Plaintiff argues that discovery of these returns is necessary to determine whether defendant was under financial pressure to increase his workload beyond the point where he could render satisfactory treatment to his patients. This argument, however, overlooks the important interest in preserving the confidentiality of federal tax returns.

Federal income tax returns are confidential communications between the taxpayer and the government. 26 U.S.C. §§ 6103, 7213(a) (1970)[2] insure that tax returns are protected from unauthorized disclosure while in the hands of government officials. The reason for this protection is straightforward. Unless taxpayers are assured that the personal information contained in their tax returns will be kept confidential, they likely will be discouraged from reporting all of their taxable income to the detriment of the government. The opposite is also true. Unless confidentiality is guaranteed, taxpayers will likely refrain from using all of the tax-saving measures to which they are lawfully entitled.

Admittedly, 26 U.S.C. §§ 6103 and 7213(a) only protect tax returns from unauthorized disclosure while in the hands of the government. And, even there, the protection is not unqualified. But the courts have broadly construed these provisions to embody a general federal policy against indiscriminate disclosure of tax returns from whatever source. Typical is the decision in Federal Savings & Loan Insurance Corporation v. Krueger, 55 F.R.D. 512 (N.D.Ill.1972). In that case, plaintiff was

---

2. Nothing in the 1976 amendments to the tax code diminishes the confidential nature of federal tax returns. In fact, the opposite appears true. See 26 U.S.C.A. § 6103 (1977 Supp.).

denied discovery of defendant's federal tax returns on the grounds that the statutory policy against disclosure applies with equal force to protect tax returns in the hands of private litigants who do not waive the protection by making an issue of their income.[3]

    *   *   *

Other courts have taken a less generous view of the statutory protection given to federal tax returns. E.g., Heathman v. United States District Court, 503 F.2d 1032, 1039 (9th Cir.1974); Trans World Airlines, Inc. v. Hughes, 29 F.R.D. 523, 524 (S.D.N.Y.1961), aff'd, 332 F.2d 602 (2d Cir.1964), cert. dismissed, 380 U.S. 249, 85 S.Ct. 934, 13 L.Ed.2d 818 (1965). But even these decisions have recognized that tax returns are discoverable only "in appropriate circumstances," as where access to tax returns is necessary to replace "lost, destroyed or otherwise unavailable" sources of information or to determine accurately the relationship of co-defendants in a "tangled network of individuals, corporations and other legal entities." Heathman v. United States District Court, supra, 503 F.2d at 1032, 1033.

Under either line of authority, defendant Howard's tax returns are not properly discoverable. Here, as in *Krueger,* defendant has not made an issue of his income. Plaintiff has. And, unlike in *Heathman,* access to defendant's tax returns here is not essential to discovering relevant information that is not obtainable by other means. If, as plaintiff asserts, she bases her request for defendant's tax returns on the need to learn about the intensity of defendant's workload, her request can be met less intrusively by examining defendant's appointment book which the Court has ordered produced in an accompanying order.

    *   *   *

When asked to produce records of patients on whom he performed surgery of the kind he performed on plaintiff, defendant Howard refused on the grounds of privilege. Under District of Columbia law, the medical records of patients are privileged from disclosure while in the hands of medical practitioners. D.C.Code § 14–307(a)[4] forbids doctors "without the consent of the person afflicted, or of his legal representative, to disclose any information, confidential in its nature, that he has acquired in attending a patient in a professional capacity. . . ." Insofar as the medical records in question necessarily reflect

---

3. The Court is aware that defendant's income may be in issue where punitive damages are sought. See, e.g., Hughes v. Groves, 47 F.R.D. 52, 55 (D.Mo.1969). In the instant case, however, a review of the complaint fails to indicate that plaintiff is seeking punitive damages.

4. D.C.Code § 14–307(a) provides:

In the Federal courts in the District of Columbia and District of Columbia courts a physician or surgeon may not be permit-

ted, without the consent of the person afflicted, or of his legal representative, to disclose any information, confidential in its nature, that he has acquired in attending a patient in a professional capacity and that was necessary to enable him to act in that capacity, whether the information was obtained from the patient or from his family or from the person or persons in charge of him.

communications made by patients to defendant Howard in confidence, they fall squarely within the bounds of the statutory protection.

The Court is of the opinion that the purpose of the statutory privilege would be better served by . . . ordering defendant to turn over only the names and addresses of patients on whom he performed the treatment in question. With this information, plaintiff could then inquire of these individuals to determine whether *they* are willing to have their medical records disclosed in connection with this litigation. This procedure, in the Court's estimation, would adequately carry out the statutory purpose of preventing the *unconsented* disclosure of confidential medical information. Cf. Connell v. Washington Hospital Center, 50 F.R.D. 360 (D.D.C.1970) (names of hospital patients held properly discoverable).

* * *

DISCOVERABILITY OF FEDERAL TAX RETURNS

Although specific statutory provisions bar the Government and those who prepare tax returns from disclosing data from the returns, there is no recognized privilege covering such information. Thus, copies in the hands of the taxpayer are subject to discovery in various circumstances. See St. Regis Paper Co. v. United States, 368 U.S. 208, 218–19, 82 S.Ct. 289, 295–96, 7 L.Ed.2d 240 (1961). At the same time, "there is a public policy against unnecessary disclosure, in order that taxpayers can be encouraged to file accurate returns." See Credit Life Ins. Co. v. Uniworld Ins. Co., Ltd., 94 F.R.D. 113, 120 (S.D.Ohio 1982).

In diversity actions Rule 501 of the Federal Rules of Evidence refers the federal courts to applicable state law to determine whether a privilege exists. If there is no state privilege covering tax returns, the only issue is whether the federal policy previously mentioned applies to bar disclosure of the returns. If there is a state privilege, the question is whether federal law will override the privilege. In Mitsui & Co. (U.S.A.) Inc. v. Puerto Rico Water Resources Auth., 79 F.R.D. 72 (D.P.R.1978), the federal district court ordered plaintiff to produce in New York tax returns and related documents in the possession of its accountants. The accountants (non-parties) moved for a protective order based on the Puerto Rican accountant's privilege. The district judge ruled that New York law applied to the issue of privilege. There being no accountant-client privilege in New York, the only limit on discovery was the federal policy against overly free disclosure of tax returns.

Circumstances that may overcome the federal policy against disclosure include: (1) the taxpayer-party has put in issue the amount of income received; (2) "appropriate circumstances" exist (Heathman v. United States District Court, 503 F.2d 1032, 1035 (9th Cir.1974), for example, an issue as to the relationship between various entities can be resolved by reference to tax returns; or (3) business deductions claimed on a tax return are directly probative of a fact in issue. See Shaver v. Yacht Outward Bound, 71 F.R.D. 561 (N.D.Ill.1976).

GRAY v. BOARD OF HIGHER EDUCATION, CITY OF NEW YORK

United States Court of Appeals, Second Circuit, 1982.
692 F.2d 901.

OAKES, CIRCUIT JUDGE:

Dr. S. Simpson Gray appeals from an interlocutory order denying him compelled discovery in a civil rights action alleging racial discrimination, brought under 42 U.S.C. §§ 1981, 1983 and 1985. Dr. Gray taught for five years in the City University of New York system, always at the rank of Instructor. He seeks at this stage to discover the vote of two of the named defendants on his unsuccessful applications for promotion and for reappointment with tenure for the 1979–80 academic year. Furthermore, Dr. Gray "made clear during oral argument on the motion for certification [that] he regards the question of how these individuals voted as only the opening wedge, to be followed by the factors motivating them." The United States District Court for the Southern District of New York, Lawrence W. Pierce, Judge, held that the confidentiality of the faculty peer review system should be protected. . . .

Dr. Gray, a black educator, was employed at LaGuardia Community College in September 1974 at the Instructor level. . . .

The first year, Dr. Gray received a satisfactory college level performance rating based on peer observations and evaluations and an excellent student evaluation. He was, however, not advanced. In his second academic year, his peer observation and evaluation by defendant Dr. Muelig was reported as unsatisfactory. Consequently, the President of LaGuardia, defendant Dr. Shenker, wrote Gray that his third year reappointment would be conditional. Dr. Gray first filed a written rebuttal of the unsatisfactory evaluation as unfounded and racially motivated, and later filed a grievance, resulting in a rescission of the letter and an unconditional reappointment.

At the end of Gray's second year at LaGuardia, his request for promotion to the rank of Assistant Professor was denied by defendant Dr. Rose Palmer, then Chairman of the LaGuardia Business Division. Gray maintains that he continued to receive excellent student evaluations and that he worked for the success of several College programs and activities, in particular the Teaching Application and Reinforcement Program (TAR). During Gray's third year at LaGuardia, the 1976–77 academic year, he again sought promotion to the rank of Assistant Professor, but, allegedly, the Chairman of the newly established Accounting-Managerial Studies Department, defendant Dr. Miller, advised that it was not a good time for Gray to apply because ill-will had been expressed by some of the Personnel and Budget Committee members and administrative staff. At the start of Gray's fourth year at LaGuardia, 1977–78, he was removed as Chairman of the TAR Program Departmental Committee, a position he had held since 1974. He alleges that defendant Dr. Moed caused his removal.

During the academic year 1978–79, the college advised Gray that he would be considered for the Certificate of Continuous Employment (CCE), the tenure equivalent for instructors. In addition to four years' teaching experience at LaGuardia, Gray by then held a Juris Doctor degree as well as his M.B.A. He again applied for but was denied a promotion to Assistant Professor. Gray contends that he requested a statement of reasons and that none was given. He alleges that several other departmental faculty members lacking his credentials were given the rank of Assistant Professor. Plaintiff filed an appeal based on his promotional denial by the college-wide Personnel and Budget (P & B) Committee. Defendant Mary E. Ryan, Director of Personnel, denied this appeal.

Both a departmental and college-wide P & B Committee voted on Gray's request for promotion and for reappointment. He received a favorable 3–2 vote from his department, but the college-wide P & B Committee rejected his application. The present motion to compel discovery is addressed to defendants Moed and Miller, who served on the latter committee. Dr. Miller also served as Chairman of Gray's department. Gray seeks to discover their votes and presumably discussions in connection therewith and argues that this evidence is material and indispensable to his case. Miller and Moed refused to answer questions and cross-moved for a protective order on the grounds that their secret votes, as well as the discussions surrounding the vote, were "privileged under both a First Amendment qualified academic privilege, and under the contract between the Professional Staff Congress and the Board of Higher Education."

* * *

The spectrum of views presented by the briefs in this case ranges from that of the Equal Employment Opportunity Commission (EEOC) ("The approach taken by the district court in restricting discovery in this case . . . would virtually foreclose proof of intentional discrimination in university promotion and tenure cases . . .." Brief at 2) to that of private universities as *amici* ("Compelling disclosure of tenure votes and confidential peer evaluations imposes significant state burdens on the university's academic freedom 'to determine for itself who may teach' . . .." Brief of the Trustees of Columbia University et al. at 4). And of course the parties themselves take diametrically opposite views on the issue of privilege, qualified or otherwise.

In resolving the tensions between the opposed needs of disclosure and confidentiality we are reminded that the discovery rules are to be accorded broad and liberal treatment, particularly where proof of intent is required. Herbert v. Lando, 441 U.S. 153, 170–75, 99 S.Ct. 1635, 1645–48, 60 L.Ed.2d 115 (1979). To sustain a privilege there must be "a public good transcending the normally predominant principle of utilizing all rational means for ascertaining truth." Trammel v. United States, 445 U.S. 40, 50, 100 S.Ct. 906, 912, 63 L.Ed.2d 186 (1980). While we have the flexibility to adopt rules of privilege on a case-by-case basis * * * we prefer the balancing approach taken by the district court, 92 F.R.D. at 90; we simply strike the balance in this case differently.

The district court minimized the importance of the appellants' discovery needs in connection with the votes of P & B Committee members because it was "not clear" how knowing the votes themselves could aid Dr. Gray's case. Closer examination of the elements of Gray's case, however, makes Gray's need for the votes transparently evident. . . .

[T]he Supreme Court has now decided that a finding of intent is necessary in suits like this one under 42 U.S.C. § 1981, General Building Contractors Association, Inc. v. Pennsylvania, ___ U.S. ___, 102 S.Ct. 3141, 3146–50, 73 L.Ed.2d 835 (1982). . . . Moreover, to establish his Fourteenth Amendment claim that his civil rights were denied, Dr. Gray must show that the discrimination he suffered was intentional. Washington v. Davis, 426 U.S. 229, 96 S.Ct. 2040, 48 L.Ed. 2d 597 (1976); see, e.g., Arlington Heights v. Metropolitan Housing Development Corp., 429 U.S. 252, 264–68, 97 S.Ct. 555, 562–65, 50 L.Ed. 2d 450 (1977). But Dr. Gray has not been told defendants' votes, much less been given reasons for the committee's decision. Dr. Gray might prove LaGuardia's intent to discriminate if he could establish that Miller or Moed harbored a racial animus against him and that this was manifested in votes against his reappointment and tenure—but to begin with he would, of course, have to know the votes. Or, he could establish that the reasons given by the P & B Committee for its actions were pretexts for its refusal to rehire and tenure him—if the committee had given reasons.[8] Once Gray has established a prima facie case, the burden shifts to defendants, note 8 supra, to articulate with reasonable specificity the reasons for the denial of tenure and to produce some evidence in support thereof. If defendants fail to do so the court will be required to enter judgment for Gray. If they discharge that burden, the burden will shift back to Gray to prove discrimination either directly (i.e., by persuading the court that a discriminatory reason more likely than not motivated the defendants) or indirectly (i.e., by showing that the proffered nondiscriminatory reason is mere pretext). At that point Gray's need for disclosure may turn on the nature of the reason or reasons put forth by defendants. If the defendants claim that the tenure denial was based on evaluations of Gray's performance discussed at the P & B meeting, then certainly Gray will be hamstrung if denied disclosure. If, in contrast, defendants claim that Gray was denied

---

8. Only if defendants explicate the reasons for the denial of reappointment with tenure can Gray proceed to meet his burden of proof that the nondiscriminatory motives advanced by the defendants are merely pretextual. This McDonnell Douglas Corp. v. Green, 411 U.S. 792, 93 S.Ct. 1817, 36 L.Ed.2d 668 (1973), analysis, though first developed in Title VII cases, applies equally in cases brought under 42 U.S.C. § 1981. [Citations omitted.]

tenure, say, because of poor student evaluations, a record of tardiness and missed classes, or failure to meet a requirement of publication, then disclosure may not be necessary, for if these reasons were pretextual that can be proven without it. [Citations omitted.]

Our problem is that we are obliged to rule not at trial but on discovery, when the precise litigating posture has not yet become known. Consequently we do not pass on the question how far discovery may go and particularly do not do so in connection with confidential communications from persons outside the college. However, the foregoing analysis seems to indicate that a college could defeat the demand for disclosure by disclaiming a defense that will require disclosure to rebut. An approach like this, of trying to find out what plaintiff's needs really are, has been used with respect to the newsman's privilege.
. . .

Merely by furnishing an after-the-fact statement of reasons the defendants cannot fill the void left by the Committee's conclusory decision, especially in light of the fixed policy against giving such reasons. But if unable to engage in discovery, Dr. Gray cannot prove intent, and without proof of intent, he has no case. . . . The district court and appellees have argued that if the courts allow this protected sphere to be invaded, candid peer evaluation will be chilled, the harmony of faculty relations will be disturbed, and academic freedom will be threatened by government intrusion into the life of colleges and universities.

These concerns, all of them real ones, are taken into account by the policy and procedure proposed to us by the American Association of University Professors (AAUP). . . .

That AAUP Statement, insofar as it is applicable here, concludes that faculty members, upon request, should be informed in writing of the reasons for a decision against reappointment. Recognizing the latitude that must be given the institution acting through its faculty, but balancing academic freedom against standards of fairness, the Statement seeks to take into account the confusion that can occur between the limited rights of probationary faculty members and the due process rights guaranteed to tenured faculty, but nevertheless determines that reasons must be given the faculty member denied reappointment or tenure who requests them. This is to permit the rejected probationer to remedy identified shortcomings, to correct erroneous information on which the peer review committee based its decision, as well as perhaps to realize that the decision resulted from institutional considerations unrelated to his or her competence. A statement of reasons also may serve to avoid arbitrariness or lack of consideration in the decision-making body itself. See generally Drown v. Portsmouth School District, 435 F.2d 1182, 1184–85 (1st Cir.1970).

We believe the position of the AAUP on the precise matter before us to be carefully designed to protect confidentiality and encourage a candid peer review process. It strikes an appropriate balance between academic freedom and educational excellence on the one hand and individual rights to fair consideration on the other, so that courts may steer the "careful course between excessive intervention in the affairs of the university and the unwarranted tolerance of unlawful behavior," mentioned in Powell v. Syracuse University, 580 F.2d 1150, 1154 (2d Cir.), cert. denied, 439 U.S. 984, 99 S.Ct. 576, 58 L.Ed.2d 656 (1978).

Rather than adopting a rule of absolute disclosure, in reckless disregard of the need for confidentiality, or adopting a rule of complete privilege that would frustrate reasonable challenges to the fairness of hiring decisions, our decision today holds that absent a statement of reasons, the balance tips toward discovery and away from recognition of privilege. * * *

NOTES

1. In a female instructor's sex discrimination suit for denial of promotion the court ordered a professor to reveal how he voted. The court discerned no privilege to withhold the relevant information. In re Dinnan, 661 F.2d 426 (5th Cir.1981).

2. In E.E.O.C. v. Franklin & Marshall College, 775 F.2d 110 (3d Cir.1985), a professor who was denied tenure charged the College with discrimination based on his French national origin. The E.E.O.C. issued a subpoena duces tecum and brought an enforcement action when the College resisted disclosure of peer review materials. Finding a congressional intent to give broad scope to relevance in Title VII investigations, the court said it declined to follow either the Second Circuit's "balancing approach" or the Seventh Circuit's "qualified academic privilege" view, elaborated in E.E.O.C. v. University of Notre Dame Du Lac, 715 F.2d 331 (7th Cir.1983), cert. denied 476 U.S. 1163, 90 L.Ed.2d 729, 106 S.Ct. 2288 (1986). The Supreme Court unanimously affirmed. University of Pennsylvania v. E.E.O.C., ___ U.S. ___, 110 S.Ct. 577, 107 L.Ed.2d 571 (1990).

3. May members of the legislature be deposed for the purpose of determining their subjective motives for enacting laws attacked in the litigation for violating the plaintiff's constitutional rights? The Supreme Court has indicated the legislators may be called to testify only in extraordinary circumstances and, even then, their testimony may be blocked by their claim of privilege. See City of Las Vegas v. Foley, 747 F.2d 1294 (9th Cir.1984).

NOTE ON PRIVILEGES

The priest-penitent privilege recognizes the human need to disclose to a spiritual counselor, in total and absolute confidence, what are believed to be flawed acts or thoughts, and to receive priestly consolation and guidance in return. The lawyer-client privilege rests on the need for the advocate and counselor to know all that relates to the client's reasons for seeking representation if the professional mission is to be carried out. Similarly, the physician must know all that a patient can articulate in order to identify and to treat disease; barriers to full disclosure would impair diagnosis and treatment. Trammel v. United States, 445 U.S. 40, 100 S.Ct. 906, 63 L.Ed.2d 186 (1980).

Another type of privilege is the "deliberative process" privilege. The rationale supporting it is that the "deliberative and decision-making processes of government officials are held confidential to preserve the free expression, integrity and independence of those responsible for making the determinations that enable government to operate." Kinoy v. Mitchell, 67 F.R.D. 1, 11 (S.D.N.Y.1975). It is limited to evaluations and expressions of opinions and recommendations on policy matters. In re "Agent Orange" Prod.Liab.Litig., 97 F.R.D. 427, 434 (E.D.N.Y.1983). Unlike the "absolute" state secrets privilege the deliberative process privilege is qualified.

UPJOHN CO. v. UNITED STATES

Supreme Court of the United States, 1981.
449 U.S. 383, 101 S.Ct. 677, 66 L.Ed.2d 584.

JUSTICE REHNQUIST delivered the opinion of the Court.*

We granted certiorari in this case to address important questions concerning the scope of the attorney-client privilege in the corporate context and the applicability of the work-product doctrine in proceedings to enforce tax summonses. . . . We . . . conclude that the attorney-client privilege protects the communications involved in this case from compelled disclosure and that the work-product doctrine does apply in tax summons enforcement proceedings.

I

Petitioner Upjohn manufactures and sells pharmaceuticals here and abroad. In January 1976 independent accountants conducting an audit of one of petitioner's foreign subsidiaries discovered that the subsidiary made payments to or for the benefit of foreign government officials in order to secure government business. The accountants so informed Mr. Gerard Thomas, petitioner's Vice President, Secretary, and General Counsel. Thomas is a member of the Michigan and New York Bars, and has been petitioner's General Counsel for 20 years. He consulted with outside counsel and R.T. Parfet, Jr., petitioner's Chairman of the Board. It was decided that the company would conduct an internal investigation of what were termed "questionable payments." As part of this investigation the attorneys prepared a letter containing a questionnaire which was sent to "All Foreign General and Area Managers" over the Chairman's signature. The letter began by noting recent disclosures that several American companies made "possibly illegal" payments to foreign government officials and emphasized that the management needed full information concerning any such payments made by Upjohn. The letter indicated that the Chairman had asked Thomas, identified as "the company's General Counsel," "to conduct an investigation for the purpose of determining the nature and

---

* Some footnotes omitted; others renumbered.

magnitude of any payments made by the Upjohn Company or any of its subsidiaries to any employee or official of a foreign government." The questionnaire sought detailed information concerning such payments. Managers were instructed to treat the investigation as "highly confidential" and not to discuss it with anyone other than Upjohn employees who might be helpful in providing the requested information. Responses were to be sent directly to Thomas. Thomas and outside counsel also interviewed the recipients of the questionnaire and some 33 other Upjohn officers or employees as part of the investigation.

On March 26, 1976, the company voluntarily submitted a preliminary report to the Securities and Exchange Commission on Form 8–K disclosing certain questionable payments. A copy of the report was simultaneously submitted to the Internal Revenue Service, which immediately began an investigation to determine the tax consequences of the payments. Special agents conducting the investigation were given lists by Upjohn of all those interviewed and all who had responded to the questionnaire. On November 23, 1976, the Service issued a summons pursuant to 26 U.S.C. § 7602 demanding production of:

> "All files relative to the investigation conducted under the supervision of Gerard Thomas to identify payments to employees of foreign governments and any political contributions made by the Upjohn Company or any of its affiliates since January 1, 1971 and to determine whether any funds of the Upjohn Company had been improperly accounted for on the corporate books during the same period."

> "The records should include but not be limited to written questionnaires sent to managers of the Upjohn Company's foreign affiliates, and memorandums or notes of the interviews conducted in the United States and abroad with officers and employees of the Upjohn Company and its subsidiaries." App. 17a–18a.

The company declined to produce the documents specified in the second paragraph on the grounds that they were protected from disclosure by the attorney-client privilege and constituted the work product of attorneys prepared in anticipation of litigation. On August 31, 1977, the United States filed a petition seeking enforcement of the summons under 26 U.S.C. §§ 7402(b) and 7604(a) in the United States District Court for the Western District of Michigan. That court adopted the recommendation of a Magistrate who concluded that the summons should be enforced. Petitioner appealed to the Court of Appeals for the Sixth Circuit which rejected the Magistrate's finding of a waiver of the attorney-client privilege, 600 F.2d 1223, 1227, n. 12, but agreed that the privilege did not apply "[t]o the extent that the communications were made by officers and agents not responsible for directing Upjohn's actions in response to legal advice . . . for the simple reason that the communications were not the 'client's.' " . . .

II

Federal Rule of Evidence 501 provides that "the privilege of a witness . . . shall be governed by the principles of the common law as they may be interpreted by the courts of the United States in light of reason and experience." The attorney-client privilege is the oldest of the privileges for confidential communications known to the common law. 8 J. Wigmore, Evidence § 2290 (McNaughton rev. 1961). Its purpose is to encourage full and frank communication between attorneys and their clients and thereby promote broader public interests in the observance of law and administration of justice. The privilege recognizes that sound legal advice or advocacy serves public ends and that such advice or advocacy depends upon the lawyer being fully informed by the client. . . .

The Court of Appeals, however, considered the application of the privilege in the corporate context to present a "different problem," since the client was an inanimate entity and "only the senior management, guiding and integrating the several operations, . . . can be said to possess an identity analogous to the corporation as a whole." . . .

The control group test adopted by the court below . . . frustrates the very purpose of the privilege by discouraging the communication of relevant information by employees of the client to attorneys seeking to render legal advice to the client corporation. The attorney's advice will also frequently be more significant to noncontrol group members than to those who officially sanction the advice, and the control group test makes it more difficult to convey full and frank legal advice to the employees who will put into effect the client corporation's policy. . . .

The narrow scope given the attorney-client privilege by the court below not only makes it difficult for corporate attorneys to formulate sound advice when their client is faced with a specific legal problem but also threatens to limit the valuable efforts of corporate counsel to ensure their client's compliance with the law. . . .

The Court of Appeals declined to extend the attorney-client privilege beyond the limits of the control group test for fear that doing so would entail severe burdens on discovery and create a broad "zone of silence" over corporate affairs. Application of the attorney-client privilege to communications such as those involved here, however, puts the adversary in no worse position than if the communications had never taken place. The privilege only protects disclosure of communications; it does not protect disclosure of the underlying facts by those who communicated with the attorney:

> "[T]he protection of the privilege extends only to *communications* and not to facts. A fact is one thing and a communication concerning that fact is an entirely different thing. The client cannot be compelled to answer the question, 'What did you say or write to the attorney?' but may not refuse to disclose any relevant fact within his knowledge merely because

he incorporated a statement of such fact into his communication to his attorney." Philadelphia v. Westinghouse Electric Corp., 205 F.Supp. 830, 831 (E.D.Pa.1962).

Needless to say, we decide only the case before us, and do not undertake to draft a set of rules which should govern challenges to investigatory subpoenas.

We conclude that the narrow "control group test" sanctioned by the Court of Appeals in this case cannot, consistent with "the principles of the common law as . . . interpreted . . . in the light of reason and experience," Fed.Rule Evid. 501, govern the development of the law in this area.

[The portion of the Court's opinion discussing the work product issue is reproduced below in part.]

NOTE

There is a vast literature on the *Upjohn* problem. An extensive empirical study of the effects of the attorney-client privilege on the behavior of attorneys and corporate executives, middle-managers and other employees is reported in Alexander, The Corporate Attorney–Client Privilege: A Study of the Participants, 63 St. John's L.Rev. 191 (1989). See, also, Waldman, Beyond Upjohn: The Attorney–Client Privilege in the Corporate Context, 28 Wm. & Mary L.Rev. 473 (1987); Sexton, A Post–Upjohn Consideration of the Corporate Attorney–Client Privilege, 57 N.Y.U.L.Rev. 443 (1982).

SECTION 5. WORK PRODUCT AND TRIAL PREPARATION MATERIALS UNDER RULE 26(b)(3)

HICKMAN v. TAYLOR
Supreme Court of the United States, 1947.
329 U.S. 495, 67 S.Ct. 385, 91 L.Ed. 451.

MR. JUSTICE MURPHY delivered the opinion of the Court.*

This case presents an important problem under the Federal Rules of Civil Procedure as to the extent to which a party may inquire into oral and written statements of witnesses, or other information, secured by an adverse party's counsel in the course of preparation for possible litigation after a claim has arisen. Examination into a person's files and records, including those resulting from the professional activities of an attorney, must be judged with care. It is not without reason that various safeguards have been established to preclude unwarranted excursions into the privacy of a man's work. At the same time, public policy supports reasonable and necessary inquiries. Properly to balance these competing interests is a delicate and difficult task.

* Footnotes omitted.

On February 7, 1943, the tug "J.M. Taylor" sank while engaged in helping to tow a car float of the Baltimore & Ohio Railroad across the Delaware River at Philadelphia. The accident was apparently unusual in nature, the cause of it still being unknown. Five of the nine crew members were drowned. Three days later the tug owners and the underwriters employed a law firm, of which respondent Fortenbaugh is a member, to defend them against potential suits by representatives of the deceased crew members and to sue the railroad for damages to the tug.

A public hearing was held on March 4, 1943, before the United States Steamboat Inspectors, at which the four survivors were examined. This testimony was recorded and made available to all interested parties. Shortly thereafter, Fortenbaugh privately interviewed the survivors and took statements from them with an eye toward the anticipated litigation; the survivors signed these statements on March 29. Fortenbaugh also interviewed other persons believed to have some information relating to the accident and in some cases he made memoranda of what they told him. At the time when Fortenbaugh secured the statements of the survivors, representatives of two of the deceased crew members had been in communication with him. Ultimately claims were presented by representatives of all five of the deceased; four of the claims, however, were settled without litigation. The fifth claimant, petitioner herein, brought suit in a federal court under the Jones Act on November 26, 1943, naming as defendants the two tug owners, individually and as partners, and the railroad.

One year later, petitioner filed 39 interrogatories directed to the tug owners. The 38th interrogatory read: "State whether any statements of the members of the crews of the Tugs 'J.M. Taylor' and 'Philadelphia' or of any other vessel were taken in connection with the towing of the car float and the sinking of the Tug 'John M. Taylor.' Attach hereto exact copies of all such statements if in writing, and if oral, set forth in detail the exact provisions of any such oral statements or reports."

Supplemental interrogatories asked whether any oral or written statements, records, reports or other memoranda had been made concerning any matter relative to the towing operation, the sinking of the tug, the salvaging and repair of the tug, and the death of the deceased. If the answer was in the affirmative, the tug owners were then requested to set forth the nature of all such records, reports, statements or other memoranda.

The tug owners, through Fortenbaugh, answered all of the interrogatories except No. 38 and the supplemental ones just described. While admitting that statements of the survivors had been taken, they declined to summarize or set forth the contents. They did so on the ground that such requests called "for privileged matter obtained in preparation for litigation" and constituted "an attempt to obtain indirectly counsel's private files." It was claimed that answering these requests "would involve practically turning over not only the complete files, but also the telephone records and, almost, the thoughts of counsel."

. . . The District Court for the Eastern District of Pennsylvania, sitting *en banc,* held that the requested matters were not privileged. 4 F.R.D. 479. The court then decreed that the tug owners and Fortenbaugh, as counsel and agent for the tug owners, forthwith "answer Plaintiff's 38th interrogatory and supplementary interrogatories; produce all written statements of witnesses obtained by Mr. Fortenbaugh, as counsel and agent for Defendants; state in substance any fact concerning this case which Defendants learned through oral statements made by witnesses to Mr. Fortenbaugh whether or not included in his private memoranda and produce Mr. Fortenbaugh's memoranda containing statements of fact by witnesses or to submit these memoranda to the Court for determination of those portions which should be revealed to Plaintiff." Upon their refusal, the court adjudged them in contempt and ordered them imprisoned until they complied.

The Third Circuit Court of Appeals, also sitting *en banc,* reversed the judgment of the District Court. 153 F.2d 212. It held that the information here sought was part of the "work product of the lawyer" and hence privileged from discovery under the Federal Rules of Civil Procedure. The importance of the problem, which has engendered a great divergence of views among district courts, led us to grant certiorari. . . .

There is an initial question as to which of the deposition-discovery rules is involved in this case. . . .

But, under the circumstances, . . . [it] matters little at this late stage whether Fortenbaugh fails to answer interrogatories filed under Rule 26 or under Rule 33 or whether he refuses to produce the memoranda and statements pursuant to a subpoena under Rule 45 or a court order under Rule 34. . . .

In urging that he has a right to inquire into the materials secured and prepared by Fortenbaugh, petitioner emphasizes that the deposition-discovery portions of the Federal Rules of Civil Procedure are designed to enable the parties to discover the true facts and to compel their disclosure wherever they may be found. It is said that inquiry may be made under these rules, epitomized by Rule 26, as to any relevant matter which is not privileged; and since the discovery provisions are to be applied as broadly and liberally as possible, the privilege limitation must be restricted to its narrowest bounds. On the premise that the attorney-client privilege is the one involved in this case, petitioner argues that it must be strictly confined to confidential communications made by a client to his attorney. And since the materials here in issue were secured by Fortenbaugh from third persons rather than from his clients, the tug owners, the conclusion is reached that these materials are proper subjects for discovery under Rule 26.

As additional support for this result, petitioner claims that to prohibit discovery under these circumstances would give a corporate defendant a tremendous advantage in a suit by an individual plaintiff. Thus in a suit by an injured employee against a railroad or in a suit by an insured person against an insurance company the corporate defendant could pull a dark veil of secrecy over all the pertinent facts it can collect after the claim arises merely on the assertion that such facts were gathered by its large staff of attorneys and claim agents. At the same time, the individual plaintiff, who often has direct knowledge of the matter in issue and has no counsel until some time after his claim arises could be compelled to disclose all the intimate details of his case. By endowing with immunity from disclosure all that a lawyer discovers in the course of his duties, it is said, the rights of individual litigants in such cases are drained of vitality and the lawsuit becomes more of a battle of deception than a search for truth.

But framing the problem in terms of assisting individual plaintiffs in their suits against corporate defendants is unsatisfactory. Discovery concededly may work to the disadvantage as well as to the advantage of individual plaintiffs. Discovery, in other words, is not a one-way proposition. It is available in all types of cases at the behest of any party, individual or corporate, plaintiff or defendant. The problem thus far transcends the situation confronting this petitioner. And we must view that problem in light of the limitless situations where the particular kind of discovery sought by petitioner might be used.

We agree, of course, that the deposition-discovery rules are to be accorded a broad and liberal treatment. No longer can the time-honored cry of "fishing expedition" serve to preclude a party from inquiring into the facts underlying his opponent's case. Mutual knowledge of all the relevant facts gathered by both parties is essential to proper litigation. To that end, either party may compel the other to disgorge whatever facts he has in his possession. The deposition-discovery procedure simply advances the stage at which the disclosure can be compelled from the time of trial to the period preceding it, thus reducing the possibility of surprise. . . .

We also agree that the memoranda, statements and mental impressions in issue in this case fall outside the scope of the attorney-client privilege and hence are not protected from discovery on that basis. It is unnecessary here to delineate the content and scope of that privilege as recognized in the federal courts. For present purposes, it suffices to note that the protective cloak of this privilege does not extend to information which an attorney secures from a witness while acting for his client in anticipation of litigation. Nor does this privilege concern the memoranda, briefs, communications and other writings prepared by counsel for his own use in prosecuting his client's case; and it is equally unrelated to writings which reflect an attorney's mental impressions, conclusions, opinions or legal theories.

But the impropriety of invoking that privilege does not provide an answer to the problem before us. Petitioner has made more than an ordinary request for relevant, non-privileged facts in the possession of his adversaries or their counsel. He has sought discovery as of right of oral and written statements of witnesses whose identity is well known and whose availability to petitioner appears unimpaired. He has sought production of these matters after making the most searching inquiries of his opponents as to the circumstances surrounding the fatal accident, which inquiries were sworn to have been answered to the best of their information and belief. Interrogatories were directed toward all the events prior to, during and subsequent to the sinking of the tug. Full and honest answers to such broad inquiries would necessarily have included all pertinent information gleaned by Fortenbaugh through his interviews with the witnesses. Petitioner makes no suggestion, and we cannot assume, that the tug owners or Fortenbaugh were incomplete or dishonest in the framing of their answers. In addition, petitioner was free to examine the public testimony of the witnesses taken before the United States Steamboat Inspectors. We are thus dealing with an attempt to secure the production of written statements and mental impressions contained in the files and the mind of the attorney Fortenbaugh without any showing of necessity or any indication or claim that denial of such production would unduly prejudice the preparation of petitioner's case or cause him any hardship or injustice. For aught that appears, the essence of what petitioner seeks either has been revealed to him already through the interrogatories or is readily available to him direct from the witnesses for the asking.

The District Court, after hearing objections to petitioner's request, commanded Fortenbaugh to produce all written statements of witnesses and to state in substance any facts learned through oral statements of witnesses to him. Fortenbaugh was to submit any memoranda he had made of the oral statements so that the court might determine what portions should be revealed to petitioner. All of this was ordered without any showing by petitioner, or any requirement that he make a proper showing, of the necessity for the production of any of this material or any demonstration that denial of production would cause hardship or injustice. The court simply ordered production on the theory that the facts sought were material and were not privileged as constituting attorney-client communications.

In our opinion, neither Rule 26 nor any other rule dealing with discovery contemplates production under such circumstances. That is not because the subject matter is privileged or irrelevant, as those concepts are used in these rules. Here is simply an attempt, without purported necessity or justification, to secure written statements, private memoranda and personal recollections prepared or formed by an adverse party's counsel in the course of his legal duties. As such, it falls outside the arena of discovery and contravenes the public policy underlying the orderly prosecution and defense of legal claims. Not even the most liberal of discovery theories can justify unwarranted inquiries into the files and the mental impressions of an attorney.

Historically, a lawyer is an officer of the court and is bound to work for the advancement of justice while faithfully protecting the rightful interests of his clients. In performing his various duties, however, it is essential that a lawyer work with a certain degree of privacy, free from unnecessary intrusion by opposing parties and their counsel. Proper preparation of a client's case demands that he assemble information, sift what he considers to be the relevant from the irrelevant facts, prepare his legal theories and plan his strategy without undue and needless interference. That is the historical and the necessary way in which lawyers act within the framework of our system of jurisprudence to promote justice and to protect their clients' interests. This work is reflected, of course, in interviews, statements, memoranda, correspondence, briefs, mental impressions, personal beliefs, and countless other tangible and intangible ways—aptly though roughly termed by the Circuit Court of Appeals in this case as the "work product of the lawyer." Were such materials open to opposing counsel on mere demand, much of what is now put down in writing would remain unwritten. An attorney's thoughts, heretofore inviolate, would not be his own. Inefficiency, unfairness and sharp practices would inevitably develop in the giving of legal advice and in the preparation of cases for trial. The effect on the legal profession would be demoralizing. And the interests of the clients and the cause of justice would be poorly served.

We do not mean to say that all written materials obtained or prepared by an adversary's counsel with an eye toward litigation are necessarily free from discovery in all cases. Where relevant and nonprivileged facts remain hidden in an attorney's file and where production of those facts is essential to the preparation of one's case, discovery may properly be had. Such written statements and documents might, under certain circumstances, be admissible in evidence or give clues as to the existence or location of relevant facts. Or they might be useful for purposes of impeachment or corroboration. And production might be justified where the witnesses are no longer available or can be reached only with difficulty. Were production of written statements and documents to be precluded under such circumstances, the liberal ideals of the deposition-discovery portions of the Federal Rules of Civil Procedure would be stripped of much of their meaning. But the general policy against invading the privacy of an attorney's course of preparation is so well recognized and so essential to an orderly working of our system of legal procedure that a burden rests on the one who would invade that privacy to establish adequate reasons to justify production through a subpoena or court order. That burden, we believe, is necessarily implicit in the rules as now constituted.

* * *

But as to oral statements made by witnesses to Fortenbaugh, whether presently in the form of his mental impressions or memoranda, we do not believe that any showing of necessity can be made under the circumstances of this case so as to justify production. Under ordinary conditions, forcing an attorney to repeat or write out all that witnesses have told him and to deliver the account to his adversary gives rise to grave dangers of inaccuracy and untrustworthiness. No legitimate purpose is served by such production. The practice forces the attorney to testify as to what he remembers or what he saw fit to write down regarding witnesses' remarks. Such testimony could not qualify as evidence; and to use it for impeachment or corroborative purposes would make the attorney much less an officer of the court and much more an ordinary witness. The standards of the profession would thereby suffer.

Denial of production of this nature does not mean that any material, non-privileged facts can be hidden from the petitioner in this case. He need not be unduly hindered in the preparation of his case, in the discovery of facts or in his anticipation of his opponents' position. Searching interrogatories directed to Fortenbaugh and the tug owners, production of written documents and statements upon a proper showing and direct interviews with the witnesses themselves all serve to reveal the facts in Fortenbaugh's possession to the fullest possible extent consistent with public policy. Petitioner's counsel frankly admits that he wants the oral statements only to help prepare himself to examine witnesses and to make sure that he has overlooked nothing. That is insufficient under the circumstances to permit him an exception to the policy underlying the privacy of Fortenbaugh's professional activities. If there should be a rare situation justifying production of these matters, petitioner's case is not of that type.

We fully appreciate the wide-spread controversy among the members of the legal profession over the problem raised by this case. It is a problem that rests on what has been one of the most hazy frontiers of the discovery process. But until some rule or statute definitely prescribes otherwise, we are not justified in permitting discovery in a situation of this nature as a matter of unqualified right. When Rule 26 and the other discovery rules were adopted, this Court and the members of the bar in general certainly did not believe or contemplate that all the files and mental processes of lawyers were thereby opened to the free scrutiny of their adversaries. And we refuse to interpret the rules at this time so as to reach so harsh and unwarranted a result.

We therefore affirm the judgment of the Circuit Court of Appeals.

Affirmed.

MR. JUSTICE JACKSON, concurring. The narrow question in this case concerns only one of thirty-nine interrogatories which defendants and their counsel refused to answer. . . .

The interrogatory asked whether statements were taken from the crews of the tugs involved in the accident, or of any other vessel, and demanded "Attach hereto exact copies of all such statements if in writing, and if oral, set forth in detail the exact provisions of any such oral statements or reports." The question is simply whether such a demand is authorized by the rules relating to various aspects of "discovery."

The primary effect of the practice advocated here would be on the legal profession itself. But it too often is overlooked that the lawyer and the law office are indispensable parts of our administration of justice. Law-abiding people can go nowhere else to learn the ever changing and constantly multiplying rules by which they must behave and to obtain redress for their wrongs. The welfare and tone of the legal profession is therefore of prime consequence to society, which would feel the consequences of such a practice as petitioner urges secondarily but certainly.

* * *

To consider first the most extreme aspect of the requirement in litigation here, we find it calls upon counsel, if he has had any conversations with any of the crews of the vessels in question or of any other, to "set forth in detail the exact provision of any such oral statements or reports." Thus the demand is not for the production of a transcript in existence but calls for the creation of a written statement not in being. But the statement by counsel of what a witness told him is not evidence when written. Plaintiff could not introduce it to prove his case. What, then, is the purpose sought to be served by demanding this of adverse counsel?

Counsel for the petitioner candidly said on argument that he wanted this information to help prepare himself to examine witnesses, to make sure he overlooked nothing. He bases his claim to it in his brief on the view that the Rules were to do away with the old situation where a law suit developed into "a battle of wits between counsel." But a common law trial is and always should be an adversary proceeding. Discovery was hardly intended to enable a learned profession to perform its functions either without wits or on wits borrowed from the adversary.

The real purpose and the probable effect of the practice ordered by the district court would be to put trials on a level even lower than a "battle of wits." I can conceive of no practice more demoralizing to the Bar than to require a lawyer to write out and deliver to his adversary an account of what witnesses have told him. Even if his recollection were perfect, the statement would be his language, permeated with his inferences. Every one who has tried it knows that it is almost impossible so fairly to record the expressions and emphasis of a witness that when he testifies in the environment of the court and under the influence of the leading question there will not be departures in some respects. Whenever the testimony of the witness would differ from the "exact" statement the lawyer had delivered, the lawyer's statement would be whipped out to impeach the witness. Counsel producing his adversary's "inexact" statement could lose nothing by saying, "Here is a contradiction, gentlemen of the jury. I do not know whether it is my adversary or his witness who is not telling the truth, but one is not." Of course, if this practice were adopted, that scene would be repeated over and over again. The lawyer who delivers such statements often would find himself branded a deceiver afraid to take the stand to support his own version of the witness's conversation with him, or else he will have to go on the stand to defend his own credibility—perhaps against that of his chief witness, or possibly even his client.

    *   *   *

Having been supplied the names of the witnesses, petitioner's lawyer gives no reason why he cannot interview them himself. If an employee-witness refuses to tell his story, he, too, may be examined under the Rules. He may be compelled on discovery, as fully as on the trial, to disclose his version of the facts. But that is his own disclosure—it can be used to impeach him if he contradicts it and such a deposition is not useful to promote an unseemly disagreement between the witness and the counsel in the case.

    *   *   *

I agree to the affirmance of the judgment of the Circuit Court of Appeals which reversed the district court.

———

UPJOHN CO. v. UNITED STATES

Supreme Court of the United States, 1981.
449 U.S. 383, 101 S.Ct. 677, 66 L.Ed.2d 584.

[The facts and a portion of the opinion appear at p. 740 supra.]

The Government concedes, wisely, that the Court of Appeals erred and that the work-product doctrine does apply to IRS summonses. Brief for Respondents 16, 48. . . .

Rule 26 accords special protection to work product revealing the attorney's mental processes. The Rule permits disclosure of documents and tangible things constituting attorney work product upon a showing of substantial need and inability to obtain the equivalent without undue hardship. This was the standard applied by the Magistrate, 78–1 USTC ¶ 9277, p. 83,604. Rule 26 goes on, however, to state that "[i]n ordering discovery of such materials when the required showing has been made, the court shall protect against disclosure of the mental impressions, conclusions, opinions or legal theories of an attorney or other representative of a party concerning the litigation." Although this language does not specifically refer to memoranda based on oral statements of witnesses, the *Hickman* court stressed the danger that compelled disclosure of such memoranda would reveal the attorney's mental processes. It is clear that this is the sort of material the draftsmen of the Rule had in mind as deserving special protection. See Notes of Advisory Committee on 1970 Amendment to Rules, 28 U.S.C. App., p. 442 . . ..

Based on the foregoing, some courts have concluded that *no* showing of necessity can overcome protection of work product which is based on oral statements from witnesses. See, e.g., In re Grand Jury Proceedings, 473 F.2d 840, 848 (C.A.8 1973) (personal recollections, notes, and memoranda pertaining to conversation with witnesses); In re Grand Jury Investigation, 412 F.Supp. 943, 949 (E.D.Pa.1976) (notes of conversation with witness "are so much a product of the lawyer's thinking and so little probative of the witness's actual words that they are absolutely protected from disclosure"). Those courts declining to adopt an absolute rule have nonetheless recognized that such material is entitled to special protection. See, e.g., In re Grand Jury Investigation, 599 F.2d 1224, 1231 (C.A.3 1979) ("special considerations . . . must shape any ruling on the discoverability of interview memoranda . . .; such documents will be discoverable only in a 'rare situation' "); cf. In re Grand Jury Subpoena, 599 F.2d 504, 511–512 (C.A.2 1979).

We do not decide the issue at this time. It is clear that the Magistrate applied the wrong standard when he concluded that the Government had made a sufficient showing of necessity to overcome the protections of the work-product doctrine. The Magistrate applied the "substantial need" and "without undue hardship" standard articulated in the first part of Rule 26(b)(3). The notes and memoranda sought by the Government here, however, are work product based on oral statements. If they reveal communications, they are, in this case, protected by the attorney-client privilege. To the extent they do not reveal communications, they reveal the attorneys' mental processes in evaluating the communications. As Rule 26 and *Hickman* make clear, such work product cannot be disclosed simply on a showing of substantial need and inability to obtain the equivalent without undue hardship.

While we are not prepared at this juncture to say that such material is always protected by the work-product rule, we think a far stronger showing of necessity and unavailability by other means than was made by the Government or applied by the Magistrate in this case would be necessary to compel disclosure. Since the Court of Appeals thought that the work-product protection was never applicable in an enforcement proceeding such as this, and since the Magistrate whose recommendations the District Court adopted applied too lenient a standard of protection, we think the best procedure with respect to this aspect of the case would be to reverse the judgment of the Court of Appeals for the Sixth Circuit and remand the case to it for such further proceedings in connection with the work-product claim as are consistent with this opinion.

Accordingly, the judgment of the Court of Appeals is reversed, and the case remanded for further proceedings.

BROWN v. SUPERIOR COURT IN & FOR MARICOPA CY.

Supreme Court of Arizona, 1983.
137 Ariz. 327, 670 P.2d 725.

FELDMAN, JUSTICE.

Petitioners, Robert A. Brown and Mary Ellen Brown and Robert A. Brown Enterprises, Inc. (Brown), bring this special action against respondent insurers (Continental) and several of their employees, alleging that the trial judge abused his discretion and acted contrary to law in denying Brown's motion to compel production. Having concluded that the petition presents important issues of first impression in this state and that remedy by appeal is inadequate, we accepted jurisdiction. Ariz. Const. art. 6, § 5, and Ariz.R.Sp.Act. 4, 17A A.R.S.

The action arose out of a fire loss to Brown's businesses, Cameo Label and Printing Company and Progressive Rent-a-Car, on August 16, 1980. Brown was insured by Continental for fire damage and various extended coverages. After some negotiation, the physical damage loss was paid, but the company refused to pay the claim based on business interruption, loss of accounts receivable and loss of valuable papers (referred to hereafter as the "loss of earnings claim"). The issues pertaining to the loss of earnings claim were arbitrated by agreement of the parties, but Brown refused to accept the award of the arbitrator. Brown then filed an action in superior court on June 30, 1982, alleging that Continental and its agents had acted in bad faith and breached the implied covenant of good faith and fair dealing contained in the insurance policies which covered Brown's property. The bad-faith allegations pertained only to the handling of Brown's claim for loss of earnings.

On the same day the complaint was filed, Brown served Continental and the other defendants with a request for production pursuant to Ariz.R.Civ.P. 34. The portion of the request at issue in this case sought production of the entire claims file compiled by Continental in handling both the physical damages and loss of earnings claim.[1] Continental

---

1. The items sought were the following:

3. The *complete* and entire claims file and other documents on the Plaintiffs, including, but not limited to, the following:

(a) The file folder or folders themselves;

(b) All inter-office memoranda or other forms of written communication to or from any employee of Defendants relating to the initial processing of the Plaintiffs' claims when Defendants first received said claims;

(c) All inter-office memoranda or other forms of written communication to or from any employee of Defendants relating to the continued processing or denial of the Plaintiffs' claims;

(d) All written communication from Plaintiffs to Defendants, including all proof of loss forms and claim forms;

(e) All written communications between Defendants and any third party concerning the processing, acceptance or denial of the Plaintiffs' claims;

(f) All medical and investigative reports concerning Plaintiffs and the Plaintiffs' claims, and all written communications between Defendants and any third party concerning said report or reports;

(g) All written communications from Defendants to Plaintiffs concerning processing and denial of the Plaintiffs' claims;

(h) All photographs, motion pictures, tape recordings, or other products of inves-

objected to production of the file, claiming . . . the file . . . contained the mental impressions, conclusions, opinions and legal theories of the insurer's agents and attorneys which were absolutely immune from discovery . . ..

Brown moved for an order compelling production of the file. The trial judge ordered Continental to submit the entire claims file for *in camera* inspection by the court, along with an itemization of the documents and a statement explaining Continental's position with respect to each item. . . . [The court also ordered Brown to submit an itemization of documents sought from the claims file, along with a statement of legal authority supporting Brown's position on each of those items. The Browns reported to the court that they were unable to submit such a document because it was not possible for them to determine which documents would be helpful by consulting an inventory prepared by Continental.]

After reviewing the files, the trial court denied the motion to compel in its entirety . . ..

[Rejecting the line of authority holding the insured's reports discoverable as records obtained in the ordinary course of business, the court considered the view advanced in Fireman's Fund Insurance Co. v. McAlpine, 120 R.I. 744, 391 A.2d 84, 89–90:]

> In our litigious society, when an insured reports to his insurer that he has been involved in an incident involving another person, the insurer can reasonably anticipate that some action will be taken by the other party. The seeds of prospective litigation have been sown, and the prudent party, anticipating this fact, will begin to prepare his case. . . . Although a claim may be settled short of the instigation of legal action, there is an ever-present possibility of a claim's ending in litigation. The recognition of this possibility provides, in any given case, the impetus for the insurer to garner information regarding the circumstances of a claim.

391 A.2d at 89–90.

We find this view equally unsatisfactory. The fact that an event has occurred which may require an insurance company to provide payments under its contract with an insured will certainly not *always* transform an insurance company's activities into preparation for litiga-

---

tigation concerning Plaintiffs taken by or on behalf of Defendants, relating to the processing or denial of the claims listed above;

(i) All other written documents pertaining to the processing of the above claims in the possession of Defendant;

(j) All documents in the claims file, including telephone messages, claim worksheets, copies of checks or drafts, memoranda of telephone calls or conferences, legal or medical researches, etc.;

(k) This request includes evidence of written communication between the Defendants and their attorneys, pursuant to United States Auto Ass'n. v. Werley, 526 P.2d 28 (Alaska 1974);

(*l*) If there are files kept by more than one office or department of the Defendants (i.e., home office and regional claims office), this request is for *all* such files.

[Footnote renumbered Eds.]

tion. This is particularly true where, as here, the claim asserted is not a liability claim against a third party's insurer, but rather a casualty claim against the claimant's own insurer. To adopt such an approach would undoubtedly give too broad an application of Rule 26(b)(3), simply because in many circumstances, although claims are expected, litigation is only problematical. *See Spaulding v. Denton,* supra [68 F.R.D. 342 (D.Del.1975)]; *Garfinkle v. Arcata National Corp.,* 64 F.R.D. 688 (S.D.N.Y.1974).

Faced with two absolute, but unsatisfactory, rules on this question, we feel it is necessary to examine the purposes behind the protection afforded trial preparation materials and develop a test which will best effectuate these purposes. The primary reasons for the protection given by Rule 26(b)(3) to materials prepared in anticipation of litigation are to maintain the adversarial trial process and to ensure that attorneys are adequately prepared for trial by encouraging written preparation. See Hickman v. Taylor, 329 U.S. 495, 510–12, 67 S.Ct. 385, 393–94, 91 L.Ed. 451 (1947); Coastal States Gas Corp. v. Department of Energy, 617 F.2d 854, 864 (D.C.Cir.1980). Counsel should not be permitted or encouraged to try a case on "wits borrowed from [an] adversary." *Hickman,* 329 U.S. at 516, 67 S.Ct. at 396 (Jackson, J., concurring). Further, an attorney or party's agent should not be deterred from adequately preparing for trial because of the fear that their efforts will be freely disclosed to opposing counsel. *Hickman,* 329 U.S. at 511, 67 S.Ct. at 393. On the other hand, the rules should be construed to allow discovery of all relevant information, so that issues may be tried on the true facts. Any formula adopted to help determine whether material fits within Rule 26(b)(3) protection should attempt to reconcile these divergent views.

Unfortunately, the cases are in considerable confusion in attempting to define the phrase "prepared in anticipation of litigation." The confusion is well described as follows:

> Courts have attempted to explain exactly what anticipation of litigation means, but such efforts have not helped to resolve the issue. For example, some courts indicate that a party . . . anticipates litigation where there is a "substantial probability" of "imminent" litigation or when there is a "prospect" of litigation. Another requirement is that there be "some possibility" of litigation; however, a "mere possibility" of litigation is not enough. Other courts have stated that there must be an "eye" towards litigation or that litigation need only be a reasonable "contingency." These methods for redefining the word anticipation do little more than say that litigation is anticipated when litigation is anticipated.

Note, Work Product Discovery: A Multifactor Approach to the Anticipation of Litigation Requirement in Federal Rule of Civil Procedure 26(b)(3), 66 Iowa L.Rev. 1277, 1277–78 (1981) (footnotes omitted). See also Fontaine v. Sunflower Beef Carrier, Inc., 87 F.R.D. 89, 92 (E.D.Mo.

1980); In re Grand Jury Investigation, 599 F.2d 1224, 1229 (3d Cir.1979)

. . .

*   *   *

Even if discovery is permitted, Continental maintains that mental impressions and legal theories of their counsel, agents or other representatives are contained in the file and are absolutely protected from disclosure. Continental asserts that the plain language of Rule 26(b)(3) requires absolute immunity for these materials because the rule provides "the court *shall* protect against disclosure of the mental impressions, conclusions, opinions, or legal theories of an attorney or other representative of a party concerning the litigation." (Emphasis supplied.) Indeed, some courts have held that without exception such material is immune from discovery. See Duplan Corp. v. Moulinage et Retorderie de Chavanoz, 509 F.2d 730 (4th Cir.1974); In re Grand Jury Proceedings, 473 F.2d 840 (8th Cir.1973). We left this issue open in Longs Drug Stores v. Howe, 134 Ariz. 424, 430 n. 7, 657 P.2d 412, 418 n. 7 (1983).

Recognizing that mental impressions and the like are afforded greater protection under Rule 26(b)(3), Longs, 134 Ariz. at 428, 657 P.2d at 416, we do not believe such protection can be absolute in a case presenting issues similar to the one at bench. As we explained above, the reasons the insurance company denied the claim or the manner in which it dealt with it are central issues to Brown's claim of bad faith. Thus, the strategy, theories, mental impressions and opinions of Continental's agents concerning the loss of earnings claim are directly at issue. When mental impressions and the like are directly at issue in a case, courts have permitted an exception to the strict protection of Rule 26(b)(3) and allowed discovery. . . .

We emphasize, however, that this exception will only be permitted where the material sought to be discovered is central to a party's claim or defense. Accordingly, we find the trial court abused its discretion in refusing to permit discovery of the mental impressions, opinions, conclusions or legal theories of Continental's representatives which pertain to the loss of earnings claim and are contained in the claims file. . . .

NOTE

A perceptive analysis of the courts' erosion of protection for core work product and undesirable consequences calls for judicial guidelines to fortify the protection. See Ward, The Litigator's Dilemma: Waiver of Core Work Product Used in Trial Preparation, 62 St. John's L.Rev. 515 (1988).

OBTAINING TRIAL PREPARATION MATERIALS UNDER RULE 26(b)(3)

The codification of the *Hickman* principle in the 1970 amendment did not end the problems of discovering materials prepared in anticipation of litigation or in preparation for trial. Apart from such obvious grounds as the unavailability or demonstrable hostility of a witness, other factors and circumstances that courts have recognized as constituting the grounds contemplated by the rule for obtaining litigation-related materials from the other side can be identified.

(1) Serious inconsistencies between a deposition or statement in possession of the examining party and a statement obtained by the other party are plus factors for discovery of the statements. See Harper & Row Publishers, Inc. v. Decker, 423 F.2d 487 (7th Cir.1970).

(2) A statement by a witness given to one side at or close to the time of the occurrence is ordinarily discoverable by the other side. See Fontaine v. Sunflower Beef Carrier, Inc., 87 F.R.D. 89 (D.C.E.D.Mo., 1980); Hamilton v. Canal Barge Co., Inc., 395 F.Supp. 975 (E.D.La.1974).

(3) If the cost of duplicating the materials sought were "prohibitive", discovery would be allowed, but costliness alone does not satisfy the "undue hardship" requirement. See In re LTV Sec. Litig., 89 F.R.D. 595, 616 (N.D.Tex.1981) (discovery denied).

(4) When the discovering party seeks documents or materials that are unique, such as photographs of a since-altered accident scene, the case is a strong one for permitting discovery. See Rackers v. Siegfried, 54 F.R.D. 24 (W.D.Mo.1971) (discovery of diagrams of accident scene allowed because police report was inaccurate and no other materials available).

The provision in Rule 26(b)(3) according special protection to materials that reveal the mental processes of the attorney or other representative who produced them has also caused the courts difficulties. *Compare* Handgards, Inc. v. Johnson & Johnson, 413 F.Supp. 926 (N.D. Cal.1976) (discovery of lawyers' mental impressions allowed because principal issue was whether defendant initiated prior suits knowing that they would be unsuccessful on the merits) *with* Duplan Corp. v. Moulinage et Retorderie de Chavanoz, 509 F.2d 730 (4th Cir.1974), cert. denied 420 U.S. 997, 95 S.Ct. 1438, 43 L.Ed.2d 680 (1974) (work product material containing opinions immune from discovery even though the litigation in which it developed had been terminated). See, generally, Special Project, The Work Product Doctrine, 68 Cornell L.Rev. 760, 821–831 (1983).

Appellate courts have said that the district courts possess broad "discretion" to determine whether the requisite showing has been made to penetrate the conditional immunity afforded by Rule 26(b)(3). See, e.g., In re Int'l Sys. & Controls Corp. Sec. Litig., 693 F.2d 1235, 1240 (5th Cir.1982). In that case the appellate court outlined the factors the district judge should weigh in deciding the issue. Is the court of appeals suggesting that the decision as to whether the factors were present or absent is for the district court alone? If not, what is meant?

LANGDON v. CHAMPION

Supreme Court of Alaska, 1988.
752 P.2d 999.

BURKE, JUSTICE.

In this appeal, petitioners Joanne and Ronald Langdon (Langdon) ask us to reverse an order of the superior court denying their motion to compel production of respondent Champion's insurance adjustors' investigative reports and files (files). Most, if not all, of the materials sought were compiled prior to commencement of suit and involvement of an attorney for Champion. The question we must resolve, therefore, is whether information in an insurance adjustor's files, prepared or obtained prior to any active participation of counsel, is protected from discovery by either the attorney-client privilege or the work product doctrine.

We conclude that statements made by an insured to an insurer are not protected by the attorney-client privilege unless it can be shown that the insurer, in receiving such communications, was acting at the express direction of counsel for the insured. Similarly, we conclude that materials contained in an insurer's files shall be presumed to have been compiled in the ordinary course of business, and, thus, outside the scope of the work product doctrine, absent a showing that the materials were prepared at the request or under the supervision of the insured's attorney.

* * *

The action below was a personal injury suit filed by Langdon against Champion on July 9, 1986. The facts material to the issue presented here are not in dispute.

The alleged tort occurred on November 26, 1984. Champion's insurance company, State Farm, and its adjustor, Mr. Ron Lee, became aware of Langdon's claims as early as September 9, 1985. On September 11, 1985, Champion gave a recorded statement to his insurance adjustor. This statement was transcribed on August 12, 1986. Actual correspondence between Langdon's attorney and Mr. Lee commenced on October 23, 1985, and continued until Langdon filed her complaint. The case was assigned to defense counsel by letter dated July 16, 1986.

On July 21, 1986, Langdon made a Request for Production of any recorded or written statements by Champion, investigative reports, including those of the insurance adjustor, and the complete insurance adjustor's file. Champion objected to production based upon the attorney-client privilege and the work product doctrine. Langdon then filed a Motion to Compel Production which [the] superior court judge denied without comment, citing Civil Rule 26(b)(3). We granted Langdon's petition for review of this order.

* * *

A shrinking majority of states prohibit discovery of statements made by an insured to his insurer. Most of these courts base their decision on provisions in the insurance policy which require the insurer to defend the insured and the insured to cooperate in the investigation. See, e.g., Gene Compton's Corp. v. Superior Court, 205 Cal.App.2d 365, 23 Cal.Rptr. 250, 252–56 (1962); Grand Union Co. v. Patrick, 247 So.2d 474, 475 (Fla.App.1971); People v. Ryan, 30 Ill.2d 456, 197 N.E.2d 15, 17–18 (1964) . . ..

These courts reason that because the insured has delegated the conduct of the defense to the insurance company, "the insured may properly assume that the communication is made to the insurer as an agent for the dominant purpose of transmitting it to an attorney for the protection of the interests of the insured." *Ryan,* 197 N.E.2d at 17. These courts are also concerned that communication between the insured and the insurer would be inhibited or that the insured would be faced with the dilemma of either refusing to cooperate with his insurer in violation of his policy or face possible civil or criminal exposure if the communication was disclosed. . . .

A substantial and growing minority of state courts, on the other hand, have concluded that statements made to an insurer by the insured are generally not protected by the attorney-client privilege. . . .

Courts adopting this view reason that communications between insured and insurer are not in the same class as communications between client and attorney, because the insurer may use its information for purposes inimical to the interests of the insured. . . . [*Butler,* 544 P.2d at 207; *DiCenzo,* 723 P.2d at 177;] *Jacobi,* 127 N.W.2d at 76. In the words of the Wisconsin Supreme Court:

When the insured makes . . . a statement he is ordinarily fulfilling a condition of his policy, requiring him to notify the insurer of the occurrence and circumstances of the accident and to cooperate with the insurer. If the statement be false, the insurer may use it against the insured as foundation for a claim of non-cooperation. If the statement discloses facts giving rise to some other defense against the insurer's liability under the policy, the insurer is doubtless free to make use of those facts.

We find the growing minority and federal rule most persuasive. In our opinion, the cases according protection to statements between insurers and insureds have extended the attorney-client privilege into areas in which it was never intended to apply. Moreover, the minority rule is more in line with our policy favoring liberal discovery . . .

We therefore hold that the attorney-client privilege does not extend to statements made by an insured to his insurer, except in those cases where it can be shown that the adjustor received the communication at the express direction of counsel for the insured. Only in the latter instance do we think it can fairly be said that the adjustor is acting as "one employed to assist the lawyer in the rendition of professional legal services," thus making him a "representative of the lawyer" within the meaning of Evidence Rule 503(a)(4).

In the case at bar, the statement Langdon seeks to discover was made nearly a year before the involvement of Champion's attorney. When Champion's insurance adjustor took this statement, he was not acting at the direction of Champion's attorney. Accordingly, Champion's statement is not protected by the attorney-client privilege.

* * *

In order for materials to fall within the ambit of Civil Rule 26(b)(3) and, thus, qualify for "work product" protection, three requirements must be met. The material involved must be (1) a document or other tangible thing, (2) prepared in anticipation of litigation or for trial, and (3) prepared by or for the opposing party's attorney or representative. Alaska R.Civ.P. 26(b)(3); Wright & Miller § 2024, at 196–97. See also 4 J. Moore, J. Lucas & G. Grotheer, Moore's Federal Practice ¶ 26.64[1]–.64[4], at 26–348 to 26–389. If these requirements are met, the party seeking discovery must then show substantial need and undue hardship before he will be entitled to such materials. Alaska R.Civ.P. 26(b)(3).

We have not had occasion in the past to formulate rules or guidelines for determining when materials were prepared in "anticipation of litigation" and, thus, entitled to "work product" protection. In other jurisdictions, it seems generally accepted that materials prepared in the "ordinary course of business" are not prepared in anticipation of litigation and, thus, do not fall within the work product rule. E.g., Wright & Miller § 2024, at 197–99. Beyond this, there is little agreement. Indeed, the cases are in considerable confusion, leading one commentator to observe:

> Courts have attempted to explain exactly what anticipation of litigation means, but such efforts have not helped to resolve the . . . issue. For example, some courts indicate that a party . . . anticipates litigation where there is a "substantial probability" of "imminent" litigation or when there is a "prospect" of litigation. Another requirement is that there be "some possibility" of litigation; however, a "mere possibility" of litigation is not enough. Other courts have stated that there must be an "eye" towards litigation or that litigation need only be a reasonable "contingency." These methods for redefining the word anticipation do little more than say that litigation is anticipated when litigation is anticipated.

Note, Work Product Discovery: A Multifactor Approach to the Anticipation of Litigation Requirement in Federal Rule of Civil Procedure 26(b)(3), 66 Iowa L.Rev. 1277, 1277–78 (1981) (footnotes omitted). Accord In re Grand Jury Investigation, 599 F.2d 1224, 1229 (3d Cir. 1979); Brown v. Superior Court, 137 Ariz. 327, 670 P.2d 725, 732–33 (1983); Clermont, Surveying Work Product, 68 Cornell L.Rev. 755, 755–56 (1982–83).

Out of this quagmire two general positions have emerged. The majority of courts dealing with the problem have taken the position that litigation is not "anticipated" until the expectation of litigation is such that an attorney has become involved in the dispute and has prepared the documents himself or has requested their preparation. . . . Under this rule, unless the insurer's investigation has been performed at the request or under the direction of an attorney, the materials resulting from the investigation are "*conclusively presumed* to have been made in the ordinary course of business and not in anticipation of litigation." Henry Enterprises [v. Smith, 225 Kan. 615, 592 P.2d 915, 920 (1979)]. (emphasis added).

A second position, taken by a minority of courts, is that virtually all insurance carrier investigations are made in anticipation of litigation and, thus, an insurer's files fall within the ambit of Civil Rule 26(b)(3). . . . According to these courts, all statements and information secured by an insurer, after an occurrence which might give rise to a claim against it or its insured, are protected from discovery unless "substantial need" and "undue hardship" can be shown. . . .

The minority rule, we believe, is flawed because it presumes too much. Simply because an event has occurred which may require an insurer to provide payments under its contract with an insured does not automatically transform an insurer's activities into preparation for litigation. . . ..

. . . [W]e hold that materials contained in an insurer's files shall be conclusively presumed to have been compiled in the ordinary course of business, absent a showing that they were prepared at the request or under the supervision of the insured's attorney. Prior to such attorney involvement, materials held by insurers are subject to discovery without regard to any work product restrictions.

Turning to the facts in the case at bar, it would appear that all of the materials requested in this case were prepared prior to any involvement of counsel. However, the court below made no specific finding on the issue, and we cannot say with complete certainty that there are no documents which might qualify for work product protection under the standard we announce today. Accordingly, we REVERSE the trial court's order denying Langdon's motion to compel and REMAND with instructions that the court order production of all materials not prepared at the request or under the supervision of an attorney for Champion.

———

NOTE

Is it an ethical practice for counsel to an insurance company to direct that all investigation materials be prepared under counsel's supervision? Why?

———

SECTION 6. PARTIES' AND WITNESS' OWN STATEMENTS

McDOUGALL v. DUNN
United States Court of Appeals, 4th Circuit, 1972.
468 F.2d 468.

[While a passenger in a car driven by defendant, the plaintiff suffered serious brain injuries, resulting in amnesia. Plaintiff served interrogatories and requests for admissions upon the defendant. Answers to the interrogatories were made by defendant's counsel, defendant being at the time in a distant state.

[Defendant virtually conceded negligence in the answers and admissions and made plain that his defense would be based on plaintiff's contributory negligence. The defense was bottomed on the allegation that the plaintiff had joined with the defendant and another in consuming two bottles of vodka in a short space of time not long before the accident. Plaintiff moved to require the defendant to produce statements the latter and the other passenger had made to the defendant's insurance company after the accident. After trial and a verdict for the defendant, the plaintiff appealed, contending primarily that the district court erred in upholding the defendant's answers to interrogatories as given under oath by defense counsel rather than by the defendant personally.

[The Court of Appeals said it would be reluctant to reverse on that "somewhat technical point alone", but found a more serious error in the denial of production of the statements to defendant's insurer.]

RUSSELL, CIRCUIT JUDGE. The theory on which the defendant resisted the motion to produce was that the statements given represented materials "prepared in anticipation of litigation or for trial" and were discoverable only upon a showing of good cause as defined in Rule 26(b) (3), incorporated in the 1970 Rules Amendments. This contention was accepted by the District Court. We are not at all convinced that the statements demanded met the definition of materials embraced within Section (b)(3) of Rule 26. The statements sought for production were secured by a claim adjuster of the insurance carrier of the defendant more than two and one half years before any claim was made or suit begun or before the plaintiff had retained counsel. The statements were secured by the claim adjuster in the regular course of his duties as an employee of the insurance company and presumably were incorporated in the files of the company. . . .

It seems manifest that . . . the plaintiff was entitled to the discovery of the defendant's and the third occupant's statements, taken by the defendant's insurance carrier. The plaintiff himself was helpless to reconstruct the events leading up to the accident or to secure contemporaneous statements from the other occupants of the car. It was almost a year before he was discharged from the hospital and, even then, he was handicapped with a loss of memory. More than two years passed before he engaged counsel and brought suit. Thus, neither he nor his counsel had any opportunity to interview immediately after the accident either the defendant or the third occupant of the car. For a "fresh and contemporaneous" account of the vital facts on defendant's plea of contributory negligence, which incidentally was the crucial issue in the case, the plaintiff was dependent on the statements procured by the defendant's insurance carrier. By denial of access to such statements, which were presumably made available to defendant's counsel after suit was filed, and which were used by such counsel in preparing answers to interrogatories and in preparing for trial, the plaintiff and his counsel were seriously prejudiced in the trial, of the cause and "sustained a disadvantage affecting the fundamental issues of liability". This prejudice was magnified by the very sketchiness of the defendant's answers to interrogatories, a sketchiness which . . . the Trial Court adverted to during the hearing on the motion for a new trial. . . .

The plaintiff, it is true, did not appeal from the order denying discovery but contented himself with raising the sufficiency and validity of defendant's answers to interrogatories. Appellate courts are not, though, powerless to correct errors in the trial, even if not raised by appeal, "where injustice might otherwise result . . . .. Rules of practice and procedure are devised to promote the ends of justice, not to defeat them. A rigid and undeviating judicially declared practice under which courts of review would invariably and under all circumstances decline to consider all questions which had not previously been specifically urged would be out of harmony with this policy. Orderly rules of procedure do not require sacrifice of the rules of fundamental justice." Washington Gas Light Co. v. Virginia Electric & Pow. Co., 438 F.2d 248, 250–251 (4th Cir.1971) . . ..

RIGHT TO SEE ONE'S OWN STATEMENT

Rule 26(b)(3) accords any potential witness, whether a party or not, the right to obtain a copy of a statement previously made by that person concerning the action or its subject matter. This affords an alternative avenue of discovery to obtain the kind of witness' statements that qualify as trial preparation materials or work product, the main concern of the *Hickman-Taylor* decision. Through this avenue a party may obtain a copy of a previously-given witness' statement if the witness is cooperative enough to request it from the one to whom it was given.

Before copies of witness' statements became obtainable under the 1970 amendment, the argument for withholding them was that a "certain amount of surprise is often the catalyst which precipitates the truth." Margeson v. Boston & Maine Railroad, 16 F.R.D. 200, 201 (D.Mass.1954). The amendment allows for both the catalytic force of surprise and the desire to uncover evidence. Seemingly, the court may order a party or witness to give his deposition before he sees his earlier statement. Cf. Parla v. Matson Navigation Co., 28 F.R.D. 348 (S.D.N.Y. 1961); Smith v. Central Linen Service Co., 39 F.R.D. 15 (D.Md.1966); McCoy v. General Motors Corp., 33 F.R.D. 354 (W.D.Pa.1963).

SECTION 7. EXPERTS

AGER v. JANE C. STORMONT HOSPITAL & TRAINING SCHOOL FOR NURSES, ETC.

United States Court of Appeals, Tenth Circuit, 1980.
622 F.2d 496.

BARRETT, CIRCUIT JUDGE.

Lynn R. Johnson, counsel for plaintiff Emily Ager, appeals from an order of the District Court adjudging him guilty of civil contempt. Jurisdiction vests by reason of 28 U.S.C.A. § 1826(b).

Emily was born April 4, 1955, at Stormont-Vail Hospital in Topeka, Kansas. During the second stage of labor, Emily's mother suffered a massive rupture of the uterine wall. The ensuing loss of blood led to Mrs. Ager's death. Premature separation of the placenta from the uterine wall also occurred, resulting in fetal asphyxia. Following Emily's delivery, it was discovered that she evidenced signs of severe neurological dysfunction. Today, she is mentally impaired and a permanently disabled quadraplegic with essentially no control over her body functions.

In March, 1977, Emily's father filed, on her behalf, a complaint for the damages sustained at her birth . . . caused by the negligence and carelessness of the defendants [Stormont-Vail Hospital and Dr. Dan L. Tappen, the attending physician] . . . After joining the issues, Dr. Tappen propounded a series of interrogatories to the plaintiff. The specific interrogatories at issue here are:

1. Have you contacted any person or persons, whether they are going to testify or not, in regard to the care and treatment rendered by Dr. Dan Tappen involved herein?

2. If the answer to the question immediately above is in the affirmative, please set forth the name of said person or persons and their present residential and/or business address.

3. If the answer to question # 1 is in the affirmative, do you have any statements or written reports from said person or persons?

[R., Vol. I, p. 1].

    . . . the Magistrate ordered the plaintiff to answer the interrogatories:

Interrogatories No. 1, 2 and 3 should be answered with the single exception, if the plaintiff has contacted an expert who was informally consulted in preparation for trial, but who was never retained or specifically employed and will not be called as a witness, it will not be necessary for the plaintiff to supply the name and address of such person or persons or to set forth any statement or report which such person or persons may have made.

[R., Vol. I, p. 15].

Plaintiff's counsel answered the interrogatories in part, but failed to provide any information concerning consultative experts not expected to testify at trial. Plaintiff apparently based the refusal to answer on her contention that an expert who advises a party that his opinion will not aid the party in the trial of the case falls within the definition of experts informally consulted but not retained or specially employed. At defendant's suggestion, the Magistrate ordered plaintiff to provide further answers to the interrogatories, specifically defining the terms retained or specially employed:

In the generally accepted meaning of the term in everyday usage, "retained" or "specially employed" ordinarily implies some consideration, a payment or reward of some kind, as consideration for being "retained" or "specially employed." It follows, therefore, that if a medical expert is consulted for the purpose of rendering advice or opinion on a hospital chart, or a physician's medical records pertaining to a case, and is paid or makes a charge for such service, he has been "retained" or "specially employed" within the meaning of the Rule. If [such an] expert is not to be called as a witness, he would be subject to the provisions of Rule 26(b)(4)(B) and, as shown by *Baki,* supra, [Baki v. B.F. Diamond Construction Co., 71 F.R.D. 179 (D.Md.1976)] there would be routine access to the names and addresses of such experts; but if they are not to be called as witnesses, facts known or opinions held by such experts would be subject to the requirements of Rule 26(b)(4)(B). However, if the consultation with the medical expert was strictly on an informal basis and such expert was not "retained" or "specially employed," the identity of such expert need not be disclosed.

[R., Vol. I, pp. 24–25].

Rather than complying with the Magistrate's order, Ager sought review by the District Court pursuant to 28 U.S.C.A. § 636(b)(1)(A). The District Court denied plaintiff's motion for review as untimely. On reconsideration, the Court affirmed the Magistrate's order. . . .

Plaintiff's counsel filed a formal response to the Court's order and refused to comply. The Court thereafter entered a civil contempt order against Johnson.[1] Johnson was committed to the custody of the United

---

1. At the contempt hearing, Johnson agreed to accept any sanctions on behalf of

plaintiff for failing to disclose the identities

States Marshal until his compliance with the Court's order. Execution of the custody order was stayed pending appeal, after Johnson posted a recognizance bond. The Court specifically found that the appeal was not frivolous or taken for purposes of delay.

The issues on appeal are whether: (1) the District Court erred in adjudging Johnson guilty of civil contempt; and (2) a party may routinely discover the names of retained or specially employed consultative non-witness experts, pursuant to Fed.Rules Civ.Proc., rule 26(b)(4) (B), 28 U.S.C.A., absent a showing of exceptional circumstances justifying disclosure.

The Contempt Power

When a recalcitrant witness fails to obey the duly issued orders of a court, he may be cited for contempt, either criminal, civil or both. Whether the adjudication of contempt "survives the avoidance of [the] underlying order depends on the nature of the contempt decree. If the contempt is criminal it stands; if it is civil it falls." [Citations omitted.]

The primary purpose of a criminal contempt is to punish defiance of a court's judicial authority. Accordingly, the normal beneficiaries of such an order are the courts and the public interest. Norman Bridge Drug Co. v. Banner, 529 F.2d 822 (5th Cir.1976). On the other hand, civil contempt is characterized by the court's desire "to *compel* obedience of the court order or to compensate the litigant for injuries sustained from the disobedience." Id. at p. 827. The remedial aspects outweigh the punitive considerations. Thus, the primary beneficiaries of such an order are the individual litigants. . . .

[The court decided that the contempt order would be valid if the order to compel discovery upon which it was based was itself valid.]

Validity of the Underlying Order

*   *   *

Fed.Rules Civ.Proc., rule 26, 28 U.S.C.A., governs the scope of discovery concerning experts or consultants. Subdivision (b)(4) separates these experts into four categories, applying different discovery limitations to each. . . .

A.   Discovery of Experts Informally Consulted, But Not Retained or Specially Employed

No provision in Fed.Rules Civ.Proc., rule 26(b)(4), 28 U.S.C.A., expressly deals with non-witness experts who are informally consulted by a party in preparation for trial, but not retained or specially employed in anticipation of litigation. The advisory committee notes to the rule indicate, however, that subdivision (b)(4)(B) "precludes discovery against experts who [are] informally consulted in preparation for

of plaintiff's consultative witnesses. [Some
footnotes omitted. Eds.]

trial, but not retained or specially employed." We agree with the District Court that this preclusion not only encompasses information and opinions developed in anticipation of litigation, but also insulates discovery of the identity and other collateral information concerning experts consulted informally. [Citations omitted.]

. . . Ager urges that "an expert 'would be considered informally consulted if, for any reason, the consulting party did not consider the expert of any assistance', and that '[a] consulting party may consider the expert of no assistance because of his insufficient credentials, his unattractive demeanor, or his excessive fees.'" . . . This view is, of course, at odds with the Trial Court's ruling that:

> The commonly accepted meaning of the term "informally consulted" necessarily implies a consultation without formality. If one makes an appointment with a medical expert to discuss a case or examine records and give advice or opinion for which a charge is made and the charge is paid or promised—what is informal about such consultation? On the other hand, an attorney meets a doctor friend at a social occasion or on the golf course and a discussion occurs concerning the case—no charge is made or contemplated—no written report rendered—such could clearly be an "informal consultation."

[R., Vol. I, p. 25]. . . .

We decline to embrace either approach in its entirety. In our view, the status of each expert must be determined on an *ad hoc* basis. Several factors should be considered: (1) the manner in which the consultation was initiated; (2) the nature, type and extent of information or material provided to, or determined by, the expert in connection with his review; (3) the duration and intensity of the consultative relationship; and, (4) the terms of the consultation, if any (e.g. payment, confidentiality of test data or opinions, etc.). Of course, additional factors bearing on this determination may be examined if relevant.

Thus, while we recognize that an expert witness' lack of qualifications, unattractive demeanor, excessive fees, or adverse opinions may result in a party's decision not to use the expert at trial, nonetheless, there are situations where a witness is retained or specifically employed in anticipation of litigation prior to the discovery of such undesirable information or characteristics. On the other hand, a telephonic inquiry to an expert's office in which only general information is provided may result in informal consultation, even if a fee is charged, provided there is no follow-up consultation.

The determination of the status of the expert rests, in the first instance, with the party resisting discovery. Should the expert be considered informally consulted, that categorization should be provided in response. The propounding party should then be provided the opportunity of requesting a determination of the expert's status based on an *in camera* review by the court. Inasmuch as the District Court failed to express its views on this question, we deem it appropriate to remand rather than attempt to deal with the merits of this issue on appeal. . . . If the expert is considered to have been only informally consulted in anticipation of litigation, discovery is barred.

B. Discovery of the Identities of Experts Retained or Specially Employed

Subdivision (b)(4)(B) of rule 26 specifically deals with non-witness experts who have been retained or specially employed by a party in anticipation of litigation. The text of that subdivision provides that "facts or opinions" of non-witness experts retained or specially employed may only be discovered upon a showing of "exceptional circumstances under which it is impracticable for the party seeking discovery to obtain facts or opinions on the same subject by other means." Inasmuch as discovery of the identities of these experts, absent a showing of exceptional circumstances, was not expressly precluded by the text of subdivision (b)(4)(B), the District Court found the general provisions of rule 26(b)(1) controlling. . . .

[The court noted the split of authority regarding the need to show exceptional circumstances before names of non-testifying retained experts may be discovered.]

The advisory committee notes indicate that the structure of rule 26 was largely developed around the doctrine of unfairness—designed to prevent a party from building his own case by means of his opponent's financial resources, superior diligence and more aggressive preparation. Dr. Tappen contends that "[d]iscoverability of the identity of an expert retained or specially employed by the other party but who is not to be called to testify hardly gives the discovering party a material advantage or benefit at the expense of the opposing party's preparation. Once those identities are disclosed, the discovering party is left to his own diligence and resourcefulness in contacting such experts and seeking to enlist whatever assistance they may be both able and willing to offer." Brief of appellee at pp. 12–13. The drafters of rule 26 did not contemplate such a result:

> Subdivision (b)(4)(B) is concerned only with experts retained or specially consulted in relation to trial preparation. Thus the subdivision precludes discovery against experts who were informally consulted in preparation for trial, but not retained or specially employed. As an ancillary procedure, a party may *on a proper showing* require the other party to *name* experts retained or specially employed, but not those informally consulted. [Emphasis supplied].

We hold that the "proper showing" required to compel discovery of a non-witness expert retained or specially employed in anticipation of litigation corresponds to a showing of "exceptional circumstances under which it is impracticable for the party seeking discovery to obtain facts or opinions on the same subject by other means." Fed.Rules Civ.Proc., rule 26(b)(4)(B), 28 U.S.C.A.

There are several policy considerations supporting our view. Contrary to Dr. Tappen's view, once the identities of retained or specially employed experts are disclosed, the protective provisions of the rule concerning facts known or opinions held by such experts are subverted. The expert may be contacted or his records obtained and information normally non-discoverable, under rule 26(b)(4)(B), revealed. Similarly, although perhaps rarer, the opponent may attempt to compel an expert retained or specially employed by an adverse party in anticipation of trial, but whom the adverse party does not intend to call, to testify at trial. . . . The possibility also exists, although we do not suggest it would occur in this case, or that it would be proper, that a party may call his opponent to the stand and ask if certain experts were retained in anticipation of trial, but not called as a witness, thereby leaving with the jury an inference that the retaining party is attempting to suppress adverse facts or opinions. Finally, we agree with Ager's view that "[d]isclosure of the identities of [medical] consultative experts would inevitably lessen the number of candid opinions available as well as the number of consultants willing to even discuss a potential medical malpractice claim with counsel . . .".

In sum, we hold that the identity, and other collateral information concerning an expert who is retained or specially employed in anticipation of litigation, but not expected to be called as a witness at trial, is not discoverable except as "provided in Rule 35(b) or upon a showing of exceptional circumstances under which it is impracticable for the party seeking discovery to obtain facts or opinions on the same subject by other means." . . .

The order of the District Court adjudging Lynn R. Johnson guilty of civil contempt is vacated. The cause is remanded. On remand, the status of the non-witness experts against whom discovery is sought should be undertaken as a two-step process. First, was the expert informally consulted in anticipation of litigation but not retained or specially employed? If so, no discovery may be had as to the identity or opinions of the expert. Second, if the expert *was not* informally consulted, but rather retained or specially employed in anticipation of litigation, but not expected to testify at trial, do exceptional circumstances exist justifying disclosure of the expert's identity, opinions or other collateral information?

Vacated and remanded.

NOTES

(1) In the principal case is the court on sound ground in requiring the discovering party to show "exceptional circumstances" before learning the identity of a retained non-witness expert? Is there ever a connection between knowing the name of a retained expert and being able to show exceptional circumstances? See Day, Expert Discovery in the Eighth Circuit: An Empirical Study, 122 F.R.D. 35 (1988).

(2) In Granger v. Wisner, 134 Ariz. 377, 656 P.2d 1238 (1982), the court permitted experts to testify for one side even though they originally had been retained by the adverse party, on condition that the experts not mention the earlier retainer. Other courts have barred unconditionally the use as trial witnesses of experts formerly retained by the opposing party. Durflinger v. Artiles, 727 F.2d 888 (10th Cir.1984); Healy v. Counts, 100 F.R.D. 493 (D.Colo. 1984).

(3) On the basis of his comprehensive doctrinal and empirical research on discovery of experts, one scholar proposed to amend Rule 26(b)(4)(B) as follows:

"(B) A party may discover facts, data, opinions and grounds thereof held by an expert who has been retained, specially employed, or consulted either formally or informally, by another party or by, or for, the other party's representative and who is not expected to be called as a witness at trial, upon a showing of exceptional circumstances under which it is impracticable for the party seeking discovery to obtain facts, data, or opinions on the same subject by other means."

Graham, "Discovery of Experts Under Rule 26(b)(4) of the Federal Rules of Civil Procedure: Part Two, An Empirical Study and a Proposal", 1977 U.Ill.L.F. 169, 200. The proposal is criticized in Note, Treating Experts Like Ordinary Witnesses: Recent Trends in Discovery of Testifying Experts Under Federal Rule of Civil Procedure 26(b)(4), 66 Wash.U.L.Q. 787, 804 (1988), on the ground that "unlimited discovery is unnecessary to achieve" the goals of allowing effective cross-examination, narrowing the triable issues and preventing surprise.

SECTION 8. PARTICULAR DEVICES: RULES 35 AND 36

SCHLAGENHAUF v. HOLDER

Supreme Court of the United States, 1964.
379 U.S. 104, 85 S.Ct. 234, 13 L.Ed.2d 152.

MR. JUSTICE GOLDBERG delivered the opinion of the Court.

This case involves the validity and construction of Rule 35(a) of the Federal Rules of Civil Procedure * as applied to the examination of a defendant in a negligence action. . . .

I.

An action based on diversity of citizenship was brought in the District Court seeking damages arising from personal injuries suffered by passengers of a bus which collided with the rear of a tractor-trailer. The named defendants were The Greyhound Corporation, owner of the bus; petitioner, Robert L. Schlagenhauf, the bus driver; Contract Carriers, Inc., owner of the tractor; Joseph L. McCorkhill, driver of the

---

* The 1970 amendments modify the provisions of Rule 35(a) to make clear that a parent or guardian suing to recover damages for injury to a minor may be ordered to produce the minor for examination, but make no change in the decision of the principal case. [Eds.]

tractor; and National Lead Company, owner of the trailer. Answers were filed by each of the defendants denying negligence.

Greyhound then cross-claimed against Contract Carriers and National Lead for damage to Greyhound's bus, alleging that the collision was due solely to their negligence in that the tractor-trailer was driven at an unreasonably low speed, had not remained in its lane, and was not equipped with proper rear lights. Contract Carriers denied negligence and asserted that Schlagenhauf was "not mentally or physically capable" of driving a bus at the time of the accident.

Contract Carriers and National Lead then petitioned the District Court for an order directing petitioner Schlagenhauf to submit to both mental and physical examinations by one specialist in each of the following fields:

(1) Internal medicine;

(2) Ophthalmology;

(3) Neurology; and

(4) Psychiatry.

For the purpose of offering a choice to the District Court of one specialist in each field, the petition recommended two specialists in internal medicine, ophthalmology, and psychiatry, respectively, and three specialists in neurology—a total of nine physicians. The petition alleged that the mental and physical condition of Schlagenhauf was "in controversy" as it had been raised by Contract Carriers' answer to Greyhound's cross-claim. This was supported by a brief of legal authorities and an affidavit of Contract Carriers' attorney stating that Schlagenhauf had seen red lights 10 to 15 seconds before the accident, that another witness had seen the rear lights of the trailer from a distance of three-quarters to one-half mile, and that Schlagenhauf had been involved in a prior accident.

* * *

The District Court, on the basis of the petition filed by Contract Carriers, and without any hearing, ordered Schlagenhauf to submit to nine examinations—one by each of the recommended specialists—despite the fact that the petition clearly requested a total of only four examinations.[1]

Petitioner applied for a writ of mandamus in the Court of Appeals against the respondent, the District Court Judge, seeking to have set aside the order requiring his mental and physical examinations. The Court of Appeals denied mandamus, one judge dissenting, 321 F.2d 43.

1. After the Court of Appeals denied mandamus, the order was corrected by the District Court to reduce the number of examinations to the four requested. We agree with respondent that the issue of that error has become moot. However, the fact that the District Court ordered nine examinations is not irrelevant, together with all the other circumstances, in the consideration of whether the District Court gave to the petition for mental and physical examinations that discriminating application, which Rule 35 requires. . . . [Some footnotes omitted; others renumbered. Eds.]

We granted certiorari to review undecided questions concerning the validity and construction of Rule 35.   375 U.S. 983, 84 S.Ct. 516, 11 L.Ed.2d 471.

Rule 35 on its face applies to all "parties," which under any normal reading would include a defendant.   Petitioner contends, however, that the application of the Rule to a defendant would be an unconstitutional invasion of his privacy, or, at the least, be a modification of substantive rights existing prior to the adoption of the Federal Rules of Civil Procedure and thus beyond the congressional mandate of the Rules Enabling Act.[2]

These same contentions were raised in Sibbach v. Wilson & Co., 312 U.S. 1, 61 S.Ct. 422, 85 L.Ed. 479, by a plaintiff in a negligence action who asserted a physical injury as a basis for recovery.   The Court, by a closely divided vote, sustained the Rule as there applied.   Both the majority and dissenting opinions, however, agreed that Rule 35 could not be assailed on constitutional grounds.   Id., at 11–12, 17, 61 S.Ct., at 425–426, 428.   The division in the Court was on the issue of whether the Rule was procedural or a modification of substantive rights.   The majority held that the Rule was a regulation of procedure and thus within the scope of the Enabling Act—the dissenters deemed it substantive.   Petitioner does not challenge the holding in *Sibbach* as applied to plaintiffs.   He contends, however, that it should not be extended to defendants.   We can see no basis under the *Sibbach* holding for such a distinction.   Discovery "is not a one-way proposition."   Hickman v. Taylor, 329 U.S. 495, 507, 67 S.Ct. 385, 391, 91 L.Ed. 451.   Issues cannot be resolved by a doctrine of favoring one class of litigants over another.

We recognize that, insofar as reported cases show, this type of discovery in federal courts has been applied solely to plaintiffs, and that some early state cases seem to have proceeded on a theory that a plaintiff who seeks redress for injuries in a court of law thereby "waives" his right to claim the inviolability of his person.

However, it is clear that *Sibbach* was not decided on any "waiver" theory.   As Mr. Justice Roberts, for the majority stated, one of the rights of a person "is the right not to be injured in one's person by another's negligence, to redress infraction of which the present action was brought."   312 U.S., at 13, 61 S.Ct., at 426.   For the dissenters, Mr. Justice Frankfurter pointed out that "[o]f course the Rule is compulsive in that the doors of the federal courts otherwise open may be shut to litigants who do not submit to such a physical examination."   Id., at 18, 61 S.Ct., at 428.

These statements demonstrate the invalidity of any waiver theory. The chain of events leading to an ultimate determination on the merits begins with the injury of the plaintiff, an involuntary act on his part. Seeking court redress is just one step in this chain.   If the plaintiff is prevented or deterred from this redress, the loss is thereby forced on

2.   28 U.S.C.A. § 2072 (1958 ed.), which   enlarge or modify any substantive right. provides that the Rules "shall not abridge,   . . . "

him to the same extent as if the defendant were prevented or deterred from defending against the action.

Moreover, the rationalization of *Sibbach* on a waiver theory would mean that a plaintiff has waived a right by exercising his right of access to the federal courts. Such a result might create constitutional problems. Also, if a waiver theory is espoused, problems would arise as to a plaintiff who originally brought his action in a state court (where there was no equivalent of Rule 35) and then has the case removed by the defendant to federal court.

We hold that Rule 35, as applied to either plaintiffs or defendants to an action, is free of constitutional difficulty and is within the scope of the Enabling Act. We therefore agree with the Court of Appeals that the District Court had power to apply Rule 35 to a party defendant in an appropriate case.

IV.

There remains the issue of the construction of Rule 35. We enter upon determination of this construction with the basic premise "that the deposition-discovery rules are to be accorded a broad and liberal treatment," Hickman v. Taylor, supra, at 507, 67 S.Ct., at 392, to effectuate their purpose that "civil trials in the federal courts no longer need be carried on in the dark." Id., at 501.

. . . There is no doubt that Schlagenhauf was a "party" to this "action" by virtue of the original complaint. Therefore, Rule 35 permitted examination of him (a party defendant) upon petition of Contract Carriers and National Lead (codefendants), provided, of course, that the other requirements of the Rule were met. Insistence that the movant have filed a pleading against the person to be examined would have the undesirable result of an unnecessary proliferation of cross-claims and counterclaims and would not be in keeping with the aims of a liberal, nontechnical application of the Federal Rules. See Hickman v. Taylor, supra, at 500–501, 67 S.Ct., at 388–389.

* * *

Petitioner next contends that his mental or physical condition was not "in controversy" and "good cause" was not shown for the examinations, both as required by the express terms of Rule 35.

It is notable, however, that in none of the other discovery provisions is there a restriction that the matter be "in controversy," and only in Rule 34 is there Rule 35's requirement that the movant affirmatively demonstrate "good cause."

This additional requirement of "good cause" was reviewed by Chief Judge Sobeloff in Guilford National Bank v. Southern R. Co., 297 F.2d 921, 924 (C.A. 4th Cir.), in the following words:

"Subject to . . . [the restrictions of Rules 26(b) and 30(b) and (d)], a party may take depositions and serve interrogatories without prior sanction of the court or even its knowledge of what the party is doing. Only if a deponent refuses to answer in the belief that the question is irrelevant, can the moving party request under Rule 37 a court order requiring an answer.

"Significantly, this freedom of action, afforded a party who resorts to depositions and interrogatories, is not granted to one proceeding under Rules 34 and 35. Instead, the court must decide as an initial matter, and in every case, whether the motion requesting production of documents or the making of a physical or mental examination adequately demonstrates good cause. The specific requirement of good cause would be meaningless if good cause could be sufficiently established by merely showing that the desired materials are relevant, for the relevancy standard has already been imposed by Rule 26(b). Thus, by adding the words '. . . good cause . . .,' the Rules indicate that there must be greater showing of need under Rules 34 and 35 than under the other discovery rules."

The courts of appeals in other cases have also recognized that Rule 34's good-cause requirement is not a mere formality, but is a plainly expressed limitation on the use of that Rule. This is obviously true as to the "in controversy" and "good cause" requirements of Rule 35. They are not met by mere conclusory allegations of the pleadings—nor by mere relevance to the case—but require an affirmative showing by the movant that each condition as to which the examination is sought is really and genuinely in controversy and that good cause exists for ordering each particular examination. Obviously, what may be good cause for one type of examination may not be so for another. The ability of the movant to obtain the desired information by other means is also relevant.

Rule 35, therefore, requires discriminating application by the trial judge, who must decide, as an initial matter in every case, whether the party requesting a mental or physical examination or examinations has adequately demonstrated the existence of the Rule's requirements of "in controversy" and "good cause," which requirements, as the Court of Appeals in this case itself recognized, are necessarily related. 321 F.2d, at 51. This does not, of course, mean that the movant must prove his case on the merits in order to meet the requirements for a mental or physical examination. . . .

Of course, there are situations where the pleadings alone are sufficient to meet these requirements. A plaintiff in a negligence action who asserts mental or physical injury, cf. Sibbach v. Wilson & Co., supra, places that mental or physical injury clearly in controversy and provides the defendant with good cause for an examination to determine the existence and extent of such asserted injury. This is not only true as to a plaintiff, but applies equally to a defendant who asserts his mental or physical condition as a defense to a claim, such as,

for example, where insanity is asserted as a defense to a divorce action.
. . .

Here, however, Schlagenhauf did not assert his mental or physical condition either in support of or in defense of a claim. His condition was sought to be placed in issue by other parties. . . .

This record cannot support even the corrected order which required one examination in each of the four specialties of internal medicine, ophthalmology, neurology, and psychiatry. Nothing in the pleadings or affidavit would afford a basis for a belief that Schlagenhauf was suffering from a mental or neurological illness warranting wide-ranging psychiatric or neurological examinations. Nor is there anything stated justifying the broad internal medicine examination.

The only specific allegation made in support of the four examinations ordered was that the "eyes and vision" of Schlagenhauf were impaired. Considering this in conjunction with the affidavit, we would be hesitant to set aside a visual examination if it had been the only one ordered. However, as the case must be remanded to the District Court because of the other examinations ordered, it would be appropriate for the District Judge to reconsider also this order in light of the guidelines set forth in this opinion.

The Federal Rules of Civil Procedure should be liberally construed, but they should not be expanded by disregarding plainly expressed limitations. The "good cause" and "in controversy" requirements of Rule 35 make it very apparent that sweeping examinations of a party who has not affirmatively put into issue his own mental or physical condition are not to be automatically ordered merely because the person has been involved in an accident—or, as in this case, two accidents—and a general charge of negligence is lodged. Mental and physical examinations are only to be ordered upon a discriminating application by the district judge of the limitations prescribed by the Rule. To hold otherwise would mean that such examinations could be ordered routinely in automobile accident cases.[3] The plain language of Rule 35 precludes such an untoward result.

Accordingly, the judgment of the Court of Appeals is vacated and the case remanded to the District Court to reconsider the examination order in light of the guidelines herein formulated and for further proceedings in conformity with this opinion.

Vacated and remanded.

MR. JUSTICE BLACK, with whom MR. JUSTICE CLARK joins, concurring in part and dissenting in part.

3. From July 1, 1963, through June 30, 1964, almost 10,000 motor vehicle personal injury cases were filed in the federal district courts. Administrative Office of the United States Courts, Annual Report of the Director, C2 (1964). In the Nation at large during 1963, there were approximately 11,500,000 automobile accidents, involving approximately 20,000,000 drivers. National Safety Council, Accident Facts, 40 (1964 ed.).

. . . Unlike the Court, . . . I think this record plainly shows that there *was* a controversy as to Schlagenhauf's mental and physical health and that "good cause" *was* shown for a physical and mental examination of him, unless failure to deny the allegations amounted to an admission that they were true . . .

In a collision case like this one, evidence concerning very bad eyesight or impaired mental or physical health which may affect the ability to drive is obviously of the highest relevance. It is equally obvious, I think, that when a vehicle continues down an open road and smashes into a truck in front of it although the truck is in plain sight and there is ample time and room to avoid collision, the chances are good that the driver has some physical, mental or moral defect. When such a thing happens twice, one is even more likely to ask, "What is the matter with that driver? Is he blind or crazy?" Plainly the allegations of the other parties were relevant and put the question of Schlagenhauf's health and vision "in controversy." The Court nevertheless holds that these charges were not a sufficient basis on which to rest a court-ordered examination of Schlagenhauf. It says with reference to the charges of impaired physical or mental health that the charges are "conclusory." I had not thought there was anything strange about pleadings being "conclusory"—that is their function, at least since modern rules of procedure have attempted to substitute simple pleadings for the complicated and redundant ones which long kept the common-law courts in disrepute. I therefore cannot agree that the charges about Schlagenhauf's health and vision were not sufficient upon which to base an order under Rule 35(a), particularly since he was a party who raised every technical objection to being required to subject himself to an examination but never once denied that his health and vision were bad. In these circumstances the allegations here should be more than enough to show probable cause to justify a court order requiring some kind of physical and mental examination.

While I dissent from the Court's holding that no examination at all was justified by this record, I agree that the order was broader than required. . . .

Mr. Justice Douglas, dissenting in part.

While I join the Court in reversing this judgment, I would, on the remand, deny all relief asked under Rule 35.

I do not suppose there is any licensed driver of a car or a truck who does not suffer from some ailment, whether it be ulcers, bad eyesight, abnormal blood pressure, deafness, liver malfunction, bursitis, rheumatism, or what not. If he or she is turned over to the plaintiff's doctors and psychoanalysts to discover the cause of the mishap, the door will be opened for grave miscarriages of justice. When the defendant's doctors examine plaintiff, they are normally interested only in answering a single question: did plaintiff in fact sustain the specific injuries claimed? But plaintiff's doctors will naturally be inclined to go on a fishing expedition in search of *anything* which will tend to prove that the defendant was unfit to perform the acts which resulted in the plaintiff's injury. And a doctor for a fee can easily discover something wrong with any patient—a condition that in prejudiced medical eyes might have caused the accident. Once defendants are turned over to medical or psychiatric clinics for an analysis of their physical well-being and the condition of their psyche, the effective trial will be held there and not before the jury. There are no lawyers in those clinics to stop the doctor from probing this organ or that one, to halt a further inquiry, to object to a line of questioning. And there is no judge to sit as arbiter. The doctor or the psychiatrist has a holiday in the privacy of his office. The defendant is at the doctor's (or psychiatrist's) mercy; and his report may either overawe or confuse the jury and prevent a fair trial.

. . . A plaintiff, by coming into court and asserting that he has suffered an injury at the hands of the defendant, has thereby put his physical or mental condition "in controversy." Thus it may be only fair to provide that he may not be permitted to recover his judgment unless he permits an inquiry into the true nature of his condition.

A defendant's physical and mental condition is not, however, immediately and directly "in controversy" in a negligence suit. The issue is whether he was negligent. His physical or mental condition may of course be relevant to that issue; and he may be questioned concerning it and various methods of discovery can be used. But I balk at saying those issues are "in controversy" within the meaning of Rule 35 in every negligence suit or that they may be put "in controversy" by the addition of a few words in the complaint . . .

Neither the Court nor Congress up to today has determined that any person whose physical or mental condition is brought into question during some lawsuit must surrender his right to keep his person inviolate. Congress did, according to *Sibbach,* require a plaintiff to choose between his privacy and his purse; but before today it has not been thought that any other "party" had lost his historic immunity. Congress and this Court can authorize such a rule. But a rule suited to purposes of discovery against defendants must be carefully drawn in light of the great potential of blackmail.

     * * *

[HARLAN, J., dissented from the court's conclusion that mandamus was available to review the District Court's order.]

NOTES

(1) Assume a suit arising out of an accident in which defendant's automobile drove into the rear of plaintiff's car traveling in the same direction on a clear summer night. Under the "guidelines" of the principal opinion, should a physical examination of the defendant be ordered if:

> (a) the complaint alleges, and the answer denies, that the accident occurred because defendant was suffering at the time from mental or physical infirmity, or was drunk or in a narcotics-induced state of diminished capacity?

(b) defendant had filed an accident report stating he had "blacked out" and remembers nothing about the evening in question from the time he left work late that afternoon until he awakened in a hospital after the collision?

(c) a police report quotes a passenger in defendant's vehicle for the statement that defendant had drunk "a few beers" about an hour before the crash?

(2) In a personal injury action the issue was whether the plaintiff, who claimed emotional as well as physical injuries, could insist on the presence of her counsel at an examination conducted by defendant's psychiatrist. Held: the trial court did not abuse its discretion in rejecting the plaintiff's request. Edwards v. Superior Court of Santa Clara County, 16 Cal.3d 905, 130 Cal.Rptr. 14, 549 P.2d 846 (1976). In contrast, the same court held in Sharff v. Superior Court, 44 Cal.2d 508, 282 P.2d 896 (1955), that "plaintiff in a personal injury action may not be required to submit to a physical examination by the defendant's doctor without the presence of her attorney."

McSPARRAN v. HANIGAN

United States District Court, Eastern District of Pennsylvania, 1963.
225 F.Supp. 628.

[In an action for wrongful death the plaintiff was served with a request to admit under Rule 36 that defendant McShain occupied or had control of the premises where the fatal accident occurred. Plaintiff made the admission. During trial McShain read the admission to the jury and argued that it insulated McShain from common law liability by admitting he was a "statutory employer" liable only for workmen's compensation benefits. After a verdict for the plaintiff, McShain moved for judgment notwithstanding the verdict, relying upon plaintiff's admission.]

FREEDMAN, DISTRICT JUDGE.

* * *

Rule 36, Federal Rules of Civil Procedure, deals with requests for admission of the genuineness of documents or of the truth of matters of fact set forth in the request. It does not, however, specifically describe the effect of an admission, or its nature. Its language, however, is significant. It is not with admissions of the truth of items of *evidence* that the rule is concerned. It deals with admissions of the truth of matters of *fact*. . . .

Here the decisive issue of fact between plaintiff and McShain was whether McShain occupied or had control of the premises on which the decedent had entered to perform his work and on which the accident occurred. With full knowledge of the significance of the vital request the plaintiff admitted its truth. She evidently came to do this because in the light of what she knew of the circumstances she could not in good faith dispute it. This admission is all the more significant because it was made a week or so prior to trial, after a promised answer to the request had been delayed and had become the subject of discussion at the pre-trial conference. It is even more significant because it super-seded a denial of the same request, made more than a year earlier, which had been subjected to reconsideration.

Discussion of Rule 36 has been relatively meager and not free from obscurity, evidently because the Rule does not decree in so many words that a request which is admitted shall be deemed conclusive against the party making the admission. Curiously, although the Rule does not specify in so many words the effect of the admission in the pending litigation, it is careful to declare that the litigant's admission "is for the purpose of the pending action only and neither constitutes an admission by him for any other purpose nor may be used against him in any other proceeding". (Rule 36(b)). It seems to me that the draftsmen of the Rule simply felt it unnecessary to specify the obvious. Rule 36 serves a salutary purpose as one of the means for reducing the area of dispute at the trial. Requests for admission of relevant facts under Rule 36 would be even less useful than interrogatories to parties under Rule 33 if they were not conclusively binding on the party making the admission. For interrogatories under Rule 33 may go beyond *relevant* facts and may deal with matters which are calculated to lead to the discovery of relevant facts.

An answer to a request under Rule 36 is unlike a statement of fact by a witness made in the course of oral evidence at a trial, or in oral pre-trial depositions, or even in written answers to interrogatories. It is on the contrary a studied response, made under sanctions against easy denials, to a request to assert the truth or falsity of a relevant fact pointed out by the request for admission. The purpose of the Rule is not the discovery of information but the elimination at trial of the need to prove factual matters which the adversary cannot fairly contest. This is analogous to the older style pleading in which so-called ultimate facts were alleged under oath by the plaintiff and were conclusively taken to be true unless specifically denied by the defendant. Having adopted a simpler form of pleading the Federal Rules preserved in the request for admission the means for obtaining a conclusive admission of any relevant fact and did not limit the remedy to so-called "ultimate" facts. Were this otherwise then the much vaunted improved Federal Rules would be without a well-known and useful mode of limiting the factual disputes, and this under a system which has reduced the significance of pleadings as the means of limiting issues of fact.

Language in textbooks and decisions declaring that admissions under Rule 36 have the effect of "sworn testimony" serve to confuse the problem. In every case such language either was dictum or the problem of the binding effect of answers to requests for admission was not presented, or there were present peculiar circumstances not here involved. One case which is cited in all the subsequent decisions starts with the assumption that answers to requests for admissions "stand in the same relation to the case that sworn evidence bears", emphasizing that such answers must be sworn to and signed by the litigant himself. But the presence of the party's oath in both instances, with its sanction of the penalty for perjury, does not make an admission of a request the same in all respects as sworn testimony. For requests for admission, although answered under the oath of a party, are normally made under the direction and supervision of counsel, who has full professional realization of their significance. Therefore, their similarity to sworn testimony in one respect should not reduce their effect from conclusive admissions to merely evidential ones. . . .

The factual evidence therefore points overwhelmingly to a finding of statutory employer. This was left to the jury. But since that issue had been removed from controversy by plaintiff's admission of McShain's request no. 3, it is clear that McShain's motion for judgment notwithstanding the verdict against it must be granted.

NOTES

(1) In an FELA action the defendant won a jury verdict after producing testimony that the train that struck and injured plaintiff was operating within the railroad yard, not outside as stated in defendant's answer to a Rule 33 interrogatory. A question by the jury's foreman showed that the location of the train at the time of injury was a critical matter. On appeal plaintiff's principal argument was that the answer to the interrogatory should have bound the defendant. The court disagreed, adopting the view that when there is conflict between an interrogatory answer and other evidence, the fact-finder must decide which version is true. Freed v. Erie Lackawanna Ry., 445 F.2d 619, cert. denied 404 U.S. 1017, 92 S.Ct. 678, 30 L.Ed.2d 665 (1972). What if defendant had made the same answer in response to a Rule 36 request?

(2) What recourse is there for a party who learns after making a Rule 36 admission that the fact admitted is open to bona fide question?

(3) In an automobile collision case A serves B with requests to admit that include: "After the initial impact between the two vehicles B's truck pulled A's automobile west along the highway for about 103 feet." B's position is that the conclusion A wants admitted is a dubious and disputable one. What ought B do under the rules? Cf. Jones v. Boyd Truck Lines, 11 F.R.D. 67 (W.D.Mo.1951).

SECTION 9.   USES, ABUSES AND ENFORCEMENT PROBLEMS

DRUM v. TOWN OF TONAWANDA
United States District Court, Western District of New York, 1952.
13 F.R.D. 317.

KNIGHT, CHIEF JUDGE. Plaintiff has moved for an order compelling defendant Town of Tonawanda properly to comply with Rule 33 of the Federal Rules of Civil Procedure, 28 U.S.C.A., by answering certain interrogatories, or, in the alternative, for an order striking the answer of said defendant and granting judgment to plaintiff.

At the outset it may be stated that interrogatories serve two separate and distinct purposes: To ascertain facts and to narrow the issues. With the first function we are familiar. The second function may be attained by exacting admissions or obtaining commitments as to the position that an adverse party takes as to issues of fact. Aktiebolaget Vargos v. Clark, D.C., 8 F.R.D. 635.

On the oral argument it was conceded that defendant's answers sought to the unanswered interrogatories are all contained in depositions. Plaintiff stated that if defendant will consent to the introduction of so much of the depositions as contain such answers, without objection, plaintiff will be satisfied; that otherwise plaintiff would be compelled to expend money unnecessarily in subpoenaing and having in Court at the trial those witnesses who are members of defendant's police department and who are under its control, and whose testimony is already known to defendants.

No objection has been made by defendant that the interrogatories are improper. Defendant contends that plaintiff has all of the information and therefore is not entitled to its duplication by direct answers to the unanswered interrogatories.

Under Rule 26, Federal Rules of Civil Procedure, the defendant, though a municipal corporation, is required to comply with the rule and give answers to interrogatories. Joy Mfg. Co. v. City of New York, D.C., 30 F.Supp. 403. Of course, the deposition of a person may be used to impeach his testimony upon the trial. Lewis v. United Air Lines Transport Corporation, D.C., 27 F.Supp. 946; Federal Rules of Civil Procedure, Rule 26(d)(1). The right to take depositions may be said to be unrestricted but there are very definite restrictions on the right to use depositions. See Rule 26, supra. No basis for plaintiff to offer the depositions of defendant's witnesses, without their presence at the trial, seems to be available here.

Plaintiff contends that answers to the unanswered interrogatories will disclose nothing presently unknown to plaintiff and defendant through the depositions but the answers sought will shorten the trial and make certain that witnesses under control of defendant will not have to be subpoenaed by plaintiff and be in Court at the trial thereby creating unnecessary expense. With these contentions the Court is in accord. Otherwise the Rules of Civil Procedure, Rules 26–37, will have lost much of the effectiveness which their adoption was intended to provide.

The contention of the defendant in its answers to interrogatories filed, in its brief and upon the oral argument that it has "no officer or agent who has knowledge sufficient to furnish the information called for with respect to these interrogatories" is an avoidance of the obvious. If defendant, upon the trial, is to establish a defense known only to its policemen who are neither its officers or agents, those same persons are its witnesses for such purpose. Those witnesses might not have authority to bind the defendant with respect to its answers to the interrogatories but the knowledge of defendant's controlled employees is the knowledge of defendant's officers for the purpose of making such answers. The source of knowledge of defendant's officers is beside the point.

Plaintiff's motion is granted to the extent that defendant Town of Tonawanda should answer the unanswered interrogatories numbered 3, 4, 6, 7, 8, 9 and 10, dated October 31, 1952, and filed by plaintiff November 5, 1952.

HERTZ v. GRAHAM

United States Court of Appeals, Second Circuit, 1961.
292 F.2d 443.

MAGRUDER, CIRCUIT JUDGE. Plaintiff owned a race horse named Speedy Wave. Defendant also owned one named Star of Roses. The two horses collided on the training track at Belmont Park and both were killed instantly. Plaintiff sued Mrs. Graham for the loss of Speedy Wave. . . . The jury brought in a verdict giving damages to the plaintiff for the death of Speedy Wave. Judgment was entered pursuant to the jury verdict, from which the defendant takes the present appeal. Wesley E. Brite, an exercise boy in the employ of the plaintiff had, prior to the present litigation, recovered the sum of $80,000 in a separate action for the injuries he received in the accident (Brite v. Graham, Civil Action No. 97–240).

The testimony of Brite and of Monte D. Parke, who was employed as Mrs. Hertz's trainer, was to the effect that, on the morning of October 17, 1954, Brite, mounted on Speedy Wave, and Parke, mounted on a pony, entered the training track at Belmont Park. Their purpose was to "breeze" their horse, that is, to run it a measured distance in a given time, in this instance three-eighths of a mile in thirty-six seconds. Upon entering the track, Brite and Parke encountered defendant's exercise boy and her foreman by the inside rail holding a horse, later identified as Star of Roses, by means of a shank. Parke called out to them, "You'd better get that horse off the track before you get run over." Star of Roses was led to the outside rail, and the exercise boy mounted it, though defendant's foreman still held onto the horse. Both Brite and Parke noted that Star of Roses was in this position when Brite started to breeze Speedy Wave in a counter-clockwise direction occupying only the inside rail, as was usual for breezing. The total width of the track was, as stated by both Brite and Parke, 90 to 100 feet. Neither of them related just what happened in the meantime. Parke testified that he saw the riderless Star of Roses running in a clockwise direction along the rail about "four jumps" before the accident. Brite did not see Star of Roses until the two horses were "10 or 15 feet away" from each other, and although he attempted to avoid the accident the horses collided.

The testimony tending to show that defendant had been guilty of negligence came entirely from three depositions which the District Court admitted in evidence. These depositions by George W. Cochrane, Peter G. Griffiths and Patrick F. O'Neil had been taken in the action brought by Brite against this same defendant to recover for his injuries. These three men had worked for the defendant at one time or another and their duties had included the training of Star of Roses. Mr. Cochrane, who was an assistant trainer for Mrs. Graham from April to June of 1954, deposed that Star of Roses was a "rogue" or "outlaw" which, unlike other two-year old horses, had not been "broken" to gallop or breeze, but customarily would "duck to the left or to the right or would wheel completely around and dislodge his rider and run off." Each time Star of Roses was brought to the track without a lead pony, it succeeded in unseating its rider, said Mr. Cochrane. Griffiths, the trainer for five days in 1954, had similar experience with Star of Roses, as did O'Neil, who from June, 1953, to May, 1954, was foreman and subsequently assistant trainer. O'Neil further observed Star of Roses on October 17, 1954, shortly before the accident in question. The horse went 100 yards down the track, dislodged its rider, then wheeled and ran clockwise along the rail. According to the depositions, Mrs. Graham did not allow those responsible for the training of the race horse to use spurs or whips, nor did she take notice of advice that Star of Roses was overstimulated sexually and should be gelded. Once, Mrs. Graham awoke her trainer at midnight in order to fire him for having used a whip on Star of Roses. This trainer was said to be "one of the finest in the country."

We think it clear that there was sufficient circumstantial evidence submitted to the jury to justify a plaintiff's verdict that Mrs. Graham and her employees had been negligent and that this negligence had caused the accident. . . .

We find no error . . . in the way in which the trial judge dealt with the three depositions which defendant complains should not have been introduced into evidence. . . . [T]hese depositions were taken in the case of Brite v. Graham. In a pre-trial ruling, Judge Dawson had held that testimony and depositions from that action would be admissible even though the parties were different, "provided, however, that plaintiff meets the same requirements necessary for the reading of any deposition (Rule 26[d][3] * of the Rules of Civil Procedure)" (23 F.R.D. 17, 23, S.D.N.Y.1958). . . .

Rule 26(d)(3) permits the use in evidence of depositions when "the witness is at a greater distance than 100 miles from the place of trial or hearing . . . [or] the party offering the deposition has been unable to procure the attendance of the witness by subpoena; or . . . that such exceptional circumstances exist as to make it desirable, in the interest of justice and with due regard to the importance of presenting the

---

* Since the 1970 amendments, this provision has appeared as Rule 32(a)(3), with no change in substance. [Eds.]

testimony of witnesses orally in open court, to allow the deposition to be used." Plaintiff introduced Cochrane's deposition and read it into evidence without objection from the defendant. Before it was introduced and read to the jury, defendant's counsel had told the court that he had "some motions" which he would like to address to the court with respect to the "lack of admissibility" of the depositions. But when asked directly whether there was "any objections to reading this deposition of Cochrane," he said he was concerned only with the form of some of the questions and answers. After reading the deposition, he indicated that "there is nothing there that I would object to."

The next day defendant's attorney objected to the introduction of the two other depositions, by Griffiths and O'Neil. These were taken in 1957 and showed on their face that the persons making them resided outside the jurisdiction. Griffiths was living in Long Beach, California; O'Neil's permanent residence was in Chicago, Illinois. When asked when he would be in New York, O'Neil answered that he did not know. In colloquy, plaintiff's counsel said that he had inquired and had made "every attempt possible" but had been unable to locate Griffiths and O'Neil. Parke, who was familiar with the habitués of the track, confirmed this. Therefore, Judge Levet's "finding" that Griffiths and O'Neil were "at a greater distance than 100 miles from the place of trial or hearing" is unassailable. There was no evidence from which this court could conclude differently (see Frederick v. Yellow Cab Co. of Phila., 200 F.2d 483 (3d Cir.1952)). The court, upon assurance of counsel that he had been unable to locate Griffiths and O'Neil allowed the two depositions to be read into the record, subject to a motion to strike if the plaintiff failed to verify that the witnesses were not around. At that time no mention was made of Cochrane's deposition. The presentation of the evidence to the jury was completed on that day. When the trial was resumed, plaintiff's counsel said he had found out that Cochrane in fact had been seen at Belmont. This was corroborated by the testimony of Parke. At this juncture defendant moved to have Cochrane's deposition stricken, but the court ruled that defendant had waived her objection by failing to object in a more timely way. Instructions were then given to the jury by the trial judge and the trial was completed.

The trial court acted within its discretion in letting in the deposition. It is true that Rule 46, F.R.C.P., has obviated the necessity of formal exceptions or rulings, but a timely objection would have given the court an opportunity to make a ruling at a time when the plaintiff could have complied without prolonging the trial. "[D]ue regard to the importance of presenting the testimony of witnesses orally in open court," as stated in Rule 26(d)(3), did not require that Cochrane's deposition be stricken after it had been read into evidence without objection. There is to be sure no suggestion that the testimony in the depositions was unreliable. Defendant's witnesses testified solely as to the amount of damages.

* * *

The judgment of the District Court is affirmed.

NOTES

(1) What is the intendment of Judge Magruder's statement that the trial court acted in its "discretion" in allowing the Cochrane deposition? Would the issue have been different if the trial court had ruled "as a matter of law" that the deposition was admissible? If there is any significance in according "discretion," what is it, and why is it given?

(2) A California resident brought suit in the Southern District of New York against her former husband to collect loans she claimed to have made. She did not attend the trial. Her lawyer offered to read her deposition as proof. On appeal, her right to do so was upheld with this observation: "The tactical burden assumed by plaintiff in proceeding to trial in her absence . . . is likely to limit frequent resort to this course. . . ." See Richmond v. Brooks, 227 F.2d 490, 492 (2d Cir.1955). But cf. Jobse v. Connolly, 60 Misc.2d 69, 302 N.Y.S.2d 35 (Civ.Ct.1969). What of the defendant's right to cross-examine? What of the argument that the deposition should be excluded because "the absence of the witness was procured by the party offering" the deposition—that is, that the plaintiff "procured" her own absence?

(3) Is a party permitted to introduce into evidence its own responses to written interrogatories? See United Bank Ltd. v. Cambridge Sporting Goods, 41 N.Y.2d 254, 263–265, 392 N.Y.S.2d 265, 273–274, 360 N.E.2d 943 (1976).

(4) At the trial, after the defendant has testified, been cross-examined, and left the witness stand, may the plaintiff read in evidence parts of defendant's deposition? See Pingatore v. Montgomery Ward & Co., 419 F.2d 1138, 1142 (6th Cir.1969); Merchants Motor Freight v. Downing, 227 F.2d 247, 250 (8th Cir. 1955).

THE MYTH OR REALITY OF "DISCOVERY ABUSE"

In 1976 a national conference on the administration of justice prompted a thoughtful observer to conclude:

> "There is a very real concern in the legal community that the discovery process is now being overused. Wild fishing expeditions, since any material which might lead to the discovery of admissible evidence is discoverable, seem to be the norm. Unnecessary intrusions into the privacy of the individual, high costs to the litigants, and correspondingly unfair use of the discovery process as a lever toward settlement have come to be part of some lawyers' trial strategy." [1]

In 1977 an American Bar Association committee for the Study of Discovery Abuse made a set of proposals for change in the Federal Rules of Civil Procedure. Among them were that (1) the number of interrogatories should be limited to 30 unless court approval were obtained for the additional ones; and (2) the scope of permissible

----

1. Erickson, The Pound Conference Recommendations: A Blueprint for the Justice System in the Twenty-First Century, 76 F.R.D. 277, 288 (1978).

discovery under Rule 26(b) should be narrowed by modifying the scope from "relevant to the subject matter" of the action to "relevant to the issues raised by the claims or defenses of any party." Neither proposal was adopted. Both were predicated on the empirically untested assumption that "overdiscovery" in the form of excessively broad inquiries was the commonest type of abuse. Other observers had reached a different conclusion and it led to a different proposed corrective:

> "It is probably true that some discovery may seem excessive to a responding party or to a court because it appears to reach beyond the issues, subject matter, or claims and defenses fairly raised or presented in the case as made by the pleadings. But it is also true that very often when discovery is viewed as excessive by responding parties and courts it is so regarded not because it is irrelevant to issues in the case but because, even though relevant, it is duplicative, redundant, or simply disproportionately costly in relation to the values at stake in the litigation. In short, much of the truly abusive discovery that occurs is discovery that is too deep rather than too broad.
>
> If that point is sound, discovery improvement efforts should be directed not toward narrowing the definition of what is relevant, but rather toward protecting responding parties from redundant, duplicative and "disproportionate" discovery by reducing the number of inquiries that may be made concerning matters otherwise properly subject to discovery."

(Rosenberg & King, Curbing Discovery Abuse in Civil Litigation: Enough is Enough, 1981 B.Y.U.L.Rev. 579, 586.)

The 1983 amendments to Rule 26 accepted the redundancy-disproportionality definition of discovery abuse. The extent and nature of abuse are difficult to measure for they involve subjective judgments. One party's zealous investigation is the other side's abuse. To be sure, some plaintiffs start suit for the very purpose of coercing tribute from defendants who sustain the greater expenses discovery entails; and some defendants use discovery and its costs to bludgeon plaintiffs into giveaway settlements. Still, there is a consensus that discovery abuse is widespread enough and serious enough to warrant corrective measures. Are the 1983 changes well-conceived to curb abuse? They utilize the rules/sanctions approach to encouraging desired litigation behavior. Whether this is the best approach only time and experience will tell. The problem of procedural-rule enforcement is considered more fully in Chapter 12.

NATIONAL HOCKEY LEAGUE v. METROPOLITAN HOCKEY CLUB

Supreme Court of the United States, 1976.
427 U.S. 639, 96 S.Ct. 2778, 49 L.Ed.2d 747.

PER CURIAM.

This case arises out of the dismissal, under Fed.Rule Civ.Proc. 37, of respondents' antitrust action against petitioners for failure to timely answer written interrogatories as ordered by the District Court. The Court of Appeals for the Third Circuit reversed the judgment of dismissal, finding that the District Court had abused its discretion. The question presented is whether the Court of Appeals was correct in so concluding.   Rule 37(b)(2) provides in pertinent part as follows:

> "If a party . . . fails to obey an order to provide or permit discovery . . . the court in which the action is pending may make such orders in regard to the failure as are just, and among others the following:
>
> . . .
>
> "(C) An order striking out pleadings or parts thereof, or staying further proceedings until the order is obeyed, or dismissing the action or proceeding or any part thereof, or rendering a judgment by default against the disobedient party."

This Court held in *Societe Internationale v. Rogers*, 357 U.S. 197, 212, 78 S.Ct. 1087, 1096, 2 L.Ed.2d 1255 (1958), that Rule 37

> "should not be construed to authorize dismissal of [a] complaint because of petitioner's noncompliance with a pretrial production order when it has been established that failure to comply has been due to inability, and not to willfulness, bad faith, or any fault of petitioner."

While there have been amendments to the Rule since the decision in *Rogers*, neither the parties, the District Court, nor the Court of Appeals suggested that the changes would affect the teachings of the quoted language from that decision.

The District Court, in its memorandum opinion directing that respondents' complaint be dismissed, summarized the factual history of the discovery proceeding in these words:

> "After seventeen months where crucial interrogatories remained substantially unanswered despite numerous extensions granted at the eleventh hour and, in many instances, beyond the eleventh hour, and notwithstanding several admonitions by the Court and promises and commitments by the plaintiffs, the Court must and does conclude that the conduct of the plaintiffs demonstrates the callous disregard of responsibilities counsel owe to the Court and to their opponents. The practices of the plaintiffs exemplify flagrant bad faith when after being expressly directed to perform an act by a date certain, *viz.*, June

14, 1974, they failed to perform and compounded that noncompliance by waiting until five days afterwards before they filed any motions. Moreover, this action was taken in the face of warnings that their failure to provide certain information could result in the imposition of sanctions under Fed.R.Civ.P. 37. If the sanction of dismissal is not warranted by the circumstances of this case, then the Court can envisage no set of facts whereby that sanction should ever be applied." 63 F.R.D. 641, 656 (1974).

The Court of Appeals, in reversing the order of the District Court by a divided vote, stated:

"After carefully reviewing the record, we conclude that there is insufficient evidence to support a finding that MGB's failure to file supplemental answers by June 14, 1974 was in flagrant bad faith, willful or intentional." 531 F.2d 1188, 1195 (1976).

The Court of Appeals did not question any of the findings of historical fact which had been made by the District Court, but simply concluded that there was in the record evidence of "extenuating factors." The Court of Appeals emphasized that none of the parties had really pressed discovery until after a consent decree was entered between petitioners and all of the other original plaintiffs except the respondents approximately one year after the commencement of the litigation. It also noted that respondents' counsel took over the litigation, which previously had been managed by another attorney, after the entry of the consent decree, and that respondents' counsel encountered difficulties in obtaining some of the requested information. The Court of Appeals also referred to a colloquy during the oral argument on petitioners' motion to dismiss in which respondents' lead counsel assured the District Court that he would not knowingly and willfully disregard the final deadline.

While the Court of Appeals stated that the District Court was required to consider the full record in determining whether to dismiss for failure to comply with discovery orders, see Link v. Wabash R. Co., 370 U.S. 626, 633–634, 82 S.Ct. 1386, 1390, 8 L.Ed.2d 734 (1962), we think that the comprehensive memorandum of the District Court supporting its order of dismissal indicates that the court did just that. That record shows that the District Court was extremely patient in its efforts to allow the respondents ample time to comply with its discovery orders. Not only did respondents fail to file their responses on time, but the responses which they ultimately did file were found by the District Court to be grossly inadequate.

The question, of course, is not whether this Court, or whether the Court of Appeals, would as an original matter have dismissed the action; it is whether the District Court abused its discretion in so doing. E.g., C. Wright & A. Miller, Federal Practice and Procedure: Civil § 2284, p. 765 (1970); General Dynamics Corp. v. Selb Mfg. Co., 481

F.2d 1204, 1211 (C.A.8 1973); Baker v. F & F Investment, 470 F.2d 778, 781 (C.A.2 1972). Certainly the findings contained in the memorandum opinion of the District Court quoted earlier in this opinion are fully supported by the record. We think that the lenity evidenced in the opinion of the Court of Appeals, while certainly a significant factor in considering the imposition of sanctions under Rule 37, cannot be allowed to wholly supplant other and equally necessary considerations embodied in that Rule.

There is a natural tendency on the part of reviewing courts, properly employing the benefit of hindsight, to be heavily influenced by the severity of outright dismissal as a sanction for failure to comply with a discovery order. It is quite reasonable to conclude that a party who has been subjected to such an order will feel duly chastened, so that even though he succeeds in having the order reversed on appeal he will nonetheless comply promptly with future discovery orders of the district court.

But here, as in other areas of the law, the most severe in the spectrum of sanctions provided by statute or rule must be available to the district court in appropriate cases, not merely to penalize those whose conduct may be deemed to warrant such a sanction, but to deter those who might be tempted to such conduct in the absence of such a deterrent. If the decision of the Court of Appeals remained undisturbed in this case, it might well be that *these* respondents would faithfully comply with all future discovery orders entered by the District Court in this case. But other parties to other lawsuits would feel freer than we think Rule 37 contemplates they should feel to flout other discovery orders of other district courts. Under the circumstances of this case, we hold that the District Judge did not abuse his discretion in finding bad faith on the part of these respondents, and concluding that the extreme sanction of dismissal was appropriate in this case by reason of respondents' "flagrant bad faith" and their counsel's "callous disregard" of their responsibilities. Therefore, the petition for a writ of certiorari is granted and the judgment of the Court of Appeals is reversed.

So ordered.

MR. JUSTICE BRENNAN and MR. JUSTICE WHITE dissent.

MR. JUSTICE STEVENS took no part in the consideration or decision of this case.

NOTES

1. Reread Rule 37(b)(2), quoted at the outset of the opinion in the principal case. It does not in terms bestow "discretion" on the district court. What nevertheless led the Supreme Court to hold that the district court was clothed with discretionary power? When is an appellate court entitled to find that the lower court committed an abuse of discretion?

2. Holding "two bites at the apple" sufficient, the court of appeals affirmed the district court's refusal to set aside a second successive jury verdict for the defendant, but upheld a $42,085 sanction against the defendant for "serious violations" of the discovery rules and other abuses. These included obstruction of a deposition by misrepresentations. See Perkinson v. Gilbert/Robinson, Inc., 821 F.2d 686 (D.C.Cir.1987).

SECURITIES AND EXCHANGE COMMISSION v. BANCA DELLA SVIZZERA ITALIANA

United States District Court, Southern District of New York, 1981.
92 F.R.D. 111.

MILTON POLLACK, DISTRICT JUDGE.

Plaintiff, Securities Exchange Commission ("SEC"), moves this Court for an appropriate order pursuant to Fed.R.Civ.P. 37 for the failure and refusal of defendant, Banca Della Svizzera Italiana ("BSI") to provide the SEC with information relative to the identities of the principals for whom it purchased stock and stock options on American exchanges in St. Joe Minerals Corporation ("St. Joe"), a New York corporation which produces natural resources.

* * *

This action alleges insider trading on the part of BSI and its principals in the purchase and sale of call options for the common stock as well as the common stock itself of St. Joe. The options were traded through the Philadelphia Stock Exchange and the stock was traded on the New York Stock Exchange both of which are registered national exchanges. The purchases in question were made immediately prior to the announcement on March 11, 1981 of a cash tender offer by a subsidiary of Joseph E. Seagram & Sons, Inc. ("Seagram"), an Indiana corporation for all of the common stock of St. Joe at $45 per share. Prior to the announcement of the tender offer St. Joe stock traded on the market at $30 per share, (approximately).

. . . These transactions resulted in a virtually overnight profit just short of $2 million.

Promptly on noticing the undue activity in the options market, the SEC investigated and based on its findings brought this suit. The SEC contends that there is a strong probability that the purchasers were unlawfully using material non-public information which could only have been obtained or misappropriated from sources charged with a confidential duty not to disclose information prior to the public announcement of the tender offer.

The SEC applied for and obtained a Temporary Restraining Order against the Irving Trust Company which held the proceeds of the sales of the options and of the common stock in BSI's bank account with Irving Trust. The Temporary Restraining Order also directed immediate discovery proceedings including the requirment that "insofar as permitted by law" BSI should disclose within three business days the identity of its principals. The effect of the Temporary Restraining Order was to immobilize the profits derived from the questioned transactions.

The SEC endeavored by one or another procedural means, here and abroad, to obtain the identity of those who, along with the bank, were involved in the particular options purchases. No disclosure was forthcoming. Explanatory but uninformative letters so far as concerned the identity of the principals were received by the SEC from time to time. The SEC served formal interrogatories which were refined at the Court's suggestion to target the demanded disclosure in simplest terms. Conferences were held with the Court at which explanations were supplied and it was made clear at these that if need be an appropriate order enforceable by appropriate but, to the bank, unpalatable sanctions, might follow any continued impasse. Nonetheless, BSI declined to furnish the requested information voluntarily, adhering to its assertion of banking secrecy law. Eight months elapsed in the efforts to obtain the requisite disclosure by cooperative measures.

The bank regularly suggested, in the interim, a variety of alternative means by which the SEC might proceed to seek the disclosure. Some of these were doomed to failure in the opinion of the bank's own experts. It appeared to the Court that the proposals would only send the SEC on empty excursions, with little to show for them except more delay, more expense, more frustration, and possibly also, the inexorable operation of time bars against the claims by statutory limits for the assertion thereof. The proposed alternatives were not viable substitutes for direct discovery.

The matter came before the Court for crystallization on November 6, 1981 and after hearing counsel, the Court announced an informal opinion that it had determined to enter an order requiring disclosure, to be followed by severe contempt sanctions if it was not complied with. One week was fixed for submission of the order by the SEC. Apparently, the decision of the Court had a catalytic effect. A waiver of Swiss confidentiality was secured by the bank and reported to the Court. Also reported was that the bank had furnished some but not all the answers to the demanded interrogatories. A further period was requested to endeavor to complete the requisite responses with leave to show that any omissions were either not within the bank's ability to respond or were due to inappropriate demands. This moved finality forward to November 20, 1981.

* * *

Any discussion of the issue posed here must begin with the Supreme Court's opinion in Societe Internationale Pour Participations Industrielles et Commerciales, S.A. v. Rogers, 357 U.S. 197, 78 S.Ct. 1087, 2 L.Ed.2d 1255 (1958) which is the Court's latest decision on the subject. *Societe* holds that the good faith of the party resisting discovery is a key factor in the decision whether to impose sanctions when foreign law prohibits the requested disclosure.

In *Societe* a Swiss holding company was suing for the return of property seized by the Alien Property Custodian during World War II. The district court dismissed plaintiff's complaint as a sanction for its refusal to comply with the Court's order to produce bank records, despite a finding that the Swiss government had constructively seized the documents [1] and that plaintiff had shown good faith efforts to comply with the production order. Id. at 201–02, 78 S.Ct. at 1090. The Court of Appeals affirmed.

The Supreme Court reversed. It held that where plaintiff was prohibited by Swiss law from complying with the discovery order and there was no showing of bad faith, the sanction of dismissal without prejudice was not justified. The Court indicated that a party who had made deliberate use of foreign law to evade American law might be subject to sanctions.

> [T]he Government suggests that petitioner stands in the position of one who deliberately courted legal impediments to production of the Sturzenegger records, and who thus cannot now be heard to assert its good faith after this expectation was realized. Certainly these contentions, if supported by the facts, would have a vital bearing on justification for dismissal of the action, but they are not open to the Government here. The findings below reach no such conclusions. . . . Id. at 208–09, 78 S.Ct. at 1093–94.

Under *Societe,* then, a foreign law's prohibition of discovery is not decisive of the issue. A noncomplying party's good or bad faith is a vital factor to consider.

* * *

In any event the Second Circuit has clearly moved to a more flexible position. In two later cases, both affirming decisions of this Court, the Court of Appeals adopted a balancing test approach in which a foreign law's prohibition is but one of many factors to consider.

In the first of these, United States v. First National City Bank, 396 F.2d 897 (2d Cir.1968), the Court of Appeals upheld this Court's decision in In re First National City Bank, 285 F.Supp. 845 (S.D.N.Y.1968) holding Citibank in contempt for its failure to comply with a subpoena duces tecum in an on-going grand jury inquiry into antitrust violations that presumably had occurred in this country. . . . This Court found that German public law did not prohibit disclosure and that moreover Citibank had not shown good faith in its attempts to comply. 285 F.Supp. at 847–48.

The Court of Appeals accepted these findings. In affirming, it emphasized that the risk or absence of foreign criminal liability did not resolve the issue. It noted first that "[a] state having jurisdiction to prescribe or enforce a rule of law is not precluded from exercising its

---

1. The Swiss Federal Attorney "confiscated" the documents, which confiscation left possession in private hands and really amounted to a specific prohibition of the documents' release. Id. at 200–01, 78 S.Ct. at 1089–90.

jurisdiction *solely* because such exercise requires a person to engage in conduct subjecting him to liability under the law of another state having jurisdiction with respect to that conduct." 396 F.2d at 901, quoting Restatement (Second), Foreign Relations Law of the United States, § 39(1) (1965) (Restatement of Foreign Relations) (emphasis supplied by the Court of Appeals). It then balanced the interests at stake, looking for guidance to § 40 of the Restatement of Foreign Relations.[2] It looked particularly at the national interests of the United States and Germany and the hardship if any that Citibank would face in complying.

As part of its balancing, the Court of Appeals stressed that the antitrust laws "have long been considered cornerstones of this nation's economic policies, have been vigorously enforced and the subject of frequent interpretation by our Supreme Court." Id. at 903. It further found noteworthy that neither the United States Department of State nor the German government had expressed any view in the case. Finally, in assessing the civil liability which Citibank alleged it might suffer, the Court said:

> [Citibank] must confront the choice . . . the need to "surrender to one sovereign or the other the privileges received therefrom" or, alternatively a willingness to accept the consequences. Id. at 905 (citation omitted).
>
> * * *

. . . [T]he Second Circuit has moved away from the position that a foreign law's prohibition of discovery is an absolute bar to compelling disclosure. It is worthy of note that in adopting a more flexible approach, this Circuit is squarely in line with other circuits and district courts that have considered the matter. . . .

Application of the Law to the Facts of this Case

BSI claims that it may be subject to criminal liability under Swiss penal and banking law if it discloses the requested information. However, this Court finds the factors in § 40 of the Restatement of Foreign Relations to tip decisively in favor of the SEC. Moreover, it holds BSI to be "in the position of one who deliberately courted legal impediments . . . and who thus cannot now be heard to assert its good faith after

---

2. § 40 reads as follows:

§ 40. Limitations on Exercise of Enforcement Jurisdiction

Where two states have jurisdiction to prescribe and enforce rules of law and the rules they may prescribe require inconsistent conduct upon the part of a person, each state is required by international law to consider, in good faith, moderating the exercise of its enforcement jurisdiction, in the light of such factors as

(a) vital national interests of each of the states,

(b) the extent and the nature of the hardship that inconsistent enforcement actions would impose upon the person,

(c) the extent to which the required conduct is to take place in the territory of the other state,

(d) the nationality of the person, and

(e) the extent to which enforcement by action of either state can reasonably be expected to achieve compliance with the rule prescribed by that state.

this expectation was realized." *Societe,* supra at 208–09, 78 S.Ct. at
1093–94. BSI acted in bad faith. It made deliberate use of Swiss
nondisclosure law to evade in a commercial transaction for profit to it,
the strictures of American securities law against insider trading.
Whether acting solely as an agent or also as a principal (something
which can only be clarified through disclosure of the requested information), BSI invaded American securities markets and profited in some
measure thereby. It cannot rely on Swiss nondisclosure law to shield
this activity.

1. The vital national interests at stake

The first of the § 40 factors is the vital national interest of each of
the States. The strength of the United States interest in enforcing its
securities laws to ensure the integrity of its financial markets cannot
seriously be doubted. That interest is being continually thwarted by
the use of foreign bank accounts. Congress, in enacting legislation on
bank record-keeping, expressed its concern over the problem over a
decade ago:

> Secret foreign bank accounts and secret foreign financial insti-
> tutions have permitted a proliferation of "white collar" crime
> . . . [and] have allowed Americans and others to avoid the
> law and regulations concerning securities and exchanges . . ..
> The debilitating effects of the use of these secret institutions on
> Americans and the American economy are vast.

> H.R.Rep. No. 975, 91 Cong., 2d Sess. 12, reprinted in [1970] U.S.
> Code Cong. & Admin.News 4394, 4397.

                          *   *   *

The Swiss government, on the other hand, though made expressly
aware of the litigation, has expressed no opposition. In response to
BSI's lawyers inquiries, the incumbent Swiss Federal Attorney General,
Rudolf Gerber, said only that a foreign court could not change the rule
that disclosure required the consent of the one who imparted the secret
and that BSI might thus be subject to prosecution. The Swiss government did not "confiscate" the Bank records to prevent violations of its
law, as it did in *Societe.* NEITHER THE UNITED STATES NOR THE
SWISS GOVERNMENT has suggested that discovery be halted. Rather, the Assistant Legal Adviser for Economic and Business Affairs for
the Department of State explicitly has said in an affidavit that:

> . . . the Department of State does not object to the efforts of the
> Commission to obtain this information through civil discovery under
> the exclusive jurisdiction of this court. . . .

2. Hardship considerations and the element of good faith

The second factor of § 40 of the Restatement of Foreign Relations
is the extent and nature of the hardship that inconsistent enforcement
actions would impose upon the party subject to both jurisdictions. It is
true that BSI may be subject to fines and its officers to imprisonment

under Swiss law. However, this Court notes that there is some flexibility in the application of that law. . . . A party's good or bad faith is an important factor to consider, and this Court finds that BSI, which deposited the proceeds of these transactions in an American bank account in its name and which certainly profited in some measure from the challenged activity, undertook such transactions fully expecting to use foreign law to shield it from the reach of our laws. Such "deliberate courting" of foreign legal impediments will not be countenanced.

3. The remaining § 40 factors

The last three of the § 40 Restatement of Foreign Relations Law factors—the place of performance, the nationality of the resisting party, and the extent to which enforcement can be expected to achieve compliance with the rule prescribed by that state—appear to be less important in this Circuit. . . . Last, with respect to enforcement, this Court believes that an appropriate formal order directing the demanded disclosure, to the extent that compliance has been incomplete, will serve as the requisite foundation for any further actions that may be needed in the form of sanctions and should serve to bring home the obligations a foreign entity undertakes when it conducts business on the American securities exchanges.

SOCIETE NATIONALE INDUSTRIELLE AEROSPATIALE v. U.S. DISTRICT COURT OF SOUTHERN DISTRICT IOWA

Supreme Court of the United States, 1987.
482 U.S. 522, 107 S.Ct. 2542, 96 L.Ed.2d 461.*

JUSTICE STEVENS delivered the opinion of the Court.

[In a personal injury action, plaintiff sought to discover pursuant to the Federal Rules of Civil Procedure. The French defendant resisted discovery, arguing that discovery could be obtained only pursuant to the Hague Convention on the Taking of Evidence Abroad in Civil or Commercial Matters, ratified by both the United States and France, and that discovery not pursuant to the Hague Convention was prohibited by a French penal statute. The lower court ordered discovery pursuant to the Federal Rules and the Eighth Circuit affirmed. The question of whether the Hague Convention was exclusive had given rise to sharply different views.]

. . . [T]he text of the Evidence Convention, as well as the history of its proposal and ratification by the United States, unambiguously supports the conclusion that it was intended to establish optional procedures that would facilitate the taking of evidence abroad. . . .

An interpretation of the Hague Convention as the exclusive means for obtaining evidence located abroad would effectively subject every

---

* Some footnotes omitted; others renumbered.

American court hearing a case involving a national of a contracting State to the internal laws of that State. Interrogatories and document requests are staples of international commercial litigation, no less than of other suits, yet a rule of exclusivity would subordinate the court's supervision of even the most routine of these pretrial proceedings to the actions or, equally, to the inactions of foreign judicial authorities. . . . The Hague Convention, however, contains no . . . plain statement of a pre-emptive intent. We conclude accordingly that the Hague Convention did not deprive the District Court of the jurisdiction it otherwise possessed to order a foreign national party before it to produce evidence physically located within a signatory nation.

. . . [I]t appears clear to us that the optional Convention procedures are available whenever they will facilitate the gathering of evidence by the means authorized in the Convention. Although these procedures are not mandatory, the Hague Convention does "apply" to the production of evidence in a litigant's possession in the sense that it is one method of seeking evidence that a court may elect to employ. . . .

Petitioners contend that even if the Hague Convention's procedures are not mandatory, this Court should adopt a rule requiring that American litigants first resort to those procedures before initiating any discovery pursuant to the normal methods of the Federal Rules of Civil Procedure. See, e.g., Laker Airways, Ltd. v. Pan American World Airways, 103 F.R.D. 42 (D DC 1984); Philadelphia Gear Corp. v. American Pfauter Corp., 100 F.R.D. 58 (ED Pa.1983). . . .

. . . [W]e cannot accept petitioners' invitation to announce a new rule of law that would require first resort to Convention procedures whenever discovery is sought from a foreign litigant. Assuming, without deciding, that we have the lawmaking power to do so, we are convinced that such a general rule would be unwise. In many situations the Letter of Request procedure authorized by the Convention would be unduly time consuming and expensive, as well as less certain to produce needed evidence than direct use of the Federal Rules. A rule of first resort in all cases would therefore be inconsistent with the overriding interest in the "just, speedy, and inexpensive determination" of litigation in our courts. See Fed.Rule Civ.Proc. 1.

Petitioners argue that a rule of first resort is necessary to accord respect to the sovereignty of states in which evidence is located. It is true that the process of obtaining evidence in a civil law jurisdiction is normally conducted by a judicial officer rather than by private attorneys. Petitioners contend that if performed on French soil, for example, by an unauthorized person, such evidence-gathering might violate the "judicial sovereignty" of the host nation. Because it is only through the Convention that civil law nations have given their consent to evidence-gathering activities within their borders, petitioners argue, we have a duty to employ those procedures whenever they are available. . . . We find that argument unpersuasive. If such a duty were to be inferred from the adoption of the Convention itself, we believe it would have been described in the text of that document. Moreover, the concept of international comity [1] requires in this context a more particularized analysis of the respective interests of the foreign nation and the requesting nation than petitioners' proposed general rule would generate.[2] We therefore decline to hold as a blanket matter that comity requires resort to Hague Evidence Convention procedures without prior scrutiny in each case of the particular facts, sovereign interests, and likelihood that resort to those procedures will prove effective. . . .

American courts, in supervising pretrial proceedings, should exercise special vigilance to protect foreign litigants from the danger that unnecessary, or unduly burdensome, discovery may place them in a disadvantageous position. Judicial supervision of discovery should always seek to minimize its costs and inconvenience and to prevent improper uses of discovery requests. When it is necessary to seek evidence abroad, however, the District Court must supervise pretrial proceedings particularly closely to prevent discovery abuses. For example, the additional cost of transportation of documents or witnesses to or from foreign locations may increase the danger that discovery may be sought for the improper purpose of motivating settlement, rather than finding relevant and probative evidence. Objections to "abusive" discovery that foreign litigants advance should therefore receive the most careful consideration. In addition, we have long recognized the demands of comity in suits involving foreign states, either as parties or as sovereigns with a coordinate interest in the litigation. See Hilton v. Guyot, 159 U.S. 113, 16 S.Ct. 139, 40 L.Ed. 95 (1895). American courts should therefore take care to demonstrate due respect for any special problem confronted by the foreign litigant on account of its nationality or the location of its operations, and for any sovereign interest expressed by a foreign state. We do not articulate specific rules to guide this delicate task of adjudication. . . .

In the case before us, the Magistrate and the Court of Appeals correctly refused to grant the broad protective order that petitioners

1. Comity refers to the spirit of cooperation in which a domestic tribunal approaches the resolution of cases touching the laws and interests of other sovereign states. . . .

2. The nature of the concerns that guide a comity analysis are suggested by the Restatement of Foreign Relations Law of the United States (Revised) § 437(1)(c) (Tent. Draft No. 7, 1986) (approved May 14, 1986). While we recognize that § 437 of the Restatement may not represent a consensus of international views on the scope of the District Court's power to order foreign discovery in the face of objections by foreign states, these factors are relevant to any comity analysis:

"(1) the importance to the . . . litigation of the documents or other information requested;

"(2) the degree of specificity of the request;

"(3) whether the information originated in the United States;

"(4) the availability of alternative means of securing the information; and

"(5) the extent to which noncompliance with the request would undermine important interests of the United States, or compliance with the request would undermine important interests of the state where the information is located." Ibid.

requested. The Court of Appeals erred, however, in stating that the Evidence Convention does not apply to the pending discovery demands. This holding may be read as indicating that the Convention procedures are not even an option that is open to the District Court. It must be recalled, however, that the Convention's specification of duties in executing States creates corresponding rights in requesting States; holding that the Convention does not apply in this situation would deprive domestic litigants of access to evidence through treaty procedures to which the contracting States have assented. Moreover, such a rule would deny the foreign litigant a full and fair opportunity to demonstrate appropriate reasons for employing Convention procedures in the first instance, for some aspects of the discovery process.

Accordingly, the judgment of the Court of Appeals is vacated, and the case is remanded for further proceedings consistent with this opinion.

[The opinion of JUSTICE BLACKMUN, with whom JUSTICE BRENNAN, JUSTICE MARSHALL, and JUSTICE O'CONNOR joined concurring in part and dissenting in part, is omitted.]

NOTE

Is the Supreme Court's solution likely to reduce the litigation that has resulted from the United States' ratification of the Evidence Convention? A similar problem has arisen under The Hague Convention on the Service Abroad of Judicial and Extrajudicial Documents in Civil or Commercial Matters of November 15, 1965, entered into force for the United States on February 10, 1969, 20 U.S.T. 361, T.I.A.S. 6638. The Supreme Court wrestled with the question in Volkswagenwerk A.G. v. Schlunk, 486 U.S. 694, 108 S.Ct. 2104, 100 L.Ed.2d 722 (1988), p. 331 supra.

DISCOVERY IN ARBITRATION PROCEEDINGS

Is discovery available to parties who have agreed to submit their dispute to arbitration? As to arbitrability, probably so, but with regard to the merits of the controversy being arbitrated, the heavy weight of authority in the federal courts answers in the negative. See Mississippi Power Co. v. Peabody Coal Co., 69 F.R.D. 558 (S.D.Miss.1976); Recognition Equipment, Inc. v. NCR Corp., 532 F.Supp. 271 (N.D.Tex.1981).

Some federal courts have ordered discovery in "exceptional circumstances," as in Ferro Union Corp. v. SS Ionic Coast, 43 F.R.D. 11 (S.D. Tex.1967), where the ship's crew was about the leave the country, perhaps forever; or in Vespe Contracting Co. v. Anvan Corp., 399 F.Supp. 516 (E.D.Pa.1975), where defendant's activities at a construction site were obliterating evidence. See also Cavanaugh v. McDonnell & Co., 357 Mass. 452, 258 N.E.2d 561 (1970); Balfour, Guthrie & Co. v. Commercial Metals Co., 93 Wn.2d 199, 607 P.2d 856 (1980); Katz v. Burkin, 3 A.D.2d 238, 160 N.Y.S.2d 159 (1957). In Bigge Crane & Rigging Co. v. Docutel Corp., 371 F.Supp. 240 (S.D.N.Y.1973), the court lowered the strict standard, allowing discovery on the ground it was "particularly necessary in a case where the claim is for payment for work done and virtually completed, and the nature of any defense is unknown." (Id. at 246.) The court made the point that discovery would not delay arbitration proceedings and relied on International Association of Heat & Frost Insulators Asbestos Workers, Local 66, AFL–CIO v. Leona Lee Corp., 434 F.2d 192 (5th Cir.1970), upholding discovery to the extent necessary to present the dispute to arbitration as effectuating the federal policy favoring arbitration. The Leona Lee case has not attracted a following. See generally Note, Relaxing the Standard for Court-Ordered Discovery in Aid of Commercial Arbitration, 50 Fordham L.Rev. 1448 (1982); Willenken, The Often Overlooked Use of Discovery in Aid of Arbitration, 35 Bus.Law. 173 (1979).

THE FREEDOM OF INFORMATION ACT
AS A DISCOVERY TOOL

The Freedom of Information Act, 5 U.S.C.A. § 552, although not designed for pretrial discovery, has been used for that purpose. The statute gives the public access to non-exempted federal agency records, a very broad range of material. It is not necessary to be involved in litigation to invoke FOIA.

The scope of FOIA is different from the scope of pretrial discovery under the federal rules. At times it is possible to get material through FOIA that would be non-discoverable because privileged. See Washington Post Co. v. United States Dep't. of Health and Human Servs., 690 F.2d 252 (D.C.Cir.1982); but cf. Association for Women in Science v. Califano, 566 F.2d 339 (D.C.Cir.1977). Further, trial-preparation immunity and attorney-client privilege are not applied as vigorously under FOIA as under the discovery rules, even though they are formally exempted under FOIA. See Toran, Information Disclosure in Civil Actions: The Freedom of Information Act and the Federal Discovery Rules, 49 Geo.Wash.L.Rev. 843, 862 (1982); Note, The Applicability and Scope of the Attorney-Client Privilege in the Executive Branch of the Federal Government, 62 B.U.L.Rev. 1003, 1016 (1982). Litigants can use FOIA without meeting scope limitations with regard to relevance or redundancy. Moreover, information can be obtained under FOIA without the opposing attorney's being aware of it.

Chapter Twelve

THE RIGHT TO A JURY

SECTION 1. COMMON LAW BACKGROUND

MAITLAND AND MONTAGUE, A SKETCH OF ENGLISH LEGAL HISTORY *
46–58 (1915).

Legal Forms in the Twelfth Century. Let us try to put before our eyes a court of the twelfth century; it may be a county court, or a hundred-court, or a court held by some great baron for his tenants. It is held in the open air—perhaps upon some ancient moothill, which ever since the times of heathenry has been the scene of justice. An officer presides over it—the sheriff, the sheriff's bailiff, the lord's steward. But all or many of the free landowners of the district are bound to attend it; they owe "suit" to it, they are its suitors, they are its doomsmen; it is for them, and not for the president, "to find the dooms." He controls the procedure, he issues the mandates, he pronounces the sentence; but when the question is what the judgment shall be, he bids the suitors find a doom. All this is very ancient, and look where we will in Western Europe we may find it. But as yet we have not found the germ of trial by jury. These doomsmen are not "judges of fact." There is no room for any judges of fact. If of two litigants the one contradicts the other flatly, if the plain "You did" of the one is met by the straightforward "You lie" of the other, here is a problem that man cannot solve. He is unable as yet to weigh testimony against testimony, to cross-examine witnesses, to piece together the truth out of little bits of evidence. He has recourse to the supernatural. He adjudges that one or other of the two parties is to prove his case by an appeal to God.

The Oath. The judgment precedes the proof. The proof consists, not in a successful attempt to convince your judges of the truth of your assertion, but in the performance of a task that they have imposed upon you: if you perform it, God is on your side. The modes of proof are two, oaths and ordeals. In some cases we may see a defendant allowed to swear away a charge by his own oath. More frequently he will have to bring with him oath-helpers—in later days they are called "compurgators"—and when he has sworn successfully, each of these oath-helpers in turn will swear "By God that oath is clean and true."

* Footnotes omitted.

749

The doomsmen have decreed how many oath-helpers, and of what quality, he must bring.   . . .

The Ordeal. But when crime is laid to a man's charge he will not always be allowed to escape with oaths. Very likely he will be sent to the ordeal. The ordeal is conceived as the "judgment of God." Of heathen origin it well may be, but long ago the Christian Church has made it her own, has prescribed a solemn ritual for the consecration of those instruments—the fire, the water—which will reveal the truth. The water in the pit is adjured to receive the innocent and to reject the guilty. He who sinks is safe, he who floats is lost. The red-hot iron one pound in weight must be lifted and carried three paces. The hand that held it is then sealed up in a cloth. Three days afterwards the seal is broken. Is the hand clean or is it foul? that is the dread question. A blister "as large as half a walnut" is fatal. How these tests worked in practice we do not know. We seldom get stories about them save when, as now and again will happen, the local saint interferes and performs a miracle. We cannot but guess that it was well to be good friends with the priest when one went to the ordeal.

Trial by Battle. Then the Norman conquerors brought with them another ordeal—the judicial combat. An ordeal it is, for though the Church has looked askance at it, it is no appeal to mere brute force; it is an appeal to the God of Battles. Very solemnly does each combatant swear to the truth of his cause; very solemnly does he swear that he has eaten nothing, drunk nothing "whereby the law of God may be debased or the devil's law exalted."

When a criminal charge is made—"an appeal of felony"—the accuser and the accused, if they be not maimed nor too young, nor too old, will have to fight in person. When a claim for land is made, the plaintiff has to offer battle, not in his own person, but in the person of one of his men. This man is in theory a witness who will swear to the justice of his lord's cause. In theory he ought not to be, but in practice he often is, a hired champion who makes a profession of fighting other people's battles.   . . .

Growth of King's Courts. But long ago the Frankish kings had placed themselves outside the sphere of this ancient formal and sacral procedure. They were standing in the shoes of Roman governors, even of Roman emperors. For themselves and their own affairs they had a prerogatival procedure. If their rights were in question, they would direct their officers to call together the best and oldest men of the neighbourhood to swear about the relevant facts. The royal officers would make an inquisition, hold an inquest, force men to swear that they would return true answers to whatever questions might be addressed to them in the king's name. They may be asked whether or no this piece of land belongs to the king; they may be asked in a general way what lands the king has in their district . . .. This privilege that the king has he can concede to others; he can grant to his favourite churches that their lands shall stand outside the scope of the clumsy and hazardous procedure of the common courts; if their title to those lands be challenged, a royal officer will call upon the neighbours to declare the truth—in other words, to give a verdict. It is here that we see the germ of the jury.

. . . Thenceforward the inquest was part of the machinery of government; it could be employed for many different purposes whenever the king desired information. He could use it in his own litigation, he could place it at the service of other litigants who were fortunate enough or rich enough to obtain this favour from him. But throughout the reigns of our Norman kings it keeps its prerogatival character.

The King's Assizes. Then Henry II., bent upon making his justice supreme throughout his realm, put this royal remedy at the disposal of all his subjects. This he did not by one general law, but piecemeal, by a series of ordinances known as "assizes," . . . .. For example, when there was litigation about the ownership of land, the defendant, instead of accepting the plaintiff's challenge to fight, was allowed to "put himself upon the king's grand assize.", Thereupon the action, which had been begun in some feudal court, was removed into the King's court; and twelve knights, chosen from the district in which the land lay, gave a verdict as to whether the plaintiff or the defendant had the better right.

In other cases—for example, when the dispute was about the possession, not the ownership, of land—less solemn forms of the inquest were employed: twelve free and lawful men, not necessarily knights, were charged to say whether the defendant had ejected the plaintiff. Before the twelfth century was at an end, the inquest in one form or another—sometimes it was called an assize, sometimes a jury—had become part of the normal procedure in almost every kind of civil action. . . .

[B]efore the Middle Ages were over, trial by jury had become the only form of trial for civil actions that had any vitality. . . .

The Earliest Jury-Trial. We have spoken of "trial by jury." That term naturally calls up before our minds a set of twelve men called into court in order that they may listen to the testimony of witnesses, give a true verdict "according to the evidence," and, in short, act as judges of those questions of fact that are in dispute. But it is very long after Henry II.'s day before trial by jury takes this form. Originally the jurors are called in, not in order that they may hear, but in order that they may give, evidence. They are witnesses. They are the neighbours of the parties; they are presumed to know before they come into court the facts about which they are to testify. They are chosen by the sheriff to represent the neighbourhood—indeed, they are spoken of as being "the neighbourhood," "the country"—and the neighbourhood, the country will know the facts.

In the twelfth century population was sparse, and men really knew far more of the doings of their neighbours than we know nowadays. It was expected that all legal transactions would take place in public; the conveyance of land was made in open court, the wife was endowed at the church-door, the man who bought cattle in secret ran a great but just risk of being treated as a thief; every three weeks a court was held in the village, and all the affairs of every villager were discussed. The verdict, then, was the sworn testimony of the countryside; and if the twelve jurors perjured themselves, the verdict of another jury of twenty-four might send them to prison and render them infamous for ever.

In course of time, and by slow degrees—degrees so slow that we can hardly detect them—the jury put off its old and acquired a new character. Sometimes, when the jurors knew nothing of the facts, witnesses who did know the facts would be called in to supply the requisite information. As human affairs grew more complex, the neighbours whom the sheriff summoned became less and less able to perform their original duty, more and more dependent upon the evidence given in their presence by those witnesses who were summoned by the parties. In the fifteenth century the change had taken place, though in yet later days a man who had been summoned as a juror, and who sought to escape on the ground that he already knew something of the facts in question, would be told that he had given a very good reason for his being placed in the jury-box. We may well say, therefore, that trial by jury, though it has its roots in the Frankish inquest, grew up on English soil; and until recent times it was distinctive of England and Scotland, for on the Continent of Europe all other forms of legal procedure had been gradually supplanted by that which canonists and civilians had constructed out of ancient Roman elements.

NOTES

(1) At early common law, the appropriate method of fact finding depended on the particular action brought. This gave rise to many problems sought to be solved by Rule 2 of the Federal Rules of Civil Procedure. The materials which follow suggest some of the reasons Rule 2 does not supply the whole answer.

(2) Proof by ordeal was abolished by the Lateran Council of 1215. But trial by battle was not formally abolished until 1819, and wager of law not until 1833. Even before their formal abolition, trial by wager and battle had become rare. See Maitland, The Forms of Action at Common Law, 17–18 (1962); 1 Pollock & Maitland, The History of English Law, 149–150 (2nd ed. 1968). In fact, as Maitland writes, "a long chapter in that history [i.e., the history of the forms of action] might be entitled 'Dodges to evade Wager of Battle', a still longer chapter, 'Dodges to evade Wager of Law' ". Eventually, these dodges developed into trial by jury in the form in which it was received in the United States.

SECTION 2. RECEPTION IN THE UNITED STATES

SECOND PRELIMINARY REPORT OF NEW YORK ADVISORY COMMITTEE ON PRACTICE AND PROCEDURE
Leg.Doc. No. 13, 564–69 (1958).

* * *

II. JURY TRIALS AND THE ONE FORM OF ACTION *

A. The Constitutional Right to Jury Trial

The right to jury trial in civil actions is protected in the Federal courts by the Constitution of the United States [1] and in the state courts by the constitutions of many states including New York.[2] The usual constitutional provision is that the right to trial by jury "shall remain inviolate forever" [3] ["but a jury trial may be waived by the parties in all civil cases in the manner to be prescribed by law"].

[Unlike the federal constitution, which preserves the right to jury trial as of 1791, the date of adoption of the bill of rights, New York's Constitution] effected a "freezing" of the right to jury trial as of 1894. Accordingly, the right to jury trial is constitutionally protected, first, in actions of the type in which trial by jury was used as a matter of right [4] at the time of the adoption of the first Constitution in 1777 and, second, in those in which a right to trial by jury was created by a statute enacted between 1777 and the adoption of the 1894 Constitution.

The first group includes actions for a sum of money only (except that a reference is permitted of certain actions involving a long account); actions of ejectment; for dower; for waste; for abatement of and damages for a nuisance, and to recover a chattel. The second group includes divorce; [5] annulment on a ground other than incapacity of one of the parties; partition; an action by the attorney-general

---

* Some footnotes omitted; others renumbered.

1. U.S. Const. amend. VII. ["In suits at Common law, where the value in controversy shall exceed twenty dollars, the right of trial by jury shall be preserved. . . ."] The Federal Constitutional provision does not affect the state courts. Lee v. Tillotson, 24 Wend. 337 (N.Y.S.Ct.1840). . . .

2. Arizona, California, Connecticut, Idaho, Indiana, Kansas, Minnesota, Missouri, Montana, Nebraska, New Mexico, New York, North Dakota, Ohio, Oklahoma, South Carolina, South Dakota, Utah, Washington and Wyoming are all states which have merged systems of law and equity but preserved the right to trial by jury by constitutional provision. Note, The Right to Jury Trial under Merged Procedures, 65 Harv.L.Rev. 453 (1952).

3. Clark, Code Pleading 91 (2d ed. 1947).

4. The "use" referred to has been held to mean as a matter of right. Sheppard v. Steele, 43 N.Y. 52, 57 (1870); Matter of Gurland, 286 App.Div. 704, 146 N.Y.S.2d 830 (1955), appeal dismissed 309 N.Y. 969, 132 N.E.2d 331 (1956). Although there was in 1777 no statute specifying the cases in which the right to trial by jury existed, the policy of trial by jury was clearly established early in the history of the colony and its use was regulated by custom. 4 Lincoln, Constitutional History of New York 38–41 (1906); Malone v. Saints Peter and Paul's Church, 172 N.Y. 269, 64 N.E. 961 (1902).

5. The issue of adultery is triable by jury. Conderman v. Conderman, 44 Hun 181 (N.Y.S.Ct.1887) (citing 2 N.Y.Rev.Laws

against an alleged usurper of an office, franchise or corporate right; an action by the attorney-general to annul a corporation; an action by the attorney-general to vacate letters patent; an application for an alternate mandamus order; and proceedings to determine the validity of a will admitted to probate by a surrogate.

The right to a jury trial in these actions cannot be abolished except by constitutional amendment. There has only been one such amendment [in New York]. In 1913, the constitutional right to jury trial of claims arising out of injury to employees in the course of their employment was abolished.[6]

B.   Statutes Defining the Jury Right

There are two forms of statutes defining the right to a jury: those merely restating the historical test of actions formerly triable by jury, and those enumerating the kinds of action so triable.

The New York statute, of the second type, has been the model for most code states. Section 425 of the civil practice act (formerly section 968 of the Code of Civil Procedure) [now N.Y.—McKinney's CPLR 4101] provides:

Issues of fact triable by a jury. In each of the following actions an issue of fact must be tried by a jury unless a jury trial is waived or a reference is directed:

1.   An action in which the complaint demands judgment for a sum of money only.

2.   An action of ejectment; for dower; for waste; for a nuisance; to recover a chattel; or for determination of a claim to real property under article fifteen of the real property law.

*   *   *

The other type of statute is exemplified by the Connecticut statute which provides that jury trial may be had in certain appeals from probate and in "civil actions involving such an issue of fact as, prior to January 1, 1880, would not present a question properly cognizable in equity." The Federal rule is simpler still. . . .[7]

NOTES

(1) Could the legislature avoid the right to trial by jury by assigning the task of assessing appropriate fines to an administrative agency? See Atlas

197 (1813)); Moot v. Moot, 214 N.Y. 204, 108 N.E. 424 (1915); see N.Y.Civ.Prac.Act § 1149.

6. N.Y. Const. art. I, § 19 (1894, as amended 1913). The amendment presently appears in N.Y. Const. art. I, § 18. It was the result of the decision of the Court of Appeals in Ives v. South Buffalo Ry., 201 N.Y. 271, 94 N.E. 431 (1911), holding un-

constitutional the Workmen's Compensation Act of 1910. Although basing its decision on other grounds, the Court of Appeals indicated in its opinion that the Act probably deprived the employer of his constitutional right to have a jury assess the amount of his liability.

7. Fed.R.Civ.P. 38(a).

Roofing Co. v. Occupational Safety & Health Review Commission, 430 U.S. 442, 97 S.Ct. 1261, 51 L.Ed.2d 464 (1977), p. 777 infra. If it could, would that make sense?

(2) Cf. Damsky v. Zavatt, 289 F.2d 46, 49–51 (2d Cir.1961), in which Judge Friendly, in determining that the defendant in action by the government for the recovery of taxes was entitled to a trial by jury, traced the history of the Court of Exchequer from the 12th century to 1791. Judge Clark, in his dissent, thought a denial of a jury in tax collection cases "more consistent with a modern age and a modern procedure" (at 59).

(3) See Pernell v. Southall Realty, 416 U.S. 363, 94 S.Ct. 1723, 40 L.Ed.2d 198 (1974), in which the court felt compelled to discuss in detail the history of common law writs to obtain possession of real property before holding that the Seventh Amendment guarantees a jury trial in an ejectment action in the District of Columbia.

(4) Parsons v. Bedford, 28 U.S. (3 Pet.) 433, 445–447, 7 L.Ed. 732, 736 (1830) (Story, J.): "The trial by jury is justly dear to the American people. It has always been an object of deep interest and solicitude, and every encroachment upon it has been watched with great jealousy. . . . One of the strongest objections originally taken against the constitution of the United States, was the want of an express provision securing the right of trial by jury in civil cases. As soon as the constitution was adopted, this right was secured by the seventh amendment of the constitution proposed by congress; and which received an assent of the people, so general, as to establish its importance as a fundamental guarantee of the rights and liberties of the people. This amendment declares, that 'in suits at common law, where the value in controversy shall exceed twenty dollars, the right of trial by jury shall be preserved; and no fact, once tried by a jury, shall be otherwise re-examinable in any court of the United States, than according to the rules of the common law.' At this time, there were no states in the Union, the basis of whose jurisprudence was not essentially that of the common law, in its widest meaning; and probably, no states were contemplated, in which it would not exist. The phrase 'common law,' found in this clause, is used in contradistinction to equity, and admiralty and maritime jurisprudence. The constitution had declared, in the third article, 'that the judicial power shall extend to all cases in law and equity arising under this constitution, the laws of the United States, and treaties made or which shall be made under their authority,' &c., and to all cases of admiralty and maritime jurisdiction. It is well known, that in civil causes in courts of equity and admiralty, juries do not intervene, and that courts of equity use the trial by jury only in extraordinary cases, to inform the conscience of the court. When, therefore, we find, that the amendment requires that the right of trial by jury shall be preserved, in suits at common law, the natural conclusion is, that this distinction was present to the minds of the framers of the amendment." . . .

(5) Some protagonists of the civil jury tend to grow lyrical in its praise. See, e.g., Belli, Ready for the Plaintiff 240 (1956): "If one were to ask me, 'Where, who, what, would portray the face of America?' rather than speak of a President, of a national capital, of a Washington Monument, of a flag or memorial, I could say, 'Look upon the faces of those twelve jurors!' " See also Hart, Long Live the American Jury (1964). Others would rather abolish the civil jury here and now. Prominent among the opponents of the civil jury are: James, Trial by Jury and the New Federal Rules of Procedure, 45 Yale L.J.

1022 (1936); Frank, Courts on Trial (1949); Peck, Do Juries Delay Justice? 18 F.R.D. 455 (1956); and Desmond, Should It Take 34 Months for a Trial?, N.Y. Times Mag., p. 29, Dec. 8, 1963; and former Chief Justice Burger, Thinking the Unthinkable, 31 Loyola L.Rev. 205 (1985).

(6) The University of Chicago undertook a comprehensive review of the American jury. The principal work it produced was Kalven & Zeisel, The American Jury (1971).

ROSENBERG, THE TRIAL JUDGES' VERDICT ON THE CIVIL JURY

Trial Judges' Journal, Jan. 1966, p. 5.

Among state trial judges—whether new to the bench or seasoned by years of service—the verdict on the civil jury is overwhelmingly "not guilty" of deserving extinction or major curtailment.

* 　 * 　 *

This clear preference of the trial judges is an intriguing factor in the perennial battle over retention or abolition of the civil jury. It means that however much the value of the jury may be doubted by appellate judges, lawyers and law teachers, however much they may call it outmoded in a rubber-tired, split-second society, they must pause and reckon with a contrary conclusion by the men who sit with the jury day after day and presumably measure its performance against their own evaluation of the case. Why are these men so overwhelmingly favorable toward the jury?

It is not, we can be sure from their responses, because of any strong belief that jurors reach results that are more just than judges would produce. Of all those surveyed only a handful credited the jury with better results; indeed, a much larger group was convinced that judges give a better brand of justice. The strong hold the jury has on the judges apparently has to do with collateral matters, not the quality of its verdicts. To uncover the underlying reasons the questionnaires gave the respondents a chance to check two "chief advantages of the civil jury" in a list of six items, and two "chief faults" in a list of seven. In addition, they were asked to volunteer the single most urgent change they would recommend to improve the civil jury in their home state.

* 　 * 　 *

Some writers have suggested that trial judges admire the jury for the bluntly selfish reason that it spares the judge from having to answer hard questions, such as the value of pain and suffering, or closely balanced issues of negligence. Only a small minority of the judges supported that hypothesis, as can be seen in Table 1.

NOTES

(1) For a follow-up on the Rosenberg survey, see Note, With Love in Their Hearts but Reform on Their Minds: How Trial Judges View the Civil Jury, 4 Colum.J. of L. & Soc.Prob. 178 (1968).

(2) In considering the current attitude of the courts toward the jury, to what extent is an evaluation of its effect on endemic delays in the courts relevant? Note that there is a wide difference of opinion on estimates of the added time needed for a jury trial. *Compare* Zeisel, Kalven & Buchholz, Delay in the Court, 71, n. 1 (1959) (Judge Peck reports 250% longer); id. at 81 (authors' estimate 40% longer) *with* Hazard, Book Review, 48 Calif.L.Rev. 360, 369–70 (1960) (California time studies showing a 300% difference). It has even been suggested that English bench trials in negligence cases are more time consuming than jury trials. See Heuston, The Law of Torts in 1960, 6 J.Soc. Pub.Teach.Law N.S. 26, 29 (1961); James, Summary of Colloquy on Torts, id. at 34, 35–36.

(3) In England, a trial by jury in civil cases occurs only in exceptional circumstances. See Section 6(1) of the Administration of Justice (Miscellaneous Provisions) Act, 1933:

> "Subject as hereinafter provided, if, on the application of any party to an action to be tried in the King's Bench Division of the High Court made not later than such time before the trial as may be limited by rules of Court, the Court or a Judge is satisfied that—
>
>> (a) a charge of fraud against that party; or
>>
>> (b) a claim in respect of libel, slander, malicious prosecution, false imprisonment, seduction or breach of promise of marriage
>
> is in issue, the action shall be ordered to be tried with a jury unless the Court or Judge is of opinion that the trial thereof requires any prolonged examination of documents or accounts or any scientific or local investigation which cannot conveniently be made with a jury; but, save as aforesaid, any action to be tried in that Division may, in the discretion of the Court or a judge, be ordered to be tried, with or without a jury:
>
> Provided that the provisions of this section shall be without prejudice to the power of the Court or a Judge to order, in accordance with rules of Court, that different questions of fact arising in any action to be tried by different modes of trial, and where any such order is made the provisions of this section requiring trial with a jury in certain cases shall have effect only as respects questions relating to any such charge or claim as aforesaid".

(4) Increasingly, legislators are concluding that a jury trial is not appropriate for settling all private disputes. The two most important areas in which the right to a jury trial has been curtailed are workmen's compensation and no-fault insurance. How do such limitations square with the jury trial guarantees of the federal and state constitutions? See Ives v. South Buffalo R., 201 N.Y. 271, 94 N.E. 431 (1911), holding the New York workmen's compensation system unconstitutional.

> ". . . If these provisions relating to compensation are to be construed as definitely fixing the amount which an employer must pay in every case where his liability is established by statute, there can be no doubt that they constitute a legislative usurpation of one of the functions of the common-law jury . . . . This part of the statute, in its present form, has given use to conflicting views among the members of the court, and, since the disposition of the question which it suggests is not necessary to the decision of the case, we do not decide it." Id., at 291–292, 94 N.E. at 438.

As a result of the doubts raised by the Ives case, the New York Constitution was amended to permit workmen's compensation to supplant the common law jury trial. N.Y.—McKinney's Const. Art. I, § 18.

(5) The no-fault automobile injury laws raise somewhat similar problems. Beginning with Pinnick v. Cleary, 360 Mass. 1, 271 N.E.2d 592 (1971), state courts have held the plans do not violate state constitutional rights to trial by jury. The court in Pinnick did not even bother to discuss the jury issue. See also Opinion of the Justices, 113 N.H. 205, 304 A.2d 881 (1973) (upholding the New Hampshire plan despite jury right curtailment); Manzanares v. Bell, 214 Kan. 589, 522 P.2d 1291, 1312 (1974) (holding that while a jury trial is required at common law, the legislature may modify the common law); Lasky v. State Farm Insurance Co., 296 So.2d 9, 22 (Fla.1974). See generally Keeton and O'Connell, Basic Protection for the Traffic Victim, 493–504 (1965).

(6) The right to a jury trial may be waived by failure to make a timely demand. Fed.R.Civ.P. 38(d). May a party bargain away the right to a jury trial before the action is commenced? The Supreme Court has held that this practice is not per se unconstitutional. In D.H. Overmyer Co., Inc. of Ohio v. Frick Co., 405 U.S. 174, 186, 92 S.Ct. 775, 782, 31 L.Ed.2d 124, 134 (1972), the Court approved a confession of judgment note which operated not only as a jury waiver but as a waiver of any trial, noting that there was no "unequal bargaining power or overreaching." On "cognovit" note practice, see also p. 234 supra. Cf. Fuentes v. Shevin, 407 U.S. 67, 95, 92 S.Ct. 1983, 2002, 32 L.Ed. 2d 556, 578 (1971), rehearing denied 409 U.S. 902, 93 S.Ct. 177, 34 L.Ed.2d 165 (1972) (pre-judgment repossession of goods sold on an installment sale contract; the court noted "no showing whatever that the appellants were actually aware or made aware of the significance of the fine print now relied upon as a waiver of constitutional rights.").

NOTE ON THE SIX–PERSON JURY

For a full history of the twelve-person jury and approval of the use of a six person jury, see Colgrove v. Battin, 413 U.S. 149, 93 S.Ct. 2448, 37 L.Ed.2d 522 (1973). Reduction in the size of civil juries from twelve to six has been widespread. See, e.g., N.Y.—McKinney's CPLR § 4104.

In *Colgrove,* the Court declared: ". . . four very recent studies have provided convincing empirical evidence of the correctness of the *Williams* [Williams v. Florida, 399 U.S. 78, 90 S.Ct. 1893, 26 L.Ed.2d 446 (1970) (sustaining six-person juries in certain criminal cases)] conclusion that 'there is no discernible difference between the results reached by the two different-sized juries.'" 413 U.S. at 159 n. 15, 93 S.Ct. at 2453, 37 L.Ed.2d at 530. Zeisel and Diamond, "Convincing Empirical Evidence" on the Six Member Jury, 41 U.Chi.L.R. 281 (1974), take a contrary position, suggesting that a smaller jury has a substantive effect.

Rosenblatt and Rosenblatt, Six-Member Juries in Criminal Cases? Legal and Psychological Considerations, 47 St. Johns L.Rev. 615, 627 (1973) (footnotes omitted):

"The chief argument in favor of a jury of twelve as opposed to one of six members has been that of increased resources. The more people that hear a set of arguments and weigh evidence, the greater the probability that the group will reach a correct solution. This argument has been supported by psychological studies of group problem solving situations that are analogous, but not identical, to the task of the jury. For example, groups were superior to individuals working alone for problems that required the overcoming of prejudices and the detection of errors in recall. Groups of 12 or 13 surpassed those of six or seven in the quality of solutions to a human relations problem.

"The superiority of group to individual and of a larger group to a smaller group can be predicted on a purely statistical basis. Pooling of individual judgments reduces random error. The distribution of pooled judgments will be closer to the true value than will that of individual judgments. 'Four judgments are better than one for the same non-social reasons that four thermometers are better than One.'

"On the same purely statistical basis, Hans Zeisel has argued that an experienced lawyer will be better able to predict the verdict in a given case for a 12-member than for a six-member jury. The 12-member jury will be less of a 'gamble' because its verdicts will be less variable. That is, the distribution of pooled judgments of larger groups will be closer to the true value than that of smaller groups due to greater elimination of random error, hence they will vary less."

Extensive reference to other views on the issue of "effectiveness of a jury of six" are collected in Colgrove, 413 U.S. at 159 n. 15, 93 S.Ct. 2453, 37 L.Ed.2d 530. See also, The Six Man Jury: A Discussion Before the Judicial Conference of the Fourth Circuit, June 29–July 2, 1972, 59 F.R.D. 180 (1972). Nearly all United States District Courts have adopted local rule requiring or authorizing six-person juries in civil cases. The soundness of using the local-rule procedure to accomplish a reduction in jury size has been questioned. See, J.B. Weinstein, Reform of Federal Rule-Making Procedures (1976). While Colgrove seems to have eliminated constitutional impediments to a six-person jury in the federal courts, a twelve-person jury may be mandatory under a state's constitutional provision. See, e.g., Burciaga, The Twelve Member Jury in Illinois—Can it be Reduced?, 63 Ill.B.J. 16 (1974).

In Ballew v. Georgia, 435 U.S. 223, 98 S.Ct. 1029, 55 L.Ed.2d 234 (1978), the Supreme Court held unconstitutional trial by a five-person jury of a criminal case in a state court. It also held unconstitutional conviction by a nonunanimous six-person jury in a state court criminal case. Burch v. Louisiana, 441 U.S. 130, 99 S.Ct. 1623, 60 L.Ed.2d 96 (1979). On the size of the jury, see also Kaye, And Then There Were 12: Statistical Reasoning, the Supreme Court, and the Size of the Jury, 68 Calif.L.Rev. 1004 (1980); Lermack, No Right Number? Social Science Research and the Jury Size Cases, 54 N.Y.U.L.Rev. 951 (1979);

Note, Impact of Jury Size on Court System, 12 Loyola U.L.Rev. 1102 (1979).

SECTION 3. PROBLEMS CREATED BY THE MERGER OF LAW AND EQUITY

SECOND PRELIMINARY REPORT OF NEW YORK ADVISORY COMMITTEE ON PRACTICE AND PROCEDURE
Leg.Doc. No. 13, 564–69 (1958).

* * *

II. JURY TRIALS AND THE ONE FORM OF ACTION *
* * *

C. Problems Arising Under the Merged Procedure

The constitutional right to trial by jury presented a major problem in the merger of law and equity. In the early days of the Code, the more conservative New York judges took the view that the problem was insuperable . . .

And as late as 1917, in Jackson v. Strong,[1] the Court of Appeals declared: "The inherent and fundamental difference between actions at law and suits in equity cannot be ignored." The more recent view is that the constitutional right to trial by jury although presenting difficulties, does not make necessary a separate system of law and equity; for the right to jury trial affects only the trial of the case and has no effect upon the pleading stage.[2]

Although generally accepting the recent view, the New York courts have nevertheless had serious problems in achieving a unified system of legal and equitable relief. These problems have arisen in part because the abolition of law and equity as living systems of separate principles has required the courts to classify actions according to a distinction fixed at a date when the substantive law was less developed and litigation less complex. Moreover, an increasing number of cases in which issues appear in new combinations are extremely difficult to fit wholly into one category or the other.[3]

. . . [F]ive specific problems . . . have plagued the New York courts since the adoption of the Code: first, the case where a plaintiff asks for money damages only in the kind of action that would otherwise

---

* Some footnotes omitted; others renumbered.

1. 222 N.Y. 149, 154, 118 N.E. 512, 513 (1917).

2. Clark, Code Pleading 91–94 (2d ed. 1947); Clark, The Union of Law and Equity, 25 Colum.L.Rev. 1 (1925); Pike and Fischer, Pleadings and Jury Rights in the New Federal Procedure, 88 U. of Pa.L.Rev. 645 (1940). But see McCaskill, Jury Demands in the New Federal Procedure, 88 U. of Pa.L.Rev. 315 (1940).

3. See Note, The Right to Jury Trial under Merged Procedures, 65 Harv.L.Rev. 453 (1952).

have been tried by a court of equity; second, the case where a plaintiff seeks equitable relief but is entitled to money damages only, either because he cannot prove that he is entitled to equitable relief or because equitable relief is impractical or impossible; third, the case where a plaintiff joins legal and equitable claims; fourth, the case where a defendant in an equitable action interposes a legal counterclaim; and fifth, the case where a defendant in a legal action interposes an equitable defense or equitable counterclaim.

BEACON THEATRES, INC. v. WESTOVER, 359 U.S. 500, 79 S.Ct. 948, 3 L.Ed.2d 988 (1959). Plaintiff, alleging that the defendant had improperly threatened suit under the antitrust laws, sought declaratory relief and an injunction preventing defendant from bringing suit. Defendant counterclaimed for treble damages and claimed trial by jury. The Ninth Circuit held that the trial court could properly exercise its discretion to try the equitable claim first, even though the plaintiff might subsequently invoke collateral estoppel to preclude a jury trial of the same issues arising under defendant's counterclaim. The Supreme Court reversed (at 510–511):

> "If there should be cases where the availability of declaratory judgment or joinder in one suit of legal and equitable causes would not in all respects protect the plaintiff seeking equitable relief from irreparable harm while affording a jury trial in the legal cause, the trial court will necessarily have to use its discretion in deciding whether the legal or equitable cause should be tried first. Since the right to jury trial is a constitutional one, however, while no similar requirement protects trials by the court, that discretion is very narrowly limited and must, wherever possible, be exercised to preserve jury trial. . . . This long standing principle of equity dictates that only under the most imperative circumstances, circumstances which in view of the flexible procedures of the Federal Rules we cannot now anticipate, can the right to a jury trial of legal issues be lost through prior determination of equitable claims."

DAIRY QUEEN, INC. v. WOOD

Supreme Court of the United States, 1962.
369 U.S. 469, 82 S.Ct. 894, 8 L.Ed.2d 44.

MR. JUSTICE BLACK delivered the opinion of the Court.*

The United States District Court for the Eastern District of Pennsylvania granted a motion to strike petitioner's demand for a trial by jury in an action now pending before it on the alternative grounds that either the action was "purely equitable" or, if not purely equitable,

----

* Footnotes omitted.

whatever legal issues that were raised were "incidental" to equitable issues, and in either case, no right to trial by jury existed. The petitioner then sought mandamus in the Court of Appeals for the Third Circuit to compel the district judge to vacate this order. When that court denied this request without opinion, we granted certiorari because the action of the Court of Appeals seemed inconsistent with protections already clearly recognized for the important constitutional right to trial by jury in our previous decisions.

At the outset, we may dispose of one of the grounds upon which the trial court acted in striking the demand for trial by jury—that based upon the view that the right to trial by jury may be lost as to legal issues where those issues are characterized as "incidental" to equitable issues—for our previous decisions make it plain that no such rule may be applied in the federal courts. . . .

. . . after the adoption of the Federal Rules, attempts were made indirectly to undercut that right [i.e., the right to trial by jury] by having federal courts in which cases involving both legal and equitable claims were filed decide the equitable claim first. The result of this procedure in those cases in which it was followed was that any issue common to both the legal and equitable claims was finally determined by the court and the party seeking trial by jury on the legal claim was deprived of that right as to these common issues. This procedure finally came before us in Beacon Theatres, Inc., v. Westover, a case which, like this one, arose from the denial of a petition for mandamus to compel a district judge to vacate his order striking a demand for trial by jury.

. . . The holding in *Beacon Theatres* was that where both legal and equitable issues are presented in a single case, "only under the most imperative circumstances, circumstances which in view of the flexible procedures of the Federal Rules we cannot now anticipate, can the right to a jury trial of legal issues be lost through prior determination of equitable claims." That holding, of course, applies whether the trial judge chooses to characterize the legal issues presented as "incidental" to equitable issues or not. Consequently, in a case such as this where there cannot even be a contention of such "imperative circumstances," *Beacon Theatres* requires that any legal issues for which a trial by jury is timely and properly demanded be submitted to a jury. There being no question of the timeliness or correctness of the demand involved here, the sole question which we must decide is whether the action now pending before the District Court contains legal issues.

The District Court proceeding arises out of a controversy between petitioner and the respondent owners of the trademark "DAIRY QUEEN" with regard to a written licensing contract made by them in December 1949, under which petitioner agreed to pay some $150,000 for the exclusive right to use that trademark in certain portions of Pennsylvania. The terms of the contract provided for a small initial payment with the remaining payments to be made at the rate of 50% of all amounts received by petitioner on sales and franchises to deal with the trademark and, in order to make certain that the $150,000 payment would be completed within a specified period of time, further provided for minimum annual payments regardless of petitioner's receipts. In August 1960, the respondents wrote petitioner a letter in which they claimed that petitioner had committed "a material breach of that contract" by defaulting on the contract's payment provisions and notified petitioner of the termination of the contract and the cancellation of petitioner's right to use the trademark unless this claim default was remedied immediately. When petitioner continued to deal with the trademark despite the notice of termination, the respondents brought an action based upon their view that a material breach of contract had occurred.

The complaint filed in the District Court alleged, among other things, that petitioner had "ceased paying . . . as required in the contract;" that the default "under the said contract . . . [was] in excess of $60,000.00;" that this default constituted a "material breach" of that contract; that petitioner had been notified by letter that its failure to pay as alleged made it guilty of a material breach of contract which if not "cured" would result in an immediate cancellation of the contract; that the breach had not been cured but that petitioner was contesting the cancellation and continuing to conduct business as an authorized dealer; that to continue such business after the cancellation of the contract constituted an infringement of the respondents' trademark; that petitioner's financial condition was unstable; and that because of the foregoing allegations, respondents were threatened with irreparable injury for which they had no adequate remedy at law. The complaint then prayed for both temporary and permanent relief, including: (1) temporary and permanent injunctions to restrain petitioner from any future use of or dealing in the franchise and the trademark; (2) an accounting to determine the exact amount of money owing by petitioner and a judgment for that amount; and (3) an injunction pending accounting to prevent petitioner from collecting any money from "Dairy Queen" stores in the territory.

In its answer to this complaint, petitioner raised a number of defenses, including: (1) a denial that there had been any breach of contract, apparently based chiefly upon its allegation that in January 1955 the parties had entered into an oral agreement modifying the original written contract by removing the provision requiring minimum annual payments regardless of petitioner's receipts thus leaving petitioner's only obligation that of turning over 50% of all its receipts; (2) laches and estoppel arising from respondents' failure to assert their claim promptly, thus permitting petitioner to expend large amounts of money in the development of its right to use the trademark; and (3) alleged violations of the antitrust laws by respondents in connection with their dealings with the trademark. Petitioner indorsed upon this answer a demand for trial by jury in accordance with Rule 38(b) of the Federal Rules of Civil Procedure.

Petitioner's contention, as set forth in its petition for mandamus to the Court of Appeals and reiterated in its briefs before this Court, is that insofar as the complaint requests a money judgment it presents a claim which is unquestionably legal. We agree with that contention. The most natural construction of the respondents' claim for a money judgment would seem to be that it is a claim that they are entitled to recover whatever was owed them under the contract as of the date of its purported termination plus damages for infringement of their trademark since that date. Alternatively, the complaint could be construed to set forth a full claim based upon both of these theories—that is, a claim that the respondents were entitled to recover both the debt due under the contract and damages for trademark infringement for the entire period of the alleged breach including that before the termination of the contract. Or it might possibly be construed to set forth a claim for recovery based completely on either one of these two theories—that is, a claim based solely upon the contract for the entire period both before and after the attempted termination on the theory that the termination, having been ignored, was of no consequence, or a claim based solely upon the charge of infringement on the theory that the contract, having been breached, could not be used as a defense to an infringement action even for the period prior to its termination. We find it unnecessary to resolve this ambiguity in the respondents' complaint because we think it plain that their claim for a money judgment is a claim wholly legal in its nature however the complaint is construed. As an action on a debt allegedly due under a contract, it would be difficult to conceive of an action of a more traditionally legal character. And as an action for damages based upon a charge of trademark infringement, it would be no less subject to cognizance by a court of law.

The respondents' contention that this money claim is "purely equitable" is based primarily upon the fact that their complaint is cast in terms of an "accounting," rather than in terms of an action for "debt" or "damages." But the constitutional right to trial by jury cannot be made to depend upon the choice of words used in the pleadings. The necessary prerequisite to the right to maintain a suit for an equitable accounting, like all other equitable remedies, is, as we pointed out in *Beacon Theatres,* the absence of an adequate remedy at law. Consequently, in order to maintain such a suit on a cause of action cognizable at law, as this one is, the plaintiff must be able to show that the "accounts between the parties" are of such a "complicated nature" that only a court of equity can satisfactorily unravel them. In view of the powers given to District Courts by Federal Rule of Civil Procedure 53(b) to appoint masters to assist the jury in those exceptional cases where the legal issues are too complicated for the jury adequately to handle alone, the burden of such a showing is considerably increased and it will indeed be a rare case in which it can be met. But be that as it may, this is certainly not such a case. A jury, under proper instructions from the court, could readily determine the recovery, if any, to be had here, whether the theory finally settled upon is that of breach of contract, that of trademark infringement, or any combination of the two. The legal remedy cannot be characterized as inadequate merely because the measure of damages may necessitate a look into petitioner's business records.

Nor is the legal claim here rendered "purely equitable" by the nature of the defenses interposed by petitioner. Petitioner's primary defense to the charge of breach of contract—that is, that the contract was modified by a subsequent oral agreement—presents a purely legal question having nothing whatever to do either with novation, as the district judge suggested, or reformation, as suggested by the respondents here. Such a defense goes to the question of just what, under the law, the contract between the respondents and petitioner is and, in an action to collect a debt for breach of a contract between these parties, petitioner has a right to have the jury determine not only whether the contract has been breached and the extent of the damages if any but also just what the contract is.

* * *

Reversed and remanded.

MR. JUSTICE STEWART concurs in the result.

MR. JUSTICE FRANKFURTER took no part in the decision of this case.

MR. JUSTICE WHITE took no part in the consideration or decision of this case.

MR. JUSTICE HARLAN, whom MR. JUSTICE DOUGLAS joins, concurring. [Omitted.]

NOTES

(1) Does the Supreme Court reject application of the clean-up doctrine (a) in a case in which the doctrine would have been applied by a court of equity at the historically decisive moment and (b) in a modern merged action that could not have been brought in a court of equity? What reasons, historical or other, does the Court advance for its holding?

(2) If a case presents legal as well as equitable issues, may or must the whole case be tried to a jury? In Fitzgerald v. United States Lines Co., 374 U.S. 16, 83 S.Ct. 1646, 10 L.Ed.2d 720 (1963), plaintiff asserted a claim for damages under the Jones Act and for maintenance and cure under admiralty principles. The first claim was legal and triable to a jury, and the second was not. In holding that the whole case should be tried to a jury, the Court stated (374 U.S. at 21, 83 S.Ct. at 1650): "Only one trier of fact should be used for the trial of what is essentially one lawsuit to settle one claim split conceptually into separate parts because of historical developments."

(3) On the clean-up doctrine, see also Levin, Equitable Clean-Up and the Jury: A Suggested Orientation, 100 U.Pa.L.Rev. 320 (1951). What are the policy considerations underlying the doctrine? In systems that have introduced the unitary action, can these policies be given effect in cases other than those in which the doctrine was applied at the constitutionally decisive time in history?

(4) In an action for civil penalties and injunctive relief under the Clean Water Act, is there a constitutional right to trial by jury on both liability for,

and amount of, the civil penalty? In Tull v. United States, 481 U.S. 412, 107 S.Ct. 1831, 95 L.Ed.2d 365 (1987), the Supreme Court said yes. Should it have sought to apply the clean-up doctrine?

———

ROSS v. BERNHARD

Supreme Court of the United States, 1970.
396 U.S. 531, 90 S.Ct. 733, 24 L.Ed.2d 729.

MR. JUSTICE WHITE delivered the opinion of the Court.*

The Seventh Amendment to the Constitution provides that in "[s]uits at common law, where the value in controversy shall exceed twenty dollars, the right of trial by jury shall be preserved." Whether the Amendment guarantees the right to a jury trial in stockholders' derivative actions is the issue now before us.

Petitioners brought this derivative suit in federal court against the directors of their closed-end investment company, the Lehman Corporation and the corporation's brokers, Lehman Brothers. They contended that Lehman Brothers controlled the corporation through an illegally large representation on the corporation's board of directors, in violation of the Investment Company Act of 1940, 54 Stat. 789, 15 U.S.C. § 80a–1 *et seq.,* and used this control to extract excessive brokerage fees from the corporation. The directors of the corporation were accused of converting corporate assets and of "gross abuse of trust, gross misconduct, willful misfeasance, bad faith, [and] gross negligence." Both the individual defendants and Lehman Brothers were accused of breaches of fiduciary duty. It was alleged that the payments to Lehman Brothers constituted waste and spoliation, and that the contract between the corporation and Lehman Brothers had been violated. Petitioners requested that the defendants "account for and pay to the Corporation for their profits and gains and its losses." Petitioners also demanded a jury trial on the corporation's claims.

On motion to strike petitioners' jury trial demand, the District Court held that a shareholder's right to a jury on his corporation's cause of action was to be judged as if the corporation were itself the plaintiff. Only the shareholder's initial claim to speak for the corporation had to be tried to the judge. . . . Convinced that "there are substantial grounds for difference of opinion as to this question and . . . an immediate appeal would materially advance the ultimate termination of this litigation," the District Court permitted an interlocutory appeal. 28 U.S.C. § 1292(b). The Court of Appeals reversed, holding that a derivative action was entirely equitable in nature, and no jury was available to try any part of it. . . .

We reverse the holding of the Court of Appeals that in no event does the right to a jury trial preserved by the Seventh Amendment

* Some footnotes omitted; others renumbered.

extend to derivative actions brought by the stockholders of a corporation. We hold that the right to jury trial attaches to those issues in derivative actions as to which the corporation, if it had been suing in its own right, would have been entitled to a jury.

The Seventh Amendment preserves to litigants the right to jury trial in suits at common law—

> "not merely suits, which the *common* law recognized among its old and settled proceedings, but suits in which *legal* rights were to be ascertained and determined, in contradistinction to those where equitable rights alone were recognized, and equitable remedies were administered. . . . In a just sense, the amendment then may well be construed to embrace all suits, which are not of equity and admiralty jurisdiction, whatever may be the peculiar form which they may assume to settle legal rights." Parsons v. Bedford, Breedlove & Robeson, 3 Pet. 433, 447, 7 L.Ed. 732 (1830).

However difficult it may have been to define with precision the line between actions at law dealing with legal rights and suits in equity dealing with equitable matters, Whitehead v. Shattuck, 138 U.S. 146, 151, 11 S.Ct. 276, 277, 34 L.Ed. 873 (1891), some proceedings were unmistakably actions at law triable to a jury. The Seventh Amendment, for example, entitled the parties to a jury trial in actions for damages to a person or property, for libel and slander, for recovery of land, and for conversion of personal property. Just as clearly, a corporation, although an artificial being, was commonly entitled to sue and be sued in the usual forms of action, at least in its own State. See Paul v. Virginia, 8 Wall. 168, 19 L.Ed. 357 (1869). . . .

The common law refused, however, to permit stockholders to call corporate managers to account in actions at law. The possibilities for abuse, thus presented, were not ignored by corporate officers and directors. Early in the 19th century, equity provided relief both in this country and in England. Without detailing these developments, it suffices to say that the remedy in this country, first dealt with by this Court in Dodge v. Woolsey, 18 How. 331, 15 L.Ed. 401 (1856), provided redress not only against faithless officers and directors but also against third parties who had damaged or threatened the corporate properties and whom the corporation through its managers refused to pursue. The remedy made available in equity was the derivative suit, viewed in this country as a suit to enforce a *corporate* cause of action against officers, directors, and third parties. As elaborated in the cases, one precondition for the suit was a valid claim on which the corporation could have sued; another was that the corporation itself had refused to proceed after suitable demand, unless excused by extraordinary conditions. Thus the dual nature of the stockholder's action: first, the plaintiff's right to sue on behalf of the corporation and, second, the merits of the corporation claim itself.

Derivative suits posed no Seventh Amendment problems where the action against the directors and third parties would have been by a bill in equity had the corporation brought the suit. Our concern is with cases based upon a legal claim of the corporation against directors or third parties. Does the trial of such claims at the suit of a stockholder and without a jury violate the Seventh Amendment?

* * *

. . . What can be gleaned from this Court's opinions is not inconsistent with the general understanding, reflected by the state court decisions and secondary sources, that equity could properly resolve corporate claims of any kind without a jury when properly pleaded in derivative suits complying with the equity rules.

* * *

. . . The Seventh Amendment question depends on the nature of the issue to be tried rather than the character of the overall action.[1] See Simler v. Conner, 372 U.S. 221, 83 S.Ct. 609, 9 L.Ed.2d 691 (1963). The principle of these cases bears heavily on derivative actions.

We have noted that the derivative suit has dual aspects: first, the stockholder's right to sue on behalf of the corporation, historically an equitable matter; second, the claim of the corporation against directors or third parties on which, if the corporation had sued and the claim presented legal issues, the company could demand a jury trial. . . . The heart of the action is the corporate claim. If it presents a legal issue, one entitling the corporation to a jury trial under the Seventh Amendment, the right to a jury is not forfeited merely because the stockholder's right to sue must first be adjudicated as an equitable issue triable to the court. *Beacon* and *Dairy Queen* require no less.

If under older procedures, now discarded, a court of equity could properly try the legal claims of the corporation presented in a derivative suit, it was because irreparable injury was threatened and no remedy at law existed as long as the stockholder was without standing to sue and the corporation itself refused to pursue its own remedies. Indeed, from 1789 until 1938, the judicial code expressly forbade courts of equity from entertaining any suit for which there was an adequate remedy at law.[2] This provision served "to guard the right of trial by jury preserved by the Seventh Amendment and to that end it should be liberally construed." Schoenthal v. Irving Trust Co., 287 U.S. 92, 94, 53 S.Ct. 50, 51, 77 L.Ed. 185 (1932). If, before 1938, the law had borrowed from equity, as it borrowed other things, the idea that stockholders

---

1. As our cases indicate, the "legal" nature of an issue is determined by considering, first, the pre-merger custom with reference to such questions; second, the remedy sought; and, third, the practical abilities and limitations of juries. Of these factors, the first, requiring extensive and possibly abstruse historical inquiry, is obviously the most difficult to apply. See

James, Right to a Jury Trial in Civil Actions, 72 Yale L.J. 655 (1963).

2. The Judicial Code of 1911, § 267, 36 Stat. 1163, re-enacting the Act of Sept. 24, 1789, § 16, 1 Stat. 82, provided: "Suits in equity shall not be sustained in any court of the United States in any case where a plain, adequate, and complete remedy may be had at law."

could litigate for their recalcitrant corporation, the corporate claim, if legal, would undoubtedly have been tried to a jury.

Of course, this did not occur, but the Federal Rules had a similar impact. Actions are no longer brought as actions at law or suits in equity. Under the Rules there is only one action—a "civil action"—in which all claims may be joined and all remedies are available. Purely procedural impediments to the presentation of any issue by any party, based on the difference between law and equity, were destroyed. In a civil action presenting a stockholder's derivative claim, the court after passing upon the plaintiff's right to sue on behalf of the corporation is now able to try the corporate claim for damages with the aid of a jury. Separable claims may be tried separately, Fed.Rule Civ.Proc. 42(b), or legal and equitable issues may be handled in the same trial. Fanchon & Marco, Inc. v. Paramount Pictures, Inc., 202 F.2d 731 (C.A.2d Cir. 1953). The historical rule preventing a court of law from entertaining a shareholder's suit on behalf of the corporation is obsolete; it is no longer tenable for a district court, administering both law and equity in the same action, to deny legal remedies to a corporation, merely because the corporation's spokesmen are its shareholders rather than its directors. . . .

Derivative suits have been described as one kind of "true" class action. Id., § 562.1. We are inclined to agree with the description, at least to the extent it recognizes that the derivative suit and the class action were both ways of allowing parties to be heard in equity who could not speak at law.[3] . . .

In the instant case we have no doubt that the corporation's claim is, at least in part, a legal one. The relief sought is money damages. There are allegations in the complaint of a breach of fiduciary duty, but there are also allegations of ordinary breach of contract and gross

---

3. Other equitable devices are used under the rules without depriving the parties employing them of the right to a jury trial on legal issues. For example, although the right to intervene may in some cases be limited, United States for Use and Benefit of Browne & Bryan Lumber Co. v. Massachusetts Bonding & Ins. Co., 303 F.2d 823 (C.A. 2d Cir.1962); Dickinson v. Burnham, 197 F.2d 973 (C.A. 2d Cir.), cert. denied 344 U.S. 875, 73 S.Ct. 169, 97 L.Ed. 678 (1952), when intervention is permitted generally, the intervenor has a right to a jury trial on any legal issues he presents. See 3B J. Moore, Federal Practice ¶ 24.16[7] (2d ed. 1969); 5 id., ¶ 38.38[3]. A similar development seems to be taking place in the lower courts in interpleader actions. Before merger interpleader actions lay only in equity, and there was no right to a jury even on issues that might, under other circumstances, have been tried to a jury. Liberty Oil Co. v. Condon Nat. Bank, 260 U.S. 235, 43 S.Ct. 118, 67 L.Ed. 232 (1922). This view continued for some time after merger, see Bynum v. Prudential Life Ins. Co., 7 F.R.D. 585 (D.C.E.D.S.C.1947), but numerous courts and commentators have now come to the conclusion that the right to a jury should not turn on how the parties happen to be brought into court. See Pan American Fire & Cas. Co. v. Revere, 188 F.Supp. 474 (D.C.E.D.La.1960); Savannah Bank & Trust Co. v. Block, 175 F.Supp. 798 (D.C.S.D.Ga.1959); Westinghouse Elec. Corp. v. United Elec. Radio & Mach. Workers of America, 99 F.Supp. 597 (D.C.W.D.Pa.1951); John Hancock Mut. Life Ins. Co. v. Yarrow, 95 F.Supp. 185 (D.C.E.D.Pa.1951); 2 W. Barron & A. Holtzoff, Federal Practice and Procedure § 556 (Wright ed. 1961); 3A J. Moore, Federal Practice ¶ 22.14[4] (2d ed. 1969). But see Pennsylvania Fire Ins. Co. v. American Airlines, Inc., 180 F.Supp. 239 (D.C.E.D. N.Y.1960); Liberty Nat. Life Ins. Co. v. Brown, 119 F.Supp. 920 (D.C.M.D.Ala. 1954).

negligence. The corporation, had it sued on its own behalf, would have been entitled to a jury's determination, at a minimum, of its damages against its broker under the brokerage contract and of its rights against its own directors because of their negligence. Under these circumstances it is unnecessary to decide whether the corporation's other claims are also properly triable to a jury. Dairy Queen, Inc. v. Wood, 369 U.S. 469, 82 S.Ct. 894, 8 L.Ed.2d 44 (1962). The decision of the Court of Appeals is reversed.

It is so ordered.

Decision of Court of Appeals reversed.

MR. JUSTICE STEWART, with whom THE CHIEF JUSTICE and MR. JUSTICE HARLAN join, dissenting.

In holding as it does that the plaintiff in a shareholder's derivative suit is constitutionally entitled to a jury trial, the Court today seems to rely upon some sort of ill-defined combination of the Seventh Amendment and the Federal Rules of Civil Procedure. Somehow the Amendment and the Rules magically interact to do what each separately was expressly intended not to do, namely, to enlarge the right to a jury trial in civil actions brought in the courts of the United States.

. . . Today the Court tosses aside history, logic and over 100 years of firm precedent to hold that the plaintiff in a shareholder's derivative suit does indeed have a constitutional right to a trial by jury. This holding has a questionable basis in policy [4] and no basis whatever in the Constitution.

* * *

NOTES

(1) Is the Court's analysis compatible with the historical test? Does it make sense in the light of the circumstance that the Court's principal ground for regarding the action as legal was that the relief sought was money?

(2) In Dasho v. Susquehanna Corp., 461 F.2d 11 (7th Cir.1972), cert. denied 408 U.S. 925, 92 S.Ct. 2496, 33 L.Ed.2d 336 (1972), the court held *Ross* did not establish new law, but merely resolved an old conflict and thus would be applied retroactively.

(3) The problem treated in *Ross* arises whenever equity has made available a new procedural device for determining what is basically a legal question. Other examples include interpleader, see, e.g., Comment, 39 Tex.L.Rev. 632 (1961), and class actions, see, e.g., Syres v. Oil Workers Int. Union, Local 23, 257 F.2d 479 (5th Cir.), cert. denied 358 U.S. 929, 79 S.Ct. 315, 3 L.Ed.2d 302 (1958).

(4) There is some evidence that at the time of the freezing of the federal jury right by the adoption of the Seventh Amendment, courts of equity in England were only gradually acquiring the power to decide contested issues of fact without a jury. See Chesin & Hazard, Chancery Procedure and the Seventh Amendment: Jury Trial of Issues in Equity Cases Before 1791, 83 Yale

---

4. See, e.g., Frank, Courts on Trial 110–111 (1949). Certainly there is no consensus among commentators on the desirability of jury trials in civil actions generally. Particularly where the issues in the case are complex—as they are likely to be in a derivative suit—much can be said for allowing the court discretion to try the case itself. See discussion in 5 J. Moore, Federal Practice ¶ 38.02[1].

L.J. 999 (1974). In Langbein, Fact Finding in the English Court of Chancery: A Rebuttal, 83 Yale L.J. 1620 (1974), this view is recognized as having "a potential for mischief in our courts." The article seeks to limit the Chesin-Hazard thesis to questions of fact in cases involving fraud. What would be the effect of a general judicial acceptance of the view that, at the time of the freezing, equity had only limited fact finding powers? Should new historical evidence have much weight in reversing two hundred years of court construction? How much weight should current trends in judicial administration have?

(5) Local No. 92 International Association of Bridge, Structural & Ornamental Iron Workers v. Norris, 383 F.2d 735 (5th Cir.1967), was a suit by union members under 29 U.S.C.A. § 501 against union officials for breach of fiduciary obligations. An accounting was demanded. The master determined that defendants had received money not duly authorized and properly paid out of the funds of the local. The court held that, even though contemplating an award of money, the relief of an accounting by a fiduciary was traditionally equitable in nature and there was no right to a jury trial. But cf. Rowan v. Howard Sober, Inc., 384 F.Supp. 1121 (E.D.Mich.1974), in which union members, seeking monetary and injunctive relief, charged both their employer and their union with collusion in the bargaining process and breach of the collective bargaining agreement and in which the court ruled that it would decide on the injunction after a jury decided legal claims.

(6) Jury rights in civil rights actions raise difficult constitutional questions. Courts have consistently held that no jury right exists under Title VII of the Civil Rights Act of 1964 (discrimination in employment). See, e.g., Johnson v. Georgia Highway Express, 417 F.2d 1122 (5th Cir.1969), which involved a claim by black workers on which the Georgia employer sought a jury. See also Annot., Award of Back Pay under EEOA, 21 A.L.R.Fed. 472, 508 (1974). By contrast, in an action based on Title VIII of the Civil Rights Act of 1964 (discrimination in housing), the Supreme Court held a jury was available as of right to either party. Curtis v. Loether, 415 U.S. 189, 94 S.Ct. 1005, 39 L.Ed.2d 260 (1974). Mr. Justice Marshall said (footnotes omitted):

> We think it is clear that a damage action under § 812 is an action to enforce "legal rights" within the meaning of our Seventh Amendment decisions. See, e.g., Ross v. Bernhard, supra, 396 U.S., at 533, 542, 90 S.Ct., at 735, 740; Dairy Queen, Inc. v. Wood, supra, 369 U.S., at 476–477, 82 S.Ct., at 899. A damage action under the statute sounds basically in tort—the statute merely defines a new legal duty, and authorizes the courts to compensate a plaintiff for the injury caused by the defendants' wrongful breach. As the Court of Appeals noted, this cause of action is analogous to a number of tort actions recognized at common law. More important, the relief sought here—actual and punitive damages—is the traditional form of relief offered in the courts of law.

In connection with a jury right under Title VII, he noted:

> We need not, and do not, go so far as to say that any award of monetary relief must necessarily be 'legal' relief. See, e.g., Mitchell v. Robert DeMario Jewelry, Inc., 361 U.S. 288, 80 S.Ct. 332, 4 L.Ed.2d 323 (1960); Porter v. Warner Holding Co., 328 U.S. 395, 60 S.Ct. 1086, 90 L.Ed. 1332 (1946). A comparison of Title VIII with Title VII of the Civil Rights Act of 1964, where the Courts of Appeals have held that jury trial is not required in an action for reinstatement and backpay, is instructive, although we of course express no view on the jury trial issue in that context. In Title VII cases the Courts of Appeals have

characterized backpay as an integral part of an equitable remedy, a form of restitution. But the statutory language on which this characterization is based—

> "the court may enjoin the respondent from engaging in such unlawful employment practice, and order such affirmative action as may be appropriate, which may include, but is not limited to, reinstatement or hiring of employees, with or without back pay . . ., or any other equitable relief as the court deems appropriate," 42 U.S.C. § 2000e–5(g) (Supp. II 1972)—

contrasts sharply with § 812's simple authorization of an action for actual and punitive damages. In Title VII cases, also, the courts have relied on the fact that the decision whether to award backpay is committed to the discretion of the trial judge. There is no comparable discretion here: if a plaintiff proves unlawful discrimination and actual damage, he is entitled to judgment for that amount. Nor is there any sense in which the award here can be viewed as requiring the defendant to disgorge funds wrongfully withheld from the plaintiff. Whatever may be the merit of the 'equitable' characterization in Title VII cases, there is surely no basis for characterizing the award of compensatory and punitive damages here as equitable relief.

415 U.S. at 195–197, 94 S.Ct. at 1009–10, 39 L.Ed.2d at 267–68.

While *Curtis* was pending in the Supreme Court, one court held that a jury trial is available in an action under the Age Discrimination Act of 1967. Chilton v. National Cash Register, 370 F.Supp. 660 (S.D.Ohio 1974). See generally Note, The Right to Jury Trial Under Title VII of the Civil Rights Act of 1964, 37 U.Chi.L.Rev. 167 (1969).

In Lorillard v. Pons, 434 U.S. 575, 98 S.Ct. 866, 55 L.Ed.2d 40 (1978), the Supreme Court held that Congress, "by providing specifically for 'legal relief' . . . intended that there would be jury trial on demand to 'enforc[e]' . . . liability for amounts deemed to be unpaid wages or unpaid overtime compensation."

(7) Is there any right to trial *without* a jury? See Note, Right to Trial by Court, 74 Harv.L.Rev. 1176 (1961); Anno. 64 A.L.R.2d 506, 584 (1959). In United Press Associations v. Charles, 245 F.2d 21 (9th Cir.1957) neither party made a timely request for a jury; later the district court denied defendant's motion for a jury trial under Federal Rule 39(b); but seven months later, on its own initiative, the district court ordered a jury trial. Plaintiff's appeal from the judgment entered on the jury's verdict was dismissed, the court holding that plaintiff had waived any error for the reason that it neglected its "duty to refuse to go to trial before a jury, if it intended to rely upon this procedural objection" (p. 25): "Appellant, as it needs must, then argues that it could not waive the point, because the trial judge had no power to grant trial by jury. This proposition is amusing and certainly paradoxical. The drafters of the Rules announce that the right of a party to jury trial shall be preserved inviolate. But the Rules provide he can waive such right. United Press claims that these provisions have metamorphosed the right of a party to have a trial by jury, which can be waived, into a right of the opposite party to trial by the judge alone, which cannot be waived. Such abracadabra is not only impotent, but utterly unconvincing."

Dissenting, Judge Pope said (pp. 30, 31):

"My objection to the result here reached is based primarily upon the fact that the only judicial officer qualified or authorized to determine the issues of fact presented in this case has never done so. If this were a case properly triable to a jury whose verdict would have the same effect as if trial by jury were a matter of right, I would have no difficulty in concluding that the judgment here must be affirmed. But the Federal Rules of Civil Procedure which settle the question whether this case was one for determination by the court, or by a jury, are too clear for argument or doubt, and when the trial ended the duty to decide rested squarely on the court.

* * *

"The jury trial which the court may order under Rule 39(b), may only be ordered 'upon motion'. This is made doubly plain by the provision in Rule 39(c) that the advisory jury there provided for may be ordered 'upon motion *or of its own initiative*'. (Emphasis added.) In my view, therefore, the judge could not summon a jury for trial of the issues in the manner of a common law jury. It does not aid the appellees to argue, as they do, that the court had the right of its own motion to call an advisory jury, for there was no compliance with the mandatory requirements of Rule 52(a) that in such a case 'the court shall find the facts specially.'"

See also Jolin v. Oster, 55 Wis.2d 199, 205, 198 N.W.2d 639, 642 (1972), in which the court wrote:

While appellant argues most vigorously that this action was improperly tried as an action at law, the prejudice which attaches to such an alleged error is not obvious. Although appellant contends that the action should not have been tried to a jury, it is clear that even in an action in equity the court may, on the motion of a party or on its motion, submit questions of fact to an advisory jury. Inasmuch as the court in this case approved the jury's determination, it would appear that the submission of the case to a jury would be harmless error, if it was error.

DI MENNA v. COOPER & EVANS CO.

Court of Appeals of New York, 1917.
220 N.Y. 391, 115 N.E. 993.

CARDOZO, J.* The action is brought to foreclose a mechanic's lien. The plaintiff, a sub-contractor, furnished labor and materials to the defendant Cooper & Evans Company, which had a contract with the city of New York for a public improvement. The complaint alleges that the defendant undertook to make advances to the plaintiff during the progress of the work; that it kept its promise for a time; but that in August, 1910, it refused to make further advances, discharged the plaintiff and terminated the contract. The value of the labor and material supplied at that time, in excess of payments already received, is placed at $3,650.43. Judgment is demanded that the plaintiff be

* Footnotes omitted.

declared to have a lien upon the moneys due to the contractor from the city of New York; that the lien be enforced, and "that the plaintiff have personal judgment against the defendant Cooper & Evans Company for the amount of his claim, together with interest and costs." The city of New York, which was joined as a defendant, served an answer which put in issue the existence of the lien. The contractor's answer denied the material allegations of the complaint, and set up a counterclaim in which it stated that the plaintiff had wrongfully abandoned the contract to the defendant's damage in the sum of $11,671.41. To this counterclaim the plaintiff made a reply which was in substance a general denial.

Upon these pleadings the plaintiff moved that issues be stated for trial by jury. The Special Term denied the motion, but the Appellate Division reversed (155 App.Div. 501, 140 N.Y.S. 680). Its order directed that the following issues be tried by jury:

"1. Is the plaintiff entitled to a money judgment against the defendant, Cooper & Evans Company, and if so, for how much?

"2. Is the defendant Cooper & Evans Company entitled to a money judgment against the plaintiff, and if so, for how much?"

These issues were brought on for trial before JUDGE NEWBURGER and a jury. A special verdict was rendered by which it was found that the plaintiff was entitled to recover from Cooper & Evans Company $4,137.97, and that Cooper & Evans Company was not entitled to recover anything from the plaintiff. A motion to set aside the verdict was denied.

The plaintiff then brought on the remaining issues for trial at Special Term. He took the position that the jury's verdict was conclusive; the defendant took the position that it was merely advisory. The court accepted the former view. Upon proof of the verdict the conclusion was announced that the plaintiff must prevail. The court was asked by the contractor's counsel to determine the issues for itself, irrespective of the verdict. It refused to do so. It ruled, however, that there remained open the question of the existence of the lien. After that ruling the city of New York proved that the notice of lien had been filed too late. This made it invalid, and so the court held. Equitable relief was accordingly refused, but the plaintiff was given a personal judgment against the contractor for the sum found due by the jury.

In determining the force to be attributed to the jury's verdict, the complaint and the counterclaim are to be distinguished.

We are unwilling to hold that the *plaintiff's* cause of action was triable by a jury as of right upon the plaintiff's demand. An action to foreclose a lien is one of equitable cognizance [citations omitted]. Until the enactment of recent statutes the rule was that if the plaintiff did not prove a lien, equity was without power to give judgment for the moneys due to him [citations omitted]. The action may be retained, and common-law relief awarded. We do not doubt that a *defendant* by timely demand may preserve his right, in the event of failure of the lien, to trial by jury of the other issues [citations omitted]. The fact that the plaintiff has combined with a prayer for equitable relief an alternative claim for a money judgment, cannot deprive the defendant of the jury trial assured to him by the Constitution. But a different question is presented where it is the *plaintiff* who seeks a jury. The form of action in such a case is that of his own selection. The law does not require him to demand a personal judgment in the event of the failure of his lien. "It is intended to afford him a privilege—not to subject him to compulsion" (Koeppel v. Macbeth, 97 App.Div. 299, 301, 89 N.Y.S. 969). If he takes advantage of that privilege, he elects that the whole controversy, in all its aspects, may be determined by the court. To hold otherwise would do violence to the plain purpose of the statute. One cannot be heard to urge as a breach of one's constitutional right the concession of a remedy which one has one's self demanded. The rule is fundamental that where a plaintiff seeks legal and equitable relief in respect of the same wrong, *his* right to trial by jury is lost. If any right remains, it is the right of the defendant. [Citations omitted.] There is a dictum in the Hawkins case which suggests that either party may be entitled to have the issues framed (82 App.Div. 72, 78, 81 N.Y.S. 794). No such question, however, was involved, for the claim to trial by jury was there made by the defendant. When the case came here, we were careful to state that we placed our affirmance on other grounds [citations omitted]. The question, therefore, is still an open one. We think our conclusion ought to be that as to the plaintiff's cause of action the jury's verdict was advisory [citations omitted].

A different question arises when we come to the counterclaim. This was more than a counterclaim in name only [citations omitted]. It was an independent cause of action, which, if sustained, would have given the defendant a judgment for upwards of $11,000. It was, therefore, triable by jury as of right [citations omitted]. As to that branch of the case the verdict was conclusive. It was conclusive that the plaintiff had not abandoned the contract without cause, and that the defendant was at fault in refusing to permit him to go on. All that was left for the plaintiff to prove was the value of the work and the order for some extra items.

In these circumstances the defendant's motion that the court determine the issues irrespective of the jury's verdict must be held to be too general to sustain the claim of error. There was no attempt to point out the minor issues that were still open. There was a general demand that the verdict be treated as advisory in its entirety. The court did not err in refusing to yield to that demand. No other exception is available to bring the question before us. We are not at liberty to look into the record to see whether apart from the verdict there is sufficient evidence either of the extra items or of value. The findings have been unanimously affirmed, and we must presume that the evidence sustains them (Const. art. 6, § 9; Code Civ.Proc. § 191, subd. 4).

* * *

The judgment should be . . . affirmed, without costs in this court to either party.

NOTES

(1) Is the decision in the principal case correct under the historical test? See James & Hazard, Civil Procedure § 8.7 (3d ed.1985).

(2) N.Y.—McKinney's CPLR § 4102(c) provides:

". . . A party shall not be deemed to have waived the right to trial by jury of the issues of fact arising upon a claim, by joining it with another claim with respect to which there is no right to trial by jury and which is based upon a separate transaction; or of the issues of fact arising upon a counterclaim, cross-claim or third party claim, by asserting it in an action in which there is no right to trial by jury."

Would this provision, if applicable at the time, have required a different disposition in the principal case? See James & Hazard, Civil Procedure § 8.7 n. 40 (3d ed.1985).

(3) What is the proper balance between the right to a jury and the doctrine of collateral estoppel? The Fifth Circuit has held that a litigant may not be bound in a subsequent jury action by an earlier non-jury determination. Rachal v. Hill, 435 F.2d 59 (5th Cir.1970), cert. denied 403 U.S. 904, 91 S.Ct. 2203, 29 L.Ed.2d 680 (1971). The Second Circuit has held that an earlier non-jury determination will preclude a later jury trial of the same issue, and, to preserve the litigant's right to a jury, it has granted mandamus to compel the district court to try the jury action first when a jury action and a non-jury action are pending simultaneously. Goldman, Sachs and Co. v. Edelstein, 494 F.2d 76 (2d Cir.1974). See generally Note, Application of the Doctrine of Collateral Estoppel Principles in Derogation of the Right to Jury Trials, 1974 Duke L.J. 970.

SECTION 4. LIMITATIONS UPON THE RIGHT TO A JURY

A. SPECIAL TYPES OF ACTIONS

Increasingly, legislators are concluding that a jury trial is not appropriate for settling all private disputes. The two most important areas in which the right to a jury trial has been curtailed are workmen's compensation and no-fault insurance. How do such limitations square with the jury trial guarantees of the federal and state constitutions? See Ives v. South Buffalo R., 201 N.Y. 271, 94 N.E. 431 (1911), holding the New York workmen's compensation system unconstitutional:

". . . If these provisions relating to compensation are to be construed as definitely fixing the amount which an employer must pay in every case where his liability is established by statute, there can be no doubt that they constitute a legislative

usurpation of one of the functions of the common-law jury
. . .. This part of the statute, in its present form, has given
use to conflicting views among the members of the court, and,
since the disposition of the question which it suggests is not
necessary to the decision of the case, we do not decide it." Id.,
at 291–292, 94 N.E. at 438.

As a result of the doubts raised by the *Ives* case, the New York
Constitution was amended to permit workmen's compensation to supplant the common law jury trial. N.Y.—McKinney's Const. Art. I,
§ 18.

The no-fault automobile injury laws raise somewhat similar problems. Beginning with Pinnick v. Cleary, 360 Mass. 1, 271 N.E.2d 592
(1971), state courts have held the plans do not violate state constitutional rights to trial by jury. The court in *Pinnick* did not even bother to
discuss the jury issue. See also Opinion of the Justices, 113 N.H. 205,
304 A.2d 881 (1973) (upholding the New Hampshire plan despite jury
right curtailment); Manzanares v. Bell, 214 Kan. 589, 522 P.2d 1291,
1312 (1974) (holding that while a jury trial is required at common law,
the legislature may modify the common law); Lasky v. State Farm
Insurance Co., 296 So.2d 9, 22 (Fla.1974). See generally Keeton and
O'Connell, Basic Protection for the Traffic Victim, 493–504 (1965).

B. PUBLIC RIGHTS

Another important area in which the Supreme Court has upheld
the absence of a right to trial by jury is that of newly created "public
rights". In Atlas Roofing Company, Inc. v. Occupational Safety and
Health Review Commission, 430 U.S. 442, 87 S.Ct. 1261, 51 L.Ed.2d 464
(1977), the Supreme Court ruled that Congress could assign the adjudication of the new "public rights" created by OSHA to an administrative
agency without violating the constitutional right to trial by jury.
There is, however, some doubt as to the extent of congressional power.
Thus, in Chauffeurs, Teamsters Local 391 v. Terry, ___ U.S. ___, 110
S.Ct. 1339, 108 L.Ed.2d 519 (1990), the Supreme Court found that rights
created by the Labor Management Relations Act were similar to
common law rights. Accordingly, it held that the right to a trial by
jury attached to litigation concerning the duty of fair representation.

C. BANKRUPTCY

Claims in bankruptcy present special problems. One way of justifying the absence of a right to trial by jury with respect to claims
asserted by a trustee in bankruptcy would be to qualify such claims as
based on "public rights". However, in Granfinanciera, S.A. v.
Nordberg, ___ U.S. ___, 109 S.Ct. 2782, 106 L.Ed.2d 26 (1989), the
Supreme Court, in an action brought by a trustee to avoid an allegedly

fraudulent transfer of money, although admitting that "the issue admits of some debate", ruled that the trustee's right "seems to us more accurately characterized as a private rather than a public right." The majority at the same time indicated that "public rights" were not necessarily limited to right asserted by or against a governmental authority. This precipitated a separate opinion by Justice Scalia who stated that, in his view, a public right "must at a minimum arise between the government and others." Since the Court also ruled that the action at issue in 18th-century England was brought "at law", it reversed the lower court's ruling that the defendant did not have a right to trial by jury. In doing so, it distinguished its ruling from that made in Katchen v. Landy, 382 U.S. 323, 86 S.Ct. 467, 15 L.Ed.2d 391 (1966), in which it had held that a claimant who had filed claims against a bankrupt estate and was met with the trustee's counterclaim that payments made by the claimant constituted avoidable preferences, had no right to trial by jury on the trustee's claim. The distinction, the Court ruled, lay in the circumstance that, in *Granfinanciera,* the defendant had not submitted a claim against the estate. Since the defendant had not filed such a claim, the trustee's fraudulent conveyance action did not arise "as part of the process of allowance and disallowance of claims" and was not "integral to the restructuring of debtor-creditor relations. Justice White wrote a vigorous dissent, in which Justices Blackmun and O'Connor joined. He noted that actions to avoid fraudulent conveyances could generally be brought in equity, that bankruptcy proceedings were equitable in nature, and that, in any event, the trustee's rights were public rights. To what extent, after these decisions, is there a right to trial by jury as to claims asserted in bankruptcy? On this problem, see Warner, Katchen Up in Bankruptcy, the New Jury Trial Right, 63 Am.Bank L.J. 1 (1989). Both the majority and the dissenters agreed to "leave for another day" the question of whether the defendant could properly be deprived of its right to trial by jury by the Foreign Sovereign Immunity Act of 1976, 28 U.S.C.A. § 1330(a), which provides that (an instrumentality of) a foreign state has no right to trial by jury in an action in which it cannot claim sovereign immunity. On this question, see Smit, The Foreign Sovereign Immunities Act of 1976. A Plea for Drastic Surgery, 1980 A.S.I.L. 49; Restatement of Foreign Relations Law (Revised) § 455 (1986).

D. PRELIMINARY ISSUES

The general judicial tendency is to rule that the right to trial by jury does not extend to questions preliminary to the merits, such as factual questions determining susceptibility to adjudicatory authority, applicable law, and the like? See Reese, Smit, and Reese, The Role of ~e Jury in Choice of Law, 25 Case Western L.Rev. 82 (1974).

E. COMPLEXITY

A number of courts have denied a right to trial by jury in cases regarded as too complex for a jury. See, e.g., In re Boise Cascade Securities Litigation, 420 F.Supp. 99 (W.D.Wash.1976); Bernstein v. Universal Pictures, Inc., 79 F.R.D. 59 (S.D.N.Y.1978); In re Japanese Electronic Products Antitrust Litigation, 631 F.2d 1069 (3d Cir.1980). The arguments in favor of denying a right to trial by jury are that, historically, the chancellor kept complex cases in chancery and that trial by jury of a case too complex for a jury would deny due process. The problem has evoked conflicting commentatorial comment. *Compare* Arnold, An Historical Inquiry into the Right to Trial by Jury in Complex Civil Litigation, 128 U.Pa.L.Rev. 829 (1980) (no historical foundation for denying jury trial) *with* Campbell & Le Poiderin, Complex Cases and Jury Trials: A Reply to Professor Arnold, 128 U.Pa.L. Rev. 965 (1980); Devlin, Jury Trial of Complex Cases: English Practice at the Time of the Seventh Amendment, 80 Colum.L.Rev. 43 (1980) (chancellor kept complex cases). See also Note, Complex Jury Trials, Due Process, and the Doctrine of Unconstitutional Complexity, 18 Colum.J.L. & Soc.Probs. 1 (1983); Note, The Right to a Jury Trial in Complex Civil Litigation, 92 Harv.L.Rev. 898 (1979); Note, Preserving the Right to Jury Trial in Complex Civil Cases, 32 Stan.L.Rev. 99 (1979). Thus far, the Supreme Court has not spoken on the problem. In In re Financial Securities Litigations, 609 F.2d 411 (9th Cir.1979), in which the Ninth Circuit reversed a lower court ruling denying a jury trial on the ground of complexity, the Supreme Court denied certiorari. 446 U.S. 929, 100 S.Ct. 1866, 64 L.Ed.2d 281 (1980). It has been argued that the Supreme Court should delay ruling on the problem until it has been studied further and addressed by the lower courts in additional cases. Lempert, Civil Juries and Complex Cases: Let's Not Rush to Judgment, 80 Mich.L.Rev. 68 (1981). It has also been argued that, in complex cases, it would be constitutional to select a special jury of persons judged able to cope with complex issues. Comment, The Case for Special Juries in Complex Civil Litigation, 89 Yale L.J. 1155 (1980).

F. THE NON-JURY FIRST STAGE

In Pittsburgh Corning Corp. v. Bradley, 499 Pa. 291, 453 A.2d 314 (1982), the Pennsylvania Supreme Court ruled constitutional, on the ground that a de novo jury trial remained available, an order that, in an effort to eliminate backlogs, directed non-jury trials in some 1,850 asbestos injury cases. Similarly, courts have upheld as constitutional preliminary reference to arbitration.

G. COLLATERAL ESTOPPEL

To what extent can the doctrine of collateral estoppel defeat the right to trial by jury? In Parklane Hosiery Co. v. Shore, 439 U.S. 322, 99 S.Ct. 645, 58 L.Ed.2d 552 (1979), p. 996, infra, the Supreme Court held that determinations in a bench-tried case precluded later litigation concerning the same issues in a dispute to which the right to a jury trial attached. This holding is, however, apparently limited to cases in which the second litigation was not pending at the time of the first trial. In Lytle v. Household Manufacturing, Inc., ___ U.S. ___, 110 S.Ct. 1331, 108 L.Ed.2d 504 (1990), both legal and equitable claims were asserted initially. After dismissal of the legal issues, the equitable case was tried without a jury. The legal claims were reinstated on appeal, and the Supreme Court held that the earlier bench trial did not preclude relitigation of issues common to both cases.

Part V

THE RISING ART OF JUDICIAL ADMINISTRATION

Chapter Thirteen

JUDICIAL ADMINISTRATION IN CIVIL COURT

SECTION 1. EXORCISING COURT DELAY

Chief Justice Earl Warren warned repeatedly that maladministration was undermining American justice: "As long as people cannot have their rights adjudicated, it makes little difference whether the substantive law is good or bad." See Burke, Recent Milestones for Effective Justice, 45 F.R.D. 69, 74 (1968). Excessive delay in the movement of cases to a determination has been one of the worst symptoms of maladministration of the courts.

JONES, ED., THE COURTS, THE PUBLIC AND THE LAW EXPLOSION
30–35, 37, 46–49, 51–55, 58 (1965).*

On the twelfth day of 1965 a *New York Times* headline made it official that courts spiritual are also burdened by an affliction well known to courts temporal. It said:

Pope Paul Exhorts Matrimonial Courts to Reduce Delay

The dispatch reported that the Pontiff, in opening the judicial year of the Sacred Roman Rota, warned that "culpable delay" in the tribunal's dispensing of justice is "in itself an act of injustice." The court members, he urged, must strive to avoid delays in handling matrimonial cases.

If the pace of justice lags in the Sacred Rota in Rome, it is a fair surmise that it also limps at times in the courts of Islam and Israel and everywhere else. It is also a fair guess that the spiritual courts, like their secular opposites, are not encountering lagging justice for the first

* The excerpts are from Chapter 2, Rosenberg, Court Congestion: Status, Causes and Proposed Remedies.

time in their history. Court congestion—delay, strictly speaking—is not something that came in with sputnik. Hammurabi denounced it; Shakespeare immortalized it: Hamlet, in compiling his dolorous list of the burdens of man, sandwiched the "law's delay" between the "pangs of dispriz'd love" and the "insolence of office." English Chancery delay made Bleak House one of the best known edifices in English literature and made Dickens a leading law reformer. Paradoxically, German court delay, scholars tell us, led Goethe to give up the law for letters.

For all its long, disreputable history and its ubiquity, court delay as a problem never before reached the pinnacle of notoriety it has achieved in this generation in this country. In the nineteenth and early twentieth centuries there had been sporadic commissions of inquiry into court delay, which even then was recognized as a chronic disease. These flurries of interest tended in the main to agitate changes in the general rules of procedure; then they subsided. The present furor is different both in its intensity and its stress on specifics and betterment of court administration as the key approaches.

By about 1950 the impact on courts of the explosions of the human and the case populations became manifest. Manifest at the same time was the ascendancy of a new philosophy of the role of judges, holding that it is as much a part of judicial responsibility to administer the courts effectively as to decide the cases wisely. . . . In 1958 the Chief Justice of the United States used crisis language to describe the situation:

> Interminable and unjustifiable delays in our courts are today compromising the basic legal rights of countless thousands of Americans and, imperceptibly, corroding the very foundations of constitutional government in the United States.
>
> * * *

Besides permitting evidence to deteriorate, memories to dull, witnesses to vanish or die, and besides forcing parties into unfair settlements, delay is said to nurture a sense of injustice because of long periods of "denial and uncertainty." When a man suffers deprivation of money this year, the wrong is not erased by paying him his due in three years. Delay breeds cynicism about justice. We become used to the wrong and accept it.

Everyone understands in a general way what is meant by delay in reference to the court process: the period of waiting litigants must endure as they take their place in a long queue inching its way toward judgment. Although it is the vogue to equate "delay" with "congestion," I prefer to reserve the latter term to describe the condition of a court with a huge volume of cases, regardless of whether or not they experience delay as they wend their way to termination. A good example of "speedy congestion" is to be found in metropolitan traffic courts, where a hundred alleged violators may pack into one courtroom and be adjudicated guilty with hardly more delay than it takes to tell. High-volume courts may find it positively useful to accumulate masses of cases on their trial dockets in order to prevent breakdowns or gaps in the flow of cases to courtrooms. In the interests of efficiency, some courts may purposely create congestion. No court would deliberately create delay.

Defining and Measuring Delay

Colloquial meanings aside, the term "delay" in the context of courts and court calendars is used in two different senses. One refers to the waiting time exacted of litigants who are ready and eager to go ahead when the court is not because other cases have priority. That is court-system delay. The other kind is the delay which the lawyers create through their own unreadiness or unwillingness to proceed. That is lawyer-caused delay.

COURT–SYSTEM DELAY

With regard, first, to "systemic" delay, it is an oddity of the subject that there is no shorthand way of stating with meaningful accuracy how much of it exists in the federal and state courts of the country.

It would be simple if each jurisdiction decreed that all cases entering its courtroom must form a single line, advance in the sequence of their filing and receive a trial in regular turn. That does not happen. No court can make the statement: "Delay in this court is one year; every case assigned for trial today was filed just twelve months ago." That would be a clear and uniform measure of delay, but it is an ideal we must do without.

*　*　*

But since it is true in every civil court that the vast majority of suits are terminated short of trial, it turns out that none of the routinely compiled figures on delay deal with the larger part of the case population. It is as if life expectancy tables for humans were based on only those who died with their boots on.

Besides differences of view regarding the proper point to begin and the proper cases to count when measuring delay, opinions split on how long the delay must last in order to be rated "excessive." In the personal-injury field—where delay is mainly centered—some lawyers urge that a lapse of a year, far from being excessive, may be indispensable because a serious injury does not show its full extent and effects for a year or more. . . .

[For] personal injury suits . . . a meaningful measure of delay must convey two dimensions. It must not only tell how long the "normal" or "average" delay is for cases that persist all the way to trial. It must also disclose what percentage of all injured suitors who ultimately received payment had to wait x months, 2x months, 3x months, and so on, for their money. The figures must tell us how many people waited how long for reparation.

For New York City those figures, and more, are available as a result of research by the Columbia University Project for Effective

Justice. They show that in a recent year, of 193,000 persons who tried to get compensated for negligently caused injuries, about 23,000 had to wait more than twenty-four months for payment. That was 14 per cent of those who ultimately recovered something. Giving further depth to the figures is the finding that the more disabling the plaintiff's injuries (and hence the greater his probable need for quick payment), the longer his wait was likely to be. In Michigan, research by a University team has developed a similar pattern—longer delay for serious than for trivial injuries.

It seems clear, in summary, that most statistics on court-system delay do no more than feel the patient's forehead, without regard to whether he has been standing in the sun or the meat cooler. The trouble is that the skin temperature readings are then treated as if they were diagnostically infallible. Worse, they form the basis for prescribing powerful nostrums, some of which are themselves likely to give the patient hot flushes and high fever.

DILATORY LAWYERS

Even in a court which dispatches its business promptly, vintage cases are often uncorked at trial. The aging was done by the litigants or their lawyers. . . .

It is important to understand that to the extent that delay is not attributable to court system failures but to dilatory lawyers, the corrective measures must be different. An analogue from the daily life of subway riders may elucidate.

Suppose that at rush travel hours people must wait their turn to board subway trains because there are more passengers on the platforms than the trains can accommodate. To spare the passengers lengthy waiting, it is theoretically possible to add more trains, lengthen platforms, or even increase tracks. But if one reason that delays arise is that the passengers are slow about moving into the trains, or across the platforms, or if they hold open the doors for latecomers, the mere abolition of system delay will not solve the passenger-caused delays.

*   *   *

Prospects

The prospects are better than the record of meager concrete accomplishment might suggest. To start with, we now have gotten a more realistic view of what a formidable problem confronts us. False hopes of quick cures have given way to realization that steady efforts on many fronts are needed. We have a new and advancing methodology for research, not alone into problems of court efficiency, but into how to improve in basic ways the quality of the processes of justice.

We have learned humility. Ahead, the prospect is not for a sudden breakthrough that will permit all civil courts to dispense instant justice. We shall have to learn to live and cope with court delay as we must with pathology in other human processes. . . .

NOTES

(1) Fewer than 5% of the civil actions filed in the federal courts persist to trial. Average delay obviously is greater in the tried cases than in those that are disposed of short of trial. Furthermore, cases that reach trial may well require different procedures than those which terminate without trial. All in all, it would be helpful to separate the probably trial-bound cases from the others if this could be done with a fair measure of predictability. In early empirical studies of personal injury actions in New York City the Columbia University Project for Effective Justice found a strong positive correlation between the size and "durability" of cases; that is, large-stake cases were much more likely to persist to trial than small-stake cases. See Rosenberg and Sovern, Delay and the Dynamics of Personal Injury Litigation, 50 Colum.L.Rev. 1115 (1959). A study that analyzed 25 major accidents involving United States airlines between 1970 and 1984 reported a similar size-durability correlation:

> "Economic theory suggests—and the results show—that the higher the stakes, the more likely that cases will result in suits and trials and will take longer to resolve. The best measure of stakes is the economic loss that a victim's survivors have suffered. . . ." (See Annual Report, 1989–1990, Institute for Civil Justice 26.)

(2) Shakespeare was right to have Hamlet name the law's delay as one of humankind's major vexations. It has stubbornly resisted one delay-killing panacea after another. As the drug abuse culture propels hordes of cases into the courts, the "local legal culture" takes over to assure that the civil-case queue stalls. Church, Justice Delayed: The Pace of Litigation in Urban Trial Courts (1978). See, also, ABA Action Commission to Reduce Court Costs and Delay, Attacking Litigation Costs and Delay (1984); Mahoney, Changing Times in Trial Courts (1988); Grossman et al., Measuring the Pace of Civil Litigation in Federal and State Trial Courts, 65 Judicature 86 (1981).

ROSENBERG, FRANK TALK ON IMPROVING THE ADMINISTRATION OF JUSTICE
47 Texas L.Rev. 1029 (1969).

This problem [reform in judicial administration] can be attacked in a simplistic way, of which a good example is "Ten Cures for Court Congestion," a famous list of unsuccessful prescriptions concocted in the mid-fifties. It can also be approached in a realistic way, with due recognition that justice is delivered by a network of mechanisms, rules, and actors that is more complicated than a mission to the moon; and more fallible, since the factor of human judgment cannot be programmed out, judgment being exactly what is wanted. In this complex maze the strands of substantive law interweave endlessly with the procedural ones. The men and machinery of justice function inseparably. The quantity of court work influences the quality of dispositions, and perhaps vice versa.

. . . Judicial administration is concerned with handling this huge tide of disputes seeking court-dispensed justice; and with improving the process of dispensing it.

Looking at the judicial process in functional terms, we can distinguish three areas of performance. One is adjudication, the classic work of deciding issues and pronouncing judgment in individual cases. Another is general administration, the task in any given court of devising and regulating channels for the smooth movement, consideration, and disposition of cases or issues. Finally, there is the job of managing personnel, records, and equipment by systematic, efficient, and up-to-date methods. In a nutshell, these three functions have to do with the decisions, case flow, and office procedures of a particular court.

To select those features of judicial administration is not to suggest that they are the whole picture. Substantive and procedural rules obviously have an impact on how effectively a court functions. So does the court system at large. If the system is loose and badly administered, a smooth-running court may be thrown off stride. If it is cohesive and well administered, a lagging court may be helped to regain the pace.

A. *Effective Judges*

At the top of any list of factors determining a court's effectiveness is the judge himself. . . . This is true with regard to the function of adjudication: the surest recipe for good judgments is good judges. It is also true with regard to administration: in John Frank's epigram, "Superjudges don't have backlogs."

There was a time when backlogs and administrative capacity were not criteria one spoke of in discussing a judge's stature. Who cared whether Cardozo could have run a pretrial conference or whether Holmes could have kept the trial lists moving? Those were the days before the explosions of population and litigation brought matters to the point when last year the United States district courts found themselves 92,000 cases in arrears. The past two decades have seen the rise of a new philosophy of the judge's role, holding it as much a part of his duty to administer the courts effectively as to decide the cases wisely. Today concern for administration is more than reputable; it is crucial.

[The author here referred briefly to judicial education as a way to improve the performance of low-producing judges. Then he examined a three-pronged plan to attract better lawyers to judicial service: lifting judicial salaries to a level competitive with those of "good" practicing lawyers; using a selection system that produces better judges; and possibly bringing judges into the civil service.]

. . . Nonpartisan selection on merit is needed—whether or not it demonstrably produces better judges—as a way of erasing the mistrust of judges that widely discolors the image of justice in this nation. Recently, Howard James, a journalist whose prize-winning book, *Crisis in the Courts,* was based on cross-country investigation, testified before a United States Senate subcommittee: "The most distressing thing that

I found . . . was the number of judges and lawyers who would tell me, 'Do not trust this judge'. . . ." [1]

Mistrust of judges is unlikely to diminish as long as they are selected by political leaders, as many are; or as long as they periodically go through the charade of running for office under partisan banners, without platforms or issues, as many do. Courts flourish on public confidence and fail without it. To enjoy trust, judicial office must be filled by a process that is not only clean and sound in fact, but is perceived by the public to be clean and sound.

Civil service status for judges does not sound enticing, . . . [because] judges who have never engaged in the practice of law may turn out to be too remote and antiseptic in the administration of their courts. Drawing judges from the bar assures that they will be in close touch with the visions and foibles of the active professionals. This enhances the prospect of useful give and take.

*   *   *

B. *Effective Application of Judicial Resources*

The bleakest fact on the landscape of judicial administration is that the creation in recent years of a large number of new judgeships has not resulted in keeping the courts abreast of their workload. . . .

The favored demand-reducing measures are to cut the intake of cases by blocking off some of the roads to the courthouse and by eliminating . . . "decision points" in lawsuits that do get to court.[*]

With regard to . . . a reduction in the number of "decision points" in cases, optimism is not in order. The value of simplifying legal controversies is clear, but how to achieve this is not. Today we find ourselves in a time and temper in which law aims insistently to reach the merits and individualize justice in every case. This is not a mood that makes for eliminating issues.

A more hopeful prospect of balancing the supply-demand equation lies in efforts to increase the efficiency of courts in scheduling, calendaring, and processing their cases. Progress has been painfully slow so far, but there are signs that help is near. It will come from the findings and insights of researchers who have been hard at work for more than a decade on the mysteries of litigation dynamics. Efforts to plug the serious information gap that has afflicted judicial administration have started to pay off, so far in seemingly negative ways.

Mainly, the research to date has served to explode old myths and folklore about highly touted procedural panaceas, whose impact often turns out to be wholly different from the effect that was advertised. An example is the report of the field survey on federal pretrial

1. *Hearings on S. 1033 Before the Sub-comm. on Improvements in Judicial Machinery of the Senate Comm. on the Judiciary,* 90th Cong., 1st Sess. 188 (1967). [Some footnotes omitted; others renumbered.]

* The term "decision point" was coined by John P. Frank in *American Law: The Case for Radical Reform* (1969). [Eds.]

discovery conducted by the Columbia University Project for Effective Justice.[4] This cast doubt upon dogmatic assertions that pretrial discovery palliates court delay by producing more settlements and shorter trials than would otherwise have come about. The evidence is that discovery does, indeed, liquidate some issues that would otherwise have been litigated, but at the same time it produces new issues that might not have arisen if the parties had not uncovered their adversary's evidence and leads. The consequence appears to be a stand-off.

* * *

C. Efficient Management

For well known reasons, law plods instead of galloping toward change. Yet, even a plodding gait should have carried judicial administration a bit closer to modern management practices and capacities than it has. True it is that court administration "is a new profession in the United States, and its practitioners are hard to come by," [5] but the skills can be imported from business and industry, once their importance is conceded. Quill-penned records and green-eye-shaded clerks waste time and energy needlessly in an age when efficient office technology is commonplace.

Management studies of courts could help greatly by proposing suitable systems of information collection and analysis, efficient workspace arrangements, labor-saving equipment, and rational ways of allocating responsibilities to court personnel. They can breathe new vigor and vitality into judicial administration, and there is no reason why they should not be utilized. The streamlining of clerical routines does not pose the slightest threat to the integrity or humanity of the adjudicative function.

With some American courts facing a crisis of overabundance and with justifiable alarms being sounded in high places about excessive delay of justice, an extra effort is needed to keep a sense of proportion about suggestions for improvement. In this society courts have to be the showcases of justice. In them society puts its decencies on display and demonstrates that even profoundly disturbing disputes can be conducted and decided with fairness and dignity. Courts thus hold up a *beau ideal* for the conduct of legal disputes, not in order to entice all such disputes into the courtroom for resolution, but so that litigants will know how society means to deal with them if they come before its solemn tribunals. Then, hopefully, they will take their stands according to the process they anticipate.

Present and proposed procedures must be evaluated in the light of the great aspirations we have for our courts. To strike a balance between the ideal and the necessities is the difficult task of those who

4. Columbia University Project for Effective Justice, Field Survey of Federal Pretrial Discovery (unpublished). See also W.A. Glaser, *Pretrial Discovery and the Adversary Process* (1968).

5. J. Frank, *American Law: The Case for Radical Reform* (1969).

offer concrete proposals for reforming judicial administration. These standards are germane:

(1) The procedure must be "effective." It must get the job done in accordance with the substantive values the system insists upon.

(2) It must operate "efficiently." In producing the desired effects, the procedure must be parsimonious. It should not cost more than necessary in manpower and money.

(3) Any change made should be minimally disruptive. It should not produce an intolerable level of side effects, such as uncertainty, disorganization or impairment of existing practices or personnel.

(4) The proposal should be perceived as fair and humane. For example, it would be intolerable merely in the interests of efficiency for a criminal court to urge prosecutors and defendants to increase the number of guilty pleas in order to save the judges' time.

(5) The change must be forthright. The courts should not do by indirect means what they would be unable or unwilling to do directly.

BETTER RULES OR BETTER ADMINISTRATION?

If instead of being regulated by rules, the course of a civil litigation is increasingly committed to the managerial control of trial-level judges, will even-handedness suffer? Will the adversary process be weakened to an undesirable extent? These are momentous questions and they provoke sharp divisions of opinion, as illustrated in the comments that follow by Professor Judith Resnik and Steven Flanders. The problem is one that affects state courts as well as federal, for at least 30 states and the District of Columbia and Puerto Rico have adopted civil rules that are substantially identical to the federal rules. (See McKusick, State Courts' Interest in Federal Rulemaking: A Proposal for Recognition, 36 Maine L.Rev. 253 (1983).) In very few states are the procedural systems wholly unlike the federal rules.

ROSENBERG, THE FEDERAL CIVIL RULES AFTER
HALF A CENTURY
36 Maine L.Rev. 243 (1984).

* * *

Cadillac-style procedures are not needed to process bicycle-size lawsuits, yet that is what the rules often appear to require. With few exceptions (such as the 1983 amendment to Rule 16 permitting district courts to exempt from elaborate pre-trial procedures categories of actions they deem "inappropriate"),[13] the rules are monolithic and

---

13. Amendments to the Federal Rules of Civil Procedure, Rule 16, 97 F.R.D. 166, 168 (1983).

indiscriminately applicable to all kinds of suits. When that involves exposing small and medium-size cases to the expansive discovery weapons the rules provide, the possibilities for abuse are obvious. When the weapons are backed up by the Supreme Court's charge that "[m]utual knowledge of all the relevant facts gathered by both parties is essential to proper litigation," [14] the danger is intensified. The point is simply that for many or possibly most cases wide-open discovery under the rules is too heavy and powerful an instrument.

The rules' relative insensitivity to the great variety of cases in the district courts' dockets is paralleled by their failure to reflect a realization that only a small fraction of the filed suits reach trial. The rules proceed as if the opposite situation obtained, for they appear built around the pleadings-trial-appeal model of case processing. If that were the course that most cases actually follow there would be good reason to gear all the procedures to that model. However, the pleadings-trial-appeal image of federal litigation is a reality for less than ten percent of the lawsuits commenced. All the others will end short of trial, the majority of them by settlement. Federal procedure in its 1938 form and even as it developed through the years is not well-designed to ease, encourage, or speed the settlement process for the great mass of cases destined to end that way. The time has come to consider whether the rules should be made less of a monolithic one-for-all system by taking account of differences in the cases in three respects: by categories, by individual features, and by their settlement propensities. However, more rules, even better rules, may not be the best hope for improving the litigation process.

III

One of the difficulties with rules is that they do not enforce themselves. Efforts to encourage compliance with them almost always consist of writing still more rules. To vindicate these frequently requires additional court proceedings and creates another round of litigation involving substantial costs in money, energy, and time for both the courts and the parties. Rather than devise additional rules propelled by threats of sanctions and penalties, a modern procedural system should try to develop incentives and rewards of positive kinds to encourage lawyers to act in harmony with the system's goals. Essentially, it should look for ways to reward compliance rather than punish non-compliance. The incentive approach is not only more pleasant, it is more efficient, for it does not require enforcement activities, satellite litigation, or other extra steps. Perhaps the courts should create honor rolls or other forms of recognition for practitioners who conduct lawsuits in exemplary fashion.

There is growing interest throughout the country in improving judicial management techniques in the trial courts. Although there

---

14. Hickman v. Taylor, 329 U.S. 495, 507 (1947).

have been criticisms of "managerial judges" as allegedly subverting important values of the adversarial process,[15] in my opinion close monitoring of cases by the courts is indispensable. Except to avoid censure or penalties, lawyers are not likely to subordinate their clients' needs to the system's needs even if spurred by the best-conceived incentives. Judicial management is essential. Experience suggests it can be made most effective by creating different supervisory modes for different types of cases. This permits simple, streamlined procedures to be used in cases that do not need the more elaborate processes that the rules countenance, encourage, or at times mandate. Particularly, it would allow paring down pre-trial discovery in appropriate cases.

The key point is that different categories of cases have different processing needs. These are identifiable, classifiable, and usable in putting them through the judicial process. Taking account of these needs, a tracking system channels cases to a particular forum (in or out of the courts), a special division of a court, or gives the case special handling within the same part of the court.

Routing cases through different channels by tracking procedures steers away from the procedural philosophy that was ascendant when the Federal Rules of Civil Procedures made their appearance. As noted earlier, the premise at that time was that all types of cases require basically the same procedural treatment after allowing for limited and specific exceptions such as admiralty and bankruptcy proceedings. In the two decades that followed, the prevailing view favored uniform procedural handling of nearly all types of cases from the time they entered the court system to the moment they came to a close. Many states embraced that view as they adapted their procedural codes to the federal rules model.

Toward the late 1950's a counter trend set in. More and more multi-judge federal district courts moved to the so-called individual assignment system, which involved start-to-finish processing of a case by the same judge in place of the so-called central calendar system which involved rotating cases *ad hoc* through different parts of the court as motions were made and rulings became necessary. Handling a case from start to finish allowed the judge to tailor the procedures to the case. The practice of treating cases differently grew quickly. If a conference appeared a useful way to design a schedule for pre-trial discovery in a particular case, the judge could call one. If the issues needed clarifying or if discovery arrangements had to be specified, the judge could notify the lawyers and take the steps that were necessary. In time, it became clear to many federal courts that selective treatment was a better way of processing many civil suits than following the rules' "all pigs is pigs" approach.

Selective treatment of cases by distinct categories is not a wild or wicked idea or even a novelty in judicial administration. Perhaps a

15. See Resnik, *Managerial Judges,* 96 Harv.L.Rev. 374 (1982).

majority of the country's court systems have long-standing practices of channeling criminal and civil suits along separate tracks. Many courts have recognized the value of picking out protracted cases for special treatment from the outset. The cases are assigned to a particular judge for all purposes, with benefits in efficiency and quality in processing the cases. Commonly, in state courts different types of civil suits are routed through different divisions of the court system and processed by different procedures from the run of cases. Custody disputes and will contest cases are common examples of this. A newer approach is to track subtypes of categories of cases into special channels. Selections are made on the basis of a variety of criteria and by applying diverse sorting methods. This opens important vistas of improved judicial administration of civil cases, for it allows tailoring the process to special purposes.

These purposes are manifold. Some are peculiarly beneficial to litigants, others are of interest mainly to courts, and some bring both sets of benefits. The particular purposes a court aims to realize will determine which types of tracking procedures it adopts.

From the litigants' standpoint, a monolithic procedure that shows no regard for the diverse needs of the cases is unjustifiable. It incorrectly assumes that the full-dress adversary process and a single set of procedures are useful in all cases and circumstances. That is either too much of a good thing or is simply inefficacious for the particular type of dispute. For instance, parties to disputes over small sums may prefer informal, inexpensive processing to full-scale pleading, discovery, and trial procedures. A complicated environmental or patent dispute may attach greatest importance to obtaining decision-makers who are experts in the subject matter of the lawsuit, as arbitrators often are, even at the price of doing without the traditional safeguards of the judicial process. There are business disputes that give first priority to speed in resolution or to privacy. When special considerations of those kinds enter they often eclipse the standard litigation values that are embodied in the rules.

Another purpose of tracking cases is to speed their disposition. A common example of a fast-track practice is found in small claims courts: an immediate hearing is offered to litigants in return for waiver of a regular court trial and appeal. Speed in disposition is the trade-off for surrender of entitlement to the full-blown judicial process. Of course, success for that sort of program depends on attracting enough volunteers to make a significant dent in the caseload.

Still regarded from the litigants' viewpoint, another aim of tracking is to avoid subjecting a case to useless and wasteful processing. If the issues are simple, the amount involved relatively small, and the litigants in accord on the best way to proceed, a court that follows a uniform practice of putting every case through one conference for scheduling purposes, then another for discovery, and a third for issue-narrowing is needlessly running up expenses for the parties and squandering the judge's time. On the other hand, in complex cases the enumerated steps may be the very ones needed to clarify issues, reduce the case to essentials, and spare elaborate preparation on matters that turn out to be irrelevant.

From the court's standpoint, tracking has other potential benefits. Efficiency is one of the main ones. Tracking can promote conservation of judicial energies by improving the odds that the cases to which the court gives close attention are the kinds that benefit most from detailed supervision. A second goal of court administration is to improve the quality of the judicial process. Close supervision can achieve this by measures that promote clarity in the issues and preparedness of the lawyers and that discourage the tactics of ambush and surprise. A third judicial goal in tracking cases is to curb excessive delay. Experience shows that an effective delay-lessening measure is to move cases through the court process at a constant, predictable pace, rather than by alternating slow-fast, accordian-like movements. Tracking allows a court to control the flow of the docket at a more constant pace.

RESNIK, MANAGERIAL JUDGES AND COURT DELAY: THE UNPROVEN ASSUMPTIONS
23 The Judges' Journal 8 (1984).*

In growing numbers, federal judges are adopting an increasingly managerial stance. Judges not only adjudicate the merits of issues presented to them by litigants but also meet with parties in chambers to encourage settlement of disputes and to supervise case preparation. As managers, judges learn about cases much earlier than they have in the past, and they negotiate with parties about the course, timing, and scope of pretrial activities.

When acting as pretrial managers, judges typically initiate contact with the parties to a lawsuit. In federal courts, under the new amendments to Rule 16 of the Federal Rules of Civil Procedure, within 120 days of the filing of a complaint, judges are obliged to issue scheduling orders, detailing the timing for pretrial motions, amendment of pleadings, and discovery. Nearly all cases receive pretrial attention under Rule 16, and some judges have already adopted the supervisory stance contemplated by the recent amendments.

Managerial meetings are usually informal and contrast sharply with the highly stylized structure of the courtroom. Pretrial conferences often occur in chambers; the participants may sit around tables, and the judge may wear business dress. The informal judge-litigant contact provides judges with information beyond that traditionally within their ken. Conference topics are wide-ranging, the judges' concerns broad. The supposedly rigid structure of evidentiary rules, designed to insulate decision-makers from extraneous or impermissible

---

* Footnotes omitted.

information, is not relevant to case management. Managerial judges are not silent auditors of retrospective events told by witnesses; judges instead become part of the tales.

* * *

In part because of their new oversight role, and in part because of increasing caseloads, many judges became concerned about the volume of their work. To reduce the pressure, judges turned to efficiency experts, who suggested judicial management as an important technique of calendar control. Under the experts' guidance, judges have increasingly experimented with schemes for speeding the resolution of cases and for persuading litigants whenever possible to settle rather than try cases. During the past decade, enthusiasm for the managerial movement has become widespread. What began as an experiment has become obligatory in virtually all cases in federal courts and is increasingly common in state courts as well.

In the rush to conquer the mountain of work, few have considered whether reliance upon trial judges for informal dispute resolution and for case management is a positive step, and whether judicial management can accomplish the many goals set for it. Little empirical evidence exists to support the claim that judicial management works— either to settle cases or to provide cheaper, quicker, or fairer dispositions.

Proponents of judicial management have also failed to consider the systemic effects of the shift in the judicial role. Management is a new form of judicial activism, a behavior that usually attracts substantial criticism. Judicial management may be teaching judges to value their statistics, such as the number of case dispositions, more than they value the quality of those dispositions. Further, because managerial judging is less visible than traditional adjudication and is usually unreviewable until after final judgments have been rendered, managerial judging gives trial courts more authority and at the same time provides litigants with fewer procedural safeguards to protect them from abuse of that authority. In sum, judicial management merits our close attention and our study before we embrace it as the slogan for the courts of the 1980s.

QUESTIONABLE BENEFITS

Managerial judging's proponents believe that their system of management improves the use of judicial resources. They argue that, with judges in charge of the litigation system, court resources are better allocated, case dispositions speeded and delay reduced while the quality of judicial decision-making is unimpaired. No one can oppose efforts to curtail exploitation of the judicial system and make dispute resolution quick and inexpensive. I do, however, question the extent to which managerial judging contributes to these worthy aims and whether it is wise to rely upon judges to achieve these goals.

Proponents of managerial judging typically assume that management enhances efficiency in three respects. They claim that case management decreases delay, produces more dispositions, and reduces litigation costs. But close examination of the currently available information reveals little support for a firm conclusion that judicial management is responsible for efficiency gains in federal district courts.

* * *

Moreover, judicial management itself imposes costs. Judges' time is one of the most expensive resources in the courthouse. Rather than concentrate all of their energies on deciding motions, charging juries, and drafting opinions, managerial judges must meet with parties, develop litigation plans, and compel obedience to their new management rules. Managerial judges have more data sheets to complete, more conferences to attend, and ever more elaborate local procedural rules to draft and debate. Even when some of these tasks are delegated to staff, administrative structures must be put into place and then supervised. Although litigants and judges can contain some costs by relying on conference calls and written exchanges, they still must spend substantial amounts of time and money. Further, because many cases settle without judicial intervention, management may require judges to supervise lawsuits that would not have consumed any judicial resources.

We are not yet able to reach any firm conclusions on whether and how management reduces costs. Until we have data on the number of judge-hours that management consumes and on its cost to the parties, we cannot calculate the net costs of managerial judging and thereby learn whether we have conserved resources. And, if we include in our equation the additional costs discussed below—of the possible increase in erroneous decisions and the loss of public participation—our calculation becomes even more complex.

In sum, I am skeptical of claims that judicial management increases court productivity at reduced costs. Data are not available to support most of these conclusions, and intuition does not compel them. Moreover, managerial proponents have rarely addressed or included in their assessments the effects of judicial management on the nature of adjudication.

Possible Risks

Transforming the judge from adjudicator to manager substantially expands the opportunities for judges to use—or to abuse—their powers. When deciding how much time to allow parties to prepare their cases, when running settlement conferences, when insisting, as some judges do, on *ex parte* meetings with each side, the trial judge sits unsupervised, virtually beyond review. Judges can create rules for the pretrial phase of lawsuits that parties have no way of challenging; with the individual calendar system in the federal courts, parties must be careful not to offend the one judge who is assigned a case at filing and presides over it until its disposition.

In addition to enhancing the power of judges, management tends to undermine traditional constraints on the use of that power. Judges, when creating management rules, need not submit their ideas to the discipline of written justification or to outside scrutiny. Many decisions are made privately; some are off the record; virtually all are beyond appellate review.

Furthermore, no explicit norms or standards guide judges in their decisions about what to demand of litigants. What does "good," "skilled," or "judicious" management entail? Other than their own intuitions, judges have little to inform them. Few institutional constraints inhibit judges during the informal pretrial phase. During pretrial management, judges are restrained only by personal beliefs about the proper role of judge-managers.

Some may argue that judges are familiar with the problems of courts and the world of litigation, that judges are qualified to respond to the ills of courts and can easily diagnose the needs of a given case. But awareness of the problems does not necessarily qualify judges to design the solutions, especially on an individual and *ad hoc* basis. As familiar adages discouraging self-medication by doctors and self-representation by lawyers suggest, self-interest often makes professionals less objective, less dispassionate, and less able to do what is best for themselves or others.

The Threat to Impartiality. A major technique of management is to rely on the private, informal meetings between judges and lawyers to discuss discovery schedules and to explore settlement proposals— meetings beyond the constraints of the formal courtroom setting. But substantial risks inhere in the informality. The extensive information that judges receive during pretrial conferences is not filtered by the rules of evidence. Some of the information is received *ex parte,* a process that deprives the opposing party of the opportunity to contest the validity of the information received. Moreover, judges are often in close contact with attorneys during the course of management. Such interactions may become occasions for the development of intense feelings about the case or the parties—feelings of admiration, kinship, or antipathy. Management may be a fertile field for the growth of personal bias.

Moreover, judges with supervisory obligations may gain stakes in the cases they manage. Their prestige may ride on "efficient" management, as calculated by the speed and number of dispositions. Competition and peer pressure may tempt judges to rush litigants because of reasons unrelated to merits of the disputes. Reported opinions, as well as attorneys' anecdotes, substantiate the fact that some judges have elevated efficiency and management goals over considerations of fairness.

Unreviewable power, casual contact, and interest in outcome (or in aggregate outcomes) have not traditionally been associated with the "due process" decision-making model. These features do not evoke images of reasoned adjudication, images that form the very basis of both our faith in the judicial process and our enormous grant of power to judges. The literature of managerial judges refers only occasionally to the values of due process: the accuracy of decision making, the adequacy of reasoning, and the quality of adjudication. Instead, commentators and training sessions for trial judges emphasize speed, court control, and quantity. Federal trial judges boast of the number of cases terminated, the number of arguments held, the number of motions decided. The accumulation of such data may cause—or reflect—a subtle shift in the values that shape the judiciary's comprehension of its own mission.

Case processing is no longer viewed as a means to an end; instead, it appears to have become the desired goal. Quantity has become all important; quality is occasionally mentioned and then ignored. Some commentators regard deliberation and the writing of opinions as an obstacle to efficiency. Proponents of management may be forgetting the quintessential judicial obligations of conducting a reasoned inquiry, articulating the reasons for decision, and subjecting those reasons to appellate review—characteristics that have long defined judging and distinguished it from other tasks.

CONCLUSION

I argue for reflection before we plunge headlong into judicial management. I do not mean to suggest that adjudication must be frozen into earlier forms or that more efficient decisionmaking is an unworthy aim. Rather, as we reorient the judicial system to accommodate contemporary demands, I believe that we should preserve the core of adjudication.

To help judges remain impartial, we should design rules to limit the flow of untested information to them. To ensure that judges have the patience for deliberation, we should refrain from giving them too many distracting new responsibilities. To hold judges accountable for the quality—not merely the quantity—of their actions, we should require them to act in public and to state reasons for their decisions. In sum, we should not simply embrace the new management ethic; we must think carefully about what role judges should take and then craft rules to enable judges to act accordingly.

FLANDERS, BLIND UMPIRES—A RESPONSE TO PROFESSOR RESNIK
35 Hastings L.J. 505 (1984).

In this Commentary, I wish to reassure Professor Resnik's readers, as well as others who are interested in the direction of the civil litigation system. Resnik exaggerates the extent of any judicial activity that is inconsistent with due process. More important, she confuses genuinely questionable approaches, which have long been understood to be questionable and thus are rare in practice, with established practices that are generally recognized as acceptable and even essential. By muddling almost every managerial technique that a trial judge might use with the special and well-understood concerns that attend an aggressive judicial insistence on settlement, Resnik does a disservice: she suggests that all judicial case management, however unexceptionable, is inconsistent with due process or with traditional images of justice. The corresponding service that she performs—focusing attention upon important changes in the roles and responsibilities of trial judges—is largely vitiated.

*   *   *

We must also remind ourselves that encouraging settlements is a policy problem of paramount importance. In a system founded upon the adversary relationship, in which lawyers are trained to fight, not to negotiate, suggestion of settlement is often taken as a sign of weakness. A settlement is in many respects the closest thing to a truly final judgment that can emerge from litigation. A settlement is not normally appealable, and it normally embodies a commitment by the parties to work together in some manner, a stance that may forestall future litigation. Thus, while Professor Resnik is correct in reminding us that judicial settlement efforts can get judges into trouble and that not all settlement approaches work, it does not follow that efforts to encourage and achieve just settlements should be rolled back or even slowed down. In any event, Resnik's unsupported misconceptions of the nature and scope of judicial involvement in the settlement process in the federal courts renders her second model as useless as her first model, if not more.

THE CORE OF MANAGERIAL ACTIVISM

As I deny that Professor Resnik accurately describes what "managerial judges" do, it must fall to me to correct the picture. Why, and in what ways, do federal judges commit their valuable time to the "management" of cases before them? I submit that the subjects of Resnik's two models, institutional reform cases and aggressive settlement efforts, are marginal examples of management activity. There are relatively few institutional reform cases, and few judges use aggressive settlement tactics. Working in a complex world that yields many different types of cases, federal judges have established appropriately diverse procedures that are individually tailored to accommodate different circumstances and policy preferences, as well as local legal practices and expectations. These practices include: (1) mechanisms to screen cases early for jurisdictional or recusal problems; (2) tailor-made schedules that will bring each case to the earliest possible resolution; (3) close supervision of discovery; and (4) the well-known components of rule 16 of the Federal Rules of Civil Procedure, before its recent modification, that bear on the scope and conduct of the trial.

In summarizing the diverse mechanisms used by judges and their staffs in the management of civil cases, one should distinguish the complex cases (e.g., many securities, patent, or antitrust cases, and class actions) from the more routine contract disputes, personal injury matters, and small-scale disputes involving government agencies (e.g., social security and tax cases) that predominate in the ordinary litigation environment. Both complex and routine cases are managed extensively, but different mechanisms are involved.

* * *

Why We Cannot Have Blind Umpires

Professor Resnik, it appears, seeks a return to what she calls a "classical view of the judicial role," a system in which judges know little or nothing of the cases they try. She is far more radical than she imagines in suggesting so thorough a re-assertion of an "umpireal" role, or what I call a system of blind umpires. Even if trial judges are removed from all the components of case management that are discretionary, they will be far from uninformed. In a criminal trial, they will know a great deal about any evidence that was suppressed. In a class action, they will be familiar with the strategy and financing of the suit, as well as the hidden agendas the lawyers may have. In many cases, earlier decisions they have made regarding injunctions, motions to strike, and motions for summary judgment will have informed them substantially. It is hard to believe that Resnik means for us to do away with all of these devices along with the discretionary devices. Even should she desire merely to move them to another judge, this would be no solution because many cities have only one federal judge available at a particular time.

The desire for a naive judge is not only fantasy, it is foolish. On the bench, the trial judge *must* rely on broad knowledge of the action at bar. For example, I am told that the most common issue in evidentiary rulings is relevance. Ruling requires knowledge of the lawyers' strategies, and the full contour of the case being developed. There simply is no reason to impoverish the judicial process by vain pursuit of an ideal that Professor Resnik believes once obtained in our past.

AMERICAN BAR ASSOCIATION, STANDARDS RELATING TO COURT ORGANIZATION (1974)

1.00 Aims of Court Organization.

The organization of a court system should serve the courts' basic task of determining cases justly, promptly, and economically. To this end, the organizational structure should facilitate the selection and assignment of competent judicial and auxiliary personnel, sound financial administration, efficient use of manpower, facilities, and equipment, and continuous planning for the future.

* * *

1.20 Competent and Independent Judges: General Principle.

The quality of a court system is determined chiefly by the quality of its judges. Judges should be selected on the basis of ability, character, training, and experience, by a procedure that assures that selection is made on a merit basis. Judges should be selected either by executive nomination, subject to approval by a judicial confirmation commission, or by executive appointment from nominations made by a judicial nominating commission. Election of judges should be abolished.

Judges should enjoy security in office in accordance with the principle of judicial independence. Questions concerning the incompetence of judges, or their physical or mental disability or fitness to serve, should be investigated by a board of judicial inquiry with final authority in such matters resting in the highest court of the jurisdiction. Judges should be compensated at levels that reflect the importance of their office and that are periodically reevaluated in light of changing economic conditions. Adequate retirement pensions should be provided for judges, and their retirement should be compulsory at age 70. Judges should be afforded opportunity to participate without cost to themselves in educational and training programs designed to enhance their professional proficiency. Regular judges should be assisted in the performance of their judicial responsibilities by legally trained and professionally experienced judicial officers serving such functions as magistrate, commissioner, or referee. Judicial officers should be selected, retained, and compensated according to merit procedures.

1.21 Selection of Judges.

Persons should be selected as judges on the basis of their personal and professional qualifications for judicial office. Their concept of judicial office and views as to the role of the judiciary may be pertinent to their qualification as judges, but selection should not be made on the basis of partisan affiliation.

(a) Personal and professional qualifications. All persons selected as judges should be of good moral character, emotionally stable and mature, patient, courteous, and capable of deliberation and decisiveness when required to act on their own reasoned judgment. They should have a broad general and legal education and should have been admitted to the bar. They should have had substantial experience in the practice, administration, or teaching of law for a term of years commensurate with the judicial office to which they are appointed. In addition to these qualifications:

(i) Trial judges. Persons selected as trial judges should have had substantial experience, preferably as judges or judicial officers in other trial courts, or as trial advocates, and in any event should have had experience in the preparation, presentation, or decision of legal argument and matters of proof according to rules of procedure and evidence.

(ii) Appellate judges. The selection of appellate judges should be guided by the aim of having an appellate bench composed of individuals having a variety of practical and scholarly viewpoints, including some with substantial experience as a trial judge. Persons selected as appellate judges preferably should have high intellectual gifts and experience in developing and expressing legal ideas and facility in exchanging views and adjusting differences of opinion.

(b) Procedures for selecting judges. Judges should be selected through a procedure in which for each judicial vacancy as it occurs (including the creation of a new judicial office) a judicial nominating commission nominates at least three qualified candidates, of whom the chief executive appoints one to office.

* * *

1.25 Continuing Judicial Education.

Judges should maintain and improve their professional competence through continuing professional education. Court systems should operate or support judges' participation in training and education, including programs of orientation for new judges and refresher education for experienced judges in developments in the law and in technique in judicial and administrative functions. Where it will result in greater convenience or economy, such programs should be operated jointly by several court systems, or regionally or nationally. Provision should be made to give judges the opportunity to pursue advanced legal education and research.

NOTES

(1) Is the recommended procedure for selecting judges right in eliminating the voters from the process of choosing or continuing the judge in office? Under the so-called Missouri Plan, after a relatively brief period of probationary service the judge runs in a "retention election" in which there is no opponent and the question for the voters is: "Shall Judge _____ be retained in office for the balance of the full term?" Is that a desirable process? Why?

(2) Despite a growing trend toward "merit selection" (see pp. 786–787 supra), most states still require that all or many of their judges be elected. Since judges cannot make campaign promises of the usual kind, is there any point or purpose to their running for office in contested elections. Does it follow that judges should not be accountable to the electorate in any manner? If there is to be accountability, by what means should it be achieved?

MAREK v. CHESNY

Supreme Court of the United States, 1985.
473 U.S. 1, 105 S.Ct. 3012, 87 L.Ed.2d 1.*

CHIEF JUSTICE BURGER delivered the opinion of the Court.

We granted certiorari to decide whether attorney's fees incurred by a plaintiff subsequent to an offer of settlement under Federal Rule of Civil Procedure 68 must be paid by the defendant under 42 U.S.C. § 1988, when the plaintiff recovers a judgment less than the offer.

I

Petitioners, three police officers, in answering a call on a domestic disturbance, shot and killed respondent's adult son. Respondent, in his own behalf and as administrator of his son's estate, filed suit against the officers in the United States District Court under 42 U.S.C. § 1983 and state tort law.

Prior to trial, petitioners made a timely offer of settlement "for a sum, including costs now accrued and attorney's fees, of ONE HUNDRED THOUSAND ($100,000) DOLLARS." Respondent did not accept the offer. The case went to trial and respondent was awarded $5,000 on the state-law "wrongful death" claim, $52,000 for the § 1983 violation, and $3,000 in punitive damages.

Respondent filed a request for $171,692.47 in costs, including attorney's fees. This amount included costs incurred after the settlement offer. Petitioners opposed the claim for post-offer costs, relying on Federal Rule of Civil Procedure 68, which shifts to the plaintiff all "costs" incurred subsequent to an offer of judgment not exceeded by the Ultimate recovery at trial. Petitioners argued that attorney's fees are part of the "costs" covered by Rule 68. The District Court agreed with petitioners and declined to award respondent "costs, including attorney's fees, incurred after the offer of judgment." 547 F.Supp. 542, 547 (N.D.Ill.1982). The parties subsequently agreed that $32,000 fairly represented the allowable costs, including attorney's fees, accrued prior to petitioner's offer of settlement. Respondent appealed the denial of post-offer costs.

The Court of Appeals reversed. 720 F.2d 474 (CA7 1983). The court rejected what it termed the "rather mechanical linking up of Rule 68 and section 1988." Id., at 478. It stated that the District

* Footnotes omitted.

Court's reading of Rule 68 and § 1988, while "in a sense logical," would put civil rights plaintiffs and counsel in a "predicament" that "cuts against the grain of section 1988." Id., at 478, 479. Plaintiffs' attorneys, the court reasoned, would be forced to "think very hard" before rejecting even an inadequate offer, and would be deterred from bringing good-faith actions because of the prospect of losing the right to attorney's fees if a settlement offer more favorable than the ultimate recovery were rejected. Id., at 478–479. The court concluded that "[t]he legislators who enacted section 1988 would not have wanted its effectiveness blunted because of a little known rule of court." Id., at 479.

We granted certiorari, 466 U.S. 949, 104 S.Ct. 2149, 80 L.Ed.2d 536. We reverse.

II

Rule 68 provides that if a timely pretrial offer of settlement is not accepted and "the judgment finally obtained by the offeree is not more favorable than the offer, the offeree must pay *the costs incurred after the making of the offer.*" (Emphasis added.) The plain purpose of Rule 68 is to encourage settlement and avoid litigation. Advisory Committee Note on Rules of Civil Procedure, Report of Proposed Amendments, 5 F.R.D. 433, 483, n. 1 (1946), 28 U.S.C.App., p. 637; Delta Air Lines, Inc. v. August, 450 U.S. 346, 352, 101 S.Ct. 1146, 1150, 67 L.Ed.2d 287 (1981). The Rule prompts both parties to a suit to evaluate the risks and costs of litigation, and to balance them against the likelihood of success upon trial on the merits. This case requires us to decide whether the offer in this case was a proper one under Rule 68, and whether the term "costs" as used in Rule 68 includes attorney's fees awardable under 42 U.S.C. § 1988.

A

The first question we address is whether petitioners' offer was valid under Rule 68. Respondent contends that the offer was invalid because it lumped petitioners' proposal for damages with their proposal for costs. Respondent argues that Rule 68 requires that an offer must separately recite the amount that the defendant is offering in settlement of the substantive claim and the amount he is offering to cover accrued costs. Only if the offer is bifurcated, he contends, so that it is clear how much the defendant is offering for the substantive claim, can a plaintiff possibly assess whether it would be wise to accept the offer. He apparently bases this argument on the language of the Rule providing that the defendant "may serve upon the adverse party an offer to allow judgment to be taken against him for the money or property or to the effect specified in his offer, *with costs then accrued*" (emphasis added).

The Court of Appeals rejected respondent's claim, holding that "an offer of the money or property or to the specified effect is, by force of the rule itself, 'with'—that is, plus 'costs then accrued,' whatever the amount of those costs is." 720 F.2d, at 476. We, too, reject respondent's argument. We do not read Rule 68 to require that a defendant's offer itemize the respective amounts being tendered for settlement of the underlying substantive claim and for costs.

*   *   *

This construction of the Rule best furthers the objective of the Rule, which is to encourage settlements. If defendants are not allowed to make lump-sum offers that would, if accepted, represent their total liability, they would understandably be reluctant to make settlement offers. As the Court of Appeals observed, "many a defendant would be unwilling to make a binding settlement offer on terms that left it exposed to liability for attorney's fees in whatever amount the court might fix on motion of the plaintiff." 720 F.2d, at 477.

Contrary to respondent's suggestion, reading the Rule in this way does not frustrate plaintiffs' efforts to determine whether defendants' offers are adequate. At the time an offer is made, the plaintiff knows the amount in damages caused by the challenged conduct. The plaintiff also knows, or can ascertain, the costs then accrued. A reasonable determination whether to accept the offer can be made by simply adding these two figures and comparing the sum to the amount offered. Respondent is troubled that a plaintiff will not know whether the offer on the substantive claim would be exceeded at trial, but this is so whenever an offer of settlement is made. In any event, requiring itemization of damages separate from costs would not in any way help plaintiffs know in advance whether the judgment at trial will exceed a defendant's offer.

Curiously, respondent also maintains that petitioners' settlement offer did not exceed the judgment obtained by respondent. In this regard, respondent notes that the $100,000 offer is not as great as the sum of the $60,000 in damages, $32,000 in pre-offer costs, and $139,692.47 in claimed post-offer costs. This argument assumes, however, that post-offer costs should be included in the comparison. The Court of Appeals correctly recognized that post-offer costs merely offset part of the expense of continuing the litigation to trial, and should not be included in the calculus. Id., at 476.

B

The second question we address is whether the term "costs" in Rule 68 includes attorney's fees awardable under 42 U.S.C. § 1988. By the time the Federal Rules of Civil Procedure were adopted in 1938, federal statutes had authorized and defined awards of costs to prevailing parties for more than 85 years. See Act of Feb. 26, 1853, 10 Stat. 161; see generally Alyeska Pipeline Service Co. v. Wilderness Society, 421 U.S. 240, 95 S.Ct. 1612, 44 L.Ed.2d 141 (1975). . . .

*   *   *

The authors of Federal Rule of Civil Procedure 68 were fully aware of these exceptions to the American Rule. . . .

In this setting, given the importance of "costs" to the Rule, it is very unlikely that this omission was mere oversight; on the contrary, the most reasonable inference is that the term "costs" in Rule 68 was intended to refer to all costs properly awardable under the relevant substantive statute or other authority. In other words, all costs properly awardable in an action are to be considered within the scope of Rule 68 "costs." Thus, absent congressional expressions to the contrary, where the underlying statute defines "costs" to include attorney's fees, we are satisfied such fees are to be included as costs for purposes of Rule 68. . . .

Here, respondent sued under 42 U.S.C. § 1983. Pursuant to the Civil Rights Attorney's Fees Awards Act of 1976, 90 Stat. 2641, as amended, 42 U.S.C. § 1988, a prevailing party in a § 1983 action may be awarded attorney's fees "as part of the costs." Since Congress expressly included attorney's fees as "costs" available to a plaintiff in a § 1983 suit, such fees are subject to the cost-shifting provision of Rule 68. This "plain meaning" interpretation of the interplay between Rule 68 and § 1988 is the only construction that gives meaning to each word in both Rule 68 and § 1988.

Rather than "cutting against the grain" of § 1988, as the Court of Appeals held, we are convinced that applying Rule 68 in the context of a § 1983 action is consistent with the policies and objectives of § 1988. Section 1988 encourages plaintiffs to bring meritorious civil rights suits; Rule 68 simply encourages settlements. There is nothing incompatible in these two objectives.

III

Congress, of course, was well aware of Rule 68 when it enacted § 1988, and included attorney's fees as part of recoverable costs. The plain language of Rule 68 and § 1988 subjects such fees to the cost-shifting provision of Rule 68. Nothing revealed in our review of the policies underlying § 1988 constitutes "the necessary clear expression of congressional intent" required "to exempt . . . [the] statute from the operation of" Rule 68. Califano v. Yamasaki, 442 U.S. 682, 700, 99 S.Ct. 2545, 2557, 61 L.Ed.2d 176 (1979). We hold that petitioners are not liable for costs of $139,692 incurred by respondent after petitioners' offer of settlement.

The judgment of the Court of Appeals is Reversed.

[JUSTICES POWELL and REHNQUIST concurred in separate opinions.]

[The dissenting opinion of JUSTICE BRENNAN, concurred in by JUSTICES MARSHALL and BLACKMUN, is omitted.]

The Advisory Committee on the Federal Rules of Civil Procedure in 1983 and 1984 recommended two versions of a revision of Rule 68.

Both formulations would have authorized either side to make an offer of settlement and would have penalized a party who improperly rejected an offer that was more favorable than the result of the trial. In the earlier proposed revision the penalty would have required paying the other side's costs, including attorney's fees. In the later proposal, the penalty would have been a sanction that *could* include attorneys' fees. Each proposal produced vigorous opposition, mainly by the plaintiffs' civil rights and personal injury bars, and was withdrawn from the rule-making process. See Simon, The Riddle of Rule 68, 54 George Washington L.Rev. 1 (1985); a comprehensive analysis of the problem and proposed remedies; Burbank, Proposals to Amend Rule 68—Time to Abandon Ship, 19 U.Mich.J.L.Ref. 425 (1986).

SECTION 2. SYSTEMATIC REGULATION OF PRETRIAL STAGES

Easy pleading and broad discovery raise risks that lawsuits may sprawl wastefully if left unsupervised in their pretrial stages. This prospect is especially unattractive when rising caseloads compel courts to function efficiently or break down. The result has been wide acceptance by judges of responsibility to regulate proceedings in civil cases from the start to the end of the suit. Enhancing the judges' interest in controlling pretrial skirmishing in the case has been the spread in federal district courts of the individual calendar system. This replaced the central calendar system in multi-judge districts, an arrangement which rotated judges through parts or terms of court after a short period of service.

The 1983 overhaul of Rule 16 embraced the view that the district judge's duties include monitoring the pretrial processing of cases that might otherwise fall prey to drift, costly churning, or otherwise unproductive proceedings. Questions have arisen over how far the judge's monitoring efforts should go. District judges were accorded inherent power to require litigants to attend a pretrial settlement conference even though represented by attorneys. G. Heileman Brewing Co. v. Joseph Oat Corp., 871 F.2d 648 (7th Cir.1989) (en banc; 6–5 majority). On the other hand, the court of appeals reversed a district judge's order imposing a sanction on a defendant who settled at trial instead of earlier as the judge had urged. He had warned at the pretrial conference that if settlement occurred after trial started at a figure comparable to the one then being discussed he would impose sanctions against the dilatory party. Kothe v. Smith, 771 F.2d 667 (2d Cir.1985).

On the general philosophy of Rule 16, see Rosenberg, Federal Rules of Civil Procedure in Action, 137 U.Pa.L.Rev. 2197, 2207–09 (1989).

McCARGO v. HEDRICK

United States Court of Appeals, Fourth Circuit, 1976.
545 F.2d 393.

CRAVEN, CIRCUIT JUDGE:

This is an appeal by Pauline McCargo from the district court's sua sponte dismissal of her consolidated actions for failure to prosecute. For the reasons stated below, we reverse.

I.

McCargo's suits against Hedrick, Buch, and Green were consolidated in the Northern District of West Virginia on January 19, 1973. Both suits claim that plaintiff's horse racing license in West Virginia was wrongfully revoked. After the pleadings were closed, and after the 120-day discovery period had expired, there arose under Local Rule 2.08 a duty for counsel to "confer and . . . meaningfully and effectively express and commit themselves in a written statement on matters and issues involved in and controlling determination of the action." The district court extended the deadline for the meeting of counsel to November 27, 1973, and later extended the time for submitting the proposed pretrial order to February 28, 1974.

Counsel were not prompt but filed it about a month later, on April 4, 1974. It was ten pages long. That is not surprising since it was necessarily cut from the pattern of Rule 2.08, which itself runs 11 and a half single-spaced pages. Even so it was not complete. On September 26, 1974, the United States Magistrate instructed counsel that certain amendments to the proposed pretrial order were needed and required their submission by November 18, 1974. This date was extended, and on April 23, 1975, the second proposed pretrial order was filed. The magistrate measured it against Local Rule 2.08 and found it wanting. He returned it to the lawyers on May 13, 1975, with a four-page-plus letter of transmittal.

[The magistrate made detailed suggestions which he characterized as "by no means exhaustive" for the preparation of a third pretrial order.]

By October 9, 1975, the third proposed amended order had not been filed, and no extension of time had been sought from the court. On that date the district court notified the parties that the consolidated actions would be dismissed with prejudice pursuant to Local Rule 2.09 [for non-prosecution] unless good cause for retention was shown within 30 days. The reason cited for the proposed dismissal was that there had been "no manifest interest and action shown in [the suit's] prosecution" and that the case had been on the court docket for more than 12 months.

McCargo's attorney responded to this notice on October 21, 1975, stating that counsel for the parties had been trying to amend the pretrial order pursuant to the magistrate's instructions. He explained, however, that preparation of the amended order had been delayed due to defendants' failure to provide him their lists of documentary evidence. He then moved the court to retain the case on the docket.

By order dated December 4, 1975, the district court sua sponte dismissed the consolidated actions with prejudice and removed them from the docket. He attached to the order the second 13-page proposed amended pretrial order that had been tendered by counsel and stated that it failed to comply with the suggestions made by the magistrate at the pretrial conference and in his May 13, 1975, letter. The district court later denied McCargo's motion to reconsider the order of dismissal.

II.

A district court may dismiss an action for lack of prosecution, either upon motion by a defendant pursuant to Federal Rule of Civil Procedure 41(b) or on its own motion. Reizakis v. Loy, 490 F.2d 1132 (4th Cir.1974). Because dismissal is such a harsh sanction, however, it "should be resorted to only in extreme cases." Dyotherm Corp. v. Turbo Machine Co., 392 F.2d 146, 149 (3d Cir.1968). In deciding whether a case should be dismissed, a district court must consider conflicting policies: "[a]gainst the power to prevent delays must be weighed the sound public policy of deciding cases on their merits." *Reizakis,* 490 F.2d at 1135.

In *Reizakis* this court listed factors that must be taken into consideration in determining whether dismissal was proper under Rule 41(b).[3] First is the degree of personal responsibility on the part of the plaintiff. Dismissal should be ordered " 'only in the face of a clear record of delay or contumacious conduct by the plaintiff.' " 490 F.2d at 1135. Second is the amount of prejudice to the defendant caused by the delay. "[G]enerally lack of prejudice to the defendant, though not a bar to dismissal, is a factor that must be considered in determining whether the trial court exercised sound discretion." Id. The court in *Reizakis* also considered whether the record indicated a " 'drawn out history' of 'deliberately proceeding in a dilatory fashion' " and whether the trial court had considered sanctions less drastic than dismissal. To the same effect is Bush v. United States Postal Service, 496 F.2d 42 (4th Cir. 1974).

When these factors are applied to the present case, the balance tips in favor of a trial on the merits rather than dismissal for want of prosecution. There is no indication in the record that McCargo was personally responsible for her lawyer's delay in filing the third proposed pretrial order or that she or her lawyer was deliberately engaging in dilatory tactics. On the contrary, the record shows that on June

3. A local rule on the subject is, of course, superfluous. The power is an inherent one and is also authorized by Rule 41(b). Link v. Wabash R.R., 370 U.S. 626, 82 S.Ct. 1386, 8 L.Ed.2d 734 (1962).

6, 1974, counsel for McCargo wrote the court requesting an expedited pretrial hearing and the setting of the trial on the earliest possible date. Exhibit A, Appellant's Brief. Nor is there any evidence that the defendants were prejudiced by the delay. In fact, the record shows that on at least one occasion counsel for the defendants requested an extension of time for drafting the proposed order and, furthermore, that defendants never complained about the delay or sought dismissal as a result of it. Finally, the district court's order dismissing the consolidated actions does not indicate that any less drastic sanctions were first considered. For these reasons, and another one fully discussed below, we conclude that the district court abused its discretion in dismissing the consolidated actions.

III.

The facts of this case illustrate the burden put upon litigants and their counsel by a pretrial procedure that appears to have become an end in itself. Rule 16 of the Federal Rules of Civil Procedure was and is a great idea. It authorizes the district courts to conduct a *conference* with counsel for the purpose of *aiding* in the disposition of the case, i.e., to make the trial easier. The idea is to help the lawyers and the litigants—not to exhaust them.

Wisely, Rule 16 is not compulsory. If the judge views the case as a simple one, he is not compelled to spin the judicial wheels and may simply order the case calendared for trial. If he should decide that a pretrial conference will be helpful in the disposition of the action, Rule 16 tells him and the lawyers briefly and simply the business to be conducted. The agenda is spelled out: (1) simplification of the issues, (2) necessity or desirability of amendments to the pleadings, (3) the possibility of obtaining admissions of fact and admissions of authenticity of documents, (4) limitation of the number of expert witnesses, (5) advisability of referring issues to a special master. The last item on the agenda is "such other matters as may aid in the disposition of the action." "Such other" suggests matters similar to the other five items on the conference agenda. And "matters" are specifically limited to those that may *aid* in the disposition of the case.

A.

Local Rule 2.08 breaks the promise of Rule 16. A lawyer reading Rule 16 for the first time must surely be pleased. He is offered the aid of the court in the disposition of his case. He is told that an experienced judge (or magistrate) stands ready to help him frame the issues. If his pleadings are inept, presumably they can be fixed. He will not have to bring the heavy bound volumes of deeds from the register of deeds' office; apparently the court will see if some Xerox copies will suffice.

But when the same lawyer turns to Local Rule 2.08, he will discern that what has been given by Rule 16 has been taken away. The first sentence is falsely reassuring. It merely says that Local Rule 2.08 implements Rule 16. As we shall see, it does not. The second sentence is not so clear. It says that the local rule "designs the basic patterns and instructions for pre-trial development . . . ." The third sentence begins the departure from Rule 16. It suggests that compliance with Local Rule 2.08, which is said to implement Rule 16, cannot be easily accomplished and instead will require "initiative, ingenuity and industry" on the lawyers' part to "determine the quality of pre-trial proceedings." The very next sentence tells him that the court means to get the sort of proposed pretrial orders it wants: "appropriate sanctions will be employed as may be necessary."

Then Rule 2.08 "implements" Rule 16 with a vengeance.

> [C]ounsel . . . shall confer and shall meaningfully and effectively express and commit themselves in a written statement on matters and issues involved in and controlling determination of the action. . . . Preliminary to the conference, counsel . . . shall be preparing in typewritten form and shall have available at the conference precise and responsive statements of their materials to be included in the total written statement to be produced by the conference as herein required. . . . While the materials . . . will necessarily vary . . ., the following itemization of issues and matters will provide the design and pattern of the statement and will be followed in order, wherever appropriate, and may be supplemented, in the imagination, ingenuity and wisdom of counsel by other materials relevant and pertinent to a just and prompt determination of the action.

By now counsel must be looking back at Rule 16 somewhat wistfully. He has only begun, however, with Local Rule 2.08. The opening paragraph of the written statement he is compelled to submit is prescribed. It recites that counsel have "maturely discussed and considered the matters" and that the "materials . . . are arranged, wherever appropriate, in compliance with the statement outline contained in Rule 2.08 . . . ." It is not immediately clear where the statement outline appears in the rule, but we think it relates to the next eight questions propounded by Local Rule 2.08. . . .

[The opinion here reviewed at length and with obvious impatience several additional provisions of Rule 2.08.]

Compliance with Local Rule 2.08 and its prescribed format produced in this case a proposed pretrial order 13 pages in length. By way of contrast, we reproduce in the margin a typical form of pretrial order consisting of two pages in its entirety, which we think is sufficient to accomplish the purposes of Rule 16.

B.

The early optimism that accompanied the adoption of Rule 16 has given way to criticism as lawyers have encountered rules such as Local

Rule 2.08. Judge Pollack of the Southern District of New York has listed objections to pretrial procedures that are frequently voiced:

> (1) They represent a mere compilation of legalistic contentions and pleadings without any real analysis of the particular case, (2) they result in formal agreements on minutiae which have no significant effect on the result of the case, (3) they represent a burdensome chore in cases plainly destined to be settled before trial, and (4) they are ceremonial, ritualistic exercises with little actual impact or actual value to the bar or the trier of fact.

65 F.R.D. 475, 477 (1975).

Good pretrial practice has also been described. It is always simple. Professor Moore, for example, states that "[t]he chief purposes of the pre-trial conference are to define and simplify the issues, to lessen surprise at trial and the risk of judicial error, to conclude stipulations on matters of evidence, and to promote settlements." 3 J. Moore Federal Practice ¶ 16.02, at 1106 (3d ed. 1974). The Handbook for Effective Pretrial Procedure, adopted by the Judicial Conference of the United States in 1964, identifies the purpose of pretrial procedure as being the "strip[ping of] each case to its essentials." The Handbook states that this goal is achieved by stipulating undisputed matters, specifying issues with particularity, and formulating an efficient trial plan so as to avoid technical objections and the introduction of unnecessary evidence. 37 F.R.D. 255, 272 (1965).

Local Rule 2.08 is a distortion of such purposes. Simplicity has been forgotten. The theory seems to be that if two pages are good, four must be better, and ten or 13 or 21 may prevent a trial altogether, as happened here. Rule 16 was never meant to make lawyers try a case on paper instead of in a courtroom. In fact, it contemplates that the district judge himself will dictate the pretrial order. Of course, the court may seek the aid of counsel in preparing the order, but Rule 16 should not be implemented in such a manner that the pretrial procedure itself is more difficult and time consuming than the actual trial.

Ours is an adversary system of justice. Local Rule 2.08 is inquisitorial in tone and purpose. In our system lawyers worry about the whereabouts of witnesses. The court does not. Lawyers worry about proof. The court does not—except in the rare case of collusion. Lawyers get the case ready for trial. The court does not. Local Rule 2.08 subordinates the role of the lawyer to that of the administering magistrate, reducing counsel to the role of clerical assistants who are to anticipate imaginatively what other matters ought to be embraced within an endless pretrial order.

The pretrial order format which is a part of Local Rule 2.08 requires: statement of contentions and position of each party litigant, statement of plaintiff's facts controverted by others, statement of defendant's facts controverted by others, statement of issues of law uncontroverted and uncontested, statement of issues of law controverted, and summary statement of issues of fact and law to be resolved. Pleading *trespass de bonis asportatis* and *quare clausum fregit* would be easier. The Federal Rules of Civil Procedure freed us from common law pleading. Under the guise of "implementing" Rule 16, Local Rule 2.08 puts back into a pretrial order that which was so painfully removed from the complaint and the answer less than 40 years ago.

The Second Circuit was faced with a case remarkably similar to this one in Padovani v. Bruchhausen, 293 F.2d 546 (1961). The plaintiff petitioned the court of appeals for a writ of mandamus directing the district court to vacate its order that had precluded plaintiff from introducing certain testimony or relying on certain theories of law. The district court had issued this preclusion order after adjudging each of three pretrial statements submitted by plaintiff to be insufficient. The Second Circuit, citing its "overriding responsibility to see that justice is done between litigants," granted the writ. In an opinion by Judge Clark, an eminent scholar of civil procedure before he became a judge, the court concluded that the pretrial procedure utilized by the district court was not only unauthorized but was "at odds with the purpose and intent of F.R. 16."

> That rule calls for a *conference* of counsel with the court to *prepare* for, not to avert, trial, leading to an order which shall recite the "agreements made by the parties as to any of the matters considered." It is subordinate and conciliatory, rather than compulsive, in character.

293 F.2d at 548.

The detailed information required by the district judge in *Padovani* is the same in scope and format as that required of McCargo by Local Rule 2.08 . . . . Padovani v. Bruchhausen, 293 F.2d 546, 548–49 (2d Cir. 1961).

We similarly conclude that the pretrial procedures embodied in Local Rule 2.08 and utilized by the district court in this case are at odds with the purposes of Rule 16. Rule 83 of the Federal Rules of Civil Procedure authorizes each district court to make rules governing its practice "not inconsistent" with the Federal Rules of Civil Procedure. We accordingly hold that Local Rule 2.08 is void and of no effect as being inconsistent with Rule 16 of the Federal Rules of Civil Procedure. See 12 C. Wright & A. Miller, Federal Practice and Procedure: Civil § 3153, at 225 (1973). Our so holding does not impair the judicial power of the district court. This is so because local rules are not a source of power but are instead a manifestation of it. Our striking down Local Rule 2.08 does not diminish the lawful power of the district court to fully implement, either by local rule or by practice, Rule 16 of the Federal Rules of Civil Procedure, so long as its local rule or practice is not inconsistent with Rule 16.

Reversed.

BRENNAN, REMARKS ON PRE–TRIAL, 17 F.R.D. 479 (1955).

I know that in some states some judges conceive of a pretrial conference as a device for forcing settlement. There could be no greater mistake and no conduct better devised to bring the administration of justice into disrepute. [The New Jersey] Manual of Pretrial Practice expressly enjoins the trial judges that the conference can never be an instrument for forcing adjustments. Coercion in any degree is intolerable. But it is a fact that our percentage of settlements, particularly in the negligence field, has increased enormously under the influence of pretrial conference procedures. Back in 1947 under the old regime we recorded settlements in 45% of the cases disposed of and a high proportion of those settlements were not accomplished until the trial was well under way. That is to be compared with our record in the court year 1953–1954, when 78% were disposed of by settlement, dismissal or discontinuance.   . . .

Our experience is that a very small percentage of settlements are reached at the pretrial conference itself. They usually come before the day, a few weeks later, when the case is in the weekly call for assignment of a trial date or at the call on the trial day before assignment of the case to a trial judge. But I repeat that settlements are a mere incident of the pretrial conference, resulting from the new view that counsel and the litigants have of their cases after the pretrial conference. Settlements are indeed a valuable by-product of the procedures, but definitely they are not the primary end sought by them.

ROSENBERG, THE PRETRIAL CONFERENCE AND EFFECTIVE JUSTICE
16–18, 28–29, 67–70, 106, 128–129 (1964).

Past efforts at fact inquiries to gauge the impact of the pretrial conference have yielded equivocal data because of problems of method. The usual approach has been to gather statistics and opinions on what happened after the pretrial procedure was introduced in the court under study. But even those who have conducted such inquiries have recognized the fatal weakness of this method, namely that it does not disclose whether pretrial, the factor being examined, is responsible for the results observed, or to what extent. Since many factors and variables, often changing from year to year, impinge upon the operation of court processes, research efforts in which these factors continue to assert unknown influences on the process cannot serve as predicates for decision. The data produced are more likely to be interesting than reliable. This difficulty is not limited to the problem of evaluating pretrial. Any effort to test the impact of law in action encounters similar problems.

Thus, the "before-and-after" approach and "side-by-side" comparisons, although useful as research techniques, have distinct limitations, and by far the most satisfactory method of researching law in action is to introduce a scientific "control" at the beginning of the program. With the active aid of the Supreme Court of New Jersey, an officially controlled experiment was possible in this research. The Project designed a test program that would determine what the pretrial conference does or does not do in personal injury cases by controlling its application. Personal injury cases were selected as the subjects because their volume and nature made them the largest question mark in the pretrial picture. The test was limited to injury cases alone in order to keep out unknown factors that might confuse the findings or make the results ambiguous. The proposal was that the Supreme Court of New Jersey issue a special order applicable to personal injury cases in the Superior and County courts, relaxing the across-the-board feature of the mandatory rule so that during the period of the test there would be a compulsory pretrial only in each alternate case and none in the other cases. The purpose of setting up the test in that way was to produce two groups of cases that would be alike in all relevant ways except for the single factor of exposure to pretrial. The concept was that as the exposed group and the unexposed group of cases made their way through the court process any observed difference in performance and results in the two groups would reflect the impact of the pretrial conference. In research parlance the not-pretried group would serve as a "control" for the pretried group. From the research standpoint this plan would have been the ideal one to measure in the simplest and clearest way the impact of the pretrial conference on cases subjected to it.

However, the Supreme Court of New Jersey thought it necessary and wise to relax the experimental design to a certain extent. The rule actually promulgated in late 1959, effective in January, 1960, departed from the ideal design sketched above by providing as to the group of cases not scheduled for pretrial that if either attorney or both attorneys expressed a desire for a pretrial conference one would be held in that case. The lawyer-chosen cases would then be entered on the pretrial conference docket and would proceed to a conference exactly as if they had been set down on the mandatory pretrial list from the beginning. In other words they would be integrated into the same schedule, processed by the same judges, and handled in exactly the same manner as the mandatorily pretried cases. This modification in the test design had certain consequences for the analysis and interpretation of the findings, and we discuss them later in this report.

The test was conducted in seven New Jersey counties, which based on available statistics, were thought to handle a good cross section of the civil litigation of the entire state. . . . Together they processed in the test period about 50 per cent of all the civil law cases disposed of in the New Jersey Superior and County courts. In order to assure useful results from a technical viewpoint, on the advice of the Columbia University Bureau of Applied Social Research, it was decided to draw a systematic sample of 3,000 cases. To obtain the sample, the procedure now described was followed.

Starting on January 4, 1960, as all personal injury cases on the calendar of the Superior and County courts in the seven test counties reached the point at which they would normally be scheduled for a pretrial conference, they were randomly segregated into two groups. Cases 1, 3, 5, 7, etc., were sent regular notice of pretrial and the usual procedure of holding a conference was followed. Cases 2, 4, 6, 8, etc., were, on the other hand, not scheduled for the conference as a matter of course. Instead, a special form was sent to the attorneys in those cases announcing that the mandatory pretrial conference requirement had been lifted, but that a pretrial conference could be requested if desired.
. . .

SUMMING UP THE TEST FINDINGS

What if one were able to state the test findings categorically, as if they conclusively proved exactly what they seem to say and as if there were no need to qualify the observations to take account of possible statistical infirmities? . . .

Does pretrial improve trial and the trial process?

(1) "Pretrial eliminates some appeals and reduces the chance of reversal in cases that are appealed."

Not Supported: No correlation appeared between pretrial and the frequency of appeals, or between pretrial and the frequency of reversal in appealed cases.

(2) "Pretrial eliminates motions for new trials and reduces the chance that such motions will be granted if made."

Partly Supported: Pretrial did not affect the frequency with which new trials were sought, but reduced the likelihood of their success.

(3) "Pretrial increases the chance that the case will be well presented at trial."

Supported: In pretried cases that reached trial the attorneys were more frequently well prepared and the theories and issues more often emerged clearly.

(4) "In pretried cases the evidence is more frequently well presented."

Supported: Pretrial reduced the frequency with which trial evidence was offered on extraneous or undisputed issues and also reduced the frequency with which too much or too little evidence was offered.

(5) "Pretrial eliminates unnecessary witnesses."

Not Supported: Pretrial did not have any effect on the frequency of calling unneeded witnesses.

(6) "Pretrial eliminates trial surprise."

Supported: In pretried cases trial lawyers agreed, whether they were for plaintiff or defendant, that they were less frequently surprised at trial than they were in not-pretried cases.

(7) "In the opinion of judges and lawyers, pretrial promotes fair trial."

Supported: Frequently pretrial judges forecast, and trial judges and trial counsel gave as their opinion that pretrial had favorable impact on trial quality.

(8) "Pretrial improves the settlement process."

Supported: The level of mutual knowledge of the litigants was more frequently high in pretried cases.

Does pretrial improve the efficiency of the court process?

(1) "Pretrial reduces the frequency with which cases require trial."

Not Supported: Pretrial did not lead to fewer cases reaching trial.

(2) "Pretrial abbreviates the trial in cases that do not settle before trial."

Not Supported: Pretrial did not reduce the hours spent in the trial of cases that required trial.

(3) "Pretrial shortens trials by increasing the frequency of jury waivers."

Not Supported: Pretrial did not increase, but actually decreased, the frequency of jury waivers.

(4) "Pretrial shortens the time required to settle cases that do not reach trial."

Not Supported: Pretrial did not decrease the time lapse from filing to disposition for settled cases.

(5) "Pretrial judges believe that pretrial will frequently eliminate trials."

Not Supported: Pretrial judges infrequently predicted that the pretrial would eliminate the need for trial.

(6) "Pretrial judges believe that a pretrial conference will frequently reduce the length of trials."

Not Supported: Pretrial judges opined that a pretrial conference infrequently reduced the length of time required for trial.

(7) "Pretrial saves judge time overall by eliminating or shortening trials."

Not Supported: Pretrial consumed appreciable judge time without compensating saving.

Does pretrial have an impact on the outcome of the cases?

(1) "Pretrial does not affect the overall frequency with which plaintiffs recover."

Supported: Plaintiffs recovered something in all but a small fraction of the cases, whether or not there was a pretrial.

(2) "Pretrial does not alter the amount plaintiffs recover in cases in which defendant has to pay something."

Not Supported: Pretrial did alter the amount of plaintiffs' recoveries, appreciably increasing the average and median amount.

(3) "Pretrial increases the probability that the jury will find on the liability issue in the way the judge thinks it ought to."

Not Supported: The judge and jury agreed on the liability issue in not-pretried cases as often as in pretried cases.

(4) "Pretrial increases the probability that the jury will make a damage award with which the judge agrees."

Not Supported: The probability of the judge's agreeing with the jury went down in pretried cases.

*   *   *

THE TEST FINDINGS IN ESSENCE

Three major findings emerged from the controlled experiment. They can be expressed as a gain, a loss, and a difference, all attributable to the impact of across-the-board pretrial compared with lawyers'-choice pretrial.

1. The *gain* was in improving the quality of the trial process in some pretried cases that reached the trial stage. The evidence of this is not of conclusive quality, but it is strong enough to credit. We believe it points to a distinct likelihood that in an appreciable fraction of the pretried cases the quality of the trial process was improved in the following respects: lawyer preparedness was promoted; a clear presentation of the opposed theories of the case was more common; improper gaps and repetition in the evidence were eliminated; and tactical surprise was curbed.

2. The *loss* was in absorbing appreciable quantities of judge time by the across-the-board pretrials with no compensating saving in the trial time demands the cases make. At the very least, it seems clear that the efficiency of the court was reduced rather than enhanced by requiring . . . that each case go through a pretrial conference instead of leaving it to the lawyers to choose the cases to be pretried. . . . [In the all-pretried group 24 per cent of the cases reached trial, compared with 22 per cent in the other group.]

3. The *difference* in outcome that appears on comparing the two groups of cases was a completely unexpected result. [Average amounts recovered were noticeably higher in the group of cases which had all been through a pretrial conference than in the other group. This is ironical because it was mainly defendants (by two to one) who opted for pretrial when given the choice.]

Of all the variables that bear on how a pretrial conference runs and what it achieves, the key factor is the judge himself—what he is, what he does, and how he does it. Since the judge's personal qualities are the least likely elements to yield to change, attention has focused instead upon improving his techniques. In scores of seminars for trial judges conducted across the country in the past three years, a prominent feature of the program regularly has been "judicial techniques" in pretrial conferences. Many experts on pretrial share the belief that certain techniques are especially effective to assure a successful conference, and that these should be diligently applied. For that reason it was a natural part of this research effort to attempt to isolate particular techniques and to determine how they work in New Jersey negligence cases, and in general. . . .

THE JUDGE AT PRETRIAL

This is a suggested guide to the judge conducting a pretrial conference in which the object is to prepare a personal injury case for trial. Its aim is to stimulate the judge to creative involvement in the conduct of the conference and not to supply a definitive check list of automatic dos and don'ts. Central to its use is that the points set out below are suggestions, not commands. The relevance or the utility of some of the suggestions depends on how the state has resolved many underlying issues of policy and principle relating to pretrial.

1. *Are there ways to increase the specificity of the factual elements of the case?*

Experienced pretrial judges assert that it is often useful in trying to pin down both the agreed facts and the disputed factual issues, not to rest on counsel's general statements, but to probe for specific details. Can the plaintiff be induced to specify the particular respects in which he claims the defendant was guilty of negligence in operating his car, maintaining the premises, or manufacturing the allegedly dangerous product?

2. *Is there a chance to eliminate sham issues from the case?*

If the defendant has pleaded contributory negligence, nonownership of the vehicle, or lack of consent, is the defendant prepared to suggest lines of evidence in support of the plea? If the plaintiff claims permanent injuries, has he indicated the nature of the medical proof in support of his claim? If the appellate courts have ruled invalid a claim or defense, is there any proper way to rid the case of it even though no formal motion made prior to the pretrial conference?

3. *Are there issues of fact or law counsel have not tendered that are certain to arise?*

If at the end of the conference the case is to be ready for trial on the basis of the pretrial order, the judge must contribute more than a referee function. If the attorneys have made light of the pretrial proceeding because they hope the case will not reach trial or because they are unwilling to do the needed work of preparation, can the judge supply the omitted effort by drawing on his experience and ingenuity? For example, does he see an issue of breach of warranty in a case that as presented raises only an issue of negligence?

4. *Are there unique features in the case that call for special procedures?*

Can a partial judgment be awarded to dispose of some of the claims, defenses, or issues? Can provision be made for inspection of premises, sites, or "things" in order to promote further stipulations or admissions? Will it serve a useful purpose because of unusually complex problems of law, including admissibility of crucial evidence, to direct the filing of special briefs in advance of trial? Shall parties be ordered added or dropped in the interests of a complete and just resolution of the controversy?

5. *With regard to trial arrangements, are there opportunities for useful planning?*

Can any of the documents, such as hospital charts or medical reports, be marked in evidence by stipulation? Will it be useful to obtain from counsel the names of witnesses to be called at the trial [if this is permitted in the state]? Will it be right to obtain disclosure of the substance of trial witnesses' testimony?

NOTES

(1) Did the decision of the Supreme Court of New Jersey to permit attorneys an "optional" pretrial conference if their cases were not in the compulsory group impair the validity of the experiment? To what sources does one turn to determine the impact of such a departure from an ideal research design?

(2) In declining to conduct a "pure" experiment, the New Jersey court was concerned that compulsory differential treatment of civil litigants for purposes of a research experiment might violate constitutional principles of equal protection. Is that a serious problem? See Experimentation in the Law: Report of the Federal Judicial Center Advisory Committee on Experimentation in the Law (Federal Judicial Center 1981); Zeisel, Kalven & Buchholz, Delay in the Court, ch. 21, The Case for the Official Experiment (1959).

JUDICIAL ACTIVISM AT PRETRIAL CONFERENCE

The adversarial motive has been the heart-beat of common law litigation. By long tradition, the lawyers, not the judges, are the ones to initiate, develop and advance the issues, arguments or evidence upon which decision turns. However, modern procedural principles tend to subordinate all other considerations to the urge to reach the merits of the case. They may impel the trial judge to try to aid the less astute or less prepared advocate. How strongly does this tendency push the judge who conducts a pretrial conference?

At pretrial may the judge presume to strike denials or defenses that seem without support in evidence or law? Is it permissible to raise or phrase the issues as the judge sees fit, overriding objections of both counsel? May each side be required to disclose the names of trial witnesses it means to call? Assuming the power is present, should the judge use it? Neither the appellate courts nor the legislatures have provided answers to those questions and trial judges differ sharply among themselves about them.

NOTES

(1) Here, too, varying circumstances and varying equities produce decisions that are difficult to reconcile. A district judge has been held by the Supreme Court of the United States to have power to render a default judgment against a plaintiff whose lawyer repeatedly failed to attend a pretrial conference. Link v. Wabash Railroad, 370 U.S. 626, 82 S.Ct. 1386, 8 L.Ed.2d 734 (1962); and to eliminate issues the parties have agreed to drop, even though one of them refuses to give his formal assent. See Life Music, Inc. v. Edelstein, 309 F.2d 242, 243 (2d Cir.1962). But compare Gamble v. Pope & Talbot, Inc., 307 F.2d 729 (3d Cir.1962), ruling the district court without power to fine for contempt a lawyer who refused to appear for a pretrial conference.

(2) A pretrial order supposedly prescribes the future course of conduct of the litigation. What in practice is its binding force as against inconsistent assertions in the pleadings or on the trial? In Plastino v. Mills, 236 F.2d 32, 33–34 (9th Cir.1956), the order recited that "the pleadings now pass out of the case," but after trial the appeals court found the order "so badly drawn that it would have been far better to have proceeded to trial on the pleadings" and directed that it be set aside along with the trial judge's findings and conclusions.

PACIFIC INDEMNITY CO. v. BROWARD COUNTY

United States Court of Appeals, Fifth Circuit, 1972.
465 F.2d 99.*

GEWIN, CIRCUIT JUDGE. This appeal presents the Case of the Forgotten Issue and raises the interesting problem of what happens in a diversity suit where the litigants raise an issue in their pleadings and then forget about the question until after the case has gone to the jury. The district court treated the absence of proof on the issue to be a failure of proof of a material element of the cross-claim of Florida Airmotive Sales, Inc. (Airmotive) against Broward County and granted judgment notwithstanding the verdict in favor of the County on the cross-claim. We affirm.

The suit was instituted by Pacific Indemnity Company as property damage insurer and subrogee of the Donzi Marine Corporation for damages in the sum of $389,000 for the destruction by fire of four aircraft owned by Donzi and insured by Pacific Indemnity. Pacific Indemnity sued both Broward County, which owned the hangar in

* Footnotes omitted.

which the aircraft were housed at the time of the fire, and Airmotive which rented the hangar from the County and had in turn leased space in the hangar to Donzi.

Airmotive filed a cross-claim against the County seeking indemnity from any loss from the suit by Pacific Indemnity and also seeking damages for the destruction of Airmotive's own aircraft and other property caused by the fire. The County replied to Airmotive's cross-claim, incorporating motions to dismiss, and asserting a counter-cross-claim against Airmotive for indemnity from loss arising from the suit by Pacific Indemnity and also seeking damages for the loss of the hangar.

Pre-trial motions disposed of both indemnity claims and that part of the County's claim for the loss of the hangar based on contractual indemnity. Pursuant to a stipulation between the parties a pre-trial order was entered. The cause was tried before a jury on the main claim of Pacific Indemnity and the remaining issues of negligence and damages raised by Airmotive's cross-claim and the County's counter-cross-claim. The jury returned verdicts in favor of Pacific Indemnity against the county for $389,000 and in favor of Airmotive as to Pacific Indemnity's claim against it. The jury also found in favor of Airmotive on its cross-claim against the County, awarding damages of $150,000, and against the County on its counter-cross-claim against Airmotive.

Following the entry of judgment on Airmotive's cross-claim, the County filed a motion for judgment n.o.v. and for a new trial. After a hearing on the motion the trial court granted the County's motion for judgment n.o.v., vacated the judgment in favor of Airmotive on its cross-claim, and entered judgment for the County. Airmotive appeals from that judgment.

Although the parties raise other questions on appeal, we reach only the problem of the interplay between the substantive law of Florida and Rule 16 F.R.Civ.P. concerning pre-trial orders.

Of central importance here is Florida Statute § 95.08, FSA:

"Every claim against any county shall be presented to the board of county commissioners within one year from the time said claim shall become due, and shall be barred if not so presented."

In count one of their amended cross-claim Airmotive specifically pleaded that notice had been given to the County in accordance with the statute. In count two Airmotive realleged by reference a number of the specific allegations of count one, including the allegation of notice to the County. In reply the County specifically denied the allegation of notice contained in count one, denied all of the specific allegations of count two and included as to both counts a general denial of all allegations of the cross-claim not specifically admitted. In addition the County in its reply separately moved to dismiss both counts of Airmotive's cross-claim because, inter alia, Airmotive had failed to give the County notice of the claims within the time required by the statute.

Thereafter during the entire pre-trial proceedings, which included two motions by the County for summary judgment on Airmotive's cross-claim, through the pre-trial hearing and order, up until the close of all evidence at trial, no specific mention of the issue of notice was made by either the County or Airmotive. Under the district court's local rules the parties were required in their pre-trial stipulation to set forth the facts as to which there was no disagreement, the remaining issues for determination and all undisposed motions. Airmotive's allegation of notice to the County was not set forth as a stipulated fact, and neither party included the question in their list of issues to be determined. The stipulation did indicate that the County's motions to dismiss the cross-claim which were based on the absence of notice remained to be acted on by the court. At the pre-trial hearing all pending motions to dismiss were denied.

At the trial of the cause, no mention was made of the issue of statutory notice until the conclusion of all of the evidence, when the County moved for a directed verdict on Airmotive's cross-claim because, inter alia, Airmotive had failed to introduce any proof of compliance with the statutory notice provisions. That motion was denied. However, following trial the County sought and was granted judgment n.o.v. on Airmotive's cross-claim for the same reason.

*   *   *

Rule 16 F.R.Civ.P. gives the trial court broad discretion in conducting pre-trial procedures in order to narrow the issues, reduce the field of fact controversy for resolution, and to simplify the mechanics of the offer and receipt of evidence. Laird v. Air Carrier Engine Service, Inc., 263 F.2d 948, 953 (5th Cir.1959). Certainly the pre-trial order is most useful in this regard, and when entered does control the subsequent course of the action unless modified at trial to prevent manifest injustice. Rule 16 F.R.Civ.P. . . .

Although the pre-trial order may supersede the pleadings it does not operate in the same manner to frame the issues as the earlier pleadings. . . .

Nothing in Rule 16 F.R.Civ.P. nor in the local rule involved here suggests that a party waives or admits an issue as to which his opponent has the burden of proof by failing to include the issue in his pre-trial stipulated list of remaining issues.

The failure to indicate in the pre-trial order that an issue remains to be resolved at trial usually precludes the offer of proof on the issue at trial—to the detriment of the party who has the burden to prove the issue. This common-sense rule has been followed where the plaintiff pleads a theory of recovery in his complaint, but fails to preserve the theory in the pre-trial order, Fernandez v. United Fruit Co., 200 F.2d 414 (2d Cir.1952), cert. den. 345 U.S. 935, 73 S.Ct. 797, 97 L.Ed. 1363 (1953), and where the defendant pleads a number of affirmative defenses which he fails to preserve during pre-trial, Shell v. Strong, 151 F.2d 909 (10th Cir.1945). In this manner the pre-trial order permits the parties and the court to prepare for trial with the assurance that they know what issues they must be ready to meet.

In the present case Airmotive had the burden to prove as part of its cause of action against the County that the statutory notice had been given as alleged. When the question was not admitted nor preserved for trial in the pre-trial order the County had grounds for a technical objection in the event Airmotive attempted to prove notice at trial. However the court in the exercise of its discretion to prevent manifest injustice under Rule 16 F.R.Civ.P. could have amended the pre-trial order during trial to permit proof on the question. Alternatively, the court could have ordered a limited new trial under Rule 59 F.R.Civ.P. where, as in these circumstances, the issue was in good faith overlooked by all concerned. But to hold, as Airmotive contends, that the County waived statutory notice because the County failed to remind Airmotive in the pre-trial stipulation that Airmotive still had to prove that it had given the County notice would strain the logic of our adversarial system and would destroy much of the usefulness of a pre-trial order as a device to reduce and limit issues at trial.

Airmotive did not ask the trial court for a new trial following the entry of the judgment n.o.v. and has stated to this court that it does not seek a new trial. Airmotive failed to prove a material element of its cause of action by cross-claim against the County. Accordingly, the judgment of the district court, notwithstanding the verdict, is affirmed.

NOTES

(1) Could the court on its own motion have invoked Rule 15 to aid Airmotive? If the trial judge had become aware of Airmotive's failure to offer proof of notice, should it have pointed out the problem to Airmotive's counsel and invited a motion to amend? Why?

(2) What will be the effect upon enforcement of the sanctions provided in Rule 16 if the court undertakes to relieve a client from counsel's derelictions at the pretrial conference and related trial proceedings? Presumably, if the court does not come to the rescue, the client's recourse will be suit against the lawyer for malpractice. Is that a satisfactory solution? What difficulties does it present?

WALLIN v. FULLER

United States Court of Appeals, Fifth Circuit, 1973.
476 F.2d 1204.

WISDOM, CIRCUIT JUDGE. This case presents the question whether a trial court should instruct a jury on a theory of liability not mentioned in the pretrial order but supported by evidence introduced at the trial without objection. The district court declined so to instruct the jury. We reverse and remand for a new trial.

Carl Wallin was killed on August 16, 1970, when his Volkswagen, which he was driving, collided with a Pontiac driven by Allen Fuller on a two-lane highway near Lowndesboro, Alabama. Wallin held a policy of insurance with Nationwide Mutual Insurance Company, which contained a standard uninsured motorist clause. Fuller was an uninsured motorist within the meaning of this clause. Marsha Lee Wallin, widow of Carl Wallin, brought suit in federal district court seeking a declaratory judgment against Nationwide under the policy, alleging that Fuller's negligence had caused the collision.

On September 20, 1971, the district court held a pretrial hearing and entered an order specifying the issues agreed upon by the plaintiff, Mrs. Wallin, and defendant, Nationwide. The plaintiff's theory of recovery, as recited in the pretrial order, was that Fuller negligently drove onto his left side of the highway, thus causing the collision with Wallin's car. The defendant denied that Fuller had been negligent. Further, the defendant contended that Wallin had been contributorily negligent in pulling out onto *his* left-hand side of the highway to pass another car when there was insufficient room to pass.

Most of the plaintiff's case at the trial was devoted to showing that the collision had occurred in Wallin's right-hand lane, and that Fuller therefore had been on the wrong side of the road. Mrs. Wallin, the plaintiff, identified photographs which she had taken showing that the left side had been torn off Wallin's Volkswagen. The plaintiff also submitted the testimony of two investigating officers, who stated that the point of impact was on Wallin's right side of the road.

The defense offered the deposition of George Mayes, who had been riding in Fuller's car at the time of the accident, and called Fuller himself to the stand. Both Mayes and Fuller testified that Wallin had pulled out to pass, and that the cars had collided while Wallin was still in the left lane and Fuller was in his right lane.

The testimony of both Mayes and Fuller revealed a possibility that, even if Wallin had been contributorily negligent, Fuller might have been guilty of subsequent negligence or wanton conduct. Under Alabama law a showing of subsequent negligence or wantonness defeats a defense of contributory negligence.[1] Counsel for the defendant made no objection to the admission of any of this testimony at the trial. Mayes, the passenger, testified at his deposition that Fuller did not slow down when he first became aware that Wallin was trying to pass; that he finally shouted at Fuller to slam on his brakes; and that Fuller then applied his brakes and skidded into Wallin.[2] The defense took the

---

1. See, e.g., Birmingham Ry., Light & Power Co. v. Jung, 161 Ala. 461, 49 So. 434 (1909).

[One footnote omitted and one renumbered. Eds.]

2. At his deposition, Mayes testified in part on direct examination by defendant's attorney:

"Q Now what did Fuller do when he saw the Volkswagen there?

"A You mean what he did right then?

"Q Yeah, what did Fuller do from the time that you saw that Volkswagen?

"A What he did looked like he wasn't never going to hit on his brakes or nothing.

"Q Who?

"A I told him, I said, 'Slam on your brakes. Do something.' I say, 'Don't

deposition of Mayes on September 8, 1971, before the pretrial hearing. The plaintiff's attorney was present at this deposition, but made no mention of the issues of subsequent negligence and wanton conduct either at the pretrial hearing or when the deposition was introduced into evidence at the trial.

Fuller, called as a witness by the defense, gave testimony on cross-examination by the plaintiff's attorney that tended to corroborate Mayes's version of the events.[3] On recross, asked by the plaintiff's attorney whether the accident would not have happened if he had slowed down the least little bit, Fuller replied: "I guess not." Counsel for the defendant made no objection to any of this examination by the plaintiff's lawyer.

Neither attorney drew the court's attention to the fact that this testimony might show subsequent negligence or wanton conduct, or to the fact that the pretrial order precluded these issues, until after both sides had rested. The defendant then submitted requested written charges to the court. The plaintiff's attorney objected to one of these charges on the ground that it failed to include the issues of subsequent

you see the man over in our lane?' He hit his brakes and we skidded right on into him."

 * * *

On cross-examination by the plaintiff's attorney:

"Q All right. Now, when the Volkswagen pulled out onto the Fuller side of the road Fuller didn't even see it, did he? At least he didn't act like he saw it, did he?

"A He didn't act like he saw it. He say 'What's the man trying to do?' I say, 'You see what he's trying to do, he's trying to go around.' I say, 'Don't you see him?'

"Q And you are the one told him to put on his brakes, aren't you?

"A You say I the one told him to put on his brakes?

"Q Yes.

"A Well, I tell you like this—

"Q (Interrupting) Fuller didn't even put on his brakes until you told him to, did he?

"A Till I told him to?

"Q Yes.

"A Well, he was going to slam on his brakes, that's what he say.

"Q He said he was going to but he still hadn't done it until you told him to, had he?

"A Well, I told him to hit his brakes, yes.

"Q When you told him to hit his brakes that's when he hit his brakes?

"A That's when he hit his brakes.

"Q He didn't hit his brakes until you told him to, did he?

"A But he seen the car.

"Q He seen the car but he didn't hit his brakes until you told him to?

"A That's right."

 * * *

"Q And you said slam on the brakes?

"A Yeah, I said, 'Slam on your brakes. What you going to do, run into him?' That's when he slammed on his brakes."

3. On cross-examination Fuller testified in part as follows:

Q Did you see him when he first started to pull out?

A Yes, sir.

Q All right. Did you slow down when you saw him first start to pull out?

A No, sir.

Q You did not. Is Mayes correct when he said you kept driving until he said what you going to do, drive into him?

A That's right.

Q That's right. You just kept going 60 miles an hour in the rain, didn't you?

A Yes, sir.

 * * *

negligence and wanton conduct, and requested leave to amend the pleadings to include these issues. The trial court denied leave to amend, applying the standard of Rule 16 of the Federal Rules of Civil Procedure that, where the issues have been narrowed by a pretrial order, amendment will be permitted only when necessary to prevent "manifest injustice." The court proceeded to submit the case to the jury without instructions as to the legal effect of subsequent negligence or wanton conduct. The jury found for the defendant. The court then denied the plaintiff's motion for a new trial, and the plaintiff brought this appeal.

The pretrial conference serves the purposes of expediting litigation and eliminating surprise at the trial. Rule 16 of the Federal Rules of Civil Procedure establishes that the pretrial order ordinarily governs the course of the trial. Under the Rule 16 "manifest injustice" standard, the question whether to permit amendment of the pretrial order in the course of the trial is generally a matter within the discretion of the trial judge, and an appellate court will intervene only if the trial judge has acted arbitrarily. See Ely v. Reading Co., 424 F.2d 758 (3 Cir. 1970); McKey v. Fairbairn, 345 F.2d 739 (D.C.Cir.1965); Case v. Abrams, 352 F.2d 193 (10 Cir. 1965).

Unbending adherence to the strictures of Rule 16 would, however, frustrate another broad policy of the Federal Rules favoring liberality of amendment. This policy is principally embodied in Rule 15, which deals with amendments to the pleadings.[4] It is unlikely that the pretrial order under Rule 16 was intended to make the pleadings, and therefore Rule 15, obsolete. . . . Rule 15(b) provides that when issues outside the pleadings are tried by express or implied consent of the parties, "they *shall* be treated in all respects as if they had been raised in the pleadings." (Emphasis added.) Amendment is thus not merely discretionary but mandatory in such a case. 3 J. Moore, ¶ 15.13[2] at 996.

The trial court erred in applying Rule 16 rather than Rule 15(b). Under the standards of Rule 15(b) the defendant impliedly consented to the trial of issues outside the pretrial order, and the pleadings should therefore have been amended. A substantial quantity of evidence tending to establish subsequent negligence or wanton conduct was brought before the jury, through the deposition of Mayes and the testimony of Fuller, without objection by defense counsel. Indeed, both Mayes and Fuller were defense witnesses, and Fuller was himself a defendant. Cf. Vogrin v. Hedstrom, 220 F.2d 863, (8 Cir.1955) cert. den. 1955, 350 U.S. 845, 76 S.Ct. 86, 100 L.Ed. 753. Having deposed Mayes well in advance of the trial, defense counsel cannot complain of having been unaware that the evidence might tend to establish subsequent negligence and wantonness. In these circumstances the failure of the

---

4. In addition to Rule 15, Rule 54(c) states that "every final judgment shall grant the relief to which the party in whose favor it is rendered is entitled, even if the party has not demanded such relief in his pleadings." Rule 1 requires that the rules be construed to secure the "just" determination of every action.

defense to seek to limit the evidence during the trial in accordance with the pretrial order establishes consent to the trial of these issues. . . .

The defendant, Nationwide Mutual, argues that the testimony of Mayes and Fuller was relevant to the issues of negligence and contributory negligence, and that therefore the admission of this evidence without objection cannot establish consent to the trial of any other issues. It is true that part of this testimony tended to rebut the plaintiff's theory that the collision occurred on Wallin's right side of the road, and tended to show that Wallin might have been contributorily negligent in pulling out to pass. But the testimony as to Fuller's failure to apply his brakes, and the conversation between Mayes and Fuller, was not relevant to the plaintiff's theory of recovery, which was founded solely on the theory that Fuller was on the wrong side of the road. Nor did it establish or rebut the contention that Wallin was contributorily negligent. This evidence was much more strongly relevant to the theories of subsequent negligence and wanton conduct, and this should have been apparent to defense counsel. . . .

Certainly the plaintiff's attorney should have raised these issues at the pretrial conference. He attended the deposition of Mayes, and was thus well aware before the pretrial conference that there was some evidence of subsequent negligence and wanton conduct. Where a party is aware of an issue before a pretrial conference, his failure to raise it there may in some circumstances be grounds for denying later amendment. See McKey v. Fairbairn, 345 F.2d 739 (D.C.Cir.1965); Marble v. Batten & Co., 36 F.R.D. 693 (D.D.C.1964).

But the failure of the plaintiff's counsel in this case to raise these issues before or during the trial is offset by the failure of the defendant's attorney to attempt to exclude any of the evidence. We find no reason to conclude that the plaintiff's attorney was acting in bad faith by trying to smuggle in issues for the purpose of surprising the defense at the trial. . . .

We therefore hold that the district court erred in applying the standards of Rule 16 rather than Rule 15(b), and that under Rule 15(b) the plaintiff was entitled to amendment. The judgment of the district court is reversed and the case is remanded for a new trial.

Part VI

ADJUDICATION AND ITS EFFECTS

Chapter Fourteen

TRIAL

SECTION 1. STEPS IN A TRIAL

A. INTRODUCTION

The purpose of trial is to resolve disputed issues of fact on the basis of evidence offered. Since triers are usually concerned with past events of which they themselves have no direct knowledge, their interpretation of the evidence will depend to a considerable extent on their training and prior experience, their reasoning powers, and emotions.

A trial is unnecessary if only questions of law are at issue, for these are resolved on the basis of considerations of fairness and substantive policy, not by evidence tending to show the truth or falsity of disputed material propositions. The concept of the common law trial, with its elaborate rules regarding evidence, burdens of proof and presumptions, rests on the premise that a fact issue is readily distinguishable from a law issue. Nevertheless, the pleadings and other materials you have already studied should have suggested that distinguishing between "fact" and "law" is often difficult and that characterization of an issue in one category or another may vary depending upon the procedural context.

In the United States, though no longer in Great Britain, the trier of fact in a civil action is usually a jury. The major focus of this chapter will be upon jury trials, which introduce complications not present in trial by a judge alone.

The first point to notice about the modern jury is its passive role: Evidence is presented to it, not imported by it. Next, there is the persistent ambiguity about the jury's proper role: Shall it decide the issues committed to it as rationally as a judge might resolve them, or according to lay notions of justice? The third point, a factor which seriously complicates the jury's function, is that the theoretical line separating issues of fact from questions of law dissolves in practice and produces difficult questions as to the relative roles of the court and the jury. For example, whether a sleeping potion is a "poison" may seem at first to present simply a question of fact for competent experts; but imbed the issue in a suit for life insurance benefits under a policy which excludes coverage in case of death by poison, and the issue may seem one of law involving construction of the insurance contract.

The sequence of steps in a trial is sometimes controlled by detailed codes, statutes and rules, and at other times is regulated by the court *ad hoc* under its "inherent powers."

Trial before a jury is quite different from trial before a judge alone. The jury must be selected from a panel of eligible persons; the lawyers almost always present opening statements, invoke the rules governing evidence, and make motions and closing arguments; the judge must instruct the jurors on the applicable law; and the jury must reach and render its verdict in prescribed fashion. A non-jury trial will not, of course, require selecting or charging a jury; is quite likely to omit opening statements and closing arguments; many evidentiary objections will go unvoiced; and there is more opportunity for continuances and supplementary stages to produce additional evidence and legal argument.

A jury trial presents abundant opportunity for collision between the judge's role as director of proceedings and oracle of the law and the jury's role as trier of the facts. Since the jury deliberates in secret and usually announces only a general verdict, an aggressive judge may try to sway the jury during the trial and to shape the outcome before the jury retires. If the verdict differs from the judge's view of the case, the judge may wish to set aside. This natural conflict between the power of the judge and the prerogative of the jury creates many of the problems treated in this chapter.

B. THE VOIR DIRE

Read 28 U.S.C.A. §§ 1861, 1862, 1865(b), 1866(c), and 1870 in the Supplement.

The voir dire is the process by which a jury (or, more exactly, a "petit jury") is selected from among the persons called for jury duty (the "venire"). In federal court, this process is controlled by Rule 47(a) of the Federal Rules of Civil Procedure, which empowers the court to permit the parties to conduct an examination of the prospective jurors. States' rules differ: some require the judge to conduct the voir dire, see, e.g., Cal.Rule Sup.Ct. 228; others give the attorneys control, see, e.g., N.Y.—McKinney's CPLR 4107. But in all judicial systems there is tension among the various goals of the process: creating an objectively impartial jury; using jurors whom the parties subjectively trust; finding jurors competent to understand highly complex evidence.

McDONOUGH POWER EQUIPMENT, INC.
v. GREENWOOD

Supreme Court of the United States, 1984.
464 U.S. 548, 104 S.Ct. 845, 78 L.Ed.2d 663.

JUSTICE REHNQUIST delivered the opinion of the Court.*

Respondents, Billy Greenwood and his parents, sued petitioner McDonough Power Equipment, Incorporated to recover damages sustained by Billy when his feet came in contact with the blades of a riding lawn mower manufactured by petitioner. The United States District Court for the District of Kansas entered judgment for petitioner upon a jury verdict and denied respondents' motion for new trial. On appeal, however, the Court of Appeals for the Tenth Circuit reversed the judgment of the District Court and ordered a new trial. It held that the failure of a juror to respond affirmatively to a question on *voir dire* seeking to elicit information about previous injuries to members of the juror's immediate family had "prejudiced the Greenwoods' right of peremptory challenge," . . . and that a new trial was necessary to cure this error. We granted certiorari, . . . and now hold that respondents are not entitled to a new trial unless the juror's failure to disclose denied respondents their right to an impartial jury.

During the *voir dire* prior to the empaneling of the six-member jury, respondents' attorney asked prospective jurors the following question:

"Now, how many of you have yourself or any members of your immediate family sustained any severe injury, not necessarily as severe as Billy, but sustained any injuries whether it was an accident at home, or on the farm or at work that resulted in any disability or prolonged pain and suffering, that is you or any members of your immediate family?" . . .

Ronald Payton, who eventually became a juror, did not respond to this question, which was addressed to the panel as a whole. After a trial which extended over a three-week period, the jury found for petitioner McDonough. Four days after judgment was entered for petitioner, respondents moved under local Rule 23A for permission to approach the members of the jury. In support of their motion respondents asserted that they were "of information and belief" that juror Payton's son may have been injured at one time, a fact which had not been revealed during *voir dire*. . . . The District Court ruled that respondents had failed to show just cause to approach the jury. . . .

Undeterred, the next day respondents filed a second motion for permission to approach the jury, attaching an affidavit from respondent John Greenwood,[1] who asserted that in the course of his employment as

* Some footnotes omitted; others renumbered.

1. It is not clear from the opinion of the Court of Appeals whether the information stated in Greenwood's affidavit was known to respondents or their counsel at the time of the *voir dire* examination. If it were, of course, respondents would be barred from

a Navy recruiter, he had reviewed the enlistment application of juror Payton's son. In that application Payton's son stated that he had been injured in the explosion of a truck tire. The District Court granted respondents permission to approach juror Payton regarding the injuries allegedly sustained by his son. The District Court directed that the inquiry should be brief and polite and made in a manner convenient to the juror. The District Court noted that it was not "overly impressed with the significance of this particular situation." . . . No provision was made to record the inquiry of juror Payton.

On the same day that the District Court granted respondents permission to approach juror Payton, respondents moved for a new trial, asserting 18 grounds in justification, including the District Court's alleged error in denying respondents' motion to approach the jury. This was the only instance when respondents even tangentially referred the District Court to the juror's failure to respond as a ground for a new trial. Shortly after the parties placed a telephone conference call to juror Payton, the District Court denied respondents' motion for a new trial, finding that the "matter was fairly and thoroughly tried and that the jury's verdict was a just one, well-supported by the evidence." . . . The District Court was never informed of the results of the examination of juror Payton, nor did respondents ever directly assert before the District Court that juror Payton's non-disclosure warranted a new trial.

On appeal, the Court of Appeals proceeded directly to the merits of respondents' claim that juror Payton's silence had prejudiced their right to exercise peremptory challenges, rather than remanding the case back to the District Court for a hearing.[2] The Court of Appeals

later challenging the composition of the jury when they had chosen not to interrogate juror Payton further upon receiving an answer which they thought to be factually incorrect. See Johnson v. Hill, 274 F.2d 110, 115–116 (CA8 1960).

2. Although neither party challenges the propriety of the Court of Appeals having disposed of the question on the merits, we believe that the proper resolution of the legal issue should be made by the District Court. . . . Nevertheless, we address the issue in order to correct the legal standard the District Court should apply upon remand.

Both parties apparently agree that during the telephone conversation with juror Payton, he related that his son had received a broken leg as the result of an exploding tire. Counsel for respondents in their brief to the Court of Appeals recalled Payton saying that "it did not make any difference whether his son had been in an accident and was seriously injured," "that having accidents are a part of life," and that "all his children have been involved in accidents." Brief for appellants in 80–1698 (CA10), p. 7. Counsel for petitioners recall Payton as saying that he "did not regard [his son's broken leg] as a 'severe' injury and as he understood the question [the injury] did not result in any 'disability or prolonged pain and suffering.' As far as Mr. Payton is concerned he answered counsel's question honestly, and correctly, by remaining silent." Brief for appellee in 80–1698 (CA10), p. 18.

Nevertheless, the manner in which the parties presented the issue of juror Payton's failure to respond on *voir dire* was highly unorthodox. While considerations of judicial economy might have motivated the Court of Appeals in this case to proceed directly to the issue of the effect of juror Payton's non-disclosure, in cases in which a party is asserting a ground for new trial, the normal procedure is to remand such issues to the district court for resolution. Although petitioner does not dispute respondents' version of the telephone call to juror Payton, it is foreseeable that in another such case, the parties could present

simply recited the recollections of counsel for each party of their conference telephone call with juror Payton contained in their appellate briefs, stating that the "unrevealed information" indicated probable bias "because it revealed a particularly narrow concept of what constitutes a serious injury." . . . The Court of Appeals assumed that juror Payton had answered in good faith, but stated:

> "Good faith, however, is irrelevant to our inquiry. If an average prospective juror would have disclosed the information, and that information would have been significant and cogent evidence of the juror's probable bias, a new trial is required to rectify the failure to disclose it." Ibid. (citation omitted).

This Court has long held that " '[a litigant] is entitled to a fair trial but not a perfect one,' for there are no perfect trials." Brown v. United States, 411 U.S. 223, 231–232, 93 S.Ct. 1565, 1570–1571, 36 L.Ed.2d 208 (1973), quoting Bruton v. United States, 391 U.S. 123, 135, 88 S.Ct. 1620, 1627, 20 L.Ed.2d 476 (1968), and Lutwak v. United States, 344 U.S. 604, 619, 73 S.Ct. 481, 490, 97 L.Ed. 593 (1953). Trials are costly, not only for the parties, but also for the jurors performing their civic duty and for society which pays the judges and support personnel who manage the trials. It seems doubtful that our judicial system would have the resources to provide litigants with perfect trials, were they possible, and still keep abreast of its constantly increasing case load. Even this straightforward products liability suit extended over a three-week period.

We have also come a long way from the time when all trial error was presumed prejudicial and reviewing courts were considered "citadels of technicality." Kotteakos v. United States, 328 U.S. 750, 759, 66 S.Ct. 1239, 1245, 90 L.Ed. 1557 (1946), quoting Kavanagh, Improvement of Administration of Criminal Justice by Exercise of Judicial Power, 11 A.B.A.J. 217, 222 (1925). The harmless error rules adopted by this Court and Congress embody the principle that courts should exercise judgment in preference to the automatic reversal for "error" and ignore errors that do not affect the essential fairness of the trial. See *Kotteakos*, 328 U.S., 759–760, 66 S.Ct., 1245–1246. For example, the general rule governing motions for a new trial in the district courts is contained in Federal Rule Civil Procedure 61, which provides:

> "No error . . . or defect in any ruling or order or in anything done or omitted by the court or by any of the parties is ground for granting a new trial or for setting aside a verdict . . . unless refusal to take such action appears to the court inconsistent with substantial justice. The court at every stage of the proceeding *must* disregard any error or defect in the

the appellate court with a continuing, difficult factual dispute. Appellate tribunals are poor substitutes for trial courts for developing a record or resolving factual controversies.

proceeding which does not affect the substantial rights of the parties." (emphasis added)

While in a narrow sense Rule 61 applies only to the district courts, see Fed.Rule Civ.Proc. 1, it is well-settled that the appellate courts should act in accordance with the salutary policy embodied in Rule 61. See, e.g., Keaton v. Atchison, Topeka & Santa Fe R. Co., 321 F.2d 317, 319 (CA7 1963); Box v. Swindle, 306 F.2d 882, 887 (CA5 1962); De Santa v. Nehi Corp., 171 F.2d 696, 698 (CA2 1948). Congress has further reinforced the application of Rule 61 by enacting the harmless error statute, 28 U.S.C. § 2111, which applies directly to appellate courts and which incorporates the same principle as that found in Rule 61. See Tipton v. Socony Mobil Oil Co., 375 U.S. 34, 37, 84 S.Ct. 1, 3, 11 L.Ed.2d 4 (1963); United States v. Borden Co., 347 U.S. 514, 516 and n. 5, 74 S.Ct. 703, 705 and n. 5, 98 L.Ed. 903 (1954).

The ruling of the Court of Appeals in this case must be assessed against this background. One touchstone of a fair trial is an impartial trier of fact—"a jury capable and willing to decide the case solely on the evidence before it." Smith v. Phillips, 455 U.S. 209, 217, 102 S.Ct. 940, 946, 71 L.Ed.2d 78 (1982). *Voir dire* examination serves to protect that right by exposing possible biases, both known and unknown, on the part of potential jurors. Demonstrated bias in the responses to questions on *voir dire* may result in a juror being excused for cause; hints of bias not sufficient to warrant challenge for cause may assist parties in exercising their peremptory challenges. The necessity of truthful answers by prospective jurors if this process is to serve its purpose is obvious.

The critical question posed to juror Payton in this case asked about "injuries . . . that resulted in any disability or prolonged pain or suffering." . . . Juror Payton apparently believed that his son's broken leg sustained as a result of an exploding tire was not such an injury. In response to a similar question from petitioner's counsel, however, another juror related such a minor incident as the fact that his six-year-old son once caught his finger in a bike chain. . . . Yet another juror failed to respond to the question posed to juror Payton, and only the subsequent questioning of petitioner's counsel brought out that her husband had been injured in a machinery accident. . . .

The varied responses to respondents' question on *voir dire* testify to the fact that jurors are not necessarily experts in English usage. Called as they are from all walks of life, many may be uncertain as to the meaning of terms which are relatively easily understood by lawyers and judges. Moreover, the statutory qualifications for jurors require only a minimal competency in the English language. 28 U.S.C. § 1865. Thus, we cannot say, and we doubt that the Court of Appeals could say, which of these three jurors was closer to the "average juror" in his response to the question, but it is evident that such a standard is difficult to apply and productive of uncertainties.

To invalidate the result of a three-week trial because of a juror's mistaken, though honest response to a question, is to insist on something closer to perfection than our judicial system can be expected to give. A trial represents an important investment of private and social resources, and it ill serves the important end of finality to wipe the slate clean simply to recreate the peremptory challenge process because counsel lacked an item of information which objectively he should have obtained from a juror on *voir dire* examination. Whatever the merits of the Court of Appeals' standard in a world which would redo and reconstruct what had gone before upon any evidence of abstract imperfection, we think it is contrary to the practical necessities of judicial management reflected in Rule 61 and § 2111. We hold that to obtain a new trial in such a situation, a party must first demonstrate that a juror failed to answer honestly a material question on *voir dire,* and then further show that a correct response would have provided a valid basis for a challenge for cause. The motives for concealing information may vary, but only those reasons that affect a juror's impartiality can truly be said to affect the fairness of a trial.

Generally, motions for a new trial are committed to the discretion of the district court. Montgomery Ward & Co. v. Duncan, 311 U.S. 243, 251, 61 S.Ct. 189, 194, 85 L.Ed. 147 (1940). The Court of Appeals was mistaken in deciding as it did that respondents were entitled to a new trial. In the event that the issue remains relevant after the Court of Appeals has disposed of respondents' other contentions on appeal, the District Court may hold a hearing to determine whether respondents are entitled to a new trial under the principles we state here. The judgment of the Court of Appeals is reversed.

JUSTICE BLACKMUN, with whom JUSTICE STEVENS and JUSTICE O'CONNOR join, concurring.

    *   *   *

JUSTICE BRENNAN, with whom JUSTICE MARSHALL joins, concurring in the judgment.

I agree with the Court that the Court of Appeals employed an erroneous legal standard to determine whether a new trial was required in this case, and that the Court of Appeals compounded that error by failing to remand the case to the District Court for a hearing and decision on the motion for new trial in the first instance. I concur only in the judgment, however, because I have difficulty understanding the import of the legal standard adopted by the Court.

The Court of Appeals ordered a new trial because Ronald Payton, who later was chosen as jury foreman, incorrectly answered an important question posed to prospective jurors on *voir dire.* Specifically, although asked whether any family members had "sustained any injuries . . . that resulted in any disability or prolonged pain or suffering," Payton failed to disclose a previous injury his son had incurred in a truck-tire explosion. The court concluded that, because the information available to counsel during *voir dire* was erroneous,

Payton's failure to respond "prejudiced the Greenwoods' right of per-emptory challenge." Greenwood v. McDonough Power Equipment, Inc., 687 F.2d 338, 342 (CA10 1982). It therefore held that the Greenwoods' motion for a new trial should have been granted, and entered judgment granting the motion.

I agree with the Court that a finding that less-than-complete information was available to counsel conducting *voir dire* does not by itself require a new trial. I cannot join, however, in the legal standard asserted by the Court's opinion. In my view, the proper focus when ruling on a motion for new trial in this situation should be on the bias of the juror and the resulting prejudice to the litigant. More specifical-ly, to be awarded a new trial, a litigant should be required to demon-strate that the juror incorrectly responded to a material question on *voir dire,* and that, under the facts and circumstances surrounding the particular case, the juror was biased against the moving litigant. See, e.g., McCoy v. Goldston, 652 F.2d 654, 659–660 (CA6 1981).

. . . Whether the juror answered a particular question on *voir dire* honestly or dishonestly, or whether an inaccurate answer was inadvertent or intentional, are simply factors to be considered in this latter determination of actual bias. I therefore cannot agree with the Court when it asserts that a new trial is not warranted whenever a prospective juror provides an honest answer to the question posed.

. . . .

*   *   *

NOTES

(1) On the *voir dire* examination generally, see Bermant & Shapard, The Voir Dire Examination, Juror Challenges, and Adversary Advocacy (Federal Judicial Center, 1978); Kalven and Zeisel, The American Jury (1966). Cf. Nesson, The Evidence or the Event? On Judicial Proof and the Acceptability of Verdicts, 98 Harv.L.Rev. 1357 (1985), who notes that, in general, litigation rules compromise truth-seeking in order to maximize public acceptance of the fruits of the process.

(2) How can the *voir dire* be used to gauge how the jurors will discharge their duties? Lawyers have engaged specialists, such as psychologists and sociologists, in helping them predict jury conduct. Does this put the pecunious litigant at an advantage? See also Suggs & Sales, Using Communication Clues to Evaluate Prospective Jurors During the Voir Dire, 20 Ariz.L.Rev. 629 (1978); Zeiglir, Young Adults As A Cognizable Jump in Jury Selections, 76 Mich.L.Rev. 1045 (1978); Sonaike, The Influence of Jury Deliberations on Juror Perception of Trial, Credibility and Damage Awards, 1978 B.Y.U.L.Rev. 889; V. Hans and N. Vidmar, Judging the Jury (1986).

(3) Because stress has been placed upon insuring that the jury (or at least the venire from which it is drawn) represents a cross section of the community, claims of discriminatory selection have been considered seriously. In criminal cases, these challenges are often based on the Sixth Amendment's guarantee of an impartial jury, but a similar policy can be found in the Seventh and Fourteenth Amendments, and in statutory law. Thus, in Thiel v. Southern Pacific Co., 328 U.S. 217, 66 S.Ct. 984, 90 L.Ed. 1181 (1946), the Supreme Court

found it unconstitutional to exclude persons who worked for a daily wage from jury lists; in Taylor v. Louisiana, 419 U.S. 522, 95 S.Ct. 692, 42 L.Ed.2d 690 (1975), a similar exclusion of women was rejected; in Batson v. Kentucky, 476 U.S. 79, 106 S.Ct. 1712, 90 L.Ed.2d 69 (1986), the use of peremptory challenges to exclude members of the defendant's ethnic group was held unconstitutional. See also McCoin, Sex Discrimination in the Voir Dire Process: The Rights of Prospective Female Jurors, 58 S.Cal.L.Rev. 1225 (1985). To a certain extent, the cross-section requirement interferes with the convenience of prospective jurors. Thus, in Duren v. Missouri, 439 U.S. 357, 99 S.Ct. 664, 58 L.Ed.2d 579 (1979), the Court refused to permit the exclusion of women upon simple request. Should students be allowed to defer jury service until vacation or graduation?

(4) Another problem with voir dire is that an extensive questioning process frames the issues for the jurors and tends to commit them to particular outcomes, while truncating questioning increases the possibility of bias. See Note, Voir Dire—Prevention of Prejudicial Questioning, 50 Minn.L.Rev. 1088 (1966); Levit, et al., Expediting Voir Dire: An Empirical Study, 44 S.Cal.L.Rev. 916 (1971); Jennison, District of Columbia Survey: Trial Court Discretion in Conducting the Voir Dire Subjected to More Stringent Scrutiny, 33 Cath.U.L. Rev. 1121 (1984).

(5) The Report of the Committee on Juries of the Judicial Council of the Second Circuit (1984) reports on seven experiments conducted in the Circuit. The experiments involved use of the following practices:

(1) attorney participation in the voir dire;

(2) questioning of a prospective juror on voir dire in the absence of the other panel members;

(3) pre-instructing the jury;

(4) allowing jurors to submit questions to witnesses;

(5) affirmatively advising jurors that they may take notes;

(6) furnishing the jury with a copy of the judge's charge; and

(7) providing the jury with a tape recording of the charge.

Which of these practices are worthy of adoption? See Sand and Reiss, A Report on Seven Experiments Conducted by District Judges in the Second Circuit, 60 N.Y.U.L.Rev. 423 (1985).

(6) In a diversity case, which law, federal or state, controls the *voir dire*? See Perry v. Allegheny Airlines, Inc., 489 F.2d 1349 (2d Cir.1974).

(7) Based on a questionnaire distributed to 5000 New York City jurors in 1971, Simon, The Juror in New York City: Attitudes and Experiences, 61 A.B.A. Journal 207 (1975), reports: "The responding jurors spent an average of 61.8 per cent of their time in the waiting room, 16.7 per cent in jury selection, 17.3 per cent in court during trial and 4.2 per cent in jury deliberations." In the federal courts, more careful scheduling of trial starts and use of telephone arrangements have decreased inconvenience and wasted time. The saving is said to run into many millions of dollars each year. See, e.g., Wilson, Use of Jurors, 62 F.R.D. 211 (1974).

C. ORDER OF TRIAL

REVISED STATUTES OF NEBRASKA 1943

25-1107. Order of trial. When the jury has been sworn the trial shall proceed in the following order, unless the court for special reasons otherwise directs:

(1) The plaintiff must briefly state his claim, and may briefly state the evidence by which he expects to sustain it.

(2) The defendant must then briefly state his defense, and may briefly state the evidence he expects to offer in support of it.

(3) The party who would be defeated if no evidence were given on either side must first produce his evidence; the adverse party will then produce his evidence.

(4) The parties will then be confined to rebutting evidence unless the court, for good reasons in furtherance of justice, permits them to offer evidence in their original case.

(5) When the evidence is concluded, either party may request instructions to the jury on points of law, which shall be refused or given by the court; which instructions shall be reduced to writing if either party requires it.

(6) The parties may then submit or argue the case to the jury. In argument, the party required first to produce his evidence shall have the opening and conclusion. If several defendants have separate defenses and appear by different counsel, the court shall arrange their relative order.

(7) The court may again charge the jury after the argument is concluded.

NOTE

Most states have statutes or court rules that, like the Nebraska statute excerpted above, control the order of proceedings in the course of the trial. The actual ordering of events varies from jurisdiction to jurisdiction, with some states allowing for greater flexibility than others. In some jurisdictions, there are few or scanty rules on the subject. In these places, custom or the presiding judge controls the order of presentation. For a discussion of the strategic advantages of various orderings, see Lawson, Order of Presentation as a Factor in Jury Persuasion, 56 Ky.L.J. 523 (1968).

The issues that relate to the conduct of the trial—the competence of witnesses, the admissability of evidence, the relevance of various proof offers—is covered in the course on Evidence. At this stage, however, it is important to note that although the jury's access to information is largely controlled by the rules of evidence, the view that it takes of the evidence depends, in large part, on how it is instructed.

JAMES, JR., SUFFICIENCY OF THE EVIDENCE AND JURY–CONTROL DEVICES AVAILABLE BEFORE VERDICT

47 Virginia Law Review 218, 236–240 (1961).

It is the common law tradition that in all civil jury trials the judge has the right and duty to instruct the jury upon the substantive law, applicable to all the ultimate issues made by the pleadings and the proof.[1] This duty was not dependent on the making of any requests to charge by parties[2]—to this extent it represents a departure from notions of party presentation and prosecution and an instance of judicial responsibility for seeing that certain steps in the litigation process are taken, and properly taken. In this tradition the judge often sums up the evidence in the course of his charge and indicates just how the legal rules should be applied to the various factual findings permissible under the evidence.[3] Moreover, he may also *comment* on the weight of the evidence and indicate his own opinion concerning the credibility of witnesses and the relative strength of competing permissible inferences, provided always that he makes it clear to the jury that it is their province to decide such questions of weight and credibility.[4]

Because of the judge's position of prestige and respect in the trial his charge can be used to exert a good deal of psychological influence on the jurors, who are laymen and sometimes inexperienced and impressionable. This influence is enhanced by the timing of the charge—it occurs after arguments of counsel and is the last significant event at the trial before the jury's deliberation. All this was not regarded as a disadvantage of the procedure but rather as an essential safeguard against the jury's possible ignorance and undue susceptibility to appeals to the "passional elements" in their nature. "It is not too much to say of any period, in all English history," says Thayer, "that it is impossible to conceive of trial by jury as existing there in a form which

1. Thayer [A Preliminary Treatise on Evidence at the Common Law (1898), cited hereinafter as Thayer] 112–14; Farley, Instructions to Juries—Their Rôle in the Judicial Process, 42 Yale L.J. 194 (1932). [Some footnotes renumbered; others omitted.]

2. For modern cases which follow the common law in this respect see Cipollone v. D'Alessandro-Crognale, Inc., 333 Mass. 469, 131 N.E.2d 754 (1956); McNeill v. McDougald, 242 N.C. 255, 87 S.E.2d 502 (1955); Shiers v. Cowgill, 157 Neb. 265, 59 N.W.2d 407 (1953); Reithof v. Pittsburgh Rys., 361 Pa. 489, 65 A.2d 346 (1949); Perlman v. Haigh, 90 N.H. 404, 10 A.2d 228 (1939); Investors Syndicate v. Thompson, 172 Ga. 203, 158 S.E. 20 (1931).

A general description of the patterns in use in America, based on correspondence with trial lawyers, appears in Arnold & James, Cases on Trials, Judgments and Appeals 676–79 (1936).

3. See 9 Wigmore § 2551; Wright, Instructions to the Jury: Summary Without Comment, 1954 Wash.U.L.Q. 177. According to Professor Wright 19 American states permit a factual summary either with or without comment. Id., at 206–07.

4. See Quercia v. United States, 289 U.S. 466, 53 S.Ct. 698 (1933); Sheahan v. Barry, 27 Mich. 217, 226–27 (1873); 9 Wigmore § 2551; Sunderland, The Inefficiency of the American Jury, 13 Mich.L.Rev. 302, 305 (1915). See generally Wright, The Invasion of Jury: Temperature of the War, 27 Temp.L.Q. 137 (1953).

would withhold from the jury the assistance of the court in dealing with the facts." [5]

The basic features of instructions to the jury which have just been described are found today in the federal courts and those of several of the states.[6]   But the nineteenth century witnessed a popular political movement which led to, among other things, an aggrandizement of the importance and stature of the jury (as the popular branch of the tribunal) and to a corresponding diminution of the importance and stature of the judge.   Among the results of this movement, several are pertinent to the present subject matter: (1) statutes and even constitutional provisions forbidding judges to comment upon the evidence; (2) rules and statutes relieving the court of its traditional duty to take the initiative in covering the whole law of the case in its charge, and requiring the court to charge only upon points expressly covered by specific requests to charge; (3) and rules requiring the charge to be given *before* final arguments of counsel.[7]

The most extreme steps to reduce the judge's function are to be found in Mississippi where the judge is forbidden to give any charge upon points not requested by counsel and the clerk simply marks the parties' request as "given" or "refused." [8]   The granted requests are then read to the jury by the attorneys before they argue the case.

These steps towards diminution of judicial responsibility and control have been widely condemned by commentators and there are some indications that the tide has turned the other way.[9]

Because of the differences in practice just described it is difficult to make valid generalizations about what a charge should and should not contain.   The rules that follow are, however, widely applied.

The charge should tell the jury which questions are for them to decide and which are not.   Usually this means that the judge tells the jury what the issues are and what rule or rules of substantive law they should apply to the various possible findings of fact they might make under the evidence.   And the judge should explain to the jury which party has the burden of proof (persuasion burden) on each issue and the measure to which they must be persuaded before that burden is met. The court usually tells the jury that questions of the credibility of witnesses are for them to decide.   It may also give them some guide for drawing rational inferences of fact.

5.   Thayer 188 n. 2.

6.   The present status of the rules in the various states may be found in the following articles: Wright, Adequacy of Instructions to the Jury, 53 Mich.L.Rev. 505, 813 (1955) (pts. 1–2); Wright, supra notes 3 and 4.

7.   As in Wyoming, Nevada, Kansas, Nebraska and Utah.   See Wright, supra note 3, at 183–89.   Compare Blatt, Judge's

Charge to Jury Should Precede Arguments of Counsel, 33 J.Am.Jud.Soc'y 56 (1949), with Hartshorne, The Timing of the Charge to the Jury, 33 J.Am.Jud.Soc'y 90 (1949).

8.   Miss.Code Ann. § 1530 (1942); Producers Gin Ass'n v. Beck, 215 Miss. 263, 60 So.2d 642 (1952); see Arnold & James, op. cit. supra note 2, at 677.

9.   Wright, supra note 4.

. . . . It is error to leave to the jury an issue which is not properly in the case under the evidence and the pleadings, except where the pleadings are treated as amended to accommodate an issue litigated by consent,[10] or the like.

The court may determine that on one permissible version of the facts there would be no question of evaluation properly for the jury, while on another permissible version there would be such a question for them. Suppose, for example, one witness puts the speed of defendant's automobile at twenty miles an hour, another at forty. If the judge believes that the former speed could not reasonably be found negligent under the circumstances, while the latter might, he should give a conditionally binding instruction on the point. He should tell them that if they find the speed to have been twenty miles an hour they must find the driver free from negligence in this particular, but that if they find the speed to have been forty miles an hour, they should then go on to determine whether that was a reasonable speed under all the circumstances.

It constitutes error to give a binding instruction where the matter of evaluation is properly for the jury.

Where it is a question for the court what the construction of a writing is, or whether given facts constitute probable cause in malicious prosecution, the court will—if the case is for the jury at all—tell them that the written words have such and such meaning, or that such and such facts do (or do not) constitute probable cause.

If the case is one in which parol evidence is admissible as an aid in construing a contract, it is up to the jury to resolve any conflicts revealed by the parol evidence and also to resolve any question of construction "if, when all the evidence is in, both written and oral, fairminded men might reasonably arrive at different conclusions" upon it.

The charge must not assume the existence or the nonexistence of a fact in issue.

All jurisdictions allow for the filing by the parties of requests to charge. A rule or statute usually prescribes a time for filing such requests (e.g., at the close of the evidence) and requires them to be in writing. Other requirements, separately numbered paragraphs, citation of supporting authority, et cetera, may also be imposed.

The importance of requests to charge varies among the different jurisdictions, inversely with the duty of the court to instruct fully upon the ultimate issues. . . .

Most jurisdictions require a party to make specific objections to the charge as a condition to appellate review of statements or omissions in the charge.[11] Such objections are generally made at the close of the charge before the jury retires.[12] The provision to this effect in Rule 51

---

10. As under Fed.R.Civ.P. 15(b).

11. See 1 Branson §§ 170–75.

12. Id. at 471.

of the Federal Rules of Civil Procedure is to be read in connection with Rule 46 which dispenses with the need for formal exceptions wherever a party makes known to the court what he wants the court to do and why, or "his objection to the action of the court and his grounds therefor." Taking these two rules together, courts of appeals have held that points clearly raised in proper requests to charge need not be repeated by objection at the close of a charge which failed to give such a request. . . .

NOTES

(1) But cf. Wright, Law of Federal Courts 629–30 (4th ed. 1983) (claim of error for giving improper instructions precluded unless proper objection is made before the jury retires).

(2) See Fed.R.Civ.P. 51. In Turner Construction Co. v. Houlihan, 240 F.2d 435, 439 (1st Cir.1957), the court said: "The first sentence of Rule 51 permits, but does not require the filing of requests for instructions. If none are filed, the court must nevertheless charge the jury on the broad general fundamental rules of law applicable to the principal issues of fact in the case. . . . If specific instructions on particular matters are wanted they must be timely requested, and a request for detailed instructions made after the charge has been given comes too late to comply with the specific provision of the Rule . . .". Robinson, A Proposal For Limiting The Duty of The Trial Judge to Instruct The Jury Sua Sponte, 11 San Diego L.R. 325 (1974), suggests that, in order to reduce the number of reversals for a faulty charge, the judge ought be relieved of his duty to charge on the whole law involved in the case and instead charge only as a direct result of counsel's requests. Is this sound?

(3) Is it reversible error for the court to fail to comply with the requirement in Rule 51 that he make known his rulings on requests to charge before counsel make their summations to the jury? See Luther v. Maple, 250 F.2d 916 (8th Cir.1958). Availability of quick methods of reproduction have led some judges to make copies of the proposed charge. Counsel and the court can then go over the charge line by line and work out all changes. This results, in many instances, in full agreement. See 1 Weinstein & Berger, Weinstein's Evidence 107[01] (1989).

(4) Most challenges to jury instructions center on whether they reflect the law that the jury is to apply. Much less litigated, but equally important, is the question whether the jury actually understands the instructions it has been given. Much of the empirical evidence suggests that jurors often do not comprehend the instructions, either because the law and/or facts are complicated or because the instructions are poorly written. See Steele and Thornburg, Jury Instructions: A Persistent Failure to Communicate, 67 N.C.L.Rev. 77 (1988), which summarizes several of these studies. Among the problems noted by the authors are (1) confusion between the criminal concept of reasonable doubt and the usual civil proof standard, preponderance of the evidence; (2) inability to comprehend the method ordered for computing damages; (3) failure to understand the concept of allocating fault in comparative fault jurisdictions; (4) inability to differentiate the concept of proximate cause from the notion of entire cause.

(5) To eliminate challenges to the substance of jury instructions, several states have standardized the instructions on common issues and either require

their courts to use these instructions or encourage them to do so[. See, e.g. 12 Okl.St. § 577.1 (1987) (requiring use of Oklahoma Uniform Jury Instructions); R. Nieland, Pattern Jury Instructions: A Critical Look at a Modern Movement to Improve the Jury System 3 (1979). Pattern jury instructions could be drafted to enhance comprehensibility, see A. Elwork, B. Sales & J. Alfini, Making Jury Instructions Understandable (1982); Imwinkelried & Schwed, Guidelines for Drafting Understandable Jury Instructions: An Introduction to the Use of Psycholinguistics, 23 Crim.L.Bull. 135 (1987). But pattern instructions cannot be regarded as a panacea. Hard cases may present unique problems that are not covered in the instructions and the instructions may lag behind substantive changes in the law. Furthermore, the instructions may bind the court's hands in unhelpful ways. For example, in Teaney v. City of St. Joseph, 548 S.W.2d 254 (Mo.App.1977), a clarification of the instructions by the trial court was deemed a failure to follow the pattern instruction. For further discussion of these questions, see Smith, Effective Instructions to the Federal Jury in Civil Cases—A Consideration in Microcosm, 18 Syr.L.Rev. 559 (1967); Stevens, Pattern Jury Instructions: Some Suggestions on Use and the Problem of Presumptions, 41 Wash.L.Rev. 282 (1966); Devitt, Ten Practical Suggestions about Federal Jury Instructions, 38 F.R.D. 75 (1965); Corbox, Pattern Jury Instructions—Their Function and Effectiveness, 32 Ins.Counsel J. 57 (1965); Dooley, Jury Instructions: An Appraisal by a Plaintiff's Attorney, (1963) U.Ill. L.F. 586; Fowler, Jury Instructions: An Appraisal by a Defendant's Attorney, (1963) U.Ill.L.F. 612.

SECTION 2. BURDENS OF PROOF

The term burden of proof is often used interchangeably with burden of persuasion and burden of producing evidence. Thus, the definitions of the Model Code of Evidence (Rule 1(2), (3)) declares:

> "Burden of producing evidence of a fact means the burden which is discharged when sufficient evidence is introduced to support a finding that the fact exists.

> "Burden of persuasion of a fact means the burden which is discharged when the tribunal which is to determine the existence or non-existence of the fact is persuaded by sufficient evidence to find that the fact exists."

In contrast, the Uniform Rules of Evidence (Rule 1(4), (5)) (1954 ed.) states:

> "(4) 'Burden of proof' means the obligation of a party to meet the requirements of a rule of law that the fact be proved either by a preponderance of the evidence or by clear and convincing evidence or beyond a reasonable doubt, as the case may be. Burden of proof is synonymous with 'burden of persuasion.'

> "(5) 'Burden of producing evidence' means the obligation of a party to introduce evidence when necessary to avoid the

risk of a directed verdict or peremptory finding against him on
a material issue of fact."

NOTES

(1) James, Jr., Burdens of Proof, 47 Va.L.Rev. 51, 58–61 (1961) *:

"There is no satisfactory test for allocating the burden of proof in either
sense on any given issue. The allocation is made on the basis of one or more of
several variable factors. Before considering these, however, we should note
three formal tests which have some currency but are not very helpful.

"1. It is often said that the party who must establish the affirmative
proposition has the burden of proof on the issue. But language can be
manipulated so as to state most propositions either negatively or affirmatively
. . . .

"2. It is sometimes said that the burden of proof is upon the party to
whose case the fact in question is essential, and so it is, but this test simply
poses another question: to which party's case is the fact essential? And the
second question is no easier to answer than the first; indeed it is but a
restatement of the same question.

"3. It is often said that the party who has the burden of pleading a fact
must prove it. This is in large part true and where there is clear authority on
the pleading rule this is a fairly good, though not infallible, indication that the
rule of burden of proof will parallel it. . . .

"Another rule for allocating the burden of proof would put it on the party
having the readier access to knowledge about the fact in question. This, it will
be noted, is not merely a formal rule. It refers rather to one of the considerations which should and do in fact influence the allocation of the burden of
proof. But it is not the only consideration and it is by no means always
controlling. It is an every day occurrence in litigation that a party has the
burden to prove what his opponent's conduct was. Examples are negligence,
contributory negligence, and breach of contract, in many common situations.
In these instances the consideration arising from greater access to evidence is
overcome by a feeling that charge of wrongdoing should in fairness be proven
by the party making it.

"Another factor to be considered is the extent to which a party's contention
departs from what would be expected in the light of ordinary human experience. . . .

"Substantive considerations may also be influential. For real or supposed
reasons of policy the law sometimes disfavors claims and defenses which it
nevertheless allows. Where that is the case procedural devices like burden of
proof are often used as handicaps, to use Judge Clark's felicitous phrase,
against the disfavored contention."

(2) There is a tendency to place the burden on the party who "has peculiar
knowledge or control of the evidence as to such matter." Allstate Finance
Corp. v. Zimmerman, 330 F.2d 740, 744 (5th Cir.1964) (who removed fixtures
from building sold in tax sale); Nemeth v. Pankost, 224 Cal.App.2d 351, 36 Cal.
Rptr. 600, 604 (3d Dist.1964) (in suit by salesman for commission, broker, if it
disputed assertion that it received a commission, should have produced its
records to show receipt or lack of receipt of commission). But "in view of the

* Footnotes omitted.

availability . . . of modern discovery" devices which enable evidence to be ferreted out before trial, this consideration is less important than it once was. Tortora v. General Motors Corp., 373 Mich. 563, 130 N.W.2d 21 (1964) (employer's knowledge of prior record of driving violations).

(3) As to the related problem of presumptions, see Rule 302, Federal Rules of Evidence: "In civil actions and proceedings, the effect of a presumption respecting a fact which is an element of a claim or defense as to which state law supplies the rule of decision is determined in accordance with state law."; 1 Weinstein & Berger, Weinstein's Evidence 302[01] (1989). It has been suggested that a state engaged in compiling pattern jury instructions has an excellent opportunity for "defining and classifying all known presumptions in a practical and meaningful manner" so that "[l]itigants should not be put to the expense of providing a forum . . . for the case to case classification of particular presumptions." Stevens, Pattern Jury Instructions: Some Suggestions on Use and the Problem of Presumptions, 41 Wash.L.Rev. 282, 287 (1966). This has been the California approach. See West's Ann.Cal.Evidence Code §§ 601 et seq. (1966). Does the allocation of burdens of proof lend itself to standardized treatment?

(4) In most civil cases the plaintiff is required to prove each material element of the case by a preponderance of the evidence. Considerable conflict and confusion are to be found in the appellate search for an acceptable definition of the term.

One group of cases rejects the idea that a jury need find only the facts to be more probable than not. In Frazier v. Frazier, 228 S.C. 149, 89 S.E.2d 225, 235 (1955), the court declared: "A 'preponderance of the evidence' . . . is that evidence which convinces us as to its truth." In Lampe v. Franklin American Trust Co., 339 Mo. 361, 384, 96 S.W.2d 710, 723 (1936), the court in approving a trial judge's refusal to charge that the jury should find a fact if they believed it to be more probable than not, said: "They [the jury] must not attempt to base a verdict upon what facts may be 'more probable' if they cannot decide what facts are true." Similar pronouncements are found in Pullman Palace Car Co. v. Adams, 120 Ala. 581, 599, 24 So. 921 (1898); Dunbar v. McGill, 64 Mich. 676, 31 N.W. 578 (1887); Toledo St. Louis & Western Railroad Co. v. Howe, 191 F.776, 782 (7th Cir.1911). These statements in a charge obviously can not be taken literally by the jury. Will it mean to them that the court is requiring a very high degree of proof?

Another line of cases places its emphasis on probabilities. In Burnett v. Reyes, 118 Cal.App.2d 878, 880, 256 P.2d 91, 93 (1953), the court stated: "[T]he burden was upon the plaintiff to prove his case by preponderance of the evidence and [that] means that the greater probability lies in favor of the decision." See also Darrow v. Fleischner, 117 Conn. 518, 520, 169 A. 197, 198 (1933), requiring a "reasonable belief that it is more probable than otherwise that the fact in issue is true."

(5) For an application of probability theory to the problem of measure of persuasion, see Ball, The Moment of Truth: Probability Theory and Standards of Proof, 14 Vand.L.Rev. 807 (1961); Finkelstein and Fairley, A Bayesian Approach to Identification Evidence, 83 Harv.L.Rev. 489 (1970); Tribe, Trial by Mathematics: Precision and Ritual in Legal Process, 84 Harv.L.Rev. 1329 (1971); Symposium: Probability and Inference in the Law of Evidence, 66 B.U.L.Rev. 771 (1986).

(6) In diversity cases, is the burden of proof determined by state or federal law? In Palmer v. Hoffman, 318 U.S. 109, 63 S.Ct. 477, 87 L.Ed. 645 (1943), the argument was made that Fed.R.Civ.P. 8(c) allocated the burden of proving contributory negligence to the defendant. The Supreme Court, however, rejected the argument, holding that 8(c) covers only the burden of pleading; the burden of proof depends on state law.

SANTOSKY v. KRAMER

Supreme Court of the United States, 1981.
455 U.S. 745, 102 S.Ct. 1388, 71 L.Ed.2d 599.*

JUSTICE BLACKMUN delivered the opinion of the Court.

Under New York law, the State may terminate, over parental objection, the rights of parents in their natural child upon a finding that the child is "permanently neglected." N.Y.Soc.Serv.Law §§ 384–b. 4.(d), 384–b.7.(a) (McKinney Supp.1981–1982) (Soc.Serv.Law). The New York Family Court Act § 622 (McKinney 1975 and Supp.1981–1982) (Fam.Ct.Act) requires that only a "fair preponderance of the evidence" support that finding. Thus, in New York, the factual certainty required to extinguish the parent-child relationship is no greater than that necessary to award money damages in an ordinary civil action.

Today we hold that the Due Process Clause of the Fourteenth Amendment demands more than this. Before a State may sever completely and irrevocably the rights of parents in their natural child, due process requires that the State support its allegations by at least clear and convincing evidence.

* * *

Petitioners John Santosky II and Annie Santosky are the natural parents of Tina and John III. In November 1973, after incidents reflecting parental neglect, respondent Kramer, Commissioner of the Ulster County Department of Social Services, initiated a neglect proceeding under Fam.Ct.Act § 1022 and removed Tina from her natural home. About 10 months later, he removed John III and placed him with foster parents. On the day John was taken, Annie Santosky gave birth to a third child, Jed. When Jed was only three days old, respondent transferred him to a foster home on the ground that immediate removal was necessary to avoid imminent danger to his life or health.

In October 1978, respondent petitioned the Ulster County Family Court to terminate petitioners' parental rights in the three children. Petitioners challenged the constitutionality of the "fair preponderance of the evidence" standard specified in Fam.Ct.Act § 622. The Family Court Judge rejected this constitutional challenge, ..., and weighed the evidence under the statutory standard. While acknowledging that the Santoskys had maintained contact with their children, the judge found those visits "at best superficial and devoid of any real emotional

---

* Footnotes omitted.

content." . . . After deciding that the agency had made " 'diligent efforts' to encourage and strengthen the parental relationship," . . ., he concluded that the Santoskys were incapable, even with public assistance, of planning for the future of their children. . . . The judge later held a dispositional hearing and ruled that the best interests of the three children required permanent termination of the Santoskys' custody. . . .

Petitioners appealed, again contesting the constitutionality of § 622's standard of proof. The New York Supreme Court, Appellate Division, affirmed, . . .

The New York Court of Appeals then dismissed petitioners' appeal to that court "upon the ground that no substantial constitutional question is directly involved." App. 55. We granted certiorari to consider petitioners' constitutional claim. 450 U.S. 993, 101 S.Ct. 1694, 68 L.Ed.2d 192 (1981).

* * *

The fundamental liberty interest of natural parents in the care, custody, and management of their child does not evaporate simply because they have not been model parents or have lost temporary custody of their child to the State. . . . When the State moves to destroy weakened familial bonds, it must provide the parents with fundamentally fair procedures.

. . . [T]he nature of the process due in parental rights termination proceedings turns on a balancing of the "three distinct factors" specified in Mathews v. Eldridge, 424 U.S. 319, 335, 96 S.Ct. 893, 903, 47 L.Ed.2d 18 (1976): the private interests affected by the proceeding; the risk of error created by the State's chosen procedure; and the countervailing governmental interest supporting use of the challenged procedure. . . .

In Addington v. Texas, 441 U.S. 418, 99 S.Ct. 1804, 60 L.Ed.2d 323 (1979), the Court, by a unanimous vote of the participating Justices, declared: "The function of a standard of proof, as that concept is embodied in the Due Process Clause and in the realm of factfinding, is to 'instruct the factfinder concerning the degree of confidence our society thinks he should have in the correctness of factual conclusions for a particular type of adjudication.' " Id., at 423, 99 S.Ct. at 1808, quoting In re Winship, 397 U.S. 358, 370, 90 S.Ct. 1068, 1075, 25 L.Ed.2d 368 (1970) (Harlan, J., concurring). Addington teaches that, in any given proceeding, the minimum standard of proof tolerated by the due process requirement reflects not only the weight of the private and public interests affected, but also a societal judgment about how the risk of error should be distributed between the litigants.

Thus, while private parties may be interested intensely in a civil dispute over money damages, application of a "fair preponderance of the evidence" standard indicates both society's "minimal concern with the outcome," and a conclusion that the litigants should "share the risk of error in roughly equal fashion." 441 U.S., at 423, 99 S.Ct., at 1808.

When the State brings a criminal action to deny a defendant liberty or life, however, "the interests of the defendant are of such magnitude that historically and without any explicit constitutional requirement they have been protected by standards of proof designed to exclude as nearly as possible the likelihood of an erroneous judgment." Ibid. The stringency of the "beyond a reasonable doubt" standard bespeaks the "weight and gravity" of the private interest affected, id., at 427, 99 S.Ct., at 1810, society's interest in avoiding erroneous convictions, and a judgment that those interests together require that "society impos[e] almost the entire risk of error upon itself." Id., at 424, 99 S.Ct., at 1808. See also In re Winship, 397 U.S., at 372, 90 S.Ct., at 1076 (Harlan, J., concurring).

The "minimum requirements [of procedural due process] being a matter of federal law, they are not diminished by the fact that the State may have specified its own procedures that it may deem adequate for determining the preconditions to adverse official action." Vitek v. Jones, 445 U.S. 480, 491, 100 S.Ct. 1254, 1262, 63 L.Ed.2d 552 (1980). . . . Moreover, the degree of proof required in a particular type of proceeding "is the kind of question which has traditionally been left to the judiciary to resolve." Woodby v. INS, 385 U.S. 276, 284, 87 S.Ct. 483, 487, 17 L.Ed.2d 362 (1966). "In cases involving individual rights, whether criminal or civil, '[t]he standard of proof [at a minimum] reflects the value society places on individual liberty.'" Addington v. Texas, 441 U.S., at 425, 99 S.Ct., at 1809, quoting Tippett v. Maryland, 436 F.2d 1153, 1166 (CA4 1971) (opinion concurring in part and dissenting in part), cert. dism'd sub nom. Murel v. Baltimore City Criminal Court, 407 U.S. 355, 92 S.Ct. 2091, 32 L.Ed.2d 791 (1972).

This Court has mandated an intermediate standard of proof— "clear and convincing evidence"—when the individual interests at stake in a state proceeding are both "particularly important" and "more substantial than mere loss of money." Addington v. Texas, 441 U.S., at 424, 99 S.Ct., at 1808. Notwithstanding "the state's 'civil labels and good intentions,'" id., at 427, 99 S.Ct. at 1810, quoting In re Winship, 397 U.S., at 365–366, 90 S.Ct., at 1073–1074, the Court has deemed this level of certainty necessary to preserve fundamental fairness in a variety of government-initiated proceedings that threaten the individual involved with "a significant deprivation of liberty" or "stigma." 441 U.S., at 425, 426, 99 S.Ct., at 1808, 1809. See, e.g., Addington v. Texas, supra (civil commitment); Woodby v. INS, 385 U.S., at 285, 87 S.Ct. at 487 (deportation); Chaunt v. United States, 364 U.S. 350, 353, 81 S.Ct. 147, 149, 5 L.Ed.2d 120 (1960) (denaturalization); Schneiderman v. United States, 320 U.S. 118, 125, 159, 63 S.Ct. 1333, 1336, 1353, 87 L.Ed. 1796 (1943) (denaturalization).

* * *

In parental rights termination proceedings, the private interest affected is commanding; the risk of error from using a preponderance standard is substantial; and the countervailing governmental interest favoring that standard is comparatively slight. Evaluation of the three

Eldridge factors compels the conclusion that use of a "fair preponderance of the evidence" standard in such proceedings is inconsistent with due process.

In government-initiated proceedings to determine juvenile delinquency, . . . this Court has identified losses of individual liberty sufficiently serious to warrant imposition of an elevated burden of proof. Yet juvenile delinquency adjudications, civil commitment, deportation, and denaturalization, at least to a degree, are all *reversible* official actions. Once affirmed on appeal, a New York decision terminating parental rights is *final* and irrevocable. See n. 1, supra. Few forms of state action are both so severe and so irreversible.

Thus, the first *Eldridge* factor—the private interest affected—weighs heavily against use of the preponderance standard at a state-initiated permanent neglect proceeding. . . .

          * * *

Under Mathews v. Eldridge, we next must consider both the risk of erroneous deprivation of private interests resulting from use of a "fair preponderance" standard and the likelihood that a higher evidentiary standard would reduce that risk. See 424 U.S., at 335, 96 S.Ct., at 903. Since the factfinding phase of a permanent neglect proceeding is an adversary contest between the State and the natural parents, the relevant question is whether a preponderance standard fairly allocates the risk of an erroneous factfinding between these two parties.

          * * *

At such a proceeding, numerous factors combine to magnify the risk of erroneous factfinding. Permanent neglect proceedings employ imprecise substantive standards that leave determinations unusually open to the subjective values of the judge. See Smith v. Organization of Foster Families, 431 U.S., at 835, n. 36, 97 S.Ct., at 2105, n. 36. In appraising the nature and quality of a complex series of encounters among the agency, the parents, and the child, the court possesses unusual discretion to underweigh probative facts that might favor the parent. Because parents subject to termination proceedings are often poor, uneducated, or members of minority groups, id., at 833–835, such proceedings are often vulnerable to judgments based on cultural or class bias.

The State's ability to assemble its case almost inevitably dwarfs the parents' ability to mount a defense. . . .

The disparity between the adversaries' litigation resources is matched by a striking asymmetry in their litigation options. Unlike criminal defendants, natural parents have no "double jeopardy" defense against repeated state termination efforts. If the State initially fails to win termination, as New York did here, see n. 4, supra, it always can try once again to cut off the parents' rights after gathering more or better evidence. Yet even when the parents have attained the level of fitness required by the State, they have no similar means by which they can forestall future termination efforts.

Coupled with a "fair preponderance of the evidence" standard, these factors create a significant prospect of erroneous termination. . . .

Raising the standard of proof would have both practical and symbolic consequences. Cf. Addington v. Texas, 441 U.S., at 426, 99 S.Ct., at 1809. The Court has long considered the heightened standard of proof used in criminal prosecutions to be "a prime instrument for reducing the risk of convictions resting on factual error." In re Winship, 397 U.S., at 363, 90 S.Ct., at 1072. An elevated standard of proof in a parental rights termination proceeding would alleviate "the possible risk that a factfinder might decide to [deprive] an individual based solely on a few isolated instances of unusual conduct [or . . . idiosyncratic behavior." Addington v. Texas, 441 U.S., at 427, 99 S.Ct., at 1810. "Increasing the burden of proof is one way to impress the factfinder with the importance of the decision and thereby perhaps to reduce the chances that inappropriate" terminations will be ordered. Ibid.

* * *

. . . [A] stricter standard of proof would reduce factual error without imposing substantial fiscal burdens upon the State. As we have observed, 35 States already have adopted a higher standard by statute or court decision without apparent effect on the speed, form, or cost of their factfinding proceedings. . . .

. . . We cannot believe that it would burden the State unduly to require that its factfinders have the same factual certainty when terminating the parent-child relationship as they must have to suspend a driver's license.

* * *

Like civil commitment hearings, termination proceedings often require the factfinder to evaluate medical and psychiatric testimony, and to decide issues difficult to prove to a level of absolute certainty, such as lack of parental motive, absence of affection between parent and child, and failure of parental foresight and progress. . . . The substantive standards applied vary from State to State. Although Congress found a "beyond a reasonable doubt" standard proper in one type of parental rights termination case, another legislative body might well conclude that a reasonable-doubt standard would erect an unreasonable barrier to state efforts to free permanently neglected children for adoption.

A majority of the States have concluded that a "clear and convincing evidence" standard of proof strikes a fair balance between the rights of the natural parents and the State's legitimate concerns. . . . We hold that such a standard adequately conveys to the factfinder the level of subjective certainty about his factual conclusions necessary to satisfy due process. We further hold that determination of the precise burden equal to or greater than that standard is a matter of state law properly left to state legislatures and state courts. Cf. Addington v. Texas, 441 U.S., at 433, 99 S.Ct., at 1813.

We, of course, express no view on the merits of petitioners' claims. . . . [We] vacate the judgment of the Appellate Division and remand the case for further proceedings not inconsistent with this opinion.

*   *   *

JUSTICE REHNQUIST, with whom CHIEF JUSTICE, JUSTICE WHITE, and JUSTICE O'CONNOR join, dissenting.

*   *   *

In determining the propriety of a particular standard of proof in a given case, . . . it is not enough simply to say that we are trying to minimize the risk of error. Because errors in factfinding affect more than one interest, we try to minimize error as to those interests which we consider to be most important. As Justice Harlan explained in his well-known concurrence to In re Winship:

> "In a lawsuit between two parties, a factual error can make a difference in one of two ways. First, it can result in a judgment in favor of the plaintiff when the true facts warrant a judgment for the defendant. The analogue in a criminal case would be the conviction of an innocent man. On the other hand, an erroneous factual determination can result in a judgment for the defendant when the true facts justify a judgment in plaintiff's favor. The criminal analogue would be the acquittal of a guilty man.
>
> The standard of proof influences the relative frequency of these two types of erroneous outcomes. If, for example, the standard of proof for a criminal trial were a preponderance of the evidence rather than proof beyond a reasonable doubt, there would be a smaller risk of factual errors that result in freeing guilty persons, but a far greater risk of factual errors that result in convicting the innocent. Because the standard of proof affects the comparative frequency of these two types of erroneous outcomes, the choice of the standard to be applied in a particular kind of litigation should, in a rational world, reflect an assessment of the comparative social disutility of each." 397 U.S., at 370–371, 90 S.Ct., at 1076.

When the standard of proof is understood as reflecting such an assessment, an examination of the interests at stake in a particular case becomes essential to determining the propriety of the specified standard of proof. Because proof by a preponderance of the evidence requires that "[t]he litigants . . . share the risk of error in a roughly equal fashion," Addington v. Texas, supra, at 423, 99 S.Ct., at 1808, it rationally should be applied only when the interests at stake are of roughly equal societal importance. The interests at stake in this case demonstrate that New York has selected a constitutionally permissible standard of proof.

*   *   *

. . . I believe that the Court today errs in concluding that the New York standard of proof in parental-rights termination proceedings violates due process of law. The decision disregards New York's earnest efforts to *aid* parents in regaining the custody of their children and a host of procedural protections placed around parental rights and interests. The Court finds a constitutional violation only by a tunnel-vision application of due process principles that altogether loses sight of the unmistakable fairness of the New York procedure.

Even more worrisome, today's decision cavalierly rejects the considered judgment of the New York Legislature in an area traditionally entrusted to state care. The Court thereby begins, I fear, a trend of federal intervention in state family law matters which surely will stifle creative responses to vexing problems. Accordingly, I dissent.

SECTION 3. VERDICTS

A. TYPES

SKIDMORE v. BALTIMORE & OHIO RAILROAD CO.

Court of Appeals of the United States, Second Circuit, 1948.
167 F.2d 54.

[Action under Federal Employers' Liability Act for personal injuries.]

. . . Defendant's counsel . . . asked that the jury be required to return a special verdict, answering the following questions: "(1) Was the defendant guilty of negligence which caused or contributed to the injury of the plaintiff? (If your answer to question (1) is 'No' you should answer no further questions and you should return this paper to the Court.) (2) If the answer to question (1) is 'Yes,' was Buzzy Skidmore, the plaintiff herein, guilty of negligence which contributed to his injuries? (3) If the answer to question (1) is 'Yes,' and the answer to question (2) is 'No,' state in writing the amount of damages sustained by the plaintiff. (4) If the answers to both question (1) and (2) are 'Yes,' state in terms of percentage what proportion of the entire causal negligence is attributable to defendant and to Buzzy Skidmore separately. (__% by defendant) (__% by Skidmore). (5) If the answers to questions (1) and (2) are 'Yes,' what is the total amount of damage (without the jury making any percentage computation in dollars and cents) sustained by Buzzy Skidmore." This request was refused, and defendant's counsel excepted. In his charge, the judge covered the subject matter of the denied request, but directed the jury to bring in a general verdict. No exception was taken to the charge. The jury returned a verdict for plaintiff in the amount of $30,000. Defendant moved for a directed verdict or a new trial; the motion was denied. From a judgment on the verdict, defendant has appealed.

Before L. HAND, SWAN and FRANK, CIRCUIT JUDGES.

FRANK, CIRCUIT JUDGE. . . .

2. Defendant argues that the judge erred in denying its request for a special verdict. We cannot agree.

Undeniably, the verdict affords no satisfactory information about the jury's findings. But almost every general verdict sheds similar or even greater darkness. Such verdicts account for much (not all) of the criticism of the civil jury. . . .

But what many persons regard as its major defects can be mitigated. One device which will help to achieve that end is the special or fact verdict. Those who resent any reform which invades the jury's province should be reassured by the historians who teach that the special verdict is no new-fangled idea, but one almost as old as the jury itself, older indeed than the modern jury. In those early days, Morgan tells us, jurors often successfully insisted upon the right to render such verdicts against the desires of the judges, who wanted general verdicts.[1] To be sure, in this country, during the latter part of the eighteenth and the early part of the nineteenth centuries, the right to return a general verdict was highly esteemed as the jury's prerogative, especially in criminal cases; the judges then instructed the juries that they were to decide both "the law" and the facts, not being bound by the opinion of the trial judge. Most jurisdictions later repudiated that doctrine. The courts and legal writers declared that, if juries had the right to ignore the judges' instructions as to the applicable legal rules, the "law" would "become as variable as the prejudices, the inclinations and the passions of men"; "the parties would suffer from an arbitrary decision"; "decisions would depend entirely upon juries uncontrolled by any settled, fixed, legal principle," and would be "according to what the jury in their own opinion suppose the law is or ought to be"; our "government" would "cease to be a government of laws and become a government of men"; "jurors would become not only judges but legislators as well"; the "law" would "be as fluctuating and uncertain as the diverse opinions of different juries in regard to it"; jurors would be "superior to the national legislature, and its laws . . . subject to their control" so that a "law of Congress" would "be in operation in one state and not in another."

Yet no amount of brave talk can do away with the fact that, when a jury returns an ordinary general verdict, it usually has the power utterly to ignore what the judge instructs it concerning the substantive legal rules, a power which, because generally it cannot be controlled, is indistinguishable for all practical purposes, from a "right." Practically, then, for all we may say about the jury's duty when it renders a

1. Morgan, A Brief History of Special Verdicts and Special Interrogatories, 32 Yale L.J. (1923) 575, 588. [Some footnotes have been omitted in whole or part; others have been renumbered.]

verdict, we now do have the very conditions which we were warned would result if the jury had the right to decide legal propositions: cases are often decided "according to what the jury suppose the law is or ought to be"; the "law," when juries sit, is "as fluctuating and uncertain as the diverse opinion of different juries in regard to it"; and often jurors are "not only judges but legislatures as well." Indeed, some devotees of the jury system praise it precisely because, they say, juries, by means of general verdicts, can and often do nullify those substantive legal rules they dislike, thus becoming ad hoc ephemeral (un-elected) legislatures (a state of affairs singularly neglected by most writers on jurisprudence, who would do well to modify their ideas by recognizing what might be called "juriesprudence"). Surprisingly, that sort of defense of the general verdict is not seldom voiced by lawyers who, in the next breath, demand strict adherence to the legal precedents.

"Competent observers," writes Judge Rossman, "who have interviewed the jurors in scores of jury trials, declare that, in many cases where the general verdict was employed, principal issues received no consideration whatever from the jury." [2] The general verdict, then, has some strange characteristics. As Sunderland puts it,[3] "The peculiarity of the general verdict is the merger into a single indivisible residuum of all matters, however numerous, whether of law or fact. It is a compound made by the jury which is incapable of being broken up into its constituent parts. No judicial reagents exist for either a qualitative or a quantitative analysis. The law supplies the means for determining neither what facts were found, nor what principles of law were applied, nor how the application was made. There are therefore three unknown elements which enter into the general verdict: (a) the facts; (b) the law; (c) the application of the law to the facts. And it is clear that the verdict is liable to three sources of error, corresponding to these three elements. It is also clear that if error does occur in any of these matters it cannot be discovered, for the constituents of the compound cannot be ascertained. No one but the jurors can tell what was put into it and the jurors will not be heard to say. The general verdict is as inscrutable and essentially mysterious as the judgment which issued from the ancient oracle of Delphi. Both stand on the same foundation—a presumption of wisdom. The court protects the jury from all investigation and inquiry as fully as the temple authorities protected the priestess who spoke to the suppliant votary at the shrine. It is quite probable that the law is wise in not permitting jurors to testify as to how they compounded their verdict, for all stability would disappear if such inquiries were open. . . . As to the second element in the general verdict, the *law,* it is a matter upon which the jury is necessarily ignorant. The jurors are taken from the body of the county, and it is safe to say that the last man who would be called or allowed to sit would be a lawyer. They are secondhand dealers in law, and must get it from the judge. They can supply nothing themselves; they are a

---

2. Rossman, The Judge-Jury Relationship in the State Courts, 3 F.R.D. 98, 108.

3. Sunderland, Verdicts, General and Special, 29 Yale L.J. (1920) 253.

mere conduit pipe through which the court supplies the law that goes into the general verdict. But while the jury can contribute nothing of value so far as the law is concerned, it has infinite capacity for mischief, for twelve men can easily misunderstand more law in a minute than the judge can explain in an hour. Indeed, can anything be more fatuous than the expectation that the law which the judge so carefully, learnedly and laboriously expounds to the laymen in the jury box become operative in their minds in its true form? One who has never studied a science cannot understand or appreciate its intricacies, and the law is no exception to this rule. The very theory of the jury and its general verdict is thus predicated upon a premise which makes practically certain an imperfect or erroneous view of the principles of law which are to be compounded into the verdict. The instructions upon the law given by the court to the jury are an effort to give, in the space of a few minutes, a legal education to twelve laymen upon the branch of the law involved in the case. Law cannot be taught in any such way. As to this element, accordingly, the general verdict is almost necessarily a failure. As to the third element in the general verdict—*the application of the law to the facts,* we find the same difficulty as in the case of the first element—a merging of the law into the verdict in such a way that it is impossible to tell how or whether the jury applied the law. They may have applied it in a wholly wrong way, or they may have failed to apply it at all. No analysis of the verdict can be made which will throw any light on the process. Since the case can ordinarily go to the jury only if a verdict either way is legally possible, whatever the jury does is presumed to be right, and this presumption excludes any inquiry from the jurors themselves. Cases may arise where the verdict shows on its face a failure to properly apply the law, usually as relating to the measure of damages, but in the vast majority of cases the verdict is a complete mystery throwing a mantle of impenetrable darkness over the operations of the jury. Whether the jurors deliberately and openly threw the law into the discard, and rendered a verdict out of their own heads, or whether they applied the law correctly as instructed by the court, or whether they tried to apply it properly but failed for lack of understanding,— these are questions respecting which the verdict discloses nothing. So far, therefore, as the third element goes, the general verdict is an unknown and unknowable mystery, with the balance of probability against it. . . . We come, then, to this position, that the general verdict . . . confers on the jury a vast power to commit error and do mischief by loading it with technical burdens far beyond its ability to perform, by confusing it in aggregating instead of segregating the issues, and by shrouding in secrecy and mystery the actual results of its deliberations. . . . The record must be absolutely flawless, but such a result is possible only by concealing, not by excluding mistakes. This is the great technical merit of the general verdict. It covers up all the shortcomings which frail human nature is unable to eliminate from the trial of a case. In the abysmal abstraction of the general verdict concrete details are swallowed up, and the eye of the law, searching anxiously for the realization of logical perfection, is satisfied. In short, the general verdict is valued for what it does, not for what it is. It serves as the great procedural opiate, . . . draws the curtain upon human errors and soothes us with the assurance that we have attained the unattainable."

The general verdict enhances, to the maximum, the power of appeals to the biases and prejudices of the jurors, and usually converts into a futile ritual the use of stock phrases about dispassionateness almost always included in judges' charges. . . .

* * *

Perhaps the least desirable feature of the general verdict, a feature which the fact verdict wipes out, is this: The theory of the general verdict involves the assumption that the jury fully comprehends the judge's instructions concerning the applicable substantive legal rules. Yet, often the judge must state those rules to the jury with such niceties that many lawyers do not comprehend them, and it is impossible that the jury can. Judge Bok notes that "juries have the disadvantage . . . of being treated like children while the testimony is going on, but then being doused with a kettleful of law during the charge that would make a third-year law student blanch."[4] Nevertheless, the patently fictitious assumption that the jurors have more legal wisdom than third-year law-students requires the upper court to reverse when a trial judge fails to state the pertinent substantive rules with sufficient particularity. Such faulty instructions, it has been said, "are the greatest single source of reversible error." Judge Rossman says: "The general verdict is responsible for the elaborate instructions given to the jury. . . . The necessity for [these] instructions creates pitfalls which may trap the trial judge and which in turn may result in new trials, appeals and reversals." In many instances, such a reversal means merely another trial at which the judge will intone to another uncomprehending jury a revised version of those legal rules. There results an

---

4. Bok, I, Too, Nicodemus (1946).

There are at least three theories of how the general-verdict-jury system works: (1) According to a naive theory, the judge conclusively determines the pertinent substantive legal rules, and the jury confines itself to finding the facts. (2) A more sophisticated theory runs thus: The judge has one function and the jury two. The judge announces authoritatively the pertinent rules of law. The jury (a) ascertain the facts and (b) apply to these facts the rules of law laid down by the judge and (c) thus arrive at their general verdict. The judge, that is, supplies the major premise, consisting of the abstract rules of law; the jury determine the minor premise from the evidence, and then work out the syllogism to its logical conclusion in the verdict which they report to the judge. Some of those who accept this theory assert that juries often circumvent the legal rules by misfinding the facts; the facts, it is said, are "found in order to reach the result." [See, e.g., Pound, Introduction to the Philosophy of Law (1921) 133; cf. 121.] That thesis assumes that the jurors, understanding what the judge told them about the substantive legal rules, proceed with consummate skill and cunning to devise the exact finding of facts which, when correlated with those rules, will logically compel the judgment the jurors desire. (3) A more realistic theory maintains that jurors often do not understand the judge's instructions and simply bring in an unexplained verdict for the party they favor. See Frank, Law and The Modern Mind (1930) Part One, Chapter 16, and Appendix V.

enormous waste of time and money. Indeed, the prospect of a prolonged new trial undoubtedly often induces a litigant of modest means to accept an unfair settlement. The fact verdict provides an obvious escape from these wasteful or unfair consequences of the general verdict.

The finding of facts, says Sunderland, "is much better done by means of the special verdict. Every advantage, which the jury is popularly supposed to have over the court as a trier of facts, is retained, with the very great additional advantage that the analysis and separation of the facts in the case which the court and the attorney must necessarily effect in employing the special verdict, materially reduces the chance of error. It is easy to make mistakes in dealing at large with aggregates of facts. The special verdict compels detailed consideration. But above all it enables the public, the parties and the court to see what the jury has really done. . . . The morale of the jury also is aided by throwing off the cloak of secrecy, for only through publicity is there developed the proper feeling of responsibility in public servants. So far, then, as the facts go, they can be much more effectively, conveniently, and usefully tried by abandoning the general verdict and substituting the special verdict. . . . The special verdict is devised for the express purpose of escaping the sham of false appearances." [5]

When using a special verdict, the judge need not—should not—give any charge about the substantive legal rules beyond what is reasonably necessary to enable the jury to answer intelligently the questions put to them. As, accordingly, the jury is less able to know whether its findings will favor one side or the other, the appeal to the jurors' cruder prejudices will frequently be less effective. "A perverse verdict may still be returned, granted a jury clever enough to appreciate the effect of its answers, and to shape them to harmonize with its general conclusions. But it is much more difficult . . . and by requiring the jury to return the naked facts only we may fairly expect to escape the results of sympathy, prejudice and passion." That may be too sanguine a hope; but the fact verdict may often reduce the more undesirable sway of emotions. It is suggested, too, that a special verdict "searches the conscience of the individual juror, as a general verdict does not," because "such are the contradictions in human nature that many a man who will unite in a general verdict for a large and unwarranted sum of money will shrink from a specific finding against his judgment and sense of right and wrong." Judge Rossman writes, "Bearing in mind that in the judge-jury relationship both members of the team are entitled to fair treatment may we not ask ourselves: Is it fair to require a jury to employ a general verdict? Since recourse to the special verdict is available, is it right to demand that a juror swear that he will obey the instructions (which the lawyers frequently say they are not sure of until they have been transcribed) and return a general verdict in obedience thereto?"

5. Sunderland, loc. cit. . . .

True, the common-law type of special verdict, when utilized in this country, frequently caused so many complications that it fell into disrepute. But in three states, North Carolina, Wisconsin and Texas, the special-verdict practice in civil cases was so modified as to avoid most of those complications. The Wisconsin and Texas procedures, apparently the most effective, seem to have been the model for Rule 49(a) of the Federal Civil Rules of Procedure, 28 U.S.C.A., following section 723c, which authorizes the trial judge to dispense with a general verdict and, instead, to require the return of special written findings. Rule 49(b) also authorizes the judge to call for a general verdict accompanied by written interrogatories. But, unlike the Texas trial judge, the federal district judge, under the Rule, has full, uncontrolled discretion in the matter: He may still require merely the old-fashioned general verdict.

Accordingly, we cannot hold that a district judge errs when, as here, for any reason or no reason whatever, he refuses to demand a special verdict, although we deem such a verdict usually preferable to the opaque general verdict. Perhaps some day soon Rule 49 will be amended to make compulsory either special verdicts or written interrogatories in civil jury cases. Meanwhile, we can but hope that, in such cases, the district judges will require one or the other, on their own motion or when asked to do so.

The fact verdict will furnish no panacea. Among other things, as previously noted, it will still be true that, in a relatively simple case, the jury will still be able to foresee what answers to the questions will produce a judgment for the side it favors. . . .

Affirmed.

L. HAND, CIRCUIT JUDGE (concurring). I concur in holding that there was evidence to support the verdict, and that it was not an error to refuse to take a special verdict along with the general verdict. I also concur in thinking that it would be desirable to take special verdicts more often. True, it would often expose the general verdict to defeat by showing how irrational had been the operation of the juror's minds. However, like my brother Frank, I am not among those who appear to esteem the system just because it gives rein to the passional element of our nature, however inevitably that may enter all our conclusions. I should like to subject a verdict, as narrowly as was practical, to a review which should make it in fact, what we very elaborately pretend that it should be: a decision based upon law. In criminal prosecutions there may be, and in my judgment there are, other considerations which intervene to make such an attempt undesirable.

SWAN, CIRCUIT JUDGE (concurring).

I concur in affirmance of judgment.

NOTES

(1) In Nunez v. Superior Oil Co., 572 F.2d 1119 (5th Cir.1978), the court ruled that the question of whether the defendant was "justified" in failing to

pay royalties under a contract was a question for the jury rather than the court. What other questions that call for judgmental evaluation should be left to the jury? See ABA Standards Relating to Trial Courts § 2.10, Commentary: "The traditional province of the jury in civil cases [includes] . . . determining standards of conduct that the law itself defines as those that an ordinary reasonable person would observe". See also James & Hazard, Civil Procedure § 7.10 (3d ed. 1985).

(2) When special issues of fact are submitted to the jury, should they be told what the effect of their answers will be? See Ryan, Are Instructions Which Inform the Jury of the Effect of Their Answers Inimical to Justice? 1940 Wis.L.Rev. 400; Stout, Our Special Issue System, 36 Texas L.Rev. 44 (1957); Green, Blindfolding the Jury, 33 Texas L.Rev. 273 (1955); Gay, "Blindfolding" the Jury: Another View, 34 Texas L.Rev. 368 (1956); Green, A Rebuttal, id. at 382; Gay, A Rejoinder, id. at 514; Green, A Reply to Mr. Gay's Rejoinder, id. at 681; Note, Informing the Jury of the Effects of Its Answers to Special Verdict Questions—The Minnesota Experience, 58 Minn.L.Rev. 903 (1974) (Minnesota is the only state permitting the jury to be informed of the effect of its answers). See also Kalven, A Report on the Jury Project of the University of Chicago Law School, 24 Ins.Counsel J. 368, 370, 372 (1957). Occasionally, duller but persuasive members will misapprehend the impact of their answers causing a result contrary to the jury's intention but in accord with substantive law. See, e.g., Trousdale v. Texas & New Orleans Railroad, 154 Tex. 231, 276 S.W.2d 242 (1955). Ten jurors voted no and two yes to a finding—one of twenty-seven issues submitted—that defendant had been negligent. The minority agreed to vote no, when they were assured by another juror "that he did not think that the railroad would have to be found negligent for the plaintiff to be awarded the money."

(3) In Hoffman v. Jones, 280 So.2d 431 (Fla.1973), the Florida Supreme Court abandoned the common-law defense of contributory negligence and endorsed comparative negligence. The court noted:

> "In accomplishing these purposes the trial court is authorized to require special verdicts to be returned by the jury and to enter such judgments as may truly reflect the intent of the jury as expressed in any verdict or verdicts which may be returned." Id., at 439.

See Finz, Does the Trend in our Substantive Law Dictate an Expanded Use of the Special Verdict, 37 Albany L.Rev. 229 (1973); Cadena, Comparative Negligence and the Special Verdict, 5 St. Mary's L.J. 688 (1974).

(4) May a jury disregard the court's instruction, refuse to agree on a special verdict, and return only a general verdict? See State Department of Highways v. Hurt, 63 Tenn.App. 689, 478 S.W.2d 775, 783 (1971) (yes) (dictum).

(5) See also Annot., Submission of Special Interrogatories in Connection with General Verdict under Federal Rule 49(b), and State Counterparts, 6 A.L.R.3d 408 (1966).

B. ATTACKING A GENERAL VERDICT

The materials that follow are limited to problems involving claimed misconduct or error by the jurors. Errors by the court, such as misdirecting the jury on the applicable law, are treated in Section 1. Errors by counsel, such as misconduct, are not specifically treated.

To be valid, a general verdict must be based upon sufficient evidence, be reached by the requisite number of jurors, be the result of a process of deliberation, be consistent with respect to similarly situated parties, and be correct in certain formal aspects. In considering the effect of jurors' misconduct, it is important to distinguish two problems—first, the types of irregularities or errors which may infect their verdict and, second, the evidence that may properly be received to establish the defects.

———

BAXTER v. TANKERSLEY
Court of Appeals of Kentucky, 1967.
416 S.W.2d 737.

* * *

Appellant contends vigorously that the jury verdict is invalid, inasmuch as the nine jurors who signed the verdict fixing damages were not the same nine jurors who found that appellant was the sole cause of the accident. Appellant relies upon Section 248 of the Constitution, KRS 29.330, and CR 48, all of which require a less than unanimous verdict to be signed by all of the jurors who agree with the verdict. Appellant states that since only six of the jurors who signed the liability verdict also signed the damages verdict, the damages verdict was in fact signed only by six jurors.

Counsel for appellant failed to call the attention of the Court to KRS 29.335, which provides as follows:

> "The verdict shall be written, signed by the foreman, and read by the clerk to the jury, and the inquiry made, whether or not it is their verdict. If more than one-fourth disagree, the jury must be sent out for further deliberation; but if no disagreement be expressed, and neither party require the jury to be polled, the verdict is complete and the jury discharged from the case."

Appellant has cited several cases from foreign jurisdictions such as Clark v. Strain, 212 Or. 357, 319 P.2d 940; Nelson v. Superior Court, 26 Cal.App.2d 119, 78 P.2d 1037; and McCauley v. International Trading Company, 268 Wis. 62, 66 N.W.2d 633. All of these cases hold that, where a jury is required to return a special and general verdict and the two verdicts are not signed by the same jurors, and where counsel for the objecting party has not waived the polling of the jury and made timely objection, the jury's verdicts must be set aside.

It is the law in Kentucky, as in other jurisdictions, that failure to poll the jury waives irregularities in a jury verdict but does not waive a void jury verdict. See Davis v. Stone, 172 Ky. 696, 189 S.W. 937. That case points out the rule as to certainty and definiteness in a verdict and citing from 38 Cyc. 1877, points out that a verdict is bad which is so uncertain or indefinite as not to base a legal judgment thereon or is inconsistent and illogical.

In order to hold Baxter liable for all of the damages incurred by Shuttleworth and Tankersley's estate, at least nine members of the jury who rendered the verdict for damages against Baxter had also to render a verdict finding him to be the sole cause of the accident. Although the trial judge entered judgment on the date of the return of the verdict, apparently the form of the verdict was not made known to him on that date but two days later. This seems a little odd in view of the fact that the judgment recites the two verdicts, but according to counsel for appellants this mistake must have resulted because the signatures of the members of the jury approving the verdicts were not read by the Court. Possibly the unfortunate mix-up was due to the fact that the verdict was returned late on Saturday afternoon, and to the further fact that the trial judge had no reason to anticipate under the instructions which he had given that there would be such a verdict as was returned here. Nevertheless, we believe that the verdict reached by the jury is void and a new trial shall be granted. See Davis v. Stone, supra, and Anderson's Ex'x v. Hockensmith, Ky., 322 S.W.2d 489 (1959).

The judgment is reversed and the action remanded for a new trial.

NOTES

(1) Constitutions and statutes in all states contain guarantees of trial by jury in civil cases, but many of them have modified the common-law rule requiring unanimity among jurors in civil cases. See Winters, Majority Verdicts in the United States, 26 J.Am.Jud.Soc'y 87 (1942). The necessary majority varies from any to five-sixths of the jury. In some states, only the lowest trial courts are included; a handful require the consent of the parties for such a verdict. Ibid. See also Fed.R.Civ.Proc. 48. The major justification for the change is that it reduces the number of disagreements, thereby avoiding new trials. In New York the change apparently did result in a reduction in disagreements. In the Supreme Court, for example, the percentage of disagreement dropped from approximately five percent to about three percent. See, e.g., Fifth Annual Report, New York Judicial Council 36 (1939); Third Annual Report, New York Judicial Conference 182 (1958). See also the discussion of six person juries in Chapter 12 supra.

(2) Kalven, A Report on the Jury Project of the University of Chicago Law School, 24 Ins.Counsel J. 368, 372–73 (1957): . . . The study discloses that in some 71% of the cases the jury was not unanimous on the first ballot and that in some 36% the split was at least 8 to 4. What then is the ultimate fate of the minority view? Does it ever prevail? Does it hang the jury? Or does it always slowly yield? In 90% of the cases in which a majority voted guilty on the first ballot, the verdict was guilty; in 97% of the cases in which the majority voted not guilty on the first ballot, the verdict was not guilty. In the few cases in which the jury was evenly split on the first ballot the final verdicts were guilty in 60% of the instances and not guilty in 40%.

"A second preliminary result is that the only instances of hung juries were in cases where the initial vote showed a substantial minority."

GUINN v. MILLARD TRUCK LINES, INC.

Supreme Court of Iowa, 1965.
257 Iowa 671, 134 N.W.2d 549.

LARSON, JUSTICE. In an action for damages arising out of an intersection-collision between an automobile operated by the plaintiff Mildred Guinn and a truck-tractor operated by the defendant Jack Coleman and owned by Millard Truck Lines, Inc., in separate counts Mildred Guinn and Shirley Guinn, age 11 years, her passenger, each sought compensation for personal injuries, and the plaintiff-husband Douglas Guinn sought compensation for property damage, medical and hospital expenses of his wife and daughter, and loss of consortium.

Defendants' motions for directed verdict, duly made, were overruled, and the trial court submitted the issues of defendants' negligence, plaintiff's freedom from contributory negligence, and proximate cause and damages on each count. The jury returned a verdict in favor of Mildred Guinn in the amount of $4,000.00, in favor of Shirley Guinn in the amount of $6,000.00, and in favor of defendants on the $4,950.00 claim of Douglas Guinn.

When the trial court overruled defendants' motion for judgment notwithstanding the verdict in favor of Mildred Guinn and Shirley Guinn, and denied their motion for a new trial as to those causes, defendants appealed. Mr. Guinn does not appeal. We find no error in the court's ruling on defendants' motions.

* * *

The serious injuries suffered by Mrs. Guinn are not disputed, nor was the reasonableness of the $905.65 medical and hospital expenses incurred by Mr. Guinn for the care and treatment of Mrs. Guinn and his daughter Shirley. Mrs. Guinn's injuries consisted of a broken pelvis, lacerations, a chest bone displacement, and two cracked ribs. She was confined to the hospital for about three weeks, and her permanent disability was estimated at 20 per cent. Shirley received lacerations on the head, arm and leg, all of which will produce permanent scars. The property damage to the jointly-owned automobile was established at $125.00.

. . . The real nub of this controversy is not the sufficiency of the evidence to sustain the verdicts for plaintiffs, but whether, in view of the verdict against the claim of the plaintiff husband of Mildred, the trial court erred in not granting a new trial to defendants, as set forth in Division I of their brief. Of course the evidence as to defendants' liability as to each plaintiff was the same, but the items of damage each asked were different. Mr. Guinn's claim was liquidated and admitted in regard to medical expense and personal property damage. Thus, if it can be fairly said that the jury's sole error was in failing to award him damages, these verdicts would not be irreconcilable.

The problem is new in this jurisdiction, and the decisions in jurisdictions which have considered the matter are not in accord either as to results or reasoning. See Anno. 36 A.L.R.2d 1333.

Perhaps we should first determine whether this court should attempt to analyze and interpret verdicts of this nature which appear to conflict, or whether we should simply classify them as inconsistent and summarily order a new trial of all the issues involved if there is an appeal by either party. The original decisions appear to adopt the old common law rule of refusing to grant partial retrials and summarily grant a new trial to all. Other recent well-reasoned decisions seem to favor the practice of analyzing and interpreting different jury verdicts where several claims of recovery are made in one action, and upon both reason and logic we prefer this procedure.

Appellants cite a number of cases from New Jersey, New York, Tennessee, and Pennsylvania, which seem to hold that where a verdict is rendered in favor of the plaintiff-wife for injuries, and denies recovery to a husband in the same action for his medical and hospital expenses, the verdicts are absolutely irreconcilable and require a new trial on both claims, especially where the husband and the defendants appeal. The reasoning underlying these decisions is that the inconsistent verdicts "demonstrate the unfitness of the jury to determine the respective rights and obligations of the parties." [Citations omitted.] In Berry v. Foster, supra, the court's statement in Gray v. Brooklyn Heights R. Co., 175 N.Y. 448, 450, 67 N.E. 899, 900, was approved as follows: "When, however, the two actions are thus tried together and inconsistent verdicts are rendered, we incline to the view that sound practice requires both verdicts be set aside at once, without attempting, by analysis of the evidence or otherwise, to discover whether either should be allowed to stand. No other course is safe, for it cannot be told with reasonable certainty what facts the jury found."

On the other hand, appellees point to a line of cases from California and Florida which do attempt to analyze the verdicts, and therefore often reach different results. In the leading case of Chance v. Lawry's, Inc., 58 Cal.2d 368, 24 Cal.Rptr. 209, 374 P.2d 185, the plaintiff-wife was awarded $15,000.00 damages against the defendant. On her husband's claim of damage for loss of consortium, services and medical expense, the jury returned a verdict against him. There too the husband was not present when his wife was injured and he did not appeal. As to the defendants' contention that the verdicts were inconsistent and the verdict in favor of the plaintiff-wife should be set aside, the court said: "Negligence of the defendants and plaintiff-wife's freedom from negligence were the primary issues to be determined by the jury. The verdict for plaintiff-wife indicates the jury's determination as to these issues. Of course, had the jury returned a verdict in favor of the husband for medical expenses incurred and *against* the plaintiff-wife, then a reversal would be proper since the husband's cause of action is derivative. [Citations omitted.] But here the jury's verdict clearly implies that they found defendants were negligent and that Mrs.

Chance was free from contributory negligence. That being so it would be contrary to common sense and the efficient administration of justice to require a new trial on the issue of liability toward Mrs. Chance. . . . But while Mr. Chance, who has not appealed, may have 'grounds for complaint because of the findings upon . . . [his] cause of action' defendants assuredly have none." [Citations omitted.]

In the California cases it is held significant that plaintiff-wife's right to recovery was not dependent on recovery by her husband, and here it is not disputed that the right of action of Mrs. Guinn and of Shirley Guinn are each independent of Mr. Guinn's right. Of course, his right of action for Mrs. Guinn's hospital and medical expenses was derivative, and had the jury found Mrs. Guinn contributorily negligent for that claim, he could not recover. Restatement of Torts, § 494.

We are inclined to accept the California view as the procedure most likely to secure justice and avoid needless repetitions and expensive litigation.

VII. The verdicts appealed from in favor of Mildred and Shirley Guinn were not contrary to the evidence and the court's instructions, and were not necessarily inconsistent with the verdict rendered in favor of the defendants on Mr. Guinn's cause of action. The record does not sustain the appellants' claim that the jury did not know what it was doing, but rather discloses it did, and in so doing simply committed an error in failing to make some award to Mr. Guinn.

The jury first made an award on both forms of verdict submitted by the court, meaning only a misunderstanding of the ministerial function given them. It clearly appears from these completed forms and the record that it intended to give Mr. Guinn no damages, nothing more. On Form No. 5 the jury indicated no amount as the verdict for plaintiff Douglas Guinn. On Form No. 6 it found for the defendants on Mr. Guinn's claim. The court in an attempt to clear up this matter, polled the jury, and all members agreed it was their intention to return a verdict for defendants on the husband's claim. While this final declaration does not help too much, we think these proceedings show quite clearly the denial of recovery was based on the damage claim, not on the liability issue.

Under these circumstances, had Mr. Guinn appealed, the Florida and perhaps the California court would order a new trial on the issue of the husband's damage, and in one court the suggestion was made that the apparent error could be corrected by a court-rendered judgment for the damages suffered if liquidated and admitted.

. . . Although we are not faced with . . . a partial retrial problem here, we conclude, upon a review of the whole case, it appears that the jury has settled the question of liability fairly and upon sufficient evidence, and that the issue of Mr. Guinn's damages was so disassociated from other questions that in the interest of justice its determination of Mildred and Shirley's causes should stand. Since the husband did not complain of the obvious error as to him, the other parties and the public should not under these circumstances be burdened with a retrial of all issues anew. We cannot correct that jury error here by setting aside verdicts for Mr. Guinn's wife and daughter, and to decide the jury was not aware of the issues because it refused to grant him damages seems unjust and needless and penalizes the truly innocent parties.

It is the correction of error and not a new trial to which the aggrieved party is primarily entitled. Of course a partial new trial may be granted as a means by which that end may be accomplished. Robinson v. Payne, supra. In Feldhahn v. Van DeVenter, 253 Iowa 1194, 115 N.W.2d 862, this court recently ordered a new trial as to damages only. While we have recognized the modern device of granting partial retrials, we have also said this device must be exercised "with caution". Larimer v. Platte, 243 Iowa 1167, 1176, 53 N.W.2d 262. Nevertheless, it appears when there are separate verdicts or judgments, and there is no danger of complications, this procedure is becoming widely sanctioned by statute, court rule, and decision. See C.J.S. New Trial § 11 a, page 89; 39 Am.Jur., New Trial, § 22. It is especially adaptable where liability of defendant is definitely established. It is not applicable here because Mr. Guinn did not appeal, and of course it would not be applicable in states where a jury may mitigate the damage under the comparative negligence doctrine.

IX. There is no merit in defendants' contention that the verdicts were rendered as a result of compromise. True, if established, a compromise would taint the verdicts, but mere speculation will not sustain such a charge. The fact that the jury deliberated 24 hours, failed to give Mrs. Guinn more than a small part of her claim, and gave Mr. Guinn nothing, does not constitute a showing sufficient to raise an inference of compromise. . . .

Finding no reversible error, the judgments must be affirmed.

Affirmed.

GARFIELD, C.J., and HAYS, LARSON, PETERSON, THORNTON, SNELL and MOORE, JJ., concur.

STUART and THOMPSON, JJ., dissent.

STUART, JUSTICE (dissenting).

* * *

The jury could not properly have found the husband had not been damaged. Therefore they could not, under the law, do what they did do in this case. If the driver and passenger were entitled to recover, so was the husband. If the husband was not entitled to recover neither were the driver or passenger. The majority opinion does not recognize the second possibility.

* * *

THOMPSON, J., joins in this dissent.

NOTES

(1) A situation analogous to *Guinn* arises in master-servant cases where the jury exculpates the servant who performed the alleged negligent acts but finds against the master who is only derivatively liable. See, e.g., Friedman v. Lundberg, 4 Utah 2d 368, 294 P.2d 705 (1956).

(2) If the jury in the principal case had found in favor of Mr. Guinn but against Mrs. Guinn, would Mrs. Guinn have been able to complain of the inconsistent verdict if neither Mr. Guinn nor the defendant appealed? In Pigage v. Chism, 237 Ark. 873, 377 S.W.2d 32, 33 (1964), where the jury denied an award to the injured minor but awarded damages to the parents whose right of action was solely derivative, the court, in affirming, held that "the appellant [the minor] cannot benefit from the inconsistent verdicts . . . since he was the primary or principal party and the verdict in his case is the controlling verdict."

(3) A note in 79 Harv.L.Rev. 439 (1965) which discusses the principal case concludes that inconsistency always requires reversal of the judgment appealed and suggests that where only one of two consolidated cases is appealed, a rule should be adopted permitting a retrial in the nonappealed case after reversal of the appealed case. Would the adoption of this suggestion change the result in Pigage v. Chism, Note 2 supra?

(4) In Kansas City So. Railway v. Marrow, 326 P.2d 817 (Okl.1958), the jury resolved a claim against joint tortfeasors by bringing in separate verdicts against each defendant in different amounts. This attempt by the jury to apportion liability considered by the substantive law to be "joint" was rejected by the court.

(5) When special verdicts are used, inconsistencies among the answers give rise to problems. For an example of special verdict answers so inconsistent as to cause a new trial when read with colloquy between judge and jury, see Griffin v. Matherne, 471 F.2d 911 (5th Cir.1973), rehearing denied 474 F.2d 1347 (5th Cir.). In Wagner v. International Harvester Co., 611 F.2d 224 (8th Cir.1979), the jury returned a special verdict finding defendant negligent in the design, testing, and manufacturing of the left foot decelerator of a tractor, but failed to return a special verdict on whether the tractor was defective. The Court ruled the answers reconcilable.

(6) In Nollenberger v. United Air Lines, Inc., 216 F.Supp. 734 (S.D.Cal. 1963), a wrongful death case, the trial court found that the answers to the special interrogatories were inconsistent with the amount of damages awarded by the general verdict. Consequently, the judge used the answers to the special interrogatories as the basis for recalculating and increasing the amount of damages. The Court of Appeals vacated the judgments and remanded to the District Court "for the purpose of permitting renewed motions for new trials on the issue of damages unless appellees . . . notify this court . . . of their . . . consent to entry of judgment in the amounts awarded in the general verdicts." United Air Lines v. Weiner, 335 F.2d 379, 409–10 (9th Cir.1964). It noted:

    *   *   *

> "The district court stated that after repeated efforts by mathematical calculation to harmonize and reconcile the answers to the eleven special interrogatories with the general verdict, no harmony resulted. This may be so. But nothing in the law compelled the jury to calculate

its damage awards according to a fixed mathematical formula using only the factors contained in the eleven special findings "The jury was admonished to award damages in accordance with all the instructions of the court. No party specified as error the giving of any of the instructions . . . [T]he answers to the eleven special interrogatories do not exhaust all of the factors of damage included within the instructions . . ."

The judge had instructed the jury that in weighing pecuniary loss they could consider, inter alia, the disposition of the decedent and his inclination to support the plaintiffs; the special interrogatories related solely to matters such as life and earning expectancy, income tax due on prospective earnings, and the proper discount rate.

Could the trial court have cured the deficiency in any way? Can an interrogatory be framed asking the jury to put a dollar value on all the other permissible factors in a case? Or would the jury have to be asked separately as to each factor?

To what extent is the decision of the Court of Appeals explicable by the federal rule on additur discussed at p. 892 infra?

HONIGSBERG v. NEW YORK CITY TRANSIT AUTHORITY

Civil Court of the City of New York, New York County, 1964.
43 Misc.2d 1, 249 N.Y.S.2d 296.

PATRICK J. PICARIELLO, JUDGE. Defendant moves to set aside the jury's verdict as against the law and the evidence, and "because of the way the verdict was rendered".

In view of the latter contention urged by the defendant, it behooves the Court to recount the colloquy which took place in the courtroom both before and after the jury returned with its verdict.

"(The Jury returned to the courtroom, at which time the following occurred:)

"THE COURT: You have a request?

"THE FOREMAN: We are at a loss, since we have a difference of opinion as to your charge. Some maintain . . .

"THE COURT: Just what portion of the charge is there a difference of opinion on?

"THE FOREMAN: Whether or not it can be broken down into a degree of guilt or . . ..

"FIFTH JUROR: On awarding of the amount . . ..

"THE FOREMAN: No, no. I forget the word you used.

"THE COURT: Are you referring to contributory negligence?

"THE FOREMAN: Yes. Can it be determined on the degree of negligence, or must it be absolutely on one side or the other?

"THE COURT: If you find that the plaintiff in this case was in any way negligent, then you must find a verdict for the defendant.

"THE FOREMAN: If we find that the defendant was in any way negligent?

"THE COURT: No. You must find that the defendant was negligent.

"THE FOREMAN: Was negligent?

"THE COURT: Was negligent in the manner in which it maintained the subway stairway.

"THE FOREMAN: But there is no degree?

"THE COURT: Was negligent, period. I have already described to you what we mean by negligence. However, notwithstanding the defendant's negligence, if you so find, should you find that the plaintiff was in any wise negligent, in other words, if her conduct was not that of a careful and prudent person in descending the stairs, and if her conduct in any way contributed to the happening of the accident, no matter how slight it might have been, then you must dismiss the complaint.

"THE FOREMAN: It is clear to me, sir, because that was my contention.

"THE COURT: Suppose I read to you that portion of my charge which has to do with plaintiff's contributory negligence.

. . .

"THE JURY RENDERS ITS VERDICT:

"COURT OFFICER: Mr. Foreman, have you reached a verdict?

"MR. FOREMAN: We did reach a verdict.

"COURT OFFICER: What is that verdict?

"THE FOREMAN: We found in favor of the plaintiff.

"COURT OFFICER: And the amount?

"THE FOREMAN: It was decided upon by the Jury, an average method—the lady, I am sorry, I can't recall her name.

"THE COURT: Just tell us the results.

"THE FOREMAN: $3,000 for her.

"THE COURT: Yes.

"THE FOREMAN: $500 for the gentleman.

"MR. MANNES: May I have the jury polled?

(The jury was polled. The verdict was unanimous.)

"COURT OFFICER: So say all of you.

"MR. MANNES: Your Honor, please, having heard the Foreman render his verdict, I believe it would be incumbent upon the Court to have the Foreman state again whether it was his report that there was an average verdict—it was done by averaging.

"THE COURT: Is that the way the verdict was arrived at?

"THE FOREMAN: No, sir. The verdict was not arrived at by averaging. The amount of money was arrived at by averaging.

"MR. MANNES: That is what I thought. Thank you very much.

"THE COURT: Thank you very much, ladies and gentlemen. You have discharged your duties.

"THE FOREMAN: The verdict was unanimous.

"THE COURT: It is quite obvious.

(The Jury left)

"MR. MANNES: For the record: first, generally, the defendant moves to set aside the verdict pursuant to all the sections of the CPLR except as to inadequacy. As to that, I move for setting aside the verdict as excessive, more particularly in view of the jury's rendering of the report; and then, in the requestioning of the jury by the court at my request on behalf of the defendant, in view of the fact that that was made by averaging, it certainly was irregular—something a jury is not either permitted to do or should do—which is an indication—strictly in view of the fact of the timing, their questioning—it indicates nothing more than sympathy and a compromise verdict, and this is not the proper way in which a verdict should be arrived at. It was not arrived at on the actual merits of the case, upon which they should really have arrived at it—either yes or no.

"In view of that, I move to set aside the verdict as against the law and the evidence, and because of the way the verdict was rendered."

The Court shall first proceed to consider the contention raised by the defendant that the verdict was compromised.

* * *

Apart from the consideration that the foreman indicated in answer to the question posed by the Court that "the verdict was not arrived at by averaging. The amount of money was arrived at by averaging," there is nothing in the rendition of the verdict, nor in the verdict itself, which even remotely suggests a compromise.

Since the deliberations of jurors are secret and have always been considered sacrosanct in perpetuating our form of jurisprudence, as indeed they should be, and, ordinarily cannot be shown by jurors' testimony nor can jury rooms be invaded to show that verdict rendered was indeed a compromise, the question arises, well then, how can a compromise verdict be detected and set aside?

* * *

The verdict rendered in this case is neither irreconcilably inconsistent nor are the amounts so disproportionate on all the evidence in this case as to warrant a finding that the same was compromised.

* * *

There was nothing in the foreman's report of the verdict, as rendered, which indicates that it was not the result of sound judgment, dispassionate consideration and conscientious reflection. Moreover, since the jurors, individually polled, answered affirmatively whether foreman's report of same meant that they had unanimously found a verdict in favor of the plaintiffs, as indicated, (supra) and verdict was accordingly so recorded, the verdict so recorded was the only verdict and foreman's statement reporting as to how or in what manner it was found was not the verdict. And also, there was no indication in this case, either in considering the record, the verdict itself or its rendition, that the jury had decided by lot whether the verdict shall have been for the plaintiff or the defendant. Mitchell v. Ehle, 10 Wend. 595.

Defendant also urges the setting aside of the verdict on the ground that it had been "averaged."

* * *

A "quotient verdict" is nothing more than a verdict by chance, is illegal, and must be set aside. North Tex. Producers Ass'n v. Jenkins, Tex.Civ.App., 342 S.W.2d 192, 195. It is one resulting from agreement whereby each juror writes down amount of damages to which he thinks party is entitled and such amounts are then added together and divided by number of jurors. [Citations "omitted.] " However, as an essential element of "quotient verdict," jurors must agree to be bound by the quotient. Wilson v. Gardner, 10 Utah 2d 89, 348 P.2d 931, 934. It is not the setting down of an amount by each of the jurors as to what he thought was fair and reasonable to award plaintiff under the circumstances as damages that is objectionable or improper. [Citations omitted.] It is rather the advance agreement to be bound by average and adherence to such agreement after a quotient is arrived at that renders the verdict illegal. [Citations "omitted.]"

So that the test is whether the jury agreed beforehand to be bound by the result of the arithmetic. See, Fortson v. Hester, 252 Ala. 143, 39 So.2d 649, 651. Therefore, a "quotient verdict"—that is, a verdict based upon the average judgment of all the jurors—is not illegal, where it does not affirmatively appear that there was an agreement beforehand to abide by the average of the amounts the jurors were in favor of awarding. State ex rel. Senter v. Cowell, Supra. The legal presumption is that no such arrangement was made. Thus, a party objecting to the verdict on the ground that it was a quotient verdict must show that it was arrived at by improper means, in that the jury in advance agreed upon a method, and agreed to be bound by the result. . . . It is not enough that the quotient be arrived at in the manner indicated (the foreman reported that his verdict had been "averaged" in this case), but in addition thereto there must be proof of an agreement among the jurors that the verdict be determined in said manner (which was totally lacking in this case). [Citations omitted]

. . . We can arrive at no other conclusion but that a great deal of "arithmeticking" goes on in the jury room in situations of this kind.

For the determination of each member of the jury is susceptible to and influenced by his own individual experience relative to pain and suffering and to his own ability to sustain, endure and tolerate it. Some may be impervious to it, and at the hands of these jurors, the plaintiff may not fare too well; others may be highly susceptible and sensitive to it, and the hands of these jurors the defendant may not fare too well. Each is individually affected thereby and the same becomes patent, is a determinative and controlling factor and is reflected in their dollar evaluation of the same.

To anticipate each of the individual jurors to come forth and produce an identical dollar evaluation for pain and suffering under these circumstances borders on folly and fantasy. . . . As was stated by Herrick, J., in the case of Hamilton v. Owego Water Works, 22 App. Div. 573, 578, 48 N.Y.S. 106, 108 (obiter dictum, affirmed on appeal on other issues) 163 N.Y. 562, 57 N.E. 1111. "If every juror persisted in voting for the exact amount he thought was proper to be awarded, we would very seldom reach a verdict in the class of damage cases I have referred to." The learned jurist was referring to cases involving the recovery of unliquidated damages.

Motion denied.

NOTES

(1) How can it be established that the jury agreed to a quotient verdict in a jurisdiction adhering to the majority rule on impeaching verdicts? In E.L. Farmer & Co. v. Hooks, 239 F.2d 547 (10th Cir.1956), cert. denied 353 U.S. 911, 77 S.Ct. 669, 1 L.Ed.2d 665 (1957), defendant's claims representative retrieved from the wastebasket in the jury room scraps of paper which bore figures yielding a quotient when divided by twelve of $114,295, the amount of the verdict for plaintiff. The court upheld the judgment entered on the verdict, citing decisions barring jurors' self-impeachment for facts which "inhere in the verdict" and concluding that no showing had been made that the jurors had entered into an agreement in advance that the quotient reached would be their verdict without subsequent consideration.

(2) In Ehalt v. McCarthy, 104 Utah 110, 138 P.2d 639 (1943), the court frowned on an instruction informing the jury it might use an average as the basis of discussion provided it did not agree in advance to be bound by the average. "The court should not put in the minds of the jurymen guides which short cut full discussion of comparative judgments."

(3) Does the prohibition against quotient verdicts apply to burdens of proof? In Clark v. Foster, 87 Idaho 134, 391 P.2d 853 (1964) each juror placed his opinion of the percentage of negligence attributable to the defendant on a piece of paper. The foreman added up the percentages, divided by 12, and arrived at a figure of 47% . Consequently, the jury, which had agreed to be bound, held that the defendant was not negligent since the percentage was below 50%. Comparative negligence does not exist in Idaho. A new trial was granted.

(4) If a judge sitting without a jury indicates that he has fixed damages on the basis of an averaging of the amounts testified to, ought his award be reversed? In Beasley v. Beasley, 256 Ala. 647, 57 So.2d 69 (1952), the court

affirmed, declaring that the trial judge's "processes" were not open to review. See also Foster v. City of Augusta, 174 Kan. 324, 256 P.2d 121 (1953).

FEDERAL RULES OF EVIDENCE FOR UNITED STATES COURTS AND MAGISTRATES RULE 606

. . . (b) Inquiry into validity of verdict or indictment. Upon an inquiry into the validity of a verdict or indictment, a juror may not testify as to any matter or statement occurring during the course of the jury's deliberations or to the effect of anything upon that or any other juror's mind or emotions as influencing the juror to assent to or dissent from the verdict or indictment or concerning the juror's mental processes in connection therewith, except that a juror may testify on the question whether extraneous prejudicial information was improperly brought to the jury's attention or whether any outside influence was improperly brought to bear upon any juror. Nor may a juror's affidavit or evidence of any statement by the juror concerning a matter about which the juror would be precluded from testifying be received for these purposes.

NOTES

(1) For a discussion of the federal rule, see 3 Weinstein & Berger, Weinstein's Evidence 606[04] (1989) (footnotes omitted):

Several types of jury conduct may present special difficulties. For instance, juror bias manifested in prejudiced comments during the deliberation may be viewed in a variety of ways. Where the comments indicate that the juror had preconceived notions of liability or guilt or personal knowledge about the facts in issue, the statements may be admissible not because they are not prohibited by Rule 606(b), but as tending to prove that the juror lied on the voir dire, a separate question from that of impeachment of verdicts. . . . But what should be done in terms of Rule 606(b) if a juror has stated that he does not trust convicts, after evidence of a conviction is used to impeach pursuant to Rule 609, or has commented adversely on the religion of a witness, or has referred in an uncomplimentary manner to the length of the defendant's hair, and proof of these statements is offered on a motion for a new trial? Can proof of these statements or some of these statements be separated from proof of the effect these statements had on the minds of the jurors, or are the two so inextricably interwoven that the entire testimony should be rejected under the Rule? The line may be very difficult to draw. Generally, it seems better to draw it in favor of juror privacy; in the heat of juror debate all kinds of statements may be made which have little effect on outcome, though taken out of context they seem damning and absurd.

(2) In Krause v. Rhodes, 570 F.2d 563 (6th Cir.1977), cert. denied 435 U.S. 924, 98 S.Ct. 1488, 55 L.Ed.2d 517 (1978), a new trial was granted upon evidence by a juror that he had been threatened and assaulted during the trial by a person interested in the litigation. But in Mashpee Tribe v. New Seabury Corp., 592 F.2d 575 (1st Cir.1979), cert. denied 444 U.S. 866, 100 S.Ct. 138, 62

L.Ed.2d 90 (1979), a new trial was denied upon a juror's evidence that he had received threatening phone calls on the ground that the calls had not affected the juror's vote.

(3) The fact that one juror took into the jury room two books not in evidence entitled, "How to Serve on a Jury" and "Impression of an Average Juryman," from which he read to his fellow jurors was not ground for a new trial. Sineri v. Smilkstein & Sons, 205 Misc. 745, 132 N.Y.S.2d 475 (1954), affirmed 285 App.Div. 959, 139 N.Y.S.2d 260 (2d Dep't 1955). See also United States v. Gordon, 253 F.2d 177 (7th Cir.1958) (Grand Jury handbook). Such examples of scholarship by jurors while they are in the jury room are relatively rare and are not encouraged. The jury is also normally dissuaded from note taking although some judges permit this practice. Report of Committee of United States District Judges, The Jury System in the Federal Courts, 26 F.R.D. 409, 457–59, 538 (1961). One commentator has suggested that "the possibility of a juror isolating a comment from the judge's oral charge and misconstruing it in his written notes is far greater than it would be if an exact copy of the court's charge were provided for the jury." Smith, Effective Instructions to the Federal Jury in Civil Cases—A Consideration in Microcosm, 18 Syr.L.Rev. 559, 569 (1967). See also Petroff, The Practice of Jury Note Taking—Misconduct, Right or Privilege? 18 Okl.L.Rev. 125 (1965); Note, Taking Note of Note-Taking, 10 Colum.J.L.Soc. p. 565 (1974); Sand and Reiss, A Report on Seven Experiments Conducted by District Courts in the Second Circuit, 60 N.Y.U.L.Rev. 423 (1985).

(4) Further scholarship on the question of jury misconduct includes Note, Racial Slurs by Jurors as grounds for Impeaching a Jury's Verdict, 1985 Wisc.L. Rev. 1481; Note, Gender Dynamics and Jury Deliberations, 96 Yale L.J. 593 (1987); Note, Pre–Deliberations, Jury Misconduct, Evidential Incompetence, and Jury Responsibility, 98 Yale L.J. 187 (1988) (discussing, among other matters, cocaine use).

SECTION 4. ERRORS LEADING TO NEW TRIALS

A. THE TRIAL JUDGE'S POWER: GROUNDS

The power of the trial judge to grant a new trial is one of his most effective devices to control the jury. It has other uses as well: to set at naught misbehavior of counsel, to rectify the judge's own errors, and, in general, to prevent miscarriage of justice. For a grant of a new trial because of counsel's misconduct, see Draper v. Airco, Inc., 580 F.2d 91 (3d Cir.1978). Statutes or court rules commonly specify grounds for the grant of a new trial; but at times, as in Rule 59, Federal Rules of Civil Procedure, the grounds must be found in case precedents. The materials in this section are concerned for the most part with the court's power to order a new trial as a means of keeping the jury within the bounds of reason in weighing the evidence, a sensitive question because of constitutional barriers to usurping the jury's function as trier of the facts. Other aspects of the power are illustrated in other sections of this volume. For example, the award of a new trial for fraud or newly discovered evidence is treated in connection with Judgments, infra, and for misconduct of the jury in section 3 of this chapter.

Besides illustrating the contest between the power of the trial judge and jury, these materials raise the question of the breadth of power of appellate courts to supervise the trial judge's action in granting or denying a new trial.

A point constantly to be borne in mind in considering the roles of the trial and appellate courts in American procedural systems is that neither tribunal sits to assure perfection in litigated proceedings. For federal district courts Rule 61 of the Federal Rules of Civil Procedure lays down the command to disregard errors in the proceedings if they were harmless. Thus, no error in admitting or excluding evidence or in any other order during the trial will result in a new trial unless to disregard it would be "inconsistent with substantial justice" and would "affect the substantial rights of the parties." See also Rule 103(a) of the Federal Rules of Evidence, providing that "Error may not be predicated upon a ruling which admits or excludes evidence unless a substantial right is affected." 1 Weinstein & Berger, Weinstein's Evidence 103[01] (1989).

Similarly for appellate courts in the federal system, 28 U.S.C.A. § 2111, the "harmless error" statute, provides: "On the hearing or any appeal or writ of certiorari in any case, the court shall give judgment after an examination of the record without regard to errors or defects which do not affect the substantial rights of the parties." Note, however, the doctrines which permit reversal for "plain error" and "constitutional error" "affecting substantial rights although they were not brought to the attention of the trial court." Rule 103(d) of the Federal Rules of Evidence. 1 Weinstein & Berger, Weinstein's Evidence 103[08] (1989).

AETNA CASUALTY & SURETY CO. v. YEATTS

United States Court of Appeals, Fourth Circuit, 1941.
122 F.2d 350.

PARKER, CIRCUIT JUDGE. This is the second appeal in a suit originally instituted to obtain a declaratory judgment with respect to the coverage of a policy of indemnity insurance. Aetna Casualty & Surety Co. v. Yeatts, 4 Cir., 99 F.2d 665. Following our first decision, the defendant Yeatts filed an amended answer alleging that consent judgment had been entered in the suit for damages filed against him in the state court and asking recovery thereof, together with costs, interest and attorney's fees, against the insurance company, plaintiff in the suit for declaratory judgment. The company denied liability on the ground that the defendant Yeatts was engaged in the performance of a criminal abortion at the time he incurred the liability for which the recovery was had against him, and that such liability was expressly excluded from the coverage of the policy. The question as to whether the defendant Yeatts was engaged in such criminal conduct was submitted to the jury, and from verdict and judgment in his favor the plaintiff brings this appeal.

There was testimony below from which the jury would have been amply justified in finding in favor of the plaintiff insurance company on the issue submitted; but the defendant himself was examined as a witness and, if his testimony is believed, he was guilty of no criminal act. No motion for directed verdict was made by the plaintiff, nor was the sufficiency of the evidence to sustain a finding in favor of the defendant challenged in any other way before verdict. After verdict, plaintiff moved for judgment non obstante veredicto and also for a new trial, on the ground that the verdict was contrary to the credible evidence in the case; and exceptions directed to denial of these motions constitute the only points presented by the appeal.

Even if a motion for directed verdict had been made by plaintiff, it is clear that same should have been denied as should, also, any motion for judgment non obstante veredicto based thereon; for it is too well settled to warrant discussion that, on such motion, the evidence must be taken in the light most favorable to the party against whom the directed verdict is asked and that all conflicts must be resolved in his favor. But here there was no motion for directed verdict to serve as a basis for the motion for judgment non obstante veredicto; and such judgment can be entered on the ground of the insufficiency of the evidence only where motion for directed verdict has been duly made. Rules of Civil Procedure, 50(b) [citations omitted]. In addition, it is well settled that, where the sufficiency of the evidence has not been challenged in this or some other appropriate way during trial, we have no power to review its sufficiency on appeal. [Citation omitted.] As said by Judge Sibley in Baten v. Kirby Lumber Corporation, supra [103 F.2d 274], "Rule of Civil Procedure 50, 28 U.S.C.A. following section 723c, does not do away with but emphasizes the necessity of a motion for a directed verdict to raise the legal question whether the evidence is sufficient."

The motion to set aside the verdict and grant a new trial was a matter of federal procedure, governed by Rule of Civil Procedure 59 and not subject in any way to the rules of state practice. On such a motion it is the duty of the judge to set aside the verdict and grant a new trial, if he is of opinion that the verdict is against the clear weight of the evidence, or is based upon evidence which is false, or will result in a miscarriage of justice, even though there may be substantial evidence which would prevent the direction of a verdict. The exercise of this power is not in derogation of the right of trial by jury but is one of the historic safeguards of that right. Smith v. Times Pub. Co., 178 Pa. 481, 36 A. 296, 35 L.R.A. 819; Bright v. Eynon, 1 Burr. 390; Melin v. Taylor, 3 B.N.C. 109, 132 Eng.Reports 351. The matter was well put by Mr. Justice Mitchell, speaking for the Supreme Court of Pennsylvania in Smith v. Times Publishing Co., supra [178 Pa. 481, 36 A. 298], as follows: "The authority of the common pleas in the control and revision of excessive verdicts through the means of new trials was firmly settled in England before the foundation of this colony and has always existed here without challenge under any of our constitutions. It is a power to examine the whole case on the law and the evidence, with a view to securing a result, not merely legal, but also not manifestly against justice,—a power exercised in pursuance of a sound judicial discretion, *without which the jury system would be a capricious and intolerable tyranny,* which no people could long endure. This court has had occasion more than once recently to say that it was *a power the courts ought to exercise unflinchingly."* (Italics supplied.)

In the same case Mr. Justice Williams, in a concurring opinion, traces the history of the exercise of this power and sums up his conclusion as follows:

" 'Trial by jury' therefore meant, at the time of Magna Charta, the investigation and decision of an issue of fact between parties litigant by 12 men, sitting as jurors, under the advice and legal direction of a law judge. When the verdict is rendered by the jury, it is to the court of which they are a part. It is recorded upon the minutes of the court, and becomes a part of the record of the trial; but it does not thereby become a judgment of the court, unless the judge is satisfied with it, and specially or by general order or rule so directs. He has a responsibility for the result no less than the jury, for it is his duty to see that right and justice are done, so far as this may be practicable in the particular case. If he is not satisfied with the verdict, it is his duty to set it aside, and grant a new trial before another jury. This was the settled practice in England as early as 1665. Forsyth, Jury Tr. 164. Lord Holt states that the practice of granting new trials, as a means of correcting the mistakes and relieving against the misconduct of juries, was in use much earlier than 1665, but accounts for its exercise not appearing in the books for the reason that, prior to that date, the action of the courts upon motions was not reported.

* * *

"As early, therefore, as 1665, the courts at Westminster did precisely what we have done in this case, and for the same reason. The right of trial by jury was not then supposed to give to a successful party the right to insist on an advantage due to the mistake or the willful misconduct of the jury, no matter how grossly unjust and oppressive the result might be; but the supervisory control of the court in banc, sitting as a court of review, was promptly exercised to relieve against the miscarriage of justice. The exercise of this power was then thought to be in aid of trial by jury. Lord Mansfield, in Bright v. Eynon, 1 Burrows, 390, described the effect of thus granting a new trial as 'no more than having the cause more deliberately considered by another jury, when there is reasonable doubt, or perhaps a certainty, that justice has not been done.' The function of the jury was well defined by Chief Justice Holt in Ash v. Ash, Holt, 701, nearly 100 years before the Declaration of Independence: 'The jury are to try the cause with the assistance of the judge.' They are not, and have never been, independent of the court of which they are a part but their verdicts must meet the approval, or at least they must not offend the sense of justice, of the presiding judge, who, as the late Justice Grier, of the supreme court of the United States, was fond of saying, was by virtue of his position 'the thirteenth juror.'"

In 1757, Lord Mansfield in Bright v. Eynon, supra, had this to say with respect to the exercise of the power:

"Trials by jury in civil causes, could not subsist now without a power, *somewhere*, to grant new trials. . . . There are numberless *causes* of false verdicts, *without* corruption or bad intention of the jurors. They may have heard too much of the matter before the trial; and imbibed prejudices without knowing it. The cause may be intricate: the examination may be so long as to distract and confound their attention. Most general verdicts include *legal consequences* as well as propositions of fact: in drawing these consequences the jury may mistake, and infer directly contrary to law. The parties may be *surprised* by a case falsely made at the trial, which they had no reason to expect, and therefore could not come prepared to answer. If *unjust* verdicts obtained under these and a thousand like circumstances, were to be conclusive for ever, the determination of civil property, in this method of trial, would be very precarious and unsatisfactory. It is absolutely *necessary to justice*, that there should, upon many occasions, be opportunities of *reconsidering* the cause by a new trial."

       *   *   *

To the federal trial judge, the law gives ample power to see that justice is done in causes pending before him; and the responsibility attendant upon such power is his in full measure. While according due respect to the findings of the jury, he should not hesitate to set aside their verdict and grant a new trial in any case where the ends of justice so require.

The distinction between the rules to be followed in granting a new trial and directing a verdict were stated by us with some care in Garrison v. United States, 4 Cir., 62 F.2d 41, 42, from which we quoted with approval in the later case of Roedegir v. Phillips, 4 Cir., 85 F.2d 995, 996, as follows: "Where there is substantial evidence in support of plaintiff's case, the judge may not direct a verdict against him, even though he may not believe his evidence or may think that the weight of the evidence is on the other side; for, under the constitutional guaranty of trial by jury, it is for the jury to weigh the evidence and pass upon its credibility. He may, however, set aside a verdict supported by substantial evidence where in his opinion it is contrary to the clear weight of the evidence, or is based upon evidence which is false; for, even though the evidence be sufficient to preclude the direction of a verdict, it is still his duty to exercise his power over the proceedings before him to prevent a miscarriage of justice. See Felton v. Spiro [6 Cir.], 78 F. 576. Verdict can be directed only where there is no substantial evidence to support recovery by the party against whom it is directed or where the evidence is all against him or so overwhelmingly so as to leave no room to doubt what the fact is.　Gunning v. Cooley, 281 U.S. 90, 50 S.Ct. 231, 74 L.Ed. 720.　Verdict may be set aside and new trial granted, when the verdict is contrary to the clear weight of the evidence, or whenever in the exercise of a sound discretion the trial judge thinks this action necessary to prevent a miscarriage of justice."

It is equally well settled, however, that the granting or refusing of a new trial is a matter resting in the sound discretion of the trial judge, and that his action thereon is not reviewable upon appeal, save in the most exceptional circumstances. [Citations omitted.]　The rule and the reason therefor is thus stated by Mr. Justice Brandeis in Fairmont Glass Works v. Cub Fork Coal Co., supra [287 U.S. 474, 53 S.Ct. 254, 77 L.Ed. 439]: "The rule that this Court will not review the action of a federal trial court in granting or denying a motion for a new trial for error of fact has been settled by a long and unbroken line of decisions; and has been frequently applied where the ground of the motion was that the damages awarded by the jury were excessive or were inadequate.　The rule precludes likewise a review of such action by a Circuit Court of Appeals.　Its early formulation by this Court was influenced by the mandate of the Judiciary Act of 1789, which provided in section 22 that there should be 'no reversal in either (circuit or Supreme) court on such writ of error . . . for any error in fact.'　Sometimes the rule has been rested on that part of the Seventh Amendment which provides that 'no fact tried by a jury, shall be otherwise re-examined in any court of the United States than according to the rules of the common law'.　More frequently the reason given for the denial of review is that the granting or refusing of a motion for a new trial is a matter within the discretion of the trial court."

While an examination of the record has led us to the conclusion that the trial judge might very properly have granted the motion for new trial, we cannot say that his denial of the motion amounted to an abuse of discretion on his part or that there are present any of the special circumstances which would subject his action to review by this court.　The judgment appealed from will accordingly be affirmed.

Affirmed.

NOTES

(1) Mills v. Mealey, 274 F.Supp. 4, 7 (W.D.Va.1967):

"Nevertheless, in spite of having the authority to set aside a verdict and grant a new trial, a district court should not forget the importance of the province of the jury.　In recent years the tendency has been to enlarge the sphere of the jury, especially in personal injury tort cases [citation omitted].　This means, among other things, that where a jury resolves conflicting evidence, a federal district court should not grant a new trial merely because the court may not have found the facts as the jury did, merely because the court disagrees with the results if a reasonable basis exists in support of the jury's conclusion. Aetna Casualty and Surety Co. v. Yeatts, 122 F.2d 350 (4th Cir.1941)."

Do you agree that the *Aetna* case stands for the statement quoted above?

(2) If, in a jury-tried case, the presiding judge sits as a "thirteenth juror," taking into account such evanescent "evidence" as witness demeanor, how can the appellate court determine from the cold record the correctness of the trial judge's conclusion that the jury's verdict was against the "clear weight of the evidence"? See generally Wright, The Doubtful Omniscience of Appellate Courts, 41 Minn.L.Rev. 751 (1957).

(3) The District of Columbia Circuit has ruled that, in order to protect the right to trial by jury, orders granting a new trial must be given considerably closer scrutiny on appeal than orders denying a new trial. Vander Zee v. Karabatosos, 589 F.2d 723 (D.C.Cir.1978), cert. denied 441 U.S. 962, 99 S.Ct. 2407, 60 L.Ed.2d 1066 (1979). The Fifth Circuit has endorsed this approach. Evers v. Equifax, Inc., 650 F.2d 793 (5th Cir.1981); Conway v. Chemical Leaman Tank Lines, Inc., 610 F.2d 360 (5th Cir.1980).

(4) Fireman's Fund Insurance Co. v. Aalco Wrecking Co., Inc., 466 F.2d 179, 187 (8th Cir.1972), cert. denied 410 U.S. 930, 93 S.Ct. 1371, 35 L.Ed.2d 592 (1973), suggested that the trial judge may be in a better position than the appellate court to grant a new trial when evidence is erroneously admitted or excluded or error is detected in the instructions. It further declared the appellate court should exercise "a closer degree of scrutiny and supervision . . . in order to protect the litigant's right to a jury trial" if the case is one in which the trial court found the verdict contrary to the weight of the evidence. Is that view correct?

(5) Cf. Mead v. Wiley Methodist Episcopal Church, 23 N.J.Super. 342, 358–59, 93 A.2d 9, 16 (1952): "The verdicts returned followed the sixth trial of these cases. Previously, there were four successive verdicts for the plaintiffs and the second successive verdict after the pretrial order of November 19, 1948, had limited the issue to the single question as to whether Rose or Joslin was driving the car. The judgment in the fifth trial was reversed on error of the trial court. . . . Regardless of what factual finding we might reach as the result of our review of the evidence, we are not permitted, under the cases, to substitute our judgment for that of the jury on a fact issue. To do so would be an invasion of the prerogative of the jury and would defeat the constitutional right of trial by jury to which the plaintiffs are entitled."

(6) Several states have enacted limitations on the number of concurring verdicts which may be set aside as against the weight of the evidence. See Note, Concurring Verdicts as a Limitation Upon Grant of New Trial for Insufficiency of the Evidence, 90 U.Pa.L.Rev. 84 (1941).

B. NEW TRIAL ON LESS THAN ALL THE ISSUES

GASOLINE PRODUCTS CO., INC. v. CHAMPLIN REFINING CO.

Supreme Court of the United States, 1931.
283 U.S. 494, 51 S.Ct. 513, 75 L.Ed. 1188.*

Mr. Justice Stone delivered the opinion of the Court.

Petitioner brought suit in the District Court for Maine, to recover royalties alleged to be due under a contract by which it licensed respondent to use two "Cross cracking units," structures adapted to the use of the "Cross cracking process" for increasing the production of gasoline from crude oil. Respondent pleaded, by way of counterclaim, in two separate counts, a contract by petitioner to construct a "Cross vapor treating tower" for treatment of gasoline, produced by the cracking units, necessary to make it marketable. The consideration for this contract was alleged to be the execution of the license contract already referred to and of two related contracts, one by a third party for the construction of the cracking units, and another by which petitioner guaranteed that they would work. Performance of these contracts is admitted.

Both counts of the counterclaim were based on the same series of transactions. The first alleged a contract arising from an oral proposal by petitioner's vice president in January, 1926, to construct for respondent a Cross vapor system treating tower, the cost of which was to be repaid by respondent to petitioner if the tower functioned in a satisfactory manner. This proposal was alleged to have been accepted by the execution of the other contracts. The second count alleged a written proposal of like tenor by petitioner to respondent, accepted by respondent on February 6, 1926, and confirmed by the later execution of the other contracts. Both counts charged that, by reason of petitioner's failure to construct the treating system, and pending the construction of a substitute system by respondent, the latter was compelled to store large quantities of the cracked gasoline awaiting treatment, resulting in four principal items of damage: The expenses of storage; depreciation of the gasoline by evaporation and other causes; the loss incident to shutting down respondent's plant because of the lack of treating apparatus; and the loss of anticipated profits from the sale of gasoline.

The jury returned a verdict on petitioner's cause of action, and a verdict for respondent on the counterclaim, leaving a balance in petitioner's favor for which the District Court gave judgment. The Court of Appeals for the First Circuit reversed because of errors in the charge of the trial court with respect to the measure of damages on the counterclaim; but, in directing a new trial, it restricted the issues to the

* Footnotes omitted.

determination of damages only. 39 F.(2d) 521, following in this respect its earlier decisions [citations omitted]. This Court granted certiorari . . . to review the single question whether the court below erred in thus limiting the new trial, upon a petition setting up a conflict of the decision with that of the Court of Appeals for the Third Circuit in McKeon v. Central Stamping Co., 264 F. 385. See also, Kean v. National City Bank (C.C.A.) 294 F. 214, 226.

Petitioner contends that the withdrawal from consideration of the jury, upon the new trial, of the issue of liability on the contract set up in the counterclaim, is a denial of its constitutional right to a trial by jury. The Seventh Amendment provides: "In suits at common law, where the value in controversy shall exceed twenty dollars, the right of trial by jury shall be preserved, and no fact tried by a jury shall be otherwise re-examined in any Court of the United States, than according to the rules of the common law." It is argued that as, by the rules of the common law in force when the amendment was adopted, there could be no new trial of a part only of the issues of fact, a resubmission to the jury of the issue of damages alone is a denial of the trial by jury which the amendment guarantees.

It is true that at common law there was no practice of setting aside a verdict in part. If the verdict was erroneous with respect to any issue, a new trial was directed as to all. This continued to be the rule in some states after the adoption of the Constitution; but in many it has not been followed, notwithstanding the presence in their Constitutions of provisions preserving trial by jury. The Massachusetts courts early modified it to permit a new trial of less than all the issues of fact when they were clearly separable. [Citations omitted] The rule as thus modified has been generally accepted in the New England States [citations omitted], and consistently followed by the Court of Appeals for the First Circuit.

Lord Mansfield, in applying the common-law rule where the verdict, correct as to one issue, was erroneous as to another, said: ". . . For form's sake, we must set aside the whole verdict. . . ." Edie v. East India Co., 1 W.Bl. 295, 298. But we are not now concerned with the form of the ancient rule. It is the Constitution which we are to interpret; and the Constitution is concerned, not with form, but with substance. All of vital significance in trial by jury is that issues of fact be submitted for determination with such instructions and guidance by the court as will afford opportunity for that consideration by the jury which was secured by the rules governing trials at common law. See Herron v. Southern Pacific Co., 283 U.S. 91, 51 S.Ct. 383, 75 L.Ed. 857, decided April 13, 1931. Beyond this, the Seventh Amendment does not exact the retention of old forms of procedure. See Walker v. New Mexico & Southern Pacific R. Co., 165 U.S. 593, 596, 17 S.Ct. 421, 41 L.Ed. 837. It does not prohibit the introduction of new methods for ascertaining what facts are in issue (see Ex parte Peterson, 253 U.S. 300, 309, 40 S.Ct. 543, 64 L.Ed. 919), or require that an issue once correctly determined, in accordance with the constitutional command, be tried a second time, even though justice demands that another distinct issue, because erroneously determined, must again be passed on by a jury.

If, in the present case, the jury has found, in accordance with the applicable legal rules, the amount due to petitioner on the contract for royalties and all the elements fixing its liability on the treating plant contract, there is no constitutional requirement that those issues should again be sent to a jury merely because the exigencies of the litigation require that a separable issue be tried again. Such is not the effect of Slocum v. New York Life Insurance Co., 228 U.S. 364, 33 S.Ct. 523, 57 L.Ed. 879, which decided only that an appellate federal court may not direct judgment non obstante veredicto, solely because the verdict given is not sustained by the evidence, but in that event must order a new trial. There it was held that the Seventh Amendment does not permit the entry of judgment on a trial at law before a jury upon an issue of fact, without the verdict of the jury. Here we hold that, where the requirement of a jury trial has been satisfied by a verdict according to law upon one issue of fact, that requirement does not compel a new trial of that issue even though another and separable issue must be tried again.

As the issues arising upon petitioner's cause of action on the royalty contract are clearly separable from all others and the verdict as to them already given is free from error, it need not be disturbed. But the question remains whether the issue of damages is so distinct and independent of the others, arising on the counterclaim, that it can be separately tried. The verdict on the counterclaim may be taken to have established the existence of a contract and its breach. Nevertheless, upon the new trial, the jury cannot fix the amount of damages unless also advised of the terms of the contract; and the dates of formation and breach may be material, since it will be open to petitioner to insist upon the duty of respondent to minimize damages.

But it is impossible from an inspection of the present record to say precisely what were the dates of formation and breach of the contract found by the jury, or its terms. Different dates are alleged in the counterclaim as that of the contract—one, February 6, 1926; the other, the date of final execution of the related contracts, fixed by some of the testimony at March 20th. No date was set for performance, and what the jury, by its verdict, found to be the reasonable time for performance, is not disclosed by the record.

The contract alleged was to construct a single treating tower; but there was a sharp conflict in the testimony as to whether the oral proposal was for one, two, or three towers. To pass on the claim for loss of profits, the jury must know whether the contract to construct was the extent of the undertaking, and, if so, the number of towers to be built, or whether petitioner also agreed that the plant, whatever the number of towers, was to be adequate to treat all gasoline produced by respondent. In addition, the jury must know whether there was a guaranty that the treating system would work satisfactorily, or, if not, whether in fact it would have done so. But the present verdict, awarding as damages on the counterclaim less than the total of the items claimed by respondent, exclusive of alleged loss of profits, cannot be taken as establishing any of these material facts.

Where the practice permits a partial new trial, it may not properly be resorted to unless it clearly appears that the issue to be retried is so distinct and separable from the others that a trial of it alone may be had without injustice. [Citations omitted.] Here the question of damages on the counterclaim is so interwoven with that of liability that the former cannot be submitted to the jury independently of the latter without confusion and uncertainty, which would amount to a denial of a fair trial. See Simmons v. Fish, supra. There should be a new trial of all the issues raised by the counterclaim.

Reversed.

DEVINE v. PATTESON

United States Court of Appeals, Sixth Circuit, 1957.
242 F.2d 828, cert. den. 355 U.S. 821, 2 L.Ed.2d 36.

ALLEN, CIRCUIT JUDGE. . . . The complaint averred that defendant maliciously, intentionally, and without just cause stated to the United States District Attorney that plaintiff had violated certain laws of the United States. At the trial of the malicious prosecution case plaintiff testified that the actual expense to which he was personally subjected in contesting the prosecution, consisting mainly of attorneys' fees and traveling expenses, amounted to over $19,000. This was not disputed. Defendant did not take the stand and no evidence was introduced to the contrary. The jury returned a verdict for plaintiff, allowing compensatory damages in the sum of $500.00 and punitive damages in the sum of $1.00.

*   *   *

Plaintiff's appeal attacks only the amount of the verdict. He contends that, as the jury found defendant liable for malicious prosecution, it was required to consider the elements of damage shown by the uncontradicted testimony as to the extensive legal and traveling expenses incurred in the criminal prosecution. Plaintiff contends that the jury's failure to consider the uncontradicted evidence is so inconsistent with its verdict on liability as to require reversal and a new trial upon that feature of the case as a matter of law.

*   *   *

Since the verdict was less than the amount of the loss shown and not disputed, the motion for new trial should have been granted. We see no essential difference between physical damage suffered in a personal injury case and professional and psychological damage suffered in the trial of a criminal case. While there was controversy as to defendant's liability, there was no controversy as to the necessity of plaintiff's incurring the expenses listed, nor as to the fact that they were actually incurred. The award of $500 was around ¹⁄₄₀ of the actual and specific damages proved and nothing was allowed for the undisputed injury shown to have been suffered by plaintiff in his professional reputation, standing, and loss of practice.

While in general the granting of a new trial is a matter of discretion with the court, it is not so when the verdict is inconsistent on its face. Pugh v. Bluff City Excursion Company [6 Cir., 177 F. 399], supra. The jury found plaintiff was entitled to recover. In view of the undisputed evidence as to expense caused by the wrongful prosecution it is evident that the jury did not comply with the instructions of the court.

As to punitive damages the award is peculiarly within the discretion of the jury. We cannot say that the discretion was abused, and we do not set aside the verdict of $1.00. . . .

The District Court erred in not granting a new trial limited to the question of compensatory damages. Federal Rules of Civil Procedure, rule 59(a), 28 U.S.C.A.; Chesevski v. Strawbridge & Clothier, D.C., 25 F.Supp. 325; Barron and Holtzoff, Federal Practice and Procedure, Vol. 3, § 1304, and § 1307. . . .

A majority of the court thinks it would be unjust to a plaintiff who has proved to the satisfaction of the jury that he was subjected to malicious prosecution to have to retry the question, not only of damages, but also of liability. If the issues are as we think, separate and distinct, conceivably plaintiff might be compelled to pay a second very large amount for legal expenses in order to collect the amounts expended in the first suit. A majority of the court considers that the issue of damages here is entirely separate from other issues presented. If the issue of compensatory damages is retried defendant will have a second opportunity to contest the claimed legal and other expenses which in the instant case he did not contradict. This is not unjust to him nor does it in any way affect the question of liability. Whether plaintiff spent $500, $5,000, or $19,000 in fighting the indictment has no bearing upon whether defendant maliciously and without probable cause secured plaintiff's indictment. The amount of the expense has no probative connection with the issue of liability, hence the issue may be retried singly.

We think this conclusion is in accord with the applicable law. While a new trial should cover the issue of liability as well as of damages if these issues are so interwoven as to be inseparable, we think this case does not call for the application of that rule. The majority of the cases cited in the dissenting opinion are personal injury cases. In this type of controversy, obviously the imponderables arising from cases which present highly emotional features are omnipresent. In a number of the cases cited there was an issue, not only of negligence but of contributory negligence. [Citations omitted.] The Fourth Circuit in Southern Railway Company v. Neese, 216 F.2d 772, held that the issues of damage and liability were separate and distinct. This case was reversed by the Supreme Court, 350 U.S. 77, 76 S.Ct. 131, 100 L.Ed. 60. However, in both decisions, that of the Circuit Court and that of the Supreme Court, the verdict as to liability was sustained.

In the Madden case, [Southern Railway Co. v. Madden, 235 F.2d 198 (4th Cir.1956)], as to the issue of liability the Fourth Circuit found that prejudicial error existed in the admission of testimony and in the charge of the court. Quoting from and following an opinion by Chief Justice Rugg in Simmons v. Fish, 210 Mass. 563, 97 N.E. 102, the court held in effect that it was obvious in the Madden case that no jury had decided the issue of liability against the railway company on "justifiable grounds."

Here defendant's contention as to liability is that the undisputed facts demonstrated the existence of probable cause. This issue was correctly submitted to the jury, which found in favor of the plaintiff and the finding is supported by the record. Reversible error exists only in the amount of the verdict. [Citations omitted.]

The judgment as to compensatory damages is set aside and a new trial is ordered upon that issue only. The judgment in all other respects is affirmed.

MILLER, CIRCUIT JUDGE (dissenting). I am in agreement with the statement in the majority opinion of the general rule that under certain conditions where the issue of damages is entirely separate from the issue of liability, a new trial may be granted limited to the issue of damages only. This Court has so held. Thompson v. Camp, 6 Cir., 167 F.2d 733. But as stated in that case, the court should proceed with caution, with a careful regard for the rights of both parties, and only in those cases where it is plain that the error which has crept into one element of the verdict did not in any way affect the determination of any other issue. The error in that case was an error in the instructions dealing with the question of damages and had no bearing on the issue of liability. In my opinion, the rule is not applicable to the present case.

It is, of course, true as stated in the majority opinion, that as an abstract question of law whether the plaintiff spent $500, $5,000 or $19,000 in fighting the indictment has no bearing upon whether defendant maliciously and without probable cause secured plaintiff's indictment. This would be a complete answer to the issue here involved if the jury followed this principle of law in reaching its verdict. It seems to me that the jury not only refused to follow the law and the evidence on the question of damages, which is the basis of the ruling that a new trial should be granted, but also at the same time refused to follow this principle of law which requires that questions of liability and damage be independently determined. I do not think we can reasonably say with any degree of certainty that the jury refused to follow the law on the question of damages but did follow the law on the question of liability. Verdicts which are obviously compromise verdicts show rather conclusively that as a practical matter, and in disregard of the rule of law to the contrary, the questions of the amount of damages and determination of liability are closely interwoven. This appears to me to be such a case.

It seems clear to me that this was a compromise verdict, that most of the jurors in this case were not in favor of returning a verdict for the plaintiff, and would not have agreed to a verdict for the plaintiff if it would result in awarding to him any substantial amount. If the jury had unanimously been in favor of a verdict for the plaintiff, the amount of the verdict would undoubtedly have been many times greater. The evidence to sustain such an amount was undisputed. There was no reason appearing in the record why as reasonable jurors they would not have followed the evidence on this issue *if* they were satisfied that the defendant wronged the plaintiff as claimed. To me, the obvious answer as to why the verdict was only $500 is not that they failed or refused to follow the evidence on the question of damages, but that most of the jurors were not satisfied that there should be a verdict in any amount against the defendant. With a few jurors strongly favoring a verdict in a substantial amount, and in order to reach a verdict and avoid a new trial those jurors opposed to a verdict for the plaintiff agreed to return a verdict for him if it was limited to a relatively small amount. This appears to me to be a more logical analysis of the verdict than to say that the twelve jurors were unanimously in favor of a verdict for the plaintiff, but arbitrarily refused to follow the law and evidence on the question of damages. In the present case it is at least probable that the questions of liability and the amount of damages were, as a practical matter, so closely interwoven that if a new trial is to be granted, it should be granted in its entirety and not limited to the question of damages only. [Citations omitted.] Unless it *clearly* appears that the issue of damages was distinct and separable from the issue of liability, a new trial on the issue of damages alone should not be granted. Gasoline Products Co. v. Champlin Refining Co., 283 U.S. 494, 500, 51 S.Ct. 513, 75 L.Ed. 1188; [citation omitted].

The point is well illustrated by the case of Bass v. Dehner, D.C., 21 F.Supp. 567, where the Court granted a new trial because the damages were inadequate but refused to limit the new trial to the question of damages only. On the retrial the jury returned a verdict for the defendant. . . .

NOTES

(1) Compromise verdicts can be avoided before the fact by the "split trial" procedure which in negligence suits involves separate trial of the liability issue and, if liability is found, a later trial on the damage issue. The split trial practice had long been used in common law actions wherein defenses such as release or res judicata were pleaded in bar of the action. See, e.g., Schollmeyer v. Sutter, 2 Misc.2d 215, 151 N.Y.S.2d 795 (S.Ct.1956). But see Berner v. British Commonwealth Pacific Airlines, Limited, 346 F.2d 532 (2d Cir.1965) (jury verdict for defendant; two years later judge set aside verdict and granted

judgment for plaintiff as to liability, ordering new trial as to damages only or conditional new trial on all issues if judgment n.o.v. were reversed on appeal; jury assessed damages exceeding $900,000; appellate court reversed judgment n.o.v. and reinstated jury verdict, finding grant of new trial an abuse of discretion). A special local court rule permitting the split practice in personal injury trials to save time and expense of damage proof in the event of a defendant's verdict on liability was adopted in the United States District Court for the Northern District of Illinois in 1959. It was unsuccessfully attacked as an impairment of the right to trial by jury in Hosie v. Chicago & North Western Railroad, 282 F.2d 639 (7th Cir.1960). May a different jury hear the damage proof in the event of a verdict of liability? For a critique of split trials, see Weinstein, Routine Bifurcation of Jury Negligence Trials: An Example of the Questionable Use of Rule Making Power, 14 Vand.L.Rev. 831 (1961). For an article favoring split trials, see Zeisel and Callahan, Split Trials and Time-Saving: A Statistical Analysis, 76 Harv.L.Rev. 1600 (1963).

(2) Dunn v. White, 206 Kan. 278, 479 P.2d 215 (1970). A new trial, limited to the issue of damages only, was ordered when it appeared that the jury had explicitly considered the probability of the defendant's insurance coverage and the size of the plaintiff's attorney's fees. Were the jurors properly permitted to impeach their verdict?

C. CONDITIONAL NEW TRIAL—REMITTITUR AND ADDITUR

GRUNENTHAL v. LONG ISLAND RAILROAD

Supreme Court of United States, 1968.
393 U.S. 156, 89 S.Ct. 331, 21 L.Ed.2d 309.

MR. JUSTICE BRENNAN delivered the opinion of the Court.

Petitioner was working for respondent as foreman of a track gang when a 300-pound railroad tie being lifted by the gang fell and severely crushed his right foot. He sued respondent for damages under the Federal Employers' Liability Act, 35 Stat. 65, as amended, 45 U.S.C.A. § 51 et seq., and a jury in the District Court for the Southern District of New York awarded him $305,000.[1] The trial judge denied the railroad's motion to set the award aside as excessive. The railroad appealed the denial to the Court of Appeals for the Second Circuit, and that court, one judge [Hays] dissenting, ordered the District Court to grant the railroad a new trial unless the petitioner would agree to remit $105,000 of the award. 388 F.2d 480 (1968). We granted certiorari, 391 U.S. 902, 88 S.Ct. 1651, 20 L.Ed.2d 416 (1968).[2] We reverse.

---

1. Petitioner's complaint sought damages of $250,000. This was amended with leave of the trial judge to $305,000 after the jury returned its verdict in that amount. [Some footnotes omitted, others renumbered.]

2. All 11 courts of appeals have held that nothing in the Seventh Amendment precludes appellate review of the trial judge's denial of a motion to set aside an award as excessive.

Petitioner argues that the Court of Appeals exceeded its appellate powers in reviewing the denial of the railroad's motion, either because such review is constitutionally precluded by the provision of the Seventh Amendment that "no fact tried by a jury, shall be otherwise reexamined in any Court of the United States, than according to the rules of the common law," or because such review is prohibited by the Federal Employers' Liability Act itself. We have no occasion in this case to consider that argument, for assuming, without deciding, that the Court of Appeals was empowered to review the denial and invoked the correct standard of review, the action of the trial judge, as we view the evidence, should not have been disturbed. See Neese v. Southern R. Co., 350 U.S. 77, 76 S.Ct. 131, 100 L.Ed. 60 (1955).

The trial judge filed an unreported opinion. [The opinion was subsequently reported at 292 F.Supp. 813 (D.C.S.D.N.Y.1967).] He considered that in deciding the railroad's motion he "must indulge . . . in a fairly accurate estimate of factors to which the jury gave attention, and favorable response, in order to arrive at the verdict announced." He concluded that the motion should be denied because, applying that standard, the relevant evidence weighed heavily in favor of the jury's assessment. His instructions to the jury had limited the items of damages to wages lost before trial, compensation for loss of future earnings, and past and continuing pain and suffering. His opinion detailed the items of evidence which in his view, were sufficient to support the jury in finding that (1) wages lost before trial amounted to approximately $27,000, (2) loss of future wages based on petitioner's present salary of $6,000 per annum plus likely increases over a life expectancy of 27.5 years would amount to $150,000 present value, and (3) "an amount approaching $150,000 [would be appropriate] for plaintiff's pain and suffering—past and future." The judge conceded that the aggregate award seemed generous, but he concluded nevertheless that it was "not generous to a fault or outside the bounds of legal appropriateness." He emphasized that "the trial record here has many unusual features, the most outstanding one being the noncontroversial nature of the defense as to damages. The jury, impressed by the uncontroverted proof adduced by plaintiff, may well have adopted *in toto* its full significance and drawn such normal and natural inferences therefrom as the law endorses."

The Court of Appeals regarded its inquiry as limited to determining whether the trial judge abused his discretion in denying the railroad's motion. Its guide for that determination, the court stated, was the standard of review announced in its earlier decision in Dagnello v. Long Island R. Co., 289 F.2d 797, 806 (1961): "[W]e appellate judges [are not to decide whether we would have set aside the verdict if we were presiding at the trial, but whether the amount is so high that it would be a denial of justice to permit it to stand. We must give the benefit of every doubt to the judgment of the trial judge; but surely there must be an upper limit and whether that has been surpassed is not a question of fact with respect to which reasonable men may differ, but a question of law."

We read *Dagnello*, however, as requiring the Court of Appeals in applying this standard to make a detailed appraisal of the evidence bearing on damages. Indeed this re-examination led to the conclusion in *Dagnello* that it was not a denial of justice to permit the jury's award to stand. If the Court of Appeals made a similar appraisal of the evidence in this case, the details are not disclosed in the majority opinion. Beyond attaching unexplained significance to petitioner's failure in his complaint "to ask for damages in such a large sum as $305,000," the relevant discussion is limited to the bald statement that "giving Grunenthal the benefit of every doubt, and weighing the evidence precisely in the same manner as we did in *Dagnello* . . . we cannot in any rational manner consistent with the evidence arrive at a sum in excess of $200,000." 388 F.2d, at 484. We have therefore made our own independent appraisal of the evidence. We conclude that the trial judge did not abuse his discretion in finding "nothing untoward, inordinate, unreasonable or outrageous—nothing indicative of a runaway jury or one that lost its head."

The liability and damage issues were tried separately before the same jury. The evidence at the trial on damages consisted of stipulated hospital and employment records, a stipulation that petitioner's life expectancy was 27.5 years, and the oral testimony of the petitioner, his medical expert, and an official of his railroad union. The railroad offered no witnesses.

Petitioner was 41 years of age at the time of his injury and had been in the railroad's employ for over 20 years. The railroad concedes in its brief that he was earning approximately $6,000 annually and that the jury could properly find that he was entitled to $27,000 for wages already lost over the four and one-half year period between injury and judgment. The railroad further concedes that an award of $100,000 for loss of future wages would not be improper, this on the premise that invested in federal securities that sum would realize $6,000 annually. The trial judge on the other hand appraised the evidence on future earnings as sufficient to support an award of $150,000 for loss of future wages in light of the "convincing testimony not refuted . . . demonstrating the steady wage increases in recent time for work equivalent to that rendered by plaintiff, and the strong likelihood that similar increases would continue."

We cannot say that the trial judge's view that the jury might properly have awarded $150,000 for loss of future earnings is without support in the evidence. The judge had instructed the jury without objection from the railroad that it was free to find on the evidence that the injury so disabled the petitioner "that it in effect closed out his working career." Although petitioner's medical witness testified that the condition of his foot would not prevent petitioner from engaging in "sedentary work," petitioner's unchallenged evidence of his unsuccessful efforts to obtain and keep jobs of that kind might reasonably have led the jury to decide that petitioner's chances of obtaining or holding any employment were most doubtful. Petitioner testified that his applications for work had often been turned down: "[W]hen they found out I had a bad foot they wouldn't take a chance." On one occasion when he obtained employment as a salesman during the Christmas rush, "I worked there for about four or five days but I couldn't stand it." Moreover, the railroad refused to employ him for any kind of work when he failed a medical examination given him by a railroad physician; after being told, "You failed the medical and we can't take you back," petitioner said he began receiving a "disability pension from the railroad."

Since the jury's award for lost future earnings may properly have been as high as $150,000, its award for pain and suffering might have been as low as $128,000 rather than the $150,000 deemed permissible by the trial judge. In any event we cannot say that the trial judge's opinion that the jury might have awarded the higher $150,000 amount is without support in the record. Petitioner's injury caused his hospitalization at five different times over a period of less than two years. His foot was so badly crushed that serious infection developed. The wounds did not heal properly and skin grafts were made from his right thigh about a year after his injury. Several months later gangrene set in and his doctors were concerned that the "foot was about to die." A sympathectomy was performed, consisting of an incision of the abdomen to reach the spinal column and the sympathetic ganglia along the spine "to remove [the] controls which maintain the closing down of the blood vessels." This operation was successful but six months later petitioner was forced to submit to yet another operation to remove a piece of bone over the ball of the great toe. Petitioner's medical witness testified that there is still a hazard of more surgery because "this is just a mess of bones"—"the metatarsal has been completely crushed"—"the joint is completely lost"—"the overall black appearance of the bone"—"indicates decalcification or demineralization"—"the nourishment to the foot is so bad that the skin shows the unhealthy condition of the foot." Petitioner testified that "I always have a pain, it is like a dull toothache, to this day," and that "I just take it for granted now. It doesn't bother me now." The jury might well have concluded that petitioner suffered and would continue to suffer great pain, although he had learned to live with it. As Judge Hays noted, 388 F.2d, at 485, the trial judge referred to "the total absence of exaggeration" in petitioner's testimony describing "the excruciating physical pain and mental anguish" he had endured since the accident. "On the record here," said the trial judge, "[the jury] had good and sufficient reason to regard and assess [the plaintiff's pain and suffering—past and future] as excruciating, deep-seated, unrelenting and debilitating—the inducing cause of his constant misery."

We therefore conclude that the action of the trial judge should not have been disturbed by the Court of Appeals.

The judgment of the Court of Appeals is reversed and the case is remanded to that court with direction to enter a judgment affirming the judgment of the District Court.

It is so ordered.

Reversed and remanded.

* * *

Mr. Justice Stewart, dissenting.

NOTES

(1) Can the plaintiff conditionally accept the remittitur in the event he is unsuccessful on appeal in attacking it? The Supreme Court has said no. Donovan v. Penn Shipping, 429 U.S. 648, 97 S.Ct. 835, 51 L.Ed.2d 112 (1977). So has the Pennsylvania Supreme Court. Corabi v. Curtis Publishing Co., 437 Pa. 143, 262 A.2d 665 (1970).

The older rule is that the plaintiff, having consented to the reduction, is estopped from questioning it. See, e.g., Woodworth v. Chesbrough, 244 U.S. 79, 37 S.Ct. 583, 61 L.Ed. 1005 (1917); McDaniel v. Hancock, 328 Mich. 78, 43 N.W.2d 68 (1950). New York provides by statute for an appeal by a remitting plaintiff. N.Y.—McKinney's CPLR 5501(a)(5). See Note, Remittitur Practice in the Federal Courts, 76 Colum.L.Rev. 299 (1976). In Plesko v. Milwaukee, 19 Wisc.2d 210, 120 N.W.2d 130, 135 (1963), the court adopted the rule that, if the defendant appeals, the plaintiff may cross-appeal on the amount of damages:

(2) When the plaintiff refuses to accept a remittitur, may judgment be entered in the reduced amount? The Supreme Court of Pennsylvania followed this course in Dornon v. McCarthy, 412 Pa. 595, 195 A.2d 520 (1963). A dissent found the majority's action unprecedented and "constitutionally inhibited." Id. at 601, 195 A.2d at 523. On this decision, see Note in 113 U.Pa.L.Rev. 137 (1964) which doubts the constitutionality of this decision and states that the best justification for the decision is that "[i]f a court may set aside a verdict because it is unreasonable, it should be able to set aside just part of a verdict on the same ground, allowing that part of it which is reasonable to stand." Id. at 140.

(3) Remittitur has been ruled an especially appropriate alternative to a new trial of the whole case in complex and lengthy litigation. United States v. 47.14 Acres of Land, 674 F.2d 722 (8th Cir.1982).

(4) May remittitur be granted on condition that the defendant engage in socially useful activity? In O'Gilvie v. International Playtex, Inc., 821 F.2d 1438 (10th Cir.1987), the verdict on a product liability claim was in the amount of $1,525,000 compensatory damages and $10,000,000 punitive damages. The District Court ordered a remittitur on condition that the defendant stop selling the tampons that the jury had found caused toxic shock syndrome. The appellate court held this an improper use of remittitur.

(5) It has been claimed that huge awards in product liability cases have hurt the competitive position of American companies, and that judges should make greater use of devices like remittitur to keep awards in line, see, e.g., Leebron, Final Moments: Damages for Pain and Suffering Prior to Death, 64 N.Y.U.L.Rev. 256 (1989).

FISCH v. MANGER

Supreme Court of New Jersey, 1957.
24 N.J. 66, 130 A.2d 815.

The opinion of the court was delivered by JACOBS, J.

The plaintiff suffered serious injuries in an automobile accident and, after trial, received a jury verdict in the sum of $3,000. He applied for a new trial because of the inadequacy of the verdict but his application was denied when the defendants consented that the damages awarded to the plaintiff be increased to the sum of $7,500. The plaintiff appealed and we thereafter certified on our own motion.

* * *

The plaintiff's actual expenditures to doctors and nurses and for drugs and hospitalization exceeded $2,200. And although he received most of his normal earnings despite his temporary incapacity, there was a loss of wages approximating $620. While the jury's verdict of $3,000 just about took care of the plaintiff's actual monetary losses, it awarded substantially nothing for his suffering and permanent injuries. Its gross inadequacy was recognized by the trial judge who pointed out that "there was no dispute but that the plaintiff suffered excruciating pain, and was rendered totally helpless for a considerable period of time." On June 28, 1956 the trial judge wrote to the parties advising that unless the defendants filed a consent in writing that the verdict be increased from $3,000 to $7,500 "then the verdict heretofore rendered will be set aside and a new trial granted limited to damages only." The consent was filed by the defendants and on June 30, 1956 a formal order was entered dismissing the plaintiff's motion for a new trial. Though it was unnecessary, the plaintiff obtained leave to appeal from the Appellate Division. [Citations omitted.]

The first point which he urges in support of his appeal is that once the trial court had concluded that the damages awarded by the verdict were inadequate it had no legal power whatever to condition the grant of a new trial upon the defendants' failure to consent to a prescribed increase in the verdict. [Citations omitted.] Much has appeared in the law reviews in support of the practices of *remittitur* and *additur* as enlightened aids in securing substantial justice between the parties without the burdensome costs, delays and harassments of new trials. See Carlin, "Remittiturs and Additurs," 49 W.Va.L.Q. 1 (1942); Note, "Correction of Damage Verdicts by Remittitur and Additur," 44 Yale L.J. 318 (1934); Note, "Additur in California," 40 Cal.L.Rev. 276 (1952); Note, "Additur and Remittitur," 26 Va.L.Rev. 836 (1940). Cf. Millar, "Notabilia of American Civil Procedure," 50 Harv.L.Rev. 1017, 1052 (1937); Scott, Fundamentals of Procedure in Actions at Law 119–131 (1922). The term *remittitur* is used to describe an order denying the defendant's application for new trial on condition that the plaintiff consent to a specified reduction in the jury's award, whereas the term *additur* is used to describe an order denying the plaintiff's application for a new trial on condition that the defendant consent to a specified increase in the jury's award. While it is now recognized that the two practices are logically and realistically indistinguishable, *remittiturs* have been recognized almost everywhere, whereas *additurs* are still outlawed in some, though by no means all, of the states. Compare O'Connor v. Papertsian, 309 N.Y. 465, 131 N.E.2d 883 (1956), where the New York Court of Appeals unanimously sustained an Appellate Division order which denied a new trial upon the defendant's consent to increase the $1,000 awarded by the jury to the sum of $2,500, with Dorsey v. Barba, 38 Cal.2d 350, 240 P.2d 604 (1952), where the Supreme Court of California (with Justice Traynor dissenting) held that although its courts could properly deny new trials upon consents by plaintiffs to reductions, they could not properly do so upon consents by defendants to increases. See 25 Fordham L.Rev. 150 (1956); 31 N.Y.U.L.Q. 1537 (1956); 40 Cal.L.Rev., supra; 10 Wash. & Lee L.Rev. 46 (1953).

The English precedents prior to the American Revolution are somewhat obscure and they are discussed in the majority and minority opinions in Dimick v. Schiedt, 293 U.S. 474, 55 S.Ct. 296, 302, 79 L.Ed. 603 (1935). There Justice Sutherland, speaking for a majority of five (with Justice Stone, joined by Chief Justice Hughes and Justices Brandeis and Cardozo, dissenting) held that although *remittitur* is permissible in the federal courts, *additur* is prohibited by the force of the provision in the Seventh Amendment that "the right to trial by jury shall be preserved, and that no fact tried by a jury shall be otherwise re-examined by any court of the United States, than according to the rules of the common law." In Belt v. Lawes (1884), 12 Q.B. 356, the court sustained the denial of a new trial upon the plaintiff's consent to accept a lesser amount than that awarded by the jury; on appeal, Brett, M.R. not only approved the practice followed below but suggested that the court would also have power "to say that the damages given are too small, but that if the defendant will agree to their being increased to such a sum as may be stated, a new trial shall be refused." Cf. Armytage v. Haley (1843) 4 Q.B. 917, 114 Eng.Rep. 1143. In later case of Watt v. Watt (1905), A.C. 115 the court took an opposite position and rejected the view that a court could condition a denial of a new trial on the plaintiff's acceptance of a reduced verdict. Lord Davey acknowledged that a contrary practice had grown up and that it generally served substantial justice; but he considered that there was a lack of common law power and referred to various judicial dicta to the effect that a jury's award of damages could not be reduced "without the consent of both parties." However, Justice Sutherland in the Dimick case did not follow the result in the Watt case and declined to upset the *remittitur* practice, first approved by Justice Story in Blunt v. Little, 3 Fed.Cas.No. 1,578 (C.C.Mass 1822), and since reaffirmed in many federal decisions. [Citations omitted.]

In his dissenting opinion in the Dimick case, Justice Stone pointed out that the Seventh Amendment was concerned with substance rather than form and that the Supreme Court had often declined to construe it as perpetuating in changeless form the minutiae of trial practice as it existed in the English courts in 1791; he referred to the many jury procedures unknown to the common law but now well established in federal practice; he considered wholly impersuasive the suggested differentiation between the settled *remittitur* practice which the majority continued and the *additur* practice which it rejected; and he concluded with the following remarks (293 U.S. at page 496, 55 S.Ct. at page 305, 79 L.Ed. at page 616):

"Appellate federal courts, although without common-law precedent, have not hesitated to resort to the *remittitur* where, by its use, the necessity of a new trial could justly be avoided. [Citations omitted.] The trial judge who denies a motion for a new trial, because the plaintiff has consented to reduce, or a defendant has consented to increase, the amount of the recovery, does no more than when, sitting in equity, he withholds relief upon the compliance with a condition, the performance of which will do substantial justice. [Citation omitted.]

"To me it seems an indefensible anachronism for the law to reject the like principle of decision, in reviewing on appeal denials of motions for new trial, where the plaintiff has consented to decrease the judgment or the defendant has consented to increase it by the proper amount, or to apply it in the one case and reject it in the other. It is difficult to see upon what principle the denial of a motion for a new trial, which for centuries has been regarded as so much a matter of discretion that it is not disturbed when its only support may be a bad or inadequate reason, may nevertheless be set aside on appeal when it is supported by a good one: That the Defendant has bound himself to pay an increased amount of damages which the court judicially knows is within the limits of a proper verdict."

The majority opinion in *Dimick* has been the subject of much criticism and it is doubtful whether the Supreme Court would still subscribe to it; in any event, the Seventh Amendment differs somewhat from our constitutional provision and has no application to proceedings in our state courts. [Citations omitted.] We must look primarily to our own history and precedents in ascertaining whether the highly desirable practices of *remittitur* and *additur* may be adhered to in our State without infringement of Art. I, par. 9 of the 1947 Constitution.

* * *

. . . [W]e are satisfied that the practices of *remittitur* and *additur* violate none of our constitutional interdictions and, if fairly invoked, serve the laudable purpose of avoiding a further trial where substantial justice may be attained on the basis of the original trial. See Meszaros v. Gransamer, 23 N.J. 179, 128 A.2d 449 (1957). Accordingly, we reject the first point urged by the plaintiff and come now to his meritorious contention that, in any event, the prescribed increase to

$7,500 was "grossly inadequate and should be set aside." Notwithstanding earlier doubts (Nelson v. Eastern Air Lines, Inc., 128 N.J.L. 46, 55, 24 A.2d 371 (E. & A.1941)), there is now no question as to the power of our appellate courts to reverse a trial court's refusal to grant a new trial (whether or not conditioned on *remittitur* or *additur*) where it is satisfied that there has been "an abuse of discretion" (Esposito v. Lazar, supra; Elvin v. Public Service Coordinated Transport, supra), or, in the more modern terminology, " 'a manifest denial of justice.' " [Citations omitted.] In the instant matter, we believe that the trial judge had a mistaken notion of the evidence which led to his prescribing the scanty sum of $7,500. He stated that the plaintiff was not entitled to a "great sum, because he certainly did have a back condition before this accident occurred"; but the evidence in the record points to the view that whatever "back condition" the plaintiff had as a result of the 1950 accident had cleared up and had no relation to the very severe injuries resulting from the 1953 accident. Under these highly special circumstances, we believe that the trial court's action should not be permitted to stand and that the interests of justice will best be served by permitting a second jury to pass on the issue of damages. The separable issue of liability was clearly and properly decided against the defendants; under the evidence it could hardly have been determined otherwise and need not be submitted for redetermination. R.R. 4:61–1; Dahle v. Goodheer [38 N.J.Super. 210, 118 A.2d 547 (App.Div.1955)], supra.

Reversed, with direction for a new trial on the issue of damages.

* * *

HEHER, J. (concurring in result).

* * *

MR. JUSTICE OLIPHANT joins in this opinion.

NOTES

(1) Novak v. Gramm, 469 F.2d 430, 433 (8th Cir.1972) ("rule laid down in *Dimick,* although a close question of law at the time, has since become a firmly entrenched rule").

(2) There is a split of state court authority on the validity of additur. Despite the unfriendly reception given Dimick v. Schiedt in the law reviews, its reasoning was echoed by the California Supreme Court in Dorsey v. Barba, 38 Cal.2d 350, 240 P.2d 604 (1952), noted in 40 Calif.L.Rev. 276 (1952), and the Montana Supreme Court in State Highway Commission v. Schmidt, 143 Mont. 505, 391 P.2d 692 (1964). The Washington court will allow additur "only where there has been no conflict as to the quantum of special damages and the special damages can be computed from the record with certainty." Cox v. Charles Wright Academy, 70 Wn.2d 173, 422 P.2d 515, 519 (1967). See Note, Additur and Remittitur in Federal and State Courts, 3 Cumberland-Samford.L.Rev. 150 (1972); Note, Judgments: New Mexico and The Additur, 2 N.M.L.Rev. 101 (1972); Note, Power of the Trial Court to Grant Additur, 40 Tenn.L.Rev. 753 (1973); Note, Statutory Authorization of Additur and Remittitur, 43 Miss.L.J. 107 (1972).

(3) James & Hazard, Civil Procedure 398, n. 54 (3d ed. 1985), suggests that if the verdict "represents a compromise then the additur is just as inappropriate as a new trial on the damages issue only." Does this criticism apply to remittitur? How does the court know whether the inadequate verdict is the result of a compromise?

(4) For many years Wisconsin followed a unique practice, approved in Campbell v. Sutliff, 193 Wis. 370, 214 N.W. 374 (1927), of combining remittitur and additur in ordering conditional new trials. The trial court might determine the minimum and maximum amounts a properly instructed, unprejudiced jury might return; and customarily gave the defendant 20 days to exercise his option to pay the higher figure; failing which, plaintiff would have 10 days to accept the lower figure; if not, a new trial would be ordered. See Recent Decisions—Appeal—Waiver, 33 Notre Dame Law. 644 (1958). In Powers v. Allstate Insurance Co., 10 Wis.2d 78, 102 N.W.2d 393 (1960), noted 44 Marq.L. Rev. 398 (1961), the practice was rejected, the court holding that in an excessive verdict case the plaintiff should be offered the option of remitting the excess above such sum as the court determined to be the "reasonable amount" of his damages, rather than the minimal amount. Instead of fixing the figure at a "reasonable" amount, should the court on remittitur award plaintiff the "maximum" amount permissible on the theory the jury intended him to have at least that much? See International Paper Co. v. Busby, 182 F.2d 790 (5th Cir.1950).

SECTION 5. WITHDRAWING THE CASE FROM THE JURY

A. DIRECTED VERDICT

Of the means of withdrawing a case from the jury's consideration the directed verdict is the most dramatic and emphatic. Professor Blume, Origin and Development of the Directed Verdict, 48 Mich.L.Rev. 555, 583 (1950), reports the following Texas newspaper item, headlined "Obedient Jury": When a federal judge instructed a jury to return a verdict of innocent in a car theft case, the foreman dutifully announced: "We find the boy that stole that car not guilty, your honor."

It is clear that the purpose of the directed verdict is to prevent lawlessness by the jury—to preempt its nullification of the substantive law. It is also plain that the jury has no constitutional right to disregard the law in reaching a verdict. The problem is to devise a workable definition of the respective roles of the trial judge and the jury. On the surface, the "law-fact" dichotomy offers an appealingly simple standard, but it proves too slippery to handle: courts are fond of saying that the question of whether there is enough evidence to find a particular fact is itself a question of law.

In federal courts the process of taking a case from the jury must square with the jury trial guarantees of the Seventh Amendment. Rule 50 of the Federal Rules of Civil Procedure assumes that directing a verdict is a permissible practice, but it affords no guides for the trial judge's exercise of the power. The cases too are spectacularly devoid of a satisfactory standard, though not for lack of dealing with the question. State procedural codes and court decisions have been no more successful in articulating a reliable guide. Is the effort hopeless? In New York, the view is that "attempts to delineate by statute the court's power to direct a verdict have confused rather than clarified the problem." Second Preliminary Report, Advisory Committee on Practice and Procedure, N.Y.Leg.Doc. No. 13, 305–308 (1958).

GALLOWAY v. UNITED STATES

Supreme Court of the United States, 1943.
319 U.S. 372, 63 S.Ct. 1077, 87 L.Ed. 1458.

MR. JUSTICE RUTLEDGE delivered the opinion of the Court.*

Petitioner seeks benefits for total and permanent disability by reason of insanity he claims existed May 31, 1919. On that day his policy of yearly renewable term insurance lapsed for nonpayment of premium.[1]

The suit was filed June 15, 1938. At the close of all the evidence, the District Court granted the Government's motion for a directed verdict. Judgment was entered accordingly. The Circuit Court of Appeals affirmed. 9 Cir., 130 F.2d 467. Both courts held the evidence legally insufficient to sustain a verdict for petitioner. He says this was erroneous and, in effect, deprived him of trial by jury, contrary to the Seventh Amendment.

[The majority's detailed analysis of the evidence has been omitted. It stressed that petitioner, who claimed incipient insanity before the decisive date of May 13, 1919, that matured into complete insanity in subsequent years, had failed to introduce evidence of his condition in a period of some eight years in which he married, and concluded that, as a consequence, there was insufficient evidence on which to base the required finding of mental disability.]

* Some footnotes omitted; others renumbered.

1. The contract was issued pursuant to the War Risk Insurance Act and insured against death or total permanent disability. (Act of Oct. 6, 1917, c. 105, § 400, 40 Stat. 398, 409.) Pursuant to statutory authority (Act of May 20, 1918, c. 77, § 13, 40 Stat. 555), T.D. 20 W.R., promulgated March 9, 1918, provided:

"Any impairment of mind or body which renders it impossible for the disabled person to follow continuously any substantially gainful occupation shall be deemed . . . to be total disability.

"Total disability shall be deemed to be permanent whenever it is founded upon conditions which render it reasonably certain that it will continue throughout the life of the person suffering from it. . . ." (Regulations and Procedure, U.S. Veterans Bureau, Part I, p. 9.) [Some footnotes have been omitted; others have been renumbered.]

I.

Certain facts are undisputed. Petitioner worked as a longshoreman in Philadelphia and elsewhere prior to enlistment in the Army November 1, 1917. . . .

* * *

Petitioner concededly is now totally and permanently disabled by reason of insanity and has been for some time prior to institution of this suit. It is conceded also that he was sound in mind and body until he arrived in France in April, 1918.

The theory of his case is that the strain of active service abroad brought on an immediate change, which was the beginning of a mental breakdown that has grown worse continuously through all the later years. Essential in this is the view it had become a total and permanent disability not later than May 31, 1919.

The evidence to support this theory falls naturally into three periods, namely, that prior to 1923; the interval from then to 1930; and that following 1930. It consists in proof of incidents occurring in France to show the beginnings of change; testimony of changed appearance and behavior in the years immediately following petitioner's return to the United States as compared with those prior to his departure; the medical evidence of insanity accumulated in the years following 1930; and finally the evidence of a physician, given largely as medical opinion, which seeks to tie all the other evidence together as foundation for the conclusion, expressed as of 1941, that petitioner's disability was total and permanent as of a time not later than May of 1919.

* * *

[The description of testimony of witnesses as to petitioner's conduct in the first period has largely been omitted.]

Dr. Wilder was the key witness. He disclaimed specializing in mental disease, but qualified as having given it "special attention."* He first saw petitioner shortly before the trial, and examined him "several times." He concluded petitioner's ailment "is a schizophrenic branch or form of praecox." Dr. Wilder heard the testimony and read the depositions of the other witnesses, and examined the documentary

---

* The court relied upon cross-examination. In qualifying the witness as an expert the record indicates (record on appeal p. 60):

"Q. Doctor, since leaving medical college what experience have you had from the standpoint of neuro-psychiatry?

"A. Well, my first service was at the Napa State Hospital; that was in nineteen hundred one, two and three. In 1903 I was licensed by the State Commission of Lunacy, as the law required in this State at that time—I was licensed to advise superior judges about commitments to the Asylum, and I served under that authorization until the law was changed, the old Commission of Lunacy was abolished. I have been called by superior judges ever since for thirty-five years. I have been qualified as an expert of the Superior Courts of half a dozen of our counties here, and qualified in the District Court, Federal Court here on a number of cases.

"Q. As a psychiatrist?

"A. Yes sir." [Footnote added.]

evidence. Basing his judgment upon this material, with inferences drawn from it, he concluded petitioner was born with "an inherent instability," though he remained normal until he went to France; began there "to be subjected to the strain of military life, then he began to go to pieces." In May, 1919, petitioner "was still suffering from the acuteness of the breakdown . . . He is going down hill still, but the thing began with the breakdown . . . ." Petitioner was "definitely insane, yes, sir," in 1920 and "has been insane at all times, at least since July, 1918, the time of this episode on the Marne"; that is, "to the point that he was unable to adapt himself. I don't mean he has not had moments when he could not [sic] perform some routine tasks," but "from an occupational standpoint . . . he has been insane." He could follow "a mere matter of routine," but would have no incentive, would not keep a steady job, come to work on time, or do anything he didn't want to do. Dr. Wilder pointed to petitioner's work record before he entered the service and observed: "At no time after he went into the war do we find him able to hold any kind of a job. He broke right down." He explained petitioner's enlistment in the Navy and later in the Army by saying, "It would have been no trick at all *for a man who was reasonably conforming* to get into the Service." (Emphasis added.)

However, the witness knew "nothing whatever except his getting married" about petitioner's activities between 1925 and 1930, and what he knew of them between 1922 and 1925 was based entirely on O'Neill's testimony and a paper not of record here. Dr. Wilder at first regarded knowledge concerning what petitioner was doing between 1925 and 1930 as not essential. "We have a continuing disease, quite obviously beginning during his military service, and quite obviously continuing in 1930, and *the minor incidents* don't seem to me—" (Emphasis added.) Counsel for the government interrupted to inquire, "Well, if he was continuously employed for eight hours a day from 1925 to 1930 would that have any bearing?" The witness replied, "It would have a great deal." Upon further questioning, however, he reverted to his first position, stating it would not be necessary or helpful for him to know what petitioner was doing from 1925 to 1930: "I testified from the information I had."

* * *

We have then the two incidents in France, followed by O'Neill's testimony of petitioner's changed condition in 1919 and its continuance to 1922. There is also the testimony of Commander Platt and Lt. Col. James E. Matthews as to his service in the Navy and the Army, respectively, during 1920–1922. Neither thought petitioner was insane or that his conduct indicated insanity. Then follows a chasm of eight years. The only evidence [2] we have concerning this period is the fact that petitioner married his present guardian at some time within it, an act from which in the legal sense no inference of insanity can be drawn.

---

2. Apart from O'Neill's vague recollection of petitioner's return to Philadelphia on one occasion.

*   *   *

Inference is capable of bridging many gaps. But not, in these circumstances, one so wide and deep as this. Knowledge of petitioner's activities and behavior from 1922 or 1925 to 1930 was peculiarly within his ken and that of his wife, who has litigated this cause in his and presumably, though indirectly, in her own behalf. His was the burden to show continuous disability. What he did in this time, or did not do, was vital to his case. Apart from the mere fact of his marriage, the record is blank for five years and almost blank for eight. For all that appears, he may have worked full time and continuously for five and perhaps for eight, with only a possible single interruption.

No favorable inference can be drawn from the omission. It was not one of oversight or inability to secure proof. That is shown by the thoroughness with which the record was prepared for all other periods, before and after this one, and by the fact petitioner's wife, though she married him during the period and was available, did not testify. The only reasonable conclusion is that petitioner, or those who acted for him, deliberately chose, for reasons no doubt considered sufficient (and which we do not criticize, since such matters, including tactical ones, are for the judgment of counsel), to present no evidence or perhaps to withhold evidence readily available concerning this long interval, and to trust to the genius of expert medical inference and judicial laxity to bridge this canyon.

In the circumstances exhibited, the former is not equal to the feat, and the latter will not permit it. . . .

*   *   *

Finally, the objection appears to be directed generally at the standards of proof judges have required for submission of evidence to the jury. But standards, contrary to the objection's assumption, cannot be framed wholesale for the great variety of situations in respect to which the question arises. Nor is the matter greatly aided by substituting one general formula for another. It hardly affords help to insist upon "substantial evidence" rather than "some evidence" or "any evidence," or vice versa. The matter is essentially one to be worked out in particular situations and for particular types of cases. Whatever may be the general formulation, the essential requirement is that mere speculation be not allowed to do duty for probative facts, after making due allowance for all reasonably possible inferences favoring the party whose case is attacked. The mere difference in labels used to describe this standard, whether it is applied under the demurrer to the evidence or on motion for a directed verdict, cannot amount to a departure from "the rules of the common law" which the Amendment requires to be followed. If there is abuse in this respect, the obvious remedy is by correction on appellate review.

*   *   *

Accordingly, the judgment is affirmed.

MR. JUSTICE BLACK, with whom MR. JUSTICE DOUGLAS and MR. JUSTICE MURPHY concur, dissenting:

The Seventh Amendment to the Constitution provides:

"In suits at common law, where the value in controversy shall exceed twenty dollars, the right of trial by jury shall be preserved, and no fact tried by a jury shall be otherwise re-examined in any Court of the United States, than according to the rules of the common law."

The Court here re-examines testimony offered in a common law suit, weighs conflicting evidence, and holds that the litigant may never take this case to a jury. The founders of our government thought that trial of fact by juries rather than by judges was an essential bulwark of civil liberty. For this reason, among others, they adopted Article III, § 2 of the Constitution, and the Sixth and Seventh Amendments. Today's decision marks a continuation of the gradual process of judicial erosion which in one-hundred-fifty years has slowly worn away a major portion of the essential guarantee of the Seventh Amendment.

I.

[The opinion here discusses the history of the Seventh Amendment.]

In 1789, juries occupied the principal place in the administration of justice. They were frequently in both criminal and civil cases the arbiters not only of fact but of law. . . .

The principal method by which judges prevented cases from going to the jury in the Seventeenth and Eighteenth Centuries was by the demurrer to the evidence, under which the defendant at the end of the trial admitted all facts shown by the plaintiff as well as all inferences which might be drawn from the facts, and asked for a ruling of the Court on the "law of the case." . . . The power of federal judges to comment to the jury on the evidence gave them additional influence. [Citation omitted.] The right of involuntary non-suit of a plaintiff, which might have been used to expand judicial power at jury expense was at first denied federal courts. [Citations omitted.]

As Hamilton had declared in The Federalist, the basic judicial control of the jury function was in the court's power to order a new trial.[3] In 1830, this Court said: "The only modes known to the common law to re-examine such facts, are the granting of a new trial by the court where the issue was tried, or to which the record was properly returnable; or the award of a *venire facias de novo,* by an appellate court, for some error of law which intervened in the proceedings." Parsons v. Bedford [28 U.S. (3 Pet.), 433, 7 L.Ed. 732], supra, at 448.[4]

3. A method used in early England of reversal of a jury verdict by the process of attaint which required a review of the facts by a new jury of twenty-four and resulted in punishment of the first jury for its error, had disappeared. Plucknett, A Concise History of the Common Law (2d ed.), 121.

4. It is difficult to describe by any general proposition the circumstances under which a new trial would be allowed under early practice, since each case was so de-

That retrial by a new jury rather than factual reevaluation by a court is a constitutional right of genuine value was restated as recently as Slocum v. New York Life Insurance Co., 228 U.S. 364, 33 S.Ct. 523, 57 L.Ed. 879, Ann.Cas.1914D, 1029.

A long step toward the determination of fact by judges instead of by juries was the invention of the directed verdict.[5] In 1850, what seems to have been the first directed verdict case considered by this Court, Parks v. Ross, 11 How. 362, was presented for decision. The Court held that the directed verdict serves the same purpose as the demurrer to the evidence, and that since there was "no evidence whatever" [6] on the critical issue in the case, the directed verdict was approved. The decision was an innovation, a departure from the traditional rule restated only fifteen years before in Greenleaf v. Birth, 9 Pet. 292, 299 (1835), in which this Court had said: "Where there is no evidence tending to prove a particular fact, the court are bound so to instruct the jury, when requested; but they cannot legally give any instruction which shall take from the jury the right of weighing the evidence and determining what effect it shall have."

This new device contained potentialities for judicial control of the jury which had not existed in the demurrer to the evidence. In the first place, demurring to the evidence was risky business, for in so doing

---

pendent on its peculiar facts. The early Pennsylvania rule was put as follows: "New trials are frequently necessary, for the purpose of attaining complete justice; but the important right of trial by jury requires they should never be granted without solid and substantial reasons; otherwise the province of jurymen might be often transferred to the judges and *they* instead of the jury, would become the real triers of the facts. A reasonable doubt, barely, that justice has not been done, especially in cases where the value or importance of the cause is not great, appears to me to be too slender a ground for them. But, whenever it appears with a reasonable certainty, that actual and manifest injustice is done, or that the jury have proceeded on an evident mistake, either in point of law, or fact, or contrary to strong evidence, or have grossly misbehaved themselves, or given extravagant damages; the Court will always give an opportunity, by a new trial, of rectifying the mistakes of the former jury, and of doing complete justice to the parties." Cowperthwaite v. Jones, Phila.Ct.Cmn.Pleas 1790, 2 Dall. 55, 1 L.Ed. 287. . . . The number of new trials permitted in a given case were usually limited to two or three; see e.g. Louisville & N.R. Co. v. Woodson, 134 U.S. 614, 10 S.Ct. 628, 33 L.Ed. 1032. The power of the judge was thus limited to his authority to return the case to a new jury for a new decision.

5. I do not mean to minimize other forms of judicial control. In a summary of important techniques of judicial domination of the jury, Thayer lists the following: control by the requirement of a "reasonable judgment"—i.e., one satisfactory to the judge; control of the rules of "presumption," cf. the dissenting opinion in New York Life Insurance Co. v. Gamer, 303 U.S. 161, 172, 58 S.Ct. 500, 503, 82 L.Ed. 726, 114 A.L.R. 1218; the control of the "definition of language"; the control of rules of practice, and forms of pleading ("It is remarkable how judges and legislatures in this country are unconsciously travelling back towards the old result of controlling the jury, by requiring special verdicts and answers to specific questions. Logic and neatness of legal theory have always called loud, at least in recent centuries, for special verdict. . . . Considerations of policy have called louder for leaving to the jury a freer hand." 218); the control of "mixed questions of law and fact"; the control of factual decisions by appellate courts. Thayer on Evidence (1898 ed.) p. 208 et seq.

6. Counsel seeking the directed verdict said: "This prerogative of the court is never exercised, but in cases where the evidence is so indefinite and unsatisfactory, that nothing but wild, irrational conjecture, or licentious speculation, could induce the jury to pronounce the verdict which is sought at their hands." Parks v. Ross, supra, 11 How. at 372, 13 L.Ed. 730.

the party not only admitted the truth of all the testimony against him but also all reasonable inferences which might be drawn from it; and upon joinder in demurrer the case was withdrawn from the jury while the court proceeded to give final judgment either for or against the demurrant. [Citations omitted.] Imposition of this risk was no mere technicality; for by making withdrawal of a case from the jury dangerous to the moving litigant's cause, the early law went far to assure that facts would never be examined except by a jury. Under the directed verdict practice, the moving party takes no such chance, for if his motion is denied, instead of suffering a directed verdict against him, his case merely continues into the hands of the jury. The litigant not only takes no risk by a motion for a directed verdict, but in making such a motion gives himself two opportunities to avoid the jury's decision; for under the federal variant of judgment notwithstanding the verdict, the judge may reserve opinion on the motion for a directed verdict and then give judgment for the moving party after the jury has formally found against him. In the second place, under the directed verdict practice the courts soon abandoned the "admission of all facts and reasonable inferences" standard referred to, and created the so-called "substantial evidence" rule which permitted directed verdicts even though there was far more evidence in the case than a plaintiff would have needed to withstand a demurrer.

The substantial evidence rule did not spring into existence immediately upon the adoption of the directed verdict device. For a few more years [7] federal judges held to the traditional rule that juries might pass finally on facts if there was "any evidence" to support a party's contention. The rule that a case must go to the jury unless there was "no evidence" was completely repudiated in Improvement Co. v. Munson, 1971, 14 Wall. 442, 447, 448, 20 L.Ed. 867, upon which the Court today relies in part. There the Court declared that "some" evidence was not enough—there must be evidence sufficiently persuasive to the judge so that he thinks "a jury can properly proceed." The traditional rule was given an ugly name, "the scintilla rule," to hasten its demise. For a time, traces of the old formula remained, as in Randall v. B. & O. R. Co., 109 U.S. 478, 3 S.Ct. 322, 27 L.Ed. 1003, but the new spirit prevailed. See for example Pleasants v. Fant [89 U.S. (22 Wall.) 116, 22 L.Ed. 780 (1874)], supra, and Commissioners of Marion County v. Clark, 94 U.S. 278, 4 Otto 278, 24 L.Ed. 59. The same transition from jury supremacy to jury subordination through judicial decisions took place in state courts.

Later cases permitted the development of added judicial control.[8] New and totally unwarranted formulas, which should surely be eradicated from the law at the first opportunity, were added as recently as

---

7. In the period of the Civil War, the formula changed slightly but its effect was the same—if the evidence so much as "tended to prove the position" of the party, the case was for the jury. [Citations omitted.]

8. One additional device was the remittitur practice which gives the court a method of controlling jury findings as to damages. [Citation omitted.]

1929 in Gunning v. Cooley, 281 U.S. 90, 50 S.Ct. 231, 74 L.Ed. 720, which, by sheerest dictum, made new encroachments on the jury's constitutional functions. There it was announced that a judge might weigh the evidence to determine whether he, and not the jury, thought it was "overwhelming" for either party, and then direct a verdict. Cf. Pence v. United States, 316 U.S. 332, 340, 62 S.Ct. 1080, 86 L.Ed. 1510. Gunning v. Cooley, 281 U.S. at 94, 50 S.Ct. at page 233, 74 L.Ed. 720, also suggests quite unnecessarily for its decision, that "When a plaintiff produces evidence that is consistent with an hypothesis that the defendant is not negligent, and also with one that he is, his proof tends to establish neither." This dictum, which assumes that a judge can weigh conflicting evidence with mathematical precision and which wholly deprives the jury of the right to resolve that conflict, was applied in Pennsylvania Railroad Co. v. Chamberlain, 288 U.S. 333, 53 S.Ct. 391, 77 L.Ed. 819. With it, and other tools, jury verdicts on disputed facts have been set aside or directed verdicts authorized so regularly as to make the practice commonplace, while the motion for directed verdict itself has become routine. [Citations omitted.]

Even Gunning v. Cooley, 281 U.S. at 94, 50 S.Ct. at page 233, 74 L.Ed. 720, acknowledged that "issues that depend on the credibility of witnesses . . . are to be decided by the jury".[9] Today the Court comes dangerously close to weighing the credibility of a witness and rejecting his testimony because the majority do not believe it.

The story thus briefly told depicts the constriction of a constitutional civil right and should not be continued. Speaking of an aspect of this problem, a contemporary writer saw the heart of the issue: "Such a reversal of opinion [as that of a particular state court concerning the jury function], if it were isolated, might have little significance, but when many other courts throughout the country are found to be making the same shift and to be doing so despite the provisions of statutes and constitutions there is revealed one aspect of that basic conflict in the legal history of America—the conflict between the people's aspiration for democratic government, and the judiciary's desire for the orderly supervision of public affairs by judges."

The language of the Seventh Amendment cannot easily be improved by formulas. The statement of a district judge in Tarter v. United States, D.C., 17 F.Supp. 691, 692, 693, represents, in my opinion, the minimum meaning of the Seventh Amendment:

"The Seventh Amendment to the Constitution guarantees a jury trial in law cases, where there is substantial evidence to support the claim of the plaintiff in an action. If a single witness testifies to a fact

9. In Ewing Lessee v. Burnet, 11 Pet. 41, 51, 9 L.Ed. 624 this Court said: "It was also their [the jury's] province to judge of the credibility of the witnesses, and the weight of their testimony, as tending, in a greater or less degree, to prove the facts relied on; as these were matters with which the court could not interfere, the plaintiff's right to the instruction asked, must depend upon the opinion of the court, on a finding by the jury in favour of the defendant, on every matter which the evidence conduced to prove; giving full credence to the witnesses produced by him, and discrediting the witness for the plaintiff."

sustaining the issue between the parties, or if reasoning minds might reach different conclusions from the testimony of a single witness, one of which would substantially support the issue of the contending party, the issue must be left to the jury. Trial by jury is a fundamental guaranty of the rights of the people, and judges should not search the evidence with meticulous care to deprive litigants of jury trials."

The call for the true application of the Seventh Amendment is not to words, but to the spirit of honest desire to see that constitutional right preserved. Either the judge or the jury must decide facts and, to the extent that we take this responsibility, we lessen the jury function. Our duty to preserve this one of the Bill of Rights may be peculiarly difficult, for here it is our own power which we must restrain. We should not fail to meet the expectation of James Madison, who, in advocating the adoption of the Bill of Rights, said: "Independent tribunals of justice will consider themselves in a peculiar manner the guardians of those rights; . . . they will be naturally led to resist every encroachment upon rights expressly stipulated for in the Constitution by the declaration of right." So few of these cases come to this Court that, as a matter of fact, the judges of the District Courts and the Circuit Courts of Appeals are the primary custodians of the Amendment. As for myself, I believe that a verdict should be directed, if at all, only when, without weighing the credibility of the witnesses, there is in the evidence no room whatever for honest difference of opinion over the factual issue in controversy. I shall continue to believe that in all other cases a judge should, in obedience to the command of the Seventh Amendment, not interfere with the jury's function. Since this is a matter of high constitutional importance, appellate courts should be alert to insure the preservation of this constitutional right even though each case necessarily turns on its peculiar circumstances.

*   *   *

All of this evidence, if believed, showed a man, healthy and normal before he went to the war, suffering for several years after he came back from a disease which had the symptoms attributed to schizophrenia and who was insane from 1930 until his trial. Under these circumstances, I think that the physician's testimony of total and permanent disability by reason of continuous insanity from 1918 to 1938 was reasonable. The fact that there was no direct testimony for a period of five years, while it might be the basis of fair argument to the jury by the Government, does not, as the Court seems to believe, create a presumption against the petitioner so strong that his case must be excluded from the jury entirely. Even if during these five years the petitioner was spasmodically employed, we could not conclude that he was not totally and permanently disabled. Berry v. United States, 312 U.S. 450, 455, 61 S.Ct. 637, 639, 85 L.Ed. 945. It is not doubted that schizophrenia is permanent even though there may be a momentary appearance of recovery.

*   *   *

NOTES

(1) Compare the test for directing a verdict in *Galloway* with the standard announced in Equitable Life Assurance Society v. Fry, 386 F.2d 239, 245 (1967): "[A] fact issue must be submitted to the jury if reasonable men could differ on the conclusions reached from the evidence presented." Are these standards dependent on the scope of the Seventh Amendment's guarantee of trial by jury?

(2) Comment, Directed Verdicts and the Right To Trial by Jury in Federal Courts, 42 Tex.L.Rev. 1053, 1060, 1063 (1964):

> "Much of the confusion with respect to the test for directed verdicts in federal court appears to result from an effort to state in precise language a notion which is not susceptible of exact formulation. The difficulties, however, are not wholly linguistic . . . [T]he critical issue is one of policy, and not merely a task of elucidating the meaning of language defining when a directed verdict is proper. Should the federal courts favor greater discretion and determination by the court of disputed fact issues, or should the parties be given the benefit of a more liberal construction of the seventh amendment and thereby greater latitude for the jury to determine disputed fact issues?"

BURNS, ADMINISTRATRIX v. PENN CENTRAL CO.

United States Court of Appeals, Second Circuit, 1975.
519 F.2d 512.

SMITH, CIRCUIT JUDGE: Teresa M. Burns, widow of George V. Burns and administratrix of her deceased husband's estate, appeals from the judgment of the United States District Court for the Southern District of New York, Whitman Knapp, Judge, dismissing her action for the wrongful death of her husband during the performance of his duties as a trainman for the Penn Central Company. This suit authorized by the Federal Employers' Liability Act, 45 U.S.C. §§ 51–60, was tried before a jury but, following the jury's inability to agree upon a verdict, Judge Knapp ultimately determined that the defendant was entitled to judgment as a matter of law and granted the railroad's motion for a directed verdict. We conclude that the evidence offered at trial by the plaintiff was sufficient for purposes of the FELA to entitle her to a final adjudication of her claim by a jury and therefore reverse the judgment of the district court and remand for a new trial.

On March 15, 1969, the decedent Burns, a longtime employee of the defendant, was working as a brakeman on a passenger run which passed over the 138th Street Bridge in Manhattan and, en route downtown, stopped to load and unload passengers at a station on 125th Street. As was customary for trainmen to do on this run, Burns opened the side and then trapdoor of one of the cars once the train had passed over the 138th Street Bridge. This action prepared the train for the entrance and departure of passengers at the 125th Street station. To prevent, as prescribed by company rules, attempts by passengers to board or leave the train between stations, Burns followed the also customary practice of assuming a position on the bottom step in the open doorway. With the train slowly approaching the 125th Street station, a rifle shot from the vicinity of 128th Street found Burns in this exposed posture and killed him instantaneously. Unbeknown to Burns and the other employees on the train, there had in the last ten months been four stonings of passenger cars within three blocks of the site of Burns' slaying and an additional four stonings within 25 blocks. The defendant's records, however, evidence its knowledge of these stonings. Whether, in light of this knowledge of the stonings and the general conditions in the Harlem area, the defendant was obliged to take measures to ensure that its employees were not, as Burns in fact was, unwittingly victimized is the subject of the complaint under review.

As early as 1955, Judge Jerome Frank was able to observe that "the more recent Supreme Court decisions make it clear that, under that Act [the FELA], the jury's power to draw inferences is greater than in common-law actions." Cahill v. New York, New Haven & Hartford R.R., 224 F.2d 637, 640 (2d Cir.1955) (Frank, J., dissenting), rev'd, 350 U.S. 898, 76 S.Ct. 180, 100 L.Ed. 790, reh. den. 350 U.S. 943, 100 L.Ed. 823 (per curiam), order of reversal recalled and amended, case remanded, 351 U.S. 183, 76 S.Ct. 758, 100 L.Ed. 1075 (1956) (per curiam). Two years later the Supreme Court set forth the test for FELA claims to go to a jury in a manner which left little doubt that Judge Frank's characterization was right:

> Under this statute the test of a jury case is simply whether the proofs justify with reason the conclusion that employer negligence played *any* part, *even the slightest,* in producing the injury or death for which damages are sought.

Rogers v. Missouri Pacific R.R., 352 U.S. 500, 506, 77 S.Ct. 443, 1 L.Ed. 2d 493 (1957) reh. den. 353 U.S. 943, 77 S.Ct. 459, 1 L.Ed.2d 515 (emphasis added). In Gallick v. Baltimore & Ohio R.R., 372 U.S. 108, 83 S.Ct. 659, 9 L.Ed.2d 618 (1963), the Court then offered a compelling and memorable illustration of the breadth of the applicable test by upholding a verdict allowing a railroad crew foreman to recover for serious injury sustained as the result of a bite by an insect which the jury could infer had come from or been attracted by a fetid pool which the jury could infer the railroad company had been negligent to maintain.

In the instant case, the defendant maintains, and the district court agreed, that there was no negligence because the injury was not foreseeable. As *Gallick*, supra, attests, foreseeability of harm is no less a matter generally left to the jury's broad decision than any other part of the requisite proof to recover under the FELA. Furthermore, although the criminal nature of the act causing injury may well bear on the jury's assessment of the defendant's ability to foresee that injury of this type might result from its acts or omissions, a jury is not constrained to find that harm caused by a third party's unlawful conduct was not foreseeable. See Lillie v. Thompson, 322 U.S. 459, 68 S.Ct. 140, 92 L.Ed. 73 (1947) (per curiam) (cause of action under FELA stated by complaint alleging negligence in providing plaintiff telegraph operator assaulted in office by late-night intruder with inadequately lit and unguarded place of employment). At the outset, then, we dismiss any suggestions that the issue framed by this case in any way summoned greater intervention by the trial court than typically sanctioned in FELA cases.

Thus, unless, as in Inman v. Baltimore & Ohio R.R., 361 U.S. 138, 140, 80 S.Ct. 242, 4 L.Ed.2d 198 (1959) (flagman killed by drunken motorist at well-lit intersection with all regular railroad crossing signals in working order and no record of similar accidents at site), "the evidence here was so thin that, on a judicial appraisal, the conclusion must be drawn that negligence on the part of the railroad could have played no part in petitioner's [here, decedent's] injury," the district court's decision that a jury verdict was dispensable was contrary to established law. Plainly, in the instant case, the evidence offered by the plaintiff to support a jury finding that the defendant could have foreseen the type of injury incurred and therefore was negligent in the fulfillment of its duties to its employee under the FELA was not so miniscule as to compel such a conclusion. Based on the railroad's actual knowledge of stonings in the vicinity in recent months and its constructive (and indubitably actual) knowledge of the generally dangerous conditions prevailing in the neighborhood in which the fatality transpired, the jury would have acted well within its authority under the FELA by returning a verdict for Mrs. Burns. In view of governing Supreme Court precedent, then, the judgment for the defendant railroad must be reversed.

Nor does a recent decision of this court, Hartel v. Long Island R.R., 476 F.2d 462 (2d Cir.1973), cert. den., 414 U.S. 980, 94 S.Ct. 273, 38 L.Ed.2d 224, require, as the district court erroneously assumed, a different result. The case is easily distinguished in light of its peculiar facts. A ticket agent for the railroad arrived at the Mineola station, where he regularly worked, to be met by three men intent on holding him up. In attempting to flee, Hartel was shot and killed. His widow then sought to recover a damages award against the railroad under the FELA. In order to prove that the assault suffered by her husband was actually, or reasonably should have been, foreseen by the railroad, Mrs. Hartel sought to introduce into evidence proof that in the past four years there had been ten robberies or attempted robberies at stations run by the defendant within approximately 5–30 miles of the Mineola station. The district court refused to allow this proof, Hartel v. Long Island R.R., 356 F.Supp. 1192 (S.D.N.Y.1972), aff'd 476 F.2d 462 (1974), cert. den. 414 U.S. 980, 94 S.Ct. 273, 38 L.Ed.2d 224, and a divided panel of this court upheld the district court's ruling on the ground that the prior incidents offered to establish the defendant's ability to foresee Hartel's misfortune did not occur at the "exact locus of the incident giving rise to the litigation." Hartel v. Long Island R.R., supra, 476 F.2d 462 at 464. In contrast, in the instant case, the evidence of the recent stonings was obviously relevant to the jury's assessment of foreseeability because those incidents occurred at "substantially the same place" as the one prompting the litigation under review. See Cahill v. New York, New Haven & Hartford R.R., 236 F.2d 410, 411 (2d Cir.1956) (per curiam), cert. den. 352 U.S. 972, 77 S.Ct. 362, 1 L.Ed.2d 325 (1957), (cited approvingly in *Hartel,* supra, 476 F.2d 462 at 464). Mrs. Burns is entitled, then, nothing in *Hartel* to the contrary, to a jury verdict premised upon a record including proof of incidents of a similar nature within recent months transpiring in the general vicinity of the accident.[1]

Finally, with regard to a question raised below which may recur on remand, we reject the appellant's suggestion that she is entitled to have the jury consider possible contributory negligence on the decedent's part regardless of the proof on that issue. Judge Knapp ruled in the course of the trial that Mr. Burns was not contributorily negligent as a matter of law. Though one might have thought that the appellant would welcome such a ruling, she contests it on the assumption that a jury will be more willing to bring in a verdict for the plaintiff if it is able to assess a lesser damages award than full compensation for the wrongful death would entail. Thus, by finding Mr. Burns contributorily negligent to some degree, the jury could, in calculating damages under the comparative negligence formula applicable in FELA actions, adjust the *ad damnum* to a sum with which it would be more comfortable. In simplest terms, the appellant would like a trial in which the jury would be fully unconstrained from returning a verdict contrary to law. While we recognize that juries have the power to decide a case in a manner which compromises the court's instruction on the law, we by no means recognize that juries have any right to ignore the law. The Supreme Court settled this long ago in *Sparf* and Hansen v. United States, 156 U.S. 51, 15 S.Ct. 273, 39 L.Ed. 343 (1895), when it upheld the trial court's instruction to the jury that it could find murder, or no murder, but not manslaughter because there was no evidence that would reduce any homicide which was committed below the level of murder. See also Berra v. United States, 351 U.S. 131, 134, 76 S.Ct. 685, 100 L.Ed. 1013 (1956).

The judgment for the defendant railroad is therefore reversed and the case remanded to the district court for proceedings in conformity with this opinion.

Reversed and remanded.

1. In ordering a new trial, we therefore have no occasion to consider the merits of the *Hartel* decision, as the plaintiff urges us to do. We do wish to note, however, that the consistency of *Hartel* with controlling Supreme Court cases in this area is not free from doubt. One member of the *Hartel* panel vigorously so argued, 476 F.2d 462 at 466–67 (Hays, J., dissenting), and two members of the Supreme Court, dissenting from the Supreme Court's denial of certiorari in *Hartel,* have since voiced a similar view, 414 U.S. 980 at 980–82 (Douglas & Brennan, JJ., dissenting). Perhaps also significant in this regard is the dissent by three judges of this court from the denial of rehearing *en banc* in *Hartel.* [Some footnotes omitted. This footnote renumbered.]

NOTES

(1) Should the test for a directed verdict be different in different kinds of cases? Is this a substantive or procedural issue or both? Are multiple standards constitutionally proper? Cf. Simler v. Conner, 372 U.S. 221, 222, 83 S.Ct. 609, 610, 9 L.Ed.2d 691 (1963) ("Only through a holding that the jury-trial right is to be determined according to federal law can the uniformity in its exercise which is demanded by the Seventh Amendment be achieved."). Is uniformity in the granting or denying of directed verdicts an inexorable consequence of a federal constitutional standard? Would there be constitutional obstacles to differing tests for directed verdicts based on the source of the evidence in question—whether adduced by the proponent or opponent of the motion—or on the nature of the evidence—whether testimonial or documentary, whether circumstantial or direct? See Cooper, Directions for Directed Verdicts: A Compass for Federal Courts, 55 Minn.L.Rev. 903, 921–927 (1971).

(2) In a diversity case is the standard for directing a verdict to be found in state law or in federal? In Byrd v. Blue Ridge Rural Electric Cooperative, Inc., 356 U.S. 525, 537–38, 78 S.Ct. 893, 900–901, 2 L.Ed.2d 953 (1958), p. 366, supra, the majority declared that the Erie-Tompkins policy of "achievement of uniform enforcement of the right" yields to "a strong federal policy against allowing state rules to disrupt the judge-jury relationship in the federal courts"—one "favoring jury decisions of disputed fact questions." The reasoning was spelled out in Phipps v. N.V. Nederlandsche Amerikaansche S.M., 259 F.2d 143 (9th Cir.1958): "The standard for directing a verdict in a federal court is governed by federal law as it involves questions of the relation of the 7th amendment to a federal trial, and more particularly the function of a federal court in respect of a federal jury." There has not, as yet, been a direct holding by the Supreme Court. Several circuits tend toward a state test. See Comment, Directed Verdicts and the Right to Trial by Jury in Federal Courts, 42 Tex.L.Rev. 1053, 1054–58 (1964). See Cooper, Directions for Directed Verdicts: A Compass for Federal Courts, 55 Minn.L.Rev. 903, 972–989 (1971).

(3) In New York, the attempt to formulate a workable standard for directing a verdict has had a bizzare history, in part recounted in the leading case of Blum v. Fresh Grown Preserve Corp., 292 N.Y. 241, 54 N.E.2d 809 (1944). Until the adoption of the N.Y.—McKinney's CPLR in 1962, the statutory formula for directing a verdict in New York was "A trial court may direct a verdict when it would be required to set aside a contrary verdict for legal insufficiency of evidence." N.Y. Civil Practice Act, § 457–a. Draftsmen of the N.Y.—McKinney's CPLR acknowledged that the standard must be sought in case law since they provided no standard other than that "the moving party is entitled to judgment as a matter of law." N.Y.—McKinney's CPLR § 4401. See 4 Weinstein, Korn and Miller, New York Civil Practice ¶¶ 4401.12–4401.15.

(4) At least one state severely restricts the power of the trial judge to direct a verdict. Barber v. Stephenson, 260 Ala. 151, 156, 69 So.2d 251, 255–56 (1953) (only a "scintilla", "a mere glimmer" of evidence is necessary to reach the jury).

(5) For an excellent discussion of directed verdict standards, see Currie, Thoughts on Directed Verdicts and Summary Judgments, 45 U.Chi.L.Rev. 72 (1977).

(6) May the court direct a verdict for the party having the burden of proof? For an affirmative answer, see Baltimore Gas & Electric Co. v. United States F. & G. Co., 166 F.Supp. 703, 710 (D.Md.1958), reversed on other grounds in 269

F.2d 138 (4th Cir.1959); United States v. Grannis, 172 F.2d 507 (4th Cir.1949). See also James, Jr., Sufficiency of the Evidence and Jury-Control Devices Available Before Verdict, 47 Va.L.Rev. 218 (1961). Not all courts agree. Cf. Giles v. Giles, 204 Mass. 383, 90 N.E. 595 (1910) (oral testimony relied on). See Note, The Power of the Court to Determine Witness Credibility: A Problem in Directing a Verdict for the Proponent of the Evidence, 107 U.Pa.L.Rev. 217 (1958).

(7) After the plaintiff's opening statement, the trial court has power to direct a verdict for the defendant if the statement shows no right to recover, but only after resolving all doubts in plaintiff's favor. Knapp v. Wabash R. Co., 375 F.2d 983 (8th Cir.1967). See also Winter v. Unaitis, 123 Vt. 372, 375, 189 A.2d 547, 549 (1963) ("[W]hen an opening statement is made by a plaintiff a directed verdict thereon cannot be sustained unless by some form of judicial admission the very basis of the action is destroyed, or shown to be lacking.") See Annot., Dismissal, Nonsuit, Judgment or Direction of Verdict on Opening Statement of Counsel in Civil Action, 5 A.L.R.3d 1405 (1966). What is the relationship between the standards for granting a motion to dismiss under Rule 41(b) of the Federal Rules of Civil Procedure and the motion for a directed verdict pursuant to Rule 50(a)? See, e.g., Kingston v. McGrath, 232 F.2d 495 (9th Cir.1956). When may each motion be used? In a non-jury case, what relationship does Rule 56 (summary judgment) bear to the directed verdict standard?

(8) Plaintiff was injured when he slipped on the clubhouse floor at defendant's golf course. At the conclusion of the plaintiff's proof, both plaintiff and defendant moved for a directed verdict. The trial court thereupon discharged the jury, concluded the trial, and granted defendant's motion for a directed verdict. On appeal, the court wrote: "We do not have the usual appeal before us that involves the granting of defendant's motion for a directed verdict. . . . Both parties having asked for a directed verdict, counsel cannot now complaint that there was an issue of fact for the jury. The court properly dismissed the jury and considered both the issues of fact and law." Pais v. Pontiac, 372 Mich. 582, 127 N.W.2d 386, 387 (1964).

The rule that cross-motions for directed verdicts waive a jury trial was once the majority rule. See Annot. 69 A.L.R. 634 (1930). Now, however, this rule is followed in only a small minority of states. See Note, Motion for a Directed Verdict by Both Parties, 24 Ark.L.Rev. 599 (1971).

(9) In federal court, the judge has power to seek information that has not been introduced by the parties. The court can take judicial notice of information whose truth cannot be seriously questioned, see Rule 201 Federal Rules of Evidence; 1 Weinstein & Berger, Weinstein's Evidence, 201[01]–[09] (1989). The court can call witnesses, see Rule 614, Federal Rules of Evidence; 3 Weinstein's Evidence, 614[01]–[06] supra. It can also appoint expert witnesses, Rule 706, Federal Rules of Evidence; 3 Weinstein & Berger, 706–7, supra. See Frankel, The Search for Truth: An Umpireal View, 123 U.Pa.L.Rev. 1031 (1975).

B. JUDGMENT NOTWITHSTANDING THE VERDICT

NEELY v. MARTIN K. EBY CONSTRUCTION CO.
Supreme Court of the United States, 1967.
386 U.S. 317, 87 S.Ct. 1072, 18 L.Ed.2d 75.

MR. JUSTICE WHITE delivered the opinion of the Court.

Petitioner brought this diversity action in the United States District Court for the District of Colorado alleging that respondent's negligent construction, maintenance, and supervision of a scaffold platform used in the construction of a missile silo near Elizabeth, Colorado, had proximately caused her father's fatal plunge from the platform during the course of his employment as Night Silo Captain for Sverdrup & Parcel . . . At the close of the petitioner's evidence and again at the close of all the evidence, respondent moved for a directed verdict. The trial judge denied both motions and submitted the case to a jury, which returned a verdict for petitioner for $25,000.

Respondent then moved for judgment notwithstanding the jury's verdict or, in the alternative, for a new trial, in accordance with Rule 50(b), Federal Rules of Civil Procedure. The trial court denied the motions and entered judgment for petitioner on the jury's verdict. Respondent appealed, claiming that its motion for judgment *n.o.v.* should have been granted. Petitioner, as appellee, urged only that the jury's verdict should be upheld.

The Court of Appeals held that the evidence at trial was insufficient to establish either negligence by respondent or proximate cause and reversed the judgment of the District Court "with instructions to dismiss the action." Without filing a petition for rehearing in the Court of Appeals, petitioner then sought a writ of certiorari, presenting the question whether the Court of Appeals could, consistent with the 1963 amendments to Rule 50 of the Federal Rules [1] and with the Seventh Amendment's guarantee of a right to jury trial, direct the trial court to dismiss the action. Our order allowing certiorari directed the parties' attention to whether Rule 50(d) and our decisions in Cone v. West Virginia Pulp & Paper Co., 330 U.S. 212, 67 S.Ct. 752, 91 L.Ed. 849; Globe Liquor Co. v. San Roman, 332 U.S. 571, 68 S.Ct. 246, 92 L.Ed. 177; and Weade v. Dichmann, Wright & Pugh, Inc., 337 U.S. 801, 69 S.Ct. 1326, 93 L.Ed. 1704, permit this disposition by a court of appeals despite Rule 50(c)(2), which gives a party whose jury verdict is set aside by a trial court 10 days in which to invoke the trial court's discretion to order a new trial. We affirm.

Under Rule 50(b), if a party moves for a directed verdict at the close of the evidence and if the trial judge elects to send the case to the

---

1. Principally, the amendments added new subdivisions (c) and (d) to Rule 50. [Some footnotes omitted; others renumbered.]

jury, the judge is "deemed" to have reserved decision on the motion. If the jury returns a contrary verdict, the party may within 10 days move to have judgment entered in accordance with his motion for directed verdict. This procedure is consistent with decisions of this Court rendered prior to the adoption of the Federal Rules in 1938. Compare Baltimore & Carolina Line, Inc. v. Redman, 295 U.S. 654, 55 S.Ct. 890, 79 L.Ed. 1636, with Slocum v. New York Life Ins. Co., 228 U.S. 364, 33 S.Ct. 523, 57 L.Ed. 879, and Aetna Ins. Co. v. Kennedy, 301 U.S. 389, 57 S.Ct. 809, 81 L.Ed. 1177. And it is settled that Rule 50(b) does not violate the Seventh Amendment's guarantee of a jury trial. Montgomery Ward & Co. v. Duncan, 311 U.S. 243, 61 S.Ct. 189, 85 L.Ed. 147.

The question here is whether the Court of Appeals, after reversing the denial of a defendant's Rule 50(b) motion for judgment notwithstanding the verdict, may itself order dismissal or direct entry of judgment for defendant. . . .

This brings us to Federal Rules 50(c) and 50(d), which were added to Rule 50 in 1963 to clarify the proper practice under this Rule. Though Rule 50(d) is more pertinent to the facts of this case, it is useful to examine these interrelated provisions together. Rule 50(c) governs the case where a trial court has granted a motion for judgment n.o.v. Rule 50(c)(1) explains that, if the verdict loser has joined a motion for new trial with his motion for judgment n.o.v., the trial judge should rule conditionally on the new trial motion when he grants judgment n.o.v. If he conditionally grants a new trial, and if the court of appeals reverses his grant of judgment n.o.v., Rule 50(c)(1) provides that "the new trial shall proceed unless the appellate court has otherwise ordered." On the other hand, if the trial judge conditionally denies the motion for new trial, and if his grant of judgment n.o.v. is reversed on appeal, "subsequent proceedings shall be in accordance with the order of the appellate court." As the Advisory Committee's Note to Rule 50(c) makes clear, Rule 50(c)(1) contemplates that the appellate court will review on appeal both the grant of judgment n.o.v. and, if necessary, the trial court's conditional disposition of the motion for new trial.[2] This review necessarily includes the power to grant or to deny a new trial in appropriate cases.

Rule 50(d) is applicable to cases such as this one where the trial court has denied a motion for judgment n.o.v. Rule 50(d) expressly preserves to the party who prevailed in the district court the right to urge that the court of appeals grant a new trial should the jury's verdict be set aside on appeal. Rule 50(d) also emphasizes that "nothing in this rule precludes" the court of appeals "from determining that the appellee is entitled to a new trial, or from directing the trial court

---

2. The Advisory Committee explains: "If the motion for new trial has been conditionally granted . . . [t]he party against whom the judgment n.o.v. was entered below may, as appellant, beside seeking to overthrow that judgment, also attack the conditional grant of the new trial. And the appellate court, if it reverses the judgment n.o.v., may in an appropriate case also reverse the conditional grant of the new trial and direct that judgment be entered on the verdict." 31 F.R.D. 645. [Citations omitted.]

to determine whether a new trial shall be granted." Quite properly, this Rule recognizes that the appellate court may prefer that the trial judge pass first upon the appellee's new trial suggestion. Nevertheless, consideration of the new trial question "in the first instance" is lodged with the court of appeals. And Rule 50(d) is permissive in the nature of its direction to the court of appeals: as in Rule 50(c)(1), there is nothing in Rule 50(d) indicating that the court of appeals may not direct entry of judgment *n.o.v.* in appropriate cases.

Rule 50(c)(2), n. 2, supra, is on its face inapplicable to the situation presented here. That Rule regulates the verdict winner's opportunity to move for a new trial if the *trial court* has granted a Rule 50(b) motion for judgment *n.o.v.* In this case, the trial court denied judgment *n.o.v.* and respondent appealed. Jurisdiction over the case then passed to the Court of Appeals, and petitioner's right to seek a new trial in the trial court after her jury verdict was set aside became dependent upon the disposition by the Court of Appeals under Rule 50(d).

As the Advisory Committee explained, these 1963 amendments were not intended to "alter the effects of a jury verdict or the scope of appellate review," as articulated in the prior decisions of this Court. 31 F.R.D. 645. In Cone v. West Virginia Pulp & Paper Co., supra, the defendant moved for a directed verdict, but the trial judge sent the case to the jury. After a jury verdict for the plaintiff, the trial court denied defendant's motion for a new trial. On appeal, the Court of Appeals reversed and ordered the entry of judgment *n.o.v.* This Court reversed the Court of Appeals on the ground that the defendant had not moved for judgment *n.o.v.* in the trial court, but only for a new trial, and consequently the Court of Appeals was precluded from directing any disposition other than a new trial. See also Globe Liquor Co. v. San Roman, supra. In Johnson v. New York, N.H. & H.R. Co., 344 U.S. 48, 73 S.Ct. 125, 97 L.Ed. 77, this Court held that a verdict loser's motion to "set aside" the jury's verdict did not comply with Rule 50(b)'s requirement of a timely motion for judgment *n.o.v.* and therefore that the Court of Appeals could not direct entry of judgment *n.o.v.* And in Weade v. Dichmann, Wright & Pugh, Inc., supra, where a proper motion for judgment *n.o.v.* was made and denied in the trial court, we modified a Court of Appeals decision directing entry of judgment *n.o.v.* because there were "suggestions in the complaint and evidence" of an alternative theory of liability which had not been passed upon by the jury and therefore which might justify the grant of a new trial. 337 U.S., at 808–809, 69 S.Ct., at 1330.

The opinions in the above cases make it clear that an appellate court may not order judgment *n.o.v.* where the verdict loser has failed strictly to comply with the procedural requirements of Rule 50(b), or where the record reveals a new trial issue which has not been resolved. Part of the Court's concern has been to protect the rights of the party whose jury verdict has been set aside on appeal and who may have valid grounds for a new trial, some or all of which should be passed upon by the district court, rather than the court of appeals, because of the trial judge's first-hand knowledge of witnesses, testimony, and issues—because of his "feel" for the overall case. . . .

But these considerations do not justify an ironclad rule that the court of appeals should never order dismissal or judgment for defendant when the plaintiff's verdict has been set aside on appeal. Such a rule would not serve the purpose of Rule 50 to speed litigation and to avoid unnecessary retrials. Nor do any of our cases mandate such a rule.

There are, on the one hand, situations where the defendant's grounds for setting aside the jury's verdict raise questions of subject matter jurisdiction or dispositive issues of law which, if resolved in defendant's favor, must necessarily terminate the litigation. . . . In such situations, . . . there can be no reason whatsoever to prevent the court of appeals from ordering dismissal of the action or the entry of judgment for the defendant.

On the other hand, where the court of appeals sets aside the jury's verdict because the evidence was insufficient to send the case to the jury, it is not so clear that the litigation should be terminated. . . . The erroneous exclusion of evidence which would have strengthened his case is an important possibility. Another is that the trial court itself caused the insufficiency in plaintiff-appellee's case by erroneously placing too high a burden of proof on him at trial. But issues like these are issues of law with which the courts of appeals regularly and characteristically must deal. The district court in all likelihood has already ruled on these questions in the course of the trial and, in any event, has no special advantage or competence in dealing with them. They are precisely the kind of issues that the losing defendant below may bring to the court of appeals without ever moving for a new trial in the district court. Cf. Globe Liquor Co. v. San Roman, 332 U.S. 571, 574, 68 S.Ct. 246, 247, 92 L.Ed. 177. Likewise, if the plaintiff's verdict is set aside by the trial court on defendant's motion for judgment *n.o.v.*, plaintiff may bring these very grounds directly to the court of appeals without moving for a new trial in the district court.[3] Final action on these issues normally rests with the court of appeals.

In our view, therefore, Rule 50(d) makes express and adequate provision for the opportunity—which the plaintiff-appellee had without this rule—to present his grounds for a new trial in the event his verdict is set aside by the court of appeals. If he does so in his brief—or in a petition for rehearing if the court of appeals has directed entry of judgment for appellant—the court of appeals may make final disposition of the issues presented, except those which in its informed discretion should be reserved for the trial court. If appellee presents no new trial issues in his brief or in a petition for rehearing, the court of appeals may, in any event, order a new trial on its own motion or refer

---

3. The Advisory Committee's Note to Rule 50(c)(2) explains: "Even if the verdict-winner makes no motion for a new trial, he is entitled upon his appeal from the judgment n.o.v. not only to urge that that judgment should be reversed and judgment entered upon the verdict, but that errors were committed during the trial which at the least entitle him to a new trial." 31 F.R.D. 646.

the question to the district court, based on factors encountered in its own review of the case. Compare Weade v. Dichmann, Wright & Pugh, Inc., supra.

In the case before us, petitioner won a verdict in the District Court which survived respondent's motion for judgment *n.o.v.* In the Court of Appeals the issue was the sufficiency of the evidence and that court set aside the verdict. Petitioner, as appellee, suggested no grounds for a new trial in the event her judgment was reversed, nor did she petition for rehearing in the Court of Appeals, even though that court had directed a dismissal of her case. Neither was it suggested that the record was insufficient to present any new trial issues or that any other reason required a remand to the District Court. Indeed, in her brief in the Court of Appeals, petitioner stated, "This law suit was fairly tried and the jury was properly instructed." . . .

Petitioner's case in this Court is pitched on the total lack of power in the Court of Appeals to direct entry of judgment for respondent. We have rejected that argument and therefore affirm. It is so ordered.

Affirmed.

MR. JUSTICE DOUGLAS and MR. JUSTICE FORTAS, while agreeing with the Court's construction of Rule 50, would reverse the judgment because in their view the evidence of negligence and proximate cause was sufficient to go to the jury.

MR. JUSTICE BLACK, dissenting.

I dissent from the Court's decision in this case for three reasons: First, I think the evidence in this case was clearly sufficient to go to the jury on the issues of both negligence and proximate cause. Second, I think that under our prior decisions and Rule 50, a court of appeals, in reversing a trial court's refusal to enter judgment *n.o.v.* on the ground of insufficiency of the evidence, is entirely powerless to order the trial court to dismiss the case, thus depriving the verdict winner of any opportunity to present a motion for new trial to the trial judge who is thoroughly familiar with the case. Third, even if a court of appeals has that power, I find it manifestly unfair to affirm the Court of Appeals' judgment here without giving this petitioner a chance to present her grounds for a new trial to the Court of Appeals as the Court today for the first time holds she must.

* * *

NOTE ON DIRECTED VERDICT PRACTICE

According to the terms of Rule 50(b), a party may move for judgment notwithstanding the verdict only when it has moved for a directed verdict "at the close of the evidence." This requirement can be explained historically. In its early decisions, the Supreme Court construed the directed verdict motion as a device for withdrawing the question it presented from jury consideration and for thus preserving it for judicial determination after the jury had rendered its verdict.

Since this question was not submitted to the jury, the Supreme Court found its later determination not to violate the Seventh Amendment, which forbids re-examination of the jury verdict otherwise than at common law. See James & Hazard, Civil Procedure § 7.22 (2d ed. 1977). However, at present, the requirement makes little sense, especially since appellate courts have urged trial courts not to grant directed verdict motions, but to rule on the question they present after the jury has returned its verdict. The advantage of this procedure is obvious. If it is followed, an appellate court that disagrees with the trial court's ruling on whether the evidence can support the verdict can simply reinstate the verdict rather than be required to order a new trial. It may cause no wonder that, since the requirement makes little sense (it can, at most, be argued that a directed verdict motion serves notice on the opponent that the evidence is asserted to be wanting and may need supplementation), and may induce premature judicial disposition, the majority of states have abolished it. Their statutes or rules now provide that, after verdict, the court may enter judgment notwithstanding the verdict when this appears appropriate.

This procedure, first adopted in Minnesota in 1895, has generally been upheld over constitutional objections by state courts. See Millar, Civil Procedure of the Trial Court in Historical Perspective, 323–30 (1952); Carlin, Judgment Non Obstante Verdicts, 51 W.Va.L.Rev. 14 (1948).

In the federal courts, the tendency has been towards flexible application of Rule 50(b)'s requirement. See, e.g., Ohio-Sealy Mattress Manufacturing Co. v. Sealy, Inc., 585 F.2d 821 (7th Cir.1978), cert. denied 440 U.S. 930, 99 S.Ct. 1267, 59 L.Ed.2d 486 (1979); Quinn v. Southwest Wood Products, Inc., 597 F.2d 1018 (5th Cir.1979) (permitting d.v. motion to be made and entered upon the record after jury had retired for deliberations); and Bonner v. Coughlin, 657 F.2d 931 (7th Cir.1981) (ruling sufficient a d.v. motion made at the close of the plaintiff's case when the trial judge reserved ruling on it); Ebker v. Tom Jay International, Ltd., 739 F.2d 812 (2d Cir.1984).

NOTES

(1) What difficulties may a court encounter in attempting to decide a motion for judgment n.o.v. and a motion for a new trial at the same time? Cf. Gordon Mailloux Enterprises, Inc. v. Firemen's Insurance Co., of Newark, New Jersey, 366 F.2d 740, 741–42 (9th Cir.1966). In Borras v. Sea-Land Service, Inc., 586 F.2d 881 (1st Cir.1978), the court, in reversing the grant of judgment n.o.v., also reversed the conditional grant of a new trial on the ground that the lower court's erroneous ruling on the n.o.v. motion had tainted its conditional ruling in favor of a new trial.

(2) May a party assert in a motion for judgment n.o.v. a ground not asserted in his motion for a directed verdict? Lewis v. Mears, 189 F.Supp. 503, 509 (W.D.Pa.1960), affirmed 297 F.2d 101 (1961), cert. denied 369 U.S. 873, 82 S.Ct. 1142, 8 L.Ed.2d 276 (1962).

(3) After trial of a personal injury action, the jury, by way of a special verdict, found damages in the amount of $3,000, but no liability. The plaintiff

moved for a new trial asserting various errors relevant only to the issue of liability. The defendant asked the court to disregard the jury verdict of no liability and to enter judgment n.o.v. against her. The defendant's motion was granted and the plaintiff appealed. Held: Affirmed. The right to move to disregard jury findings is not limited to the party against whom the unsupported issue is found. The court did not rely upon a waiver theory, but applied the same test it would have applied had the plaintiff moved for judgment n.o.v. Guckian v. Fowler, 453 S.W.2d 323 (Tex.Civ.App.1970). What should the result be in a federal court?

––––––

Proposed Amendments to Rule 50

Proposed amendments to the Federal Rules of Civil Procedure approved by the Advisory Committee on Civil Rules on April 29, 1989, if adopted, would change Rules 50 and 56. Amended Rule 50 would no longer speak of a "directed verdict" or "judgment notwithstanding the verdict", but of "judgment as a matter of law." Amended Rule 56 would speak not only of "summary judgment," but also of "summary establishment of fact and law." Amended Rule 50 would permit the court to render judgment as a matter of law on its own motion "during a trial". However, it would retain the fiction that a motion for judgment as a matter of law at the close of the evidence is deemed to preserve for determination after the jury's verdict the legal questions raised by the motion and would not appear to permit the court to render judgment as a matter of law after the jury's verdict unless a motion for such a judgment were made at the trial. Should the amendment go further and authorize the court to render judgment as a matter of law after the jury's verdict, regardless of whether a motion for such a judgment was made at the trial? Under the proposed amendment, could the court raise the question of whether judgment as a matter of law should be granted on its own motion at the trial and then, again on its own motion, reserve its decision in order to permit it to render it after the jury's verdict? Note that the proposed amendment retains the language "Whenever a motion for judgment as a matter of law made at the close of the evidence is denied or for any reason is not granted. . . ."

––––––

NEW YORK CIVIL PRACTICE LAW AND RULES

§ 4401. Motion for Judgment During Trial.

Any party may move for judgment with respect to a cause of action or issue upon the ground that the moving party is entitled to judgment as a matter of law, after the close of the evidence presented by an opposing party with respect to such cause of action or issue, or at any time on the basis of admissions. Grounds for the motion shall be specified. The motion does not waive the right to trial by jury or to present further evidence even where it is made by all parties.

§ 4404. Post-Trial Motion for Judgment and New Trial.

(a) Motion after trial where jury required. After a trial of a cause of action or issue triable of right by a jury, upon the motion of any party or on its own initiative, the court may set aside a verdict or any judgment entered thereon and direct that judgment be entered in favor of a party entitled to judgment as a matter of law or it may order a new trial of a cause of action or separable issue where the verdict is contrary to the weight of the evidence, in the interest of justice or where the jury cannot agree after being kept together for as long as is deemed reasonable by the court.

(b) Motion after trial where jury not required. After a trial not triable of right by a jury, upon the motion of any party or on its own initiative, the court may set aside its decision or any judgment entered thereon. It may make new findings of fact or conclusions of law, with or without taking additional testimony, render a new decision and direct entry of judgment, or it may order a new trial of a cause of action or separable issue.

NOTE

In New York, the Appellate Division may enter judgment n.o.v. without any "advice" from the trial court by way of conditional ruling. See, e.g., Guido v. The Delaware, Lackawanna & Western Railroad, 5 A.D.2d 754, 803, 170 N.Y.S.2d 48 (4th Dep't 1958).

SECTION 6. VOLUNTARY DISMISSAL

A plaintiff's lawyer sometimes finds herself faced with sure defeat and wishing she had not commenced her action when or where or on quite the grounds she chose. A voluntary nonsuit would present no problem if she could abandon the action and sue again without prejudice or penalty. To give such a privilege to the plaintiff would accord with the law's policy of not compelling a party to sue against her will, but it is open to abuse, for example, as a tool of oppression or as a trick to learn the defendant's secrets. Without an empowering statute or rule, has a court power to refuse or condition plaintiff's voluntary discontinuance of her action?

LITTMAN v. BACHE & CO.

United States Court of Appeals, Second Circuit, 1958.
252 F.2d 479.

WATERMAN, CIRCUIT JUDGE. The question presented by this appeal is whether the plaintiff-appellant had an unconditional right to dismiss this action before service by the defendant of an answer or of a motion for summary judgment. The answer lies in construction of Rule 41(a)

Fed.Rules Civ.Proc., 28 U.S.C., which rule we previously have construed in Harvey Aluminum, Inc., v. American Cyanamid Co., 2 Cir., 1953, 203 F.2d 105, cert. den. 345 U.S. 964, 73 S.Ct. 949, 97 L.Ed. 1383.

Appellant commenced this action by the filing of a complaint on March 18, 1957, served upon the defendant on the following day. The District Court granted a three-week extension of time, or until April 29, within which the defendant might answer or otherwise move with respect to the complaint. Within this extended time, by motion dated April 26 the defendant obtained an order directing plaintiff to show cause why the action should not be transferred to the Southern District of Florida pursuant to 28 U.S.C.A. § 1404(a). On May 7 the District Court granted the motion despite plaintiff's objections, and directed that the transfer order be settled upon two days' notice. The following day plaintiff obtained an order returnable May 14 directing the defendant to show cause why the motion to transfer should not be reargued, and, upon reargument, denied. The date for the settlement of the transfer order was therefore set over until May 14. On May 13 the plaintiff filed a notice of voluntary dismissal. Defendant moved to vacate the dismissal and after hearing argument, the District Court, on May 16, entered an order directing that the action be transferred to the Southern District of Florida, and that the plaintiff's notice of dismissal, be vacated. The plaintiff appealed from these orders. Upon motion of the defendant to dismiss the appeal we held, 2 Cir., 246 F.2d 490, that the § 1404(a) order was not appealable, but that an appeal would lie from the order vacating plaintiff's notice of dismissal.

Voluntary dismissal of actions commenced in the District Court is governed by Rule 41(a) which, insofar as pertinent, provides that "an action may be dismissed by the plaintiff without order of the court (i) by filing a notice of dismissal at any time before service by the adverse party of an answer or of a motion for summary judgment, whichever first occurs . . ." The Rule was intended to limit the right of dismissal to an early stage of the proceedings, thereby curbing the abuse of the right which had previously been possible. See 5 Moore's Federal Practice 1007 (2d Ed. 1951). In furtherance of the purpose underlying the Rule, we held in Harvey Aluminum, Inc., v. American Cyanamid Co., supra [203 F.2d 108] that under the circumstances of that case the notice of dismissal filed by the plaintiff was properly vacated even though no "paper labeled 'answer' or 'motion for summary judgment' " had been served by the defendant. There the dismissal had been attempted by the plaintiff after an adverse ruling on its motion for an injunction *pendente lite.* The injunction had been denied after several days of argument and testimony before the District Court. We noted that the merits of the controversy were squarely raised and the district court in part based its denial of the injunction on its conclusion that the plaintiffs' chance of success was "remote, if not completely nil." 203 F.2d 105, 107. Cf. Butler v. Denton, 10 Cir., 1945, 150 F.2d 687; Love v. Silas Mason Co., D.C.W.D.La.1946, 66 F.Supp. 753. These decisions rest on the ground that prior to filing of the voluntary dismissal the parties had joined issue on the merits of the controversy, irrespective of the status of the formal pleadings. Where, on the other hand, issue has not been joined prior to notice of dismissal, the courts have held that the dismissal may not be vacated. Kilpatrick v. Texas & P. Ry. Co., 2 Cir., 1948, 166 F.2d 788; Wilson & Co. v. Fremont Cake & Meal Co., D.C.D.Neb.1949, 83 F.Supp. 900; cf. Pennsylvania R. Co. v. Daoust Construction Co., 7 Cir., 1952, 193 F.2d 659.

The present case is akin to the latter group of decisions. The only issue that was raised before the District Court was whether to grant defendant's motion to transfer the action to the Southern District of Florida. The merits of the controversy were never before the court. To be sure, both parties were familiar with the subject matter of the litigation, but this was clearly insufficient to deprive plaintiff of his right to a voluntary dismissal. We hold that the District Court erred in vacating the dismissal. See White v. Thompson, D.C.N.D.Ill.1948, 80 F.Supp. 411; Toulmin v. Industrial Metal Protectives, D.C.D.Del.1955, 135 F.Supp. 925.

Reversed.

LUMBARD, CIRCUIT JUDGE (dissenting). I would affirm. I agree with the majority that the issues had not been joined on the merits so as to allow the District Court to treat the stage of the proceedings as equivalent to an answer or motion for summary judgment. If Harvey Aluminum, Inc., v. American Cyanamid Co., 2 Cir., 1953, 203 F.2d 105, cert. den. 345 U.S. 964, 73 S.Ct. 949, 97 L.Ed. 1383 and the other cases cited by Judge Herlands stand only for that proposition and if that is the sole exception to the literal language of Rule 41(a)(1), the decision should be reversed. I believe, however, that Harvey means that we need not allow the literal language of the Rules to defeat the interests of justice and sound judicial administration. Cf. Hormel v. Helvering, 1941, 312 U.S. 552, 557, 61 S.Ct. 719, 85 L.Ed. 1037; Bucy v. Nevada Const. Co., 9 Cir., 1942, 125 F.2d 213, 216.

The facts set out by Judge Herlands show, and the thrust of his opinion is, that the plaintiff presumed upon the Court in an attempt to shift his forum. The plaintiff filed the notice of dismissal after he had been defeated on the motion to transfer and after he had expressly requested and received a delay in transfer for the purpose of reargument. On the same day that he dismissed he initiated an action in the New York courts. The District Court has an area of discretion to prevent trifling tactics of this nature. The action of the majority seems to me to lose sight of the larger objective in the process of embracing a technicality.

It seems apparent that the plaintiff, not having achieved the result for which he hoped on the motion to transfer the action to Florida, has now changed his tune as to his citizenship and has started an action in the Supreme Court of New York County on the theory that he is a New York citizen. Thus the merry-go-round goes around again and under the removal statute the parties may be knocking on the door of the Federal Courthouse once more.

Rule 1 of the Federal Rules of Civil Procedure enjoins us to construe the rules "to secure the just, speedy, and inexpensive determination of every action." I think the injunction applies to this kind of forum shopping which multiplies expense and delay. The District Court had the power to vacate the voluntary dismissal under such circumstances as took place here. Exercising this power in such a proper case was not an abuse of discretion and I would affirm.

NOTES

(1) At common law, the plaintiff had an unfettered right to a nonsuit. "The plaintiff had a right to be nonsuited at any stage of the proceedings he might prefer, and thereby reserve to himself the power of bringing a fresh action for the same subject matter; and this right continued to the last moment of the trial, even till after verdict rendered, or, where the case was tried by the court without the intervention of a jury, until the judge had pronounced his judgment. [Citation omitted.] Consequently, if he was not satisfied with the damages given by the jury, he might become nonsuit." Washburn v. Allen, 77 Me. 344, 346 (1885).

(2) In most states, the right to a voluntary nonsuit is now governed by statute or court rule. "The problem confronting the legislators in drafting their nonsuit statutes has been to decide at which point the plaintiff's right to halt the proceedings without prejudice should cease; or rather, at which point the defendant should have his right to final litigation protected by the discretion of the trial judge. There are, obviously, numerous places in the proceedings of a trial which the legislature could conveniently choose. And, for the most part, the various jurisdictions have shown their individuality by striking variations in the time limit imposed upon the plaintiff—one state denying the right only after verdict is entered, others more stringent, to the most strict of all where the plaintiff's right is limited to the time before receipt of the defendant's answer." Note, The Right of a Plaintiff to Take a Voluntary Nonsuit or to Dismiss His Action Without Prejudice, 37 Va.L.Rev. 969, 970–71 (1951). See also Annot., Time when Voluntary Nonsuit or Dismissal May be Taken as of Right under Statute Authorizing at Any Time Before "Trial," "Commencement of Trial," "Trial of the Facts," or the Like, 1 A.L.R.3d 711 (1965).

(3) Where plaintiff has an absolute right to dismissal without prejudice, what is to prevent him from repeatedly bringing new actions and dismissing them voluntarily for the purpose of harassing the defendant? See Renfroe v. Johnson, 142 Tex. 251, 177 S.W.2d 600 (1944). Is this a problem under Federal Rule 41? See also Chapter 16, infra, on the res judicata effect of dismissals.

SECTION 7. SPECIAL PROBLEMS IN TRIALS
WITHOUT A JURY

HANSON, FINDINGS OF FACT AND CONCLUSIONS OF
LAW, AN OUTMODED RELIC OF THE
STAGE COACH DAYS

32 American Bar Association Journal 52 (1946).

Until the Supreme Court of the United States in 1938 promulgated its "Rules of Procedure for the District Courts of the United States" only one-fourth of the states of the Union (eleven to be exact) required findings of fact and conclusions of law as the basis of a judgment in a jury-waived case. Additionally, seven other states required findings unless they were waived by counsel on both sides. In the other thirty states, as in England, it was sufficient, as it always was in the old Chancery decrees, for the trial court to recite in a judgment that it found the merits with the prevailing party without any special finding on the issues that had been joined. At common law and under the old English Chancery practice special findings on the issues joined was a procedure wholly unknown.

The doctrine that a court should make findings of fact and conclusions of law as the basis of a judgment in a case tried by a court without a jury stems from the fertile pen of David Dudley Field, who was largely responsible for the so-called "Field" Procedure Code presented to the New York legislature in the early part of 1848, and to the California legislature in 1851 by David Dudley Field's brother, Stephen J. Field. Both states adopted the practice Code, but New York early repealed the provision here involved; California did not and never has. Moreover, the provision shortly thereafter received the approval of most of the legislatures of the so-called Pacific slope and western states, and its habitat today is almost exclusively there, aside from its use in the Federal Courts.

At this moment the Advisory Committee appointed by the Supreme Court of the United States to revise the federal rules is on record in its second preliminary draft to expand the doctrine further so as to require findings by the court in actions tried with an *advisory jury* and in cases tried to the court without a jury where a *nonsuit or directed verdict* s granted. Moreover, the Advisory Committee in its own notes to Rule 52 insists that the *findings should be prepared by the judge and not by counsel* and that in setting forth the findings there "is no necessity for overelaboration of detail or particularization of facts." In view of the changes contemplated by the Committee and the observations thus made by it, it seems appropriate at this time to consider whether the doctrine of special findings should or should not be abolished in the federal rules and by the states that still adhere to the doctrine.

When we marshal the arguments in favor of the requirement that a judge sitting without a jury should make special findings of fact and conclusions of law as a basis of a judgment we find there are only two: 1. They "aid in defining for future cases the precise limitations of the issues and the determination thereon" and are "an important factor in the proper application of the doctrine of *res judicata* and estoppel by judgment."

2. They aid an appellate court on review in affording a clear understanding of the basis of the decision below, so that the appellate court and the parties as well can determine whether the case has been decided upon the evidence and the law or *whether* on the contrary upon arbitrary or extra-legal considerations.

The first argument is obviously the weaker of the two. In the first place it is clear that in only a negligible number out of every 1000 cases decided is there any occasion to plead the judgment as *res judicata* or as an estoppel by judgment in another case. Secondly, where it is necessary to do so, the controlling test with respect to *res judicata* is not the findings but the identity of the causes of action; in the case of estoppel by judgment, the rule is that the judgment in the first action operates, quite apart from the findings, as an estoppel only as to the points or the questions actually litigated and determined and not as to matters not litigated in the former action. Hence, as a practical matter, the first argument mentioned possesses little, if any, merit. . . .

Today the pressure to get cases to trial in the metropolitan centers is such that the judges cannot take time out after they have completed a trial to prepare the findings in it. Theoretically, that is what should be done, but practically it cannot be done, unless there is a very large increase in judicial personnel. It is not to be expected that taxpayers or legislatures will invite such increase or grant it. Consequently, the trial judges must of necessity leave the preparation of special findings and the conclusions of law to counsel for the prevailing party. Sometimes—and indeed too often—the findings and conclusions reach the trial judge weeks after he has tried the case. In the meantime he may have tried a dozen or more cases of considerable importance with numerous witnesses before him, to say nothing of a series of comparatively short cases and defaults. Accordingly, after the proposed findings are submitted to him, he must in odd moments taken from current trials, endeavor to recall the evidence so as to determine if the findings presented accord with the views he previously announced from the bench. Moreover, it is not uncommon for losing counsel to ask and to be given an opportunity to go over the findings with the court. This may now and then be helpful but often it leads only to additional confusion.

Cases generally are decided by judges from the bench at the conclusion of the trial with the reasons given for the decision. This, it would seem, should be enough. Where the cases are taken under submission it is believed that the prevailing practice is either to write a more or less short memorandum or letter to counsel setting forth the reasons for the decision, or for the judge to recall counsel and then announce from the bench the decision and the reasons for it, as is the English practice. The latter practice is, of course, preferable and should be encouraged. The litigant layman is much better satisfied when he hears from the lips of the judge the reasons why he is not entitled to the decision. The fact that thirty states of the Union appear to get along very well without special findings is in itself something of an argument against the system of special findings. Moreover, where special findings are prepared by prevailing counsel—a system which appears to be a necessity for courts with large calendars—there is always the temptation for the successful counsel to make the findings as strong as possible in favor of his client, and, indeed, at times even to "pad" them.[1] Even so, too little pruning is or can be done by the trial judge who is busily engaged in the trial of other cases. The fact is that judges generally have too little time and too often stenographic facilities are not immediately at hand. To correct the findings by hand and return them to counsel for rewriting means further delay and, therefore, generally it is not done. Hence, findings instead of being an open sesame to losing counsel on an appeal, too often are framed to avoid a reversal and therefore are nothing more or less than a trap for the unwary. But it must be admitted there are times when findings are also pitfalls for the successful party because of failures in form or substance of little or no moment.

When we analyze the contention that special findings are an aid to a reviewing court we soon discover that it is at best a broad generalization and largely a myth. . . . If we look straight at the statement that findings are an aid on review, because they disclose the basis of the decision below (the only reason ever urged) we quickly ascertain that special findings, in and of themselves are an aid only where the appeal is on the judgment-roll alone. On such an appeal it may be urged that the findings are deficient in form, inconsistent, inadequate, insufficient, or otherwise do not support the judgment. But the aid which a reviewing court gets from such specific findings it can and does procure as succinctly on appeals in states where the system of special findings does not prevail. Moreover, contentions on appeal such as that the findings are not material to the issues as made by the pleadings, or are outside the issues, require reference to the pleadings, and if the contention is that the findings are not sustained by the evidence, it is crystal

---

1. In 2 Hayne, New Trial and Appeal, § 245, p. 1362, it is said:

"In practice the successful party is usually directed to draft the findings and too often the judge signs the draft presented to him without sufficient examination. This practice cannot be too strongly condemned. It results in the preparation by the attorney of findings favorable to himself on every issue while the judge may have decided in his favor on only some of the issues. In view of the rule that a finding of fact will not be disturbed if there be a substantial conflict in the evidence, this practice results in the grossest injustice to the losing party. It is the duty of the judge to make his own findings." [This footnote renumbered; others omitted.]

clear that the court must read the evidence on the point to adjudicate upon it.

In the states where special findings are not required, the appellate courts assume that all the essential facts to support the judgment were found by the trial judge. If it is contended that there is no evidence or insufficient evidence to sustain an essential fact, generally counsel for the respondent or appellee is required to state the evidence of the fact which he contends is sufficient, and to refer to the page and line in the record for his statement. This system it would seem is simpler, less verbose, and more to the point than that of special findings.

The system of findings may be an *aid to counsel*, where he contends that the facts do not justify the judgment, as he can then appeal on the judgment-roll alone, where otherwise he could not. But the aid he thus gets is of no aid to the reviewing court. Moreover, as a practical matter we need to remind ourselves that the appeals taken on a judgment-roll alone, in states where the special finding system prevails, are almost infinitesimal, when compared to appeals supported by a transcript of the record or a bill of exceptions.

Aside from the fact that special findings waste precious time of judges and counsel, the cost to litigants and even taxpayers seems to be wholly disproportionate to the value such findings may now and then have. In California, which possibly may be regarded as representative of other jurisdictions, only 13% of the cases, in which findings are made, are appealed. . . .

It is submitted that special findings have never been worth the price and that they should have gone out as they came in—in the stage coach days. The answer to the problem in jury waived or equity cases is not special findings, but better and more competent trial judges.

NOTES

(1) For similar views, see Tunstall, Findings of Fact and Conclusions of Law: Their Use and Some Abuses, 38 A.B.A.J. 413 (1952); Sunderland, Findings of Fact and Conclusions of Law in Cases Where Juries Are Waived, 4 U.Chi.L.Rev. 218, 229–232 (1937); Yankwich, Findings in the Light of the Recent Amendments to the Federal Rules of Civil Procedure, 8 F.R.D. 271, 291–95 (1946); Note, 31 Wash.L.Rev. 261 (1956). But see Clark & Stone, Review of Findings of Fact, 4 U.Chi.L.Rev. 190, 205 (1937); Trelease, Wyoming Practice, 12 Wyo.L.Rev. 202, 213 (1958). Cf. United States v. Forness, 125 F.2d 928, 942 (2d Cir.1942) ("as every judge knows, to set down in precise words the facts as he finds them is the best way to avoid carelessness in the discharge of that duty").

(2) The requirement of Rule 52 is mandatory; the parties may not agree to dispense with findings of fact. Berguido v. Eastern Air Lines, Inc., 369 F.2d 874 (3d Cir.1966), cert. denied 390 U.S. 996, 88 S.Ct. 1194, 20 L.Ed.2d 95 (1968).

(3) In a footnote to Montgomery v. Goodyear Aircraft Co., 392 F.2d 777, 779 (2d Cir.), cert. denied 393 U.S. 841, 89 S.Ct. 121, 21 L.Ed.2d 112 (1968), the Second Circuit advised its trial judges that:

"It would be more helpful to us on review, however, and would give us greater certainty that the result was correct and reached after careful and thoughtful consideration of all factors, if detailed findings and conclusions were reached by the judge himself rather than wholesale adoption of those submitted by counsel. See Matton Oil Transfer v. The Dynamic, 123 F.2d 999 (2d Cir.1941).

(4) For a while, the Court of Appeals for the Federal Circuit accorded the record closer scrutiny when the district court had adopted the findings prepared by one of the parties, Lindemann Maschinenfabrik GmbH v. American Hoist & Derrick Co., 730 F.2d 1452, 1457 (Fed.Cir.1984). However, it abandoned this practice after the Supreme Court announced that the same standard of review applies to all factual findings, Anderson v. Bessemer City, 470 U.S. 564, 105 S.Ct. 1504, 84 L.Ed.2d 518 (1985), see Hybritech v. Monoclonal Antibodies, Inc., 802 F.2d 1367, 1375 (Fed.Cir.1986).

TILLMAN v. BASKIN

Supreme Court of Florida, 1972.
260 So.2d 509.

ERVIN, JUSTICE. We have for review on petition for writ of certiorari the decision of the District Court of Appeal, Fourth District, in Tillman v. Baskin, 242 So.2d 748 (Fla.App.1971), quashed 260 So.2d 509.

At the close of the plaintiff's case in this nonjury, gross negligence action, the trial judge granted the defendants' motion for directed verdict and entered a final judgment in their favor. On appeal, the Fourth District Court affirmed. The District Court held the motion was properly granted, even though the evidence would not have supported such a motion in a jury trial. In this connection the District Court said:

"As concerns the evidence, it was adequate to withstand such motion under the criteria that obtains in jury trials,"

which indicates plaintiff's evidence made out a prima facie case.

The District Court distinguished jury and nonjury trials, saying,

"In non-jury trials, a motion for directed verdict is tantamount to a motion for involuntary dismissal under Rule 1.420(b), 30 F.S.A. [Footnote omitted.] *Thus, the trial judge as trier of the fact was governed by different criteria and was entitled to weigh the evidence, resolve conflicts and pass upon the credibility of the witnesses.* If in this light the court finds that plaintiff's evidence is insufficient to merit judgment, the court may enter judgment at that point for the defendant." (Emphasis supplied.)

* * *

Rule 1.420(b) F.R.C.P., 30 F.S.A., the involuntary dismissal rule, provides in part:

"After a party seeking affirmative relief in an action *tried by the court without a jury* has completed the presentation of his evidence, any other party may move for a dismissal on the ground that upon the facts and the law the party seeking affirmative relief *has shown no right to relief,* without waiving his right to offer evidence if the motion is not granted. The court as trier of the facts may then determine them and render judgment against the party seeking affirmative relief or may decline to render any judgment until the close of all the evidence." (Emphasis supplied.)

The District Court properly concluded that in a nonjury trial a Rule 1.420(b) F.R.C.P. motion for involuntary dismissal is the proper method by which a defendant may obtain a verdict in his favor following the presentation of the plaintiff's case. Rule 1.480 F.R.C.P., motions for directed verdicts, accomplish the same goal in jury trials.

The issue before this Court is whether the lower appellate court also properly concluded that under the involuntary dismissal rule the trial judge in a nonjury case may weigh the evidence and rule in the defendant's favor before the defendant presents his evidence even though the plaintiff has established a prima facie case.

An affirmative answer to this question would create an important difference between involuntary dismissals and their jury-trial counterparts, directed verdicts. It is clear that a judge in ruling on a latter motion may not weigh the evidence.

The question posed by this case has been considered by courts in other jurisdictions with rules of civil procedure similar to ours. Since it was amended in 1946, Federal Rule of Civil Procedure 41(b), which is virtually identical to Florida's Rule 1.420(b), has been interpreted by federal courts as permitting a trial judge to "weigh the evidence, consider the law, and find for the defendant at the close of the plaintiff's case." 5 J. Moore, Moore's Federal Practice 1158 (2d ed. 1971). In the past, several of this state's district courts of appeal have followed this holding. . . .

Federal courts apparently feel justified in permitting their trial judges to weigh evidence following the presentation of a plaintiff's prima facie case, because such a holding enables judges "to expedite the trial of cases," and "dispose of cases at the earliest opportunity." Bach v. Friden Calculating Mach. Co., 148 F.2d 407, 410 (6th Cir.1945). Their interpretation of the rule regarding involuntary dismissals, however, has not been universally accepted. Professor Roscoe Steffen of the University of Chicago Law School has called it "a misbegotten offspring of an unseemly desire for speed and hurry [which] has no place in our system of justice." 27 U.Chicago L.Rev. 94, 125 (1959). The Supreme Court of Alaska also has rejected the federal interpretation, stating:

"Where plaintiff's proof has failed in some aspect the motion should, of course, be granted. Where plaintiff's proof is overwhelming, application of the rule is made easy and the motion should be denied. But where plaintiff has presented a prima facie case based on unimpeached evidence we are of the opinion that the trial judge should not grant the motion even though he is the trier of the facts and may not himself feel at that point in the trial that the plaintiff has sustained his burden of proof. We believe that in the latter situation the trial judge should follow the alternative offered by the rule wherein it is provided that he '. . . may decline to render any judgment until the close of all the evidence', and deny the motion. If, after denial of the motion, the defendant declines to present any evidence, the judge must, of course, then exercise his own judgment in applying the law to the facts presented and rule on the motion and decide the case." Rogge v. Weaver, 368 P.2d 810, 813 (Alaska 1962). *Accord,* Arbenz v. Bebout, 444 P.2d 317 (Wyo.1968).

We agree. There is nothing in Rule 1.420(b) making mandatory a weighing of the facts before the end of all the testimony. Fairness and justice demand that this not be done where the plaintiff has presented a prima facie case in his favor. We prefer the rule enunciated by the Supreme Court of Alaska to that followed by the federal courts. It is inconceivable that a trial judge can fairly find for a defendant after hearing nothing more than testimony from a plaintiff establishing a prima facie case in that plaintiff's favor. When a prima facie case is made by plaintiff, fairness would appear to require that the trial judge weigh it in the light of the strength or weakness of the defendant's defense evidence, if any, as in the case of a jury trial. We hold that a trial judge cannot weigh evidence when ruling on a defendant's Rule 1.420(b) F.R.C.P. motion for involuntary dismissal following the presentation of a prima facie case by a plaintiff.

The decision of the District Court of Appeal, Fourth District, is quashed and the cause is remanded to the trial court for new trial.

It is so ordered.

CARLTON, ADKINS and DEKLE, JJ., concur.

ROBERTS, C.J., concurs in judgment only.

BOYD, J., and RAWLS, DISTRICT COURT JUDGE, dissent.

NOTES

(1) On the clearly erroneous test of Rule 52, see Pullman-Standard v. Swint, 456 U.S. 273, 102 S.Ct. 1781, 72 L.Ed.2d 66 (1982), reversing the appellate court's finding of discriminatory intent on the ground that the appellate court had made its own determination based on evidence not considered by the trial court rather than review the trial court's finding.

(2) Note, Improper Evidence in Nonjury Trials: Basis for Reversal? 79 Harv.L.Rev. 407, 409, 412, 414, 415 (1965): *

"The presumption approach presents the apparent anomaly of allowing a judge to admit improper evidence and then presuming that he has not considered it in making his decision. It is patently absurd to *assume* that a

* Footnotes omitted.

judge who mistakenly thought that certain evidence was admissible later knew enough to disregard it in arriving at his decision . . .

"An alternative more frequently suggested by commentators than by courts is for the appellate court to presume that the judge appraised all of the admitted evidence in a sensible manner. Here the premise is not that the judge can disregard improper material that might sway a jury, but rather that a judge can give all evidence its proper weight in a manner that is beyond the capability of an unskilled jury . . .

"Any theory that attempts to lay down a system of nonjury rules of evidence should be centrally concerned with the judge's special competence as contrasted with that of a jury. It is thus essential that a particular theory take into account the different classes of evidence and a judge's special competence with respect to each class. However, the various rationales that appellate courts use with respect to nonjury trials do not recognize and provide for the different types of evidence . . . Short of a concerted undertaking to write a system of nonjury rules, the most satisfactory solution is probably to apply the jury rules of evidence to all trials."

For an espousal of the position that in a non-jury trial the judge should evaluate the sufficiency of the evidence in the same manner as in a jury trial, see Steffen, The Prima Facie Case in Non-Jury Trials, 27 U.Chi.L. Rev. 94 (1959); but cf. Allred v. Sasser, 170 F.2d 233 (7th Cir.1948).

(3) The Fifth Circuit has ruled that admission of improper evidence in a bench-tried case should lead to reversal only if the competent evidence is insufficient to support the judgment or if it is clear that the court made an essential finding on the basis of incompetent evidence that it could not have made without that evidence. Goodman v. Highland Insurance Co., 607 F.2d 665 (5th Cir.1979).

(4) Davis, An Approach to Rules of Evidence for Nonjury Cases, 50 A.B.A.J. 723, 726 (1964): "Anglo-American exclusionary rules of evidence are unique in the world. Lawyers of other lands are unable to understand why relevant evidence that has probative force should be barred from consideration. Our only excuse is that we use juries and don't trust the juries to consider all relevant and probative evidence. But our only excuse does not even purport to reach the . . . trials without juries."

Chapter Fifteen

JUDGMENTS

SECTION 1. FORM, ENTRY, AND DOCKETING OF JUDGMENT

A judgment is a distinctive legal document and it carries serious consequences, some of which are examined in this chapter and the next one. In federal practice, Rule 54 permits the court to render the relief to which the prevailing litigant is entitled, whether or not it was demanded, except that a judgment by default must not differ in kind from the relief prayed for. See Chapter 9 supra.

"A judgment is the sentence of the law given by the court as the result of proceedings instituted therein for the redress of an injury. [A] final judgment . . . terminates the controversy and either merges itself into or bars the plaintiff's claim. It thus itself becomes the generating source of new rights and liabilities of the parties. Under the constitution it is entitled to full faith and credit in every American jurisdiction. It may become a lien upon the losing party's land within the court's territorial jurisdiction and thus affect the title thereto. These considerations and many others which readily come to mind indicate the necessity of a final judgment being clear and unambiguous in its meaning and effect." Allegheny County v. Maryland Casualty Co., 132 F.2d 894, 897 (3d Cir.1943), cert. denied 318 U.S. 787, 63 S.Ct. 981, 87 L.Ed. 1154.

The issues discussed in this chapter deal in part with a party's ability to have the case that has just been litigated reexamined in the course of entering or enforcing the judgment. This "direct" review of the proceedings must be compared with the procedure that is the focus of the next chapter, which is the party's right to relitigate issues, claims and defenses in separate (collateral) proceedings. The competing interests in both cases are, on the one hand, the judicial system's concern with reaching the correct and most just result; on the other hand, the interest in repose—in forcing the parties to come to terms with their circumstances, in conserving the resources of the courts and the judgment winner, in bringing an end to litigation.

NOTES

(1) Some codes, rules and decisions take the position that "there are two steps to convert an adjudication into an effective judgment: (1) the judgment must be set forth in writing and signed by the judge; and (2) the judgment so set forth must be entered in the civil docket by the clerk of the court." Before then, the judgment is of no effect "for any purpose". Bloodworth v. Thompson, 230 Ga. 628, 629, 198 S.E.2d 293, 294 (1973).

Compare State v. Bridenhager, 257 Ind. 544, 546, 276 N.E.2d 843, 844 (1972), modified on other grounds upon rehearing 257 Ind. 699, 279 N.E.2d 794 (1972): Although . . . for many purposes, a judgment, until entered is not complete, perfect and effective . . . it, nevertheless is effective between the parties from the time of rendition."

(2) In Ferrara v. Jordan, 134 Cal.App.2d Supp. 917, 286 P.2d 589 (1955), an appeal was dismissed because the "judgment" read: "It is adjudged that the defendants Orvin Jordan and Eleanor Jordan have and recover from the plaintiff, Nicholas Ferrara, costs in the sum of $8.25." The court said there was no judgment from which an appeal could be taken, but simply an award of costs.

(3) In a personal injury action the jury fixed recovery at $36,000, "to be paid at $150 per month for 20 years." Neither party objected to the form of the verdict, the court accepted it and the jury was discharged. Reversing the trial court's order of a lump-sum $36,000 verdict, the Supreme Court held that in the circumstances the verdict should have stood, with interest at 6 per cent from the due date of each instalment. M & P Stores, Inc. v. Taylor, 326 P.2d 804 (Okl.1958). How can such a judgment be enforced? Cf. Roach v. Roach, 164 Ohio St. 587, 132 N.E.2d 742, 59 A.L.R.2d 685 (1956).

(4) In Department of Public Assistance v. Reustle, 358 Pa. 111, 56 A.2d 221 (1948), the plaintiff had filed a judgment against "Rosie Reustle" in 1939. In 1941, Reustle conveyed real property, held under the name of "Rosie C. Reustle" to the Di Paolas. The plaintiff obtained a declaratory judgment that the Dipolas hold title subject to the 1939 judgment lien. The court ruled that the omission of the middle initial did not *ipso facto* invalidate the judgment if the name docketed designated the defendant accurately enough to lead a reasonably careful searcher to conclude the defendant was intended.

(5) New York Civil Rights Law section 61 provides that a petition for a change of name "must also specify whether or not . . . there are any judgments or liens of record against the petitioner or actions or proceedings pending to which the petitioner is a party." Other states have comparable provisions.

SECTION 2. RELIEF FROM JUDGMENT

ATCHISON, TOPEKA AND SANTA FE RAILWAY v. BARRETT

United States Court of Appeals, Ninth Circuit, 1957.
246 F.2d 846.

BARNES, CIRCUIT JUDGE. Plaintiff recovered a judgment in the District Court under the provisions of the Federal Employers' Liability Act, for head injuries suffered on March 11, 1955, while working as a waiter aboard one of appellant's trains. The distinctive manifestation of plaintiff's alleged injury was a jerking or twisting of the head, medically described as a "spasmodic torticollis." This occurred with varying frequency, usually every few seconds. It apparently was pronounced enough during the trial to impress the jury, for it awarded him $12,500. Plaintiff had lost no time from work after the accident, and sought no medical care for over a month after it. The jerking allegedly started about three months after the accident.

Plaintiff was observed by defendant's counsel after the trial, and the jerking or twitching appeared to have stopped. Plaintiff was placed under observation by under-cover operatives employed by the defendant, who took some motion pictures indicating that the twitching or jerking was no longer evident, at least during a two hour period. Plaintiff discovered he was being "tailed," and the jerking again manifested itself. After the time to file a motion for new trial had expired, under-cover operators for the defendant again took motion pictures which indicated plaintiff had apparently recovered from the twitching.

By deposition taken before trial, plaintiff testified he had no control over the twitching, that he was seldom without it, though unaware whether or not he was twitching. If defendant was not suspicious of plaintiff's claims immediately upon their being made, it most assuredly was after the medical expert of its choice made his report to the defendant, subsequent to his examination of plaintiff on April 10, 1956.[1] The defendant's medical expert was not called as a witness. Very understandably, this decision was dictated by sound trial strategy. But sometimes trial strategy involves calculated risks.

The motion pictures in evidence were viewed by the trial court, and by this Court. The entire seven Exhibits show plaintiff for approximately fourteen minutes of film coverage during four and one-half hours of personal observation on several days. The pictures raise grave suspicion of the legitimacy of plaintiff's complaint, but they are far from conclusive.

Another unusual factor in the case was the strong interest displayed in it by Dr. Darrington Weaver, who was present during at least part of the trial, and aided plaintiff in collecting the judgment after trial. He had referred plaintiff to a specialist, but had neither treated nor prescribed for plaintiff. Dr. Weaver is not unknown to the negligence trial bar of Los Angeles County. In 1942 he had been convicted on thirteen counts contained in two informations of violating § 556 of the California Insurance Code, one count of subornation of perjury, one count of perjury, and one count of forgery. For the amazing story, see People v. Weaver, 56 Cal.App.2d 732, 133 P.2d 818.

Relying on the record now on appeal, as briefly highlighted above, counsel for appellant moved to vacate and set aside the judgment

1. ". . . it would appear that as a result of the accident . . . the patient sustained a contusion of the scalp without losing consciousness. The evolution of his symptoms was gradual and unquestionably was aggravated by resentment toward an official in the Commissary Department of the Railway. The clinical picture is not that of spasmodic torticollis but rather of habit spasms. In my opinion Mr. Barrett's symptoms are due entirely to mental causes. In this case settlement of litigation may be expected to be followed by his prompt recovery." [This footnote has been renumbered; others have been omitted.]

pursuant to Rule 60(b) of the Federal Rules of Civil Procedure, on the grounds that the judgment had been obtained by fraud, misrepresentation and other misconduct. This motion was denied by the trial court.

The trial judge stated, when denying appellant's motion below, that though "there are some strange things in it," he could not be sure that the jury would return a different verdict had "these facts" been presented to it.

Appellant urges the trial court erred (a) in failing to find "fraud, misrepresentation and other misconduct"; (b) in failing to find "other reasons" justifying relief from the judgment; (c) in applying the criteria applicable for determining a motion for a new trial, rather than criteria for relief from judgment under Rule 60(b).

We can agree with many of the principles of law cited, and maintained for, by appellant. Judgments obtained through fraud, misrepresentation or other misconduct should be vacated, by use of Rule 60(b) of the Federal Rules of Civil Procedure. That rule is remedial and should be liberally construed. Where perjury has played some part in influencing the court or jury to render a judgment, the effect of the perjury will not be weighed on a motion to set aside the judgment.

The difficulty here, is the factual question—was there perjury? And was the judgment obtained by fraud, misrepresentation or other misconduct of plaintiff?

A psychosomatic injury may be as real as one induced by trauma. "Litigation neurosis" is accepted as a medical fact, particularly by those neurological physicians and practitioners of psychosomatic medicine most closely associated with forensic medicine.

Can we say the action of the trial court was an abuse of discretion? We are frank to state that had the able trial judge determined that fraud or other misconduct existed to grant appellant relief under Rule 60(b), we would not have disturbed that conclusion, on the record before us. While the remedial statute is to be liberally construed, there still exists a definite burden on the moving party to prove the existence of the fraud, or other misconduct, or other cause for relief. Parker v. Checker Taxi Co., 7 Cir., 1956, 238 F.2d 241; Federal Deposit Ins. Corp. v. Alker, 3 Cir., 1956, 234 F.2d 113.

*   *   *

Such a motion for relief is directed to the sound discretion of the trial court, and particularly to the discretion of the trial judge who "presided in the litigation in which the judgment (now alleged as fraudulent) was entered." Independence Lead Mines v. Kingsbury, 9 Cir., 175 F.2d 983, 988. Discretion is peculiarly and properly left in the trial court in matters of this kind. Not only must there be clear and convincing evidence of fraud, but it must be such as prevented the losing party from fully and fairly presenting his case or defense. Independence Lead Mines v. Kingsbury, supra, at page 988; Toledo Scale Co. v. Computing Scale Co., 261 U.S. 399, 421, 43 S.Ct. 458, 67

L.Ed. 719. The trial judge saw and heard the plaintiff; saw his twitchings, what they were and what they were not, as did the jury. He saw or heard the other matters relied on by appellant; he felt the "climate" of the trial. The trial judge found no fraud nor misrepresentation. [Tr. p. 180] The Court of Appeals should not and will not substitute its judgment for that of the trial court, nor reverse the lower court's determination save for an abuse of discretion. . . .

Our research fails to disclose a single case in this Circuit where this Court has reversed a trial judge on a matter of this kind. We should not commence innovation on the factual basis of this case. We cannot say the District Court did not exercise a sound legal discretion.

Affirmed.

NOTES

(1) On what reasoning and on what grounds is the trial court accorded discretion to grant or withhold relief in the principal case? What circumstances lead to a finding of "abuse of discretion"? Is appellate review of discretionary rulings subject to different standards than review of legal rulings? Cf. Skidmore v. Baltimore & Ohio Railroad, p. 851, supra.

(2) Consult Rules 59 and 60 of the Federal Rules of Civil Procedure. When should relief be sought under Rule 59 and when under Rule 60(b)? In what circumstances may relief be sought by a plenary action in equity?

(3) Clause (b)(5) of Fed.R.Civ.P. 60 allows a re-opening of a judgment upon showing that "a prior judgment upon which it was based has been reversed." Consider Lubben v. Selective Service System, 453 F.2d 645 (1st Cir.1972): The district court had granted a final judgment barring plaintiff's induction into the armed services. The government appealed, but later withdrew the appeal. When the precedential support for the district court's decision was over-ruled by the Supreme Court, the government sought to re-open the judgment under Rule 60(b). The district court re-opened and vacated its earlier judgment. On appeal, held: reversed. The change of applicable law would not support a motion under Rule 60(b). The judgment was not "void," only "erroneous." Note that, while the appeal from the judgment is pending, a change in the law will be recognized.

See also Ackermann v. United States, 340 U.S. 193, 71 S.Ct. 209, 95 L.Ed. 207 (1950): The Supreme Court refused to allow petitioner, who had not appealed from the original judgment, to re-open his denaturalization case. Petitioner had sought to re-open the case, after his brother-in-law had his identical case reversed on appeal. In a dissent by Justice Black, concurred in by Justices Frankfurter and Douglas, the minority complained that the decision "neutralizes the humane spirit of the Rule," 340 U.S. at 202, 71 S.Ct. at 209, 95 L.Ed. at 213.

(4) It is generally said that a judgment in violation of due process is void within the meaning of Rule 60(b)(4). See, e.g., Aguchak v. Montgomery Ward, 520 P.2d 1352 (Alaska 1974) (failure to inform debtor in small claims action that he could file a written pleading; failure of due process).

NEW YORK LIFE INSURANCE CO. v. NASHVILLE TRUST CO.

Supreme Court of Tennessee, 1956.
200 Tenn. 513, 292 S.W.2d 749.

BURNETT, J. The bill in this cause was filed by the Insurance Company against the Trust Company and others, as defendants, seeking to recover of the Trust Company certain funds which it holds as successor trustee to the Nashville Trust Company, which was the beneficiary under two life insurance policies, as described in the bill, issued on the life of Thomas C. Buntin and payable to the Nashville Trust Company as trustee under a trust instrument dated February 16, 1928.

The beneficiaries under the trust agreement are made individual defendants to this suit and are the former wife of Thomas C. Buntin and their three children.

Thomas C. Buntin, the insured, who was likewise an insurance man, disappeared from his home in Nashville, Tennessee, and subsequently a suit was brought by the Nashville Trust Company against the complainant Insurance Company, appellant, in which a judgment was rendered against the Company for the full amount of the policies. This case is reported in 178 Tenn. 437, 159 S.W.2d 81, and is styled, New York Life Insurance Company v. Nashville Trust Company. As a result of this suit, on March 10, 1942, the Insurance Company paid to the trustee $59,438.40, from which certain expenses and costs were paid and the net balance paid to the trustee and later turned over to the successor trustee, defendant in the present suit.

Thomas C. Buntin, the insured upon which that money was paid, was found alive on June 3, 1953, and his identity verified June 12, 1953. This suit was brought immediately thereafter and is for the purpose of recovering the net balance of the funds in the hands of the successor trustee.

The relief sought in this suit is based on five grounds: (1) mistake, (2) fraud, (3) that the defendants have been unjustly enriched, (4) newly discovered evidence and (5) that the defendant trustee holds the funds in its hands as constructive trustee for the Insurance Company.

To this bill the defendants demurred which with the original and amended demurrers substantially raise these points, to wit:

1. That whatever right of action the complainant has is barred either by the six or ten year statute of limitations;

2. That the judgment in the Circuit Court action between the same parties is res judicata on the merits;

3. That no actionable mistake has been made;

4. That all facts as to fraud were in the original proceeding and cannot be attacked in this proceeding;

5. That there are not sufficient allegations of fraud pleaded;

6. That no facts are pleaded which show a mistake;

7. That there is no charge of fraud against either the trustee or beneficiary.

The Chancellor sustained the defendant's demurrers and dismissed the bill. He kept in force an injunction to enjoin the successor trustee from paying out the money pending this litigation. . . .

[W]e think the demurrers should have been overruled. We think that the fraud committed here by Buntin is extrinsic. True, it is very closely allied to what is known as intrinsic fraud wherein all the courts, insofar as we have been able to find, have followed U.S. v. Throckmorton, 98 U.S. 61, 25 L.Ed. 93; Pico v. Cohn, 91 Cal. 129, 25 P. 970, 27 P. 537, 13 L.R.A. 336. We are committed to this rule if the fraud is intrinsic as is shown by Keith v. Alger, 114 Tenn. 1, 85 S.W. 71. We feel though that fraud in the instant case, for the reasons hereinafter stated, more or less brings it within the rule of Hazel-Atlas Glass Co. v. Hartford-Empire Co., 322 U.S. 238, 64 S.Ct. 997, 88 L.Ed. 1250, wherein the well-recognized rule of the Throckmorton case and others was recognized again by the Supreme Court of the United States.

In the first place it is conceded by all that the money now sought by the appellant is money being held by a successor trustee. . . . This money was paid on a contract that Thomas C. Buntin had with the Life Insurance Company wherein they agreed to pay the principal amount of these policies "upon receipt of due proof of the death of Thomas C. Buntin". As is shown by the reported opinion, which was prepared by the late Chief Justice Grafton Green, the proof in that lawsuit and the inferences there along with the seven-year presumption statute, (which is simply the common-law rule of evidence and has no more force than any other evidence which might turn out to be untrue, D'Arusment v. Jones, 72 Tenn. 251) warranted this Court, in that case, in finding under such circumstantial evidence that the insured died prior to March 8, 1933, the expiration date of the insurance. In that case great weight and great store was put on the fact of the wills being sent home from St. Louis to two of his relatives; the unstability [sic] of Buntin himself; the suicide of Buntin's father and things of that kind which clearly convinced this Court, in that lawsuit, that Buntin was dead.

It now, twenty years after the policies had matured in 1933, turns out that Buntin is alive, is married again and is raising another family. The trial court in the reported case did not consider that Buntin was committing any fraud on them. The question there was whether or not Buntin was dead. Under the facts and circumstances introduced in that case the court and jury, affirmed by the appellate courts as was shown by the reported opinion, concluded that he was dead. It is true that the Insurance Company offered certain proof to the effect that he had been seen here and there (all of which later turned out to be incorrect), but this was not a showing of fraud, it was merely a showing or an attempt to show, that subsequent to the time that the policies lapsed, Buntin was seen alive. It now turns out that he has committed a *gross fraud upon the Court* as well as upon the Insurance Company. By his acts then, which no one knew anything of until twenty years later and after this judgment became final, he fooled this Court and caused it to reach a mistake of fact (that Buntin was dead) when as a matter of fact he was alive.

In 31 Am.Jur., Sec. 654, page 232, it is said:

"Fraud which induces an adversary to withdraw his defense, or *prevents him from presenting an available defense* or cause of action in the action in which the judgment is obtained, has been *regarded as a proper ground* for equitable relief against the judgment." (Emphasis ours.)

There are then cited a number of cases from many jurisdictions in the United States. In this instant case Buntin by hiding out committed a fraud on this Court and by his action prevented the available defense to the Insurance Company that he was actually alive. This was not discovered until 1953.

. . . Atlas Glass Co. v. Hartford-Empire Co., [322 U.S. 238, 64 S.Ct. 1000, 88 L.Ed. 1250] . . .

. . . was a suit wherein the Supreme Court of the United States set aside a judgment, or authorized the Circuit Court of Appeals to or directed them to, which judgment had been entered by them some ten years prior thereto and the term had expired, etc., which brought the judgment as contended under the rules of the Throckmorton case and others. The bill was filed to set aside the judgment as having been obtained by fraud. The fraud consisted of a conspiracy entered into by the attorneys and officials of one of the companies to have published in a trade journal an article which would describe the process under consideration as a remarkable advance in the art of fashioning certain glass machinery. The Circuit Court on the strength of this article held that the patent was valid and the District Court was reversed. At the time the matter was tried in the District Court the Hazel-Atlas Glass attorneys received information that one Clark and one of Hartford's attorneys had several years previously admitted that the Hartford lawyer was the true author of the publication. Hazel-Atlas attorneys did not at that time attempt to verify the truth of the hearsay story but relied on and won the case on other grounds. After the Circuit Court opinion reversed the District Court on this ground, investigation was made which determined the true state of affairs. The mandate of the Circuit Court was entered in 1932. In 1941 the present suit, just quoted from above, was commenced with the result that due to the fraud therein committed the suit was reversed. Picture the related acts of Buntin in this case and the facts of the case just quoted from. We cannot see that the fraud in the case last above quoted from is as extrinsic as is the fraud in the instant case, Buntin case. *The fraud of Buntin was not discovered until many years after the money was paid and the judgment was rendered and it was this fraud which was discovered later on that is now the question. That fraud was not before the Court and is not the basis of the opinion as heretofore reported.* 178 Tenn. 437, 159 S.W.2d 81.

The rationale of these decisions [refusing relief for fraud called "intrinsic"] is that in the course of a trial the adversary has the opportunity by a cross-examination to show perjury or forgery and that in every case there is likely to be a difference of opinion among the witnesses which may be shown by rigid cross-examination. The rationale further is that where there has been a fair trial, the parties have had a fair opportunity to present the situation, then the final judgment is final and cannot be reopened for very good and obvious reasons. But *in the instant case there was not a fair and honest opportunity to present things which were discovered twenty years later.* No one would doubt certainly, if it could have been discovered at the time this case was originally tried, that Buntin was alive that there would have been any judgment rendered in it then. We would guess that if Buntin had been found then he would have been held in contempt of Court to the limit of its severity. Is it right that he can now come in court, years later and say: "Well, I've got your money, do what you want to about it, there is nothing you can do with me about it or anything else"? Is it right then that someone else, that he has made beneficiary under his policy, should keep this money? It certainly seems to us that it should go back where it belongs, that part which is left and that those who are not entitled to it should not be allowed further to participate in it.

* * *

Clearly the plea of res judicata should have been overruled. The issue in the case now is whether or not Tom Buntin by active extrinsic fraud has defrauded the Courts and Insurance Company, thereby causing the Courts to say that money should be paid to the beneficiaries of Buntin. And also that by his deliberately and wilfully keeping himself hidden out he has simulated death and has manufactured a chain of circumstances and evidence which was calculated to and did persuade the Courts of this State that he had committed suicide. In the case heretofore tried the issue was whether or not under the facts there he was dead. The issue in the law case decided twenty-odd years ago was "whether or not Buntin had died prior to March 8, 1933, (the date the policy expired without value) was the issue in the previous trial". It certainly seems to us that this is an independent action and does not involve any retrial of the issues disposed of in the former case. . . .

We are likewise very confident that the statute of limitations did not run herein. The fraud of Buntin was not known until he was found in 1953.

* * *

[Separate concurring opinions of TOMLINSON, J., and NEIL, CH.J., omitted.]

SWEPSTON, J., dissenting. My dissent in this case is based solely upon that part of the majority opinion which relates to the question of whether this fraud was intrinsic or extrinsic.

I think the majority opinion reflects a great deal of study on 'the part of the writer and I think his conclusion would be justified by the opinion in the Hazel-Atlas Glass Company, decided by the United States Supreme Court, except that it is out of line with our own case. "Extrinsic fraud is said to consist of conduct or occurrences extrinsic or collateral to the issues examined and determined in the action", as distinguished from those things which are a part of the internal chain composing the process of adjudication.

Likewise the fraudulent conduct of Buntin in setting the stage to make it appear that his death had occurred was intrinsic evidence because, although the Insurance Company offered evidence to the contrary, this Court reached the conclusion on the strength of Buntin's very conduct among other things that he was in fact dead.

It is suggested by one member of the Court that the evidence in the instant case is both intrinsic and extrinsic. According to the above definition of the two it is impossible for such a statement to be correct. The evidence is extrinsic in the sense that it occurred outside the courtroom but that is not within the definition of extrinsic evidence; it must be extrinsic because it was conduct or occurrences collateral to the issues examined in Court.

* * *

For these reasons I am of opinion that we should let the dead past bury its dead, as in fact Thomas Buntin was dead within the contemplation of the insurance contract and the laws of Tennessee.

[Separate dissenting opinion of PREWITT, J., omitted.]

[Opinion on rehearing omitted.]

RESTATEMENT, SECOND, JUDGMENTS *

§ 70. Judgment Procured by Corruption, Duress, or Fraud

(1) Subject to the limitations stated in § 74, a judgment in a contested action may be avoided if the judgment:

(a) Resulted from corruption of or duress upon the court or the attorney for the party against whom the judgment was rendered, or duress upon that party, or

(b) Was based on a claim that the party obtaining the judgment knew to be fraudulent.

(2) A party seeking relief under Subsection (1) must:

(a) Have acted with due diligence in discovering the facts constituting the basis for relief;

(b) Assert his claim for relief from the judgment with such particularity as to indicate it is well founded and prove the allegations by clear and convincing evidence; and

(c) When his claim is based on falsity of the evidence on which the judgment was based, show that he had made a reasonable effort in the original action to ascertain the truth of the matter.

Comment:

*   *   *

c. Fraud: Extrinsic and intrinsic, and similar distinctions. Defining the circumstances under which the conclusiveness of a judgment can be overcome on account of fraud is especially difficult. The question presented by a charge of fraud is whether a judgment that is fair on its face should be examined in its underpinnings concerning the very matters it purports to resolve. Reexamination of those matters typically involves testimonial conflicts, often the same that were presented in the original action. Such conflicts are easy to propound and difficult to resolve with confidence. The definitional task is therefore to state criteria that cannot so easily be met as to create open opportunity for relitigation, but which are not so demanding that plain cases of fraud cannot be remedied.

From an early date some decisions permitted a judgment to be attacked on the ground that it was based on perjured or fabricated evidence. The only qualification was that the application for relief show clearly and persuasively that the evidence had indeed been perjured or fabricated. Since in the early days the procedure of seeking relief was a separate suit in equity, the complaint was permitted and required to go into detail concerning the evidence of the fraud and the reason it had not been discovered at the time of trial. Later decisions, however, attempted to draw distinctions in terms other than the positiveness with which the fraud could be shown, and these have led to much confusion.

The most widely recognized distinction was between "extrinsic" and "intrinsic" fraud. In its core meaning, "extrinsic" fraud meant fraud that induced a party to default or to consent to judgment against him. See § 68. "Intrinsic" fraud meant knowing use of perjured testimony or otherwise fabricated evidence. But this distinction was obliterated by decisions in which it was reasoned that offering fabricated evidence "prevented" the other party from contesting the proposition for which the fabricated evidence was offered as proof. Hence, in many jurisdictions the distinction between "extrinsic" and "intrinsic" fraud was accepted nominally but not in substance. Moreover, it was never satisfactorily explained why a litigant misled into defaulting should be more fully protected than one who suffered judgment by reason of deception committed in open court.

*   *   *

d. Elements required for relief from fraud. Four elements must be established to obtain relief. First, it must be shown that the fabrication or concealment was a material basis for the judgment and was not merely cumulative or relevant only to a peripheral issue. Second, the party seeking relief must show that he adequately pursued means for discovering the truth available to him in the original action. Under modern procedure in trial courts of general jurisdiction in cases involving substantial stakes, abundant devices exist for discovering an opposing party's proof and subjecting it to investigation prior to trial and adequate incentive usually exists to use such devices. Hence in such circumstances, only a well concealed or unforeseeable fraud is likely to survive a reasonably diligent effort to ascertain the truth. On the other hand, in cases involving limited stakes, it may be unreasonably costly to pursue intensive discovery or investigation when there is no indication that the other side may offer fabricated evidence. Furthermore, in some situations a litigant is entitled to be passive and unquestioning with respect to the proofs of another party. Thus, the cases allowing relief from fraud practiced by a trustee often advert to the fact that a beneficiary should not have to anticipate a trustee's deliberate falsification of the accounts he presents to the court.

Third, the applicant must show due diligence after judgment, in that he discovered the fraud as soon as might reasonably have been expected. This is an application of the general principle of due diligence, see § 74.

Finally, the party seeking relief must demonstrate, before being allowed to present his case, that he has a substantial case to present, and must offer clear and convincing proof to establish that the evidence underlying the judgment was indeed fabricated or concealed. This heavy burden of proof is an important measure of protection against attacks on honestly procured judgments. It also transforms the issue from a retrial of a question previously litigated to a search for something approaching incontestable proof as to truth of the underlying matter in issue.

NOTES

(1) For a strong defense of the distinction between intrinsic and extrinsic fraud, see Schwartz v. Merchant Mortgage Co., 272 Md. 305, 322 A.2d 544 (1974). But compare the well-known critique and rejection of the principle in Shammas v. Shammas, 9 N.J. 321, 88 A.2d 204 (1952) (Judge, now Justice, Brennan).

(2) What is "fraud" under Rule 60(b) of the Federal Rules of Civil Procedure? 62 F.R.D. 357 (E.D.Pa.1974) (false answers to interrogatories do not amount to fraud on the court). Is it confined to corruption of the judge or other court officials? What of perjurious testimony? Does it matter that a lawyer was involved? See Restatement, Second, Judgments § 70, Comment d.

(3) A mule stepped in front of plaintiff's moving car, causing injuries to plaintiff. Defendant, who could neither read nor write, upon being served with a citation, came to court to explain that the mule was not his; he left his address with the clerk, on the understanding that the clerk would inform him when his case was called. The clerk did not do so and a default judgment was taken on the basis of plaintiff's statements to the trial judge that defendant

admitted the mule was his. When defendant found that his bank had been garnished, he retained counsel to have the judgment set aside. What should be the result? Alexander v. Hagedorn, 148 Tex. 565, 226 S.W.2d 996 (1950). The case created a furor and one leading newspaper arranged a testimonial dinner to solicit funds for defendant's legal costs.

(4) Judgment was entered on a directed verdict in favor of the insurer because the "Iron Safe clause" of the policy required two copies of inventory to be kept in a fireproof safe and only one copy was there at the time of the fire. Seven months after judgment plaintiff discovered that fortuitously a second copy of the inventory survived the fire. The judgment was reopened on the ground of newly discovered evidence "in order that judgments may reflect the true merits of the case" and to serve "the ends of justice." Serio v. Badger Mutual Insurance Co., 266 F.2d 418, 421 (5th Cir.1959), cert. denied 361 U.S. 832, 80 S.Ct. 81, 4 L.Ed.2d 73. Should this same doctrine have applied if the insurance company "discovered" a release in its files after judgment rendered in favor of the insured?

(5) Can a state rule according absolute verity to recitations in a judgment prevent an inquiry showing that, contrary to the judgment, service was not properly made and thus jurisdiction never acquired? See O'Boyle v. Bevil, 259 F.2d 506 (5th Cir.1958), cert. denied 359 U.S. 913, 79 S.Ct. 590, 3 L.Ed.2d 576 (1959).

(6) While courts have only limited power to modify their judgments upon substantive grounds, when the error is "clerical", the modification may be made pursuant to Rule 60(a) of the Federal Rules of Civil Procedure or similar state rules. See Reavley and Orr, Trial Court's Power to Amend Its Judgments, 25 Baylor L.Rev. 191, 195 (1973).

(7) Should a court have power to modify a judgment upon substantive grounds when the law upon which it was based has changed? The general rule is that after the time for appeal has expired, there is no power to alter the decision. In that way, parties are encouraged to pursue their appeals. At the same time, the legal system is not burdened with reconsidering every case that has gone before each time it announces a new rule of law. But what about changes that occur during the time when the case could be appealed? Some courts take the position that it is senseless to require the parties to pursue an appeal when the trial court can easily correct the error. See, e.g., Schildhaus v. Moe, 335 F.2d 529 (2d Cir.1964); Watson v. Symons Corp., 121 F.R.D. 351 (N.D. Ill.1988) (modifying judgment in light of Supreme Court opinion when opposing counsel had relied on lower court opinion without notifying the Illinois court that the case was pending before the Supreme Court). Many federal courts, however, do not see Rules 59 or 60 as providing them with this authority, Silk v. Sandoval, 435 F.2d 1266 (1st Cir.1971), cert. denied 402 U.S. 1012, 91 S.Ct. 2189, 29 L.Ed.2d 435.

SECTION 3. ENFORCEMENT OF JUDGMENTS

RIESENFELD, COLLECTION OF MONEY JUDGMENTS IN AMERICAN LAW—A HISTORICAL INVENTORY AND A PROSPECTUS

42 Iowa L.Rev. 155, 156–72 (1957).

GENERAL CLASSIFICATION OF COLLECTION TECHNIQUES AND THE IMPACT OF THE COMMON LAW TRADITION

In classifying the legal effects of a final personal judgment for the recovery of money it might be helpful to distinguish between its intrinsic effects as authoritative and conclusive disposition of the cause of action and the litigated issues between the parties pertaining thereto and the extrinsic attributes which are bestowed thereon by the common law (and the classical statutes that are deemed to have become part of it) for the purpose of enabling the judgment creditor to proceed to a forced but orderly collection. The latter effects may be divided into three great categories, *viz.:*

(1) *Executability* (by means of assorted writs or process).

(2) *Actionability* (by constituting a cause of action for an action of debt or civil action in general).

(3) *Creation of lien* (by "encumbering" specifically defined interests in land of the debtor).

. . . [E]quity also added to the arsenal of collection remedies by entertaining creditors' suits to compel or facilitate the satisfaction of judgments in cases calling for such intervention.

The *common law,* in its mature or classical stage, provided for the execution of money judgments by means of two principal writs known by the names of *fieri facias* and *elegit.* The former writ, which was of uncertain but ancient origin, commanded the sheriff to cause the judgment to be satisfied out of the judgment debtor's goods and chattels and was executed by seizure and sale. *Elegit,* on the other hand, was an innovation introduced by the Statute of Westminster II in the course of the great reform legislation of Edward I [1285, 13 Edw 1, c. 18] and authorized the judgment creditor to obtain satisfaction not only out of his debtor's goods and chattels, but also out of the use of a moiety of his lands. The goods and chattels were transferred to the judgment creditor at a reasonable price, while the use of half of the lands was assigned to him in the form of a tenancy for a term determined by an appraisal of its annual value (so-called tenancy by *elegit*).

*   *   *

The *executability* of a money judgment at common law by means of a suitable writ—whether *levari facias, fieri facias* or *elegit*—was limited in time. According to English practice in the eighteenth century the judgment creditor was entitled to sue out a writ of execution upon "signing final judgment" without awaiting its formal entry in the judgment roll or its docketing and lost such right upon the expiration of a year and a day, counted from such signing date. The reason for this limitation was the presumption that after such time the judgment was satisfied. This presumption could be overcome. . . .

The *actionability* of the judgment, consequently, was originally extremely important in view of the limited executability. The subsequent availability of *scire facias* reduced the importance of the actionability of domestic judgments. Still there were certain procedural considerations why the actionability of domestic judgments remained of practical utility. . . .

In the course of time *equity* came to intervene in aid of execution in situations where the legal process available to the creditor was either frustrated through fraud or concealment on the side of the debtor or was inadequate for other reasons. . . .

While it was said by a famous eighteenth century writer that a creditor was "favored in equity against the debtor and others claiming from him . . ." the truth is that equity's intervention in his favor was slow, haphazard, vacillating and in need of frequent legislative prodding. Perhaps the two most important statutes prompting equitable aid to creditors were the two acts directed against fraudulent dispositions of assets, *viz.* the Statute against Fraudulent Conveyances and the Statute against Fraudulent Devises. . . .

During the latter part of the seventeenth century, at the latest, equity also commenced to lend its discovery procedure to creditors for the purpose of ascertaining whether assets were fraudulently conveyed or concealed. . . .

[Gradually the two writs for execution of money judgments coalesced and a single writ developed. Another evolution was the creation over time of the judgment lien, enforceable in four different ways.]

* * *

In some states judgment liens are only enforceable by writ of execution, whereas others permit only foreclosure in equity; a third class of jurisdictions gives to the creditor the choice between foreclosure in equity and enforcement through execution, while a fourth group ordinarily requires enforcement by writ of execution, but permits foreclosure where such writ is unavailable.*

NOTES

(1) For an empirical study of the taking and enforcement of consumer credit judgments, see Due Process Denied: Consumer Default Judgments in New York City, 10 Colum.J.L.Soc.P. 370 (1974). The study finds, among other things, that at times large commercial creditors file false affidavits of personal

---

* This paragraph was footnote 115 in the original. Other footnotes have been omitted.

service after actually making only "sewer service." When that happens, the first actual notice to debtor comes in the form of a wage garnishment. For an overview of constitutional limitations on pre- and post-judgment collection practices, see Countryman, The Bill of Rights and the Bill Collector, 15 Ariz. L.R. 521 (1973).

(2) In 1971, Maine replaced its traditional judgment collection machinery, including executions against property and garnishments, with a new approach centered around a debtor disclosure hearing and an individualized judicial determination of how the judgment is to be satisfied.

At the hearing, the court first determines if the debtor has sufficient non-exempt property to satisfy the judgment. If so, he is ordered, on pain of contempt, to turn over this property to the creditor. If sufficient property is not available, the court makes an inquiry into the financial resources of the debtor and orders installment payments out of income. In making this order, the court is not bound by a legislative formula, but is free to consider individually the debtor's position. Upon three consecutive defaults in the installment payments, the court can order the employer to make the payments directly to the creditor. See Ch. 502, 14 § 3121 and ff.; Post-judgment Procedures for Collection of Small Debts: The Maine Solution, 25 Maine L.Rev. 43 (1973).

––––––––––

COUNTRYMAN, CASES & MATERIALS ON DEBTOR AND CREDITOR
pp. 77–79 (1964) *

Imprisonment for debt in the United States followed the English practice until the early nineteenth century. Thus there were in Massachusetts, Maryland, New York, and Pennsylvania in 1830 from three to five times as many persons imprisoned for debt as for crime. For the decade 1820–1830 the Suffolk County Jail in Boston alone contained 11,818 imprisoned debtors from a total population ranging from 43,000 to 63,000.

A wave of reform in the 1830's led to state constitutional provisions forbidding imprisonment for debt. Today such prohibitions appear in the constitutions of nearly all states and in the statutes of several where the constitution is silent. . . . But many of the constitutional prohibitions are expressly or by interpretation limited to contract debtors. Hanson v. Isaak, 72 S.D. 311, 33 N.W.2d 561 (1948); Notes, 37 Yale L.J. 509 (1928), 1 N.C.L.Rev. 229 (1923), 31 Yale L.J. 439 (1922), 4 Calif.L.Rev. 331 (1916). Many of those so limited contain exceptions for absconding contract debtors or those guilty of fraud, Notes, 3 Vill.L. Rev. 79 (1957), 22 Minn.L.Rev. 424 (1938), and in the fraud cases "evidence may be conclusive which would be far from sufficient in a criminal prosecution." Other constitutions, not confined to contract debtors, contain exceptions for specific types of torts. Note, 42 Iowa L.Rev. 306 (1957). In some states body execution is available only where the judgment cannot be collected by execution against the

* Footnotes omitted.

debtor's property, Note, 31 Mich.L.Rev. 731 (1933), and proceedings against property may be forbidden while the debtor is imprisoned, Tappan v. Evans, 11 N.H. 311 (1840); Moran v. Toth, 196 Misc. 860, 95 N.Y.S.2d 237 (1949). Whatever the area of constitutional prohibition, it applies to detention of the debtor on body attachment while the suit is pending, as well as to his detention after judgment on body execution. Note, 26 Colum.L.Rev. 1007 (1926).

In most states the debtor "carries the jail keys in his own pocket" in the sense that he may obtain a release by paying the judgment or by complying with a state insolvency act under which his nonexempt property is placed at the disposal of all of his creditors and he takes a "poor debtor's oath." Notes, 42 Iowa L.Rev. 306 (1957), 1952 Wis.L.Rev. 764, 7 U.Chi.L.Rev. 137 (1939), 13 Chi.-Kent.L.Rev. 279 (1935), 37 Yale L.J. 509 (1928). But in some states, where "malice is the gist of the action" or the judgment is for specified torts, the debtor who does not pay the judgment must serve a minimum term. Colo.Rev.Stat. § 77-9-4 (1953) (in discretion of court, not exceeding one year); Ill.Ann.Stat., C. 72, § 2, C. 77, § 68 (Smith-Hurd, 1935) (six months); Pa.Stat.Ann., tit. 39, § 257 (Purdon, 1954) (sixty days); R.I.Gen.Laws §§ 9-25-7, 9-25-8, 10-13-2 (1956) (in discretion of court); Vt.Stat.Ann., tit. 12, §§ 3673, 3691, 3692 (1958) (same). In only a few states is there a specified maximum period of imprisonment, although failure of the creditor to pay the debtor's board bill in states where that is required may be a ground for release. Notes, 42 Iowa L.Rev. 306 (1957), 23 id. 126 (1937). In Illinois the defendant receives a credit of $1.50 per day for time served, Ill.Ann.Stat., C. 72, § 33 (Smith-Hurd, 1935), but the board bill which the creditor is required to pay is added to the costs of the suit, § 31. And see People v. Lohman, 13 Ill.App.2d 335, 142 N.E.2d 156 (1957), indicating that the board bill is $3.50 per week.

REEVES v. CROWNSHIELD

Court of Appeals of New York, 1937.
274 N.Y. 74, 8 N.E.2d 283.

FINCH, J. The uncollectibility of money judgments has ever been a subject of concern to bench and bar. A large part of the statute law of this State is designed to enable a judgment creditor to obtain satisfaction upon his money judgment. That a large percentage of these money judgments have remained uncollectible has been confirmed by statistical surveys. (Study of Civil Justice in New York [Survey of Litigation in New York], Johns Hopkins University Institute of Law [1931.) Many debtors who were in a position to pay have evaded their legal obligations by unlawful and technical means. Discontent with this situation resulted in agitation for reform in collection procedure. (Levien, The Collection of Money Judgments, New York Legislative Document, No. 50 F [1934].) Finally, in 1935, upon the recommendation of the Judicial Council, a law was enacted creating a new mode of enforcing the payment of judgments (Laws of 1935, ch. 630).

Section 793 of the Civil Practice Act * now provides that, in addition to the garnishee provisions of the old law, the court may make an order directing a judgment debtor to make payments in installments out of the income which he receives. Such orders must be made upon notice to the judgment debtor and after he has had an opportunity to show inability to pay, and with due regard to the reasonable requirements of the judgment debtor and his family, as well as of payments required to be made by him to other creditors. Section 801 of the Civil Practice Act provides that refusal to pay after such an order of the court is punishable as a contempt. Statutes somewhat similar are to be found in Massachusetts, England and Nova Scotia (General Laws, Mass., ch. 224, § 16; Debtor's Act, 1869, § 5 [32 & 33 Victoria, ch. 62], see Annual Practice [1937], p. 764; Nova Scotia Rev.Stat. [1923, vol. 2 ch. 232, § 29.)

This new procedure was invoked against the appellant, in an attempt to collect a judgment for approximately $400. The examination in supplementary proceedings disclosed that he was employed by the Federal government as a steamship inspector at a salary of $230 per month, less a small pension deduction. He has no children, and the whereabouts of his wife are unknown. Aside from $48 a month paid as rent and his living expenses, he has no financial obligations. The court ordered the appellant to pay installments of $20 per month until the judgment was satisfied. Upon his failure to pay, he was held in contempt and fined the sum of $20, commitment being provided for in default of payment.

An appeal was taken directly to this court from the City Court of New York City on the ground that a constitutional question was involved.

By stipulation it was provided that the appeals from the order directing payment, and the order adjudging the appellant in contempt, were to be consolidated and treated as one appeal. A final order in supplementary proceedings is appealable to this court, since it is a final order in a special proceeding. (Civ.Prac.Act, §§ 773, 774.) The order in the case at bar is a final order in a special proceeding. (Civ.Prac.Act, § 801.)

The judgment debtor challenges the constitutionality of section 793 and section 801 on the ground that in effect they provide for imprisonment for debt. It is admitted that neither the State nor the Federal Constitutions contain provisions expressly prohibiting imprisonment for debt, and that the statutory provision forbidding imprisonment for debt found in section 21 of the New York Civil Rights Law (Cons.Laws, ch. 6) excepts cases otherwise specially prescribed by law. It is asserted, however, that imprisonment for debt is barred by the due process

* Now redistributed to diverse sections of the N.Y.C.P.L.R. See especially N.Y.C.P. L.R. § 5226 providing for orders to pay in instalments. [Footnote by eds.]

clauses of the State and Federal Constitutions. No cases so holding are cited, but reliance is had upon vague dicta found in Bailey v. Alabama, 219 U.S. 219, 244, 31 S.Ct. 145, 55 L.Ed. 191, and Henderson v. Mayor of New York, 92 U.S. 259, 268, 23 L.Ed. 543. Whatever doubt there may exist as to whether imprisonment for debt without regard to ability to pay may be treated as a deprivation of liberty without due process of law (Eikenberry & Co. v. Edwards, 67 Iowa 619, 25 N.W. 832, 56 Am. Rep. 360), there can be no doubt that imprisonment for failure to obey an order of a court to make payment out of income, which order is made with due regard to the needs of the debtor and his family, is not violative of the due process clause.

"In one form or another prohibitions against imprisonment for debt are found in most, if not all, of our state constitutions. Usually these prohibitions allow exceptions in cases of fraud, willful injury to persons or property, or fines or penalties imposed by law. Courts, in construing such provisions, have frequently been called upon to determine to what extent they invalidated statutes authorizing civil executions against a body of a judgment debtor. Their manifest intent is to exempt from imprisonment the honest debtor who is poor, and in good faith unable to pay his debts. This shield of protection should not, therefore, be allowed to be interposed for the benefit of debtors who, being able to pay, yet seek to avoid doing so by assigning or concealing their effects, or by eluding judicial process. Consequently, courts have generally, and quite properly, upheld the validity of statutes authorizing the imprisonment of a debtor after the return of an execution unsatisfied and proof that he has property legally applicable to the discharge of his liabilities. The imprisonment in such a case is not for debt, but for the neglect and refusal to perform a moral and legal duty, the performance resting in the ability of the debtor.

* * *

"The amelioration of the condition of poor debtors has also proceeded through the enactment of insolvency laws. But in construing legislation having this end in view, courts cannot keep too constantly in mind the fundamental theory upon which it is based, namely, that none of the exemptions thereby afforded debtors should enable them to avoid the payment of debts when able to pay them." (3 Freeman on The Law of Executions [3d ed.], p. 2394 et seq.)

In the case at bar the judgment debtor has not complained that the order directing the payment of $20 per month is unjust, inequitable or harsh. His position is an arbitrary refusal to pay. It is based upon the ground that the courts are powerless to compel him to pay out of his income an amount fixed after deducting the sum necessary for his reasonable needs.

The Legislature has seen fit to provide a creditor with a direct remedy for the collection of his just debts. A refusal to recognize such an order by the judgment debtor entitles the creditor to move to have him punished for contempt. Without this right, there would be no power in the court to enforce its order. To compel the judgment debtor to obey the order of the court is not imprisonment for debt, but only imprisonment for disobedience of an order with which he is able to comply. His refusal is contumacious conduct, the same as a refusal to obey any other lawful order of the court.

* * *

The argument that the imprisonment of the debtor for failure to comply with the order to pay will result in interference with the Federal agency which employs him cannot be sustained. Certainly his Federal position does not exempt him from imprisonment for crimes which he may commit. It is equally clear that it does not give him the privilege to disobey with impunity the orders of a State court.

It follows that the orders appealed from should be affirmed, with costs.

NOTES

(1) Article 52 of the N.Y.—McKinney's CPLR, Enforcement of Money Judgments, contains an extensive and elaborate engine for extracting satisfaction from a judgment debtor, including the levers of arrest and contempt in some circumstances. Cf. §§ 5210, 5250; Report of Committee on Law Reform, Civil Arrest and Execution Against the Person, 11 The Record 402 (1956); Note, Present Status of Execution Against the Body of the Judgment Debtor, 42 Iowa L.Rev. 306 (1957).

(2) Despite serious efforts at reform, the enforcement of money judgments remains an unsavory business in New York, as elsewhere. Does hope lie more with the lawyers than the laws? See Third Preliminary Report of New York Advisory Committee on Practice and Procedure, N.Y.Leg.Doc. No. 17, at 234 (1959):

> "Whether [enforcement] procedure is used to take advantage of and to unmercifully harass honest debtors without assets or means to acquire them or whether it is used to permit judgment debtors with the ability to pay judgments to flout the law and defraud their creditors depends, in the ultimate analysis, upon the integrity of the bar and the seriousness with which the court views the questions involved in the collection of judgments."

(3) A judgment debtor can postpone his doom for astonishingly long periods if he is resolute of purpose and nimble of foot. The modern classic is James v. Powell, 19 N.Y.2d 249, 279 N.Y.S.2d 10, 225 N.E.2d 741 (1967)—to mention but one of its numerous contributions to New York's corpus juris. Representative Adam Clayton Powell was held in 1963 to have defamed Mrs. Ethel James and was cast in a $46,000 judgment. After prevailing in the highest court of the state, Mrs. James set out to collect her judgment. Congressman Powell invoked a wide range of defenses, maneuvers and evasive tactics to avoid discovery of his assets, arrest, examination, attachment, execution or any other collection remedy. Scores of proceedings and many judges later, Mr. Powell, in about 1968, began paying on the judgment.

(4) Extensive symposia on collection and enforcement problems appear in: 1951 U.Ill.L.F. 1, 42 Iowa L.Rev. 155 (1957) and 5 St. Mary's L.J. 715 (1974).

HICKS v. FEIOCK

Supreme Court of the United States, 1988.
485 U.S. 624, 108 S.Ct. 1423, 99 L.Ed.2d 721.

JUSTICE WHITE delivered the opinion of the Court.*

* * *

I.

On January 19, 1976, a California state court entered an order requiring respondent, Phillip Feiock, to begin making monthly payments to his ex-wife for the support of their three children. Over the next six years, respondent only sporadically complied with the order, and by December 1982 he had discontinued paying child support altogether. His ex-wife sought to enforce the support orders. On June 22, 1984, a hearing was held in California state court on her petition for ongoing support payments and for payment of the arrearage due her. The court examined respondent's financial situation and ordered him to begin paying $150 per month commencing on July 1, 1984. . . .

Respondent apparently made two monthly payments but paid nothing for the next nine months. He was then served with an order to show cause why he should not be held in contempt on nine counts of failure to make the monthly payments ordered by the court. At a hearing on August 9, 1985, petitioner made out a *prima facie* case of contempt against respondent by establishing the existence of a valid court order, respondent's knowledge of the order, and respondent's failure to comply with the order. Respondent defended by arguing that he was unable to pay support during the months in question. This argument was partially successful, but respondent was adjudged to be in contempt on five of the nine counts. He was sentenced to five days in jail on each count, to be served consecutively, for a total of 25 days. This sentence was suspended, however, and respondent was placed on probation for three years. As one of the conditions of his probation, he was ordered once again to make support payments of $150 per month. As another condition of his probation, he was ordered, starting the following month, to begin repaying $50 per month on his accumulated arrearage, which was determined to total $1650. [On appeal, the state appellate court held that the legislative presumptions applied by the trial court violate the Due Process Clause of the Fourteenth Amendment, which forbids a court from employing certain presumptions that affect the determination of guilt or innocence in criminal proceedings.]

II.

Three issues must be decided to resolve this case, [The first two involve interpretation of state law. The] third is whether this contempt proceeding was a criminal proceeding or a civil proceeding, i.e., whether the relief imposed upon respondent was criminal or civil in

* Footnotes omitted.

nature [for the purpose of deciding whether the strictures of the Due Process Clause apply].

*   *   *

III.

A.

The question of how a court determines whether to classify the relief imposed in a given proceeding as civil or criminal in nature, for the purposes of applying the Due Process Clause and other provisions of the Constitution, is one of long standing, and its principles have been settled at least in their broad outlines for many decades. . . .

[T]he critical features are the substance of the proceeding and the character of the relief that the proceeding will afford. "If it is for civil contempt the punishment is remedial, and for the benefit of the complainant. But if it is for criminal contempt the sentence is punitive, to vindicate the authority of the court." Gompers v. Bucks Stove & Range Co., 221 U.S. 418, 441, 31 S.Ct. 492, 498, 55 L.Ed. 797 (1911). The character of the relief imposed is thus ascertainable by applying a few straightforward rules. If the relief provided is a sentence of imprisonment, it is remedial if "the defendant stands committed unless and until he performs the affirmative act required by the court's order," and is punitive if "the sentence is limited to imprisonment for a definite period." Id., at 442, 31 S.Ct. at 498. If the relief provided is a fine, it is remedial when it is paid to the complainant, and punitive when it is paid to the court, though a fine that would be payable to the court is also remedial when the defendant can avoid paying the fine simply by performing the affirmative act required by the court's order.

. . .

    *   *   *

B.

In repeatedly stating and following the rules set out above, the Court has eschewed any alternative formulation that would make the classification of the relief imposed in a State's proceedings turn simply on what their underlying purposes are perceived to be. Although the purposes that lie behind particular kinds of relief are germane to understanding their character, this Court has never undertaken to psychoanalyze the subjective intent of a State's laws and its courts, not only because that effort would be unseemly and improper, but also because it would be misguided. In contempt cases, both civil and criminal relief have aspects that can be seen as either remedial or punitive or both: when a court imposes fines and punishments on a contemnor, it is not only vindicating its legal authority to enter the initial court order, but it also is seeking to give effect to the law's purpose of modifying the contemnor's behavior to conform to the terms required in the order. . . .

    *   *   *

IV.

*   *   *

Applying the traditional rules for classifying the relief imposed in a given proceeding requires the further resolution of one factual question about the nature of the relief in this case. Respondent was charged with nine separate counts of contempt, and was convicted on five of those counts, all of which arose from his failure to comply with orders to make payments in past months. He was sentenced to five days in jail on each of the five counts, for a total of 25 days, but his jail sentence was suspended and he was placed on probation for three years. If this were all, then the relief afforded would be criminal in nature. But this is not all. One of the conditions of respondent's probation was that he begin making payments on his accumulated arrearage, and that he continue making these payments at the rate of $50 per month. At that rate, all of the arrearage would be paid before respondent completed his probation period. Not only did the order therefore contemplate that respondent would be required to purge himself of his past violations, but it expressly states that "[i]f any two payments are missed, whether consecutive or not, the entire balance shall become due and payable." Order of the California Superior Court for Orange County (Aug. 9, 1985), App. 39. What is unclear is whether the ultimate satisfaction of these accumulated prior payments would have purged the determinate sentence imposed on respondent. Since this aspect of the proceeding will vary as a factual matter from one case to another, depending on the precise disposition entered by the trial court, and since the trial court did not specify this aspect of its disposition in this case, it is not surprising that neither party was able to offer a satisfactory explanation of this point at argument. Tr. of Oral Arg. 42–47. If the relief imposed here is in fact a determinate sentence with a purge clause, then it is civil in nature [and the Due Process Clause does not apply].

The state court did not pass on this issue because of its erroneous view that it was enough simply to aver that this proceeding is considered "quasi-criminal" as a matter of state law. . . . Yet the Due Process Clause does not necessarily prohibit the State from employing this presumption as it was construed by the state court, if respondent would purge his contempt judgment by paying off his arrearage. In these circumstances, the proper course for this Court is to vacate the judgment below and remand for further consideration. . . . If on remand it is found that respondent would purge his sentence by paying his arrearage, then this proceeding is civil in nature and there was no need for the state court to reinterpret its statute to avoid conflict with the Due Process Clause.

*   *   *

JUSTICE O'CONNOR filed a dissenting opinion in which Chief Justice Rehnquist and Justice Scalia joined (omitted).

JUSTICE KENNEDY took no part in the consideration or decision of the case.

NOTES

(1) Perhaps the clearest definition of civil contempt was formulated by In re Nevitt, 117 Fed. 448, 461 (8th Cir.1902), as quoted in Penfield Co. v. SEC, 330 U.S. 585, 590, 67 S.Ct. 918, 921, 91 L.Ed. 1117 (1947):

> "A conditional penalty, by contrast, is civil because it is specifically designed to compel the doing of some act. 'One who is fined, unless by a day certain he [does the act ordered], has it in his power to avoid any penalty. And those who are imprisoned until they obey the order, "carry the keys of their prison in their own pockets." ' "

(2) "Woman Held 17 Months on Civil Charge Seeks Release From Unlimited Sentence", New York Times, June 20, 1975, at 39, col. 1. The 52 year old wheelchair bound appellant sought release on the ground that she was unable to produce her foster child as ordered by the court because she did not know where he was. The suit was brought by the boy's natural mother who, after 13 years, sought custody. The Appellate Division affirmed the dismissal of her habeas corpus writ: "She has certainly not made the kind of effort that a mother would normally make if her son's whereabouts were unknown to her." People ex rel. Feldman v. Warden, 46 A.D.2d 256, 362 N.Y.S.2d 171 (1st Dept. (1974)), affirmed mem. 36 N.Y.S.2d 846, 370 N.Y.S.2d 913, 331 N.E.2d 691 (1975).

As a result of the case, a bill was introduced in the state legislature limiting civil contempt sentences to no more than one year.

(3) Child support orders are notoriously difficult to enforce. To facilitate enforcement outside the state in which an order was entered, all the states have enacted the Uniform Reciprocal Enforcement of Support Act, 9A U.L.A. 647–746. In addition, the federal government has made available to child support enforcement agencies certain tax return information that would otherwise be kept confidential, 26 U.S.C.A. § 6103(l)(6) (including the address, social security number, filing status, income and number of dependents claimed). It has also been suggested that states formally adopt criminal penalties for nonsupport, see, e.g., Note, Criminal Nonsupport and a Proposal for an Effective Felony–Misdemeanor Distinction, 37 Hast.L.J. 1075 (1986).

(4) Courses in Conflict of Laws ordinarily examine in greater detail the principles that underlie recognition and enforcement of judgments of sister states or foreign nations. For short and lucid treatments, see Reese, The Status in This Country of Judgments Rendered Abroad, 50 Colum.L.Rev. 783 (1950); Reese and Johnson, The Scope of Full Faith and Credit to Judgments, 49 Colum.L.Rev. 153 (1949); Smit, International Res Judicata and Collateral Estoppel in the United States, 9 U.C.L.A.L.Rev. 44 (1962). Among the questions that arise are: What defenses are open to a judgment due full faith and credit? Which issues are precluded and which persons are bound? To what extent must the enforcing court award the same remedies as those given by the rendering court? Cf. In re Fotochrome, Inc., 377 F.Supp. 26 (E.D.N.Y.1974), affirmed 517 F.2d 512 (2d Cir.1975) (Japanese arbitral award was given greater recognition than an award in an American jurisdiction in the same situation; defenses under treaties and state and federal statutes based primarily upon due process were available when entry of judgment in this country was sought).

(5) Judgments of federal courts are easily enforced in other districts because of availability of simple registration procedures under 28 U.S.C.A. § 1963. In a small but growing group of states the Uniform Enforcement of Foreign Judgments Act has been adopted and provides an accelerated type of summary judgment, preceded by registration of the sister state's judgment. Many other states allow a judgment of another jurisdiction to be used as the basis for a summary judgment motion, with a limited number of collateral issues raisable to deny quick recognition to the former judgment.

LIENS AND PRIORITIES

Debtors' difficulties have a tendency to come not singly but in legions. A race of diligence among the creditors results, with first-in-time often determining first-in-right. However, other circumstances also enter into the question of how creditors line up and for what shares of the debtor's assets. A comprehensive discussion of the situation in New York before adoption of the N.Y.—McKinney's C.P.L.R. is found in Distler and Schubin, Enforcement Priorities and Liens: The New York Judgment Creditor's Rights in Personal Property, 60 Colum. L.Rev. 458 (1960).

When the debtor owns real property, the creditor commonly gets the protection of a lien upon filing his judgment. This prevents an effective transfer of good title as long as the judgment continues unpaid and in force.

Chapter Sixteen

RES JUDICATA (FORMER ADJUDICATION)

SECTION 1. ESSENTIAL DISTINCTIONS

"Res judicata" is composed of two concepts, commonly termed claim preclusion and issue preclusion. Both are related to the doctrine of stare decisis, which was encountered earlier. All of these doctrines are used to foreclose parties from litigating their claims, or relitigating questions of law or fact, because of prior activity within the judicial system. All stem from the principle that one aim of the adjudicatory process is to achieve repose—an end to disputes—irrespective of whether a more correct result might be achieved by further litigation: *interest reipublicae ut sit finis litium.* As the growing volume of litigation threatens to overwhelm the courts, these doctrines have taken on new significance. Not only do they force the parties to make their peace and insure uniform treatment, they also allocate precious judicial resources to those with the most compelling claims to them. They assure that litigants receive one—but only one—full, fair opportunity to present their cases in court.

A. *Stare decisis.* The doctrine of stare decisis is so well ingrained in the common law that it is rarely discussed in cases. However, in 1989, after the composition of the Supreme Court was altered significantly by President Reagan's appointees, the scope of the doctrine was expressly addressed.

PATTERSON v. McLEAN CREDIT UNION

Supreme Court of the United States, 1989.*
491 U.S. ___, 109 S.Ct. 2363, 105 L.Ed.2d 132.

JUSTICE KENNEDY delivered the opinion of the Court. Petitioner Brenda Patterson, a black woman, was employed by respondent McLean Credit Union as a teller . . .. In July 1982, she was laid off. After the termination, petitioner commenced this action in District Court. She alleged that respondent, in violation of 42 U.S.C. § 1981, had harassed her, failed to promote her to an intermediate accounting clerk position, and then discharged her, all because of her race. . . .

We granted certiorari to decide whether petitioner's claim of racial harassment in her employment is actionable under § 1981, and whether the jury instruction given by the District Court on petitioner's § 1981 promotion claim was error . . . . After oral argument on these

---

* Footnotes omitted.

issues, we requested the parties to brief and argue an additional question:

> "Whether or not the interpretation of 42 U.S.C. § 1981, adopted by this Court in Runyon v. McCrary, 427 U.S. 160, 96 S.Ct. 2586, 49 L.Ed.2d 415 (1976) [prohibiting racial discrimination in the making and enforcement of private contracts], should be reconsidered."

We now decline to overrule our decision in Runyon. . . .

* * *

The Court has said often and with great emphasis that "the doctrine of stare decisis is of fundamental importance to the rule of law." Welch v. Texas Dept. of Highways and Public Transportation, 483 U.S. 468, 494, 107 S.Ct. 2941, ___, 97 L.Ed.2d 389 (1987). Although we have cautioned that "stare decisis is a principle of policy and not a mechanical formula of adherence to the latest decision," Boys Markets, Inc. v. Retail Clerks, 398 U.S. 235, 241, 90 S.Ct. 1583, 1587, 26 L.Ed.2d 199 (1970), it is indisputable that stare decisis is a basic self-governing principle within the Judicial Branch, which is entrusted with the sensitive and difficult task of fashioning and preserving a jurisprudential system that is not based upon "an arbitrary discretion." The Federalist, No. 78, p. 490 (H. Lodge ed. 1988) (A. Hamilton). See also Vasquez v. Hillery, 474 U.S. 254, 265, 106 S.Ct. 617, 625, 88 L.Ed.2d 598 (1986) (stare decisis ensures that "the law will not merely change erratically" and "permits society to presume that bedrock principles are founded in the law rather than in the proclivities of individuals").

Our precedents are not sacrosanct . . . . Nonetheless, we have held that "any departure from the doctrine of stare decisis demands special justification." Arizona v. Rumsey, 467 U.S. 203, 212, 104 S.Ct. 2305, 2311, 81 L.Ed.2d 164 (1984). We have said also that the burden borne by the party advocating the abandonment of an established precedent is greater where the Court is asked to overrule a point of statutory construction. Considerations of stare decisis have special force in the area of statutory interpretation, for here, unlike in the context of constitutional interpretation, the legislative power is implicated, and Congress remains free to alter what we have done. . . .

. . . In cases where statutory precedents have been overruled, the primary reason for the Court's shift in position has been the intervening development of the law, through either the growth of judicial doctrine or further action taken by Congress. Where such changes have removed or weakened the conceptual underpinnings from the prior decision, or where the later law has rendered the decision irreconcilable with competing legal doctrines or policies, the Court has not hesitated to overrule an earlier decision. . . . Our decision in Runyon has not been undermined by subsequent changes or development in the law.

Another traditional justification for overruling a prior case is that a precedent may be a positive detriment to coherence and consistency

in the law, either because of inherent confusion created by an unworkable decision, . . . or because the decision poses a direct obstacle to the realization of important objectives embodied in other laws . . . . In this regard, we do not find Runyon to be unworkable or confusing.
. . .

Finally, it has sometimes been said that a precedent becomes more vulnerable as it becomes outdated and after being " 'tested by experience, has been found to be inconsistent with the sense of justice or with the social welfare.' " Runyon, 427 U.S., at 191 (Stevens, J., concurring), quoting B. Cardozo, The Nature of the Judicial Process 149 (1921). Whatever the effect of this consideration may be in statutory cases, it offers no support for overruling Runyon. In recent decades, state and federal legislation has been enacted to prohibit private racial discrimination in many aspects of our society. Whether Runyon's interpretation of § 1981 as prohibiting racial discrimination in the making and enforcement of private contracts is right or wrong as an original matter, it is certain that it is not inconsistent with the prevailing sense of justice in this country. To the contrary, Runyon is entirely consistent with our society's deep commitment to the eradication of discrimination based on a person's race or the color of his or her skin. . . .

We decline to overrule Runyon and acknowledge that its holding remains the governing law in this area.

* * *

JUSTICE BRENNAN filed an opinion concurring in the judgment in part and dissenting in part, in which Justices Marshall and Blackmun joined, and in which Justice Stevens joined in part (omitted).

JUSTICE STEVENS filed an opinion concurring in the judgment in part and dissenting in part (omitted).

NOTES

(1) The principle of stare decisis burdens a stranger to the former adjudication with an adverse determination of the question of law adjudicated. What are the justifications for foreclosing McLean Credit from its day in court on the question of how § 1981 ought to be interpreted?

(2) The Court carefully limited its conclusions on stare decisis to matters of statutory interpretation. Although the principle also applies to judge-made law, *Patterson* expressly distinguished holdings on constitutional law. What policies favor a different view of constitutional adjudication?

(3) Special problems are presented by decisions of appellate courts when there is no majority opinion. Although the result should affect other litigants similarly situated, the lack of an agreed rationale makes it difficult to know exactly who those litigants are. See Note, The Precedential Value of Supreme Court Plurality Decisions, 80 Colum.L.Rev. 756 (1980).

———

B. *Claim Preclusion.* This doctrine forecloses parties who have had a day in court from trying their cases afresh. It holds that the same parties cannot re-assert against each other claims or defenses that they have already litigated, or logically could have litigated, after a valid, final judgment has been entered between them. These three requirements—(1) the sameness of the claims, (2) the identicality of the parties, and (3) the validity and finality of the judgment—will be explored fully in the next section.

———————

C. *Issue Preclusion.* This doctrine holds that even when the claims in a second litigation are not the same as the claims in an earlier lawsuit, parties who have had their day in court should not be allowed to ask the court to reexamine issues of law or fact that were actually and necessarily decided in a case that concluded in a valid, final judgment. The requirements for issue preclusion—(1) the issues were actually litigated, (2) the decision was necessary to the judgment, (3) the parties were the same, and (4) the judgment was valid and final—will be examined in Section 3, following Claim Preclusion.

Unlike stare decisis, which must be applied flexibly to keep the law responsive to social needs, claim and issue preclusion are often used more rigidly, when the requirements for their application are met. But both are sometimes tempered by the realization that litigation is a fallible process and that it may sometimes be wise to give the parties a second chance. The principles that call for mitigation of claim and issue preclusion are discussed in Section 4. Section 5 examines the special problems that arise when a court is called upon to examine the res judicata effect of a decision rendered by a different judicial system.

Before beginning, note that, as *Patterson* discussed the effect of *Runyon v. McCrary,* each of the cases in this chapter discusses at least one prior adjudication. Since (unlike the situation in *Patterson*) the cases often have the same caption, it is helpful to diagram them, calling the case that is first in time "A" and the second, "B," etc. Record the identity of the parties, the capacity in which they brought the earlier lawsuit(s), the claims, and which party won. Then note who in the later litigation is arguing for preclusion.

SECTION 2. CLAIM PRECLUSION

The nomenclature here is confusing. First, this branch of res judicata law is sometimes itself referred to as "res judicata." Some modern courts and the Restatement of Judgments have, however, adopted the term "claim preclusion" to distinguish this specific concept from the general notion of foreclosure by prior adjudication. Second, the doctrine is sometimes said to consist of two prongs, bar and merger, although both have precisely the same effect, namely to preclude parties from litigating claims that were, or could have been, litigated before. It will be helpful to get used to referring to the concept as claim preclusion.

———————

RESTATEMENT, SECOND, JUDGMENTS *

§ 17. Effects of Former Adjudication—General Rules

A valid and final personal judgment is conclusive between the parties, except on appeal or other direct review, to the following extent:

(1) If the judgment is in favor of the plaintiff, the claim is extinguished and merged in the judgment and a new claim may arise on the judgment (see § 18);

(2) If the judgment is in favor of the defendant, the claim is extinguished and the judgment bars a subsequent action on that claim (see § 19);

(3) A judgment in favor of either the plaintiff or the defendant is conclusive, in a subsequent action between them on the same or a different claim, with respect to any issue actually litigated and determined if its determination was essential to that judgment (see § 27).

§ 18. Judgment for Plaintiff—The General Rule of Merger

When a valid and final personal judgment is rendered in favor of the plaintiff:

(1) The plaintiff cannot thereafter maintain an action on the original claim or any part thereof, although he may be able to maintain an action upon the judgment; and

(2) In an action upon the judgment, the defendant cannot avail himself of defenses he might have interposed, or did interpose, in the first action.

§ 19. Judgment for Defendant—The General Rule of Bar

A valid and final personal judgment rendered in favor of the defendant bars another action by the plaintiff on the same claim.

A. SAME CLAIM

CLANCEY v. McBRIDE

Supreme Court of Illinois, 1929.
338 Ill. 35, 169 N.E. 729.

DE YOUNG, J. Two automobiles, one driven by Marie Clancey and the other by Thomas G. McBride, collided at the intersection of Wisconsin avenue with Randolph street in the village of Oak Park, in Cook county. Marie Clancey was injured and her automobile was damaged in the collision. To recover compensation for the damage to her car, she sued McBride before a justice of the peace. After a trial, judgment was rendered in her favor for $275 and McBride satisfied the judgment.

Subsequently she instituted suit in the superior court of Cook county against McBride to recover damages for her personal injuries. The defendant interposed as a bar to the action the rendition of the judgment by the justice of the peace and its subsequent satisfaction, but the court excluded this defense. The jury awarded the plaintiff $2,000; the court required a remittitur of $500 and rendered judgment for $1,500 and costs against the defendant. He prosecuted an appeal to the Appellate Court for the First District. The Appellate Court (251 Ill. App. 157) held that, since a single tortious act caused both the damage to the plaintiff's automobile and the injuries to her person, she could maintain only one suit for the damages which ensued, and consequently that the judgment rendered by the justice of the peace for the property damage constituted a bar to the instant suit. Accordingly that court reversed the judgment of the superior court and remanded the cause, with directions to enter judgment for the defendant. Upon the petition of the plaintiff, this court granted a writ of certiorari, and the record is here for a further review.

The plaintiff in error contends, in substance, that the common law recognizes distinct and separate rights in respect to the person and his property; that separate actions may be brought to recover damages for injuries to the first and damage to the second, although both resulted from the same tortious act, and, hence, that a judgment for the property damage is not a bar to a subsequent suit to recover damages for the personal injuries. The defendant in error asserts, on the contrary, that by the great weight of American authority, a single tort resulting in personal injuries and property damage gives rise to one indivisible claim or cause of action; that all damages must be assessed and recovered in a single action, and that, if successive suits are brought for constituent elements of the entire claim, a judgment on the merits in one suit will be available as a bar to the prosecution of the other suits, although the court which rendered the judgment was one whose jurisdiction was limited and did not possess the power to adjudicate upon other elements of the claim.

The only question raised is whether a tortious act which causes personal injury and property damage gives rise to a single cause of action or to a cause of action for each of the two rights infringed. A number of courts have declared that a single wrongful act, which causes injury or damage with respect to different rights, creates but one cause of action, since it grows out of the act itself and not out of its results, and that the injury and damage occasioned by the act are merely items of a single claim proceeding from the same wrong. [Citations omitted.] In England and in certain states, it has been held that injury to the person and damage to property resulting from the same wrongful act give rise to a distinct cause of action for each of the rights infringed. Brunsden v. Humphrey, L.R. 14 Q.B.Div. 141; Reilly v. Sicilian Asphalt Paving Co., 170 N.Y. 40, 62 N.E. 772, 773, 57 L.R.A. 176, 88 Am.St.Rep. 636. . . .

A single negligent act from which personal injury and property damage ensue simultaneously does not necessarily make its consequences inseparable or result in a single grievance. If two persons are injured by the same tortious act, two grievances result and two actions are maintainable. Likewise, if the same negligent act causes injury to a person and damage to the property of another in his custody, two causes of action arise—one in favor of the person injured and the other to the owner of the damaged property. On the other hand, if a horse and vehicle owned by the same person are damaged by the wrongful act of another, the owner will have a single cause of action for the damage to both. If, however, as the result of such an act, the owner is injured and his vehicle is damaged, two separate and distinct wrongs are inflicted upon him for two of his rights, first, the right to the uninterrupted enjoyment of his body and limbs, and second, the right to have his property kept free from damage, are invaded. While both wrongs result from a single tortious act, yet the consequences of that act, it seems, give rise to a distinct cause of action for the vindication of each of the violated rights.

Lord Justice Bowen, in Brunsden v. Humphrey, supra, observed that "it certainly would appear unsatisfactory to hold that the damage done in a carriage accident to a man's portmanteau was the same injury as the damage done to his spine." The Court of Appeals of New York, in Reilly v. Sicilian Asphalt Paving Co., supra, said: "If, while injury to the horse and vehicle of a person gives rise to but a single cause of action, injury to the vehicle and its owner gives rise to two causes of action, it must be because there is an essential difference between an injury to the person and an injury to property, that makes it impracticable, or at least very inconvenient, in the administration of justice, to blend the two. We think there is such a distinction." Illustrations of the distinction are not wanting. The plaintiff cannot assign his right of action for an injury to his person. . . . Such a right of action cannot be reached by a creditor's suit; nor does a trustee in bankruptcy take title to it. A right of action for a tort causing damage to property, on the contrary, is assignable; creditors may seize it by a bill in equity; it will pass to a trustee in bankruptcy, and an indemnifier will acquire it by subrogation. . . . If the personal injury result in death, a cause of action arises by statute for the benefit of the widow and the next of kin of the decedent, while the right to recover for the damage to property is preserved for the benefit of the decedent's estate. The evidence establishing an injury to the person cannot be the same as the evidence showing damage to property for the determination of the character and extent of the plaintiff's personal injuries differs essentially from the ascertainment of his property damage. Other issues peculiar to each right or claim, such, for example, as the title to the property damaged, may also be raised. The periods of limitation too are different, since an action for damages for an injury to the person must be commenced within two years, while an action to recover for damage to property may be brought within five years next after the cause of action accrued.

The differences in the rules governing assignability and subrogation, in the methods of enforcement, in the evidence required to sustain, in the distribution of the proceeds, and in the periods of limitation, above stated, militate against the doctrine that out of a single wrongful act only one cause of action to redress injury to the person and damage to property can arise. To cite a single instance, it would be highly impracticable, if not impossible, to determine a case involving claims for personal injury and property damage, where the right of action for the damage to property had passed to a receiver on a creditor's bill or to a trustee in bankruptcy without treating the latter claim as an independent cause of action. The differences noted among others, justify the conclusion that, where injury to the person and damage to property are caused by the same negligent act, different rights are infringed for the vindication of which distinct causes of action exist. Manifestly these causes of action accruing to the same person may be joined in a single suit in a court of competent jurisdiction. The recovery of a judgment, however, for the damage to property is not a bar to a subsequent action to recover damages for injuries to the person. Brunsden v. Humphrey, supra; Reilly v. Sicilian Asphalt Paving Co., supra; Ochs v. Public Service Railway Co., supra; Watson v. Texas & Pacific Railway Co., supra.

The judgment of the Appellate Court is reversed, and the judgment of the superior court is affirmed. . . .

NOTES

(1) What was the *Clancey* court's test for what constitutes the "same claim?" Some courts have looked at the number of "rights" the defendant has allegedly injured; others, at the number of "wrongs" the defendant has committed; still others at the number of legal theories propounded by the plaintiff. Sometimes, courts have looked at whether the same evidence is used to prove both cases. If different evidence is needed, the claims are not considered the same.

(2) What values are protected by each of these rules? Does it matter which rule is used, so long as the parties are acquainted with it at the time they begin the first litigation? See Rush v. City of Maple Heights, 167 Ohio St. 221, 147 N.E.2d 599 (S.Ct.Ohio 1958), which demonstrates what happens when the doctrine of stare decisis is not applied to the judge-made rule of claim preclusion.

RESTATEMENT, SECOND, JUDGMENTS *

§ 24. Dimensions of "Claim" for Purposes of Merger or Bar— General Rule Concerning "Splitting"

(1) When a valid and final judgment rendered in an action extinguishes the plaintiff's claim pursuant to the rules of merger or bar (see §§ 18, 19), the claim extinguished includes all rights of the plaintiff to remedies against the defendant with respect to all or any part of the transaction, or series of connected transactions, out of which the action arose.

(2) What factual grouping constitutes a "transaction," and what groupings constitute a "series," are to be determined pragmatically, giving weight to such considerations as whether the facts are related in time, space, origin, or motivation, whether they form a convenient trial unit, and whether their treatment as a unit conforms to the parties' expectations or business understanding or usage.

§ 25. Exemplifications of General Rule Concerning Splitting

The rule of § 24 applies to extinguish a claim by the plaintiff against the defendant even though the plaintiff is prepared in the second action

(1) To present evidence or grounds or theories of the case not presented in the first action, or

(2) To seek remedies or forms of relief not demanded in the first action.

NOTES

(1) It has been said that the Restatement's test is very close to the definition of a "case" offered in United Mine Workers v. Gibbs, pp. 210, 211, supra. Is this fortuitous, or are there reasons why the tests should be analogous?

(2) Note that under the Restatement test, the plaintiff in *Clancey* would not have been able to bring separate actions for personal injury and property damage, any more than she would have been able to bring a separate action for each finger and toe that was injured in the accident. Constraining her to one action is a significant benefit to a litigation system that is heavily overworked; it also conserves the resources of McBride. Perhaps for this reason, the Restatement test is enjoying success in jurisdictions all over the United States, including, as next principal case demonstrates, the federal courts.

(3) Once a transactional test like the Restatement's is accepted, the claims of the defendant may also logically fall within the concept of the "same claim." Should a defendant be bound to assert all its claims in an action brought at the place and time chosen by the plaintiff? Should the judicial system be forced to expend resources on the same transaction twice in order to protect the defendant's right to be in control of its own lawsuit? See Fed.R.Civ.P. 13(a). Review

the materials at pp. 420–426, supra. Cf. Cummings v. Dresher, 18 N.Y.2d 105, 271 N.Y.S.2d 976, 218 N.E.2d 688 (1966); Jocie Motor Lines, Inc. v. Johnson, 231 N.C. 367, 57 S.E.2d 388 (1950); Phoenix Insurance Co. v. Haney, 235 Miss. 60, 108 So.2d 227 (1959), cert. denied 360 U.S. 917, 79 S.Ct. 1435, 3 L.Ed.2d 1534 (1959), noted 73 Harv.L.Rev. 1410 (1960); Horne v. Woolever, 170 Ohio St. 178, 163 N.E.2d 378 (1959). See Wright, Estoppel by Rule: The Compulsory Counterclaim Under Modern Pleading, 39 Iowa L.Rev. 255 (1954).

(4) Would a result foreclosing Clancey have been just if Clancey had been insured for property damage, and the first action had been brought on her behalf by the insurance company? In Vasu v. Kohlers, Inc., 145 Ohio St. 321, 61 N.E.2d 707 (1945), the Ohio court allowed an insured to maintain an action after the property damage suit brought by his insurance company had reached final judgment. One explanation is that the insurance company's choice of forum, timing, and strategy might not match that of the insured, and the insured has little leverage to force the insurance company to do things his way. This question of *who* should be foreclosed is the topic of the next subsection.

B. SAME PARTIES—PRIVITY

NEVADA v. UNITED STATES

Supreme Court of the United States, 1983.
463 U.S. 110, 103 S.Ct. 2906, 77 L.Ed.2d 509.

JUSTICE REHNQUIST delivered the opinion of the Court.*

* * *

I.

Nevada has, on the average, less precipitation than any other State in the Union. . . . The present litigation relates to water rights in the Truckee River, one of the three principal rivers flowing through west central Nevada. It rises in the High Sierra in Placer County, Cal., flows into and out of Lake Tahoe, and thence down the eastern slope of the Sierra Nevada mountains. It flows through Reno, Nev., and after a course of some 120 miles debauches into Pyramid Lake, which has no outlet.

* * *

The origins of the cases before us are found in two historical events involving the Federal Government in this part of the country. First, in 1859 the Department of the Interior set aside nearly half a million acres in what is now western Nevada . . . as the Pyramid Lake Indian Reservation. The Reservation includes Pyramid Lake, and land surrounding it, the lower reaches of the Truckee River, and the bottom land alongside the lower Truckee.

Then, with the passage of the Reclamation Act of 1902, 32 Stat. 388, the Federal Government was designated to play a more prominent role in the development of the West. That Act directed the Secretary of the Interior to withdraw from public entry arid lands in specified Western States, reclaim . . . 200,000 acres in western Nevada, which ultimately became the Newlands Reclamation Project. The Project was

---

* Some footnotes omitted.

designed to irrigate a substantial area in the vicinity of Fallon, Nev., with waters from both the Truckee and the Carson Rivers.

* * *

. . . Before the works contemplated by the Project went into operation, . . . the United States filed a complaint in the United States District Court for the District of Nevada in March 1913, commencing what became known as the *Orr Ditch* litigation. The Government, for the benefit of both the Project and the Pyramid Lake Reservation, asserted a claim to 10,000 cubic feet of water per second for the Project and a claim to 500 cubic feet per second for the Reservation. The complaint named as defendants all water users on the Truckee River in Nevada. The Government expressly sought a final decree quieting title to the rights of all parties.

* * *

[A]lmost 10 years later [and several judicial proceedings], in the midst of a prolonged drought, . . . settlement negotiations were commenced. . . . The United States still acted on behalf of the Reservation's interests, but the Project was now under the management of the Truckee–Carson Irrigation District (TCID). [After further negotiations,] a settlement agreement was signed on July 1, 1935. The District Court entered a final decree adopting the agreement on September 8, 1944. No appeal was taken. . . .

On December 21, 1973, the Government instituted the action below seeking additional rights to the Truckee River for the Pyramid Lake Indian Reservation; the Pyramid Lake Paiute Tribe was permitted to intervene in support of the United States. The Government named as defendants all persons presently claiming water rights to the Truckee River and its tributaries in Nevada. The defendants include the defendants in the *Orr Ditch* litigation and their successors, approximately 3,800 individual farmers that own land in the Newlands Reclamation Project, and TCID. The District Court certified the Project farmers as a class and directed TCID to represent their interests.

In its complaint the Government purported not to dispute the rights decreed in the *Orr Ditch* case. Instead, it alleged that *Orr Ditch* determined only the Reservation's right to "water for irrigation," . . . not the claim now being asserted for "sufficient waters of the Truckee River . . . [for] the maintenance and preservation of Pyramid Lake, [and for] the maintenance of the lower reaches of the Truckee River as a natural spawning ground for fish." [7] . . .

---

7. Between 1920 and 1940 the surface area of Pyramid Lake was reduced by about 20,000 acres. The decline resulted in a delta forming at the mouth of the Truckee that prevented the fish indigenous to the lake, the Lahontan cutthroat trout and the cui-ui, from reaching their spawning grounds in the Truckee River, resulting in the near extinction of both species. Efforts to restore the fishery have occurred since that time. Pyramid Lake has been stabilized for several years and, augmented by passage of the Washoe Project Act of 1956, § 4, 70 Stat. 777, the lake is being restocked with cutthroat trout and cui-ui. Fish hatcheries operated by both the State of Nevada and the United States have been one source for replenishing the lake. In 1976 the Marble Bluff Dam and Fishway was completed enabling the fish to bypass the delta to their spawning grounds in the Truckee. Both the District Court and

The defendants below asserted res judicata as an affirmative defense, saying that the United States and the Tribe were precluded by the *Orr Ditch* decree from litigating this claim. Following a separate trial on this issue, the District Court sustained the defense and dismissed the complaint in its entirety.

*   *   *

II.

*   *   *

To determine the applicability of res judicata to the facts before us, we must decide first if the "cause of action" which the Government now seeks to assert is the "same cause of action" that was asserted in *Orr Ditch;* we must then decide whether the parties in the instant proceeding are identical to or in privity with the parties in *Orr Ditch*. We address these questions in turn.[10]

A.

Definitions of what constitutes the "same cause of action" have not remained static over time. Compare Restatement of Judgments § 61 (1942) with Restatement (Second) of Judgments § 24 (1982).[12] . . . We find it unnecessary in these cases to parse any minute differences which these differing tests might produce, because whatever standard may be applied the only conclusion allowed by the record in the *Orr Ditch* case is that the Government was given an opportunity to litigate the Reservation's entire water rights to the Truckee, and that the Government intended to take advantage of that opportunity.

Court of Appeals observed that "these restoration efforts 'appear to justify optimism for eventual success.'" 649 F.2d, at 1294. See Nevada App. 184a.

10. The policies advanced by the doctrine of res judicata perhaps are at their zenith in cases concerning real property, land and water. . . . As this Court explained over a century ago in *Minnesota Co. v. National Co.*, 3 Wall. 332, 18 L.Ed. 42 (1866):

"Where questions arise which affect titles to land it is of great importance to the public that when they are once decided they should no longer be considered open. Such decisions become rules of property, and many titles may be injuriously affected by their change. . . . [W]here courts vacillate and overrule their own decisions . . . affecting the title to real property, their decisions are retrospective and may affect titles purchased on the faith of their stability. Doubtful questions on subjects of this nature, when once decided, should be considered no longer doubtful or subject to change." *Id.*, at 334. . . .

12. Under the first Restatement of Judgments § 61 (1942), causes of action were to be deemed the same "if the evidence needed to sustain the second action would have sustained the first action." In the Restatement (Second) of Judgments (1982), a more pragmatic approach . . . was adopted . . . .

The Tribe argues that the first Restatement of Judgments standard should control because it was the prevailing standard at the time of Orr Ditch. While we find that the result would be the same under either version of the Restatement of Judgments, we nevertheless point out that the Tribe is somewhat mistaken in this argument. Although the "same evidence" standard was "[o]ne of the tests" used at the time, *The Haytian Republic*, 154 U.S. 118, 125, 14 S.Ct. 992, 994, 38 L.Ed. 930 (1894), it was not the only one. For example, in *Baltimore S.S. Co. v. Phillips*, 274 U.S. 316, 47 S.Ct. 600, 71 L.Ed. 1069 (1927), the Court concluded:

"A cause of action does not consist of facts, but of the unlawful violation of a right which the facts show." . . .

In its amended complaint in *Orr Ditch*, the Government averred
. . . .:

"16. On or about or prior to the 29th day of November, 1859, the Government of the United States, having for a long time previous thereto recognized the fact that certain Pah Ute and other Indians were residing upon and using certain lands in the northern part of the said Truckee River Valley and around said Pyramid Lake . . . and the said Government being desirous of protecting said Indians and their descendants in their homes, fields, pastures, fishing, and their use of said lands and waters, . . . did reserve said lands from any and all forms of entry or sale and for the sole use of said Indians . . . ."

This cannot be construed as anything less than a claim for the full . . . rights that were due the Pyramid Lake Indian Reservation.

* * *

B.

Having decided that the cause of action asserted below is the same cause of action asserted in the *Orr Ditch* litigation, we must next determine which of the parties before us are bound by the earlier decree. As stated earlier, the general rule is that a prior judgment will bar the "parties" to the earlier lawsuit, "and those in privity with them," from relitigating the cause of action. Cromwell v. County of Sac, 94 U.S. (4 Otto) 351, 352, 24 L.Ed. 195 (1876).

There is no doubt but that the United States was a party to the *Orr Ditch* proceeding, acting as a representative for the Reservation's interests and the interests of the Newlands Project, and cannot relitigate the Reservation's . . . water rights with those who can use the *Orr Ditch* decree as a defense. . . . We also hold that the Tribe, whose interests were represented in *Orr Ditch* by the United States, can be bound by the *Orr Ditch* decree.[14] This Court left little room for an argument to the contrary in Heckman v. United States, 224 U.S. 413, 32 S.Ct. 424, 56 L.Ed. 820 (1912), where it plainly said that "it could not, consistently with any principle, be tolerated that, after the United States on behalf of its wards had invoked the jurisdiction of its courts . . . these wards should themselves be permitted to relitigate the question." Id., at 446, 32 S.Ct., at 435. See also Restatement (Second) of Judgments § 41(1)(d) (1982). We reaffirm that principle now.[15]

14. We, of course, do not pass judgment on the quality of representation that the Tribe received. In 1951 the Tribe sued the Government before the Indian Claims Commission for damages, basing its claim of liability on the Tribe's receipt of less water for the fishery than it was entitled to. Northern Paiute Tribe v. United States, 30 Ind.Cl.Comm'n 210 (1973). In a settlement the Tribe was given $8 million in return for its waiver of further liability on the part of the United States.

15. This Court held in Hansberry v. Lee, 311 U.S. 32, 44, 61 S.Ct. 115, 119, 85 L.Ed. 22 (1940), that persons vicariously represented in a class action could not be bound by a judgment in the case where the representative parties had interests that impermissibly conflicted with those of persons represented. See also Restatement

We then turn to the issue of which defendants in the present litigation can use the *Orr Ditch* decree against the Government and the Tribe. There is no dispute but that the *Orr Ditch* defendants were parties to the earlier decree and that they and their successors can rely on the decree. The Court of Appeals so held, and we affirm.

The Court of Appeals reached a different conclusion concerning TCID and the Project. . . . [It] stated that . . . "[a]s a general matter, a judgment does not conclude parties who were not adversaries under the pleadings," and that in "representative litigation we should be especially careful not to infer adversity between interests represented by a single litigant." 649 F.2d, at 1309. Since the pleadings in *Orr Ditch* did not specifically allege adversity between the claims asserted on behalf of the Newlands Project and those asserted on behalf of the Reservation, the Court of Appeals ruled that the decree did not conclude the dispute between them.

* * *

[W]e disagree with the Court of Appeals . . . . It has been held that the successors in interest of parties who are not adversaries in a stream adjudication nevertheless are bound by a decree establishing priority of rights in the stream. . . . This rule seems to be generally applied in stream adjudications in the Western States, where these actions play a critical role in determining the allocation of scarce water rights, and where each water rights claim by its "very nature raise[s] issues inter se as to all such parties for the determination of one claim necessarily affects the amount available for the other claims." . . .

* * *

We hold that under the circumstances described above, the interests of the Tribe and the Project landowners were sufficiently adverse so that both are now bound by the final decree entered in the *Orr Ditch* suit.

We turn finally to those defendants below who appropriated water from the Truckee subsequent to the *Orr Ditch* decree. These defendants, we believe, give rise to a difficult question, but in the final analysis we agree with the Court of Appeals that they too can use the *Orr Ditch* decree

(Second) of Judgments § 42(1)(d) (1982). The Tribe seeks to take advantage of this ruling, arguing that the Government's primary interest in Orr Ditch was to obtain water rights for the Newlands Reclamation Project and that by definition any water rights given to the Tribe would conflict with that interest. We reject this contention.

[T]he Government stands in a different position than a private fiduciary where Congress has decreed that the Government must represent more than one interest. When the Government performs such duties it does not by that reason alone compromise its obligation to any of the interests involved.

* * *

The record suggests that the [Bureau of Indian Affairs] alone may have made the decision not to press claims for a fishery water right, for reasons which hindsight may render questionable, but which did not involve other interests represented by the Government. For instance, in a 1926 letter to a federal official on the Pyramid Lake Reservation, the Commissioner of Indian Affairs explained: "We feel that their ultimate welfare depends in part on their being able to hold their own in a civilized world . . . they should look forward to a different means of livelihood, in part at least, from their ancestral one, of fishing and hunting." . . .

against the plaintiffs below. While mutuality has been for the most part abandoned in cases involving collateral estoppel, see Parklane Hosiery Co. v. Shore, 439 U.S. 322, 99 S.Ct. 645, 58 L.Ed.2d 552 (1979); Blonder–Tongue Laboratories, Inc. v. University of Illinois Foundation, 402 U.S. 313, 91 S.Ct. 1434, 28 L.Ed.2d 788 (1971), it has remained a part of the doctrine of res judicata. Nevertheless, exceptions to the res judicata mutuality requirement have been found necessary, . . . and we believe that such an exception is required in these cases.

Orr Ditch was an equitable action to quiet title, an *in personam* action. But as the Court of Appeals determined, it "was no garden variety quiet title action." 649 F.2d, at 1308. As we have already explained, everyone involved in *Orr Ditch* contemplated a comprehensive adjudication of water rights intended to settle once and for all the question of how much of the Truckee River each of the litigants was entitled to. Thus, even though quiet title actions are *in personam* actions, water adjudications are more in the nature of *in rem* proceedings. Nonparties such as the subsequent appropriators in these cases have relied just as much on the *Orr Ditch* decree in participating in the development of western Nevada as have the parties of that case. We agree with the Court of Appeals that under "these circumstances it would be manifestly unjust . . . not to permit subsequent appropriators" to hold the Reservation to the claims it made in *Orr Ditch;* "[a]ny other conclusion would make it impossible ever finally to quantify a reserved water right." 649 F.2d, at 1309.[16]

      *   *   *

JUSTICE BRENNAN filed a concurring opinion [omitted].

NOTE ON PERSONS BOUND AS PRIVIES

The usual rule is that claim preclusion applies only between parties and their "privies," but when does privity exist? According to the traditional definition, a privy is one who claims an interest in the subject-matter affected by the judgment *through* or *under* one of the parties, either by inheritance, succession or purchase. This approach restricts preclusion to situations involving transfers of property, too

---

16. The Tribe makes the argument that even if res judicata would otherwise apply, it cannot be used in these cases because to do so would deny the Tribe procedural due process. The Tribe argues that in Orr Ditch they were given neither the notice required by Mullane v. Central Hanover Bank & Trust Co., 339 U.S. 306 (1950), nor the full and fair opportunity to be heard required by Hansberry v. Lee, 311 U.S. 32 (1940) . . . .. Mullane, which involved a final accounting between a trustee and beneficiaries, is of course inapposite. Hansberry was based upon an impermissible conflict in a class action between the representatives of the class and certain class

members; we have already said that such a conflict did not exist in these cases and that in any event this litigation is governed by different rules than those that apply in private representative litigation. . . . In these cases, the Tribe, through the Government as their representative, was given adequate notice and a full and fair opportunity to be heard. If in carrying out their role as representative, the Government violated its obligations to the Tribe, then the Tribe's remedy is against the Government, not against third parties. As we have noted earlier, the Tribe has already taken advantage of that remedy. . . .

narrow a view in the res judicata field. The concept has therefore been made broader, as the principal case demonstrates.

a. *Representatives.* In the principal case, the Pyramid Lake Paiute Tribe was precluded, even though it did not participate in Orr Ditch, because the United States represented its interests. Similarly, trustees, guardians, and executors are sometimes said to hold a relationship of privity with the parties they protect. As in *Nevada*, see n. 14 of the opinion, if these representatives do not conduct the litigation competently, the beneficiary's remedy is against the representative; a new lawsuit cannot be brought against the adversary, who, after all, has already shouldered the burden of fighting the suit that was brought by the representative.

Note that for claim preclusion to apply the representative must be bringing the action on behalf of the beneficiary, see, e.g. Virginia v. Johnson, 7 Va.App. 614, 376 S.E.2d 787 (1989), which held that a child is not barred from bringing a paternity action by a previous paternity action brought by the child's mother on the ground that the mother's interests and the child's are not aligned. Had the child been represented in the first action by a guardian ad litem appointed by the court, it would have been precluded.

b. *Class Actions.* Review Hansberry v. Lee, supra. There it is assumed that ordinarily the actions of the named representatives of a class preclude relitigation by members of the class. In that case, however, the class members were permitted to bring a new lawsuit. Why did the *Hansberry* Court think it permissible to require the adversary to relitigate? Is *Hansberry* distinguishable from *Nevada* on the ground that the inadequacy of the representation was so obvious at the time of the first lawsuit that it is not unfair to require the adversary to litigate again? This result benefits the judicial system because it gives the parties some incentive to make sure that their adversaries are competently represented.

c. *Coparties.* The general rule is that the judgment between adversaries does not preclude later litigation among former coparties. In other words, in the action, A v. B + C, C's claims against B will not be precluded in later litigation, even if the jurisdiction follows the Restatement test and C's claims are transactionally related to the action against A. For an example, examine Fed.R.Civ.P. 13(g) and the notes on cross claims.

In *Nevada*, on the other hand, the Tribe and TCID were nominally coparties, but this rule was not followed—TCID was able to foreclose the Tribe from relitigating the question of water rights. The stress, however, is on "nominally:" the Court in essence held that since a water rights adjudication is a zero-sum game, everyone involved is the adversary of everyone else.

d. *Nonparties.* To many observers, the most surprising holding in Nevada was the last one: that subsequent users of the Truckee River, who were not involved in *Orr Ditch*, could nonetheless use the *Orr*

Ditch judgment to preclude the Tribe. If nonparties can use claim preclusion in this way—to benefit from prior adjudication concluded in their favor, should they also sometimes find themselves on the other end of the stick—bound to a judgment adverse to their interests? A few cases have raised this possibility:

(1) Montana v. United States, 440 U.S. 147, 99 S.Ct. 970, 59 L.Ed.2d 210 (1979). The first action, a challenge to the constitutionality of a Montana tax levied on the construction of United States' property, was brought in state court by Peter Kiewit Sons' Co., the government contractor who paid the tax. When Kiewit lost, the United States instituted its own action on the same claim in federal court. Finding that the United States had directed the first litigation by requiring Kiewit to file the suit, by reviewing and approving the complaint and appeal strategy, by paying the attorneys' fees and costs, and by appearing as an amicus, the Supreme Court held the Government "plainly had a sufficient 'laboring oar' in the conduct of the state-court litigation to actuate principles of estoppel," id. at 155. Consequently, the second action was precluded.

(2) Provident Tradesman v. Patterson, p. 441, supra. At p. 445, in the middle paragraph, the Court addressed the question whether Dutcher, an insured car owner, could draw on his policy after it was exhausted through the payment of claims asserted against the person who drove his car. The Court stated:

> "At that point it might be argued that Dutcher should be bound by the previous decision because, although technically a nonparty, he had purposely bypassed an adequate opportunity to intervene. We do not now decide whether such an argument would be correct under the circumstances of this case."

This language has tantalized litigants, particularly defendants in mass tort cases, who have argued that since procedural rules generally permit people affected by litigation to intervene as parties (see, e.g., Fed.R.Civ.P. 24), and since resources are conserved if mass actions are litigated all at once, victims who fail to intervene should be precluded from bringing separate suits later. The Supreme Court was, however, first asked to reconsider its dictum in *Provident Tradesman* in a very different context:

MARTIN v. WILKS

Supreme Court of the United States, 1989.
490 U.S. ___, 109 S.Ct. 2180, 104 L.Ed.2d 835.

CHIEF JUSTICE REHNQUIST delivered the opinion of the Court.*

* * *

The litigation . . . began in 1974, when the Ensley Branch of the NAACP and seven black individuals filed separate class-action complaints against Birmingham Alabama (the City) and the Jefferson

---

* Footnotes omitted.

County Personnel Board (the Board). They alleged that both had engaged in racially discriminatory hiring and promotion practices in various public service jobs in violation of Title VII of the Civil Rights Act of 1964, 42 U.S.C. § 2000e et seq., and other federal law. After a bench trial on some issues, but before judgment, the parties entered into two consent decrees, one between the black individuals and the City and the other between them and the Board. These proposed decrees set forth an extensive remedial scheme, including long-term and interim annual goals for the hiring of blacks as firefighters. The decrees also provided for goals for promotion of blacks within the department.

The District Court entered an order provisionally approving the decrees and directing publication of notice of the upcoming fairness hearings. . . . Notice of the hearings, with a reference to the general nature of the decrees, was published in two local newspapers. At that hearing, the Birmingham Firefighters Association (BFA) appeared and filed objections as amicus curiae. After the hearing, but before final approval of the decrees, the BFA and two of its members also moved to intervene on the ground that the decrees would adversely affect their rights. The District Court denied the motions as untimely and approved the decrees. . . . Seven white firefighters, all members of the BFA, then filed a complaint against the City and the Board seeking injunctive relief; the District Court denied relief. . . .

[The Eleventh Circuit affirmed.]

A new group of white firefighters, the Wilks respondents, then brought suit against the City and the Board in district court. They too alleged that, because of their race, they were being denied promotions in favor of less qualified blacks in violation of federal law. The Board and the City admitted to making race conscious employment decisions, but argued the decisions were unassailable because they were made pursuant to the consent decrees. A group of black individuals, the Martin petitioners, were allowed to intervene in their individual capacities to defend the decrees.

[The District Court granted a motion to dismiss the complaint]. On appeal, the Eleventh Circuit reversed. . . .

We granted certiorari, and now affirm the Eleventh Circuit's judgment. All agree that "[i]t is a principle of general application in Anglo-American jurisprudence that one is not bound by a judgment in personam in a litigation in which he is not designated as a party or to which he has not been made a party by service of process." . . . This rule is part of our "deep-rooted historic tradition that everyone should have his own day in court." 18 C. Wright, A. Miller, & E. Cooper, Federal Practice and Procedure § 4449, p. 417 (1981). . . .

Petitioners argue . . . that respondents were aware that the underlying suit might affect them and if they chose to pass up an opportunity to intervene, they should not be permitted to later litigate the issues in a new action. . . .

We begin with the words of Justice Brandeis in Chase National Bank v. Norwalk, 291 U.S. 431, 54 S.Ct. 475, 78 L.Ed. 894 (1984):

"The law does not impose upon any person absolutely entitled to a hearing the burden of voluntary intervention in a suit to which he is a stranger. . . . Unless duly summoned to appear in a legal proceeding, a person not a privy may rest assured that a judgment recovered therein will not affect his legal rights." Id. at 441, 54 S.Ct., at 479.

While these words were written before the adoption of the Federal Rules of Civil Procedure, we think the Rules incorporate the same principle; a party seeking a judgment binding on another cannot obligate that person to intervene; he must be joined. [Thus,] the drafters cast Rule 24, governing intervention, in permissive terms. . . . They determined that the concern for finality and completeness of judgments would be "better [served] by mandatory joinder procedures." 18 Wright § 4452, p. 453. Accordingly, Rule 19(a) provides for mandatory joinder in circumstances where a judgment rendered in the absence of a person may "leave . . . persons already parties subject to a substantial risk of incurring . . . inconsistent obligations. . . ." Rule 19(b) sets forth the factors to be considered by a court in deciding whether to allow an action to proceed in the absence of an interested party.

Joinder as a party, rather than knowledge of a lawsuit and an opportunity to intervene, is the method by which potential parties are subjected to the jurisdiction of the court and bound by a judgment or decree. The parties to a lawsuit presumably know better than anyone else the nature and scope of relief sought in the action, and at whose expense such relief might be granted. It makes sense, therefore, to place on them a burden of bringing in additional parties where such a step is indicated, rather than placing on potential additional parties a duty to intervene when they acquire knowledge of the lawsuit. . . .

* * *

Petitioners contend that a different result should be reached because the need to join affected parties will be burdensome and ultimately discouraging to civil rights litigation. Potential adverse claimants may be numerous and difficult to identify; if they are not joined, the possibility for inconsistent judgments exists. Judicial resources will be needlessly consumed in relitigation of the same question.

Even if we were wholly persuaded by these arguments as a matter of policy, acceptance of them would require a rewriting rather than an interpretation of the relevant Rules. But we are not persuaded that their acceptance would lead to a more satisfactory method of handling cases like this one. . . .

. . . Rule 19's provisions for joining interested parties are designed to accommodate the sort of complexities that may arise from a decree affecting numerous people in various ways. We doubt that a mandatory intervention rule would be any less awkward. . . .

* * *

Petitioners also urge [support from] the congressional policy favoring voluntary settlement of employment discrimination claims . . .. But once again it is essential to note just what is meant by "voluntary settlement." A voluntary settlement in the form of a consent decree between one group of employees and their employer cannot possibly "settle," voluntarily or otherwise, the conflicting claims of another group of employees who do not join in the agreement. . . .

Insofar as the argument is bottomed on the idea that it may be easier to settle claims among a disparate group of affected persons if they are all before the Court, joinder bids fair to accomplish that result as well as a regime of mandatory intervention.

* * *

Affirmed.

JUSTICE STEVENS filed a dissenting opinion in which JUSTICES BRENNAN, MARSHALL and BLACKMUN joined (omitted).

C. VALID, FINAL JUDGMENT

The issue in *Martin* should be distinguished from the question whether a consent decree should have claim preclusive effect as between the parties that entered into it. Put more broadly, should any disposition short of a final judgment on the merits, after plenary consideration and appeal, be considered final for res judicata purposes?

KEIDATZ v. ALBANY

Supreme Court of California, 1952.
39 Cal.2d 826, 249 P.2d 264.*

TRAYNOR, J. In this action to recover damages for fraud, plaintiffs alleged that they were induced to buy a newly-constructed home from defendants by certain false and fraudulent representations respecting the character of the construction of the house and its location on the described real property. They further alleged that the representations were known by defendants to be false and were made to induce plaintiffs to purchase the property and that the contract price of $6,500 exceeded the value of the property by $3,000. In their answer defendants denied the allegations of fraud and pleaded affirmatively that plaintiffs' action was barred by two former adjudications between the parties. Defendants then made a motion for summary judgment supported by affidavits setting out the following undisputed facts: in 1949, plaintiffs brought an action to rescind the contract for fraud and failure of consideration. A demurrer to the second amended complaint was sustained with leave to amend. Plaintiffs failed to amend within the time allowed, and judgment was entered for defendants for costs. Thereafter plaintiffs unsuccessfully sought relief from the judgment under section 473 of the Code of Civil Procedure. No appeal was taken,

* Footnote omitted.

however, from the judgment or from the order denying relief under section 473. Approximately four months after the judgment in the rescission action was entered, plaintiffs brought this action for damages for fraud. The trial court granted defendants' motion for summary judgment and plaintiffs have appealed.

Plaintiffs contend that their unsuccessful attempt to secure rescission of the contract does not bar their present action for damages for fraud. Defendants, on the other hand, contend that the former judgment is res judicata of all issues presented here. Since the former judgment was entered after a general demurrer had been sustained with leave to amend, it is necessary to determine the scope of the doctrine of res judicata in such circumstances. The procedural effect of such a judgment appears to be *sui generis*. It is a judgment on the merits to the extent that it adjudicates that the facts alleged do not constitute a cause of action, and will accordingly, be a bar to a subsequent action alleging the same facts. [Citations omitted.] Moreover, even though different facts may be alleged in the second action, if the demurrer was sustained in the first action on a ground equally applicable to the second, the former judgment will also be a bar. [Citations omitted.] If, on the other hand, new or additional facts are alleged that cure the defects in the original pleading, it is settled that the former judgment is not a bar to the subsequent action whether or not plaintiff had an opportunity to amend his complaint. (. . . Restatement, Judgments, § 50, Comments c and e; 30 Cal.L.Rev. 487; Anno., 106 A.L.R. 437, 444.)

In plaintiffs' first action they sought rescission of the contract. In addition to alleging certain fraudulent representations whereby they were induced to enter into the contract, they alleged that they had offered to restore everything of value they had received, and sought the return of the payments they had made. It appeared from the complaint, however, that the alleged defects in construction became apparent to plaintiffs over a year before they sought to rescind, and defendants successfully demurred on the ground that the action was barred by laches and by failure to rescind promptly. [Citations omitted.] Whether or not the complaint states a cause of action for rescission, the demurrer should have been overruled if a cause of action for damages was stated. [Citations omitted. Plaintiffs' complaint did not, however, allege that the property was worth less than the price they agreed to pay for it (Civ.Code, § 3343), and accordingly, it did not state a cause of action for damages for fraud. [Citations omitted.] In the present action, plaintiffs have added this allegation that was absent from their former complaint, and accordingly, under the rule hereinabove stated, the former judgment is not a bar to this action.

Defendants contend however, that Wulfjen v. Dolton, 24 Cal.2d 891 [151 P.2d 846], establishes the rule that a party claiming to have been defrauded must seek all the relief to which he may be entitled in one action and that he may not, after having failed in an action to rescind a contract for fraud, thereafter bring a second action for damages. In the

Wulfjen case, however, the judgment in the rescission action had not been entered on demurrer, but had followed a full trial on the merits, and the court applied the rule that such a judgment is res judicata not only as to issues actually raised, but as to issues that could have been raised in support of the action. [Citation omitted.] As has been pointed out above, however, it has been the settled rule in this state that a judgment entered on demurrer does not have such broad res judicata effect. The rule respecting such judgments is illustrative of the line that has been drawn beyond which a plaintiff may not go if he hopes thereafter to start again. It is analogous to the rule that was applicable to nonsuits before section 581c was added to the Code of Civil Procedure in 1947. A judgment of nonsuit was not on the merits, and a plaintiff could start anew and recover judgment if he could prove sufficient facts in the second action. [Citations omitted.] Section 581c now provides that a judgment of nonsuit operates as an adjudication upon the merits unless the court otherwise specifies. In view of the liberal rules relating to amendments to the pleadings, it has been forcefully advocated that the same policy reflected in section 581c should apply to judgments on demurrer, and that a plaintiff should be required to set forth all the facts relating to his dispute in one action. (See McFarland, J. dissenting in Newhall v. Hatch, 134 Cal. 269, 276 [66 P. 266, 55 L.R.A. 673]; Von Moschzisker, Res Judicata, 38 Yale L.J. 299, 319–320; Clark on Code Pleading [2d ed.] § 84, p. 531; 30 Cal.L.Rev. 487, 490–491.) On the other hand less prejudice is suffered by a defendant who has had only to attack the pleadings, than by one who has been forced to go to trial until a nonsuit is granted, and the hardship suffered by being forced to defend against a new action, instead of against an amended complaint, is not materially greater. [Citations omitted.] We do not feel, however, that at this time we should reweigh the conflicting arguments over the wisdom of the rule we apply. Since it is a settled rule of procedure upon which parties are entitled to rely in conducting their litigation, any change therein should be made by the Legislature and not by this court.

Since the judgment must be reversed, it is unnecessary to decide whether it was proper in this case for defendants to proceed by motion for summary judgment under section 437c of the Code of Civil Procedure rather than under the provisions of section 597 of that code.

The judgment is reversed.

NOTES

(1) A judgment "based merely on rules of procedure rather than on rules of substantive law" was not on the merits and thus not preclusive according to the first Restatement of Judgment (§ 49, Comment a). The drafters of the Second Restatement rejected this approach and abandoned the "on the merits" terminology. Litigation must come to an end at some point, "even though the substantive issues have not been tried, especially if the plaintiff has failed to avail himself of opportunities to pursue his remedies in the first proceeding, or has deliberately flouted orders of the court" (§ 19, Comment a).

Rule 41 (or a corresponding state rule) has a considerable impact in determining the effect of dismissals. Rule 41(b) provides in part that unless the court specifically orders otherwise, a dismissal other than for lack of jurisdiction, improper venue and failure to join a party under Rule 19 operates as an adjudication on the merits. The enumerated exceptions also serve to prevent a judgment for the defendant from operating as a bar, according to Restatement, Second, Judgments § 20.

(2) In assigning res judicata effect to a judgment on demurrer, does it make any difference what the ground of the demurrer was? See Restatement, Second, Judgments § 20. Which of the following grounds operate as a bar: lack of capacity to sue; failure to join an essential party; omission from the complaint of a material allegation; faulty major premise for the action; presence in the complaint of a complete defense; failure to prosecute; limitations or laches; statute of frauds?

(3) Will the answer to the preceding questions change depending on whether the defendant prevailed in the first action by a demurrer, motion to dismiss under Rule 12(b), summary judgment, directed verdict, or posttrial motion?

(4) The recent trend, motivated perhaps by the Second Restatement of Judgments, has been to weaken the "on the merits" requirement, and to find actions barred by dismissals based on a variety of dilatory defenses. Consider, for example, an action that accrued on Jan. 1, 1987. If plaintiff brings the action in jurisdiction X, with a 1–year statute of limitations on Jan. 2, 1988, she will suffer a dismissal because the action is time-barred in X. What if, on Jan. 3, 1988, she brings a new action on the same claim in jurisdiction Y, which has a 2–year statute of limitations: is the new action claim precluded? See Shoup v. Bell & Howell Co., 872 F.2d 1178 (4th Cir.1989) (holding, over a strong dissent, that a dismissal on statute of limitation grounds is a dismissal that bars further litigation, even in a forum where the action would not have been time-barred). Is such an approach justifiable?

(5) "The national trend seems clearly toward enlarging the scope of judgments on demurrer so as to be preclusionary of not only those things actually litigated but also any others which could have been adjudicated at the time." Note, Judgments—Res Judicata—Judgment on Demurrer, 29 So.Cal.L.Rev. 502, 511 (1956); see also Comment, Conclusiveness of a Judgment on a Demurrer, 19 J.B.A.Kan. 159 (1950). This may be a consequence of the principle that on a successful demurrer leave to amend is routinely given whenever it appears that the defect in the complaint is curable by supplying a new allegation or revising a weak one. If the plaintiff declines the privilege of amending, he can expect little charity the second time around. Cf. Hacker v. Beck, 325 Mass. 594, 91 N.E.2d 832 (1950).

(6) May a litigant base a plea of res judicata on a judgment from which an appeal is pending? The Restatement, Second, Judgments answers in the affirmative, "unless what is called an appeal actually consists of a trial de novo" (§ 13, Comment f). Inconsistent judgments may pose problems, for instance, if the first judgment is reversed on appeal. In that event the second judgment is not automatically nullified (§ 16), but may be set aside in appropriate proceedings (see R. 60(b)).

SECTION 3. ISSUE PRECLUSION

Again, the nomenclature is confusing because the older literature refers to the doctrine of issue preclusion by other terms, such as "collateral estoppel" and "partial res judicata." The Restatement, Second, and modern courts generally use the term issue preclusion.

It is important to keep the difference between claim preclusion and issue preclusion clear. Claim preclusion applies to matters that were—or could have been—litigated in the first action. For example, under the Restatement, litigating about the property damage incurred in a car accident precludes litigation about the personal injuries, even if the question of injuries was never mentioned in the property damage action. In issue preclusion, only issues that were fully litigated are precluded in later lawsuits, and then only if the issues were vigorously contested: actually and necessarily decided in litigation in which their importance was recognized. In this sense, issue preclusion is narrower than claim preclusion. However, once it is found that an issue was fully litigated previously, issue preclusion will apply even when the claims and subject matter of the second lawsuit are different from the first. In addition, parties who were not involved in the first lawsuit may be allowed to use issue preclusion. In that sense, issue preclusion has much broader application than claim preclusion.

RESTATEMENT, SECOND, JUDGMENTS *

§ 27. Issue Preclusion—General Rule

When an issue of fact or law is actually litigated and determined by a valid and final judgment, and the determination is essential to the judgment, the determination is conclusive and in a subsequent action between the parties, whether on the same or a different claim.

A. ACTUALLY LITIGATED

CROMWELL v. COUNTY OF SAC

Supreme Court of the United States, 1876.
94 U.S. (4 Otto) 351, 24 L.Ed. 195.

Error to the Circuit Court of the United States for the District of Iowa.

*   *   *

MR. JUSTICE FIELD delivered the opinion of the court.

This was an action on four bonds of the county of Sac, in the State of Iowa, each for $1,000, and four coupons for interest, attached to them, each for $100. The bonds were issued in 1860, and were made payable to bearer, in the city of New York, in the years 1868, 1869, 1870, and 1871, respectively, with annual interest at the rate of ten per cent a year.

To defeat this action, the defendant relied upon the estoppel of a judgment rendered in favor of the county in a prior action brought by one Samuel C. Smith upon certain earlier maturing coupons on the same bonds, accompanied with proof that the plaintiff Cromwell was at the time the owner of the coupons in that action, and that the action was prosecuted for his sole use and benefit.

The questions presented for our determination relate to the operation of this judgment as an estoppel against the prosecution of the present action, and the admissibility of the evidence to connect the present plaintiff with the former action as a real party in interest.

In considering the operation of this judgment, it should be borne in mind, as stated by counsel, that there is a difference between the effect of a judgment as a bar or estoppel against the prosecution of a second action upon the same claim or demand, and its effect as an estoppel in another action between the same parties upon a different claim or cause of action. In the former case, the judgment, if rendered upon the merits constitutes an absolute bar to a subsequent action. It is a finality as to the claim or demand in controversy, concluding parties and those in privity with them, not only as to every matter which was offered and received to sustain or defeat the claim or demand, but as to any other admissible matter which might have been offered for that purpose. Thus, for example, a judgment rendered upon a promissory note is conclusive as to the validity of the instrument and the amount due upon it, although it be subsequently alleged that perfect defences actually existed, of which no proof was offered, such as forgery, want of consideration, or payment. If such defences were not presented in the action, and established by competent evidence, the subsequent allegation of their existence is of no legal consequence. The judgment is as conclusive, so far as future proceedings at law are concerned, as though the defences never existed. The language, therefore, which is so often used, that a judgment estops not only as to every ground of recovery or defence actually presented in the action, but also as to every ground which might have been presented, is strictly accurate, when applied to the demand or claim in controversy. Such demand or claim, having passed into judgment, cannot again be brought into litigation between the parties in proceedings at law upon any ground whatever.

But where the second action between the same parties is upon a different claim or demand, the judgment in the prior action operates as an estoppel only as to those matters in issue or points controverted, upon the determination of which the finding or verdict was rendered. In all cases, therefore, where it is sought to apply the estoppel of a judgment rendered upon one cause of action to matters arising in a suit upon a different cause of action, the inquiry must always be as to the point or question actually litigated and determined in the original action, not what might have been thus litigated and determined. Only upon such matters is the judgment conclusive in another action.

* * *

Various considerations, other than the actual merits, may govern a party in bringing forward grounds of recovery or defence in one action, which may not exist in another action upon a different demand, such as the smallness of the amount or the value of the property in controversy, the difficulty of obtaining the necessary evidence, the expense of the litigation, and his own situation at the time. A party acting upon considerations like these ought not to be precluded from contesting in a subsequent action other demands arising out of the same transaction.

* * *

* * *

If, now, we consider the main question presented for our determination by the light of the views thus expressed and the authorities cited, its solution will not be difficult. It appears from the findings in the original action of Smith, that the county of Sac, by a vote of its people, authorized the issue of bonds to the amount of $10,000, for the erection of a court-house; that bonds to that amount were issued by the county judge, and delivered to one Meserey, with whom he had made a contract for the erection of the court-house; that immediately upon receipt of the bonds the contractor gave one of them as a gratuity to the county judge; and that the court-house was never constructed by the contractor, or by any other person pursuant to the contract. It also appears that the plaintiff had become, before their maturity, the holder of twenty-five coupons, which had been attached to the bonds; but there was no finding that he had ever given any value for them. The court below held, upon these findings, that the bonds were void as against the county, and gave judgment accordingly. The case coming here on writ of error, this court held that the facts disclosed by the findings were sufficient evidence of fraud and illegality in the inception of the bonds to call upon the holder to show that he had given value for the coupons; and, not having done so, the judgment was affirmed. Reading the record of the lower court by the opinion and judgment of this court, it must be considered that the matters adjudged in that case were these: that the bonds were void as against the county in the hands of parties who did not acquire them before maturity and give value for them, and that of the plaintiff, not having proved that he gave such value, was not entitled to recover upon the coupons. Whatever illegality or fraud there was in the issue and delivery to the contractor of the bonds affected equally the coupons for interest attached to them. The finding and judgment upon the invalidity of the bonds, as against the county, must be held to estop the plaintiff here from averring to the contrary. But as the bonds were negotiable instruments, and their issue was authorized by a vote of the county, and they recite on their face a compliance with the law providing for their issue, they would be held as valid obligations against the county in the hands of a *bona fide* holder taking them for value before maturity, according to repeated decisions of this court upon the character of such obligations. If, therefore, the plaintiff received the bond and coupons in suit before maturity for value, as he offered to prove, he should have been permitted to show that fact. There was nothing adjudged in the former action in the finding that the plaintiff had not made such proof in that case which can preclude the present plaintiff from making such proof here. The fact that a party may not have shown that he gave value for one bond or coupon is not even presumptive, much less conclusive, evidence that he may not have given value for another and different bond or coupon. The exclusion of the evidence offered by the plaintiff was erroneous, and for the ruling of the court in that respect the judgment must be reversed and a new trial had.

Upon the second question presented, we think the court below ruled correctly. Evidence showing that the action of Smith was brought for the sole use and benefit of the present plaintiff was, in our judgment, admissible. The finding that Smith was the holder and owner of the coupons in suit went only to this extent, that he held the legal title to them, which was sufficient for the purpose of the action, and was not inconsistent with an equitable and beneficial interest in another.

Judgment reversed, and cause remanded for a new trial.

NOTES

(1) In the first action, Smith v. County, the County established that the bonds were issued fraudulently and that Cromwell, whom Smith represented, had not paid value for the obligations that he held. Since only bona fide purchasers for value can obtain payment on fraudulently issued bonds, the County prevailed.

Cromwell then brought the second action on other coupons. Again, the County argued that the bonds were fraudulently issued and that Cromwell was not a bona fide purchaser for value. These issues—fraudulent issuance, bona fide purchase for value—were the ones that were litigated on Cromwell's behalf by Smith, and Smith lost. As in claim preclusion, a party's representative binds the party. Accordingly, why was Cromwell allowed to go forward with the second case? Is there anything that the County could have done in the first lawsuit to prevent the second action?

(2) Useful discussions of collateral estoppel are: Cleary, Res Judicata Reexamined, 57 Yale L.J. 339 (1948); Currie, Civil Procedure: The Tempest Brews, 53 Calif.L.Rev. 25 (1965); Currie, Mutuality of Collateral Estoppel: Limits of the Bernhard Doctrine, 9 Stan.L.Rev. 281 (1957); Polasky, Collateral Estoppel—Effects of Prior Litigation, 39 Iowa L.Rev. 217 (1954); Scott, Collateral Estoppel by Judgment, 56 Harv.L.Rev. 1 (1942); Note, Developments in the Law—Res Judicata, 65 Harv.L.Rev. 818 (1952); Weinstein, Revision of Procedure: Some Problems in Class Actions, 9 Buff.L.Rev. 433, 448–54 (1960); Moore and Currier, Mutuality and Conclusiveness of Judgments, 35 Tul.L.Rev. 301 (1961).

(3) The party asserting res judicata has the burden of establishing that it applies. Cf. Rule 8(c). For that purpose he may rely upon the record underlying the former adjudication, as well as the pleadings and formal judgment or orders.

(4) Other questions to consider in determining whether an issue was "actually litigated" concern the burden and standard of proof. For an example of the burden-of-proof problem, if in the first action the plaintiff bears the burden of proving "X" and in the second action the defendant bears the burden of proving "not X," the X issue will not be considered "actually litigated" for issue preclusion purposes. This is because a decision on the issue in the defendant's favor in the first action means only that the plaintiff failed to sustain the burden of proving "X;" the judgment says nothing about whether the defendant will be able to sustain the burden of proving "not X."

The standard of proof question is illustrated by considering a criminal action (for example, for smuggling contraband into the country), followed by a civil action (for example, for forfeiture of contraband smuggled into the country) raising the same issue (e.g., is the material contraband?). A loss by the government in the first action means that it could not sustain the burden of proving beyond a reasonable doubt that the material was contraband. But in the second action, the government has only to make its case by a preponderance of evidence, a much easier proposition. Since the government was not given the chance to make the easier case in the first action, it will not be precluded. What if the civil action was brought before the criminal action? What if the defendant lost in the first action?

———

B. NECESSARY TO THE JUDGMENT

CAMBRIA v. JEFFERY
Supreme Judicial Court of Massachusetts, 1940.
307 Mass. 49, 29 N.E.2d 555.

LUMMUS, J.   Two automobiles, one owned by the plaintiff Cambria and operated by his servant, the other owned and operated by the defendant Jeffery, had a collision.

Jeffery brought in a District Court an action of tort for alleged negligence against Cambria to recover for bodily injury and damage to Jeffery's automobile. The judge found that the collision was caused by negligence of both operators, and therefore judgment was rendered in favor of the then defendant Cambria.

Afterwards the present action of tort, for alleged negligence of Jeffery causing damage to Cambria's automobile, was tried. The jury returned a verdict in favor of the plaintiff Cambria for $838.35; but the judge under leave reserved (G.L.[Ter.Ed.] c. 231, § 120) entered a verdict for the defendant Jeffery on the ground that the earlier judgment had adjudicated that the present plaintiff Cambria through his servant was guilty of contributory negligence, and reported the case.

A fact merely found in a case becomes adjudicated only when it is shown to have been a basis of the relief, denial of relief, or other ultimate right established by the judgment. [Citations omitted.]

The earlier judgment was in effect that Jeffery could not recover against Cambria. The sole basis for that judgment was the finding that Jeffery was guilty of contributory negligence. The further finding that Cambria's servant was negligent had no effect, and could have none, in producing that judgment. Therefore that judgment did not adjudicate that Cambria's servant was negligent.

Verdict under leave reserved set aside.

Judgment upon the verdict returned by the jury.*

NOTES

(1) This is where diagraming cases becomes especially important. In the first action, *Jeffery* v. *Cambria*, contributory negligence was a complete defense, so Cambria could argue that he was not negligent and that Jeffery was. Why should the court in the second suit not be permitted to regard both issues as precluded? The problem is that only one of the two issues was necessary to the judgment. Which was it?

(2) The preclusive doctrines are all based on the notion that once a party has a day in court on a matter, that is all that the party deserves. The adjudicatory system should devote its resources to resolving the disputes of parties who have not yet had a chance to litigate, and the adversary is entitled to repose. Since Jeffery had his day on the question of his and Cambria's negligence, why doesn't this logic apply here? What interests are protected by the added requirement that the decision be necessary to the judgment?

(3) Notice that in jurisdictions that use the Restatement test for "same claim," and that apply claim preclusion to defendants as well as plaintiffs, the *Cambria* problem would not arise. Cambria's injuries and Jeffery's injuries were part of the same transaction. Accordingly, Cambria's failure to assert his injuries as a counterclaim in the first action would have precluded him from asserting those claims in a subsequent lawsuit. Reconsider Note (3), p. 963.

(4) Consider an action by Patentee against alleged Infringer. At trial, Infringer prevails, the court holding that the patent is invalid and besides, the defendant's activity did not constitute infringement. The defendant then alters her activities, and now clearly practices the invention that is the subject of the patent. Patentee sues again. The defendant now admits infringement, but claims the patentee is issue precluded on the ground that the patent was already held invalid. What result?

The problem here is that in the first case either holding (invalidity and no infringement) fully supports the judgment for the Infringer. When it is impossible to tell *which* of two issues was the one upon which the first court relied, most jurisdictions hold that neither is precluded in later litigation. See Russell v. Place, 94 U.S. (4 Otto) 606, 24 L.Ed. 214 (1876). However, in a few jurisdictions, both issues would be considered precluded. In jurisdictions that would not find preclusion, is there anything the infringer could have done in the first case to prevent relitigation?

* But cf. Cummings v. Dresher, 18 N.Y.2d 105, 271 N.Y.S.2d 976, 218 N.E.2d 688 (1966), where the court was apparently confused by a bizarre response of the jury in the first action and allowed collateral estoppel effect to a non-essential finding.

(5) Notice the difference between the hypothetical case in Note (4) and *Cambria*. In the former either holding would sustain the judgment and the usual rule is that neither is foreclosed. In *Cambria*, there were also two findings, but only one was actually necessary to the judgment. Accordingly, one issue is foreclosed, but the other is not. A third variation occurs in jury trials, when the jury is asked to return a general verdict. If there was more than one claim or defense, it is often impossible to know what was actually decided. In such cases, there is no preclusion on any issue.

(6) Consider a car accident involving A, B, and C. A sues B, claiming B is negligent and A is free of contributory negligence. B impleads C on the theory that the entire accident was C's fault, and that C owes B for whatever B is found to owe to A. In addition, B asserts her own claim against C for the damage done to B's car. On a special verdict, the court finds that all three parties were guilty of negligence and denies recovery to A on his claim against B, and to B on her claim against C.

C now brings his own lawsuit against B, claiming that B's negligence proximately caused C's injuries and that C was free from contributory negligence. Is C precluded from litigating the question of his freedom from contributory negligence by the fact that he was found negligent in the first action? Was that finding necessary to the first judgment? Is B precluded from denying her negligence? Was the finding that B was negligent necessary to the first judgment? What difference would it make if B had impleaded C, but had not asserted an independent claim against C?

In complicated cases such as this one, it is sometimes helpful to ask whether the party who is to be precluded could have appealed the first decision. Generally, issues that were not necessary to a judgment turn out not, as a practical matter, to be appealable either. For example, in this case, the answer to whether C is precluded is no: once the court decided that A was contributorily negligent, B was not liable to A, so C was not liable to B on the impleader, irrespective of whether C was negligent. Similarly, once the court decided B was contributorily negligent, C was not liable on B's claim irrespective of whether C was negligent. The same conclusion could have been reached by simply asking whether C could, as a practical matter, have appealed the first judgment. The answer again is no: C won and hence, had no reason to appeal.

———

THE EVERGREENS v. NUNAN, 141 F.2d 927, 928–31 (2d Cir.), cert. denied 323 U.S. 720, 65 S.Ct. 49, 89 L.Ed. 579 (1944): The Tax Court in A–2 assessed income tax deficiencies against A, and the question of A's basis for computing taxable gains was in issue. The Tax Court, disregarding the finding of the Board of Tax Appeals in A–1, independently appraised the value of A's "partially improved" lots. The taxpayer appealed, contending that the Board's order established the value of his "fully improved" lots, and that the value of his "partially improved" lots had to be found by using this established value and deducting the cost of improvements. Judge Learned Hand declared that "in ascertaining which facts, of those decided in the first suit, are conclusively established, the court in the second suit may go beyond the judgment roll. . . . The next question is whether, after the court in the second suit has learned what the court in the first suit actually did decide, the judgment conclusively establishes for any purpose any other facts than those which were 'ultimate' in the first suit; that is to say, whether any facts decided in the first which were only 'mediate data' in that suit, are conclusively established in the second suit. Some courts hold that only facts 'ultimate' in the first suit are conclusively established . . . On the other hand, other courts refuse to distinguish between 'ultimate' facts and 'mediate data' decided in the first suit, so long as they were necessary to the result.

"The important question here is not . . . whether 'mediate data' in the first suit are as conclusively established as 'ultimate' facts in that suit. On the contrary, we are to decide what are the purposes in the second suit for which anything decided in the first suit—whether 'ultimate facts', or 'mediate data' therein—are conclusively established. Do the 'ultimate' facts, or the 'mediate data' decided in the first suit conclusively establish in the second, anything but facts 'ultimate' in that suit? Do they also establish 'mediate data' in that suit: i.e. premises from which to deduce the existence of any of the facts 'ultimate' in that suit? . . . Being free to decide . . . we do not hesitate to hold that, even assuming arguendo that 'mediate data,' decided in the first suit, conclusively established facts, 'ultimate' in the second, no fact decided in the first whether 'ultimate' or a 'mediate datum,' conclusively establishes any 'mediate datum' in the second, or anything except a fact 'ultimate' in that suit."

Besides requiring a party asserting collateral estoppel to show that the issue in question was essential to the former judgment, the cases often declare that he must show it was "ultimate" or "material" in both the former and the present suit. This is designed to restrict the preclusive effect of the former judgment on a different cause of action to fully and seriously contested issues to avoid unfairness to the loser. The problem is to devise a workable test to determine whether an issue is "ultimate."

One test is whether the fact must be *pleaded* or is simply "evidentiary." See King v. Chase, 15 N.H. 9 (1844). But that merely substitutes another unworkable and repudiated logic-chopping inquiry without advancing a solution. Judge Learned Hand propounded a famous but also unworkable test in The Evergreens v. Nunan: "ultimate" facts for estoppel purposes are those "upon whose combined occurrence the law raises the duty, or the right, in question." "Evidentiary" facts are those from which the existence of an "ultimate" fact can be inferred.

Attempts to draw lines between an "evidentiary" fact or "mediate datum" (as Judge Hand put it) and "ultimate" issues have not been more conspicuously successful in the field of estoppel than in the field of pleading.

NOTE

The so-called "*Evergreens*" rule is another spin often put on the "necessary to the judgment" requirement. Most courts have not, however, been able to follow Judge Hand's logic in the case. Instead, they have responded to his concern that "Defeat in one suit might entail results beyond all calculation by either party; a trivial controversy might bring utter disaster in its train. There is no reason for subjecting the loser to such extravagant hazards . . ." To deal with the problem, many jurisdictions ask whether the importance of the issue on which preclusion is sought was foreseeable at the time of the first lawsuit. If the importance could not have been foreseen, the parties may not have argued about the issue vigorously, and accordingly, they are not foreclosed from later relitigation. See Note, Res Judicata—Matters Concluded—Prior Determination of Denial of Permission to Drive in Action Under Insurance Policy is Conclusive Evidence of Lack of Permission in Action Under New York Statute, 74 Harv.L.Rev. 421, 423 (1960). Is that test simple or merely simplistic? Cf. Rosenberg, Collateral Estoppel in New York, 44 St. Johns L.Rev. 165 (1969).

C. SAME PARTIES—PRIVITY

This requirement started out as equivalent to the privity requirement in claim preclusion: both doctrines applied only between the parties who were involved in the first litigation, or their representatives. In the issue preclusion context, this requirement underlies the concept of "mutuality." Under the doctrine of mutuality, a prior determination can be preclusive in favor of a person only if that person would have been precluded to the same extent had the earlier determination been the opposite.

NEENAN v. WOODSIDE ASTORIA TRANSPORTATION CO.

Court of Appeals of New York, 1933.
261 N.Y. 159, 184 N.E. 744.

Appeal, by permission, from a judgment of the Appellate Division of the Supreme Court in the second judicial department, entered May 2, 1932, unanimously affirming a judgment in favor of plaintiff entered upon a verdict.

* * *

CRANE, J. On February 7, 1929, at the corner of Seventeenth avenue and Jamaica avenue, in the borough of Queens, New York City, a collision occurred between the automobile owned and operated by John J. Huppmann and a bus of the Woodside Astoria Transportation Co., Inc. Huppmann sued the transportation company for damages and proved that the collision was due solely to the negligence of its driver to which no carelessness on his part contributed. He recovered a judgment of $2,153.75 against the company.

Later, a passenger in the bus, Mary Neenan, sued both Huppmann and the Woodside Astoria Transportation Co., Inc., for the damages due to personal injuries received in the collision and, strange as it may seem, recovered a judgment of $1,500 against both defendants. Huppmann sought to introduce the judgment roll in his action against the transportation company but of course it was not *res judicata* as to the passenger, Mary Neenan, as she was not a party to that action. She was free to prove that Huppmann was also negligent. If this were not so a responsible party might by collusion shift the liability upon an irresponsible person who cared little about a judgment against him. A plaintiff may hold all joint tort feasors. There was no error in excluding the judgment roll in the action of Mary Neenan.

* * *

POSTAL TELEGRAPH CABLE CO. v. NEWPORT, 247 U.S. 464, 476, 38 S.Ct. 566, 570–71, 62 L.Ed. 1215 (1918): "The doctrine of *res judicata* rests at bottom upon the ground that the party to be affected, or some other with whom he is in privity, has litigated or had an opportunity to litigate the same matter in a former action in a court of competent jurisdiction. . . . And as a State may not, consistently with the Fourteenth Amendment, enforce a judgment against a party named in the proceedings without a hearing or an opportunity to be heard . . ., so it cannot, without disregarding the requirement of due process, give a conclusive effect to a prior judgment against one who is neither a party nor in privity with a party therein."

NOTE

The first action was brought by the sole beneficiary to recover death benefits on an accident insurance policy on plaintiff's husband, who had died of a cerebral hemorrhage 48 hours after his automobile collided with a taxicab. Recovery was denied on a finding that death resulted from natural causes, not an accident. In the present action for wrongful death against the taxi driver and owner, the same plaintiff sues on behalf of herself and her children. On the defendants' plea of res judicata, what result? See Smith v. Hood, 396 F.2d 692 (D.C.Cir.1968). If the children cannot be bound, what about absent members of a class in a class action?

BERNHARD v. BANK OF AMERICA NATIONAL TRUST & SAVINGS ASSOCIATION

Supreme Court of California, 1942.
19 Cal.2d 807, 122 P.2d 892.

TRAYNOR, JUSTICE. . . . Mrs. Sather died in November, 1933. Cook qualified as executor of the estate and proceeded with its administration. After a lapse of several years he filed an account at the instance of the probate court accompanied by his resignation. The account made no mention of [certain] money transferred by Mrs. Sather to the San Dimas Bank; and Helen Bernhard, Beaulah Bernhard, Hester Burton, and Iva LeDoux, beneficiaries under Mrs. Sather's will, filed objections to the account for this reason. After a hearing on the objections the court settled the account, and as part of its order declared that the decedent during her lifetime had made a gift to Charles O. Cook of the amount of the deposit in question.

After Cook's discharge, Helen Bernhard was appointed administratrix with the will annexed. She instituted this action against defendant, the Bank of America, successor to the San Dimas Bank, seeking to recover the deposit on the ground that the bank was indebted to the estate for this amount because Mrs. Sather never authorized its withdrawal. In addition to a general denial, defendant pleaded two affirmative defenses: (1) That the money on deposit was paid out to Charles O. Cook with the consent of Mrs. Sather and (2) that this fact is res judicata by virtue of the finding of the probate court in the proceeding to settle Cook's account that Mrs. Sather made a gift of money in question to Charles O. Cook and "owned no sums of money whatsoever" at the time of her death. Plaintiff demurred to both these defenses, and objected to the introduction in evidence of the record of the earlier proceeding to support the plea of res judicata. . . . The trial court overruled the demurrers and objection to the evidence, and gave judgment for defendant on the ground that Cook's ownership of the money was conclusively established by the finding of the probate court. Plaintiff has appealed, denying that the doctrine of res judicata is applicable to the instant case or that there was a valid gift of the money to Cook by Mrs. Sather.

Plaintiff contends that the doctrine of res judicata does not apply because the defendant who is asserting the plea was not a party to the previous action nor in privity with a party to that action and because there is no mutuality of estoppel.

The doctrine of res judicata precludes parties or their privies from relitigating a cause of action that has been finally determined by a court of competent jurisdiction. Any issue necessarily decided in such litigation is conclusively determined as to the parties or their privies if it is involved in a subsequent lawsuit on a different cause of action. See cases cited in 2 Freeman, Judgments, 5th Ed., sec. 627; 2 Black, Judgments, 2d Ed., sec. 504; 34 C.J. 742 et seq.; 15 Cal.Jur. 97. The rule is based upon the sound public policy of limiting litigation by preventing a party who has had one fair trial on an issue from again drawing it into controversy. See cases cited in 38 Yale L.J. 299; 2 Freeman, Judgments, 5th Ed., sec. 626; 15 Cal.Jur. 98. The doctrine also serves to protect persons from being twice vexed for the same cause. Ibid. It must, however, conform to the mandate of due process of law that no person be deprived of personal or property rights by a judgment without notice and an opportunity to be heard. Coca Cola Co. v. Pepsi-Cola Co., 6 W.W.Harr. 124, 36 Del. 124, 172 A. 260. See cases cited in 24 Am. and Eng.Encyc., 2d ed., 731; 15 Cinn.L.Rev. 349, 351; 82 Pa.L.Rev. 871, 872.

Many courts have stated the facile formula that the plea of res judicata is available only when there is privity and mutuality of estoppel. See cases cited in 2 Black, Judgments, 2d Ed., secs. 534, 548, 549; 1 Freeman, Judgments, 5th Ed., secs. 407, 428; 35 Yale L.J. 607, 608; 34 C.J. 973, 988. Under the requirement of privity, only parties to the former judgment or their privies may take advantage of or be bound by it. Ibid. A party in this connection is one who is "directly interested in the subject matter, and had a right to make defense, or to control the proceeding, and to appeal from the judgment." 1 Greenleaf, Evidence, 15th Ed., sec. 523. See cases cited in 2 Black, Judgments, 2d Ed., sec. 534; 15 R.C.L. 1009; 9 Va.L.Reg., N.S., 241, 242; 15 Cal.Jur. 190; 34 C.J. 992. A privy is one who, after rendition of the judgment, has acquired an interest in the subject matter affected by the judgment through or under one of the parties, as by inheritance, succession, or purchase. See cases cited in 2 Black, Judgments, 2d Ed., sec. 549; 35 Yale L.J. 607, 608; 34 C.J. 973, 1010, 1012; 15 R.C.L. 1016. The estoppel is mutual if the one taking advantage of the earlier adjudication would have been bound by it, had it gone against him. See cases cited in 2 Black, Judgments, 2d Ed., secs. 534, 548; 1 Freeman, Judgments, 5th Ed., sec. 428; 35 Yale L.J. 607, 608; 34 C.J. 988; 15 R.C.L. 956.

The criteria for determining who may assert a plea of res judicata differ fundamentally from the criteria for determining against whom a plea of res judicata may be asserted. The requirements of due process of law forbid the assertion of a plea of res judicata against a party unless he was bound by the earlier litigation in which the matter was decided. Coca Cola Co. v. Pepsi-Cola Co., supra. See cases cited in 24 Am. & Eng.Encyc., 2d Ed., 731; 15 Cinn.L.Rev. 349, 351; 82 Pa.L.Rev. 871, 872. He is bound by that litigation only if he has been a party thereto or in privity with a party thereto. Ibid. There is no compelling reason, however, for requiring that the party asserting the plea of res judicata must have been a party, or in privity with a party, to the earlier litigation.

No satisfactory rationalization has been advanced for the requirement of mutuality. Just why a party who was not bound by a previous action should be precluded from asserting it as res judicata against a party who was bound by it is difficult to comprehend. See 7 Bentham's Works, Bowring's Ed., 171. Many courts have abandoned the requirement of mutuality and confined the requirement of privity to the party against whom the plea of res judicata is asserted. Coca Cola Co. v. Pepsi-Cola Co., supra; Liberty Mutual Insur. Co. v. George Colon & Co., 260 N.Y. 305, 183 N.E. 506; Atkinson v. White, 60 Me. 396; Eagle, etc., Insur. Co. v. Heller, 149 Va. 82, 140 S.E. 314, 57 A.L.R. 490; Jenkins v. Atlantic Coast Line R. Co., 89 S.C. 408, 71 S.E. 1010; United States v. Wexler, D.C., 8 F.2d 880. See Good Health Dairy Products Corp. v. Emery, 275 N.Y. 14, 9 N.E.2d 758, 112 A.L.R. 401. The commentators are almost unanimously in accord. 35 Yale L.J. 607; 9 Va.L.Reg.(N.S.) 241; 29 Ill.L.Rev. 93; 18 N.Y.U.L.Q.R. 565, 570; 12 Corn.L.Q. 92. The courts of most jurisdictions have in effect accomplished the same result by recognizing a broad exception to the requirements of mutuality and privity, namely, that they are not necessary where the liability of the defendant asserting the plea of res judicata is dependent upon or derived from the liability of one who was exonerated in an earlier suit brought by the same plaintiff upon the same facts. See cases cited in

35 Yale L.J. 607, 610; 9 Va.L.Reg.,N.S., 241, 245–247; 29 Ill.L.Rev. 93, 94; 18 N.Y.U.L.Q.R. 565, 566, 567; 34 C.J. 988, 989. Typical examples of such derivative liability are master and servant, principal and agent, and indemnitor and indemnitee. Thus, if a plaintiff sues a servant for injuries caused by the servant's alleged negligence within the scope of his employment, a judgment against the plaintiff on the grounds that the servant was not negligent can be pleaded by the master as res judicata if he is subsequently sued by the same plaintiff for the same injuries. Conversely, if the plaintiff first sues the master, a judgment against the plaintiff on the grounds that the servant was not negligent can be pleaded by the servant as res judicata if he is subsequently sued by the plaintiff. In each of these situations the party asserting the plea of res judicata was not a party to the previous action nor in privity with such a party under the accepted definition of a privy set forth above. Likewise, the estoppel is not mutual since the party asserting the plea, not having been a party or in privity with a party to the former action, would not have been bound by it had it been decided the other way. The cases justify this exception on the ground that it would be unjust to permit one who has had his day in court to reopen identical issues by merely switching adversaries.

In determining the validity of a plea of res judicata three questions are pertinent: Was the issue decided in the prior adjudication identical with the one presented in the action in question? Was there a final judgment on the merits? Was the party against whom the plea is asserted a party or in privity with a party to the prior adjudication? In re Estate of Smead, 219 Cal. 572, 28 P.2d 348; Silva v. Hawkins, 152 Cal. 138, 92 P. 72, and People v. Rodgers, 118 Cal. 393, 46 P. 740, 50 P. 668, to the extent that they are inconsistent with this opinion, are overruled.

In the present case, therefore, the defendant is not precluded by lack of privity or of mutuality of estoppel from asserting the plea of res judicata against the plaintiff. Since the issue as to the ownership of the money is identical with the issue raised in the probate proceeding, and since the order of the probate court settling the executor's account was a final adjudication of this issue on the merits (Cal.Prob.Code, sec. 931 [formerly Cal.Code Civ.Proc., sec. 1637]; see cases cited in 12 Cal. Jur. 62, 63; 15 Cal.Jur. 117, 120), it remains only to determine whether the plaintiff in the present action was a party or in privity with a party to the earlier proceeding. The plaintiff has brought the present action in the capacity of administratrix of the estate. In this capacity she represents the very same persons and interests that were represented in the earlier hearing on the executor's account. In that proceeding plaintiff and the other legatees who objected to the executor's account represented the estate of the decedent. They were seeking not a personal recovery but, like the plaintiff in the present action, as administratrix, a recovery for the benefit of the legatees and creditors of the estate, all of whom were bound by the order settling the account. Cal.Prob.Code, sec. 931. See cases cited in 12 Cal.Jur. 62, 63. The plea of res judicata is therefore available against plaintiff as a party to the former proceeding, despite her formal change of capacity. "Where a party though appearing in two suits in different capacities is in fact litigating the same right, the judgment in one estops him in the other." 15 Cal.Jur. 189; Williams v. Southern Pacific Co., 54 Cal.App. 571, 202 P. 356; Stevens v. Superior Court, 155 Cal. 148, 99 P. 512; In re Estate of Bell, 153 Cal. 331, 95 P. 372. . . .

The judgment is affirmed.

* * *

NOTE

Rejecting the *Bernhard* doctrine, the court in Spettigue v. Mahoney, 8 Ariz. App. 281, 445 P.2d 557, 562 (1968), said: "The adversary system prevails in many aspects of the life of man but contest rules seldom provide that one contestant must be declared the loser to a competitor that he has never met on the field of contest."

EROSION OF MUTUALITY

In the days when the mutuality principle was regarded as the embodiment of evenhandedness, the courts had to struggle hard to carve exceptions. A "derivative liability" exception, holding that a judgment exonerating a person whose liability could be established only by finding another party liable also served to exonerate the latter, was for many courts a more satisfactory escape from the strict mutuality doctrine than the Bernhard exception. However, it soon generated an oddity of its own which made another expansion of collateral estoppel acceptable.

The oddity became apparent in automobile accident cases in which the owner or employer was sued in the first action and prevailed on a finding of no negligence. Might the driver or servant then use that finding defensively in A–2? To preserve mutuality, the Restatement of Judgments § 96(2) (1942) answered in the negative, restricting the derivative liability exception to the case wherein the indemnitor-driver had been exonerated first. However, the weight of judicial authority apparently recognized that the same insurance company would pay if either the driver or owner was ultimately held liable, and expanded the exception. See, e.g., Giedrewicz v. Donovan, 277 Mass. 563, 179 N.E. 246 (1931); Davis v. Perryman, 225 Ark. 963, 286 S.W.2d 844 (1956); Silva v. Brown, 319 Mass. 466, 66 N.E.2d 349 (1946); Fightmaster v. Tauber, 43 Ohio App. 266, 183 N.E. 116 (1932); Jones v. Valisi, 111 Vt. 481, 18 A.2d 179 (1941); Wolf v. Kenyon, 242 App.Div. 116, 273 N.Y.S. 170 (3d Dep't 1934).

As time passed, it occurred to the courts that the derivative liability rationalization was unnecessary in everyday accident cases, such as those in which a passenger first sued the auto's owner and, failing to prove negligence, then sued the driver. The *Bernhard* rule, embodying the "successive-plaintiff" exception to mutuality, permitted the driver to plead collateral estoppel with no concern for mutuality and the courts readily applied the exception in automobile cases. See Lober v. Moore, 417 F.2d 714 (D.C.Cir.1969). In Blonder-Tongue Laboratories, Inc. v. University of Illinois Foundation, 402 U.S. 313, 91 S.Ct. 1434, 28 L.Ed.2d 788 (1971), on remand 334 F.Supp. 47 (D.Ill.1972), affirmed 465 F.2d 380 (7th Cir.1972), cert. denied 409 U.S. 1061, 93 S.Ct. 559, 34 L.Ed.2d 513 (1973), the Supreme Court dispensed with mutuality in the successive-plaintiff situation, holding that a patentee whose patent had been held invalid in a suit against alleged infringer B was precluded from relitigating the question of validity in a suit against alleged infringer C.

Meanwhile, the weakening of mutuality proceeded on still another front, illustrated by Eagle, Star and British Dominions Insurance Co. v. Heller, 149 Va. 82, 140 S.E. 314 (1927). Heller was convicted of intentionally burning his inventory of goods for the insurance proceeds. The insurer was permitted to set up the prior finding as collateral estoppel in Heller's suit on the policy, even though it was not, of course, in privity with any party to the criminal action and even though Heller had by no means sued as plaintiff in the first proceeding. The rationale was simple: every litigant is entitled to one opportunity to try his case on the merits, but to only one, and Heller had used up his turn. See, also, S.T. Grand, Inc. v. New York, 32 N.Y.2d 300, 344 N.Y.S.2d 938, 298 N.E.2d 105 (1973).

Although courts still strongly resisted abandoning mutuality when a stranger sought to use a first-action finding "offensively," the judicial erosion of its foundations had set the stage for the final assault on the mutuality citadel. It was made in a cement mix truck.

B.R. De WITT, INC. v. HALL
Court of Appeals of New York, 1967.
19 N.Y.2d 141, 278 N.Y.S.2d 596, 225 N.E.2d 195.

SCILEPPI, JUDGE. In September, 1961, defendant Hall's jeep collided with and damaged a cement mix truck owned by plaintiff and operated by one Farnum. Farnum sued defendant for personal injuries, recovering a $5,000 verdict after a jury trial. In May, 1964, about two months after the termination of the Farnum v. Hall lawsuit, plaintiff sued Hall for property damage to its truck in the amount of $8,250. After issue was joined, plaintiff moved for summary judgment under CPLR 3212 upon the ground that the judgment in Farnum v. Hall was "*res judicata* of the issues" in the present action (except, of course, damages). . . . Summary judgment was granted. . . .

The Appellate Division, Fourth Department, reversed in a memorandum decision. . . . The majority in the Appellate Division held that only a *defendant* may raise a prior judgment as conclusive of the issues decided therein, citing Elder v. New York & Pennsylvania Motor

Express (284 N.Y. 350, 31 N.E.2d 188, 133 A.L.R. 176). The dissenters were of the opinion that, since Hall has had his day in court and litigated fully and lost on the only issues raised in the present case, the judgment in the first action is conclusive against him. This appeal comes here by permission of the Appellate Division, which certified the question: "Was the order of Special Term [granting plaintiff summary judgment] entered January 18, 1965, properly made?"

. . . . While it is true that most of the relevant cases in this area in New York have arisen under circumstances wherein the defendant sought to use the prior adjudication against the plaintiff, there seems to be no reason in policy or precedent to prevent the "offensive" use of a prior judgment. In fact, there have been cases in this court that have allowed the affirmative use of a prior judgment to establish a right to recover (see Liberty Mut. Ins. Co. v. Colon & Co., 260 N.Y. 305, 183 N.E. 506; United Mut. Fire Ins. Co. v. Saeli, 297 N.Y. 611, 175 N.E.2d 626).
. . .

The main support for defendant's argument is the so-called rule of mutuality of estoppel, that is, unless both parties are bound by the prior judgment, neither may use it. This rule has been so undermined as to be inoperative.

These two cases, *Colon* and *Good Health*, did much to undermine, if not destroy, the doctrine of mutuality. In 1942 in a perceptive and, as later events proved, far-reaching decision, the Supreme Court of California decided the case of Bernhard v. Bank of America (19 Cal.2d 807, 122 P.2d 892 [Traynor, J., now Chief Justice]). There the court, noting that other jurisdictions had abandoned the requirement of mutuality of estoppel and had confined the requirement of privity to the party against whom the plea of *res judicata* is asserted (citing, *inter alia*, *Colon* and *Good Health*, supra), held that the plea of *res judicata* may be raised when the earlier action resulted in a final judgment on the merits; where the party against whom the plea is asserted was a party or the privy of a party in the prior action and when the two actions present identical issues.

The criteria established in *Bernhard* (supra) have been absorbed into our law. . . .

To recapitulate, we are saying that the "doctrine of mutuality" is a dead letter. While we have not expressly so held, the trend of our decisions leads to this conclusion (see 5 Weinstein-Korn-Miller, N.Y.Civ. Prac., par. 5011.42). This view finds support in other States (Bernhard v. Bank of America, supra; Coca Cola Co. v. Pepsi-Cola Co., 6 W.W. Harr. 134, 36 Del. 124, 172 A. 260; DePolo v. Greig, 338 Mich. 703, 62 N.W.2d 441; Gammel v. Ernst & Ernst, 245 Minn. 249, 72 N.W.2d 364, 54 A.L.R.2d 316; Lustik v. Rankila, 269 Minn. 515, 131 N.W.2d 741; Cantrell v. Burnett & Henderson Co., 187 Tenn. 552, 216 S.W.2d 307; cf. First Nat. Bank of Cincinnati v. Berkshire Life Ins. Co., 176 Ohio St. 395, 199 N.E.2d 863; see, also, Ordway v. White, 14 A.D.2d 498, 217 N.Y.S.2d 334; but see Reardon v. Allen, 88 N.J.Super. 560, 213 A.2d 26) and Federal courts (see, e.g., Zdanok v. Glidden Co., 327 F.2d 944 [2d Cir.]; Graves v. Associated Transp., 344 F.2d 894 [4th Cir.] ; cf. Berner v. British Commonwealth Pacific Airlines, 346 F.2d 532 [2d Cir.]).

In this case, where the issues, as framed by the pleadings, were no broader and no different than those raised in the first lawsuit; where the defendant here offers no reason for not holding him to the determination in the first action; where it is unquestioned (and probably unquestionable) that the first action was defended with full vigor and opportunity to be heard; and where the plaintiff in the present action, the owner of the vehicle, derives his right to recovery from the plaintiff in the first action, the operator of said vehicle, although they do not technically stand in the relationship of privity, there is no reason either in policy or precedent to hold that the judgment in the *Farnum* case is not conclusive in the present action (see Currie, Mutuality of Collateral Estoppel, 9 Stan.L.Rev. 281; Currie, Civil Procedure: The Tempest Brews, 53 Calif.L.Rev. 25; Thornton, Further Comment on Collateral Estoppel, 28 Brooklyn L.Rev. 250).

Accordingly, the order of the Appellate Division should be reversed; the certified question "Was the order of Special Term entered January 18, 1965, properly made?" answered in the affirmative; and the order of Special Term reinstated.

BREITEL, JUDGE (dissenting).

*   *   *

Stated concretely, the issue in this case is whether a defendant truck owner cast in judgment in a personal injury action brought by the driver of the other automobile involved is bound by that judgment on the issues of liability in the subsequent action by the owner of the other automobile to recover for property damage. There is, of course, no unity of litigation interest between the two plaintiffs and the practical risks of litigation in a personal injury action and a property damage action are different. Perhaps, more important, in this age of widespread liability insurance there is no certainty of identity in the liability carriers for personal injury claims and property damage claims, and, of course, the law may not generally take direct notice of that difference. This is particularly true with respect to commercial or industrial owners of fleets of vehicles. Hence, there is little probability of equal commitment of time, money, and talent in the different litigations. A converse situation could be even more grievous in effect, namely where the prior judgment may have been for the relatively small amount of property damage incurred, and it is sought to give that judgment binding effect in a personal injury action involving claims for huge sums.

These are some of the practical disadvantages in a too facile extension of the doctrine of *res judicata* in hitherto unexplored areas. As for the offsetting disadvantage of duplicating the trial of issues in litigation, this does not weigh heavily in measuring the balance of convenience. The present rules in this area have subsisted for a long time and there is no great amount of such duplicated litigation.

Above all, the problems in this area turn on broad questions of policy and practicality as all questions of essential justice do. That means that the correct course is not discovered by ignoring the practical effects and concentrating on formal relations of parties and formalistic findings of identical issues and the identity of but one side of the two actions compared. This, of course, has nothing to do with mutuality of estoppel which itself was a doctrine carried too far by being analyzed solely on an abstract basis.

* * *

FULD, C.J., and BURKE and KEATING, JJ., concur with SCILEPPI, J.

BREITEL, J., dissents in an opinion in which VAN VOORHIS and BERGAN, JJ., concur.

NOTES

(1) The court's reliance on the *Colon* and *Saeli* cases seems strained. In the *Colon* case privity probably existed between the plaintiff in the later action and the one in the earlier suit. In the *Saeli* case the Court of Appeals affirmed without opinion in circumstances so complex procedurally that the decision went almost unnoticed in later cases. Comprehensive discussions of DeWitt v. Hall are found in King, Collateral Estoppel and Motor Vehicle Accident Litigation in New York, 36 Ford L.Rev. 1 (1967); Rosenberg, Collateral Estoppel in New York, 44 St. John's L.Rev. 165 (1969); Semmel, Collateral Estoppel, Mutuality and Joinder of Parties, 68 Colum.L.Rev. 1457 (1968); Vestal, Preclusion/Res Judicata Variables: Nature of the Controversy, 1965 Wash.U.L.Q. 158; Developments in the Law—Res Judicata, 65 Harv.L.Rev. 818 (1952).

(2) Under the *De Witt* ruling, what issues are open in A–2 to the loser in A–1 when a stranger pleads collateral estoppel? In Cobbs v. Thomas, 55 Misc. 2d 800, 286 N.Y.S.2d 943 (1968), affirmed 31 A.D.2d 719, 296 N.Y.S.2d 557 (2d Dep't 1969), a front seat passenger was not allowed to use the finding of driver negligence, established in a back seat passenger's suit.

(3) A number of states have rejected the *De Witt* result, clinging to the requirement of mutuality. A common pattern is the sequence of suits by different passengers against the same auto driver. If passenger # 1 wins, passenger # 2 is, in the anti-*DeWitt* states, not allowed to use the prior determination offensively. See Howell v. Vito's Trucking and Excavating Co., 386 Mich. 37, 191 N.W.2d 313 (1971); Standage Ventures, Inc. v. State, 114 Ariz. 480, 562 P.2d 360 (1977); Keith v. Schiefen-Stockham Insurance Agency, Inc., 209 Kan. 537, 498 P.2d 265 (1972); Armstrong v. Miller, 200 N.W.2d 282 (N.D.1972). Paralleling the *DeWitt* approach is Desmond v. Kramer, 96 N.J. Super. 96, 232 A.2d 470 (1967) (after 14 bus passengers recovered by proving negligence on the part of the bus and two drivers, another passenger was allowed to use the determination offensively against the same defendants). In Bahler v. Fletcher, 257 Or. 1, 474 P.2d 329 (1969), a stranger to the first litigation was allowed to use preclusively a finding of breach of a home remodeling contract in an earlier suit against the contractor.

THE DECLINE OF MUTUALITY AND THE
RISE OF MASS LITIGATIONS

Ever since the citadel of mutuality began to show weak spots, writers have composed horror stories about the day when collateral estoppel could be used offensively by strangers. With the arrival of that day, at least in New York, courts around the country are encountering interesting problems, real and imagined. Most have declined to join New York in pronouncing mutuality dead.

"If . . . [collateral estoppel] can be used offensively, then it is to a plaintiff's advantage, when there are several persons injured in a single accident, to use his superior powers to keep his claim out of the legal arena until there has been another plaintiff's judgment arising out of the same events. . . . We are reluctant to adopt a rule which would incline a plaintiff to maneuver to advance on the calendar another plaintiff's case with more jury-appeal . . . ." Spettigue v. Mahoney, 8 Ariz.App. 281, 287–88, 445 P.2d 557, 563–64 (1968).

Is the fear of an "After you, Gaston!" tableau realistic? Are some plaintiffs' lawyers likely to wave others ahead, preferring to hold their admittedly greater talents in reserve for the damage questions? If this is a serious prospect, is it undesirable?

Or is the serious problem that of "what standard the court in the second action should apply if it undertakes to determine whether the first action was litigated 'with full vigor and opportunity to be heard' "? See Semmel, Collateral Estoppel, Mutuality and Joinder of Parties, 68 Colum.L.Rev. 1457, 1469 (1968). Is Professor Semmel on sound ground in urging that instead of testing the availability of collateral estoppel by reference to the opponent's chance to litigate fully in the prior action, the test should be in terms of who was at fault in not using joinder procedures to avoid the second suit?

PARKLANE HOSIERY CO. v. SHORE

Supreme Court of the United States, 1979.
439 U.S. 322, 99 S.Ct. 645, 58 L.Ed.2d 552.

MR. JUSTICE STEWART delivered the opinion of the Court.

This case presents the question whether a party who has had issues of fact adjudicated adversely to it in an equitable action may be collaterally estopped from relitigating the same issues before a jury in a subsequent legal action brought against it by a new party.

The respondent brought this stockholder's class action against the petitioners in a federal district court. The complaint alleged that the petitioners, Parklane Hosiery Company, Inc. (Parklane) and 12 of its officers, directors, and stockholders, had issued a materially false and misleading proxy statement in connection with a merger.[1] The proxy statement, according to the complaint, had violated §§ 14(a), 10(b), and 20(a) of the Securities Exchange Act of 1934, 48 Stat. 895, 891, 899, as amended, 15 U.S.C. §§ 78n(a), 78j(b) and 78t(a), as well as various rules and regulations promulgated by the Securities and Exchange Commission (SEC). The complaint sought damages, recission of the merger, and recovery of costs.

Before this action came to trial, the SEC filed suit against the same defendants in a federal district court, alleging that the proxy statement that had been issued by Parklane was materially false and misleading in essentially the same respects as those that had been alleged in the respondent's complaint. Injunctive relief was requested. After a four-day trial, the District Court found that the proxy statement was materially false and misleading in the respects alleged, and entered a declaratory judgment to that effect. Securities and Exchange Commission v. Parklane Hosiery Co., 422 F.Supp. 477. The Court of Appeals for the Second Circuit affirmed this judgment. 558 F.2d 1083.

The respondent in the present case then moved for partial summary judgment against the petitioners, asserting that the petitioners were collaterally estopped from relitigating the issues that had been resolved against them in the action brought by the SEC. The District Court denied the motion on the ground that such an application of collateral estoppel would deny the petitioners their Seventh Amendment right to a jury trial. The Court of Appeals for the Second Circuit reversed, holding that a party who has had issues of fact determined against him after a full and fair opportunity to litigate in a nonjury trial is collaterally estopped from obtaining a subsequent jury trial of these same issues of fact. 565 F.2d 815. The appellate court concluded that "the Seventh Amendment preserves the right to jury trial only with respect to issues of fact, [and] once those issues have been fully and fairly adjudicated in a prior proceeding, nothing remains for trial, either with or without a jury." Id., at 819. Because of an intercircuit conflict, we granted certiorari. 435 U.S. 1006, 98 S.Ct. 1875, 56 L.Ed.2d 387.

I

The threshold question to be considered is whether, quite apart from the right to a jury trial under the Seventh Amendment, the petitioners can be precluded from relitigating facts resolved adversely to them in a prior equitable proceeding with another party under the general law of collateral estoppel. Specifically, we must determine

---

1. The amended complaint alleged that the proxy statement that had been issued to the stockholders was false and misleading because it failed to disclose: (1) that the President of Parklane would financially benefit as a result of the company going private; (2) certain ongoing negotiations that could have resulted in financial benefit to Parklane, and (3) that the appraisal of the fair value of Parklane stock was based on insufficient information to be accurate. [Some footnotes have been omitted. Eds.]

whether a litigant who was not a party to a prior judgment may nevertheless use that judgment "offensively" to prevent a defendant from relitigating issues resolved in the earlier proceeding.

* * *

The present case . . . involves offensive use of collateral estoppel—a plaintiff is seeking to estop a defendant from relitigating the issues which the defendant previously litigated and lost against another plaintiff. In both the offensive and defensive use situations, the party against whom estoppel is asserted has litigated and lost in an earlier action. Nevertheless, several reasons have been advanced why the two situations should be treated differently.

First, offensive use of collateral estoppel does not promote judicial economy in the same manner as defensive use does. Defensive use of collateral estoppel precludes a plaintiff from relitigating identical issues by merely "switching adversaries." Bernhard v. Bank of America Nat. Trust & Savings Assn., 19 Cal.2d 807, 813, 122 P.2d 892, 895 (1942). Thus defensive collateral estoppel gives a plaintiff a strong incentive to join all potential defendants in the first action if possible. Offensive use of collateral estoppel, on the other hand, creates precisely the opposite incentive. Since a plaintiff will be able to rely on a previous judgment against a defendant but will not be bound by that judgment if the defendant wins, the plaintiff has every incentive to adopt a "wait and see" attitude, in the hope that the first action by another plaintiff will result in a favorable judgment. E.g., Nevarov v. Caldwell, 161 Cal. App.2d 762, 767–768, 327 P.2d 111, 115 (1968); Reardon v. Allen, 88 N.J.Super. 560, 571–572, 213 A.2d 26, 32 (1965). Thus offensive use of collateral estoppel will likely increase rather than decrease the total amount of litigation, since potential plaintiffs will have everything to gain and nothing to lose by not intervening in the first action.[13]

A second argument against offensive use of collateral estoppel is that it may be unfair to a defendant. If a defendant in the first action is sued for small or nominal damages, he may have little incentive to defend vigorously, particularly if future suits are not foreseeable. Evergreens v. Nunan, 2nd Cir., 141 F.2d 927, 929; cf. Berner v. British Commonwealth Pac. Airlines, 2nd Cir., 346 F.2d 532 (application of offensive collateral estoppel denied where defendant did not appeal an adverse judgment awarding damages of $35,000 and defendant was later sued for over $7 million). Allowing offensive collateral estoppel may also be unfair to a defendant if the judgment relied upon as a basis for the estoppel is itself inconsistent with one or more previous judgments in favor of the defendant.[14] Still another situation where it might be unfair to apply offensive estoppel is where the second action

13. The Restatement (Second) of Judgments (Tent. Draft No. 2, 1975) § 88(3), provides that application of collateral estoppel may be denied if the party asserting it "could have effected joinder in the first action between himself and his present adversary."

14. In Professor Currie's familiar example, a railroad collision injures 50 passengers all of whom bring separate actions against the railroad. After the railroad wins the first 25 suits, a plaintiff wins in suit 26. Professor Currie argues that offensive use of collateral estoppel should not

affords the defendant procedural opportunities unavailable in the first action that could readily cause a different result.[15]

C

We have concluded that the preferable approach for dealing with these problems in the federal courts is not to preclude the use of offensive collateral estoppel, but to grant trial courts broad discretion to determine when it should be applied.[16] The general rule should be that in cases where a plaintiff could easily have joined in the earlier action or where, either for the reasons discussed above or for other reasons, the application of offensive estoppel would be unfair to a defendant, a trial judge should not allow the use of offensive collateral estoppel.

*   *   *

II

The question that remains is whether, notwithstanding the law of collateral estoppel, the use of offensive collateral estoppel in this case would violate the petitioners' Seventh Amendment right to a jury trial.

*   *   *

The Seventh Amendment has never been interpreted in the rigid manner advocated by the petitioners. On the contrary, many procedural devices developed since 1791 that have diminished the civil jury's historic domain have been found not to be inconsistent with the Seventh Amendment. See Galloway v. United States, 319 U.S. 372, 388–393, 63 S.Ct. 1077, 1086–1088, 87 L.Ed. 1458 (a directed verdict does not violate the Seventh Amendment); Gasoline Products Co. v. Champlin Refining Co., 283 U.S. 494, 497–498, 51 S.Ct. 513–514, 75 L.Ed. 1188 (retrial limited to question of damages does not violate the Seventh Amendment even though there was no practice at common law for setting aside a verdict in part); Fidelity & Deposit Co. v. United

---

be applied so as to allow plaintiffs 27 through 50 automatically to recover. B. Currie, Mutuality of Estoppel: Limits of the *Bernhard* Doctrine, 9 Stan.L.Rev. 281, 304 (1957). See Restatement (Second) of Judgments (Tentative Draft No. 2, 1975) § 88(4).

15. If, for example, the defendant in the first action was forced to defend in an inconvenient forum and therefore was unable to engage in full scale discovery or call witnesses, application of offensive collateral estoppel may be unwarranted. Indeed, differences in available procedures may sometimes justify not allowing a prior judgment to have estoppel effect in a subsequent action even between the same parties, or where defensive estoppel is asserted against a plaintiff who has litigated and lost. The problem of unfairness is particu-

larly acute in cases of offensive estoppel, however, because the defendant against whom estoppel is asserted typically will not have chosen the forum in the first action. See Restatement (Second) of Judgments (Tentative Draft No. 2, 1975) § 88(2) and Comment d.

16. This is essentially the approach of the Restatement (Second) of Judgments (Tent. Draft No. 2, 1975) § 88, which recognizes that "the distinct trend if not the clear weight of recent authority is to the effect that there is no intrinsic difference between 'offensive' as distinct from 'defensive' issue preclusion, although a stronger showing that the prior opportunity was adequate may be required in the former situation than the later." Reporter's Note, at 99.

States, 187 U.S. 315, 319–321, 23 S.Ct. 120, 121–122, 47 L.Ed. 194 (summary judgment does not violate the Seventh Amendment).[23]

The law of collateral estoppel, like the law in other procedural areas defining the scope of the jury's function, has evolved since 1791. Under the rationale of the *Galloway* case, these developments are not repugnant to the Seventh Amendment simply for the reason that they did not exist in 1791. Thus if, as we have held, the law of collateral estoppel forecloses the petitioners from relitigating the factual issues determined against them in the SEC action, nothing in the Seventh Amendment dictates a different result, even though because of lack of mutuality there would have been no collateral estoppel in 1791.

The judgment of the Court of Appeals is

Affirmed.

*   *   *

Mr. Justice Rehnquist, dissenting.

. . . In my view, it is "unfair" to apply offensive collateral estoppel where the party who is sought to be estopped has not had an opportunity to have the facts of his case determined by a jury. Since in this case petitioners were not entitled to a jury trial in the Securities and Exchange Commission (SEC) lawsuit, I would not estop them from relitigating the issues determined in the SEC suit before a jury in the private action. I believe that several factors militate in favor of this result.

First, the use of offensive collateral estoppel in this case runs counter to the strong federal policy favoring jury trials, even if it does not, as the majority holds, violate the Seventh Amendment. . . .

Second, I believe that the opportunity for a jury trial in the second action could easily lead to a different result from that obtained in the first action before the court and therefore that it is unfair to estop petitioners from relitigating the issues before a jury. This is the position adopted in the Restatement (Second) of Judgments, which disapproves of the application of offensive collateral estoppel where the defendant has an opportunity for a jury trial in the second lawsuit that was not available in the first action. . . .

[§ 88(2), Comment d, p. 92 (Tent. Draft No. 2 1975.]

NOTE

(1) Although in some jurisdictions mutuality has died, so that nonparties can assert issue preclusion (defensively and offensively), one core requirement

---

23. The petitioners' reliance on Dimick v. Schiedt, 293 U.S. 474, 55 S.Ct. 296, 79 L.Ed. 603, is misplaced. In the *Dimick* case the Court held that an increase by the trial judge of the amount of money damages awarded by the jury violated the *second* clause of the Seventh Amendment, which provides that "no fact tried by a jury, shall be otherwise reexamined in any Court of the United States, than according to the rules of the common law." Collateral estoppel does not involve the "re-examination" of any fact decided by a jury. On the contrary, the whole premise of collateral estoppel is that once an issue has been resolved in a prior proceeding, there is no further factfinding function to be performed.

has remained: only parties who have had a day in court can be precluded. But as with claim preclusion, attempts have been made to circumvent this requirement, particularly in mass tort litigation where winning defendants have tried to preclude relitigation of their liability by other victims, see, e.g., In re Multidistrict Civil Actions Involving the Air Crash Disaster Near Dayton Ohio, On March 9, 1967, 350 F.Supp. 757 (S.D.Ohio 1972), reversed sub nom. Humphreys v. Tann, 487 F.2d 666 (6th Cir.1973), cert. denied 416 U.S. 956, 94 S.Ct. 1970, 40 L.Ed.2d 307 (1974). In this case, the district court held a victim of an aircrash precluded from relitigating the issue of the aircraft owner's liability on the ground that a similar action brought by another party had been concluded in favor of the aircraft owner. According to the district court, consolidation of the two actions pursuant to the multidistrict rules meant that in some sense, the second victim participated in the first litigation. He had, for example, allowed the other victim to try his case first. Nonetheless, the Sixth Circuit reversed, giving each victim a separate day in court.

(2) Another interesting attempt to expand the doctrine is illustrated by Hardy v. Johns–Manville Sales Corp., 509 F.Supp. 1353 (E.D.Tex.1981), reversed 681 F.2d 334 (5th Cir.1985). In that case, Hardy sued Johns–Manville and other asbestos producers, including Forty–Eight Insulations, for proximately causing his pulmonary asbestosis. Hardy had been an insulation worker and although he did not know which manufacturer's insulation he had worked with, he invoked the doctrine of enterprise liability to sue all major producers. A similar theory had prevailed in Borel v. Fibreboard Paper Products Corp., 493 F.2d 1076 (5th Cir.1973), in which Johns–Manville, but not Forty–Eight Insulations, was joined. Hardy attempted to preclude both defendants from relitigating the issues of proximate cause and the sufficiency of the warnings and precautions they used, arguing that Johns–Manville had had its day in court on these issues in *Borel*, and since Forty–Eight Insulations was involved in the enterprise for liability purposes, it should also be bound by the *Borel* decision. The district court so held, but was reversed on appeal, the Fifth Circuit finding that the enterprise liability theory did not extend to finding that Johns–Mansville's day in court counted as Forty–Eight's.

D. VALID AND FINAL JUDGMENT

Review the materials in the claim preclusion section on the validity and finality of the judgment. Should the standards be the same for issue preclusion and claim preclusion? Remember that in issue preclusion, courts look carefully at whether the issue was fully ventilated and necessarily decided in litigation in which the parties could foresee the future importance of the issue.

––––

NOTES

(1) When the second suit involves a "different" cause of action, the issues that might have been raised, but were not, remain open. Cf. Restatement, Second, Judgments § 18(2). Logically, a defendant who defaults entirely in the first action should be free in a later suit on a different cause to raise any claim or defense he has. The so-called "New York doctrine" (see Jordahl v. Berry, 72 Minn. 119, 124, 75 N.W. 10, 12 (1898)) nevertheless imposes collateral estoppel,

frequently with harsh results. See Note, Collateral Estoppel in Default Judgments: The Case for Abolition, 70 Colum.L.Rev. 522 (1970) and Note (2), infra.

(2) A, a doctor, sued his patient, B, for the value of his services. B defaulted. In A–2, B sued for malpractice. Does the judgment for the doctor preclude further litigation? Ruling in the affirmative are Blair v. Bartlett, 75 N.Y. 150 (1878); Gates v. Preston, 41 N.Y. 113 (1869); Note, Collateral Estoppel by Judgment, 52 Colum.L.Rev. 647, 654–56 (1952). The same doctrine has been applied to a tenant's default in a landlord's suit based on nonpayment of rent (Reich v. Cochran, 151 N.Y. 122, 45 N.E. 367 (1896)) and even to an injured motorist's default in an action against him for trivial property damages (Roberts v. Strauss, 108 N.Y.S.2d 733 (Sup.Ct.1951)). See Rosenberg, Collateral Estoppel in New York, 44 St. John's L.Rev. 165, 171–77 (1969).

(3) What about the effects of "consent" judgments, such as those entered when B's automobile liability insurer settles A's claim for property damage and personal injuries? Will B be precluded from proving that he was not negligent and that A was? See Sanatar v. Hyder, 17 Misc.2d 286, 176 N.Y.S.2d 467 (Sup. Ct.1958); but cf. Biggio v. Magee, 272 Mass. 185, 172 N.E. 336 (1930) and Macheras v. Syrmopoulos, 319 Mass. 485, 66 N.E.2d 351 (1946). The Massachusetts decisions led to curative legislation which in effect provides that a victim of automobile injury will not be precluded from suit for his damages unless he himself signs the settlement entered into with adverse parties. Mass.Gen.Laws Ann. ch. 231, § 140A (1959). See James, Jr., Consent Judgments as Collateral Estoppel, 108 U.Pa.L.Rev. 173 (1959).

(4) There has been considerable controversy concerning the preclusionary effect of administrative adjudications. Because such actions often use different procedures and adjudicators than do courts, there is an argument against considering relitigation foreclosed. However in an issue preclusion case, University of Tennessee v. Elliott, 478 U.S. 788, 106 S.Ct. 3220, 92 L.Ed.2d 635 (1986), the Supreme Court held that "giving preclusive effect to administrative factfinding serves the value underlying general principles of collateral estoppel: enforcing repose. This value, which encompasses both the parties' interest in avoiding the cost and vexation of repetitive litigation and the public's interest in conserving judicial resources, . . . is equally implicated whether factfinding is done by a federal or state agency." Should the same result apply to claim preclusion as well? See Gjellum v. Birmingham, 829 F.2d 1056 (11th Cir.1987) (no).

(5) In addition to claiming that an agency adjudication is not of high enough quality to preclude later litigation on the issues decided, the appellant in Elliott had also claimed that the policies underlying the civil rights laws are such that adjudication by the State of Tennessee should not preclude reexamination in federal court. The question of what policies mitigate the effect of preclusionary principles is the subject of the next section.

SECTION 4. BRAKES ON THE MOMENTUM OF
RES JUDICATA

Although the pressures are strong to preclude relitigation of formerly adjudicated claims, defenses and issues, these pressures do not operate unopposed. Potent countervailing policies sometimes intervene to turn aside the force of res judicata. Some of the opposing policies are broad and general, relying on principles such as evenhandedness and fairness. Other policies are of narrower, more specific application. They take their strength from substantive values that the law sometimes places ahead of avoiding repetitive litigation. When one of these policies comes into play, the courts may decline to apply the normal rules of res judicata.

RESTATEMENT, SECOND, JUDGMENTS *

§ 26. Exceptions to the General Rule Concerning Splitting

(1) When any of the following circumstances exists, the general rule of § 24 does not apply to extinguish the claim, and part or all of the claim subsists as a possible basis for a second action by the plaintiff against the defendant:

(a) The parties have agreed in terms or in effect that the plaintiff may split his claim, or the defendant has acquiesced therein; or

(b) The court in the first action has expressly reserved the plaintiff's right to maintain the second action; or

(c) The plaintiff was unable to rely on a certain theory of the case or to seek a certain remedy or form of relief in the first action because of the limitations on the subject matter jurisdiction of the courts or restrictions on their authority to entertain multiple theories or demands for multiple remedies or forms of relief in a single action, and the plaintiff desires in the second action to rely on that theory or to seek that remedy or form of relief; or

(d) The judgment in the first action was plainly inconsistent with the fair and equitable implementation of a statutory or constitutional scheme, or it is the sense of the scheme that the plaintiff should be permitted to split his claim; or

(e) For reasons of substantive policy in a case involving a continuing or recurrent wrong, the plaintiff is given an option to sue once for the total harm, both past and prospective, or to sue from time to time for the damages incurred to the date of suit, and chooses the latter course; or

(f) It is clearly and convincingly shown that the policies favoring preclusion of a second action are overcome for an extraordinary reason, such as the apparent invalidity of a continuing restraint or condition having a vital relation to personal liberty or the failure of the prior litigation to yield a coherent disposition of the controversy.

(2) In any case described in (f) of Subsection (1), the plaintiff is required to follow the procedure set forth in §§ 78–82.

COMMISSIONER v. SUNNEN

Supreme Court of the United States, 1948.
333 U.S. 591, 68 S.Ct. 715, 92 L.Ed. 898.*

Opinion of the Court by MR. JUSTICE MURPHY, announced by MR. JUSTICE RUTLEDGE.

The taxpayer had entered into several non-exclusive agreements whereby the corporation was licensed to manufacture and sell various devices on which he had applied for patents. In return, the corporation agreed to pay to the taxpayer a royalty equal to 10% of the gross sales price of the devices. . . . Two of the agreements were in effect throughout the taxable years 1937–1941, while the other two were in existence at all pertinent times after June 20, 1939.

The taxpayer at various times assigned to his wife all his right, title and interest in the various license contracts. She was given exclusive title and power over the royalties accruing under these contracts. All the assignments were without consideration and were made as gifts to the wife, those occurring after 1932 being reported by the taxpayer for gift tax purposes. The corporation was notified of each assignment.

In 1937 the corporation, pursuant to this arrangement, paid the wife royalties in the amount of $4,881.35 on the license contract made in 1928; no other royalties on that contract were paid during the taxable years in question. The wife received royalties from other contracts totaling $15,518.68 in 1937, $17,318.80 in 1938, $25,243.77 in 1939, $50,492.50 in 1940, and $149,002.78 in 1941. She included all these payments in her income tax returns for those years, and the taxes she paid thereon have not been refunded.

Relying upon its own prior decision in Estate of Dodson v. Commissioner, 1 T.C. 416, the Tax Court held that, with one exception, all the royalties paid to the wife from 1937 to 1941 were part of the taxable income of the taxpayer. 6 T.C. 431. The one exception concerned the royalties of $4,881.35 paid in 1937 under the 1928 agreement. In an earlier proceeding in 1935, the Board of Tax Appeals dealt with the taxpayer's income tax liability for the years 1929–1931; it concluded that he was not taxable on the royalties paid to his wife during those years under the 1928 license agreement. This prior determination by the Board caused the Tax Court to apply the principle of *res judicata* to bar a different result as to the royalties paid pursuant to the same agreement during 1937.

The Tax Court's decision was affirmed in part and reversed in part by the Eighth Circuit Court of Appeals. 161 F.2d 171. Approval was given to the Tax Court's application of the *res judicata* doctrine to exclude from the taxpayer's income the $4,881.35 in royalties paid in 1937 under the 1928 agreement. But to the extent that the taxpayer

---

* Footnotes omitted.

had been held taxable on royalties paid to his wife during the taxable years of 1937–1941, the decision was reversed on the theory that such payments were not income to him. Because of that conclusion, the Circuit Court of Appeals found it unnecessary to decide the taxpayer's additional claim that the *res judicata* doctrine applied as well to the other royalties (those accruing apart from the 1928 agreement) paid in the taxable years. We then brought the case here on certiorari, the Commissioner alleging that the result below conflicts with prior decisions of this Court.

If the doctrine of *res judicata* is properly applicable so that all the royalty payments made during 1937–1941 are governed by the prior decision of the Board of Tax Appeals, the case may be disposed of without reaching the merits of the controversy. We accordingly cast our attention initially on that possibility, one that has been explored by the Tax Court and that has been fully argued by the parties before us.

It is first necessary to understand something of the recognized meaning and scope of *res judicata,* a doctrine judicial in origin. The general rule of *res judicata* applies to repetitious suits involving the same cause of action. It rests upon considerations of economy of judicial time and public policy favoring the establishment of certainty in legal relations. [The court here set forth the basic distinctions between total res judicata and partial preclusion, as enunciated in Cromwell v. County of Sac.]

These same concepts are applicable in the federal income tax field. Income taxes are levied on an annual basis. Each year is the origin of a new liability and of a separate cause of action. Thus if a claim of liability or non-liability relating to a particular tax year is litigated, a judgment on the merits is *res judicata* as to any subsequent proceeding involving the same claim and the same tax year. But if the later proceeding is concerned with a similar or unlike claim relating to a different tax year, the prior judgment acts as a collateral estoppel only as to those matters in the second proceeding which were actually presented and determined in the first suit. Collateral estoppel operates, in other words, to relieve the government and the taxpayer of "redundant litigation of the identical question of the statute's application to the taxpayer's status." Tait v. Western Md. R. Co., 289 U.S. 620, 624, 53 S.Ct. 706, 707, 77 L.Ed. 1405.

But collateral estoppel is a doctrine capable of being applied so as to avoid an undue disparity in the impact of income tax liability. A taxpayer may secure a judicial determination of a particular tax matter, a matter which may recur without substantial variation for some years thereafter. But a subsequent modification of the significant facts or a change or development in the controlling legal principles may make that determination obsolete or erroneous, at least for future purposes. If such a determination is then perpetuated each succeeding year as to the taxpayer involved in the original litigation, he is accorded a tax treatment different from that given to other taxpayers of the same class. As a result, there are inequalities in the administration of the revenue laws, discriminatory distinctions in tax liability, and a fertile basis for litigious confusion. Compare United States v. Stone & Downer Co., 274 U.S. 225, 235–236, 47 S.Ct. 616, 71 L.Ed. 1013. Such consequences, however, are neither necessitated nor justified by the principle of collateral estoppel. That principle is designed to prevent repetitious lawsuits over matters which have once been decided and which have remained substantially static, factually and legally. It is not meant to create vested rights in decisions that have become obsolete or erroneous with time, thereby causing inequities among taxpayers.

And so where two cases involve income taxes in different taxable years, collateral estoppel must be used with its limitations carefully in mind so as to avoid injustice. It must be confined to situations where the matter raised in the second suit is identical in all respects with that decided in the first proceeding and where the controlling facts and applicable legal rules remain unchanged. Tait v. Western Md. R. Co., supra. If the legal matters determined in the earlier case differ from those raised in the second case, collateral estoppel has no bearing on the situation. See Travelers Ins. Co. v. Commissioner, 2 Cir., 161 F.2d 93. And where the situation is vitally altered between the time of the first judgment and the second, the prior determination is not conclusive. See State Farm Ins. Co. v. Duel, 324 U.S. 154, 162, 65 S.Ct. 573, 577, 89 L.Ed. 812; 2 Freeman on Judgments (5th ed. 1925) § 713. As demonstrated by Blair v. Commissioner, 300 U.S. 5, 9, 57 S.Ct. 330, 331, 81 L.Ed. 465, a judicial declaration intervening between the two proceedings may so change the legal atmosphere as to render the rule of collateral estoppel inapplicable. But the intervening decision need not necessarily be that of a state court, as it was in the Blair case. While such a state court decision may be considered as having changed the facts for federal tax litigation purposes, a modification or growth in legal principles as enunciated in intervening decisions of this Court may also effect a significant change in the situation. Tax inequality can result as readily from neglecting legal modulations by this Court as from disregarding factual changes wrought by state courts. In either event, the supervening decision cannot justly be ignored by blind reliance upon the rule of collateral estoppel. . . .

Of course, where a question of fact essential to the judgment is actually litigated and determined in the first tax proceeding, the parties are bound by that determination in a subsequent proceeding even though the cause of action is different. See The Evergreens v. Nunan, 141 F.2d 927 (2 Cir.). And if the very same facts and no others are involved in the second case, a case relating to a different tax year, the prior judgment will be conclusive as to the same legal issues which appear, assuming no intervening doctrinal change. But if the relevant facts in the two cases are separable, even though they be similar or identical, collateral estoppel does not govern the legal issues which recur in the second case. Thus the second proceeding may involve an instrument or transaction identical with, but in a form separable from, the one dealt with in the first proceeding. In that situation, a court is free in the second proceeding to make an independent examination of the legal matters at issue. It may then reach a different result or, if consistency in decision is considered just and desirable, reliance may be placed upon the ordinary rule of *stare decisis*. Before a party can invoke the collateral estoppel doctrine in these circumstances, the legal matter raised in the second proceeding must involve the same set of events or documents and the same bundle of legal principles that contributed to the rendering of the first judgment. Tait v. Western Md. R. Co., supra. . . .

It is readily apparent in this case that the royalty payments growing out of the license contracts which were not involved in the earlier action before the Board of Tax Appeals and which concerned different tax years are free from the effects of the collateral estoppel doctrine. That is true even though those contracts are identical in all important respects with the 1928 contract, the only one that was before the Board, and even though the issue as to those contracts is the same as that raised by the 1928 contract. For income tax purposes, what is decided as to one contract is not conclusive as to any other contract which is not then in issue, however similar or identical it may be. . . .

A more difficult problem is posed as to the $4,881.35 in royalties paid to the taxpayer's wife in 1937 under the 1928 contract. Here there is complete identity of facts, issues and parties as between the earlier Board proceeding and the instant one. The Commissioner claims, however, that legal principles developed in various intervening decisions of this Court have made plain the error of the Board's conclusion in the earlier proceeding, thus creating a situation like that involved in Blair v. Commissioner, supra. This change in the legal picture is said to have been brought about by such cases as Helvering v. Clifford, 309 U.S. 331, 60 S.Ct. 554, 84 L.Ed. 788; Helvering v. Horst, 311 U.S. 112, 61 S.Ct. 144, 85 L.Ed. 75; Helvering v. Eubank, 311 U.S. 122, 61 S.Ct. 149, 85 L.Ed. 81; Harrison v. Schaffner, 312 U.S. 579, 61 S.Ct. 759, 85 L.Ed. 1055; Commissioner v. Tower, 327 U.S. 280, 66 S.Ct. 532, 9 L.Ed. 670; and Lusthaus v. Commissioner, 327 U.S. 293, 66 S.Ct. 539, 90 L.Ed. 679. These cases all imposed income tax liability on transferors who had assigned or transferred various forms of income to others within their family groups, although none specifically related to the assignment of patent license contracts between members of the same family. It must therefore be determined whether this Clifford-Horst line of cases represents an intervening legal development which is pertinent to the problem raised by the assignment of the 1928 agreement and which makes manifest the error of the result reached in 1935 by the Board. . . .

The principles which have thus been recognized and developed by the Clifford and Horst cases, and those following them, are directly applicable to the transfer of patent license contracts between members of the same family. They are guideposts for those who seek to determine in a particular instance whether such an assignor retains sufficient control over the assigned contracts or over the receipt of income by the assignee to make it fair to impose income tax liability on him.

Moreover, the clarification and growth of these principles through the Clifford-Horst line of cases constitute, in our opinion, a sufficient change in the legal climate to render inapplicable, in the instant proceeding, the doctrine of collateral estoppel relative to the assignment of the 1928 contract. . . .

NOTES

(1) In United States v. Stone & Downer Co., 274 U.S. 225, 47 S.Ct. 616, 71 L.Ed. 1013 (1927), the Court declined to accord preclusive effect to a former judgment giving an importer a duty-free classification on certain goods. Other importers were held subject to tax on the same type of goods. Would it have been just to allow one importer a competitive advantage over others because of a one-time favorable ruling? Restatement, Second, Judgments § 28(2) excepts issues of law from preclusion when the earlier action is based on claims that are "substantially unrelated" to the present ones or a new determination is called for to avoid "inequitable administration of the laws."

(2) Does all the talk in the *Sunnen* and *Stone & Downer* decisions boil down to the simple point that res judicata will not be applied in tax or customs cases? Must the taxpayer be content with stare decisis? Contrast the *Moser* case, infra.

(3) United States v. Moser, 266 U.S. 236, 242, 45 S.Ct. 66, 67, 69 L.Ed. 262 (1924), was an action to recover an installment of pension pay. The issue was whether an adjudication that by attending the Naval Academy Moser "served during the Civil War" precluded the same question in a later suit for a subsequent installment, the competent court having meanwhile reached an opposite result on sounder reasoning in the case of a similarly situated officer named Jasper. The Government argued that the question was one of law to which the doctrine of res judicata does not apply. The court agreed that it "does not apply to unmixed questions of law" and "the parties in a subsequent action upon a different demand are not estopped from insisting that the law is otherwise, merely because the parties are the same in both cases. But a *fact, question* or *right* distinctly adjudged in the original action cannot be disputed in a subsequent action, even though the determination was reached upon an erroneous view or by an erroneous application of the law. . . . A determination in respect of the status of an individual upon which his right to recover depends is as conclusive as a decision upon any other matter." Is there any help in the court's attempted distinctions?

UNITED STATES v. MENDOZA

Supreme Court of the United States, 1984.
464 U.S. 154, 104 S.Ct. 568, 78 L.Ed.2d 379.

JUSTICE REHNQUIST delivered the opinion of the Court.*

*   *   *

In 1942, Congress amended the Nationality Act, § 701 of which provided that noncitizens who served honorably in the Armed Forces of

* Some footnotes omitted.

the United States during World War II were exempt from some of the usual requirements for nationality. In particular, such veterans were exempt from the requirement of residency within the United States and literacy in the English language. Congress later provided by amendment that all naturalization petitions seeking to come under § 701 must be filed by December 31, 1946. Act of Dec. 28, 1945, § 202(c), 59 Stat. 658. Section 702 of the Act provided for the overseas naturalization of aliens in active service who were eligible for naturalization under § 701 but who were not within the jurisdiction of any court authorized to naturalize aliens. In order to implement that provision, the Immigration and Naturalization Service from 1943 to 1946 sent representatives abroad to naturalize eligible alien servicemen.

Respondent Mendoza served as a doctor in the Philippine Commonwealth Army from 1941 until his discharge in 1946. Because Japanese occupation of the Philippines had made naturalization of alien servicemen there impossible before the liberation of the Islands, the INS did not designate a representative to naturalize eligible servicemen there until 1945. Because of concerns expressed by the Philippine Government to the United States, however, to the effect that large numbers of Filipinos would be naturalized and would immigrate to the United States just as the Philippines gained their independence, the Attorney General subsequently revoked the naturalization authority of the INS representative. Thus all naturalizations in the Philippines were halted for a 9–month period from late October 1945 until a new INS representative was appointed in August 1946.

Respondent's claim for naturalization is based on the contention that conduct of the Government deprived him of due process of law in violation of the Fifth Amendment to the United States Constitution, because he was present in the Philippines during part, but not all, of the 9–month period during which there was no authorized INS representative there. The naturalization examiner recommended denial of Mendoza's petition, but the District Court granted the petition without reaching the merits of Mendoza's constitutional claim. The District Court concluded that the Government could not relitigate the due process issue because that issue had already been decided against the Government in In re Naturalization of 68 Filipino War Veterans, 406 F.Supp. 931 (N.D.Cal.1975) (hereinafter *68 Filipinos*), a decision which the Government had not appealed.

*　*　*

. . . Collateral estoppel, like the related doctrine of res judicata, serves to "relieve parties of the cost and vexation of multiple lawsuits, conserve judicial resources, and, by preventing inconsistent decisions, encourage reliance on adjudication." Allen v. McCurry, 449 U.S. 90, 94, 101 S.Ct. 411, 66 L.Ed.2d 308 (1980). In furtherance of those policies, this Court in recent years has broadened the scope of the doctrine of collateral estoppel beyond its common-law limits. Ibid. It has done so by abandoning the requirement of mutuality of parties, Blonder–Tongue Laboratories, Inc. v. University of Illinois Foundation, 402 U.S. 313, 91 S.Ct. 1434, 28 L.Ed.2d 788 (1971), and by conditionally approving the "offensive" use of collateral estopped by a nonparty to a prior lawsuit. Parklane Hosiery, 439 U.S. 322, 99 S.Ct. 645, 58 L.Ed.2d 552 (1979).

In Standefer v. United States, 447 U.S. 10, 24, 100 S.Ct. 1999, 2008, 64 L.Ed.2d 689 (1980), however, we emphasized the fact that Blonder–Tongue and Parklane Hosiery involved disputes over private rights between private litigants. We noted that "[i]n such cases, no significant harm flows from enforcing a rule that affords a litigant only one full and fair opportunity to litigate an issue, and [that] there is no sound reason for burdening the courts with repetitive litigation." 447 U.S., at 24. Here, as in Montana v. United States, 440 U.S. 147, 99 S.Ct. 970, 59 L.Ed.2d 210 (1979), the party against whom the estoppel is sought is the United States; but here, unlike in Montana, the party who seeks to preclude the Government from relitigating the issue was not a party to the earlier litigation.

We have long recognized that "the Government is not in a position identical to that of a private litigant," INS v. Hibi, 414 U.S. 5, 8, 94 S.Ct. 19, 21, 38 L.Ed.2d 7 (1973) (per curiam), both because of the geographic breadth of Government litigation and also, most importantly, because of the nature of the issues the Government litigates. It is not open to serious dispute that the Government is a party to a far greater number of cases on a nationwide basis than even the most litigious private entity; in 1982, the United States was a party to more than 75,000 of the 206,193 filings in the United States District Courts. Administrative Office of the United States Courts, Annual Report of the Director 98 (1982). In the same year the United States was a party to just under 30% of the civil cases appealed from the District Courts to the Court of Appeals. Id., at 79, 82. Government litigation frequently involves legal questions of substantial public importance; indeed, because the proscriptions of the United States Constitution are so generally directed at governmental action, many constitutional questions can arise only in the context of litigation to which the Government is a party. Because of those facts the Government is more likely than any private party to be involved in lawsuits against different parties which nonetheless involve the same legal issues.

A rule allowing nonmutual collateral estoppel against the Government in such cases would substantially thwart the development of important questions of law by freezing the first final decision rendered on a particular legal issue. Allowing only one final adjudication would deprive this Court of the benefit it receives from permitting several courts of appeals to explore a difficult question before this Court grants certiorari. See E.I. du Pont de Nemours & Co. v. Train, 430 U.S. 112, 135 n. 26, 97 S.Ct. 965, 978 n. 26, 51 L.Ed.2d 204 (1977); see also Califano v. Yamasaki, 442 U.S. 682, 702, 99 S.Ct. 2545, 2558 (1979). Indeed, if nonmutual estoppel were routinely applied against the Government, this Court would have to revise its practice of waiting for a conflict to develop before granting the Government's petitions for certiorari. See this Court's Rule 17.1.

The Solicitor General's policy for determining when to appeal an adverse decision would also require substantial revision. . . . Unlike a private litigant, who generally does not forgo an appeal if he believes that he can prevail, the Solicitor General considers a variety of factors, such as the limited resources of the Government and the crowded dockets of the courts, before authorizing an appeal. Brief for United States 30–31. The application of nonmutual estoppel against the Government would force the Solicitor General to abandon those prudential concerns and to appeal every adverse decision in order to avoid foreclosing further review.

In addition to those institutional concerns traditionally considered by the Solicitor General, the panoply of important public issues raised in governmental litigation may quite properly lead successive administrations of the Executive Branch to take differing positions with respect to the resolution of a particular issue. . . .

. . . But for the very reason that such policy choices are made by one administration, and often reevaluated by another administration, courts should be careful when they seek to apply expanding rules of collateral estoppel to Government litigation. The Government, of course, may not now undo the consequences of its decision not to appeal the District Court judgment in the *68 Filipinos* case; it is bound by that judgment under the principles of res judicata. But we now hold that it is not further bound in a case involving a litigant who was not a party to the earlier litigation.

*   *   *

. . . The conduct of Government litigation in the courts of the United States is sufficiently different from the conduct of private civil litigation in those courts so that what might otherwise be economy interests underlying a broad application of collateral estoppel are outweighed by the constraints which peculiarly affect the Government. . . . The doctrine of res judicata, of course, prevents the Government from relitigating the same cause of action against the parties to a prior decision,[8] but beyond that point principles of nonmutual collateral estoppel give way to the policies just stated.

*   *   *

Reversed.

---

8. In Nevada v. United States, 463 U.S. 110, 103 S.Ct. 2906, 77 L.Ed.2d 509 (1983), we applied principles of res judicata against the United States as to one class of claimants who had not been parties to an earlier adjudication, id., at 143–144, but we recognized that this result obtained in the unique context of "a comprehensive adjudication of water rights intended to settle once and for all the question of how much of the Truckee River each of the litigants was entitled to." Id., at 143.

On the same day that *Mendoza* was decided, the Court decided the next case:

UNITED STATES v. STAUFFER CHEMICAL CO.

Supreme Court of the United States, 1984.
464 U.S. 165, 104 S.Ct. 575, 78 L.Ed.2d 388.

JUSTICE REHNQUIST delivered the opinion of the Court.*

In March 1980, when the Environmental Protection Agency (EPA) tried to inspect one of respondent Stauffer Chemical Co.'s Tennessee plants using private contractors in addition to full-time EPA employees, Stauffer refused to allow the private contractors to enter the plant. Stauffer argues that private contractors are not "authorized representatives" as that term is used in § 114(a)(2) of the Clean Air Act, 84 Stat. 1687, 42 U.S.C. § 7414(a)(2) (1976 ed., Supp. V). Stauffer also argues that the Government should be estopped from relitigating the question of whether private contractors are "authorized representatives" under the statute because it has already litigated that question against Stauffer and lost in connection with an attempted inspection of one of Stauffer's plants in Wyoming. The Court of Appeals agreed with Stauffer on the merits and also on the collateral-estoppel issue. Without reaching the merits, we affirm the Court of Appeals' holding that the Government is estopped from relitigating the statutory issue against Stauffer.

*   *   *

The Government . . . argues here, as it did in United States v. Mendoza, ante, p. 154, that the application of collateral estoppel in Government litigation involving recurring issues of public importance will freeze the development of the law. But we concluded in United States v. Mendoza that that argument is persuasive only to prevent the application of collateral estoppel against the Government in the absence of mutuality. When estoppel is applied in a case where the Government is litigating the same issue arising under virtually identical facts against the same party, as here, the Government's argument loses its force. The Sixth Circuit's decision prevents EPA from relitigating the § 114(a)(2) issue with Stauffer, but it leaves EPA free to litigate the same issue in the future with other litigants.

The Government also argues that because EPA is a federal agency charged with administering a body of law nationwide, the application of collateral estoppel against it will require EPA to apply different rules to similarly situated parties, thus resulting in an inequitable administration of the law. For example, EPA points to the situation created by the recent decision in Bunker Hill Company Lead & Zinc Smelter v. EPA, 658 F.2d 1280 (1981), where the Ninth Circuit accepted EPA's argument that § 114(a)(2) authorizes inspections by private contractors. EPA argues that if it is foreclosed from relitigating the statutory issue with Stauffer, then Stauffer plants within the Ninth Circuit will benefit from a rule precluding inspections by private contractors while plants

_____
* Some footnotes omitted.

of Stauffer's competitors will be subject to the Ninth Circuit's contrary rule. . . . Whatever the merits of EPA's argument, for the purpose of deciding this case, it is enough to say that the issue of whether EPA would be estopped in the Ninth Circuit is not before the Court. Following our usual practice of deciding no more than is necessary to dispose of the case before us, we express no opinion on that application of collateral estoppel.

We therefore find the Government's arguments unpersuasive in this case as justifications for limiting otherwise applicable rules of estoppel. . . .

Affirmed.

WHITE, J. (concurring in the result). I agree with the majority that within the Tenth Circuit Stauffer is insulated from further litigation with the EPA on the private contractor issue. . . .

*   *   *

Preclusion was justified, however, only because the Sixth Circuit had not previously ruled on the Clean Air Act issue. Stauffer argues that Stauffer I also immunizes it in the Ninth Circuit, which has adopted a different rule than the Tenth on the merits. See Bunker Hill Co. Lead & Zinc Smelter v. EPA, 658 F.2d 1280 (CA9 1981). Under this view private contractors may join EPA inspections of all plants in that Circuit except those owned by Stauffer. The majority does not address this contention, considering it "more than is necessary to dispose of the case before us." Ante. I do address it, however, for it is only because today's result does not afford Stauffer the blanket protection it seeks that I concur in the judgment.

*   *   *

. . . In general, persons present in several circuits must conduct themselves in accordance with varying rules, just as they are subject to different state laws. Other companies with plants in several circuits do not enjoy a favorable rule nationwide, like Stauffer, nor do they have to put up with an unfavorable rule nationwide, like Bunker Hill. A split in the circuits cannot justify abandonment of all efforts at evenhanded and rational application of legal rules. Nor is the mere fact that these companies happen to have been involved in litigation elsewhere sufficient reason for uniquely favored or disfavored status.

Such misapplication of collateral estoppel has been condemned by this Court before. For example, in United States v. Stone & Downer Co., 274 U.S. 225, 47 S.Ct. 616, 71 L.Ed. 1013 (1927), it had been established in a prior action that certain imports were duty free. In a later suit involving the classification of similar goods imported by the same defendant, the Court of Customs Appeals refused to apply collateral estoppel and this Court affirmed. Application of the doctrine would mean that an importer, having once obtained a favorable judgment, would be able to undersell others, while an importer having lost a case would be unable to compete. "Such a result would lead to inequality in the administration of the customs law, to discrimination and to great injustice and confusion." Id., at 236, 47 S.Ct., 619. The same concerns were evident in Commissioner v. Sunnen, 333 U.S. 591, 68 S.Ct. 715, 92 L.Ed. 898 (1948). There the Court noted the inequality that would flow from blanket application of collateral estoppel in the tax area. A taxpayer is not entitled to the benefit of his judgment if there has been "a subsequent . . . change or development in the controlling legal principles." Id., at 599. Otherwise, he would enjoy preferential treatment. Such discrimination is to be avoided, because collateral estoppel "is not meant to create vested rights in decisions that have become obsolete or erroneous with time, thereby causing inequities among taxpayers." Ibid.

There is no real difference between those cases and this one. In each, the prior litigant escapes strictures that apply to others solely because he litigated the issue once before and prevailed. As the Restatement points out, "[r]efusal of preclusion is ordinarily justified if the effect of applying preclusion is to give one person a favored position in current administration of a law." Restatement (Second) of Judgments § 28, Comment c (1982).[1]

Cases like Sunnen and Stone & Downer merely recognize that collateral estoppel on issues of law, which is a narrow, flexible, judge-made doctrine, becomes intolerable if the rule of law at issue is too far removed from the prevailing legal rules. Even Stauffer concedes that a decision from this Court on the merits would so affect the "controlling law" that it would lose the entire benefit of the initial judgment in its favor. Similarly, no one contends that if Congress amended the statute to make the opposite result plain, Stauffer could continue to rely on the original judgment. And presumably if the Tenth Circuit were to reverse itself, en banc, and hold that private contractors could make EPA inspections, then Stauffer would no longer be able to keep them out on the authority of Stauffer I. Finally, it is apparent that if, for example, Stauffer has plants in Canada, it cannot impose the Tenth Circuit's inspection requirements on the Canadian authorities. Why then should Stauffer be able to use the decisions of the Sixth and Tenth Circuits to estop the Government in the Ninth Circuit, where the opposite rule prevails? The decisions of those other Circuits are not the "controlling law" in the Ninth; the controlling law in the Ninth is exactly to the contrary. There is no difference between this situation and that where the law within a particular jurisdiction has changed since the initial decision.

* * *

1. According to the Restatement, relitigation of an issue is not precluded if "[t]he issue is one of law and (a) the two actions involve claims that are substantially unrelated, or (b) a new determination is warranted in order to take account of an intervening change in the applicable legal context or otherwise to avoid inequitable administration of the laws . . . .." Restatement (Second) of Judgments § 28 (1982). Even if part (a) is inapplicable in the circumstances of this case, it seems clear to me that both prongs of part (b) apply to litigation in a circuit where the prevailing legal rule is different from that established in earlier litigation in another jurisdiction.

In sum, I concur in the judgment of the Court. I do so with the view that preclusion is inappropriate in circuits that have adopted, or later adopt, the contrary legal rule.

NOTES

(1) Is the *Mendoza* Court correct in thinking that the United States is in a unique position relative to other litigants? With huge backlogs in most appellate courts and in the Supreme Court, is it not the case that all litigants should be encouraged to think twice before seeking review of their cases?

(2) *Stauffer* was greeted with appreciation for straightening out some of the distinctions the Court had made in earlier cases. Thus, the Court had said that "estoppel" did not apply to "unmixed questions of law" arising in "successive actions involving unrelated subject matter," United States v. Moser, 266 U.S. 236, 242, 45 S.Ct. 66, 67, 69 L.Ed. 262 (1924), and that it had no application when the facts in the successive actions were "separable," Commissioner v. Sunnen, 333 U.S. 591, 601–602, 68 S.Ct. 715, 721, 92 L.Ed. 898 (1948). In *Stauffer,* however, the court recognized that both doctrines are confusing. As to the "mixed questions" concept, the Court said:

> "[W]e are frank to admit uncertainty as to its application. The exception seems to require a determination as to whether an 'issue of fact' or an 'issue of law' is sought to be relitigated and then a determination as to whether the 'issue of law' arises in a successive case that is so unrelated to the prior case that relitigation of the issue is warranted. Yet we agree that, for the purpose of determining when to apply an estoppel, '[w]hen the claims in two separate actions between the same parties are same or are closely related . . . it is not ordinarily necessary to characterize an issue as one of fact or of law for purposes of issue preclusion. . . . In such a case, it is unfair to the winning party and an unnecessary burden on the courts to allow repeated litigation of the same issue in what is essentially the same controversy, even if the issue is regarded as one of 'law'. Restatement (Second) of Judgments § 28, Comment b (1982)."

In short, issue preclusion applies to facts, and to mixed questions of fact and law and at times to issues of law. It does not, however, apply when so much time has passed between the two cases that the controlling law has changed significantly. When the law has changed, it is not unfair to require the winning party to defend its position a second time. The question when the law has changed significantly will, of course, be difficult to answer in some cases. But it is an easier inquiry than the "mixed question" doctrine of *Moser*.

As to the "separable facts" doctrine, the *Stauffer* Court said:

> "Whatever applicability that interpretation may have in the tax context, see Commissioner v. Sunnen, 333 U.S. 591, 601–602 (1948) (refusing to apply an estoppel when two tax cases presenting the same issue arose from 'separable facts'), we reject its general applicability outside of that context."

(3) The governmental entities involved in the principal cases, the INS and EPA, illustrate a common practice among federal administrative agencies. When a court of appeals decides a case against them, they will decide whether to "acquiesce" in the decision. If they do, then they will abide by it throughout the country. If they decide not to acquiesce they will follow the decision only

within the rendering court's territorial jurisdiction. Some agencies—including at times the Social Security Administration—have taken a more aggressive position: if they disagree with a court of appeals decision, they will follow it only with respect to the actual litigant in the case. Other litigants who wish to enjoy the benefit of the decision must bring their own challenges and, under *Mendoza,* rely only on the doctrine of stare decisis. See Estreicher & Revesz, Nonacquiescence by Federal Administrative Agencies, 98 Yale L.J. 679 (1989); Diller and Morewetz, Intracircuit nonacquiescence and the breakdown of the Rule of Law: A Response to Estreicher and Revesz, 99 Yale L.J. 801 (1990).

ALLEN v. McCURRY

Supreme Court of the United States, 1980.
449 U.S. 90, 101 S.Ct. 411, 66 L.Ed.2d 308.

JUSTICE STEWART delivered the opinion of the Court.

At a hearing before his criminal trial in a Missouri court, the respondent, Willie McCurry, invoked the Fourth and Fourteenth Amendments to suppress evidence that had been seized by the police. The trial court denied the suppression motion in part, and McCurry was subsequently convicted after a jury trial. The conviction was later affirmed on appeal. State v. McCurry, 587 S.W.2d 337 (Mo.App. 1979). Because he did not assert that the state courts had denied him a "full and fair opportunity" to litigate his search and seizure claim, McCurry was barred by this Court's decision in Stone v. Powell, 428 U.S. 465, 96 S.Ct. 3037, 49 L.Ed.2d 1067, from seeking a writ of habeas corpus in a federal district court. Nevertheless, he sought federal-court redress for the alleged constitutional violation by bringing a damages suit under 42 U.S.C. § 1983 against the officers who had entered his home and seized the evidence in question. We granted certiorari to consider whether the unavailability of federal habeas corpus prevented the police officers from raising the state courts' partial rejection of McCurry's constitutional claim as a collateral estoppel defense to the § 1983 suit against them for damages. 444 U.S. 1070, 100 S.Ct. 1012, 62 L.Ed.2d 571.

In April 1977, several undercover police officers, following an informant's tip that McCurry was dealing in heroin, went to his house in St. Louis, Mo., to attempt a purchase. Two officers, petitioners Allen and Jacobsmeyer, knocked on the front door, while the other officers hid nearby. When McCurry opened the door, the two officers asked to buy some heroin "caps." McCurry went back into the house and returned soon thereafter, firing a pistol at and seriously wounding Allen and Jacobsmeyer. After a gun battle with the other officers and their reinforcements, McCurry retreated into the house; he emerged again when the police demanded that he surrender. Several officers then entered the house without a warrant, purportedly to search for other persons inside. One of the officers seized drugs and other contraband that lay in plain view, as well as additional contraband he found in dresser drawers and in auto tires on the porch.

McCurry was charged with possession of heroin and assault with intent to kill. At the pretrial suppression hearing, the trial judge excluded the evidence seized from the dresser drawers and tires, but denied suppression of the evidence found in plain view. McCurry was convicted of both the heroin and assault offenses.

McCurry subsequently filed the present § 1983 action for $1 million in damages against petitioners Allen and Jacobsmeyer, other unnamed individual police officers, and the city of St. Louis and its police department. The complaint alleged a conspiracy to violate McCurry's Fourth Amendment rights, an unconstitutional search and seizure of his house, and an assault on him by unknown police officers after he had been arrested and handcuffed. The petitioners moved for summary judgment. The District Court apparently understood the gist of the complaint to be the allegedly unconstitutional search and seizure and granted summary judgment, holding that collateral estoppel prevented McCurry from relitigating the search-and-seizure question already decided against him in the state courts. 466 F.Supp. 514 (ED Mo.1978).

The Court of Appeals reversed the judgment and remanded the case for trial. 606 F.2d 795 (CA8 1979). . . .

In recent years, this Court has reaffirmed the benefits of collateral estoppel in particular, finding the policies underlying it to apply in contexts not formerly recognized at common law. Thus, the Court has eliminated the requirement of mutuality in applying collateral estoppel to bar relitigation of issues decided earlier in federal-court suits, Blonder-Tongue Laboratories, Inc. v. University of Illinois Foundation, 402 U.S. 313, 91 S.Ct. 1434, 28 L.Ed.2d 788, and has allowed a litigant who was not a party to a federal case to use collateral estoppel "offensively" in a new federal suit against the party who lost on the decided issue in the first case, Parklane Hosiery Co. v. Shore, 439 U.S. 322, 99 S.Ct. 645, 58 L.Ed.2d 552. But one general limitation the Court has repeatedly recognized is that the concept of collateral estoppel cannot apply when the party against whom the earlier decision is asserted did not have a "full and fair opportunity" to litigate that issue in the earlier case. . . .

The federal courts generally have also consistently accorded preclusive effect to issues decided by state courts. . . .

. . . Congress has specifically required all federal courts to give preclusive effect to state-court judgments whenever the courts of the State from which the judgments emerged would do so:

> "[J]udicial proceedings [of any court of any State] shall have the same full faith and credit in every court within the United States and its Territories and Possessions as they have by law or usage in the courts of such State . . .." 28 U.S.C. § 1738.[1]

1. This statute has existed in essentially unchanged form since its enactment just after the ratification of the Constitution, Act of May 26, 1790, ch. 11, 1 Stat. 122, and its re-enactment soon thereafter, Act of Mar. 27, 1804, ch. 56, 2 Stat. 298–299. [This footnote has been renumbered; others are omitted. Eds.]

* * *

This Court has never directly decided whether the rules of res judicata and collateral estoppel are generally applicable to § 1983 actions. . . .

Because the requirement of mutuality of estoppel was still alive in the federal courts until well into this century, see Blonder-Tongue Laboratories, Inc. v. University of Illinois Foundation, supra, at 322–323, 91 S.Ct., at 1439–1440, the drafters of the 1871 Civil Rights Act, of which § 1983 is a part, may have had less reason to concern themselves with rules of preclusion than a modern Congress would. Nevertheless, in 1871 res judicata and collateral estoppel could certainly have applied in federal suits following state-court litigation between the same parties or their privies, and nothing in the language of § 1983 remotely expresses any congressional intent to contravene the common-law rules of preclusion or to repeal the express statutory requirements of the predecessor of 28 U.S.C. § 1738. . . .

Moreover, the legislative history of § 1983 does not in any clear way suggest that Congress intended to repeal or restrict the traditional doctrines of preclusion. The main goal of the Act was to override the corrupting influence of the Ku Klux Klan and its sympathizers on the governments and law enforcement agencies of the Southern States, see Monroe v. Pape, 365 U.S. 167, 174, 81 S.Ct. 473, 477, 5 L.Ed.2d 492, and of course the debates show that one strong motive behind its enactment was grave congressional concern that the state courts had been deficient in protecting federal rights, Mitchum v. Foster, 407 U.S. 225, 241–242, 92 S.Ct. 2151, 2161–2162, 32 L.Ed.2d 705; Monroe v. Pape, supra, at 180, 81 S.Ct., at 480. But in the context of the legislative history as a whole, this congressional concern lends only the most equivocal support to any argument that, in cases where the state courts have recognized the constitutional claims asserted and provided fair procedures for determining them, Congress intended to override § 1738 or the common-law rules of collateral estoppel and res judicata. Since repeals by implication are disfavored, Radzanower v. Touche Ross & Co., 426 U.S. 148, 154, 96 S.Ct. 1989, 1993, 48 L.Ed.2d 540, much clearer support than this would be required to hold that § 1738 and the traditional rules of preclusion are not applicable to § 1983 suits.

* * *

The actual basis of the Court of Appeals' holding appears to be a generally framed principle that every person asserting a federal right is entitled to one unencumbered opportunity to litigate that right in a federal district court, regardless of the legal posture in which the federal claim arises. But the authority for this principle is difficult to discern. It cannot lie in the Constitution, which makes no such guarantee, but leaves the scope of the jurisdiction of the federal district courts to the wisdom of Congress. And no such authority is to be found in § 1983 itself. For reasons already discussed at length, nothing in the language or legislative history of § 1983 proves any congressional intent to deny binding effect to a state-court judgment or decision when the state court, acting within its proper jurisdiction, has given the parties a full and fair opportunity to litigate federal claims, and thereby has shown itself willing and able to protect federal rights. And nothing in the legislative history of § 1983 reveals any purpose to afford less deference to judgments in state criminal proceedings than to those in state civil proceedings. There is, in short, no reason to believe that Congress intended to provide a person claiming a federal right an unrestricted opportunity to relitigate an issue already decided in state court simply because the issue arose in a state proceeding in which he would rather not have been engaged at all.

*   *   *

The only other conceivable basis for finding a universal right to litigate a federal claim in a federal district court is hardly a legal basis at all, but rather a general distrust of the capacity of the state courts to render correct decisions on constitutional issues. It is ironic that Stone v. Powell provided the occasion for the expression of such an attitude in the present litigation, in view of this Court's emphatic reaffirmation in that case of the constitutional obligation of the state courts to uphold federal law, and its expression of confidence in their ability to do so.

. . .

. . . Accordingly, the judgment is reversed, and the case is remanded to the Court of Appeals for proceedings consistent with this opinion.

It is so ordered.

JUSTICE BLACKMUN, with whom JUSTICE BRENNAN and JUSTICE MARSHALL join, dissenting.

. . . Although the legislators of the 42d Congress did not expressly state whether the then existing common-law doctrine of preclusion would survive enactment of § 1983, they plainly anticipated more than the creation of a federal statutory remedy to be administered indifferently by either a state or a federal court. The legislative intent, as expressed by supporters and understood by opponents, was to restructure relations between the state and federal courts. Congress deliberately opened the federal courts to individual citizens in response to the States' failure to provide justice in their own courts. Contrary to the view presently expressed by the Court, the 42d Congress was not concerned solely with procedural regularity. Even where there was procedural regularity, which the Court today so stresses, Congress believed that substantive justice was unobtainable. The availability of the federal forum was not meant to turn on whether, in an individual case, the state procedures were adequate. Assessing the state of affairs as a whole, Congress specifically made a determination that federal oversight of constitutional determinations through the federal courts was necessary to ensure the effective enforcement of constitutional rights.

* * *

The following factors persuade me to conclude that this respondent should not be precluded from asserting his claim in federal court. First, at the time § 1983 was passed, a nonparty's ability, as a practical matter, to invoke collateral estoppel was nonexistent. One could not preclude an opponent from relitigating an issue in a new cause of action, though that issue had been determined conclusively in a prior proceeding, unless there was "mutuality." Additionally, the definitions of "cause of action" and "issue" were narrow. As a result, and obviously, no preclusive effect could arise out of a criminal proceeding that would affect subsequent *civil* litigation. Thus, the 42d Congress could not have anticipated or approved that a criminal defendant, tried and convicted in state court, would be precluded from raising against police officers a constitutional claim arising out of his arrest.

Also, the process of deciding in a state criminal trial whether to exclude or admit evidence is not at all the equivalent of a § 1983 proceeding. The remedy sought in the latter is utterly different. In bringing the civil suit the criminal defendant does not seek to challenge his conviction collaterally. At most, he wins damages. In contrast, the exclusion of evidence may prevent a criminal conviction. A trial court, faced with the decision whether to exclude relevant evidence, confronts institutional pressures that may cause it to give a different shape to the Fourth Amendment right from what would result in civil litigation of a damages claim. . . .

A state criminal defendant cannot be held to have chosen "voluntarily" to litigate his Fourth Amendment claim in the state court. The risk of conviction puts pressure upon him to raise all possible defenses. He also faces uncertainty about the wisdom of forgoing litigation on *any* issue, for there is the possibility that he will be held to have waived his right to appeal on that issue. The "deliberate bypass" of state procedures, which the imposition of collateral estoppel under these circumstances encourages, surely is not a preferred goal. To hold that a criminal defendant who raises a Fourth Amendment claim at his criminal trial "freely and without reservation submits his federal claims for decision by the state courts," . . . is to deny reality. . . .

NOTES

(1) Note that *Allen* also raises the question whether a criminal defendant's actions during his criminal trial should preclude later civil litigation. Could not an argument to that effect be based on footnote 15 in Parklane Hosiery Co. v. Shore, p. 996, supra?

(2) Could McCurry have avoided issue preclusion? See Haring v. Prosise, 462 U.S. 306, 103 S.Ct. 2368, 76 L.Ed.2d 595 (1983). By pleading guilty, the criminal defendant avoided putting the propriety of the police's conduct in

issue. Accordingly, he was allowed to bring a civil action challenging the constitutionality of their actions.

(3) *Allen* involves yet another question, which is when does litigation in one legal system (here, a state court) preclude litigation in a second system (here, a federal court). This is the subject of the next section.

SECTION 5.   INTERSYSTEM PRECLUSION

There are two issues here. First, are courts in one legal system required to treat claims as precluded because of litigation that occurred in another judicial system? Second, if preclusionary rules do apply, ought the second legal system use its own rules or those of the system that entertained the original action? There are three permutations to the intersystem preclusion question for courts within the United States:

Read 29 U.S.C. § 1738 in the Supplement. Which of these variations does that section treat?

A.   STATE/STATE PRECLUSION

Section 1738, which was enacted pursuant to the authority given Congress by Art. IV, § 1 of the Constitution, clearly applies to the situation successive suits in the courts of two states; a state suit followed by a federal suit; and a federal suit followed by a state suit in which a party who previously litigated in one state court ("state X") brings a related action in the court of another state ("state Y"). The provision, which directs "every court within the United States" to accord full faith and credit to the "judicial proceedings" of "any court of any such State, Territory or Possession of the United States," requires the second court to give the same preclusive effect to the judgment that the first court would have given it. In general, therefore, state Y must apply the res judicata law of state X. See Note, Collateral Estoppel in Multistate Litigation, 68 Colum.L.Rev. 1590 (1968).

THOMPSON v. THOMPSON

Supreme Court of the United States, 1988.
484 U.S. 174, 108 S.Ct. 513, 98 L.Ed.2d 512.

Justice Marshall delivered the opinion of the Court.*

* * *

. . . . This case arises out of a jurisdictional stalemate that came to pass notwithstanding the strictures of the Parental Kidnaping Prevention Act (PKPA or Act) of 1980, 28 U.S.C. § 1738A. In July 1978, respondent Susan Clay (then Susan Thompson) filed a petition in Los Angeles Superior Court asking the court to dissolve her marriage to petitioner David Thompson and seeking custody of the couple's infant son, Matthew. The court initially awarded the parents joint custody of Matthew, but that arrangement became infeasible when respondent

---

* Footnotes omitted.

decided to move from California to Louisiana to take a job. The court then entered an order providing that respondent would have sole custody of Matthew once she left for Louisiana. This state of affairs was to remain in effect until the court investigator submitted a report on custody, after which the court intended to make a more studied custody determination. . . .

Respondent and Matthew moved to Louisiana in December of 1980. Three months later, respondent filed a petition in Louisiana state court for enforcement of the California custody decree, judgment of custody, and modification of petitioner's visitation privileges. By order dated April 7, 1981, the Louisiana court granted the petition and awarded sole custody of Matthew to respondent. Two months later, however, the California court, having received and reviewed its investigator's report, entered an order awarding sole custody of Matthew to petitioner. Thus arose the current impasse.

In August 1983, petitioner brought this action in the District Court for the Central District of California. Petitioner requested an order declaring the Louisiana decree invalid and the California decree valid, and enjoining the enforcement of the Louisiana decree. Petitioner did not attempt to enforce the California decree in a Louisiana state court before he filed suit in federal court [seeking to enforce the PKPA. The Court granted certiorari to determine whether the Act creates a private right of action in federal court to determine the validity of two conflicting custody decrees.]

In determining whether to infer a private cause of action from a federal statute, our focal point is Congress' intent in enacting the statute. . . . Cort v. Ash, 422 U.S. 66, 78, 95 S.Ct. 2080, 2088, 45 L.Ed. 2d 26 (1975). . . .

We examine initially the context of the PKPA with an eye toward determining Congress' perception of the law that it was shaping or reshaping. . . . At the time Congress passed the PKPA, custody orders held a peculiar status under the full faith and credit doctrine, which requires each State to give effect to the judicial proceedings of other States, see U.S. Const., Art. IV, § 1; 28 U.S.C. § 1738. The anomaly traces to the fact that custody orders characteristically are subject to modification as required by the best interests of the child. As a consequence, some courts doubted whether custody orders were sufficiently "final" to trigger full faith and credit requirements, see e.g., Hooks v. Hooks, 771 F.2d 935, 948 (CA6 1985); McDougald v. Jenson, 596 F.Supp. 680, 684–685 (N.D.Fla.1984), aff'd 786 F.2d 1465 (CA11), cert. denied, 479 U.S. 1001, 107 S.Ct. 207, 93 L.Ed.2d 137 (1986), and this Court had declined expressly to settle the question. See Ford v. Ford, 371 U.S. 187, 192, 83 S.Ct. 273, 276, 9 L.Ed.2d 240 (1962). Even if custody orders were subject to full faith and credit requirements, the Full Faith and Credit Clause obliges States only to accord the same force to judgments as would be accorded by the courts of the State in which the judgment was entered. Because courts entering custody orders generally retain the power to modify them, courts in other States were no less entitled to change the terms of custody according to their own views of the child's best interest. See New York ex rel. Halvey v. Halvey, 330 U.S. 610, 614–615, 67 S.Ct. 903, 906, 91 L.Ed. 1133 (1947). For these reasons, a parent who lost a custody battle in one State had an incentive to kidnap the child and move to another State to relitigate the issue. This circumstance contributed to widespread jurisdictional deadlocks like this one, and more importantly, to a national epidemic of parental kidnaping. . . .

A number of States joined in an effort to avoid these jurisdictional conflicts by adopting the Uniform Child Custody Jurisdiction Act (UCCJA), 9 U.L.A. §§ 1–28 (1979). The UCCJA prescribed uniform standards for deciding which State could make a custody determination and obligated enacting States to enforce the determination made by the State with proper jurisdiction. The project foundered, however, because a number of States refused to enact the UCCJA while others enacted it with modification. In the absence of uniform national standards for allocating and enforcing custody determinations, noncustodial parents still had reason to snatch their children and petition the courts of any of a number of haven States for sole custody.

The context of the PKPA therefore suggests that the principal problem Congress was seeking to remedy was the inapplicability of full faith and credit requirements to custody determinations. Statements made when the Act was introduced in Congress forcefully confirm that suggestion. The sponsors and supporters of the Act continually indicated that the purpose of the PKPA was to provide for nationwide enforcement of custody orders made in accordance with the terms of the UCCJA. . . .

* * *

The significance of Congress' full faith and credit approach to the problem of child snatching is that the Full Faith and Credit Clause, in either its constitutional or statutory incarnations, does not give rise to an implied federal cause of action. Rather, the clause "only prescribes a rule by which courts, Federal and state, are to be guided when a question arises in the progress of a pending suit as to the faith and credit to be given by the court to the public acts, records, and judicial proceedings of a State other than that in which the court is sitting." Minnesota v. Northern Securities Co., 195 U.S. 48, 72, 24 S.Ct. 598, 605, 48 L.Ed. 870 (1904). . . . Because Congress' chief aim in enacting the PKPA was to extend the requirements of the Full Faith and Credit Clause to custody determinations, the Act is most naturally construed to furnish a rule of decision for courts to use in adjudicating custody disputes and not to create an entirely new cause of action. It thus is not compatible with the purpose and context of the legislative scheme to infer a private cause of action. See Cort v. Ash, 422 U.S., at 78, 95 S.Ct., at 2088.

The language and placement of the statute reinforce this conclusion. The PKPA, 28 U.S.C. § 1738A, is an addendum to the full faith and credit statute, 28 U.S.C. § 1738. This fact alone is strong proof that the Act is intended to have the same operative effect as the full faith and credit statute.

*   *   *

JUSTICE O'CONNOR filed an opinion concurring in part in the judgment (omitted).

JUSTICE SCALIA filed an opinion concurring in the judgment (omitted).

B. STATE/FEDERAL PRECLUSION

By its terms, § 1738 also applies to this "vertical" choice of law question, unless some mitigating principle comes into play. *Allen v. McCurry*, p. 1016, supra, presented several unsuccessful arguments for opposing the application of issue preclusion. The next case is its claim preclusion analogue.

MARRESE v. AMERICAN ACADEMY OF ORTHOPAEDIC SURGEONS

Supreme Court of the United States, 1985.
470 U.S. 373, 105 S.Ct. 1327, 84 L.Ed.2d 274.

JUSTICE O'CONNOR delivered the opinion of the Court.*

This case concerns the preclusive effect of a state court judgment in a subsequent lawsuit involving federal antitrust claims within the exclusive jurisdiction of the federal courts. The Court of Appeals for the Seventh Circuit, sitting en banc, held as a matter of federal law that the earlier state court judgments barred the federal antitrust suit. 726 F.2d 1150 (1984). Under 28 U.S.C. § 1738, a federal court generally is required to consider first the law of the State in which the judgment was rendered to determine its preclusive effect. Because the lower courts did not consider state preclusion law in this case, we reverse and remand.

I

Petitioners are board-certified orthopaedic surgeons who applied for membership in respondent American Academy of Orthopaedic Surgeons (Academy). Respondent denied the membership applications without providing a hearing or a statement of reasons. In November 1976, petitioner Dr. Treister filed suit in the Circuit Court of Cook County, State of Illinois, alleging that the denial of membership in the Academy violated associational rights protected by Illinois common law. Petitioner Dr. Marrese separately filed a similar action in state court. Neither petitioner alleged a violation of state antitrust law in his state court action; nor did either petitioner contemporaneously file

_____

* Some footnotes omitted.

a federal antitrust suit. The Illinois Appellate Court ultimately held that Dr. Treister's complaint failed to state a cause of action, Treister v. American Academy of Orthopaedic Surgeons, 78 Ill.App.3d 746, 33 Ill. Dec. 501, 396 N.E.2d 1225 (1979), and the Illinois Supreme Court denied leave to appeal. 79 Ill.2d 630 (1980). After the Appellate Court ruled against Dr. Treister, the Circuit Court dismissed Dr. Marrese's complaint.

In March 1980, petitioners filed a federal antitrust suit in the United States District Court for the Northern District of Illinois based on the same events underlying their unsuccessful state court actions. As amended, the complaint alleged that respondent Academy possesses monopoly power, that petitioners were denied membership in order to discourage competition, and that their exclusion constituted a boycott in violation of § 1 of the Sherman Act, 15 U.S.C. § 1. . . . [After various appellate proceedings,] the Court of Appeals held that claim preclusion barred the federal antitrust suit and reversed the contempt order because the discovery order was invalid. 726 F.2d 1150 (1984). . . .

We granted certiorari limited to the question whether the Court of Appeals correctly held that claim preclusion requires dismissal of the federal antitrust action, 467 U.S. 1258, 104 S.Ct. 3553, 82 L.Ed.2d 854 (1984), and we now reverse.

* * *

III

* * *

The preclusive effect of a state court judgment in a subsequent federal lawsuit generally is determined by the full faith and credit statute, which provides that state judicial proceedings "shall have the same full faith and credit in every court within the United States . . . as they have by law or usage in the courts of such State . . . from which they are taken." 28 U.S.C. § 1738. This statute directs a federal court to refer to the preclusion law of the State in which judgment was rendered. "It has long been established that § 1738 does not allow federal courts to employ their own rules of res judicata in determining the effect of state judgments. Rather, it goes beyond the common law and commands a federal court to accept the rules chosen by the State from which the judgment is taken." Kremer v. Chemical Construction Corp., 456 U.S. 461, 481–482, 102 S.Ct. 1883, 1897, 72 L.Ed.2d 262 (1982); see also Allen v. McCurry, 449 U.S. 90, 96, 101 S.Ct. 411, 415, 66 L.Ed.2d 308 (1980). Section 1738 embodies concerns of comity and federalism that allow the States to determine, subject to the requirements of the statute and the Due Process Clause, the preclusive effect of judgments in their own courts. See *Kremer,* supra, 456 U.S., at 478, 481–483, 102 S.Ct., at 1897–1898. Cf. Riley v. New York Trust Co., 315 U.S. 343, 349, 62 S.Ct. 608, 612, 86 L.Ed. 885 (1942) (discussing preclusive effect of state judgment in proceedings in another State).

The fact that petitioners' antitrust claim is within the exclusive jurisdiction of the federal courts does not necessarily make § 1738 inapplicable to this case. Our decisions indicate that a state court judgment may in some circumstances have preclusive effect in a subsequent action within the exclusive jurisdiction of the federal courts. Without discussing § 1738, this Court has held that the issue preclusive effect of a state court judgment barred a subsequent patent suit that could not have been brought in state court. Becher v. Contoure Laboratories, Inc., 279 U.S. 388, 49 S.Ct. 356, 73 L.Ed. 752 (1929). . . .

More generally, *Kremer* indicates that § 1738 requires a federal court to look first to state preclusion law in determining the preclusive effects of a state court judgment. Cf. Haring v. Prosise, 462 U.S. 306, 314, and n. 8, 103 S.Ct. 2368, 2373, and n. 8, 76 L.Ed.2d 595 (1983); Smith, Full Faith and Credit and Section 1983; A Reappraisal, 63 N.C.L.Rev. 59, 110–111 (1984). The Court's analysis in *Kremer* began with the finding that state law would in fact bar relitigation of the discrimination issue decided in the earlier state proceedings. 456 U.S., at 466–467, 102 S.Ct., at 1889–1890. That finding implied that the plaintiff could not relitigate the same issue in federal court unless some exception to § 1738 applied. Ibid. *Kremer* observed that "an exception to § 1738 will not be recognized unless a later statute contains an express or implied repeal." Id., at 468, 102 S.Ct., at 1890; see also Allen v. McCurry, supra, 449 U.S., at 99, 101 S.Ct., at 417. Title VII does not expressly repeal § 1738, and the Court concluded that the statutory provisions and legislative history do not support a finding of implied repeal. 456 U.S., at 476, 102 S.Ct., at 1894. We conclude that the basic approach adopted in *Kremer* applies in a lawsuit involving a claim within the exclusive jurisdiction of the federal courts.

To be sure, a state court will not have occasion to address the specific question whether a state judgment has issue or claim preclusive effect in a later action that can be brought only in federal court. Nevertheless, a federal court may rely in the first instance on state preclusion principles to determine the extent to which an earlier state judgment bars subsequent litigation. Cf. FDIC v. Eckhardt, 691 F.2d 245, 247–248 (CA6 1982) (applying state law to determine preclusive effect on claim within concurrent jurisdiction of state and federal courts). *Kremer* illustrates that a federal court can apply state rules of issue preclusion to determine if a matter actually litigated in state court may be relitigated in a subsequent federal proceeding. See 456 U.S., at 467, 102 S.Ct., at 1890.

With respect to matters that were not decided in the state proceedings, we note that claim preclusion generally does not apply where "[t]he plaintiff was unable to rely on a certain theory of the case or to seek a certain remedy because of the limitations on the subject matter jurisdiction of the courts . . . ." Restatement (Second) of Judgments § 26(1)(c) (1982). If state preclusion law includes this requirement of prior jurisdictional competency, which is generally true, a state judgment will *not* have claim preclusive effect on a cause of action within the exclusive jurisdiction of the federal courts. Even in the event that a party asserting the affirmative defense of claim preclusion can show that state preclusion rules in some circumstances bar a claim outside the jurisdiction of the court that rendered the initial judgment, the federal court should first consider whether application of the state rules would bar the particular federal claim.

Reference to state preclusion law may make it unnecessary to determine if the federal court, as an exception to § 1738, should refuse to give preclusive effect to a state court judgment. The issue whether there is an exception to § 1738 arises only if state law indicates that litigation of a particular claim or issue should be barred in the subsequent federal proceeding. To the extent that state preclusion law indicates that a judgment normally does not have claim preclusive effect as to matters that the court lacked jurisdiction to entertain, lower courts and commentators have correctly concluded that a state court judgment does not bar a subsequent federal antitrust claim. See 726 F.2d, at 1174 (Cudahy, dissenting) (citing cases); 692 F.2d, at 1099 (Stewart, J., dissenting); Restatement, supra, § 25(1), Comment *e;* id., § 26(1)(c), Illustration 2; 18 C. Wright, A. Miller, & E. Cooper, Federal Practice and Procedure § 4470, pp. 687–688 (1981). Unless application of Illinois preclusion law suggests, contrary to the usual view, that petitioners' federal antitrust claim is somehow barred, there will be no need to decide in this case if there is an exception to § 1738.[3]

The Court of Appeals did not apply the approach to § 1738 that we have outlined. Both the plurality opinion, see 726 F.2d, at 1154, and an opinion concurring in part, see id., at 1163–1164 (Flaum, J.), express the view that § 1738 allows a federal court to give a state court judgment greater preclusive effect than the state courts themselves would give to it. This proposition, however, was rejected by *Migra v. Warren City School Dist. Bd. of Ed.,* 465 U.S. 75, 104 S.Ct. 892, 79 L.Ed.2d 56 (1984), a case decided shortly after the Court of Appeals announced its decision in the instant case. In *Migra,* a discharged schoolteacher filed suit under 42 U.S.C. § 1983 in federal court after she prevailed in state court on a contract claim involving the same underlying events. The

---

3. The Chief Justice notes that preclusion rules bar the splitting of a cause of action between a court of limited jurisdiction and one of general jurisdiction, and suggests that state requirements of jurisdictional competency may leave unclear whether a state court action precludes a subsequent federal antitrust claim. Post, at 1336–1337. The rule that the judgment of a court of limited jurisdiction concludes the entire claim assumes that the plaintiff might have commenced his action in a court *in the same system of courts* that was competent to give full relief. See Restatement (Second) of Judgments § 24, Comment *g* (1982). Moreover, the jurisdictional competency requirement generally is understood to imply that state court litigation based on a state statute analogous to a federal statute, e.g., a state antitrust law, does not bar subsequent attempts to secure relief in federal court if the state court lacked jurisdiction over the federal statutory claim. Id., § 26(1)(c), Illustration 2. Although a particular State's preclusion principles conceivably could support a rule similar to that proposed by The Chief Justice, post, at 1337, where state preclusion rules do not indicate that a claim is barred, we do not believe that federal courts should fashion a federal rule to preclude a claim that could not have been raised in the state proceedings.

Federal District Court dismissed the § 1983 action as barred by claim preclusion. The opinion of this Court emphasized that under § 1738, state law determined the preclusive effect of the state judgment. Id., at 81, 104 S.Ct., at 896. Because it was unclear from the record whether the District Court's ruling was based on state preclusion law, we remanded for clarification on this point. Id., at 87, 104 S.Ct., at 899. Such a remand obviously would have been unnecessary were a federal court free to give greater preclusive effect to a state court judgment than would the judgment rendering State. See id., at 88, 104 S.Ct., at 900 (White, J., concurring).

We are unwilling to create a special exception to § 1738 for federal antitrust claims that would give state court judgments greater preclusive effect than would the courts of the State rendering the judgment. Cf. Haring v. Prosise, 462 U.S., at 317–318, 103 S.Ct., at 2375 (refusing to create special preclusion rule for § 1983 claim subsequent to plaintiff's guilty plea. . . .

If we had a single system of courts and our only concerns were efficiency and finality, it might be desirable to fashion claim preclusion rules that would require a plaintiff to bring suit initially in the forum of most general jurisdiction, thereby resolving as many issues as possible in one proceeding. See Restatement (Second) of Judgments § 24, Comment g (1982); C. Wright, A. Miller, & E. Cooper, supra, § 4407, p. 51; id. § 4412, p. 93. The decision of the Court of Appeals approximates such a rule inasmuch as it encourages plaintiffs to file suit initially in federal district court and to attempt to bring any state law claims pendent to their federal antitrust claims. Whether this result would reduce the overall burden of litigation is debatable, see 726 F.2d at 1181–1182 (Cudahy, J., dissenting); C. Wright, A. Miller, & E. Cooper, supra, § 4407, pp. 51–52, and we decline to base our interpretation of § 1738 on our opinion on this question.

More importantly, we have parallel systems of state and federal courts, and the concerns of comity reflected in § 1738 generally allow States to determine the preclusive scope of their own courts' judgments. See Kremer, 456 U.S., at 481–482, 102 S.Ct., at 1897; Allen v. McCurry, 449 U.S., at 96, 101 S.Ct., at 415; cf. Currie, Res Judicata: The Neglected Defense, 45 U.Chi.L.Rev. 317, 327 (1978) (state policies may seek to limit preclusive effect of state court judgment). These concerns certainly are not made less compelling because state courts lack jurisdiction over federal antitrust claims. We therefore reject a judicially created exception to § 1738 that effectively holds as a matter of federal law that a plaintiff can bring state law claims initially in state court only at the cost of forgoing subsequent federal antitrust claims. . . .

In this case the Court of Appeals should have first referred to Illinois law to determine the preclusive effect of the state judgment. Only if state law indicates that a particular claim or issue would be barred, is it necessary to determine if an exception to § 1738 should apply. Although for purposes of this case, we need not decide if such an exception exists for federal antitrust claims, we observe that the more general question is whether the concerns underlying a particular grant of exclusive jurisdiction justify a finding of an implied partial repeal of § 1738. Resolution of this question will depend on the particular federal statute as well as the nature of the claim or issue involved in the subsequent federal action. Our previous decisions indicate that the primary consideration must be the intent of Congress. See *Kremer,* 456 U.S., at 470–476, 102 S.Ct., at 1891–1894 (finding no congressional intent to depart from § 1738 for purposes of Title VII); cf. Brown v. Felsen, 442 U.S. 127, 138, 99 S.Ct. 2205, 2212, 60 L.Ed.2d 767 (1979) (finding congressional intent that state judgments would not have claim preclusive effect on dischargeability issue in bankruptcy).

* * *

The judgment of the Court of Appeals is reversed, and the case is remanded for further proceedings consistent with this opinion.

It is so ordered.

JUSTICE BLACKMUN and JUSTICE STEVENS took no part in the consideration or decision of this case.

CHIEF JUSTICE BURGER [concurred in the judgment.]

NOTES

(1) As in the state/state situation, *Marrese* requires the Y court (federal court) to apply the res judicata law of another judicial system, that of state X. But what will the federal court find when it inquires into state X's law? Is a state likely to have taken a position on whether it would preclude causes of action like the one brought by Marrese? Since these actions are within the exclusive jurisdiction of the federal court, is it conceivable that the state would ever have considered the issue? See Burbank, Interjurisdictional Preclusion, Full Faith and Credit and Federal Common Law: A General Approach, 71 Cornell L.Rev. 733 (1986). One possibility is that the federal court will look at the res judicata effect that the state gives to judgments rendered by its own courts of limited jurisdiction, such as small claims court or housing court.

(2) In his concurring opinion in *Marrese,* Chief Justice Burger made the point discussed in Note (1), and then argued that federal courts should have the power to decide the effect they give to state court judgments. On the one hand, it seems peculiar that a state should control the docket in federal courts by deciding whether relitigation can occur there. On the other hand, it would be very difficult to litigate in an environment in which the effect of the judgment becomes clear only when it is known where relitigation will occur.

(3) In the principal case, Marrese had an adequate remedy under Illinois law, which has its own antitrust law. But in many cases, Congress preempts the states from legislating in a field in which Congress has created federal rights: should the same result hold in such a case? What, for example, if P filed a suit against D in state court, claiming unfair competition under state law. After judgment, P files, in federal court, a patent infringement action against D arising from the same practices on which the state claim was based. Patent infringement is within the exclusive jurisdiction of the federal courts and states are not permitted to write law comparable to patent law—yet if the Restatement's transactional test is used, the patent dispute is part of the "same

claim" as the unfair competition action. Would it be just to foreclose P from enforcing the patent because of litigation that occurred in a court that could not have entertained the patent claim? On the other hand, perhaps claim and issue preclusion doctrine should be used to force the parties to choose the right court in the first place; to bring their lawsuits in a forum that can hear all their claims. Cf. Dreyfuss, The Federal Circuit: A Case Study in Specialized Courts, 64 N.Y.U.L.Rev. 1 (1989).

(4) Could Marrese—or the patentee in Note (3)—have avoided claim preclusion? Cf. England v. Louisiana Board of Medical Examiners, 375 U.S. 411, 84 S.Ct. 461, 11 L.Ed.2d 440 (1964) (permitting a party to reserve a federal claim pending state court resolution of state claims).

(5) Review Finley v. United States, p. 206, supra, where the plaintiff was required to sue separately different defendants in state and federal courts. What happens if one of those cases goes to judgment against Finley? Will nonmutual issue preclusion apply?

(6) If the federal court had been sitting in diversity, should it apply state preclusion law because of the *Erie* doctrine? See McConnell v. Travellers Indemnity Co., 346 F.2d 219 (5th Cir.1965); Forrester v. Southern Railway, 268 F.Supp. 194 (N.D.Ga.1967). Cf. Angel v. Bullington, 330 U.S. 183, 67 S.Ct. 657, 91 L.Ed. 832 (1947). See also Carrington, Collateral Estoppel and Foreign Judgments, 24 Ohio St.L.J. 381 (1963); Note, Erie and the Preclusive Effect of Federal Diversity Judgments, 85 Colum.L.Rev. 1505 (1985).

(7) Do the same principles that apply to claim preclusion also apply to issue preclusion?

———

C. FEDERAL/STATE PRECLUSION

Since § 1738 speaks only of the judicial proceedings of a "State, Territory or Possession of the United States," it does not define the effect of a federal court proceeding in later adjudication. Nonetheless, it is generally thought that the state should apply federal law. Is this because of the Supremacy Clause, the Full Faith and Credit Clause, or general principles? See Degnan, Federalized Res Judicata, 85 Yale L.J. 741 (1976).

NOTE

What effect should courts within the United States give to the judgments of other countries? Is there reason to give these judgments less effect than they would have where rendered? See Smit, International Res Judicata and Collateral Estoppel in the United States, 9 U.C.L.A.L.Rev. 44 (1962).

Part VII

EFFORTS TO CONTROL DECISION MAKERS

Chapter Seventeen

APPELLATE REVIEW

SECTION 1. GENERAL CONSIDERATIONS

Appellate courts in our system serve a number of functions. Their extensive power within the judicial system is obvious: Through stare decisis their decisions shape the law and control future cases in the jurisdiction and, by the sanction of reversal, they compel trial courts to follow the law as they have laid it down; they attempt to insure that, so far as possible in conformance with substantive and procedural rules, justice is done in individual cases; and, increasingly, they directly promulgate rules controlling court procedure and administer the judicial system through judicial conferences. Appellate courts also have important powers with respect to administrative agencies. Finally, there is the political aspect of appellate court power in our constitutional system, requiring the courts to balance the conflicting demands of separate branches of government and of local, state and national interests. See, e.g., Freund, A Supreme Court in a Federation: Some Lessons from Legal History, 53 Colum.L.Rev. 597 (1953). Have our appellate courts assumed too many burdens?

The federal courts have been feeling the pressure of a rapidly expanding work load. See Wright, The Overloaded Fifth Circuit: A Crisis in Judicial Administration, 42 Tex.L.Rev. 949, 976–77 (1964). Believing that "[t]he entire system is already taxed to—or beyond—its capacity" the author advocated "imaginative and fundamental alterations in the structure" of the federal courts, specifically suggesting:

    1. The more extensive assignment of judges who are not fully occupied to sit with busier courts.

    2. Increased use of per curiam opinions.

    3. Additional law clerks and secretarial help for the judges.

    4. Curtailment, or abolition, of diversity jurisdiction.

    5. Appeal as of right only when a particular amount is in controversy.

6. Refusal of interlocutory appeals.

7. Creation of specialized courts to review decisions of administrative agencies, and to hear other specialized areas of litigation.

8. Limitation of the scope of review to errors of law, rather than factual matters.

Various states' appellate courts are also under great pressure from increased filings. Before management techniques can be improved it is necessary to come to grips with the following basic preliminary questions:

1. What are the functions of state appellate courts?

2. Why are more appeals being taken today?

3. Where does all the appellate judge time go?

4. How can we conserve appellate time or use it more effectively?

Appellate courts of last resort may have all or some of the following functions:

1. Correct errors made below, but not all of them;

2. Enunciate and harmonize the decisional law of the State;

3. Increase public confidence in the impartiality of court justice by bringing a broader set of values to bear on the case than a solo trial judge can;

4. Assure greater detachment, perspective, and opportunity for reflection than exist below;

5. Spread responsibility more widely, making mistakes more tolerable to the people affected.

All these functions have to do with adjudication and give no indication of the growing number of other duties being given to state appellate judges, such as rule making, the general administration of the court system, personnel administration, planning the expansion and modernization of physical facilities, passing on qualifications and discipline of judges and lawyers, producing nominees for public positions, formulating budgets, and public relations.

The causes for the sharp increase in the volume of appeals have not been definitely established, except for criminal appeals. There, such factors as the provision of publicly paid counsel for indigent persons, the removal of financial impediments to appeal for persons without means, and the turbulent state of criminal procedural law have combined to stimulate appeals in the vast majority of convictions. Among other reasons offered are: the relative shrinkage in the cost of appealing in relation to the pretrial and trial costs of lawsuits; favorable interest rates, making it attractive for parties who have lost money judgments to hold on to the money by taking a hopeless appeal; and lowered predictability of appellate outcomes for a number of reasons.

To determine the causes of delay in appellate courts and where the judges' time went the American Judicature Society surveyed state appellate judges in 1968. The judges voted heavily for two delay factors:

    1. Too many cases are heard as a matter of right; particularly, too many duplicate appeals are prosecuted.

    2. Too many opinions must be written.

The judges also provided information on the allocation of their time, which was roughly as follows:

    1. Writing opinions consumed one third of the total outlay of time on average.

    2. Slightly over one fourth of their time was spent on research.

    3. Non-adjudicative duties took up from 10 to 25 per cent of their time—call it about one fifth.

    4. Approximately 15 per cent—or one sixth of their time—was absorbed by hearing oral arguments.

The following remedies for coping with excessive caseload demands were suggested by the judges:

    1. More auxiliary personnel, especially court administrators;

    2. Curbing the right of appeal in some cases;

    3. An intermediate appellate court system;

    4. Appointment instead of election of judges, which would save time of campaigning;

    5. Limiting the length of briefs;

    6. More affirmances without opinions.

For a succinct treatment of the basic structural and procedural issues confronting federal and state appellate courts in the last quarter of the twentieth century, see P. Carrington, D. Meador and M. Rosenberg, Justice on Appeal (1976). Drawing on that treatment, a comprehensive investigation of the work of the appellate courts in New York declared:

Features of an appellate system that are said to be imperative in achieving fairness for litigants include these four elements:

- a party should have one right of appeal of an adverse decision on a substantial claim of right, and the appeal should be to an impartial multi-judge appellate court;
- the parties are entitled to present arguments to the appellate court, both through written briefs and oral presentation, and the individual judges should inform themselves fully on the material issues, evidence and law;
- the appellate court's decision process should reflect both the individual thinking of each judge and the effects of consultation among the judges; and

- the appellate court should disclose in writing the reasons underlying its decision.

Complementing these litigant-oriented goals are a set of system-oriented goals:

- to provide a uniform and coherent enunciation and application of the law;

- to decide expeditiously and by a process involving the fewest steps consonant with a sound process;

- to maintain working conditions in the appellate courts designed to attract lawyers of high quality and standing; and

- to establish procedures that foster the judge's humane concern for individual litigants.

See R. MacCrate, J. Hopkins and M. Rosenberg, Appellate Justice in New York 8–9 (1982).

SUNDERLAND, A SIMPLIFIED SYSTEM
OF APPELLATE PROCEDURE
17 Tenn.L.Rev. 651–658 (1943).

* * *

Method and Scope of Review

At the common law all questions of fact were decided by juries, and a review of the facts could be had by what was called the attaint. This was the common-law predecessor of the new trial, but it took place before a superior jury of twenty-four who reviewed the action of the twelve. It was like an appeal from a single judge to a bench of judges, and involved the idea of a superior grade of tribunal whose decision would, for that reason, be of higher quality. But it was primarily a proceeding against the jury rather than against the verdict. The attainted jury was punished by imprisonment and fine for its false verdict, although the false verdict was at the same time, and as a useful incident, replaced by the true verdict of the higher jury.

Questions of law, on the other hand, were decided by the judges, and a proceeding very much like the attaint was developed to reach false judgments. In the 1200's proceedings in error against judgments took the form of semi-criminal proceedings against the judges, and Holdsworth tells us that even to the present day the writ of error is deemed to commence a new suit for no better reason than because, seven hundred years ago, it really was a new proceeding directed against the judge, and was based upon a new cause of action arising out of the wrongful act committed by him in rendering his false judgment. To this day, also, we employ formal assignment of error because seven hundred years ago the judge was held to be entitled to know what were the charges against him,[1] and the assignments of error are still regarded in many of our states as the appellant's pleading in the court of errors, just as they were regarded seven hundred years ago.

The same theory of review applied to both verdicts and judgments, and the jury, in the one case and the judge in the other, became defendants before a superior tribunal in a proceeding very much like an accusation of perjury.

It was not until the days of Edward I, who reigned from 1272 to 1307 and in whose reign our present bill of exceptions was first invented and authorized, that the idea arose of a complaint against a judgment which was not an accusation against the judge.

The common-law proceeding in error did not operate as a review of the merits of the judgment. The question never arose as to whether the judgment was just or unjust, nor did the proceeding ever involve an inquiry as to what the true judgment ought to be. The sole question was, Did the judge commit an error? Such error might be great or small; its consequences might be serious or trifling, but an error was an error and the judgment must fall.

Prior to the invention of the bill of exceptions, in 1285, no review could be had except for errors apparent on the face of the record, and it might therefore be said, with sufficient accuracy, that so far as the knowledge of the reviewing court was permitted to extend, no errors could be deemed to have legal existence except those which appeared on the face of the record itself. The problem before the court of errors was, in that case, very simple, for if any alleged error was found to exist, the judgment was merely reversed, and that was the end of the whole controversy in that court.

When, however, bills of exceptions were authorized, a wholly new problem arose. The errors brought up by that device did not immediately control the judgment, as did the errors in the judgment roll, but only affected the minds of the jury. But the extent and character of that influence could not be shown to the reviewing court. They could tell if an error had been made in admitting or excluding evidence, or in any other matter involved in the trial before the jury, but they could not tell what effect it had had upon the verdict. In such a situation there was nothing to do but send the case back for a new trial, so that another verdict could be obtained free from the error which had vitiated the first one.

The remand of cases for new trials was therefore a necessary incident in the use of juries. So long as the jury had the exclusive right to weigh the evidence and find the facts, no error of law which was related in any material respect to either of those functions could be cured in any other way. The judges of the higher court could not

1. 1 Holdsworth Hist.Eng.Law (3rd ed.) 214. [Some footnotes omitted; others renumbered.]

undertake to adjust the verdict so as to eliminate the error, without depriving the parties of their right to trial by jury.

But in spite of the use of new trials, there was one part of the case which could never be reviewed at all, and that was the part which dealt with questions of fact. The very essence of a proceeding in error involved the conception of wrong judicial conduct on the part of the judge. He had no control over the conclusions which the jury might draw from the evidence, and if they went wrong it was sufficient to say that it was no fault of his. Therefore no error could be assigned upon any matter of fact.

Summarizing the scope of this common law system of review, it may be said that it dealt best with the least important class of questions, namely, controlling errors of law which appeared upon the judgment roll, that it dealt rather clumsily, by means of new trials, with those incidental errors of law which affected the course of the trial and influenced the conduct of the jury; and that it dealt not at all with pure errors of fact.

Continental Europe had had a very different experience from that of England. There, both law and fact were determined by the same persons, and the theory of a divided tribunal, one part to try the facts and the other to declare the law, had never become established. Under such a system there was no serious obstacle to a full review of a judgment by other judges, who could be as free to reconsider the facts as they were to pass on the law. This enabled the appellate tribunal to dispose of the whole controversy, and render the judgment which ought to have been rendered, and there was no occasion whatever for ignoring questions of fact or for sending back cases for new trials, or even for refusing to hear new evidence if justice could thereby be done. . . .

The continental notion of a unified tribunal, capable of dealing at the same time with the law and the facts, was adopted in England in the courts of chancery, so that in reviewing equity cases there was no need for resorting to the clumsy and ineffective procedure in error. If the upper court had the power to determine the merits of the case, it became less important to know whether an error had been committed than to know how it could be rectified. In a proceeding in error the entire aim of the review was to affirm or deny the existence of the error; in a true appeal that problem became merely preliminary to the really basic question of what the right decree should be.

    *   *   *

The two methods were bound to influence each other.

These various influences produced the following results:

A law case was reviewed only for errors, by means of a new suit. Since a jury was always employed, and therefore the judge made no decisions on issues of fact, the only errors he could commit were errors of law. Hence the review was limited to matters of law. New points could not be raised, and new evidence could not be introduced even for the purpose of showing that there ought to be a new trial.

An equity case was likewise reviewed only for errors, but it was by means of a continuation of the original suit. Since a jury was not employed, and the judge decided all the issues, both of law and fact, he might commit error as to either one. Hence the review embraced all matters, both of law and fact. But new points, as in law cases, could not be raised, and new evidence could not be introduced.

This was the appellate system that we inherited from England. It was technical, rigid, steeped in tradition, and unrealistic. Its faults and limitations were so plain that their elimination would have presented no difficulties. Nevertheless, in most of our states we are still operating under concepts which for seven hundred years have had no actual basis for existence.

The first step in simplifying the methods of review should be to abolish the wholly useless and fictitious doctrine that an appellate proceeding in a law action is a new suit and to frankly recognize its true nature as a mere continuation of the original action. This will remove one more of the distinctions between proceedings at law and in equity which have produced nothing but trouble and confusion.

The next step in simplification should be to abolish the doctrine that a review either at law or in equity is a mere proceeding in error, which must be confined to the precise points raised and passed upon, and the precise evidence introduced in, the trial court. It is quite true that in most cases every important question affecting the merits of the controversy is presented and decided, and all important evidence is brought in, so that an assignment of errors based on exceptions will usually constitute an adequate review. But there are numerous cases where questions not raised below are seen later to be vital to the merits, and the rights of the parties cannot be protected unless those questions can be considered by the reviewing court. Sometimes an adequate consideration of such questions would require the opening of the case for further evidence. Under such circumstances it should be within the power of the appellate court to receive such evidence and give it the weight to which it is entitled.

* * *

England abandoned this doctrine nearly three quarters of a century ago, and provided that all appeals to the court of appeal should be by way of rehearing, which was held to mean that the appellate court might render such a judgment as the judge of first instance should have rendered if the case had been heard before him on the date on which the appeal was heard. The court of appeal is given all the powers of amendment that the trial court has, with full discretionary power to receive further evidence upon questions of fact, such evidence to be either by oral examination in court by affidavit or by deposition taken before an examiner. It is given express power to draw inferences of fact and to give any judgment and make any order as the case may require.

A few of our states have followed this course. California has a statutory provision that additional evidence can be taken in non-jury cases in the appellate court as to facts occurring at any time prior to the decision of the appeal, and this provision contains a direction that it shall be liberally construed, to the end that cases may be fully disposed of on appeal without further proceedings below unless justice requires a new trial. Similar statutes are found in Kansas and New Jersey.

. . .

The final step in simplifying the methods and scope of review should be to abolish the old forms and names of appellate proceedings which embody the taboos and traditions which encumber appellate procedure, and substitute a single, universal method, identical for every case.

Its form should be as simple as possible, a mere notice of appeal filed in the trial court. This should constitute the sole jurisdictional requirement, as is now provided under Federal Rule 73(a). And even this requirement should be subject to the discretionary power of the appellate court to authorize a delayed appeal where extraordinary circumstances would justify it. This is the present rule in Michigan.

. . .

NOTES

(1) In recent years the number of cases appealed in the state and federal courts has been increasing dramatically. See Friendly, Averting the Flood by Lessening The Flow, 59 Cornell L.Rev. 634 (1974); Rosenberg, Enlarging the Federal Courts' Capacity to Settle the National Law, 10 Gonzaga L.Rev. 709 (1975); Rosenberg, Planned Flexibility to Meet Changing Needs of the Federal Appellate System, 59 Cornell L.R. 576 (1974). See Lilly & Scalia, Appellate Justice: A Crisis in Virginia? 57 Va.L.R. 3 (1971).

(2) Various proposals have been considered for reducing the burden on the courts of appeals. In the federal system, these suggestions include inserting a new tier of review between the Supreme Court and the Circuit Courts, and establishing specialized courts with unique expertise to deal with complex subject matter, see, e.g., Commission on Revision of the Federal Court Appellate System, Structure and Internal Procedures: Recommendations for Change, reprinted in 67 F.R.D. 195 (1975). See also J. Sexton and S. Estreicher, Redefining the Supreme Court's Role (1986); R. Posner, The Federal Courts (1985); Posner, Will the Federal Courts of Appeals Survive Until 1984? An Essay on Delegation and Specialization of the Judicial Function, 56 S.Cal.L.Rev. 756 (1983).

SECTION 2. TIMELINESS AND PERFECTING THE APPEAL

Timeliness usually refers to the period within which a notice of appeal must be filed and the appeal perfected. Sometimes, the normal course of appellate review is too slow to protect litigants' rights. Appellate courts have developed informal methods of expediting appeals and granting stays when speed is vital, as, for example, in election matters. See Rule 8, Federal Rules of Appellate Procedure. For a curious instance of a dispute about the power of individual Justices to grant stays in an action brought to enjoin the bombing in Cambodia, see Holtzman v. Schlesinger, 414 U.S. 1304, 94 S.Ct. 1, 38 L.Ed.2d 18 (1973); 414 U.S. 1316, 94 S.Ct. 8, 38 L.Ed.2d 28 (1973); Schlesinger v. Holtzman, 414 U.S. 1321, 94 S.Ct. 11, 38 L.Ed.2d 33 (1973).

See Rules 1, 3, 4, 5, 10, 11, 12, and 26 of the Federal Rules of Appellate Procedure.

NOTES

(1) Lateness in filing a notice of appeal is generally termed a "jurisdictional" defect. Accordingly, the appellate court is without power to hear the appeal under any circumstance, cf. Pittsburgh Towing Co. v. Mississippi Valley Barge Line, Co., 385 U.S. 32, 87 S.Ct. 195, 17 L.Ed.2d 31 (1966) (decided under Supreme Court's former appellate jurisdiction). However, lateness as to other aspects of the appellate timetable as, for instance, in serving briefs or docketing the case, is not generally so characterized. See, e.g., In re Hanley's Estate, 23 Cal.2d 120, 142 P.2d 423 (1943), in which the appeal was dismissed because the notice had been filed late, even though the appealing party's attorney was misled by opposing counsel as to the date of filing of the order appealed from.

(2) Statutes in some jurisdictions authorize trial courts to certify late appeals for a reasonable time after judgment, and some courts reach the same result by interpreting statutes allowing extensions of time to appeal to be invoked after the extension period has expired. See, e.g., In Dewees v. Cedarbaum, 381 P.2d 830 (Okl.1963) (provision allowing a three month appeal period to be extended to six months could be applied retroactively after the expiration of three months). See Comment, Ad Hoc Relief for Untimely Appeals, 65 Colum.L.Rev. 97 (1965).

(3) The moment when the time to appeal starts running varies. In New York it begins when the winner below serves upon the appellant a notice of entry of the judgment to be appealed. N.Y.—McKinney's CPLR § 5513. Compare Fed.R.Civ.P. 77(d). If the clerk of the lower court fails to notify appellant of entry of the judgment, is the time to appeal extended? See Wanless v. Louisiana Real Estate Board, 243 La. 801, 147 So.2d 395, (1962) (contrary to Louisiana constitution to have period begin running before notice is actually given or delivered).

(4) In connection with filing a "notice of appeal", the first step to secure appellate review, question may arise as to which document is the "judgment." See, e.g., Merlands Club, Inc. v. Messall, 238 Md. 359, 208 A.2d 687 (1965) (appeal dismissed where taken from judgment nisi which did not become final for three days).

(5) It is generally necessary that the appellant file an appeal bond to secure payment of costs to his adversary upon affirmance or dismissal. Sometimes the size of the bond can be prohibitively high, see, e.g., Pennzoil Co. v. Texaco, Inc., 481 U.S. 1, 107 S.Ct. 1519, 95 L.Ed.2d 1 (1987) (bond in excess of $13 billion). If appellant wishes to stay execution of the judgment below, a timely supersedeas bond, such as prescribed in Rule 7 of the Federal Rules of Appellate Procedure,

may be necessary. In addition, as the record of proceedings had below, or an abstract of it, will have to be made available to the appellate court.

SECTION 3. WHO MAY APPEAL

IN RE BARNETT

United States Circuit Court of Appeals, Second Circuit, 1942.
124 F.2d 1005.

Before L. HAND, CLARK and FRANK, CIRCUIT JUDGES.

FRANK, CIRCUIT JUDGE. The District Court, reversing an order of the referee, declared that an instrument by which Cecilia Barnett, the bankrupt, assigned to her mother, Clara Essenfeld, her testate and intestate interest in her father's estate, was invalid as to her trustee in bankruptcy. In 1935, her father had made a will, leaving to her 15% of his residuary estate. The following year she assigned to her mother, in consideration of $5,000 paid by her father, all her rights, in intestacy or under any will previously or thereafter made, to her father's estate. Some four years later, on August 29, 1940, she filed a voluntary petition in bankruptcy and was adjudicated. On the following day her father died, and his 1935 will was admitted to probate soon thereafter.

The trustee in bankruptcy petitioned for an order directing the bankrupt to execute an instrument assigning her interest in her father's estate to the trustee, free and clear of the claims of Clara Essenfeld, and restraining her father's executors from recognizing the assignment to Mrs. Essenfeld and from making payments pursuant to it. The bankrupt and Mrs. Essenfeld contested the application on the merits; the executors appeared, but did not oppose. The referee held the assignment was valid as against the trustee, and denied his application. The judge reversed and granted the requested order. The bankrupt has appealed.

No appeal was prayed by the other parties. But the attorney for the bankrupt signed his brief, filed in this court, as attorney both for the bankrupt and her mother Mrs. Essenfeld. He apparently believed that the rights of the mother were before this court. No objection to his thus signing his brief was made by the trustee. Going below the surface appearances and viewing the situation realistically, as the Supreme Court admonishes us to do, it is obvious that the mother assumed that the order, so far as it affected her, would be dealt with by us on this appeal.

In the brief which he filed here, counsel for the bankrupt and her mother, seemingly believing that the District Court had correctly decided that the assignment was invalid as against the trustee, asserted that the order was erroneous on another ground not argued in the trial court, i.e., that the consideration paid to the bankrupt by her father operated as an ademption. The trustee strenuously argued that we should not consider that new issue. Although we are inclined to agree that, if the assignment were invalid, there was an effective ademption, we prefer not to decide the case on that basis. We do not feel that we are precluded from deciding on a ground not pressed by counsel. Such a course, however, is undesirable where not necessary; it is usually better if possible, to consider a case as it was presented to the lower court.[1] If the trustee opposed our consideration of the ground relied upon by the lower court merely because it was abandoned on appeal by his adversary, we would still feel free to consider it; where, as here, the trustee expressly urges that only the original theory is open to us, we are of course doubly justified in preferring to rest upon that theory rather than upon the new one. . . .

. . . We now turn to the trustee's contention that the appeal must be dismissed because the bankrupt, sole appellant, was not affected by the decree and hence is not a proper party appellant. It is true, as the bankrupt admits in her brief, that the adjudication as between the trustee in bankruptcy and the assignee, is not, as such, her concern. But the trustee petitioned for, and the District Court granted, an order requiring the bankrupt to execute an instrument assigning her rights to the trustee in bankruptcy. That this order is appealable there can be no doubt, for if the assignment was valid, then the District Court lacked power to compel the bankrupt to execute an assignment. This is true regardless of whether such an assignment would deprive the bankrupt of any substantial property rights. For a citizen cannot be wrongfully compelled by a court to do any involuntary act, and therefore, if the District Court's order was in error, it should be reversed. . . .

As previously observed, the other parties adversely affected by the lower court's order did not pray an appeal. Had they done so, it is clear, from our opinion, that we would have held the order erroneous as to them. We are clear that we have the power to order a reversal as to them even though they did not appeal, and that we should do so under the circumstances here disclosed. The anomalous position of the parties otherwise, and the quite naturally embarrassing questions which would confront the state court if the order, stigmatized by us as erroneous, remains partially in effect, are patent. . . .

We have jurisdiction in the premises. Several courts have recognized that, where reversal of a judgment wipes out all basis for recovery against a non-appealing, as well as against an appealing, defendant, the reversal may operate to the benefit of both. [Citations omitted.]

---

1. For that reason it has been held that an appellate court may properly remand a case for further proceedings, "if the case has been tried on a wrong theory" and the correct theory was not considered by the parties either in the pleadings or in their arguments on appeal. Finefrock v. Kenova Mine Car Co., 22 F.2d 627, 634 (4 Cir.); see, also Underwood v. Commissioner, 56 F.2d 67, 73 (4 Cir.). [Some footnotes omitted; others renumbered.]

In such a case as this, we should, then, consider the parties to the order below as before this court, at least to the extent that where modification of the judgment affecting them is necessary in order to afford proper and adequate relief to appellant, they are bound thereby. And we should make every effort to achieve such a result here since, as already observed, it is obvious that the bankrupt's mother, one of the parties below, and for whose benefit, the bankrupt's assignment to her father was made, assumed that a reversal of the order would mean a reversal as to her. The executors are mere stakeholders, and to reverse as to the bankrupt and her mother, leaving outstanding an order enjoining the executors, would be to frustrate the relief afforded by our decision. In declining to make a narrow disposition of this appeal, which will afford only inadequate relief to the parties and leave in effect a truncated order, we are in part guided by the fact that a court of bankruptcy is a court of equity, and that once a court of equity has taken jurisdiction of a case, it will endeavor, in order to do justice, to dispose harmoniously of all its aspects. It is established doctrine, furthermore, that in disposing of a case before it, an appellate court has a broad power "to make such disposition . . . as justice requires." [2]

We recognize that, . . . we are adopting a procedure rejected by some courts. But adherence to a stricter procedure in such cases seems to us to derive from an excessive veneration for what Wigmore and others have properly criticized as the "sporting theory of justice."
. . .

That theory stems from the original function of trials in courts as substitutes for private wars. That function, to be sure, is still of prime importance. Chambers v. Baltimore & O.R. Co., 207 U.S. 142, 148, 28 S.Ct. 34, 52 L.Ed. 143. But we think that courts, in civilized communities, should do more than decide cases, one way or another, without regard to considerations of justice, merely to prevent private brawls and breaches of the peace. Government having, through its courts, established, in large areas, a monopoly of dispute-deciding, should try, as far as possible, to decide cases correctly—both by ascertaining the actual facts, as near as may be, and then by applying correct legal rules in an effort to do justice to the parties affected by their decisions. And not merely the parties, but the public as well, are interested that justice shall be done. . . .

As Wigmore says, the judge should "cease to be merely an umpire at the game of litigation. Often he is little more. . . . The right to use a rule of procedure or evidence precisely as one plays a trump card, or draws to three aces, or holds back a good horse till the home stretch, is a distinctive result of the common-law moral attitude toward parties in litigation." [3] Thanks to such criticisms, there has developed, inter alia, the doctrine of "harmless error," which, to the chagrin of those

2. State of Minnesota v. National Tea Co., 309 U.S. 551, 555, 60 S.Ct. 676, 679, 84 L.Ed. 920; Dorchy v. Kansas, 264 U.S. 286, 289, 44 S.Ct. 323, 68 L.Ed. 686.

3. Wigmore, Evidence, 3d Ed. 1940, I, 374; VI, 374–376.

devoted to a conception of litigation as a game of skill, has led to a marked reduction of reversals based upon procedural errors which do no real harm.

Of course, courts should be exceedingly cautious in disturbing (at least retrospectively) precedents in reliance on which men may have importantly changed their positions. Other deviations from traditions, which have no such hurtful consequences, but which, relating solely to procedure, improve the administration of justice, may win adverse criticism from those members of the bar who regard all procedural changes as wrong because, as Wigmore puts it, they interfere with the "mere mental convenience of the profession." Wigmore notes that "such a naive confession as that of Lord Ellenborough we do not often receive, but its significance is radical: 'If that rule were to be changed, a lawyer who was well stored with these rules would be no better than any other man is without them.' " [4]

Nothing we have said is to be taken as disparaging the contentious mode of procedure, which has demonstrable values: It aids courts in effectively discharging their basic function of deciding disputes because, in the clash of wits between the contending parties, factual and legal aspects of a case, which might otherwise be ignored, are brought sharply to the court's attention. For that reason, the federal courts are forbidden by the Constitution to give decisions except in respect of actual "cases or controversies." But while a court must often rely chiefly on the arguments of opposing counsel, and while, as a consequence, inadequate arguments may sometimes lead courts to overlook points which counsel have not pressed (so that, indeed, the decision may have little value as a precedent), the occasional resulting incompleteness or error in a decision should not be cherished as a virtue. A court, striving to do justice between the parties, should not put on blinders and ignore matters which counsel overlook. We do not, however, mean to suggest that there are no limits to the extent to which a court may relieve a party from the procedural mistakes of his lawyer; thus, for instance, we would be powerless here if no party had appealed. . . .

The trustee, in his brief and initially in his oral argument, sought to sustain the order in its entirety, including that part of the order which directed the bankrupt to execute an assignment to the trustee. Subsequently, in the course of the oral argument, however, a member of this court asked the trustee's counsel whether he would consent to a deletion of that part of the order, and he said he would. That consent, thus prompted, was, in effect, no more than a belated attempt to accomplish a voluntary dismissal, at least in part, of the trustee's action, for we may treat his petition to the referee, to have the bankrupt make the assignment, as the equivalent of an action. Such an attempt voluntarily to dismiss does not, without approval by this court, render the case moot. By Rule 41 of the Federal Rules of Civil

4. Wigmore, The Judicial Function, in Science of Legal Method (1917) XXVI, XXXVIII–XXXIX. . . .

Procedure, an action in the District Court may be dismissed, after an answer has been filed, only by permission of the court. The very purpose of the rule is to provide that the mere effort of a plaintiff to withdraw his suit should not make the case moot. . . .

We have already said that the rights of the bankrupt's mother are before us on this appeal by the bankrupt. When the voluntary dismissal was attempted, the time for the mother to pray an appeal had expired and that dismissal, if permitted, would therefore trap her. Because of that fact and the general importance of the issue presented, and because the judgment below is a broad adjudication of a status which may affect later proceedings in the state court, we decline to permit the deletion of the order without a determination of the real question before us.

The order appealed from is reversed, and the District Court is directed to affirm the order of the referee so far as it "in all respects denied" the prayer of the trustee's application herein.

L. HAND, CIRCUIT JUDGE (dissenting). When the trustee upon the argument consented to the deletion of the clause in the order directing the bankrupt to execute an assignment by way of further assurance, the appeal became moot as to her. In no event could she have any interest in the property; if her assignment to her mother was valid, her mother was the owner; if it was invalid, the trustee was. I agree that she had the right to appeal from the provision which directed her to execute the assignment—idle formality though it was—and that the appellee's consent did not deprive us of jurisdiction. The question is not what we can, but what we should, do; ordinarily no court decides a question which has ceased to have any real importance for the parties. Indeed, my brothers would not do so here, I apprehend, if they did not also reverse the order so far as it declared that the trustee was entitled to the property as against the widow.

The real question is therefore whether upon the bankrupt's appeal we may, and should, reverse that part of the order also; i.e., whether that appeal opened it up for all purposes. . . . The most common occasion for dispensing with the need of an appeal is when the reversal in favor of the appellant puts the appellee in a worse position than he was before. Thus if one joint obligor appeals and succeeds, the other who has not, loses both his right of contribution and the protection that exists in the rule that the release of one joint obligor releases all. . . .

I believe that we should hold that it is not enough that the law was misunderstood by the lower court, and that it is precisely to raise such questions that the right of appeal is provided. I feel very confident that the bar so understands it and is not misled when we do not disturb judgments in the interest of appellees. Particularly is this appropriate in the case at bar, where the widow has not so much as intimated that she is not content with the order, unless we are to account it such an intimation that the attorney for the bankrupt signs the brief in this court as attorney for her as well as for the bankrupt. It is a sound instinct that confines courts to the decision of disputes and does not seek to redress grievances of which the parties do not complain.

Since for the foregoing reasons I think the appeal should be dismissed, I have not considered the validity of the assignment. Indeed, I should not have done so in any event, because even the bankrupt does not challenge the correctness of the ruling below, but now asserts no more than that the testator's payment was an ademption of the legacy. I quote from her brief: "Appellant rests her case squarely upon the sole proposition that there has been an ademption of her legacy." Again: "We therefore take no issue with the propositions of law and the authorities cited in support thereof as set forth in the opinion of the Court below." Thus, we are insisting upon deciding the case on a point which the only appellant has expressly abandoned, on behalf of a party who has not appealed at all. I am sorry, but I cannot go along with that result.

NOTES

(1) In Fenton v. Thompson, 352 Mo. 199, 176 S.W.2d 456 (1944), plaintiff was allowed to take a voluntary nonsuit after submission of the case to the jury but before verdict. Defendant was held to be "aggrieved" for appeal purposes, since the voluntary dismissal was without prejudice to plaintiff's bringing a new action. See also Adair County v. Urban, 364 Mo. 746, 268 S.W.2d 801 (1954), holding defendant could appeal from an order setting aside a judgment for damages in plaintiff's favor and granting a third trial of the issues.

(2) A defendant is not aggrieved by an erroneous judgment in favor of a co-defendant. Consequently, in some jurisdictions, where the case against one tortfeasor is dismissed in error and a judgment rendered against the other, the latter may neither appeal the dismissal nor obtain contribution from him towards satisfying the judgment. See, e.g., Guy F. Atkinson Co. v. Consani, 223 Cal.App.2d 342, 35 Cal.Rptr. 750 (1st Dist.1963). That seems wrong, does it not?

(3) Should nonparties ever be permitted to appeal a decision? The Federal Rules of Appellate Procedure permit the substitution of parties upon death and for other good causes, Rule 43, and give the United States a right to be heard when the constitutionality of an act of Congress is drawn into question, Rule 44. Otherwise, the right is severely limited, see, e.g., Marino v. Ortiz, 484 U.S. 301, 108 S.Ct. 586, 98 L.Ed.2d 629 (1988) (affirming by an equally divided court the denial of a nonparty's motion to appeal a consent decree). See also Walker v. City of Mesquite, 858 F.2d 1071 (5th Cir.1988) (holding that non-named class members lack standing to appeal entry of consent decree).

(4) How should nonparties protect themselves? Review the materials on intervention, p. 459, supra, and Martin v. Wilks, p. 971, supra. Does the amicus curiae practice help? See Rule 37 of the Rules of the Supreme Court of the United States.

SECTION 4. FINAL JUDGMENT RULE

The work load of some appellate courts is so heavy a serious question is whether their work can be handled with adequate attention to important cases. The legislatures and the courts have been forced to resort to a variety of procedural limitations and shortcuts, such as restricting appealability, eliminating oral argument and cutting down on the frequency of full-scale explanation of the courts' reasons for deciding as they do. See P. Carrington, D. Meador and M. Rosenberg, Justice on Appeal (1976). Limiting appeals has been the device most relied upon for keeping work loads manageable. This section on the final judgment rule and on the next section on certiorari discussed procedural problems in keeping the work load at a proper level and in insuring sound selection of cases for consideration on appeal.

The final judgment rule is the generally prevailing rule in most American jurisdictions, although a few states, notably New York, allow appeals from most interlocutory orders to the intermediate appellate courts. In reading the materials in the following two sections, consider

(1) the effect the final judgment rule (or lack of one) has on each case;

(2) whether a mechanical rule is preferable to vesting discretion in the trial or appellate court to grant appeals; and

(3) whether these matters should be treated by statute or court rules.

The concept that an appeal to a higher level of a court system should wait until a final decision has issued at the first level of the system commands wide support. It makes sense to prevent cases from going to appellate courts in fragments, prematurely, or more than once. The finality requirement is designed to avoid those evils. However, postponing appeal until a case has been fully prepared and completely tried not infrequently produces extravagant waste: the legal premise on which the trial court processed the case all the way through trial may have been erroneous; and all the wasted processing could have been avoided if the case had been appealed and the faulty premise corrected in the early stages of the proceeding. This problem calls for an entirely pragmatic solution—to devise methods to identify first-level decisions that should be reviewed on appeal promptly and without having to abide until the very end of the trial-court process. The approach to the finality-appealability puzzle in federal practice is to stake out a strong position for finality, but to soften the requirement by allowing exceptions of various kinds. Section 1291 of the Judicial Code lays down the basic principle by making finality a literal prerequisite to the "jurisdiction" of the courts of appeals. Judicial decisions then loosen the requirement by allowing immediate appeal of decisions on many collateral matters that do not in any sense dispose finally of the litigation.

In Section 1291 of the Judicial Code Congress has designated categories of orders that are appealable even though non-final—that is, interlocutory. In Section 1292(b) Congress has designed a certification procedure by which district courts can, in effect, recommend interlocutory decisions for immediate appeal, subject to the discretion of the court of appeals. An analogous process for dispatching non-final orders in multiclaim and multiparty cases for immediate review is provided in Rule 54(b) of the Federal Rules of Civil Procedure. Finally, the All-Writs Act, Section 1651 of the Judicial Code, erects a flexible set of end-around mechanisms for appealing interlocutory orders. Of these, mandamus is by far the best known and most used.

HOBERMAN v. LAKE OF ISLES

Supreme Court of Errors of Connecticut, 1952.
138 Conn. 573, 87 A.2d 137.

INGLIS, ASSOCIATE JUSTICE. This action was brought to foreclose a mortgage. The answer denied the execution of the mortgage and alleged that the loan purporting to be secured had not been made. Judgment was entered for the defendants. Thereafter the plaintiff filed his motion for a new trial pursuant to Practice Book, § 229. The court found that material testimony relating to the execution of the mortgage given by the defendant Girden on the trial of the case was false. It concluded that for that reason the judgment must be opened and a new trial had in order to avoid injustice or judicial error and entered an order granting the motion. From that order this appeal has been taken. The only questions raised or argued on the appeal related to the propriety of the order. The appeal, however, necessarily raises another and more fundamental question, namely, whether the order is one from which an appeal lies.

Section 8003 of the General Statutes authorizes an appeal only from a final judgment or from a decision granting a motion to set aside a verdict. The jurisdiction of this court is therefore limited to appeals which are within either of those two categories. Since it is a matter of jurisdiction, this court may and should upon its own motion reject any purported appeal which is not within the statute even though the question has not been raised by a motion to erase. . . .

The present appeal is clearly not one from a decision granting a motion to set aside a verdict. The sole question, therefore, is whether the order granting the motion for a new trial is a final judgment under the statute. In determining whether a decision of a trial court is a final judgment, we have uniformly applied the test laid down in Banca Commerciale Italiana Trust Co. v. Westchester Artistic Works, Inc., 108 Conn. 304, 307, 142 A. 838, 839: "The test lies, not in the nature of the judgment, but in its effect as concluding the rights of some or all of the parties. If such rights are concluded, so that further proceedings after the entry of the order or decree of the court cannot affect them, then the judgment is a final judgment from which an appeal lies." In State v. Kemp, 124 Conn. 639, 643, 1 A.2d 761, 762, we said: "We did not use the word 'rights' in [the Banca] opinion in an inclusive sense. There are many rulings in the course of an action by which rights are determined which are interlocutory in their nature and reviewable only upon an appeal taken from a judgment later rendered."

Proceedings upon a motion to open a judgment and for a new trial are interlocutory. The rule requires such a motion to be filed within six days after the rendition of the judgment. It contemplates that action on the motion shall be taken while the court has power to modify its judgment, that is, during the term in which the judgment is rendered or while the court has the power by virtue of the fact that the motion is pending. See Morici v. Jarvie, 137 Conn. 97, 104, 75 A.2d 47. The granting of the motion does not determine any of the substantive rights of the parties. See Magill v. Lyman, 6 Conn. 59, 61. It determines merely that the parties must retry the issues in order to obtain a final adjudication of those rights. After the retrial is had and judgment is entered, on appeal from that judgment the granting of the motion for a new trial may be assigned as error. Ferguson v. Sabo, 115 Conn. 619, 623, 162 A. 844.

The effect of the granting of such a motion is analogous to that of an order of the Superior Court remanding a case to a workmen's compensation commissioner to hear further evidence, correct the finding and enter a new award. Such an order, we have held, is not appealable to this court. Burdick v. United States Finishing Co., 128 Conn. 284, 22 A.2d 629. An order restoring to the docket a case which was previously withdrawn provides an even closer analogy. Such an order deprives the defendant of the equivalent of a judgment in his favor and compels him to relitigate the issue. Yet we have held that the granting of a motion to restore is not a final judgment from which an appeal lies. Lusas v. St. Patrick's Roman Catholic Church Corporation, 123 Conn. 166, 167, 193 A. 204, 111 A.L.R. 763.

* * *

So far as the right of appeal is concerned, there is a distinction between an order granting a motion for a new trial and a judgment entered upon a petition for a new trial, which may be instituted at any time within three years after a judgment is rendered. See General Statutes, § 8322. The latter is appealable. Palverari v. Finta, 129 Conn. 38, 41, 26 A.2d 229; Husted v. Mead, 58 Conn. 55, 68, 19 A. 233. The difference is in at least two essential particulars. In the first place, a petition for a new trial is instituted by writ and complaint served upon the adverse party in the same manner as in any other new action. Although the action so started is collateral to the action in which the new trial is sought, it nevertheless is a distinct suit in itself. The judgment rendered therein is, therefore, the termination of the suit. It is the final judgment in the action. See State v. Kemp, 124 Conn. 639, 644, 1 A.2d 761. On the other hand, a motion for a new trial is filed in a case already pending and is merely a step in the procedure leading to the final judgment in that case. In the second place, claimed errors committed in rendering judgment on a petition for a new trial are not reviewable on an appeal from the judgment rendered in the action in which a new trial is sought. This consideration is given as the basis of the decision in both the Palverari case and the Husted case. The same is not true of a decision by the trial court on the less formal motion for a new trial. As is pointed out above, errors claimed in connection therewith may be assigned on the appeal from the judgment in the case in which the motion was made.

The order for a new trial from which this appeal was taken was purely interlocutory. It was entered at a time when the trial court still had control over and power to modify the judgment which it had rendered. The order did not finally conclude any of the rights of the parties which were in litigation. It, therefore, is not a final judgment from which an appeal lies. This court is without jurisdiction and the appeal must be dismissed. When an appeal is dismissed for lack of jurisdiction no costs are taxable. . . .

The appeal is dismissed without taxable costs to either party.

NOTES

(1) In 7 Weinstein, Korn & Miller, New York Civil Practice ¶ 5701.03 the authors note that CPLR 5701, which permits parties to "obtain immediate review as of right from almost any order made during the course of an action . . . represents an extreme position among American jurisdictions . . ." A 1982 study of the State's appellate system revealed, however, that despite the delays and expenses generated by the provision, there were also significant benefits for the Appellate Division's supervisory and error-review role. See R. MacCrate, J. Hopkins, and M. Rosenberg, Appellate Justice in New York (1982).

(2) Compare Mills v. Alabama, 384 U.S. 214, 86 S.Ct. 1434, 16 L.Ed.2d 484 (1966), involving the right to publish an editorial on election day. Although the highest state court had sent the case back for a new trial and 28 U.S.C.A. § 1257 permits only review of "Final judgments . . . rendered by the highest court of a State in which a decision could be had," the court assumed jurisdiction and reversed. Is this case explicable on the ground that the "chilling effect" on free speech of the statute will continue during the long period when the case is processed by the state courts? Should the definition of finality depend upon such considerations?

(3) In Mercantile National Bank v. Langdeau, 371 U.S. 555, 83 S.Ct. 520, 522, 9 L.Ed.2d 523 (1963), the court prior to trial entertained an appeal to determine which state court had proper venue in an action against two national banks. The court argued "that it serves the policy underlying the requirement of finality in 28 U.S.C.A. § 1257 to determine now in which state court appellants may be tried rather than to subject them, and appellee, to long and complex litigation which may all be for naught if consideration of the preliminary question of venue is postponed until the conclusion of the proceedings." The dissent argued that a determination that venue is proper "being tantamount to a denial of a motion to dismiss is a classic example of an interlocutory

ruling that is only a step toward ultimate disposition and is not in itself reviewable as a final judgment." Id. at 572, 83 S.Ct. at 529.

(4) In Local No. 438 Construction & General Laborers' Union v. Curry, 371 U.S. 542, 83 S.Ct. 531, 9 L.Ed.2d 514 (1963), the Supreme Court reviewed the granting of a temporary injunction in a labor matter by the Supreme Court of Georgia. The court held that even though the injunction was only temporary, the finality requirement was satisfied because "[w]hat we . . . have here is a judgment of the Georgia court finally and erroneously asserting its jurisdiction to deal with a controversy which is beyond its power and instead is within the exclusive domain of the National Labor Relations Board." Id. at 548, 83 S.Ct. at 535–36.

(5) In reading the cases, infra, consider whether the criterion of finality is the same when the Supreme Court reviews a state court judgment as when a federal court judgment is being reviewed. See Note, The Requirement of a Final Judgment or Decree for Supreme Court Review of State Courts, 73 Yale L.J. 515 (1964).

(6) In Budinich v. Becton Dickinson and Co., 486 U.S. 196, 108 S.Ct. 1717, 100 L.Ed.2d 178 (1988), the Supreme Court held that a judgment could be appealed despite the fact that the lower court had expressly ordered argument on the question of attorneys' fees, reasoning that:

"As a general matter, at least, we think it indisputable that a claim for attorney's fees is not part of the merits of the action to which the fees pertain. Such an award does not remedy the injury giving rise to the action, and indeed is often available to the party defending against the action. At common law, attorney's fees were regarded as an element of 'costs' awarded to the prevailing party, see 10 C. Wright, A. Miller, & M. Kane, Federal Practice and Procedure: Civil § 2665 (1983), which are not generally treated as part of the merits judgment, cf. Fed.Rule Civ.Proc. 54(d) ('[e]ntry of the judgment shall not be delayed for the taxing of costs'). Many federal statutes providing for attorney's fees continue to specify that they are to be taxed and collected as 'costs,' see Marek v. Chesny, 473 U.S. 1, 43–48, 105 S.Ct. 3012, 3035–3037, 87 L.Ed. 2d 1 (1985) (Brennan, J., dissenting) (citing 63 such statutes)."

Read 28 U.S.C.A. §§ 1291 and 1292, which appear in the Supplement.

BACHOWSKI v. USERY, 545 F.2d 363, 367 (3d Cir.1976) (per Adams, J.):

"The requirement that only final judgments are reviewable in the federal courts dates back to the beginnings of the federal judicial system. The Judiciary Act of 1789 provided for review only of final judgments and decrees, whether at law or in equity. And indeed, this limitation can trace its roots to the practice of the English common law courts that entertained appeals solely from the final disposition of a completed controversy.

"Until the last decade of the nineteenth century, the final judgment statutes provided the sole authorization for review within the federal judicial system. Congress began to realize, however, that rigid application of the final judgment rule in all cases might inflict irreparable harm upon litigants in certain instances, and might actually have the effect of unnecessarily prolonging the litigation. Its response, however, was not an abrogation of the general rule of finality, but rather a careful delineation of narrow categories of interlocutory orders that would be appealable. These initial enactments, now codified in 28 U.S.C. § 1292(a), encompassed limited types of interlocutory orders that would be appealable, the most familiar of which are orders granting, continuing or denying a preliminary injunction.

"Although these statutes ameliorated, to some degree, the hardships caused by the final judgment rule, there were other instances where the underlying concerns of serious harm and wasted effort, which section 1292(a) spoke to, were also present. At the instance of the Judicial Conference of the United States, Congress enacted 28 U.S.C. § 1292(b). Unlike earlier statutes permitting certain substantive classes of interlocutory appeals, section 1292(b) established a procedure for judicial identification of cases where the grant of an interlocutory appeal might aid in promptly resolving litigation. This would be done by a process whereby the district judge and the court of appeals would each certify a case as comporting with specified criteria. The certification procedure is not mandatory; indeed, permission to appeal is wholly within the discretion of the courts, even if the criteria are present.

"Thus, the reaction of the Congress to the rigors occasionally imposed by the final judgment rule has been very cautious. Congress has retained the finality doctrine as the general rule of appealability, in recognition of the rule's general contribution to the maintenance of an orderly judicial system. But it has also provided limited exceptions to the rule of finality so as to relieve any hardship that remorseless application of the rule might create."

COOPERS & LYBRAND v. LIVESAY

Supreme Court of the United States, 1978.
437 U.S. 463, 98 S.Ct. 2454, 57 L.Ed.2d 351.

MR. JUSTICE STEVENS delivered the opinion of the Court.*

The question in this case is whether a district court's determination that an action may not be maintained as a class action pursuant to Fed. Rule Civ.Proc. 23 is a "final decision" within the meaning of 28 U.S.C. § 1291 and therefore appealable as a matter of right. Because there is a conflict in the Circuits over this issue, we granted certiorari and now hold that such an order is not appealable under § 1291.

* Some footnotes omitted; others renumbered.

Petitioner, Coopers & Lybrand, is an accounting firm that certified the financial statements in a prospectus issued in connection with a 1972 public offering of securities in Punta Gorda Isles for an aggregate price of over $18 million. Respondents purchased securities in reliance on that prospectus. In its next annual report to shareholders, Punta Gorda restated the earnings that had been reported in the prospectus for 1970 and 1971 by writing down its net income for each year by over $1 million. Thereafter, respondents sold their Punta Gorda securities and sustained a loss of $2,650 on their investment.

Respondents filed this action on behalf of themselves and a class of similarly situated purchasers. They alleged that petitioner and other defendants had violated various sections of the Securities Act of 1933 and the Securities Exchange Act of 1934. The District Court first certified, and then, after further proceedings, decertified the class.

Respondents did not request the District Court to certify its order for interlocutory review under 28 U.S.C. § 1292(b). Rather, they filed a notice of appeal pursuant to § 1291. The Court of Appeals regarded its appellate jurisdiction as depending on whether the decertification order had sounded the "death knell" of the action. After examining the amount of respondents' claims in relation to their financial resources and the probable cost of the litigation, the court concluded that they would not pursue their claims individually. The Court of Appeals therefore held that it had jurisdiction to hear the appeal and, on the merits, reversed the order decertifying the class. Livesay v. Punta Gorda Isles, Inc., 550 F.2d 1106.

Federal appellate jurisdiction generally depends on the existence of a decision by the District Court that "ends the litigation on the merits and leaves nothing for the court to do but execute the judgment." Catlin v. United States, 324 U.S. 229, 233, 65 S.Ct. 631, 633, 89 L.Ed. 911. An order refusing to certify, or decertifying, a class does not of its own force terminate the entire litigation because the plaintiff is free to proceed on his individual claim. Such an order is appealable, therefore, only if it comes within an appropriate exception to the final-judgment rule. In this case respondents rely on the "collateral order" exception articulated by this Court in Cohen v. Beneficial Industrial Loan Corp., 337 U.S. 541, 69 S.Ct. 1221, 93 L.Ed. 1528, and on the "death knell" doctrine adopted by several Circuits to determine the appealability of orders denying class certification.

*   *   *

To come within the "small class" of decisions excepted from the final-judgment rule by *Cohen*, the order must conclusively determine the disputed question, resolve an important issue completely separate from the merits of the action, and be effectively unreviewable on appeal from a final judgment. Abney v. United States, 431 U.S. 651, 658, 97 S.Ct. 2034, 2039, 52 L.Ed.2d 651; United States v. MacDonald, 435 U.S. 850, 855, 98 S.Ct. 1547, 1549, 56 L.Ed.2d 18. An order passing on a request for class certification does not fall in that category. First, such an order is subject to revision in the District Court. Fed.Rule Civ.Proc. 23(c)(1). Second, the class determination generally involves considerations that are "enmeshed in the factual and legal issues comprising the plaintiff's cause of action." Mercantile Nat. Bank v. Langdeau, 371 U.S. 555, 558, 83 S.Ct. 520, 522, 9 L.Ed.2d 523. Finally, an order denying class certification is subject to effective review after final judgment at the behest of the named plaintiff or intervening class members. United Airlines, Inc. v. McDonald, 432 U.S. 385, 97 S.Ct. 2464, 53 L.Ed.2d 423. For these reasons, as the Courts of Appeals have consistently recognized, the collateral-order doctrine is not applicable to the kind of order involved in this case.

II

Several Circuits, including the Court of Appeals in this case, have held that an order denying class certification is appealable if it is likely to sound the "death knell" of the litigation. The "death knell" doctrine assumes that without the incentive of a possible group recovery the individual plaintiff may find it economically imprudent to pursue his lawsuit to a final judgment and then seek appellate review of an adverse class determination. Without questioning this assumption, we hold that orders relating to class certification are not independently appealable under § 1291 prior to judgment.

In addressing the question whether the "death knell" doctrine supports mandatory appellate jurisdiction of orders refusing to certify class actions, the parties have devoted a portion of their argument to the desirability of the small-claim class action. Petitioner's opposition to the doctrine is based in part on criticism of the class action as a vexatious kind of litigation. Respondents, on the other hand, argue that the class action serves a vital public interest and, therefore, special rules of appellate review are necessary to ensure that district judges are subject to adequate supervision and control. Such policy arguments, though proper for legislative consideration, are irrelevant to the issue we must decide.

There are special rules relating to class actions and, to that extent, they are a special kind of litigation. Those rules do not, however, contain any unique provisions governing appeals. The appealability of any order entered in a class action is determined by the same standards that govern appealability in other types of litigation. Thus, if the "death knell" doctrine has merit, it would apply equally to the many interlocutory orders in ordinary litigation—rulings on discovery, on venue, on summary judgment—that may have such tactical economic significance that a defeat is tantamount to a "death knell" for the entire case.

Though a refusal to certify a class is inherently interlocutory, it may induce a plaintiff to abandon his individual claim. On the other hand, the litigation will often survive an adverse class determination. What effect the economic disincentives created by an interlocutory order may have on the fate of any litigation will depend on a variety of factors.[1] Under the "death knell" doctrine, appealability turns on the court's perception of that impact in the individual case. Thus, if the court believes that the plaintiff has adequate incentive to continue, the order is considered interlocutory; but if the court concludes that the ruling, as a practical matter, makes further litigation improbable, it is considered an appealable final decision. . . .

A threshold inquiry [as to whether some class members' claims are large enough to warrant individual litigation] may, it is true, identify some orders that would truly end the litigation prior to final judgment; allowing an immediate appeal from those orders may enhance the quality of justice afforded a few litigants. But this incremental benefit is outweighed by the impact of such an individualized jurisdictional inquiry on the judicial system's overall capacity to administer justice.

The potential waste of judicial resources is plain. The district court must take evidence, entertain argument, and make findings; and the court of appeals must review that record and those findings simply to determine whether a discretionary class determination is subject to appellate review. And if the record provides an inadequate basis for this determination, a remand for further factual development may be required. Moreover, even if the court makes a "death knell" finding and reviews the class-designation order on the merits, there is no assurance that the trial process will not again be disrupted by interlocutory review. For even if a ruling that the plaintiff does not adequately represent the class is reversed on appeal, the district court may still refuse to certify the class on the ground that, for example, common questions of law or fact do not predominate. Under the "death knell" theory, plaintiff would again be entitled to an appeal as a matter of right pursuant to § 1291. And since other kinds of interlocutory orders may also create the risk of a premature demise, the potential for multiple appeals in every complex case is apparent and serious.

Perhaps the principal vice of the "death knell" doctrine is that it authorizes *indiscriminate* interlocutory review of decisions made by the trial judge. The Interlocutory Appeals Act of 1958, 28 U.S.C. § 1292(b), was enacted to meet the recognized need for prompt review of certain nonfinal orders. However, Congress carefully confined the availability of such review. Nonfinal orders could never be appealed as a matter of right. Moreover, the discretionary power to permit an interlocutory appeal is not, in the first instance, vested in the courts of appeals. A party seeking review of a nonfinal order must first obtain the consent of the trial judge. This screening procedure serves the dual purpose of ensuring that such review will be confined to appropriate cases and avoiding time-consuming jurisdictional determinations in the court of

---

1. E.g., the plaintiff's resources; the size of his claim and his subjective willingness to finance prosecution of the claim; the probable cost of the litigation and the possibility of joining others who will share that cost; and the prospect of prevailing on the merits and reversing an order denying class certification.

appeals.[2] Finally, even if the district judge certifies the order under § 1292(b), the appellant still "has the burden of persuading the court of appeals that exceptional circumstances justify a departure from the basic policy of postponing appellate review until after the entry of a final judgment." Fisons, Ltd. v. United States, 458 F.2d 1241, 1248 (CA7 1972). The appellate court may deny the appeal for any reason, including docket congestion. By permitting appeals of right from class-designation orders after jurisdictional determinations that turn on questions of fact, the "death knell" doctrine circumvents these restrictions.

Accordingly, we hold that the fact that an interlocutory order may induce a party to abandon his claim before final judgment is not a sufficient reason for considering it a "final decision" within the meaning of § 1291.[3] The judgment of the Court of Appeals is reversed with directions to dismiss the appeal.

It is so ordered.

NOTES

(1) "Since the attempts to imprison the appealability of orders granting or denying class action designation within judicially-created formulae have proved to be failures and, in my judgment, will continue to be so, we should return to the earlier wisdom." See Parkinson v. April Industries, Inc., 520 F.2d 650 (2d Cir.1975) (Friendly, J., concurring).

2. H.R.Rep. No. 1667, 85th Cong., 2d Sess. 5–6 (1958).

"We also recognize that such savings may be nullified in practice by indulgent extension of the amendment to inappropriate cases or by enforced consideration in Courts of Appeals of many ill-founded applications for review. The problem, therefore, is to provide a procedural screen through which only the desired cases may pass, and to avoid the wastage of a multitude of fruitless applications to invoke the amendment contrary to its purpose. . . .

" . . . Requirement that the Trial Court certify the case as appropriate for appeal serves the double purpose of providing the Appellate Court with the best informed opinion that immediate review is of value, and at once protects appellate dockets against a flood of petitions in inappropriate cases. . . . [A]voidance of ill-founded applications in the Courts of Appeals for piecemeal review is of particular concern. If the consequence of change is to be crowded appellate dockets as well as any substantial number of unjustified delays in the Trial Court, the benefits to be expected from the amendment may well be outweighed by the lost motion of preparation, consideration, and rejection of unwarranted applications for its benefits."

3. Respondents also suggest that the Court's decision in Gillespie v. United States Steel Corp., 379 U.S. 148, 85 S.Ct. 308, 13 L.Ed.2d 199 supports appealability of a class-designation order as a matter of right. We disagree. In *Gillespie,* the Court upheld an exercise of appellate jurisdiction of what it considered a marginally final order that disposed of an unsettled issue of national significance because review of that issue unquestionably "implemented the same policy Congress sought to promote in § 1292(b)," id., at 154, and the arguable finality issue had not been presented to this Court until argument on the merits, thereby ensuring that none of the policies of judicial economy served by the finality requirement would be achieved were the case sent back with the important issue undecided. In this case, in contrast, respondents sought review of an inherently nonfinal order that tentatively resolved a question that turns on the facts of the individual case; and, as noted above, the indiscriminate allowance of appeals from such discretionary orders is plainly inconsistent with the policies promoted by § 1292(b). If *Gillespie* were extended beyond the unique facts of that case, § 1291 would be stripped of all significance.

(2) "Finality as a condition of review is an historic characteristic of federal appellate procedure. It was written into the first Judiciary Act and has been departed from only when observance of it would practically defeat the right to any review at all." Cobbledick v. United States, 309 U.S. 323, 324–25, 60 S.Ct. 540, 541, 84 L.Ed. 783 (1940). For a classic description of the history of the final judgment rule and a criticism of its use to prevent congestion in appellate courts, see Crick, The Final Judgment Rule as a Basis for Appeal, 41 Yale L.J. 539 (1931). See also Redish, The Pragmatic Approach to Appealability in the Federal Courts, 75 Colum.L.Rev. 89 (1975); Note, Interlocutory Appeals in the Federal Courts Under 28 U.S.C.A. § 1292(b), 88 Harv.L.Rev. 607 (1975).

(3) Decisions denying settlement of class actions are normally appealable, but not under § 1291. Rather, the Supreme Court has reasoned that if the settlement contemplated an injunction, the practical effect of the denial is the same as refusal to grant an injunction. Such actions are immediately appealable under § 1292(a)(1), see Carson v. American Brands, Inc., 450 U.S. 79, 101 S.Ct. 993, 67 L.Ed.2d 59 (1981).

(4) North Dakota State Board of Pharmacy v. Snyder's Drug Stores, Inc., 414 U.S. 156, 94 S.Ct. 407, 38 L.Ed.2d 379 (1973). Plaintiff was denied a pharmacy license and sued to invalidate the state statute requiring all holders of pharmacy licenses to be either registered pharmacists or corporations controlled by registered pharmacists. The North Dakota Supreme Court held the statute violative of the federal constitution and remanded to the Board of Pharmacy "for an administrative hearing [on the other grounds for the application's denial] *sans* the constitutional issue . . ." Snyder's Drug Stores, Inc. v. North Dakota State Board of Pharmacy, 202 N.W.2d 140, 145 (N.D.1972), reversed 414 U.S. 156, 94 S.Ct. 407, 38 L.Ed.2d 379 (1973), on remand 219 N.W.2d 140 (1974). The Board appealed. The United States Supreme Court found the requisite jurisdiction. "It would appear that, as a matter of North Dakota procedure, the only way in which the Board could preserve the constitutional issue would be to defy its own State Supreme Court and deny the application on the grounds of failure to meet ownership requirements . . ." and "there is no suggestion that the remaining litigation may raise other federal questions." These factors placed the case within the "penumbral area" of finality.

FIRESTONE TIRE & RUBBER CO. v. RISJORD

Supreme Court of the United States, 1981.
449 U.S. 368, 101 S.Ct. 669, 66 L.Ed.2d 571.

JUSTICE MARSHALL delivered the opinion of the Court.

This case presents the question whether a party may take an appeal, pursuant to 28 U.S.C. § 1291, from a district court order denying a motion to disqualify counsel for the opposing party in a civil case. The United States Court of Appeals for the Eighth Circuit held that such orders are not appealable, but made its decision prospective only and therefore reached the merits of the challenged order. We hold that orders denying motions to disqualify counsel are not appealable final decisions under § 1291, and we therefore vacate the judgment of the Court of Appeals and remand with instructions that the appeal be dismissed for lack of jurisdiction.

I

Respondent is lead counsel for the plaintiffs in four product-liability suits seeking damages from petitioner and other manufacturers of multipiece truck tire rims for injuries caused by alleged defects in their products. The complaints charge petitioner and the other defendants with various negligent, willful, or intentional failures to correct or to warn of the supposed defects in the rims. Plaintiffs seek both compensatory and exemplary damages. . . .

Petitioner was at all relevant times insured by Home Insurance Co. (Home) under a contract providing that Home would be responsible only for some types of liability beyond a minimum "deductible" amount. Home was also an occasional client of respondent's law firm. [The firm included Home in a list of its clients in the Martindale-Hubbell Law Director and occasionally represented the insurer on matters unrelated to the multipiece rim litigation. Home does not pay respondent or his firm a retainer.] Based on these facts, petitioner in May 1979 filed a motion to disqualify respondent from further representation of the plaintiffs. Petitioner argued that respondent had a clear conflict of interest because his representation of Home would give him an incentive to structure plaintiffs' claims for relief in such a way as to enable the insurer to avoid any liability. This in turn, petitioner argued, could increase its own potential liability. Home had in fact advised petitioner in the course of the litigation that its policy would cover neither an award of compensatory damages for willful or intentional acts nor any award of exemplary or punitive damages. The District Court entered a pretrial order requiring that respondent terminate his representation of the plaintiffs unless both the plaintiffs and Home consented to his continuing representation. Id., at 157, 160.

In accordance with the District Court's order, respondent filed an affidavit in which he stated that he had informed both the plaintiffs and Home of the potential conflict and that neither had any objection to his continuing representation of them both. He filed supporting affidavits executed by the plaintiffs and by a representative of Home. Because he had satisfied the requirements of the pretrial order, respondent was able to continue his representation of the plaintiffs. Petitioner objected to the District Court's decision to permit respondent to continue his representation if he met the stated conditions, and therefore filed a notice of appeal pursuant to 28 U.S.C. § 1291.

Although it did not hear oral argument on the appeal, the Eighth Circuit decided the case en banc and affirmed the trial court's order permitting petitioner to continue representing the plaintiffs. . . . We granted certiorari, 446 U.S. 934, 100 S.Ct. 2150, 64 L.Ed.2d 786 (1980), to resolve a conflict among the Circuits on the appealability question.

* * *

Because the litigation from which the instant petition arises had not reached final judgment at the time the notice of appeal was filed, the order denying petitioner's motion to disqualify respondent is appealable under § 1291 only if it falls within the *Cohen* doctrine. [Cohen v. Beneficial Industrial Loan Corp., 337 U.S. 541, 69 S.Ct. 1221, 93 L.Ed. 1528 (1949).] The Court of Appeals held that it does not, and 5 of the other 10 Circuits have also reached the conclusion that denials of disqualification motions are not immediately appealable "collateral orders." We agree with these courts that under *Cohen* such an order is not subject to appeal prior to resolution of the merits.

An order denying a disqualification motion meets the first part of the "collateral order" test. It "conclusively determine[s] the disputed question," because the only issue is whether challenged counsel will be permitted to continue his representation. In addition, we will assume, although we do not decide, that the disqualification question "resolve[s] an important issue completely separate from the merits of the action," the second part of the test. Nevertheless, petitioner is unable to demonstrate that an order denying disqualification is "effectively unreviewable on appeal from a final judgment" within the meaning of our cases.

In attempting to show why the challenged order will be effectively unreviewable on final appeal, petitioner alleges that denying immediate review will cause it irreparable harm. It is true that the finality requirement should "be construed so as not to cause crucial collateral claims to be lost and potentially irreparable injuries to be suffered," Mathews v. Eldridge, 424 U.S. 319, 331, n. 11, 96 S.Ct. 893, 901, n. 11, 47 L.Ed.2d 18 (1976). In support of its assertion that it will be irreparably harmed, petitioner hints at "the possibility that the course of the proceedings may be indelibly stamped or shaped with the fruits of a breach of confidence or by acts or omissions prompted by a divided loyalty," . . . and at "the effect of such a tainted proceeding in frustrating public policy." . . . But petitioner fails to supply a single concrete example of the indelible stamp or taint of which it warns. The only ground that petitioner urged in the District Court was that respondent might shape the products-liability plaintiffs' claims for relief in such a way as to increase the burden on petitioner. Our cases, however, require much more before a ruling may be considered "effectively unreviewable" absent immediate appeal.

To be appealable as a final collateral order, the challenged order must constitute "a complete, formal and, in the trial court, final rejection," Abney v. United States, supra, at 659, 97 S.Ct. at 2040, of a claimed right "where denial of immediate review would render impossible any review whatsoever," United States v. Ryan, 402 U.S. 530, 533, 91 S.Ct. 1580, 1582, 29 L.Ed.2d 85 (1971). Thus we have permitted appeals prior to criminal trials when a defendant has claimed that he is about to be subjected to forbidden double jeopardy, Abney v. United States, supra, or a violation of his constitutional right to bail, Stack v. Boyle, 342 U.S. 1, 72 S.Ct. 1, 96 L.Ed. 3 (1951), because those situations, like the posting of security for costs involved in *Cohen*, "each involved an asserted right the legal and practical value of which could be destroyed if it were not vindicated before trial." United States v. MacDonald, 435 U.S. 850, 860, 98 S.Ct. 1547, 1552, 56 L.Ed.2d 18 (1978). By way of contrast, we have generally denied review of pretrial discovery orders, see, e.g., United States v. Ryan, supra; Cobbledick v. United States, supra. Our rationale has been that in the rare case when appeal after final judgment will not cure an erroneous discovery order, a party may defy the order, permit a contempt citation to be entered against him, and challenge the order on direct appeal of the contempt ruling. See Cobbledick v. United States [309 U.S. 323, 60 S.Ct. 540, 84 L.Ed. 783 (1940)] at 327, 60 S.Ct. at 542. We have also rejected immediate appealability under § 1291 of claims that "may fairly be assessed" only after trial, United States v. MacDonald, supra, at 860, and those involving "considerations that are 'enmeshed in the factual and legal issues comprising the plaintiff's cause of action.'" Coopers & Lybrand v. Livesay, 437 U.S., at 469, 98 S.Ct., at 2458, quoting Mercantile National Bank v. Langdeau, 371 U.S. 555, 558, 83 S.Ct. 520, 522, 9 L.Ed.2d 523 (1963).

An order refusing to disqualify counsel plainly falls within the large class of orders that are indeed reviewable on appeal after final judgment, and not within the much smaller class of those that are not. The propriety of the district court's denial of a disqualification motion will often be difficult to assess until its impact on the underlying litigation may be evaluated, which is normally only after final judgment. The decision whether to disqualify an attorney ordinarily turns on the peculiar factual situation of the case then at hand, and the order embodying such a decision will rarely, if ever, represent a final rejection of a claim of fundamental right that cannot effectively be reviewed following judgment on the merits. In the case before us, petitioner has made no showing that its opportunity for meaningful review will perish unless immediate appeal is permitted. On the contrary, should the Court of Appeals conclude after the trial has ended that permitting continuing representation was prejudicial error, it would retain its usual authority to vacate the judgment appealed from and order a new trial. That remedy seems plainly adequate should petitioner's concerns of possible injury ultimately prove well founded. As the Second Circuit has recently observed, the potential harm that might be caused by requiring that a party await final judgment before it may appeal even when the denial of its disqualification motion was erroneous does not "diffe[r] in any significant way from the harm resulting from other interlocutory orders that may be erroneous, such as orders requiring discovery over a work-product objection or orders denying motions for recusal of the trial judge." Armstrong v. McAlpin, 625 F.2d 433, 438 (1980), cert. pending, No. 80–431. But interlocutory orders are not appealable "on the mere ground that they may be erroneous." Will v. United States, 389 U.S. 90, 98, n. 6, 88 S.Ct. 269, 275, n. 6, 19 L.Ed.2d 305 (1967). Permitting wholesale appeals on that ground not only would constitute an unjustified waste of scarce judicial resources, but also would transform the limited exception carved out in *Cohen* into a license for broad disregard of the finality rule imposed by Congress in § 1291. This we decline to do.

. . . We therefore hold that because the Court of Appeals was without jurisdiction to hear the appeal, it was without authority to decide the merits. Consequently, the judgment of the Eighth Circuit is vacated, and the case is remanded with instructions to dismiss the appeal for want of jurisdiction. See DiBella v. United States, 369 U.S., at 133, 85 S.Ct. at 661.

So ordered.

NOTES

(1) Would an order granting a motion to disqualify counsel be appealable under the *Cohen* doctrine? Would such an order qualify for a § 1292(b) certification?

(2) On what reasoning is the finality requirement treated as "jurisdictional." Should it be?

GULFSTREAM AEROSPACE CORP. v. MAYACAMAS CORP.

Supreme Court of the United States, 1988.
485 U.S. 271, 108 S.Ct. 1133, 99 L.Ed.2d 296.

JUSTICE MARSHALL delivered the opinion of the Court.*

The primary issue in this case is whether a district court denying a motion to stay or dismiss an action when a similar suit is pending in state court is immediately appealable.

I

Petitioner Gulfstream Aerospace Corporation and respondent Mayacamas Corporation entered into a contract under which respondent agreed to purchase an aircraft manufactured by the petitioner. Respondent subsequently refused to make payments due, claiming that petitioner, by increasing the production and availability of its aircrafts, had frustrated respondent's purpose in the transaction, which was to sell the aircraft when demand was high. Petitioner thereupon filed suit against respondent for breach of contract in the Superior Court of Chatham County, Georgia. Respondent, declining to remove this action to federal court, filed both an answer and a counterclaim. In addition, approximately one month after the commencement of petitioner's state-court suit, respondent filed a diversity action against petitioner in the United States District Court for the Northern District of California. This action alleged breach of the same contract that formed the basis of petitioner's state-court suit.

Petitioner promptly moved for a stay or dismissal of the federal-court action pursuant to the doctrine of Colorado River Water Conser-

---

* Footnotes omitted.

vation Dist. v. United States, 424 U.S. 800, 96 S.Ct. 1236, 47 L.Ed.2d 483 (1976). In *Colorado River,* we held that in "exceptional" circumstances, a federal district court may stay or dismiss an action solely because of the pendency of similar litigation in state court. Id., at 818, 96 S.Ct. at 1246; see Moses H. Cone Memorial Hospital v. Mercury Construction Corp., 460 U.S. 1, 13–19, 103 S.Ct. 927, 935–938, 74 L.Ed.2d 765 (1983). Petitioner argued that the circumstances of this case supported a stay or dismissal of the federal-court action under *Colorado River.* The District Court disagreed. Finding that "the facts of this case fall short of those necessary to justify" the discontinuance of a federal-court proceeding under *Colorado River,* the District Court denied petitioner's motion. . . .

The Court of Appeals dismissed the appeal for lack of jurisdiction, holding that neithcr § 1291 nor § 1292(a)(1) allowed an immediate appeal from the District Court's order. See 806 F.2d 928, 929–930 (1987). The Court of Appeals then declined to treat petitioner's notice of appeal as an application for mandamus on the ground that the District Court's order would not cause "serious hardship or prejudice" to petitioner. Id., at 930. Finally, the Court of Appeals stated that even if the notice of appeal were to be treated as an application for mandamus, petitioner did not have a right to the writ because "[i]t was well within the district court's discretion to deny" petitioner's motion. Id., at 930–931.

We granted certiorari, 481 U.S. 1068, 107 S.Ct. 2458, 95 L.Ed.2d 868 (1987), to resolve a division in the Circuits as to whether a district court's denial of a motion to stay litigation pending the resolution of a similar proceeding in state court is immediately appealable. We now affirm.

II

Petitioner's principal contention in this case is that the District Court's order denying the motion to stay or dismiss the federal-court litigation is immediately appealable under § 1291. That section provides for appellate review of "final decisions" of the district courts. This Court long has stated that as a general rule a district court's decision is appealable under this section only when the decision "ends the litigation on the merits and leaves nothing for the court to do but execute the judgment." Catlin v. United States, 324 U.S. 229, 233, 65 S.Ct. 631, 633, 89 L.Ed. 911 (1945). The order at issue in this case has no such effect: indeed, the order ensures that litigation will continue in the District Court. In Cohen v. Beneficial Industrial Loan Corp., 337 U.S. 541, 69 S.Ct. 1221, 93 L.Ed. 1528 (1949), however, we recognized a "small class" of decisions that are appealable under § 1291 even though they do not terminate the underlying litigation. Id., at 546, 69 S.Ct., at 1225. We stated in *Cohen* that a district court's decision is appealable under § 1291 if it "finally determine[s] claims of right separable from, and collateral to, rights asserted in the action, too important to be denied review and too independent of the cause itself to require that appellate consideration be deferred until the whole case is adjudicated." Ibid. Petitioner asserts that the District Court's decision in this case falls within *Cohen's* "collateral order" doctrine.

Since *Cohen*, we have had many occasions to revisit and refine the collateral-order exception to the final-judgment rule. We have articulated a three-pronged test to determine whether an order that does not finally resolve a litigation is nonetheless appealable under § 1291. See Coopers & Lybrand v. Livesay, 437 U.S. 463, 98 S.Ct. 2454, 57 L.Ed.2d 351 (1978); see also, e.g., Richardson–Merrell Inc. v. Koller, 472 U.S. 424, 431, 105 S.Ct. 2757, 2761, 86 L.Ed.2d 340 (1985); Firestone Tire & Rubber Co. v. Risjord, 449 U.S. 368, 375, 101 S.Ct. 669, 674, 66 L.Ed.2d 571 (1981). First, the order must "conclusively determine the disputed question." Coopers & Lybrand v. Livesay, supra, 437 U.S., at 468, 98 S.Ct. at 2458. Second, the order must "resolve an important issue completely separate from the merits of the action." Ibid. Third and finally, the order must be "effectively unreviewable on appeal from a final judgment." Ibid. (footnote omitted). If the order at issue fails to satisfy any one of these requirements, it is not appealable under the collateral-order exception to § 1291.

This Court held in Moses H. Cone Memorial Hospital v. Mercury Construction Corp., 460 U.S. 1, 103 S.Ct. 927, 74 L.Ed.2d 765 (1983), that a district court order granting a stay of litigation pursuant to *Colorado River* meets each of the three requirements of the collateral-order doctrine and therefore is appealable under § 1291.

Application of the collateral-order test to an order denying a motion to stay or dismiss an action pursuant to *Colorado River,* however, leads to a different result. We need not decide whether the denial of such a motion satisfies the second and third prongs of the collateral-order test—the separability of the decision from the merits of the action and the reviewability of the decision on appeal from final judgment— because the order fails to meet the initial requirement of a conclusive determination of the disputed question. A district court that denies a *Colorado River* motion does not "necessarily contemplate" that the decision will close the matter for all time. In denying such a motion, the district court may well have determined only that it should await further developments before concluding that the balance of factors to be considered under *Colorado River* . . . warrants a dismissal or stay. The district court, for example, may wish to see whether the state-court proceeding becomes more comprehensive than the federal-court action or whether the former begins to proceed at a more rapid pace. Thus, whereas the granting of a *Colorado River* motion necessarily implies an expectation that the state court will resolve the dispute, the denial of such a motion may indicate nothing more than that the district is not completely confident of the propriety of a stay or dismissal at that time. Indeed, given both the nature of the factors to be considered under *Colorado River* and the natural tendency of courts to attempt to eliminate matters that need not be decided from their dockets, a district court usually will have occasion to revisit and reassess an order denying a stay in light of events occurring in the normal course of litigation. Because an order denying a *Colorado River* motion is "inherently tentative" in this critical sense—because it is not "made with the expectation that it will be the final word on the subject addressed"—the order is not a conclusive determination within the meaning of the collateral-order doctrine and therefore is not appealable under § 1291.

III

Petitioner argues in the alternative that the District Court's order in this case is immediately appealable under § 1292(a)(1), which gives the courts of appeals jurisdiction of appeals from interlocutory orders granting or denying injunctions. An order by a federal court that relates only to the conduct or progress of litigation before that court ordinarily is not considered an injunction and therefore is not appealable under § 1292(a)(1). See Switzerland Cheese Assn., Inc. v. E. Horne's Market, Inc., 385 U.S. 23, 25, 87 S.Ct. 193, 195, 17 L.Ed.2d 23 (1966); International Products Corp. v. Koons, 325 F.2d 403, 406, (CA2 1963) (Friendly, J.). Under the *Enelow–Ettelson* doctrine, however, certain orders that stay or refuse to stay judicial proceedings are considered injunctions and therefore are immediately appealable. Petitioner asserts that the order in this case, which denied a motion for a stay of a federal-court action pending the resolution of a concurrent state-court proceeding, is appealable under § 1292(a)(1) pursuant to the *Enelow–Ettleson* doctrine.

The line of cases we must examine to resolve this claim began some fifty years ago, when this Court decided Enelow v. New York Life Ins. Co., 293 U.S. 379, 55 S.Ct. 310, 79 L.Ed. 440 (1935). At the time of that decision, law and equity remained separate jurisprudential systems in the federal courts. The same judges administered both these systems, however, so that a federal district judge was both a chancellor in equity and a judge at law. In *Enelow,* the plaintiff sued at law to recover on a life insurance policy. The insurance company raised the affirmative defense that the policy had been obtained by fraud and moved the District Court to stay the trial of the law action pending resolution of this equitable defense. The District Court granted this motion, and the plaintiff appealed. This Court likened the stay to an injunction issued by an equity court to restrain an action at law. The Court stated:

"[T]he grant or refusal of . . . a stay by a court of equity of proceedings at law is a grant or refusal of an injunction within the meaning of [the statute.] And, in this aspect, it makes no difference that the two cases, the suit in equity for an injunction and the action at law in which proceedings are stayed, are both pending in the same court, in view of the established distinction between 'proceedings at law and proceedings in equity in the national courts . . . .'"

* * *

"It is thus apparent that w~~h~~equire, that an equitable de-
. . . requiring, or refusing court, exercising what is essential-
fense shall first be tried, t~~'~~ly an equitable juris-ion, in effect grants or refuses an
injunction restrair-~~'~~ proceedings at law precisely as if the
court had acted ~~'~~pon a bill of complaint in a separate suit for
the same p~~'~~~~'~~ose." Id., at 382–383, 55 S.Ct., at 311.

The Court ~~t~~~~'~~~~s~~ concluded that the District Court's order was appealable unde~~'~~ § 1292(a)(1).

~~i~~i Ettelson v. Metropolitan Life Ins. Co., 317 U.S. 188, 63 S.Ct. 163,
~~&~~~~r~~ L.Ed. 176 (1942), the Court reaffirmed the rule of *Enelow*, notwithstanding that the Federal Rules of Civil Procedure had fully merged
law and equity in the interim. . . .

The historical analysis underlying the results in *Enelow* and *Ettelson* has bred a doctrine of curious contours. Under the *Enelow–
Ettelson* rule, most recently restated in Baltimore Contractors, Inc. v.
Bodinger, 348 U.S. 176, 75 S.Ct. 249, 99 L.Ed. 233 (1955), an order by a
federal court staying or refusing to stay its own proceedings is appealable under § 1292(a)(1) as the grant or denial of an injunction if two
conditions are met. First, the action in which the order is entered
must be an action that, before the merger of law and equity, was by its
nature an action at law. Second, the order must arise from or be based
on some matter that would then have been considered an equitable
defense or counterclaim. If both conditions are satisfied, the historical
equivalent of the modern order would have been an injunction, issued
by a separate equity court, to restrain proceedings in an action at law.
If either condition is not met, however, the historical analogy fails.
When the underlying suit is historically equitable and the stay is based
on a defense or counterclaim that is historically legal, the analogy fails
because a law judge had no power to issue an injunction restraining
equitable proceedings. And when both the underlying suit and the
defense or counterclaim on which the stay is based are historically
equitable, or when both are historically legal, the analogy fails because
when a chancellor or a law judge stayed an action in his own court, he
was not issuing an injunction, but merely arranging matters on his
docket. Thus, unless a stay order is made in a historically legal action
on the basis of a historically equitable defense or counterclaim, the
order cannot be analogized to a pre-merger injunction and therefore
cannot be appealed under § 1292(a)(1) pursuant to the *Enelow–Ettelson*
doctrine.

The parties in this case dispute whether the *Enelow–Ettelson* rule
makes the District Court's decision to deny a stay immediately appealable under § 1292(a)(1). . . .

We decline to address the issue of appealability in these terms;
indeed, the sterility of the debate between the parties illustrates the
need for a more fundamental consideration of the precedents in this
area. This Court long has understood that the *Enelow–Ettelson* rule is

deficient in utility and sense. In the two cases we have decided since *Ettelson* relating to the rule, we criticized its perpetuation of "outmoded procedural differentiations" and its consequent tendency to produce incongruous results. Baltimore Contractors, Inc. v. Bodinger, supra, 348 U.S., at 184, 75 S.Ct. at 254; see Morgantown v. Royal Ins. Co., 337 U.S. 254, 257–258, 69 S.Ct. 1067, 1069–1070, 93 L.Ed. 1347 (1949). We refrained then from overruling the *Enelow* and *Ettelson* decisions, but today we take that step. A half century's experience has persuaded us, as it has persuaded an impressive array of judges and commentators, that the rule is unsound in theory, unworkable and arbitrary in practice, and unnecessary to achieve any legitimate goals. . . .

The case against perpetuation of this sterile and antiquated doctrine seems to us conclusive. We therefore overturn the cases establishing the *Enelow–Ettelson* rule and hold that orders granting or denying stays of "legal" proceedings on "equitable" grounds are not automatically appealable under § 1292(a)(1). This holding will not prevent interlocutory review of district court orders when such review is truly needed. Section 1292(a)(1) will, of course, continue to provide appellate jurisdiction over orders that grant or deny injunctions and orders that have the practical effect of granting or denying injunctions and have "serious, perhaps irreparable, consequence." Carson v. American Brands, Inc., 450 U.S. 79, 84, 101 S.Ct. 993, 996, 67 L.Ed.2d 59 (1981), quoting Baltimore Contractors, Inc. v. Bodinger, supra, 348 U.S., at 181, 75 S.Ct., at 252. As for orders that were appealable under § 1292(a)(1) solely by virtue of the *Enelow–Ettelson* doctrine, they may, in appropriate circumstances, be reviewed under the collateral-order doctrine of § 1291, see Moses H. Cone Memorial Hospital v. Mercury Construction Corp., 460 U.S. 1, 103 S.Ct. 927, 74 L.Ed.2d 765 (1983), and the permissive appeal provision of § 1292(b), as well as by application for writ of mandamus. Our holding today merely prevents interlocutory review of district court orders on the basis of historical circumstances that have no relevance to modern litigation. Because we repudiate the *Enelow–Ettelson* doctrine, we reject petitioner's claim that the District Court's order in this case is appealable under § 1292(a)(1) pursuant to that doctrine.

IV

Petitioner finally contends that if the order denying the motion for a stay or dismissal is not appealable, the Court of Appeals should have issued a writ of mandamus directing the District Court to vacate the order and grant the motion. In making this argument, petitioner points primarily to respondent's decision to eschew removal of the state-court action in favor of bringing a separate suit in federal court. Petitioner asserts that in the absence of "imperative circumstances" not present in this case, a district court must respond to this kind of conduct by staying or dismissing the action brought in that court. Brief for Petitioner 23. Refusal to do so, petitioner concludes, is a "demonstrable abuse of discretion" warranting the issuance of a writ of mandamus. Id., at 5.

This Court repeatedly has observed that the writ of mandamus is an extraordinary remedy, to be reserved for extraordinary situations. See, e.g., Kerr v. United States District Court, 426 U.S. 394, 402, 96 S.Ct. 2119, 2123–2124, 48 L.Ed.2d 725 (1976). The federal courts traditionally have used the writ only "to confine an inferior court to a lawful exercise of its prescribed jurisdiction or to compel it to exercise its authority when it is its duty to do so." Roche v. Evaporated Milk Assn., 319 U.S. 21, 26, 63 S.Ct. 938, 941, 87 L.Ed. 1185 (1943). In accord with this historic practice, we have held that only "exceptional circumstances amounting to a judicial 'usurpation of power'" will justify issuance of the writ. Will v. United States, 389 U.S. 90, 95, 88 S.Ct. 269, 273, 19 L.Ed.2d 305 (1967), quoting De Beers Consol. Mines, Ltd. v. United States, 325 U.S. 212, 217, 65 S.Ct. 1130, 1133, 89 L.Ed. 1566 (1945). Moreover, we have held that the party seeking mandamus has the "burden of showing that its right to issuance of the writ is 'clear and indisputable.'" Bankers Life & Cas. Co. v. Holland, 346 U.S. 379, 384, 74 S.Ct. 145, 148, 98 L.Ed. 106 (1953), quoting United States v. Duell, 172 U.S. 576, 582, 19 S.Ct. 286, 287, 43 L.Ed. 559 (1899).

Petitioner has failed to satisfy this stringent standard. This Court held in Colorado River that a federal court should stay or dismiss an action because of the pendency of a concurrent state-court proceeding only in "exceptional" circumstances, 424 U.S., at 818, 96 S.Ct. at 1246–1247, and with "the clearest of justifications," id., at 819, 96 S.Ct. at 1247. Petitioner has failed to show that the District Court clearly overstepped its authority in holding that the circumstances of this case were not so exceptional as to warrant a stay or dismissal under Colorado River. . . .

V

The District Court's order denying petitioner's motion to stay or dismiss respondent's suit because of the pendency of similar litigation in state court was not immediately appealable under § 1291 or § 1292(a)(1). In addition, the District Court's order did not call for the issuance of a writ of mandamus. Accordingly, the judgment of the Court of Appeals is affirmed.

It is so ordered.

JUSTICE KENNEDY took no part in the consideration or decision of this case.

JUSTICE SCALIA, concurring.

I join the Court's opinion, but write separately principally to express what seems to me a necessary addition to the analysis in Part II. While I agree that the present order does not come within the Cohen exception to the final-judgment rule under § 1291, I think it oversimplifies somewhat to assign as the reason merely that the order is "inherently tentative." A categorical order otherwise qualifying for *Cohen* treatment does not necessarily lose that status, and become "nonfinal," merely because the court may contemplate—or even, for that matter, invite—renewal of the aggrieved party's request for relief at a later date. The claim to *immediate* relief (in this case, the right to be free of the obstruction of a parallel federal proceeding) is categorically and irretrievably denied. The court's decision *is* "the final word on the subject" insofar as the time period between the court's initial denial and its subsequent reconsideration of the renewed motion is concerned. Thus, it is inconceivable that we would hold denial of a motion to dismiss an indictment on grounds of absolute immunity (an order that is normally appealable at once, see Nixon v. Fitzgerald, 457 U.S. 731, 102 S.Ct. 2690, 73 L.Ed.2d 349 (1982)), to be nonfinal and unappealable, simply because the court announces that it will reconsider the motion at the conclusion of the prosecution's case.

In my view, invocation of the *Cohen* exception makes sense in the present case because not only (1) the motion is likely to be renewed and reconsidered, but also (2) the relief will be just as effective, or nearly as effective, if accorded at a later date—that is, the harm caused during the interval between initial denial and reconsideration will not be severe. Moreover, since these two conditions will almost always be met when the asserted basis for an initial stay motion is the pendency of state proceedings, the more general conclusion that initial orders denying *Colorado River* motions are never immediately appealable is justified.

I note that today's result could also be reached by application of the rule adopted by the First Circuit, that to come within the *Cohen* exception the issue on appeal must involve "an important and unsettled question of controlling law, not merely a question of the proper exercise of the trial court's discretion." Boreri v. Fiat, S.P.A., 763 F.2d 17, 21 (1985), quoting United States v. Sorren, 605 F.2d 1211, 1213 (1979). See also, e.g., Sobol v. Heckler, Congressional Committee, 709 F.2d 129, 130–131 (1983); Midway Mfrg. Co. v. Omni Video Games, Inc., 668 F.2d 70, 71 (1981); In re Continental Investment Corp., 637 F.2d 1, 4 (1980). This approach has some support in our opinions, see Cohen v. Beneficial Industrial Loan Corp., 337 U.S. 541, 546, 69 S.Ct. 1221, 1225–1226, 93 L.Ed. 1528 (1949); Coopers & Lybrand v. Livesay, 437 U.S. 463, 468, 98 S.Ct. 2454, 2457–2458, 57 L.Ed.2d 351 (1978), as well as in policy, see Donlon Industries v. Forte, 402 F.2d 935, 937 (CA2 1968) (Friendly, J.) (when an issue is reviewable only on an abuse-of-discretion basis the "likelihood of reversal is too negligible to justify the delay and expense incident to an [immediate] appeal and the consequent burden on hardpressed appellate courts"); *Midway Mfrg. Co.,* supra, at 72 (questions of discretion "are less likely to be reversed and offer less reason for the appellate court to intervene"). This rationale has not been argued here, and we should not embrace it without full adversarial exploration of its consequences. I do think, however, that our finality jurisprudence is sorely in need of further limiting principles, so that

Cohen appeals will be, as we originally announced they could be, a "small class [of decisions] . . . too important to be denied review." 337 U.S., at 546, 69 S.Ct., at 1225–1226.

NOTE

(1) After *Gulfstream* was decided, Congress attempted to clarify the appealability of orders staying litigation pending arbitration for all arbitrations subject to federal arbitration law, see 9 U.S.C.A. § 15.

(2) In a suit growing out of the hi-jacking of the cruise ship Achille Lauro, the shipowner defendant moved to dismiss on the basis of a forum-selection clause in each passenger ticket obligating the passenger to bring any suit connected with the passage in Naples, Italy, and not elsewhere. The Court held that the district court's order denial dismissal was not appealable under the *Cohen v. Beneficial Loan* doctrine. Lauro Lines v. Chasser, 490 U.S. ___, 109 S.Ct. 1976, 104 L.Ed.2d 548 (1989). See also J.B. Stringfellow, Jr. v. Concerned Neighbors in Action, 480 U.S. 370, 107 S.Ct. 1177, 94 L.Ed.2d 389 (1987), holding that orders denying intervention as of right and imposing restrictions on permissive intervention are not immediately appealable under *Cohen*.

(3) In Van Cauwenberghe v. Biard, 486 U.S. 517, 108 S.Ct. 1945, 100 L.Ed. 2d 517 (1988), the district court had denied a motion to dismiss based on an extradited person's claim that he was immune from civil service of process. In addition, the court had denied a motion to dismiss on the ground of forum non conveniens. Review of both orders was sought, but in both cases, the Supreme Court held that an immediate appeal was not available under § 1291. The Court, however, left open the possibility that the second order might be reviewable under § 1292(b).

MULAY PLASTICS, INC. v. GRAND TRUNK WESTERN RAILROAD CO.

United States Court of Appeals, Seventh Circuit, 1984.
742 F.2d 369.

POSNER, CIRCUIT JUDGE.

We have consolidated these two appeals (and one mandamus petition) to consider what is likely to be a recurrent question under the recent amendments to the Federal Rules of Civil Procedure (effective August 1, 1983) strengthening the powers and responsibilities of federal district judges to mete out sanctions for procedural abuse: the immediate appealability of orders imposing such sanctions. The issues have been fully briefed, and are ripe for disposition.

In *Mulay*, 102 F.R.D. 130, the district judge ordered the appellant to pay the appellee $3,820.70 as a sanction for failing to produce relevant evidence in connection with the appellee's motion for summary judgment. The motion was denied, and the case is continuing. The order to pay is not final in the sense of winding up a lawsuit, and is appealable if at all only under the "collateral order" doctrine of Cohen v. Beneficial Industrial Loan Corp., 337 U.S. 541, 546–47, 69 S.Ct. 1221, 1225–26, 93 L.Ed. 1528 (1949). That doctrine allows the immediate appeal of some orders which, while not injunctions and so not appealable under 28 U.S.C. § 1292(a)(1), have the same effect as injunctions: they inflict irreparable harm. See Illinois v. F.E. Moran, Inc., 740 F.2d at 533 (7th Cir.1984); In re UNR Industries, Inc., 725 F.2d 1111, 1117–18 (7th Cir.1984). But an order to pay money as a sanction for abuse of discovery usually does not—and in this case did not—inflict irreparable harm on the party (Grand Trunk) ordered to pay. If, on appeal from the final judgment in this case, Grand Trunk convinces this court that the sanction should not have been imposed, it will get its money back then. See, e.g., Kordich v. Marine Clerks Ass'n, 715 F.2d 1392, 1393 (9th Cir.1983) (per curiam); Eastern Maico Distributors, Inc. v. Maico Fahrzeugfabrik, G.m.b.H., 658 F.2d 944, 947 (3d Cir.1981). There is no argument either that the appellee, a substantial corporation, will not be good for the trifling sum of money involved, if ultimately ordered to return it, or that the appellant, also a substantial corporation, will suffer a liquidity crisis by being deprived of this amount during the interim.

As there is nothing irreparable about the harm that the order to pay has done the appellant, appeal under the *Cohen* doctrine is not permissible. This is the usual conclusion reached in cases where parties try to appeal sanctions imposed during the discovery process, before a final judgment is entered. See, e.g., Eastern Maico Distributors, Inc. v. Maico Fahrzeugfabrik, G.m.b.H., supra, 658 F.2d at 947; In re Underwriters at Lloyd's, 666 F.2d 55, 58 (4th Cir.1981). It is true that Ohio v. Arthur Andersen & Co., 570 F.2d 1370, 1372 (10th Cir. 1978), is *contra*, but it has not been followed in any other circuit, and the force of its reasoning is weakened by the failure to refer to the irreparable-harm requirement of the *Cohen* doctrine. It is also true that judgments of criminal contempt, sometimes entered as sanctions for abuse of discovery, are appealable. United States v. Ryan, 402 U.S. 530, 532–33, 91 S.Ct. 1580, 1581–82, 29 L.Ed.2d 85 (1971). But if someone is adjudged guilty of a crime, he ought to be able to appeal as soon as possible; the general interest in expediting criminal proceedings is engaged even by a contempt proceeding. Apart from criminal contempt and some other exceptional cases, well illustrated by Knorr Brake Corp. v. Harbill, Inc., 738 F.2d 223 at 226 (7th Cir.1984), where the sanction was against nonparties, and In re UNR Industries, Inc., 736 F.2d 1136 at 1137 n. 2 (7th Cir.1984), where the appeal was from an order in bankruptcy, an area where interlocutory appeals traditionally are liberally allowed, see In re Saco Local Development Corp., 711 F.2d 441, 444 (1st Cir.1983), sanctions for abuse of discovery, like other discovery orders, are not appealable orders in the federal system, unless the party sanctioned can bring his appeal within the *Cohen* doctrine by showing that all the elements of the doctrine are present.

Magnavox [the companion appeal] is a virtually identical case: . . . and it adds nothing that the appellant here has also asked for a writ of mandamus to direct the district judge to vacate the award. Mandamus may not be used to get around the limitations on the appealability of interlocutory orders. Allied Chemical Corp. v. Daiflon, Inc., 449 U.S. 33, 101 S.Ct. 188, 66 L.Ed.2d 193 (1980) (per curiam). It also adds nothing that the judge certified his order awarding sanctions for an immediate appeal under Rule 54(b) of the Federal Rules of Civil Procedure. The rule allows an immediate appeal in some circumstances from an order finally disposing of a separate "claim for relief," but this has been held to mean a substantive claim, see Swanson v. American Consumer Industries, Inc., 517 F.2d 555, 560–61 (7th Cir. 1975); Seigal v. Merrick, 619 F.2d 160, 164 n. 7 (2d Cir.1980); Redding & Co. v. Russwine Construction Corp., 417 F.2d 721, 726 n. 33 (D.C.Cir. 1969); Atkins, Kroll (Guam), Ltd. v. Cabrera, 277 F.2d 922, 924 (9th Cir. 1960), and the separate claim here was not substantive. The language of Rule 54(b) leaves little room for doubt that it indeed is limited to substantive claims . . . ..

The appeals in these two cases are Dismissed, and the petition for mandamus is denied. Costs in this court are awarded to the appellees.

SEARS, ROEBUCK & CO. v. MACKEY

Supreme Court of the United States, 1956.
351 U.S. 427, 76 S.Ct. 895, 100 L.Ed. 1297.

MR. JUSTICE BURTON delivered the opinion of the Court.

This action, presenting multiple claims for relief, was brought by Mackey and another in the United States District Court for the Northern District of Illinois, Eastern Division, in 1953. The court expressly directed that judgment be entered for the defendant, Sears, Roebuck & Co., on two, but less than all, of the claims presented. It also expressly determined that there was no just reason for delay in making the entry. After Mackey's notice of appeal from that judgment to the Court of Appeals for the Seventh Circuit, Sears, Roebuck & Co. moved to dismiss the appeal for lack of appellate jurisdiction. The Court of Appeals upheld its jurisdiction and denied the motion, relying upon 28 U.S.C.A. § 1291 and Rule 54(b) of the Federal Rules of Civil Procedure, as amended in 1946. 218 F.2d 295. Because of the importance of the issue in determining appellate jurisdiction and because of a conflict of judicial views on the subject, we granted certiorari. 348 U.S. 970. For the reasons hereafter stated, we sustain the Court of Appeals and its appellate jurisdiction.

Although we are here concerned with the present appealability of the judgment of the District Court and not with its merits, we must examine the claims stated in the complaint so as to consider adequately the issue of appealability.

The complaint contains six counts. We disregard the fifth because it has been abandoned and the sixth because it duplicates others. The claims stated in Counts I and II are material and have been dismissed without leave to amend. The claim contained in Count III and that in amended Count IV are at issue on the answers filed by Sears, Roebuck & Co. The appeal before us is from a judgment striking out Counts I and II without disturbing Counts III and IV, and the question presented is whether such a judgment is presently appealable when the District Court, pursuant to amended Rule 54(b), has made "an express determination that there is no just reason for delay" and has given "an express direction for the entry of judgment."

In Count I, Mackey, a citizen of Illinois, and Time Saver Tools, Inc., an Illinois corporation owned by Mackey, are the original plaintiffs and the respondents here. Sears, Roebuck & Co., a New York corporation doing business in Illinois, is the original defendant and the petitioner here. Mackey charges Sears with conduct violating the Sherman Antitrust Act in a manner prejudicial to three of Mackey's commercial ventures causing him $190,000 damages for which he seeks $570,000 as treble damages. His first charge is unlawful destruction by Sears, since 1949, of the market for nursery lamps manufactured by General Metalcraft Company, a corporation wholly owned by Mackey. Mackey claims that this caused him a loss of $150,000. His second charge is unlawful interference by Sears, in 1952, with Mackey's contract to sell, on commission, certain tools and other products of the Vascoloy-Ramet Corporation, causing Mackey to lose $15,000. His third charge is unlawful destruction by Sears, in 1952, of the market for a new type of carbide-tipped lathe bit and for other articles manufactured by Time Saver Tools, Inc., resulting in a loss to Mackey of $25,000. Mackey combines such charges with allegations that Sears has used its great size to monopolize commerce and restrain competition in these fields. He asks for damages and equitable relief.

In Count II, Mackey claims federal jurisdiction by virtue of diversity of citizenship. He incorporates the allegations of Count I as to the Metalcraft transactions and asks for $250,000 damages for Sears' wilful destruction of the business of Metalcraft, plus $50,000 for Mackey's loss on obligations guaranteed by him.

In Count III, Mackey seeks $75,000 in a common-law proceeding against Sears for unlawfully inducing a breach of his Vascoloy commission contract.

In Count IV, Time Saver seeks $200,000 in a common-law proceeding against Sears for unlawfully destroying Time Saver's business by unfair competition and patent infringement.

The jurisdiction of the Court of Appeals to entertain Mackey's appeal from the District Court's judgment depends upon 28 U.S.C.A. § 1291, which provides that "The courts of appeals shall have jurisdiction of appeals from *all final decisions* of the district courts of the United States. . . ." (Emphasis supplied.)

If Mackey's complaint had contained only Count I, there is no doubt that a judgment striking out that count and thus dismissing, in its entirety, the claim there stated would be both a final and an appealable decision within the meaning of § 1291. Similarly, if his complaint had contained Counts I, II, III and IV, there is no doubt that a judgment striking out all four would be a final and appealable decision under § 1291. The controversy before us arises solely because, in this multiple claims action, the District Court has dismissed the claims stated in Counts I and II, but has left unadjudicated those stated in Counts III and IV.

Before the adoption of the Federal Rules of Civil Procedure in 1939, such a situation was generally regarded as leaving the appellate court without jurisdiction of an attempted appeal. It was thought that, although the judgment was a final decision on the respective claims in Counts I and II, it obviously was not a final decision of the whole case, and there was no authority for treating anything less than the whole case as a judicial unit for purposes of appeal.[1] This construction of the judicial unit was developed from the common law which had dealt with litigation generally less complicated than much of that of today.

With the Federal Rules of Civil Procedure, there came an increased opportunity for the liberal joinder of claims in multiple claims actions. This, in turn, demonstrated a need for relaxing the restrictions upon what should be treated as a judicial unit for purposes of appellate jurisdiction. Sound judicial administration did not require relaxation of the standard of finality in the disposition of the individual adjudicated claims for the purpose of their appealability. It did, however, demonstrate that, at least in multiple claims actions, some final decisions, on less than all of the claims, should be appealable without waiting for a final decision on *all* of the claims. Largely to meet this need, in 1939, Rule 54(b) was promulgated in its original form through joint action of Congress and this Court. It reads as follows:

"(b) JUDGMENT AT VARIOUS STAGES. When more than one claim for relief is presented in an action, the court at

---

1. At common law, a writ of error did not lie to review a judgment that failed to adjudicate every cause of action asserted in the controversy. See Holcombe v. McKusick, 20 How. 552; United States v. Girault, 11 How. 22; Metcalfe's Case, 11 Co.Rep. 38a, 77 Eng.Rep. 1193. The rule generally followed in the federal courts was that, in a case involving a single plaintiff and a single defendant, a judgment was not appealable if it disposed of some, but less than all, of the claims presented. See Collins v. Miller, 252 U.S. 364, 40 S.Ct. 347, 64 L.Ed. 616; Sheppy v. Stevens, 200 F. 946 (C.A.2d Cir.). In cases involving multi-

ple parties where the alleged liability was joint, a judgment was not appealable unless it terminated the action as to all the defendants. See Hohorst v. Hamburg-American Packet Co., 148 U.S. 262, 13 S.Ct. 590, 37 L.Ed. 443. But if, in a multiple party case, a judgment finally disposed of a claim that was recognized to be separate and distinct from the others, that judgment, under some circumstances, was appealable. See Republic of China v. American Express Co., 190 F.2d 334 (C.A. 2d Cir.). [Some footnotes omitted; others renumbered.]

any stage, upon a determination of the issues material to a particular claim and all counterclaims arising out of the transaction or occurrence which is the subject matter of the claim, may enter a judgment disposing of such claim. The judgment shall terminate the action with respect to the claim so disposed of and the action shall proceed as to the remaining claims. In case a separate judgment is so entered, the court by order may stay its enforcement until the entering of a subsequent judgment or judgments and may prescribe such conditions as are necessary to secure the benefit thereof to the party in whose favor the judgment is entered."

It gave limited relief. The courts interpreted it as not relaxing the requirement of a "final decision" on each individual claim as the basis for an appeal, but as authorizing a limited relaxation of the former general practice that, in multiple claims actions, *all* the claims had to be finally decided before an appeal could be entertained from a final decision upon any of them. Thus, original Rule 54(b) modified the single judicial unit theory but left unimpaired the statutory concept of finality prescribed by § 1291. However, it was soon found to be inherently difficult to determine by any automatic standard of unity which of several multiple claims were sufficiently separable from others to qualify for this relaxation of the unitary principle in favor of their appealability. The result was that the jurisdictional time for taking an appeal from a final decision on less than all of the claims in a multiple claims action in some instances expired earlier than was foreseen by the losing party. It thus became prudent to take immediate appeals in all cases of doubtful appealability and the volume of appellate proceedings was undesirably increased.

Largely to overcome this difficulty, Rule 54(b) was amended, in 1946, to take effect in 1948. Since then it has read as follows:

"(b) JUDGMENT UPON MULTIPLE CLAIMS. *When more than one claim for relief is presented in an action,* whether as a claim, counterclaim, cross-claim, or third-party claim, *the court may direct the entry of a final judgment upon one or more but less than all of the claims only upon an express determination that there is no just reason for delay and upon an express direction for the entry of judgment.* In the absence of such determination and direction, any order or other form of decision, however designated, which adjudicates less than all the claims shall not terminate the action as to any of the claims, and the order or other form of decision is subject to revision at any time before the entry of judgment adjudicating all the claims." (Emphasis supplied.)

In this form, it does not relax the finality required of each decision, as an individual claim, to render it appealable, but it does provide a practical means of permitting an appeal to be taken from one or more final decisions on individual claims, in multiple claims actions, without waiting for final decisions to be rendered on *all* the claims in the case. The amended rule does not apply to a single claim action nor to a multiple claims action in which all of the claims have been finally decided. It is limited expressly to multiple claims actions in which "one or more but less than all" of the multiple claims have been finally decided and are found otherwise to be ready for appeal.

To meet the demonstrated need for flexibility, the District Court is used as a "dispatcher." It is permitted to determine, in the first instance, the appropriate *time when each "final decision"* upon "one or more but less than all" of the claims in a multiple claims action is ready for appeal. This arrangement already has lent welcome certainty to the appellate procedure. Its "negative effect" has met with uniform approval. The effect so referred to is the rule's specific requirement that for "one or more but less than all" multiple claims to become appealable, the District Court must make both "an express determination that there is no just reason for delay" and "an express direction for the entry of judgment." A party adversely affected by a final decision thus knows that his time for appeal will *not* run against him until this certification has been made.

In the instant case, the District Court made this certification, but Sears, Roebuck & Co. nevertheless moved to dismiss the appeal for lack of appellate jurisdiction under § 1291. The grounds for such a motion ordinarily might be (1) that the judgment of the District Court was not a decision upon a "claim for relief," (2) that the decision was not a "final decision" in the sense of an ultimate disposition of an individual claim entered in the course of a multiple claims action, or (3) that the District Court abused its discretion in certifying the order.

In the case before us, there is no doubt that each of the claims dismissed is a "claim for relief" within the meaning of Rule 54(b), or that their dismissal constitutes a "final decision" on individual claims. Also, it cannot well be argued that the claims stated in Counts I and II are so inherently inseparable from, or closely related to, those stated in Counts III and IV that the District Court has abused its discretion in certifying that there exists no just reason for delay. They certainly *can* be decided independently of each other.

Petitioner contends that amended Rule 54(b) attempts to make an unauthorized extension of § 1291. We disagree. It could readily be argued here that the claims stated in Counts I and II are sufficiently independent of those stated in Counts III and IV to satisfy the requirements of Rule 54(b) even in its original form. If that were so, the decision dismissing them would also be appealable under the amended rule. It is nowhere contended today that a decision that would have been appealable under the original rule is not also appealable under the amended rule, provided the District Court makes the required certification.

While it thus might be possible to hold that in this case the Court of Appeals had jurisdiction under original Rule 54(b), there at least would be room for argument on the issue of whether the decided claims were separate and independent from those still pending in the District Court.[2] Thus the instant case affords an excellent illustration of the value of the amended rule which was designed to overcome that difficulty. Assuming that the requirements of the original rule are not met in this case, we nevertheless are enabled to recognize the present appellate jurisdiction of the Court of Appeals under the amended rule. The District Court *cannot,* in the exercise of its discretion, treat as "final" that which is not "final" within the meaning of § 1291. But the District Court *may,* by the exercise of its discretion in the interest of sound judicial administration, release for appeal final decisions upon one or more, but less than all, claims in multiple claims actions. The timing of such a release is, with good reason, vested by the rule primarily in the discretion of the District Court as the one most likely to be familiar with the case and with any justifiable reasons for delay. With equally good reason, any abuse of that discretion remains reviewable by the Court of Appeals.

Rule 54(b), in its original form, thus may be said to have modified the single judicial unit practice which had been developed by court decisions. The validity of that rule is no longer questioned. In fact, it was applied by this Court in Reeves v. Beardall, 316 U.S. 283, 62 S.Ct. 1085, 86 L.Ed. 1478 without its validity being questioned.

Rule 54(b), in its amended form, is a comparable exercise of the rulemaking authority of this Court. It does not supersede any statute controlling appellate jurisdiction. It scrupulously recognizes the statutory requirement of a "final decision" under § 1291 as a basic requirement for an appeal to the Court of Appeals. It merely administers that requirement in a practical manner in multiple claims actions and does so by rule instead of by judicial decision. By its negative effect, it operates to restrict in a valid manner the number of appeals in multiple claims actions.

We reach a like conclusion as to the validity of the amended rule where the District Court acts affirmatively and thus assists in properly timing the release of final decisions in multiple claims actions. The amended rule adapts the single judicial unit theory so that it better meets the current needs of judicial administration. Just as Rule 54(b), in its original form, resulted in the release of some decisions on claims in multiple claims actions before they otherwise would have been released, so amended Rule 54(b) now makes possible the release of more of such decisions subject to judicial supervision. The amended rule preserves the historic federal policy against piecemeal appeals in many cases more effectively than did the original rule.

---

2. In the instant case, the claim dismissed by striking out Count I is based on the Sherman Act, while Counts III and IV do not rely on, or even refer to, that Act. They are largely predicated on common-law rights. The basis of liability in Count I is independent of that on which the claims in Counts III and IV depend. But the claim in Count I does rest in part on some of the facts that are involved in Counts III and IV. The claim stated in Count II is clearly independent of those in Counts III and IV.

Accordingly, the appellate jurisdiction of the Court of Appeals is sustained, and its judgment denying the motion to dismiss the appeal for lack of appellate jurisdiction is

Affirmed.

[Concurring opinion of MR. JUSTICE FRANKFURTER, whom MR. JUSTICE HARLAN joined, omitted.]

NOTES

(1) See United States v. Crow, Pope & Land Enterprises Inc., 474 F.2d 200 (5th Cir.1973), in which the court refused to review the district court's holding that a portion of the Chattahoochee River was not navigable, and therefore the government was not entitled to an injunction prohibiting pollution of the river. There remained the question of whether the river was a tributary of a navigable waterway. The government argued this was a separate claim. The Court stated:

> While we recognize that, for purposes of Rule 54(b) of the Federal Rules of Civil Procedure, a separate claim need not be predicated on acts entirely distinct from those on which all of the other asserted claims in the action are bottomed, a mere variation in legal theories is insufficient.

Id. at 202. The court therefore refused to review the tributary argument.

(2) Notice that in footnote 2 to the principal opinion the Court conceded that the claim in count I rested "in part" on facts "involved" in counts III and IV. Does this mean that it arose out of the "same transaction or occurrence?" Court of appeals judges, despite the 1946 amendment, have been less willing than appears in the Sears, Roebuck case to permit a Rule 54(b) certification. See, e.g., Baca Land & Cattle Co. v. New Mexico Timber, Inc., 384 F.2d 701, 702 (10th Cir.1967) ("[B]ecause each theory of the appellants arises out of the same transaction or occurrence, the pragmatic approach which all circuits apply directs us to conclude that the trial court's ruling is not appealable."); Seaboard Machinery Corp. of Delaware v. Seaboard Machinery Corp. of New Jersey, 267 F.2d 178 (2d Cir.1959); Schwartz v. Eaton, 264 F.2d 195 (2d Cir. 1959).

LA BUY v. HOWES LEATHER CO.

Supreme Court of the United States, 1957.
352 U.S. 249, 77 S.Ct. 309, 1 L.Ed.2d 290.

MR. JUSTICE CLARK delivered the opinion of the Court.

These two consolidated cases present a question of the power of the Courts of Appeals to issue writs of mandamus to compel a District Judge to vacate his orders entered under Rule 53(b) of the Federal Rules of Civil Procedure referring antitrust cases for trial before a master. The petitioner, a United States District Judge sitting in the Northern District of Illinois, contends that the Courts of Appeals have no such power and that, even if they did, these cases were not appropriate ones for its exercise. The Court of Appeals for the Seventh Circuit has decided unanimously that it has such power and, by a divided court, that the circumstances surrounding the references by the petitioner required it to issue the mandamus about which he complains. 226 F.2d 703. The importance of the question in the administration of the Federal Rules of Civil Procedure, together with the uncertainty existing on the issue among the Courts of Appeals, led to our grant of a writ of certiorari. 350 U.S. 964, 76 S.Ct. 439. We conclude that the Court of Appeals properly issued the writs of mandamus.

History of the Litigation.—These petitions for mandamus, filed in the Court of Appeals, arose from two antitrust actions instituted in the District Court in 1950. Rohlfing involves 87 plaintiffs, all operators of independent retail shoe repair shops. The claim of these plaintiffs against the six named defendants—manufacturers, wholesalers, and retail mail order houses and chain operators—is identical. The claim asserted in the complaint is a conspiracy between the defendants "to monopolize and to attempt to monopolize" and fix the price of shoe repair supplies sold in interstate commerce in the Chicago area, in violation of the Sherman Act. The allegations also include a price discrimination charge under the Robinson-Patman Act. Shaffer involves six plaintiffs, all wholesalers of shoe repair supplies, and six defendants, including manufacturers and wholesalers of such supplies and a retail shoe shop chain operator. The allegations here also include charges of monopoly and price fixing under the Sherman Act and price discrimination in violation of the Robinson-Patman Act. Both complaints pray for injunctive relief, treble damages, and an accounting with respect to the discriminatory price differentials charged.

The record indicates that the cases had been burdensome to the petitioner. In Rohlfing alone, 27 pages of the record are devoted to docket entries reflecting that petitioner had conducted many hearings on preliminary pleas and motions. The original complaint had been twice amended as a result of orders of the court in regard to misjoinders and severance; 14 defendants had been dismissed with prejudice; summary judgment hearings had resulted in a refusal to enter a judgment for some of the defendants on the pleadings; over 50 depositions had been taken; and hearings to compel testimony and require the production and inspection of records were held. It appears that several of the hearings were extended and included not only oral argument but submission of briefs, and resulted in the filing of opinions and memoranda by the petitioner. It is reasonable to conclude that much time would have been saved at the trial had petitioner heard the case because of his familiarity with the litigation.

The References to the Master.—The references to the master were made under the authority of Rule 53(b) of the Federal Rules of Civil Procedure. The cases were called on February 23, 1955, on a motion to reset them for trial. Rohlfing was "No. 1 below the black line" on the trial list, which gave it a preferred setting. All parties were anxious for an early trial, but plaintiffs wished an adjournment until May. The petitioner announced that "it has taken a long time to get this case at issue. I remember hearing more motions, I think, in this case than any case I have ever sat on in this court." The plaintiffs estimated that the trial would take six weeks, whereupon petitioner stated he did not know when he could try the case "if it is going to take this long." He asked if the parties could agree "to have a Master hear" it. The parties ignored this query and at a conference in chambers the next day petitioner entered the orders of reference *sua sponte*.[1] The orders declared that the court was "confronted with an extremely congested calendar" and that "exception [sic] conditions exist for this reason" requiring the references. The cases were referred to the master "to take evidence and to report the same to this Court, together with his findings of fact and conclusions of law." It was further ordered in each case that "the Master shall commence the trial of this cause" on a certain date and continue with diligence, and that the parties supply security for costs. While the parties had deposited some $8,000 costs, the record discloses that all parties objected to the references and filed motions to vacate them. Upon petitioner's refusal to vacate the references, these mandamus actions were filed in the Court of Appeals seeking the issuance of writs ordering petitioner to do so. These applications were grounded on 28 U.S.C.A. § 1651(a), the All Writs Act.[2] In his answer to the show cause orders issued by the Court of Appeals, petitioner amplified the reasons for the references, stating "that the cases were very complicated and complex, that they would take considerable time to try," and that his "calendar was congested." Declaring that the references amounted to "a refusal on his [petitioner's] part, as a judge, to try the causes in due course," the Court of Appeals concluded that "in view of the extraordinary nature of these causes" the references must be vacated "if we find that the orders were beyond the court's power under the pertinent rule." 226 F.2d at 705, 706. And it being so found, the writs issued under the authority of the All Writs Act. It is not disputed that the same principles and considerations as to the propriety of the issuance of the writs apply equally to the two cases.

*   *   *

Affirmed.

1. The fact that the master is an active practitioner would make the comment of Chief Justice Vanderbilt with regard to the effect of references appropriate here. In his work, Cases and Materials on Modern Procedure and Judicial Administration (1952), at pages 1240–1241, he states:

"There is one special cause of delay in getting cases on for trial that must be singled out for particular condemnation, the all-too-prevalent habit of sending matters to a reference. There is no more effective way of putting a case to sleep for an indefinite period than to permit it to go to a reference with a busy lawyer as referee.

Only a drastic administrative rule, rigidly enforced, strictly limiting the matters in which a reference may be had and requiring weekly reports as to the progress of each reference will put to rout this inveterate enemy of dispatch in the trial of cases." [Some footnotes omitted; others renumbered.]

2. "(a) The Supreme Court and all courts established by Act of Congress may issue all writs necessary or appropriate in aid of their respective jurisdictions and agreeable to the usages and principles of law."

MR. JUSTICE BRENNAN, with whom MR. JUSTICE FRANKFURTER, MR. JUSTICE BURTON and MR. JUSTICE HARLAN join, dissenting.

The issue here is not whether Judge La Buy's order was reviewable by the Court of Appeals. The sole question is whether review should have awaited final decision in the cause or whether the order was reviewable before final decision by way of a petition under the All Writs Act for the issuance of a writ of mandamus addressed to it. I do not agree that the writ directing Judge La Buy to vacate the order of reference was within the bounds of the discretionary power of the Court of Appeals to issue an extraordinary writ under the All Writs Act.

. . .

The view now taken by this Court that the All Writs Act confers an independent appellate power, although not so broad as "to authorize the indiscriminate use of prerogative writs as a means of reviewing interlocutory orders," in effect engrafts upon federal appellate procedure a standard of interlocutory review never embraced by the Congress throughout our history, although it is written into the English Judicature Act and is followed in varying degrees in some of the States. That standard allows interlocutory appeals by leave of the appellate court. It is a compromise between conflicting viewpoints as to the extent that interlocutory appeals should be allowed. The federal policy of limited interlocutory review stresses the inconvenience and expense of piecemeal reviews and the strong public interest in favor of a single and complete trial with a single and complete review. The other view, of which the New York practice of allowing interlocutory review as of right from most orders is the extreme example, perceives danger of possible injustice in individual cases from the denial of any appellate review until after judgment at the trial.

The polestar of federal appellate procedure has always been "finality," meaning that appellate review of most interlocutory actions must await final determination of the cause at the trial level. "Finality as a condition of review is an historic characteristic of federal appellate procedure. It was written into the first Judiciary Act and has been departed from only when observance of it would practically defeat the right to any review at all." Cobbledick v. United States, 309 U.S. 323, 324–325, 60 S.Ct. 540, 541, 84 L.Ed. 783. The Court's action today shatters that statutory policy. I protest, not only because we invade a domain reserved by the Constitution exclusively to the Congress, but as well because the encouragement to interlocutory appeals offered by this decision must necessarily aggravate further the already bad condition of calendar congestion in some of our District Courts and also add to the burden of work of some of our busiest Courts of Appeals. More petitions for interlocutory review, requiring the attention of the Courts of Appeals, add, of course, to the burden of work of those courts. Meanwhile final decision of the cases concerned is delayed while the District Courts mark time awaiting action upon the petitions. Rarely does determination upon interlocutory review terminate the litigation. Moreover, the District Court calendars become longer with the addition of new cases before older ones are decided. This, then, interposes one more obstacle to the strong effort being made to better justice through improved judicial administration.

* * *

NOTES

(1) Plaintiff, publisher of an underground newspaper called "The Daily Rag" sued the Postal Service for injunctive relief preventing interference with mail processing of the newspaper. Plaintiff asked the court for an order authorizing non-stenographic recording of several depositions pursuant to Rule 30(b)(4). Upon the district court's refusal, plaintiff moved for a writ of mandamus from the Court of Appeals. Relying heavily on Schlagenhauf v. Holder, 379 U.S. 104, 85 S.Ct. 234, 13 L.Ed.2d 152 (1964), p. 766 supra, the court concluded that "mandamus lies in this case because the issue of discovery is one of first impression and is important to the administration of discovery." See Colonial Times, Inc. v. Gasch, 509 F.2d 517 (D.C.Cir.1975).

(2) Schlagenhauf v. Holder, p. 719, supra, reached the Supreme Court via a writ of certiorari to review the Court of Appeal's denial of a writ of mandamus against the District Court Judge which sought to have set aside the order requiring a physical and mental examination. The court held that because there was a "basic, undecided question" "the Court of Appeals had power to determine all of the issues presented by the petition for mandamus." But the court added as a caveat that:

> "This is not to say, however, that, following the setting of guidelines in this opinion, any further allegation that the District Court was in error in applying these guidelines to a particular case makes mandamus an appropriate remedy. The writ of mandamus is not to be used when 'the most that would be claimed is that the district courts have erred in ruling on matters within their jurisdiction.'" Id. at 112, 85 S.Ct. at 239.

(3) Erie Bank v. United States District Court for District of Colorado, 362 F.2d 539, 540–41, 1 A.L.R.Fed. 811, 814 (10th Cir.1966):

> "The motion to dismiss the counterclaim, filed in the action below by the bank, goes to the jurisdiction of the court to further proceed as to the counterclaim. This court . . . held that in an interpleader suit, where the plaintiff asserts no claim to the interpleaded fund, a counterclaim cannot be asserted by one of the claimants to the fund against the plaintiff because they are not 'opposing parties' within the meaning of Rule 13, F.R.Civ.P. The facts presented here fall squarely within that decision and the bank's motion to dismiss the counterclaim should have been granted. It should also be noted, in support of petitioner's position, that both the bank and National Dental Plan, Inc., are Colorado corporations, so there can be no diversity jurisdiction of the counterclaim in the federal court. To deny the motion to dismiss, allow the parties to exhaust discovery and then permit the bank to renew the motion at the pre-trial conference compels petitioner here to expend time and money on discovery, answer interrogatories uselessly and participate in a pre-trial conference that is unnecessary for the proper disposition of the alleged counterclaim. We believe all of the circumstances presented make this an exceptional case and justifies resort to the prerogative writs."

(3) It may at times be difficult to determine whether the proper mode of review is by mandamus or by interlocutory appeal. In A. Olinick & Sons v. Dempster Brothers, Inc., 365 F.2d 439, 2 A.L.R.Fed. 558 (2d Cir.1966), the court considered this problem in the context of which method could be used to review the disposition of a United States Code, Title 28, § 1404(a) transfer motion for erroneous evaluation of proper factors. After noting a conflict in the circuits, the court held that an interlocutory appeal pursuant to § 1292(b) would be improper because "the correctness of such an evaluation can only with difficulty be described as a 'controlling question of law'; and review of such an evaluation is not likely to advance the termination of the litigation since, even if the evaluation were incorrect, no reviewing court would be likely after a trial on the merits to order a transfer or retransfer for a new trial on the merits." (365 F.2d at 443).

Having concluded that an interlocutory appeal would be improper, the court, after reviewing the case on its merits and finding that the District Court had not abused its discretion, denied the petition for mandamus, stating that mandamus lies "only to redress a clear-cut abuse of discretion." (Id. at 445.)

(5) On procedural aspects of applications for extraordinary writs, see Fed. R.App.P. 21.

(6) What would be a more rational plan for dealing with the finality-appealability problem?

SECTION 5.   CERTIORARI

ROGERS v. MISSOURI PACIFIC RAILROAD

Supreme Court of the United States, 1957.
352 U.S. 500, 77 S.Ct. 443, 1 L.Ed.2d 493.

MR. JUSTICE BRENNAN delivered the opinion of the Court.*

A jury in the Circuit Court of St. Louis awarded damages to the petitioner in this action under the Federal Employers' Liability Act. The Supreme Court of Missouri reversed upon the ground that the petitioner's evidence did not support the finding of respondent's liability. This Court granted certiorari to consider the question whether the decision invaded the jury's function.

[The Court's review of the evidence is omitted.]

We think that the evidence was sufficient to support the jury finding for the petitioner. . . .

The Congress when adopting the law was particularly concerned that the issues whether there was employer fault and whether that fault played any part in the injury or death of the employee should be decided by the jury whenever fair-minded men could reach these conclusions on the evidence. . . .

* Footnotes omitted.

Cognizant of the duty to effectuate the intention of the Congress to secure the right to a jury determination, this Court is vigilant to exercise its power of review in any case where it appears that the litigants have been improperly deprived of that determination. Some say the Act has shortcomings and would prefer a workmen's compensation scheme. The fact that Congress has not seen fit to substitute that scheme cannot relieve this Court of its obligation to effectuate the present congressional intention by granting certiorari to correct instances of improper administration of the Act and to prevent its erosion by narrow and niggardly construction. Similarly, once certiorari is granted, the fact that the case arises under the Federal Employers' Liability Act cannot in any wise justify a failure on our part to afford the litigants the same measure of review on the merits as in every other case.

*   *   *

Reversed.

MR. JUSTICE BURTON concurs in the result.

MR. JUSTICE REED would affirm the judgment of the Supreme Court of Missouri. . . .

MR. JUSTICE FRANKFURTER, dissenting.

*   *   *

At the outset . . . I should deal briefly with a preliminary problem. It is sometimes said that the "integrity of the certiorari process" as expressed in the "rule of four" (that is, this Court's practice of granting certiorari on the vote of four Justices) requires all the Justices to vote on the merits of a case when four Justices have voted to grant certiorari and no new factor emerges after argument and deliberation. There are two reasons why there can be no such requirement. Last Term, for example, the Court disposed of 1,361 petitions for certiorari. With such a volume of certiorari business, not to mention the remainder of the Court's business, the initial decision to grant a petition for certiorari must necessarily be based on a limited appreciation of the issues in a case, resting as it so largely does on the partisan claims in briefs of counsel. [Citations omitted.] The Court does not, indeed it cannot and should not try to, give to the initial question of granting or denying a petition the kind of attention that is demanded by a decision on the merits. The assumption that we know no more after hearing and deliberating on a case than after reading the petition for certiorari and the response is inadmissible in theory and not true in fact. . . . The course of argument and the briefs on the merits may disclose that a case appearing on the surface to warrant a writ of certiorari does not warrant it, [citation omitted] or may reveal more clearly that the only thing in controversy is an appraisal of facts on which this Court is being asked to make a second guess, to substitute its assessment of the testimony for that of the court below.

But there is a more basic reason why the "integrity of the certiorari process" does not require me to vote on the merits of these cases.

The right of a Justice to dissent from an action of the Court is historic. Of course self-restraint should guide the expression of dissent. But dissent is essential to an effective judiciary in a democratic society, and especially for a tribunal exercising the powers of this Court. Not four, not eight, Justices can require another to decide a case that he regards as not properly before the Court. The failure of a Justice to persuade his colleagues does not require him to yield to their views, if he has a deep conviction that the issue is sufficiently important. Moreover, the Court operates ultimately by majority. Even though a minority may bring a case here for oral argument, that does not mean that the majority has given up its right to vote on the ultimate disposition of the case as conscience directs. This is not a novel doctrine. As a matter of practice, members of the Court have at various times exercised this right of refusing to pass on the merits of cases that in their view should not have been granted review.

This does not make the "rule of four" a hollow rule. I would not change the practice. No Justice is likely to vote to dismiss a writ of certiorari as improvidently granted after argument has been heard, even though he has not been convinced that the case is within the rules of the Court governing the granting of certiorari. In the usual instance, a doubting Justice respects the judgment of his brethren that the case does concern issues important enough for the Court's consideration and adjudication. But a different situation is presented when a class of cases is systematically taken for review. Then a Justice who believes that such cases raise insignificant and unimportant questions—insignificant and unimportant from the point of view of the Court's duties—and that an increasing amount of the Court's time is unduly drained by adjudication of these cases cannot forego his duty to voice his dissent to the Court's action.

The "rule of four" is not a command of Congress. It is a working rule devised by the Court as a practical mode of determining that a case is deserving of review, the theory being that if four Justices find that a legal question of general importance is raised, that is ample proof that the question has such importance. This is a fair enough rule of thumb on the assumption that four Justices find such importance on an individualized screening of the cases sought to be reviewed. The reason for deference to a minority view no longer holds when a class of litigation is given a special and privileged position.

* * *

To relieve the Court of this burden of reviewing the large volume of insignificant litigation under the Federal Employers' Liability Act was one of the principal reasons for passage of the Act of September 6, 1916, 39 Stat. 726. [Citations omitted.] In thus freeing the Court from unrestricted access to it of cases that have no business here, Congress assimilated Federal Employers' Liability Act litigation to those other categories of cases—e.g., diversity, patent, admiralty, criminal cases—that Congress had in 1891, 26 Stat. 826, 828, withdrawn from this Court's obligatory jurisdiction. Believing review in the state appellate systems or in the newly created Circuit Courts of Appeals sufficient, it made the lower courts' decisions final also in this class of litigation in all but the unusual cases raising significant legal questions. Thereafter such cases could be reviewed by the Supreme Court only on certiorari to "secure uniformity of decision" between the Circuit Courts of Appeals and "to bring up cases involving questions of importance which it is in the public interest to have decided by this Court of last resort. The jurisdiction was not conferred upon this Court merely to give the defeated party in the Circuit Court of Appeals another hearing. . . . These remarks, of course, apply also to applications for certiorari to review judgments and decrees of the highest courts of States." Magnum Co. v. Coty, 262 U.S. 159, 163–164, 43 S.Ct. 531, 532, 533, 67 L.Ed. 922. (See also Hamilton-Brown Shoe Co. v. Wolf Brothers & Co., 240 U.S. 251, 257–258, 36 S.Ct. 269, 271, 272, 60 L.Ed. 629. Certiorari jurisdiction "is a jurisdiction to be exercised sparingly, and only in cases of peculiar gravity and general importance, or in order to secure uniformity of decision.") The statement for the Court by Mr. Chief Justice Taft in the Coty case indicates the strict criteria governing certiorari policy observed by the Court, except occasionally in FELA cases, previous to the Act of 1925, by which Congress put the Court's docket for all practical purposes in its own keeping. (For a more detailed history of the origin of certiorari jurisdiction, see Frankfurter and Landis, Business of The Supreme Court, cc. II, III, V, and VII.)

The vast extension of discretionary review by the Supreme Court on writ of certiorari contained in the Judges Bill of 1925, 43 Stat. 936, led the Court to promulgate formal rules, and not rely on admonitions in opinions, regarding conditions under which petitions for certiorari would be granted. The present Rule 19 of the Revised Rules of the Supreme Court contains the substance of the original Rule 35(5) of the Revised Rules of 1925, 266 U.S. 645, 681, and perhaps in view of the issue in these cases it is not unwarranted to set forth the full text of that rule:

"1. A review on writ of certiorari is not a matter of right, but of sound judicial discretion, and will be granted only where there are special and important reasons therefor. The following, while neither controlling nor fully measuring the court's discretion, indicate the character of reasons which will be considered:

"(a) Where a state court has decided a federal question of substance not theretofore determined by this court, or has decided it in a way probably not in accord with applicable decisions of this court.

"(b) Where a court of appeals has rendered a decision in conflict with the decision of another court of appeals on the same matter; or has decided an important state or territorial question in a way in conflict with applicable state or territorial law; or has decided an important question of federal law which has not been, but should be, settled by this court; or has decided a federal question in a way in conflict with applicable decisions of this court; or has so far departed from the accepted and usual course of judicial proceedings, or so far sanctioned such a departure by a lower court, as to call for an exercise of this court's power of supervision.

"2. The same general considerations outlined above will control in respect of petitions for writs of certiorari to review judgments of the Court of Claims, of the Court of Customs and Patent Appeals, or of any other court whose determinations are by law reviewable on writ of certiorari."

Of course, cases raising questions that are not evidentiary, questions that fairly involve the construction or scope of the statute are appropriate for review here. [Citations omitted.] But the ordinary negligence case under the Federal Employers' Liability Act does not satisfy the criteria that define the "special and important reasons" when a writ of certiorari will be granted. . . .

. . . [T]he petitioner brought suit for damages, alleging negligence on the part of respondent railroad in providing an unsafe place to work and an unsafe method for doing his work. Petitioner was engaged in burning weeds on respondent's right of way with a hand torch. He heard a whistle indicating an approaching train. He ran thirty to thirty-five yards along the track from the fire and, thinking himself far enough from the fire danger, stood near a drainage culvert watching the passing train for "hotboxes." The train caused the fire to come "right up in [his] face." Petitioner backed away with his arm over his face and fell down the incline of the culvert. There was considerable testimony concerning the circumstances of the accident, the methods of burning weeds, the duties of railroad workers, the condition of the right of way, in particular the condition of the culvert, and petitioner's knowledge of those conditions. Respondent's motions for a directed verdict at the close of petitioner's case and at the close of all the evidence were denied. The case was submitted to the jury, which returned a verdict for petitioner.

On appeal, the Missouri Supreme Court reversed. 284 S.W.2d 467. Considering the evidence from a standpoint most favorable to the petitioner, it held that there was insufficient evidence of negligence on the part of respondent, and that even if there were sufficient evidence of negligence, there was no evidence to show that such negligence contributed to petitioner's injury.

    *   *   *

In all good conscience, what "special and important" reason for granting certiorari do the facts . . . disclose? . . .

In any event, the Court . . . has merely reviewed evidence that has already been reviewed by two lower courts, and in so doing it ignores its own strictures to the bar that "We do not grant a certiorari to review evidence and discuss specific facts." United States v. Johnston, 268 U.S. 220, 227, 45 S.Ct. 496, 497, 69 L.Ed. 925. [Citations omitted.] Constant complaints have been made by successive Chief Justices about the large number of frivolous petitions that are filed each Term, "frivolous" meaning that the issues are not deserving of consideration for review when judged by the Court's instructions to the bar. See the remarks of Chief Justice Taft, in 35 Yale L.J. 1, 3–4; Chief Justice Hughes, in 20 A.B.A.J. 341; Chief Justice Vinson, in 69 S.Ct. V, VI–VII. If the Court does not abide by its Rules, how can it expect the bar to do so? Standards must be enforced to be respected. If they are merely left as something on paper, they might as well be written on water.

* * *

. . . Finally, one cannot acquit the encouragement given by this Court for seeking success in the lottery of obtaining heavy verdicts of contributing to the continuance of this system of compensation whose essential injustice can hardly be alleviated by the occasional "correction" in this Court of ill-success.

* * *

The Court finds justification for granting certiorari in an alleged conflict of these decisions of the Courts of Appeals for the Second, Sixth, and Seventh Circuits and the Supreme Court of Missouri with the applicable decisions of this Court. All that can fairly be said is that these courts found that there was not evidence to bring these cases within the recognized rules for submitting a case to the jury. In none of them is there any intimation or atmospheric indication of unwillingness to enforce the governing rules of the Act as laid down by this Court. These rules are well known. That there should be differences of opinion in their application is almost inevitable. But once Congress in 1916 commanded that the ordinary Federal Employers' Liability Act case, like other essentially private litigation, should reach a final decision in the Courts of Appeals or the state appellate tribunals, this Court should never have granted certiorari to assess the evidence in any of them. I would not continue a bad practice to aid a few plaintiffs because there was once a bad practice that aided a few defendants. One still does not commit two wrongs to "do right."

This is not the supreme court of review for every case decided "unjustly" by every court in the country. The Court's practice in taking these Federal Employers' Liability Act cases discriminates against other personal injury cases, for example those in the federal courts on diversity jurisdiction. Similar questions of negligence are involved there and the opportunity for swallowing up more of the Supreme Court's energy is very great indeed. While 1,332 cases were commenced under the Federal Employers' Liability Act in the Federal District Courts in the fiscal year 1956 and 2,392 cases under the Jones Act, 11,427 personal injury cases were begun under the diversity jurisdiction in the District Courts. Annual Report of the Director of the Administrative Office of the United States Courts—1956, pp. 52–53.

The Court may well have had this discrimination in mind when it granted certiorari in the diversity case of Gibson v. Phillips Petroleum Co., 352 U.S. 874, 77 S.Ct. 16, 1 L.Ed.2d 77, and decided it on the merits. A few more such decisions and a flood of petitions from this source may confidently be expected. Whether or not it be true that we are a litigious people, it is a matter of experience that clients, if not lawyers, have a strong urge to exhaust all possibility of further appeal, particularly when judicially encouraged to do so. Disappointed litigants and losing lawyers like to have another go at it, and why should they not try when certiorari was granted in cases like these?

*   *   *

. . . And experience leaves no doubt, though the fact cannot be established statistically, that by granting review in these cases, the Court encourages the filing of petitions for certiorari in other types of cases raising issues that likewise have no business to be brought here. Moreover, the considerations governing discharge of the Court's function involve only in part quantitative factors. Finally, and most important, granting review in one or two cases that present a compassionate appeal on this ground and one or two that present a compassionate appeal on that ground and one or two that present a compassionate appeal on a third ground inevitably makes that drain upon the available energy of the Court that is so inimical to the fullest investigation of, the amplest deliberation on, the most effective opinion-writing and the most critical examination of draft opinions in, the cases that have unquestioned claims upon the Court.

*   *   *

It is, I believe, wholly accurate to say that the Court will be enabled to discharge adequately the vital, and, I feel, the increasingly vital, responsibility it bears for the general welfare only if it restricts its reviewing power to the adjudication of constitutional issues or other questions of national importance, including therein settlement of conflict among the circuits. Surely it was this conviction, born of experience, that led the Court to ask of Congress that of the great mass of litigation in the state and federal courts only those cases should be allowed to be brought here that this Court deemed fit for review. Such was the jurisdictional policy accepted by Congress when it yielded to the Court's realization of the conditions necessary for its proper functioning.

*   *   *

The judgments of this Court are collective judgments. Such judgments are especially dependent on ample time for private study and reflection in preparation for discussion in Conference. Without adequate study, there cannot be adequate reflection; without adequate reflection, there cannot be adequate discussion; without adequate discussion, there cannot be that full and fruitful interchange of minds that is indispensable to wise decisions and persuasive opinions by the Court. Unless the Court vigorously enforces its own criteria for granting review of cases, it will inevitably face an accumulation of arrears or will dispose of its essential business in too hurried and therefore too shallow a way.

I would dismiss all four writs of certiorari as improvidently granted.

[Opinion of Mr. Justice Harlan omitted.]

NOTES

(1) The juxtaposition of the rule-of-four for granting certiorari with the five votes required on the merits results in some peculiar situations, for five justices can sometimes use their merit votes to summarily decide cases to which the other four would accord plenary review. See Revesz and Karlan, Nonmajority Rules and the Supreme Court, 136 U.Pa.L.Rev. 1067 (1988). See also Harlan, Manning the Dikes: Some Comments on Statutory Certiorari Jurisdiction and Jurisdictional Statement Practice of the Supreme Court of the United States, 13 The Record of the Assoc. of the Bar 541 (1958); Brown, Process of Law, Foreword to the Supreme Court 1957 Term 77, 78–79 (1958); Leiman, The Rule of Four, 57 Colum.L.Rev. 975 (1957); Note, Certiorari Policy in Cases Arising Under the FELA, 69 Harv.L.Rev. 1441 (1956).

(2) In 1988, Congress responded to the Supreme Court's docket crisis by substantially eliminating its mandatory jurisdiction. Before passage of P.L. 100–352, 102 Stat. 662, the Supreme Court was required to review all decisions of highest state courts when federal law was invalidated or state law upheld against constitutional challenges. In addition, the Supreme Court was required to review federal decisions that invalidated state statutes on federal grounds. Both provisions were motivated by a concern for structural bias: that state courts would have less sympathy for federal law than the Constitution contemplates and that federal courts would treat state law with less deference than is constitutionally required. On the theory that these structural concerns are less problematic in the modern era, Congress made review in both situations (and in some others) discretionary with the Supreme Court.

RULES GOVERNING THE NEW JERSEY COURTS (1989)

2:12–1. Certification on Motion of the Supreme Court

The Supreme Court may on its own motion certify any action or class of actions for appeal.

2:12–2. Certification of Appeals Pending Unheard in Appellate Division

(a) Filing and Service of Motion. A motion for certification of an appeal pending unheard in the Appellate Division shall be served and filed with the Supreme Court and the Appellate Division within 10 days after the filing of all briefs with the Appellate Division. . . .

2:12–4. Grounds for Certification

Certification will be granted only if the appeal presents a question of general public importance which has not been but should be settled by the Supreme Court or is similar to a question presented on another appeal to the Supreme Court; if the decision under review is in conflict with any other decision of the same or a higher court or calls for an exercise of the Supreme Court's supervision and in other matters if the interests of justice requires. Certification will not be allowed on final judgments of the Appellate Division except for special reasons.

RULES OF THE SUPREME COURT OF THE UNITED STATES

Rule 11

CERTIORARI TO A UNITED STATES COURT OF APPEALS BEFORE JUDGMENT

A petition for a writ of certiorari to review a case pending in a United States court of appeals, before judgment is given in that court, will be granted only upon a showing that the case is of such imperative public importance as to justify deviation from the normal appellate practice and to require immediate settlement in this Court.

Examples of cases reviewed prior to judgment include Youngstown Sheet & Tube Co. v. Sawyer, 343 U.S. 579, 72 S.Ct. 863, 96 L.Ed. 1153 (1952) (which reviewed President Truman's decision to take over the Nation's steel mills during the Korean War) and United States v. Nixon, 418 U.S. 683, 94 S.Ct. 3090, 41 L.Ed.2d 1039 (1974) (which considered the President's duty to obey a subpoena for tape recordings made in the Executive Office).

NEW YORK STATE CONSTITUTION, ARTICLE VI

§ 3. a. The jurisdiction of the court of appeals shall be limited to the review of questions of law except where the judgment is of death, or where the appellate division, on reversing or modifying a final or interlocutory judgment in an action or a final or interlocutory order in a special proceeding, finds new facts and a final judgment or a final order pursuant thereto is entered; but the right to appeal shall not depend upon the amount involved.

b. Appeals to the court of appeals may be taken in the classes of cases hereafter enumerated in this section;

* * *

In civil cases and proceedings as follows:

(1) As of right, from a judgment or order entered upon the decision of an appellate division of the supreme court which finally determines an action or special proceeding wherein is directly involved the construction of the constitution of the state or of the United States, or where one or more of the justices of the appellate division dissents from the decision of the court, or where the judgment or order is one of reversal or modification.

(2) As of right, from a judgment or order of a court of record of original jurisdiction which finally determines an action or special proceeding where the only question involved on the appeal is the validity of a statutory provision of the state or of the United States under the constitution of the state or of the United States; and on any such appeal only the constitutional question shall be considered and determined by the court.

(3) As of right, from an order of the appellate division granting a new trial in an action or a new hearing in a special proceeding where the appellant stipulates that, upon affirmance, judgment absolute or final order shall be rendered against him.

(4) From a determination of the appellate division of the supreme court in any department, other than a judgment or order which finally determines an action or special proceeding, where the appellate division allows the same and certifies that one or more questions of law have arisen which, in its opinion, ought to be reviewed by the court of appeals, but in such case the appeal shall bring up for review only the question or questions so certified; and the court of appeals shall certify to the appellate division its determination upon such question or questions.

* * *

(6) From a judgment or order entered upon the decision of an appellate division of the supreme court which finally determines an action or special proceeding but which is not appealable under paragraph (1) of this subdivision where the appellate division or the court of appeals shall certify that in its opinion a question of law is involved which ought to be reviewed by the court of appeals. Such an appeal may be allowed upon application (a) to the appellate division, and in case of refusal, to the court of appeals, or (b) directly to the court of appeals. Such an appeal shall be allowed when required in the interest of substantial justice.

* * *

(8) The legislature may abolish an appeal to the court of appeals as of right in any or all of the cases or classes of cases specified in paragraph (1) of this subdivision wherein no question involving the construction of the constitution of the state or of the United States is directly involved, provided, however, that appeals in any such case or class of cases shall thereupon be governed by paragraph (6) of this subdivision.

NOTES

(1) Speaking of the easy standards for appealing to the Court of Appeals, a 1982 study concluded:

(1) Successive or "double" appeals are prosecuted too frequently because the standards for appealing as a matter of right are too easy and lax. The result is frequent waste of two kinds.

First, no particular benefit enures to the public from double-appeal practice. Many of the appeals of right to the Court of Appeals are merely reruns of the Appellate Division appeal. The appellant makes no claim that the appeal will have broader social significance than correcting an error in the adverse judgment. Such appeals—and they are common—do not present the Court of Appeals with any opportunity to advance its chief function of law-declaring.

Second, from the perspective of the Court of Appeals, the high volume of obligatory appeals (approximately 75% of its caseload) has the effect of substantially restricting the number of appeals it can choose to hear. Undoubtedly, the Court (whose caseload exceeds that of all but one or two courts of last resort) is obliged to forego review in some cases that would involve the law-declaring function in a significant way.

The Court of Appeals' institutional review function is distorted by the provisions of law that prevent it from controlling its own docket. The larger part of its workload comes to it, either by categorical provisions according litigants a mandatory right of appeal in a wide range of circumstances, or by the dispensation of the Appellate Division or individual judges of that court. We believe the Court of Appeals should be given much broader control of its docket, as is commonly the prerogative of courts of last resort throughout the country where there is an intermediate appellate court in the jurisdiction.

(2) While urging that the control of the Court of Appeals over its own docket should be enlarged we suggest that the standards by which it exercises its control be made more predictable. To do this effectively, the decisive factors or criteria in passing on motions for leave to appeal need to be made more explicit and more prominent.

See R. MacCrate, J. Hopkins and M. Rosenberg, Appellate Justice in New York 10–11.

(2) Am.Jud.Soc'y, Solutions for Appellate Court Congestion and Delay: Analysis and Bibliography 14–15 (1963):

"Some cases which are within the final jurisdiction of the intermediate court and which are not appealable as a matter of right to the highest court, may, nevertheless, be subject to review by the highest court on certiorari, or writ of error from the highest court or on certification from the intermediate court. Such provision is commonly made for the following types of cases: cases in which members of the intermediate court do not arrive at a unanimous decision; cases where two intermediate courts are in conflict on the same question of law; cases where a new question of law is decided erroneously by the intermediate court; and cases where the second appeal is deemed necessary in the discretion of either court.

*   *   *

"There are two important problems with the tri-level judiciary. One is the problem of uniformity of the application of law by intermediate courts which sit in several districts of a state. Of course discretionary review by the highest court is a guard against inconsistent applications of law, but the discretionary review also produces multiple appeals and increased litigation, the initial problem which intermediate courts were designed to solve. Second there is the problem of increased litigation on questions of jurisdiction between the two appellate courts."

(3) Note that Rule 38 of the Federal Rules of Appellate Procedure provides for damages for delay and that Rule 39 gives the court some discretion in awarding costs. Neither of these rules, however, has had significant effect in limiting appeals.

SECTION 6. SCOPE OF REVIEW

STURM v. CHICAGO & NORTH WESTERN RAILROAD

United States Court of Appeals, Eighth Circuit, 1946.
157 F.2d 407.

PER CURIAM. Gustav C. Sturm (who will be referred to as plaintiff), while employed by the defendant Railway Company (appellee) as a brakeman in Chicago, Illinois, fell from the top of a box car and was injured. He brought this action under the Federal Employers' Liability Act, 45 U.S.C.A. §§ 51–60, to recover damages for his injuries. In his complaint the plaintiff charged that the Railway Company was negligent in failing to equip the car from which he fell with an efficient hand brake as required by the Federal Safety Appliance Act of 1910, § 2, 45 U.S.C.A. § 11, and that his injuries were the proximate result of such negligence. The Railway Company denied that the brake was inefficient and that its alleged failure to operate properly caused the plaintiff's injuries. The issues were tried to a jury. The evidence of the plaintiff tended to prove that the brake was inefficient and inoperative and that his injuries were due to its failure to operate. The evidence of the defendant tended to show that the brake was efficient and that the plaintiff's injuries could not have resulted from a defect in the brake. Neither party moved for a directed verdict at the close of the evidence. The issues were submitted to the jury. There were no requests for instructions. No exceptions were taken to the trial court's charge. The jury returned a verdict for the defendant, upon which a judgment was entered. The plaintiff has appealed from the judgment.

It is obvious that this appeal presents no question which is reviewable by this court. No ruling of the trial court is challenged. The question of the sufficiency of the evidence to support the verdict is not subject to review, since that question was not presented to the trial court by a motion for a directed verdict or any other equivalent action. Emanuel v. Kansas City Title & Trust Co., 8 Cir., 127 F.2d 175, 176, and cases cited. This court is without power to retry this case. It cannot concern itself with the credibility of witnesses or the weight of evidence. Booth v. Gilbert, 8 Cir., 79 F.2d 790, 792, 793; Elzig v. Gudwangen, 8 Cir., 91 F.2d 434, 444; Dierks Lumber & Coal Co. v. Mabry, 8 Cir., 128 F.2d 1005, 1007; Tennant v. Peoria & P.U. Ry. Co., 321 U.S. 29, 35, 64

S.Ct. 409, 88 L.Ed. 520. The verdict of the jury, whether right or wrong, was completely determinative of the issues of fact tried and submitted.

The judgment is affirmed.

HEWLETT ARCADE v. FIVE TOWNS REFRIGERATION CORP.

Supreme Court of New York, Appellate Division, Second Department, 1957.
3 A.D.2d 728, 159 N.Y.S.2d 771.

MEMORANDUM BY THE COURT. Action in the County Court, Nassau County, by the owner of a building to recover damages for injuries to the building, alleged to have been caused by the explosion of an oil burner therein, against Eugene J. Brandt & Co., Inc., which had contracted with the owner to service the oil burning equipment in the building, and Five Towns Refrigeration Corp., which had been employed by Brandt to service said equipment. Brandt served a cross complaint on Five Towns for judgment over. The jury rendered a verdict in favor of the owner, Hewlett Arcade, Inc., against Brandt, in favor of Five Towns against Hewlett, and in favor of Five Towns against Brandt on its cross complaint. Brandt appeals from the judgment entered thereon.

Appeal from judgment insofar as it is in favor of respondent Five Towns against respondent Hewlett dismissed, without costs.

As to such portion of the judgment, Brandt has no right to appeal. Ward v. Iroquois Gas Corp., 258 N.Y. 124, 179 N.E. 317; Leider v. Gramatan Associates, 272 App.Div. 947, 72 N.Y.S.2d 19. Consequently, in the absence of an appeal by Hewlett from such portion, we have no alternative but to allow it to stand.

Judgment, insofar as it is in favor of respondent Hewlett against appellant, Brandt, and insofar as it is in favor of respondent Five Towns against appellant, reversed and a new trial ordered between respondent Hewlett and appellant on the complaint, and between appellant and respondent Five Towns on the cross complaint, with costs to abide the event.

The trial court instructed the jury that they might find liability against either appellant or respondent Five Towns, or against both of them. Under the circumstances here such charge was erroneous. The resulting exoneration from liability of respondent Five Towns is inconsistent with the resulting imposition of liability upon its co-defendant, the appellant herein. If the repair work was improperly performed, the ultimate and primary responsibility was obviously that of respondent Five Towns, which actually did the work under its contract with appellant, and appellant's liability was secondary or derivative, cf. Pangburn v. Buick Motor Co., 211 N.Y. 228.

However, that question was not preserved for review since there was no exception to the charge, which consequently became the law of the case. The trial court did charge, however, that in order to recover against appellant, respondent Hewlett was required to prove a failure on appellant's part to use the care required by law, or to do what a reasonably prudent person would do under the circumstances. Such a finding, implicit in the verdict, has no support in the evidence. If appellant is liable to respondent Hewlett, it may only be so held on the theory that it had assumed, by its contract with that respondent, a personal and nondelegable duty to service and keep in repair the oil burner, which duty could not be discharged by delegating it to an independent contractor. See May v. 11½ East 49th Street Co., 269 App. Div. 180, 182, 54 N.Y.S.2d 860, 862; Blumenthal v. Prescott, 70 App. Div. 560, 75 N.Y.S. 710; Paltey v. Egan, 200 N.Y. 83, 91, 93 N.E. 267, 269. No such theory of liability was submitted to the jury.

The new trial is ordered for the purpose of determining appellant's liability to respondent Hewlett under the contract between them, and for the purpose of determining the liability of respondent Five Towns to appellant under the contract between them, in the event that appellant be held liable to respondent Hewlett.

For the purposes of the new trial only, all findings of fact implicit in the jury's verdict are reversed.

NOTES

(1) The problem of preserving the trial court's ruling for appellate review by a timely and proper objection has recurred in this book. See, e.g., Palmer v. Hoffman, p. 845, Note (6), supra; Federal Rules of Evidence, p. 1097, infra.

(2) On the other hand, not every incorrect ruling below will result in reversal because of the doctrine of "harmless error." See, e.g., Fuentes v. Tucker, p. 607, supra; cf. Fed.R.Civ.P. 61. See 28 U.S.C.A. § 2111.

(3) See Sunderland, A Simplified System of Appellate Procedure, 17 Tenn. L.Rev. 651, 658–661 (1943), suggesting abandonment of "The notion that assignment of error constitutes the jurisdictional foundation for the appeal in the same sense that pleadings constitute the jurisdictional basis of the proceedings below."

MILLER v. AVIROM

United States Court of Appeals, District of Columbia Circuit, 1967.
384 F.2d 319.*

SPOTTSWOOD W. ROBINSON, III, CIRCUIT JUDGE. Appellee, a licensed real estate broker, sued appellant in the District Court for a commission allegedly earned by appellee's negotiation of an offer, which appellant refused to accept, for the purchase of an apartment building. The District Judge, sitting without a jury, entered a judgment in appellee's favor on findings that appellant had orally listed the proper-

* Footnotes omitted.

ty with appellee for sale on specified terms and for an agreed commission, and that appellee had produced a purchaser ready, able and willing to buy on the conditions so established.

Appellant resisted the action in the District Court principally on the ground that he never authorized appellee's activities, but also asserted the statute of frauds defensively. The case as submitted to us tenders two claims of error, one contesting the sufficiency of the proof to support the finding that the prospective purchaser was financially able to consummate his offer. We have scrutinized the evidence and, the standard for our review considered, are satisfied that the finding should not be disturbed.

Appellant's second and main argument on appeal is that the arrangements for the sale and payment of a commission were void because they were made orally. He directs our attention in this connection to provisions in the statute regulating the licensing of real estate brokers and salesmen. As appellant reads them, the offering of realty for sale without the written consent of the owner or his authorized agent is both a ground for suspension or revocation of a license and an occasion for initiation of a criminal prosecution. On this analysis appellant insists that an oral sale listing is illegal, and cannot provide the basis for recovery of a commission.

Other courts in this jurisdiction have considered the legislation to which appellant adverts too restricted in its reach to achieve this result, but we have not ourselves previously had occasion to measure the statute's impact upon the problem. By our current appraisal, the question appellant poses is sufficiently substantial to command serious attention if properly presented for our decision. But because the issue was neither raised nor decided in the District Court, we do not address it on this appeal or intimate any view as to how it should be resolved.

In our jurisprudential system, trial and appellate processes are synchronized in contemplation that review will normally be confined to matters appropriately submitted for determination in the court of first resort. Questions not properly raised and preserved during the proceedings under examination, and points not asserted with sufficient precision to indicate distinctly the party's thesis, will normally be spurned on appeal. Canons of this tenor reflect, not obeisance to ritual, but "considerations of fairness to the court and the parties and of the public interest in bringing litigation to an end after fair opportunity has been afforded to present all issues of law and fact." The injunction that trial ventilation precede appellate exploration best subserves that policy without appreciable imposition upon the litigants. "It requires them to deal fairly and frankly with each other and with the trial tribunal with respect to their controversies. It prevents the trial of cases piecemeal or in installments. It tends to put an end to litigation." We think that sound judicial administration embraces importantly the elimination of expenditures of time and energy—by parties as well as courts—incidental to potentially unnecessary appeals.

Appellant nowhere claimed that the licensing statute was involved until the litigation reached this court. Previously represented by different counsel, he did not advance that proposition in his pleadings or when the case was heard on the merits, nor are such singular omissions explained. Certainly appellant's secondary reliance upon the statute of frauds did not define for the District Court's decision the far-reaching contention his present approach incorporates. And it is settled that judicial action sought on one ground at trial does not suffice to enable a party to invoke another on appeal.

Sometimes even the salutary principle under discussion must give way in peculiar circumstances, but this is a course to be pursued sparingly and only in exceptional situations. Appellant has brought to our attention nothing to distinguish this case from a host of others in which that principle was conventionally applied. The dispensation appellant would have us grant "is a right to prevent a clear miscarriage of justice apparent from the record, and not a right to afford a defeated litigant another day in court because he thinks that if he were given the opportunity to try his case again upon a different theory he might prevail."

Affirmed.

NOTES

(1) "To say that appellate courts must decide between two constructions proffered by the parties, no matter how erroneous both may be, would be to render automatons of judges, forcing them merely to register their reactions to the arguments of counsel at the trial level. It is quite true that an appellate court should not, and will not, consider different theories or new questions, if proof might have been offered to refute or overcome them had they been presented at the trial . . . Here, the issue involved the meaning of the written contract between the parties. The writing was in the record; each party had full opportunity to adduce all pertinent evidence bearing on its construction; and there is no claim or suggestion that either party would or could have offered any further evidence. In that state of the record the Appellate Division was not limited to a choice between the opposing constructions contended for, at the trial . . ." Rentways, Inc. v. O'Neill Milk & Cream Co., 308 N.Y. 342, 349, 126 N.E.2d 271, 274, (1955).

(3) Even when its rules permit a court to notice "plain error" on the record, if the aggrieved party deliberately chooses to disregard the error, so may the court. Barr v. Mateo, 100 U.S.App.D.C. 319, 244 F.2d 767 (1957).

(4) "[A]ppeals have to be taken from final judgments, not from judicial rationales. And court judgments may of course be supported by sound judicial argumentation—or not at all if they are legally correct. Judges have at least the solace of knowing that only judicial deeds—not judicial words—may constitute legal error." Cook v. Hirschberg, 258 F.2d 56, 57 (2d Cir.1958) (Clark, J.). Consistent with this theory, the Supreme Court has held "[T]he appellee may, without taking a cross-appeal, urge in support of a decree any matter appearing in the record, although his argument may involve an attack upon the reasoning of the lower court or an insistence upon a matter overlooked or ignored by it."

United States v. American Railway Express Co., 265 U.S. 425, 435, 44 S.Ct. 560, 564, 68 L.Ed. 1087 (1924).

(5) Does violation of a state pleading rule requiring reference to specific sections of a statute challenged as unconstitutional prevent an appellate court from deciding that the entire statute is invalid on its face? See Staub v. City of Baxley, 355 U.S. 313, 78 S.Ct. 277, 2 L.Ed.2d 302 (1958).

SANTOSKY v. KRAMER
Supra, p. 845.

RULES OF EVIDENCE FOR UNITED STATES COURTS AND MAGISTRATES 1975

Rule 103. Rulings on Evidence

(a) **Effect of Erroneous Ruling.** Error may not be predicated upon a ruling which admits or excludes evidence, unless a substantial right of the party is affected, and

(1) **Objection.** In case the ruling is one admitting evidence, a timely objection or motion to strike appears of record, stating the specific ground of objection; or

(2) **Offer of Proof.** In case the ruling is one excluding evidence, the substance of the evidence was made known to the court by offer or was apparent from the context within which questions were asked.

(b) **Record of Offer and Ruling.** The court may add any other or further statement which shows the character of the evidence, the form in which it was offered, the objection made, and the ruling thereon. It may direct the making of an offer in question and answer form.

(c) **Hearing of Jury.** In jury cases, proceedings shall be conducted, to the extent practicable, so as to prevent inadmissible evidence from being suggested to the jury by any means, such as making statements or offers of proof or asking questions in the hearing of the jury.

(d) **Plain Error.** Nothing in this rule precludes taking notice of plain errors affecting substantial rights although they were not brought to the attention of the court.

McKELVY v. BARBER
Supreme Court of Texas, 1964.
381 S.W.2d 59.

WALKER, JUSTICE. Our opinion delivered in this cause on March 4, 1964, is withdrawn and the following is substituted therefor:

Jim C. McKelvy, petitioner, brought this suit against Dr. Forrest C. Barber, respondent, to recover damages alleged to have resulted from negligent medical treatment. Respondent's motion for instructed verdict at the conclusion of all the evidence was granted by the trial court, and the Court of Civil Appeals affirmed. 368 S.W.2d 38. As the case reaches us, the appeal presents two procedural problems and two questions of substantive law. We have concluded that respondent was not entitled to a peremptory instruction on any of the grounds asserted in his motion, and the cause will be remanded for a new trial.

Petitioner injured his finger in the course of his employment by American Manufacturing Company. He was taken by the Personnel Director to the office of respondent, who treated the injury. Petitioner later developed tetanus and was totally and permanently disabled at the time of trial. He settled with Pacific Employers Insurance Company, the compensation carrier for American, prior to the institution of this suit.

While respondent's motion for instructed verdict contains twenty numbered paragraphs, it actually asserts two basic and independent grounds for granting a peremptory instruction in his favor. These are: (1) that there is no evidence to support a finding that the tetanus was proximately caused by any negligence on respondent's part; and (2) that since the undisputed evidence shows that respondent was acting as the agent, servant or employee of American and its compensation carrier in treating petitioner, he is immune from liability by virtue of the provisions of Article 8306, § 3, Vernon's Ann.Tex.Civ.Stat. The judgment of the trial court merely recites that specific grounds were set forth in the motion for instructed verdict, and that the court was of the opinion that the motion was well taken and should be granted. To reverse the judgment of the trial court under these circumstances, it was necessary for petitioner to assume the appellate burden of establishing that the peremptory instruction cannot be supported on either of the grounds set out in the motion. If he has waived the right to question either of such grounds or if either is sound, the judgment of the trial court must be affirmed.

Petitioner was not required to file a motion for new trial as a prerequisite to an appellate attack on the action of the trial court in granting a peremptory instruction. Rule 324, Texas Rules of Civil Procedure. His brief as appellant in the Court of Civil Appeals contains three points of error which assert that there is evidence to support findings that the tetanus was proximately caused by respondent's negligence. Since he did not have a point of error complaining of the action of the trial court in sustaining the motion for instructed verdict on the second ground mentioned above, respondent says that petitioner has waived any complaint he might have had with respect thereto. We do not agree.

[The Court points out that the Court of Civil Appeals affirmed on an invalid ground without considering the grounds warranting reversal.]

*   *   *

A careful and seasoned appellate practitioner would have included in his application for writ of error a point asserting that the Court of Civil Appeals erred in failing to consider and sustain the points of error dealing with negligence and causation. Respondent says, in effect, that the failure to do so here requires us to affirm the judgment of the trial court no matter how erroneous it may be. That approach might save the Supreme Court some time, but it is also calculated to entrap the inexperienced appellate advocate. The attack in this Court is upon the judgment of the Court of Civil Appeals. That judgment rests squarely upon a single holding, which has been brought forward for review. When it is determined, as we have in this instance, that the conclusion reached by the intermediate court is unsound, it would certainly be proper to remand the cause to that court for a ruling on the points of error not previously considered by it. Since these points present only law questions, however, we can and do dispose of them now instead of requiring the parties to go back to the Court of Civil Appeals and then possibly return here with a second application for writ of error. In our opinion the evidence raises issues of negligence and causation that can be resolved only by the trier of fact, and the trial court erred in granting respondents' motion for instructed verdict.

In Jecker v. Western Alliance Ins. Co., Tex.Sup., 369 S.W.2d 776, and Rogers v. Winters, 161 Tex. 451, 341 S.W.2d 417, the Court of Civil Appeals reversed and rendered judgment for the appellant. After concluding that the holding of the intermediate court on the question considered by it was unsound, we refused to pass on other points of the appellant in that court which might have entitled the appellant to a reversal and remand or modification of the trial court's judgment. It was reasoned that such complaints would, if sustained, result in an alteration of the judgment of the Court of Civil Appeals, and therefore could not be considered unless brought to this Court by crosspoint. These holdings of Jecker and Rogers . . . will not be followed in the future.

The judgments of the courts below are reversed, and the cause is remanded to the district court for a new trial.

NOTES

(1) In Parker v. Washington, 421 P.2d 861 (Okl.1966), the court reversed a long line of previous cases to hold that it need not confine its review to the specific reasons assigned by the trial court in granting a new trial but instead could review the entire record and, rather than reversing if the trial court had erred in its reasoning, could affirm on other grounds.

(2) In Home Indemnity Co. v. Reynolds & Co., 38 Ill.App.2d 358, 187 N.E.2d 274, 277, 278 (1st Dist.1962), the court was faced with the problem of whether "a party, whose motion for summary judgment is denied, [has] the right to have the denial of that motion reviewed after the case goes to trial and a verdict is returned against it." The motion had not been reviewable immediately because of the final judgment rule in Illinois. The court concluded that even if

the motion had been improperly denied it could not be reviewed. Pointing out that the evidence at the time of the motion and at the time of the trial differed, the court noted that if the judgment were set aside "a decision based on less evidence would prevail over a verdict reached on more evidence and judgment would be taken away from the victor and given to the loser despite the victor having the greater weight of evidence."

(3) Hurwitz v. Directors Guild of America, Inc., 364 F.2d 67, 69–70 (2d Cir. 1966):

> "This appeal reaches us in a curious posture. The plaintiffs' motion for a preliminary injunction is moot to the extent that it sought to interfere with the DGA elections completed in September 1965. However, the plaintiffs also requested a mandatory preliminary injunction compelling DGA to admit them to membership in the surviving union *pendente lite*. The district court's denial of this portion of plaintiff's motion is not moot, since plaintiffs have continued to refuse to sign the oath and DGA has contrived to refuse them membership.

> "As it is our opinion that the DGA loyalty oath is *per se* an unreasonable requirement for union membership, an initial question is whether this court may go beyond review of the denial of a preliminary injunction and direct entry of a judgment for plaintiff on the merits.

> ". . . As a general rule, when an appeal is taken from the grant or denial of a preliminary injunction, the reviewing court will go no further into the merits than is necessary to decide the interlocutory appeal . . . However, this rule is subject to a general exception—the appellate court may dismiss the complaint on the merits if its examination of the record upon an interlocutory appeal reveals that the case is entirely void of merit . . .

> "Such an exception serves the obvious interest of economy of litigation, and this interest is equally served if the appellate court directs a verdict for plaintiff in an appropriate case. We have found no case reaching this result, but this is not surprising since it is the rare case that contains no triable issue of fact, and it is rarer still that this would result in a judgment for the plaintiff at the pre-trial stage . . . Finding no reason why the cautious exercise of such a power would be undesirable, we conclude that we may direct the entry of a judgment for the plaintiffs here."

(4) One difficult problem for the appellate court is how far it should go by way of dictum to point out to the trial court, when a trial is necessary, various rules that may prevent further errors and retrials. A recent interesting example is Nader v. General Motors Corp., 25 N.Y.2d 560, 307 N.Y.S.2d 647, 255 N.E.2d 765 (1970). Do you agree with the majority opinion or with the concurrence? What position would you prefer if you were a litigant, a trial judge, a taxpayer paying for the court system? Would your judgment in this case be affected by the fact that the Court of Appeals of New York is predicting what the courts of the District of Columbia will hold is the law of their district?

(5) Fed.R.Civ.P. 52(a) sets forth the scope of review in federal courts. Until 1985, the second sentence read: "Findings of fact shall not be set aside unless clearly erroneous, and due regard shall be given to the opportunity of the trial court to judge the credibility of witnesses." The major thrust of the provision was to distinguish between legal issues, which are reviewable without deference to the district court, and factual findings, which can be set aside only in special

circumstances. However, some courts took the sentence to mean that factual findings based on evidence other than live witnesses—i.e., documents—should be accorded the same plenary review given to legal conclusions. The theory was that the trial court is in a better position than the appellate court to determine credibility, so its decisions on oral testimony should not usually be disturbed, but that the appellate court is just as able as the trial court to evaluate documents, and accordingly should have the authority to reject the trial court's decision. See generally Lundgren v. Freeman, 307 F.2d 104 (9th Cir.1962). In 1985, the sentence was revised to make clear that factual findings based on both oral and documentary evidence are accorded the same scope of review. The Supreme Court has been firm in its commitment to Rule 52(a). See, e.g., Pullman–Standard, Inc. v. Swint, 456 U.S. 273, 102 S.Ct. 1781, 72 L.Ed. 2d 66 (1982).

(6) Congress has created a few specialized courts to deal with highly technical matters such as tax and patent law. In part, the decision to create these courts was motivated by the desire to relieve docket pressure in the regional circuits; in part, by a desire to capture the benefits of expertise. Should Rule 52(a) apply when a specialized appellate court reviews the factual findings of a generalist district court? See Dennison Manufacturing Co. v. Panduit Corp., 475 U.S. 809, 106 S.Ct. 1578, 89 L.Ed.2d 817 (1986) (the Court of Appeals for the Federal Circuit, which has exclusive jurisdiction over cases arising under the patent laws, must apply Rule 52(a) to the factual decisions of the regional district courts). If the allocation of responsibility in Rule 52(a) stems from a perception about the relative competence of the trial and appellate courts, does Rule 52(a) make sense in this context? See Dreyfuss, The Federal Circuit: A Case Study in Specialized Courts, 64 N.Y.U. L.Rev. 1 (1989).

(7) On the difference in scope of review on appeal from a judge's decision compared to a jury verdict, see Brochin and Sandler, Appellate Review of Facts in New Jersey, Jury and Non-Jury Cases, 12 Rut.L.Rev. 482 (1958); see also Note, Proof of the Law of Foreign Countries: Appellate Review and Subsequent Litigation, 72 Harv.L.Rev. 318 (1958); 7 Weinstein, Korn & Miller, New York Civil Practice, ¶¶ 5501.19–5501.22.

(8) The difficult problem of enunciating the proper standard in judicial review of administrative action lies beyond the scope of this course. See generally Jaffee, Judicial Control of Administrative Action, chs. 14–16 (1965); 4 Davis, Administrative Law Treatise, ch. 23 (1983).

SECTION 7. REHEARING

UNITED STATES v. OHIO POWER CO.
Supreme Court of the United States, 1957.
353 U.S. 98, 77 S.Ct. 652, 1 L.Ed.2d 683.

PER CURIAM. On June 11, 1956, we unanimously vacated *sua sponte* our order of December 5, 1955, (350 U.S. 919, 76 S.Ct. 192, 100 L.Ed. 805) denying the timely petition for rehearing in this case, 351 U.S. 980, 76 S.Ct. 1044, 100 L.Ed. 1495, so that this case might be disposed of consistently with the companion cases of United States v. Allen-Bradley Co., 352 U.S. 306, 77 S.Ct. 343, 1 L.Ed.2d 347, and National Lead Co. v. Commissioner, 352 U.S. 313, 77 S.Ct. 347, 1 L.Ed. 2d 352, in which we had granted certiorari the same day, viz. June 11, 1956. 351 U.S. 981, 76 S.Ct. 1052, 100 L.Ed. 1496. If there is to be uniformity in the application of the principles announced in those two companion cases, the judgment below in the instant case cannot stand. Accordingly we now grant the petition for rehearing, vacate the order denying certiorari, grant the petition for certiorari, and reverse the judgment of the Court of Claims on the authority of United States v. Allen-Bradley Co., supra, and National Lead Co. v. Commissioner, supra.

We have consistently ruled that the interest in finality of litigation must yield where the interests of justice would make unfair the strict application of our rules. This policy finds expression in the manner in which we have exercised our power over our own judgments, both in civil and criminal cases. [Citations omitted.]

Reversed.

MR. JUSTICE BRENNAN and MR. JUSTICE WHITTAKER took no part in the consideration or decision of this case.

MR. JUSTICE HARLAN, whom MR. JUSTICE FRANKFURTER and MR. JUSTICE BURTON join, dissenting.

The Court's action in overturning the judgment of the Court of Claims in this case, nearly a year and a half after we denied certiorari, and despite the subsequent denial of two successive petitions for rehearing, is so disturbing a departure from what I conceive to be sound procedure that I am constrained to dissent.

This is a tax case involving the right of the War Production Board to certify that only part of the actual cost of wartime facilities, constructed by a taxpayer at the instance of the Government, was necessary in the national defense and hence subject to accelerated amortization under § 124(f) of the Internal Revenue Code of 1939. Claiming that the War Production Board had no power to certify less than the full cost of such facilities, the Ohio Power Company sued the Government in the Court of Claims to recover an alleged overpayment of taxes, asserting that it was entitled to accelerated amortization of the full cost of wartime facilities which it had constructed, and not merely of that part of the cost which the War Production Board had certified as necessary in the interest of national defense. The Court of Claims, sustaining this contention, entered judgment in favor of the taxpayer on March 1, 1955.

On August 12, 1955, the Government petitioned for certiorari, its time for filing having been duly extended. We denied the petition on October 17, 1955. 350 U.S. 862, 76 S.Ct. 104, 100 L.Ed. 765. On November 10, 1955, the Government filed a timely petition for rehearing, requesting that its consideration be deferred until the case of Commissioner v. National Lead Co., involving this same tax question, had been decided by the Court of Appeals for the Second Circuit. We denied this petition on December 5, 1955. 350 U.S. 919, 76 S.Ct. 192, 100 L.Ed. 805. On February 14, 1956, the Court of Appeals decided National Lead in favor of the Government, and on April 3, 1956, the Court of Claims, in Allen-Bradley Co. v. United States, decided the same tax question favorably to the taxpayer, as it had already done in the Ohio Power case. This, then, provided the Government with the "conflict" which had been lacking at the time when the Court denied its petition for certiorari in the present case. On this basis the Government, on May 3, 1956, petitioned for certiorari in Allen-Bradley, and at the same time petitioned for leave to file a second petition for rehearing in the Ohio Power case. On May 28, 1956, the Court denied that petition because it was both long out of time and "consecutive," [1] 351 U.S. 958, 76 S.Ct. 844, 100 L.Ed. 1480, and thus for the third time refused to take the case. Nevertheless, two weeks thereafter, on June 11, 1956, the Court, incident to its grants of certiorari in the Allen-Bradley and National Lead cases, vacated *sua sponte* its order of December 5, 1955 denying the Government's original timely petition for rehearing in the Ohio Power case. 351 U.S. 980, 76 S.Ct. 1044, 100 L.Ed. 1495. And today the Court grants that petition, some 16 months after it had originally been denied, and reverses the Court of Claims' judgment in favor of the taxpayer.

I.

In my opinion, today's order reversing the Court of Claims violates our own Rules. That order is based upon the Court's order of June 11, 1956, which vacated the order of December 5, 1955 denying the Government's first petition for rehearing of the denial of certiorari. This June 11 order thus purported to continue consideration of the original petition for rehearing, which is now granted. Under our Rules, I think the order of June 11 was improvidently issued. Had the Government, just prior to June 11, 1956, petitioned to vacate the order of December 5, 1955, the petition would have violated Rule 58 of our Revised Rules, whether considered as, in effect, a petition for rehearing of that order, in which case it would have been out of time, or as a petition for rehearing of the original denial of certiorari, in which case it would have been both out of time and "consecutive." To say that the order of June 11 could escape Rule 58 because it was made on the Court's initiative seems to me to involve the most hypertechnical sort of reasoning.

1. Rule 58, par. 2, of this Court's Revised Rules provides: "A petition for rehearing of orders on petitions for writs of certiorari may be filed with the clerk . . . subject to the requirements respecting time . . . as provided in paragraph 1 of this rule." Paragraph 1 of Rule 58 provides: "A petition for rehearing of judgments or decision other than those denying or granting certiorari, may be filed with the clerk . . . within twenty-five days after judgment or decision, unless the time is shortened or enlarged by the court or a justice thereof." There was, of course, no enlargement of the time here. Paragraph 4 of Rule 58 provides: "Consecutive petitions for rehearings, and petitions for rehearing that are out of time under this rule, will not be received." [Some footnotes renumbered; others omitted.]

If we are to follow our Rules the order of June 11, and with it today's order, must fall, for this litigation must be considered to have been closed on December 5, 1955, when the Court denied the Government's first petition for rehearing.

II.

Rule 58, by marking the end of a case in this Court, is intended to further the law's deep-rooted policy that adjudication must at some time become final. I think we should follow it. Prior to 1948, the outside limit of rules of finality in the federal courts was the end of the term, because, except for the extraordinary writs, federal courts were considered to have no power to deal with their judgments after the end of the term at which they were rendered. Bronson v. Schulten, 104 U.S. 410, 415, 26 L.Ed. 797. In 1948 Congress abolished the "end of term" rule by a statute, 28 U.S.C.A. § 452, which was expressly made applicable to this Court. 28 U.S.C.A. § 451. The effect of § 452 was to leave the federal courts untrammeled in establishing their own rules of finality. But the history of § 452 indicates that the courts were to have no power to re-examine their judgments otherwise than in accordance with their established rules of statutes. Section 452 was modeled on Rule 6(c) of the Federal Rules of Civil Procedure. See the Reviser's Note to § 452, 28 U.S.C.A., p. 4142. As originally promulgated in 1938, Rule 6(c) had referred only to the "expiration of a term" and not to its "continued existence." In 1944 this Court held that a District Court had inherent power to vacate a judgment and enter a new one, with the effect of extending a party's right to appeal, notwithstanding such action was not authorized by any rule of the District Court, because the term had not yet expired. Hill v. Hawes, 320 U.S. 520, 524, 64 S.Ct. 334, 336, 88 L.Ed. 283, 149 A.L.R. 736. Thereafter, Rule 6(c) was amended to provide that the "*continued existence or* expiration" of the term should not affect the power of a court. The purpose was "to prevent reliance upon the continued existence of a term as a source of power to disturb the finality of a judgment upon grounds other than those stated in these rules." Advisory Committee on Rules of Civil Procedure, Report of Proposed Amendments to Rules, H.R.Doc. No. 473, 80th Cong., 1st Sess. 50 (1946). The "continued existence or" language of amended Rule 6(c) was taken bodily into § 452.

The history of § 452 thus casts grave doubt, to say the least, on the power of the Court to do what it has done in this case, for its action was certainly not taken "upon grounds . . . stated in [its] rules." [2] I recognize in 1954, the Court has been asked on 40 occasions to grant rehearing out of time of orders denying certiorari, and, with the exception of [the three criminal cases previously discussed] cases that may fairly be described as unique, and that are certainly unlike this

---

2. Text writers have disagreed as to the effect of § 452. Compare Wiener, The Supreme Court's New Rules, 68 Harv.L.Rev. 20, 84–86 (1954), with Stern & Gressman, Supreme Court Practice (2d ed. 1954), 349, 355.

one, each time it has refused. In 13 of the 40 cases, relief was denied despite the claimed development of a conflict. [Citations omitted.]

This history of past practice justifies the assertion that the Court has exercised its inherent power with a sharp eye to the "principle that litigation must at some definite point be brought to an end," Federal Trade Commission v. Minneapolis-Honeywell Regulator Co., 344 U.S. 206, 213, 73 S.Ct. 245, 249, 97 L.Ed. 245, and, in recent years at least, has acted only where it felt that the interests of justice plainly outweighed considerations of finality.

What about this case? There is nothing to distinguish it from any other suit for a money judgment in which a conflict turns up long after certiorari and rehearing have been denied. The most that can be said in justification of the Court's action is that otherwise Ohio Power would not have to pay taxes which Allen-Bradley and National Lead must pay as a result of the much later decisions in their cases. Yet the Court twice faced and rejected that very possibility many months ago, (1) when it denied the Government's timely petition for rehearing, despite the request that consideration of it be deferred until the Court of Appeals had decided the National Lead case, and (2) when it denied the Government's second, and untimely, petition for rehearing in the face of the conflict with National Lead. And in any event, this is surely not the kind of injustice that warrants overriding the policy of finality of adjudication. What has happened here is commonplace; indeed it arises in every instance where the Court grants certiorari to settle any but the most recent conflict. Perhaps out-of-time action may be justified in some instances where the time interval between a finally decided case and a subsequent contrary decision of this Court is short. But we do not have that situation here, where more than 15 months elapsed between the denial of certiorari in Ohio Power (October 17, 1955) and our decisions in Allen-Bradley and National Lead (January 22, 1957), and where in the interval the Court had twice denied rehearing, with the very factors before it which are now said to justify its present action. If the rules of finality are to have real significance in this Court, I submit that by every token the taxpayer here was entitled to believe that its case had been irrevocably closed.

There is an additional reason why this case should not now be reopened. Had this case come to us from the Tax Court, our Court would have had no power to do what it has done, it being well established that when certiorari has been denied the power of this Court to affect decisions of the Tax Court ends with the denial of a petition for rehearing, or, where no such petition has been filed, with the running of the 25-day period within which rehearing may be sought. [Citations omitted.] . . . The undesirability of according different treatment to tax cases arising from different sources scarcely requires comment. For me, this consideration alone is a sufficient reason for denying relief in this case.

For the reasons given I must dissent. I can think of nothing more unsettling to lawyers and litigants, and more disturbing to their confidence in the evenhandedness of the Court's processes, than to be left in the kind of uncertainty which today's action engenders, as to when their cases may be considered finally closed in this Court.

NOTES

(1) Sometimes the rehearing petition, though denied, permits the appellate court to clarify its prior decision. A notable example is Simpson v. Loehmann, 21 N.Y.2d 990, 290 N.Y.S.2d 914, 238 N.E.2d 319 (1969), where the Court of Appeals appreciably limited its decision in Seider v. Roth, 17 N.Y.2d 111, 269 N.Y.S.2d 99 (1966), in an attempt to insulate it against constitutional attack.

(2) On petitions for rehearing, see also Fed.R.App.P. 40.

––––––––

Read Federal Rules of Appellate Procedure, Rule 35.

NOTES

(1) In banc hearings provide a means for a court that sits in panels to avoid conflicts and to develop rules in important areas that may be better reasoned, obtain the support of all members of the court, and have a more powerful stare decisis impact. Like three judge district courts, they require considerable extra expenditure of judge time and cause added delay. They are, therefore, infrequently utilized in most courts that do not sit as a single panel regularly.

(2) On determinations in banc, see 28 U.S.C.A. § 46(c). Counsel must be given the opportunity to suggest an in banc hearing, but the decision to allow or deny it is completely within the power of the judges with authority to vote on the question. Western Pacific Railway Corp. v. Western Pacific Railway Co., 345 U.S. 247, 73 S.Ct. 656, 97 L.Ed. 986 (1953). See also In Banc Hearings in the Federal Courts of Appeals, 40 N.Y.U.L.Rev. 563, 726 (1965).

(3) After an in banc hearing limited to a single issue, the case was returned to the original panel to consider the other issues on appeal not originally reached. Farrand Optical Co., Inc. v. United States, 317 F.2d 875 (2d Cir.1963). One judge dissented on the grounds that the in banc court supplants the panel and must hear all undetermined issues. The case is noted in 77 Harv.L.Rev. 767 (1964).

(4) In a case involving successive appeals to the same court, to what extent—beyond the normal application of *stare decisis*—is the court bound by its prior interpretation of the law? See United States v. Lewis, 475 F.2d 571, 574 (5th Cir.1973), rehearing denied 472 F.2d 1405 (5th Cir.) ("a panel of this Court cannot overrule a prior decision of the Circuit, en banc consideration being required.").

(5) Walters v. Moore-McCormack Lines, Inc., 312 F.2d 893 (2d Cir.1963): "The most important criterion for granting an in banc hearing is whether the case involves an issue likely to affect many other cases."

––––––––

SECTION 8. EXTRAORDINARY REMEDIES

At common law, the King employed so-called prerogative writs to test the propriety of various kinds of official, including judicial and quasi-judicial, action. The best known of these writs were mandamus, certiorari, prohibition, quo warranto, and habeas corpus. Habeas corpus ad subjiciendum was used to compel production of a person imprisoned on a criminal charge or in private detention; quo warranto, to inquire into the authority by which a public grant or franchise was exercised; certiorari, to review orders and convictions of inferior adjudicatory and administrative bodies; prohibition, to prevent inferior tribunals from exceeding their adjudicatory powers; and mandamus, to compel the performance of a public duty. See DeSmith, The Prerogative Writs, 11 Cambridge L.J. 40 (1951). See also Henderson, Foundations of English Administrative Law: Certiorari and Mandamus in the Seventeenth Century 46–81 (1963); Jenks, The Prerogative Writs in English Law, 32 Yale L.J. 523 (1923).

The prerogative writs of the English law have evolved into what are often called extraordinary remedies today. The writ of habeas corpus ad subjiciendum is preserved in state as well as federal law. See Article I(a)(2) of the U.S. Constitution; N.Y.—McKinney's CPLR §§ 7001–7012. Although it is used principally to test the legality of imprisonment by criminal mandate, it is usually available to test the legality of any custody, including that of a child or of someone committed to an institution. See, e.g., Gardner v. Allen, 311 Ky. 147, 223 S.W.2d 723 (1949). The contemporary use of quo warranto is exemplified by People v. Rosehill Cemetery Co., 3 Ill.2d 592, 122 N.E.2d 283 (1954), in which the plaintiff brought a quo warranto action on the ground that the defendant exceeded its charter by selling monuments for profit. "Mandamus" as a method of avoiding the final judgment rule is discussed at pp. 1076–1080, supra. "Certiorari" as a method of controlling an appellate court's calendar is discussed at pp. 1081–1088, supra.

ADMINISTRATIVE PROCEDURE ACT
5 U.S.C.A. (1967).

§ 702. Right of Review

A person suffering legal wrong because of agency action, or adversely affected or aggrieved by agency action within the meaning of a relevant statute, is entitled to judicial review thereof.

§ 703. Form and Venue of Proceeding

The form of proceeding for judicial review is the special statutory review proceeding relevant to the subject matter in a court specified by statute or, in the absence or inadequacy thereof, any applicable form of legal action, including actions for declaratory judgments or writs of prohibitory or mandatory injunction or habeas corpus, in a court of competent jurisdiction. . . . Except to the extent that prior, adequate, and exclusive opportunity for judicial review is provided by law, agency action is subject to judicial review in civil or criminal proceedings for judicial enforcement.

§ 706. Scope of Review

To the extent necessary to decision and when presented, the reviewing court shall decide all relevant questions of law, interpret constitutional and statutory provisions, and determine the meaning or applicability of the terms of an agency action. The reviewing court shall—

(1) compel agency action unlawfully withheld or unreasonably delayed; and

(2) hold unlawful and set aside agency action, findings, and conclusions found to be—

(A) arbitrary, capricious, an abuse of discretion, or otherwise not in accordance with law;

(B) contrary to constitutional right, power, privilege, or immunity;

(C) in excess of statutory jurisdiction, authority, or limitations, or short of statutory right;

(D) without observance of procedure required by law;

(E) unsupported by substantial evidence in a case subject to sections 556 and 557 of this title or otherwise reviewed on the record of an agency hearing provided by statute; or

(F) unwarranted by the facts to the extent that the facts are subject to trial de novo by the reviewing court.

In making the foregoing determinations, the court shall review the whole record or those parts of it cited by a party, and due account shall be taken of the rule of prejudicial error.

NOTES

(1) In Degge v. Hitchcock, 229 U.S. 162, 33 S.Ct. 639, 57 L.Ed. 1135 (1913), the Supreme Court held that a fraud order, issued by the Postmaster General after notice and a hearing, could not be reviewed by certiorari. Has the Federal Administrative Procedure Act changed the law in this respect? Authoritative commentators have stated that "no lawyer has been sufficiently incompetent or sufficiently foolhardy to find out whether Degge v. Hitchcock has been overruled by the Administrative Procedure Act". Gellhorn & Byse, Administrative Law 407 (4th ed. 1960). What other means of attack would a more competent or prudent lawyer use?

(2) Most federal regulatory statutes provide in terms for limited judicial review of administrative action. The reviewing tribunal is usually a federal

court of appeals. On these forms of specific statutory review, see 3 Davis, Administrative Law Treatise ch. 23 (1983).

(3) In 1962, the Congress enacted 28 U.S.C.A. § 1361, which provides: "The district courts shall have original jurisdiction of any action in the nature of mandamus to compel an officer or employee of the United States or any agency thereof to perform a duty owed to the plaintiff." Section 1391(e), simultaneously enacted (but subsequently amended), greatly liberalizes venue and competence in such an action. What is the significance of these enactments within the general context of means of review of administrative action available in the federal courts?

NEW YORK CIVIL PRACTICE LAW AND RULES

Proceeding Against Body or Officer

§ 7801. Nature of Proceeding. Relief previously obtained by writs of certiorari to review, mandamus or prohibition shall be obtained in a proceeding under this article. Wherever in any statute reference is made to a writ or order of certiorari, mandamus or prohibition, such reference shall, so far as applicable, be deemed to refer to the proceeding authorized by this article. Except where otherwise provided by law, a proceeding under this title shall not be used to challenge a determination:

1. which is not final or can be adequately reviewed by appeal to a court or to some other body or officer or where the body or officer making the determination is expressly authorized by statute to rehear the matter . . .; or

2. which was made in a civil action or criminal matter unless it is an order summarily punishing a contempt committed in the presence of the court.

* * *

§ 7803. Questions Raised. The only questions that may be raised in a proceeding under this title are

1. whether the body or officer failed to perform a duty enjoined upon it by law; or

2. whether the body or officer proceeded, is proceeding or is about to proceed without or in excess of jurisdiction; or

3. whether a determination was made in violation of lawful procedure, was affected by an error of law or was arbitrary and capricious or an abuse of discretion, including abuse of discretion as to the measure or mode of penalty or discipline imposed; or

4. whether a determination made as a result of a hearing held, and at which evidence was taken, pursuant to direction by law is, on the entire record, supported by substantial evidence.

NOTE

The availability of a particular extraordinary remedy may depend on the statutory provision regulating its use. See, e.g., Drummey v. State Board of Funeral Directors, 13 Cal.2d 75, 87 P.2d 848 (1939) (because of constitutional limitations, only mandamus, not certiorari, available to review quasi-judicial act by administrative authority).

Chapter Eighteen

REPRISE: ALTERNATIVE METHODS OF CIVIL DISPUTE RESOLUTION, PARTICULARLY ARBITRATION

SECTION 1. INTRODUCTION

Chapter 1 surveys the forces and objectives that have impelled the movement to find non-court methods of resolving civil disputes. These methods include traditional mechanisms such as mediation, conciliation, negotiation, and arbitration; and also new-comers such as "minitrials," "rent-a-judge" programs and summary jury trials. Of all the alternatives, old and new, the one that comes closest to the normal adjudicative process is arbitration.

Voluntary arbitration, requiring the consent of the parties either before or after the dispute arises, has a long history and holds an increasingly secure place in the law. Compulsory arbitration as a means of shunting cases out of the court channels that lead to trial is a newer alternative. The materials that follow are concerned with both types of arbitration. Because arbitration is so close to adjudication in many of its major characteristics, it serves as a mirror that reflects the strengths and weaknesses of court processes.

SECTION 2. COURT–ANNEXED ARBITRATION

E. ROLPH, INTRODUCING COURT–ANNEXED ARBITRATION

The Institute for Civil Justice p. v (1984).

Traditionally, arbitration has been a dispute resolution process available on a private basis. Disputants agree to submit cases to and comply with the judgment of chosen arbitrators. In recent years, courts have developed a variation called *court-ordered* or *court-annexed arbitration*. Court-annexed arbitration is a court-run dispute resolution process to which cases that meet some specified criteria are involuntarily assigned. Operating under special rules, arbitrators hear the case and render awards. However, their awards are not binding. To avoid the possibility of abridging constitutional or statutory protections granting litigants the right to a jury trial, parties may always appeal an arbitrator's award by requesting and receiving a trial *de novo*

1111

(a new trial, without regard to the prior arbitration hearing or outcome) back on the traditional adjudicative track.

In the last decade, court-annexed arbitration has gained remarkable popularity as a means of disposing of small civil cases. Pennsylvania adopted the first contemporary program in 1952. For many years, it remained the only one in the country. Since 1970, however, more than ten states have joined Pennsylvania, and several more are currently considering legislative proposals to enact arbitration statutes. Within those states, arbitration can be found in over 100 local courts.

These programs enjoy broad support from a variety of constituencies. Legislatures and courts adopting such programs hope to solve their growing congestion and budget problems. They reason that, by diverting smaller civil cases to a presumably faster and cheaper dispute resolution process, courts can handle their remaining cases more expeditiously, and spend less money overall. Furthermore, at least one legislature adopted arbitration because it promised to give litigants a more convenient and congenial form of dispute resolution. In most states that have adopted arbitration, the Bar has also supported it, if sometimes reluctantly, hoping it will reduce the time a lawyer must spend on arbitrated cases as well as reduce court delay generally. And finally, the fragmentary evidence available suggests that litigants themselves are reasonably happy with the new procedure. With this base of support, it is reasonable to surmise that court-annexed arbitration is becoming a permanent feature of the judicial landscape.

NOTE

On court-annexed arbitration, see Levin, Court Annexed Arbitration, 16 Mich.J.Law Reform 537 (1983); Adler, Hensler & Nelson, Simple Justice: How Litigants Fare in the Pittsburgh Court Arbitration Program (1983); Nejelski & Zelden, Court–Annexed Arbitration in the Federal Courts: The Philadelphia Story, 42 M.D.L.Rev. 787 (1983); Hensler, Court–Annexed Arbitration in the State Trial Court System (Institute for Civil Justice, 1984).

SECTION 3. VOLUNTARY ARBITRATION

A. INTRODUCTION

At common law, courts refused to enforce arbitration agreements. The commonly advanced reason was that private parties could not oust the courts of the jurisdiction the law gave them. The judicial resistance to arbitration remained so strong that special statutes were enacted to overcome it. This was achieved on the federal level by the Federal Arbitration Act, which was first enacted in 1925 and appears in its present form in 9 U.S.C.A. §§ 2–11 (1970 and Supp.1989). A second chapter was added to the Federal Act in 1970, when the United States ratified the New York Convention on the Recognition of Foreign Arbitral Awards. 9 U.S.C.A. §§ 201–208 (1970 and Supp.1989).

Needed reform on the state level was brought about by widespread adoption of the Uniform Arbitration Act, 9 U.L.A. 76 (1957), which was first approved by the Conference of Commissioners on Uniform State Laws in 1925.

On the struggle for enforceability of arbitration agreements, see Kulukundis Shipping Co. v. Amtorg Trading Corp., 126 F.2d 978, 980–85 (2d Cir.1942).

The general thrust of both the federal and the state arbitration statutes is to declare agreements to arbitrate, whether of present or future disputes, binding when in writing. Arbitral awards may be set aside or vacated only on very narrow grounds, including fraud, corruption or the use of undue means, evident partiality or misconduct of an arbitrator, excess of power, or failure to accord procedural due process. See, e.g., 9 U.S.C.A. §§ 2, 10, 11; N.Y.—McKinney's CPLR 7501, 7511.

In recent years, a number of states, including California, Connecticut, Florida, Georgia and Texas, have adopted special international arbitration statutes. Largely modeled upon UNCITRAL Model Arbitration Law, they seek to provide a legal regime that is likely to attract international arbitration. On those statutes, see Comment, 1 Am.Rev. Int.Arb. 140 (1990).

At present, the overwhelming majority of commercial disputes are settled by arbitration rather than litigation. See Mentschikoff, The Significance of Arbitration—A Preliminary Inquiry, 17 Law & Contemp.Prob. 698 (1952). On commercial arbitration generally, see Domke, The Law and Practice of Commercial Arbitration (2d ed. by Willner).

Labor arbitration has achieved special prominence. The Supreme Court has distilled a special federal common law from the provisions of the Labor Management Relations Act of 1947, 29 U.S.C.A. § 185, which provides for enforcement of labor agreements to arbitrate. Textile Workers Union of America v. Lincoln Mills of Alabama, 353 U.S. 448, 77 S.Ct. 912, 1 L.Ed.2d 972 (1957). See generally Updegraff, Arbitration and Labor Relations (1970).

B. ARBITRABILITY

---

1. As Determined by the Arbitration Agreement

PRIMA PAINT CORP. v. FLOOD & CONKLIN MANUFACTURING CO.

Supreme Court of the United States, 1967.
388 U.S. 395, 87 S.Ct. 1801, 18 L.Ed.2d 1270.

Mr. Justice Fortas delivered the opinion of the Court.*

This case presents the question whether the federal court or an arbitrator is to resolve a claim of "fraud in the inducement," under a contract governed by the United States Arbitration Act of 1925, where there is no evidence that the contracting parties intended to withhold that issue from arbitration.

The question arises from the following set of facts. On October 7, 1964, respondent, Flood & Conklin Manufacturing Company, a New Jersey corporation, entered into what was styled a "Consulting Agreement," with petitioner, Prima Paint Corporation, a Maryland corporation. This agreement followed by less than three weeks the execution of a contract pursuant to which Prima Paint purchased F & C's paint business. The consulting agreement provided that for a six-year period F & C was to furnish advice and consultation "in connection with the formulae, manufacturing operations, sales and servicing of Prima Trade Sales accounts." These services were to be performed personally by F & C's chairman, Jerome K. Jelin, "except in the event of his death or disability." F & C bound itself for the duration of the contractual period to make no "Trade Sales" of paint or paint products in its existing sales territory or to current customers. To the consulting agreement were appended lists of F & C customers, whose patronage was to be taken over by Prima Paint. In return for these lists, the covenant not to compete, and the services of Mr. Jelin, Prima Paint agreed to pay F & C certain percentages of its receipts from the listed customers and from all others, such payments not to exceed $225,000 over the life of the agreement. The agreement took into account the possibility that Prima Paint might encounter financial difficulties, including bankruptcy, but no corresponding reference was made to possible financial problems which might be encountered by F & C. The agreement stated that it "embodies the entire understanding of the parties on the subject matter." Finally, the parties agreed to a broad arbitration clause, which read in part:

> "Any controversy or claim arising out of or relating to this Agreement, or the breach thereof, shall be settled by arbitra-

---

* Some footnotes omitted; others renumbered.

tion in the City of New York, in accordance with the rules then obtaining of the American Arbitration Association . . . ."

The first payment by Prima Paint to F & C under the consulting agreement was due on September 1, 1965. None was made on that date. Seventeen days later, Prima Paint did pay the appropriate amount, but into escrow. It notified attorneys for F & C that in various enumerated respects their client had broken both the consulting agreement and the earlier purchase agreement. Prima Paint's principal contention, so far as presently relevant, was that F & C had fraudulently represented that it was solvent and able to perform its contractual obligations, where as it was in fact insolvent and intended to file a petition under Chapter XI of the Bankruptcy Act, 52 Stat. 905, 11 U.S.C. § 701 et seq., shortly after execution of the consulting agreement. Prima Paint noted that such a petition was filed by F & C on October 14, 1964, one week after the contract had been signed. F & C's response, on October 25, was to serve a "notice of intention to arbitrate." On November 12, three days before expiration of its time to answer this "notice," Prima Paint filed suit in the United States District Court for the Southern District of New York, seeking rescission of the consulting agreement on the basis of the alleged fraudulent inducement. The complaint asserted that the federal court had diversity jurisdiction.

Contemporaneously with the filing of its complaint, Prima Paint petitioned the District Court for an order enjoining F & C from proceeding with the arbitration. F & C cross-moved to stay the court action pending arbitration. F & C contended that the issue presented— whether there was fraud in the inducement of the consulting agreement—was a question for the arbitrators and not for the District Court. Cross-affidavits were filed on the merits. On behalf of Prima Paint, the charges in the complaint were reiterated. Affiants for F & C attacked the sufficiency of Prima Paint's allegations of fraud, denied that misrepresentations had been made during negotiations, and asserted that Prima Paint had relied exclusively upon delivery of the lists, the promise not to compete, and the availability of Mr. Jelin. They contended that Prima Paint had availed itself of these considerations for nearly a year without claiming "fraud," noting that Prima Paint was in no position to claim ignorance of the bankruptcy proceeding since it had participated therein in February of 1965. They added that F & C was revested with its assets in March of 1965.

The District Court, 262 F.Supp. 605, granted F & C's motion to stay the action pending arbitration, holding that a charge of fraud in the inducement of a contract containing an arbitration clause as broad as this one was a question for the arbitrators and not for the court. For this proposition it relied on Robert Lawrence Co. v. Devonshire Fabrics, Inc., 271 F.2d 402 (C.A.2d Cir.1959), cert. granted, 362 U.S. 909, 80 S.Ct. 682, 4 L.Ed.2d 618, dismissed under Rule 60, 364 U.S. 801 (1960). The Court of Appeals for the Second Circuit dismissed Prima Paint's appeal, 2 Cir., 360 F.2d 315. It held that the contract in question evidenced a transaction involving interstate commerce; that under the controlling *Robert Lawrence Co.* decision a claim of fraud in the inducement of the contract generally—as opposed to the arbitration clause itself—is for the arbitrators and not for the courts; and that this rule—one of "national substantive law"—governs even in the face of a contrary state rule.[1] We agree, albeit for somewhat different reasons, and we affirm the decision below.

The key statutory provisions are §§ 2, 3, and 4 of the United States Arbitration Act of 1925. Section 2 provides that a written provision for arbitration "in any maritime transaction or a contract evidencing a transaction involving commerce . . . shall be valid, irrevocable, and enforceable, save upon such grounds as exist at law or in equity for the revocation of any contract." Section 3 requires a federal court in which suit has been brought "upon any issue referable to arbitration under an agreement in writing for such arbitration" to stay the court action pending arbitration once it is satisfied that the issue is arbitrable under the agreement. Section 4 provides a federal remedy for a party "aggrieved by the alleged failure, neglect, or refusal of another to arbitrate under a written agreement for arbitration," and directs the federal court to order arbitration once it is satisfied that an agreement for arbitration has been made and has not been honored. In Bernhardt v. Polygraphic Co., 350 U.S. 198, 76 S.Ct. 273, 100 L.Ed. 199 (1956), this Court held that the stay provisions of § 3, invoked here by respondent F & C, apply only to the two kinds of contracts specified in §§ 1 and 2 of the Act, namely those in admiralty or evidencing transactions in "commerce." Our first question, then, is whether the consulting agreement between F & C and Prima Paint is such a contract. We agree with the Court of Appeals that it is. . . .

Having determined that the contract in question is within the coverage of the Arbitration Act, we turn to the central issue in this case: whether a claim of fraud in the inducement of the entire contract is to be resolved by the federal court, or whether the matter is to be referred to the arbitrators. The courts of appeals have differed in their approach to this question. The view of the Court of Appeals for the Second Circuit, as expressed in this case and in others, is that—*except where the parties otherwise intend*—arbitration clauses as a matter of federal law are "separable" from the contracts in which they are embedded, and that where no claim is made that fraud was directed to the arbitration clause itself, a broad arbitration clause will be held to encompass arbitration of the claim that the contract itself was induced by fraud. The Court of Appeals for the First Circuit, on the other

---

1. Whether a party seeking *rescission* of a contract on the ground of fraudulent inducement may in New York obtain judicial resolution of his claim is not entirely clear. Compare Exercycle Corp. v. Maratta, 9 N.Y.2d 329, 334, 214 N.Y.S.2d 353, 174 N.E.2d 463, 465 (1961), and Amerotron Corp. v. Maxwell Shapiro Woolen Co., 3 A.D.2d 899, 162 N.Y.S.2d 214 (1957), aff'd, 4 N.Y.2d 722, 148 N.E.2d 319 (1958), with Fabrex Corp. v. Winard Sales Co., 23 Misc. 2d 26, 200 N.Y.S.2d 278 (1960). In light of our disposition of this case, we need not decide the status of the issue under New York law.

hand, has taken the view that the question of "severability" is one of state law, and that where a State regards such a clause as inseparable a claim of fraud in the inducement must be decided by the court. Lummus Co. v. Commonwealth Oil Ref. Co., 280 F.2d 915, 923–924 (C.A. 1st Cir.), cert. denied, 364 U.S. 911, 81 S.Ct. 274, 15 L.Ed.2d 225 (1960).

With respect to cases brought in federal court involving maritime contracts or those evidencing transactions in "commerce," we think that Congress has provided an explicit answer. That answer is to be found in § 4 of the Act, which provides a remedy to a party seeking to compel compliance with an arbitration agreement. Under § 4, with respect to a matter within the jurisdiction of the federal courts save for the existence of an arbitration clause, the federal court is instructed to order arbitration to proceed once it is satisfied that "the making of the agreement for arbitration or the failure to comply [with the arbitration agreement] is not in issue." Accordingly, if the claim is fraud in the inducement of the arbitration clause itself—an issue which goes to the "making" of the agreement to arbitrate—the federal court may proceed to adjudicate it. But the statutory language does not permit the federal court to consider claims of fraud in the inducement of the contract generally. Section 4 does not expressly relate to situations like the present in which a stay is sought of a federal action in order that arbitration may proceed. But it is inconceivable that Congress intended the rule to differ depending upon which party to the arbitration agreement first invokes the assistance of a federal court. We hold, therefore, that in passing upon a § 3 application for a stay while the parties arbitrate, a federal court may consider only issues relating to the making and performance of the agreement to arbitrate. In so concluding, we not only honor the plain meaning of the statute but also the unmistakably clear congressional purpose that the arbitration procedure, when selected by the parties to a contract, be speedy and not subject to delay and obstruction in the courts. There remains the question whether such a rule is constitutionally permissible. The point is made that, whatever the nature of the contract involved here, this case is in federal court solely by reason of diversity of citizenship, and that since the decision in Erie R. Co. v. Tompkins, 304 U.S. 64, 58 S.Ct. 817, 82 L.Ed. 1188 (1938), federal courts are bound in diversity cases to follow state rules of decision in matters which are "substantive" rather than "procedural," or where the matter is "outcome determinative." Guaranty Trust Co. of New York v. York, 326 U.S. 99, 65 S.Ct. 1464, 89 L.Ed. 2079 (1945). The question in this case, however, is not whether Congress may fashion federal substantive rules to govern questions arising in simple diversity cases. See Bernhardt v. Polygraphic Co., supra, 350 U.S. at 202, and concurring opinion, at 208, 76 S.Ct. at 275 and at 279. Rather, the question is whether Congress may prescribe how federal courts are to conduct themselves with respect to subject matter over which Congress plainly has power to legislate. The answer to that can only be in the affirmative.

*   *   *

Affirmed.

MR. JUSTICE HARLAN, concurring.

SHARON STEEL CORP. v. JEWELL COAL AND COKE CO., 735 F.2d 775 (3d Cir.1984). A contract whereby Jewell would supply Sharon with 120,000 tons of coke per year for a five-year period included (1) a complicated pricing formula keyed to, *inter alia,* labor costs, equipment, trucking, black lung expense, etc., (2) a *"force majeure"* clause excusing performance upon the occurrence of specified factors that rendered "performance commercially impracticable", and (3) an arbitration clause covering only disputes involving price and any claims of commercial impracticability. After depressed conditions in the steel industry lowered the market price of coke to a point well below that called for by the agreement, Sharon repudiated, relying on commercial impracticability. After Jewell had filed suit in a U.S. District Court in Virginia to enforce the contract, Sharon sued in a Court in Pennsylvania to compel arbitration. The lower court interpreted the contract as not embracing a drop in market price as an instance of commercial impracticability, and accordingly denied the application to compel arbitration.

On appeal from this ruling, the Third Circuit reversed:

"This [i.e., the lower court's] is a reasonable interpretation of the contract, and it may well prove to be the correct one. However, we do not believe that it was appropriate for the district court to make it. So long as the appellant's claim of arbitrability was plausible, interpretation of the contract should have been passed on to the arbitrator. Cf. United Steelworkers v. Warrier & Gulf Navigation Co., 363 U.S. 574, 582–83, 80 S.Ct. 1347, 1352–53, 4 L.Ed.2d 1409 (1960) ('[a]n order to arbitrate . . . should not be denied unless it may be said with positive assurance that the arbitration clause is not susceptible of an interpretation that covers the asserted dispute. Doubts should be resolved in favor of coverage'); quoted in Bristol Farmers Market v. Arlen Realty, 589 F.2d 1214, 1218–19 (3d Cir.1978). See also, Stateside Machinery Co. v. Alperin, 591 F.2d 234, 240 (3d Cir.1979) ('doubtful issues regarding the applicability of an arbitration clause are to be decided in favor of arbitration.'); United Engineering and Foundry Employees v. United Engineering & Foundry Co., 389 F.2d 479, 481–2 (3d Cir.1967).

" . . .

"The heart of the problem in this case is the fact that the question of arbitrability is intertwined with the merits of the commercial impracticability claim. But the Federal Arbitration Act gives the arbitrator the power to determine the scope of the arbitration clause as well as the substantive merits of the claim. See Acevedo Maldonado v. PPG Industries, 514 F.2d 614, 617 (1st Cir.1975) ("the arbitrator must ultimately pass on the outer boundaries of what is arbitrable.") If anything, a case in which the scope of arbitrability affects the merits of the claim is a stronger candidate for an arbitration. For the district court to hold that the dispute is not arbitrable because the parties did not intend a particular circumstance to trigger the exculpatory clause that, in turn, triggers the arbitration proceedings, would risk a collateral estoppel on the substantive claim. That would be an undesirable result, especially where, as here, the court's purported ruling on the arbitration clause relied almost entirely on the pleadings.

" . . .

"We therefore hold that in this case the arbitrability of appellant's claim—as well as the substantive merits—properly belonged to the arbitration panel specified in the contract. . . ."

NOTES

(1) In the principal case, did the Court apply federal law? What were the constitutional and statutory bases for the court's adjudicatory authority over the subject matter? If the proceeding is in the federal court on the basis of diversity of citizenship, and the Federal Act is not applicable by its terms, the federal court must apply the applicable state law. Bernhardt v. Polygraphic Co. of America, Inc., 350 U.S. 198, 76 S.Ct. 273, 100 L.Ed.2d 199 (1956).

(2) In Matter of Rederi (Dow Chemical Co.), 25 N.Y.2d 576, 307 N.Y.S.2d 660, 255 N.E.2d 774 (1970), the New York Court of Appeals ruled that the timeliness of a claim in arbitration, which under the provisions of the CPLR is a threshold question to be determined by the court, had to be left to the arbitrators under the provisions of the Federal Act. See, generally, Siegel, New York Practice §§ 869–872 (1978).

2. THE ARBITRABILITY OF THE SUBJECT MATTER OF THE DISPUTE

NOTE ON ARBITRABILITY OF THE SUBJECT MATTER

Questions of arbitrability of the subject matter arise when the subject matter of the dispute involves interests of persons other than parties to the agreement. Thus, in family matters, such as custody, alimony, guardianship, and the like, the courts have been reluctant to find the dispute arbitrable. See, e.g., Bowmer v. Bowmer, 50 N.Y.2d 288, 428 N.Y.S.2d 902, 406 N.E.2d 760 (1980) (notwithstanding broadly worded arbitration clause, modification of separation agreement not arbitrable); Nestel v. Nestel, 38 A.D.2d 942, 331 N.Y.S.2d 241 (2d Dep't 1972) (arbitrators in custody dispute may not hear minor children in camera); Agur v. Agur, 32 A.D.2d 16, 298 N.Y.S.2d 772 (2d Dep't 1969) (refusing to compel arbitration of custody dispute). But see Hirsch v.

Hirsch, 37 N.Y.2d 312, 372 N.Y.S.2d 71, 333 N.E.2d 371 (1975) (enforcing arbitration award terminating alimony).

Similarly, some courts have held that arbitrators lack the power to award punitive damages. Garrity v. Lyle Stuart, Inc., 40 N.Y.2d 354, 386 N.Y.S.2d 831, 353 N.E.2d 793 (1976).

The materials that follow deal with the interplay between arbitration and regulatory statutes, such as the antitrust and securities laws.

PERRY v. THOMAS

Supreme Court of the United States, 1987.
482 U.S. 483, 107 S.Ct. 2520, 96 L.Ed.2d 426.*

JUSTICE MARSHALL delivered the opinion of the Court.

In this appeal we decide whether § 2 of the Federal Arbitration Act (Act), 9 U.S.C. § 1 et seq., which mandates enforcement of arbitration agreements, pre-empts § 229 of the California Labor Code, which provides that actions for the collection of wages may be maintained "without regard to the existence of any private agreement to arbitrate." Cal.Lab.Code Ann. § 229 (West 1971).

I

Appellee, Kenneth Morgan Thomas, brought this action in California Superior Court against his former employer, Kidder, Peabody & Co. (Kidder, Peabody), and two of its employees, appellants Barclay Perry and James Johnston. His complaint arose from a dispute over commissions on the sale of securities. Thomas alleged breach of contract, conversion, civil conspiracy to commit conversion, and breach of fiduciary duty, for which he sought compensatory and punitive damages. After Thomas refused to submit the dispute to arbitration, the defendants sought to stay further proceedings in the Superior Court. Perry and Johnston filed a petition in the Superior Court to compel arbitration; Kidder, Peabody invoked diversity jurisdiction and filed a similar petition in Federal District Court. Both petitions sought arbitration under the authority of §§ 2 and 4 of the Federal Arbitration Act.

The demands for arbitration were based on a provision found in a Uniform Application for Securities Industry Registration form, which Thomas completed and executed in connection with his application for employment with Kidder, Peabody. That provision states:

> "I agree to arbitrate any dispute, claim or controversy that may arise between me and my firm, or a customer, or any other person, that is required to be arbitrated under the rules, constitutions or by-laws of the organizations with which I register . . .." App. 33a.

Rule 347 of the New York Stock Exchange, Inc. (1975) (NYSE), with which Thomas registered, provides that

---

* All but one of the footnotes omitted.

"[a]ny controversy between a registered representative and any member or member organization arising out of the employment or termination of employment of such registered representative by and with such member or member organization shall be settled by arbitration, at the instance of any such party . . . ." Id., at 34a.

Kidder, Peabody sought arbitration as a member organization of the NYSE. Perry and Johnston relied on Thomas' allegation that they had acted in the course and scope of their employment and argued that, as agents and employees of Kidder, Peabody, they were beneficiaries of the arbitration agreement.

Thomas opposed both petitions on the ground that § 229 of the California Labor Code authorized him to maintain an action for wages, defined to include commissions, despite the existence of an agreement to arbitrate. He relied principally on this Court's decision in Merrill Lynch, Pierce, Fenner & Smith, Inc. v. Ware, 414 U.S. 117, 94 S.Ct. 383, 38 L.Ed.2d 348 (1973), which had also considered the validity of § 229 in the face of a pre-emption challenge under the Supremacy Clause, U.S. Const., Art. VI, cl. 2. . . .

The Superior Court denied appellants' petition to compel arbitration. . . .

*   *   *

In an unpublished opinion, the Court of Appeal affirmed. . . .

The California Supreme Court denied appellants' petition for review. Id., at 144a. We noted probable jurisdiction, 479 U.S. 982, 107 S.Ct. 567, 93 L.Ed.2d 572 (1986), and now reverse.

II

"Section 2 is a congressional declaration of a liberal federal policy favoring arbitration agreements, notwithstanding any state substantive or procedural policies to the contrary. The effect of the section is to create a body of federal substantive law of arbitrability, applicable to any arbitration agreement within the coverage of the Act." Moses H. Cone Memorial Hospital v. Mercury Construction Corp., 460 U.S. 1, 24, 103 S.Ct. 927, 941, 74 L.Ed.2d 765 (1983). Enacted pursuant to the Commerce Clause, U.S. Const., Art. I, § 8, cl. 3, this body of substantive law is enforceable in both state and federal courts. Southland Corp. v. Keating, 465 U.S. 1, 11–12, 104 S.Ct. 852, 858–59, 79 L.Ed.2d 1 (1984) (§ 2 held to pre-empt a provision of the California Franchise Investment Law that California courts had interpreted to require judicial consideration of claims arising under that law). As we stated in *Keating*, "[i]n enacting § 2 of the federal Act, Congress declared a national policy favoring arbitration and withdrew the power of the states to require a judicial forum for the resolution of claims which the contracting parties agreed to resolve by arbitration." Id., at 10, 104 S.Ct. 858. "Congress intended to foreclose state legislative attempts to undercut the enforceability of arbitration agreements." Id., at 16, 104

S.Ct. 861 (footnote omitted). Section 2, therefore, embodies a clear federal policy of requiring arbitration unless the agreement to arbitrate is not part of a contract evidencing interstate commerce or is revocable "upon such grounds as exist at law or in equity for the revocation of any contract." 9 U.S.C. § 2. "We see nothing in the Act indicating that the broad principle of enforceability is subject to any additional limitations under state law." *Keating,* supra, at 11, 104 S.Ct. 858.

* * *

. . . [T]he present appeal addresses the pre-emptive effect of the Federal Arbitration Act, a statute that embodies Congress' intent to provide for the enforcement of arbitration agreements within the full reach of the Commerce Clause. Its general applicability reflects that "[t]he preeminent concern of Congress in passing the Act was to enforce private agreements into which parties had entered. . . ." *Byrd,* 470 U.S., at 221, 105 S.Ct., at 1242. We have accordingly held that these agreements must be "rigorously enforce[d]." Ibid.; see Shearson/ American Express, Inc. v. McMahon, 482 U.S. 220, 226, 107 S.Ct. 2332, 2337, 96 L.Ed.2d 185 (1987); Mitsubishi Motors Corp. v. Soler Chrysler–Plymouth, Inc., 473 U.S. 614, 626, 105 S.Ct. 3346, 3354, 87 L.Ed.2d 444 (1985). This clear federal policy places § 2 of the Act in unmistakable conflict with California's § 229 requirement that litigants be provided a judicial forum for resolving wage disputes. Therefore, under the Supremacy Clause, the state statute must give way.

* * *

Our holding that § 2 of the Arbitration Act preempts § 229 of the California Labor Code obviates any need to consider whether our decision in *Byrd,* supra, 470 U.S., at 221, 105 S.Ct., at 1242, would have required severance of Thomas' ancillary claims for conversion, civil conspiracy, and breach of fiduciary duty from his breach of contract claim. We likewise decline to reach Thomas' contention that Perry and Johnston lack "standing" to enforce the agreement to arbitrate any of these claims, since the courts below did not address this alternative argument for refusing to compel arbitration. However, we do reject Thomas' contention that resolving these questions in appellants' favor is a prerequisite to their having standing under Article III of the Constitution to maintain the present appeal before this Court. As we perceive it, Thomas' "standing" argument simply presents a straightforward issue of contract interpretation: whether the arbitration provision inures to the benefit of appellants and may be construed, in light of the circumstances surrounding the litigants' agreement, to cover the dispute that has arisen between them. This issue may be resolved on remand; its status as an alternative ground for denying arbitration does not prevent us from reviewing the ground exclusively relied upon by the courts below.*

---

* We also decline to address Thomas' claim that the arbitration agreement in this case constitutes an unconscionable, unenforceable contract of adhesion. This issue was not decided below and may likewise be considered on remand.

III

The judgment of the California Court of Appeal is reversed, and the case is remanded for further proceedings not inconsistent with this opinion.

It is so ordered.

. . . JUSTICE STEVENS, dissenting. [B]ecause I share JUSTICE O'CONNOR'S opinion that the States' power to except certain categories of disputes from arbitration should be preserved unless Congress decides otherwise, I would affirm the judgment of the California Court of Appeal.

JUSTICE O'CONNOR, dissenting.

The Court today holds that § 2 of the Federal Arbitration Act (Act), 9 U.S.C. § 1 et seq., requires the arbitration of respondent's claim for wages despite clear state policy to the contrary. This Court held in Southland Corp. v. Keating, 465 U.S. 1, 104 S.Ct. 852, 79 L.Ed.2d 1 (1984), that the Act applies to state court as well as federal court proceedings. Because I continue to believe that this holding was "unfaithful to congressional intent, unnecessary, and in light of the [Act's] antecedents and the intervening contraction of federal power, inexplicable," id., at 36, 104 S.Ct., at 871 (O'Connor, J., dissenting), I respectfully dissent.

Even if I were not to adhere to my position that the Act is inapplicable to state court proceedings, however, I would still dissent. We have held that Congress can limit or preclude a waiver of a judicial forum, and that Congress' intent to do so will be deduced from a statute's text or legislative history, or "from an inherent conflict between arbitration and the statute's underlying purposes." Shearson/American Express, Inc. v. McMahon, 482 U.S. 220, 227, 107 S.Ct. 2332, 2337, 96 L.Ed.2d 185 (1987). As Justice Stevens has observed, the Court has not explained why state legislatures should not also be able to limit or preclude waiver of a judicial forum:

> "We should not refuse to exercise independent judgment concerning the conditions under which an arbitration agreement, generally enforceable under the Act, can be held invalid as contrary to public policy simply because the source of the substantive law to which the arbitration agreement attaches is a State rather than the Federal Government. I find no evidence that Congress intended such a double standard to apply, and I would not lightly impute such an intent to the 1925 Congress which enacted the Arbitration Act." Southland Corp. v. Keating, supra, 465 U.S., at 21, 104 S.Ct. at 863.

Under the standards we most recently applied in Shearson/American Express, Inc. v. McMahon, supra, there can be little doubt that the California legislature intended to preclude waiver of a judicial forum; it is clear, moreover, that this intent reflects an important state policy.

Section 229 of the California Labor Code specifically provides that actions for the collection of wages may be maintained in the state courts "without regard to the existence of any private agreement to arbitrate." Cal.Lab.Code Ann. § 229 (West 1971). The California legislature thereby intended "to protect the worker from the exploitative employer who would demand that a prospective employee sign away in advance his right to resort to the judicial system for redress of an employment grievance," and § 229 has "manifested itself as an important state policy through interpretation by the California courts." Merrill Lynch, Pierce, Fenner & Smith v. Ware, 414 U.S. 117, 131, 132–133, 94 S.Ct. 383, 391, 392, 38 L.Ed.2d 348 (1973).

In my view, therefore, even if the Act applies to state court proceedings, California's policy choice to preclude waivers of a judicial forum for wage claims is entitled to respect. Accordingly, I would affirm the judgment of the California Court of Appeal.

NOTES

(1) Is the dissent correct? See Smit, Mitsubishi: It Is Not What It Seems To Be, 4 J.Int.Arb. 7 (1987).

(2) The California Arbitration Act, unlike its federal counterpart, allows a court to stay arbitration pending resolution of related litigation. In Volt Information Sciences, Inc. v. Stanford University, 489 U.S. 468, 109 S.Ct. 1248, 103 L.Ed.2d 488 (1989), the Supreme Court held that the Federal Arbitration Act does not preempt the California statute so as to preclude a court stay in a case in which the parties have agreed that their arbitration agreement will be governed by California law.

(3) For lower court decisions dealing with preemption by the Federal Arbitration Act, see Securities Industry Ass'n v. Connolly, 883 F.2d 1114 (1st Cir.1989) (holding a state statute barring brokers from requiring customers to sign arbitration agreements preempted); Saturn Distribution Corp. v. Williams, 717 F.Supp. 1147 (E.D.Va.1989) (ruling statute that gave automobile dealers the right to delete arbitration clause from franchise agreement not preempted).

MITSUBISHI MOTORS CORP. v. SOLER CHRYSLER–PLYMOUTH, INC.

United States Court of Appeals, First Circuit, 1983.
723 F.2d 155, cert. granted 469 U.S. 916, 105 S.Ct. 291, 83 L.Ed.2d 227 (1984).

[Mitsubishi initiated an arbitration proceeding, claiming that Soler had breached its dealership agreement by failing to take delivery of 966 vehicles. In proceedings brought in the U.S. district court to compel Soler to proceed to arbitration, Soler claimed that Mitsubishi had violated the antitrust laws and that it was entitled to terminate the dealership agreement for that reason; it also counterclaimed for damages under the Sherman Act. The district court ordered arbitration of the antitrust defense and counterclaims. Soler appealed. The principal issues on appeal were (1) whether the arbitration agreement purported to cover the antitrust claims and, if so, (2) whether the lower court could properly compel arbitration of those claims. The court found the antitrust claims embraced by the agreement and then proceeded to the second issue:]

We divide our discussion into three areas. First we consider whether recognition of the antitrust exception to arbitrability is compatible with the Convention on the Recognition and Enforcement of Foreign Arbitral Awards [reprinted following 9 U.S.C. § 201 (Supp. 1982)] ("Convention"), which was adopted by a United Nations conference in 1958, consented to by the United States in 1970, and implemented when Congress passed Chapter 2 of the United States Arbitration Act, 9 U.S.C. § 201 et seq. Finding that it is compatible, we next consider whether, as the district court held, Scherk v. Alberto–Culver Co., 417 U.S. 506, 94 S.Ct. 2449, 41 L.Ed.2d 270 (1974), proscribes application of the *American Safety Equipment* doctrine to the contract in this case. Concluding that *Scherk* does not so proscribe, we reach the final inquiry: since Soler's antitrust claims against Mitsubishi must be decided by a court, should the district court stay all arbitration pending a judicial decision? We answer this by concluding that decisions as to separability of issues, likelihood of success of the antitrust claims, and timing are within the informed discretion of the district court.

A. The Convention and the Antitrust Exception

We begin by noting a rarity in our jurisprudence, the overriding of a strong policy in favor of arbitration as evidenced by the Federal Arbitration Act, 9 U.S.C. § 1 et seq., by a judicially created rule excepting antitrust claims. This ruling, the reasons marshalled for it, and the unanimity of its acceptance in the field of domestic contracts are solid evidence of the strength of the policy on nonarbitrability. The most complete exegesis is found in the decision establishing the exception, *American Safety Equipment, . . .* [391 F.2d 821 (2d Cir.1968)]. The reasoning is fourfold: (1) governance of the realm of antitrust law, so vital to the successful functioning of a free economy, is delegated by statute to both government and private parties, the latter being given special incentive to supplement efforts of the former, the work of both being equally the grist of judicial decisions, 391 F.2d at 826; (2) the strong possibility that contracts which generate antitrust disputes may be contracts of adhesion militates against automatic forum determination by contract, id. at 827; (3) antitrust issues are—an understatement—"prone to be complicated, and the evidence extensive and diverse", id., and, we may add, the economic data subject to rigorous analysis dictated by a growing and increasingly sophisticated jurisprudence, with the subject correspondingly ill-adapted to strengths of the arbitral process, i.e., expedition, minimal requirements of written rationale, simplicity, resort to basic concepts of common sense and simple equity; and (4) the notion, suggestive of the proposition that issues of war and peace are too important to be vested in the generals, that decisions as to antitrust regulation of business are too important to be lodged in arbitrators chosen from the business community—particularly those from a foreign community that has had no experience with or exposure to our law and values. Id.

So far as we have ascertained, all other circuits that have had occasion to consider the doctrine of *American Safety Equipment* have embraced it. Applied Digital Technology, Inc. v. Continental Casualty Co., 576 F.2d 116, 117 (7th Cir.1978); Cobb v. Lewis, 488 F.2d 41, 47 (5th Cir.1974); Helfenbein v. International Industries, Inc., 438 F.2d 1068, 1070 (8th Cir.1971); Power Replacements, Inc. v. Air Preheater Co., 426 F.2d 980, 983–84 (9th Cir.1970). We conclude, therefore, that the nonarbitrability of antitrust issues in domestic contract disputes is established as solid and sound doctrine.

Before endeavoring to parse the Convention, we pause to examine whether there are factors which suggest that the exception be confined to disputes between United States citizens. We begin by noting that the antitrust laws apply to restraints not merely of interstate but also of foreign commerce. 15 U.S.C. § 1. Although the presence of foreign parties is a factor that should be considered in deciding to take jurisdiction of a case involving foreign conduct, it is not dispositive. Timberlane Lumber Co. v. Bank of America, 549 F.2d 597 (9th Cir. 1976); Mannington Mills, Inc. v. Congoleum Corp., 595 F.2d 1287 (3d Cir.1979).

More importantly, we consider two questions. The first is: is the American antitrust ethic and system of law so "parochial" that insistence on the application of the nonarbitrability of antitrust issues to international agreements would be anathema to other countries and would incite retaliation? We have in mind the admonition in The Bremen v. Zapata Off–Shore Co., 407 U.S. 1, 9, 92 S.Ct. 1907, 1912, 32 L.Ed.2d 513 (1972), to abjure parochial considerations.

We doubt that other nations are ignorant of the primary we accord to antitrust law. A typical reference to our ideological topography is the Court's statement in United States v. Topco Associates, Inc., 405 U.S. 596, 610, 92 S.Ct. 1126, 1135, 31 L.Ed.2d 515 (1972):

> "Antitrust laws in general, and the Sherman Act in particular, are the Magna Carta of free enterprise. They are as important to the preservation of economic freedom and our free-enterprise system as the Bill of Rights is to the protection of our fundamental personal freedoms."

We are advised by the United States that the Federal Republic of Germany also accords high status to its antitrust rule and prohibits agreements entrusting future such disputes solely to arbitration. We also note the policy of the European Economic Community, as embodied in the Treaty of Rome, in Articles 85–90, to forbid practices restricting or distorting competition. In any event, whether or not other nations agree with United States law and attitudes relating to competition, it is extremely doubtful that they would describe them as "parochial" in the sense of being petty provincialisms.

The obverse question, whether any policy reason supports the application of the rule against arbitration of antitrust issues to agreements involving American companies and foreign suppliers and sellers, is also easily answered. In an increasingly interdependent and interrelated commercial world, where the multinational corporation with ties to several countries is becoming more prevalent, see Scherk v. Alberto–Culver Co., 417 U.S. 506, 533, 94 S.Ct. 2449, 2463, 41 L.Ed.2d 270 (1974) (Douglas, J., dissenting), the insulation of agreements with some international coloration from the antitrust exception would go far to limit it to the most minor and insignificant of business dealings. Indeed, suppliers and sellers could achieve immunity from antitrust law threats and sanctions by the simple expedient of co-opting some foreign or international entity into the arrangement. Specifically, the sovereign sway of antitrust law and policy in the United States economy would be hopelessly fragmented if, say, all domestic manufacturers with overseas partners, suppliers, or financers could force all their dealers and distributors to arbitrate their antitrust claims.

We conclude that the nonarbitrability of antitrust issues is an American doctrine that is alive, well, justified both in its conception and in its application to at least the kind of international agreement we confront in this case—an agreement governing the sales and distribution of vehicles *in the United States*. What remains for us to do is to see how such law and policy fit, if at all, with the Convention.

[The reasoning leading to the court's conclusion that application of the antitrust exception to arbitrability would not be incompatible with the Convention is omitted.]

* * *

B.   Does Scherk v. Alberto–Culver Co. Compel Arbitration?

* * *

In *Scherk* an American company selling toiletries in the United States and abroad acquired three European manufacturing companies from German defendant Fritz Scherk. The negotiations, the signing of the sales contract (which included a clause providing for arbitration of "any controversy or claim . . . [arising] out of this agreement or the breach thereof"), and the closing had been accomplished largely in European countries. The plaintiff company discovered that the critical trademarks, which defendant had warranted to be unencumbered, were indeed substantially encumbered, and brought suit in federal court, alleging that the defendant had misrepresented the status of the trademarks in violation of § 10(b) of the Securities Exchange Act of 1934.

Defendant moved that the action in federal court be dismissed or that it be stayed pending arbitration pursuant to the contract clause. Plaintiff, relying on Wilko v. Swan, 346 U.S. 427, 74 S.Ct. 182, 98 L.Ed. 168 (1953), argued that the arbitration clause was inapplicable to its securities claim. In *Wilko,* the Court had held that an arbitration clause in a domestic contract could not deprive a securities buyer of his right to the judicial remedy provided in the Securities Act of 1933, since § 14 of the 1933 Act specifically prohibited any "condition, stipulation, or provision" waiving the Act's protection.

A 5–4 majority of the Court declined to apply the *Wilko* holding to the contract in *Scherk*. While *Wilko* had addressed the validity of an arbitration clause in a domestic contract, the Court noted that the agreement in *Scherk* was "truly international", involving "the sale of business enterprises organized under the laws of and primarily situated in European countries, whose activities were largely, if not entirely, directed to European markets". 417 U.S. at 515, 94 S.Ct. at 2455. The Court had held two terms earlier that a forum-selection clause in an international contract would be respected by the United States courts "unless enforcement is shown by the resisting party to be 'unreasonable' under the circumstances". The Bremen v. Zapata Off–Shore Co., 407 U.S. 1, 10, 92 S.Ct. 1907, 1913, 32 L.Ed.2d 513 (1972). In *Scherk,* the Court observed that "[a]n agreement to arbitrate before a specified tribunal is, in effect, a specialized kind of forum-selection clause". 417 U.S. at 517, 94 S.Ct. at 2456. The Court had already decided that arbitration of the Scherk contract was not "unreasonable".

In reaching this decision, the Court held that a "parochial refusal by the courts of one country to enforce an international arbitration agreement" would not only frustrate the orderly and predictable resolutions that the parties had intended to achieve with their forum-selection clause, but would also invite "mutually destructive jockeying" for advantage. Id. at 516–17, 94 S.Ct. at 2455–56. The supposed counterweight to these harmful results—the benefit of having securities claims heard in American courts—was without substance; for if one party resorted to American courts to have arbitration enjoined, "an opposing party [might] by speedy resort to a foreign court block or hinder access to the American court of the purchaser's choice". Id. at 518, 94 S.Ct. at 2456.

We have several reasons for finding that *Scherk* does not control the case now before us. . . .

      *   *   *

Perhaps the major difference between *Scherk* and the case at hand lies in the different policies at issue. In *Wilko,* the Court observed that the securities laws were "[d]esigned to protect investors", 346 U.S. at 431, 74 S.Ct. at 184, and that arbitration clauses impermissibly deprive investors of this protection by restricting the "wider choice of courts and venue" provided by the securities laws. Id. at 435, 74 S.Ct. at 186. The Court declined in *Scherk* to extend this reasoning to international contracts: first, because it found that the private investor's ability to choose an American judicial forum at the time the dispute arose was illusory, since the other party could block the forum choice in a foreign court; and second, because it found that the private investor's interest in choosing his forum ahead of time was greater in an international contract, where the forum and substantive law that would govern any specific dispute absent an arbitration clause were so uncertain. 471 U.S. at 516–18, 94 S.Ct. at 2455–56. In short, the Court engaged in a balancing test, weighing the policy considerations of giving the investor the full protection of the securities laws against the policy considerations of giving the investor the certainty of an arbitration clause; and it decided that the individual investor would be better served by enforcement of the arbitration clause.

The policy underlying the antitrust laws, however, is not to protect individual companies, but to protect *competition*. In *American Safety Equipment*, the Second Circuit observed:

> "A claim under the antitrust laws is not merely a private matter. The Sherman Act is designed to promote the national interest in a competitive economy; thus, the plaintiff asserting his rights under the Act has been likened to a private attorney-general who protects the public's interest [citations omitted]. Antitrust violations can affect hundreds of thousands—perhaps millions—of people and inflict staggering economic damage . . .. We do not believe that Congress intended such claims to be resolved elsewhere than in the courts". 391 F.2d at 826–27.

Although it is true that an investor like Scherk who brings an action under the securities laws serves the public interest by policing the securities market, the securities laws are designed primarily to protect a fairly small "special interest" group: those investors in a particular security who read and are influenced by information in the company's prospectuses or financial reports. Antitrust laws, on the other hand, protect the general public by preserving a competitive atmosphere that keeps prices down in an entire industry or in a group of related industries. The strength of the public interest in private enforcement of antitrust laws is illustrated by the fact that successful antitrust plaintiffs are allowed to recover treble damages, while securities plaintiffs may only recover their actual damages. If we engage in a *Scherk*-type balancing exercise, therefore, we must weigh the private party's interest in the arbitration of international contract disputes against the public's interest in the preservation of economic order in the United States. Such a balancing exercise can have only one result: to enforce the private arbitration clause at the expense of public policy would be "unreasonable". Cf. *Zapata*, 407 U.S. at 10, 92 S.Ct. at 1913.

Appellant has argued briefly that, since the antitrust issues "permeate" the claims in arbitration, the arbitration proceedings should be stayed. Applied Digital Technology, Inc. v. Continental Casualty Co., 576 F.2d 116 (7th Cir.1978); Cobb v. Lewis, 488 F.2d 41 (5th Cir.1974). Appellee counters with Kelly v. Kosuga, 358 U.S. 516, 79 S.Ct. 429, 3 L.Ed.2d 475 (1959), and Kaiser Aluminum & Chemical Sales, Inc. v. Avondale Shipyards, Inc., 677 F.2d 1045 (5th Cir.1982). The district court, however, has not had the occasion to decide whether the matters are sufficiently separable to justify separate and contemporaneous treatment. Moreover, the district court has not, because of its application of *Scherk* to this case, been called upon to assess the likelihood of success of the antitrust claims, a relevant factor in deciding whether or not to stay arbitration. See N.V. Maatschappij Voor Industriele Waarden v. A.O. Smith Corp., 532 F.2d 874 (2d Cir.1976). Such cases as Fuchs Sugars & Syrups, Inc. v. Amstar Corp., 602 F.2d 1025 (2d Cir. 1979), Continental T.V. Inc. v. G.T.E. Sylvania Inc., 694 F.2d 1132 (9th Cir.1982), and our own Auburn News Company, Inc. v. Providence Journal Co., 659 F.2d 273 (1st Cir.1981), may be relevant. See also American Bar Association Section of Antitrust Law, Monograph 9, Refusals to Deal and Exclusive Distributorships, at 28 n. 110.

The district court may now, in the light of our holding that Soler's antitrust claims against Mitsubishi are not arbitrable, focus on such matters as permeation and likelihood of success and decide whether both arbitrable and nonarbitrable matters should proceed on their own course or whether one set of problems should await resolution of the other. For example, the claim that Mitsubishi had "good cause" to terminate its dealership arrangement with Soler is part of Mitsubishi's case in chief, which will be submitted to arbitration. If the district court believes that Soler's antitrust claims are separable and that the interests of judicial economy would be served by staying a determination of these claims pending arbitration, it will be able to allow the arbiter to make an initial determination on the "good cause" issue. If the arbiter finds that good cause existed, the district court may not need to reach the antitrust issues; if the arbiter finds that Mitsubishi did not have good cause to terminate the contract, the district court may then need to decide whether the termination was caused by a violation of the antitrust laws. We leave the method of decision, including specifically whether or not to entertain further evidence and/ or argument, to the district court.

NOTES

(1) In the principal case, should the court have left to the arbitrators the decision on whether the arbitration clause covered the antitrust claims and, if so, whether it could do so validly? See Prima Paint Corp. v. Flood and Conklin Manufacturing Co., 388 U.S. 395, 87 S.Ct. 1801, 18 L.Ed.2d 1270 (1967), p. 1114, supra; Sharon Steel Corp. v. Jewell Coal and Coke Co., 735 F.2d 775 (3d Cir. 1984), p. 1118, supra.

(2) In the principal case, if there had been no arbitration agreement and Mitsubishi had brought its action against Soler in the district court, would the antitrust violations claimed by Soler have been entertained as a defense? See Kaiser Steel Corp. v. Mullins, 455 U.S. 72, 102 S.Ct. 851, 70 L.Ed.2d 833 (1982) (antitrust claim cannot be heard as defense to an action for breach of otherwise valid contractual provisions).

(3) Southland Corp. v. Keating, 465 U.S. 1, 104 S.Ct. 852, 79 L.Ed.2d 1 (1984). In a class action alleging violation of California's Franchise Investment Act, the defendant defended on the ground that an arbitration clause in the franchise agreements required arbitration of the claims pursued. The Califor-

nia Supreme Court held that the class action aspect was no bar to arbitration, but that claims under the California Act were for judicial determination only. The Supreme Court reversed, holding that the claims were arbitrable under the Federal Arbitration Act and that state law could not make exceptions to that Act.

(4) Moses H. Cone Memorial Hospital v. Mercury Construction Corp., 460 U.S. 1, 103 S.Ct. 927, 74 L.Ed.2d 765 (1983). The hospital sought to stay arbitration in a state court on the ground that arbitration was time-barred. Mercury sued in the federal court to compel arbitration. The district court stayed the federal proceedings pending resolution of the issue in the state court. The Fourth Circuit reversed and directed arbitration. The Supreme Court affirmed: The policy of the Federal Act is the rapid and unobstructed enforcement of arbitration agreements. The stay was at odds with this policy.

(5) Shearson/American Express, Inc. v. McMahon, 482 U.S. 220, 107 S.Ct. 2332, 96 L.Ed.2d 185 (1987) holds arbitrable claims under the Racketeer Influenced and Corrupt Organization Act (RICO) and Section 10(b) of the Securities Exchange Act of 1934. Does this decision overrule Wilko v. Swan, referred to in the principal case?

(6) In the principal case, the Supreme Court affirmed the ruling that antitrust claims are arbitrable. 473 U.S. 614, 105 S.Ct. 3346, 87 L.Ed.2d 444 (1985). On this decision, see Smit, Mitsubishi: It Is Not What It Seems To Be, 4 J.Int.Arb. 7 (1987).

C. THE PROCEEDINGS BEFORE THE ARBITRATORS

The statutory regulation of the proceedings before the arbitrators is very limited. More detailed rules are provided by the various institutions that are active in the fields of arbitration. See, e.g., the Commercial Arbitration Rules of the American Arbitration Association (April 1, 1982) and the Rules for the ICC Court of International Arbitration (1989). The parties may provide in their agreement for rules that are to govern the proceedings. Even under institutional rules, the arbitrators have considerable leeway in determining how the proceedings are to be conducted.

Arbitration may give rise to special problems. It may be claimed that arbitrators are disqualified, consolidation with other proceedings may be desired, provisional judicial relief may be needed, and questions may arise as to the availability of pre-trial discovery. All of these and similar problems are of great practical interest. On these problems, see, generally, Siegel, New York Practice §§ 596–599 (1978).

D. THE AWARD AND ITS ENFORCEMENT

The statutory and judicial tendency has been to limit rather strictly attacks upon arbitral awards. In American practice, awards frequently do not provide reasoning. This may render attacks on them particularly difficult. How, for example, can a court determine whether the arbitrators have gone beyond the dispute submitted to them or have based their decision on improper grounds if their award fails to disclose how they arrived at their conclusions? Many foreign countries require, upon penalty of nullity, that arbitral awards be reasoned. See, e.g., Dutch Code of Civil Procedure § 1057(3)(c), § 1065(1)(d); Zivilprozessordnung § 1041(1)(5) (West–Germany). Should American statutes be amended to impose a similar requirement?

The United States has acceded to the New York Convention on the Recognition and Enforcement of Foreign Arbitral Awards, which has been implemented by the Federal Arbitration Act, 9 U.S.C.A. §§ 201–208. On this Convention, see generally van den Berg, The New York Arbitration Convention of 1958 (1981); 1 Gaja, International Commercial Arbitration: New York Convention III (1984). The Convention limits narrowly the grounds upon which enforcement of an award may be denied.

PARSONS & WHITTEMORE OVERSEAS CO., INC. v. SOCIETE GENERALE DE L'INDUSTRIE DU PAPIER (RAKTA)

United States Court of Appeals, Second Circuit, 1974.
508 F.2d 969.

J. Joseph Smith, Circuit Judge:

Parsons & Whittemore Overseas Co., Inc., (Overseas), an American corporation, appeals from the entry of summary judgment on . . . the counterclaim by Societe Generale de L'Industrie du Papier (RAKTA), an Egyptian corporation, to confirm a foreign arbitral award holding Overseas liable to RAKTA for breach of contract. . . . Jurisdiction is based on 9 U.S.C. § 203, which empowers federal district courts to hear cases to recognize and enforce foreign arbitral awards, and 9 U.S.C. § 205, which authorizes the removal of such cases from state courts, as was accomplished in this instance. We affirm the district court's confirmation of the foreign award.

In November 1962, Overseas consented by written agreement with RAKTA to construct, start up and, for one year, manage and supervise a paperboard mill in Alexandria, Egypt. The Agency for International Development (AID), a branch of the United States State Department, would finance the project by supplying RAKTA with funds with which to purchase letters of credit in Overseas' favor. Among the contract's terms was an arbitration clause, which provided a means to settle differences arising in the course of performance, and a "force majeure" clause, which excused delay in performance due to causes beyond Overseas' reasonable capacity to control.

Work proceeded as planned until May, 1967. Then, with the Arab–Israeli Six Day War on the horizon, recurrent expressions of Egyptian hostility to Americans—nationals of the principal ally of the Israeli enemy—caused the majority of the Overseas work crew to leave Egypt.

On June 6, the Egyptian government broke diplomatic ties with the United States and ordered all Americans expelled from Egypt except those who would apply and qualify for a special visa.

Having abandoned the project for the present with the construction phase near completion, Overseas notified RAKTA that it regarded this postponement as excused by the force majeure clause. RAKTA disagreed and sought damages for breach of contract. Overseas refused to settle and RAKTA, already at work on completing the performance promised by Overseas, invoked the arbitration clause. Overseas responded by calling into play the clause's option to bring a dispute directly to a three-man arbitral board governed by the rules of the International Chamber of Commerce. After several sessions in 1970, the tribunal issued a preliminary award, which recognized Overseas' force majeure defense as good only during the period from May 28 to June 30, 1967. . . .

Subsequent to the final award, Overseas in the action here under review sought a declaratory judgment to prevent RAKTA from collecting the award out of a letter of credit issued in RAKTA's favor by Bank of America at Overseas' request. . . . RAKTA . . . counterclaimed to confirm and enter judgment upon the foreign arbitral award. Overseas' defenses to this counterclaim, all rejected by the district court, form the principal issues for review on this appeal. Four of these defenses are derived from the express language of the applicable United Nations Convention on the Recognition and Enforcement of Foreign Arbitral Awards (Convention), 330 U.N.Treaty Ser. 38, and a fifth is arguably implicit in the Convention. These include: enforcement of the award would violate the public policy of the United States, the award represents an arbitration of matters not appropriately decided by arbitration; the tribunal denied Overseas an adequate opportunity to present its case; the award is predicated upon a resolution of issues outside the scope of the contractual agreement to submit to arbitration; and the award is in manifest disregard of law. In addition to disputing the district court's rejection of its position on the letter of credit, RAKTA seeks on appeal modification of the court's order to correct for an arithmetical error in the sum entered for judgment, as well as an assessment of damages and double costs against Overseas for pursuing a frivolous appeal.

* * *

In 1958 the Convention was adopted by 26 of the 45 states participating in the United Nations Conference on Commercial Arbitration held in New York. For the signatory states, the New York Convention superseded the Geneva Convention of 1927, 92 League of Nations Treaty Ser. 302. The 1958 Convention's basic thrust was to liberalize procedures for enforcing foreign arbitral awards: While the Geneva Convention placed the burden of proof on the party seeking enforcement of a foreign arbitral award and did not circumscribe the range of available defenses to those enumerated in the convention, the 1958 Convention clearly shifted the burden of proof to the party defending against enforcement and limited his defenses to seven set forth in Article V. See Contini, International Commercial Arbitration, 8 Am.J. Comp.L. 283, 299 (1959). Not a signatory to any prior multilateral agreement on enforcement of arbitral awards, the United States declined to sign the 1958 Convention at the outset. The United States ultimately acceded to the Convention, however, in 1970 . . ..

A. *Public Policy*

Article V(2)(b) of the Convention allows the court in which enforcement of a foreign arbitral award is sought to refuse enforcement, on the defendant's motion or *sua sponte,* if "enforcement of the award would be contrary to the public policy of [the forum] country." . . .

. . . The general pro-enforcement bias informing the Convention and explaining its supersession of the Geneva Convention points toward a narrow reading of the public policy defense. . . . Additionally, considerations of reciprocity—considerations given express recognition in the Convention itself—counsel courts to invoke the public policy defense with caution lest foreign courts frequently accept it as a defense to enforcement of arbitral awards rendered in the United States.

We conclude, therefore, that the Convention's public policy defense should be construed narrowly. Enforcement of foreign arbitral awards may be denied on this basis only where enforcement would violate the forum state's most basic notions of morality and justice. . . .

Under this view of the public policy provision in the Convention, Overseas' public policy defense may easily be dismissed. Overseas argues that various actions by United States officials subsequent to the severance of American–Egyptian relations—most particularly, AID's withdrawal of financial support for the Overseas–RAKTA contract— required Overseas, as a loyal American citizen, to abandon the project. Enforcement of an award predicated on the feasibility of Overseas' returning to work in defiance of these expressions of national policy would therefore allegedly contravene United States public policy. In equating "national" policy with United States "public" policy, the appellant quite plainly misses the mark. To read the public policy defense as a parochial device protective of national political interests would seriously undermine the Convention's utility. This provision was not meant to enshrine the vagaries of international politics under the rubric of "public policy." Rather, a circumscribed public policy doctrine was contemplated by the Convention's framers and every indication is that the United States, in acceding to the Convention, meant to subscribe to this supranational emphasis. . . .

To deny enforcement of this award largely because of the United States' falling out with Egypt in recent years would mean converting a defense intended to be of narrow scope into a major loophole in the Convention's mechanism for enforcement. We have little hesitation, therefore, in disallowing Overseas' proposed public policy defense.

B. *Non–Arbitrability*

Article V(2)(a) authorizes a court to deny enforcement, on a defendant's or its own motion, of a foreign arbitral award when "[t]he subject matter of the difference is not capable of settlement by arbitration under the law of that [the forum] country." . . .

. . . The mere fact that an issue of national interest may incidentally figure into the resolution of a breach of contract claim does not make the dispute not arbitrable. Rather, certain *categories* of claims may be non-arbitrable because of the special national interest vested in their resolution. Cf. American Safety Equipment Corp., supra, 391 F.2d 821 at 826–827. Furthermore, even were the test for non-arbitrability of an ad hoc nature, Overseas' situation would almost certainly not meet the standard, for Overseas grossly exaggerates the magnitude of the national interest involved in the resolution of its particular claim. Simply because acts of the United States are somehow implicated in a case one cannot conclude that the United States is vitally interested in its outcome. . . .

The court below was correct in denying relief to Overseas under the Convention's non-arbitrability defense to enforcement of foreign arbitral awards. There is no special national interest in judicial, rather than arbitral, resolution of the breach of contract claim underlying the award in this case.

*   *   *

[The Court's rejection of Overseas' other defenses is omitted.]

Affirmed.

APPENDIX

BURNHAM v. SUPERIOR COURT OF CALIFORNIA

Supreme Court of the United States, 1990.
___ U.S. ___, 110 S.Ct. 2105, ___ L.Ed.2d ___.

JUSTICE SCALIA announced the judgment of the Court.*

The question presented is whether the Due Process Clause of the Fourteenth Amendment denies California courts jurisdiction over a nonresident, who was personally served with process while temporarily in that State, in a suit unrelated to his activities in the State.

I

Petitioner Dennis Burnham married Francie Burnham in 1976, in West Virginia. In 1977 the couple moved to New Jersey, where their two children were born. In July 1987 the Burnhams decided to separate. They agreed that Mrs. Burnham, who intended to move to California, would take custody of the children. Shortly before Mrs. Burnham departed for California that same month, she and petitioner agreed that she would file for divorce on grounds of "irreconcilable differences."

In October 1987, petitioner filed for divorce in New Jersey state court on grounds of "desertion." Petitioner did not however, obtain an issuance of summons against his wife, and did not attempt to serve her with process. Mrs. Burnham, after unsuccessfully demanding that petitioner adhere to their prior agreement to submit to an "irreconcilable differences" divorce, brought suit for divorce in California State court in early January 1988.

In late January, petitioner visited southern California on business, after which he went north to visit his children in the San Francisco Bay area, where his wife resided. He took the older child to San Francisco for the weekend. Upon returning the child to Mrs. Burnham's home on January 24, 1988, petitioner was served with a California court summons and a copy of Mrs. Burnham's divorce petition. He then returned to New Jersey.

Later that year, petitioner made a special appearance in the California Superior court, moving to quash the service of process on the ground that the court lacked personal jurisdiction over him because his only contacts with California were a few short visits to the State for the purpose of conducting business and visiting his children. The Superior Court denied the motion, and the California Court of Appeal denied mandamus relief, rejecting petitioner's contention that the Due Process Clause prohibited California court from asserting jurisdiction over him because he lacked "minimum contacts" with the State. The court held

* Footnotes omitted.

1136

it to be "a valid jurisdictional predicate for in personam jurisdiction" that the "defendant [was] present in the forum state and personally served with process." . . . We granted certiorari . . .

II

A

The proposition that the judgment of a court lacking jurisdiction is void traces back to the English Year Books, see Bowser v. Collins, Y.B. Mich. 22 Edw. 4, f. 30, pl. 11, 145 Eng.Rep. 97 (1482), and was made settled law by Lord Coke in Case of the Marshalsea, 10 Co.Rep. 68b, 77 Eng.Rep. 1027, 1041 (K.B.1612). Traditionally that proposition was embodied in the phrase coram non judice, "before a person not a judge"—meaning, in effect, that the proceeding in question was not a judicial proceeding because lawful judicial authority was not present, and could therefore not yield a judgment. American courts invalidated, or denied recognition to, judgments that violated this common-law principle long before the Fourteenth Amendment was adopted. See, e.g., Grumon v. Raymond, 1 Conn. 40 (1814). . . . In Pennoyer v. Neff, 95 U.S. 714, 732 (1878), we announced that the judgment of a court lacking personal jurisdiction violated the Due Process Clause of the Fourteenth Amendment as well.

To determine whether the assertion of personal jurisdiction is consistent with due process, we have long relied on the principles traditionally followed by American courts in marking out the territorial limits of each State's authority. . . . In what has become the classic expression of the criterion, we said in International Shoe Co. v. Washington, 326 U.S. 310 (1945), that a State court's assertion of personal jurisdiction satisfies the Due Process Clause if it does not violate " 'traditional notions of fair play and substantial justice.' " Id., at 316, quoting Milliken v. Meyer, 311 U.S. 457, 463 (1940). . . . Since International Shoe, we have only been called upon to decide whether these "traditional notions" permit States to exercise jurisdiction over absent defendants. . . . The question we must decide today is whether due process requires a similar connection between the litigation and the defendant's contacts with the State in cases where the defendant is physically present in the State at the time process is served upon him.

B

Among the most firmly established principles of personal jurisdiction in American tradition is that the courts of a State have jurisdiction over nonresidents who are physically present in the State. The view developed early that each State had the power to hale before its courts any individual who could be found within its borders, and that once having acquired jurisdiction over such a person by properly serving him with process, the State could retain jurisdiction to enter judgment against him, no matter how fleeting his visit. See, e.g., Potter v. Allin,

2 Root 63, 67 (Conn.1793); Barrell v. Benjamin, 15 Mass. 354 (1819). That view had antecedents in English common-law practice, which sometimes allowed "transitory" actions, arising out of events outside the country, to be maintained against seemingly nonresident defendants who were present in England. . . . See, e.g., Mostyn v. Fabrigas, 98 Eng.Rep. 1021 (K.B.1774). . . .

* * *

This American jurisdictional practice is, moreover, not merely old; it is continuing. . . . We do not know of a single State or federal statute, or a single judicial decision resting upon State law, that has abandoned in-State service as a basis of jurisdiction. Many recent cases reaffirm it. See Hutto v. Plagens, 254 Ga. 512, 513, 330 S.E.2d 341, 342 (1985). . . .

C

Despite this formidable body of precedent, petitioner contends, in reliance on our decisions applying the International Shoe standard, that in the absence of "continuous and systematic" contacts with the forum, . . . a non-resident defendant can be subjected to judgment only as to matters that arise out of or relate to his contacts with the forum. This argument rests on a thorough misunderstanding of our cases.

* * *

Nothing in International Shoe or the cases that have followed it . . . offers support for the . . . proposition petitioner seeks to establish today: that a defendant's presence in the forum is not only unnecessary to validate novel, nontraditional assertions of jurisdiction, but is itself no longer sufficient to establish jurisdiction. That proposition is unfaithful to both elementary logic and the foundations of our due process jurisprudence. The distinction between what is needed to support novel procedures and what is needed to sustain traditional ones is fundamental. . . .

* * *

The short of the matter is that jurisdiction based on physical presence alone constitutes due process because it is one of the continuing traditions of our legal system that define the due process standard of "traditional notions of fair play and substantial justice." That standard was developed by analogy to "physical presence," and it would be perverse to say it could now be turned against that touchstone of jurisdiction.

D

* * *

It goes too far to say, as petitioner contends, that Shaffer [v. Heitner, 433 U.S. 186 (1977)] compels the conclusion that a State lacks jurisdiction over an individual unless the litigation arises out of his activities in the State. Shaffer, like International Shoe, involved jurisdiction over an absent defendant, and it stands for nothing more than the proposition that when the "minimum contact" that is a substitute for physical presence consists of property ownership it must, like other minimum contacts, be related to the litigation. Petitioner wrenches out of its context our statement in Shaffer that "all assertions of state-court jurisdiction must be evaluated according to the standards set forth in International Shoe and its progeny." 433 U.S., at 212. When read together with the two sentences that preceded it, the meaning of this statement becomes clear:

> "The fiction that an assertion of jurisdiction over property is anything but an assertion of jurisdiction over the owner of the property supports an ancient form without substantial modern justification. Its continued acceptance would serve only to allow state-court jurisdiction that is fundamentally unfair to the defendant.
>
> "We *therefore conclude* that all assertions of state-court jurisdiction must be evaluated according to the standards set forth in International Shoe and its progeny." Ibid. (emphasis added).

Shaffer was saying, in other words, not that all bases for the assertion of in personam jurisdiction (including, presumably, in-state service) must be treated alike and subjected to the "minimum contacts" analysis of International Shoe; but rather than quasi in rem jurisdiction, that fictional "ancient form," and in personam jurisdiction, are really one and the same and must be treated alike—leading to the conclusion that quasi in rem jurisdiction, i.e., that form of in personam jurisdiction based upon a "property ownership" contact and by definition unaccompanied by person, in-state service, must satisfy the litigation-relatedness requirement of International Shoe. . . .

It is fair to say, however, that while our holding today does not contradict Shaffer, our basic approach to the due process question is different. We have conducted no independent inquiry into the desirability or fairness of the prevailing in-state service rule, leaving that judgment to the legislatures that are free to amend it; for our purposes, its validation is its pedigree. . . . Shaffer did conduct such an independent inquiry, asserting that " 'traditional notions of fair play and substantial justice' can be as readily offended by the perpetuation of ancient forms that are no longer justified as by the adoption of new procedures that are inconsistent with the basic values of our constitutional heritage." 433 U.S., at 212. Perhaps that assertion can be sustained when the "perpetuation of ancient forms" is engaged in by only a very small minority of the States. Where, however, as in the present case, a jurisdictional principle is both firmly approved by tradition and still favored, it is impossible to imagine what standard we could appeal to for the judgment that it is "no longer justified." While in no way receding from or casting doubt upon the holding of Shaffer or any other case, we reaffirm today our time-honored approach. . . . For new procedures, hitherto unknown, the Due Process Clause requires analysis to determine whether "traditional notions of fair play and substantial justice" have been offended. International Shoe, 326 U.S., at 316. But a doctrine of personal jurisdiction that dates back to the adoption of the Fourteenth Amendment and is still generally observed unquestionably meets that standard.

III

A few words in response to JUSTICE BRENNAN'S concurrence:

* * *

The subjectivity, and hence inadequacy, of this approach [which utilizes "contemporary notions of due process"] becomes apparent when the concurrence tries to explain why the assertion of jurisdiction in the present case meets its standard of continuing-American-tradition-plus-innate-fairness. Justice Brennan lists the "benefits" Mr. Burnham derived from the State of California—that fact that, during the few days he was there, "his health and safety [were] guaranteed by the State's police, fire, and emergency medical services; he [was] free to travel on the State's roads and waterways; he likely enjoy[ed] the fruits of the State's economy.". . . Three days worth of these benefits strike us a powerfully inadequate to establish, as an abstract matter, that it is "fair" for California to decree the ownership of all Mr. Burnham's worldly goods acquired during the ten years of his marriage, and the custody over his children. We daresay a contractual exchange swapping those benefits for that power would not survive the "unconscionability" provision of the Uniform Commercial Code. . . .

* * *

The difference between us and Justice Brennan has nothing to do with whether "further progress [is] to be made" in the "evolution of our legal system.". . . It has to do with whether changes are to be adopted as progressive by the American people or decreed as progressive by the Justices of this Court. Nothing we say today prevents individual States for limiting or entirely abandoning the in-state-service basis of jurisdiction. . . .

* * *

Because the Due Process Clause does not prohibit the California courts from exercising jurisdiction over petitioner based on the fact of in-state service of process, the judgment is Affirmed.

JUSTICE WHITE, concurring in part and concurring in the judgment.

I join in Part I and Parts II–A, II–B, and II–C of Justice Scalia's opinion and concur in the judgment of affirmance. The rule allowing jurisdiction to be obtained over a non-resident by personal service in the forum state, without more, has been and is so widely accepted throughout this country that I could not pssibly strike it down. . . . Although the Court has the authority under the Amendment to examine even traditionally accepted procedures and declare them invalid, e.g., Shaffer v. Heitner, 433 U.S. 186 (1977), there has been no showing here or elsewhere that as a general proposition the rule is so arbitrary and lacking in common sense in so many instances that it should be held violative of Due Process in every case. Furthermore, until such a showing is made, which would be difficult indeed, claims in individual cases that the rule would operate unfairly as applied to the particular non-resident involved need not be entertained. At least this would be the case where presence in the forum state is intentional, which would almost always be the fact. Otherwise, there would be endless, fact-specific litigation in the trial and appellate courts, including this one. . . .

JUSTICE BRENNAN, with whom JUSTICE MARSHALL, JUSTICE BLACKMUN, and JUSTICE O'CONNOR join, concurring in the judgment. . . .*

I agree with Justice Scalia that the Due Process Clause of the Fourteenth Amendment generally permits a state court to exercise jurisdiction over a defendant if he is served with process while voluntarily present in the forum State. It do not perceive the need, however, to decide that a jurisdictional rule that "'has been immemorially the actual law of the land,'" . . . automatically comports with due process simply by virtue of its "pedigree." . . . Unlike Justice Scalia, I would undertake an "independent inquiry into the . . . fairness of the prevailing in-state service rule.". . .

I

I believe that the approach adopted by JUSTICE SCALIA's opinion today—reliance solely on historical pedigree—is foreclosed by our decisions in International Shoe Co. v. Washington, 326 U.S. 310 (1945), and Shaffer v. Heitner, 433 U.S. 186 (1977). In International Shoe, we held that a state court's assertion of personal jurisdiction does not violate the Due Process Clause if it is consistent with "'traditional notions of fair play and substantial justice.'" 326 U.S., at 316, quoting Milliken v. Meyer, 311 U.S. 457, 463 (1940). In Shaffer, we stated that "*all* assertions of state-court jurisdiction must be evaluated according to the standards set forth in International Shoe and its progeny." 433 U.S., at 212 (emphasis added). The critical insight of Shaffer is that all rules of jurisdiction, even ancient ones, must satisfy contemporary notions of due process. No longer were we content to limit our jurisdictional analysis to pronouncements that "[t]he foundation of jurisdiction is physical power," McDonald v. Mabee, 243 U.S. 90, 91 (1917), and that "every State possesses exclusive jurisdiction and sovereignty over persons and property within its territory." Pennoyer v. Neff, 95 U.S. 714, 722 (1878). While acknowledging that "history must be considered as supporting the proposition that jurisdiction based solely on the presence of property satisfie[d] the demands of due process," we found that this factor could not be "decisive." 433 U.S., at 211–212. We recognized that "'[t]raditional notions of fair play and substantial justice' can be as readily offended by the perpetuation of ancient forms that are no longer justified as by the adoption of new procedures that are inconsis-

* Footnotes omitted.

tent with the basis values of our constitutional heritage." Id., at 212 (citations omitted). . . .

* * *

II

Tradition, though alone not dispositive, is of course relevant to the question whether the rule of transient jurisdiction is consistent with due process.

* * *

[H]owever murky the jurisprudential origins of transient jurisdiction, the fact that American courts have announced the rule for perhaps a century (first in dicta, more recently in holdings) provides a defendant voluntarily present in a particular State today "clear notice that [he] is subject to suit" in the forum. World–Wide Volkswagen Corp. v. Woodson, 444 U.S. 286, 297 (1980). . . .

By visiting the forum State, a transient defendant actually "avail[s]" himself, Burger King [Corp. v. Rudzewicz, 471 U.S. 462] 476 [(1985)], of significant benefits provided by the State. His health and safety are guaranteed by the State's police, fire, and emergency medical services; he is free to travel on the State's roads and waterways; he likely enjoys the fruits of the State's economy as well. Moreover, the Privileges and Immunities Clause of Article IV prevents a state government from discriminating against a transient defendant by denying him the protections of its law or the right of access to its courts. Without transient jurisdiction, an asymmetry would arise: a transient would have the full benefit of the power of the forum State's courts as a plaintiff while retaining immunity from their authority as a defendant. . . .

The potential burdens on a transient defendant are slight. " '[M]odern transportation and communications have made it much less burdensome for a party sued to defend himself' " in a State outside his place of residence. Burger King, 471 U.S., at 474, quoting McGee v. International Life Insurance Co., 355 U.S. 220, 223 (1957). That the defendant has already journeyed at least once before to the forum—as evidenced by the fact that he was served with process there—is an indication that suit in the forum likely would not be prohibitively inconvenient. Finally, any burdens that do arise can be ameliorated by a variety of procedural devices. For these reasons, as a rule the exercise of personal jurisdiction over a defendant based on his voluntary presence in the forum will satisfy the requirements of due process.

In this case, it is undisputed that petitioner was served with process while voluntarily and knowingly in the State of California. I therefore concur in the judgment.

JUSTICE STEVENS, concurring in the judgment.

. . . For me, it is sufficient to note that the historical evidence and consensus identified by Justice Scalia, the considerations of fairness identified by Justice Brennan, and the common sense displayed by

Justice White, all combine to demonstrate that this is, indeed, a very easy case. . . .* Accordingly, I agree that the judgment should be affirmed.

* Perhaps the adage about hard cases making bad law should be revised to cover easy cases.

*

INDEX

PLEADING—Cont'd
Alternative and hypothetical pleading, 573–574.
Certification, 566–572.
Inconsistency, 573–574.
Sanctions, 566–572.
Verification, 563–566.
Hypothetical, 573–574.
Inconsistent, 573–574.
Libel or slander, 588.
Nature and function of, 543–551.
Negative pregnant, 610–611.
Objectives of, 543–545.
Particularity in specific actions, 588.
Responsive pleadings, 32–33, 557, 604–614, 619.
Denials and defenses, 557, 604–611.
Sufficiency of, 609–611.
Specificity, 577–579, 581.
Substantive law basis, 551–557.
Supplemental, 616, 625.
Verifications, 563–566.
Waiver of defenses and objections, 611–614.

POLITICAL QUESTIONS
See Justiciability.

PRE-TRIAL CONFERENCE
See also Judicial Administration.
Amendment to order, 823–827.
Columbia project, 813–819.
Default judgment, 820.
Effectiveness of, 813–820.
Extent of judicial authority, 819–820.
Function of, 34–35, 806, 813–820.
Order, excluded issue, 820–827.
Amendment of, 823–827.
Settlements, 813.

PROCESS
See Service of Process.

PROOF
See Burden of Proof.

PROVISIONAL REMEDIES
Attachment and garnishment, 119–145.
New York statute, 120–121.
Wages, 121–125.
Preliminary injunction, 119, 145–151.
Damages, 151.
Notice of pendency, 120, 125, 151–152.
Receivership, 119, 125.

QUASI IN REM JURISDICTION
See Adjudicatory Authority.

REAL PARTY IN INTEREST
Generally, 400–405.
History, 402.
Insurance carrier, 400–402, 403–405.

REMEDIES
See also Equity; Extraordinary Remedies; Forms of Action; Provisional Remedies.
Assumpsit, 68–69, 80.
Attorney's fees, 111–118.
Declaratory judgment, 99–111.
Discretion, 110–111.
Federal act, 102.
Federal question adjudicatory authority, 189–194, 195–199.
German, 111.
History, 100–102.
Justiciability, 100–102, 103–110, 176–177.
Right to jury trial in, 103.
Uniform Act, 102.
Ejectment, 85–86, 752, 754, 755.
Final remedies, 61–118.
Current remedies, 78–118.
Historical remedies,
American, 76–77.
English, 61–76.
Formulary system, 61–63.
Personal actions, 65–70.
Procedures, 70–72.
Real actions, 64–65.
Royal and ecclesiastical courts, 63–64.
Injunctive relief, 90–99, see Injunction.
Money judgment, 79–81, 943–949.
Tort, 80–81.
Recovery of property, 81–89.
Detinue, 65–66, 81, 83–84.
Ejectment, 85–89.
Equitable replevin, 84–85.
Replevin, 65, 81–83, 84–85.
Specific performance, 95–98.
Trover, 69–70, 83.

REMITTITUR, 886–895.

REMOVAL OF ACTIONS, 219–221.

REPLY, 33.

RES JUDICATA
Generally, 955–1030.
Appeal pending, 977.
Bar and merger, see Claim preclusion, this topic.
Basic distinctions, 955–958.
Cause of action, see Same claim, this topic.
Claim preclusion, 957–977.
Privity, 964–974.
Same claim, 959–964, 966–967, 1003.
Valid judgment, 974–978.
Collateral estoppel, see Issue preclusion, this topic.
Compulsory counterclaim, 417–426, 991.
Consent decree, effect, 964–969, 971–974.
Constitutional issues, 505–511, 780, 987, 996–1000.
Countervailing policies, 1004–1021.
Change in legal climate, 1004–1008.

†